The Letters of William Lloyd Garrison

EDITED BY

WALTER M. MERRILL AND LOUIS RUCHAMES

PUBLISHER'S NOTE

A word of explanation about the cooperation of the editors of this edition. Some time before 1960, each of the editors, unknown to the other, had embarked on the task of editing Garrison's letters. Each had secured a publisher: Professor Merrill, Harvard University Press; Professor Ruchames, University of Massachusetts Press. On learning accidentally of one another's efforts, the editors decided to cooperate in issuing one edition. The University of Massachusetts Press and Harvard University Press, after discussions, concluded that the latter should assume responsibility for publishing the work.

In arriving at their decision to cooperate, the editors agreed to combine the letters which each had gathered separately as well as to unite in a systematic search for letters that had thus far been overlooked. Repositories of manuscript letters, including libraries, state and local historical societies, and manuscript dealers, in the United States and abroad, were checked. In a number of instances, collections of uncatalogued letters were also searched and several hundred new letters have been discovered and incorporated in the collections.

In the allocation of responsibilities, the editors have divided the material by periods as follows:

1822–1835 — Walter M. Merrill	1850–1860 — Louis Ruchames
1836–1840 — Louis Ruchames	1861–1869 — Walter M. Merrill
1841–1849 — Walter M. Merrill	1870–1879 — Louis Ruchames

Garrison at the age of forty-seven

The Letters of
William Lloyd Garrison

Volume IV

FROM DISUNIONISM TO THE BRINK OF WAR

1850-1860

EDITED BY LOUIS RUCHAMES

The Belknap Press of Harvard University Press
Cambridge, Massachusetts
and London, England

1975

To my cousins,

Zalman and Miriam Arkin,
of Mizkeret Batya, Israel,

whose pioneering spirit and devotion to their people
helped build present-day Israel
and are the surest guarantees of its future

ACKNOWLEDGMENTS

I wish to express my deepest appreciation to the many persons — librarians, curators, scholarly predecessors, colleagues, autograph dealers, research assistants, typists, historical societies, universities, and friends — who have contributed to the preparation of this volume.

I am deeply indebted to the following institutions for furnishing photocopies of Garrison letters included in this volume and for permission to publish them: American Antiquarian Society, Worcester, Massachusetts; Arlington Historical Society, Arlington, Massachusetts; Arthur and Elizabeth Schlesinger Library on the History of Women in America, Radcliffe College, Cambridge, Massachusetts; Birmingham University Library, Birmingham, England; Boston Public Library, Boston, Massachusetts; Brown University Library, Providence, Rhode Island; Chicago Historical Society, Chicago, Illinois; Colby Junior College, Department of Social Studies Archives, New London, New Hampshire; College of the Holy Cross, Worcester, Massachusetts; Columbia University Library, New York City; Essex Institute, Salem, Massachusetts; Friends Historical Library of Swarthmore College, Swarthmore, Pennsylvania; Haverford College Library, Haverford, Pennsylvania; Houghton Library, Harvard University, Cambridge, Massachusetts; Huntington Library, San Marino, California; Indiana Historical Society Library, Indianapolis, Indiana; Library of Congress, Washington, D.C.; Lynn Historical Society, Lynn, Massachusetts; Maine Historical Society, Portland, Maine; Massachusetts Historical Society, Boston, Massachusetts; Morristown National Historic Park, Morristown, New Jersey; New Hampshire Historical Society, Concord, New Hampshire; New-York Historical Society, New York City; New York Public Library, New York City; Oberlin College Library, Oberlin, Ohio; Ohio State University Libraries, Columbus, Ohio; Rush Rees Library, University of Rochester, Rochester, New York; Smith College Library, Northampton, Massachusetts; Society for the Preservation of Old Webster, Webster, New Hampshire; Taconic Foundation, New York City; University of California Library, Berkeley, California; University of Pennsylvania Library, Philadelphia, Pennsylvania;

Acknowledgments

Wellesley College Library, Wellesley, Massachusetts; Wichita State University Library, Wichita, Kansas; William Clements Library, University of Michigan, Ann Arbor, Michigan; Worcester Historical Society, Worcester, Massachusetts; Yale University Library, New Haven, Connecticut. I am indebted, similarly, to the following owners of Garrison letters for the use of letters in their possession: Mr. and Mrs. John W. Coolidge, Jr., Marblehead, Massachusetts; Mr. James Lawton, Brookline, Massachusetts; Mr. Forman M. Lebold, Chicago, Illinois; Colonel Richard Maass, White Plains, New York; Mr. Ralph G. Newman, Chicago, Illinois.

The following persons were most helpful in providing information and research assistance: Daniel Aaron, Harvard University; John Alden, Boston Public Library; M. Y. Ashcroft, County Record Office, Northallerton, Yorkshire, England; D. Barlow, British Transport Historical Records, Paddington, England; Roy P. Basler, Library of Congress; W. E. Bigglestone, Oberlin College Archives; C. W. Black, The Mitchell Library, Glasgow, Scotland; John B. Blake, National Library of Medicine, Bethesda, Maryland; Dennis R. Bodem, Michigan State Archives; J. D. Cadwell, Essex County Historical Association, Windsor, Canada; Ruth E. Cannard, Jackson Homestead, Newton, Massachusetts; Wayne S. Carpenter, Lenawee County Historical Society, Adrian, Michigan; George A. Carter, Municipal Library, Warrington, England; Marian K. Chubb, West Orange, New Jersey; J. W. Cockburn, City Librarian, Edinburgh, Scotland; William D. Coughlan, Abington, Massachusetts; Alice C. Dalligan, Detroit Public Library; Margaret Deas, National Library of Scotland, Edinburgh, Scotland; Merton Dillon, Ohio State University; Elizabeth B. Downey, Rochester Historical Society, Rochester, New York; Herbert Finch, Cornell University Library; Frances Forman, Cincinnati Historical Society; John Hope Franklin, University of Chicago; Doris A. Frazier, Lenawee County Historical Society, Adrian, Michigan; Roger W. Fromm, New York State Archives, Cooperstown, New York; Eleanor Garrison, Santa Barbara, California; Lloyd K. Garrison, New York City; Gerald W. Gillette, The Presbyterian Historical Society, Philadelphia, Pennsylvania; Emily N. Haggerty, Essex Institute, Salem, Massachusetts.

Also, J. D. S. Hall, Rhodes House Library, Oxford, England; Virginius C. Hall, Jr., Virginia Historical Society; Olive S. Harrison, Furman University Library, Greenville, South Carolina; Virginia Hawley, The Western Reserve Historical Society, Cleveland, Ohio; James J. Heslin, New-York Historical Society, New York City; H. Hobart Holly, Braintree, Massachusetts; James Hurley, The Long Island Historical Society, Brooklyn, New York; Shirley Iversen, Rochester Public Library, Rochester, New York; Elizabeth G. Jack,

Acknowledgments

The Library, University of Glasgow; Marion Jarrett, Drexel University; William L. Joyce, American Antiquarian Society, Worcester, Massachusetts; Karl Kabelac, University of Rochester Library, Rochester, New York; Elizabeth B. Knox, The New London County Historical Society, New London, Connecticut; Aaron Kramer, Dowling College, Oakdale, Long Island; Richard C. Kugler, Old Dartmouth Historical Society Whaling Museum, New Bedford, Massachusetts; Mrs. N. B. Lacy, New Hampshire Historical Society, Concord, New Hampshire; Dorothy B. Lapp, Chester County Historical Society, West Chester, Pennsylvania; James Lawton, Boston Public Library; Mildred Leavitt, New England Historic Genealogical Society; Stephanie Loeb, Museum of Fine Arts, Boston, Massachusetts; Kenneth A. Lohf, Columbia University Library; Anne G. McGuffee, Historical Society of Vicksburg and Warren County, Mississippi; William McNitt, Michigan Historical Collections, University of Michigan; Pamela McNulty, The Marine Historical Association, Mystic, Connecticut; Clyde Maffin, The Ontario County Historical Society, Canandaigua, New York; R. E. Marston, Central Library, Warwick, England; Elizabeth R. Martin, The Ohio Historical Society.

Also, Eleanor Mayer, Friends Historical Library of Swarthmore College; Dianne Melnychuk, The George Arents Research Library, Syracuse University; Nyle Miller, Kansas State Historical Society; Eva Moseley, Arthur and Elizabeth Schlesinger Library on the History of Women in America, Radcliffe College; Dorothy Mozley, Springfield City Library, Springfield, Massachusetts; Mary-Elizabeth Murdock, Smith College Library; Alice J. Nearing, Drexel University; Reidun D. Nuquist, Vermont Historical Society; Merrilyn R. O'Connell, The Oneida Historical Society, Utica, New York; Ellen M. Oldham, Boston Public Library; Helen A. Patterson, Mercer County Historical Society, Mercer, Pennsylvania; Dorothy Porter, Howard University; Mary Jo Pugh, Michigan Historical Collections, University of Michigan; Benjamin Quarles, Morgan State College, Baltimore, Maryland; Richard B. Reed, Bowdoin College Library; Douglas C. Riach, Dublin, Ireland; Hester Rich, Maryland Historical Society; Stephen T. Riley, Massachusetts Historical Society; Priscilla Ritter, Massachusetts Historical Society; Marjarie Robertson-Coe Maurer, Philadelphia Historical Commission; Eric Robinson, University of Massachusetts–Boston; T. Roth, The Historical Society of Pennsylvania; Allen D. Russell, Plymouth, Massachusetts; H. Russell, Local History Library, Belfast, Ireland; Mary R. Shannon, Rochester Historical Society, Rochester, New York; Elizabeth Shenton, Schlesinger Library, Radcliffe College; Patricia Siemiontkowski, Philadelphia Historical Commission; Diana Small, New England Historic Genealogical Society; Mildred Steinbach, Frick

Acknowledgments

Art Reference Library, New York City; Sheldon Stern, University of Massachusetts–Boston.

Also, Lynn P. Stoddard, Battle Creek Historical and Archeological Society, Battle Creek, Michigan; Marjorie Stuff, National Library of Medicine, Bethesda, Maryland; Carolyn H. Sung, Bethesda, Maryland; Rosemary Taylor, University of London, Institute of Historical Research; Juliette Tomlinson, Connecticut Valley Historical Museum, Springfield, Massachusetts; Stanley Tongue, Shoreditch District Library, London, England; Kenneth Twinn, Dr. Williams's Library, London, England; Holly B. Ulseth, Detroit Historical Commission; J. W. Vitty, Belfast Library and Society for Promoting Knowledge, Belfast, Ireland; Nicholas B. Wainwright, The Historical Society of Pennsylvania; Conrad F. Weitzel, Ohio Historical Society; B. A. Walsh, Rensselaer County Historical Society, Troy, New York; Walter M. Whitehill, Boston Athenæum; Robin W. Winks, Yale University; Richard N. Wright, Onondaga Historical Association, Syracuse, New York; Bertram Wyatt-Brown, Case Western Reserve University; Nancy Zurich, Drexel University.

I am indebted to the University of Massachusetts for the major portion of the financial support which I have received as well as for assistance and encouragement in numerous other forms.

Professor Walter M. Merrill, who is editing alternate volumes of the Garrison letters, has been of great help in the process of gathering letters, exchanging information, including transcriptions, photocopies, and lists, and in many editorial matters.

Mrs. Carl A. Pitha of the Harvard University Press has provided valuable assistance.

My colleagues at the University of Massachusetts–Boston, Professors Paul Boller, Thomas N. Brown, Paul Gagnon, Dorothy Marshall, Richard Powers, and Robert Steamer, have been a source of continuing encouragement and support. Mr. Thor B. Olson has been helpful in many ways.

My wife, Miriam, has again borne stoically and with love the trials of completing this volume.

Mrs. Dorothy Koval has again provided the splendid assistance which has made her a mainstay of this project. Words can only feebly express my gratitude.

L. R.

July 1975
Boston, Massachusetts

CONTENTS

Contents

Contents

IV   THE KANSAS-NEBRASKA ACT — THE CONFLICT INTENSIFIES: 1854   289

V   THE RADICALIZATION OF MASSACHUSETTS — WARFARE IN KANSAS: 1855   327

Contents

Contents

Contents

VIII THE REMOVAL OF JUDGE LORING: 1858   501

Contents

Contents

X ILLNESS, MORE CONVENTIONS, AND
GARRISONIAN ANTISLAVERY REDEFINED: 1860   666

Contents

LIST OF ILLUSTRATIONS

Frontispiece

William Lloyd Garrison at the age of forty-seven. Part of a group picture with Wendell Phillips, from a daguerreotype taken in May 1852 at Rochester, New York. Reproduced from *Life*, III, facing page 358.

Following page 96

Wendell Phillips, William Lloyd Garrison, and George Thompson in 1851 From a daguerreotype taken that year.
Courtesy of Boston Public Library.

The Pennsylvania Anti-Slavery Society, 1851. Left to right, front row: Oliver Johnson, Mrs. Margaret Jones Burleigh, Benjamin C. Bacon, Robert Purvis, Lucretia Mott, James Mott; back row: Mary Grew, Edward M. Davis, Haworth Wetherald, Abby Kimber, J. Miller McKim, Sarah Pugh. From Ira V. Brown, *The Negro in Pennsylvania History*, Pennsylvania History Studies No. 11, The Pennsylvania Historical Association, University Park, Pennsylvania, 1970.
Courtesy of The Pennsylvania Historical Association and the Historical Society of Pennsylvania.

Theodore Parker in 1853. From John White Chadwick, *Theodore Parker, Preacher and Reformer*, Boston and New York, 1900, frontispiece.

Louis Kossuth. From P. C. Headley, *The Life of Louis Kossuth*, Auburn, 1852, frontispiece.

Following page 414

Elizabeth Pease, about 1851. From a daguerreotype. Reproduced from *Life*, III, facing page 322.

Helen Benson Garrison, about 1853. From a daguerreotype taken that year. Reproduced from *Life*, II, frontispiece.

Charles Fox Hovey, about 1852. From a daguerreotype. Reproduced from *Life*, III, facing page 282.

Charles Sumner, at the age of forty-two. An engraving from an 1853 daguerreotype. From Edward L. Pierce, *Memoir and Letters of Charles Sumner*, Boston, 1881, I, frontispiece.

EDITORIAL STATEMENT

THIS VOLUME contains all the available letters written by Garrison from the beginning of 1850 to the end of 1860. The originals were either in Garrison's own handwriting, or appeared in newspapers under Garrison's name, or have been found in typescripts or handwritten copies prepared by others from the originals. The exact source is indicated in the notes.

The letters are arranged in one-year periods, with the exception of 1850–1851, with each year prefaced by a short essay which provides a context for understanding the letters of that year. Where there are two or more letters per day, they are arranged in alphabetical order according to the surname of the recipient, unless there is some indication of temporal priority.

1. Each letter is numbered according to its position in the sequence of letters.

2. The name of the recipient, in its usual spelling, is printed at the head of each letter. Titles are excluded from the caption unless their presence helps to differentiate two persons of the same name.

3. Each letter is given a date line using Garrison's original words, the editor having supplied additional information, as in conjectural dates and place names, in square brackets. Where Garrison noted the place and date at the close of a letter, these are also included, in brackets, at the beginning.

4. The salutation is uniformly placed and follows Garrison's original wording.

5. The editor has sought to provide an accurate text of each letter as presented in its source. Obvious slips in punctuation, the misspelling of a word, or the inadvertent repetition of a word or phrase have been silently corrected.

6. The complimentary close and signature are presented as in the source, but uniformly placed.

7. Postscripts are uniformly placed after Garrison's signature.

Editorial Statement

Marginal notations intended as postscripts are similarly placed, with a note indicating their original position in the manuscript.

8. Certain editorial situations are indicated by the following symbols:

⟨Cancellation⟩

[. . .] Unrecoverable matter. If the material is more than four or five words long, its nature and extent are explained in the notes.

[   ] Editorial insertion.

[   ] Garrison's brackets.

☞ ☜ Garrison's method of emphasis.

Descriptive Notes

1. The source of the letter is provided immediately following the text; abbreviations used are ALS for "autograph letter signed," and AL for "autograph letter" unsigned. A source other than an autograph is always described.

2. Known previous publications of a letter, whether in whole or in part, have been indicated.

3. Efforts have been made to identify all recipients.

Notes

1. Notes, numbered consecutively, are placed immediately after the descriptive notes.

2. The editor has attempted to identify persons referred to in the texts of the letters and to explain references and allusions not immediately clear in their contexts. Whenever possible, Garrison's quotations have been identified. The Contents and the Index of Recipients should serve as convenient guides.

3. The King James version of the Bible is the one always cited.

ABBREVIATIONS AND SHORT TITLES

BDAC. James L. Harrington, *Biographical Directory of the American Congress, 1774–1961* (Washington, D.C.: Government Printing Office, 1961).

HEUSH. Harper's Encyclopedia of United States History. New Edition Revised and Enlarged. Based upon the Plan of Benson John Lossing. Preface by Woodrow Wilson (New York and London: Harper & Brothers, 1901–1912).

Letters, I. *The Letters of William Lloyd Garrison,* vol. I, *I Will Be Heard! 1822–1835,* Walter M. Merrill, ed. (Cambridge, Mass.: The Belknap Press of Harvard University Press, 1971).

Letters, II. *The Letters of William Lloyd Garrison,* vol. II, *A House Dividing Against Itself, 1836–1840,* Louis Ruchames, ed. (Cambridge, Mass.: The Belknap Press of Harvard University Press, 1971).

Letters, III. *The Letters of William Lloyd Garrison,* vol. III, *No Union With Slaveholders, 1841–1849,* Walter M. Merrill, ed. (Cambridge, Mass.: The Belknap Press of Harvard University Press, 1973).

Life. W. P. and F. J. Garrison, *William Lloyd Garrison, 1805–1879: The Story of His Life, Told by His Children* (New York: 1885–1889), 4 volumes.

NCAB. National Cyclopaedia of American Biography (New York: James T. White and Co., 1898–1968).

Notable American Women. Edward T. James, Janet Wilson James, and Paul S. Boyer, eds., *Notable American Women 1607–1950* (Cambridge, Mass.: The Belknap Press of Harvard University Press, 1971), 3 volumes.

Quarles, *Black Abolitionists.* Benjamin Quarles, *Black Abolitionists* (New York, 1969).

Ruchames, *The Abolitionists.* Louis Ruchames, *The Abolitionists: A Collection of Their Writings* (New York: Capricorn Edition, 1964).

Union List of Newspapers. Winifred Gregory, ed., *American Newspapers, 1821–1936: A Union List of Files Available in the United States and Canada* (New York: H. W. Wilson & Co., 1937).

Union List of Serials. Edna Brown Titus, ed., *Union List of Serials in Libraries of the United States and Canada,* 3d edition (New York: H. W. Wilson & Co., 1965), 5 volumes.

Weld-Grimké Letters. Gilbert H. Barnes and Dwight L. Dumond, eds., *Letters of Theodore Dwight Weld, Angelina Grimké Weld and Sarah Grimké, 1822–1844* (Gloucester, Mass.: 1965).

I THE YEAR OF THE COMPROMISE – THE FUGITIVE SLAVE ACT AND ITS AFTERMATH: 1850–1851

THE OVERSHADOWING ISSUE of 1850 was the compromise legislation introduced by Henry Clay in January, Daniel Webster's Seventh of March speech in favor of the compromise and, following the death of President Zachary Taylor in July after a little more than a year in office, the final enactment of the legislation which received President Millard Fillmore's signature in September. Of the various sections of the law, it was the Fugitive Slave Act that was of most direct and crucial concern to the abolitionists and the black population of the United States, and that evoked their greatest resistance.

The tension created by the debate over the compromise, combined with the periodic threats of secession by the South if its demands were not granted, resulted in a recrudescence of hatred and violence in certain northern quarters toward the abolitionists. The annual meeting of the American Anti-Slavery Society on May 7 and 8, in New York City, evoked editorials in James Gordon Bennett's New York *Herald* and other New York newspapers demanding that the meeting be prohibited and encouraging mob violence during the convention. Mob action and harassment of the speakers did occur under the leadership of Isaiah Rynders, a Tammany tough, and finally resulted in a somewhat premature ending of the convention on the second day.

In November, George Thompson, the English abolitionist and Garrison's close friend who had last been in the United States in 1835, when he left rather precipitously with a mob at his heels, arrived in the United States. The reception for him at Faneuil Hall on November 15 was broken up by a mob and was adjourned to Worcester, where it was held without difficulty and with the blessings of the city officials. As Garrison's *Life* observes, "Thompson was the great central fact in

1

Mr. Garrison's life and public activity during the eight months of the Englishman's stay in America." Thompson spoke at numerous anti-slavery meetings, often with Garrison. Of these, one of the most exciting was a soirée in Cochituate Hall in Boston, on January 24, 1851, in celebration of the twentieth anniversary of the founding of *The Liberator*, at which Wendell Phillips, Edmund Quincy, Henry Wilson, Theodore Parker, Thompson, and others spoke. Perhaps equally exciting was the farewell soirée for Thompson in Boston on June 16, with more than a thousand plates spread, prior to his sailing on the *America* for England on June 25, 1851.

The Fugitive Slave Law, which the federal government and the southern states insisted upon enforcing, met with the resistance of the abolitionists, blacks, and large sections of the northern public who were outraged by the injustice of the law. Vigilance committees were organized in Boston and other cities to warn blacks of the presence of southern planters looking for their slaves, and to help fugitive slaves, of whom there were hundreds in Boston alone, reach Canada. There were four especially prominent fugitive slave cases in 1851. The first was the rescue of Shadrach from a Boston courtroom on February 15, 1851, and his subsequent escape to Canada. The second was the rendition on Saturday, April 12, of Thomas Sims to Savannah, Georgia, with the city of Boston providing a police escort and using the militia to prevent any rescue. The third was the Christiana, Lancaster County, Pennsylvania encounter in September, in which a slaveholder, Edward Gorsuch, and his son were slain while trying to apprehend their alleged runaway slaves. The last was the Jerry rescue in Syracuse, New York, on October 1, 1851. The last noteworthy event involving Garrison, in 1851, was the appearance at the end of the year of a volume of more than four hundred pages entitled *Selections from the Writings and Speeches of William Lloyd Garrison*, published by R. F. Wallcut, publication date 1852.

1

TO SAMUEL J. MAY

Boston, Jan. 13, 1850.

MY DEAR FRIEND:

Among the obstacles interposing to prevent my attendance at the Anti-Slavery Convention in Syracuse,[1] on Tuesday next, is bodily indisposition. It is worth going the long distance to see *you*, personally, — you, for whom I entertain a most ardent friendship and the highest esteem — you, who were among the first in Boston, nearly twenty years ago, to give me strengthening words of encouragement and open countenance, at that time of unspeakable value — you, who have never been ashamed to avow, nor afraid to defend, the sacred principles which lie at the basis of the anti-slavery cause — as well as to commune with the other choice spirits, who are to be present at Freedom's gathering in your city this week. Happily, where so many able advocates of the slave are to congregate, my presence is of no consequence whatever. That the occasion will be one of transcendant interest, and of no ordinary importance, at this great crisis, I feel certain; and that the proceedings will be characterized by the boldest enunciation of truth, the most radical avowal of sentiment, the most earnest inculcation of duty, I will not entertain a doubt. In a struggle like ours, nothing is gained by indirectness of assault, or circumlocution of language. Like the apostles of old, we must use great plainness of speech; like the reformers of all ages, we must call things by their right names; like Jesus, we must we willing to make ourselves of no reputation, as without conflict there can be no victory — without the cross, no crown.

The existence of slavery in this country, in the seventy-fourth year of our national independence, is the most inexcusable of crimes. For a people, holding it to be a self-evident truth, that all men are created equal, and endowed by their Creator with an inalienable right to liberty, to be literally trafficking in the bodies and souls of millions of the human race, and bending all their energies to perpetuate this terrible system, is the most extraordinary paradox in the records of human depravity. Their case admits of no extenuation, of no apology; they are condemned out of their own mouths (in the emphatic language of O'Connell) [2] as the 'greatest of liars and the vilest of hypocrites.' [3] Truly, 'their feet run to evil, and they make haste to shed innocent blood.' [4] But their guilt is intensely aggravated by their claiming to be a Christian people — believers in Him who came to be the Redeemer and Savior of men, not their enslaver — 'to preach deliverance to the captive, and the opening of prison to them that are bound.' [5] It is enough to send a shudder throughout the universe. When I think of what slavery is — the extinction of every virtue, the nourishment of every vice, the abrogation of all holy precepts and divine commands, the exaltation of the slave-master above the living God, the overthrow of the sacred institution of marriage, the merciless and systematic robbery of the poor and needy, the extinction of mind and the ruin of the soul — its yokes and fetters, its whips and bloodhounds, its thumb-screws and branding-irons — and that this heathenish and frightful system is upheld and defended, in whole or in part, by all the leading religious and political influences in the land — by Catholics, Episcopalians, Presbyterians, Baptists, Methodists, and other sects — by Whigs, Democrats, and (at least so far as the pro-slavery compromises of the Constitution are concerned) even Free Soilers — I feel how utterly impotent is language to describe the sins of the American people. Every eulogy they pronounce upon liberty is a sentence of condemnation upon themselves; every denunciation of tyranny that falls from their lips is a woe invoked upon their own heads; every celebration of their own deliverance from bondage is public demonstration to the world of their unparalleled ingratitude and duplicity.

I know of no other method of putting down slavery, (a bloody insurrection out of the question,) except by making slaveholding, in all cases, a most despicable and wicked act. The affirmation must be, without respect of persons, — EVERY SLAVEHOLDER IS A MANSTEALER, — and he must be put on a level with the basest of men. The church that will receive him as a Christian brother, must be excommunicated as heretical in the worst sense. The government that is framed to accommodate his tyranny, and that accords to him power in proportion to the number of his victims, ceases to deserve allegiance, and must be overthrown. There must be no union with slaveholders, religiously or politically. It seems to me impossible to utter a plainer proposition. On the part of the South, the condition of union has been, and is, that we of the North shall give absolute protection and encouragement to the slave system; to this hour, that condition has been complied with; a refusal to comply with it dissolves the union inevitably and necessarily. The time has come to preach disunion on the highest moral and religious grounds. The Constitution of the United States is 'a covenant with death and an agreement with hell.'[6] In the name of God, of Christ, of Humanity, of Liberty, it must be repudiated by all who revere God, love Christ, regard Humanity, and cherish Liberty. It remains to be seen how the people of the North will meet this issue. As for the vaporing of the South about a separation, in case the Wilmot Proviso [7] is passed, (in any case, I am inclined to believe,) it is empty as the whistling wind — 'full of sound and fury, signifying nothing.'[8] The South knows that the dissolution of the Union will be abolition of slavery; and her threats are only to intimidate Northern cowardice and servility. I am for the abolition of slavery, therefore for the dissolution of the Union.

Yours, uncompromisingly for Freedom,

WM. LLOYD GARRISON.

Printed in *The Liberator*, February 8, 1850.

Samuel J. May, the veteran abolitionist, Unitarian minister, and one of Garrison's oldest and closest friends, was at this time minister of a Unitarian church in Syracuse, New York, serving there from 1845 to 1867. (See *Letters*, II, xxvi–xxvii, for a biographical sketch of May, and Letters, I, II, and III, *passim.*)

1. This was to be a convention of the abolitionists of the state of New York on Tuesday, January 15, 1850. The announcement of the convention in *The Liberator*, January 4, 1850, explained the purpose of the convention, as follows: "The present aspect of national affairs in regard to the question of Slavery; the present position of political parties in relation to those affairs; the present position which Abolitionists, who have preserved their faith inviolate, hold to those parties; and the relation which Abolitionists sustain to each other and the cause, demand that such a Conveniton be held in this State; that it be held during the present session of Congress; and that it shall represent the entire strength of that portion of our people who are hostile, not only to the extension of Slavery into new Territories, but to its existence anywhere; who are determined not only to resist its establishment on the coast of the Pacific, or in the valleys of New Mexico, but are equally determined on its extirpation on the Atlantic coast and in the valley of the Mississippi. . . . The warning cry of No UNION WITH SLAVEHOLDERS and their abettors was never more needed than at this moment, and has never been so heeded as it will be in the present crisis."

2. Daniel O'Connell (1775–1847), the Irish patriot and orator, was known as "the Liberator." He and Garrison became good friends. He joined other British antislavery leaders in signing the protest against the American Colonization Society which Garrison brought from his first visit to England in 1833, he favored the admission of women to the World's Antislavery Convention in London in 1840, and, at the end of 1841, his name headed the "Address of the Irish People to their Countrymen and Countrywomen in America" signed by 60,000 persons, which urged the American Irish to treat Negroes as equals and to join with the abolitionists in combatting slavery. (*Life*, I, 360–361, 376–377; II, 379–380; III, 43.)

3. From O'Connell's speech delivered at Exeter Hall, London, on Saturday morning, July 13, 1833, on the occasion of Garrison's first visit to England. For a description of the address and a quotation from it, see *Life*, I, 376–377.

4. Proverbs 1:16, slightly altered.

5. Isaiah 61:1 (the King James version; the Jewish Publication Society version has "eyes" instead of "prison").

6. Isaiah 28:15.

7. The Wilmot Proviso was introduced in the House by David Wilmot, a Democrat of Pennsylvania, in August 1846 and February 1847, as an amendment to bills requested by President James K. Polk, for the purchase of Mexican territory outside of Texas. The amendment provided that "neither slavery nor involuntary servitude shall ever exist in any part of said territory, except for crime, whereof the party shall first be duly convicted." The amendment passed the House, but failed both times in the Senate. Thereafter, until the Civil War, the Wilmot Proviso was brought up and debated from time to time, whenever new territories were to be organized.

8. Shakespeare, *Macbeth*, V, v, 27.

2

TO HELEN E. GARRISON

New York, May 7, 1850,
Tuesday Morning.

My Dear Wife:

I arrived here safely yesterday afternoon at 4 o'clock,[1] in company with Phillips,[2] Francis and Edmund Jackson,[3] Mr. May[4] and his mother,[5] Mr. Hovey,[6] and other dear anti-slavery friends. The rain, which was pouring down so copiously when we left Boston, accompanied us nearly all the distance, an immense quantity having fallen over a wide tract of country.

At Springfield, I was happy to see Mr. McKinley,[7] who had just returned from Northampton, and was on his way to this city. He greatly relieved my mind by informing me that brother George[8] had not been ill, though he gave no reason why G. had not written or visited Boston, and I did not care to press him on business matters. Some of the family had been vaccinated, and accordingly a little unwell. He said that George intended to see you in the course of two or three days, and perhaps would be in New York before the termination of our anniversary meetings.

In the course of another hour, I shall be on my way to our meeting at the Tabernacle,[9] "bound in the spirit," as Paul said of old, "not knowing the things that shall befall me there," saving that "bonds and afflictions abide with me, in every city"; though "none of these things move me, neither count I my life dear unto me,"[10] in comparison with the sacred cause to which I have so long been consecrated. That our meeting will be a stormy one, I have very little doubt — perhaps brutal and riotous in the extreme; — for Bennett,[11] in each number of his infamous Herald, for a week, has been publishing the most atrocious and inflammatory articles respecting us, avowedly to have us put down by mobocratic violence; and it will be strange indeed, if, with his almost omnipotent influence over all the mobocratic elements in this city, we are permitted to meet without imminent personal peril. Bennett has aimed to hold me up as a special object of vengeance; and thus I am doomed to go, under circumstances of peculiar trial and danger. It is evident that, as long as our meetings are held, he is determined to set the mob upon us; with what temporary success, will soon appear.[12] As to the final result of all this, there can be no doubt. It is the prerogative of the God whom we serve to cause the wrath of man to praise him, and the remainder of wrath to restrain.

Here I must pause. We are all in the hands of a good Father, for time and eternity.

2 o'clock, P.M.

Well, we have had our meeting,[13] and, thus far, thank God, all goes well, even triumphantly with us; notwithstanding the desperate efforts of the New York papers to get up a ferocious mob against us. Not that we have not had a very tumultuous, nay, even stormy time; the ocean of feeling has been lashed into a fury, but the proud waves were stayed, and a song of deliverance is in our mouths. I have not time, of course, to give you the particulars. The Tabernacle was crowded beyond all precedent. Every thing proceeded, for a time, very peaceably. I read a portion of the Scriptures — [14] prayer was offered by Henry Grew [15] — and I proceeded to make my speech about the religion of the country; [16] when, at last, the pent up feelings of the mobocrats broke out, and with the notorious Capt. Rynders [17] at their head, they came rushing on to the platform, yelling, cheering, swearing, &c. &c. But, after much tumult, and many interruptions, I got through with my speech — then Mr. Furness made a capital speech [18] — then an opponent spoke [19] — then Douglass [20] & Saml. Ward [21] —and we wound up with electrical effect. Wendell [Phillips] had no time to speak. But the mail will close instanter. No part of this for the press. The N. Y. papers will tell the story to-morrow.[22]

Lovingly yours,

W. L. G.

ALS: Garrison Papers, Boston Public Library; it is also printed, in part, in *Life*, III, 284–286.

For further information about Garrison's wife, the former Helen Eliza Benson, see the introductory sketch of the Benson family in Volume II.

1. Garrison and his friends were in New York to attend the sixteenth annual meeting of the American Anti-Slavery Society, called for Tuesday, May 7, 1850, to continue for three days, at the Broadway Tabernacle in New York City. The call to the meeting was signed by Garrison as president of the society, and by Wendell Phillips and Sydney Howard Gay as secretaries. (*The Liberator*, April 26, 1850.)

2. Wendell Phillips was Garrison's friend and co-worker (see *Letters*, I, II, and III, *passim*).

3. Francis Jackson, Garrison's close friend and collaborator, was at this time vice-president and treasurer of the American Anti-Slavery Society and president of both the annual New England Anti-Slavery Convention and the Massachusetts Anti-Slavery Society (see biographical sketch in Letters, II, xxv). His brother, Edmund Jackson (b. Newton, Massachusetts, January 9, 1795; d. Boston, April 15, 1875), was a well-to-do soap and candle manufacturer, a Garrisonian abolitionist who contributed frequently to *The Liberator*. (Abner Forbes and J. W. Greene, *The Rich Men of Massachusetts*, 2d ed., Boston, 1852, p. 37; *Life*, III, 114; IV, 387.)

4. The Reverend Samuel May, Jr. (b. Boston, April 11, 1810; d. Leicester,

Massachusetts, November 24, 1899), cousin of Samuel J. May, graduated from Harvard College in 1829, studied theology with Samuel J. May, and graduated from Harvard Divinity School in 1833; he was minister of the Unitarian Congregational Church at Leicester, Massachusetts, from 1834 to 1846 when his antislavery activities led to his resignation. He had entered the antislavery movement early in his ministry, had attended the 1840 annual meeting of the American Anti-Slavery Society as a Garrisonian, and had become the general agent of the Massachusetts Anti-Slavery Society in June 1847, a position which he held until the close of the antislavery struggle. He served in the Massachusetts House of Representatives in 1875, was a member of the Leicester School Board, a trustee of Leicester Academy, and librarian of the Leicester Library. He was an ardent disunionist and Garrison's supporter until the very end. In 1866, he collected more than $30,000 as a national testimonial to Garrison. Garrison's sons dedicated the *Life* to May with the following inscription: "To Samuel May, of Leicester, Massachusetts, who freed from toil and care the declining years of William Lloyd Garrison, this work is gratefully and affectionately inscribed." (Samuel May, John Wilder May, John Joseph May, *A Genealogy of the Descendants of John May*, Boston, 1878, pp. 31–32; *Life*, I, 423; II, 348; III, 187, 224; IV, 396 *et passim.*)

5. Mary Goddard May (b. Brookline, Massachusetts, December 15, 1787; d. Boston, March 17, 1882) was the second daughter of Joseph and Mary Goddard of Brookline. At fourteen, she was taken into the home of her uncle, Nathaniel Goddard of Boston. She married Samuel May (1776–1870) of Boston in 1809. He was a merchant and manufacturer, as well as a philanthropist. He was overseer of the poor in Boston for many years, an officer of the Boston Dispensary; he helped establish the Massachusetts Asylum for the Blind and was one of the original proprietors of the Boston Athenaeum. Mary Goddard May was an early sponsor of the temperance, antislavery, and woman's rights movements, a supporter of Garrison and an associate of Maria Weston Chapman, Lydia Maria Child, and other antislavery women. (*A Genealogy of the Descendants of John May*, pp. 15–16; *Life*, IV, 396.)

6. Charles Fox Hovey (b. South Brookfield, Massachusetts, February 28, 1807; d. Boston, April 28, 1859) was described by Edmund Quincy as follows in 1848 in a private letter: "A rich, money-making merchant [of Boston], at the same time a thorough-going Garrisonian. He came into the cause some three years ago, by the way of Democracy, Free Trade, Hard Money, No Monopoly, Freedom of Public Land, etc. Finding out that all the political parties were equally selfish and unprincipled, and really wishing to do some good in the world, he bethought himself of anti-slavery, and the first thing he did was to call and make Mrs. Chapman's acquaintance, and give her fifty dollars for the Fair. Having thus come in at the gate and not over the wall, he was soon in line with us, and is now as thoroughly one of the *Cab* as if he had always belonged to it. He is a member of the American and Mass. Boards, and is always ready with his money, and has no reverences of any kind. He began by being a Come-outer. He is one of the best of fellows. A thorough man of business, managing a very large concern and making plenty of money, without being the slave of business or money." (Quoted in *Life*, III, 220–221n, from MS. October 3, 1848; see also IV, 386.)

Hovey was a descendant of Daniel Hovey, one of the earliest settlers of Ipswich, Massachusetts. On coming to Boston in 1829, he became a bookkeeper in the store of Howe, Dorr & Co., and thereafter proved himself to be one of the most enterprising and successful merchants of Boston. His obituary in *The Liberator*, May 6, 1859, notes: "He went many times to Europe on business, and resided several years in Paris and Rome. His summer residence was for many years in Gloucester, and for the last five years in Framingham. He died at his mansion-house in Kingston-street, Boston, on the evening of the 28th April, 1859, aged 52 years and two months, leaving a wife and four sons." See also the "Tribute of Respect" to Hovey adopted in a series of resolutions by the Board of Managers of the Massachusetts Anti-Slavery Society on Tuesday, May 3, 1859, as well as the texts of the eulogies by Garrison and Wendell Phillips, at his funeral on May 2, 1859. (*The Liberator*, May 6, 1859.)

7. Unidentified.

8. George W. Benson was the brother of Garrison's wife, Helen. George and his family were then living in Northampton, Massachusetts. For a biography of George Benson, see the introductory biographical sketch in Volume II.

9. "The Tabernacle was a Congregational place of worship, on the northeast corner of Broadway and Anthony (now Worth) Street. The revivalist [C. G.] Finney had formerly preached there. It was a large hall, nearly square, on the ground floor, with a gentle descent from the entrance. The platform faced this entrance, with tiers of seats rising rearward to the organ, and then merging with those of the gallery, which rested on four great pillars." (*Life*, III, 286.)

10. Acts 20:22–24, slightly altered.

11. James Gordon Bennett (1795–1872) was a newspaper editor; born in Scotland, he came to New York in 1822. After a variety of newspaper ventures, in 1835 he founded the New York *Herald*, of which he became the proprietor and editor. Bennett had an instinct for sensational news, which soon gave his paper great popularity. He was proslavery in his views, violently antiabolitionist, and so reactionary that he even regarded colonizationists as "species of abolitionists." He helped to incite more than one riot against the abolitionists. (*Life*, III, 281–286, 306, 393; Leonard L. Richards, "*Gentlemen of Property and Standing,*" *Anti-Abolition Mobs in Jacksonian America*, New York, 1970, pp. 9–10, 16, 18, 29.)

12. *The Liberator* (May 10, 1850) reprinted several editorial extracts from the *Herald*. One such extract read, in part, as follows:

"The merchants, men of business, and men of property, in this city, should frown down the meetings of these mad people, if they would save themselves. What right have all the religious lunatics of the free states to gather in this commercial city for purposes which, if carried into effect, would ruin and destroy its prosperity? Will the men of sense allow meetings to be held in this city, which are calculated to make our country the arena of blood and murder, and render our city an object of horror to the whole South? We hope not. Public opinion should be regulated. These abolitionists should not be allowed to misrepresent New York. . . . All who are opposed to having our city disgraced should go there, speak their views, and prevent it."

13. For a very good, detailed account of the meeting that afternoon and of the entire convention, see *Life*, III, 281–300. The accounts in John L. Thomas, *The Liberator: William Lloyd Garrison* (Boston and Toronto, 1963), pp. 362–366, and Walter Merrill, *Against Wind and Tide, A Biography of William Lloyd Garrison* (Cambridge, Massachusetts, 1963), pp. 257–261, are based, essentially, upon the account in *Life*.

14. Garrison, as president of the American Anti-Slavery Society and, therefore, "the central figure of the meetings," "was resolved to avoid all outward singularity. For this reason he abandoned for good the turn-down collar which he had clung to through all the changes of fashion, and put on the stand-up collar of the day. Surrounded on the platform by the flower of the Massachusetts Board and by the speakers agreed upon, he entered calmly upon his duties to the Society and to the vast assembly about him. In front, he saw a most respectable company of men and women; behind and above him he felt the organized and impending mob." (*Life*, III, 286. The observation about the change in collar was related by Garrison to his son William. *Ibid.*)

The portion of the Scriptures that he read consisted of numerous excerpts from different books of the Bible. It opened with Isaiah 3:13: "The Lord standeth up to plead, and standeth to judge the peoples" (*The Liberator*, May 24, 1850). A part of the portion read is to be found in *Life*, III, 287, reprinted from *The Liberator* of May 24.

15. The Reverend Henry Grew (b. Birmingham, England, December 25, 1781; d. Philadelphia, August 8, 1862), a "conservative abolitionist" of Philadelphia, was

a delegate from Philadelphia to the World's Anti-Slavery Convention in London in 1840, where he opposed the seating of women, although his daughter Mary was also a delegate to the convention. At the end of 1840, he withdrew his subscription to *The Liberator*. *Weld-Grimké Letters*, I, 477n, characterizes him as a minister in the Society of Friends. However, in a letter published in the *National Anti-Slavery Standard*, on May 23, 1850, Grew writes to Sydney H. Gay, "some editors have erroneously stated that I am 'of the Society of Friends.' I am connected, I hope, with all the true friends of God and Man, but with no religious sect." An obituary notice in *The Liberator* of August 15, 1862 read: "For thirty years, our revered friend was the uncompromising advocate of 'the cause of all such as are appointed to destruction' in our land, and both with his voice and pen vindicated the safety and duty of immediate and unconditional emancipation. He was of a deeply religious nature, eminently conscientious and upright in all his ways, warm in his sympathies for suffering humanity in its various phases, generous in the distribution of his charities, and truly a good man, whose constant aim it was to glorify God and bless his fellow-men. In all theological matters he was an independent thinker, true to his convictions, however unpopular they might be, anxious only to know and cherish the truth, and a preacher of practical righteousness. He was widely known, revered and beloved." (*Life*, II, 370; III, 266, 285, 298; *The Liberator*, January 1, 1841.)

16. A summary of Garrison's speech and of the events that followed appeared in the New York *Herald* on May 8, 1850. It was reprinted in the *National Anti-Slavery Standard*, May 16, 1850, with the comment that "it is a faithful and true account of the proceedings of the mob," and in *The Liberator*, May 17, 1850.

17. Isaiah Rynders (1804–1884), a Tammany Hall politician and muscle man, had been a boatman on the Hudson River, a professional gambler in the Southwest and, after returning to New York City, had become active politically in Tammany Hall. He opened a sporting house which became a Democratic "rendezvous and the headquarters of the Empire Club, an organization of roughs and desperadoes who acknowledged his 'captaincy.' " As a reward for his part in the victory of the Democrats in the presidential election of 1844, he was given the office of weigher in the New York City Custom-house, a position which he lost as a result of the Whig victory in 1848. He exhibited notable ability in breaking up meetings and creating riots as needed, and although arrested for assaulting a gentleman in a hotel was not prosecuted because of the failure of his victim and witnesses to testify against him. (*Life*, III, 290–291; IV, 409.)

18. Mr. Furness' speech was reprinted in its entirety in *The Liberator*, May 24, 1850.

The Reverend William Henry Furness (1802–1896), Boston-born and Harvard-educated, had served in Philadelphia since 1825 as minister of the Unitarian Church founded by Joseph Priestley in 1796. He became its pastor emeritus in 1875. Although his antislavery views may be traced to the mid-1820's, he first began to preach publicly against slavery in 1839 and continued to do so until its abolition. A close friend of abolitionists in Philadelphia and elsewhere, including James and Lucretia Mott, Garrison, and others, still he never joined an antislavery organization. The passage of the Fugitive Slave Act in 1850 evoked his public condemnation and the announcement that he would oppose the law, regardless of consequences. Several years later, in May 1856, Charles Sumner, after being brutally beaten on the floor of the Senate, came to Furness' home to recuperate. In 1859, after John Brown's attack on Harpers Ferry, he spoke at meetings organized in support of Brown and his family. In addition to his antislavery efforts, Furness was interested in the story of the life of Jesus as a historical figure and was one of the first American scholars to study and translate German literature. His books included *Remarks on the Four Gospels* (1836), *Jesus and his Biographers* (1838), and *A History of Jesus* (1850). (Elizabeth M. Geffen, "W. H. Furness, Philadelphia Antislavery Preacher," *The Pennsylvania Magazine of History and Biography*, 82:259–292, July 1958.)

19. A "Professor" or "Dr." Grant; the official report of the proceedings, printed in *The National Anti-Slavery Standard* (May 16, 1850), notes: "The latter part of Mr. Garrison's speech was frequently interrupted, and, during the speeches which succeeded his, the tumult increased so much that the speakers' voices were often entirely inaudible.

"The President repeatedly invited the opponents of the Society to take the platform and meet argument with argument.

"At the close of Mr. Furness' speech, Dr. Grant, a champion selected by the mob, addressed the audience in an elaborate speech designed to prove, by physiological argument, that the Negro is not a man.

"Frederick Douglass and Samuel R. Ward replied to him."

Life (III, 294) refers to "Dr. Grant" and his speech as follows: "Up rose, as per agreement, one 'Professor' Grant, a seedy-looking personage, having one hand tied round with a dirty cotton cloth. Mr. Garrison recognized him as a former pressman in the *Liberator* office. His thesis was that blacks were not men, but belonged to the monkey tribe. His speech proved dull and tiresome, and was made sport of by his own set, whom Mr. Garrison had to call to order."

20. Frederick Douglass (b. Talbot County, Maryland, February 1817; d. near Washington, D.C., February 20, 1895) was a former slave and a great Negro orator, author, and leader of his people. He had escaped from slavery in 1838 and lived in New Bedford for two or three years, where he married and worked as a day laborer. In 1841, at an antislavery meeting at Nantucket, he delivered a speech which was so well received that he was invited to be an agent of the Massachusetts Anti-Slavery Society. He accepted and remained in the post for four years. He went to Europe in 1845, lecturing in England, Ireland, Scotland, and Wales. Returning in 1847, he began publication at Rochester, New York, of *Frederick Douglass's Paper*, later changed to *The North Star*. Although the circumstances surrounding the establishment of the paper strained his relations somewhat with Garrison, the final break between the two antislavery leaders came in the early 1850's with Douglass' support of the Liberty party and his opposition to disunionism. (*Life*, III and IV, *passim*; *HEUSH.*)

21. The Reverend Samuel Ringgold Ward (b. October 17, 1817; d. 1866[?]) achieved freedom with the escape of his parents from slavery when he was aged three. Through the aid of Gerrit Smith he received a liberal education in the classics and theology. He entered the ministry in the Presbyterian church and for several years (1841–1843) he served a white congregation at South Butler, New York, and a congregation at Cortland, New York, from 1846 to 1851. Through the influence of Lewis Tappan, whom he impressed as a public speaker, he was appointed an agent of the American Anti-Slavery Society in 1839 and was soon transferred to the New York Anti-Slavery Society. From 1840 to the passage of the Fugitive Slave Law of 1850, he devoted much of his time to lecturing and preaching in the antislavery cause, primarily in western and central New York. A tall, black man, measuring six feet in height, with a strong voice and great energy, he was an impressive figure on the platform and "one of the most prominent Negroes of the critical period of our history, from 1830 to 1860." In 1851, after taking part in the rescue of a fugitive slave, Jerry, in Syracuse, he fled to Canada and became an agent of the Anti-Slavery Society of Canada. In April 1853 he traveled to England, whence he went to Jamaica (about 1855), where he remained until his death in or about 1866. He was the author of *Autobiography of a Fugitive Negro* (London, 1855) and *Reflections Upon the Gordon Rebellion* (Jamaica, 1866). (Carter G. Woodson, *Negro Orators and their Orations*, Washington, D.C., 1925, p. 193n; Carter G. Woodson and Charles H. Wesley, *The Negro in Our History*, 11th ed., further revised and enlarged, Washington, D.C., 1966, pp. 277–278.)

22. *The Liberator* (May 10, 1850) reprinted a short account of the meeting from the New York *Journal of Commerce*. In its issue of May 17, *The Liberator* devoted its first two pages to reports of the convention from various New York newspapers, and most of the third page to abolitionist accounts and evaluations of

the proceedings. The issue of May 24, 1850, included most of the official account of the proceedings and the transcript of the Reverend William Henry Furness' speech at the convention.

3

TO THE EDITOR OF THE NEW YORK *TRIBUNE*

Boston, Monday, May 13, 1850.

To the Editor of the N. Y. Tribune:

Sir — After a band of rioters has been allowed to trample with impunity upon all law and order in your city, it is not surprising that an anonymous writer, in the Tribune of Friday last,[1] should attempt to screen the city authorities from all blame in the premises. The facts are strictly these: Both the high sheriff[2] and the chief of police,[3] by their own confession, were instructed by the mayor[4] not to make any arrest, nor to do aught to suppress the disturbance, until personal violence had been committed; and in the interview which the venerable Isaac T. Hopper[5] had with the Mayor on the morning of the Tabernacle meeting, the latter declared (in substance) that no amount of uproar and outrage, short of actual assault and battery, constituted a breach of the peace, or authorized his official interference.[6] This the rioters perfectly understood, and therefore were emboldened to persevere in their most indecent and insulting conduct. How much they feared, or had reason to fear, being arrested, was shown by the fact, that at the meeting held in the Library Room on Wednesday forenoon, when they were hooting, screeching, yelling, threatening and blaspheming, almost without cessation, the inquiry was made from the chair, by request, 'Is the chief of police in the hall?' to which Rynders responded derisively, 'Oh don't! don't! you'll frighten us all to death!' — the sovereign mob responding with shouts of laughter! There were present some thirty or forty of the police, besides Mr. Matsell and the high sheriff; and then it was, in the presence of these sworn conservators of the peace of the city, and with their approbation, I announced, under protest, that the proprietors of the building felt compelled to refuse us further occupancy of it, for fear of the rioters, especially on account of the imminent peril in which the Public Library was placed.

As the presiding officer of the meeting held in the Tabernacle, I am represented by your correspondent as having said to the Chief of Police, 'We do not want Rynders removed. We have invited him, and his friend, Mr. Grant, to address us, and we are willing to hear them.'

Again I am represented as not objecting to the presence of Rynders and his followers; 'especially as the disturbance, so far from being an injury, would prove a benefit.' This is sheer caricature. Toward the close of the meeting, after two hours of violent interruption and great confusion, and during the speech of Mr. Douglass, when that gifted man had effectually put to shame his assailants by his wit and eloquence, Mr. Matsell did say to me, in a whisper, that he would remove Rynders, whenever I demanded it, in case he proceeded to commit any further violence. My reply was, that I hoped we should be able to conclude the proceedings without rendering such a step necessary. But I regarded the offer of assistance under such circumstances as little better than a mockery, and made only to save appearances.

Happily, the members of the American A. S. Society are deeply imbued with the spirit of peace as well as of liberty, and believe in overcoming evil with good; for, abandoned as they were to the insults and outrages of the mob by the city authorities, had they resorted to violence in self-defence, the most deplorable consequences might have followed.

That I uttered the calm conviction, that an assault so brutal and unjustifiable would aid, instead of injuring, the sacred cause of emancipation, true; but, of course, not with any gratification at such an outrage, in itself considered. I am fully persuaded of the truth of the scriptural declaration, that the God of justice will 'cause the wrath of man to praise him, and the remainder of wrath he will restrain.' [7]

Requesting an insertion of this correction in the Tribune, at your earliest convenience, I remain.

Yours, for all that is free, just and equal,

WM. LLOYD GARRISON.

Printed in *The Liberator*, May 17, 1850. The letter appears undated in *The Liberator*, but is reprinted in the *Pennsylvania Freeman* with the dateline "Boston, Monday, May 13, 1850."

Horace Greeley (1811–1872) was editor of the *Tribune*, which he had established in 1841 and which he edited until his death. The *Tribune* was at first Whig, then antislavery Whig, and finally Republican.

1. The item referred to appeared in the New York *Tribune* on Friday, May 10, 1850. It read, in part, as follows: ". . . On Tuesday morning, the occasion of the first interruption, the Chief of Police was sent to the building with instructions from the Mayor to preserve order and, if necessary, to remove the disturbers. The Chief, on reaching the scene, found the officers of the Society in a parley with Rynders and his gang, and inviting them to address the meeting. Rynders and his followers were shouting, calling on Mr. Grant to address the meeting. Mr. Garrison and others said that Mr. Grant should have a chance to speak, and that they invited him and other opponents to reply. The Chief of Police informed the President (Mr. Garrison) that he was there to protect them, that he would remove

the disturbers if the President desired it, and that the regular order of proceeding should not be interfered with.

". . . Mr. Garrison gave the Chief of Police to understand that he, as President of the Society, did not object to the presence of Rynders and his followers, and especially that this disturbance, so far from being an injury, should prove a benefit. Under these circumstances, what could the Chief of Police do? Mr. Garrison, as President of the Society, had the control of the house, and Mr. Garrison gave the Chief of Police to understand that the services of the Police were not wanted, and that they did not want the disturbance quelled.

"At the close of the first meeting, all persons so disposed were, and Mr. Rynders especially by name, was invited to attend their meeting in the evening.

"The Police could not then prevent Rynders and his gang from attending the meeting; and, being present at the meeting by invitation, the Police could not direct Rynders and his men in their mode of proceeding.

"The Abolitionists were told that if they wanted those disturbers excluded it should be done, and when, on Wednesday, they expressed a desire to meet by themselves without interruption from their opponents, they were fully protected. The Mayor, then, on Wednesday afternoon, gave the Chief of Police instructions to that effect, and on Wednesday night a strong force was on duty ready at a moment's notice to protect both of the Abolition meetings held that night. No disturbance was permitted to be given that night. Had Garrison on Tuesday morning taken the same ground, and said, 'We do not want these disturbers here,' they would have been removed at once. But these disturbers, having been present by invitation and encouragement, and being invited also to address the meeting, the Mayor and Chief of Police could not do otherwise than allow Rynders to remain, and prevent him and all others from acts of violence, which was effectually done."

The *Tribune*, in an editorial comment on Garrison's letter, stated, "We consider the above considerably worse than no excuse at all. . . . The fact that the Garrisonians invited their adversaries to attend and speak, and cheerfully accorded them a patient hearing, only gave the strangers a clearer, stronger right to protection and hospitality. If their adversaries had had the magnanimity of brutes they could not have interrupted and broken up the meeting of men who had treated them so graciously.

"No, there is no excuse, there can be none, for the conduct of our Authorities in suffering the meetings of Tuesday night and Wednesday to be broken up, and especially the latter, after the fair notice given of the ruffians' designs through the medium of the former. No matter what Mr. Garrison or any body else may have thought or said . . . the peace and order of our city should have been preserved, if only for the sake of the women who were subjected to beastly insult from the ribaldry of the rioters. Whoever is culpable in the premises ought to resign forthwith or be ejected from his office. We should be glad to know distinctly whether the Mayor did or did not give the requisite orders to the Chief of Police to protect the assembled people from riot and outrage. That the Chief was grossly derelict we have no doubt; we only wish to know whether he was so of his own motion or for want of the necessary orders."

2. Thomas Carnley, a resident of Carmonsville, New York, was high sheriff of New York City from 1850 to 1852. (D. T. Valentine, *Manual of the Corporation of the City of New York*, New York, 1850, 1851, 1852.)

3. George W. Matsell (b. New York City, 1807; d. there, July 25, 1877), the son of an Englishman who was a tailor, went to sea as a youth, returned and opened a bookstore on Chatham Street in New York City. He gained notoriety for the heretical nature of his books, which included the works of Thomas Paine, Frances Wright, Robert Dale Owen, and the like. His bookstore became a rendezvous for the freethinkers of the day. Active as a Democrat in politics, he was appointed a police justice. In 1845, a year after its organization, he was appointed chief of the municipal police force. He was forced to resign in 1857, following a

conflict in jurisdiction between the municipal police force and the metropolitan commissioners, and retired to a farm in Iowa, where he edited the *National Police Gazette* with William MacKellar. Emerging from private life in 1873, he returned to New York wheer he became superintendent of police from 1873 to 1875. Thereafter he practiced law until his death. (*New York Times*, July 26, 1877.)

4. Caleb S. Woodhull (b. Long Island, 1792; d. there, 1866) graduated from Yale in 1811, studied law with George W. Strong, was admitted to the New York bar as counsellor-at-law in 1817, and was elected in 1836 to the New York City Common Council, where he represented Ward 2 for eight years. He was president of the Board of Aldermen and the Common Council in 1843 and was elected mayor of New York City in the spring of 1849, continuing in office until January 1851, when he retired from political life. (Mary Gould Woodhull and Francis Bowes Stevens, *Woodhull Genealogy*, Philadelphia, 1904, pp. 324–325.)

5. Isaac Tatem Hopper (b. Deptford Township, Gloucester County, New Jersey, December 3, 1771; d. New York City, May 7, 1852) learned the tailor's trade in Philadelphia, where he lived until 1829. There he joined the Quakers and became a Hicksite. He also joined the Pennsylvania Abolition Society, becoming known as an active opponent of slavery, helper of fugitive slaves, and friend of the free Negro. His other reform and philanthropic activities included help to the poor, apprentices, prisoners, the sick, and the insane. In 1829 he moved to New York, where he managed a Hicksite bookstore. After visiting Ireland and England in 1830, he returned to New York, where he became especially active in the work of the Prison Association. He was treasurer and book-agent for the American Anti-Slavery Society from 1841 to 1845, and thereafter devoted most of his time to the Prison Association. His daughter, Abigail Hopper, married James S. Gibbons, a New York abolitionist, friend of Garrison, and an early supporter of the *National Anti-Slavery Standard*. For further information and numerous anecdotes about Hopper, see L. Maria Child, *Isaac T. Hopper, A True Life* (Boston, 1860).

Two accounts by Hopper of his interviews with the mayor and the chief of police, in an attempt to prevent disruption of the meetings, are to be found in letters to the *Tribune*, subsequently reprinted in *The Liberator*, May 31, 1850, and July 5, 1850.

6. Hopper, in his letter "To the Editor of the Tribune," dated May 16, 1850, and printed in *The Liberator*, May 31, 1850, quotes the following from his interview with the mayor:

"Mayor — I have no power to interfere unless they commit violence.

"H. — If we should adjourn to some future time, wilt thou send a sufficient force to keep those rioters out of the meeting; or if they are suffered to come in, to preserve order?

"Mayor — I have no authority to interfere unless violence is committed. I have often been called upon to interfere in political meetings, but I would not interfere in any of those cases, because I have no authority to do so.

"H. — Is every public meeting similar to ours liable to be broken up by a rabble?

"Mayor — I have no authority to prevent it."

For an additional account of the efforts of abolitionists to secure police protection for the maintenance of order at the meeting, see the letter by S. H. Gay, an officer of the American Anti-Slavery Society and editor of the *National Anti-Slavery Standard*, to the editor of the *Tribune*, undated, printed in the *Standard*, May 16, 1850.

7. Psalms 76:10.

4

TO THE EDITOR OF THE BOSTON *TRANSCRIPT*

[May 17, 1850.]

To the Editor of the Boston Transcript: —

SIR — Of the numberless public misrepresentations which are made of my sentiments and purposes, either through ignorance or malignity, it is very seldom I am induced to take the slightest notice. The pages of the Liberator, for the last nineteen years, bear witness, that I have voluntarily published hundreds of columns of the most defamatory matter against myself personally, without uttering a word in self-defence; so conscious have I been of the rectitude of my course, and the purity of my intentions. But I am moved to depart from my usual habit, in such cases, by a communication which appeared in the Transcript of Tuesday,[1] under the signature of 'SIGMA';[2] first, because the author of it claims to be a gentleman and a Christian — on what grounds I know not; and, secondly, because his attack is made in connection with a speech recently delivered by me in New York, which has been wickedly perverted or stupidly misapprehended in various quarters.

'SIGMA' is so certain that I am 'guilty of blasphemy, under the statute of this Commonwealth,' that he magnanimously declares himself to be incapacitated, alas! as a juryman to try me on that indictment. He says, 'it is well known (!) that Mr. Garrison has, upon various public occasions, discharged upon the community impudent and disgusting blasphemy'; — and, again, 'the good people of the State are forgetting, for a time, the furious and frantic abolition of Mr. Garrison, in his audacious and abominable blasphemy.' He quotes, for my admonition, the following section in the Revised Statutes of Massachusetts, printing in Italics the passage which he deems applicable to my particular transgression: —

'If any person shall wilfully blaspheme the holy name of God, by denying, cursing, or contumeliously reproaching Jesus Christ, or the Holy Ghost, or by cursing or contumeliously reproaching the Holy Word of God, contained in the Holy Scriptures, *or exposing them to contempt and ridicule,* he shall be punished by imprisonment in the State prison, not more than two years, or in the county jail, not more than one year, or by fine, not exceeding three hundred dollars, and may also be bound to good behavior.' — *Mass. Revised Statutes, Chap.* 130, *Sec.* 15.

Under this section, 'SIGMA' says he shall be pleased, on a repetition of my offence, 'to find the Grand Inquest performing a very simple and intelligible duty'!

Now, Mr. Editor, like Paul, when 'the Jews laid many and grievous complaints against him,' [3] I say — 'I have done no wrong; but If I be an offender, or have committed any thing worthy of death, I refuse not to die.' [4] At any moment I am ready for the trial, whether before Cesar or 'the Grand Inquest.'

This charge of 'blasphemy' is as old as religious persecution, and has been the pretext of bigots and formalists, in all ages, for consigning to the prison or the stake, the purest and best spirits of their times. The prophets were blasphemers — Jesus and his apostles were blasphemers — Wickliffe, and Huss, and Luther,[5] were blasphemers. In all those instances, it meant, — as it now means, — the arraignment and condemnation of the leaders of the people, — the prophets that prophesy falsely, and the priests that bear rule by their means; the impeachment of the popular religion as hollow, polluted, oppressive, inhuman, murderous; disgust at the offering of incense, the observance of the new moons and sabbaths, the calling of assemblies, the gathering of solemn meetings, the appointment of feasts, the multiplication of fastings and prayers, while 'none calleth for justice, nor any pleadeth for truth; the act of violence is in their hands; their feet run to evil, and they make haste to shed innocent blood; and *he that departeth from evil maketh himself a prey.'* [6] In this sense, and to this extent, I am a blasphemer; in such company I am not ashamed to be found. 'If they have called the master of the house Beelzebub, how much more shall they call those of his household? It is enough for the disciple that he is as his master, and the servant as his lord.' [7]

'Sigma' is an adept at the use of opprobrious epithets; but, one thing the readers of his libellous article will do me the justice to remember, and that is, he does not quote a single *sentence or word from my lips to sustain his 'blasphemous' allegation.* For more than twenty years, I have been before the public as an editor and a lecturer; and during all that time, I challenge 'Sigma' to produce any thing from my pen or lips irreverent toward God, derogatory to the character of Jesus, or hostile to pure and undefiled religion. What crime have I winked at, what popular iniquity shrunk from rebuking, what cross refused to bear, what peril avoided, what sacrifice in the cause of down-trodden humanity been unwilling to make? Has not my life been devoted to the promotion of all that is pure, lovely, beneficent, and Christ-like? And is it to my shame, or to my praise, that I have fiercely arrayed against me all that is profligate, brutal, profane, lawless, and tyrannical, on the one hand — and all that is cowardly, time-serving, bigoted and hypocritical, on the other? I am feared, execrated, anathematized, threatened by those who 'trade in slaves and the souls of men' [8] — who insult, degrade and trample upon the image of God — who systematically violate every command in the Decalogue, and every precept in the Gospel: — is this an evidence of my impiety? They have set a price upon my head: — does that prove my recreancy to the cause of liberty? I am trusted, beloved, honored, blessed by the oppressed, the forsaken, those who are 'peeled, meted out, and trodden under foot': [9] — does this indicate that I am a dangerous member of society? The patient, tender-hearted, yet persecuted Job deemed it good evidence of his acceptance with God, that he espoused the cause of the oppressed, and succored the perishing: — 'When the ear heard me, then it blessed me; and when the eye saw me, it gave witness to me: because I delivered the poor that cried, and the fatherless, and him that had none to help him. I was eyes to the blind, and feet was I to the lame. I was a father to the poor: and the cause which I knew not, I searched out. And I brake the jaws of the wicked, and plucked the spoil out of his teeth.' [10] But what was his treatment, at the hands of others? 'He teareth me in his wrath, who hateth me; he gnasheth upon me with his teeth; mine enemy sharpeneth his eyes upon me. They have gaped upon me with their mouth; they have smitten me upon the cheek reproachfully; they have gathered themselves together against me, but not for any injustice in my hands. Behold, my witness is in heaven, and my record is on high.' [11]

'SIGMA' refers to my 'late blasphemy at New York,' but makes no quotation. My speech moves his choler, and stirs within him a holy rage surpassed only by that which was expressed by that notorious profligate and rioter, 'Capt. ISAIAH RYNDERS,' who, with his nefarious confederates, day after day invaded the anti-slavery meetings in New York, uttering imprecations and threats against the non-resisting friends of the slave, and behaving in a most beastly manner.

'Rynders,' says the New York Courier and Enquirer,[12] 'seemed to be in a violent passion; probably his feelings were much wounded at hearing Daniel Webster [13] and *the Christian religion* treated with evident disrespect'!!! The patron and representative of the brothels, rum-holes and gambling hells of the 'Five Points,' [14] side by side with 'SIGMA,' rushing in furious haste to rescue the Christian religion and 'our glorious Union'!! *Par nobile fratrum!* [15]

What shall be said of the fairness or honor of the man, who takes a garbled report of a speech from a paper intensely hostile to the speaker, and, assuming it to be authentic, makes it the occasion of scattering in this community the most unjust and inflammatory comments upon it? Is this doing as he would be done by? Can any thing be more despicable? What I said at New York was comprehensively this — that the popular tests of piety, in this nation, were of no significance, and proved nothing of love to God or man, because 'the offence of the cross' [16] has ceased, and it is every where safe and reputable to embrace them. Is this 'blasphemy,' or the utterance of an undeniable fact? I said that a profession of faith in Jesus now costs nothing; for his praises are every where sung and his deeds are every where lauded, — by none more loudly than by those who enslave and imbrute their fellow-men; and, therefore, this is no longer a true test of piety. Can this be truthfully denied? Finally, I declared my faith in a Jesus who redeems, not enslaves; who binds up the broken-hearted, not crushes the weak; who goes for proclaiming liberty throughout all the land, not for perpetuating human thraldom — the Jesus who lived and suffered eighteen hundred years ago. Was that an impious sentiment? Had I not been riotously interrupted, my design was to have shown how striking has been the analogy between the Anti-Slavery movement in the United States, and the promulgation of primitive Christianity in Judea — both experiencing essentially the same treatment, despised and rejected of men, hooted by the rabble, denounced by the Scribes and Pharisees, persecuted by the rulers; their advocates accused of being 'pestilent and seditious fellows, seeking to turn the world upside down' [17] 'the filth of the earth and the offscouring of all things,' [18] — scourged, imprisoned, and in some cases put to an ignominious death, — accused of blasphemy, — 'in perils of robbers, in perils by their own countrymen, in perils in the city, in perils among false brethren,' [19] — approving themselves 'as ministers of God, in much patience, in afflictions, in necessities, in distresses, in stripes, in imprisonments, in tumults' [20] 'by evil and good report as deceivers and yet true, as unknown and yet well-known, as sorrowful yet always rejoicing, as chastened and not killed, as always delivered unto death for Jesus' sake, that the life of Jesus might be made manifest in their mortal flesh.' [21]

From time to time, old things pass away — all things become new. While, in this age and country, the recognition of Jesus, as the Messiah, subjects no one to shame, reproach or peril, eighteen centuries ago, in Judea, it cost every thing; and Jesus himself was crucified as an imposter and blasphemer. And still, in the person of THE SLAVE, is he despised, rejected.

'The cycles with their long shadows have stalked silently
    forward
Since those ancient days; many a pouch enwrapping meanwhile
Its fee, like that paid for the Son of Mary.

Look forth, Deliverer,
Look forth, First Born of the Dead,
Over the tree-tops of Paradise!
See thyself in yet continued bonds;
Toilsome and poor, thou bearest man's form again:
Thou art reviled, scourged, put into prison;
Hunted from the arrogant equality of the rest:
With slaves and swords throng the willing servants of
    authority;
Again they surround thee, mad with devilish spite —
Toward thee stretch the hands of a multitude, like vultures'
    talons;
The meanest spit in thy face — they smite thee with their palms;
Bruised, bloody and pinioned is thy body,
More sorrowful than death is thy soul.

Witness of anguish — Brother of Slaves,
Not with thy price closed the price of thine image;
And still Iscariot plies his trade.' [22]

What 'Sigma' means, by referring me to that portion of the Statute which relates to 'exposing the Holy Scriptures to contempt and ridicule,' I know not; but this I know, that, for twenty years, I have been vindicating the Bible from the foul charge of sanctioning the enslavement of a portion of the human race; and if this is to expose it to 'contempt and ridicule,' I must submit to the imputation without a murmur.

The episodes of 'Sigma' about Abner Kneeland [23] and Lord George Gordon [24] must be left without comment, as this communication is already somewhat extended. Its insertion in the Transcript I ask as a matter of simple justice.

WM. LLOYD GARRISON.

Boston, May 17, 1850.

Printed in *The Liberator*, May 24, 1850.
The letter appeared with the following heading and Biblical quotations:

REPLY TO THE 'BLASPHEMOUS' CHARGE
OF A FALSE ACCUSER.
'And, behold, certain of the scribes said within themselves, This man blasphemeth.' — *Matt.* ix.3.
'Then the high priest rent his clothes, saying, He hath spoken blasphemy: what further need have we of witnesses? Behold, now ye have heard his blasphemy. What think ye? They answered and said, He is guilty of death.' — *Matt.* xxvi, 65, 66.

The Boston *Transcript*, "the family paper," had been established in July 1830. Presenting a neat typographical appearance, "it was small, always clean, and was a general favorite in the family circle. It was lively, without any large pretensions to enterprise, carefully edited, and profitably patronized." Its first editor, Lynde M. Walter, occupied his position until 1840, when illness forced him to resign.

He died July 24, 1842. During his illness, the editor *pro tem.* was Dr. Joseph Palmer. Upon Walter's death, Miss Cornelia M. Walter, his sister, became editor. In 1846, she was succeeded by Epes Sargent, who was still editor in 1850. (Frederic Hudson, *Journalism in the United States, from 1690 to 1872*, New York and Evanston, 1969, p. 386; "Sargent, Epes," *HEUSH.*)

1. May 14, 1850.
2. The statement by "Sigma" was reprinted in *The Liberator*, May 24, 1850. "Sigma" was the pen-name of Lucius Manlius Sargent (1786–1867), of Boston and West Roxbury, a frequent contributor under that name to the Boston *Transcript*, a philanthropist and temperance advocate, and author of several books of prose and poetry. See Garrison's letter to Helen, New York, May 10, 1836, *Letters*, II, pp. 94, 95.
3. Acts 25:7.
4. Acts 25:10, 11.
5. John Wicliffe (also spelt Wycliffe, Wyclif, Wiclif and with other variations; *c.* 1324–1384) was an English scholar and reformer whose doctrines were condemned as heretical by the clergy. He deeply influenced John Huss.
   John Huss (*c.* 1373–1415) was a Bohemian religious reformer who was burnt at the stake upon refusal to recant his heretical doctrines.
   Martin Luther (1483–1546) was the founder of Protestantism.
6. Isaiah 59:4, 6–7, 15.
7. Matthew 10:25. Garrison has reversed the verses of the original.
8. Revelation 18:13.
9. Isaiah 18:2, somewhat telescoped.
10. Job 29:11–12, 15–17.
11. Job 16:9–10, 17, 19.
12. The article in the New York *Courier and Enquirer* from which Garrison quotes was reprinted in the *National Anti-Slavery Standard*, May 16, 1850. The New York *Courier and Enquirer*, next to the *National Intelligencer* at Washington, D.C., was the leading Whig newspaper. It was hostile to antislavery agitation. James Watson Webb (1802–1854) was its editor from 1827 to 1861, when it merged with the New York *World*. (Frank Luther Mott, *American Journalism*, New York, 1950, pp. 260–261.)
13. The reference is to criticism of Daniel Webster, then senator from Massachusetts, for his Seventh of March (1850) speech in support of the Compromise of 1850 and, especially, the Fugitive Slave Act.
14. A slum area in Manhattan, on the site of the former Collect Pond, in the center of the island north of City Hall, which became a red-light district, a center of crime, and hangout of the most notorious gangs in New York. (Cleveland Rogers and Rebecca B. Rankin, *New York: The World's Capital City*, New York, 1948, pp. 284–285.)
15. "Equally noble brothers."
16. Galatians 5:11.
17. A combination of Acts 17:6 and 24:5.
18. I Corinthians 4:13.
19. II Corinthians 11:26.
20. II Corinthians 6:4–5.
21. II Corinthians 6:8–9; 4:11.
22. These lines are from a poem by Walt Whitman, "Blood-Money." Emory Holloway, in his edition of *Walt Whitman: Complete Poetry and Selected Prose and Letters*, characterizes this poem as "almost the first that Whitman published in free verse" and notes that it "appeared in Horace Greeley's New York *Tribune*, Supplement, March 22, 1850. It was inspired, like Whittier's 'Ichabod,' by Webster's speech conciliating the slave states, on the 7th of March, and by the Fugitive Slave Law." (London, 1964, p. 1087n.) The complete poem is reprinted in Holloway's volume, pp. 503–504. I am grateful to Aaron Kramer, the poet, for first identifying the source of these lines.

23. Abner Kneeland (1774–1844), clergyman and editor, had founded *The Investigator* in Boston in 1832 as an organ of free thought, and had been tried and convicted for blasphemy in Boston in 1834–1838. After serving a short jail sentence, he moved to Iowa. "Sigma" had cited the case of Abner Kneeland as an example of how blasphemers like Garrison should be treated, noting that Kneeland had been sentenced to three months in prison. The result, said "Sigma," was that "Kneeland served out his time, and slunk away into pitiful obscurity — his assemblies were dissolved — his followers were scattered."

24. Lord George Gordon (1751–1793) was the leader of the "Gordon" or "no Popery" riots, provoked by the canceling of restrictions on Roman Catholics in England in 1780. The rioters held London for two weeks, and damaged much property. Although committed to the Tower on a charge of treason, he was acquitted because of insanity and died insane in Newgate gaol. Concerning Lord Gordon, "Sigma" had remarked: "*Whenever* the time shall arrive, and these *bad citizens* shall have stirred up the country to civil and a servile war, men may be found, who, like Colonel Gordon, believe that woe is, first of all, for those, by whom the offence has come."

5

TO THE EDITOR OF THE BOSTON *TRANSCRIPT*

[May 31, 1850.]

To the Editor of the Boston Transcript:

SIR — A few words in reply to the communication of 'SIGMA,' in your paper of last evening,[1] and I leave him to his chosen work of personal defamation, without further notice. His private opinion of me, whether favorable or unfavorable, is the last thing for solicitude on my part; because he who is ungovernable in temper and scurrilous in controversy, whatever may be his ability, is neither to be courted nor feared. The only inducements I had to notice his unjust and unmanly assault, (all the more unmanly because it was made anonymously,) were, in its connection with the late pro-slavery riots in New York, its tendency and apparent design to excite similar disturbances in this city during the approaching anniversary week,[2] and the opportunity it afforded me to correct certain wilful misstatements respecting the speech I delivered in the Broadway Tabernacle, to which a hundred hostile presses are giving a wide circulation.

The charge that 'Sigma' brought against me was, that, here and elsewhere, upon various occasions, I had 'discharged upon the community, impudent, disgusting, audacious and abominable blasphemy,' and ought to be indicted under a statute of this Commonwealth! My reply to this was — 'For more than twenty years I have been before the public as a writer and a lecturer; and during all that time, I challenge 'Sigma' to produce any thing from my pen or lips irreverent toward God, derogatory to the character of Jesus, or hostile to pure and undefiled religion.' How does he attempt to substantiate his charge? By *repeating the act*, of which I complained as unfair and dastardly in the extreme — viz., taking a garbled report of my New York speech 'from a paper intensely hostile to the speaker, and, assuming it to be authentic, making it the occasion of scattering in this community the most unjust and inflammatory comments upon it'! He finds that report in the Boston Daily Advertiser,[3] a paper notoriously inimical to the anti-slavery movement, as copied from the New York Commercial Advertiser,[4] a paper still more bitter and malevolent in its opposition; and by such witnesses he coolly declares 'its authenticity is established' — especially as the editor of the latter journal says he was present at the meeting, 'and, consequently, able [yes, able, but utterly indisposed] to give a correct account of the scenes enacted there'! Effrontery, like this, has seldom its parallel.

Now I assert, once more — that report is a malicious caricature, as every one who heard my remarks, possessing the least candor or regard for truth, will bear witness. I will refer to only two or three points.

1. I am represented to have said, 'There could be no piety in the Romish Church.' This I did not say — this I do not believe. I said of that Church, as such, that inasmuch as it sanctions slaveholding and slave-breeding on the part of its priesthood and lay members, in this country, the slave could not look to it for deliverance from his chains. I said the same thing of the Episcopal, Presbyterian, Baptist and Methodist Churches. Now, if the charge against these Churches is true, (and not even 'Sigma' has the hardihood to deny it,) is not the inference one of common sense? Are we — for example — to look for those in Europe who are monarchists in principle and practice, and loud in their denunciations of democratic agitators, to subvert the monarchy which they are so zealous to perpetuate, and on its ruins to establish the republic which they so much dread? In former years, 'Sigma' was an able and faithful laborer in the unpopular cause of Temperance, and cared not who called him fanatical or irreverent. At that time, (I know not what he would say now,) if any one had declared that the Church which sanctioned moderate drinking and the traffic in ardent spirits was not to be relied on to promote teetotalism, I am quite sure he would have endorsed the declaration as a self-evident truth. This was 'the head and front of my offending'[5] at New York. What 'blasphemy'!

2. I am reported to have said, comprehensively, 'The Churches had no piety, — i.e. had no members connected with them who were truly

pious. I said nothing of the kind. I merely referred to their pro-slavery features as organized bodies.

3. I am accused of having 'attacked the inspiration of the Bible.' This is utterly false, whatever may be my views of the popular notion of inspiration. But on what is this accusation based? Mark! — 'The question of inspiration, he said, was worth nothing' — nothing as a test of vital piety, I added — 'in this age.' And what is it worth? A hundred conflicting sects believe in the inspiration of the Bible, but to what purpose? Further — 'The greatest amount of immorality was compatible with the highest degree of veneration' for the book. Is not this true? 'The Bible has become the most popular book in America.' Was this to assail it? What other book is so revered, or so highly eulogized, or so systematically and gratuitously circulated? Did I refer to this fact reproachfully or complainingly? No! But only to remind all who heard me that 'it was not difficult to believe in a fashionable book, and faith in the Bible [i.e. assent to the doctrine of its inspiration] was no clue to moral conduct.' Is it? I said, moreover, that every Protestant claimed the right of private judgment as to what inspiration is, and what the Bible teaches; and, therefore, though a person says he believes in its being inspired, and in obeying its injunctions, in the last analysis it is only *his opinion* on these points that is obtained, and not absolutely what is inspiration or the book itself; and the question still remains open, 'What is inspiration? What is it that the Bible requires?' Is this to be guilty of irreverence, or only of uttering a truism?

4. I am reported to have said, 'Jesus is become obsolete'— but what I added is maliciously suppressed by the editor of the Commercial Advertiser — 'obsolete as a test of loyalty to God or love to man, because nothing is more common or more respectable than a profession of faith in him as a Savior; whereas in primitive times nothing was more odious or more perilous than such a profession, and then it was a searching test.

> 'Then to side with Truth is noble when we share her wretched crust,
> *Ere her cause bring fame and profit and 'tis prosperous to be just;*
> Then it is the brave man chooses, while the coward stands aside,
> Doubting in his abject spirit till his Lord is crucified,
> And the multitude make virtue of the faith they had denied.' [6]

5. I am reported to have said, 'Jesus believes in war, and in giving the Mexicans hell.' This is a gross misrepresentation as it stands. After

saying that Jesus, as a historical personage, is every where honored and believed on among us, I added that, in the person of Zachary Taylor,[7] he occupies the Presidential chair; for President Taylor professes to believe in Jesus, but *in a Jesus who enslaves human beings, and hands them over to him for a possession* — yes, in a Jesus who is for 'giving the Mexicans hell' — quoting the language so frequently alleged to have been uttered on the battle-field in Mexico by this military chieftain. Here, according to the Commercial Advertiser, (for the hit was palpable,) 'some one in the audience, unable longer to control his emotions, called out, "This cannot be tolerated!" and considerable excitement prevailed all over the house.' It was that most abandoned of men, Isaiah Rynders, who made that exclamation, and, with his ruffian confederates at his heels, rushed down upon the platform with horrid oaths and imprecations, threatening to knock down the speaker; thus confirming every word I had said respecting the popular religion of this nation, and its slave-holding, blood-stained President! So much for my 'sickening and disgusting blasphemies' on that occasion!

6. 'Sigma' says, 'It appears that Mr. Garrison *permitted* any one to pray that felt it to be of any use.' It was not merely a permission, but an *invitation* that was given, and in these words: — 'If any person present feels moved to offer vocal prayer to the God of the oppressed, an opportunity is now given for that purpose.' This has been the uniform practice of the American Anti-Slavery Society since its organization, in the true spirit of religious liberty, — thus giving no offence to the peculiar notions of any one, and avoiding a purely ceremonial observance. And this is deemed worthy of a sneer!

7. 'Mr Garrison read passages from the Bible, *which*, he said, *some persons considered to be the word of God.*' Surely, to make such a declaration was not 'blasphemy,' — nay, was strictly in accordance with truth. Surely, to read those passages was not an immorality! Yet my language is so represented and italicised as to imply that I spoke in a sarcastic manner; whereas what I said was this: — 'I will now read select portions of the Scriptures, *which the people of this country profess to receive as the word of God.*' This I said seriously and emphatically, for the purpose of deepening the impression upon the assembly in reading those thrilling rebukes and warnings of the prophets, relating to the oppression of the poor and needy.

I said no more in derogation of the popular religious observances of the day, than Isaiah [8] uttered against such in his times when he declared — 'To what purpose is the multitude of your sacrifices unto me? saith the Lord. When ye come to appear before me, who hath required this at your hand to tread my courts? Bring no more vain oblations: incense is an abomination unto me; the new moon and sabbaths, the calling of assemblies, I cannot away with: *it is iniquity,* EVEN THE SOLEMN MEETING. Your new moons and your appointed feasts my soul hateth: they are a trouble unto me; I am weary to bear them. And when ye spread forth your hands, I will hide mine eyes from you; yea, when ye make many prayers, I will not hear.' [9] My reasons for condemning such observances as worthless and hypo-critical are precisely those which the prophet gave for his 'blasphe-mous' conduct: — 'Ah, sinful nation, a people laden with iniquity, a seed of evil-doers! Your hands are full of blood. Wash you, make you clean; put away the evil of your doings from before mine eyes; cease to do evil; learn to do well; seek judgment, relieve the oppressed, judge the fatherless, plead for the widow.' [10]

And now, Mr. Editor, let me state an edifying fact. The speech at New York, which has been so basely misrepresented, was not a new one for the occasion, but was one that I had previously delivered, verbatim, in Plymouth, Weymouth, Abington, South Hingham, (on Sunday, in the Congregation meeting-house, at a regular church ser-vice, in the pulpit,) Salem, Portsmouth, Portland, and in various other places, (at greater length, it is true,) to large, attentive, and deeply interested audiences, composed of persons of conflicting religious and political opinions; in every instance apparently to great acceptance, and always impressively. Nothing was further from me than any thought or intention to create unnecessary excitement by repeating that speech at New York — the sole design of which was strictly philo-sophical, viz., to demonstrate how old tests, which were vital in one age, become powerless in another; how forms of iniquity change, bringing new circumstances, affecting other people, prevailing in other times, and requiring other tests of religious fidelity in their extirpation; how, to sum it all up in the very truthful and graphic verse of one of our most gifted poets —

'Once to every man and nation comes the moment to decide,
In the strife of Truth with Falsehood, for the good or evil
    side;
Some Great Cause, GOD'S NEW MESSIAH, offering each the bloom
    or blight,
Parts the goats upon the left hand, and the sheep upon the right,
And the choice goes by forever 'twixt that darkness and that
    light!' [11]

Nothing can be a wider departure from the truth, than the representation, that it was my speech that led to the riotous outbreaks in New York. I happened to be the first speaker, and in the audience was a band of ruffians lying in wait to make me, or any other speaker, 'an offender for a word' [12] — who came pre-determined to break up the meeting — stimulated by the inflammatory and murderous appeals of such infamous journals as Bennett's Herald and the New York Globe,[13] and having their reward. I utter no unmanly cries — I shrink from no just responsibility; but I have a right to protest against the foulest treatment and the most atrocious misrepresentations.

WM. LLOYD GARRISON.

Printed in *The Liberator*, May 31, 1850.

1. May 30, 1850. Sigma's communication to the *Transcript* was reprinted in *The Liberator*, May 31, 1850, beside Garrison's rejoinder.

2. The reference is to the annual New England Anti-Slavery Convention, held in Boston at the Melodeon, May 28–30, 1850.

3. The Boston *Daily Advertiser*, "the first prominent daily paper issued in New England," began publication in 1813, with W. W. Clapp as publisher, under the editorship of Horatio Bigelow, who was succeeded in 1814 by Nathan Hale, a nephew of the Revolutionary patriot spy. The *Advertiser* "was essentially a business paper. Of its twenty-four columns frequently only two or three, seldom more than five, were given to what is known as reading matter. No notice was taken of theatres or concerts, though these were duly advertised in its columns. There were no book notices and no correspondence either foreign or domestic. Literature and art were alike ignored." (Justin Winsor, ed., *The Memorial History of Boston*, Boston, 1881, 4 vols., III, 627–628; Frederic Hudson, *Journalism in the United States from 1690 to 1872*, New York and Evanston, 1969, pp. 379–382.)

4. The New York *Commercial Advertiser* was the lineal descendant of the *American Minerva*, which had been established by Noah Webster, the lexicographer, in 1793. In 1797, the name was changed to *Commercial Advertiser*, its title for more than a century. Succeeding editors included Colonel William M. Stone, a Federalist, who became its editor in 1821 and remained its editor-in-chief until shortly before his death in 1844. His successors were Francis Hall, the editor from 1844 to 1863, and William Henry Hurlbut, from 1863 to 1867. (Frank Luther Mott, *American Journalism, A History: 1690–1960*, 3d. ed., New York, 1962, pp. 134, 181, 339n; Hudson, *Journalism in the United States*, pp. 191–194.)

5. Shakespeare, *Othello*, I, iii, 80.

6. James Russell Lowell (1819–1891), American poet, author, and, for a time, abolitionist, "The Present Crisis."

7. Zachary Taylor (1784–1850), twelfth President of the United States, had commanded United States troops in the Mexican War, and was elected President on the Whig party ticket in 1848. He died on July 9, 1850, and was succeeded by Millard Fillmore.

8. Eighth century B.C. Hebrew prophet of Judaea, whose prophecies are collected in the book of the Old Testament that bears his name.

9. Isaiah 1:11–15.

10. Isaiah 1:4, 15–17.

11. James Russell Lowell, "The Present Crisis."

12. Isaiah 29:21.

13. The New York *Globe*, a daily newspaper, was an organ of Tammany Hall, and had been established in 1847 by Casper C. Childs. It continued until April 1851, when it went out of existence. (Hudson, *Journalism in the United States*, p. 576.)

6

TO SYDNEY HOWARD GAY

Boston, June 21. [1850]
Friday Noon.

Dear Gay:

Herewith you will receive the speeches of Parker Pillsbury [1] and Wendell Phillips, made at our *tremendous* Faneuil Hall meeting.[2] Mine will be forwarded by the mail to-morrow. Do as you please about publishing any of them.[3] The meeting in F. H. was the great one of the anniversary week, though the stormiest.

These speeches have not yet been read at all, since they were put in type. Perhaps you will discover some blunders affecting the sense. If so, correct *ad lib.*

Am very sorry to hear of the illness of your dear child.

Yours in haste.

W. L. G.

ALS: Columbia University Library. The year has been added on the back of the letter by another hand, probably that of one of Garrison's sons.

Sydney Howard Gay (b. Hingham, Massachusetts, 1814; d. New Brighton, Staten Island, June 25, 1888), a Garrisonian abolitionist, became a lecturing agent for the American Anti-Slavery Society in 1842 and an editor of the *National Anti-Slavery Standard*, the organ of the American Anti-Slavery Society, in 1843, remaining in that post until 1857, when he joined the New York *Tribune*. He was managing editor of the *Tribune* from 1862 to 1865 and managing editor of the Chicago *Tribune* from 1867 to 1871. In 1872–1874, he was associated with the New York *Evening Post*. In later years, he wrote a four-volume illustrated history of the United States, and a life of James Madison (Boston, 1884).

1. Parker Pillsbury (b. Hamilton, Massachusetts, 1809; d. Concord, New Hampshire, 1898), minister, antislavery leader, and author, gave up the ministry in 1840 as a result of opposition to his antislavery preaching from members of his congregation in the Congregational church at London, New Hampshire. He thereafter devoted himself to the antislavery cause as a Garrisonian abolitionist. From 1840 until the emancipation of the slaves, he served as agent for the New Hampshire, Massachusetts, and American Anti-Slavery Societies. He spoke in support of John Brown following the latter's raid on Harpers Ferry. He edited the *Herald of Freedom* at Concord, New Hampshire, in 1840 and from 1845 to 1846. For several months in 1866, he edited the *National Anti-Slavery Standard*. Besides antislavery, he was also devoted to temperance, international peace, woman's rights and political reform. His most important written work was the *Acts of the Anti-Slavery Apostles* (1883).

2. The reference is to the annual New England Anti-Slavery Convention, which convened in Boston, Tuesday morning, May 28, 1850, and continued through Thursday evening, May 30. Six of the meetings were held in the Melodeon, two in Cochituate Hall, with the final meeting, on Thursday evening, in Faneuil Hall. The speakers at that meeting were Edmund Quincy, chairman, Francis Jackson, president of the convention, Garrison, Parker Pillsbury, and Wendell Phillips. The proceedings of the convention were reported in *The Liberator*, May 31, June 7, 1850.

3. The *National Anti-Slavery Standard* published the three addresses on June 27, 1850.

7

TO SYDNEY HOWARD GAY

Boston, June 24, 1850.

Dear Gay:

Enclosed, you have the remainder of my Faneuil Hall speech: but, remember, not for insertion in the Standard, either as a matter of courtesy, or because it is forwarded to you in slips. Please exercise your own freedom, and judgment, and especially convenience.[1]

Next week, I am to publish Theodore Parker's able speech.[2] It will occupy at least a page. I will forward it to you (for I should like to see it in the Standard) as fast as we can set it up — in slips.[3]

Faithfully yours,

W. L. G.

ALS: Columbia University Library.

1. Gay did publish it in the *Standard* on June 27, 1850.
2. This was Theodore Parker's address at the New England Anti-Slavery Convention, delivered at the Melodeon, Wednesday afternoon, May 29, 1850. It appeared in *The Liberator*, July 5, 1850.

Theodore Parker (b. Lexington, Massachusetts, August 24, 1810; d. Florence, Italy, May 10, 1860), Unitarian minister, perhaps the greatest American scholar of his day, author and antislavery leader, had been minister of a Unitarian society in West Roxbury from 1837 to 1845, when he became minister of the 28th Congregational Society in Boston. He established the *Massachusetts Quarterly Review* in 1847 and was its editor for its duration of three years. Although he was interested in the antislavery movement at an early age, he did not speak or write publicly against slavery until the 1840's, when he began to write and speak almost incessantly against the institution. Following the passage of the Fugitive Slave Law of 1850, he played a major role in protecting runaway slaves in Boston and helping them reach safety in Canada. He later became a firm supporter and defender of John Brown. He died of tuberculosis in Florence, Italy, during a trip abroad undertaken for the purpose of regaining his health.
3. It appeared in its entirety in the *Standard* on July 4, 1850.

8

TO SYDNEY HOWARD GAY

Boston, July 2, 1850.

Dear Gay:

Here is the remainder of Theodore Parker's speech, as corrected by himself. I fear it will arrive too late, by one day, to enable you to insert the whole speech in this week's Standard. But it has been out of our power to send it any earlier, Mr. Parker being at West Roxbury, and his Ms. being almost illegible. *Possibly* this may arrive in season to be used this week and therefore [I] venture to send it.[1]

Yours, to serve,

Wm. Lloyd Garrison.

ALS: Columbia University Library.

1. The entire speech did arrive in time to appear on July 4, 1850.

9

TO SAMUEL MAY, JR.

Boston, July 16, 1850.

My Dear Friend:

In regard to your inquiries about my attendance at conventional meetings [1] during the month of August, I think I may venture to say, (extraordinaries excepted,) that I will endeavor to attend each of the meetings specified in your letter.[2]

The reason why G. W. B.[3] suggested the month of August for the Convention at Northampton was, simply, to keep up a steady anti-slavery fire monthly in the Town Hall. I suppose it can easily be deferred a month longer, and will endeavor to make such an arrangement when I see him.

Are not Uxbridge [4] and Woonsocket (seeing we have had a Convention at Blackstone [5]) rather too near each other to hold meetings in them two consecutive Sundays? Perhaps not. I think we ought to have one in Woonsocket,[6] certainly. Our friends in Feltonville [7] deserve to have one in that quarter.

It is strongly desired that we should have one of our meetings in Fall River, and another in Valley Falls, R.I.[8] I hope we shall do so in September.

Our meetings at Pawtucket [9] were exceedingly well attended, and evidently gave great satisfaction. Burleigh and Pillsbury [10] both spoke "in demonstration of the spirit, and with power." [11]

My meeting in Providence,[12] on Sunday evening, was a very large one, and the lecture was so well received as to be repeatedly applauded, in spite of the "holiness" of the hour. Nature will out.

In my opinion two speakers are enough at any one convention. A third one is rather an embarrassment than an aid to the others, especially if there are auxiliary speakers on the spot; and, for one, I want others to participate in the discussions, besides the agents, even at the risk of getting "bored" occasionally. I like the old primitive method of doing up these things.

If Wendell and I should go to Andover,[13] friend Pillsbury could easily be spared elsewhere, and I think to better advantage, because he would in that case have the day all to himself, and the people hearing anti-slavery truth would be proportionately multiplied. Besides, as he graduated at Andover, the rule holds good in regard to himself personally, that "a prophet hath no honor in his own country" — and there is, doubtless, a stronger prejudice against him there, on that account, than against some others. Unless Phillips can go to A., I would not attempt to hold a meeting there; for we shall have "a beggarly account of empty boxes," [14] even with all his reputation as an orator to attract hearers.

I have not yet been able to see Theodore Parker, but asked Mr. [Francis] Jackson to see him about going to Worcester,[15] last Sunday. He forgot to do so. We will try to get word to him as soon as we can. I have little hope of his being with us.[16]

I am glad you think of writing to Stetson,[17] and also to Weiss.[18] I hope they will both attend, and speak. Of course, you will proffer them their expenses.

I am happy to add, that our estimable friend Mary Grew,[19] of Philadelphia, is in this city, and will go to Worcester with us, if her health will permit, and probably be among the speakers, though it is not best to promise this.[20]

The selecting and printing of the Hymns I will attend to. I suppose you will see to the printing of the placards.

We shall not attempt any extra train of cars from Boston, I think, though we may need one in returning from Worcester, to leave at 5 o'clock, P.M., if such an arrangement can be made.

If we find that we have an abundance of speakers, the speeches must be short as convenient to do any justice to the ideas of each speaker.

[Frederick] Douglass is in Ohio; but, if he were at home, exceedingly pleasant as it would be to have him with us, I do not think a single speech would "pay" for the expenses incurred by such a journey.

With true regards to Mrs. May,[21] and trusting all the members of your family are in the enjoyment of good health I remain.

Yours, to the end, and beyond it,

Wm. Lloyd Garrison.

Saml. May Jr.

ALS: Antislavery Manuscripts, Boston Public Library.

1. The term "conventional meetings" refers to a decision by the New England Anti-Slavery Convention of May 28–30, pursuant to a resolution introduced by Samuel May, Jr., to hold "a Hundred Conventions in the New England States, for the purpose of agitating the question of slavery with regard to the particular phases it presents at this time, and especially with regard to the duty of the people of the North to refuse assistance in the rendition of fugitive slaves. . . ." (*The Liberator*, June 7, 1850.) *The Liberator* (June 21, 1850) listed the following places as the earliest convention sites: Essex (Essex County, Massachusetts), Saturday and Sunday, June 22 and 23; Blackstone (Worcester County, Massachusetts), Saturday and Sunday, June 29 and 30; Lexington (Middlesex County, Massachusetts), Sunday, June 30; Abington (Plymouth County, Massachusetts), Thursday, July 4.

2. The letter from Samuel May, Jr., to Garrison was dated Leicester, July 11, 1850. Among other things, May asked Garrison the following: "Will you inform me, as soon as convenient, what help you can give us in August? There are 4 Sundays — 4th, 11th, 18th, & 25th — Will you go to Uxbridge one day? & which wd you prefer? To Northampton, one? and when?" (Anti-Slavery Letters to Garrison and Others, Boston Public Library.)

3. George W. Benson. Apparently it was Benson who had suggested to May a convention in Northampton, Massachusetts, in August.

4. The Uxbridge (Massachusetts) convention was scheduled for August 10 and 11, with the announcement that Garrison and Charles Burleigh would attend. (*The Liberator*, August 2, 1850.) For an account of the convention, see *The Liberator*, August 16, 1850.

5. The Blackstone (Worcester County, Massachusetts) meeting was scheduled for June 29 and 30, in conjunction with the quarterly meeting of the Worcester County (South) Anti-Slavery Society. (*The Liberator*, June 28, 1850.)

6. A close perusal of *The Liberator* for June, July, August, and September does not indicate that a convention was held in Woonsocket.

7. A convention was scheduled for Feltonville (Middlesex County, Massachusetts), on August 24 and 25. (*The Liberator*, August 16, 1850.)

8. A convention in Valley Falls, Rhode Island, was scheduled for September 28 and 29. (*The Liberator*, September 13, 1850.)

9. The Pawtucket, Rhode Island, convention was held on Saturday evening and Sunday, July 13 and 14. (*The Liberator*, July 5, 1850.) For an account see *The Liberator*, July 19 and 26, 1850.

10. Charles C. Burleigh and Parker Pillsbury. (*The Liberator*, July 12, 1850.) Charles C. Burleigh was a Garrisonian antislavery agent, lecturer, and writer. For a short biographical sketch, see *Letters*, II, 72.

11. I Corinthians 2:4 (slightly altered).

12. Garrison spoke in Providence, Rhode Island, on Sunday evening, July 21. For a description and synopsis of the address, see *The Liberator*, August 2, 1850.

13. The convention at Andover (Essex County), Massachusetts, was scheduled for Saturday evening and Sunday, July 27 and 28. Garrison, Wendell Phillips, and Parker Pillsbury were originally listed as speakers. (*The Liberator*, July 19 and 26, 1850.) All three appeared and spoke. For an account of the meeting see *The Liberator*, August 2, 1850.

14. Shakespeare, *Romeo and Juliet*, V, i, 45.

15. The convention at Worcester was scheduled for Thursday, August 1, and was combined with the official, Annual First of August, West India Emancipation anniversary celebration under the sponsorship of the Massachusetts Anti-Slavery Society. (*The Liberator*, July 19, 1850.)

16. Parker was not present. (See the account of the meeting in *The Liberator*, August 9, 1850.)

17. Caleb Stetson (b. Kingston, Massachusetts, July 12, 1793; d. May 17, 1870), a Unitarian minister, scholar and abolitionist, graduated from Harvard in

1822 and taught at the newly opened Academy at Lexington until 1825. After preparing for the ministry at Cambridge, he became pastor of the First Parish Church (Unitarian) in Medford, Massachusetts, in February 1827, remaining there until 1848, when he accepted a call to the Second Unitarian Church in Scituate, Massachusetts. After ten years there, he lost his pulpit because of his antislavery preaching. Thereafter, he lived in Lexington, Massachusetts. (*The Descendants of Cornet Robert Stetson*, vol. I, no. 3, of the *Stetson Genealogy*, published by Stetson Kindred of America, Inc., n.p., 1956, p. 91; Nelson M. Stetson, compiler, *Stetson Kindred of America*, Booklet No. 5, Rockland, Mass., 1918, pp. 13–14.)

Samuel May, Jr., did write to Stetson, inviting him to address the meeting in Worcester. Stetson, however, was unable to accept the invitation because of family responsibilities. (Letter from Caleb Stetson to Samuel May, Jr., July 25, 1850, Anti-Slavery Letters to Garrison and Others, Boston Public Library.)

18. John Weiss (b. Boston, June 28, 1818; d. Boston, March 9, 1879), Unitarian minister, author, and biographer of Theodore Parker, was a graduate of Harvard College in 1837, and subsequently attended Harvard Divinity School and the University of Heidelberg. He was pastor of the Unitarian Church in Watertown, Massachusetts, from 1843 to 1845, 1846 to 1847, and 1862 to 1869; and of the First Congregational Society in New Bedford, from 1847 to 1859. He was a contributor to the *Atlantic Monthly, Christian Examiner, Galaxy* and *Radical*, and was the author of the *Life and Correspondence of Theodore Parker*, 2 vols. (1863), as well as of other works in literature. He helped to found the Free Religious Association in 1867.

As in the case of Stetson, he was unable to attend. (Letter from John Weiss to Samuel May, Jr., July 25, 1850, Anti-Slavery Letters to Garrison and Others, Boston Public Library.)

19. Mary Crew (b. Hartford, Connecticut, September 1, 1813; d. 1896) was the daughter of Henry Grew. Her family moved to Philadelphia in 1834. Soon afterward, she joined the Female Anti-Slavery Society of Philadelphia, became its secretary, and, for thirty-four years thereafter, until March 4, 1870, when the society went out of existence, wrote its annual reports. In 1840, she and her father were delegates to the World's Anti-Slavery Convention in London. She worked arduously at the Philadelphia antislavery fairs, lectured and wrote frequently on slavery, and was an assistant editor of the *Pennsylvania Freeman*. After the Civil War, she became deeply involved in the woman suffrage movement, serving as president of the Pennsylvania Woman Suffrage Association for twenty-three years. (Gertrude Bosler Biddle and Sarah Dickinson Lowrie, *Notable Women of Pennsylvania*, Philadelphia, 1942, pp. 140–141; letter from E. M. Davis to Maria W. Chapman, November 21, 1845, Weston Papers, Boston Public Library.)

20. The account in *The Liberator* does not mention Mary Grew.

21. Sarah Russell (b. January 5, 1813), the third daughter of Nathaniel P. and Sarah Tidd Russell of Boston, married Samuel May, Jr., on November 11, 1835. They had four children. (Samuel May, John Wilder May, John Joseph May, *A Genealogy of the Descendants of John May*, Boston, 1878, pp. 23, 46.)

10

TO ELIZABETH MOUNTFORT

Boston, July 19, 1850.

Esteemed Friend:

Congratulating you on the organization of the Portland Anti-Slavery Society,[1] I shall be happy to comply with the invitation ex-

tended to me, in its behalf, by you, to give a lecture at the time specified in your note, — *Deo volente.* As for any remuneration, beyond my
travelling expenses, I desire not a farthing — as I fairly owe another
visit to your city, in consequence of the liberality shown to me through
friend Newell A. Foster [2] and Mrs. Morrill [3] — to whom, and all the
other friends, I desire to be kindly remembered.

Hoping that the series of lectures contemplated will result in greatly
increasing the anti-slavery sentiment in Portland and its vicinity, I
remain,

Yours, with great respect and esteem,

Wm. Lloyd Garrison.

Elizabeth Montfort.

ALS: Portland Anti-Slavery Society Collection, Maine Historical Society.

Elizabeth Mountfort (Garrison, erroneously, omits the "u") was secretary of
the Portland Antislavery Society. She is listed in the Portland *Directory* for 1847–
1848 as a widow living at 29 Fore Street with Joseph Mountfort, a shipmaster,
and James Mountfort, a merchant. (Edward O. Schriver, *Go Free: The Antislavery
Impulse in Maine, 1833–1855*, University of Maine Study No. 91, Orono, Maine,
1970, pp. 44n, 113–114.)

1. The Portland (Maine) Anti-Slavery Society had originally been formed in
March 1833, a year and a half before the organization of the Maine Anti-Slavery
Society. Although the former organization had more or less lapsed after 1845, it
was re-formed on March 10, 1850, with a pro-Garrisonian program. Part of its
activity was the presentation of an antislavery lyceum, consisting of lectures by
outstanding antislavery lecturers, among whom were Garrison, Wendell Phillips,
and George Thompson, then visiting the United States. (Schriver, *Go Free: The
Antislavery Struggle in Maine, 1833–1855*, pp. 35–26, 123–135.)

2. Newell Abbott Foster (1814–1868), a native of Canterbury, New Hampshire, was the brother of abolitionist Stephen S. Foster. A printer by trade, he
was the chief owner of the Portland (Maine) *Daily Press*, a prominent Republican,
and a member of the state legislature for some years. He was also a well-known
spiritualist. His first wife, Eliza Jane Allison, died in 1854. In 1861, he married
Ellen French. He entered the Union army several months before the close of the
Civil War, but did not see action. (Reginald Foster, *Foster Genealogy*, Chicago,
1899, part I, p. 366.)

3. Since there are six Morrills listed in the Portland *Directory* for 1847–1848,
it is difficult to determine the identity of Garrison's friend. We also know that
Newell Foster's mother's maiden name was Morrill. (*Foster Genealogy*; Ann
Morrill Smith, *Morrill Kindred in America*, New York, 1931, II, 169, 242.)

11

TO JAMES BROWN SYME

Boston, August 9, 1850.

Dear Sir:

I am truly obliged to you for sending me the remainder of your excellent speech at the Worcester gathering [1] on the glorious First of

August. I happened to find the first six pages of your manuscript on the desk, at the close of the meeting, and took the liberty to bring them with me to Boston for publication. The whole speech would have appeared in the Liberator of this week, if I had received the latter portion of it a little earlier.[2]

It gave me great pleasure to take you by the hand in the presence of such an assembly. Welcome to America, and to all the manifold blessings of New England freedom! Aside from our revolting slave system at the South — would to God it might instantly *be* put aside, and forever! — this country has certainly no parallel on earth in regard to the comfort, intelligence, education, industry, enterprise and growth of the population. But to think of every sixth man, woman, child, of this mighty mass, registered and treated as a chattel slave, a mere animal, a piece of property! It is a horrible paradox, such as the world has never before beheld.

Now that you are here in this country to reside, you will be able to understand the philosophy of the anti-slavery movement, and the peculiarity of its features, and the spirit of its advocates, and the nature and extent of the opposition arrayed against it, far better than you or any other person could do on the other side of the Atlantic. The struggle is unique, and necessarily shakes the foundations of Church and State, because Church and State are but the vassals of the Slave Power. It is like assaulting idolatry in India.

Your reference to "John Wigham's house and garden"[3] — to "Mrs. Sarah Wigham,[4] Miss Nicholson,[5] and the noble household of 5 Grey Street," Edinburgh — moistens my eyes, and makes my heart leap within me. Never shall I forget those beloved friends while I remember any thing of Scotland. My desire to see them all again is at times so intense, that I scarcely know how to remain another day on this side of the Atlantic until it be gratified. A thousand thanks for your allusion to them, and for avowing a feeling of intimacy with me, in consequence of your acquaintance with them. Yesterday, I received a very pleasant letter from Henry Wigham, the brother of my special favorite, Eliza Wigham.[6]

Whenever you come to Boston, I shall be extremely glad to see you. My house is 65 Suffolk Street — office, 21 Cornhill.

Yours, with much respect,

Wm. Lloyd Garrison.

J. B. Syme.

ALS: American Antiquarian Society.

James Brown Syme (b. Edinburgh, Scotland, February 1821; d. Worcester, Massachusetts, August 2, 1855), born into a poverty-stricken working-class family, was physically deformed as the result of a severe beating during his childhood.

He taught school briefly in his youth, then turned to writing for *Hogg's Weekly Instructor*, a literary magazine in Edinburgh, as a means of earning a livelihood. Elihu Burritt, the American reformer, author, and editor of the *Christian Citizen*, a weekly reform journal established in Worcester in 1842, was then visiting England. Impressed by Syme's writing, Burritt asked him to contribute to the *Christian Citizen* as well as to the *Bond of Brotherhood*, a periodical tract then owned and edited by Burritt. Syme became a regular contributor to both publications, and he and Burritt became close friends. When Burritt offered him the position of associate editor of the *Christian Citizen*, Syme accepted and left for the United States on April 8, 1850, with three orphan children whom he had recently adopted and a wife whom he had recently married. After an association of about a year with the *Christian Citizen*, which ceased publication in 1851, he joined Thomas Drew in editing the *Worcester Daily Spy*. (Charles Nutt, *History of Worcester and Its People*, New York, 1919, III, 436–441.)

1. A detailed description of the proceedings appeared in *The Liberator*, August 9, 1850.

2. Syme's address was printed in *The Liberator*, August 16, 1850.

3. John Wigham, Jr. (1782–1862), of Edinburgh, Scotland, a shawl manufacturer and well known as a philanthropist and Quaker, was active in abolition and peace and other reform movements of the day. (*Letters*, III, October 24, 1846.) He was the author of a pamphlet, "To John Shank More, Professor of the Law of Scotland in Edinburgh University," printed July 10, 1851. In it, he presented his views on juvenile delinquency and the treatment of delinquents, based upon his experience as a member of the Board of Commissioners for Prisoners from 1839 to 1850. (Dr. W. Garden Blaikie, "Miss Eliza Wigham," *The Scottish Women's Temperance News*, June 1898, p. 8n. For this and other information to be found in the ensuing notes, I am indebted to J. W. Cockburn, City Librarian and Curator, Edinburgh Corporation, Libraries and Museums Department, Scotland.)

4. Sarah Nicolson Wigham was John, Jr.'s second wife. His first wife was Ann White. (Wigham Family Genealogical Table, p. 12, in "Eliza Wigham," pamphlet provided by J. W. Cockburn, which incudes Blaikie, "Miss Eliza Wigham," and, no author's name, "The Late Eliza Wigham," in *The Scottish Women's Temperance News*, December 1899.)

5. Probably Sarah's sister. (Letter from J. W. Cockburn, dated January 6, 1972.)

6. Henry and Eliza Wigham were the children of John Tertius Wigham, a cousin of John, Jr., and a shawl manufacturer of Edinburgh, Scotland, who died in 1864 at the age of eighty. Henry Wigham lived in Dublin during the latter part of his life. Eliza (1820–1899) was the most prominent reformer of the family. Raised as a Quaker whose parents were actively antislavery during the campaign to abolish slavery in the West Indies, she was sympathetic from early youth to the antislavery movement in the United States, especially to Garrisonian abolition. She knew personally Garrison, Phillips, and Frederick Douglass. She was active in the campaign for woman's suffrage as well as in the temperance cause. She was the author of a pamphlet, *The Anti-Slavery Cause in America and Its Martyrs*, published in 1863. (Pamphlet, "Eliza Wigham.")

1 2

TO SAMUEL MAY, JR.

Boston, Sept. 6, 1850.

My dear May:

Our friend Wallcut [1] forgot to hand me your letter, received by him yesterday, till this moment; and I hasten to say that I will gladly avail myself of your kind suggestion to take the half past 2 o'clock train to-morrow for Worcester, that I may have the pleasure of riding with you to Leicester, [2] according to your proposal: — that is, should this letter be received by you in season to get to Worcester without inconvenience to yourself. In case you cannot come, I will spend the afternoon at my friend Effingham L. Capron's, [3] and take the stage for L. in the evening.

Your meeting at Princeton [4] appears to have been a failure as to numbers. Ours at the Cape [5] was multitudinous, especially on Sunday, and most encouraging.

With my warm regards to Mrs. May, I remain,

Faithfully yours,

Wm. Lloyd Garrison.

N.B. My wife would be extremely happy to accompany me, but cannot see her way clear to leave the children.

S. May Jr.

ALS: Anti-Slavery Manuscripts, Boston Public Library.

1. The Reverend Robert Folger Wallcut (1797–1884) was a Unitarian clergyman at North Dennis on Cape Cod and an early antislavery man. (*Life*, II, 422n, 478; see also *Letters*, II, 401, 402.) In a letter dated October 25, 1876, Garrison writes to Edward L. Pierce that Wallcut was bookkeeper for *The Liberator* from 1846 until *The Liberator's* discontinuance in January 1866, and that in 1876 he was a clerk in the Boston Custom House (ALS: Houghton Library, Harvard University).

2. The meeting at Leicester (Worcester County, Massachusetts) was one of the One Hundred Conventions and was called for Saturday evening and Sunday, September 7 and 8. It was to be held in connection with the quarterly meeting of the Worcester County South Anti-Slavery Society. The speakers listed included Garrison, Stephen S. Foster, and Samuel May, Jr. (*The Liberator*, August 16, 1850.)

3. Effingham L. Capron (1791–1859) was a Quaker Garrisonian, one of the founders of the American Anti-Slavery Society, a nonresistant and, for many years, an officer of the Massachusetts Anti-Slavery Society. (See *Letters*, II, 113.)

4. The meeting at Princeton (Worcester County, Massachusetts) took place on Saturday evening and Sunday, August 31 and September 1. Speakers included Stephen S. Foster, Samuel May, Jr., and others. The meeting, another of the One Hundred Conventions, was held in connection with the Worcester County North Anti-Slavery Society. (*The Liberator*, August 16, 1850.) An account of the convention appeared in *The Liberator*, September 13, 1850.

5. Garrison refers to a Barnstable County Anti-Slavery Convention, one of the One Hundred, at Harwich, Massachusetts, on Friday, Saturday, and Sunday, August 30 to September 1, with Garrison and Charles C. Burleigh, among others, as speakers. (*The Liberator*, August 16, 1850.) An account of the meeting, "Convention on the Cape," appeared in *The Liberator*, September 6, 1850.

---

1 3

TO AN UNIDENTIFIED CORRESPONDENT

Boston, Sept. 27, 1850.

Dear Sir:

According to your request, I send you my autograph. You may safely have it in your possession in the Old Bay State; but, should you travel south of Mason and Dixon's line, it will scarcely be tolerated, even in a book of curiosities, by the "chivalry" in that quarter. So, be cautious!

Yours, for a free country,

Wm. Lloyd Garrison.

P.S. I have parted with all the English autographs that would be of any special value to you or they should be at your service.

ALS: John Hay Papers, Library of Congress.
Name of correspondent unknown. Although the letter is in the John Hay Papers at the Library of Congress, it seems unlikely, though not impossible, that it was written to John Hay, Lincoln's biographer and assistant secretary, who was then only twelve years old.

---

1 4

TO SAMUEL J. MAY

Northampton, Oct. 7, 1850.

Dear Friend:

On Saturday afternoon, I received a telegraphic despatch at Boston from brother George,[1] stating that our beloved and long afflicted sister Sarah[2] was rapidly failing, and requesting me to come up immediately. In the course of fifteen minutes, I was on my way to Northampton, and arrived here at 10 o'clock that night. Helen[3] had preceded me the day before. It was deemed best not to let the dear sufferer know of my arrival till the next morning, as she was not considered in immediate danger. Yesterday morning, at 9 o'clock, I went into her room, kissed her, and pressed her hand. "Kind brother!"

she exclaimed. "The kindest of sisters," I replied. But she was too weak to continue the conversation. It was evident that she was "struck with death." She spoke of being excessively tired, and said, with a characteristic smile, "It requires a great deal of patience." "Yes," I replied, "and in you patience has had its perfect work." She was greately emaciated, and so altered in appearance as scarcely to be recognizable. Her spirit was translated at 12 o'clock, and thus "entered into rest." The mortal dissolution was not attended with any apparent suffering. As long as she could speak or make any sign, it was evident that her mind was clear, serene, and ready for the change, though that change took place at a much earlier hour than she had anticipated. — Indeed, till within a few hours of her decease, she evidently did not consider herself to be near the termination of her earthly career — she had passed safely through so many severe *crises*, and was always so hopeful in regard to her ultimate restoration to health! There was nothing gloomy or repulsive to her in death — she had no forebodings in regard to a future state; but she greatly enjoyed the society of her friends, her attachments were very strong, and she desired to live only that she might "spend and be spent" [4] in the service of suffering humanity. But "the inevitable hour" [5] has come, to our great bereavement and her exceeding gain — for, who that knew her, having any appreciation of moral excellence, can doubt that hers is among "the spirits of the just made perfect"? [6]

For years, she was a silent, uncomplaining, living martyr to a cancerous affection, at once loathsome and appalling. I had not the slightest idea as to the ravages it had made, until after her death. But, while the revelation of it shocked me beyond measure, it served to heighten my admiration of the patience, fortitude, and serenity of spirit, she uniformly exhibited, under circumstances that would have filled with dismay, and rendered miserable, almost any one not made "perfect through suffering." [7]

You are not a stranger to her many good qualities and rare merits — as your acquaintance with her began at an earlier period than mine. If she had any faults or failings, I was not good enough to make the discovery. She was eminently conscientious, kind, amiable, sympathetic, disinterested, benevolent. Her sense of propriety was ever active and discriminating, without being prudish. — Hers was the exactness of virtue and the beauty of modesty. Her piety was not wordy, loud-tongued, ostentatious, occasional, but simple, quiet, permanent, "in deed and in truth." [8] In all the works and ways of God, she found rest and satisfaction.

It was extremely comforting to her to have her cherished friend and sisterly companion with her in her closing hours — our much esteemed and ever faithful Olive Gilbert,[9] who arrived here about ten days ago from central New York, and who, I believe, had the pleasure of seeing you and your beloved family on her way down. They had for many years been one in sympathy, affection, suffering, and goodness.

[. . . .]

We are glad to hear, through Miss Gilbert, that you and yours are all in good health and spirits. Much do we desire to see you all again in the flesh, but know not when to hope that time will come. In spirit, we feel that nothing divides us, and trust the union between us will prove eternal.

[. . . .]

George [. . .] and Helen, [. . . remem]brances to [. . . .]

AL: Smith College Library. The bottom of the last page, including the signature, is torn off.

1. George W. Benson was then living in Northampton, Massachusetts.
2. Sarah Benson was Garrison's sister-in-law. See the introductory biographical sketch of the Benson family in *Letters*, II, xxiii.
3. Garrison's wife, the sister of Sarah and George W. Benson.
4. II Corinthians 12:15.
5. Thomas Gray (1716–1771), *Elegy Written in a Country Churchyard*.
6. Hebrews 12:23.
7. A variation of I Peter 5:10.
8. I John 3:18.
9. Olive Gilbert (b. August 6, 1801; d. Franklin, Massachusetts, January 5, 1884) lived in Brooklyn, Connecticut, until 1872 and subsequently, for some time, in Vineland, New Jersey. She must have been a childhood friend of the Benson children. She never married. (George Gordon Gilbert and Geoffrey Gilbert, compilers, *Gilberts of New England*, Victoria, B.C., 1959, part I, p. 159.)

15

TO WILLIAM RATHBONE

Boston, Oct. 17, 1850.

William Rathbone, Esq.

Dear Sir — I take the liberty of introducing to you — knowing your courtesy to American strangers in Liverpool, irrespective of the colour of their skin — the bearer of this, Mr. William P. Powell,[1] a colored gentleman of New York, with whom I have long been acquainted, and who is highly esteeemed for his enterprising spirit, his moral integrity of character, and his many excellent qualities, by all who know him. He is well and favourably known by many of the merchants and shipmasters of New York, in which city he has long been at the head of an institution for the special benefit of coloured seamen. He takes out with him, I believe, a considerable shipment of flour. He intends visiting portions of England, Scotland and Ireland, with a view to locating himself permanently on your side of the Atlantic, for the sake of his family. He has several children, and is anxious and determined to give them a better education, under better circumstances, than he can do in America; for, although the spirit of complexional caste is very much weakened in the free States of America, through the unwearied labours and faithful testimonies of the abolitionists; yet there is much to discourage those who are identified in complexion with the slave population, and many obstacles that remain as yet wholly insurmountable.

Should Mr. Powell decide to take up his residence in England, his removal will be a great loss to us here; as such an example as he has given of true self-respect and moral worth, as a coloured man, is of great value. But he has the feelings of a loving father for the welfare, improvement and freedom of his children; and I do not wonder that he is disposed to turn his back upon the land in which there are three millions of his brethren held in chattel slavery, and the evil spirit of complexional caste is every where omnipotent — even though it be the land of his nativity.

Never has this nation been so convulsed on the subject of slavery as at the present time. The Fugitive Slave Bill, (so called,) which was passed at the late session of Congress, granting unlimited facilities as it does to slave-hunters in quest of their prey, — and striking down, as it does, the writ of habeas corpus, trial by jury, and all the safeguards of liberty, in the non-slaveholding States of this Union, — is producing a tremendous sensation, and rousing up all the human, moral and religious elements in the land against it, and against the foul system it is designed to strengthen and protect. Under this Bill, a fugitive slave, named Hamlet,[2] who had been living in safety for several years in New York, was stealthily arrested, a short time since, and summarily sent back to bondage; but was speedily redeemed by the humanity of the citizens, seven or eight hundred dollars being paid for his freedom. On his return to the city, an enthusiastic meeting of the colored and white citizens was held in the Park, to express their joy at his deliverance. At that meeting, my friend Mr. Powell had the honour to preside.

If you can give Mr. Powell any information in reply to any inquiries that he may make, it may be of service to him and will greatly oblige
Yours, with great esteem,

Wm. Lloyd Garrison.

ALS: Merrill Collection of Garrison Papers, Wichita State University, Wichita, Kansas.

William Rathbone (b. Liverpool, June 17, 1787; d. Greenbank, February 1, 1868) was the son of a prominent Liverpool merchant and reformer. A reformer in his own right, he was active in philanthropy and education, in Catholic emancipation, and in Parliamentary and municipal reform (for which he received public recognition in 1836). In 1837 he was mayor of Liverpool. In 1846–1847, during the Irish famine, he was in charge of the distribution of a relief fund from New England. A Unitarian by conviction, he was a member of the Society of Friends until 1829.

1. William P. Powell (b. New York State, 1806; d. 1875) was a grandson of Elizabeth Barjova, cook for the Continental Congress, and the son of Edward Powell, a New York slave. He was born free and spent most of his early years at sea, possibly as a cook. In October 1833, he helped form an antislavery society in New Bedford. He was then a staunch Garrisonian and a subscriber and occasional contributor to *The Liberator*. He also conducted a boarding house for sailors in New Bedford and married an Indian girl of Plymouth, Massachusetts. Moving to New York in 1839, he opened a sailors' home at 10 John Street, then at 33 Pearl Street, New York City. He conducted his business under the auspices of the American Seamen's Friends Society, with an employment bureau as an adjunct until 1851. He took a prominent part in public antislavery meetings, his home provided hospitality for many antislavery leaders, and he was very active in helping fugitive slaves. Powell sailed for England near the end of October and arrived December 12, 1850. He returned to the United States several months later, only to depart again, this time with his family, arriving in England in December 1851. He took up residence in Liverpool, secured a job in the British Custom Service, and remained for about ten years. He returned to the United States with his family in 1861 and continued his association with the sailors' home in both New Bedford and New York. The latter was almost destroyed in the Draft Riot of 1863, with Powell and his family barely escaping with their lives. He went west in 1875 and died on the way to Honolulu shortly thereafter. (G. W. Forbes, *Biographical Sketches of Eminent Negroes*, mimeographed copy, Rare Book Room, Boston Public Library, n.d.; letter datelined New Bedford, July 18, 1863, from Powell to Garrison in *The Liberator*, July 24, 1863.)

With regard to Powell's trip to England, see *The Standard*, October 24, 1850.

2. In October 1850, James Hamlet was thirty years old and a porter by occupation in New York City. While at work, on Saturday, September 28, 1850, he had been seized by two deputy United States marshals, and taken to the United States Commissioner's office where he was accused of being a fugitive slave. As related in the *National Anti-Slavery Standard* (October 3, 1850), "after a brief examination of the person so claiming him, without any rebutting testimony being admitted, without the advice of counsel as to what plea he should make to establish his right to freedom, without time being allowed for the arrival of the counsel sent for, he was delivered over by the Commissioner, as a slave, to the claimant, who immediately demanded the protection and aid of the U. S. Marshal, to insure the safe return of the party to the residence of the said claimant, in Baltimore. Hereupon handcuffs were fastened upon the wrists of Hamlet; he was hurried into a carriage by the officers in whose custody he was placed, and in a few moments was on his way to Baltimore. He left behind him a wife and three young children, who were not even aware of his arrest till he was on his way to the South."

The Negroes of New York, during the succeeding days, raised $800 for the purpose of buying Hamlet and celebrated his return home at a great mass meeting at twelve noon, on October 5, 1850, in the public park. Several thousand persons attended. (For a description of the meeting, see *The National Anti-Slavery Standard*, October 10, 1850; see also Quarles, *Black Abolitionists*, pp. 197–198.)

16

TO THE EDITOR OF THE *TIMES*

[Nov. 1, 1850.]

To the Editor of the Times:

SIR, — In the Times of this morning appears a paragraph, relating to the arrival of George Thompson, Esq.,[1] in this city, representing him as having been imported by the abolitionists for the purpose of extinguishing the fugitive slave law![2] This statement is wholly inaccurate. The visit of Mr. Thompson has no reference whatever to that law, or to any other special aspect of the slavery question. The simple fact is, that, as long ago as last winter, it was publicly announced that he intended to be here as early as the 1st of August. Circumstances having prevented his coming at that time, it was supposed that he had abandoned his purpose of visiting this country during the present year, until the receipt of a letter about three weeks ago, announcing his intention to sail by the Canada. He merely takes advantage of the interval between the sessions of Parliament to revisit us, in order to renew his acquaintance with the friends of former years; to invigorate his physical system, much worn by his indefatigable labors in the cause of British reform; and to address the people here, only when solicited to do so, on those subjects which overleap all national, all geographical boundaries.

Surely, it cannot be the intention of a Democratic journal intentionally to misrepresent or assail the man who powerfully aided in liberating eight hundred thousand British slaves from their chains; who has consecrated his best energies to the cause of universal emancipation; who has boldly grappled with the colossal power of the East India Company, and vindicated the cause of one hundred and fifty millions of the natives of India, the victims of British misrule; who, with Cobden[3] and Bright,[4] made himself conspicuous for his powerful and successful efforts for the abolition of the Corn Laws and the triumph of free trade; who is now specially engaged, in connection with the National Reform Association,[5] in behalf of the oppressed laboring classes of England, and for the extension of the elective franchise; who, three years ago, was returned to Parliament by the constituency of the Tower Hamlets, London, the largest in Great Britain, upon the most radical and reformatory principles, in the place of a scion of the Whig nobility, and the son-in-law of an English king,[6] and by a majority unequalled in the annals of British elections;

and who, in his place in Parliament, was one of only thirteen, who voted for the 'People's Charter.' [7]

WM. LLOYD GARRISON.

Boston, Nov. 1, 1850.

Printed in *The Liberator*, November 8, 1850.

The Boston *Daily Times*, a penny daily, first appeared in 1836, under the management of George Roberts and William H. Garfield, and lasted for twenty-one years. During its early years it sought to avoid politics, but by 1850 it had become Democratic. It was absorbed in 1857 by the *Herald*. (Mott, *American Journalism, A History: 1690–1960*, 3d. ed., New York, 1962, pp. 238–239.)

1. George Thompson, the great English abolitionist and Garrison's close friend for almost two decades, had last been in the United States in 1835 when he finally had to return precipitously to England as a result of the violence which he encountered. (For further biographical information, see *Letters*, II, xxix, and Volumes I and II, *passim*.) Thompson arrived in the United States, for the second time, on October 29, 1850.

2. The statement as it appeared in the *Times* read, in part, as follows: "We hear that the Abolitionists have imported Thompson as a 'star' — to extinguish the Fugitive Slave Law."

3. Richard Cobden (1804–1865), English calico merchant, manufacturer, economist, and statesman, was a vigorous advocate of free trade, which he expressed in pamphlets issued in 1835 and 1836. He was a prominent member of the Anti-Corn Law League, founded at Manchester in 1838, and sought actively the repeal of the laws placing a duty on the importation of corn. Elected to Parliament from Stockport, he delivered his maiden speech on August 25, 1841, in opposition to the corn laws. The repeal of the corn laws in 1846 was the basis of Cobden's reputation as the savior of the poor.

4. John Bright (1811–1889), English statesman and orator, helped found the Anti-Corn Law League in cooperation with Richard Cobden and others. He was elected to the House of Commons from Durham in 1843 and contributed to the repeal of the corn laws in 1846. In 1847, and again in 1852, he was elected to Parliament for Manchester. He opposed the advocates of the Crimean war and in 1858 played an important part in the admission of Jews to Parliament and in the transfer of the government of India from the East India Company to the crown.

5. In January 1849, with the decline of Chartism, Sir Joshua Walmsley, M.P. for Leicester, Joseph Hume, George Thompson, and several middle-class radicals, "formed the National Parliamentary and Financial Reform Association, designed to unite Radical Free Traders and moderate Chartists on a programme of household suffrage. Finding that this by itself would attract no working-class support, the new Association proceeded in August to widen its programme to include a lodge franchise and the abolition of the property qualification for members of Parliament." (G. D. H. Cole, *Chartist Portraits*, London, 1941, pp. 291–292.)

6. The reference is to Colonel Charles Richard Fox (b. November 6, 1796; d. April 13, 1873), a distinguished numismatist and member of Parliament. He was the natural son of Henry Richard Vassall Fox, Third Baron Holland, and Elizabeth Vassall Fox. After representing several other constituencies in Parliament, he represented Tower Hamlets from 1841 to 1847, when he was succeeded by George Thompson. In 1824, Fox married Lady Mary Fitzclarence, the second daughter of the Duke of Clarence and Mrs. Dorothea Jordan, the famous actress. The Duke of Clarence later became King William IV and reigned from 1830 to 1837. (Gerrit P. Judd IV, *Members of Parliament 1734–1832*, London, 1955, p. 200; Frederick Boase, *Modern English Biography*, Truro, 1892, I, 1094.)

7. The "People's Charter" had been drawn up in 1838 by six members of the House of Commons and representatives of the Workingmen's Association. It called

for universal male suffrage, abolition of property qualifications for a seat in Parliament, equal representation, payment of members of Parliament, and vote by ballot.

1 7

TO FRANCIS JACKSON

Anti-Slavery Office,
Dec. 31, 1850.

Friend Jackson:

The bearer of this — John Morgan [1] — says that, some years ago, he worked as a printer on the Liberator; and recently has been at Thomaston, Maine, working at his trade, but, by the failure of the newspaper establishment at that place, lost all that was due to him, and is now very destitute. He desires to get a passage to New York, if possible, as he says he can obtain a situation there, on his arrival. *This is not to solicit of you any money*, but to inquire whether it is probable you could obtain for Morgan a free pass to New York? I know nothing of his case, beyond the statement herein given by himself, but have no doubt it would be an act of charity to grant him the desired pass.

Yours, truly,

Wm. Lloyd Garrison.

Francis Jackson, Esq.

ALS: Garrison Papers, Boston Public Library.

1. John Morgan is unidentified except for the description of him by Garrison.

1 8

TO WENDELL PHILLIPS

Jan., 1851

Dear P. — There is no one to whom I can more freely unbosom myself, in any extremity, than yourself; and therefore I confidingly submit my case to your friendship.

On the first of this month, I find that I owe for the necessaries of life, during the past year, above what I have a dollar to pay with, something over two hundred dollars, — the bills running as follows, that remain unsettled: —

(In.) [1]

This deficit, it is just to state, is not all to be put down to the past year, but a portion belongs to a previous year, — as each quarter, during that entire period, has entrenched upon the receipts of the next, to meet unavoidable expenditures. Various circumstances, during the last 3 mos. — sickness in the family, incidental expenses arising from the visit of our beloved G[eorge] T[hompson], the purchase of a large parlor stove, &c. &c., — have served to make the sum total of indebtedness greater than it would have been ordinarily.

I need not protest to you, my dear Phillips, that I have not thoughtlessly or needlessly got thus straitened. If my conscience is lively in any direction, it is in regard to the use of money, especially while I occupy a dependent position. I am neither a spendthrift nor improvident, but careful and scrupulous, and ever anxious to keep out of debt. But, in spite of my best efforts in this respect, (seconded faithfully by dear Helen, whose dread of debt is of the strongest kind, and to whose economy in regard to personal expenditures & household affairs, I can bear grateful testimony,) at the beginning of this year I find myself, pecuniarily, just as I have stated above. My family is large, & with increasing age the children unavoidably augment the burden of support. My connection with the A. S. cause is such as to increase my family expenses, — i.e. to exhibit any thing like hospitality; though I endeavor to keep the number entertained at my table as much reduced as I can with civility — still the average is large. Upon myself, my expenditures are small — for personal fancy or gratification, nothing. Every thing is absorbed in "bread & butter," rent & fuel, and necessary clothing. But details like these are not needed by you to inspire confidence or remove doubt, and I will not multiply them.

In addition to my usual salary, I have received something for lecturing services; but with this incidental aid, I am still embarrassed.

Before the past year terminated, foreseeing how I was coming out, my mind was greatly exercised as to how Providence might open a way for me to meet my pecuniary liabilities. My deep indebtedness to you, and a few other beloved friends, on various occasions made me sick at heart to think of increasing it by any statement of my real situation that might lead to further assistance; especially when you all have so many calls upon your charity, in the A. S. cause in particular, and to relieve suffering humanity in general.

AL: Garrison Papers, Boston Public Library.

This letter was probably a first draft. It was written in pencil on the blank inner pages of a note from Parker Pillsbury to Garrison, dated January 1, 1851. The month and year at the top of the letter may not have been inserted by Garrison. We have not reproduced words or phrases which Garrison crossed out.

1. "(In.)" probably refers to the list of expenses on the last page of the letter, which Garrison may have meant to insert in the final copy. The list reads as follows:

"Strong's,	$14"41	Fay's,	15"97
Farwell's,	12"47	Wood,	37"25
Milk,	9"30	Geist,	26"00
Horn's,	37"50	Curtis,	15"00
Hovey,	6"56	Miss Bannun	20"00
Kingsbury,	46"86	Wallaces,	5"00"

19

TO DRS. WILLIAM CLARK AND —— PORTER

BOSTON, Jan. 23, 1851.

Drs. Clark [1] & Porter: Gentlemen — Last year, suffering much from a scrofulous diathesis, and also general bodily debility, I was induced to test the efficacy of your Anti-Scrofulous Panacea. Its renovating effect upon my system was very soon apparent in my restoration to a state of health much better than I had enjoyed for several years previous. I gained in flesh several pounds beyond the highest point I had ever attained before, and was much improved in every respect, being enabled to go through an unusual amount of mental labor and public lecturing with difficulty. I used some half a dozen bottles. Your Panacea is very pleasant to the taste, and permeates through the system in a very quickening manner. I have repeatedly recommended it in my paper, and among my friends and acquaintances, as unquestionably remedial or alleviative in the various complaints for which it is prescribed, and have known its salutary effects in several cases of Scrofula, Salt Rheum, &c. I cheerfully give you this certificate, (the first I have ever given any medical preparation,) being desirous that the merits of your Panacea may be more extensively known, and its sale widely extended.[2]

Yours, respectfully,

WM. LLOYD GARRISON.

Printed as part of an advertisement in *The Liberator*, May 2, May 16, May 23, May 30, etc., 1851.

1. For biographical information about Dr. Clark see *Letters*, II, 342–343.
2. On January 13, 1853, Edmund Quincy wrote to Richard Davis Webb of Dublin, Ireland, concerning Garrison's gullibility in the area of medicine: "He is quite ignorant of physiology and has no belief in hygiene, or in anything pertaining to the body except *quack medicines*. That he has survived all he has taken is proof of an excellent constitution. . . . You remember his puff of Dr. C——'s Anti-Scrofulous Panacea, . . . in which he said that he felt it 'permeating the whole system in the most delightful manner.' 'Permeating the system!' said Hervey Wes-

ton, with the malice of a regular practitioner; 'why, it was the first time he had taken a glass of grog, and [he] didn't know how good it was!' — some sort of spirits being the basis of all these sort of quackeries." (*Life*, IV, 323.)

It may be said in defense of Dr. Clark that he was publicly opposed to the use of alcohol in medicines and was a staunch temperance man. Either Quincy was wrong or Clark was an out-and-out scoundrel.

---

2 0

TO GEORGE THOMPSON GARRISON

Boston, February 18, 1851.

My dear Son:

You must excuse Mother for using the pen for me, as I have been for the last five days, nearly all the time, prostrate on my back, in consequence of a severe inflammatory attack of the spine. I am now a little relieved, and hope in a few days to be so far recovered as to go with Mother to Syracuse. But I may have to abandon the journey altogether. If so, you shall be informed of the fact.

I wish you to say to your school teacher, Miss Ballou,[1] that I intended to converse with her particularly with regard to your studies; but our time was so limited, and so much occupied, while we were at Hopedale, that no convenient opportunity presented itself. I had nothing special to suggest to her, but she may have thought it a little strange that I made no inquiries of her respecting your progress in learning. I think you are very fortunate in having so amiable and excellent a teacher, and trust you will feel more and more resolved to improve the present opportunity to the utmost in your power. Be not discouraged, be not discontented. You are now laying the foundations for a useful life. There is no place in the world, away from home, where I feel that you could be so well guarded as to your morals, and cared for as to your happiness, as in the Hopedale community. It is a great thing to be with those who are virtuous, upright, industrious, honest, kind, and loving, in all their dealings and actions. The instructions that you will receive, I am confident, will be such as I can heartily approve; and, if followed, cannot fail to be of everlasting benefit to you.

I do not wish you to be too anxious about earning money to help me pay for your board and schooling. Whatever work you do must, of course, be done steadily; but do not make it oppressive by your desire to relieve me. Whatever money you need, you can make use of out of your earnings, as I am confident you will spend it properly.

You will see, by the papers, that we have had another slave case in the city,[2] within a few days past, and that the slave was rescued by the colored people. There is great excitement here now, but it will probably subside in the course of a few days. The slave is by this time safely in Canada.

Mr. Thompson was very much pleased with his visit to Hopedale,[3] as well as myself. The more he is known the more he will be beloved. You see that I have named you after a great and good man.

Give my warmest regards to Mr. and Mrs. Fish,[4] Mr. and Mrs. Draper,[5] Mr. Ballou [6] and family, &c.

Yours, affectionately,

Wm. Lloyd Garrison.

LS: Merrill Collection of Garrison Papers, Wichita State University Library. The letter was dictated by Garrison to his wife, and was preceded by letters from Helen Garrison and William Lloyd Garrison, Jr. to George Thompson Garrison. "Yours, affectionately," and the signature were written by Garrison.

George Thompson Garrison (b. February 13, 1836; d. January 26, 1904), Garrison's first child, was associated with his father in publishing *The Liberator* until about 1857, when he went west. He lived for a while in Nininger, Minnesota, where he worked in a blind and sash factory, whence he went to Nebraska, where he was engaged in printing. He returned to Boston in 1859. With the advent of the Civil War, he enlisted in the army, and became a lieutenant in the Massachusetts 55th Regiment, a black outfit. He served at the front for two years. After the war, he engaged in various businesses until ill health forced him to retire. He married Annie Anthony in 1873. (Boston *Evening Transcript*, obituary, January 28, 1904; *New York Times*, obituary, January 28, 1904.)

1. Abigail Sayles Ballou (b. 1829; fl. 1888) was the daughter of Adin Ballou, Universalist clergyman, reformer, and founder of the Hopedale Community, at Hopedale, Massachusetts. She began teaching at an early age, graduated from the state Normal School at West Newton, Massachusetts, and became distinguished as an educator. On May 11, 1851, she married the Reverend William Sweetser Heywood, who had come to the Hopedale Community in 1848, had been ordained in 1849, and eventually became president of the Community. He and Abigail Ballou joined in setting up the Hopedale Home School, which they ran successfully for two years. They left Hopedale in 1864, with Heywood thereafter serving as pastor in various communities, including Scituate, Hudson, Holyoke and Boston, Massachusetts. (Adin Ballou, *An Elaborate History and Genealogy of the Ballous in America*, Providence, 1888, pp. 873–875.)

2. Shadrach, or Frederick Wilkins, was a fugitive slave from Norfolk, Virginia, who had been employed in Boston for almost a year at Taft's Cornhill Coffee House near the courthouse. He was captured at his place of work on Saturday morning, February 15, 1851, by John Capehart, an agent of his master, and nine deputy marshals, who carried him to the courthouse, where he was brought before the United States commissioner, Judge George T. Curtis.

Shadrach was defended by Richard Henry Dana, Jr., who was joined by Robert H. Morris, Charles G. Davis, Charles List, Ellis Gray Loring, and Samuel Sewall. On the motion of Shadrach's lawyers, Commissioner Curtis had granted a delay of the case until Tuesday. By the early afternoon, however, a crowd of blacks had collected, rushed into the courtroom, surrounded Shadrach, and carried him out before anyone could interfere. In a few minutes he had disappeared, ultimately arriving in Canada and freedom.

Several persons were subsequently arrested, charged with having played a part in Shadrach's rescue. These included, among others, Elizur Wright, present in the courtroom as a correspondent at the time of rescue, Robert H. Morris, Charles G. Davis, James Scott, and Robert Hayden. The latter two were Negroes who had apparently actively aided in the escape. In each of the trials, the jury was unable to reach a verdict and the cases were dismissed. (Lawrence Lader, *The Bold Brahmins: New England's War Against Slavery (1831–1863)*, New York, 1961, pp. 161–167; *Life*, III, 325–327; *The Liberator*, February 21, 1851.)

3. *The Liberator*, February 14, 1851, carried an unsigned article, by Garrison, "The Cause Advances," which noted that "we made a very pleasant and refreshing visit, with Mr. Thompson, on Sunday, to our beloved friends at the Hopedale Community, by whom we were both received in a manner only as kindred spirits can express. The usual meetings for religious improvement were held in their commodious school house during the day, and highly gratified were we to be present. In the afternoon, our cherished co-laborer in the great field of Christian Reform, Adin Ballou, made a truly felicitous address to Mr. Thompson, in behalf of all present, in the course of which he explained, in a very lucid and comprehensive manner, the principles on which the Community at Hopedale is based, and the objects it has in view, and gave the outlines of its rise and progress up to the present time — concluding by giving Mr. Thompson the right hand of fellowship as the friend and benefactor of the human race.

"Mr. Thompson responded in a very feeling manner, and was evidently much affected. He humbly disclaimed any higher merit than that of being a sincere and earnest laborer in the cause of suffering humanity; and expressed his high appreciation of the moral worth of those who surrounded him, and wished them all desirable success in their great undertaking."

4. The Reverend William Henry Fish (b. Newport, Rhode Island, March 25, 1812; d. July 8, 1880) married Anne Eliza Wright (b. Providence, Rhode Island, May 9, 1815) on June 8, 1835. He was ordained in 1838 as a minister among the Independent Restorationists of the Massachusetts Association, and first served as a minister in Millville, Massachusetts, where he remained nine years. He was a leader in forming the Hopedale Community and resided in it from 1846 to 1855. From the beginning, in 1841, he was the community's Intendent of Religion, Morals, and Missions. In 1854, Fish was an agent of the Worcester County Anti-Slavery Society. In 1855, he went to central New York on a missionary tour for the community, intending to remain but a few months, and stayed almost ten years. In 1865, at the suggestion of Samuel J. May, he was called to the First Parish Church (Unitarian) in South Scituate, Massachusetts. (Adin Ballou, *History of the Town of Milford, Worcester County, Mass.*, Boston, 1882, pp. 746–747; Adin Ballou, *History of the Hopedale Community*, Lowell, Massachusetts, 1897, pp. 15, 49, 84, 275; *The Liberator*, June 9, July 7, and 28, 1854.)

5. Ebenezer D. Draper (b. Weston, Massachusetts, June 14, 1813; d. Boston, October 19, 1887), a well-to-do manufacturer and merchant, was a partner with his brother in the firm of E. D. and G. Draper, manufacturers of temples for weaving. Ebenezer Draper married Anna Thwing in 1834. Both joined the Hopedale Fraternal Community as original members in 1841. He became its president in 1852 after Adin Ballou's resignation and contributed heavily to it in financial resources and management ability. When it became evident at the end of 1855 that the community was in debt, its liabilities exceeding its resources, he withdrew from the organization in 1856, taking with him his share of the enterprise's capital stock, which amounted to about three-fourths, at the same time guaranteeing the organization's debt, which was paid with interest. From then until 1868, he was in partnership with his brother in the Hopedale Manufacturing Company, which made them both wealthy. He was devoted to antislavery, temperance, and non-resistance. It is said that during his prosperity he made it a rule to give away each year as much or more than he expended for his living. (*Life*, IV, 367; Thomas Wall-Morgan, *The Drapers in America*, New York, 1892, pp. 100, 108–109.)

6. Adin Ballou (1803–1890), Universalist clergyman and editor of the *Practical Christian*, was a founder of the Hopedale Community in 1841 and its presi-

dent until 1852. He was the author of *Practical Christian Socialism* (1854) and other works.

---

2 1

TO WHOM IT MAY CONCERN

BOSTON, March 4, 1851.

I commend the bearer of this, Francis S. Anderson,[1] a poor, hunted, fugitive American slave, to the sympathy and kind consideration of the philanthropic and Christian people of England. Notwithstanding his amiable spirit, his upright deportment, his good intelligence, his capacity for usefulness, his Christian profession, and his connection with a Christian church as a most exemplary member thereof, on no part of the American soil, between the Atlantic and the Pacific, is he permitted to live as a rational and accountable being! Though created in the divine image, and desirous of 'glorifying God in his body and spirit, which are his,'[2] he is held by the laws of the country as a chattel personal; the property of another, and can avoid that terrible doom only by a clandestine flight from the land of his nativity. The present is a dark and perilous hour for all fugitive slaves still remaining in America. The whole power of the National Government is concentrating for their re-capture, banishment, or extermination. Houseless, penniless, every white person forbidden by heavy penalties to give them either shelter or food, they are fleeing in every direction, filled with terror, anguish and despair, and experiencing much bodily suffering. Oh, the guilt of Christian, republican America.

WM. LLOYD GARRISON.

Printed in the *National Anti-Slavery Standard*, May 1, 1851.
   The article in the *Standard* (May 1, 1851) which contains this letter is taken from the London *Inquirer*. The letter is prefixed by this paragraph:
   "MORE TROPHIES OF AMERICAN LIBERTY.
   "Two more fugitive slaves, driven from the United States, have arrived at Liverpool by one of the line of packet ships, from Boston. One of them bears with him the following touching document from William Lloyd Garrison."

and followed by the further explanation:

   "The poor fellow who bears the above, escaped from Slavery six years ago, and has ever since been a resident in the 'Free States,' earning a respectable living as a waiter, till thus compelled to leave the country, or be carried back again to bondage."
   After printing a letter from Samuel May to Francis Bishop about another fugitive slave, the article goes on:
   "The *Liverpool Mercury*, of Tuesday, says, 'The two poor men who have thus sought liberty and protection on English ground are, we regret to find, in an almost

penniless condition; and no wonder, for the Abolitionists of Boston must have to divide their charities amongst so many hunted fugitives, that when the passage money has been paid, in cases like the present, there can be but little left for subsequent necessities. Both the fugitives are anxious to proceed to London, thinking that there they will be more likely to obtain employment than in the country. We have been requested, and shall be very glad, to take charge of any subscriptions that may help them forward, and give them the means of living for a few weeks, till they can find work, as they are evidently most anxious to do, and so maintain themselves.' "

    1. Otherwise unidentified.
    2. I Corinthians 6:20.

---

2 2

TO ABBY KELLEY FOSTER

Boston, March 25, 1851.

Most persevering, most self-sacrificing, most energetic, most meritorious of coadjutors: —

In reply to your letter, urging me to be in Syracuse on the 15th of next month, to meet dear Thompson on his return from Canada, and attend with him a few anti-slavery conventions prior to the anniversary of the American A. S. Society, a just regard for my health requires me to say, that I must reluctantly decline an invitation, which, under other circumstances, would be accepted with exceeding joy, and with an "alacrity" which Nero [1] Webster desires to see exhibited in the catching of fugitive slaves. It is true, the power of locomotion between my house and office is once more granted to me, and I am relieved from the acute pain in my spine which has for several weeks kept me prostrate; but I am still extremely weak, and utterly unfit to think of engaging in any public lecturing, whether at home or abroad. Bodily, I am in a condition that makes "the grasshopper a burden"; [2] and mentally, I am far from being vigorous. Most fortunate was it that my illness began before I started on my contemplated tour; but it has deprived me of an amount of pleasure, in being the travelling companion of dear Thompson, and in witnessing the warm reception which has been every where extended to him, as well as of seeing and communing with the noble friends of our great cause in western New York, which I have no arithmetical powers to compute. If tears and lamentations could avail any thing, I could furnish them in any quantity.

I fully agree with you as to the importance of the speedy organization of a New York State A. S. Society, auxiliary to the American Society, the head quarters thereof to be located at Syracuse. This ought to be effected, if possible, before Mr. Thompson leaves for Boston. How to be present at its formation, with [Wendell] Phillips, Quincy,[3] Burleigh,[4] &c. I see not, except by an arrangement of this kind.

Let the anniversary of the American A. S. Society be held at Syracuse, at the usual time in May;[5] and in conjunction with it, let a special meeting be called to form a State Society. We should then have much of our anti-slavery strength present, and thus "kill two birds with one stone." I make this suggestion, in order to further your plans, and as presenting the only probability that either Phillips or myself will be able to visit Western New York until another season, if at that period. I make it, also, believing that it will be utterly impracticable for us to hold our annual meeting in New York. Between the upper and the nether millstone — the great "Union Committee"[6] on the one hand, and Rynders and his demon-gang on the other — we shall hardly fail of being pulverized on that occasion. In other words, it will be "chaos come again,"[7] *and more too*, as compared with last year. You are aware, I presume, that the Tabernacle has been closed against us; and Mr. Gay writes that no public hall in the city can be procured for our meeting. These are only premonitory symptoms. Even if a suitable hall could be procured, it would be impossible for us to hold a meeting. I do not like the appearance of succumbing; yet I dislike mere contumacy, for the sake of showing that we are full of pluck, quite as much. Certainly, there are occasions when common sense and true wisdom harmonize with the declaration — "If they persecute you in one city, flee ye into another."[8] It is not necessary, at this late day, for abolitionists to prove themselves courageous and mob-proof. It is not a question of principle — of yielding anything, except to the city of New York the infamy of being thoroughly under the control of mob law — but one of sound judgment, a wise forecast, and real availability. My judgment is clear, that it would be a fine stroke of policy (in the highest use of the term) to transfer the meeting to Syracuse, where we may count upon having a large, enthusiastic, and most profitable gathering. If this could be done, I would try to be with you and Mr. Thompson some two or three weeks before the meeting, (say a fortnight,) — but, otherwise, I could not think of going such a distance, and then returning exhausted to encounter the excitement of the scenes in New York city.

A few days since, a meeting of the Executive Committee was held to deliberate on this subject, at which I fully expressed my views, as I have briefly done to you. The majority, I think, incline going to New York city, as usual; but in case no place can be obtained for our meeting in that city, then to hold it in Brooklyn, if any hall or meeting-house can be there secured for that purpose, which is somewhat doubtful. By a vote of the Committee, Mr. [Samuel] May [Jr.] was instructed to visit New York and Brooklyn, and report progress. He will leave here to-morrow, and we shall know the result in the course of the present week. If we are compelled to retire from N. Y. city, I see not why we might not go to Syracuse as well as to Brooklyn, and much better too — for then we should have Thompson with us, and the organization of a State Society could be then effected.

Of course, I for one am content to be hooted at, mobbed, and personally outraged, if need be, for the cause's sake, in the great city of Babylon. Whether our meeting be allowed or not, I have no fears as to the result — not I. But, soberly and sincerely, I believe we may rightfully and efficaciously "shake off the dust" [9] from our feet upon that great focal point of Northern selfishness and pro-slavery diabolism, and do a great work at the same time in western New York. I presume, however, if any place can be procured in Brooklyn, the Executive Committee will decide to hold the annual meeting in that city, and leave western New York to take care of itself for the present. A majority of the members attach more importance to the fact of attempting to hold our meeting in that direction, than I do. In case, however, that Brooklyn will afford us no hall, the Committee will unanimously vote, I think, to hold the meeting in Syracuse. What is your opinion? What is Stephen's [10] and George [Thompson]'s?

See to it that G. T. is not utterly prostrated by excessive labor. I really fear for his life among his friends and admirers. I will try to write to him to-morrow. Love to him and your dear husband — &c. &c.

Yours, faithfully,

Wm. Lloyd Garrison.

Abby Kelley Foster.

ALS: Abigail Kelley Foster Papers, American Antiquarian Society.

Abigail Kelley Foster (b. Pelham, Massachusetts, January 15, 1810; d. Worcester, Massachusetts, January 14, 1887), Quaker, teacher, antislavery and woman's rights leader, began her antislavery activities as a reader of Garrison's *Liberator* while teaching at a Friends' school in Lynn, and served as secretary of the Lynn Female Anti-Slavery Society from 1835 to 1837. In 1838, she abandoned teaching for full-time antislavery activity with the Garrisonian abolitionists. Spurred on by the example of Angelina Grimké, she has been said to be "the first Massachusetts woman to have regularly addressed mixed audiences." It was her appointment to the executive committee of the American Anti-Slavery Society that was the occasion of the split in the society in 1840 and the secession of a substantial number of its members. During the same year, she was a delegate to the World's Anti-Slavery Convention at London. She continued as a leading Garrisonian abolitionist for the next two decades. In 1845, she married Stephen S. Foster. A serious ideological and personal dispute developed in 1859 between her and her husband, on the one hand, and Garrison on the other, leading to a coolness in their relationship which was not overcome until the 1870's. (*Notable American Women.*)

1. The reference is to Daniel Webster and his responsibility for the Fugitive Slave Law.

2. Ecclesiastes 12:5.

3. Edmund Quincy was then corresponding secretary of the Massachusetts Anti-Slavery Society, an editor of the *Standard* and, from time to time, of *The Liberator* in Garrison's absence. See the biographical sketch of Quincy in *Letters*, II, xxviii–xxix.

4. William Henry Burleigh (1812–1871), brother of Charles, was an abolitionist and temperance man. *Life*, III, 330, notes that among those present at the Syracuse Convention was Burleigh, "who had strayed into the Liberty Party fold," but then "recanted of his bitter opposition to his old abolition co-workers." For additional biographical information see *Letters*, II, 178–179.

5. *The Liberator*, on April 11, 1851, carried a notice that the seventeenth annual meeting of the American Anti-Slavery Society would be held at Syracuse, New York, on Wednesday, May 7. It explained that "Hitherto, since the formation of the Society, the Annual Meeting has been uniformly held in the City of New York, and usually in the Broadway Tabernacle. So absolute, however, is the sway of the Slave Power in that city, and such the fear of mobocratic excesses (stimulated by 'The Union Committee' on the one hand, and the lawless Rynders and his crew on the other,) that no meeting-house or hall, in that great city can be procured, either for the love of liberty or for gold, for the accommodation of the Society. Neither in the adjacent city of Brooklyn can any suitable building be obtained for this purpose."

6. The reference is probably to the "Union Safety Committee," which held a large public dinner in New York City as a Washington's Birthday celebration on February 22. The dinner was held in support of the Union and the compromise measures of 1850. (See *The Liberator*, March 7, 1851.) "Union" committees sponsored such meetings in other large cities as well. (*The Liberator*, February 7 and 21, 1851.)

7. Shakespeare, *Othello*, III, iii, 92.

8. Matthew 10:23.

9. Matthew 10:14.

10. Stephen S. Foster (1809–1881) was a New Hampshire-born Dartmouth College graduate who studied for a while at the Union Theological Seminary but abandoned the ministry for a reformer's career. He became an antislavery lecturer in 1840. He was a nonresistant whose picturesque language involved him in perhaps more riots than most other abolitionists. One of his favorite declarations, usually made in a church, was that the Methodist Episcopal Church — because of its support of slavery — was worse than any brothel in New York City. The predictable riot usually followed. In 1844, in Boston, his book, *The Brotherhood of Thieves: or, A True Picture of the American Church and Clergy: A Letter to Nathaniel Barney of Nantucket*, was published. (Ruchames, *The Abolitionists*, p. 185.)

---

2 3

TO ABBY KELLEY FOSTER

Boston, April 6, 1851.

My Dear Friend:

I received a letter from Stephen, yesterday, dated "Lockport, March 31," containing various suggestions, and wishing me to apprise you, without delay, as to the place agreed upon for the approaching annual meeting of the Parent Society, and whether my health is so far restored as to warrant the expectation of my being in Western New York in the course of the present month.

As to our annual meeting, it is settled that it cannot be held in New York city or Brooklyn. Not a hall or meeting-house can be obtained in either of these populous cities, in which to plead the cause of the most miserable portion of the human race. Mr. Willis Hall,[1] a highly respectable gentleman of Brooklyn, was quite sanguine that he could procure for us Henry Ward Beecher's Church, for at least one meeting, and a commodious hall for our subsequent gatherings; but, after making a strenuous effort, he had to inform us, on Friday, that he was utterly foiled. Of course, Ward Beecher[2] was willing, and I believe desirous, that we should have his Church for our anniversary celebration; but a majority of the Committee were unwilling to give their consent.

Since this intelligence was received, no formal meeting of the Executive Committee has been held; but, at the last meeting, it was unanimously understood, I believe, if no place could be obtained in Brooklyn, then we would decide upon going to Syracuse. Since Mr Hall has notified us of his ill success, we have consulted together informally, and are entirely agreed as to our meeting being held in S[yracuse]. So you may consider this matter settled, and give notice accordingly. Under all the circumstances, I am not sorry that, being excluded from the city of New York, we are also shut out from Brooklyn, and therefore take our appeal from the seaboard to the interior. It is true, our Eastern delegation to Syracuse will be very small, on account of the distance and expense; and the number of delegates from Pennsylvania will probably be much smaller, than it would be if the meeting were held in Brooklyn; still, I think we shall be pretty sure to have a series of crowded and thrilling meetings, and the attendance from Ohio, I trust, will be more numerous than ever it has been, especially as we shall calculate on having with us our beloved and indefatigable Thompson, whose presence will be inspiring. I trust there will be no failure of the presence of Wendell Phillips, Edmund Quincy, Francis Jackson, and other well known friends of our cause in this region, especially our eloquent and beloved friend Phillips. It is not improbable that we shall also have with us the celebrated Joseph Barker,[3] of England, from whom I rceived a letter yesterday, stating that he should leave Liverpool on the 29th March, for New York, in the royal mail steamer Africa, so that he is now probably half way across the Atlantic. On arriving at New York, he will come to Boston to spend a few days, and will then go with his

family to Ohio. He expresses a strong desire at once publicly to identify himself with our cause, in the most unequivocal manner, and says
he shall be happy to attend any of our meetings. He is the man for
the people — the working people particularly — bold, outspoken, direct, and full of electric energy. I shall do what I can to secure his
attendance at Syracuse.

Our annual meeting had better begin on Wednesday than on
Tuesday, as it will enable us in this section to leave home on Monday,
and arrive in Syracuse in good season, with the usual night rest.

And now as to my coming in advance, to hold a few meetings with
Mr. Thompson, Mr. [Frederick] Douglass, and yourself. I am almost
afraid to make any promise, lest there should be another serious disappointment. I am much better than I have been, but still weak, so
that the public lecturing field, even to be occupied but a short time,
looks very formidable to me. Besides, "I am no orator as Brutus is," [4]
and it is a perilous thing to follow in the wake or in the presence of
George Thompson. My aversion to public speaking, under almost any
circumstances, is daily increasing. But the main thing now is, my
health. Stephen desires me to join you by the 15th inst. But this I cannot do. Besides, if (as Stephen writes) G. T. is to remain in Canada
a fortnight, and then to deliver a series of lectures in Buffalo, he would
not be able to meet me till after that time. I hardly dare to promise
to come earlier than the last of this month. On the 27th, I have agreed
to attend the County meeting at Worcester; but from this I might,
perhaps, get excused, though they are extremely desirous to have
me present. Mr. May suggests that I could attend this meeting on my
way to Syracuse. Perhaps I could spend ten days or a fortnight in
your region, after the annual meeting, if G. T. could be with me. At
any rate, you may expect me (say at Syracuse) by the 1st of May.
If I can write any thing more definitely in the course of a few days,
I will do so. Remember, however, that the annual meeting is fixed.

Phillips has just told me that Theodore Parker has intimated his
willingness to be one of our speakers at the annual meeting in Syracuse, if nothing unforeseen prevents. Rely upon it, we shall bring him
with us, if we can.

I wonder that you are not entirely broken down. Heaven watch
over you to the end!

I believe the regular time for holding our annual [meeting] is
Tuesday, the 6th of May. We shall change it to Wednesday, the 7th.

Yours, everlastingly for freedom,

Wm. Lloyd Garrison.

Abby Kelley Foster.

ALS: Abigail Kelley Foster Papers, American Antiquarian Society.

1. Willis Hall (1801–1868), a lawyer, was admitted to the bar in 1827, practiced in Mobile, Alabama, from 1827 to 1831 and in New York from 1831 to 1838. He was a member of the New York Assembly in 1837 and 1842. He served as attorney-general of New York for one year, in 1838. In 1848, at the Whig convention, he supported the nomination of Henry Clay for President, and opposed Zachary Taylor as the Whig candidate. He retired from professional and political life in 1848.

2. Henry Ward Beecher (June 24, 1813–March 8, 1887), prominent Presbyterian-Congregationalist antislavery clergyman, son of Dr. Lyman Beecher and brother of Harriet Beecher Stowe, was pastor of the Plymouth (Congregational) Church of Brooklyn from 1847 until his death. Evaluating Beecher's career, his biographer emphasizes that "for conspicuousness and influence [it] has probably not been equaled by that of any other American clergyman."

3. The Reverend Joseph Barker (1806–1875), wool-spinner at Bramley, near Leeds, as well as Methodist minister and traveling preacher, was expelled from the Methodist New Connexion in 1841 after several years of membership. He was pastor for some years at Newcastle-on-Tyne, during which period he left the Methodist denomination for Unitarianism, was imprisoned in 1848 for his connection with the Chartist agitation, and went to central Ohio in 1851. He returned to England in 1860, remained there for several years and finally went back to the United States, dying in Omaha, Nebraska. He published many religious works, conducted a printing business, issued "Barker's Library," a cheap series of theological, philosophical, and ethical works, and founded several periodicals. *Life*, III, 174, writes about his first meeting with Garrison in England in 1846 that "this able but shifting character was well calculated to impress Mr. Garrison as one of the most remarkable men he had yet met." Concerning Barker's move to the United States in 1851, *Life*, III, 384, writes: "Barker had apparently taken permanent leave of his native England, having purchased a farm in Ohio and removed thither with his family. . . . Once settled, he identified himself with the abolitionists, writing copiously for *The Liberator*, and finding there admission (which Edmund Quincy denied to it in the *Liberty Bell*) for an article showing that, since the Bible sanctioned slavery, the book must be abolished as a condition precedent to emancipation." *The Liberator*, January 21, 1853, published a letter from Henry C. Wright to Garrison, dated Millwood, Knox County (Ohio), December 25, 1852, in which Wright told of a visit to Joseph Barker and his family on their 160-acre farm.

In his later years, Barker returned to orthodoxy and the church. One year before he died, he published his autobiography, *Modern Skepticism: A Journey through the Land of Doubt and Back Again*. Yuri Suhl, Ernestine Rose's biographer, writes that "his second apostasy created quite a stir in free thought and infidel circles. *The Boston Investigator*, always a hotbed of theological dispute, bristled with criticism of his defection. As far as is known Ernestine did not join in the public denunciation of him. But one could well imagine how painful her disappointment must have been." (*Ernestine Rose and the Battle for Human Rights*, New York, 1959, p. 138.) The *DNB* has additional details about Barker's return to orthodoxy.

4. Shakespeare, *Julius Caesar*, III, ii, 217.

2 4

TO GEORGE THOMPSON GARRISON

Thursday night, June 10. [1851]

My dear Son:

Be assured, I did not mean to cheat you out of the letter your mother wrote to you last week, especially as I am myself so neglectful to correspond with those I love. It may be that you have already received it from Abington, if my friend Mr. Ford was thoughtful enough to put it into the Post Office.[1]

There is nothing special to communicate in regard to city affairs. The trial of Elizur Wright,[2] on the very creditable charge of having aided in the rescue of Shadrach, the hunted fugitive slave, has terminated, like all the preceding ones, in a disagreement of the jury, so that no verdict could be rendered. Probably the case of Lewis Hayden [3] will come next, and with a similar result. Should any one be convicted, and made to suffer the penalty of the law, it will give him an honorable renown, at least in another generation, if not in this. But it is not at all probable that any such conviction will be had; nor do I believe the Court really desires it.

The meetings of the New England Anti-Slavery Convention [4] were even more spirited and interesting than usual, and almost wholly free from any manifestations of rowdyism. No doubt our evening sessions would have been as much disturbed as formerly, had it not been for the admission fee of five cents, which the disturbers either could not or would not pay for the entertainment. Mr. Mellen [5] was on hand, with his string of resolutions and *"habeas corpus,"* as heretofore; but, fortunately, Mrs. Folsom [6] was among the missing — for what cause, I know not.

I hope you continue to like your place and employment. You are very fortunate in being with so kind and worthy a man as Mr. Clark,[7] and I have no doubt you will try to discharge every duty that may devolve upon you, in the most faithful manner. I have the utmost confidence in your integrity and good behaviour. Something of homesickness you will naturally feel, for the present; but this will gradually wear off, as you make new acquaintances, and get familiar with your business. Occasionally, you can come up to the city, and see us, and some of us will reciprocate the visit from time to time; and this will be mutually very pleasant.

The annual meeting of the Essex County A. S. Society [8] is to be held in Georgetown [9] the last Sunday in this month. I shall attend to it, with Parker Pillsbury. If you would like to go down to Georgetown with me, on that occasion, you can do so, if Mr. Clark is willing, and return in the first train on Monday morning. Mr. Buffum [10] and Mr. Remond [11] will also be present at the meeting.

We are expecting from Lynn, this week, the daughter of Joseph Barker, of Ohio, to stay with us a short time before her return West. — Miss Gilbert [12] sends her kindest remembrances to you. — All the children will be very glad to see you. — Give my regards to Mr. and Mrs. Clark; and let us hear from you soon.

Your affectionate father,

Wm. Lloyd Garrison.

ALS: Merrill Collection of Garrison Papers, Wichita State University.

Garrison's letter is written at the end of a letter from Helen Garrison to their son, George Thompson Garrison. Both letters bear the same date, but Garrison's does not include the year.

1. Helen Garrison opens her letter as follows: "I wrote you a week ago and gave the letter to your father, he promised to put it in the office but forgot it, he took it to Abington and there left it. If Mr. Ford has discovered it, he has probably forwarded it to you before this."

Lewis Ford (b. April 24, 1812), of Abington, was a member of the Finance Committee of the New England Anti-Slavery Convention. (*The Liberator*, June 6, 1851.) The son of James and Parna Ford of Abington, he married Anna Dyer of Braintree, August 25, 1833 (*The Descendants of Andrew Ford*, Montpelier, Vermont, 1968, Part I, p. 102; *Vital Records of Abington, Mass.*, Boston, 1912, p. 75.)

2. Elizur Wright (1804–1885), an abolitionist who had broken with Garrison during the 1830's, edited, in 1839, the *Massachusetts Abolitionist*, an organ of Garrison's opponents. In 1851, he was an editor of the *Commonwealth*, a newspaper published in Boston, for which he was acting as correspondent when the rescue of Shadrach took place. (Ruchames, *The Abolitionists*, p. 58; see also *Letters*, II, 111.)

3. Lewis Hayden (b. Kentucky, 1816; d. Boston, April 7, 1889) was a fugitive slave from Kentucky in 1844, and became a leading black citizen in Boston. According to Benjamin Quarles, his home in downtown Boston became "the best known rendezvous for runaways" in the northeast, among whom were William and Ellen Craft. "When Harriet Beecher Stowe visited the Haydens she was surrounded by thirteen escaped slaves." It was on June 16, 1851 that the jury trying Hayden reported its inability to reach a verdict. (*Life*, III, 324, IV, 385; Quarles, *Black Abolitionists*, pp. 112, 149, 150, 164, 165, 206, 207; *The Liberator*, June 20, 1851.)

4. The New England Anti-Slavery Convention was held in Boston. It began on Tuesday, May 27, at 10 a.m. and continued in session for three days.

5. Dr. George W. F. Mellen, a chemist, of Boston, was regarded as a deranged spirit by the abolitionists, whose meetings he frequently attended. Henry B. Stanton describes Mellen as attending an abolitionist convention "clad in the military costume of the Revolution, and fancying himself to be General Washington, because he was named after him. Poor Mellen died in an asylum for the insane." (*Random Recollections*, New York, 1887, p. 70; see also *Letters*, II, 727.)

6. Another "character." See *Letters*, II, 727.

7. Aaron F. Clark of South Danvers, Massachusetts, was a selectman of Danvers from 1851 to 1852, and a trustee of the Peabody Institute in Danvers from 1852 to 1854. (Harriet Silvester Tapley, *Chronicle of Danvers*, Danvers, 1923,

pp. 162, 256, 257; *Proceedings at the Reception and Dinner in Honor of George Peabody, Esq.*, Boston, 1856, p. 144.)

8. *The Liberator*, July 4, 1851, carried the story of the meeting, noting that it was held on Saturday evening and all day Sunday, June 28 and 29, in South Danvers. Participants were Garrison, Parker Pillsbury, Charles Lenox Remond, J. N. Buffum, and others.

9. Georgetown is in Essex County, Massachusetts, about twenty miles north of South Danvers.

10. James Needham Buffum (b. North Berwick, Maine, May 6, 1807; d. Lynn, Massachusetts, June 12, 1887), a Quaker, left home at the age of sixteen to seek his fortune, and learned the trade of housebuilding at Salem, Massachusetts. After attending a Friends' school in Providence in 1827, he learned the trade of organ-building at which he worked for three years in Salem. Returning to Lynn at about 1830, he was a leading carpenter in that city for the next twenty years. He was a progressive spirit who encouraged the use of new inventions in industry and innovations in architecture and town planning. In 1831, Arnold Buffum, his distant relative, brought Garrison to his house and thus began a lifelong friendship. Thenceforth, James Buffum devoted himself to the causes of antislavery, temperance, peace, woman's rights, and labor. He sailed to Great Britain with Frederick Douglass in 1845 and spent a year there, speaking primarily on slavery. After the Civil War, he was a Massachusetts elector in the first election of Grant in 1868, was mayor of Lynn in 1869 and 1872, and represented Lynn in the state legislature in 1874. (James R. Newhall, *Centennial Memorial of Lynn*, Lynn, 1876, pp. 187–190.)

11. Charles Lenox Remond was a prominent black abolitionist of Salem, Massachusetts, a Garrisonian who advocated "no union with slaveholders," and an agent of the American Anti-Slavery Society for many years. He had joined the antislavery movement in the 1830's. (See *Letters*, II, 464.)

12. Olive Gilbert, who was then visiting the Garrisons.

---

2 5

TO ELIZABETH PEASE

Boston, June 23, 1851.

My Dear Friend:

I still remain deeply indebted to you on the score of epistolary interchange, as well as in other respects, although some time has elapsed since I received a letter from you. The return of our dear friend George Thompson, to-morrow, in the Liverpool steam-ship, presents an opportunity to send you a few lines, if nothing more, which it would be wholly inexcusable for me to lose. Hoping that you will soon have the privilege of seeing him face to face, and thus learning much about our affairs as pertaining to the anti-slavery movement that cannot be written, I shall feel comparatively easy in sending you a very brief, though I owe you a very long epistle.

It is more than eight months since George Thompson came among us, on a second visit to this country; and if you have kept the run of his movements, during that time, as detailed in the Liberator and

Standard, you need no special information in regard to it. It constitutes another era in his eventful life, and by no means an unpleasant one; for, with only one or two very slight exceptions, he has been every where received, — from Maine to Upper Canada, and from the Lakes to Pennsylvania, — in a manner truly gratifying. His labors have been almost without intermission, and though he has never failed to speak of slavery and its abettors in the strongest terms of reprobation, he has never failed to commend himself to the respect, admiration and good will of the thousands who have listened to his addresses. His presence has had a quickening and purifying influence, nationally; and it has proved how great is the change which has been wrought in public sentiment, on the subject of slavery, since his former visit. A Farewell Soiree was given to him in this city, on Monday evening last, at which more than a thousand persons sat down to supper, constituting an imposing array of intellect, moral worth, and philanthropy, such as I have never seen before on any occasion.[1] Addresses were made by Quincy,[2] Thompson, [Wendell] Phillips, Theodore Parker, [Charles] Remond, myself, and others, sketches of which will be given in the next Liberator[3] G. T[hompson] spoke at great length, and in a very happy strain. It would amply have compensated you for taking a voyage across the Atlantic, to have witnessed the scene. And, pray, when are you coming? What is such a voyage now, but a mere pleasure excursion? In twelve days, you can be with us in Boston. Only think of it, seriously, not as a matter of fancy, and see whether you cannot come over, and spend at least a few months with us. — There are multitudes longing to take you by the hand, and to extend to you their friendship and hospitality. I have no doubt your health would be benefitted by the voyage, and that you would derive much gratification from the visit. Let me know whether you dare to cherish the hope that you may yet see New England, and tread on the soil of the Pilgrim Fathers.

I have had a very strong desire (which I have smothered in my own breast, as it has been idle to cherish it, on many accounts,) to visit England this summer, and be one of the universal multitude at the World's Bazaar.[4] What a miracle of contrivance, skill and taste is the building in which it is held! It ought to be allowed to remain as long as iron and glass can defy the storms of time or the fate of empires. Whatever drawbacks there may be about this exhibition, (and I have no doubt there are many,) I am convinced that it will do much toward hastening the day of universal reconciliation, when nation shall no longer lift up sword against nation, and there shall be none to molest or make afraid.

There is to be a Peace Congress in London,[5] the third of the series begun at Paris. Several delegates will be present from this country. Those held at Paris and Frankfort were characterised by great timidity: the one in London, it is to be hoped, will be bolder in its tone, and more radical in principle. George Thompson has been elected a delegate to it on this side of the Atlantic, and will no doubt ably acquit himself on the occasion. In one aspect — in only one — war is more frightful than slavery; the latter is local and exceptional, the former is to be found as universal as our race, for the forgiveness of injuries is a point yet unattained by any kingdom, tribe or race.

I hope that Mrs. Follen,[6] Mrs. Chapman [7] and Miss Weston [8] have had the pleasure of seeing you, as I believe they are now in England. No doubt they are exerting a constant and wholesome anti-slavery influence on your side of the Atlantic, but we are longing to see them again in Boston, and to have their direct co-operation. None of their relatives or friends seem to know when they will return; but, wherever they may for the time being sojourn, they will never fail to bear an uncompromising testimony against slavery.

Our beloved Henry C. Wright [9] has been spending the past year in Indiana and Ohio, "instant in season and out of season" in bearing his testimony against cruelty, injustice and slavery, in his own peculiar manner — strong, fearless, and uncompromising. He sometimes errs in taste and judgment, (who is not fallible?) and often writes or expresses himself in a manner liable to be misapprehended; but I regard him as one of the best men living, animated by love to God and love to man in an extraordinary degree.

The £20 forwarded by you, in your last letter to me, "to help the cause along," I gave to Francis Jackson, for the American A. S. Society. You will see it acknowledged in the Standard.[10]

I have not time to write another sentence.

With unbounded regard,

Your faithful friend,

Wm. Lloyd Garrison.

Elizabeth Pease.

ALS: Garrison Papers, Boston Public Library.

Elizabeth Pease, the English Quaker and abolitionist, was the friend and correspondent of Wendell Phillips and his wife, of Garrison, Lucretia Mott, the Grimkés, and other American abolitionists. In 1853, she married Professor John Nichol of Glasgow University. For further information about Miss Pease, see *Letters*, II, 326–327.

1. The Soirée took place on June 16, in the Assembly Room over the Boston and Worcester Railroad Depot. Every seat in the hall was occupied and hundreds of persons seeking seats had to be turned away. The affair was reported in *The Liberator*, June 27, 1851.

2. Edmund Quincy had presided.

3. *The Liberator,* June 27, 1851, devoted almost three pages to the affair.

4. The World's Bazaar or World's Fair was also known as the "Great Exhibition." Held in London in 1851, it opened during the late spring and "dominated the year." It had as its purpose " 'to present a true test and living picture of the point of development at which the whole of mankind has arrived . . . and a new starting-point, from which all nations will be able to direct their further exertions.' " (Asa Briggs, *Victorian People,* Penguin Books, England, 1965, pp. 23–24; Sir John Clapham, *An Economic History of Modern Britain,* Cambridge, 1963, p. 1 *et passim*; see also a letter reprinted from the *Richmond Enquirer,* in *The Liberator,* July 18, 1851. The letter is dated London, June 2, 1851, and is headed "Letter from an American Commissioner at the World's Fair.")

5. There were actually four mid-century international peace congresses. The first was held in Brussels, Belgium, beginning on September 20, 1848. The second, in Paris, opened its sessions on August 22, 1849. The Frankfurt-on-Main, Germany, congress was held in August 1850, and the London peace congress opened its sessions on July 22, 1851, at Exeter Hall. (Merle Curti, *The American Peace Crusade,* Durham, North Carolina, 1929, pp. 168–187; *The Liberator,* August 8, 1851.)

6. Eliza Lee Follen was the widow of Dr. Charles Follen, abolitionist, scholar, and Unitarian minister who had perished in the fire aboard the steamer *Lexington* in 1840. Eliza Lee Follen, like her late husband a reformer and fervent abolitionist, was the author of several books, including a biographical memoir of Charles Follen. (See *Letters,* II. 57.)

7. Maria Weston Chapman was the pioneer abolitionist and Garrison's lifetime friend (see introductory biographical sketch in *Letters,* II, xxiv–xxv). Her husband had died on October 3, 1842, in his thirty-ninth year. Several years later, on July 19, 1848, she sailed for England with her children (her primary purpose was their education) and her sister Caroline Weston. After a seven-year residence abroad, they returned to the United States on November 24, 1855. (*Life,* III, 78–79, 229–230, 431.)

8. Caroline Weston (1808–1882). See *Letters,* II, 57.

9. See the introductory biographical sketch of Henry C. Wright in *Letters,* II, xxx–xxxi.

10. The *Standard,* June 12, 1851, acknowledged a donation of $98 from Elizabeth Pease, Darlington, England, "(by W. L. Garrison)."

---

2 6

TO SAMUEL MAY, JR.

Boston, July 16, 1851.

Dear Friend May:

As our friend Wallcut has opened this letter, (according to the discretion you left with him,) to see what are its contents, I improve the opportunity to say, that I saw some of the Hubbardston friends, at Gardner,[1] and promised them I would attend a conventional meeting in H. on Sunday, August 3rd; so you may make the arrangements accordingly. Who will be with me on the occasion? One will be sufficient, and I should like to have your company, if convenient.[2] I think two speakers are sufficient at the meetings, besides it being more economical. The collection at G. was $12.50 above the local expenses.

I am willing to go to Lowell on the 10th, but should like to make it *sine qua non* that Phillips shall go with me. We must try to bring it about, if we can.[3]

I hope to meet you at Milford on Sunday.[4]

The accompanying letter of Oliver C. Gilbert[5] has not been answered.

I will speak to friend [Francis] Jackson about seeing Twitchell[6] immediately.

My best regards to Mrs. May & family.

Faithfully yours,

Wm. Lloyd Garrison.

ALS: Antislavery Manuscripts, Boston Public Library.

1. The reference is to the quarterly meeting of the Worcester County North Anti-Slavery Society, held at Gardner, Massachusetts, on Saturday and Sunday, July 12 and 13. Garrison was one of the speakers.

2. *The Liberator*, July 25, 1851, announced that there would be a meeting at Hubbardston (Worcester County), Massachusetts, on Sunday, August 3, in commemoration of West India Emancipation. "The meeting-house of the Unitarian Society having been kindly granted for this occasion, the meeting will be held in connexion with their usual services; and will be attended by William Lloyd Garrison and Samuel May, Jr."

A description of the meeting appeared in *The Liberator*, August 8, 1851.

3. *The Liberator*, August 8, 1851, carried the following announcement:

"Our readers and friends generally, in the upper part of *Middlesex County*, are requested to notice the Convention to be held on Sunday next (10th inst.) at Lowell, to be attended by W. L. Garrison, Wendell Phillips, and James N. Buffum. We hope the neighboring towns will be largely represented."

4. On July 25, 1851, *The Liberator* announced that "four consecutive antislavery meetings were held in Milford, in this State, commencing on Saturday and closing on Sunday evening last [July 19–20] — constituting one of the One Hundred Conventions. Though there are at least half a dozen meeting-houses in that industrious and thriving village, not one of them could be obtained for the use of the Convention, only the hall of a tavern. . . ." Among the speakers were Samuel May, Jr., Lucy Stone, and Garrison.

5. Benjamin Quarles writes that "Late in 1855 an antislavery weekly gave a personal description of one O. C. Gilbert who was pocketing monies he collected for fugitive slaves. Gilbert was a large, robust man, 5 feet, 9 inches, of dark brown hue, practically bald and quite bowlegged: 'Let all the papers pass him around,' ran the warning." (*Black Abolitionists*, New York, 1969, p. 160.) In a letter dated Saratoga Springs, July 22, 1874, an O. C. Gilbert thanks Garrison for certain photographs and mentions that he never went to school in his life. A notation on the letter identifies Gilbert as an ex-fugitive slave. (Anti-Slavery Letters to Garrison and Others, Boston Public Library.)

6. Ginery Bachelor Twitchell (also Twichell) was born in Athol, Massachusetts, August 25, 1811, and died in Brookline, Massachusetts, July 23, 1883. He rose from stage driver to proprietor of several stage lines. In time he became superintendent and then president of the Boston and Worcester Railroad, as well as of other railroads. After the Civil War he served several times in the United States House of Representatives. At the time of this letter, Twitchell was superintendent

of the Boston and Worcester Railroad. (Ralph Emerson Twitchell, *Genealogy of the Twitchell Family* . . . , New York, 1929, pp. 304–308; Boston *Directory,* 1850, 1852; *BDAC.*)

---

2 7

TO ADIN BALLOU

Boston, July 24, 1851.

Esteemed Friend:

I am very glad that you are willing to preside at our First of August celebration [1] next week, because, preferring as I know you do "a less conspicuous position," it is another evidence of your regard for the cause of the fettered slave in our country. In making this self-sacrifice, you shall have our united thanks in this quarter. Francis Jackson, Edmund Quincy, and myself, have acted as chairman on so many occasions, it is really desirable that there should be a change in this respect; — and we know of no one more worthy to fill the chair, or who will preside with more commingled urbanity and dignity, benefitting so great and thrilling an occasion, than yourself.

I trust the celebration will be made memorable by the numbers in attendance, the right spirit prevailing, and the effectiveness of the addresses.

The friends in Hopedale and Milford will understand, it is hoped, that they can be carried to Worcester, and returned the same day, at half the usual price.

I am exceedingly gratified and strengthened to hear that our recent conventions in Gardner [2] and Milford [3] have evidently made a salutary impression. God grant that impression may never be effaced.

I need not say how much we were indebted to our Hopedale friends for their hospitality; nor how pleased to have been able to see you face to face, and to have taken you by the hand, (had you not been absent,) would have been

Your loving friend,

Wm. Lloyd Garrison.

ALS: Paine Collection, Massachusetts Historical Society.

1. The celebration was to take place at the City Hall in Worcester, Massachusetts. Among the announced participants were Wendell Phillips, Garrison, Edmund Quincy, William I. Bowditch, Adin Ballou, Stephen S. Foster, Parker Pillsbury, and others. (*The Liberator*, July 25, 1851.)

2. The convention at Gardner, on July 12 and 13, was under the sponsorship of the Worcester County North Anti-Slavery Society. "Five meetings were held consecutively, at which the attendance was highly encouraging, — clearly indi-

cating that, in that part of the Commonwealth, the field only needs a slight cultivation (comparatively speaking) to bring forth a plentiful harvest." The convention was one of the "Hundred Conventions" that were being held throughout the state. (*The Liberator*, July 18, 1851.)

3. Another of the "Hundred Conventions" was held at Milford, Massachusetts, on Saturday and Sunday, July 19 and 20, and consisted of four consecutive anti-slavery meetings on the two days. Garrison was present as were Samuel May, Jr., and Lucy Stone, among others. (*The Liberator*, July 25, 1851.)

---

2 8

TO ABBY KELLEY FOSTER

Boston, August 12, 1851.

My Dear Mrs. Foster:

In May last, at the anniversary of the American Anti-Slavery Society at Syracuse, I signified to various friends my desire and purpose to visit Central New York in the month of September, lecturing consecutively along the way from Albany to Buffalo. That purpose I have cherished until recently, but now abandon, in consequence of various considerations — the friends here unitedly advising me not to risk my health unnecessarily at this sickly season by such a laborious tour as it would inevitably prove. Of course, there is no lack of work to be done here, especially as we are about to lose, for a time, the few lecturing agents in the field, by their removal elsewhere. I am extremely sorry to dash to the ground any expectations that may have been raised as to my coming; and I need not be told how great will be your own disappointment at this failure on my part. But it is not an easy thing for me to leave my post, and so large a family, and be absent for several weeks. Besides, I am positively pledged to visit Eastern Pennsylvania, at the time of the annual meeting of the Penn. A. S. Society in October; and to accomplish both objects would be the prolongation of my absence from home beyond what would be either prudent or proper.

I am not insensible to the importance of moulding the popular sentiment in Central and Western New York into an anti-slavery form that shall defy the earthquake and the storm; nor to the necessity of improving our time before the coming of another Presidential simoom; and I only wish, feeble as my efforts must ever be in comparison with the strength of my desires and the necessities of our great cause, that I could multiply myself indefinitely, and be in all places at one and the same time. O the work that remains to be done! O how few are the active laborers in the field! O the strength of the Slave Power! O the guilt of our country!

My apprehensions on your account are and have long been very great. Your devotion to the cause, and self-sacrificing efforts in its behalf, have no parallel. But you are exceeding the claims of duty, I fear, and putting in peril your valuable life, partly for lack of sound discretion. All our lecturing agents err in this — they speak too often and too long — and you probably more than any other. I hear that you frequently speak from two to three hours — sometimes, where others are ready to help share the burden, and are expected to speak. This must operate to your physical prostration, and seriously affect your voice and lungs. Besides, no matter how great the ability displayed, it is a tax upon the bodily comfort of the audience beyond what is remunerative. If all our agents would abridge their speeches one half, I am satisfied the effect produced would be much greater. The "art of leaving off" at the right time, and in the right place, is one of the most difficult things to learn. In this respect, it is far easier for me to preach than to practice. I am often surprised and ashamed to think how much of the time of an audience I have been unconsciously occupying — so vast is the theme, so many are the objectives to be met and refuted, so multitudinous are the aspects of our enterprise. Ordinarily, a speech an hour long, however interesting, is long enough, and will produce the best effect. If it is to be the only speech at the time, half an hour more may sometimes be profitably occupied. We all of us ought to have our watches before us, that we may know precisely how long we have been talking. People will often remain long after they are greatly wearied by a protracted sitting, but it will be rather as a matter of courtesy than of interest.

These suggestions are made to preserve your life. It is bad economy, to say nothing more, to bring upon yourself a pressure that shall suddenly crush you to the dust, especially as nothing is gained by it in any quarter. You are a very rare and very complete woman in every thing but — a just consideration of your own health and strength. These are to be sacrificed, cheerfully and unreservedly, I admit, rather than one jot or tittle of principle; but this is not a question of principle, but of sound judgment.

Helen unites with me in tendering many thanks to you for your prompt attention to the matter in Albany. Our estimable friend Lydia Mott[1] saw it properly negotiated, with true business despatch. We shall be under additional obligations to you respecting the bequest at Winfield.[2]

Parker Pillsbury and Charles C. Burleigh leave this week for Ohio. How long they intend to be gone, or whether they will be able to lecture in Western and Central New York on their return home, I do not know.

I shall be very glad to hear from you, by letter, whenever convenient.

Yours, with great regard,

Wm. Lloyd Garrison.

Mrs. A. K. Foster.

ALS: Abigail Kelley Foster Papers, American Antiquarian Society.

1. Lydia Mott of Albany, the youngest daughter of Daniel and Amey Searing Mott, was born October 24, 1807 and died on August 20, 1875. For a sketch of her character and way of life, see Letter 162, to Helen, February 19, 1857. (*The Woman's Journal*, August 28, 1875; Thomas C. Cornell, *Adam and Ann Mott*, Poughkeepsie, New York, 1890, p. 219.) There was also another Lydia Mott, sister-in-law of James and Lucretia Mott, *ibid.*, pp. 55–58, 74, 89, 111, 213.

2. Herkimer County, New York. In the postscript to Abby Kelley Foster's letter to Garrison dated March 16, 1851, she says, "you will see the obituary of Samuel A. Green, of West Winfield, in the last Standard. He remembered you in his will in a legacy of $50. . . ." (Anti-Slavery Letters to Garrison and Others, Boston Public Library.) The obituary of Samuel A. Green appeared in the *National Anti-Slavery Standard*, March 13, 1851.

29

TO SAMUEL MAY, JR.

Boston, August 19, 1851.

My Dear Friend:

I am very sorry I missed the mail yesterday for Leicester,[1] but I have been quite unwell for a week past — so much so, that I was unable to go to East Bridgewater on Saturday.[2] Indeed, for a week past, every one of the family at home — Helen, my Aunt,[3] Frank,[4] the servant girl — has had a severe attack of the cholera morbus; though we are all now in a convalescent state, except the girl, who was taken with a fresh attack last night. I am still weak, and "good for nothing."

Just before I received your note, in regard to Willie's[5] return on Wednesday, (and I hope he will not fail to come home to-morrow, in consequence of your not hearing from me sooner,) my wife urged me to write to you, saying she thought Willie had better conclude his visit for the present. We are still anxious about the use of his thumb, and he needs continual admonition and care. We hope he has not been troublesome, beyond the care which every additional member of a family necessarily makes. Of course, you will need no special assurance of our gratitude for Mrs. May's kindness and your own. — If Willie is still with you, on the arrival of this, we think it desirable for him to return without delay, even if it will be no inconvenience whatever to you for him to remain. The complete restoration of his hand is to us an object of very great solicitude.

Please give our best regards to Mrs May and the family.

Your much obliged friend,

Wm. Lloyd Garrison.

Samuel May, Jr.

ALS: Antislavery Manuscripts, Boston Public Library.

1. Leicester, Massachusetts, May's residence.

2. Garrison had been scheduled to speak at a meeting of the Old Colony Anti-Slavery Society in East Bridgewater (Plymouth County) on Sunday, August 17. (*The Liberator*, August 8, 1851.) *The Liberator*, August 22, 1851, announced that "The Editor of the *Liberator* was unable to fulfil his engagement at East Bridgewater on Saturday and Sunday last, in consequence of sudden illness. He has been too unwell to bestow any attention on the present number of his paper. . . ."

3. Charlotte Lloyd Newell (d. October 2, 1857, in her sixty-fourth year), the youngest sister of Garrison's mother, lived with the Garrison family during the last six months of her life. She was the widow of Thomas Newell of Lowell, who died in 1828. See Letter 83, from Garrison to Charlotte Newell, dated Boston, April 7, 1854. (*Life*, I, 427; III, 464; obituary in *The Liberator*, October 2, 1857; *Vital Records of Lowell, Massachusetts*, Salem, 1930, p. 224.)

4. Garrison's son and last child, Francis Jackson (b. October 29, 1848; d. in Newtonville, Massachusetts, December 11, 1916), named for the Massachusetts abolitionist of the same name, was then almost three years old. He graduated from Boston Latin School in 1865 and assisted his father in the publication of *The Liberator*. He joined Houghton Mifflin Company, the Boston publishing house, and retired only a year before his death. He was one of the authors of Garrison's *Life*. (Obituary, *New York Times*, December 12, 1916; W. P. Garrison, *The Benson Family of Newport, Rhode Island*, New York, 1872, p. 43.)

5. Garrison's son, William Lloyd Garrison, Jr. (b. Boston, January 21, 1838; d. Lexington, Massachusetts, September 12, 1909), was then thirteen years old. He left high school before graduation to begin a business career at the age of eighteen. He lived in Lynn, Massachusetts, for seven years, where he became a bank teller; from 1862 to 1864 he was cashier of the Mattapan Bank in Dorchester, Massachusetts. In the latter year, he married Ellen Wright of Auburn, New York. During the ensuing years, he became a prominent wool merchant in Boston, and also established one of the earliest electric light stations in Brockton, Massachusetts. He retired from business activity in 1900. He became involved in public reform activities only after his father's death. His interests included Henry George's Single Tax, free trade, peace, enfranchisement of women, and anti-imperialism. For several years, he was president of the Massachusetts Single Tax League and of the American Free Trade League. (Obituary, *New York Times*, September 13, 1909; W. P. Garrison, *The Benson Family of Newport, Rhode Island*, p. 43.)

3 0

TO AN UNNAMED CORRESPONDENT

Boston, Aug. 23, 1851.

Dear Sir:

My answer to the letter of inquiry from P. B. Fessenden,[1] in your behalf, is, that I have no recollection of any such alleged fugitive slave as David Clarke; that I have given him neither any money nor letter of recommendation; and, consequently, that he is undoubtedly one who is imposing upon the benevolence of the friends of the oppressed in Maine, and obtaining money under fraudulent pretences. Every such instance ought to be promptly exposed, and in my next Liberator[2] I will do so to the public. Our anti-slavery friends cannot be too careful in bestowing their charities; as there are many imposters abroad, and the number is likely to increase rather than diminish. In all this, one thing is sa[tisfac]torily demonstrated — and that is, that the blacks belong [to] the human race, as animals are not guilty of any such misconduct. Let their traducers controvert this if they can!

It is a good legal axiom, that it is better that ninety-nine guilty persons should escape, than that one innocent person should be condemned. So, we had better be imposed upon many times, than turn away from relieving one who is actually a suffering fugitive slave. But we are bound to exercise all possible diligence to detect the unworthy, while we help the meritorious.

Yours, with much esteem,

Wm. Lloyd Garrison.

ALS: Merrill Collection of Garrison Papers, Wichita State University. There is a hole in the manuscript toward the end of the first paragraph, but the missing letters have been supplied between brackets.

1. Unidentified.
2. There is no such statement in the next *Liberator*, nor in the succeeding issue.

3 1

TO THE EDITOR OF THE
LONDON MORNING ADVERTISER

[September 19, 1851.]

Dear Sir — Your replication of August 20th[1] fills me with surprise. The conviction, that you are not animated by an unfriendly spirit, and that you take a deep interest in the Anti-Slavery Cause on this side of the Atlantic alone prompts me again to refer to the charges which you have brought against me; charges which I have specifically declared to be at variance with the truth, but which, notwithstanding my denial, you reiterate, with some additional counts.

Your first impeachment of my course was in the following language: — 'What we complain of and lament in Mr. Garrison is, that, in the advocacy of the holy enterprise in which he has embarked with his whole heart and soul, he should, *on so many occasions, gratuitously obtrude his peculiar views on religious subjects*. Why cannot he, *in his capacity of an Anti-Slavery advocate*, put his theological views in abeyance.'

To this I pleaded NOT GUILTY. I went still further: — I declared — 'No man has been — no man could have been — more scrupulous than I have felt against mixing up extraneous matters with the Anti-Slavery movement.' My final affirmation was — 'as for putting my theological notions in abeyance, in my capacity as an Anti-Slavery advocate, *having always done so, I have nothing to alter in this respect.*'

On you, therefore, I threw the *onus probandi*. The *Morning Advertiser* of the 20th ultimo brings me your reply. How do you meet my clear and explicit denial?

First, by modifying your original complaint, that I should, 'on so many occasions,' gratuitously obtrude my peculiar religious views. Now the form of your indictment reads — 'We took occasion to express our regret that he *sometimes* went out of his way, when on the Anti-Slavery platform, to advocate, or, perhaps, more properly speaking, to *enunciate* theological views *at variance with divine revelation.*[1]

The difference is that which exists between what is habitual and what is incidental. But the gravity of the charge is substantially the same. It implies not only a lack of sound discretion, but a deliberate violation of good faith, a sacrifice of personal integrity, a wanton attack upon the religious opinions of others, while professing to 'remember those in bonds as bound with them,'[2] and advocating the union of men of every sect and party for the abolition of Slavery!

My dear sir, taking this view of my course, how can you bestow such warm encomiums upon me, even as an Abolitionist? If, on the Anti-Slavery platform, I — 'on so many occasions,' or 'sometimes' — 'gratuitously' go out of my way to obtrude my peculiar religious views, views 'at variance with divine revelation,' on an assembly convened to hear the cause of the slave vindicated, how can you place any confidence in my integrity, or cherish for me the slightest respect?

For, surely, it is not an error of judgment that you deplore. 'Gratuitously' to do a censurable act, and to do it 'on so many occasions' as to compel 'many of the most earnest and sincere friends of the cause to withdraw themselves from the Anti-Slavery Cause,' is to evince a most dishonourable purpose, and a reckless and disorganizing spirit.

Here let me be understood. I do not mean to say, that, in pleading for the slave, I have never come into conflict with the religious opinions of any who have listened to me, or given a shock to their organ of veneration. This has been unavoidable — not 'gratuitously' but necessarily done — for the slave's sake. Nor do I mean to say, that, in illustrating my Anti-Slavery views, no critical eye has ever been able to detect a 'peculiar' theological tinge. Every man after his own method, and in his own style. This furnishes no just ground for 'complaint' or 'regret.' On the Anti-Slavery platform, if men of every variety of religious opinion are to be found, agreeing only in the paramount claims of the slave to his immediate and unconditional emancipation, it is to be expected that every one will speak in his own dialect, and utter his own shibboleth. Thus, a Trinitarian may allude to the Trinity — a Unitarian speak of the unity of God — a Calvinist enforce the guilt of slaveholders by the terrors of eternal damnation — a Universalist or Restorationist hint at the ultimate triumph of infinite love over all iniquity — a Presbyterian speak reverently of the pulpit — a Quaker allude to the importance of being guided by the inward light — a Baptist indicate his belief in immersion as the true outward Baptism — a believer in the holiness of the first day of the week refer to it as the Christian Sabbath — an Infidel intimate his dissent from the popular religious sentiments of the day — a military man argue and illustrate in a military vein — a peace man avow that he has no faith in the use of carnal weapons — and so on to the end of the category; and no one has a right to raise an outcry, or run from the platform, on that account. So long as such manifestations are natural, incidental, with no proselyting intention, subordinate to the great object of redeeming the slave, — even though they are made on the Anti-Slavery platform, — who, that is truly baptised into the spirit of abolitionism, will enter his protest against them? That I have exceeded this limit intentionally or consciously, I deny.

Most heartily, dear sir, do I adopt your catholic declaration: — 'In a cause so great, so sacred, so divine, — one in which the happiness here and hereafter, of millions of human beings is so deeply involved, we are prepared to merge all other considerations, and feel, for the time, as if we had no other mission on earth to fulfill.' But what obligation does this impose on you, or me, or any other occupant of the platform? To make no allusion, or do no act, religiously, which shall be regarded as heretical or erroneous by any of the company? The absurdity of such a conclusion is manifest. Is the Infidel to be justified in withdrawing, because the Bible is read and referred to as the Word of God — a divine revelation? Is the Baptist to run away, because he hears the Infidel speak of the Bible of Nature as far more sure and reliable than any parchment? Is the Catholic to lift his heel, because the Quaker exalts the inward light above every outward standard of truth and duty? Is the Quaker to stand aloof, because the Presbyterian refers to the clerical order as divinely instituted? Is the Unitarian to desert, because he has heard the doctrine of the atonement, the trinity, or total depravity, assumed as true and vital, in the course of the Anti-Slavery discussions? If so, where is the possibility of general co-operation? If not, 'the head and front of my offending hath that extent — no more.'[3] Why, then, am I singled out for censure or expostulation?

It is readily conceded by me, that great care should be taken to keep in abeyance, as far as is consistent with a free and manly spirit, religious peculiarities; but, I repeat it, unless these are offensively urged, and evidently with a design to make the Anti-Slavery Cause the medium of their promulgation, no imputations should be thrown, no clamour raised, no offence taken, at their appearance. Incidentally, according to the peculiar theological bias of the mind, they are unavoidable.

For myself, I am no partisan, no sectarian. The test of character and condition which Jesus has laid down, is to me all-sufficient — 'By their FRUITS shall ye know them.'[4] My adherence to the Anti-Slavery platform has been steadfast and loyal. The man is not living who can truthfully declare that, in this great struggle for the overthrow of the most impious and God-defying power that ever wielded the rod of despotism, I have refused to stand by his side, because dissenting from his religious or political opinions. Many have fled from me, on this ground, and become personally malignant, and have resorted to the most dastardly expedients to destroy my usefulness in the cause of the perishing bondman. Their sectarianism has overmastered their humanity; the inalienable rights of man they regard as dust in the balance, in comparison with their cherished theological dogmas. Their requirement of me, as the condition of Anti-Slavery fellowship and co-operation, has been unequal, absurd, and tyrannical — nothing less than to have no mind or conscience of my own, on any subject but that of Slavery — at least, none differing from theirs! For themselves, individually, on their own responsibility, as Presbyterians, Baptists, Methodists, &c., &c., they claim the right (which I cordially concede) to promulgate their own sectarian views, and to make as many proselytes as possible. To me they concede no such liberty! If, — *representing no association, speaking as a man, in view of my accountability to God, apart from the Anti-Slavery platform,* — I venture to enunciate religious sentiments not in accordance with their own, they immediately attempt to create all possible odium against me *as an Abolitionist,* and actively inculcate the lying declaration, that such sentiments are part and parcel of what they invidiously term 'Garrisonian Abolitionism'! It was on this ground, and in this evil spirit, that the secession was made from the American Anti-Slavery Society in 1840, and opposition to that Society is still continued; though the Constitution of the Society remains as it was originally adopted, and makes no other condition for membership than this — 'that immediate emancipation is the right of the slave and the duty of the master.' Thus, too have originated the senseless and hypocritical outcries against me as 'a Woman's Rights, Anti-Sabbath, No-Government man' — all for the express purpose of making me detestable as an Abolitionist!

My aim has been, from the beginning, to erect and uphold a platform, on which all those 'who despise fraud, and loathe rapine, and abhor blood,' might rally, and 'mingle like kindred drops into one,'[5] whatever their views on other subjects. Strangely enough, my dear sir, you accuse me of having been reckless of such unanimity of action, and quite as anxious to obtrude my heretical 'theological notions' on Anti-Slavery audiences, as to exhibit the cruelty and injustice of the slave system! And, what is still more strange, to sustain your accusation, you refer to a speech made by me at an Anti-Slavery meeting at the Crown and Anchor Tavern, in London, in 1846, at which you were an eye witness!

Your charge is without the slightest qualification — 'On that occasion, Mr. GARRISON did fiercely assail those institutions which Christians of *all* denominations hold, by common consent, to be an essential part of Christianity.' I will impute to you nothing worse than a bad memory, and very erroneous impressions. You accuse, but furnish no evidence. I deny the accuracy of your statement. The burden of proof still rests on you. Am I to be condemned on your recollection of a speech five years after its delivery? That speech was reported, more or less copiously, for several journals. The only report — it was, I believe, the fullest — I can now refer to, was that which was published in the London *Universe,* of August 21, 1846.[6] There is not a sentence or syllable in it to justify your allegation. *The special object of that speech was to remove religious prejudices and conciliate all classes in England.* If what you say of it is true, then I must have been unfortunate and bewildered to the last degree! Is it credible — supposing me to have been of sound mind — that I should have seized the very first opportunity presented to address a public audience in the British metropolis, 'fiercely to assail those institutions which constitute an essential part of Christianity,' and thus to defeat the very object of my mission to England? My dear sir, you are certainly labouring under a serious misapprehension, and doing me great injustice. — Was I not addressing a Christian assembly? Would they have tolerated, with no expression of disgust or indignation, such language as you impute to me on that occasion? Yet, was there any indication of disapprobation? Were not my remarks repeatedly cheered by that enlightened and religious auditory? If I did what you allege, why were you dumb at that meeting? The fraud, the outrage, the insult, to British intelligence and piety, demanded from you, if no other one would speak, an open and stern rebuke. Why were the religious journals silent about it?

I claim to be a Christian: why do you persist in representing me as an infidel; I am a lover of Christian institutions: why do you accuse me of seeking their overthrow? I have engaged in no reform, I have promulgated no doctrines, which I have not vindicated by an appeal to the Bible, — an appeal more frequently made than to all other books in the world besides: why do you insist that my religious views 'are not in harmony with divine revelation'? Is it a paramount regard for the triumph of the Anti-Slavery cause in America, or a perverted sectarian vision, that has led to my arraignment before the British public as a heretic?

The institutions that I assailed — 'fiercely assailed,' if you please — at the meeting alluded to, were exclusively slaveholding and Slavery sustaining institutions. Take the following extracts as a specimen:

It is said that the Abolitionists are assailing the American church; it is true. It is said that they are assailing the American clergy in a body; it is true. It is said that they are assailing the Government under which they live; it is true. It is said that they are seeking the dissolution of the Union; it is true. Why do I say this? *Because the church is the stronghold of the system; because the clergy are active defenders of the system; because the government was originally so constructed that it gives its entire support to Slavery,* so long as the slaveholder shall desire it. ° ° ° We found the political parties sanctioning Slavery. We found the religious bodies heeding not the cries and groans of the slave. Now, *we had either to denounce these bodies, or to give up the cause.* ° ° Slavery does not necessarily exist with, but in defiance of our republicanism. Never let the minions of tyranny confound republicanism and Slavery. It also exists *despite of Christianity. I want no Christianity mingled with the institutions of Slavery. I want Christianity such as Jesus practically exemplified,* — a Christianity which knows no color or clime — which comprehends us all — which makes the world our country, and all mankind our countrymen.

Thus do I dispose of your first charge.

You next declare — "He ridiculed the institution of a Christian ministry, and, if our memory be not grievously at fault, attacked the institution of a Christian Sabbath; and in doing this, he employed phraseology *which no christian could hear without a shudder.*" My dear sir, there can be no mistake here — your memory is 'grievously at fault.' I should add a stronger declaration, were it not that I believe your injustice is unintentional: nevertheless, that injustice is none the less enormous. How you can have any respect for me, (and your encomiums have been liberally bestowed,) while behaving in this manner, I do not understand. I 'employed phraseology which no Christian could hear without a shudder'! I 'ridiculed the institution of a Christian ministry, and of a Christian Sabbath'! Monstrous accusations. To sustain them, you have yet to present the first particle of evidence. Many clergymen were present at the meeting. On the platform sat Dr. OXLEY,[7] Rev. Dr. CARLISLE,[8], of Hackney, Rev. Mr. NELSON,[9] of Belfast, Rev. H. SOLLY,[10] and others. Account for it as you can, they took no exception to what fell from my lips. How could they be thus recreant to their Lord and Master? Why were not my folly and baseness promptly exposed? I appeal to them all — GEORGE THOMPSON, HENRY VINCENT,[11] WILLIAM LOVETT,[12] J. H. PARRY [13] — to the entire audience; what is safer than mere recollections or impressions, I appeal to the various printed reports of my speech — to testify to the injustice of your accusation.

It is true, the Rev. J. H. HINTON,[14] at an early stage of the proceedings, took occasion to express his lack of unity with the meeting; but this was before the delivery of my speech, and had reference only to committing himself to the pledge contained in the following resolution, which was offered by JAMES HAUGHTON, Esq., of Dublin: [15]

'That we extend the right hand of fellowship to WILLIAM LLOYD GARRISON, the undaunted and steadfast pioneer in the cause of universal emancipation; to HENRY C. WRIGHT, the unwearied advocate of the rights of humanity; and to FREDERICK DOUGLASS, the self-emancipated bondsman, and eloquent asserter of the claims of his brethren in chains; and do pledge ourselves to render all the aid in our power to these gentlemen, and their devoted coadjutors of the American Anti-Slavery Society, in the prosecution of their holy purposes for the extinction of American slavery.'

The resolution was adopted by acclamation — only four persons in the immense assembly dissenting — the Rev. Mr. HINTON, an American slave driver named Collyer,[16] (who said he had the care of six thousand slaves,) and two others, names unknown, probably *Collyer's* companions.

You are equally unfortunate, equally unjust, in your next assertion: — 'One thing he said was, that the Christian's God was his devil.' Believing in the God of Christianity, how could I have made so revolting a declaration? On a careful perusal of my speech as reported in the *Universe*, (a report which I never revised,) I can find no such expression, nor anything upon which to base your charge. Surely, it was too shocking to be overlooked by the reporters, if it fell from my lips in the manner represented by you. That I may have said, in substance, that the God who, in America, is declared to sanction the impious system of Slavery — the annihilation of the marriage institution and the sacrifices of all human rights — is my ideal of the devil, is not improbable; but that is not what you represent me to have said. It may have evinced a lack of good taste, on my part; but strong contrasts are sometimes called for, even though sure to shock the fastidious or unreflecting. It was deemed in bad taste, doubtless, not to say libellous, when Isaiah abruptly addressed the Jewish rulers and nation as follows: — 'Hear the word of the Lord, ye rulers of Sodom! Give ear to the law of our God, yet people of Gomorrah!' With Luther, I will plead in self-defence — 'If I have exceeded the bounds of moderation, the monstrous turpitude of the times has transported me.'

I now come to the subject of 'divine revelation.' You seem bent on proving me to be a heretic, either by implication, inference, or direct admission. The method you take to show that I am not 'a believer in divine revelation' is equally curious and illogical.

(1) 'Mr. Garrison does not deny that he rejects revelation.' May I not respectfully ask, what right have you to catechise me as to my religious faith? As an Abolitionist, I neither affirm nor deny any thing pertaining to revelation; for the Anti-Slavery platform is not the arena on the which to debate such a question. Beyond this, you are travelling out of the record. Is it not highly inconsistent in you to leap from that platform, and insist on my giving you categorical answers to questions relating to my theological views as a private individual? Is it not to be guilty of as great a breach of decorum as it would be in an Anti-Slavery meeting to arraign a Presbyterian or Baptist for his religious tenets? 'Mr. Garrison, or anyone else, has just as good a right to reject revelation as we have to receive it.' Certainly: what then is the difficulty? 'Our *sole ground of controversy*,' you declare, 'is, that he should introduce his peculiar views on theological points — views at variance with divine revelation — *on the Anti-Slavery platform*.' You

have yet to substantiate the accusation, and from it I cannot allow you to wander, in order to make a false issue. To your inquiry — 'If he reverentially receives the Scriptures as a revelation of the mind and will of the Deity, why does he not say so at once?' I reply, first, that I do not choose to establish a precedent of this kind, either as a matter of self-respect, or by my regard for the Anti-Slavery cause; secondly, that the question of divine revelation, or plenary scriptural inspiration, is exceedingly broad, into the discussion of which I am not willing to be drawn at present, while so much remains to be done for the deliverance of those in bondage; and, thirdly, that an affirmative answer would give you no insight into my religious opinions or practices, nor be any evidence of moral courage or true piety, because it would be on the popular side.

(2) 'Mr. Garrison further, by implication, shows that his views are not in consonance with divine revelation, by asking us what we mean by it.' What kind of reasoning is this? You evade a very pregnant question, and then claim to have made out a case — 'by implication'! This may be proof of dexterity, but it is not sound logic.

(3) 'But he still more manifestly admits that he does not receive the Bible as a Book containing a divine revelation, when he says, that the man who professes to receive the claims of the Scripture to the character of an inspired book does not therefore know what is to be made of the book,' &c. This was the inquiry I made:

'Do you know, or can you intelligently surmise, what are the religious sentiments or practices, or what is the character or conduct of any man, because he professes to receive 'the claims of the Scriptures to the character of an inspired book?' Do you know, can you imagine, what such a man will make of the book, or to what sect in religion or party in government he must belong? If not — *and certainly your answer must be in the negative* — then why attach such vital importance to that which really determines nothing?'

It seems to me that this inquiry is pertinent, sensible, and conclusive; and I feel constrained again to press it upon you, and to renew the closing interrogation, 'Why attach such vital importance to that which really determines nothing?' I would also renewedly ask, and solicit a direct reply —

'What is it that the Bible reveals, and who shall authoritatively decide that point? Is truth dependent upon the entire authenticity of any book? Are human duties, relations, responsibilities, to be ascertained by an appeal to Hebrew or Greek manuscripts — to ancient opinions, teachings, usages — or do they grow out of the nature of man, and pertain to the living present rather than to the dead past?'

(4) 'Mr. Garrison attends no place of Christian worship; and this, we hold, unless there be some peculiar circumstances in the case, to be presumptive proof that he does not recognize the authority of the Scriptures'!! My dear sir, this is quite unworthy of a man of candour. What has my attendance on public worship to do with the Anti-Slavery platform. On what ground do you presume to tell me how, when or where I shall engage in the worship of God? If you disclaim infallibility, why assume the robes? Who has certified to you, that I 'attend no place of Christian worship'? Is this *espionage* upon my private walk to be taken as additional proof of your concern for the welfare of the Anti-Slavery cause? If I ask you to define what Christian worship is, will you retort by saying that such a question proves I am an irreverent man? But the question is, nevertheless, a momentous one, covering much ground. — In the following Sonnet from my pen, published some time since, you have my views on this subject:

TRUE WORSHIP.[17]
They, who, as worshippers, some mountain climb,
   Or to some temple made with hands repair,
   As though the Godhead specially dwelt there,
And absence, in Heaven's eye, would be a crime,
Have yet to comprehend this truth sublime:
   The freeman of the Lord no chain can bear,
   His soul is free to worship every where,
Nor limited to any place or time.
No worldly sanctuary now may claim
   Man's reverence, as a consecrated pile;
Mosque, synagogue, cathedral, are the same,
   Differing in nought but architectural style:
Avaunt, then, Superstition! In God's name,
   Nor longer thy blind devotees beguile!

Whether I recognize or reject the authority of the Scriptures, in regard to public worship, let a few citations determine: — 'Then verily the first covenant had also ordinances of divine service, and a *worldly sanctuary.*' . . .[18] 'If that first covenant had been faultless, then should no place have been sought for the second.' . . .[19] 'Jesus saith unto her, Woman, believe me, the hour cometh, when ye shall neither in this mountain, nor yet at Jerusalem, worship the Father.[20] But the hour cometh, and now is, when the true worshippers shall worship the Father in spirit and in truth: for the Father seeketh such to worship him.' . . .[21] 'Howbeit, the Most High dwelleth not in temples made with hands. Heaven is my throne, and earth is my footstool: what house wil ye build me? saith the Lord: or where is the place of my rest?' [22]

Surrounded as I am by pro-Slavery churches and a pro-Slavery clergy, where would you have me attend public worship? There is one occupant of a pulpit in this city, THEODORE PARKER, who bears a bold and unfaltering testimony against Slavery and its abettors; but, religiously, he is branded as a heretic. If I listen to his ministration, will you recognise me as attending a place of Christian worship? You perceive by this, that there are 'some very peculiar circumstances' in my case! Besides, you may learn from the *Liberator*, that I generally occupy the first day of the week in addressing the people, showing them their guilt, and imploring them to combine for the deliverance of the millions in this country whom they have so long held in the galling chains of Slavery. Is not this to worship God acceptably?

What my views of the True Church are, I long since embodied in the following lines. Is this the language of 'infidelity'?

THE TRUE CHURCH.[23]

Church of the living God! in vain thy foes
　　Make thee, in impious mirth, their laughing-stock —
　　Contemn thy strength, thy radiant beauty mock:
In vain their threats, and impotent their blows,
Satan's assaults, Hell's agonizing throes!
　　For thou art built upon th'Eternal Rock,
　　Nor fear'st the thunder-storm, the earthquake shock,
And nothing shall disturb thy calm repose.
All human combinations change and die,
　　Whate'er their origin, name, form, design:
But, firmer than the pillars of the sky,
　　Thou standest ever by a power divine:
Thou art endued with immortality,
　　And cannot perish — GOD'S OWN LIFE IS THINE!

In what sense, and to what extent, I am an 'Anti-Sabbath' heretic, you and your readers may learn by reading another Sonnet from my pen, long since given to the public:

THE TRUE REST.[24]

O Thou, by whom eternal life is given,
　　Through Jesus Christ, they well-beloved Son,
As is thy will obeyed by all in heaven,
　　So let it now by all on earth be done!
Nor by th'observance of one day in seven,
　　As holy time, but of ALL DAYS AS ONE;
The soul set free — all legal fetters riven —
　　Vanished the law — the reign of grace begun!
Dear is the Christian Sabbath to my heart,
　　Bound by no forms — from times and seasons free;
The whole of life absorbing, not a part;
　　Perpetual rest and perfect liberty!
Who keeps not this steers by a Jewish chart,
　　And sails in peril on a storm-tossed sea.

Is this to depress or to elevate the standard of personal consecration to righteousness? Is it 'infidelity'? Is it not substantially the same view of the Sabbath as was taken by Tyndale, Calvin, Luther, Melancthon, Whitby, Paley, Belsham, Priestl[e]y, Roger Williams, George Fox and Robert Barclay, and by the present eminent Archbishop Whately of Dublin? 25 But what has this to do with the Anti-Slavery platform or the Anti-Slavery movement? Nothing! It is an extraneous question. I admit it!

Believe me, dear sir, that I cherish no sentiments which I am ashamed to avow; which I do not believe to be true; which I am not prepared to vindicate as in accordance with the spirit and precepts of the gospel. But I have no desire to engage in a barren theological controversy, especially in a crisis like the present. Technically, I think very little of the Christian name or profession at the present day: it has long since ceased to be odious, it has become respectable and popular. Eighteen hundred years ago, it was a badge of infamy, and decisive evidence of heresy, and cost those who assumed it reputation, ease, wealth, personal safety, and life itself. Then it was a test of character; now it is a fashionable appendage. The calumnious charge of infidelity gives me no concern, except as it operates injuriously to the cause of the slave, as his enemies well know; otherwise, I should never pause to notice it. Whatever else I may be, I am neither a slaveholder nor his apologist, but

Yours, for universal liberty, peace, and righteousness,

William Lloyd Garrison.

Printed in *The Liberator*, September 19, 1851.

The Liberator carries the legend, "Infidelity — Divine Revelation," above Garrison's letter.

The editor of the *London Morning Advertiser* was James Grant (1802–1879), who edited the *Advertiser* from 1850 to 1871. A "devout Calvinist," Grant was the author of numerous works, including many in theology. His chief work, published in three volumes in 1871–1872, was *The Newspaper Press, Its Origin and Present Position*. The *Advertiser* was begun in 1794 as a trade organ of the London Society of Licensed Victuallers and was considered a radical newspaper. In the early 1870's it was perhaps the most powerful journal in England. (James Grant, *The Newspaper Press*, London, 1871, II, 55–64; R. H. Fox Bourne, *English Newspapers*, New York, 1966, I, 285; II, *passim*.)

1. *The Liberator*, August 1, 1851, had carried an essay by Garrison, entitled "The London Morning Advertiser," in reply to an editorial article in the *London Morning Advertiser* of June 30, 1851. The *Advertiser* article, entitled "Maria Weston Chapman — William Lloyd Garrison," appeared in *The Liberator* of August 1, 1851, together with Garrison's reply.

2. Hebrews 13:3.

3. Shakespeare, *Othello*, I, iii, 67.

4. Matthew 7:20.

5. William Cowper (1731–1800), English poet, *The Task*, Book II, "The Timepiece," I, 17.

6. *The Liberator* of September 19, 1851, reprinted the report of the London *Universe* of August 21, 1846, under the title "The new Anti-Slavery League."

7. William Oxley (1779–1867) was "the venerable head of the temperance cause in London." (*Life*, III, 258–259; IV, 401.) P. T. Winskill, in *The Temperance Movement and its Workers* (London, 1893), III, 193, notes: "Dr. William Oxley of London, who was a practical teetotaler from 1794, or nearly forty years before the formation of our modern total abstinence societies, went on two voyages to the arctic regions, and his experience proved to him in a conclusive manner that his abstinence from alcoholic liquors was advantageous to him in every way. Despite all his hardships in these regions, and his life of active usefulness, he lived to the age of eighty-eight years." I am indebted to Miss Rosemary Taylor, Assistant Librarian, Institute of Historical Research, University of London, in a letter dated September 20, 1971, for this quotation.

8. The Reverend James Carlile, a Congregational minister born in Ireland, lived in Hackney, London, for many years. He may have first met Garrison in 1840 during the latter's trip to England. Carlile "became minister of Well Street Chapel, in Hackney, sometime between 1832 and 1842. The congregation of this chapel had, in 1832, split into two factions, one group leaving the parent foundation to form a new church." He was a nephew of Dr. James Carlile and contributed an Introductory Notice to a book written by the latter, *Station and Occupation of Saints in Final Glory.* (I am indebted for this information to Mr. Stanley Tongue, Archivist, Shoreditch District Library, Pitfield Street, London, England.)

A letter from Carlile to Garrison, dated Hackney, London, March 9, 1841, notes: "I have commenced the periodical about which we had some conversation when I had the pleasure of seeing you here. It is called the Christian Examiner, and Advocate of Religious and Civil Liberty! I have sent to your address nos. 1 & 2 — May I ask your opinion of it as a whole — and for any hints relating to its future management which your wisdom and experience may suggest . . ." (Anti-Slavery Letters to Garrison and Others, Boston Public Library.) There are at least nine letters to the Reverend Amos A. Phelps from Carlile, written between 1843 and 1845, in the Phelps Papers, Boston Public Library.

9. The Reverend Isaac Nelson (1802–1888), of Belfast, Ireland, was a Presbyterian clergyman who resigned his duties as clergyman in 1880 when he was elected to Parliament. He retained his seat until 1885. (Brian A. Kennedy, "The Rev. Isaac Nelson, M. P.," *The Irish News and Belfast Morning News*, June 8, 1948.) An essay on Nelson in the *Belfast Telegraph*, December 5, 1928, quotes a fellow-minister of Nelson as having remarked in 1867 about Nelson that "on the question of fellowship with slaveholders, on the revivals, on the riots in Belfast, . . . on the Civil War in America, and on fifty other matters he has taken and maintained with determined courage a solitary or nearly solitary position." I am indebted to H. Russell of the Local History Library, City of Belfast Public Libraries, for both newspaper items.

There is a letter from Nelson to Henry C. Wright, dated August 26, 1846, in the Anti-Slavery Letters to Garrison and Others, Boston Public Library.

10. The Reverend Henry Solly (b. November 17, 1813; d. February 27, 1903), a descendant of Kentish yeomen, first met Garrison in 1840 during the World's Anti-Slavery Convention in London, where they discussed nonresistance and temperance. He served as a Unitarian minister in Yeovil from 1840 to 1842, in Tavistock from 1842 to 1844, in Shepton Mallet from 1844 to 1847, and in subsequent years in Cheltenham, London, and Lancaster. He was active in the Chartist and temperance movements. In his later years, he was primarily interested in workingmen's clubs. His published works include *James Woodford, Carpenter and Chartist,* as well as poems and novels. (Henry Solly, *"These Eighty Years" or, The Story of an Unfinished Life,* London, 1893, 2 vols., *passim*; Henry Solly, *Workingmen's Social Clubs and Educational Institutes,* 2d ed., London, 1904, pp. 1–15.)

11. Henry Vincent (b. London, May 10, 1813; d. there, December 29, 1878)

was a Chartist leader and political agitator. He was imprisoned twice, in 1839 and 1840–1841. He lectured in the United States in 1866, 1867, 1869, and 1875.

12. William Lovett (1800–1877), Chartist and political agitator, helped to draft parliamentary petitions and bills in 1836–1838, was arrested and imprisoned in 1839–1840 for a memorandum against the police, published *Chartism: A New Organisation of the People* (1841), on the organization of the Chartist party, and was a member of the council of the Anti-Slavery League in 1840.

13. John Humffreys Parry (1816–1880), after working at the British Museum in the printed book department, was admitted to the bar in 1843, and became a leading criminal lawyer. After 1856, when he was appointed sergeant-at-law, he turned to civil law. He was elected a bencher of the Middle Temple in 1878. A strong liberal, he sympathized with the Chartists and helped found the Complete Suffrage Association.

14. The Reverend John Howard Hinton (1791–1873), editor of the *Anti-Slavery Reporter*, and a Baptist minister, was minister of Devonshire Square Chapel at Bishopsgate, 1837–1863, and wrote and edited theological, biographical and educational works.

15. James Haughton (b. Carlow, Ireland, May 7, 1795; d. Dublin, February 20, 1873) was a philanthropist and reformer, active in antislavery, temperance, and other reform movements. He published *Slavery Immoral* in 1847, *Memoir of T. Clarkson* in 1847, and *Plea for Teetotalism* in 1855.

16. Unidentified.

17. This sonnet by Garrison was first printed in *The Liberator*, November 19, 1841, carried the title, "Sonnet — Worship," and was dated "Boston, Nov. 15, 1841."

18. Hebrews 9:1.

19. Hebrews 8:7.

20. John 4:21.

21. John 4:23.

22. Acts 7:48–49; also, Isaiah 66:1.

23. This sonnet was first printed in *The Liberator*, November 26, 1841, and was dated "Boston, Nov. 21, 1841."

24. This sonnet first appeared in *The Liberator*, August 25, 1837, and was dated August 14, 1837.

25. William Tyndale (d. 1536), English reformer, theologian, and translator of the Bible, wrote several theological works and was burned at the stake for heresy. "He was one of the most remarkable of the Reformation leaders . . . but his translation of the bible . . . is his surest title to fame."

Melancthon (1497–1560), originally named Philipp Schwarzerd, was a German scholar and humanist, second only to Luther in the Lutheran Reformation, a friend of Erasmus and Calvin, and more conciliatory than Luther on doctrinal issues and toward other reformers.

Daniel Whitby (1638–1726), English polemical minister and theologian, wrote many theological treatises, including *The Protestant Reconciler* in 1682, in which he pleaded for concessions to nonconformists.

William Paley (1743–1805) was an English clergyman, fellow of Christ's College, Cambridge, and college lecturer; archdeacon of Carlisle; author of *Principles of Morals and Political Philosophy* (1785), of *Evidences of Christianity* (1794), his most popular book, and of *Natural Theology* (1802). He is regarded as an eighteenth-century utilitarian, "differing chiefly from Bentham" in his morality by the "introduction of the supernatural sanction."

Thomas Belsham (1750–1829) was an English Unitarian minister, professor of divinity, author of theological works. His works included *Evidences of Christianity* and *Elements of the Philosophy of the Human Mind*.

Joseph Priestley (1733–1804), English theologian and scientist, turned from Presbyterian to Unitarian, became a theological and political dissenter, and came to the United States in 1794, following destruction of his home and scientific materials because of his sympathy with the French Revolution.

Roger Williams (1603–1683), clergyman, was an advocate of religious freedom and founder of Rhode Island.

George Fox (1625–1691) was the English founder of the Society of Friends.

Robert Barclay (1648–1690) was an English Quaker apologist and author. His best known and greatest work is *An Apology for the True Christian Divinity Held by the Quakers*, published in 1678. (Louis Ruchames, ed., *Racial Thought in America*, volume I, *From the Puritans to Abraham Lincoln*, University of Massachusetts Press, 1969, p. 99n.)

Richard Whately (1787–1863) was a clergyman and author and archbishop of Dublin, Ireland, from 1831 to 1863.

---

3 2

TO SYDNEY HOWARD GAY

Boston, Sept. 27, 1851.

My dear Gay:

The accompanying bundle of newspapers, and letter, for Mr. J. P. Marquand, please keep till they are called for by him. I intended to have sent them a fortnight ago, and he may have already called for them more than once; and, not hearing from me, may have come to the conclusion that no answer to his letter was intended. He desires a copy of my Poems,[1] and most readily would I comply with his request, if I knew where to procure a copy. Not a single one, for my own reference, have I in my possession; nor is there one to be obtained in Boston. It is barely possible that there may be a stray copy at your Anti-Slavery Office; if so, please hand it to Mr. Marquand, with my respects. If you know where to send the accompanying bundle, please do so, as he may not call again at your office.

Many years ago, in Newburyport, (my birth-place,) there used to be a wealthy and distinguished citizen by the name of Marquand,[2] collector of the port. He had a son by the name of J. P. Marquand. Whether he is the gentleman who has written to me, and for whom my letter is intended, I should be glad to learn.[3]

Please give my best regards to your wife,[4] and believe me, whether in sunshine or affliction,

Yours, truly,

Wm. Lloyd Garrison.

S. H. Gay.

ALS: Columbia University Library.

1. The reference is to William Lloyd Garrison, *Sonnets and Other Poems* (Boston, Oliver Johnson, 1843), 96 pp.

2. Joseph Marquand (b. Newbury, October 16, 1748; d. September 6, 1820) was collector of customs at Newburyport from 1811 to his death. During the Revolution, he owned a large number of privateers. In 1805, he "had so many vessels coming from prosperous voyages that he is said to have cried out: 'Lord, stay Thy hand, Thy servant hath enough.'" (Claude M. Fuess, *The Story of Essex County*, New York, 1935, pp. 974–975.)

3. According to existing historical records, Joseph Marquand married Rebecca Coffin in 1776. Their son Joseph was born December 25, 1793, and died either in 1851 or in July 1854. He had a son named John Phillips Marquand, born in Newburyport, October 16, 1831, who was still alive in 1895. (John J. Currier, *History of Newburyport, Massachusetts*, Newburyport, 1909, II, 239–240, 556; Edmund J. and Horace G. Cleveland, *The Genealogy of the Cleveland and Cleaveland Families*, Hartford, Connecticut, 1899, II, 1057, 1755.)

It is probable that neither the son nor the grandson of Joseph Marquand was the J. P. Marquand who had written to Garrison. For there are two letters extant in the Anti-Slavery Letters to Garrison and Others (Boston Public Library), the first of which, signed J. P. Marquand, is dated Williamsburgh, Long Island, July 8, 1852, and is addressed to "Dear Friend" (not necessarily Garrison); the second, dated June 16, 1877, is from Josiah P. Marquand to Garrison, and in it the former mentions his friendship with George W. Benson and his having printed copies of Garrison's poem, "True Rest." In the earlier letter Marquand writes, "I received a letter from you some time since and also a bundle of newspapers for which I thank you — I have distributed the newspapers principally in this city and hope the seed sown will spring up and bring forth fruit. In the month of January last I obtained a Free Ticket to Boston & back with the intention of making you a visit but many things have prevented me from so doing. I have the ticket yet and can come at any time. . . . I am well acquainted with your friend Mr. George Benson as he lives only 2 or 3 blocks distance from my residence in Williamsburgh. . . ."

4. The former Elizabeth Johns Neall, granddaughter of Warner Mifflin, prominent Quaker reformer and antislavery man, married Gay in 1845. (See *Letters*, II, 662.)

---

3 3

TO ADELINE ROBERTS

Boston, Sept. 27, 1851.

Esteemed Friend:

I deeply participate in the disappointment that must be felt by your Society, in consequence of the declining of Mr. Parker to give one of the course of lectures you have in contemplation.[1] Of course, this is not because he lacks interest in the anti-slavery cause, or would not as readily lecture before your Society as any other; but he has already a multiplicity of engagements on hand, and is compelled to decline very many invitations extended to him in every direction. Besides, he is somewhat careful and elaborate in the preparation of his discourses, and feels that he cannot command the time to do any justice either to himself or our great cause.

You may calculate upon my being with you at the time appointed, *Deo volente.*

Hoping that the entire course of lectures may be in the highest degree promotive of the interests of the millions who are perishing for lack of knowledge, and pining in the prison-house of slavery, in our guilty country, I remain,

Yours, to break all fetters,

　　　　　　　　　　　　　　　　　Wm. Lloyd Garrison.

Adeline Roberts.

ALS: Essex Institute, Salem, Massachusetts.

Adeline Roberts of Salem, Massachusetts, the Corresponding Secretary of the Salem Female Anti-Slavery Society, was a teacher in Salem (*Salem Directory,* 1869).

1. *The Liberator,* September 26, 1851, carried an announcement that "The Seventh Course of Lectures, before the *Salem Female Anti-Slavery Society,* comprising eight in number, will be delivered on successive Sunday evenings, commencing Oct. 5th, at Lyceum Hall, at 7 o'clock." The following week's issue (October 3) carried the list of speakers, headed by Lucy Stone (October 5), with Garrison scheduled to speak last, on November 23.

---

3 4

TO J. MILLER McKIM

Boston, Oct. 4, 1851.

My Dear Friend: — A sudden cold, attended with considerable inflammation of the lungs, (aside from other considerations,) must deprive me of the pleasure of attending the Annual Meeting of the Pennsylvania Anti-Slavery Society, at West Chester, next week.[1] Whatever may be the disappointment felt at my absence, it cannot be greater than the regret I feel at the interposing of any obstacle to prevent my being with those I have known, loved and honored, for so many years, as among the earliest, most reliable, most devoted friends of a sorely afflicted and horribly outraged race.

Your Anniversary is to be held at a time of intense excitement, under circumstances peculiarly trying, in a location not very remote from the Christiana tragedy.[2] It cannot fail, therefore, to be an occasion of thrilling interest and deep solemnity. Whatever may transpire, I am confident that you all will possess your souls in patience, nor think it 'strange concerning the fiery trial which is to try you, as though some strange thing had happened unto you; but rejoice, inasmuch as ye are partakers of Christ's sufferings;'[3] 'committing the keeping of your souls to God in well-doing, as unto a faithful Creator.'[4] 'For yet a little while, and the wicked shall not be; [5] but the meek shall inherit the earth.[6] The wicked plotteth against the just, and gnasheth upon him with his teeth. The Lord shall laugh at him; for he seeth that his day is coming. The wicked have drawn out the sword, and have bent their bow, to cast down the poor and needy, and to slay such as be of upright conversation. Their sword shall enter their own heart, and their bow shall be broken.' [7] 'God is our refuge and strength, a very present help in time of trouble; therefore will we not fear, though the earth be removed, and though the mountains be carried into the midst of the sea.' [8]

Truly, 'This is a nation that obeyeth not the voice of the Lord their God, nor receiveth correction; truth is perished, and is cut off from their mouth.[9] . . . Were they ashamed when they had committed abomination? nay, they were not at all ashamed, neither could they blush.[10] . . . From the least of them even unto the greatest of them, every one is given to covetousness; and from the prophet even unto the priest, every one dealeth falsely.[11] . . . They make a man an offender for a word, and lay a snare for him that reproveth in the gate, and turn aside the just for a thing of naught.[12] . . . Their feet run to evil, and they make haste to shed innocent blood; wasting and destruction are in their paths.[13] . . . They all lie in wait for blood; they hunt every man his brother with a net. That they may do evil with both hands earnestly, the prince asketh and the judge asketh for a reward; and the great man, he uttereth his mischievous desire; so they wrap it up.[14] . . . And he that departeth from evil, maketh himself a prey.' [15]

Nevertheless, 'Strengthen ye the weak hands, and confirm the feeble knees. Say unto them that are of a fearful heart, Be strong, fear not.[16] . . . Hearken unto me,' saith the Lord, 'ye that know righteousness, the people in whose hearts is my fear; fear yet not the reproach of men, neither be ye afraid of their revilings; for the moth shall eat them up like a garment, and the worm shall eat them like wool.[17] I, even I, am he that comforteth you. Who art thou, that thou shouldst be afraid of a man that shall die, and the son of man that shall be made as grass; and forgettest the Lord thy Maker, that hath stretched forth the heavens, and laid the foundations of the earth; and hast feared continually every day because of the fury of the oppressor, as if he was ready to destroy? and where is the fury of the oppressor? The captive exile hasteneth that he may be loosed, and that he shall not die in the pit, nor that his bread should fail.[18] . . . For the oppression of the poor, for the sighing of the needy, now will I arise, saith the Lord; I will set him in safety from him that puffeth at him.[19] . . . Say ye not, A confederacy, to all them to whom this people shall say, A confederacy; neither fear ye their fear, nor be afraid. . . . Sanctify the Lord of Hosts himself; and let him be your fear, and let him be your dread.' [20]

My dear friend, I can find no language so apposite, so reliable, so descriptive, so consoling, in the present time, as that which I have quoted from a volume, professedly held by this oppressive nation in the highest veneration as the inspired word of God, which yet disregards, in the most daring manner, all its admonitions, warnings, expostulations, examples, threatenings and judgments.

More than three millions of our fellow-creatures are continually crying for deliverance from a servitude, 'one hour of which,' in the truthful words of THOMAS JEFFERSON, 'is fraught with more misery than ages of that which our fathers rose in rebellion to oppose.' [21] Their enslavement demonstrates that the guilt of this nation is unparalleled. Our duty, as abolitionists, is still to 'cry aloud and spare not,' [22] until every chain is broken. We have nothing to change — no steps to retrace — no new course to mark out — no confession to make, except that we have come short in zeal, self-sacrifice, devotedness. If the Declaration of Independence is to be cherished, we are right; if the gospel is to be obeyed, we are right; if man is man, we are right. We may safely defy the world to show wherein we have demanded any thing unreasonable for the slave, or unjust to the master. What we protest against is conduct so tremendously wrong, so awfully impious, that no language can exaggerate it — the reducing of a rational, accountable, immortal being to the condition of a beast. We deny that man can be rightfully the property of man. It is the plainest of all propositions, and needs no proof. The people that reject this are filled with a tyrannical spirit; the law that contravenes this is iniquitous, and to be disobeyed at all hazards; the government that repudiates this is essentially despotic, and forfeits all claim to respect, all right to exist. Injustice, cruelty, oppression, these are the works of the devil, not to be tolerated, but destroyed. Whoever undertakes to enforce them, whether called President, Judge, or Commissioner, ranks himself among the enemies of mankind; and must take his place in history by the side of such monsters as Caligula, Nero and Domitian. A compact made at the expense of the rights and liberties of any portion of the people is 'a covenant with death and an agreement with hell'; [23] and that covenant — so runs the promise of God — shall be annulled, and that agreement shall not stand, when judgment is laid to the line, and righteousness to the plummet; for the hail shall sweep away the refuge of lies, and the waters shall overflow the hiding place — 'Open ye the gates, that the righteous nation which keepeth the truth may enter in.[24] Trust ye in the Lord forever; for in the Lord Jehovah is everlasting strength. For he bringeth down them that dwell on high; the lofty city, he layeth it low; he layeth it low, even to the ground; he bringeth it even to the dust. The foot shall tread it down, even the foot of the poor, and the steps of needy.' [25]

I have just been cursorily reading a work, published in London in 1792, entitled, 'Thoughts and Inquiry on the Principles and Tenure of the Revealed and Supreme Law,' with reference to African Slavery, 'being humbly submitted to the British Legislature, and to the public in general,' by P. W. HALL.[26] As I have never seen a copy of it before, and as it contains many things (somewhat quaintly expressed) very pertinent to our land and times, I am tempted to occupy the remainder of my sheet with a few quotations: —

'Among the most abandoned and villanous pursuits of men, that of modern slavery has claimed the pre-eminence as most abominable. And it has appeared throughout all its long continued depression of men by men, as not only contrary to every mark of Christian virtue, but as a most horrible disgrace to human nature; and which, to the universal shame of civilized and enlightened nations, is very debasing to them who have imbrued their hands in the blood of iniquity, oppression, cruelty, and murders, by shamefully countenancing and suffering lawless ruffians, robbers, and depredators, to go out from them to various places of the earth, to rob and extirpate the inhabitants; and, for the purpose of cursed avarice, to set up a traffic in men, as if they were beasts, to capture, murder, and enslave the people of a dark complexion, and with infernal intrepidity, to carry them away with hostile force from the coast of Africa to all their colonies, which they have founded in oppression, injustice, murder and blood.

That accursed avarice and brutish wickedness has led the tyrannical oppressors, in the insolence of their infidelity and arrogance, *to form laws of iniquity for establishing combinations of villany*; and the enchantments of its venality have so prevailed over the nations, that a deprivation of every principle of justice, honesty and humanity, has so debased the understandings of men, that they have *formed systems of government, civil policy*, and laws of commerce, diametrically opposite, and contrary to the express laws of revealed religion, and every sacred right of man. ° ° ° °

The refinery of our civilization has extneded *protection and support to a combination of man-stealers and slaveholders*, contrary to all law, reason and justice; and the efficient execution of THE JUST LAW has no authority over them, *because those who ought to be the judges and administrators of the law, are the depredators and extortioners*, AND PARTNERS IN THE MATTER; and the only true law, either in its severity or wise and merciful mitigations, is not regarded. How long shall it be, O Lord God of Hosts! that the people and nations will rebel against thee, and forsake thy law?

What a covetous, wicked and iniquitous generation do we yet live in! *When thieves and oppressors can rob others and bring us gain, for our own profit*, WE LET THEM GO; but when they rob *ourselves* of some money or other trifles of temporary use, we hang them according to the equilibrium law of our land! * * * *

That audacious, tyrannical and accursed avarice which has set up its dominion over men as property, *has extended into the very concerns of the British* [*American*] *Senate,* contrary to the laws of justice and reason, bringing them into considerations and CONCESSIONS, *as if robbers, thieves, and depredators had a right to the profits of their perfidy*!

'O ye inhabitants of the British [American] nation, who have bewitched you! Have ye not followed after the idols of your avarice, and have adhered to the *arrogance of your legislative assemblies, in setting up laws and statutes,* from time to time, *as claiming an arbitrary authority to themselves,* in reversing the laws of justice and disregarding the light of His truth and the words of His command, who only could make ye wise? And as a foolish people and a rebellious nation, have you not adhered to barbarities and *laws of murder,* which even heathen nations would blush to execute? I have no reason to accuse you falsely; your own hypocrisy and arrogance will show the matter. Ye have put away that authority from you, in the science of your law, which, in other respects, ye generally profess to believe. But ye may be vain, and as long arrogant as ye will, it will not profit you in the end; and the truth, while it gives you light, will bear its own testimony against you. * * * * *

'The horrible combination of that man-degrading traffic has appeared as a monster rolled in blood, as a horrible twisting serpent seeking the vitals of its prey, and as gorging itself with the slaver of its own wickedness; and it has been suffered to go abroad, with all the power and force of villany and violence, devouring and oppressing men, and has come back with the turpitude of its cruelty and voluptuousness, in all its channels and courses, to stifle and benumb the virtues, to tarnish and corrupt the morals, and to spoil the natural generosity and urbanity of the people of this country; and, like a corroding menstruum, it has speckled the inhabitants with brutish barbarity, fretting to the bone, and with tyranny, cruelty, treachery, and covetousness, in all their occupations, in their boats, in their ships, in their houses, in their lands, and in all their situations, callings and offices of life. For a little leaven leaveneth the whole lump; and when tyranny, injustice, and oppression have any root and power in government, they do not sleep and be still, but go on in all the villanies of violence where they can find occasion, and have power to exercise its depredation. *In proportion as any government admits tyranny, injustice and oppression, the people under its jurisdiction will be tyrannical, treacherous, covetous and unjust.* And when such barbarity as the abandoned traffic of slavery is any where tolerated, and suffered with impunity, and without hindrance by the government of any nation, and where almost nothing else in comparison could be reckoned as crimes among men, may not every villain exult in his wickedness, and triumph in the guilt of his covetousness?'

These extracts, my dear friend, strike me as singularly applicable to the present crisis in our guilty land. They occupy so large a portion of my sheet as to exclude some other topics upon which I intended to expatiate — especially in reference to that most heart-rending and atrocious enactment, the Fugitive Slave Bill, to denounce and disregard which is the imperative duty of every one who fears God and regards man. If to put it beneath my feet, and to hold up those who are for executing it to the execration of the world, as the most perfidious, inhuman and lawless of men, be treason, then I glory in being a traitor, and am ready for the dungeon or halter at any moment. All carnal weapons I have long since renounced, but only to put on 'the whole armor of God,' [27] that I may 'be able to withstand in the evil day; and having done all, TO STAND.' [28]

> 'Glory to those who die in this great cause!
> Courts, judges, can inflict no brand of shame,
> Or shape of death, to shroud them from applause!
> No, manglers of the martyr's earthly frame,
> Your hangmen fingers cannot touch his fame!
> Still in our guilty land there shall be some
> True hearts, the shrine of Freedom's vestal flame:
> Long trains of ill may pass, unheeded — dumb —
> But Vengeance is behind, and Justice is to come!' [29]

Yours, for universal liberty,

WM. LLOYD GARRISON.

J. Miller McKim.

Printed in *The Liberator*, November 1, 1851.

James Miller McKim (b. Carlisle, Pennsylvania, November 14, 1810; d. West Orange, New Jersey, June 13, 1874), ordained pastor of a Presbyterian church at Womelsdorf, Pennsylvania, had been converted to abolition on reading Garrison's *Thoughts on African Colonization*. He was a participant in the founding convention of the American Anti-Slavery Society in December 1833, and left his pulpit in 1836 to become a lecturer for the society, speaking throughout Pennsylvania. He moved to Philadelphia in 1840, to be the publishing agent of the Pennsylvania Anti-Slavery Society. His position was later changed to that of corresponding secretary for the society, which he held for about twenty-five years. He remained a friend of Garrison and a leader of the American Anti-Slavery Society, participating also in the Underground Railroad and in court cases involving escaped slaves. During the Civil War, he helped found the Philadelphia Port Royal relief committee, urged and furthered the enlistment of Negro troops, and served as corresponding secretary of the Pennsylvania Freedmen's Relief Association. He was one of the founders of *The Nation* in 1865. From 1865 to 1869, he worked with the American Freedman's Union Commission, in which he sought to advance "general and impartial education at the south."

1. *The Liberator*, October 17, 1851, carried a letter dated "Marlborough, Chester Co., Pa., Oct. 10, 1851" from Oliver Johnson, describing the proceedings of the anniversary meeting of the Pennsylvania Anti-Slavery Society.

2. The event referred to took place in September 1851 at Christiana, Lancaster County, Pennsylvania. A Maryland slaveowner, Edward Gorsuch, his son, a federal marshal, and other whites, all of whom were armed, appeared one day in the vicinity of Christiana for the purpose of apprehending certain alleged fugitive slaves belonging to Gorsuch. As word spread of Gorsuch's plan, blacks of the area appeared before the house in which Gorsuch claimed the fugitives were hiding and where a number of blacks were living. What heightened the tension was the fact that certain blacks of the area had recently been abducted, apparently by

southerners, and were never seen again. When Gorsuch and his party appeared before the house in question they were met by a crowd of blacks, led by a former slave named William Parker, who were prepared to resist any attempt to drag any black back to captivity. In the crowd were two white Quakers who lived in the neighborhood, Castner Hanway and Elijah Lewis. Both were asked by the marshall to assist in the capture of the alleged fugitives. They refused. At the same time, they apparently asked the blacks not to resist forcefully. A fight broke out, resulting in the death of Gorsuch and the wounding of several blacks and whites. Some of the blacks involved in the fight fled to Rochester, where they were helped by Frederick Douglass to reach Toronto, Canada. Although Hanway, Lewis, and thirty-seven blacks were imprisoned on a charge of treason for resisting the operation of the Fugitive Slave Law, they were all eventually freed by the federal courts after spending several months in jail. (*The Liberator,* September 19, 26, October 3, 10, 17, 24, November 14, 28, December 5, 19, 1851, January 9, 1852; the best account of the case is *A History of the Trial of Castner Hanway and Others, for Treason, at Philadelphia in November, 1851, with an Introduction upon the History of the Slave Question,* by a Member of the Philadelphia Bar, Philadelphia, Uriah Hunt & Sons, 1852, 86 pp. The account in Carleton Mabee, *Black Freedom: The Nonviolent Abolitionists from 1830 Through the Civil War,* London, 1970, pp. 304–305, which summarizes the event, contains errors resulting from a failure to consult *A History of the Trial. . . .*)

3. I Peter 4:12–13.
4. I Peter 4:19, slightly emended.
5. Psalms 37:10.
6. Psalms 37:11.
7. Psalms 37:12–15.
8. Psalms 46:1–2.
9. Jeremiah 7:28.
10. Jeremiah 6:15
11. Jeremiah 6:13.
12. Isaiah 29:21.
13. Isaiah 59:7.
14. Micah 7:2–3.
15. Isaiah 59:15.
16. Isaiah 35:3–4.
17. Isaiah 51:7–8.
18. Isaiah 51:12–14.
19. Psalms 12:5.
20. Isaiah 8:12–13.
21. "Answers of Mr. Jefferson, to questions propounded to him by M. de Meusnier," in H. A. Washington, *The Writings of Thomas Jefferson* (Washington, D.C., 1854, 9 vols.), IX, 279.
22. Isaiah 58:1.
23. Isaiah 28:15.
24. Isaiah 26:2.
25. Isaiah 26:4–6.
26. The volume is listed in the Library of Congress catalogue under the following title: *Thoughts and inquiry on the principles and tenur[!] of the revealed and supreme law, shewing the utter inconsistency and injustice of our penal statutes, and the illicit traffic and practice of modern slavery . . . with some grounds of a plan for abolishing the same. To which is added a letter to a clergyman on the same subject . . .* (London, printed for J. Ridgway, 1792), 304 pp. The author has not been further identified.
27. Ephesians 6:11.
28. Ephesians 6:13.
29. Thomas Campbell (1777–1844), Scottish poet, "Stanzas to the Memory of the Spanish Patriots."

II KOSSUTH IN THE UNITED STATES: 1852

LOUIS KOSSUTH, the leader of the short-lived Hungarian revolution which had been suppressed by Austria with the aid of Russia, arrived in the United States on December 5, 1851. Arriving aboard an American warship and as the result of an invitation from the American Congress, Kossuth was greeted with adulation by American officialdom and lionized by all sections of American society. During his stay in this country, in which he delivered scores of speeches, he emphasized the need for American help for the achievement of Hungarian independence. The better to achieve his aims, he announced publicly that he would refrain from any remarks about American domestic affairs, obviously with slavery in mind. Yet he did praise American devotion to freedom. It was this which appalled the abolitionists; which, in effect, seemed to them to strengthen the hands of the slaveholder and to evince an unmitigated hypocrisy. The result was an open letter to Kossuth, first published in February in *The Liberator* and immediately thereafter as an expanded pamphlet or small book of 112 pages. The letter was written by Garrison and signed by him as president of the American-Slavery Society and by the two secretaries of the Society, Sydney Howard Gay and Wendell Phillips.

It is difficult to assess the impact of Garrison's letter. But it may be noted that after several months, the enthusiasm for Kossuth waned, other distractions occupied the American mind, and Kossuth left the United States for England in July with a somewhat disappointing sum of $90,000 for his pains, instead of the one million dollars which he had hoped for. Moreover, even his announced silence with regard to slavery failed to win him any real support in the South. Indeed, Haim Genizi, a recent student of the subject, points out that whereas Kossuth was generally received with enthusiasm in the North, at least during the early months of his stay, "in Southern cities, he was received with coolness and even hostility." Genizi's explanation is that "a study of

Kossuth's speeches and activities proves that his opinion on Freedom, Emancipation, Tyranny and political slavery, though he was careful not to mention personal slavery, aroused Southern anger against him. His association with people who were classified (truly or not) as abolitionists, his reception of a Negro delegation, his ideas on slavery, all earned for him, from the supporters of slavery, the stigma of 'abolitionist.'" [1]

What may have contributed to cooling even the North's ardor toward Kossuth was the appearance on March 20, 1852, of Harriet Beecher Stowe's *Uncle Tom's Cabin* after having been serialized in the (Washington, D.C.) *National Era.*

The novel, which took both the United States (at least the North) and the world by storm, may well have revealed to many the hollowness of Kossuth's praise of American devotion to freedom. It certainly distracted the public from Kossuth's presence and helped to remove news of him from the front pages of American newspapers. Garrison reviewed the book in *The Liberator* on March 26, and gave it great praise despite his disagreement with its favorable view of African colonization in its final pages. At the end of the year, Mrs. Stowe called on Garrison. It is reported that during their chat, "Mrs. Stowe inquired earnestly, but in no offensive spirit, 'Mr. Garrison, are you a Christian?' . . . It was met smilingly on his part, and substantially as was of old the inquiry, 'And who is my neighbor?'" (*Life*, III, 363n.)

Unfortunately, there are few Garrison letters extant for 1852 and in none of these is Harriet Beecher Stowe mentioned, although the issues of *The Liberator* were filled with items about Mrs. Stowe and her work. However, Mrs. Beecher's biographer does mention a letter (undated) from Garrison upon the appearance of *Uncle Tom's Cabin* and quotes the following sentences: "I estimate the value of anti-slavery writing by the abuse it brings. Now all the defenders of slavery have let me alone and are abusing you." [2]

The remainder of the year was marked by nominations of candidates for the November presidential election: John P. Hale as candidate of the "Free Democracy," a loose combination of Free Soil and Liberty party members, and Winfield Scott and Franklin Pierce as the respective nominees of the Whig and Democratic parties.

1. Haim Genizi, "The American Attitude Towards Louis Kossuth," in Menahem Zevi Kaddari, ed., *Bar-Ilan, Volume in Humanities and Social Sciences, Decennial Volume II (1955–1965)* (Jerusalem, 1969), p. CXVII. The quotation is from a one-page English summary of a longer essay by Genizi in Hebrew which occupies pages 173–185 in the same volume.
2. Charles Edward Stowe, *Life of Harriet Beecher Stowe Compiled from her Letters and Journals* (Boston and New York, 1891), p. 161.

During October and November, for a period of three weeks beginning on October 16, Garrison visited Pennsylvania by way of Northampton, Massachusetts, and New York, stopping at both of the latter cities, attending the Pennsylvania Anti-Slavery Society's annual convention at West Chester on October 25–27, and visiting numerous friends and speaking to a variety of meetings during the remainder of the trip.

---

3 5

TO CAROLINE C. THAYER

Boston, Jan. 5, 1852.

Esteemed Friend:

Pardon me for not instantly replying to your kind note of the first instant, which with its accompanying gifts, was received with great pleasure and heartfelt gratitude; but I desired to send you, though a very poor return indeed, the volume herewith enclosed, which was not then in the binding I wished. The selections from my writings have no literary merit, and certainly present my "fanaticism" and "infidelity" in their most offensive form; yet they seem to me exceedingly tame and commonplace, and I really marvel that such an excitement should have followed their promulgation through the Liberator. However, "what is writ is writ — would it were worthier!" I need not assure you, that I shall carefully preserve and do very highly prize the "sculptured semblance" of our beloved friend Theodore Parker, a "heretic" of no mean quality, and a brave hearted reformer of no common stature, who, though now popularly decried and rejected, is building for himself a most solid frame. May he long be preserved, perfecting himself in knowledge and in grace, and mightily aiding in the redemption of an oppressed and suffering world!

My dear little Fanny [1] was highly delighted with your New Year's presents, and desires me to send you her hearty thanks. Please give to your mother [2] and sisters [3] the best wishes of the season for me, and accept for yourself the assurances of my sincere esteem — in which my dear wife cordially joins. —

Your much obliged friend.

Wm. Lloyd Garrison

Miss Caroline C. Thayer

Transcript: Garrison Papers, Boston Public Library.

Caroline Coddington Thayer (d. Roxbury, February 15, 1891), the daughter of Nathaniel F. and Susanna T. Thayer, was "one of that 'glorious phalanx of old

Wendell Phillips, William Lloyd Garrison, and George Thompson in 1851

The Pennsylvania Anti-Slavery Society, 1851

Left to right, front row: Oliver Johnson, Mrs. Margaret Jones Burleigh, Benjamin C. Bacon, Robert Purvis, Lucretia Mott, James Mott; back row: Mary Grew, Edward M. Davis, Haworth Wetherald, Abby Kimber, J. Miller McKim, Sarah Pugh

Theodore Parker in 1853

Louis Kossuth

maids,' who was always busy with parish work," and a close friend and admirer of Theodore Parker. Although a semi-invalid for much of her life, she was nevertheless a philanthropic and public-spirited Bostonian, and an active supporter of anti-slavery and woman suffrage. Passionately fond of books, she and her sisters collected a large library which they bequeathed to the Boston Public Library. (Henry Steele Commager, *Theodore Parker*, Boston, 1936, p. 114; obituary, *Boston Evening Transcript*, February 21, 1891.)

1. Helen Frances Garrison, the Garrisons' daughter (b. December 16, 1844; d. July 5, 1928, at Dobbs Ferry, New York), met Henry Villard, of Bavaria, Germany, journalist and railroad promoter, during the Civil War when he served as a war correspondent for the *New York Tribune*. She married him on January 3, 1866. After his death in 1900, she immersed herself in woman suffrage, followed by activity in the Woman's Peace Society. For many years, she was owner of *The Nation* and *The New York Evening Post*. (W. P. Garrison, *The Benson Family of Newport, Rhode Island*, New York, 1872, p. 43; obituary, *The New York Times*, July 6, 1928.)

2. Mrs. Susanna T. (Soper) Thayer, widow of Nathaniel F. Thayer, of Boston, married him in 1803. She died on May 9, 1860, "aged 78 years and 8 months." In her obituary, Garrison writes that "deprived of her husband at middle age, the cares and responsibilities of a large family devolved upon her, which she met with surpassing fidelity and extraordinary ability. She combined with a never-failing vigilance for the welfare of her own household, a broad sympathy and an active benevolence for the poor and needy, the unfortunate and distressed, without regard to complexion or race, and was never weary in doing good." (*The Liberator*, June 1, 1860; *Columbian Centinel*, March 9, 1803.)

3. One of her sisters was Eliza Thayer. In a letter dated August 16, 1876, Garrison wrote to comfort Caroline on the death of Eliza (Garrison Papers, Boston Public Library).

36

TO LOUIS KOSSUTH

[February 1852]

To M. Louis Kossuth:

Sir — We, the undersigned, officers of the American Anti-Slavery Society, — an association now in the eighteenth year of its existence, having for its object the emancipation of an immense portion of our countrymen from a thraldom which finds no toleration in any part of Europe, and no parallel in any other quarter of the globe, — respectfully take this method to convey to you an expression of those feelings which your visit to the United States has awakened in our breasts. We would gladly have had a personal audience, and were intending to seek it, if not in New York, at least on your intended visit to Boston; but, from the tenor of your speeches, and especially since the publication of your significant Address to the People of the United States, bearing date of the 12th December, (1) we are led to infer that such an interview, if solicited, would be regarded by you as superfluous, if not intrusive. Nevertheless, for us wholly to keep silent, in the position you occupy as the professed friend of universal freedom, and the relation we sustain to the millions in slavery on our own soil as their representatives and advocates, would be doing violence to our convictions of duty — a duty we owe to you, to ill-fated Hungary, to the cause of liberty throughout the world. That duty we shall endeavor to discharge with fidelity.

Sir, we have no parade to make of our abhorrence of the despotic power of Austria and Russia, or of our sympathy with bleeding and oppressed Hungary. Words are cheap — professions are easily made. If we had not been personally ready to meet obloquy, persecution and danger, through long years of conflict, in behalf of the downtrodden of our own land, we should be ashamed to look you in the face, or take you by the hand, as a sufferer under the rod of tyranny. It is easy in America to denounce European injustice; it is not less easy in Europe to reprobate American slavery; but to be true to the principles of justice and humanity, on both sides of the Atlantic, in every land, is to be sublimely heroic.

Partly through the intercession of the American Government, you have been released from an irksome confinement in Turkey. — a confinement without injustice, and bringing with it distinguished hospitality as well as personal safety for the time being, — and now stand on the American soil, "a poor, persecuted, penniless exile," [1] "the wandering son of a bleeding nation," whose reception has been so triumphant as to be without a parallel. It is very natural, therefore, that you should feel — it is highly proper that you should express — strong emotions of gratitude both to the government and people of the United States. But neither your release, on the one hand, nor your sense of obligation, on the other, can justify you in conniving at the horrible crimes perpetrated by that people and government; nor can the condition of Hungary excuse you from being as honest and truthful here, as you have shown yourself to be heroic and self-sacrificing at home.

We frankly confess, that our solicitude for the preservation of your manhood and the integrity of your soul was extreme when we first heard of your intention to come to the United States, — knowing, as we did, that your visit must be made under circumstances calculated to blind your vision, obstruct your freedom of utterance, shake your moral firmness, and circumscribe your action. This solicitude was not diminished by the recollection, that no distinguished European, whether statesman or divine, whether patriot or philanthropist, (with hardly an exception,) had ever failed, in some way or other, to prove himself recreant to principle almost as soon as he had touched our soil, by a servile course of policy in regard to the omnipresent and omnipotent Slave Power of the land. Still, you had exhibited so much courage, voluntarily encountered so many perils, spurned so many bribes, overcome so many temptations, endured so many hardships, for the sacred cause of liberty in your native land, we were determined to hope to the last, that here it would be shown to the world, you would never sacrifice principle to expediency, nor allow a padlock to be put upon your lips. And when we read your glowing speeches in England, in which you declared — "I am a man of justice, right and liberty, and will be so my whole lifetime — little do I care what the sworn enemies of justice, right and liberty may call me — there is a common tie which binds the destiny of humanity — liberty, being the common bond of mankind, constitutes the union of heart with heart — how can men be contented without freedom? — this fair world was not created by God to be a prison to humanity, neither is it created for the jailer's sake — the principles of freedom are in harmony, and I love, I am interested in the freedom of all other countries as well as my own — to me life has no value, but only as much as I can make use of it for the liberty and independence of my country, and for the benefit of humanity — though my words and my pronunciation be bad, my heart is true to the principles of freedom and liberty, not the privileges of a class, but the freedom of all for all — my heart, as well as my arm, will ever be ready, to my last moments, to give effective success to those principles which are the very root of my life" [2] — &c., &c., we were inspired to hope and believe that, on the blood-stained soil of America, you would stand erect, cost what it might, and still "give the world assurance of a MAN," [3]

> "Who would not flatter Neptune for his trident,
> Nor Jove for his power to thunder." [4]

Alas! sir, already our hopes are in the dust!

Less than a month has elapsed since your arrival; but, during that brief period, you have made more addresses, and received more delegations, — representing various professions, societies and corporations, — than any other man living. Your addresses have been characterized by astonishing versatility and copiousness, as well as charged with the electric flame of an oriental eloquence; you have discussed a wide range of topics; you have marked out your own course, and been left unembarrassed by any distinct presentation of a mooted question; you have shown yourself no stranger to the history, growth and power of this nation; and you seem to have found among us, as a people, every thing to admire and extol, in strains of loftiest panegyric. But there is one topic that you have shunned, as though to name it would be a crime, — and that is, SLAVERY! There is one stain on our national escutcheon that your vision has failed to detect, — and that is, the blood of the almost exterminated Indian tribes, and of millions of the descendants of Africa! There is one fact that you choose to be ignorant of, — and that is, that every sixth person in this land, among a people swarming from ocean to ocean, is a fettered slave, an article of property, a marketable commodity, — to plead for those whose restoration to freedom is the most odious and the most hazardous act that can be performed!

Thus far, then, you have eyes, but see not; you have ears, but hear not [5] except what you suppose is in accordance with popular sentiment, and will be sure to further your own designs.

Landing as you did on these shores, a liberated captive, the victim of European absolutism, an exile from your native country, and asking sympathy and aid in the spirit of universal liberty; — coming here, moreover, at a period when the all-absorbing question in the land relates to the enslavement of the wretched millions already alluded to, — when the national government is prosecuting, as guilty of high treason, those who defend themselves against prowling slave-hunters and mercenary kidnappers,[6] — when the panting fugitives from Southern plantations are hunted by bloodhounds, two legged and four legged, throughout our wide domains, and can find succor and the recognition of their common humanity only as they escape to Canada, and exchange the American star-spangled banner for the British flag, — when "the propagation, preservation and perpetuation of slavery" are officially declared to be essential to the continuance of the American Union, — when a strict adherence to bloody and atrocious compromises, made in furtherance of the fiendish designs of the Slave Power, is declared to be the test of loyalty, not to the present administration, but to the government itself, — and, finally, when the most flagitious efforts are making to seize Cuba,[7] and also still other portions of distracted, ill-fated, subjugated Mexico,[8] in order to enlarge and strengthen our doubly accursed slave system, — it was natural that the uncompromising advocates of impartial liberty should look to you for at least one word of sympathy and approval, — at least an incidental expression of grief and shame at the existence of a bondage so frightful, in a land so boastful of its freedom. How, under circumstances so extraordinary and revolting, — especially as the undaunted champion of freedom, — could you expect to find neutral ground? to please alike the traffickers in human flesh, and those who execrate that traffic? to be considered as neither on one side nor the other? to be allowed to skulk behind the flimsy subterfuge of foreign non-intervention, as an excuse for remaining dumb and insensate in the immediate presence of millions of your fellow-creatures in chains, and herded with the beasts that perish? Deplorable as it is, the relation of your countrymen to the Austrian government is incomparably more hopeful, a million times less appalling, than that of our slave population to the American government; yet you invoke for the Hungarians the sympathy of the civilized world — for their prompt deliverance, you insist that both England and America should interfere, by expostulation, remonstrance and warning, — even, if need be, at the point of the bayonet and the mouth of the cannon, though both nations should thereby become doubly bankrupt, though it should cause a deluge of blood to flow! The representatives of the vast slave population of the United States ask you to join no particular party in their behalf, to give no countenance to a bloody struggle for their emancipation, but simply to recognize the shocking inconsistency and awful guilt of this nation in trampling under foot its heaven-attested declarations of freedom and equality; and what is your answer? It is, that, neither directly nor indirectly, neither by oral testimony nor overt act, will you concern yourself with any matter now in controversy on the American soil! You are a Hungarian: what is it to you, that, in this country, one hundred and fifty thousand kidnappers claim and possess as their property more than three millions of the population? You are a foreigner: why should you "meddle" with any of our "domestic institutions"? It is not for you, but for such as reside here, to exclaim, if they think the matter worth a moment's consideration: —

> "What, ho! — *our* countrymen in chains!
>   The whip on woman's shrinking flesh!
> *Our* soil yet reddening with the stains,
>   Caught from her scourging, warm and fresh!
> What! mothers from their children riven!
>   What! God's own image bought and sold!
> AMERICANS to market driven,
>   And bartered as the brutes for gold!" [9]

You are a fugitive from Austrian vengeance, as a rebel, and as the leader in a formidable insurrectionary movement: now that you want money and arms to renew the bloody struggle, why should you evince any sympathy for the hunted fugitives from Southern slaveholding barbarity, — fugitives who raise no standard of revolt, and whose only crime is in trying to gain their freedom without any injury to their merciless oppressors? Has not every nation a right to do as it pleases within its own boundaries? If cannibalism prevails in the Fejee Islands, or man-stealing in the United States, let no foreigner presume to interfere with the practice, even to the extent of a single remonstrance!

Such is the humiliating position you now occupy before the world. Sir, your honors and laudations are purchased at too great cost; you are seeking aid for Hungary by a cowardly and criminal policy, that shall turn to ashes like the apples of Sodom to the taste. While declaiming against Jesuitism as the scourge of Europe, you are acting on the jesuitical maxim, "the end sanctifies the means." Has it come to this, O Kossuth, that you are fearful, and dare not speak; selfish, and dare not pity; a Hungarian for Hungarians, and nothing for mankind? Cease, then, to declaim against timidity, against selfishness, against national indifference to human wrongs! Assume no longer the character of a champion of liberty, talk not of being animated by a divine inspiration, and quote no more reproachfully the Cain-like interrogation, "Am I my brother's keeper?"

Unquestionably, your first fatal step in this downward career was taken when, in your Turkish asylum and prison, you consented to accept the proffered interposition of this slaveholding government to obtain your liberation; which, if it did not necessarily imply, on your part, a pledge that you would not, on your arrival here, say or do aught to swell the tide of anti-slavery sentiment, or indulge in any language criminating the character of the nation, was certainly so regarded by the Executive and Congress of the United States, from considerations both of comity and gratitude. Having taken that step, all the rest have followed naturally and inevitably.

> —— "*Facilis descensus Averni,*
> *Sed revocare gradum —*
> *Hoc opus, hic labor est.*" [10]

But, sir, what right had you to enter into such an arrangement, or to impose upon yourself such an obligation? Your liberation was an object of great solicitude to yourself personally, and of vast importance to Hungary, beyond a doubt; but not the safety of a Kossuth, not even the freedom of Hungary, can atone for connivance at crime, or justify an alliance with tyrants in any quarter of the globe. Integrity is more than life — honor better than success — the Golden Rule, "Whatsoever ye would that men should do to you, do ye even so to them," of more importance than the overthrow of the house of Hapsburg.

Possibly, when in Turkey you accepted the proffered hospitality of this nation, you were ignorant of the fact, that it is the most shameless slave-holding and slave-trading nation in the world, and so made no compromise with it for favors received. Possibly, you were not at that time aware of the astounding fact, that the very same session of the American Congress which passed the resolves respecting the release of Louis Kossuth and his associates in exile, and their transportation to this country in one of its naval ships, also enacted the merciless Fugitive Slave Law [11] — a Law, which, on account of its atrocious provisions, has convulsed even this hardened republic, and sent a thrill of horror throughout all Europe. Possibly, you were not then apprised that, in one half of the American Union, the advocates of negro emancipation are outlawed, or, whenever caught, subjugated to the lynch code; that, in the other half, the wealth, the talent, the respectability, the power, the accredited piety, are combined to crush every demonstration for the extinction of slavery. But, on your arrival in England, if hitherto ignorant of these matters, you were promptly enlightened by the vigilant friends of universal freedom in that country. Private and public addresses were forwarded to you from individuals and societies, — Scotland and Ireland uniting with England in these appeals to your moral sense, — expressly in reference to the slavery question in America, warning you of your danger, imploring you to be true to your principles on her polluted soil, revealing to you the horrors of the American slave system, in some instances conjuring you not to cross the Atlantic, but to announce to the world your unwillingness to purchase favor at the sacrifice of honor. Nothing was left undone to purge your vision, enlighten your understanding, or affect your heart. It does not yet appear that you had the courtesy or courage, even in England, to make a single reply to those philanthropic and Christian appeals, or in any speech to allude to the subject of American slavery.[12]

It is plain, therefore, that you came to these shores with your eyes open, your mind intelligently informed, your conscience thoroughly probed; — came, alas! not to be faithful, but time-serving — not to temper praise with reproof, but to deal in wholesale flattery — not to maintain an erect position, but to bend the knee to "the dark spirit of slavery," so that the cause of Hungary might prosper! You are doubly criminal; for you not only omit to rebuke this nation for the glaring inconsistency of its practice with its professions, but you have already exhausted the language of eulogy upon its Union, its Constitution, its institutions, its greatness and power, its freedom and purity, its humanity and piety. In no instance do you qualify your praise, or hint at any thing to be lamented in our national career. The vanity of our countrymen is proverbial, and never has it been so skillfully or profusely administered to as by your own hand. That a candid world may see, at a glance, the prodigality of your flattery, we place in one column a few specimens culled from your various speeches; and then, in an opposite column, to show how widely at variance with the truth are your encomiums — what deeds of horror, oppression and blood are legalized in the United States — we present some of the features of our slave system: —

"May your kind anticipations of me be not disappointed! I am a plain man. I have nothing in me but honest fidelity to those principles which have made you great, and my most ardent wish is that my own country may be, if not great as yours, *at least as free and as happy*, which it will be in the establishment of the same great principles. The sounds I now hear seem to me the trumpet of resurrection for downtrodden humanity throughout the world." — [*Reply to Dr. Doane, at Staten Island.*] [13]

"The twelve hours that I have had the honor and happiness to stand on *your glorious shores* give me a happy augury of the fact that during my stay here in the United States, I shall have a pleasant duty to perform — to answer the many manifestations of the generous public spirit of the people of this country. ° ° ° Citizens, accept my fervent thanks for your generous welcome on my arrival to *your happy shores*, and my blessing upon you for the sanction of my hopes which you express. You have most truly expressed what my hopes are, when you tell me what you consider the destiny of *your glorious country* to be — when you tell me that henceforth *the spirit of liberty* shall go forth and achieve the freedom of the world. ° ° ° I confidently hope, citizens, that as you have anticipated my wishes by the expression of your generous sentiments, even so will you agree with me in the conviction, that *the spirit of liberty has not only spiritually but materially to go forth from your glorious country, in order that it may achieve the freedom of the world.* The spirit itself is the inspiring pow-

PROFESSION.

"We hold these truths to be self-evident; that all men are created equal; that they are endowed by their Creator with certain inalienable rights; that among these are life, LIBERTY, and the pursuit of happiness." — [Declaration of American Independence.]

PRACTICE.

By the census of 1790, the number of SLAVES in the United States was six hundred and ninety-seven thousand eight hundred and ninety-seven.

In 1800, eight hundred and ninety-three thousand and forty-one[.]

In 1810, one million one hundred and ninety-one thousand three hundred and sixty-four.

In 1820, one million five hundred and thirty-eight thousand and sixty-four.

In 1830, two millions and nine thousand and thirty-one.

In 1840, two millions four hundred and eighty-seven thousand three hundred and fifty-five.

In 1850, THREE MILLIONS ONE HUNDRED AND SEVENTY-SEVEN THOUSAND FIVE HUNDRED AND EIGHTY-NINE.

"Slaves shall be deemed, sold, taken, reputed and adjudged in law to be chattels personal in the hands of their owners and possessors, and their executors, administrators and assigns, to all intents, constructions and purposes whatsoever." — [Law of South Carolina. 2 Brev. Dig. 229.]

"A slave is one who is in the power of a master to whom he belongs. The master may sell him, dispose of

er to deeds, but yet no *deed* in itself; and you need not be told that those who would be free must, besides being inspired, also 'strike the blow.' Despotism and oppression never yet were beaten, except by heroic resolution, and vigorous, manly resistance. That is a sad necessity, but it is a necessity nevertheless. I have so learned it out of the great book of history. I hope the people of the United States will remember, that in the hour of *their* nation's glorious struggle, they received from Europe *more* than kind wishes and friendly sympathy. They received material aid from others in times past, and they will doubtless impart now their mighty agency in achieving the liberty of other lands."

"Citizens, I thank you that you have addressed me through your speaker, not in the language of party, but in *the language of liberty, and therefore the language of the people of the United States.*" ° ° °

"Take, for instance, *the glorious struggle you had not long ago with Mexico*, in which General Scott [14] drove out the President of that republic from his capital. Now, suppose General Santa Anna [15] had come to Washington, and driven away President Taylor, [16] would General Taylor have ceased to be the rightfully elected President of the United States, from the fact that a foreign power had, for a moment, forced him to leave his place? I believe there is not a single man in the United States who would say yes." — [*Speech at Staten Island.*] [17]

"Let me, before I go to work, have some hours of rest upon *this soil of freedom*, your happy home. Freedom and Home! what heavenly music in those two words! Alas, I have no home, and the freedom of my people is down-trodden. *Young Giant of free America*, do not tell me that thy shores are *an asylum to*

his person, his industry, and his labor: he can do nothing, possess nothing, nor acquire anything but what must belong to his master." — [Civil Code of Louisiana, Art. 35.]

"The slave is one doomed in his own person, and in his posterity, to live without knowledge, and without capacity to make any thing his own, and to toil that others may reap the fruits . . . The end is the profit of the master, his security, and the public peace . . . The power of the master must be absolute to render the submission of the slave perfect . . . In the actual condition of things, it must be so. There is no remedy. This discipline belongs to slavery." — [Opinion of the Supreme Court of North Carolina, delivered by Judge Ruffin, [18] State *vs.* Mann, 2 Dev. Rep. 263.]

"The system of slavery denies to a whole class of human beings the sacredness of marriage and of home, compelling them to live in a state of concubinage; for, in the eye of the law, no colored slave-man is the husband of any wife in particular, nor any slave-woman the wife of any husband in particular; no slave-man is the father of any children in particular, and no slave child is the child of any parent in particular." [Rev. Robert J. Breckenridge, [19] D. D. of the Presbyterian Church, himself a slave-holder in Kentucky.]

If more than seven slaves are found together in any road, without a white person, twenty lashes a piece; for visiting a plantation without a written pass, ten lashes; for letting loose a boat from where it is made fast, thirty-nine lashes for the first offence — and for the second, shall have cut off from his head one ear; for keeping or carrying a club, thirty-nine lashes; for having any article

the oppressed, and a home for the homeless exile. An asylum it is, but all the blessings of *your glorious country,* can they drown into oblivion the longing of the heart, and the fond desires, for our native land?

❅   ❅   ❅   ❅   ❅

"Even here, with this prodigious view of greatness, *freedom,* and happiness, which spreads before my astonished eyes, my thoughts are wandering towards home; and when I look over these thousands of thousands before me, the happy inheritance of yonder *freedom for which your fathers fought and bled* — and when I turn to you, citizens, to bow before the majesty of the United States, and to thank the people of New York for their generous share in my liberation, and for the unparalleled honor of this reception, I see, out of the very midst of this great assemblage, rise the bleeding image of Hungary, looking to you with anxiety whether there be in the lustre of your eyes a ray of hope for her; whether there be in the thunder of your hurrahs, a trumpet-call of resurrection. If there were no such ray of hope in your eyes, and no such trumpet-call in your cheers, then *wo to Europe's oppressed nations!* They will stand alone in the hour of need. Less fortunate than you were, they will meet no brother's hand to help them in the approaching giant struggle against the leagued despots of the world; and wo also to me. I will feel no joy even here, and the days of my stay here will turn out to be lost for my father-land — lost at the very time when every moment is teeming in the decision of Europe's destiny.

❅   ❅   ❅   ❅   ❅

"I have to thank the people, Congress and Government of the United States, for my liberation from captivity. Human tongue has no words to express the bliss which I felt when

for sale, without a ticket from his master, ten lashes; for travelling in any other than the most usual and accustomed road, when going alone to any place, forty lashes; for travelling in the night, without a pass, forty lashes; for being found in another person's negro-quarters, forty lashes; for hunting with dogs in the woods, thirty lashes; for being on horseback without the written permission of his master, twenty-five lashes; for riding or going abroad in the night, or riding horses in the day time, without leave, a slave may be whipped, cropped, or branded in the cheek with the letter R, or otherwise punished, not extending to life, or so as to render him unfit for labor — &c. &c. &c. — [Laws of the Slave States. — See 2 Brevard's Digest, Haywood's Manual, 1 Virginia Revised Code, Prince's Digest, Missouri Laws, Mississippi Revised Code.]

"If any emancipated slave (infants excepted) shall remain within the State more than twelve months after his or her right to freedom shall have accrued, he or she shall forfeit all such right, and may be apprehended and sold by the overseers of the poor, &c. for the benefit of the literary fund." — [Rev. Code of Virginia, 436.]

"Every negro or mulatto found within the State, and not having the ability to show himself entitled to freedom, may be sold, by order of the court, as a slave." — [Mississippi Rev. Code, 389.]

By T. J. WALSH & Co. — Private sale. 1 Berkshire Sow, four months old; 1 Sussex Boar Pig, 2½ months old. A Negro Man, aged about 38; a carpenter. *Titles undoubted.*

COOK AT PRIVATE SALE. — Will be sold at private sale, a mulatto

I — the down-trodden Hungary's wandering chief — saw *the glorious flag of the stripes and stars fluttering over my head* — when I first bowed before it with deep respect — when I saw around me the gallant officers and the crew of the Mississippi frigate — the most of them the worthiest representatives of true *American principles, American greatness, American generosity* — and to think that it was not a mere chance which cast the star-spangled banner around me, but that it was *your protecting will* — to know that *the United States of America, conscious of their glorious calling as well as of their power, declared by this unparalleled act to be resolved to become the protectors of human rights* — to see a powerful vessel of America coming to far Asia, to break the chains by which the mightiest despots of Europe fettered the activity of an exiled Magyar, whose very name disturbed the proud security of their sleep — to feel restored by such a protection, and in such a way, to freedom, and by freedom to activity, you may be well aware of what I have felt, and still feel, at the remembrance of this proud moment of my life. Others spoke — *you acted; and I was free!* You acted; and *at this act of yours, tyrants trembled; humanity shouted out with joy; the down-trodden people of Magyars* — the down-trodden, but not broken — raised his head with resolution and with hope, and *the brilliancy of your stars was greeted by Europe's oppressed nations as the morning star of rising liberty.* Now, gentlemen, you must be aware how boundless the gratitude must be which I feel for you. You have restored me to life — because restored to activity; and should my life, by the blessings of the Almighty, still prove useful to my fatherland, and to humanity, it will be your merit — it will be your

woman, named Mary, about 48 years of age, a good cook, washer and ironer, a fair pastry cook, perfectly honest, and very cleanly, and kind and attentive to children. If not sold on the first Monday of July next, she will then be offered at public auction. Apply to

T. E. BAKER, or
JOHN STUBBS.

COW AND CALF FOR SALE. — A prime young milch cow and calf, for sale as above. — [South Carolinian.]

ADMINISTRATOR'S SALE. — On the first Tuesday in May next, within the legal hours of sale, before the Court House in Effingham County, the following property belonging to the estate of Gideon C. Bevill, late of Chatham County, deceased: Two Timber Carriages, one Wood Flat, one Jack Screw, one Writing Desk, two Negro Men, Adam and Fraiser, 100 acres of Land, &c.

E. W. SOLOMONS, Adm'r.

35 LIKELY NEGROES FOR SALE. — The subscriber having purchased Byrd Hill's old stand, on Adams street, will keep a good lot of Negroes, fresh from North Carolina, Virginia, and Middle Tennessee. A partner is now in Richmond, Va., and will buy a lot of plough boys and small girls for the Spring trade, and will be out soon. I have ample room to accommodate traders, and board negroes, and sell on commission, &c.

BENJ. LITTLE.

NEGROES FOR SALE. — A likely young mulatto fellow, about 20 years old; a boy, black, about 28 years old; a boy, dark mulatto, 27 years of age. The above negroes are warranted

work. May you and *your glorious country* be blessed for it. ❋ ❋

"What is the motive of my being here at this very time? The motive, citizens, is, that your generous act of my liberation has raised the conviction throughout the world, that this generous act of yours is but the manifestation of your resolution to throw your weight into the balance where the fate of the European continent is to be weighed. You have raised the conviction throughout the world, that by my liberation you were willing to say, '*Ye oppressed nations of old Europe's continent, be of good cheer; the young giant of America stretches his powerful arm over the waves, ready to give a brother's hand to your future.*' So is your act interpreted throughout the world. You, in your proud security, can scarcely imagine how beneficial this conviction has already proved to the suffering nations of the European continent. You can scarcely imagine what self-confidence you have added to the resolution of the oppressed. You have knit the tie of solidarity in the destinies of nations." ❋ ❋ ❋ ❋

"Your generous act of my liberation is taken by the world for the revelation of the fact that *the United States are resolved not to allow the despots of the world to trample on oppressed humanity*. It is hence that my liberation was cheered, from Sweden down to Portugal, as a ray of hope. It is hence that even those nations which most desire my presence in Europe now, have unanimously told me, 'Hasten on, hasten on to *the great, free, rich and powerful people of the United States*, and bring over its brotherly aid to the cause of your country, so intimately connected with European liberty;' and here I stand to plead the cause of the solidarity of human rights before the great republic of the United States. Humble as I am, *God, the Almighty, has selected me to rep-

sound, and will be sold low for cash by

McKEEN & MAFFITT.

☞ Speculators in slaves are found on every Court Yard, and at every hiring ground where slaves are to be disposed of. We would therefore recommend to such of our readers as have negroes to sell, to keep a steady eye upon the market, as this species of property seems to be steadily improving in point of value. — [North Carolina paper.]

Runaway, on Wednesday last, my Mulatto Woman, Louise, about 27 years of age, 5 feet 2 inches in height, hair nearly straight, and is quite fleshy. She speaks the French and Spanish languages, and is shrewd and intelligent. I will give fifty dollars for her detention and delivery to me.

GEORGE SCHUMAKER.

$100 Reward will be given for the apprehension of my negro, Edward Kenney. He has straight hair, and complexion so nearly white, that it is believed a stranger would suppose that there was no African blood in him. He was with my boy Dick a short time in Norfolk, and offered him for sale, and was apprehended, but escaped under pretence of being a white man (!)

ANDERSON BOWLES.
Richmond, Va., Jan. 6, 1836.

Ranaway from the subscriber, working on the plantation of Col. H. Tinker, a bright mulatto boy, named Alfred. Alfred is about 18 years old, pretty well grown, has blue eyes, light flaxen hair, skin disposed to freckle. He will try to pass as freeborn.

Green County, Ala.
S. G. STEWART.

resent the cause of humanity before you. My warrant to this capacity is written in *the sympathy and confidence of all who are oppressed,* and of all who, as your elder brother, the people of Britannia, sympathise with the oppressed — my warrant to this capacity is written in the hopes and expectations you have entitled the world to entertain, by liberating me out of my prison, and by restoring me to activity." ° ° ° °

"The people of England desire the brotherly alliance of the United States to secure to every nation the sovereign right to dispose of itself, and to protect the sovereign right of nations against the encroaching arrogance of despots, and leagued to you against the league of despots, to stand, together with you, godfather to the approaching baptism of European liberty. Now, gentlemen, I have stated my position. I am a straightforward man. I am a republican. I have avowed it openly in monarchial, but free England; and I am happy to state that I have nothing lost by this avowal there. I hope I will not lose here, in republican America, by that frankness, which must be one of the chief qualities of every republican." ° ° ° °

"I profess, highly and openly, my admiration for *the glorious principle of union, on which stands the mighty pyramid of your greatness,* and upon the basis of which you have grown, in the short period of seventy-five years, to a prodigious giant, the living wonder of the world. I have the most warm wish that the star-spangled banner of the United States may for ever be floating, united and one, *the proud ensign of mankind's divine origin*; and, taking my ground on *this principle of union, which I find lawfully existing,* an established constitutional fact, it is not to a party, but to the united people of the United States, that I confidently will

$100 REWARD. — Ranaway from the subscriber, a bright mulatto man-slave, named Sam. Light sandy hair, blue eyes, ruddy complexion; is so white as very easily to pass for a free white man.　　EDWIN PECK.
Mobile, April 22, 1837.

Ranaway, on the 15th of May, from me, a negro woman, named Fanny. Said woman is 20 years old; is rather tall; can read and write, and so forge passes for herself; is very pious. She prays a great deal, and was, as supposed, (!) contented and happy (!) She is as white as most white women, with straight light hair, and blue eyes, and can pass herself for a white woman. I will give $500 for her apprehension and delivery to me. She is very intelligent.　　JOHN BALCH.
Tuscaloosa, May 29, 1845.

$200 REWARD. — Ranaway from the subscriber, last November, a white (!) negro man, about 35 years old, height about 5 feet 8 or 10 inches, blue eyes, has a yellow woolly head, very fair skin. He was lately known to be working on the railroad in Alabama, near Moore's Turn Out, and passed as a white man, by the name of Jesse Teams. I will give $500 for sufficient proof to convict, in open court, any man who carried him away.
　　　　　　　J. D. ALLEN.
P. S. Said man has a good-shaped foot and leg, and his foot is very small and hollow.
Barnwell Court House, L. C.

Ten dollars reward for my woman Siby, very much scarred about the neck and ears by whipping. — [Mobile Commercial Advertiser.]

One hundred dollars reward for my negro Glasgow, and Kate, his

address my humble requests for *aid and protection to oppressed humanity*. I will conscientiously respect your laws, but within the limits of your laws, I will use every honest exertion to gain your operative sympathy, and your financial, material and political aid for my country's freedom and independence, and entreat the realization of these hopes which your generosity has raised in me and my people's breasts, and *also in the breasts of Europe's oppressed nations.*" * * *

"As to your minister at Vienna, how can you combine the letting him stay there with your opinion of the cause of Hungary, I really don't know; but so much I know, that the present absolutistical atmosphere of Europe is not very propitious to American principles. I know a man who could tell some curious facts about this matter. But as to Mr. Hulsemann,[20] really I don't believe that he would be so ready to leave Washington. He has extremely well digested the caustic pills which Mr. Webster has administered to him so gloriously." * * *

"Having thus expounded my aim, I beg leave to state, that I came not to *your glorious shores* to enjoy a happy rest — I came not with the intention to gather triumphs of personal distinction, but as a humble petitioner, in my country's name, as its freely chosen constitutional chief, *humbly to entreat your generous aid*; and then it is to this aim that I will devote every moment of my time, with the more assiduity, the more restlessness, as every moment may bring a report of events which may call me to hasten to my place on the battle field, where the great, and I hope *the last battle will be fought between Liberty and Despotism* — a moment marked by the finger of God to be so near, that every hour of delay of your generous aid may

wife. Glasgow is 24 years old — has marks of the whip on his back. Kate is 26 — has a scar on her cheek, and several marks of a whip. — [Macon, Georgia, Messenger.]

Ranaway, Bill — has several large scars on his back from a severe whipping in early life. [Baltimore, Maryland, Republican.]

Ranaway, negro fellow John — from being whipped, has scars on his back, arms, and thighs. — [Milledgeville, Georgia, Standard of Union.]

Committed to jail, a mulatto fellow — his back shows lasting impressions of the whip, and leaves no doubt of his being a slave. — [Fayetteville, North Carolina, Observer.]

Ranaway, the negro Manuel, much marked with irons. — [New Orleans, Louisiana, Bee.]

Ranaway, the negress Fanny — had on an iron band about her neck. — [New Orleans Bee.]

Ranaway, a black woman, Betsey — had an iron bar on her right leg. — [Grand Gulf, Mississippi, Advertiser.]

Ranaway, a negro man named David — with some iron hobbles around each ankle. — [Staunton, Virginia, Spectator.]

Ranaway, the negro Hown — has a ring of iron on his left foot. Also, Grise, his wife, having a ring and chain on the left leg. — [New Orleans Bee.]

Committed to jail, a man who calls his name John — he has a clog of iron on his right foot, which will weigh four or five pounds. — [Montgomery, Alabama, Advertiser.]

prove fatally disastrous to *oppressed humanity.*" * * *

"Lafayette [21] had great claims to your love and sympathy. But I have none. I came a humble petitioner, *with no other claims than those which the oppressed have to the sympathy of free men,* who have the power to help; with the claim which the unfortunate has to the happy; and the down-trodden has to the protection of eternal justice and of human rights. In a word, I have *no other claims than those which the oppressed principle of freedom has to the aid of victorious liberty.* Then I would humbly ask, are these claims sufficient to insure your generous protection, not to myself, but to the cause of my native land — not to my native land only, but to the principle of freedom in Europe's continent, of which the independence of Hungary is the indispensable keystone. If you consider these claims not sufficient to your active and operative sympathy, then let me know at once that the hopes have failed with which Europe's oppressed nations have looked to *your great, mighty and glorious republic* — let me know at once the failure of our hopes, that I may hasten back and tell *Europe's oppressed nations,* 'Let us fight, forsaken and singlehanded, the battle of Leonidas; let us trust to God, to our right, and to our good sword; there is no other help for the oppressed nations on earth.' But if *your generous republican hearts* are animated by the high principle of freedom and of the solidarity in the destinies of humanity — if you have the will, as, to be sure, you have the power, to *support the cause of freedom against the sacrilegious league of despotism,* then give me some days of calm reflection to become acquainted with the ground upon which I stand — let me take the kind advice of some active friends on the most practical course I have to adopt

Detained at the police jail, the negro wench Myra — has several marks of lashing, and has irons on her feet. — [New Orleans paper.]

Was committed to jail, a negro boy — had on a large neck iron, with a huge pair of horns, and a large bar or band of iron on his left leg. — [Memphis, Tennessee, Times.]

Ranaway, a negro boy about twelve years old — had round his neck a chain dog-collar, with "De Yampert" engraved on it. — [Mobile, Alabama, Chronicle.]

Ranaway, a negro girl called Mary — has a small scar over her eye, a good many teeth missing; the letter A is branded on her cheek and forehead. — [Natchez, Mississippi, Courier.]

Ranaway, Mary, a black woman — has a scar on her back and right arm near the shoulder, caused by a rifle ball. — [Natchez Courier.]

Twenty dollars reward — Ranaway from the subscriber, a negro girl named Molly — 16 or 17 years of age, slim made, lately branded on her left cheek, thus, R, and a piece taken off of her ear on the same side; the same letter on the inside of both her legs. — [Charleston, S. C. Courier.]

Twenty dollars reward — Ranaway from the subscriber, a negro woman and two children; the woman is tall and black, and a few days before she went off, I burnt her with a hot iron on the left side of her face. I tried to make the letter M — and she kept a cloth over her head and face, and a fly bonnet on her head, so as to cover the burn. — [North Carolina Standard.]

— let me see if there be any preparatory steps taken in favor of that cause which I have the honor to represent; and then, let me have a new opportunity to expound before you my humble request in a practical way; and let me add, with a sigh of thanksgiving to the Almighty God, that it is *your glorious country which Providence has selected to be the pillar of freedom, as it is already the asylum to oppressed humanity.*

"I am told that I will have the high honor to review your patriotic militia. O God! how my heart throbs at the idea *to see this gallant army enlisted on the side of freedom against despotism*; the world would be free, and you the saviours of humanity. And why not? These gallant men take part in the mighty demonstration of the day, proving that I was right when I said that now-a-days even the bayonets think. Citizens of New York, *it is under your protection that I place the sacred cause of the freedom and independence of Hungary.*" ° °
— [*Reply to the Mayor's Address of Welcome at New York.*] ²²

"I am aware that your war with Mexico was carried on chiefly by volunteers . . . It is a duty to confess, that those who fought in that war have high claims to an acknowledgment of their brilliant achievements . . . I know what distinguished part the volunteers of New York took in that war — in the siege of Vera Cruz, in the battles of Cerro Gordo, Contreras, Molino del Rey, Cherubusco, and Chapultepec, and how they partook in the immense glory of entering — a handful of gallant men — the metropolis of Mexico." ²³

"History shows eminently this truth, that YOU ARE ENTITLED TO CALL YOURSELVES FREEMEN. [*Reply to the Address of Citizens of New Haven.*]

Ranaway, from the plantation of James Surgett, the following negroes: Randall — has one ear cropped; Bob — has lost one eye; Kentucky Tom — has one jaw broken. — [Southern Telegraph.]

Stolen, a negro man named Winter — has a notch cut out of the left ear, and the marks of four or five buck shot on his legs. — [Natchitoches, Louisiana, Herald.]

Committed to jail, a negro named Mike — his left ear off. — [Natchez Free Trader.]

Ranaway Bill — has a scar over one eye, also one on his leg, from the bite of a dog — has a burn on his buttock, from a piece of hot iron in the shape of T. — [New Orleans Bulletin.]

Ranaway, my slave Lewis — he has lost a piece of one ear, and a part of one of his fingers; a part of one of his toes is also lost. — [Mobile Chronicle.]

Was committed to jail a negro man, says his name is Josiah — his back very much scarred by the whip, and branded on the thigh and hips, in three or four places, thus (J. M.) — the rim of his right ear has been bit or cut off. — [Clinton, Mississippi, Gazette.]

Ranaway a negro named Henry — his left eye out, some scars from a dirk on and under his left arm, and much scarred with the whip. [Lexington, Kentucky, Observer.]

Fifty dollars reward for my fellow Edward — he has a scar on the corner of his mouth, two cuts on and under his arm, and the letter E on

"I feel that to command the sympathy of generous minds is but to show the true position of Hungary, and the ground on which its future rests. By this attention, which has marked your address, and all other addresses received since I have arrived on *these glorious shores of America*, my work and my mission in this country will be greatly facilitated, because it will not be necessary for me to try to explain my views, nor to persuade the people of the United States; for they already understand it, and *they are already persuaded that my cause merits their sympathy and support*; and they are convinced, because they have paid attention to the views, hopes, and aims of my nation." ° ° ° °

"I come here with the humble prayers of Hungary and my own, seeking for sympathy and aid, not to one party, but to the whole people of the United States. *When I see the whole people of this great confederacy* — not of one party, but of all parties — coming forward to stretch out *a friendly hand to my poor country*, I put my trust in the God of mercy and justice, that he will ere long set Hungary free, and place her in the position she ought to hold in the scale of nations. It will be sufficient reward for me, even at the sacrifice of my life, if my efforts, aided by the generosity of your nation, shall contribute to the redemption of my country, and the development of all those moral and material faculties which are necessary to the welfare of every nation." — [*Reply to the Address of a Committee of the American and Foreign Anti-Slavery Society.*] [24]

"I wish the free women of free America will help my down-trodden land to get out of that iron grasp, or to get out of those bloody fangs, and become independent and free. ° ° ° But I have a stronger motive than all these to claim your protecting

his arm. — [Charleston, South Carolina, Courier.]

One hundred dollars reward will be paid to any person who may apprehend and safely confine in any jail in this State, a certain negro man, named Alfred. And the same reward will be paid, if satisfactory evidence is given of his having been KILLED. He has one or more scars on one of his hands, caused by his having been shot. — [Wilmington, North Carolina, Advertiser.]

Ranaway, my negro man Richard. A reward of $25 will be paid for his apprehension, DEAD OR ALIVE. Satisfactory proof will only be required of his being KILLED. — [Same paper.]

Three hundred dollars reward — Ranaway from the subscriber in November last, his two negro men, named Billy and Pompey. Billy in all probability may resist; in that event, $50 will be paid for HIS HEAD. — [Charleston Courier.]

Two hundred dollars reward — Ranaway from the subscriber, a certain negro named Ben; he had but one eye. Also, one other negro, by the name of Rigdon. I will give the reward of $100 for each of the above negroes, to be delivered to me, or confined in the jail of Lenori or Jones county, or for the KILLING of them, so that I can see them. — [Newbern, North Carolina, Spectator.]

From the Wilmington, N. C. Journal.

STATE OF NORTH CAROLINA.

WHEREAS, complaint upon oath hath this day been made to us, two of the Justices of the Peace for the State and county aforesaid, by Guild-

sympathy for my country's cause. It is her nameless woes, nameless sufferings. In the name of that ocean of bloody tears which the sacrilegious hand of the tyrant wrung from the eyes of the childless mothers, of the brides who beheld the hangman's sword between them and their wedding day — in the name of all those mothers, wives, brides, daughters and sisters, who, by thousands of thousands, weep over the graves of Magyars so dear to their hearts, and weep the bloody tears of a patriot (as they all are) over the face of their beloved native land — in the name of all those torturing stripes with which the flogging hand of Austrian tyrants dared to outrage humanity in the womankind of my native land — in the name of that daily curse against Austria with which even the prayers of our women are mixed — in the name of the nameless sufferings of my own dear wife, (here the whole audience rose and cheered vehemently,) — the faithful companion of my life — of her who for months and for months was hunted by my country's tyrants, like a noble deer, not having, for months, a moment's rest to repose her wearied head in safety, and no hope, no support, no protection but at the humble threshold of the hardworking people, as noble and generous as they are poor — (applause) — in the name of my poor little children, who so young are scarcely conscious of their life, had already to learn what an Austrian prison is — in the name of all this, and what is still worse, in the name of downtrodden liberty, I claim, ladies of New York, your protecting sympathy for my country's cause. Nobody can do more for it than you. The heart of man is as soft wax in your tender hands. Mould it, ladies; mould it into the form of generous compassion for my country's wrongs, inspire it with the noble feelings of your own hearts,

ford Horn, of Edgecombe County, that a certain male slave belonging to him, named HARRY, a carpenter by trade, about 40 years old, 5 feet 5 inches high, or thereabouts, yellow complexion, stout built, with a scar on his left leg, (from the cut of an axe,) has very thick lips, eyes deep sunk in his head, forehead very square, tolerably loud voice, has lost one or two of his upper teeth, and has a very dark spot on his jaw, supposed to be a mark — hath absented himself from his master's service, and is supposed to be lurking about in this country, committing acts of felony or other misdeeds: These are, therefore, in the name of the State aforesaid, to command said slave forthwith to surrender himself, and return home to his said master; and we do hereby, by virtue of the Act of Assembly in such cases made and provided, intimate and declare that if said slave Harry doth not surrender himself, and return home immediately after the publication of these presents, that any person or persons may KILL and DESTROY the said slave by such means as he or they may think fit, without accusation or impeachment of any crime or offence for so doing, and without incurring any penalty or forfeiture thereby.

Given under our hands and seals, this 29th day of June, 1850.

JAMES T. MILLER, J. P. [Seal.]
W. C. BETTENCOUT, J. P. [Seal.]

ONE HUNDRED AND TWENTY-FIVE DOLLARS REWARD will be paid for the delivery of the said HARRY to me at Tonsott Depot, Edgecombe county, or for his confinement in any jail in the State, so that I can get him; or One Hundred and Fifty Dollars will be given for his HEAD.

He was lately heard from in Newbern, where he called himself Henry Barnes (or Burns,) and will be likely

inspire it with the consciousness of your country's power, dignity and might." * * * "All this power you have. Use it, ladies, use it in behalf of your country's glory, and for the benefit of oppressed humanity; and when you meet a cold calculator, who thinks by arithmetic when he is called to feel the wrongs of oppressed nations, convert him, ladies." — [*Address to the Ladies of New York in Tripler Hall.*] 25

"I am sure that the sympathy of Baltimore (!) will be such as to respect the cause of Hungary, for the people and the authorities act in perfect harmony together in this FREE country . . . I am not egotistical for myself, but for the great principles of liberty, which makes your country so great, so glorious, and so free, and also the land of PROTECTION for THE PERSECUTED SONS OF FREEDOM among the great brotherhood of nations." 26

"As to your glorious Constitution . . . Never forget to love it . . . Your glorious country . . . The glorious republic of the United States . . . Great, glorious and free . . . Let not the enemies of freedom grow too strong (!!) . . . Absolutism cannot tranquilly sleep while the Republican principle has such a mighty representative as your country is (!!!) . . . The United States of America is a great, glorious and free country, under Republican government . . . I believe your glorious country should every where unfurl the star-spangled banner of liberty . . . The United States number many millions of inhabitants, all attached with warm feelings to the principles of liberty . . . You took me for the representative of that principle of liberty which God has destined to become the common benefit of humanity; and it is a glorious sight to see a mighty, free,

to continue the same name, or assume that of Coppage or Farmer. He has a free mulatto woman for a wife, by the name of Sally Bozeman, who has lately removed to Wilmington, and lives in that part of the town called Texas, where he will likely be lurking.

Masters of vessels are particularly cautioned against harboring or concealing said negro on board their vessels, as the full penalty of the law will be rigorously enforced.

GUILFORD HORN.
June 29th, 1850.

Ten silver dollars reward will be paid for apprehending and delivering to me my man Moses, who ran away this morning; or I will give *five times the sum* to any person who will make due proof of his being KILLED, and never ask a question to know by whom it is done.

W. SKINNER,
Clerk of the County of Perquinous, N. C.

About the first of March last, the negro man Ransom left me without the least provocation whatever. I will give a reward of twenty dollars for said negro, if taken DEAD or ALIVE; and if KILLED in any attempt, *an advance of five dollars will be paid.*

BRYANT JOHNSON,
Crawford County, Georgia.

From the Sumpter County (Alabama) Whig.

NEGRO DOGS — The undersigned, having bought the entire pack of negro dogs, (of the Hay & Allen stock,) he now proposes to catch runaway negroes. His charges will be $3 a day for hunting, and $15 for catching, north of Livingston, near the lower Jones' Bluff road.

WILLIAM GAMBREL.
Nov. 6, 1845.

powerful people come forth to greet with such a welcome the principle of freedom, even in a poor, persecuted, penniless exile . . . Through all posterity, oppressed men will look to your memory as a token of God, that there is a hope for freedom on earth, because there is a people like you (!!) to feel its worth and to support its cause . . . Europe has many things to learn from America: it has to learn the value of free institutions, and the expansive power of freedom." [27]

"Happy art thou, free nation of America, that thou hast founded thy house upon the only solid basis of a nation's liberty! Thou hast no tyrants among thee, to throw the apple of Eros in thy Union. Thou hast no tyrants among thee, to raise the fury of hatred in thy national family — hatred of nations, that curse of humanity, that venomous instrument of despotism." [28]

"A tempest-tossed life has somewhat sharpened the eyes of my soul; and had it not even done so, still I would dare say, I know how to read your people's heart. It is so easy to read it, because it is open, like nature, and unpolluted, (!) like a virgin's heart (!!) May others shut their ears to the cry of oppressed humanity, because they regard duties but through the glass of petty interests. Your people has that instinct of justice and generosity (!) which is the stamp of mankind's heavenly origin; and it is conscious of your country's power; it is jealous of its own dignity; it knows that it has the power to restore the law of nations to the principles of justice and right; and knowing itself to have the power, it is willing to be as good as its power is great." (!) [29]

I am here on the free ground of free America (!). .

From the Madison (Louisiana) Journal.

NOTICE. — The subscriber, living on Carroway Lake, on Hoe's Bayou, in Carroll Parish, sixteen miles on the road leading from Bayou Mason to Lake Providence, is ready with a pack of dogs to hunt runaway negroes at any time. These dogs are well trained, and are known throughout the parish. Letters addressed to me at Providence will secure immediate attention. My terms are $5 per day for hunting the trails, whether the negro is caught or not. Where a twelve hours' trail is shown, and the negro not taken, no charge is made. For taking a negro, $25, and no charge made for hunting.
JAMES W. HALL.
Nov. 26, 1847.

☞ A negro woman, belonging to William Woods, Esq. of Clay county, Missouri, recently destroyed her three children, the oldest eight years of age, by drowning them in a creek. She afterwards told a negro man what she had done, and where they might be found, and then went and drowned herself. The children were found laid out, and protected by some boughs to shade their faces.

NEGROES FOR SALE. — I have again returned to this market, with eighteen or twenty likely negroes. I have located on the corner of Main and Adams streets. I have ploughboys, men, women, and girls, and some very fancy ones. I intend to keep a constant supply through the season, and will not be undersold by any in the market. My motto is, "the swift penny; the slow shilling" I never get. I will also pay the highest cash price for young negroes.
W. H. BOLTON.
Nov. 21, 1846.

Let an astonished world peruse, and reperuse, these extravagant and unqualified eulogiums upon this country from your lips, as "the land

of protection for the persecuted sons of freedom," "the glorious republic of the United States," whose "millions of inhabitants are all attached with warm feelings to the principles of liberty," with "no tyrants among them," having "the instinct of justice and generosity," as
"willing to be as good as their power is great," "the brilliancy of whose
stars is greeted by Europe's oppressed nations as the morning star of
rising liberty," whose "star-spangled banner is the proud ensign of
mankind's divine origin," whose "glorious country Providence has selected to be the pillar of freedom, as it is already the asylum to oppressed humanity," "From which the spirit of liberty has not only
spiritually but materially to go forth, in order that it may achieve the
freedom of the world," &c. &c.; and then read the blood-congealing,
soul-harrowing facts which are embodied in a parallel column, respecting the condition, liabilities and sufferings of more than three millions
of the American population — stripped of every right — having nothing
that they can call their own, except the capacity to suffer — constantly
bought and sold, in lots to suit purchasers, with cattle and swine —
lacerated, scarred, branded, mutilated — if fugitives, hunted with bloodhounds, shot down with rifles, in some instances a premium offered
for killing them, instead of returning them alive — with the eyes of
their souls bored out — under laws making it felony to teach them
how to spell the name of God, or to read Christ's Sermon on the
Mount; — and then record its verdict as to your language, conduct
and mission among us! Must not that verdict be — "Guilty of flattery
and dissimulation! Guilty of falsehood, and recreancy to principle!
Guilty of striking hands with thieves, and consenting with adulterers!
Guilty of compromising honor, justice, humanity, liberty!" Sir, dare
you, after this exposure, repeat the solemn declaration, made by you
at New York — "Humble as I am, God, the almighty, has selected me to
represent the cause of humanity before you! My warrant to this capacity is written in the sympathy and confidence of all who are oppressed!" [30] He whom God qualifies and sends forth to testify against
tyranny is faithful in the discharge of his mission; and, surely, Divine
Wisdom is never so infatuated as to send him to a nation of slave-
catchers and human flesh-mongers, to extol it as "the asylum of the
oppressed of all nations." If you were a true witness for God, instead
of suppressing the truth or dealing in flattery, you would be commissioned in this wise: — "Son of man, I send thee to the children of
Israel, to a rebellious nation that hath rebelled against me: they and
their fathers have transgressed against me, even unto this very day:
for they are impudent and hard-hearted. I do send thee unto them;
and thou shalt say unto them, Thus saith the Lord God. And they,

whether they will hear, or whether they will forbear, (for they are a rebellious house,) yet SHALL KNOW THAT THERE HATH BEEN A PROPHET AMONG THEM. And thou, son of man, be not afraid of them, neither be afraid of their words, though briers and thorns be with thee, and thou dost dwell among scorpions. Hear what I say unto thee: Be not thou rebellious, like that rebellious house." See Ezekiel, 2d chap. If you were the heaven-inspired messenger you assume to be, you would imitate the example of another ancient prophet, who claimed for himself, "Truly, I am full of power by the spirit of the Lord, and of judgment, and of might," — and who, in proof of the validity of this claim, spoke in the following terms: — "Hear, I pray you, O heads of Jacob, and ye princes of the house of Israel: Is it not for you to know judgment? Who hate the good, and love the evil; who pluck off their skin from off them, and their flesh from off their bones; who also eat the flesh of my people, and flay their skin from off them; and they break their bones, and chop them in pieces, (2) as for the pot, and as flesh within the cauldron; who abhor judgment and pervert all equity; who build up Zion with blood, and Jerusalem with iniquity; (3) yet who lean upon the Lord, and say, Is not the Lord among us? none evil can come upon us." Micah, 3d chap.

Instead of being thus true and faithful to this nation, — in comparison with whose turpitude, that of the ancient Jews whitens into virtue, — your powers of speech are tasked in framing compliments and panegyrics. Whether at New York, Baltimore, or Washington, — whether on soil nominally free, as in Pennsylvania, or on soil saturated with the blood of its slave population, as in Maryland, — your praise of the government and people, the institutions and laws of the United States, continues indiscriminate and unmeasured. In one of your speeches in England, you said — "I meet, in certain quarters, the remark that I am slippery, and evade the question. Now, on the point of sincerity, I am particularly susceptible. I have the sentiment of being a plain, honest man, and I would not be charged with having entered by stealth into the sympathies of England, without displaying my true colors." [31] Sir, is it the part of "a plain, honest man" to pursue a course so tortuous as this? Has there been nothing "slippery" in your conduct, no studied avoidance of the subject, no concealment of your real feelings and sentiments, in regard to our colossal slave system? Are you not seeking to "enter by stealth into the sympathies of" America, so as to secure her co-operation in aid of Hungary, by pandering to her vanity, and holding her up to the world not only as without blemish, but as radiant with beauty and covered with glory?

In striking contrast with your exalted estimate of this slaveholding republic was the view taken of it by the great champion of Irish liberation, and the outspoken opponent of tyranny in every quarter of the globe, the late DANIEL O'CONNELL! [32] Read the following extracts from his numerous speeches, extending over a period of twenty years: —

'I now come to America, the boasted land of freedom; and here I find slavery, which they not only tolerate, but extend, justified and defended as a legacy left them by us. It is but too true. But I would say unto them, you threw off the allegiance you owed us, because you thought we were oppressing you with the Stamp Act. You boasted of your deliverance from slavery. On what principle, then, do you now continue your fellow-men in bondage, and render that bondage even more galling by ringing in the ears of the sufferers from your tyranny, what *you* have done, what *you* have suffered, for freedom? They may retaliate upon us. They may reply by allusions to the slaveries we have established or encouraged. But what would be thought of that man who should attempt to justify the crime of sheep-stealing, by alleging that another stole sheep too? Would such a defence be listened to? Oh, no; and I will say unto you, freemen of America, and the press will convey it to you almost as swift as the wind, that God understands you; that you are HYPOCRITES, TYRANTS, AND UNJUST MEN; that you are DEGRADED AND DISHONORED; and I say unto you, dare not to stand up boasting of your freedom or your privileges, while you continue to treat men, redeemed by the same blood, as the mere creatures of your will; for so long as you do so, there is a blot on your escutcheon which all the waters of the Atlantic cannot wash out.'

✿ ✿   ✿   ✿ ✿

Of all men living, an American citizen, who is the owner of slaves, is the most despicable; he is a political hypocrite of the very worst description. *The friends of humanity and liberty, in Europe, should join in one universal cry of shame on the American slaveholders!* 'Base wretches,' should we shout in chorus — 'base wretches, how dare you profane the temple of national freedom, the sacred fane of republican rites, with the presence and sufferings of human beings in chains and slavery?' — [Speech delivered at an Anti-Slavery meeting in 1829.] [33]

I speak of liberty in commendation. Patriotism is a virtue, but it can be selfish. Give me the great and immortal Bolivar, the saviour and regenerator of his country. He found her a province, and he has made her a nation. His first act was to give freedom to the slaves upon his own estate. (Hear, hear.) In Colombia, all castes and all colors are free and unshackled. But how I like to compare him with the far-famed northern heroes! George Washington! that great and enlightened character, — the soldier and the statesman, — had but one blot upon his character. He had slaves, and he gave them liberty when he wanted them no longer. (Loud cheers.) Let America, in the fulness of her pride, wave on high her banner of freedom and its blazing stars. I point to her, and say, There is one foul blot upon it; *you have negro slavery.* They may compare their struggles for freedom to Marathon and Leuctra,[34] and point to the rifleman with his gun, amidst her woods and forests, shouting for liberty and America. In the midst of their laughter and their pride, I point them to the negro children screaming for the mother from whose bosom they have been torn. America, it is a foul stain upon your character! (Cheers.) This conduct, kept up by men who had themselves to struggle for freedom, is doubly unjust. Let them hoist the flag of liberty, with the whip and rack on one side, and the star of freedom upon the other. The Americans are a sensitive people; in fifty-four years they have increased their population from three millions to twenty millions; they have many glories that surround them, but their beams are partly shorn, for they have slaves. (Cheers.) Their hearts do not beat so strong for liberty as mine . . . . . . I will call for justice, in the name of the living God, and I shall find an echo in the breast of every human being. (Cheers.) — [Speech delivered at the annual meeting of the Cork Anti-Slavery Society, 1829.] [35]

Ireland and Irishmen should be foremost in seeking to effect the emancipation of mankind. (Cheers.) . . . . . The Americans alleged that they had not perpetrated the crime, but inherited it from England. This, however, fact as it was, was still a paltry apology for America, who, asserting liberty for herself, still used the brand and the lash against others. (Hear.) He taunted America with the continuance of slavery; and the voice with which he there uttered the taunt would be wafted on the wings of the press, until it would be heard in the remote wilds of America; it would be wafted over the waters of the Missouri and those of the Mississippi; and even the slaves upon the distant banks of the Ohio would make his words resound in the ears of their heartless masters, and tell them to their face, that they were the victims of cruelty, injustice, and foul oppression. (Cheers.) Bright as was the page of American history, and brilliant as was the emblazonment of her deeds, still, negro slavery was a black, a 'damning spot' upon it. Glorious and spendid as was the star-spangled banner of republican America, still it was stained with the deep, foul blot of human blood. — [Speech delivered at a meeting of the Dublin Anti-Slavery Society, 1830.] [36]

Man cannot have property in man. Slavery is a nuisance, to be put down, *not to be compromised with*; and to be assailed without cessation and without mercy by every blow that can be levelled at the monster . . . . . . Let general principles be asserted. And as it is the cause of religion and liberty, all that is wanted is the unwearied repetition of zealous advocacy to make it certainly triumphant. *Let every man, then, in whatever position he may be placed,* do his duty in crushing that hideous tyranny, which rends the husband from the wife, the children from the parents; which enables one human being, at his uncontrolled will, to apply the lash to the back of his fellow-man. — [Speech delivered at the London Anti-Slavery Society, 1830.] [37]

We are responsible for what we do, and also for the influence of our example. Think you that the United States of America would be able to hold up their heads among the nations, — the United States, who shook off their allegiance to their sovereign, and declared that it was the right of *every man* to enjoy freedom — of every man, whether black, white, or red; who made this declaration before the God of armies, and then, when they had succeeded in their enterprise, forgot their vow, and made slaves, and used the lash and the chain, — would they dare to take their place among the nations, if it were not that England countenances them in the practice? —

[Speech delivered at the General Meeting of the British Anti-Slavery Society, 1831.] [38]

My claim to be heard at all on this occasion is included in one sentence — I am an abolitionist. (Cheering.) I am for speedy, immediate abolition. (Renewed cheers.) I care not what caste, creed, or color, slavery may assume. I am for its total, its instant abolition. Whether it be personal or political, mental or corporeal, intellectual or spiritual, I am for its immediate abolition. (Great applause.) *I enter into no compromise with slavery.* I am for justice, in the name of humanity, and according to the law of the living God.

✿   ✿   ✿   ✿   ✿

The time has now come, when every man who has honest feelings should declare himself the advocate of abolition. He who consents to tolerate crime is a criminal; and never will I lose the slightest opportunity, whether here or in the legislature, or any where else, to raise my voice for liberty, — FOR THE EXTINCTION OF SLAVERY. (Great applause.) Humanity, justice and religion combine to call upon us to abolish this foul blot. But it is not England or Britain alone that is stained with this crime. The democratic republic of America shares in the guilt. Oh! the inconsistency of these apostles of liberty talking of freedom, while they basely and wickedly continue the slavery of their fellow-men, the negroes of Africa! A republican is naturally proud and high-minded, and we may make the pride of the North American republicans the very weapon by which to break down slavery; for, if the example of England were gone, they could not, in the face of the world, continue the odious and atrocious system one moment longer. (Cheers.) Abolish it throughout the British colonies, and away it goes in America. (Renewed cheers.)

✿   ✿   ✿   ✿   ✿

Slavery is a crime, a high crime against Heaven, and its annihilation ought not to be postponed. We have lately heard a good deal of the iniquity of the East India Company getting money from the poor, infatuated wretches who throw themselves beneath the wheel of Juggernaut's car. This is lamentable indeed; but what care I, whether the instrument of torture be a wheel or a lash? (Applause.) I am against Juggernaut, both in the East Indies and West Indies, and am determined, therefore, not to assist in perpetuating slavery. Is it possible, that where humanity, benevolence, and religion are combined, there can be doubt of success? The priests of Juggernaut are respectable persons compared with those who oppose such a combination (applause;) and I entreat you to assist in the great work by becoming its apostles. — [Speech delivered before the London Anti-Slavery Society, 1831.] [39]

I will not go to America. I have often longed to go there, in reality; but, *so long as it is tarnished by slavery, I will never pollute my foot by treading on its shores.* (Cheers.) In the course of my Parliamentary duty, a few days ago, I had to arraign the conduct of the despot of the North, for his cruelty to the men, women and children of Poland; and I spoke of him with the execration he merits. But, I confess, that although I hate him with as much hatred as one Christian man can hate another human being, viz: I detest his actions with abhorrence, unutterable and indescribable; yet there is a climax in my hatred. I would adopt the language of the poet, but reverse the imagery, and say,

'In the deepest hell, there is a depth still more profound,' [39a]

and that is to be found in the conduct of the American slave owners. (Cheers.) They are the basest of the base — the most execrable of the execrable. I thank God that upon the wings of the press, the voice of so humble an individual as myself will pass against the western breeze — that it will reach the rivers, the lakes, the mountains, and the glens of America — and that the friends of liberty there will sympathize with me, and rejoice that I here *tear down the image of liberty from the recreant hand of America,* and condemn her as the vilest of hypocrites — the greatest of liars. (Long continued cheers.)

When this country most unjustly and tyrannically oppressed its colonies, and insisted that a Parliament of borough-mongers in Westminster should have the power of putting their long fingers across the Atlantic, into the pockets of the Americans, taking out as much as they pleased, and, if they found anything, leaving what *residuum* they chose — America turned round, and appealed to JUSTICE, and she was right; appealed to HUMANITY, and she was right; appealed to her own brave sword, and she was right, and I glory in it. At that awful period, when America was exciting all the nations of the world; when she was declaring her independence, and her inhabitants pledged their lives, their fortunes, and their sacred honor, and invoked the God of charity (whom they foolishly called the God of battles, which he is not, any more than he is the God of murder) — at this awful period when they laid the foundation of their liberty, they began with these words: '*We hold these truths to be self-evident: that all men are created equal; that they are endowed by their Creator with certain inalienable rights; that amongst these are life,* LIBERTY, *and the pursuit of happiness.*' Thus the American has acknowledged what he cannot deny, viz. that God the Creator has endowed men with those things as inalienable rights. But it is not the white man, it is not the copper-colored man, nor is it the black man alone, who is thus endowed; but it is *all* men who are possessed of these inalienable rights. The man, however, who cannot vote in any State assembly without admitting this as the foundation of his liberty, has the atrocious injustice, the murderous injustice, to trample upon these inalienable rights; as it were, to attempt to rob the Creator of his gifts, and to appropriate to himself his brother man, as if he could be his slave. (Cheers.) Shame be upon America! eternal shame be upon her escutcheon! (Loud cheers.)

Shortly there will not be a slave in the British colonies. Five lines in an Act of Parliament, the other night, liberated nearly 500,000 slaves in the East Indies, at a single blow. The West Indians will be obliged to grant emancipation, in spite of the paltry attempts to prevent it; and then we will turn to America, and to every part of Europe, and require emancipation. (Cheers.) No! they must not think that they can boast of their republican institutions — that they can talk of their strength and their glory. Unless they abolish slavery, they must write themselves down LIARS, or call a general convention of the States, and blot out the first sentence of their Declaration of Indèpendence, and write in its place, '*Liberty in America means the power to flog slaves, and to work them for nothing.*' (Loud applause.) * * * *

The voice of Europe will proclaim the slave's deliverance, and will say to him, "SHED NO BLOOD, BUT TAKE CARE THAT YOUR BLOOD BE NOT SHED." *I tell the American slave owner, that he shall not have silence*; for, humble as I am, and feeble as my voice may be, yet deafening the sound of the westerly wave, and riding against the blast as thunder goes, it shall reach America, telling the black man that the time for his emancipation is come, and the oppressor that the period of his injustice is soon to terminate! (Cheers.) — [Speech delivered at the Great Anti-Colonization Meeting in London, 1833.] [40]

Mr. O'Connell presented himself to the meeting, amid the most enthusiastic cheers. After some remarks of a general nature, the Hon. and learned gentleman proceeded to speak in terms of severe censure of the conduct of the Americans, in continuing to keep in bondage the black population in many of their States. He did not wonder at the death plagues of New Orleans, or the devastation of its people, many of whom enjoyed health and vigor at morn, and were lifeless at noon, when they had committed or countenanced crimes *which could only be registered with the annals of Nicholas and the curses of Poland.*

The Hon. and learned gentleman read several extracts from an American slaveholding Act, in which it was enjoined that no judge, legislative member, barrister or preacher, should speak or write anything against slavery, under the pain of being sentenced to not less than three years, and not more than twenty-one years imprisonment, or death at the discretion of the court!!! And that no American should teach a slave to read or write, under pain of not less than three months, and not more than twelve months imprisonment. (Hear, hear.) The Hon. and learned gentleman flung this black dishonor on the star-spangled banner of America — in vain did it wave over every sea, proclaiming the honor of the boasted republic of modern times — *those who fought under it were felons to the human race,* (Hear, hear,) *traitors to liberty, to their own honor, and blasphemers of the Almighty.* 'The red arm of God,' continued the Hon. and learned gentleman, 'is bared; and let the enemies of those whom his Son died to save, the black man as well as the white man, beware of its vengeance! The lightning careers through the troubled air resistless, amidst the howling of the tempest and rolling of the thunder. O for one moment of poetic inspiration, that my words, with the fire of indignation with which my bosom burns, that my voice might be borne on the western breeze across the wide Atlantic, light on their shores and their mountains, and be wafted down the rivers of America!' — [Speech delivered at an Anti-Slavery meeting in London, 1835.] [41]

He had given the Americans some severe but merited reproofs; for which they had paid him wages in abuse and scurrility. *He was satisfied that they had done so.* He was accustomed to receive such wages in return for his labors. He had never done good, but what he was vilified for his pains; and he felt that he could not sleep soundly were such opponents to cease abusing him. (Cheers.) *He would continue to earn such wages.* (Cheers.) By the blessing of God, he would yet trample on the serpent of slave-owning cupidity, and triumph over the hiss of the foul reptile, which marked its agony, and excited his contempt. The Americans, in their conduct towards the slaves, were traitors to the cause of human liberty, and foul detractors of the democratic principle, which he had cherished throughout his political life, and blasphemers of that great and sacred name which they pretended to reverence. In reprobation of their disgraceful conduct, his public voice had been heard across the wide Atlantic. Like the thunder-storm in its strength, it had careered against the breeze, armed with the lightning of Christian truth. (Great cheering.) And let them seek to repress it as they may; let them murder and assassinate in the true spirit of Lynch law; the storm would wax louder and louder around them, till the claims of justice became too strong to be withstood, and the black man would stand up, too big for his chains. It seemed, indeed — he hoped what he was about to say was not profanation — as if the curse of the Almighty had already overtaken them. For the first time in their political history, disgraceful tumult and anarchy had been witnessed in their cities. Blood had been shed without the sanction of law, and even Sir Robert Peel [42] had been enabled — but he was here in danger of becoming political. (Cries of no, no, — go on, and cheers.) Well, then, even Sir R. Peel had been enabled to taunt the Americans with gross inconsistency and lawless proceedings. He differed from Sir Robert Peel on many points. (Laughter.) Every body knew that. (Renewed cheering.) It was no doubt presumption in him to differ from so great a man, but yet such was the fact. (Laughter.) On one point, however, he fully agreed with him. Let the proud Americans learn, that *all parties in this country unite in condemnation of their conduct*; and let them also learn that the worst of all aristocracies is that which prevails in America — an aristocracy which had been aptly denominated that of the human skin. The most insufferable pride was that shown by such an aristocracy. And yet he must confess that he could not understand such pride. He could understand the pride of noble descent. He could understand why a man should plume himself on the success of his ancestors, in plundering the people some centuries ago. He could understand the pride arising from immense landed possessions. He could even understand the pride of wealth, the fruit of honest and careful industry. Yet when he thought of the color of the skin making men aristocratic, he felt his astonishment to vie with his contempt. Many a white skin covered a black heart; yet an aristocrat of the skin was the proudest of the proud. Republicans were proverbially proud, and therefore he delighted to taunt the Americans with the superlative meanness, as well as injustice, of their assumed airs of superiority over their black fellow-citizens. (Cheers.) He would continue to hurl his taunts across the Atlantic. And, oh! — but perhaps it was his pride that dictated the hope — THAT SOME BLACK O'CONNELL MIGHT RISE AMONG HIS FELLOW SLAVES, (tremendous cheers,) who would cry AGITATE, AGITATE, (renewed cheering,) till the two millions and a half of his fellow sufferers learned the secret of their strength — learned that they were two millions and a half. (Enthusiastic cheers.) If there was one thing which more than another could excite his hatred, it was the laws which the Americans had framed to prevent the instruction of their slaves. To be seen in company with a negro who could write, was visited with imprisonment, (shame!) and to teach a slave the principles of freedom was punished with death. Were these human laws, it might be asked? Were they not laws made by wolves of the forest? No — they were made by a congregation of two-legged wolves — American wolves — monsters in human shape, who boast of their liberty and of their humanity, while they carry the hearts of tigers within them. (Cheers.) — [Speech delivered at the presentation of the Emancipation Society's Address to Mr. O'Connell, 1835.] [43]

I hate slavery in all countries — *the slavery of the Poles in Russia under their miscreant tyrant*, and the slavery of the unfortunate men of color under their fellow-men, the boasted friends of liberty in the United States. Let the slave leap up for joy when he hears of the meeting this day (cheers); let him have the prospect of freedom to cheer him in the decline of life (cheers.) *We ought to make our exertions strongly*, IMMEDIATELY *and* UNANIMOUSLY (cheers.) Remember what is taking place elsewhere. Only cast your eyes across the Atlantic, and see what is taking place on the American shores (cheers.) Behold those pretended sons of freedom — those who declared that every man was equal in the presence of his God — that every man had an inalienable right to liberty — behold them making, in the name of honor, their paltry honor, an organized resistance in Southern slave States, against the advocates of emancipation. — Behold them aiding in the robbery committed on an independent State. See how they have seized upon the territory of Texas, taking it from Mexico, Mexico having totally abolished slavery without apprenticeship, (loud cheers,) in order to make it a new market for slavery (shame!) Remember how they have stolen, cheated, swindled, robbed that country, for the audacious and horrible purpose of perpetuating negro slavery (cries of 'Shame!') Remember that there is now a treaty on foot, in contemplation at least, between the Texians and the President of the United States, and that it is only postponed till this robbery of Texas from Mexico can be completed. *Oh! raise the voice of humanity against these horrible crimes* (cheers.) There is about republicans a sentiment of pride — a feeling of self-exaltation. Let us tell these republicans, that instead of their being the highest in the scale of humanity, THEY ARE THE BASEST OF THE BASE, THE VILEST OF THE VILE (tremendous cheers.) My friends, *there is a community of sentiment all over the world*, borne on the wings of the press; and what the humble individual who is now addressing you may state, will be carried across the waves of the Atlantic; it will go up the Missouri — it will be wafted along the banks of the Mississippi — it will reach infernal Texas itself (immense cheering.) And though that pandemonium may scream at the sound, they shall suffer from the lash of human indignation applied to their horrible crime (cheers.) If they are not arrested in their career of guilt, four new States in America will be filled with slaves. O, hideous breeders of human beings for slavery! Such are the horrors of that system in the American States that it is impossible, in this presence, to describe them; the mind is almost polluted by thinking of them. Should the measures now contemplated by the Americans be accomplished, these horrors will be increased fourfold; and men, with the human soul degraded, will be in a worse state even than the physical degradation of human bodies (cheers.) — What have we to look to? Their honor — their generosity! We must expect nothing from their generosity (cheers.) Sir, I cannot restrain myself. It was only the other day I read a letter in The Morning Chronicle, from their Philadelphia correspondent. A person, whose Indian name I forget, (a voice, 'Oceola,') but who was called Powell, had carried on a war at the head of the Seminoles, and other Florida tribes, against the people of Florida. He behaved nobly, and bravely fought for his country; and he would have been deified as a hero had he fought in a civilized nation, and testimonials would have been reared to commemorate his deeds, as great and numerous as those which have been raised to a Napoleon or a Wellington; but what happens to this warrior? — Why, these Americans having made a truce with him, invited him to a conference. He comes under the protection of that truce. Thus confiding in their honor, is he allowed to return? O no! He is not allowed to return, but is taken prisoner, and carried captive to the fort (shame, shame!) O, cry out shame, and let that cry be heard across the waves of the mighty ocean (cheers.) We are the teachers of humanity, we are the friends of humanity. What does it signify to us, that the crime is not committed on British soil? *Wherever it is committed, we are its enemies* (cheers.) The American, it is true, boasts of having been the first to abolish the slave trade carried on in foreign vessels. Why, he was. But what was the consequence? Every one of his own slaves at home was made of more value to him. *It was a swindling humanity. It was worse than our twenty millions scheme.* It had the guise of humanity, but had really *the spirit of avarice and oppression* (cheers.) I, perhaps, ought to apologize for detaining you (no, no! go on!); but we are all children of the same Creator; heirs to the same promise, purchased by the blood of the same Redeemer, and what signifies of what caste, color or creed we may be (cheers)? *It is our duty to proclaim that the cause of the negro is our cause,* and that we will insist upon doing away, to the best of our human ability, the stain of slavery, *not only from every portion of this mighty empire, but from the whole face of the earth* (cheers.) If there be in the huts of Africa, or amidst the swamps of Texas, a human being panting for liberty, let it be proclaimed to him that he has friends and supporters amongst the great British nation (cheers.) — [Speech delivered at a public meeting of Anti-Slavery delegates, 1837.] [44]

It is utterly impossible that any thing should exist more horrible than the American slave breeding. The history of it is this: The Americans abolished the foreign slave trade earlier than England, but with this consolation — no small comfort to so money loving a race as the slaveholders — that by such abolition, they enhanced the price of the slaves then in America, by stopping the competition in the home market of newly imported slaves. Why, otherwise, was not the home trade stopped as well as the foreign? The reply is obvious.

To supply the home slave trade, an abominable, a most hideous, most criminal, and most revolting practice of breeding negroes exclusively for sale, has sprung up, and especially, we are told, in Virginia. There are breeding plantations for producing negroes, as there are with us breeding farms for producing calves and lambs. And as our calf and lamb breeders calculate the number of males of the flock to the females, similar calculations are made by the traffickers in human flesh. One instance was mentioned to me of a human breeding farm in America, which was supplied with two men and twelve women. Why should I pollute my page with a description of all that is immoral and infamous in such practice? But only think of the wretched mothers, whom nature compels to love their children — children torn from them forever, just at the period that they could requite their mother's love! The wretched, wretched mother! Who can depict the mother's distraction, her madness! 'But their maternal feelings are,' says a modern writer, 'treated with as much contemptuous indifference, as those of the cows and ewes whose calves and lambs are sent to the English market.'

That it is which stains the character of the American slaveholder, and leaves the breeder of slaves the most detestable of human beings; especially when that slaveholder is a republican, boasting of freedom, shouting out for liberty, and declaring, as the charter of his liberal institutions, these are self-evident truths, *'that all men are created equal — that they are endowed by their Creator with certain inalienable rights — that among these rights are* LIFE, LIBERTY, *and the* PURSUIT OF HAPPINESS.'

My sole object in my speech at Birmingham, and present object, is *to rouse the attention of England and of Europe* to all that is cruel, criminal, and, in every sense of the word, infamous, in the system of negro slavery in North America. MY DELIBERATE CONVICTION IS, that until that system is abolished, *no American slaveholder ought to be received on a footing of equality by any of the civilized inhabitants of Europe.* — [Letter of Mr. O'Connell to the Editor of the London Morning Chronicle, 1838.] [45]

I have no superfluous tears to shed for Ireland, and shall show my love of my country by continuing my exertions to obtain for her, justice and good government; but I feel that I have something Irish at my heart, *which makes me sympathize with all those who are suffering under oppression, and forces me to give to universal man, the benefit of the exertions which are the consequence.* (Cheers.) — And what adds peculiarly to the claim of Ireland for sympathy and support is, that in the great cause of suffering humanity, no voice was ever raised, but Ireland was found ready to afford relief and succor. — [Speech delivered at a meeting of the British India Society, 1839.] [46]

He then came to North America, and there, thank God, he found much reason for congratulation. There were now present forty representatives of American Abolition Societies to aid them in the great struggle for human liberty. *Let them be honored, in proportion as the slaveholders were execrated.* Oh! they had a hard battle to fight! In place of being honored as they were in this land, they had to encounter coolness and outrage; the bowie knife and lynch law threatened them; they were abolitionists at the risk of their lives (cheers.) — *Glory to them!* A year or two since, he made some observations upon the conduct of the American Minister; he charged him with breeding slaves for sale; he denied it; and, in order to prove who was right, he sent him [Mr. O'Connell] a challenge to fight a duel (laughter.) He did not accept it. Nothing would ever induce him to commit murder. God had forbidden it, and he would obey him (cheers.) The American Minister denied the charge, but he admitted that he had slaves, and he admitted that he did afterwards sell some; so let him have the benefit of such a denial (a laugh.) He added, however, that he did not believe that slaves were bred for sale in Virginia. Now, he would read some few extracts from Judge Jay's book, published in New-York, in 1839.[47] He would call Mr. Stevenson's attention to page 88 of that book, and that would prove to him not only that slave-breeding existed in Virginia, but within twenty-five miles of his own residence. [The Hon. Gentleman read several extracts, proving the practice; also several advertisements of lots of slaves wanted for ready money, for shipment to New-Orleans, and dated in Richmond, the very place of Mr. Stevenson's residence.] He had established against the Ambassador, that slave-raising did exist in Virginia — yet all these things took place in a civilized country — a civilized age — advertisements of human flesh for sale, and written in even a more contemptuous manner than if the subjects of them were cattle. The traffic in slaves from the North to the Southern States was immense. In the latter, they were put to the culture of sugar — a horrible culture, that swept off the whole in seven years — every seven years there was a new generation wanted. This was in a community calling themselves civilized. Why, *they were worse than the savage beasts of the desert*, for they only mangled when driven to it by hunger; but this horrible practice is carried on by well-fed Americans for paltry pecuniary profit — for that low and base consideration, they destroy annually their tens and twenty thousands.

These scenes took place in a country, which, in all other respects, had a fair claim to be called civilized — in a country which had nobly worked out its own freedom — in a country where the men were brave and the women beautiful. Amongst the descendants of Englishmen — even amongst such was to be found a horrible population, whose thirst for gold could only be gratified at the expense of such scenes of human suffering; a population who were insensible to the wrath of God, who were insensible to the cries and screams of mothers and children, torn from each other forever. But there was one thing they would not be insensible to — they dare not, they would not be insensible to *the contempt of Europe* (loud cheers.) *While they embraced the American Abolitionists as friends and brothers, let none of the slave-owners, dealers in human flesh, dare to set a foot upon our free soil* (cheering.) Let them call upon the Government to protest to America, that *they would not receive any slaveholding ambassador* (loud cheering.) *Let them declare that no slave-owner can be admitted into European society*; and then Calhoun and Clay, and men like them, who stand up putting forth their claims to be President of the great Republic, must yield to the public, universal opinion. He had made mention of those two men — he would only say that *Calhoun was branded with the blood issuing from the stripes of the slave, and Clay drowned in the tears of the mothers and children* (cheers.) Let the people of Europe say to slave-owners, 'MURDERERS, YOU BELONG NOT TO US, — AWAY TO THE DESERT, AND HERD WITH KINDRED SAVAGES!' (cheers.) *He begged pardon of the savage* (laughter.) Sometimes in anger he committed heinous crimes, but he was incapable of coolly calculating how long or how hard he could work a human being with a profit, — sometimes granting him a boon for the purpose of obtaining a year or two's more labor out of him. Well, are we to remain passive as hitherto? (loud cries of 'No, no!') *Let our declaration also go abroad.* Let this Society adopt it — let the benevolence and good sense of Englishmen make that declaration. If an American addresses you, *find out at once if he be a slaveholder* (hear, hear.) He may have business with you, and the less you do with him, the better (a laugh) — but the moment that is over, turn from him as if he had the cholera or the plague (cheers) — for there is a moral cholera and a political plague upon him (cheers.) HE BELONGS NOT TO YOUR COUNTRY OR YOUR CLIME — HE IS NOT WITHIN THE PALE OF CIVILIZATION OR CHRISTIANITY (cheers.) *Let us rally for the liberty of the human race* (applause) — *no matter in what country or in what clime he is found, the slave is entitled to our protection*; no matter of what caste, of what creed, of what color, he is your fellow-man — he is suffering injustice; and British generosity, which has done so much already, ought to be cheered to the task by the recollection of the success it has already attained (cheers.)

* * * I am zealous in the cause, to be sure, but inefficient — acknowledging the humility of the individual, I am still swelled by the greatness of the cause. My bosom expands, and I glory in the domestic struggle for freedom which gave me a title to stand among you, and to use that title in the best way I can, to proclaim humanity to man, and *the abolition of slavery all over the world.* — [Speech delivered at the anniversary of the British and Foreign Anti-Slavery Society, 1840.] [48]

From this spot, I wish to rouse all the high and lofty pride of the American mind. Republicanism necessarily gives a higher and prouder tone to the human mind than any other form of government. I am not comparing it with any thing else at present; but all history shows there is a pride about republicanism, which, perhaps, is a consolation to the republican for any privations he may suffer, and a compensation for many things in which he may possibly be inferior; but from this spot, I repeat, I wish to rouse all the honesty and pride of American youth and manhood; *and would that the voice of civilized Europe would aid me in the appeal,* and swell my feeble voice to one shout of honest indignation! And when these Americans point to their boasted Declaration of Independence, exclaim, 'Look at your PRAC- TICE!' Can there be faith in man, or reliance placed in human beings, who thus contrast their action with their declarations? . . . That was the first phrase of their boasted Declaration of Independence. What was the last? — 'To these principles we solemnly pledge our lives,' (invoking the name of the great God, and calling for his aid,) 'we solemnly pledge our lives, our fortunes, and our sacred honor.' It has the solemnity without the profaneness of an oath; it speaks in the presence of the living God; it pledges life, for- tune, and sacred honor to the principles they assert. How can they lay claim to 'sacred honor,' with this dark, emphatic, and diabolical violation of their principles staring them in the face? No! *America must know that all Europe is looking at her,* and that her Senate, in declaring that there is a property in human beings, has violated her oath to God, and 'sacred honor' to men. Will the American come down upon me, then, with his republicanism? I will meet him with the taunt, that he has mingled perjury with personal disgrace and dishonor, and inflicted both with a double barb into the char- acter of any man who claims property in any human being. France, and even England, might possibly adopt such a resolution without violating their national honor, because they have made no such declarations as America, and therefore she is doubly dyed in disgrace by the course she has taken, in open opposition to her own charter of Independence. * * * I rejoice to hear the present agitation is striking terror into the hearts of the slave- mongers, whose selfish interests, vile passions, and predominant pride, with all that is bad and unworthy commingled, make them willing to retain their hold of human property, and to work with the bones and blood of their fellow-creatures; whilst a species of democratic aristocracy, the filthiest aristocracy that ever entered into civilized society, is set up in the several States, an aristocracy that wishes to have property without the trouble and toil of earning it, and to set themselves above men, only to plunder them of their natural rights, and to live solely upon their labor. Thus, the gratifi- cation of every bad passion, and every base emotion of the human mind, is enlisted in defense of the slaveholder's right. When we turn our eyes upon America, we see in her Declaration of Independence, the display of the democratic elements of popular feeling against every thing like tyranny or oppression. But when I come to the District of Columbia, there I see in the capital and temple of freedom, the negro chained to his toil, and writhing beneath the lash of his taskmaster, and the negress doomed to all the horrors of slavery. There I see their infant, yet unable to understand what it is that tortures its father, or distracts its mother; while that mother is cursing its existence, because it is not a man, but a slave; and almost wishing — oh! what a wringing thought to a mother's heart — that the child might sink into an early grave, rather than become the property of an excruciating tyrant, and the instrument of wealth to others, without being able to procure comfort and happiness for itself. *That is America; that is the land of the free; these are the illustrations of the glorious principles laid down in the Declaration of American Independence!* These evils, inflicted as they are by the democratic aristocracy of the States, are worse than ever were inflicted by the most kingly aristocracy, or the most despotic tyranny I do not mean any thing offensive to our American friends present, but I do say, there is written in letters of blood upon the American escutcheon, ROBBERY AND MURDER, AND PLUNDER OF HUMAN BEINGS. *I recognize no American as a fellow-man, except those who belong to anti-slavery societies.* Those who uphold slavery are not men as we are, they are not honest as we are; and *I look upon a slaveholder as upon a pickpocket*, who violates the common laws of property and honesty.

They say, that by their Constitution they are prevented from emancipating the slaves in the slaveholding States; but I look in the Declaration of Independence, and the Constitution of 1787, and I defy them to find a single word about slavery, or any provision for holding property in man. No man can deny the personal courage of the American people. With the recollection of the battles of Bunker's Hill and Saratoga, — of which, indeed, I might be reminded by the portrait which hangs opposite to me, of one of the officers who took an active part in those conflicts, (the Earl of Moira,) with the recollection, I say, of those battles, it would be disgraceful and dishonest to deny to the American people, personal courage and bravery. There exists not a braver people upon the face of the earth. But, amongst all those who composed the Convention of 1787, there was not one man who had the moral courage — I was about to say the *immoral* courage — to insert the word SLAVERY in the Constitution. No! they did not dare pronounce the word; and if they did not dare to use the *word* slavery, are they to be allowed to adopt *the thing? Is America to shake her star-spangled banner in the breeze, and boast of liberty, while she is conscious that the banner floats over the heads of slaves?* Oh, but they call it 'persons held to labor,' that is the phrase they use in their documents; but dare anyone say that slavery is implied in those words? The term applies to any person who enters into a contract to labor, for a given period, as by the month or year, or for an equivalent; but his doing so does not constitute him a slave, surely; the very term is disgraceful to nature, and an affront to nature's God. No wonder the word was not in their Declaration; you would not look to find words of injustice and cruelty in a Declaration of honesty and humanity. I repeat it, they have not used the word. They *meant* slavery: *they intended to have slaves*, but they dared not employ the word; and 'persons held to labor' was as near as they dared approach to it. Can you conceive of a deeper crime than slavery? A crime which includes in it injustice and cruelty, which multiplies robberies and murders! Ay, there is one thing worse even than this, and that is hypocrisy added to it. Let hypocrisy be superinduced on injustice, and you have, indeed, a character fit to mingle with the murky powers of darkness; and the Americans (I speak not of them all, there are many noble exceptions,) have added hypocrisy to their other accomplishments. They say they have *no power* to emancipate the slaves; is that the real reason? It may be, that they have not power to do so in some particular States; but then, what shall be said of COLUMBIA? There they have full power. Columbia is not bound by any restriction; yet in Columbia there are slaves, and there they furnish further proof of their hypocrisy. O, say they, we are the finest gentlemen, the wisest statesmen, the most profound legislators in the world. We are ardent lovers of liberty, we detest slavery, and we lament that we have not the power to make all free. Then I whisper, Columbia! Columbia! You have the power there, you have the authority there, to remove this foul blot; you have the means and opportunities; you have, in short, every thing but *the will*: the will alone is wanting; and, with all your professions, you are hypocrites.

But I will now turn to a subject of congratulation: *I mean the Anti-Slavery Societies of America — those noble-hearted men and women*, who, through difficulties and dangers, have proved how hearty they are in the cause of abolition. I hail them all as my friends, and wish them to regard me as a brother. I wish for no higher station in the world; but *I do covet the honor of being a brother with these American abolitionists.* In this country, the abolitionists are in perfect safety: here we have fame and honor; we are lauded and encouraged by the good; we are smiled upon and cheered by the fair; we are bound together by godlike truth and charity; and though we have our differences as to points of faith, *we have no differences as to this point*, and we proceed in our useful career esteemed and honored; but it is not so with our anti-slavery friends in America; there they are vilified, there they are insulted. Why, did not very lately a body of men — of *gentlemen*, so called — of persons who would be angry if you denied them that cognomen, and would even be ready to call you out to share a rifle and a ball — did not such 'gentlemen' break in upon an Anti-Slavery Society in America; aye, upon a ladies' Anti-Slavery Society, and assault them in a most cowardly manner? And did they not denounce the members of that Society? And where did this happen? Why, in Boston — in enlightened Boston, the capital of a non-slaveholding State. In this country, the abolitionists have nothing to complain of; but in America, they are met with the bowie-knife and lynch law! Yes! in America, you have had martyrs; your cause has been stained with blood; the voice of your brethren's blood crieth from the ground, and riseth high, not, I trust, for vengeance, but for mercy upon those who have thus treated them. But *you ought not to be discouraged, or relax in your efforts.* HERE YOU HAVE HONOR. *A human being cannot be placed in a more glorious position than to take up such a cause under such circumstances.* I am delighted to be one of a Convention *in which are so many of such great and good men.* I trust that their reception will be such as that their zeal may be greatly strengthened to continue their noble struggle. I have reason to hope, that, in this assembly, a voice will be raised which will roll back in thunder to America, which will mingle with her mighty waves, and which will cause one universal shout of liberty to be heard throughout the world. *O, there is not a delegate from the Anti-Slavery Societies of America,* but ought to have his name, aye, *her* name, WRITTEN IN CHARACTERS OF

IMMORTALITY. *The Anti-Slavery Societies in America are deeply persecuted, and are deserving of every encouragement which we can possibly give them.* I would that I had the eloquence to depict their character aright; but my tongue falters, and my powers fail, while I attempt to describe them. THEY ARE THE TRUE FRIENDS OF HUMANITY, and would that I had a tongue to describe aright the mighty majesty of their undertaking! I love and honor America and the Americans. I respect their great principles; their untiring industry; their lofty genius; their social institutions; their morals, such morals as can exist with slavery — God knows they cannot be many — but I respect all in them or about them that is good. But, at the same time, I denounce and anathematize them as slaveholders, and hold them up to the scorn of all civilized Europe. I would that the government of this country would determine to have no dealings with him, and to tell the United States of America, that *they must send no more slaveholding negotiators here!*

I will tell you a little anecdote. Last year, I was accosted with great civility by a well-dressed, gentleman-like person, in the lobby of the House of Commons. He stated that he was from America, and was anxious to be admitted to the House. 'From what State do you come?' 'From Alabama.' 'A slaveholder, perhaps?' 'Yes.' 'Then,' said I, 'I beg to be excused;' and so I bowed and left him. Now, THAT IS AN EXAMPLE WHICH I WISH TO BE FOLLOWED. Have no intercourse with a slaveholder. You may, perhaps, deal with him as a man of business, but, even then, you must act with caution, as you would with a pickpocket and a robber. You ought to be very scant of courtesy towards him, at least until he has cleared himself of the foul imputation. Let us beware of too much familiarity with such men; and let us plainly and honestly tell them, as a Convention, what we think of them. I am not for the employment of force; no — let all be done by the statement of indisputable facts; by the diffusion of information; by the union of benevolent minds; *by our bold determination to expose tyranny and cruelty*; by proclaiming to the slaveholders that, so long as they have any connexion with the accursed traffic in human beings, *we hold them to be a different race.* Why should it not be so? *Why should we not shrink from them, as we would with shuddering from the approach of the vilest reptiles?* The declaration of such views and feelings from such a body of men as are now before me, will make the slaveholders tremble. My voice is feeble: but I have no doubt that what I say will reach them, and that it will have some influence upon them. They must feel that they cannot much longer hold the sway. One of the great objects of my hope is to affright the Americans by laying hold upon their pride, their vanity, their self-esteem, by commending what is excellent in them, and by showing how very far they come short in those properties upon which they boast themselves. I would have this Convention avail themselves of all such aids, and to urge them by every possible argument to abandon the horrid vice by which their character is so foully disfigured. * * * We have proof this day that there are those who love the cause of freedom in every part of the globe. And why should it not be so? *Why should not all unite in such a glorious cause?* We are all formed by the same Creator; we are alike the objects of the same watchful Providence; we are all the purchase of the same redeeming blood; we have one common Saviour; and our hearts beat high with the same immortal hopes. And why should any portion of the human race be shut out from our affection and regard? * * * O let a word go forth from this place, that we do not deem the Americans Christians, by whatever name they are called, whether Episcopalians, or Baptists, or Independents, or Methodists, or whatever other name, — that we regard them not as Christians at all, unless they cordially unite with us in this great work. We honor all that is really good in America, and would have it all on our side in this glorious struggle — in this holy cause. Let us unite and persevere, and, by the blessing of God, and the aid of good men, freedom will, ere long, wave her triumphant banner over emancipated America, and we shall unite with the whole world to rejoice in the result. — [From a speech delivered by Mr. O'Connell, on the third day of the sittings of the World's Anti-Slavery Convention, held in Freemason's Hall, London, June, 1840.] [49]

"Faithful are the wounds of a friend." [50] These, sir, are terrible denunciations; but are they not justly applied? Let no man accuse DANIEL O'CONNELL of having been inimical to the character and prosperity of this republic. The strength of his rebuke was the measure of his love. He was true to his convictions of duty. Whenever he heard our boasts of freedom and equality, and then saw us wielding the slave-driver's lash and sundering the ties of nature — buying, selling and enslaving our fellow-creatures, on a gigantic scale — making republicanism a by-word among the tyrants of the Old World, and thus perpetuating the thraldom of the oppressed millions of Europe — a mighty moral conflagration instantly kindled within him. It was then that the flames of his righteous indignation burst out in awful grandeur and with consuming power, the intensity of which spread over the Atlantic, and was felt in every section of our land. There was something sublime in the attitude of this great vindicator of human rights. If he had courted popularity in America, — that evanescent popularity which general corruption bestows upon its apologist, — if he had been intent on advancing the interests of Ireland at any sacrifice, even the sacrifice of truth and honor, — he would either have flattered our vices and extenuated our crimes, or, like yourself, have maintained an unbroken silence in regard to them. But his love of liberty was stronger than all personal considerations, — stronger than his regard even for his own stricken Ireland, — and therefore he exclaimed, on every suitable occasion, "Oh, the inconsistency of these apostles of liberty, talking of freedom, while they basely and wickedly continue the slavery of their fellow-men!"

Similar was the indignation felt and cherished by Ireland's distinguished poet, THOMAS MOORE, as expressed in the following lines: —

> "Who can, with patience, for a moment see
> The medley mass of pride and misery,
> Of whips and charters, manacles and rights,
> Of slaving blacks and democratic whites,
> And all the piebald policy that reigns

In free confusion o'er Columbia's plains?
To think that man, thou just and gentle God!
Should stand before thee with a tyrant's rod,
O'er creatures like himself, with souls from thee,
Yet dare to boast of perfect liberty!
Away! away! I'd rather hold my neck
By doubtful tenure from a Sultan's beck,
In climes where liberty has scarce been nam'd,
Nor any right but that of ruling claim'd,
Than thus to live where boasted Freedom waves
Her fustian flag in mockery over SLAVES!
Where motley laws, (admitting no degree
Betwixt the basely slav'd and madly free,)
Alike the bondage and the license suit —
The brute made ruler, and the man made brute!" [51]

Not merely at a distance from us, however, but in our immediate presence — face to face — has the same fidelity been shown to us by one born on a foreign strand. In the year 1835, the present distinguished member of Parliament for the Tower Hamlets in London, GEORGE THOMPSON, was in this country, disinterestedly laboring by Christian instrumentalities to bring slavery to an immediate end, in the spirit of peace, and without the shedding of blood — in imitation of the example of WILBERFORCE,[52] CLARKSON,[53] and other illustrious philanthropists in Great Britain, for the abolition of West India slavery. After the experience and observation of a year, — himself nearly all that time hunted for his life as though he had been a wild beast, — he registered his testimony as follows, which is substantially as applicable to our guilty nation now, as it was strictly true at that period. Read and compare it, KOSSUTH, with your laudations of us, and blush for your sycophancy!

How unutterably affecting is a view of the present aspect of the country! The enslavement of the colored population seems to be but one of a hideous host of evils, threatening in their combined influence the overthrow of the fairest prospects of this wide republic. My fears are founded upon the symptoms every where exhibited, of an approach to mob-supremacy, and consequent anarchy. In every direction, I see the minority prostrate before the majority; who, despite of law, the Constitution, and natural equity, put their heel upon the neck of the weaker portion, and perpetrate every enormity in the name of "public opinion." "Public opinion" is at this hour the demon of oppression, harnessing to the ploughshare of ruin, the ignorant and interested opposers of the truth in every section of this heaven-favored, but mob-cursed land. Where is the freedom of speech? where the right of association? where the security of national conveyances? where the inviolability of personal liberty? where the sanctity of the domestic circle? where the protection of property? where the prerogatives of the judge? where the trial by jury? Gone, or fast disappearing. The minority in every place speak, and write, and meet, and walk, at the peril of their lives. * * Were I a

134

citizen of this country, and did there seem no escape from such a dreadful state of things — if I did not, on behalf of the righteous and consistent, (for, thank God, there are thousands of such, who cease not day nor night to weep and pray for their country,) hope and believe for brighter days and better deeds, I should choose to own the dominion of the darkest despot that ever sealed the lips of truth, or made the soul of a slave tremble at his glance. If I must be a slave, if my lips must wear a padlock, if I must crouch and crawl, let it be before an hereditary tyrant. Let me see around me the symbols of royalty, the bayonets of a standing army, the frowning battlements of a Bastile. Let me breathe the air of a country where the divine right of kings to govern wrong is acknowledged and respected. Let me know what is the sovereign will and pleasure of the one man I am taught to fear and serve. Let me not see my rights, and property, and liberties, scattered to the same breeze that floats the flag of freedom. Let me not be sacrificed to the demon of despotism, while laying hold upon the horns of an altar dedicated to "FREEDOM and EQUALITY!" * * O, tell it not in St. Petersburg! publish it not in the streets of Constantinople! [54] But it will be told; it will be published. The damning fact will ring through all the haunts of despotism, and will be a cordial to the heart of Metternich, sweet music in the ears of the haughty Czar, and a prophetic note of triumph to the sovereign Pontiff. What American lip will henceforth dare to breathe a sentence of condemnation against the bulls of the Pope, or the edicts of the Autocrat? Should a tongue wag in affected sympathy for the denationalized Pole, the outlawed Greek, the wretched Serf, or any of the priest-ridden or king-ridden victims of Europe, will not a voice come thundering over the billows: —

"Base hypocrites! let your charity begin at home! Look at your own Carolinas! Go, pour the balm of consolation into the broken hearts of your two millions of enslaved children! Rebuke the murderers of Vicksburg! Reckon with the felons of Charleston! Restore the contents of rifled mail-bags! Heal the lacerations, still festering, on the ploughed backs of your citizens! Dissolve the star-chambers of Virginia! Tell the confederated assassins of Alabama and Mississippi to disband! Call to judgment the barbarians of Baltimore, and Philadelphia, and New York, and Concord, and Haverhill, and Lynn, and Montpelier; and the well-dressed mobocrats of Utica, and Salem, and Boston! Go, ye praters about the soul-destroying ignorance of Romanism, gather again the scattered schools of Canterbury and Canaan! Get the clerical minions of Southern taskmasters to rescind their 'Resolutions' of withholding knowledge from immortal Americans! Rend the veil of legal enactments, by which the beams of light divine are hidden from millions who are left to grope their way through darkness here, to everlasting blackness beyond the grave! Go, shed your 'patriotic' tears over the infamy of your country, amidst the ruins of yonder Convent! Go, proud and sentimental Bostonians, preach clemency to the respectable horde who are dragging forth for immolation one of your own citizens! Cease your anathemas against the Vatican, and screw your courage to resist the worse than papal bulls of Georgia, demanding, at the peril of your 'bread and butter,' the 'HEADS' of your citizens, and the passage of GAG-LAWS! Before you rail at arbitrary power in foreign regions, save your own citizens from the felonious interception of their correspondence; and teach the sworn and paid servants of the Republic the obligations of an oath, and the guaranteed rights of a free people! Send not your banners to Poland, but tear them into shreds, to be distributed to the mob, as halters for your sons! When, next July, you rail at mitres, and crosiers, and sceptres; and denounce the bowstring, and the bayonet, and the fagot; let your halls be decorated with plaited scourges, wet with the blood of the sons of the Pilgrims — let the tar cauldron smoke — the gibbet rear aloft its head — and cats and bloodhounds, (4) (the brute auxiliaries of Southern Liberty men,) howl and bark in unison with the demoniacal ravings of a 'gentlemanly mob' — while above the Orator of the day, and beneath the striped and starry banner, stand forth, in characters of blood, the distinctive mottoes of the age: — DOWN WITH DISCUSSION! LYNCH LAW TRIUMPHANT! SLAVERY FOREVER! HAIL, COLUMBIA!

Before you weep over the wrongs of Greece, go wash the gore out of your national shambles — appease the frantic mother robbed of her only child, the centre of her hopes, and joys, and sympathies — restore to yon desolate husband the wife of his bosom — abolish the slave marts of Alexandria, the human flesh auctions of Richmond and New Orleans — 'undo the heavy burdens,' 'break every yoke,' and stand forth to the gaze of the world, not steeped in infamy and rank with blood, but in the posture of penitence and prayer, a free and regenerated nation!'

Such, truly, are the bitter reproaches with which every breeze from a distant land might be justly freighted. How long — in the name of outraged humanity I ask, how long shall they be deserved? Are the people greedy of a world's execration? or have they any sense of shame — any blush of patriotism left? Each day the flagrant inconsistency and gross wickedness of the nation are becoming more widely and correctly known. Already, on foreign shores, the lovers of corruption and despotism are referring with exultation to the recent bloody dramas in the South, and the pro-slavery meetings and mobs of the country generally, in proof of the 'dangerous tendency of Democratic principles.' How long shall the deeds of America clog the wheels of the car of Universal Freedom? Vain is every boast — acts speak louder than words. While

> "Columbia's sons are bought and sold;"

while citizens of America are murdered without trial; while persons and property are at the mercy of a mob; while city authorities are obliged to make concessions to a bloody-minded multitude, and finally incarcerate unoffending citizens to save them from a violent death; while "gentlemen of standing and property" are in unholy league to effect the abduction and destruction of a "foreigner," the head and front of whose offending is, that he is laboring to save the country from its worst foe; while assemblages of highly respectable citizens, comprising large numbers of the clergy, and some of the judges of the land, are interrupted and broken up, and the houses of God in which they met attacked in open day by thousands of men, armed with all the implements of demolition; while the entire South presents one great scene of slavery and slaughter; and while the North deeply sympathise with their "Southern brethren," sanction their deeds of felony and murder, and obsequiously do their bidding by hunting down their own fellow-citizens who dare to plead for equal rights; and, finally, while hundreds of the ministers of Christ, of every denomination, are making common cause with the plunderer of his species; yea, themselves reducing God's image to the level of the brute, and glorying in their shame; I say, while these things exist, professions and boasts are "sounding brass;" men will learn to loathe the name of Republicanism, and deem it synonymous with mob despotism, and the foulest oppression on the face of the globe! [55]

In addition to these weighty testimonies, take that of one whose philanthropic fame fills the civilized world, whose spirit was characterised by rare meekness and simplicity, and whose language was ever chosen with the utmost precaution — the deeply lamented THOMAS CLARKSON, of England.

Slavery is the greatest evil which has ever afflicted your country. It has heaped incalculable sufferings upon the heads of a people who have never given you any cause of offense; and you have done this without any right to do it but your own will and the law of force. It has corrupted the morals of your population to a frightful extent, by familiarizing them with cruelty and injustice, by hardening their hearts, and by giving birth to erroneous opinions which lead to infidelity; and, moreover, *it has injured your national character in the eyes of the civilized nations of the world.*

You have got a slave-holding President, a slave-holding Senate, a slave-holding Congress, and a slave-holding Cabinet. You have got the very sort of men in these high offices, the most detrimental to your best interests.

In the common routine of business, in Congress, they have done, perhaps, as well as any other men could have done; but, whenever slavery has been brought before them as a matter of business, *the most malignant of what we call demons could not have done worse.* Their laws against their slaves stand on record as *the most bloody of the most savage nations upon earth;* so shocking as to produce horror and indignation in all who read them; and so shocking that one of your own judges, Stroud,[56] who first brought them together in print, is now, or was lately, buying up the unsold copies; because, as was reported, wherever the book is seen, it makes converts to the Anti-Slavery cause. Again, the men filling these offices brought forward and passed the famous gagging bills, and gave power to Postmasters to open letters and parcels, thus stopping the free liberty of speech, and of writing a man's own thoughts. And why was this tyrannical law passed? *That not a murmur against slavery might be allowed to transpire,* and that slavery might go on uninterruptedly in all its miseries and horrors as before, without censure or reproach. * * * Again, the men filling these offices caused the butchery of the Indians, and the extermination of some of their tribes, on the mere surmise that these tribes might disturb the plantations of their brother slave-holders, and afford a refuge or retreat for their fugitive slaves. Was this a proper motive for shedding torrents of blood? And will not a day of just retribution come? The same description of men made a law, that whoever aided the escape of a fugitive slave from the oppression of a cruel taskmaster, should be punished with death; though it was commanded, of old, that no fugitive slave should be restored to his master. Was not this setting up a legislation in direct opposition to the law of God? Again, the same description of men had the audacity to propose the annexation of Texas to the United States, so that both might be one territory, and under one sway. But for what purpose was this union proposed? To have a contiguous Slave Territory, where the poor fugitive could find no shelter, but must be sent back to an enraged owner, to undergo whatever torture the monster's ingenuity might think fit; and, secondly, not only to perpetuate slavery in the United States, but to extend it to another country, from which it might be spread we know not where. Was there ever a more wicked proposition than this, to transfer the whip, the chain, the iron collar, and other hideous instruments of torture, to innocent millions, yet unborn, and to an indefinite extent of country? *Could the mind of a Nero have invented a more wholesale complication of cruelty?* * * * While slavery lasts, you will have the same sort of men in office, and, of course, the same sort of wicked measures, and the same sort of evils, and perhaps worse; for, wherever arbitrary power has been once exerted successfully, it may go to precedents it has made for its continuance. What, indeed, can you hope for from a slave-holding Cabinet — a Cabinet of men who appear to have no fear of God before their eyes, whose motto seems to be expediency in preference of honor and honesty, and who have been accustomed to look upon the sin of slavery as a common custom only, and without reproach? Will God smile upon the labors of such men? Or, will he not rather take vengeance? [57]

But it is not English or Irish philanthropy, that is alone stirred with indignation, filled with astonishment, or melted into tears, in view of the revolting spectacle presented to the world by the United States as a slaveholding republic. Read, sir, the following letter to an eminent American lady, (5) now in Paris, (whose name will ever be honorably identified with the anti-slavery cause in this country, for her labors and sacrifices in its behalf,) from the distinguished VICTOR HUGO, of France: — [58]

MADAME:

I have scarcely anything to add to your letter. I would cheerfully sign every line of it. Pursue your holy work. You have with you all great souls and all good hearts.

You are pleased to believe, and to assure me, that my voice, in this august cause of slavery, will be listened to by the great American people, whom I love so profoundly, and whose destinies, I am fain to think, are closely linked with the mission of France. You desire me to lift up my voice.

I will do it at once, and I will do it on all occasions. I agree with you in thinking, that, within a definite time — that, within a time not distant, the United States will repudiate slavery with horror! Slavery in such a country! Can there be an incongruity more monstrous? Barbarism installed in the very heart of a country, which is itself the affirmation of civilization; liberty wearing a chain; blasphemy echoing from the altar; the collar of the negro chained to the pedestal of Washington! It is a thing unheard of. I say more, it is impossible. Such a spectacle would destroy itself. The light of the nineteenth century alone is enough to destroy it.

What! Slavery sanctioned by law among that illustrious people, who for seventy years have measured the progress of civilization by their march, demonstrated democracy by their power, and liberty by their prosperity! Slavery in the United States! It is the duty of this republic to set such a bad example no longer. It is a shame, and she was never born to bow her head.

It is not when slavery is taking leave of old nations, that it should be received by the new. What! When slavery is departing from Turkey, shall it rest in America? What! Drive it from the hearth of Omar, and adopt it at the hearth of Franklin? No! No! No!

There is an inflexible logic which develops more or less slowly, which fashions, which redresses according to a mysterious plan, perceptible only to great spirits, the facts, the men, the laws, the morals, the people; or better, under all human things, there are things divine.

Let those great souls who love the United States, as a country, be re-assured. The United States must renounce slavery, or they must renounce liberty. They cannot renounce liberty. They must renounce slavery, or renounce the Gospel. They will never renounce the Gospel.

Accept, Madam, with my devotion to the cause you advocate, the homage of my respect.

VICTOR HUGO.

6 Juillet, 1851, Paris.

O that to you, Louis Kossuth, it had been given to register, in a similar spirit, a similar testimony! — Mark the readiness with which Victor Hugo complied with the request made to him! Mark, too, the cogency as well as the pathos of his rebuke, and on what ground he felt justified in bestowing it! — "You desire me to lift up my voice. *I will do it at once, and I will do it on all occasions.* The destinies of the great American people, I am fain to think, are *closely linked with the mission of France.*" And are not those destinies as closely linked with the mission of Hungary? Yet you are dumb — surrounded by slaves, you are dumb — to propitiate their merciless oppressors, you are dumb! The language of the eloquent Frenchman would have come with even greater pertinency and force from your lips than from his own — "It is not when slavery is taking leave of old nations, that it should be received by the new. What! *When slavery is departing from Turkey, shall it rest in America! What! Drive it from the hearth of Omar, and adopt it at the hearth of Franklin!* No! No! No!" Still you are dumb — you "the champion of liberty"! Tell it not in Austria! Publish it not in the streets of St. Petersburg!

You have alluded, on several occasions, in terms of admiration, to the brave and generous assistance which Lafayette rendered to this country in its great struggle for independence.[59] You have quoted his example, in this particular, as a strong incitement to the people of the United States to lend their aid (now that they are powerful) to the oppressed of other lands, especially of Hungary; and thus to cancel their great indebtedness. Having won for himself their gratitude, veneration, and almost idolatrous attachment, for his gallant services, if any man had strong temptations to avoid giving them offence by "meddling" with their "domestic institutions," Lafayette was that man. But he scorned to calculate consequences, and would not be dumb. "When I am indulging in my views of American prospects and American liberty," he said, "it is mortifying to be told, that, *in that very country, a large portion of the people are slaves.* It is a dark spot

ON THE FACE OF THE NATION. Such a state of things cannot always exist." [60] It is the testimony of THOMAS CLARKSON, that LAFAYETTE said frequently, "*I would never have drawn my sword in the cause of America, if I could have conceived that thereby I was founding a land of slavery.*" [61] While you would have his example of physical bravery imitated, in the extension of our protecting hand to Hungary, will you repudiate his example of moral courage, in rebuking us for our atrocious slave system?

Not to cite any more foreign testimony, listen to the confession of a Virginian — THOMAS JEFFERSON, himself a slaveholder while he lived, although the author of the Declaration of Independence: —

The whole commerce between master and slave is a perpetual exercise of the most boisterous passions; *the most unremitting despotism on the one part, and degrading submission on the other.* With what execration should the statesman be loaded, who, permitting one half the citizens thus to trample on the rights of the other, transforms those into despots, and these into enemies, destroys the morals of the one part, and the *amor patriae* of the other! For if the slave can have a country in this world, it must be any other in preference to that in which he is born to live and labor for another; in which he must lock up the faculties of his nature, contribute as far as depends on his individual endeavors to the evanishment of the human race, or entail his own miserable condition on the endless generations proceeding from him. And can the liberties of a nation be thought secure, when we have removed their only firm basis, a conviction in the minds of the people that these liberties are the gift of God? that they are not to be violated but with his wrath? Indeed, I tremble for my country when I reflect that God is just; that his justice cannot sleep for ever; that, considering numbers, nature, and natural means only, a revolution of the wheel of fortune, an exchange of situation, is among possible events; that it may become probable by supernatural interference! The Almighty has no attribute which can take side with us in such a contest. [62] * * *

What an incomprehensible machine is man! Who can endure toil, famine, stripes, imprisonment, and death itself, in vindication of his own liberty, and the next moment be deaf to all those motives, whose power supported him through his trial, and inflict on his fellow-men a bondage, *one hour of which is fraught with more misery than ages of that which he rose in rebellion to oppose!* But we must wait with patience the workings of an overruling Providence, and hope that that is preparing the deliverance of these our suffering brethren. When the measure of their tears shall be full — when their tears shall have involved heaven itself in darkness — doubtless a God of justice will awaken to their distress, and by diffusing light and liberality among their oppressors, or at length by his exterminating thunder, manifest his attention to things of this world, and that they are not left to the guidance of blind fatality. [63]

Sir, if one hour of the bondage of the American slave is fraught with more misery than ages of that which WASHINGTON and his compatriots rose in rebellion to oppose, — if, with only half a million of slaves,

JEFFERSON trembled for his country when he reflected that God was
just, — what ought now to be the language of every true friend of freedom, whether sojourner or resident here, in full view of more than
three millions of slaves, and the general purpose to make their bondage interminable?

As further illustrative of the fatuity of your mission to this country,
and the extravagance of your encomiums upon it, read the following
lines from one of Freedom's true bards in the United States: —

> "What! shall we send, with lavish breath,
>   Our sympathies across the wave,
> Where Manhood, on the field of death,
>   Strikes for his freedom, or a grave?
> And shall the SLAVE, beneath our eye,
>   Clank o'er *our* fields his hateful chain?
> And toss his fettered arms on high,
>   And groan for Freedom's gift, in vain?
>
> Shall every flap of England's flag
>   Proclaim that all around are free,
> From 'farthest Ind' to each blue crag
>   That beetles o'er the Western Sea?
> And shall we scoff at Europe's kings,
>   When Freedom's fire is dim with us,
> And round our country's altar clings
>   The damning shade of slavery's curse?
>
> Go — let us ask of Constantine
>   To loose his grasp on Poland's throat,
> And beg the lord of Mahmoud's line
>   To spare the struggling Suliote —
> *Will not the scorching answer come*
>   *From turbaned Turk and scornful Russ,*
> '*Go*, LOOSE YOUR FETTERED SLAVES AT HOME,
>   THEN TURN, AND ASK THE LIKE OF US!'
>
> Just God! and shall we calmly rest,
>   The Christian's scorn — the heathen's mirth —
> Content to live the lingering jest
>   And by-word of a mocking Earth?
> Shall our own glorious land retain
>   That curse which Europe scorns to bear?
> *Shall our own brethren drag the chain*
>   *Which not even Russia's menials wear?*" [64]

Sir, is it not as palpable as the noon-day sun, that, whatever else
this country can do, she is not in a condition either to fight the battles
of European liberty, or to hurl her anathemas at European despots?
Is she not constantly liable to be called upon to suppress a servile in-

surrection on the part of the millions whom she is enslaving on her own soil? Is it not literally true, that "the preservation, propagation, and perpetuation of slavery is the vital and animating spirit of her national government"? Why, then, do you persist in outraging the common sense of the world, by extolling her as the abode of freedom, and the asylum of the oppressed? How can you rationally expect to receive any countenance from her, in your bloody rebellion against a tyranny not comparable in atrocity with her own? Or, if her aid can be secured to any extent, must it not be on the condition, — either expressed or understood, but certainly imperative, — that your lips will be for ever sealed respecting her transcendant criminality as the most active power in the world for the extension and perpetuation of chattel slavery? And can you comply with such a condition, without degrading your manhood?

Instead of making the afflictive state of Hungary, and her need of assistance, the justification of your silence on the subject of American slavery, you are bound, as a man of honor and a true friend of freedom, to imitate the illustrious example given by DANIEL O'CONNELL, who, when he was struggling against such overwhelming odds for the restoration to Ireland of some of her ancient rights and privileges, was proffered the most liberal pecuniary assistance on this side the Atlantic, — provided he would cease to reprove us for our traffic in human flesh. How he spurned the bribe — and how it will exalt you in the estimation of the world to scorn a similar bribe — you will learn by reading the following proceedings: — [65]

At a special meeting of the Loyal National Repeal Association, held in the Great Room, Corn Exchange, Dublin, May 9th, 1843, — JAMES HAUGHTON, Esq. in the chair, —

Mr. O'Connell said — The Association had adjourned to that day for the purpose of receiving a communication with which they had been honored from the Anti-Slavery Society of America — *a body of men whom they most entirely respect* — whose objects should be cherished in their heart's core — whose dangers enhanced their virtues — and whose persevering patriotism would either write their names on the page of temporal history, or impress them in a higher place, where eternal glory and happiness would be the reward of their exertions. (Cheers.) His impressions were so strong in favor of the Anti-Slavery Society of America, that he thought it would not be so respectful as he would desire, if he brought forward that document in the routine of business on the last day, when it could not be so much attended to as it deserved. (Hear, hear.) It was out of respect to the people who sent that document, that they had adjourned; and he might say, that personal respect for the chairman was mixed up with that consideration. (Cheers.) They could not have sent a better message, or a more sincere one; and, if he now had the kindness to make the communication, they would receive it with the respect it deserved. (Cheers.)

The Anti-Slavery Address having been read, —

Mr. O'Connell then said: — I rise with the greatest alacrity to move that that most interesting document be inserted on the minutes, and that the fervent thanks of the Repeal Association of Ireland be by acclamation voted to the writers of it. I never in my life heard any thing read, that imposed more upon my feelings, and excited a deeper sympathy and sorrow within me. I never, in fact, before knew the horrors of slavery in their genuine colors. It is a production framed in the purest effort of simplicity, but, at the same time, powerful in its sentiments, so at once to reach the human heart, and stir up the human feelings to sorrow and execration, — sorrow for the victims, and execration for the tyrants. (Loud cries of hear, hear, and cheers.) It will have its effect throughout Ireland; for the Irish people did not know what was, alas! familiar to you, Sir, and to me, — the real state of slavery in America, and of the unequalled evils it inflicts; for slavery, wherever it exists, is the bitterest potion that can be commended to the lips of man. Let it be presented in any shape, and it must disgust, for a curse inherent to it grows with it, and inflicts oppression and cruelty wherever it descends. (Hear, hear, and cheers.) We proclaim it an evil; and though, as a member of this Association, I am not bound to take up any national quarrel, still, *I do not hesitate to declare my opinions; I never paltered in my own sentiments.* (Cheers.) I never said a word in mitigation of slavery in my life; and I would consider myself the most criminal of human beings if I had done so. (Hear, and cheers.)

Yes, I will say, shame upon every man in America, who is not an anti-slavery man; shame and disgrace upon him. *I don't care for the consequences.* I will not restrain my honest indignation of feeling. I pronounce every man a faithless miscreant, who does not take a part for the abolition of slavery. (Tremendous cheering for several minutes.) It may be said that offence will be taken at these words. *Come what may from them, they are my words.* (Renewed applause.) The question never came regularly before us until now. We had it introduced collaterally; we had it mentioned by persons who were friends of ours, and who were endeavoring to maintain good relations between us and the slaveholders, but it is only now that it comes directly before us. We might have shrunk from the question by referring the document to a committee; but, *I would consider such a course unworthy of me,* enjoying as I do the confidence of the virtuous, the religious, and the humane people of Ireland; for I would be unfit to be what I would desire to consider myself, the representative of the virtues of the people, *if I were not ready to make every sacrifice for them, rather than to give the least sanction to human slavery.*

They say that the slaves are worse treated, since the cry of the Abolitionists has been raised in their favor, as it has made their masters more suspicious of them, and more severe against them; but has that any weight with me? How often was I told, during our agitation, that 'the Catholics would be emancipated but for the violence of that O'Connell.' (Laughter.) Why, one of the cleverest men in the country wrote a pamphlet in 1827, in which he stated that the Protestants of Ireland would have emancipated their Catholic countrymen long before, but for me, and fellows of my kind; and yet, two years after, I got emancipation in spite of them. (Cheers.) But it is clearly an insult to the understanding to speak so. When did tyranny relax its grip merely because it ought to do so? (Hear.) As long as there was no agitation, the masters enjoyed the persecution of their slaves in quietness; but the moment the agitation commenced, they cried out, 'Oh, it is not the slave we are flogging, but we are flogging through his back the anti-slavery men.' (Laughter.) But the subject is too serious for ridicule. I am afraid they will never give up slavery until some horrible calamity befalls their country; and I here warn them against the event, for it is utterly impossible that slavery can continue much longer. (Hear, hear.) But, good Heaven! can Irishmen be found to justify, or rather to palliate, (for no one could dare attempt to justify,) a system which shuts out the book of human knowledge, and seeks to reduce to the condition of a slave, 2,500,000 human beings; — which closes against them not only the light of human science, but the rays of divine revelation, and the doctrines which the Son of God came upon the earth to plant. The man who will do so belongs not to my kind. (Hear, hear.) Over the broad Atlantic I pour forth my voice, saying, 'Come out of such a land, you Irishmen; or, if you remain, and dare countenance the system of slavery that is supported there, we will recognize you as Irishmen no longer.' (Hear, hear, and cheers.) . . . .

I say the man is not a Christian, — he cannot believe in the binding law of the Decalogue. He may go to the chapel or the church, and he may turn up the whites of his eyes, but he cannot kneel as a Christian before his Creator, or he would not dare to palliate such an infamous system. No, America! the black spot of slavery rests upon your star-spangled banner; and no matter what glory you may acquire beneath it, the hideous, damning stain of slavery rests upon you, and a just Providence will sooner or later avenge itself for your crime. (Loud and continued cheers.) Sir, *I have spoken the sentiments of the Repeal Association.* (Renewed cheers.) There is not a man amongst the hundreds of thousands that belong to our body, or amongst the millions that will belong to it, who does not concur in what I have stated. *We may not get money from America after this declaration;* but even if we should not, *we do not want blood-stained money.* (Hear, hear.) *If they make it the condition of our sympathy, or if there be implied any submission to the doctrine of slavery on our part, in receiving their remittances, let them cease sending it at once.* But there are wise and good men every where, and there are wise and good men in America, — and that document which you have read, Sir, is a proof, among others, that there are; and I would wish to cultivate the friendship of such men; but the criminals and the abettors, — *those who commit, and those who countenance the crime of slavery, — I regard as the enemies of Ireland, and I desire to have no sympathy or support from them.* (Cheers.)

I have the honor to move that this document be inserted in full upon our minutes, and that the most grateful thanks of the Repeal Association be given to the Anti-Slavery Society of America who sent it to us, and in particular, to the two office bearers, whose names are signed to it.

At a meeting of the Loyal National Repeal Association, in Dublin, August 8, 1843, Mr. O'Connell, in the course of a powerful anti-slavery speech, said —

A disposition was evinced in America to *conciliate the opinion of that Association in favor of the horrid system of slavery,* but they refused, of course, to show any sanction to it. (Hear and cheers.)

He had taken an active part in the Anti-Slavery Society from the moment that he was competent to discover any one body of men acting for the extinction of slavery all over the world; and standing in that Association as the representative of the Irish people, who had themselves suffered centuries of persecution, because they were attached to humanity, and to what justice and reason demanded; for *if they had chosen to be silent, and had bowed to authority — if they had acquiesced in the dictates of their masters and tyrants, they would have escaped many temporary sufferings, but they would not have acquired the glory of having adhered with religious fidelity to their principles.* Standing as their representative, he could not act otherwise than he had done, *though the liberty of Ireland, the repeal of the Union itself, were to abide the result. He was bound not to look to consequences, but to justice and humanity;* and come what would, he did not hesitate to throw heart and soul into his opposition to the system that would treat human beings as brute beasts of the field. He spoke distinctly and emphatically, for as he wanted to make an impression, he used harsher words than he would have done, if he did not know that harsh words were necessary to rouse the selfish temperament of the domineering master of slaves. And he did make that sensation, and he was glad of it.

At a meeting of the Loyal National Repeal Association, held in Conciliation Hall, Dublin, Sept. 29th, 1845, Mr. O'Connell, speaking on the subject of American slavery, said —

I have been assailed for attacking the American institution, as it is called, negro slavery. I am not ashamed of that attack — I do not shrink from it. *I am the advocate of civil and religious liberty all over the globe, and wherever tyranny exists, I am the foe of the tyrant; wherever oppression shows itself, I am the foe of the oppressor; wherever slavery rears its head, I am the enemy of the system,* or the institution, call it by what name you will — (great cheering.) I am the friend of liberty in every clime, class, and color — my sympathy with distress is not confined within the narrow bound of my own green island — no, *it extends itself to every corner of the earth —* my heart walks abroad, and wherever the miserable is to be succored, and the slave is to be set free, there my spirit is at home, and I delight to dwell in its abode — (enthusiastic cheering.) It has been asked, *What business has O'Connell in interfering with American slavery?* Why, do not the Americans show us their sympathy for our struggles, and why should we not show a sympathy in efforts for liberty amongst themselves? (Cheers.) But I confess I have another strong reason for desiring to abolish slavery in America. *In no monarchy on the face of the earth is there such a thing as domestic slavery;* it is true, in some colonies belonging to monarchies, slavery exists; but *in no European country is there slavery at all —* for the Russian serf is far different from the slave of America, and therefore I do not wish that any lover of liberty should be able to draw a contrast between the democratic republics of America and the despotic States of Europe — (Hear, hear.) I am in favor of the democratic spirit, and I wish to relieve it from the horror of slavery — (cheers.) I do not wish to visit America with force and violence — I would be the last man in the world to consent to it. I would not be for making war to free the negro — at least, not for the war of knife, and lash, and sword; but I would be for the moral warfare — I would be for the arms of argument and humanity to procure the extinction of tyranny, and to hurl contempt and indignation on those who call themselves freemen, and yet keep others in slavery. I would bring elements of that kind to bear upon the system, until the very name of slavery should be regarded with horror in the republic of America — (cheers.)
❊ ❊ ❊ ❊

In the year '25, when I left my profession and went over to England, there was an anti-slavery meeting, at which I attended and spoke; and afterwards, when I went to Parliament, another meeting was appointed, greater in magnitude. The West India interest was 27 strong in the House of Commons — the Algerine bill was carried through the House by a majority of 19 — therefore, the emancipation bill was in the power of the West India interest; but when they sent a respected friend of mine — the Knight of Kerry — to me, to ask why I did not take a certain course with regard to it, what was my answer? I represent the Irish people here, and I will act as the Irish people will sanction. *Come liberty, come slavery to myself, I will never countenance slavery, at home or abroad!* (Cheers.) I said I came here on principle; the Irish people sent me here to carry out their principles; *their principles are abhorrent of slavery*; and, therefore, I will take my part at that anti-slavery meeting; *and though it should be a blow against Ireland, it is a blow in favor of human liberty, and I will strike that blow* — (cheers). So far was I from cultivating the slavery interest, that I adopted that course, though I regretted to lose their votes. But I must do them the credit to say, that I did not lose them. They acted nobly, and said they would not revenge upon Ireland my attack upon them. (Cheers.) * * * Let them blame me — in America let me be execrated by them — *let their support be taken from Ireland* — Slavery, I denounce you wherever you are — (Loud cheers.) *Come freedom, come oppression to Ireland — let Ireland be as she may* — I have my conscience clear before my God — (continued cheers.) * * *

They were told that the speech he made in that room would put an end to the remittances from America, and that the Americans would not again contribute to the funds of the Association. *If they should never get one shilling from America, his course was plain, his path was obvious.* He was attached to liberty; he was the uncompromising hater of slavery wherever it was to be found (cheers).

Such was the spirit of an O'CONNELL — brave, ingenuous, disdaining every trammel, scorning every bribe, soaring above all national and all personal considerations! — "I do not hesitate to declare my opinions. I never faltered in my own sentiments. We might have shrunk from the question of American slavery, but I would consider such a course unworthy of me. We may not get money from America after this declaration; but we do not want blood-stained money. *Those who commit, and those who countenance the crime of slavery, I regard as the enemies of Ireland, and I desire to have no sympathy or support from them.* I am not bound to look to consequences, but to justice and humanity. Wherever slavery rears its head, I am the enemy of the system. I will take my part in the anti-slavery meeting; and *though it should be a blow against Ireland,* IT IS A BLOW IN FAVOR OF HUMAN LIBERTY, AND I WILL STRIKE THAT BLOW. In America, let them execrate me — *let their support be taken from Ireland* — slavery, I denounce you, wherever you are! Come freedom, come slavery to Ireland — *let Ireland be as she may* — I have my conscience clear before my God."[66]

These are noble sentiments, and most faithful was O'CONNELL to his pledge. His love for Ireland was not less strong than yours for Hungary; but, unlike you, he disdained to act a deceptive and pusillanimous part, to secure foreign sympathy and aid in her behalf. Blush at your own craven and selfish policy, as contrasted with that pursued by Ireland's distinguished Liberator!

So much for the spirit of the sire. Now witness how closely akin to it is that of the son!

Extract from a speech delivered by John O'Connell,[67] M. P., at a meeting of the Loyal National Repeal Association, held in Dublin, Nov. 23rd, 1840: — [68]

He had to perform a duty which he had imposed upon himself, and a duty in which he was sure he would have their concurrence that he ought to discharge, to bring before the Association the atrocities practised upon the miserable slaves in the United States of America. He was of opinion they would think he ought to discharge it, because it was right that ☞ *when putting forward their claims to become a nation,* they should be able to put forth a claim upon this ground also, that THEY HAD SHOWN THEIR SYMPATHY FOR THE SLAVES.

[Here Mr. O'Connell read to the meeting several cases of slaveholding barbarity in America.]

He thought when he produced such details of atrocity as these, we would be acquitted of the charge of bringing forward a subject which was not WELL WORTHY THE ATTENTION OF THE ASSOCIATION. Nothing could be more shameful — nothing more unjust — nothing more cruel — nothing more atrocious and demoralizing — than the treatment of the black slaves in America, while the people boasted of their adhesion to universal liberty. But, not only did they suffer such enormities to be perpetrated against slaves, but against free people also. In the northern States, where slavery did not exist, the free people of color were subject to the greatest indignities. In the railway trains, there were separate places for them; in the churches, they were not permitted to sit in the same pews; nay, in the grave yards, (for they carried their dislike and contempt for the negro even there, where one would suppose all distinctions should cease,) there were separate places for the interment of negroes. (Hear.) And yet the country which did this called itself free. He alluded to this matter at present, because the American journals which arrived that day had brought intelligence that the Irish in America, and their descendants, were joining in the rally for repeal, and that meetings had been held, at which subscriptions were collected to aid the objects of that Association. (Cries of 'hear, hear,' and cheers.) Every testimony of sympathy in their struggles was grateful to their feelings; and it was delightful to know, that, among the new associations which Irishmen formed in other lands, they and their descendants were not forgetful of the older associations they had left at home. (Hear hear.) But while they hold out to us the hand of brotherhood, we tell them that they come from a suspected land, — a land that holds man in bondage; and if they have any connection with, or if they approve of that bondage, then ☞ WE REJECT THEIR PROFFER: we have neither kindred nor sympathy for them, if they participate in the most degrading, demoralizing, wicked, and atrocious system which ever was maintained by man. (Hear, hear.) Talk of freedom, indeed! they spurned their association, if they had any thing to do with this system, — nay, if they were passive observers of the atrocity; for, if it was incumbent upon this nation to express their abhorrence at what they did not themselves witness, it was doubly incumbent upon those who were witnesses of it, to oppose the system, and to TAKE PART WITH THE ABOLITIONISTS. If they did not take part against the system, they were equally culpable with those who upheld it. (Hear, hear.) Therefore, if they wish us to receive their aid and sympathy, LET THEM JOIN WITH THE ABOLITIONISTS; if not, WE SHALL REJECT AND REFUSE ALL CONNEXION WITH THEM. (Hear, hear.) It has been attempted to mix up Catholicity with the system, and the name of a distinguished individual in the southern States had been alluded to. But he would not now speak of him more than to express a hope, that the allegation was untrue; but there was no one who knew what Catholicity was, that did not know, not only that its tenets did not allow of slavery, but proclaimed that it was criminal in those who had any participation in the system. (Hear, hear, and loud cheers.)

Reply of John O'Connell, Esq., M. P., to a letter from James Haughton, Esq.

30, *Merrion Square, 27th Jan.* 1842.

MY DEAR SIR: — I beg to assure you, and the other gentlemen of the Committee, that there is no abatement of zeal on the part of the Repeal Association in the blessed cause of negro freedom. You would have easily seen this, had you been at our meeting of Monday week, when my father alluded, in strong terms, to slavery in America, and met the warmest approbation of the assembly. The most effectual means, too, of spreading abroad the knowledge and the detestation of that hideous system have been taken, by the collection together, *by order of the Association,* of all the extracts I read at former meetings on the subject of negro slavery, with a view to publish them in the form of a report, and *to distribute them with our reports.* I have prepared a short introduction to be prefixed to these extracts, and I think you will find it to speak the Association's sentiments as to slavery, in terms not to be mistaken. * * *

I trust we now stand acquitted of the charge, that our 'cry for liberty is a mere selfish affair.' We do not and did not deserve this charge. Our warmest exertions are ready to be given, and, whenever the occasion offers, *are given, freely and heartily, to every movement in favor of the liberty and happiness of any and all the branches of the universal family of man.* If we have been more before the public in our particular character as Repealers of the legislative union between England and Ireland, it is because our first duty is to our native land; but, *we have never refused nor neglected an opportunity of raising our voices in support and vindication of the rights of others*; and one of the strongest incitements that we have to labor for the restoration of our country's legislative independence is, that hers will then be the potential voice of a nation, and no longer the unheeded cry of a mendicant province, upraised in the cause of liberty and of Christianity.

I remain, my dear sir, ever faithfully yours,

JOHN O'CONNELL.

James Haughton, Esq.

Be careful to observe, that neither the elder nor the younger O'CON-

NELL spoke merely their own sentiments, but they also spoke for all Ireland — for eight millions of their own countrymen, in a state of almost unequalled physical suffering. "It was right" — nobly did they say — "that, when putting forward their claims to become a nation, they should be able to put forth a claim upon this ground also, that *they had shown their sympathies for the slaves.*" With you, they say — "Our first duty is to our native land"; but, they proudly add, what it is not now in your power to declare — "We have never refused nor neglected an opportunity of raising our voices in support and vindication of the rights of others" — even of the American slaves, across the wide Atlantic! Surely, such a people deserve to be free and independent!

But they go further. They tell the millions of their countrymen who have migrated to America, that, if they have any connection with slavery, "we have neither kindred nor sympathy for them — we reject their proffered assistance." Nay, "if they are passive observers of the atrocity, we spurn their association." Nay, more — "if they wish us to receive their aid and sympathy, *let them join with the abolitionists*; if not, we shall reject and refuse all connection with them; for it is doubly incumbent upon those who are witnesses of it, to oppose the demoralizing and atrocious system."

Sir, the analogy between the condition and aim of Hungary and Ireland, if defective in some particulars, is sufficiently close to warrant the presentation of it as an argument and an illustration. "Ireland for Ireland," was the watchword of O'CONNELL. "Hungary for Hungary," is yours. In other words, let each nation manage its own affairs, without foreign intervention. In the opinion of O'CONNELL, the Repeal of the Union which subjugated Ireland to England was as essential to the full development of Ireland, as the overthrow of the house of Hapsburg is deemed by you indispensable to the freedom and prosperity of Hungary. But there is this difference: he acted upon principle — you are inspired by a sentiment: to save Ireland, he would not consent to be gagged upon any subject — to subserve the interests of Hungary, you are willing not only to wear a padlock upon your lips, but to eulogize, as the special champions of liberty, those who require you to be silent! (6)

There are those who seek to justify your non-committal policy on the subject of American slavery. They say —

That you are here on a special mission, to the promotion of which, every thing else may justifiably give place:

That what you have done and suffered for Hungary should satisfy the most skeptical as to your abhorrence of oppression in every clime:

That your speeches are imbued with the warmest feelings of humanity, and abound with the noblest sentiments of liberty — and these should suffice:

That the freedom of Hungary will give to American slavery, as well as to European despotism, a fatal blow, and therefore that it should absorb all your powers:

That to express any sympathy for the anti-slavery movement, or any surprise or regret at the existence of slavery, in this country, would be sure to create an intense excitement, beneath the fiery billows of which, all "material aid" for Hungary would instantly disappear: hence, the middle course is the safe one — to avoid Scylla on the one hand, and Charybdis on the other:

That, if you were to give your countenance to any particular reform among us, you would be called upon to endorse every other — and thus the cause of Hungary would be inextricably entangled and mixed up with foreign or collateral issues, to its inevitable injury:

That you are managing your cause with consummate tact and judgment, and in the best manner to secure the glorious end in view, the freedom of all Europe:

That it is not to be supposed that you understand the nature or extent of our slave system, or its relations to the government, and therefore you ought not to be blamed, but rather commended, for declining to express any opinion upon the subject:

That you are acting in perfect consistency with the doctrine which you have constantly enforced as the safe rule of conduct — to wit, that it is for the people of every nation to manage their own affairs, without dictation, intermeddling, or influence from any other quarter — &c., &c., &c.

Such are the pleas made in your behalf. Doubtless, they embody the substance of your justification, as it lies in your own mind. Certainly, they are not destitute of plausibility. Let us briefly examine them in detail, and see whether they are conclusive.

I. It is conceded that you have a special work to perform, a cherished object to accomplish, of no small magnitude, in coming to these shores; and that it would be equally impertinent and unfair to seek to divert you therefrom, by committing you to any party issue or purely local interest. But in what form do you present yourself? Is it not as a penniless, homeless fugitive from oppression? Is it not as a sincere and earnest advocate of liberty? Do you not appeal to us for sympathy and "material aid" on the broad principles of absolute justice, in the spirit of a common brotherhood, and by all the claims of suffering humanity? Read your own words: — "The fact is clear, that the despotisms are leagued against the freedom of the world, [not merely of Hungary,] so that there is no hope against them but in the brotherhood of people, headed and protected by England and the United States of America." Again: — "England and America! do not forget, in your proud security, those who are oppressed! Do not grant a charter to the Czar to dispose of humanity! Do not grant a charter to despots to drown liberty in Europe's blood! Save the myriads who would and will bleed; and, by not granting this charter, be the liberators of the world!" [69] Do you object to being measured by your own standard? If you insist that it is the duty of the American people to remember the oppressed of Europe, is it impertinent to ask you not to forget the enslaved of America? When you are seen to take men-stealers fraternally by the hand, and are heard to acknowledge them as the truest friends of liberty, "whose heart is easy to read, because it is open like nature," [70] is such conduct to be allowed to pass without censure, because you have come to these shores on a "special mission?" You aspire to be " the representative of that principle of liberty, which God has destined to become the common benefit of humanity." Why, then, do you shrink from applying that principle to the case of those who are clanking their chains on our soil? You exultingly declare — "It is a glorious sight to see a mighty, free, powerful people come forth to greet with such a welcome the principle of freedom, even in a poor, persecuted, penniless exile!" But what have you to say of the spectacle of every sixth person held as a chattel among that same "mighty, free (!) and powerful people?" In England, you were not thus tongue-tied. Respecting the anti-slavery associations of that country, you could speak in the following complimentary terms: — "These associations are bound up with much of the glory of England, because it was by them that every great principle was carried in that country, from the abolition of slavery down to free trade." This you were quite ready to say in a land where there were no slaves sighing for deliverance, no slaveholders needing to be rebuked for their tyranny; evidently because you knew it would be a popular reference. But you have not the courage to bestow one word of approbation upon similar associations here, whose object, principles, doctrines and measures are essentially the same, and where the number retained in slavery is greater than the entire population of Scotland or New England; and where your commendation would make a deep impression, and be of vital importance in the mighty struggle for universal emancipation. Alas! you maintain a profound silence when you should lift up your voice in thunder tones; you speak when and where your approving utterance is of no special value. But, for Hungary, every one is bound to become an advocate or actor! For Hungary, all the burdens and horrors of a war conjointly with Austria and Russia should be cheerfully hazarded, because she is oppressed! "May others shut their ears to the cry of oppressed humanity," you exclaim, "because they regard duties but through the glass of petty interests; the American people have that instinct of justice and generosity, which is the stamp of mankind's heavenly origin"! [71] Have they indeed? How can this be reconciled with the existence of slavery and the slave trade among them, to an unparalleled extent? Despotic as Austria may be, she long since nobly decreed — "Every man, by right of nature, sanctioned by reason, must be considered a free person. *Every slave becomes free from the moment he touches the Austrian soil, or an Austrian ship.*" Compare this decree with the Slave Code and the Fugitive Slave Bill of the United States, and then repeat in the hearing of an astonished world your truthless declarations — "Happy art thou, free nation of America, that thou hast founded thy house upon the only solid basis of a nation's liberty! Thou hast no tyrants among thee, to throw the apple of Eris in thy Union!" [72] — Men, women, children, babes, constantly in the market for sale, but not a tyrant in all the land! "Europe has many things to learn from America: it has to learn the value of free institutions, and the expansive power of freedom"! [73] Sir, your praise is the most biting satire.

II. As to what you have done and suffered for Hungary, it proves how great has been your devotion to the liberties and interests of your own countrymen; but it proves nothing more. Local patriotism, courageous and self-sacrificing to the last extremity, is no anomaly in human history. To prove that it is neither selfish nor exclusive, a world-wide test must be applied to it. "Thou shalt love thy neighbor as thyself" does not mean, "Thou, a Hungarian, shalt love every other Hungarian as thyself," and there terminate: the command is of universal obligation. WASHINGTON, JEFFERSON and PATRICK HENRY as willingly perilled life, character and property, in struggling to overthrow British oppression, as you and your compatriots have done in attempting to throw off Austrian usurpation; yet, while they lived, they were slaveholders, and drew their sustenance, in part, from the unrequited toil, the tears and blood of their plundered vassals; and thus were guilty of trampling upon the principles which they professed to hold sacred. The American revolutionists counted nothing dear to them in their struggle for independence; yet, at that trying period, they held half a million of slaves in "a bondage, one hour of which was fraught with more misery than ages of that which they rose in rebellion to oppose"; [74] and their descendants are now enslaving three millions two hundred thousand, while holding it to be a self-evident truth, that all men are created equal! It is one thing for a suffering and oppressed people to combine for their own deliverance from a galling yoke; it is quite another thing for them to be regardful of the rights of others. It is comparatively easy to be the leader of millions in arms, cheered by their approving voices, and supported by their physical strength; but the case is altered when he who attempts to lead has few or none to follow him, — when those whose cause he advocates are unable to whisper a word of encouragement, — and when no turn of fortune promises station or popularity. The plea, therefore, that your patriotic efforts in Hungary have demonstrated your abhorrence of tyranny in every clime, is not valid, — especially as on this foreign soil you have been weighed in the balance, and found wanting.

III. It is true, that your speeches abound with the noblest sentiments of liberty; and these would suffice, if words were always acts, and were not as cheap as the air. But what falls from your lips, in praise of freedom, is precisely what the political demagogues and office-seekers here are continually using, but (like yourself) never applying. Nay, none surpass the slaveholders of the South in their rhetorical flourishes against despotism, and in favor of the rights of man. In a recent number of the St. Louis (Ky.) *Times,* the following definition of Democracy was published in terms of commendation:

"Democracy is a sentiment not to be appalled, corrupted, or compromised. It knows no baseness, *it cowers to no danger, it oppresses no weakness.* Destructive only of despotism, it is the sole conservator of liberty, labor and property. It is the sentiment of freedom, of equal rights, of equal obligations — the law of nature pervading the law of the land."

In the same number of the *Times,* the following, with other similar advertisements, appeared: —

CASH FOR NEGROES. — The highest price will be paid in cash for negroes, on application to the undersigned, stating age, &c.
                                        MOORE & PORTER.

At Philadelphia, Judge KANE,[75] fresh from the court before which, estimable citizens were on trial on the charge of TREASON, because they would give no co-operation in slave-catching, could attend your banquet, and unblushingly offer the following sentiment: —

"The cause of human freedom throughout the world! Its enemies are the same every where, and why should not its allies be the same?"[76]

He affected to believe that your "advent upon our shores was indicative of a new era, not only in the history of this country, but of the world" — and as though inspired by the noblest feelings for all mankind, he added, "The duties of man, originally bounded by the homestead, afterwards expanding around the social circle, had now a wider orbit than the country in which it pleased God to give him birth. *Where there was a man, there man has found a brother."* A most sentimental slave-catcher!

Presiding at the banquet given to you in Philadelphia, Hon. George M. DALLAS [77] could readily taunt Prussia with being "a vast barbaric empire," and say — "Her structure, her policy, her cunning, her super-stition, are inherently and irreconcilably adverse to human progress, rights and happiness." He could pathetically allude to your case, and ask — "Why, when wandering a defenceless exile from strand to strand, far separated from the sustaining sympathies of country, race, and home, does inexorable tyranny, with agitated eye, follow his track — while its poisoned arrows of defamation are furtively shot in ad-vance to obstruct his progress, or to deaden his appeals?" He could talk of "Despotism writhing like the huge reptile under the darts of Apollo, unconsciously recognizing the might, the majesty of Liberty." Yet, of all the Northern sycophants of the Slave Power, no one has more basely bowed the knee than himself. It is not long since he wrote to a Southern slaveholder, approving an alteration in the Constitution of the United States, so as to give ample security to the slave system against the growing spirit of freedom at the North! While, sir, in your case, he can express sympathy with "a wandering and defenceless ex-ile," whose track is followed by "inexorable tyranny," no one is more eager than himself for the recapture of every fugitive slave who en-deavors to find a hiding-place at the North!

Under the Fugitive Slave Law, already several victims have been seized and hurried from the soil of Pennsylvania, back to galling chains and a frightful servitude. That State is the "keystone of the arch" of the slave system, at least as far as the North is concerned. In no other non-slaveholding State is there less sympathy with the anti-slavery movement. Yet in your speech in Philadelphia, you could say — "The liberty of this land was not only proclaimed, but also achieved. You stand a proud, a mighty nation, unparalleled in history. But there is one word of that prophecy unfulfilled, and that word is — ALL — proclaim liberty to all the land. Now, as there is one Father only in heaven, and as there is one mankind only on earth; so all that prophecy cannot be fulfilled until other nations are at least, if not so glorious, yet as free and independent as you." [78] The adroitness with which you overlook our slave population, and apply the com-mand, "Proclaim liberty throughout all the land, *unto all the inhabi-*

tants thereof," to "other nations," instead of giving it a true and natural rendering, is equally palpable and significant. In desiring that "other nations" may be as free as ours, practically you ask that every sixth person of their entire population may be made a slave, for whose deliverance it shall be deemed a factious and criminal act to plead. And this, you declare, constitutes a basis on which we have "founded a building of human freedom, and of the development of the human intellect, and of civilization, prouder, loftier than that which humanity before you has beheld through five thousand years"! [79] Sir, something more is needed, *in this country*, than glowing generalities, to prove a man to be true to the cause of human liberty, without regard to complexion or clime.

IV. To the plea, that, by securing freedom for Hungary, you will give a powerful blow to slavery in America, it may be replied — first, even if this should follow, (which is to beg the question,) nothing can justify shuffling and double-dealing, unmerited panegyric, the substitution of falsehood for the truth; secondly, that it is paradoxical to talk of doing the best thing that can be done for your unhappy countrymen, and for the chattel slaves of this land, by striking hands in amity with the advocates and upholders of slavery; thirdly, that if the slave power of America has cause to dread your success in Hungary, then, in coming to this country for "material aid," you are convicted of extreme folly, — and in trying to propitiate that power, you are guilty of gross duplicity; and, finally, that the truth is, instead of the liberated Hungarian striking the chains from the limbs of the American slave, the existence of slavery in this republic is the all-sustaining prop of European absolutism, and the mightiest obstacle to the progress of liberty throughout the world.

V. The excuse for your silence on the subject of slavery, (so gravely reiterated as a full justification,) that, if you were to avow your real sentiments, you would excite general alarm and indignation, and quench every spark of sympathy for Hungary, it must be confessed, embodies a terrible truth; but, instead of relieving you from censure, it deepens your criminality. It shows how absolute is the sway of the slave power over this whole nation; it is a confession, that there is no substance in the welcome that you are receiving (as you flatter yourself) as "the representative of that principle of liberty which God has destined to become the common property of humanity"; and, with this consciousness of the delicacy of your position, it renders disgusting and intolerable your endless encomiums of the United States as "the land of protection for the persecuted sons of freedom among the great brotherhood of nations — great, glorious, and free" [80]

— &c., &c. Sir, what will posterity think of you? You, a homeless and penniless fugitive, but refusing to manifest any sympathy for the fugitives from an incomparably worse than Austrian despotism! You, "a humble petitioner, with no other claims than those which the oppressed have to the sympathy of freemen," [81] but deterred from acknowledging the superior claims of the American slave, who is supplicating for mercy! You, who profess to see in our "star-spangled banner, the proud ensign of mankind's divine origin," [82] but afraid to cast a glance of commiseration at the millions whose "divine origin" is practically denied under that banner! You, who make the act of your liberation, "the revelation of the fact, that the United States are resolved not to allow the despots of the world to trample on oppressed humanity," [83] but dare not in the United States say aught against the traffic "in slaves and the souls of men"! [84] And all this, to promote the interests of your own countrymen, whose condition is one of comparative freedom and happiness!

"The cause of the solidarity of human rights," which you have come "to plead before the great republic of the United States," [85] is not Hungarian, but universal. A people who aim or desire to be saved at the expense, or to the detriment of any other, is undeserving of salvation. This land is too full of compromisers and trimmers, to need your presence to teach us how to do evil, that good may come. What we need, what the world demands, is, an illustrious example of fidelity to the principles of liberty, in their application not merely to one but to all races and lands. You cannot be too true to Hungary; but you ought not, for her sake, to be false to America — and false you will be, if you fail to rebuke her for her atrocious system of slavery. The fact, that her soil is stained with blood, that there is no other institution to which she clings with so much tenacity as to that of slavery, that your welcome depends upon your silence where even the very stones cry out, that the universal sympathy which is expressed for your oppressed countrymen would instantly be turned to rage, and thus proved to be spurious — this fact alone would make you faithful and fearless, instead of timid and parasitical, if "God, the Almighty," had selected you "to represent the cause of humanity" before us.

VI. As there is, in reality, only one reason for your turning a deaf ear to the cry of imbruted humanity among us, — and that is, an apprehension of exciting popular displeasure, — it is idle to pretend that you are compelled to take this course, to avoid being mixed up with a multitude of extraneous matters that would otherwise be pressed upon your consideration. The case of millions deprived of personal liberty, and subjected to all the mutations of property, is too distinct and too awful to be put into the same category with the question of tariff, or free trade, or the extension of suffrage, or the distribution of the public lands,[86] or social re-organization, or national independence, or non-intervention, or any other question relating to individual advancement or the general welfare. In every land, men differ — widely and honestly differ — in their views respecting the science of political economy, and the best form of government, whether for transient or permanent adoption. But, as to chattelizing those upon whom the Creator has stamped his own image, "the same verdict has always been rendered — 'GUILTY!' — the same sentence has always been pronounced — 'LET IT BE ACCURSED!' — and human nature, with her million echoes, has rung it round the world in every language under heaven — 'LET IT BE ACCURSED!' His heart is false to human nature, who will not say, 'AMEN!' There is not a man on earth, who does not believe that slavery is a curse. Human beings may be inconsistent, but human nature is true to herself. She has uttered her testimony against slavery with a shriek ever since the monster was begotten; and till it perishes amidst the execrations of the universe, she will traverse the world on its track, dealing her bolts upon its head, and dashing against it her condemning brand. We repeat it, every man knows that slavery is a curse. Whoever denies this, his lips libel his heart. Try him! Clank the chains in his ears, and tell him they are for him; give him an hour to prepare his wife and children for a life of slavery; bid him make haste, and get ready their necks for the yoke, and their wrists for the coffle chains; then look at his pale lips and trembling knees, and you have nature's testimony against slavery." So isolated, therefore, is this from every other question that now awakens interest or excites agitation on our soil, that, whether you give a full and manly expression of your feelings, once for all, or only incidentally raise a commendatory voice in regard to it, it will furnish no just occasion to extort from you an opinion on any question, however important, that is strictly local in its application.

But, sir, if you are to be excused from taking one step here, in aid of suffering humanity, lest it may require others to be taken, terminating you know not where, then, certainly, it is not for you to insist on the cause of Hungary being espoused by this nation, at whatever hazard, and lead where it may! If we should interpose, in any manner, to secure freedom and independence for the oppressed of your country, why not also for the oppressed of all other countries? If we take the first step which you desire, who can predict what will be the entanglements, troubles and calamities growing out of it? What claims has Hungary upon us, that Poland, that Italy, that British

India, cannot as strongly and consistently urge? Yet you will listen to no excuses; you bid us see that justice is done, though the heavens fall; you implore us not by inaction to "grant a charter to despots to drown liberty in Europe's blood"; [87] and you base your appeal on the ground of universal humanity. Are you not condemned out of your own mouth?

VII. As to the tact displayed by you, in the management of your cause, it certainly indicates great wordly shrewdness. In England, you could eulogize the government, advocate free trade, and warmly commend the abolition of West India slavery as "bound up with much of the glory" of that country; for this was sailing with both wind and tide. In the United States, your admiration is boundless for the Union, the Constitution, the Government, even the Mexican war, unparalleled for its turpitude, because waged expressly for the extension and perpetuity of slavery. All this is congenial with the popular taste. But as for free trade, the anti-slavery enterprise, &c., these are questions of "domestic policy" with which you cannot properly meddle, because they have not yet become victorious! You will find, sir, in the end, that "honesty is the best policy," and that no amount of skilful diplomacy can be advantageously substituted for manly rectitude. Strive as you may to propitiate the slave power, by which this government is moulded and directed, it will be only to your own degradation, and without attaining the end you desire.

VIII. The plea, that, in fairness, you must be supposed to know little or nothing intelligently about slavery in this country, and therefore are excusable for declining to express any opinion concerning it, is too shallow to bear an examination. It is manifest that you need not any illumination whatever on the subject. You are not more distinguished for the fervor of your eloquence, than you are for your historical knowledge. Exhibiting, as you do, so familiar an acquaintance with American affairs, from the earliest period, it is preposterous to assume that you have yet to learn to what extent slavery is tolerated on our soil, or how far the nation, as such, is responsible for it. Before leaving the shores of England, (as has already been stated,) the information communicated to you, on this point, by philanthropic individuals and associations, was abundant. The excessive care you have taken, since your arrival here, to say and do nothing indicative of sympathy with our down-trodden bondmen, is proof not of your ignorance of their miserable condition, but that you perfectly understand how absolute and all pervading is the power which grinds them to the dust; and, consequently, how unpopular and perilous it is to plead their cause. Yet you have the assurance to say — "I am here on the free ground of free America. The United States number many millions of inhabitants, *all attached with warm feelings to the principles of liberty*"!! [88]

IX. If you are acting consistently with the course originally marked out by you, not to be identified with any movements among us, — and with the rule you have laid down, and so frequently referred to, that it is for the people of every nation to manage their own affairs, without any foreign intervention whatever, — it does not prove either the soundness of the rule or the wisdom of your conduct. For if the civil disabilities imposed upon your own countrymen are such as should excite the sympathy and elicit the remonstrances of other nations, surely the utter annihilation of the rights of millions on this boasted soil of freedom justifies, nay demands, the indignant protest of every friend of liberty throughout the world. How far you think we ought to go, in behalf of Hungary, you frankly disclose in the following admission made in your speech at the dinner given to you by the New York Bar: — [89]

"But I may be answered — 'Well, if we (the United States) make such a declaration of non-admission of the interference of Russia in Hungary, (because that is the practical meaning of the word; I will not deny,) and Russia will not respect our declaration — then we might have to go to war.' And there is the rub. Well, I am not the man to decline the consequence of my principles. I will not steal into your sympathy by slippery evasion. Yes, gentlemen, *I confess, should Russia not respect such a declaration of your country, then you are obliged, literally obliged, to go to war, or else be prepared to be degraded before mankind from your dignity.* Yes, I confess that would be the case."

For the relief, then, of these who are oppressed thousands of miles from us, it is our duty to interfere, sublimely indifferent to what may befall us, and at the risk of being "literally obliged to go to war" with the most formidable power on earth! All this is very clear to you as a fugitive from oppression, and unquestionably proper for the relief of outraged Hungarians! But when you are asked, on the ground of consistency, and by all the claims that suffering humanity can present, to "remember them that are in bonds" in this country "as bound with them," [90] you affect to regard the call as impertinent, and declare that you have no right nor wish to exert any influence in their favor! What makes your conduct the more extraordinary is, that, while you do not scruple to solicit of us "material aid" — i.e. money and arms — and to invoke us to run the risk of involving ourselves in a bloody revolutionary struggle on European soil — you shrink from giving any countenance, even of a moral kind, to a peaceful movement for the abolition of slavery in this country, the language of whose advocates is — "The principles of our revolutionary sires led them to wage war against their oppressors, and to spill human blood like water, in order to be free. Ours forbid the doing of evil that good may come, and lead us to reject, and to entreat the oppressed to reject, the use of all carnal weapons for deliverance from bondage. Their measures were physical resistance — the marshalling in arms — the hostile array — the mortal encounter. Ours shall be such only as the opposition of moral purity to moral corruption — the destruction of error by the potency of truth — the overthrow of prejudice by the power of love — and the abolition of slavery by the spirit of repentance." (7)

But, sir, it is not true that you are pursuing a non-committal course, (even if, in your case, it were justifiable to do so,) on the question of American slavery. To say that "the language of liberty is the language of the people of the United States"; that "the United States are resolved to become the protectors of human rights"; that "it is your glorious country which Providence has selected to be the pillar of freedom, as it is already the asylum to oppressed humanity"; is not this to treat the enslavement of one sixth portion of our population with entire disregard, and to feed the self-complacency of their brutal oppressors? To address, as the true friends of freedom, such men as FILLMORE, WEBSTER, CLAY and CASS,[91] — the great political props of the slave system, — is this to occupy neutral ground? To come to a slave-breeding, slave-hunting government, like ours, as qualified to testify and act against Russian usurpation, — is this to pass no judgment upon our national character, and to give it no endorsement? To call slavery "a question of domestic *policy*," — to require of every Hungarian resident on our soil "non-interference" with it as a duty, and on pain of being branded as acting "injuriously to the interest of his own country," — is this not taking sides against the slave? To declare, over and over again, "I never did or will do any thing, which, *in the remotest way*, could interfere with the matter alluded to," [92] [slavery,] — is not this to do the bidding of the slave power in the most effectual manner?

As to your theory of non-interference with the affairs of another country, it is essentially anti-christian and inhuman, as exemplified in your conduct among us; for it strikes a blow at every foreign missionary enterprise, brands the venerable apostles of Christ as intermeddlers, and virtually repeals the command, "Go ye into all the world, and preach the gospel of freedom to every creature." [93] To say or imply that, being a Hungarian, your right to assail despotism with moral weapons in any other portion of the world, terminates at the boundary line of Hungary, is to be guilty of a Jewish exclusiveness, and to adopt as valid the interrogation of Cain, "Am I my brother's keeper"?

You are now at the Seat of Government, in the city of Washington, the Capital of the United States. You have been introduced to President Fillmore, and to both houses of Congress. In your address to the President, you say,[94] "The star-spangled banner was seen casting its protection around me, announcing to the world there is a nation, alike powerful as free" — "cheered by your people's sympathy, so as freemen cheer, *not a man whatever, but a* PRINCIPLE" — and "may God, the Almighty, bless you with a long life, that you may long enjoy the happiness to see your country great, glorious and free, the corner-stone of international justice, and the column of freedom on the earth, as it is already an asylum to the oppressed"!! In your speech at the Congressional Banquet, you say: — [95]

"As once Cyneas, the Epirote, stood among the Senators of Rome, who, with an earnest word of self-conscious majesty, controlled the condition of the world, and arrested mighty kings in their ambitious march; thus, *full of admiration and reverence,* I stand before you, legislators of the new capitol — that glorious hall of your people's collective majesty. The capitol of old yet stands, but the spirit has departed from it and come over to yours, *purified by the air of liberty.* The old stands a mournful monument of the fragility of human things — *yours as a sanctuary of eternal rights.* The old beamed with the red lustre of conquest, now darkened by oppression's gloomy night — *yours beams with freedom's bright ray.* The old absorbed the world by its own centralized glory — yours protects your own nation's absorption, even by itself. The old was awful with unrestricted power — yours is glorious with having restricted it. At the view of the old, nations trembled — *at the view of yours, humanity hopes.* To the old, misfortune was only introduced with fettered hands to kneel at the triumphant conqueror's heels — to yours, the triumph of introduction is granted to unfortunate exiles, invited to the honor of a seat. And where kings and Caesars never will be hailed, for their power, might, and wealth, there the persecuted chief of a down-trodden nation is welcomed as your great Republic's guest, *precisely because he is persecuted, helpless and poor.* In the old, the terrible *vae victis* [96] was the rule — in yours, *protection to the oppressed, malediction to ambitious oppressors, and consolation to the vanquished in a just cause.* And while out of the old, a conquered world was ruled, you in yours provide for the common confederate interests of a territory larger than the conquered world of the old. There sat men boasting their will to be sovereigns of the world; *here sit men whose glory is to acknowledge the laws of Nature and of Nature's God, and to do what their sovereign, the people, wills.*"

Sir, more biting satire than this was never uttered; yet you did not mean to be satirical. Language more at variance with the truth was never spoken. As a commentary upon it, let the following scenes, which have occurred in that Capital which you insist "beams with freedom's bright ray," which is "the sanctuary of eternal rights," at "the view of which, humanity hopes," and in the legislative halls of which "sit men whose glory is to acknowledge the laws of Nature and of Nature's God," (*vide* the Slave Code of the District of Columbia (8) and the Fugitive Slave Bill!) as specimens of what has been constantly occurring therein for the last sixty years: —

The Washington Union [97] of July 3, 1845, contained an advertisement, offering for sale to the highest bidder, on the 13th of July, the following property, viz:

"One negro woman, named Elizabeth, about the age of sixty years; and one negro girl, named Caroline, about the age of twenty years — seized and levied upon as the property of Henry Miller, and sold to satisfy judicials, No. 22, October term, 1847, *in favor of the Post Master General;* also, judicials, Nos. 1, 2, 3, and 4, to June term, 1847, *in favor of the United States*, and against said Henry Miller.

> ALEXANDER HUNTER,
> *Marshal of the District of Col.*"

The National Era says: — [98]

"At the appointed time, the sale took place. Two women — a mother, aged about sixty, and a daughter of twenty — were sold *by the United States Marshal*, to satisfy *a United States claim*; and the proceeds of the sale were deposited in *the United States Treasury*, in defraying the expenditures of *the United States* Government"!!!

Read the following statement from the Washington *Spectator*,[99] of 1830: —

"Let it be known to the citizens of America, that at the very time when the procession, which contained the President of the United States and his Cabinet, was marching in triumph to the Capital, another kind of procession was marching another way; and that consisted of colored human beings, *handcuffed in pairs*, and driven along by what had the appearance of a man on horseback! A similar scene was repeated on Saturday last. A drove consisting of males and females, *chained in couples*, starting from Roly's tavern on foot for Alexandria, where with others they are to embark on board a slave ship in waiting to convey them to the South."

Take the testimony of the late Ex-President JOHN QUINCY ADAMS,[100] as given on the floor of Congress in 1838: —

"He (Mr. PICKENS, of S. C.) does not know the crushing and destruction of all the tenderest and holiest ties of nature which this system produces, but which *I have seen, with my own eyes, in this city of Washington*. Twelve months have not passed since a woman, in this District, was taken with her four infant children, and separated from her husband, who was a free man, to be sent away, I know not where. That woman in a dungeon in Alexandria, killed with her own hand two of her own children, and attempted to kill the others. The woman was asked how she could perpetrate such an act, for she had been a woman of unblemished character and religious sentiments. She replied, that wrong had been done to her and to them, that she was entitled to her freedom, though she had been sold to go to Georgia; and that she had sent her children to a better world."

Read the following advertisement, and say whether St. Petersburg or Vienna can match it for atrocity — a woman and her babe thrust into the jail at Washington, by the United States Marshal, on suspicion of being runaways, and to be sold into slavery, if not claimed, to pay their jail fees!!

NOTICE. Was committed to the jail of Washington County, District of Columbia, as a runaway, a negro woman, by the name of Polly Leiper, and her infant child William. Says she was set free by John Campbell, of Richmond, (Va.) in 1818 or 1819. The owner of the above described woman and child, if any, is requested to come and prove them, and take them away; or they will be sold for their jail fees, and other expenses, as the law directs.
                                    TENCH RINGGOLD, *Marshal.*
Washington, May 19, 1827.

Here is another advertisement of a similar character: —

NOTICE. Was committed to the jail of Washington County, District of Columbia, on the 23d of July, 1847, as a runaway, a negro woman, who calls herself Ann E. Hodges. She is nearly black, about 5 feet 5 1-4 inches high, and about 22 years of age. Had on, when committed, a slate-colored merino dress, and a brown calico sun-bonnet. She says she is free, and served her time out with a Mr. Benjamin Daltry, of Southampton, Va.; and that Messrs. Griffin & Bishop, of the same place, know her to be free. *She has two scars on the left leg, near the knee, from the bite of a dog, one on her left wrist, and one on the point of her breast-bone, occasioned by a burn.* The owner or owners of the above described negro woman are hereby required to come forward, prove her, and take her away, or *she will be sold for her prison and other expenses,* AS THE LAW DIRECTS.
                                    ROBT. BALL, *Jailer,* for
                                    A. HUNTER, *Marshal.* (9)
Washington, Aug. 23, 1847.

In 1846,[101] a number of slaves attempted to escape from the District of Columbia, the Capital which "beams with freedom's bright ray," and is "the sanctuary of eternal rights," in the schooner Pearl, commanded by Capt. Sayres, bound for a Northern port. The following is an account of their capture and treatment: — [102]

"It is as I expected: the poor negroes are taken, with captain, crew, vessel and all. This morning, as I left my boarding house, I saw coming from the street that leads to the landing, a long procession of colored people, and quite a number of soulless looking white men, marching in the direction of the Pennsylvania Avenue. I hastened to meet them, and as they came in front of the United States Hotel, the crowd became so dense that it was next to impossible for them to proceed. The captain and his crew were with them, with their hands manacled. As soon as the former became generally known to the crowd, the most intense excitement was manifested by the multitude. Oaths, that would have made even devils tremble, were poured forth, and vengeance seemed to be depicted on their countenances. '*Drag him out!*' cried some. '*Knock his d———d brains out!*' cried others. '*Shoot him! shoot the hell-hound!*' '*Lay hold of him! hang the d———d villain!*' were some of the mildest epithets that were used by this fierce-looking band of pandemonium wretches. In the mean time, some of the officers came to the poor fellow's relief, and he was hastily put into a carriage, and driven to the jail. The procession then went on towards the jail of the district, and I hastened in advance to get a view of the whole. The men were tied together with ropes, by couples. Some of them were fine looking fellows, but their countenances wore an expression of sadness. There were about thirty women in the train, but these were permitted to march in double file, without being hand-cuffed or tied. Some of them carried babes, others led children, and many were weeping over their sad fate, while ever and anon the brutes who drove them would order them to *hush* their *snivelling*; and to make their order more imposing, would raise their cudgels over their heads, as if about to strike. As they entered the gate that opens into the jail, I counted them, and found there were in all eighty-five. Some were whiter than the wretches who had them in custody, and looked far more intellectual and worthy of liberty. The throng around the jail was immense, and I could hear the most bitter imprecations against the abolitionists and the abolition paper (National Era) of the District.

The vessel in which they were taken, was boarded by the steamer at the mouth of the river, where she was lying at anchor for a favorable breeze to take them up the bay. As the steamboat hove in sight, the negroes wished to fight and defend themselves, but were not permitted to by the captain. They then suffered themselves to be quietly taken, and are in jail by virtue of laws sanctioned by the American Congress; and you, sons of the Pilgrims, will be under the necessity of contributing your mite to sustain this system of oppression. Oh! this is a glorious country. Let the star-spangled banner be flung to the breeze; let peals of victory rend the heavens; let cheers go up; for slavery has triumphed over liberty, the oppressed are retaken, and are now in chains to await their doom.

Ever since that period, SAYRES and DRAYTON, the humane captain and mate of the vessel in which these poor victims attempted to make their escape, have been languishing in prison at Washington, and there is no prospect of their liberation!

Here is an incident which occurred in Washington, a few days before your advent in that city, as related by a correspondent of the Ashtabula (Ohio) *Sentinel*, — probably the Hon. JOSHUA R. GIDDINGS: — [103]

"Yesterday, a servant man came to my room, saying a colored woman wished to speak with me. I told him to show her up. He soon returned with her. She was sobbing, and evidently in great agony of mind. I asked the cause of her grief. It was some time before she could so far compose her mind as to relate to me her misfortune; which consisted in living under the barbarous laws enacted by Congress for the government of this district. She said her husband had just been sold to a slave dealer, and taken to the baracoons of Alexandria — that his purchaser was intending to take him to Alabama in two or three days, — that she had four children at home. At this point, she burst out into a loud expression of her grief. Her sobbings were interrupted occasionally with the exclamations of 'Oh God! Oh my dear children! Oh my husband!' then appealing to me, 'Oh master, for God's sake do try to get back the father of my babes!'

"I learned that her husband's name is George Tooman. His former owner is a female, named Martha Johnwood, living east of the capitol some half a mile. George went to work this morning in the barn, at husking corn, without any suspicion of the fate which awaited him. The slave dealer and an assistant came to the barn, seized him, placed handcuffs upon him, and hurried him off to the slave pen in Alexandria.

"The woman hearing of it followed him here on foot, and returned, and then sought me in the vain hope that I should be able to assist her. The day is said by many to be the coldest known here for years, yet she has been exposed to the keen piercing winds, although I think she was thinly clad. She had not seen her children since morning, when she left them without firewood. I endeavored to soothe her feelings by expressing some faint hope that her husband might yet be redeemed — that I would make inquiry, and ascertain if I could find someone who would repurchase him, and permit him to remain in the district. It was dark when she left my room to return to her home, rendered bitter by the fate of the husband and father. The cold winds rocked the building, and howled mournfully about the corners. I reflected upon the barbarous law by which Congress has authorized and encouraged such crimes, and inflicted such misery upon the down-trodden of God's poor. 'I trembled for my country when I reflected that God was just, and that his justice will not sleep forever.' I asked myself the question, will Heaven permit such wickedness, such barbarous cruelty to go unpunished? Yet Mr. Fillmore in his message advises Congress to abide by the Compromise as a final settlement of the slave question, and leave the colored women who are wives and mothers in this district to the operations of this savage law — would leave fathers here to be sold in the manner above related — leave children here to be robbed of their parents. And the Whig caucus resolve substantially that they will lend their aid to sustain this law, which would disgrace the tyrant of Austria, and would add a deeper infamy to Haynau, the butcher of the Hungarians.

My feelings are too much excited on this subject to write coolly. I only wish the men of Ashtabula county, who, since 1848, have unintentionally sustained by their votes and influence this slave trade, could have witnessed the tears, the horror of mind, the deep anguish of that woman's heart, that they could have heard her wailings, her ejaculatory prayers for her children. Methinks they would not adhere to party dictation with so much devotion."

Here is the testimony of the Hon. HENRY L. ELLSWORTH,[104] for many years U. S. Commissioner of Patents at Washington, in a speech delivered by him at Lafayette, Indiana, in 1848: —

"I have resided ten long years in a slave territory — the District of Columbia — the little spot the nation emphatically calls her own. Would to God that I could say slavery was not there! But there it is, to greet the arrival of strangers attracted to the metropolis by business or curiosity. Yes, there it is in awful reality. In full sight of great legislators — near the Western gate of the capitol, and almost reached by its flag — the "Pen" is found, walled in and guarded, with manacles and handcuffs, the paraphernalia of a slave ship. There human beings are daily incarcerated and brought out for sale, first exposed and proved, like cattle, sound in wind and limb, and then ironed and driven to acclimate or die in the rice swamps, or on the sugar plantations of the South.

Here, too, the dignitaries of the land, (who travel at 8 dollars for every 20 miles), come to stock *their* farms.

Here, too, color is a crime; one speck of African blood consigns the unfortunate, if found at large, to the prison; and if, as does occur, his passport or manumission is lost, he is sold to slavery again! Those who have purchased their freedom live in constant fear of abduction. I have been awakened at the dead hour of night, by the supplication of a domestic, that I would save her sister, whom the men were carrying off. Knowing she was free, I went with a friend in search of the captive. We found her in custody of "two negro hunters," who showed an advertisement, $50 bounty; they claimed her as a runaway; she protested by her tears and assertions that she was not a slave. Force was threatened; it would have been resisted at all hazards. A night of horror to this girl passed away. The light of day beamed upon the facts; she was free, and proved it! How narrow her escape! If carried far away, her lips sealed in silence, when would her rescue arrive? At the grave!

Shall I tell you with what horror representatives at our court from foreign lands behold, at the seat of government, the exhibition of the principles of this free republic, where all men are by nature born equal!

Even citizens of the District have not nerve to behold the execution of their wishes. Mothers are separated from their children, and the injunction not to put asunder what God has joined together, is despised and rejected. Slaves are sent on pretence of business, and when beyond the sound of shrieks and supplication, they are seized and borne away to the *pen.*

Here it is that fathers sell their own children, and themselves rivet the manacles of slavery forever!"

Read and reflect upon the following revolting case, in the light of Christianity: —

Washington, Aug. 12, 1851.

A case of considerable interest came under my observation a few days since, which has caused some excitement and considerable talk in this District. A Presbyterian Elder, in *"good and regular standing,"* a reputed "watchman upon the walls of Zion," — among his goods and chattels is owned a young female, who is a member of the Congregational Baptist Church, which was under the pastoral charge of Rev. Mr. Samson — the church at which Secretary Corwin [105] and family worship. This female displeased her *religious* master in some way, and he — *Christian* man — forthwith gave her into the hands of the slave traders, who took her over to Alexandria, and incarcerated her with others in a slave pen, where she is to remain till a full "drove" is made up for the Southern market. When spoken to upon the subject, the grey-haired Elder excused *himself* by charging *her* with crime. The girl protested her innocence, and desired, even begged, for a trial. This poor helpless slave has a mother, who is also a slave, subject to all the rigors of the *lower law*. When apprised of the situation of her daughter, she flew to the pen, and with tears besought an interview with her only child, but she was cruelly repulsed, and told to begone!

As a specimen of the enactments adopted at Washington, by Congress, for the regulation of slavery in the District, take the following: —

To deal or barter with servants or slaves, subjects the person so doing (white person,) to a fine of two thousand pounds of tobacco, and in case of an inability to pay, then the offender, upon conviction before the proper court, is subjected to forty stripes, save one, on the bare back.

Free negroes and mulattoes, who intermarry with whites, are made slaves for life, and the whites made servants for seven years, the avails of such service to go towards the support of the public schools.

Slaves convicted of pilfering and other petit crimes, are subject to a whipping upon the bare back, not exceeding forty lashes.

Slaves caught away from their homes without a pass or permit, are subject to thirty-nine lashes, to be inflicted by any constable of the county.

If any slave shall strike a white person, and he is convicted of the same before a justice, said justice may cause one of the ears of the slave to be cropped.

Any person convicted of stealing any slave, or becoming accessory in any manner to a theft of this character, suffers death as a felon, without benefit of clergy.

Slaves guilty of rambling in the night, or running away without leave, are subject to punishment by whipping, cropping an ear, branding in the cheek the letter R, or otherwise, not extending to life.

In the year 1836, three hundred thousand men and women petitioned Congress for the abolition of slavery in the District of Columbia; but the legislators "whose glory is to acknowledge the laws of Nature and of Nature's God," [106] and whose power over the District is absolute, passed the following resolution by the following vote — yeas, 117 — nays, 68: — [107]

"Whereas, it is extremely important and desirable, that the agitation on this subject (slavery) should be finally arrested, for the purpose of restoring tranquillity to the public mind; therefore,

Resolved, That all petitions, memorials, resolutions, and propositions, relating *in any way, or to any extent whatever*, to the subject of slavery, shall, without being either printed or referred, be laid on the table, and that no farther action whatever shall be had thereon." (10)

Such are the legislators "whose glory is to acknowledge the laws of Nature and of Nature's God"!!

The "star-spangled banner" of the United States seems to excite your special admiration, though beneath it millions are groaning in bondage! To what purpose it is sometimes used, you can learn by reading the following statement of a credible eye-witness, Rev. JAMES H. DICKEY: [108]

"In the summer of 1822, as I returned with my family from a visit to the Barrens of Kentucky, I witnessed a scene such as I never witnessed before, and such as I hope never to witness again. Having passed through Paris in Bourbon county, Ky., the sound of music (beyond a little rising ground) attracted my attention. I looked forward, and saw the flag of my country waving. Supposing that I was about to meet a military parade, I drove hastily to the side of the road; and having gained the ascent, I discovered (I suppose) about forty black men all chained together after the following manner: each of them was handcuffed, and they were arranged in rank and file. A chain perhaps 40 feet long, the size of a fifth-horse-chain, was stretched between the two ranks, to which short chains were joined, which connected with the handcuffs. Behind them were, I suppose, about thirty women, in double rank, the couples tied hand to hand. A solemn sadness sat on every countenance, and the dismal silence of this march of despair was interrupted only by the sound of two violins; yes, as if to add insult to injury, the foremost couple were furnished with a violin apiece; the second couple were ornamented with cockades, while near the centre waved the Republican flag, carried by a hand *literally in chains*. I could not forbear exclaiming to the lordly driver who rode at his ease along side, 'Heaven will curse that man who engages in such traffic, and the government that protects him in it.' I pursued my journey till evening, and put up for the night; when I mentioned the scene I had witnessed. 'Ah!' (cried my landlady) 'that is my brother!' From her I learned that his name is Stone, of Bourbon county, Kentucky, in partnership with one Kinningham of Paris; and that a few days before, he had purchased a Negro woman from a man in Nicholas county. She refused to go with him; he attempted to compel her, but she defended herself. Without farther ceremony, he stepped back, and, by a blow on the side of her head with the butt of his whip, brought her to the ground; he tied her, and drove her off. I learned further, that besides the drove I had seen, there were about thirty shut up in the Paris prison for safe keeping, to be added to the company, and that they were designed for the Orleans market. And to this they are doomed for no other crime than that of a black skin and curled locks. Shall I not visit for these things, saith the Lord? Shall not my soul be avenged on such a nation as this?"

At Washington, you have had an interview with Henry Clay, (now an invalid,) and have professed to regard it as a great honor.[109] Mr. Clay holds more than sixty of his fellow creatures in slavery as his property, audaciously declaring that "that is property which the law declares to be property," even the children of God, — and that "the legislation of two hundred years has sanctioned and sanctified negro slaves as property," [110] and, therefore, they are not men! Listen to his avowal: — "I am myself a slaveholder; and I consider that kind of property as inviolable as any other in the country. I would resist as soon, and with as much firmness, encroachments upon it, as I would *encroachments upon any other kind of property*. I know there is a *visionary dogma*, which holds that negro slaves cannot be the subject of property. I shall not dwell long upon this *speculative abstrac-*

tion." [111] Again — "If I had been then, or were now a citizen of any of the planting States — the Southern or South-western States — I should have opposed, and would continue to oppose, *any scheme whatever of emancipation, gradual or immediate.*" [112] Again — "It is not true, and *I rejoice that it is not true*, that either of the two great political parties in this country has any design or aim at abolition. I should deeply lament it, if it were true." There is no man living, who has done so much for the extension and perpetuation of slavery as Mr. CLAY, or who is more inimical to the anti-slavery movement. He is the President of the American Colonization Society, an association organized by Southern slaveholders and their Northern allies for the expatriation of the free colored population of this country to Africa, *on account of their freedom and complexion,* whom it slanderously accuses of being "the most abandoned race on earth," [113] "scarcely reached in their debasement by the heavenly light," [114] "a curse and contagion wherever they reside," [115] "scorned by one class, [the whites,] and foolishly envied by another," [116] [the slaves,] "with no privilege but that of being more vicious and miserable than slaves can be," [117] "in one part of the country dull as a brutish beast, in another the wild stirrer up of sedition and insurrection," [118] "forever excluded, by public sentiment, by law, and by a physical distinction, from equality," [119] "a distinct and inferior race, repugnant to our republican (!) feelings, and dangerous to our republican (!) institutions," [120] "in this country forever debased, forever useless, forever a nuisance, from which it were a blessing for society to be rid," [121] "doomed by immovable barriers to eternal degradation," [122] "weighed down by causes, powerful, universal, inevitable, which neither legislation nor Christianity can remove, as it is *an ordination of Providence, and no more to be changed than the laws of nature,*" [123] (11) yet absurdly and audaciously maintaining, in the same breath, that "they, and they only, are QUALIFIED for colonizing Africa," [124] — "every one of whom," says Mr. CLAY, "is a missionary, carrying with him credentials in the holy cause of civilization, religion, and free institutions"!! The Colonization Society commends itself to slaveholding confidence and patronage by further declaring, that the removal of the free blacks "would prove one of the greatest securities to enable the master to keep in possession his property," [125] and would "contribute more effectually to the continuance and strength of the slave system, than any or all other methods which could possibly be devised." At the head of this cruel, unnatural and oppressive combination stands HENRY CLAY, in whose presence you, LOUIS KOSSUTH, reverently bow your head, and for the prolongation of whose life you express the most earnest solicitude!

It is the boast of Mr. Clay, that his slaves are "well fed and clad," and that "they look sleek and hearty." [126] Doubtless, the same is true of his cattle and swine. What scenes are witnessed on his plantation at Ashland, may be inferred from the following authentic incident. In 1846, one of his slaves obtained permission of the overseer to visit his wife on a distant plantation, on condition of returning an hour earlier in the morning than usual. Unluckily, he overslept his time, but presented himself at the usual hour for labor, with a humble apology. The enraged overseer levelled a blow at him with a handspike, the point of which passed along by the side of the slave's head with such force as to cut through his hat; and the scalp, from near the middle of the forehead to the back of the ear, was cut through also.

"When the wounded slave had so far recovered from the stunning effects of the blow as to be able to walk, he turned away towards Mr. Clay's mansion, to tell him of his wrongs. The overseer seeing the course he took, and guessing at his object, put the dogs after him, one of which caught him by the calf of the leg. This he choked off, and made his way to Mr. Clay's presence. There he addressed this form of speech to his master: "Massa Clay, I have worked for you now nine years, and if I haven't done my work as well as the rest of the people, and been as early at home Monday morning as massa says, I wish massa Clay tell me so, and not let the overseer cut my head so bad with the handspike." "You impudent fellow! what sent you here to tell of your working for me nine years, or any other time? Why, you black rascal, *I paid seven hundred dollars for you*! Go back and attend to your work; and I will see to settling this matter with the overseer."

Meeting with this harsh rebuff, he turned into one of the negro cabins, got his head dressed the best way he could, and hurried back to the hog-killing, where he labored through the day as well as he was able. In the course of the day, the overseer had an interview with the sage of Ashland, when these wise men and benevolent individuals came to this conclusion: "The impudent, refractory slave must be curbed and broke in by three hundred lashes, well laid on." The "Sage" directed his faithful overseer to call to his assistance Mr. Wickliffe's overseer, that between them both, "right and justice" might be done.

Some three days after this, the overseer of Mr. Wickliffe came riding up to where H. Clay's "well fed," &c., were at work, under the patriarchal guidance of his chosen overseer, when the bland salutation, "Good morning, sir," from Wickliffe's organ, was responded to by the Clay organ in the most chivalric and genteel manner possible; echoing back the bewitching "Good morning, sir. Will you be so good as to dismount, and see how we get along, sir?" Persuaded to do so by the courteous bearing of the Clay man, he dismounted, and stood erect in all his dignity before the "civil and respectfull" Ashlanders; while his brother overseer made his horse fast to a post. This done, the Clay overseer tapped the half-scalped $700 slave, (not in soon enough at the hog-killing on Monday,) significantly on the shoulder, with the alarming direction, "Come, boy, go with us; we have some business to attend to with you." This was on an extremely cold morning in December last. The overseers led the way across the fields to an old barn, near the woods. Here the victim was tied both hands together, and both feet in like manner, with ropes; after stripping the body above the hips entirely naked. This done, one end of a rope was tied fast to the rope which bound the hands, and the other end flung over a beam, upon which the two overseers flung their weight, and raised up the doomed slave to the proper height for receiving a kind, salutary whipping. To prevent the body from turning round, a rail was passed through between the legs, resting upon the rope that bound them together. All things being now ready, the Clay overseer thought of his whip for the first time, which, in his haste to shed innocent blood, he had entirely overlooked. To supply this defect, he hastened to the adjoining wood, and cut a good armful of ox-goads; the tortured slave, in the meantime, hanging in the position above mentioned, exposed to the bitter blasts of cold December. Upon his return, the work of flaying alive commenced. After striking some 150 times, Wickliffe's overseer advised him to desist, remarking, "I think he will obey you now." The infuriated Clay man had not drunk deep enough of blood yet, and renewed, and for some time continued his terrible work, till the less excited and more considerate Wickliffe man cried, "Stop, if you mean to spare the boy alive." After having been suspended three quarters of an hour, the victim of Kentucky law, and Ashland usage, was lowered down, unbound, and his clothes placed over his lacerated, bruised, mangled, and half-frozen body, and left lying in the cold barn; while the gentlemen executioners walked off to watch for other prey. The poor slave had barely strength to drag himself to some friendly negro-quarters, where his wounds could be mollified, the broken splinters of wood left sticking in his mangled body picked out, and healing remedies applied, to restore him to something like a living condition again. As soon as he was able to visit his wife, he did so, and she, filled with astonishment and horror, at beholding the condition in which he came back to her, and fully impressed as she was with the certainty of his being sold down the river, as soon as his wounds were healed, if for nothing else, to rid Ashland of a witness to its cruelty, she advised him by all means to make his escape, as soon as he could possibly bear the fatigues of travelling by night, and shape his course toward a land of freedom. In obedience to the counsellings of his wife, and the promptings of his own heart and will, he made the attempt while his wounds were in a measure yet green; and under the protection of Him who "tempers the winds to the shorn lamb," he had reached thus far on his way to a "city of refuge," when Prof. H. fell in company with him. (12) His guide through Ohio was a native born fellow-citizen of the chivalric, the gallant State of Kentucky. He, too, had drunk deep and long of that death-dealing cup, mingled in the Southern prison-house, the land of oppression. A beloved wife and child had forever been torn from his embrace by the damnable operations of Kentucky slave-law. The wife of his youth, if she yet survives, is now the *property* of a Mississippi planter, purchased for the unhallowed purpose of satisfying his "fleshly lusts, which war against the soul, and drown men in perdition." [127]

Mr. CLAY's chattel having succeeded in reaching Canada, a public meeting was held at Amherstburgh on his arrival, the official proceedings of which are herewith annexed: — [128]

THE SLAVE OF HENRY CLAY.

Amherstburgh, March 13, 1846.

A public meeting of the citizens of Amherstburgh, Canada West, met in Union Chapel, to hear an address from Lewis Richardson, a fugitive from Henry Clay, of Ashland, Kentucky. At half-past 7 o'clock, A. M., the house was called to order by Mr. L. Foster, who acted as chairman of the meeting, and J. Binga, secretary. After the object of the meeting was explained by H. Bibb,[129] of Detroit, Mr. Richardson proceeded as follows: —

"Dear Brethren, I am truly happy to meet with you on British soil, (cheers,) where I am not known by the color of my skin, but where the Government knows me as a man. I am now free from American slavery, after wearing the galling chains on my limbs 53 years; nine of which it has been my unhappy lot to be the slave of Henry Clay. It has been said by some, that Clay's slaves had rather live with him than be free; but I had rather this day have a millstone tied to my neck, and be sunk to the bottom of Detroit River, than to go back to Ashland, and be his slave for life. As late as Dec., 1845, H. Clay had me stripped and tied up, and one hundred and fifty lashes given me on my naked back; the crime for which I was so abused was, I failed to return home on a visit to see my wife, on Monday morning, before 5 o'clock. My wife was living on another place, three miles from Ashland. During the nine years living with Mr. Clay, he has not given me hat nor cap to wear, nor a stitch of bed clothes, except one small coarse blanket. Yet he has said publicly his slaves were 'fat and sleek'! But I say if they are, it is not because they are so well used by him. They have nothing but coarse bread and meat to eat, and not enough of that. They are allowanced every week. For each field hand is allowed one peck of coarse corn meal, and meat in proportion, and no vegetables of any kind. Such is the treatment that Henry Clay's slaves receive from him. I can truly say that I have only one thing to lament over, and that is my bereft wife, who is yet in bondage. If I only had her with me, I should be happy. Yet think not that I am unhappy. Think not that I regret the choice I have made. I counted the cost before I started. Before I took leave of my wife, she wept over me, and dressed the wounds on my back, caused by the lash. I then gave her the parting hand, and started for Canada. I expected to be pursued as a felon, as I had been before, and to be hunted as a fox from mountain to cave. I well knew if I continued much longer with Clay, that I should be killed by such floggings and abused by his cruel overseer in my old age. I wanted to be free before I died — and if I should be caught on the way to Canada, and taken back, it could be but death, and I might as well die with the colic as the fever. With these considerations, I started for Canada.

Such usage as this caused me to flee from under the American eagle, and take shelter under the British crown. (Cheers.) Thanks be to Heaven that I have got here at last! On yonder side of Detroit river, I was recognized as property; but on this side I am on free soil. Hail, Britannia! Shame, America! (Cheers.) A republican despotism, holding three millions of fellow-men in slavery! Oh, what a contrast between slavery and liberty! Here I stand erect, without a chain upon my limbs. (Cheers.) Redeemed, emancipated by the generosity of Great Britain. (Cheers.) I now feel as independent as ever Henry Clay felt when he was running for the White House. In fact, I feel better. He has been defeated four or five times, and I but once. But he was running for slavery, and I for liberty. I think I have beat

him out of sight. Thanks be to God that I am elected to Canada, and if I
don't live but one night, I am determined to die on free soil. Let my days
be few or many, let me die sooner or later, my grave shall be made in free
soil."

So much for the principles, conduct, character and position of
HENRY CLAY, who expresses so much sympathy for the poor Hungarians! ·

Among those who have come forward, at Washington, to welcome
you to the Capital, is Judge BAILEY.[130] On being informed, by himself,
that he was from Virginia, (true to your parasitical policy,) you exclaimed — "Virginia! the mother of statesmen!" Yes — of statesmen,
under whose iron rule nearly half a million of slaves are groaning on
the blood-stained soil of Virginia! One of these, (Mr. GHOLSON,) [131]
in his speech in the legislature of that State, Jan. 18, 1832, said: —

"It has always (perhaps erroneously) been considered, by steady and
old-fashioned people, that the owner of land had a reasonable right to its
annual profits; the owner of orchards, to their annual fruits; the owner of
brood mares, to their product; and *the owner of female slaves, to their increase.* We have not the fine-spun intelligence nor legal acumen to discuss
the technical distinctions drawn by gentlemen. The legal maxim of 'Partus
sequitur ventrem' [132] is coeval with the existence of the rights of property
itself, and is founded in wisdom and justice. It is on the justice and inviolability of this maxim, that the master foregoes the services of the female
slave; has her nursed and attended during the period of her gestation, and
raises the helpless and infant offspring. *The value of the property justifies
the expense*; and I do not hesitate to say, that *in its increase consists much
of our wealth.*"

Human flesh is now the great staple of Virginia. In the Legislature
of that State in 1832, THOMAS JEFFERSON RANDOLPH [133] declared that
Virginia had been converted into *"one grand menagerie, where men
are reared for the market like oxen for the shambles."* This same gentleman thus compared the foreign with the domestic traffic: — "The
trader (African) receives the slave, a stranger in aspect, language,
and manners, from the merchant who brought him from the interior.
But *here,* sir, individuals whom the master has known from infancy —
whom he has seen sporting in the innocent gambols of childhood —
who have been accustomed to look to him for protection, *he tears
from his mother's arms, and sells into a strange country, among a
strange people, subject to cruel taskmasters.* In my opinion, it is *much
worse.*"

Mr. C. F. MERCER [134] asserted in the Virginia Convention of 1829,[135]
"The tables of the natural growth of the slave population demonstrate,
when compared with the increase of its numbers in the Commonwealth for twenty years past, that an annual revenue of not less than

a million and a half of dollars is derived from the *exportation* of a part of this population." — *Debates, p.* 99.

The Richmond Enquirer [136] of Nov. 13, 1846, says — "Negroes have become the only *reliable staple* of the tobacco-growing sections of Virginia, *the only reliable means of liquidating debts, foreign and domestic*"! It was stated in the Virginia *Times*,[137] in 1836, that the number of slaves exported for sale 'the last twelve months,' amounted to FORTY THOUSAND; each slave averaging six hundred dollars and thus yielding a capital of TWENTY-FOUR MILLIONS"! (13.)

J. K. PAULDING,[138] the late Secretary of the Navy, gives the following picture of a scene he witnessed in Virginia: —

"The sun was shining out very hot, and in turning an angle of the road, we encountered the following group: first, a little cart drawn by one horse, in which five or six half naked black children were tumbled like pigs together. The cart had no covering, and they seemed to have been actually broiled to sleep. Behind the cart marched three black women, with head, neck and breasts uncovered, and without shoes or stockings; next came three men, bare-headed, half naked, and *chained together with an ox chain.* Last of all came a white man — a white man, Frank! — on horseback, carrying pistols in his belt, and who, as we passed him, had the impudence to look us in the face without blushing. I should like to have seen him hunted by bloodhounds. At a house where we stopped a little further on, we learned that he had bought these miserable beings in Maryland, and was marching them in this manner to some of the more Southern States. Shame on the State of Maryland! I say — and shame on the State of Virginia! and every State through which this wretched cavalcade was permitted to pass. Do they expect that such exhibitions will not dishonor them in the eyes of strangers, however they may be reconciled to them by education and habit?"

So much for "Virginia, the mother of statesmen"! — But this is not all. In the year 1831, an insurrection of slaves took place in Southampton, Virginia,[139] — like your own struggle in Hungary. What was the sequel you will learn by reading the following particulars: —

RICHMOND, (Va.) August 23, 1831.
An express reached the Governor this morning, informing him that an insurrection had broken out in Southampton, and that, by the last accounts, there are seventy whites massacred, and the militia retreating. The negroes are armed with muskets, scythes, axes, &c. &c. Our volunteers are marching to the scene of action. The Fayette Artillery and the Light Dragoons will leave here this evening for Southampton. ° ° Col. House, commanding at Fortress Monroe, at 6 o'clock this morning, embarked on board the steamer Hampton, with three companies and a piece of artillery for Suffolk. These troops were reinforced in the Roads by detachments from the U. S. ships Warren and Natchez, the whole amounting to nearly 300 men. ° ° ° Muskets, pistols, swords and ammunition, have been forwarded to Suffolk to-day, by Commodore Warrington, at the request of our civil authorities. ° ° °
We do not yet know the strength of the blacks, but think they must all perish within a few days.

AUGUST 25. Passengers by the Fayetteville stage say that, by the latest accounts, 120 negroes had been killed. ° ° Several prisoners were put to death forthwith by the enraged inhabitants. The celebrated Nelson, called by the blacks "General Nelson," Hercules or Hark, Gen. Moore and the other ringleaders, except Nat Turner, the prophet, had all been shot or taken prisoners. Turner calls himself General Turner. He pretends to be a Baptist preacher — is a great enthusiast. He stimulated his comrades to join with him, by declaring to them that he had been commissioned by Jesus Christ, and that he was acting under inspired direction in what he was going to do. He is represented, in a description of his person, to have "a scar on one of his temples; also one on the back of his neck, and a large knot on one of the bones of his right arm, near the wrist, produced by a heavy blow." ° ° ° The United States troops, at Old Point Comfort, have been ordered out to scour the Dismal Swamp, in which it is asserted from two to three thousand blacks are concealed.

A letter from Rev. G. W. Powell, under date of August 27, says that "there are thousands of troops in arms, searching in every direction, and many negroes are killed every day. *The exact number will never be ascertained.*" Eleven of the insurgents have already been tried, condemned, and executed. Thirty yet remain to be tried.

A young gentleman in Virginia, in a letter to his parents residing in New Hampshire, says — "It is truly revolting to learn, that, without trial — *in some instances, without the shadow of suspicion* — innocent colored persons were sacrificed without mercy to the excited passion and inconsiderate revenge of the whites in pursuit. One negro, I am informed, was sent on horseback, upon an errand to the next neighbor's, and commanded to go quick. While he was riding along rather fast, a company of soldiers, supposing him an enemy fleeing, let in a whole volley upon him, and killed both man and horse. Another was taken alive, and put to death by torture. *They burnt him with red hot irons — cut off his ears and nose — stabbed him — cut his ham-strings — stuck him like a hog — and, at last, cut off his head, and spiked it to the whipping post,* for a spectacle and a warning to the other negroes."

In riding in the stage from Richmond to Fredericksburg, a passenger by the name of Smith, direct from the seat of the insurrection, stated that the blacks who were taken prisoners were killed in the most barbarous manner. *Their noses and ears were cut off, the flesh of their cheeks cut out, their jaws broken asunder, and then set up as a mark to shoot at!* If a black was found out of doors, after dark, without a pass, he was immediately shot down.

WILMINGTON, N. C., Sept. 20. We have been under a very great excitement here, in consequence of an expected insurrection among our blacks. It appears, on investigation, that the plot was much deeper laid than we anticipated. ° ° ° The leaders in this plot have all been executed — Nimrod, Dan, Prince and Abraham were all shot this morning, at 6 o'clock, on Gallows Hill, and *their heads are now sticking on poles at the four corners of the town.*

SEPT. 28. Three ringleaders of the late diabolical conspiracy were executed at Onslow Court House, on Friday evening last, 23d inst, *by the people.*

It is said that four negroes who were suspected to be in the plot *were flogged to make them confess, and then hung upon their confessions!*

JERUSALEM, (Va.) Oct 31. Last night, about 9 o'clock, the news reached our little village that General Nat was taken alive. He reached this place, well guarded, to-day, at a quarter after 1 o'clock, and was committed to prison. During two hours close examination, he evinced great intelligence and much shrewdness of intellect, answering every question clearly and distinctly, and without confusion or prevarication. He seems to labor under as perfect a state of fanatical delusion (!) as ever wretched man suffered. He does not hesitate to say, that, even now, *he thinks he was right*, but admits he may possibly have been deceived. Nevertheless, he seems of the opinion, that if his time were to go over again, *he must necessarily act in the same way.*

A correspondent of the Richmond Whig says — "Nat had for some time thought closely on this subject; for I have in my possession some papers given up by his wife, *under the lash.*"

We learn, says the Petersburg *Intelligencer*, by a gentleman from Southampton, that the fanatical murderer, Nat Turner, was executed, according to his sentence, at Jerusalem, (14) on Friday last, about 1 o'clock. He exhibited the utmost composure throughout the whole ceremony; and although assured that he might, if he thought proper, address the immense crowd assembled on the occasion, declined availing himself of the privilege, and told the sheriff, in a firm voice, that he was ready. *Not a limb or a muscle was observed to move.*"

And this, O KOSSUTH, in "Virginia, the mother of statesmen" — in "the glorious republic of the United States, whose millions of inhabitants are all attached with warm feelings to the principles of liberty, with no tyrants among them"! What can equal it, in point of atrocity and horror, in the history of the Hungarian struggle with Austria and Russia combined? And where has there appeared a more heroic spirit than that of NATHANIEL TURNER, the unfortunate but indomitable slave leader in the Southampton insurrection? Is the State, is the nation, that put him to an ignominious death, the State or nation to rally in behalf of Hungary, or to arraign the Autocrat of Russia for his tyranny?

To complete this "assemblage of horrors," we present for your contemplation a few other illustrations of American slavery.

In the summer of 1845, a number of slaves attempted to escape from Maryland, that they might find liberty and protection under the British flag in Canada. If you would learn their fate, read the following statement communicated to the New York *Herald*: —

BALTIMORE, July 12, 1845.
I learn from a gentleman who was present at the arrest of a gang of runaway negroes near Rockville, Maryland, that they were treated in the most brutal manner by their captors. When surrounded by the Rockville volun-

teers, they were commanded to surrender, and because one out of forty showed a determination to resist, a whole volley of balls from rifles and pistols was poured indiscriminately among them. Those wounded are Ferdinand, slave of Wm. Browner, a ball in the left side of his neck, which will probably prove fatal; James, slave of Edwin Jones, rifle ball in his back, which will cripple him for life; David, a slave of John Hamet, part of his cheek torn away, and a ball in his back; David, another slave of John Hamet, his right arm completely shattered with a musket ball; James, a slave of Barnes' estate, perfectly riddled with balls in his side and neck, and part of his cheek torn away; Mark, do., a pistol ball in the back of his neck; James Gray, belonging to Chas. Rye, severely wounded on the side of his face; Lewis Dey, a slave of Colonel Miller, struck with a ball on the side of his face; Henry, slave of General Chapman, a ball in his back. Had their arms been loaded with fine shot, or even a little coarse salt, it would have answered every purpose; but instead of that, the deadly bullet must be used, and aim taken in every instance, as will be seen by the direction of the shot, at the head and shoulders, instead of the extremities. Some of them, on their return, even regretted that they "could not make the damn niggers resist, so that they might have had the pleasure of shooting them all down." They were all marched with ox chains, handcuffs, &c., and driven through Washington yesterday, on their way to their homes, more like a drove of hogs than human beings. In less than a week, those that escaped the balls of their captors will be on their way to the cotton fields of Louisiana, while some at least of the wounded will die of neglect.

The Natchez *Free Trader* [140] gives an account of the arrest of a fugitive negro boy, named Joseph, who confessed (probably under the lash) to having committed various revolting crimes, including murder; after which, it was deliberately resolved that THE NEGRO SHOULD BE BURNED ALIVE! The terrible scene is thus described: —

"The body was taken and chained to a tree immediately on the banks of the Mississippi, on what is called Union Point. Fagots were then collected and piled around him, to which he appeared quite indifferent. When the work was completed, he was asked what he had to say. He then warned all to take example by him, and asked the prayers of all around; he then called for a drink of water, which was handed to him; he drank it, and said: 'Now set fire — I am ready to go in peace!' The torches were lighted, and placed in the pile, which soon ignited. He watched unmoved the curling flame that grew, until it began to entwine itself around and feed upon his body; then he sent forth cries of agony painful to the ear, begging some one to blow his brains out; at the same time surging with almost superhuman strength, until the staple with which the chain was fastened to the tree (not being well secured) drew out, and he leaped from the burning pile. At that moment the sharp ringing of several rifles was heard: the body of the negro fell a corpse on the ground. He was picked up by some two or three, and again thrown into the fire, and consumed — not a vestige remaining to show that such a being ever existed."

Here is another case of human burning, as detailed in the New Orleans *Bulletin*: — [141]

ANOTHER NEGRO BURNED. — We learn from the clerk of the Highlander, that while wooding a short distance below the mouth of Red River, they were invited to stop a short time, and see another negro burned. They were informed that the fellow who was prepared for the exhibition was another of the gang recently mentioned as having committed enormities, and fled to the swamp — one of whom was burnt, as already published. The last fellow had killed a man, and carried off two women, one of whom he had violated; and for this they had him well chained, and the fagots ready, with a view of giving him a foretaste of his inevitable, ultimate end.

Take a third and final case, though the number might be indefinitely extended: —

HORRIBLE. — A correspondent of the Cincinnati *Herald* relates the following occurrence, but it seems scarcely credible. It is said to have occurred near Oakland Cottage, Mississippi: "A slaveholder, a short time previous to his death, made provisions for the liberation of his slaves. Those who were entrusted with the execution of his designs failing or refusing to carry out his last will and testament concerning the slaves, the latter became restive and impatient to enjoy their long looked for boon. At length, disappointment, expecting to be sold, and incensed at their oppressors, they set fire to the overseer's dwelling, and burnt it to the ground. A little child, which they were unable to rescue, was consumed in the flames. The slaves, eight or nine in number, were taken, and two of them hung on the spot. The others were taken into an old log-house, and chained to the floor. The house was then set on fire, and they were, by a slow fire, burned to death, in a most shocking manner, while the air was rent with their unavailing shrieks and screams."

Read the following heart-rending narrative, as given by Isaac Johnson and his wife, who have just escaped from the South, and are now in Canada. It is taken from the *Voice of the Fugitive*: — [142]

They were held as property in the State of Mississippi, a short time since, and were the parents of an only child, which was about thirteen months old. A few days before they started on the hazardous voyage to Canada, the mother learned that she was sold to a slave trader, who intended to separate her from her beloved child and husband, never more to see them on this earth. But they resolved on running away to Canada, with their child, or perish by the way. They succeeded in crossing over the line into what is called a free State, (Indiana,) with their child, where they were chased until their babe was sacrificed on the bloody altar of Slavery. On seeing that they were closely pursued, they broke and ran to a corn field — the wife first got over the fence, and the husband handed her the child, with which she ran as fast as she could. She heard the pursuer saying "stop, stop, or I will shoot you down;" and before she had proceeded far, a gun was fired, and her child was shot dead from her back — and the ball, which passed through the child's neck, cut off one corner of the mother's ear. At this moment the poor mother fell down with her lifeless babe, when she was rushed upon by two white men, who commenced trying to bind her with ropes; but when she cried for help, her husband came to her relief — the contest was desperate for a few moments; the wife and husband both fought until they brought down one of the party, and his companion fled and left him. The husband and wife, fearing that they would soon be surrounded and overpowered, and seeing that their little one was dead, and that they could do it no good, reluctantly left it lying by the villain who shot it. Fortunately for them, they soon found a depot of the underground railroad, and one of the conductors thereof was kind enough to put on an extra train, which soon landed them on a soil where "no slave can breathe." We deeply sympathize with them in their bereavement, while we think that it would be far better that ten thousand children should perish by the wayside, than for one to be taken back into Southern slavery.

After reading an occurrence like this, indulge once more (if you can) in your encomiums upon "this glorious country, which Providence has selected to be the pillar of freedom, as it is already the asylum to oppressed humanity"!

Sir, you have signified your intention to visit Boston, and doubtless feel an electric thrill at the thought of standing in Faneuil Hall, and by the granite shaft of Bunker Hill. What will you say, what can you say, in view of a recital like the following, published in the New York *Evangelist?* [143]

A Scene in Boston. — A colored girl eighteen years of age, a few years ago, escaped from slavery at the South. Through scenes of adventure and peril, almost more strange than fiction can create, she found her way to Boston. She obtained employment, secured friends, and became a consistent member of a Methodist Church. She became interested in a very worthy young man, of her own complexion, who was a member of the same church. They were soon married. Their home, though humble, was the abode of piety and contentment. Industrious, temperate and frugal, all their wants were supplied. Seven years passed away. They had two little boys, one six and the other four years of age. These children, the sons of a free father, but of a mother who had been a slave, by the laws of our Southern States, were doomed to their mother's fate. These Boston boys, born beneath the shadow of Faneuil Hall, the sons of a free citizen of Boston, and educated in the Boston free schools, were by the compromises of the Constitution admitted to be slaves, the property of a South Carolinian planter. The Boston father had no right to his own sons. The law, however, had long been considered a dead letter. The Christian mother, as she morning and evening bowed with her children in prayer, felt that they were safe from the slave-hunter, surrounded as they were by the churches, the schools, and the free institutions of Massachusetts.

The Fugitive Slave Law was enacted. It revived the hopes of the slave-owners. A young, healthy, energetic mother, with two fine boys, was a rich prize. She would make an excellent breeder. Good men began to say, "We must enforce this law; it is one of the compromises of the Constitution." Christian ministers began to preach, "The voice of the law is the voice of God. There is no higher rule of duty. We must send back the fugitive and her children, even though we take our sister from the sacramental table of our common Saviour."

The poor woman was panic-stricken. Her friends gathered around her, and trembled for her. Her husband was absent from home, a seaman on board one of our Liverpool packets. She was afraid to go out of doors, lest one from the South should see her, and recognize her. One day, as she was going to the grocery for some provisions, her quick and anxious eye caught a glimpse of a man prowling around, whom she immediately recognized as from the vicinity of her old home of slavery. Almost fainting with terror, she hastened home, and taking her two children by the hand, fled to the house of a friend. She and her trembling children were hid in the garret. In less than one hour after her escape, the officer, with a writ, came for her arrest.

It was a dark and stormy day. The rain, freezing as it fell, swept in floods through the streets of Boston. Night came, cold, black, and tempestuous. At midnight her friends took her in a hack, and conveyed her, with her children, to the house of her pastor. A prayer meeting had been appointed there, at that hour, in behalf of their suffering sister. A small group of stricken hearts were there assembled. They knelt in prayer. The poor mother, thus hunted from her home, her husband far away, sobbed, in the bitterness of her anguish, as though her heart would break. Her little children, trembling before a doom, the enormity of which they were incapable of appreciating, cried loudly and uncontrollably. The humble minister caught the contagion. His voice became inarticulate through emotion. Bowing his head, he ceased to pray, and yielded himself to the sobbings of sympathy and grief. The floods of anguish were unloosed. Groanings and lamentations filled the room. No one could pray. Before the Lord they could only weep. Other fugitives were there, trembling in view of a doom more dreadful to them than death.

After an hour of weeping, for the voice of prayer had passed away into the sublimity of unutterable anguish, they took this Christian mother and her children, in a hack, and conveyed them to one of the Cunard steamers, which fortunately was to sail for Halifax the next day. They took them in the gloom of midnight, through the tempest-swept streets, lest the slave-hunter should meet them. Her brethren and sisters of the church raised a little money from their scanty means to pay her passage, and to save her, for a few days, from starving, after her first arrival in the cold land of strangers. Her husband soon returned to Boston to find his home desolate, his wife and his children exiles in a foreign land. These facts need no word painting. I think that this narrative may be relied upon as accurate. I received the facts from the lips of one, a member of the church, who was present at that midnight "weeping meeting," before the Lord. Such is slavery in Boston, in the year 1852. Shade of Calhoun! Has the North nothing to do with slavery?

John S. C. Abbot.[144]

Brunswick, Me., Jan., 1852.

Such, sir, are the deeds perpetrated and legalized in the land to which you have come, to ask its sympathy and aid in behalf of oppressed Hungarians! Whether you have not mistaken your mission, and sullied your character, in so doing, let a candid world decide. Whatever may be the popularity of the hour, and however you may strive to propitiate the bloody power of Slavery to accomplish the end in view, your self-abasement will be in vain. Hungary has nothing to hope or expect from slaveholding America.

In behalf of the American Anti-Slavery Society,

WM. LLOYD GARRISON, *President.*

SYDNEY HOWARD GAY,　　　*Secretaries.*
WENDELL PHILLIPS,

NOTES

[These notes, (1) to (14), are Garrison's]

(1) See Appendix.[145]

(2 To show what it is in the power of every slaveholder to do with impunity, and how literal is the language of the prophet as applied to Southern slaveholding atrocities, read the following authentic narrative from the pen of the Rev. WILLIAM DICKEY,[146] a man of undoubted veracity, who was well acquainted with the circumstances he describes: —

"In the county of Livingston, Ky., near the mouth of Cumberland, lived Lilburn Lewis, a sister's son of the venerable Jefferson. He, 'who suckled at fair Freedom's breast,' was the wealthy owner of a considerable number of slaves, whom he drove constantly, fed sparingly, and lashed severely. The consequence was, they would run away. This must have given, to a man of spirit and a man of business, great anxieties until he found them, or until they had starved out, and returned. Among the rest was an ill grown boy about seventeen, who, having just returned from a skulking spell, was sent to the spring for water, and in returning let fall an elegant pitcher. It was dashed to shivers upon the rocks. This was the occasion. It was night, and the slaves all at home. The master had them collected into the most roomy negro-house, and a rousing fire made. When the door was secured, that none might escape, either through fear of him or sympathy with George, he opened the design of the interview, namely, that they might be effectually taught to stay at home and obey his orders. All things being now in train, he called up George, who approached his master with the most unreserved submission. He bound him with cords, and by the assistance of his younger brother, laid him on a broad bench or meat block. He now proceeded to chop off George by the ankles! It was with the broad axe! In vain did the unhappy victim scream and roar! He was completely in his master's power. Not a hand amongst so many durst interfere. Casting the feet into the fire, he lectured them at some length. He chopped him off below the knees! George roaring out, and praying his master to BEGIN AT THE OTHER END! He admonished them again, throwing the legs into

181

the fire! Then above the knees, tossing the joints into the fire! He again lectured them at leisure. The next stroke severed the thighs from the body. These were also committed to the flames. And so off the arms, head and trunk, until all was in the fire! Still protracting the intervals with lectures, and threatenings of like punishment, in case of disobedience, and running away, or disclosure of this tragedy. Nothing now remained but to consume the flesh and bones; and for this purpose, the fire was briskly stirred, until two hours after midnight; when, as though the earth would cover out of sight the nefarious scene, and as though the great Master in heaven would put a mark of displeasure upon such monstrous cruelty, a sudden and surprising shock of earthquake overturned the coarse and heavy black wall, composed of rock and clay, which completely covered the fire, and the remains of George. This put an end to the amusements of the evening. The negroes were now permitted to disperse, with charges to keep this matter among themselves, and never to whisper it in the neighborhood, under the penalty of a like punishment. When he retired, the lady exclaimed, 'O! Mr. Lewis, where have you been, and what have you done!' She had heard a strange pounding, and dreadful screams, and had smelled something like fresh meat burning! He said that he had never enjoyed himself at a ball so well as he had enjoyed himself that evening.

"Sure there are bolts, red with no common wrath, to blast the man.

— "Bloomingsburg, Oct. 8, 1824.   WILLIAM DICKEY."

(3) In proof that this is not only figuratively but literally true in this country, read the following statement of the Rev. J. CABLE,[147] made before the General Assembly of the Presbyterian Church: —

"What shocked me more than any thing else was, the church engaged in this jobbing of slaves. The college church which I attended, and which was attended by all the students of Hamden Sydney College and Union Theological Seminary, held slaves enough to pay their pastor, Mr. Stanton, ONE THOUSAND DOLLARS a year, of which the church members did not pay a cent, (so I understood it.) The slaves, who had been left to the church by some pious mother in Israel, had increased so as to be a large and still increasing fund. These were hired out on Christmas day of each year, the day in which they celebrate the birth of our blessed Saviour, to the highest bidder.

"There are four other churches near the College Church, that were in the same situation with this, when I was in that country, that supported the pastor, in whole or in part, in the same way, viz.: Cumberland Church, John Kirkpatrick, pastor; Briny Church, William Plummer, pastor, (since Dr. P. of Richmond;) Buffalo Church, Mr. Cochran, pastor; Pisga Church, near the peaks of Otter, J. Mitchell, pastor."

The following advertisement is from the Charleston, S. C., Courier, of Feb. 12, 1832: —

"FIELD NEGROES.

"By Thomas Gadsden. On Tuesday, the 17th inst., will be sold, at the North of the Exchange, at 10 o'clock, A.M., a prime gang of

TEN NEGROES,

accustomed to the culture of cotton and provisions, belonging to the Independent Church, in Christ's Church Parish.

"Feb. 6th."

In 1823, the Rev. Dr. Furman,[148] of South Carolina, addressed a lengthy communication to the Governor of that State, expressing the sentiments of the Baptist Church and clergy on the subject of slavery. This brief extract contains the essence of the whole: —

"The right of holding slaves is clearly established in the Holy Scriptures, both by precept and example."

Not long after, Dr. Furman died. His legal representatives thus advertised his property: —

"NOTICE.

"On the first Monday of February next, will be put up at *public auction*, before the *court house*, the *following property*, belonging to the estate of the late REV. FURMAN, viz.: —

"A plantation or tract of land, on and in the Wataree Swamp. A tract of the first quality of fine land, on the waters of Black River. A lot of land in the town of Camden. A LIBRARY of a miscellaneous character, CHIEFLY THEOLOGICAL.

27 NEGROES,

some of them very prime. Two mules, one horse, and an old wagon."

The Savannah, Ga., Republican of the 13th of March, 1845, contains an advertisement, one item of which is as follows: —

"Also, at the same time and place, the following negro slaves, to wit: Charles, Peggy, Antonnette, Davy, September, Maria, Jenny, and Isaac — levied on as property of Henry T. Hall, to satisfy a mortgage fi. fia. issued out of McIntosh Superior Court, in favor of the Board of Directors of the *Theological Seminary of the Synod of South Carolina and Georgia,* vs. said Henry T. Hall. Conditions, cash.

"C. O'NEAL,
"Deputy Sheriff, M. C."

(4) See the accounts in Southern newspapers of *"a curious mode of punishment"* recently introduced, called "CAT-HAULING." The victim is stretched upon his face, and a cat, thrown upon his bare shoul-

ders, is dragged to the bottom of the back. This is continued till the body is "lacerated."

"The Vicksburg (Miss.) Register [149] says, that Mr. Earl, one of the victims of mobocracy in Mississippi, was tortured a whole night to elicit confession. The brutal and hellish tormentors laid Mr. Earl upon his back, and drew a cat tail foremost across his body!!! He hung himself soon after in jail."

See also the accounts of the Mississippi murders given by a correspondent in the Charleston Courier,[150] dating his letter Tyger (how appropriate!) Bayou, Madison County, Miss. The following is an extract: — "Andrew Boyd, a conspirator, was required by the Committee of Safety, and Mr. Dickerson, Hiram Reynolds and Hiram Perkins (since killed) were ordered to arrest him. They discovered he was flying, and immediately commenced the pursuit, with a pack of TRAINED HOUNDS. He miraculously effected his deliverance from his pursuers, after swimming Big Black River, and running through canebrakes and swamps until night-fall, when the party called off THE DOGS. Early next morning they renewed the chase, and started Boyd one mile from whence they had called off the dogs. But he effected his escape on horse, (fortune throwing one in his way,) *the hounds* not being accustomed to that training after he quit the bush."

(5) Mrs. MARIA WESTON CHAPMAN, of Boston.

(6) "Kossuth has sacrificed the cause of liberty itself. He has consented to praise a nation whose liberty is a sham. He has consented to praise the nation which tramples Mexico under foot. He has consented to praise her, that he might save Hungary. Then rate him at his right price. The freedom of twelve millions bought the silence of Louis Kossuth for a year. A world in the scale never bought the silence of O'Connell or Lafayette for a moment. That is just the difference between him and them. O'Connell, (I was told the anecdote by Sir Thomas Fowell Buxton,) [151] in 1829, after his election to the House of Commons, was called upon by the West India interest, some fifty or sixty strong, who said, "O'Connell, you have been accustomed to act with Clarkson and Wilberforce, Lushington [152] and Brougham,[153] to speak on the platform of Freemasons' Hall, and advocate what is called the abolition cause. Mark this! If you will break loose from these associates, if you will close your mouth on the slave question, you may reckon on our undivided support on Irish matters. Whenever your country's claims come up, you shall be sure of fifty votes on your side." "No!" said O'Connell, "let God care for Ireland; I will never shut my mouth on the slave question to save her!" (Loud cheers.) He stood with eight millions whom he loved; he stood with

a peasantry at his back, meted out and trodden under foot as cruelly as the Magyar; he stood with those behind him, who had been trampled under the horses' feet of the British soldiery in 1782 and 1801; he knew the poverty and wretchedness, he knew the oppressions under which the Irish groaned; but never, for a moment, would he consent to lift Ireland — whose woes, we may well suppose, weighed heavily on the heart of her greatest son — by the sacrifice of the freedom of any other portion of the race. "When," said the friend who told me this anecdote, in conclusion, "when there were no more than two or three of us in the House of Commons, O'Connell would leave any court or any meeting to be present at the division, and vote on our side." That is the type of a man who tries, by its proper standard, the claim of all classes upon his sympathy. He did for Ireland all that God had enabled him to do; but there was one thing which God had not called upon him to do, and that was, to speak a falsehood or to belie his convictions. He did not undertake to serve his country by being silent when he knew he ought to speak, or speak in language that should convey a false impression to his hearers." — *Speech of Wendell Phillips, Esq., at the National Anti-Slavery Bazaar.*

(7) Declaration of Anti-Slavery Sentiments.[154]

(8) "The old slave laws of Virginia and Maryland, marked by the barbarity of other days, form *by Act of Congress* the slave code of the District. Of this code, a single sample will suffice. A slave convicted of setting fire to a building *shall have his head cut off, and his body divided into quarters, and the parts set up in the most public places!*" — JUDGE JAY.[155]

(9) By the report of the committee on the District of Columbia, in 1829, it appears that, in three years, 179 human beings were, *by the authority of the Federal Government,* arrested in *one* county of the District, and committed to prison on no allegation of crime, but merely on suspicion of being fugitive slaves! "The Marshal of the United States," says Judge Jay, "after deciding on the liberty or bondage of his prisoners, is allowed to take his fees in human flesh, and the condemned becomes the *property* of the very judge who sentenced him to servitude, and who carries him into the market, there to make out of him as much money as he can! [156] * * * Thus to this judge the law offers a high and tempting bribe to sell men he knows to be free, and thus he becomes a manufacturer of slaves!" [157] In one instance, at least, Mr. Ringgold's speculations appear not to have been very productive, having sold the victim for only $20, while his jail fees amounted to $84.82. No reason is assigned for this nominal price.

Very probably, it was a case similar to the one described by the Hon. Charles Miner, in his speech on the floor of the House of Representatives, in 1829.[158] "In August, 1821," said Mr. M., "a black man was taken up, and imprisoned as a runaway. He was kept confined until October, 1822, four hundred and five days. In this time, vermin, disease and misery had deprived him of the use of his limbs. He was rendered a cripple for life, and finally discharged, *as no one would buy him.*

(10) "One of the peculiar atrocities of this resolution is, that it wrests from every member of the House his constitutional right to *propose* such measures for the government of the District as justice and humanity may require. Slaves might be burned alive in the streets of the Capital; the slavers might be crowded to suffocation with human victims; every conceivable cruelty might be practised, and no one member of the local legislature could be permitted to propose even a committee of inquiry, 'relating in any way, or to any extent whatever, to the subject of slavery.'" — JUDGE JAY.

(11) See the Annual Reports of the American Colonization Society, and its official organ, the *African Repository.*

(12) This poor man stated to Prof. H., that "Henry Clay, last summer, sold ten slaves for the Southern market — and the summer before, one. Also, that summer before last, one of his slaves received an infliction of *four hundred lashes* — and a short time after, he hung himself."

(13) "A writer in the New Orleans *Argus,*[159] Sept. 1830, in an article on the culture of the sugar cane, says — 'The loss by death in bringing slaves from a northern climate, which our planters are under the necessity of doing, is not less than twenty-five per cent'!! Our tables prove the same thing. Of the 40,000 slaves annually carried South, only 29,101 are found to survive; — *a greater sacrifice of life than that caused by the middle passage*'! — [*Slavery and the Constitution, by William I. Bowitch.*] [160]

(14) "Jerusalem, where our Lord was crucified."

Printed Pamphlet: Houghton Library, Harvard College.

The pamphlet is entitled *Letter to Louis Kossuth, Concerning Freedom and Slavery in the United States. In Behalf of the American Anti-Slavery Society* (Boston, R. F. Wallcut, 1852), 112 pp. A shorter and slightly different version of the letter appeared in *The Liberator*, February 20, 1852. It occupied all of the first and last pages of the paper. It lacks the footnotes and the Appendix which accompanied the printed pamphlet. An incomplete manuscript of the letter, in Garrison's writing, varying slightly from the printed versions, is to be found in the Merrill Collection of Garrison Papers, Wichita State University Library.

Life, III, 353, notes that "This document, put forth in the name and with the sanction of the American Anti-Slavery Society, was drafted and compiled by its President; and it and the 'Thoughts on Colonization' constitute what may properly be called the 'Works of Garrison,' as distinguished from his journalistic writings or the two collections of his prose and verse."

Garrison's footnote numbers are in parentheses. All others are the editor's.

Louis Kossuth (1802–1894) was one of the leaders of the Hungarian revolution of March 1848. He became governor of the newly established Hungarian republic in April 1849, but, with the reestablishment of Austrian rule as a result of Russian intervention, he was forced to flee to Turkey several months later. In the meanwhile, the Hungarian revolution had evoked great sympathy and support in the United States, with Kossuth emerging as a national hero. On March 3, 1851, President Millard Fillmore approved a joint resolution of Congress in support of Kossuth and offering him a warship of the Mediterranean squadron to bring him from Turkey, where he had been confined and had faced the possibility of being extradited to Russia, to a safe haven. He embarked on an American man-of-war in September 1851, was brought to England where he remained for several weeks, and then came to the United States, arriving in New York on December 4, 1851. He returned to England in the spring of 1852 and lived there for eight years. Thereafter, he lived in Italy, dying in Turin on March 20, 1894. (*Life*, III, 340–344.)

Kossuth aroused the ire of many abolitionists, especially the Garrisonians, by his failure to issue any condemnation of slavery and by his explicit statement, made about a week after his arrival in New York, that he would not "meddle" in the domestic concerns of the United States. Since the statement received a great deal of attention in the press, we reprint it in its entirety.

"Having come to the United States to avail myself, for the cause of my country, of the sympathy which I had reason to believe existed in the heart of the nation, I found it my duty to declare, in the first moments of my arrival, that it is my mission to plead the independence of Hungary, and the liberty of the European Continent, before the great Republic of the United States. My principle in this respect is, that every nation has the sovereign right to dispose of its own domestic affairs, without any foreign interference; that I, therefore, shall not meddle with any domestic concerns of the United States, and that I expect it from all the friends of my cause, not to do anything in respect to myself, that could throw difficulties in my way, and, while expressing sympathy for the cause, would injure it.

"It is with regret that I must feel the necessity of again making that appeal to the public opinion of this country, and particularly to those who profess themselves to be the friends of my cause, to give one proof of their sympathy by avoiding every step which might entangle me in difficulties in respect to that rule which I have adopted, and which I again declare to be my leading principle, viz: not to mix, and not to be mixed up with whatever domestic concerns or party questions.

L. KOSSUTH.

"New York, Dec. 12, 1851."

It should be noted, however, that about three years later, *The Liberator*, May 11, 1855, indicated that Kossuth had finally begun to speak out against slavery. In a news item entitled "Kossuth Has Changed His Tune," it wrote as follows:

"Kossuth is speaking out more decidedly upon American slavery than he once did. While he had hopes of enlisting this nation under Hungary's banner, he was remarkably silent respecting the oppression of three millions of negroes in this sham-republic. But time has shown him that such a republic cannot afford to aid strangers to gain their liberties, while fostering slavery at home. In a recent letter to a gentleman residing in New York, Kossuth says:

"'O, if your nation, with all the light she has in herself, would but elevate herself for one moment to the moral height of true Republican principles; and with a noble resolution, cast away that curse from your future, and that stain from your escutcheon, *Slavery*, — how different would be the standing of America in a few years! Her brightness would efface the brightest page of mankind's history; but with that incubus paralyzing the Union, nothing ever can be expected, but convulsion at home, disrespect abroad, and a speedy decay of a national life, dying without having come of age.

" '*Hoc fonte derivata clades* — everything which is deplorable dates from that source. No foreign power should be admitted to meddle with the domestic affairs of any country; but a great, enlightened — and, above all, a Republican nation should know by herself to be faithful to right — to do what is just, and to cure the cancer gnawing on her own heart. Where the difficulties are great, there the glory of overcoming them is the greater. Small matters may be done by small men, and small nations. It is worthy of great nations to do great things. Besides, freemen should never think it a hard task to be just, or else sooner or later they will cease to be free.' "

See also the comments by Elizabeth Pease Nichol quoted in *Elizabeth Pease Nichol*, by Anna M. Stoddart (London and New York, 1899), pp. 201–202.

1. Kossuth, at a reception for him by the city authorities of New York, upon his landing at Castle Garden, in replying to the official greeting of the mayor of New York City, referred to himself as "a plain, poor, penniless exile." (*The Liberator*, December 19, 1851.) In a later address at a New York banquet he described himself as "a poor, persecuted, penniless exile." (*Ibid.*)

2. This quotation combines several statements by Kossuth, uttered on different occasions. The opening lines, until "call me," were said in a speech at Birmingham, England, on November 12, 1851. The words "liberty, being" to "heart with heart," are from a speech delivered in London, November 13, 1851. (*Authentic Life of His Excellency Louis Kossuth, Governor of Hungary . . . With a Full Report of his Speeches Delivered in England . . .*, London, 1851, pp. 113, 120.) The words from "to me life" until "benefit of humanity" were expressed in a speech in Southampton, England, on October 23, 1851. (P. C. Headley, *The Life of Louis Kossuth, Governor of Hungary . . .*, Auburn, 1852, p. 233.)

3. Shakespeare, *Hamlet*, III, iv, 62.

4. Shakespeare, *Coriolanus*, III, i, 254.

5. Psalms 115:5–6; Mark 8:18.

6. The reference is to the Fugitive Slave Law of 1850 and the federal efforts to enforce it.

7. In April 1850 and August 1851, there were landings on Cuban soil by bands of 750 and 450 men respectively, mostly southerners, who had been recruited by an adventurous Venezuelan, Narciso Lopez, who had once held important offices in Spain and Cuba. Their purpose was to create revolts, sever Cuba from Spain, and ultimately attach it to the United States. As Samuel Flag Bemis notes, Lopez "became the instrument of revolt in Cuba and the tool of the slavery expansionists in the United States." Both efforts failed. In the second, Lopez was publicly garroted in Havana, fifty others were caught and summarily shot, while 135 were imprisoned in Spain but eventually released following United States intercession. (Samuel Flag Bemis, *A Diplomatic History of the United States*, 4th ed., New York, 1955, pp. 315–322.)

8. For several years after the Mexican War, there were numerous filibustering expeditions organized in Texas and California, against Mexican territory. Samuel F. Bemis notes: "Santa Anna had inserted into the original text of the Gadsden Treaty an article for the suppression of filibusters; but the Senate significantly threw it out, and the treaty was ratified by both parties without it. The Whig Administration had made conscientious efforts to restrain the filibustering expeditions organizing in Texas and California, but found it difficult to secure convictions from local juries, or indeed to prevent the departure of some of the expeditions. In the Pierce Administration that followed, Jefferson Davis as Secretary of War

made only perfunctory efforts to stop the filibusters. Until the outbreak of the American Civil War . . . the border was a scene of chronic turbulence, filibustering, raiding, robbing and shooting." (Bemis, *Diplomatic History*, p. 326.)

9. John Greenleaf Whittier, stanza 3 of "Stanzas," *Poems* (Boston, 1856), p. 134.

10.   "Easy is the descent to Avernus . . .
                       but to retrace thy steps . . .
                       This is the task, this is the toil."
Vergil, *Aeneid*, Book VI, lines 126–130. The quotation is incomplete.

11. This was the Thirty-first Congress. Henry Clay's Compromise Resolutions, which included the Fugitive Slave Act as part of what came to be called the Compromise of 1850, were introduced in January 1850 and were signed into law by Millard Fillmore on September 18, 1850.

12. *Life* notes the following attempts in Great Britain to inform Kossuth of American slavery: "W. H. Ashurst wrote to Mr. Garrison on October 13, 1851, that a common friend, of weight, had put in his hands for Kossuth a packet describing 'with faithfulness and correctness the true state of the slave question in the States.' On November 4, James Haughton sent through Charles Gilpin a letter to Kossuth admonishing him not to go to America, and to give to the world his reasons for staying away. On November 17, Richard Webb, forwarding his mite for the Hungarian fund to the Mayor of Southampton, desired him to lay before Kossuth considerations why, in visiting America, he should not forfeit the esteem of European admirers by ignoring the existence of slavery. The Edinburgh Ladies' Emancipation Society, on November 18, and the Glasgow anti-slavery societies forwarded addresses of a like tenor. A committee of the British and Foreign Anti-Slavery Society in person ensured the conveyance to Kossuth of truthful warning. Copies of the Fugitive Slave Law and of Weld's 'Slavery as It Is' were placed in his hands. To all this intelligence he paid no heed." (III, 343–344.)

13. Dr. Augustus Sidney Doane (1808–1852), a physician who was then Commissioner of Health at Staten Island, had been delegated by the Kossuth reception committee of the Common Council of New York City to receive and entertain Kossuth and his family until arrangements were made for the official reception by the city. When Kossuth's American steamer, the *Humboldt*, arrived in New York late Thursday night, December 4, 1851, Dr. Doane hurried aboard and made a short welcoming address, to which Kossuth replied briefly. (*Report of the Special Committee Appointed by the Common Council of the City of New York, to Make Arrangements for the Reception of Gov. Louis Kossuth, the Distinguished Hungarian Patriot*, New York, 1852, pp. 20–24.) Kossuth's reply to Dr. Doane, which is printed in full in the *Report*, differs in much of its wording from Garrison's quotation, which may have been taken from newspaper accounts.

14. Winfield Scott (1786–1866) became commander-in-chief of the United States Army in 1841 and took command of the United States Army in Mexico in 1847. In a period of about six months he conquered Mexico, finally entering Mexico City, the capital of Mexico, on September 14, 1847. Santa Anna, then provisional president and generalissimo of the Mexican Army, who had been in Mexico City, fled, finally leaving the country and going to Jamaica, West Indies, in April 1848. In 1852, Scott was defeated as the Whig candidate for President by Franklin Pierce. Although still in command of the army at the outbreak of the Civil War, he retired in October, 1861. (Bemis, *Diplomatic History*, pp. 241–243.)

15. Antonio Lopez de Santa Anna (1795–1876), Mexican political-military leader, was President of Mexico in 1832–1835, 1841–1844, and 1846–1847. Despite his defeat and escape during the Mexican War, he reappeared as President and dictator in 1853–1855, but died in obscurity.

16. Zachary Taylor gained a brilliant victory over Santa Anna at Buena Vista in February 1847, which made him a national hero. He died before completing his term of office as President.

17. Except for one or two words Garrison's quotation agrees with the text in

Report, pp. 27–33. The address was delivered at Staten Island on December 5, 1851.

18. Thomas Ruffin (1787–1870) was judge of the Supreme Court of North Carolina in 1816–1818, was reelected in 1825, and was Chief Justice of the state Supreme Court from 1825 to 1852, and again from 1856 to 1858.

19. Robert J. Breckenridge (1800–1871), lawyer, legislator, and clergyman, practiced law in Kentucky for eight years, beginning in 1823; was a member of the state legislature for the succeeding four years; and after studying theology privately was ordained a minister in 1832. He was pastor of the Second Presbyterian Church of Baltimore, Maryland, for thirteen years. He was president of Jefferson College, Pennsylvania, from 1845 to 1847, then moved to Lexington, Kentucky, where he was pastor of the First Presbyterian church and superintendent of public instruction for the state. He became professor of theology at a new theological seminary at Danville, Kentucky, where he remained until his death. He was a Unionist during the Civil War. (See *Letters*, II, 165–166, 167, 263.)

20. Chevalier Hulsemann was then chargé d'affaires ad interim of the Austrian government. For the exchange between Hulsemann and Daniel Webster, the secretary of state, see Bemis, *Diplomatic History*, pp. 310–311.

21. The Marquis de Lafayette (1759–1834), the French general and member of the French nobility, was a friend of American Independence and participant in the American Revolution.

22. These are selections from "Kossuth's First Speech in New York," in reply to New York City Mayor Ambrose C. Kingsland's welcoming address, Saturday, December 6, 1851, *Report*, pp. 58–69.

23. Speech by Kossuth, at his meeting with the First Division, New York State Militia, Castle Garden, December 16, 1851. See *Report*, p. 262; *New York Times*, December 17, 1851.

24. The presentation of the address and Kossuth's reply took place on December 9, 1851. For the complete text, see *Report*, pp. 80–82.

25. The speech from which these selections were made was delivered by Kossuth on Saturday afternoon, December 20, 1851. See *Report*, pp. 348–359.

26. A selection from Kossuth's reply to a delegation from Baltimore, December 9, 1851, in *Report*, pp. 105–117. The selection only approximates the wording in *Report*, but follows exactly the version of Kossuth's reply which appeared in *The Liberator*, December 19, 1851.

27. Selections from Kossuth's address at the New York City Corporation Dinner, December 11, 1851. For the text, see *Report*, pp. 139–180, and especially 140–143, 155, 170, 178, 179. The final sentence is from a speech delivered on December 16, 1851 to the First Division New York State Militia. See *Report*, p. 261.

28. From Kossuth's speech to the Press, December 15, 1851. See *Report*, p. 242.

29. From Kossuth's speech to the Bar of New York, December 19, 1851. See text in *Report*, p. 327 and in P. C. Headley, *The Life of Louis Kossuth*, p. 437. In the former, the tenth line begins with *Many* instead of *May*. The exclamation marks are Garrison's. Both versions omit the last word of the paragraph, "great," and end the sentence after "is."

30. From Kossuth's first speech in New York, December 6, 1851; see *Report*, p. 62.

31. From Kossuth's speech at Copenhagen House in Southampton, England, on November 3, 1851. For the text see *Authentic Life . . .* , pp. 70–78, and especially p. 78. The address also appeared in *The Times* (London), November 4, 1851.

32. Daniel O'Connell had died in 1847. For additional information, see *Letters*, II, 41.

33. Both paragraphs are to be found in *Daniel O'Connell upon American Slavery: With Other Irish Testimonies* (New York, Published by the American Anti-Slavery Society, 1860), Anti-Slavery Tracts, No. 5, New Series, pp. 5–6.

34. Marathon was a plain in ancient Greece, northeast of Athens, where the Athenians defeated the Persians in 490 B.C. Leuctra was a village in ancient Greece, seven miles southwest of Thebes, where the Thebans under Epaminondas defeated Sparta in 731 B.C.

35. *Daniel O'Connell upon American Slavery*, p. 6.

36. *Ibid.*, p. 7.

37. *Ibid.*

38. *Ibid.*, pp. 7–8.

39. *Ibid.*, pp. 8–9.

39a. Garrison's version of John Milton, *Paradise Lost*, Book IV, line 76.

40. *Ibid.*, pp. 9–11.

41. *Ibid.*, pp. 11–12.

42. Sir Robert Peel, second baronet (1788–1850), English statesman, had been prime minister and chancellor of the exchequer for a few months in 1834. He became prime minister again in 1841.

43. *Daniel O'Connell upon American Slavery*, pp. 12–14.

44. *Ibid.*, pp. 14–16.

45. *Ibid.*, pp. 16–17.

46. *Ibid.*, pp. 17–18.

47. William Jay (1789–1858), of New York, second son of John Jay, the first Chief Justice of the United States Supreme Court, was a lawyer and judge and an early abolitionist. (See *Letters*, II, 99–100.) Jay wrote many books and pamphlets on slavery. The reference here is probably to *A View of the Action of the Federal Government, in Behalf of Slavery* (New York, 1839), 217 pp.

48. *Daniel O'Connell Upon American Slavery*, pp. 18–20.

49. *Ibid.*, pp. 20–26.

50. Proverbs 27:6.

51. "To the Lord Viscount Forbes. From the City of Washington," in *The Poetical Works of Thomas Moore* (Paris, 1842), p. 133. The poem is one of a group entitled "Poems Relating to America." Moore, born in Dublin in 1779, died February 25, 1852, several days after publication of Garrison's letter to Kossuth in *The Liberator*.

52. William Wilberforce (1759–1833) was the British statesman who played an important part in the abolition of the British slave trade and of slavery.

53. Thomas Clarkson (1760–1846), writer of numerous works on slavery and the slave trade, was an early antislavery agitator who played an important part in ending the British slave trade and slavery in the West Indies.

54. A paraphrase of II Samuel 1:20.

55. Letter from George Thompson to William Lloyd Garrison, dated Marblehead (Massachusetts), October 22, 1835, in *Letters and Addresses by George Thompson during His Mission in the United States* . . . (Boston, 1837), pp. 106–113.

56. George McDowell Stroud (1795–1875), of Pennsylvania, was a jurist and author of *Sketch of the Laws Relative to Slavery in the Several States* (Philadelphia, 1827; enlarged edition, 1856).

57. Letter from Thomas Clarkson "To the Christian and Well-Disposed Citizens of the Northern States of America," dated "Playford Hall, near Ipswich, August 30, 1844," printed in *The Liberty Bell, 1845* (Boston, 1845), pp. 33–51.

58. Victor Marie Hugo (1802–1885), French poet, dramatist, novelist, and man-of-letters par excellence has been justifiably described by Algernon C. Swinburne as "one of the very greatest among poets and among men." Eight years later, on December 2, 1859, Hugo raised his voice in a public letter in defense of John Brown. The text of Hugo's letter is reprinted in Louis Ruchames, *A John Brown Reader* (London and New York, 1959), pp. 268–270.

59. For one such allusion see p. 111, above.

60. I am unable to locate this quotation in Lafayette's writings. However, for an excellent short summary of Lafayette's views on slavery and his participation

in the antislavery movement, see Melvin D. Kennedy, *Lafayette and Slavery, From His Letters to Thomas Clarkson and Granville Sharp* (Easton, Pennsylvania, 1950), 44 pp.

61. This statement by Lafayette is quoted in a letter from Thomas Clarkson to Mrs. H. G. Chapman (Maria Weston Chapman), dated "Playford Hall, near Ipswich, Oct. 3, 1845," and printed in *The Liberator*, January 2, 1846. The passage referring to Lafayette reads as follows:

"I will finish my letter with a saying of one of the dearest friends I ever had, namely, General Lafayette. I was with the general often, and corresponded with him after his coming out of his dungeon at Olmutz. But the first time I knew him was when I was in Paris, the year after the French Revolution, on the subject of the slave-trade, and I assisted him materially. He was decidedly as uncompromising an enemy to the slave-trade, and slavery, as any man I ever knew. He freed all his slaves in French Cayenne, who had come to him by inheritance, in 1785, and shewed me all his rules and regulations for his estate when they were emancipated. I was with him no less than four different times in Paris. He was a real gentleman, and of soft and gentle manners. I have seen him put out of temper, but never at any time except when slavery was the subject. He has said, frequently, 'I would never have drawn my sword in the cause of America, if I could have conceived that thereby I was founding a land of slavery.' How would the people of Fayette County like to hear this? — to hear their land cursed by the man who gained it for them?"

62. From *Notes on Virginia*, Andrew A. Lipscomb, ed., *The Writings of Thomas Jefferson* (Washington, D.C., 1904), II, 225–227.

63. From "Miscellaneous Papers," Lipscomb, *Writings of Jefferson*, XVII, 103.

64. John Greenleaf Whittier, "Stanzas" (stanzas 5, 8, 9, 10), *Poems* (Boston, 1856), pp. 134–135.

65. The selections from O'Connell's speeches that follow were included in *Daniel O'Connell upon American Slavery*, pp. 27–33.

66. This statement is quoted *ibid.*, p. 4.

67. John O'Connell (1810–1858) son of Daniel O'Connell, was a barrister, an M.P. representing different constituencies from 1832 to 1851 and 1853 to 1857, and an active assistant to his father in the Irish repeal agitation. He shared his father's trial and imprisonment in 1844 and succeeded his father as head of the Repeal Association, which failed for lack of funds in 1848. In 1846, he published his father's *Life and Speeches*.

68. The following extract, including the "Reply of John O'Connell, Esq., M.P. to a letter from James Haughton, esq.," was included in *Daniel O'Connell upon American Slavery*, pp. 34–36.

69. P. C. Headley, *The Life of Louis Kossuth*, p. 360.

70. *Ibid.*, p. 437.

71. *Ibid.*

72. *Ibid.*, p. 427.

73. *Report*, p. 261.

74. Thomas Jefferson. See note 63.

75. Garrison's reference here is to the trial of Castner Hanway and others who refused to participate in the apprehension of certain fugitive slaves, described in Garrison's letter (No. 34) to J. Miller McKim, Boston, October 4, 1851, note 2. Judges John Kintzing Kane and Robert Cooper Grier presided at the trial.

John Kintzing Kane (1795–1858), a lawyer, had been living in Philadelphia since 1801 and was admitted to the bar in 1817. Although initially a Federalist, he supported Andrew Jackson in 1828 and remained, thereafter, a Democrat. In 1845, he was appointed attorney-general of Pennsylvania. He resigned the following year, to assume the post of judge of the United States district court for the eastern district of Pennsylvania, which he held for the remainder of his life. In 1856, he jailed an abolitionist for refusing to produce certain fugitive slaves.

He was active in the American Philosophical Society, holding various offices, including that of president from the beginning of 1857 until his death.

76. These remarks were reported in *The Liberator*, January 23, 1852, and are also noted in *Life*, III, 352.

77. George Mifflin Dallas (1792–1864), a lawyer, was United States senator from Pennsylvania in 1831–1833, attorney-general of Pennsylvania from 1833 to 1835, minister to Russia from 1837 to 1839. He was vice-president of the United States from 1845 to 1849, and minister to Great Britain from 1856 to 1861. (*BDAC.*) He presided over the Citizens' Banquet for Kossuth given in Philadelphia on December 26, 1851. His speech is reported in the *New York Times*, December 29, 1851.

78. These remarks were delivered at the Corporation Banquet in Philadelphia, on December 24, 1851, and were printed in the *New York Times*, December 25, 1851.

79. Kossuth's reply to Mayor Gilpin of Philadelphia, December 24, 1851, reported in the *New York Times*, December 25, 1851.

80. Somewhat adapted from Kossuth's reply to a Baltimore delegation on December 9, 1851, reprinted in *The Liberator*, December 12, 1851.

81. From Kossuth's first speech in New York, December 6, 1851, in *Report*, p. 67.

82. Kossuth's first speech in New York, *ibid.*, p. 64.

83. *Ibid.*, pp. 61–62.

84. Revelation 18:13.

85. These two quotations, as well as the last two in this paragraph, are from Kossuth's first speech in New York, *ibid.*, p. 62.

86. *Life*, III, 55n, notes: "The Homestead Bill was now looming up as an issue between north and south. Passed by the House of Representatives, it was rejected by the Senate in August, 1852, as an abolition measure (*Lib.* 22:141)."

87. Speech in London, in P. C. Headley, *The Life of Louis Kossuth*, p. 360.

88. The second sentence is from Kossuth's speech at the Municipal Banquet in New York City, December 11, 1851. The first sentence must be from another address. See *Report*, p. 178.

89. Speech to the New York bar, December 19, 1851, P. C. Headley, *The Life of Louis Kossuth*, p. 441.

90. Hebrews 13:3.

91. Millard Fillmore (1800–1874) was the thirteenth President of the United States, from July 1850, to March 1853. He had been elected vice-president in 1848 and became President after the death of President Zachary Taylor on July 9, 1850. He signed, and attempted a vigorous enforcement of, the Fugitive Slave Law of 1850.

Daniel Webster was then President Millard Fillmore's secretary of state. As senator from Massachusetts he had helped enact the Compromise of 1850, including the Fugitive Slave Law. He was to die several months later, in October 1852.

Henry Clay, the prominent southern statesman and orator, as senator from Kentucky had played the foremost part in the Compromise of 1850, including the Fugitive Slave Law. He died several months later, in June 1852.

Lewis Cass (1782–1866), a Democrat, was United States senator from Michigan in 1845–1848 and 1849–1857. He was a vigorous supporter of the Compromise of 1850, including the Fugitive Slave Law.

92. Speech at Citizens' Banquet in Philadelphia, December 26, 1851, *Report*, p. 376.

93. Mark 16:15. The words "of freedom" have been added by Garrison.

94. The three succeeding quotations are from Kossuth's speech to President Fillmore at the Executive Mansion in Washington, D.C., in December 1851. See P. C. Headley, *The Life of Kossuth*, pp. 282–283.

95. The address was delivered on January 7, 1852. See *Report*, pp. 419–420.

96. "Woe to the conquered." The conquered lost their heads.

97. The Washington *Union* was established in 1845 as the "recognized central organ of the Polk administration," under the editorship of Thomas Ritchie and John P. Heiss. (Frederic Hudson, *Journalism in the United States, from 1690 to 1872*, New York and Evanston, 1969, p. 241.)

98. *The National Era* was an antislavery newspaper, published in Washington, D.C., from 1847 to 1860, with Gamaliel Bailey as editor and John Greenleaf Whittier as contributing editor.

99. Frederic Hudson writes that the Washington *Spectator* "was under the influence of Senator Rhett," "the organ of the South Carolina section only. Martin and Heart were the publishers." The name was later changed to the *Constitution*. (*Journalism in the United States*, p. 253.)

100. John Quincy Adams was a representative from Massachusetts in 1838.

101. The correct date is 1848.

102. For a more complete account of the case by one of the principal participants, see *Personal Memoir of Daniel Drayton, for Four Years and Four Months a Prisoner (for Charity's Sake) in Washington Jail, including a Narrative of the Voyage and Capture of the Schooner Pearl* (Boston, 1855), 122 pp.

The selection that Garrison quotes was reprinted in *The Liberator* on April 28, 1848, from the Correspondence of the Boston *Daily Whig*, was dated Washington, April 18, and signed "North."

Edward Sayres and Daniel Drayton (b. New Jersey, 1802; d. New Bedford, June 24, 1857), captain and mate of the schooner *Pearl*, had taken on board at Washington, D.C., in April 1848, seventy-six slaves whom they sought to bring to freedom. They were carrying them down the Potomac when they were captured. They were tried and convicted in the District of Columbia. They were defended by Horace Mann, who had accepted the case at the suggestion of Charles Sumner. Their sentence involved heavy fines, which they were unable to pay. They remained in jail for four years when a petition on their behalf, signed by many abolitionists, was presented to Charles Sumner, who had just been elected senator from Massachusetts, for presentation to the Senate. Sumner's judgment was that a quiet but direct approach to the President, on a personal level, would be more effective than a debate in the Senate. After consulting the prisoners, and with their approval and that of their counsel, he withheld the petition and appealed directly to President Fillmore for a pardon. After requesting and receiving a brief on the case from Sumner, and after consultations with the attorney-general, Fillmore pardoned the men in August 1852. Fearing that other efforts were afoot to detain the men again, Sumner hurried to the jail and put the men in a carriage in charge of a friend who brought them to Baltimore, whence they were conveyed to the North and out of danger. For further information, see Edward L. Pierce, *Memoir and Letters of Charles Sumner, 1845–1860* (Boston, 1893), III, 156–157, 276–277. For a copy of Sumner's brief and additional facts, see *Charles Sumner: His Complete Works*, with an introduction by Hon. George F. Hoar (Boston, 1900), pp. 219–233; Benjamin Quarles, *Black Abolitionists* (New York, 1969), pp. 163, 211; Louis Filler, *The Crusade Against Slavery, 1830–1860* (New York, Evanston, and London, 1963), pp. 164–165; *Life*, IV, 367.

103. Joshua Reed Giddings (1795–1864), of Ohio, was elected in 1838 as a Whig to Congress, where he became prominent as an active abolitionist. In 1842, he was censured by the House (125 to 69) for his defense of the mutineers on the *Creole*, resigned his seat, and was reelected by a large majority. In 1843, he opposed the annexation of Texas and in 1848 refused to support the candidacy of General Taylor for the Presidency, supporting the candidate of the Free Soil party. He opposed the Compromise of 1850, including the Fugitive Slave Law. His congressional career ended in 1859, when he refused another nomination. Appointed United States consul-general in Canada in 1861 by Lincoln, he remained in that office until his death.

104. Henry Leavitt Ellsworth (b. Windsor, Connecticut, November 10, 1791;

d. Fairhaven, Connecticut, December 27, 1858) was United States commissioner of patents from July 1836, to May 1848. He was a lawyer who had lived earlier for almost ten years in Hartford, Connecticut. Immediately prior to his appointment as commissioner of patents he had been resident commissioner among the Indian tribes to the south and west of Arkansas. After 1848, he was a land agent for a while in Lafayette, Indiana, but lived at Fairhaven, Connecticut, from 1857 until his death.

105. Thomas Corwin (1794–1865) was Whig representative from Ohio in Congress from 1831 to 1840, United States senator from 1845 to 1850, and secretary of the treasury from July 23, 1850 to March 6, 1853. He was minister to Mexico from 1861 to 1864. (Robert Sobel, ed., *Biographical Dictionary of the United States Executive Branch*, 1774–1971, Connecticut, 1971, p. 68.)

106. From Kossuth's speech at the Congressional Banquet, January 7, 1852, in Washington, D.C., *Report*, p. 420.

107. This resolution was introduced into the House by a special committee, which had been appointed on February 8, 1836, under the chairmanship of Representative Henry L. Pinckney of South Carolina, to look into the antislavery petitions which had been arriving in increasing numbers. The resolution was adopted on May 26, 1836. Garrison's version varies somewhat from the original. (Albert Bushnell Hart, *Slavery and Abolition, 1831–1841*, New York and Evanston, 1906, pp. 259–260.)

108. James H. Dickey and his brother William were leading ministers in the Chillicothe, Ohio, Presbytery. James Dickey (b. Virginia, 1780; d. December 24, 1856) was originally a missionary in Tennessee, where he freed the slaves whom he and his wife had inherited, and then went to South Salem, Ohio (in 1810), where he became known for his antislavery activities. He was pastor of the Pisgah Presbyterian Church in Ross County, Ohio, from 1811 to 1818 and in later years served as minister in other towns and cities of the area as well as in Illinois. We find him in 1838 as chairman of an antislavery convention in Hennepin, Illinois, where he appoints Benjamin Lundy and two others to a committee "to prepare a memorial to the state legislature for the repeal of 'all oppressive laws growing out of slavery whether applying to slaves, free negroes, or whites. . . .'" (Merton Dillon, *Benjamin Lundy and the Struggle for Negro Freedom*, Urbana and London, 1966, p. 256; Lyle S. Evans, *A Standard History of Ross County, Ohio*, Chicago and New York, 1917, I, 476; R. C. Galbraith Jr., *The History of the Chillicothe Presbytery*, Chillicothe, Ohio, 1889, *passim*, with a character sketch on pp. 139–140; Dwight L. Dumond, *Antislavery, The Crusade for Freedom in America*, Ann Arbor, 1961, p. 91. Gilbert Barnes and Dwight L. Dumond, in the *Weld-Grimké Letters*, and Dumond in *Letters of James Gillespie Birney, 1831–1857*, Gloucester, Massachusetts, 1966, copyright 1938, American Historical Association, mention that James and William Dickey were born in South Carolina. Dumond, in *Antislavery*, states that James Dickey was born in Virginia.)

109. Kossuth met with Henry Clay on Friday, June 9, 1852 (see the account in the *New York Times*, January 12, 1852). Clay's short speech to Kossuth during their interview was apparently his last public utterance.

P. C. Headley, in *The Life of Kossuth* (pp. 286–287), describes the interview: "With a few friends, Kossuth called on Henry Clay, who is evidently approaching the dark transit to the eternal main. . . . The Magyar listened solemnly to the dying accents of the great statesman and orator, and made a brief yet feeling reply. And when Kossuth rose to depart, the emaciated form whose pallid face was lit up by the radiance that cannot fade, slowly assumed its commanding attitude before the Exile. Then taking the hand of the chief within one of his own feverish palms, he placed the other upon the shoulder of the Hungarian, and invoked the blessing of Heaven upon him. The tears flowed freely down his cheeks, and Kossuth's bosom swelled with struggling emotion, while the venerable Kentuckian added, that every day his life should be spared, his fervent prayers would ascend to Almighty God for the exile's protection and restoration to his native land. And thus they parted, to meet no more till both appear before the King of kings." For a complete account of the interview, including the text of Clay's remarks, see *Report*, pp. 574–579.

110. These two quotations are from *Speech of the Hon. Henry Clay, in the Senate of the United States, on the Subject of Abolition Petitions, February 7, 1839* (Boston, 1839), p. 28.

111. The first two sentences of this quotation, with the first person pronoun changed to the third, were quoted by Garrison in his *Thoughts on African Colonization* (originally published in Boston, 1832, reprinted in New York, 1969), p. 42, from a speech by Henry Clay as reported in the *First Annual Report* of the American Colonization Society.

112. From *Speech of the Hon. Henry Clay . . . Abolition Petitions, February 7, 1839*, p. 31.

113. *African Repository*, III, 197, as quoted in Garrison's *Thoughts on African Colonization*, p. 125.

114. *African Repository*, I, 68, *ibid.*, p. 125.

115. *African Repository*, III, 203, *ibid.*, p. 125.

116. *African Repository*, V, 238, *ibid.*, p. 126.

117. *Seventh Annual Report* of the American Colonization Society, p. 99, *ibid.*, p. 127.

118. Speeches of J. R. Townshend, Esq., and W. W. Campbell, Esq., New York City, *ibid.*, p. 128.

119. *African Repository*, I, 34, *ibid.*, p. 134.

120. *African Repository*, II, 188, *ibid.*, p. 135.

121. *African Repository*, V, 276, *ibid.*, p. 136.

122. Speeches delivered at the formation of the Young Men's Auxiliary Colonization Society in New York City, *ibid.*, p. 139.

123. Quoted in part, *ibid.*, p. 142.

124. In *Thoughts on African Colonization*, p. 144, Garrison attributes this remark to "Dr. Nott." It may have been either Eliphalet Nott, president of Union College, New York, from 1804 to 1866, or Josiah Nott (1804–1873), a leading southern physician and student of ethnology, co-author of the volume entitled *Types of Mankind . . .* (Philadelphia, 1854). For further information about both men, see Louis Ruchames, ed., *Racial Thought in America*, vol. I, *From the Puritans to Abraham Lincoln* (New York, 1969), pp. 313–314, 462–469, 481, 485, 486.

125. From a speech by John Randolph at a meeting of the American Colonization Society, January 1, 1818, quoted by Garrison in *Thoughts on African Colonization*, p. 43.

126. Both quotations are from an address by Henry Clay, "On Slavery and Abolition," delivered at Richmond, Indiana, October 1, 1842, published in Daniel Mallory, compiler and editor, *The Life and Speeches of the Hon. Henry Clay* (New York, 1843), II, 599.

127. The story of Henry Clay's slave, up to this point, is to be found in *The Liberator*, April 10, 1846, on the first page. It is reprinted from the *Cleveland* (Ohio) *American* (undated) as a letter from Q. F. Atkins to "Friend Rice," dated March 14, 1846. The Prof. H. referred to in the account is identified elsewhere in *The Liberator* as Professor Hudson. It is probable that this was Dr. Erasmus Darwin Hudson, referred to in *Letters*, II, p. 386, a physician who had been an active abolitionist from 1837 to 1849 and who devoted himself thereafter to orthopedic surgery and invention of orthopedic appliances.

128. The following account appears in *The Liberator*, April 10, 1846, on the second page, and was reprinted from the Michigan *Signal of Liberty*. The account was mistakenly dated 1845 in *The Liberator*.

129. See Letter 73 for material on Henry Bibb.

130. At first glance, the person referred to seemed to be Judge Thomas Henry Bayly, not "Bailey," (1810–1856), a lawyer, who served in the Virginia House of Representatives from 1835 to 1840, was elected judge of the Superior Court of

Law and Chancery, and served from 1842 to 1844. He was a representative from Virginia in Congress from 1844 until his death. (*BDAC.*) However, a more likely possibility is James Madison Hite Beale (1786–1866), a representative from Virginia at the same time as Judge Bayly. He was a representative from 1833 to 1837 and from 1849 to 1853. (*BDAC.*) The *New York Times*, January 3, 1852, reported that Kossuth's exclamation "Virginia! the mother of statesmen" was made to "Judge Beale" of Virginia. What makes Beale more likely is that Judge Bayly is reported in The New York Times, January 1, 1852, as having introduced a resolution in the House during a discussion of the arrangements for Kossuth's reception which emphasized that "nothing should be construed as expressive of a design to involve ourselves in entangling alliances with European powers."

131. James Herbert Gholson (1798–1848), a lawyer, was a member of the Virginia state House of Delegates in 1824–1828 and 1830–1833. He was elected to the Twenty-third Congress, as a Democrat, where he served from March 4, 1833 to March 3, 1835. (*BDAC.*) A large portion of Gholson's speech, including that cited by Garrison, is reprinted in Joseph Clarke Robert, *The Road From Monticello, A Story of the Virginia Slavery Debate of 1832* (Durham, North Carolina, 1941), pp. 65–68. According to Robert, the address was delivered on January 12, 1832.

132. "The status of the child follows that of the mother."

133. Thomas Jefferson Randolph (1792–1875) was Thomas Jefferson's favorite grandson. As Jefferson's literary executor, he published, in 1829, *The Life and Correspondence of Thomas Jefferson* (Boston, 4 vols.). He was in the Virginia legislature which met on December 5, 1831, soon after the Nat Turner revolt in the summer of 1831. In January 1832 he introduced a motion for gradual emancipation. It was during the debate on his motion that he made the remarks from which Garrison quotes. (Robert, *The Road from Monticello*, pp. 95–97 *et passim*, reprints selections from Randolph's speech which include the short quotation but not the longer one.

134. Charles Fenton Mercer (1778–1858) practiced law, was a member of the Virginia house of delegates from 1810 to 1817, a delegate to the state constitutional convention in 1829, and a representative from Virginia in Congress from 1817 to 1839. He helped originate the plan for establishing the Free State of Liberia and was vice president of the Virginia Colonization Society in 1836. (*BDAC.*)

135. A convention to revise the constitution of the state of Virginia. See *Proceedings and Debates of the Virginia State Convention of 1829–1830* (Richmond, 1830).

136. The Richmond *Enquirer*, a semiweekly, was first issued in 1804 under the editorship of Thomas Ritchie, who was also its senior proprietor. It had the support and encouragement of Thomas Jefferson and was soon recognized as one of the most important voices of the Democratic party in the country. Frank Luther Mott, speaking of the first third of the nineteenth century, refers to the *Enquirer* as "the greatest paper of the southern states in these years." Ritchie left the *Enquirer* in May 1845 — handing over its editorship and management to his two sons, William F. and Thomas Ritchie, Jr. — to edit the *Union*, the official organ of President Polk. (Mott, *American Journalism, A History: 1690–1960*, 3d. ed., New York, 1962, pp. 188–189; Hudson, *Journalism in the United States*, pp. 268–271.)

137. The Virginia *Times* was founded by Samuel Saunders in 1823. Saunders was succeeded by William Ramsey in 1843. (*Virginia Magazine of History and Biography*, Richmond, 1901, IX, 7.)

138. James K. Paulding (1779–1860), a prominent author, born in New York, lived most of his life there except for several years when he lived in Washington, D.C., under a political appointment by President Madison, and as secretary of the navy from 1839 to 1841. Associated with Washington Irving in the publication of *Salmagundi* in 1807, Paulding wrote comic history, stories in verse, novels and essays, including *Letters from the South by a Northern Man* in 1816, *Life of*

George Washington in 1835, *Slavery in the United States* in 1836. (Louis Ruchames, ed., *Racial Thought in America*, vol. I, p. 427.)

139. The reference is to the Nat Turner rebellion of August 1831.

140. The Natchez *Free Trader* was probably the *Mississippi Free Trader and Natchez Gazette*, published in Natchez, Mississippi. Established in 1838, it was issued variously as a tri- and semiweekly. It became the *Natchez Daily Free-Trader* in 1858. (*Union List of Newspapers*.)

141. The New Orleans *Commercial Bulletin* was founded in 1831. Colonel Isaac Seymour, formerly of the Georgia *Messenger*, an officer in the Mexican War, joined it in 1849 and was associated with a Colonel Hodge in its control and direction. Conservative in policy, it was the equivalent of the Boston *Courier and Advertiser* or the *Journal of Commerce* in New York. (*The Louisiana Historical Quarterly*, 30:228–293, New Orleans, 1947.)

142. *The Voice of the Fugitive* was a semiweekly, published in Windsor, Canada, from January 1, 1851, to 1853, and edited by Henry Bibb. (Dwight L. Dumond, *A Bibliography of Antislavery in America*, Ann Arbor, 1961, p. 112. See also Robin Winks, " 'A Sacred Animosity': Abolitionism in Canada," in Martin Duberman, ed., *The Antislavery Vanguard: New Essays on the Abolitionists*, Princeton, New Jersey, 1965, pp. 317, 328, 335.)

143. The New York *Evangelist* was founded by Arthur and Lewis Tappan and their Association of Gentlemen to promote religious revivals, temperance, and other reforms. Joshua Leavitt, the abolitionist, became its editor in 1831. See *Letters*, II, p. 6.

144. The Reverend John S. C. Abbott (1805–1877), a Congregational clergyman and historian. Born and raised in Brunswick, Maine, he graduated from Bowdoin College in the same class as Hawthorne and Longfellow and studied for the ministry at Andover Theological Seminary. He occupied pulpits in Worcester, Massachusetts (1829–1834), Roxbury (1835–1841), Nantucket (1841–1843), and devoted about a decade thereafter to a young ladies' seminary started by his brother in New York City. He returned to the ministry in 1861 in New Haven, Connecticut, for five years. He wrote histories of Austria, Russia, Italy, and the Civil War in the United States, and several biographies, including one of Napoleon.

145. The Appendix, which consists of pages 81–112 of the pamphlet, reprints Kossuth's "Address to the People of the United States" on p. 81.

146. William Dickey (b. December 4, 1774; d. December 5, 1857), Presbyterian minister and brother of James Dickey, was born in South Carolina and raised in southern Kentucky. He moved to Ohio in 1817 and organized the Pisgah Presbyterian Church in Bloomingburgh, Ross County, Ohio, where he remained forty years. Both he and his brother were outspoken antislavery men. (The Reverend R. C. Galbraith, Jr., *The History of the Chillicothe Presbytery*, Chillicothe, Ohio, 1889, pp. 217–219; Lyle S. Evans, *A Standard History of Ross County, Ohio*, Chicago and New York, 1917, pp. 139–140; *Weld-Grimké Letters*, I, 272n.)

147. The Reverend Jonathan Cobb, not "Cable" (b. Hartford, Washington Co., New York, June 15, 1799; d. Danville, Iowa, June 13, 1884) was a Presbyterian minister who graduated from Union Theological Seminary in Virginia and thereafter served various pastorates in Ohio, Indiana and Iowa. (I am indebted to Gerald W. Gillette, Research Historian, The Presbyterian Historical Society for this information in the form of a transcription from Moore, Miller and Lacy, *General Catalogue of the Trustees, Officers, Professors and Alumni of Union Theological Seminary in Virginia*, [1807–1924], Richmond, Whittet and Shepperson, 1924, p. 53.)

148. Dr. Richard Furman (1755–1825) was pastor of the First Baptist Church in Charleston, South Carolina, from 1787 to 1824. In 1814, he was unanimously elected the first president of the triennial convention, an organization representing all United States Baptists, and was also president of the South Carolina Baptist Convention for seven years. Furman University of South Carolina was named after him. The communication to which Garrison refers was entitled *Rev. Dr. Richard*

Furman's Exposition of the Views of the Baptists, Relative to the Coloured Population of the United States, in a Communication to the Governor of South-Carolina (Charleston, Printed by A. E. Miller, 1823), 24 pp. (Library of Congress Catalogue). Through what appears to be a typographical error, which we have corrected in the text, Garrison lists the date of the pamphlet as 1833.

149. The *Vicksburg Register* was established in 1829. In 1831, it combined with the *Mississippi Advocate* to form the *Advocate and Register*, with William Mills, editor, M. Shannon, publisher. By January 1, 1834, it reverted to *Vicksburg Register*. In 1839, under new ownership, its name was changed to Vicksburg *Whig*. (*Mississippiana: Union List of Newspapers*, Vol. 2, compiled by the Mitchell Memorial Library, Mississippi State University. I am indebted for this information to Mrs. Anne G. McGuffee, Assistant Director, Historical Society of Vicksburg and Warren County, Old Court House Museum, Vicksburg, Mississippi.)

150. The Charleston (South Carolina) *Courier* was founded in 1803 by A. S. Willington and became the city's leading mercantile newspaper. During the nullification crisis in South Carolina it represented the Unionist position. (Mott, *American Journalism*, p. 189.)

151. Thomas Fowell Buxton (1786–1845) was a Member of Parliament and one of the leaders of the British antislavery movement. (See *Letters*, II, 61.)

152. Stephen Lushington (1782–1873), English reformer and abolitionist, a barrister, was a Member of Parliament during various years from 1806 to 1841, a judge of the High Court of Admiralty, 1838–1867, and dean of arches, 1858–1867.

153. Henry Peter Brougham (1778–1868), of Edinburgh, Scotland, was Lord Chancellor of England, an outstanding statesman and writer, and an ardent supporter of the British antislavery movement. (See *Letters*, II, 40.)

154. The Declaration of Sentiments of the American Anti-Slavery Society, was written by Garrison and adopted at its first convention in December 1833, in Philadelphia. For the complete text, see Ruchames, *The Abolitionists*, pp. 78–83.

155. Judge William Jay, *A View of the Action of the Federal Government, in Behalf of Slavery* (New York, 1839), p. 28.

156. *Ibid.*, p. 43.

157. *Ibid.*, p. 35.

158. Charles Miner (1780–1865), a representative from Pennsylvania, served from March 4, 1825, to March 3, 1829 (*BDAC*).

159. The New Orleans *Argus* was published in English and French from 1824 to 1834, when it became the *Louisiana Whig* or *Le Republicain de la Louisiane*. It later merged with *L'Abeille*. (*Union List of Newspapers*.)

160. Published in Boston, by Robert Wallcut, 1849, 156 pp.

37

TO BENJAMIN FISH

Boston, Feb. 20, 1852.

My Dear Friend:

I am greatly obliged to you and the other friends in Rochester, for extending to me an invitation to visit your city at the present time, in order to advance the cause of our fettered countrymen. I regret to say that I shall not be able to comply with the invitation, though I long to see Rochester once more; but my visit to Albany and Union Village will occupy a week, and I cannot conveniently be absent from home for a longer period. At a later period, in the spring, I shall hope to be with you.

Yours, with much regard,

Wm. Lloyd Garrison.

Benjamin Fish.

ALS: Rush Rees Library, University of Rochester, N.Y.

Benjamin Fish, a merchant in Rochester, New York, built a flouring mill at Main Falls, *circa* 1834, and owned a store with John Braithwaite on State Street. About 1848 he was converted to spiritualism through the influence of the Fox sisters. He was also active in the antislavery movement in Rochester. (Major Wheeler C. Case, "In the Looking-Glass of 1834," in *Centennial History of Rochester, New York*, Rochester, 1932, vol. II, p. 185; Mrs. Elizabeth J. Varney, "Panorama of Rochester in Its Early Days," in *The Rochester Historical Society Publication Fund Series*, Rochester, 1929, vol. 8, p. 220; Jenny Marsh Parker, *Rochester, A Story Historical*, Rochester, 1884, pp. 256, 268–269.)

The Rochester City *Directory* lists him in 1834 as a merchant, in 1840 as a farmer, in 1847 and 1848 as a gardener, in 1851 as a nurseryman, and in 1853–1855 as having a nursery and land office. (Letter from Mrs. Elizabeth B. Downey, Rochester Historical Society, November 11, 1971.)

---

3 8

TO SAMUEL J. MAY

Boston, March 23, 1852.

My Dear Friend:

We have just received a final answer from Mr. Gay,[1] at New York, as to the feasibility of holding the approaching annual meeting of the American Anti-Slavery Society in that city, and being protected in so doing; and it is to the effect, that it is idle and useless for us to make any effort in that direction.

At a meeting of the Executive Committee, just concluded, it has been unanimously resolved to hold the anniversary at Syracuse, on the 11th, 12th, and 13th of May; and I therefore hasten to apprise you of this fact, trusting our decision will be acceptable to the anti-slavery friends in your region in particular, and throughout the country generally. Wendell Phillips has promised to attend the meeting, where I hope we shall again have the pleasure of meeting with Gerrit Smith.[2]

It has been in my heart and mind to write you many letters, but I am as incorrigible as ever on the score of epistolary correspondence. You are ever with me, in memory and affection. I deeply sympathize with you and your people in the loss you have jointly sustained by the destruction of your beautiful meeting-house, and trust all necessary aid will be forthcoming. Excuse my assault upon tall steeples.[3]

We are all in very good health at home, and trust that you and yours are in the full enjoyment of the same unspeakable blessing. With the most loving regards to them all, and my fervent benediction, I remain, (writing in extreme haste,)

Your old and admiring friend,

Wm. Lloyd Garrison.

Saml. J. May.

ALS: Garrison Papers, Boston Public Library.

1. Sydney Howard Gay.
2. Gerrit Smith (1797–1874) of Peterboro, New York, philanthropist, reformer and political abolitionist, remained friendly to Garrison and the Garrisonian abolitionists despite their ideological and political differences. In May 1851, when the American Anti-Slavery Society held its annual meeting in Syracuse, New York, with George Thompson, the British abolitionist, attending, Gerrit Smith had greeted them with "Joy, then, to you, William Lloyd Garrison; to you, George Thompson!" Two months earlier, Smith had publicly praised Garrison as "the most distinguished and meritorious of American abolitionists." (*Life*, III, 328–329.)
3. On March 12, 1852, *The Liberator* reported that Samuel May's church in Syracuse had been destroyed "by the falling of the steeple during a violent gale," and called for financial contributions to help in the rebuilding of the church. The article, obviously written by Garrison, also paid tribute to May as "one of the purest, best, and most philanthropic men living. . . . His was indeed a free pulpit, and mighty have been the influences for good that have emanated from it since his settlement. It was freely offered, as opportunity presented, to the friends of reform, whether men or women, and irrespective of theological opinions; and nobly did the congregation uphold this freedom."

Garrison's phrase, "my assault upon tall steeples," refers to the last paragraph of the article which noted that the church "was destroyed in consequence of its lofty steeple falling upon and crashing it to the earth. In erecting another building, let there be no such hazard again incurred, and no such waste of means. A belfry, sufficiently elevated to contain the bell, is all that is needed. Tall steeples are equally expensive and dangerous, and commonly erected through rivalry and vain-glory. George Fox entertained many and well-founded objections to them, especially in connection with religious worship; and we think his was an enlightened testimony."

3 9

TO GEORGE THOMPSON GARRISON

Thursday, June 17, 1852.

Dear George:

If your centennial celebration in Danvers had been to-day, instead of yesterday,[1] (which, you know, is always my busiest day at the office,) I would gladly have been present at it. The day, fortunately, was a very fine one, though the heat must have been very oppressive — the mercury in Boston ranging as high as 100 deg. above zero, in the shade. Short as his visit was, I presume it was very agreeable to you to see Wendell.[2] William [Garrison] went with a Sunday School celebration party to Framingham.

To day is the anniversary of the Bunker Hill battle. From our house, (far as we are off,) I can see the flags waving from the Monument in Charlestown, in honor of that event, notwithstanding the shocking fact that we have more than three millions of chattel slaves in this boasted land of freedom, and are more eager to extend and support the slave system than all the interests of freedom put together! As a nation, we are the vilest of hypocrites, as well as the worst of oppressors.

Enclosed, I send you two dollars for your use. If you can find a straw hat to suit you in Danvers, you had better buy one at once.

My best regards to Mr. and Mrs. Clark.

Your loving father,

Wm. Lloyd Garrison.

Geo. T. Garrison.

ALS: Merrill Collection of Garrison Papers, Wichita State University.

Addressed to George Thompson Garrison, c/o Aaron F. Clark, Esq., South Danvers, Massachusetts. Garrison's letter is followed by a note from Helen to George.

1. The reference is to the hundredth anniversary of the separation of Danvers from Salem. For a description of the event, see Harriet Silvester Tapley, *Chronicles of Danvers* (Danvers, 1923), pp. 161–162.

2. Wendell Phillips Garrison (June 4, 1840–February 28, 1907), Garrison's third son, graduated from Harvard in 1861, was editor of *The Nation* for forty-one years, author of *The Benson Family of Newport, Rhode Island*, and joint author with his brother, Francis Jackson Garrison, of Garrison's *Life*.

---

4 0

TO J. MILLER McKIM

Boston, July 18, 1852.

My dear McKim:

It will give me the highest satisfaction to be present at the next anniversary of the Pennsylvania Anti-Slavery Society, at Westchester,[1] in accordance with the invitation so kindly extended to me in your letter; and I trust nothing will occur to prevent my being with you at that time. — The friends of the Anti-Slavery cause, in Eastern Pennsylvania, are peculiarly dear to me, and none in the world occupy a higher place in my esteem than they. Many of them are older laborers in the field than myself, and to such I am greatly indebted for their early example, and their noble persistency to the present hour. Assure all such that my heart leaps at the thought of seeing them once more, face to face. Though your anniversary will be held at a time of intense political excitement, and therefore under somewhat unfavorable circumstances, still it is our duty to bear a faithful testimony against popular corruption, whether there be many or few to give heed to it. In one point, at least, we shall have a decided advantage: — all disguises are now thrown off by the two great political parties in the land, and they stand committed to the side of slavery, nakedly, openly, impudently, and, as they say, everlastingly! Both Scott and Pierce [2] have agreed to uphold all that was done by the Baltimore Conventions, relating to slavery; so that, by no casuistry whatever, can a vote cast for either of them be any thing else than a direct sanction to slave-holding, slave-breeding, and slave-hunting. None but those who are morally depraved or blind can give such a vote.

And now, my dear friend, a word in regard to another subject, which ought long, long since to have been explained by me. I allude to the seeming disrespect shown to your late father-in-law,[3] and apparent disregard of your feelings, by my neglecting to answer any one of several letters addressed to me by you conjointly, respecting a certain statement made in the Liberator in regard to the operatives of Lowell being required to attend public worship. Why were none of those letters answered? As truly as that I live, it was not because I did not wish or mean to give the information desired; nor because I had taken any offence at the pertinacity with which what seemed to me a very small matter was pressed by your father-in-law — (I had utterly forgotten, at the time, that he stood in any such relation to you) — but *solely* owing to my inveterate, yes, I will .say criminal habit of procrastination in regard to all my epistolary interchanges. When the first letter of inquiry was received from him, I fully intended to reply to it; but, like a hundred other instances, it got laid aside, lost sight of, buried beneath any quantity of accumulated and accumulating materials; and I forgot all about it. When the second letter came, the same thing occurred. When the third came, (in which, I believe, my silence was construed into a personal affront, and the Liberator was ordered to be discontinued,) I resolved to hunt up the information desired, and make the desired reply. But, alas! day after day passed without seeing my purpose executed; and then the whole affair passed from my mind, my memory being very poor. And it is owing to the same bad habit of procrastination, that your letters were not answered. The mischief was, that I meant to write so long an explanatory letter, that I wrote none; whereas, half a dozen lines would have been better than nothing at any stage of "this strange, eventful history." [4] I acknowledge myself immensely to blame, and that your beloved father-in-law had every reason to feel wounded (as well as yourself) at such unaccountable silence; but I solemnly declare that it was wholly unintended. There seems to have been some strange fatality about it, and I shall regret the occurrence as long as I live, especially as your father-in-law is not now living, to whom this explanation ought to have been sent long ago.

But the mail closes in a few minutes; — and I am compelled to close very abruptly. When we see each other, we will go into all the particulars. Till then, and ever more,

Yours, most affectionately, and with unbounded regard,

Wm. Lloyd Garrison.

P.S. My loving regards to your dear wife, James and Lucretia Mott,[5] Oliver Johnson,[6] Mary Grew, &c. &c.

ALS: Garrison Papers, Boston Public Library. Several lines of this letter are printed in *Life*, III, 370–371.

1. The Fifteenth Annual Meeting of the Pennsylvania Anti-Slavery Society convened at West Chester in Pennsylvania on October 25, 1852 and continued in session for several days. Garrison was an active participant in the proceedings. (*National Anti-Slavery Standard*, November 18, 1852.)

2. Winfield Scott and Franklin Pierce. Franklin Pierce (1804–1869), of New Hampshire, fourteenth President of the United States, was nominated on the forty-ninth ballot at the Democratic National Convention at Baltimore, Maryland, in June 1852. He triumphed over such competitors as Stephen Douglas and James Buchanan, who was elected President four years later. One of the resolutions adopted at the convention affirmed that the party would "live by and adhere to a faithful execution of the acts known as the compromise measures, settled by the last Congress, the act for reclaiming fugitives from service or labor included. . . ." (*The Liberator*, June 11, 1852.)

During the same month, Winfield Scott (1786–1866) was nominated as the Whig candidate for President on the fifty-third ballot. The defeated nominees were Millard Fillmore and Daniel Webster. One of the resolutions passed at the Whig Convention affirmed support of the Compromise of 1850, including the Fugitive Slave Law, as "a final settlement — of the dangerous and exciting subjects which they embrace; and so far as the Fugitive Slave Law is concerned, we will maintain the same, and insist on its strict enforcement . . . and we deprecate all future agitation of the slavery question as dangerous to our peace. . . ." (*The Liberator*, June 25, 1852.)

3. McKim's father-in-law was Micajah Speakman (1781–1852), of Wallace Township, Chester County, Pennsylvania, who was active in the antislavery movement and kept a way-station at his home for fugitive slaves. Apparently hundreds of slaves passed through his hands and those of his son, William A. Speakman. Micajah's wife, Phebe, was born in 1785 and died in 1832. Their daughter, Sarah, born March 1, 1813, married J. Miller McKim. (R. C. Smedley, *History of the Underground Railroad in Chester* . . . , Lancaster, Pennsylvania, 1883, pp. 164–167.)

The remainder of Garrison's letter is in reply to a letter from McKim, dated December 30, 1851, which is printed here in its entirety. (The original is in the Boston Public Library, Garrison Papers.

"Dear Garrison:

"I want to recall to your mind some facts which you have probably forgotten,

— or of which you possibly may have never had any knowledge. My object in doing so will be seen before I have done.

"Some 4 or 5 or 6 years ago there appeared in the 4th page of the Liberator an article reflecting severely on the clergy of Lowell & insinuating I believe that they were in the practice of peculating in true clerical way the factory girls out of their wages. My father-in-law Micajah Speakman of Chester Co. an old subscriber to the Liberator & at that time a strong advocate of it, had occasion to quote this article in a conversation with the member of Congress from his district, as a proof of some charge which he was preferring against the clergy. His opponent, the member of Congress, pronounced the article to be false. My father-in-law took an opportunity soon after this to write to you to know what authority you had for publishing it — not doubting himself however that it was true & that you would give him ample warrant for its publication. He received no answer, and wrote again. Still he received no reply. Seeing that he took it a good deal to heart, and — though attaching very little importance to the matter myself — wishing that his mind might be made easy by a word of explanation, I wrote to you myself stating the circumstances of the case. Having done this the whole subject passed out of my mind. But not so with Mr. Speakman. I have since discovered that he has ever since felt exceedingly piqued, mortified & irritated about it. He was mortified to be caught in quoting for a fact what was denied & what he was utterly unable to prove, & piqued & irritated that four different letters to you (for it appears he wrote to you again, after my letter referred to) written he says in respectful language had failed to elicit a word of reply.

"Now I think it quite possible that part of these letters may have never reached you & I have no doubt that the whole thing is susceptible of an easy explanation without making you chargeable with any wilful slight or intentional disrespect in the matter; and under ordinary circumstances I should have said nothing to you about it; but just now my father-in-law is in very poor health. He is old and fast declining, and his children are anxious to do all they can to minister to his comfort. The only medicaments that can do him good must be of a mental kind, and I know of nothing that would be more likely to be of service in this way than something that would explain your apparent disrespect to him & reinstate him in possessing his former good opinion of the Liberator & its Editor. Will you not drop me a line on this subject, a line so phrased as will do for me to put in an envelope & send to him by mail?

"Yours most truly, . . ."

4. Shakespeare, *As You Like It*, II, vii, 164.

5. James and Lucretia Mott, Quakers, were pioneer leaders in the antislavery movement. They were present at the founding convention of the American Antislavery Society and continued their devotion to the antislavery cause until emancipation. They were lifelong friends of Garrison. For a more detailed biography see *Letters*, II, xxvii–xxviii.

6. Oliver Johnson was an early friend of Garrison, one of the founders of the New England Anti-Slavery Society in 1832. He edited *The Liberator* on various occasions in Garrison's absence. In the 1840's and 1850's, he edited the *Anti-Slavery Bugle* of Salem, Ohio, the *Pennsylvania Freeman*, another antislavery newspaper, the *National Anti-Slavery Standard*, official organ of the American Anti-Slavery Society, and for some years was also associated with the New York *Tribune* as assistant to Horace Greeley. For further information, see *Letters*, II, xxv–xxvi.

41

TO SAMUEL MAY, JR.

Boston, July 19, 1852.

My Dear Friend:

I like your idea of having the First of August celebrated at Salem on the regular day,[1] and will endeavor to hold myself in readiness to attend the meeting, if you make the appointment; especially if I may count on the assistance of Pillsbury and Remond. Whether the Lyceum or the Mechanic's Hall could be obtained for a Sunday meeting, I do not know, and feel somewhat in doubt, but we can soon ascertain. Such a celebration might prevent a few from going to Framingham,[2] but it would accommodate many who could not go there in any event. As I shall not be able to hear any thing definitely from you, I suppose, before the Liberator goes to press, I think I will venture to announce, unofficially, our intention to hold such a meeting in Salem; otherwise, the notice will be too limited.

I will see to the selecting and printing of the hymns for our grand celebration,[3] and in good season, and also to the other matters referred to in your notes to Mr. Wallcut and myself, so that I do not think your presence will be needed here, though it is always so agreeable.

My head is somewhat relieved of its recent inflammatory attack, but still sore and heavy.

Yours, faithfully,

Wm. Lloyd Garrison.

Samuel May, Jr.

ALS: Antislavery Manuscripts, Boston Public Library.

1. *The Liberator*, July 23, 1852, made the following announcement: "The friends of the anti-slavery cause in Essex County will be gratified to learn, that the anniversary of West India Emancipation will be commemorated, by appropriate exercises, in Salem, on Sunday, August 1st. Probably three meetings will be held on that day, to be attended by Parker Pillsbury, Charles Lenox Remond, William Lloyd Garrison, and others." A later issue, July 30, 1852, announced the place of the meeting as Mechanic Hall.

2. On July 16, 1852, *The Liberator* had announced that the Massachusetts Anti-Slavery Society was holding its anniversary celebration of West India Emancipation in "the beautiful grove" at Framingham, on Tuesday, August 3.

3. This was the meeting in Framingham, where the list of speakers included Garrison, Edmund Quincy, Parker Pillsbury, Charles C. Burleigh, Charles L. Remond, Theodore Parker, John Pierpont, Thomas Wentworth Higginson, Henry Wilson, and several others.

4 2

TO SAMUEL MAY, JR.

Boston, July 22, 1852

My Dear Friend:

Friend Wallcut [1] meant, without fail, to send you Twitchell's agreement and arrangement with us, yesterday, but did not succeed. Accompanying this is a copy of this week's Liberator, in which you will find what you desire, as expressed in Twitchell's own language.[2]

John Pierpont has written a scathing song or hymn, on Slave Hunting, which will be among the number to be sung at the Grove.[3] To-morrow I shall put the whole series into the hands of Mr Prentiss,[4] and will endeavor to send copies to Hopedale [5] on Saturday.

I hope you will persuade Higginson [6] to attend our celebration, and speak. As the 1st of August comes on Sunday, why can he not prepare a discourse suitable for the occasion, to be delivered to his people, and re-delivered at Framingham? [7]

My head is better, but not as I desire it to be.

My regards to Mrs. May.

Yours, truly,

Wm. Lloyd Garrison.

Saml. May. Jr.

ALS: Antislavery Manuscripts, Boston Public Library.

1. Robert F. Wallcut.
2. The agreement with Ginery Bachelor Twitchell (or Twichell), who was then superintendent of the Boston and Worcester Railroad, involved the railroad facilities that were made available to the abolitionists for transportation from Boston and vicinity to Framingham, the time schedule, prices, etc. These are given in full in an editorial essay, "The Jubilee! West India Emancipation," in *The Liberator*, July 30, 1852, and in previous issues.
3. The Reverend John Pierpont's hymn was entitled "The Slave-Catcher," and was sung to the tune of "Scots Wha Hae." It was printed in full in *The Liberator*, August 6, 1852.

John Pierpont (1785–1866), Unitarian clergyman, poet, reformer, grandfather of John Pierpont Morgan, and a native of Litchfield, Connecticut, was ordained minister of the Hollis Street Church in Boston on April 14, 1819. He resigned in 1845 after a "Seven Years' War" waged by conservative members of his congregation to oust him over his reform activities. He was later pastor of the First Unitarian Society of Troy, New York (1845–1849), and of the First Congregational (Unitarian) Church of West Medford, Massachusetts (1849–1858). From 1861 until his death, he was a clerk in the Treasury Department at Washington, D.C. See also *Letters*, III, 535–536.
4. Henry James Prentiss (b. Marblehead, July 17, 1807; d. Boston, April 22, 1869), a printer since boyhood, known for his meticulousness as a printer and engaged in printing in Boston since at least 1839, was connected with the firm of Prentiss and Sawyer, as well as others at various times. He was a staunch and vocal abolitionist as well as a devoted member of the Church of the Disciples.

(C. J. F. Binney, *The History and Genealogy of the Prentice or Prentiss Family in New England* . . . , Boston, 1883, 2d. edition, pp. 88, 131; *New England Historical and Genealogical Register*, Boston, 1870, vol. XXIV, pp. 199, 200.)

5. The reference is either to the town of Hopedale, Massachusetts, adjoining Milford, or to the Hopedale Community in the same area, founded by Adin Ballou in 1840, which came to an end at about 1856.

6. Thomas Wentworth Higginson (1823–1911), Unitarian minister, author and antislavery man. A graduate of Harvard College in 1841 and the Harvard Divinity School in 1847, he was pastor of the First Congregational church in Newburyport, Massachusetts, from 1847 to 1850 and of a free church in Worcester, Massachusetts, from 1852 to 1858, when he left the ministry. Thereafter, he devoted himself primarily to literature. In 1854, he was indicted, with Theodore Parker, Wendell Phillips, and others, for murder in the attempted rescue of Anthony Burns, but was freed with the others before the case came to trial. He was a friend and supporter of John Brown. During the Civil War, in September 1862, he became captain of the 51st Massachusetts regiment, and in November was given the rank of colonel of the 1st South Carolina volunteers (later known as the 33rd U.S. colored troops), the first regiment of freed slaves in the U.S. Army.

7. The account of the celebration at Framingham, as printed in *The Liberator* (August 6, 1852), makes no mention of Higginson's participation.

4 3

TO ANNE W. WESTON

Boston, Aug. 14, 1852.

My Dear Friend:

You inquire after our worthy English friend, Rev. Francis Bishop,[1] of Liverpool. He remained only one day in Boston, and then proceeded to Philadelphia, Washington, &c., carrying with him introductory letters from me to James and Lucretia Mott, Rev. Dr. Furness,[2] Joshua R. Giddings, and others. It was his purpose to travel in the slave States, perhaps as far as Georgia, as he expressed a strong desire to have an interview with the "owner" of William and Ellen Crafts.[3] Then to return to New-York, go up the North river, and so proceed to the far West, — calculating to be in Boston about the 1st of October. He said he should try to remain in this city and vicinity, on his return, some two or three weeks. — Of course, we here will see that he is duly cared for.

I see it announced that George Thompson has been elected to Parliament from Aberdeen;[4] but, whether it is *our* G. T., or some other person, I feel somewhat in doubt; though the papers seem to think it is our friend of the Tower Hamlets. I do not know why there were groans given by T's constituents for the *Morning Advertiser*, not being aware that that journal was otherwise than friendly to his re-election.

I regret to hear that your brother [5] continues greatly debilitated, and proffer to him, and to you all, my warmest sympathies. May he soon have a favorable "crisis."

Helen and I have just returned from a visit to the bedside of our estimable friend, Catharine Sargent,[6] in Poplar Street, who is probably near the close of her earthly career. It has been ascertained that her disease is not neuralgia, but a schirrous state of the bowels, which utterly and hopelessly precludes all action of the same; so that for a week past she has tasted no food, and can only take a very little liquid to moisten her lips, &c. A considerable portion of the time she is under the influence of morphine, to soothe her extreme anguish. We found her surprisingly cheerful, nevertheless, and in the full and bright possession of her mental faculties. Her mind is serene as heaven itself, and she lies

> "Dressed for the flight, and ready to be gone,"

should this be the will of her Heavenly Father. Henrietta [7] has had the entire care of her, day and night, and it is marvellous how she has been sustained through it all. I believe that she has not yet communicated the fact to her sister, that her recovery is not practicable; but Catharine probably so regards it, and is ready for the result, turn as the scales may. She will be a great loss to Henrietta.

Helen desires me to remember her most kindly to you and all the family. At some future day, we are hoping to make our long promised visit to Weymouth, but not while you are in a state of affliction.

Yours, with the highest regards,

Wm. Lloyd Garrison

Anne W. Weston.

ALS: Weston Papers, Boston Public Library.

Anne Warren Weston (b. July 13, 1812; d. January 1, 1890), of Weymouth, Massachusetts, was the sister of Maria Weston Chapman as well as of Caroline, Deborah, and Lucia Weston. She was very active in the antislavery and nonresistance movements. A devoted Garrisonian, she helped arrange the annual fairs of the Boston Female Anti-Slavery Society and, during the 1850's, helped edit the *Liberty Bell*. She taught school at various times in Weymouth, Dorchester, and New Bedford, and also frequently took care of Maria W. Chapman's children. For some years, during the latter part of her life, she lived abroad. Her voluminous correspondence, from which this information has been gleaned, is to be found in the Weston Papers and May Papers, Boston Public Library.

1. The Reverend Francis Bishop (1813–1869), a Unitarian minister, became friendly with Garrison during the latter's visit to England in 1840 to attend the World's Anti-Slavery Convention. He was first settled as the Unitarian minister at Cheltenham, in the Severn Valley. In 1844, he settled at Exeter, as one of the ministers at George's Chapel, one of the earliest English Presbyterian churches. He married the sister of Henry Solly. By this time, he had left Exeter to take charge of the Liverpool Domestic Mission, where he did "remarkable" work as a slum missionary. He was active in the temperance as well as the antislavery movement. (Henry Solly, *"These Eighty Years,"* or, *The Story of an Unfinished*

Life, London, 1893, 2 vols., I, 328–329, 427–428, 431; II, 6 and 33; see also *Letters,* III, 463.)

2. The Reverend Dr. William Henry Furness of Philadelphia.

3. William and Ellen Craft, husband and wife, aged twenty-four and twenty-two respectively, the latter nearly white, fled from Macon, Georgia, where they were enslaved, the day after Christmas, 1848. Ellen impersonated a southern planter, with her right arm in a sling so as not to be expected to write, her jaws swathed in a muffler to disguise her lack of beard, and green glasses covering her eyes, and feigned deafness to avoid using her voice. William accompanied her as her servant. They finally reached Boston. William, who had been a carpenter in Macon, secured a job as carpenter, while Ellen worked as a seamstress. After the passage of the Fugitive Slave Bill in September, 1850, their identity was discovered and on October 25 two southerners appeared in Boston with warrants for the Crafts' arrest. They were hidden by the abolitionists at different homes, including those of Ellis Gray Loring, Lewis Hayden, and Theodore Parker. Finally, on November 11, after Parker married them according to Massachusetts law — southern law prohibited legal marriage between slaves — the Crafts were placed on board a ship to England, where they arrived safely. (*DUSH*; Lawrence Lader, *The Bold Brahmins: New England's War Against Slavery (1831–1863),* New York, 1961, pp. 139–143; Carleton Mabee, *Black Freedom: The Nonviolent Abolitionists from 1830 through the Civil War,* London, 1970, pp. 285–286.)

John Daniels, *In Freedom's Birthplace: A Study of the Boston Negroes* (Boston and New York, 1914), pp. 61–62n, writes about the Crafts' latter years: "After the war, the Crafts returned to America. For some time they lived at Cambridge, where their children were educated, and then they went back to their native state, Georgia, where they passed their old age in a comfortable home near Savannah." Daniels cites Booker T. Washington, *The Story of the Negro,* vol. I, p. 230, as his source.

4. On July 30, 1852, *The Liberator* announced that George Thompson had been defeated in the election in the Tower Hamlets, London, for member of Parliament. The George Thompson who was elected to Parliament from Aberdeen was not the abolitionist but the son of Andrew Thompson, born at Woolwich, Kent in 1804, the same year as the abolitionist. He was a merchant and shipowner, provost of Aberdeen from 1847 to 1852, a liberal and a reformer. He was first elected from Aberdeen in July 1852. (Charles R. Dod, *The Parliamentary Companion, Twentieth Year,* 2d. ed., New Parliament, London, 1852, p. 272.)

5. Hervey Eliphaz Weston (b. Weymouth, June 21, 1817; d. July 21, 1882), a physician, graduated from Yale College in 1839 and from the Harvard Medical School in 1844. He subsequently spent three years at the School of Medicine in Paris. Returning to Weymouth in 1847, he practiced medicine there for several years and afterwards in Boston. He lived in Italy from 1859 to 1869. A few years later, as the result of a spinal affliction, he became an invalid. His nonmedical interests included classical scholarship, archaeology, and numismatics. (George Nash, compiler, *Historical Sketch of the Town of Weymouth, Mass.,* Weymouth, 1885, p. 204; *A Quarter-Century Record of the Class of 1839,* Yale College, New York, 1865, p. 54. It should be noted that George W. Chamberlain, *History of Weymouth,* Weymouth, 1923, vol. II, p. 627, errs in citing Hervey's name as "Henry.")

6. Catherine Sargent (b. Gloucester, April 26, 1774; d. there, September 24, 1852) was the daughter of Epes Sargent IV, the Collector of the Port of Gloucester until 1795, when he went to New Hampshire and thence to Boston (Emma W. Sargent and Charles S. Sargent, *Epes Sargent of Gloucester and His Descendants,* Cambridge, 1923, p. 12). Miss Sargent's obituary in *The Liberator* (October 1, 1852), written by Garrison, notes that "the cause of the stricken slave, and of all identified with him by complexion, has lost one of its truest and best friends. Her sympathies were constantly affected, and her charities actively exercised, in behalf of the poor, the outcast, and the oppressed, without regard to color or race. Of a

meek and quiet spirit, her beneficence was dispensed unostentatiously, the right hand not knowing what the left did. As the coffin containing her remains was carried out of the house, to be conveyed to Mount Auburn, a colored friend who was in attendance exclaimed aloud, with touching pathos, 'There goes one of the best friends I have found in the world' — and his eye moistened as he paid the grateful tribute. He related to us some of the many cases of distress which the deceased had alleviated through her charities, entrusted to his care, and by him faithfully applied."

7. Henrietta Sargent (b. Gloucester, November 18, 1785; d. Boston, January 11, 1871) was the sister of Catherine Sargent. A pioneer in the antislavery movement, she was deeply devoted to the rights of the Negro, even before the organization of the New England Anti-Slavery Society in 1832. She was an officer in the Boston Female Anti-Slavery Society and a close friend throughout her lifetime of Garrison and his wife. A Universalist, she devoted much of her time during her later years to conducting a Bible class in the Sunday School connected with the Society of the Reverend Dr. Miner in Boston. (Sargent, *Epes Sargent of Gloucester*, p. 13.)

On October 29, 1852, *The Liberator* carried a news item stating that the Boston Female Anti-Slavery Society, at its annual meeting on October 20, had adopted two resolutions, one of which stated: "That in the death of Miss Catherine Sargent, this society deplores the loss of one of its earliest and most efficient members — of one qualified in no common degree by her clear sense of right and justice, her faith in their ultimate triumph, and her fervent love to God and man, to exemplify those characteristics which should be the distinctive traits of every Abolitionist."

44

TO SAMUEL MAY, JR.

Boston, Aug. 27, 1852.

My Dear Friend:

I have just received your note in regard to the Harwich meeting.[1] Our friends at Harwich say that they would like to have C. C. Burleigh at the meeting, and you will see, by this week's Liberator, that I have announced him to be present — though I have done so at "haphazard," not having had time to confer with him. I hope you will secure him at once. I hope to see Remond to-morrow. If not, will you engage him *positively* for Harwich, at Leicester?[2]

In great haste, with best regards to Mrs. M.,

Yours, faithfully,

Wm. Lloyd Garrison.

S. May, Jr.

ALS: Garrison Papers, Boston Public Library.

1. Harwich, Massachusetts. *The Liberator*, August 27, 1852, announced that "the friends of impartial liberty, on the Cape, will rally at their annual gathering in Harwich, on Saturday and Sunday, September 4th and 5th." Weather permitting, it was to be an open-air meeting. The speakers listed were Garrison, C. C. Burleigh, and Charles Lenox Remond.

2. Remond was scheduled to speak at Leicester, Massachusetts, on "Colonization and the American Colonization Society," on Sunday, August 29, at the Second Congregational (Unitarian) meeting-house.

45

TO SAMUEL J. MAY

Boston, Sept. 7, 1852.

My Dear Friend:

I have just returned from a visit to Cape Cod, with my face well sun-burnt, and looking as red as a boiled lobster — my nose somewhat redder than that, to the scandal of my professed teetotalism. I find another letter from you, in regard to my being with you, at Syracuse, on the 1st of October, to celebrate the "Rescue" anniversary.[1] As I have but a moment, or so, at this time, in which to answer your letter, I must be very brief. *Deo volente*, I will be with you on the occasion designated, which, I trust, will be a glorious one for our cause. Theodore Parker says he cannot go, but he will write a letter to be read to the assembly, and it will partly atone for his absence, I have no doubt.[2] Whether Wendell Phillips will be able to attend, I think is very doubtful; but you will doubtless hear from him directly. I shall use all my endeavors to secure him.[3]

Much very much do I regret that I cannot be at the Woman's Rights Convention, which is to assemble to-morrow in Syracuse;[4] but circumstances prevent. I shall be there, in spirit, from its organization to its dissolution. It has as noble an object in view, ay, and as *Christian* a one too, as was ever advocated beneath the sun. Heaven bless all its proceedings!

Yours, for all human rights,

Wm. Lloyd Garrison.

Rev. S. J. May

ALS: Garrison Papers, Boston Public Library.

1. The reference is to the rescue of an alleged fugitive slave, Jerry McHenry, also known as William Henry, then living in Syracuse, from the hands of the police, who had arrested him on October 1, 1851 for the purpose of returning him to slavery. The rescue was carried out on the same day, by a vigilance committee of between twenty and thirty picked men, including Samuel J. May and Gerrit Smith, who overpowered his police guard, cut off his shackles, and sent him to Canada and freedom.

Eighteen persons were indicted for their part in the rescue and taken to Auburn, New York. They were accompanied on their journey by one hundred sympathizers, including women. Senator William H. Seward signed his name to their bond, as did others. May, Smith, and Charles A. Wheaton, who had not been arrested, issued a public statement admitting their part in the rescue and expressing a desire to be tried for it. Public opinion was found to be so overwhelmingly in sympathy with the offenders, that after several attempts at a trial, in Buffalo, Albany, and Canandaigua, the last named as late as October 1853, the government finally decided to abandon the case. The anniversary of the rescue was thereafter celebrated for several years. (Good accounts are to be found in *Memoir of Samuel Joseph May*, Boston, 1873, pp. 218–222, and in Samuel J. May, *Some Recollections of Our Antislavery Conflict*, Boston, 1869, pp. 373–384. See also Quarles, *Black Abolitionists*, pp. 209–211.)

2. A letter from Theodore Parker was read at the meeting. (*The Liberator*, October 8, 1852.)

3. Wendell Phillips's name is not listed among the speakers or participants. (*The Liberator*, October 8, 1852.)

4. *The Liberator*, October 1 and 8, 1852, carried a detailed report of the convention.

---

4 6

TO ADELINE ROBERTS

Boston, Sept. 14, 1852.

Esteemed Friend:

I have been wishing to know how to answer your letter, in regard to Miss Holley,[1] ever since I received it; but, knowing nothing as to where a letter would reach her, I could give you no definite reply. Happily, I am now able, by conferring with Mr. May,[2] our General Agent, who has just arrived from Leicester,[3] to inform you that the desire of your Lecturing Committee shall be gratified, and, therefore, that you may announce Miss Holley to give the lecture on the evening of Oct. 10th; thus filling the only blank in your list. If the ability of Miss H., as a speaker, were widely known in Salem, she would doubtless draw a larger audience than any other speaker embraced in your programme.

Allow me to add, that while I shall be happy to give the closing lecture of the course, as set down for me, it will give me still more pleasure to have some one substituted in my place; and I hope, therefore, you will not hesitate to make the change,[4] in case some other speaker may occur to the Committee, whom it may be thought desirable to bring before a Salem audience.

Trusting the entire course will be one of surpassing interest and power, I remain,

Yours, for the freedom of all in bonds,

Wm. Lloyd Garrison.

Miss Adeline Roberts.

ALS: Essex Institute, Salem, Massachusetts.

1. Sallie Holley (February 17, 1818–January 12, 1893), born in Canandaigua, New York, was the daughter of Myron Holley, a political abolitionist and founder of the Liberty party. She was converted to Garrisonian abolitionism by Abby Kelley Foster. On her graduation from Oberlin College in 1851, she accepted an appointment as an agent of the American Anti-Slavery Society, often speaking three or four times a week, and continuing with her work until after Emancipation, indeed as late as 1870, when the Society officially disbanded. During these years, she was also a vigorous advocate of woman's rights as well as of temperance. After 1870, she joined her friend, Caroline Putnam, in conducting a school for freedmen which had been established by the latter two years earlier at Lottsburg, Northumberland County, Virginia. Miss Holley remained with the school, which became known as the Holley School, throughout the remainder of her life. (*Notable American Women.*)

2. Samuel May, Jr.

3. Leicester, Massachusetts.

4. The list of speakers, as finally printed, named Garrison as the speaker on November 21 (*The Liberator*, October 1, 1852).

---

4 7

TO SAMUEL J. MAY

Boston, Sept. 16, 1852.

My Dear Friend:

In being at your "rescue" anniversary on the 1st of October, I was hoping to be able to "kill two stones with one bird," (as some one has said, in Ireland or out of it,) — i.e. to make it incidental to my visit to Pennsylvania, to attend the annual meeting of the State A. S. Society; but as that meeting has been postponed from the first week in October to the last, I shall not be able to carry that plan into effect. I am hesitating, therefore, whether to be with you on the 1st. My presence, with the amount of talent you will not fail to have present on the occasion, can certainly be of no special value; and as the distance and the expense are both considerable, (the latter being the most weighty consideration,) my conclusion is, that I had better send a letter to be read to the meeting, and abandon the idea of being on the ground bodily. I am always pecuniarily straitened, (you know how to sympathize with me,) and at the present time a little more so than usual, and therefore do not feel able to meet the expense of such a journey; nor could I feel reconciled to taxing any of the friends of the cause in your region, as my visit would assuredly "not pay." Allow me, dear friend, to do what Theodore Parker and Wendell Phillips will do — send you an epistle as a substitute for a speech. The former will cost only three cents — the latter probably not less than sixteen dollars, besides, a week's absence from home. If I could spend any time lecturing in your State in other places, it would alter the case; but I cannot.

My spirit is exulting in view of the successful proceedings of the Woman's Rights Convention in your city.[1] This is the fifth or sixth conventional experiment on the part of the women of this country to plead their own cause, and vindicate their inalienable rights. In every instance, the result has far surpassed the most sanguine expectations. They have conducted their meetings with a dignity, a propriety, and an amount of talent, seldom equalled by the other sex. The effect upon the public mind has been very striking. The press generally has behaved remarkably well, and treated the effort respectfully, in many instances cordially. What a change, my dear friend, has been wrought since 1840, when the American Anti-Slavery Society was rent asunder, on the sole ground (at least ostensibly) that it was an intolerable outrage, and shockingly unscriptural, to place a woman on one of its committees! Where is the orthodox General Association of Massachusetts, which was once so prompt to issue its bull against the Grimkes,[2] for publicly pleading "the cause of all such as are appointed to destruction"?[3] Even the New York Observer[4] and Puritan Recorder[5] are dumb! And all this in view of the fact, that the women are claiming entire equality of rights with men — the right to be ministers, lawyers, doctors, and even legislators! Really, the age is "progressive" — and, beyond all cavil, "the world moves."

Speaking of the Grimkes, Angelina (with her children) and Sarah[6] are now spending a few weeks at the pleasant residence of Samuel Philbrick[7] in Brookline. The latter I have seen, but Angelina was too unwell the day I called to leave her room. She is suffering from the fever and ague. They both wear the Bloomer costume.[8] Theodore [Weld] is at home on his farm.[9]

I see that the seceding portion of the Liberty Party,[10] with William Goodell at its head, adjourned their meeting to assemble again at Syracuse on the "Jerry" anniversary; probably to take advantage of the gathering of the friends of the slave on that occasion. It seems to me this ought not to have been done. That day ought to be unitedly and entirely consecrated to the one great purpose contemplated by your arrangements.

By the way, the nomination of Goodell for the Presidency of the United States, by less than a baker's dozen, and without a supporter in any State except New York, and scarcely one in that, is one of the most comical incidents of the age — "a farce in one act," unequalled for its simplicity and folly. Pray, where is Goodell's common sense? where his self-respect? where his respect for the popular intelligence?

The weakness, the egotism, the presumption, manifested by such a course, are equally ludicrous and astounding. O, politics! "O, trumpery! O, Moses!"

Our friend Gerrit Smith is still "as green as grass," politically. It is laughable to read the resolutions presented by him at Canastota,[11] especially where he holds out the lure (!) to the "Free Democratic party," that they will secure his vote, and those of his score of political followers, if they will only make their platform conform to that of the Liberty Party! My gravity is utterly routed by the gravity which he assumes in waiting to learn whether Hale and Julian [12] will adopt his theory of government, before making up his mind for whom to vote! *"Ohe! jam satis!"* [13]

Helen sends her loving remembrances to you all. Mine are included, of course.

Yours, everlastingly,   Wm. Lloyd Garrison.

ALS: Garrison Papers, Boston Public Library. A substantial portion of this letter is printed in *Life*, III, 372–373.

1. September 8–10, 1852.
2. Garrison is referring to the "Pastoral Letter of the General Association of Massachusetts to the Congregational Churches under their care," issued on July 28, 1837, which, among other things, denounced those females, "who so far forget themselves as to itinerate in the character of public lecturers and teachers." The reference was to Sarah and Angelina Grimké, who were speaking throughout New England, to mixed audiences of men and women, on the subject of slavery. (See Gerda Lerner, *The Grimké Sisters from South Carolina, Rebels Against Slavery*, Boston, 1967, p. 189 ff.)
3. Proverbs 31:8.
4. The New York *Observer* was a conservative Presbyterian newspaper established in 1823 by Sidney and Richard Carey Morse. (See *Letters*, II, 381.)
5. The reference is to the Boston *Recorder*, a conservative Congregational weekly founded in 1816. (*Letters*, II, 149.)
6. The Grimké sisters, originally of South Carolina, had been active in the antislavery movement since 1835. By 1838, Angelina had married Theodore Weld, and had immediately after the marriage moved into a house in Fort Lee, New Jersey, with Theodore and her sister, Sarah. Angelina gave birth to a boy, Charles Stuart, on December 14, 1839. In March 1840 the three bought a fifty-acre farm, with a fifteen-room house, in Belleville, New Jersey, along the Passaic River. Angelina gave birth to her second son, Theodore, on January 3, 1841, and to a daughter, Sarah Grimké, on March 22, 1844. By 1851, they had formed a boarding school, named Belleville School, on the farm, with Theodore Weld as principal, and Sarah and Angelina doing the cooking, washing, and cleaning as well as helping out with the instruction. In 1854, they left Belleville for Raritan Bay Union at Eagleswood, New Jersey, a cooperative community in which the Welds and Sarah each invested $1000 in the community's stock, and where Weld accepted the position of director of the community's school, known as Eagleswood School. Although the cooperative died by the end of the second year, the Welds and Sarah continued to live there on their own land and Weld continued the school as a private venture. In 1862, Weld gave up the school and the family moved to a private home in Perth Amboy, New Jersey, then to West Newton, Massachusetts, and finally in 1864 to Hyde Park, Massachusetts, where they remained until the end of their lives. (Gerda Lerner, *The Grimké Sisters, passim.*)

7. Samuel Philbrick, a businessman and pioneering abolitionist, was a devoted friend and supporter of Garrison and for many years treasurer of the Massachusetts Anti-Slavery Society. (For additional information see *Letters*, II, 348.)

8. "A short skirt, with trousers (*Lib.* 21:76). 'Mrs. [Amelia] Bloomer was among the first to wear the dress, and stoutly advocated its adoption in her paper, the *Lily*, published at Seneca Falls, N. Y. But it was introduced by Elizabeth Smith Miller, the daughter of the great philanthropist, Gerrit Smith, in 1850' ('Hist. of Woman Suffrage,' I:127; and see also pp. 469, 844)." (*Life*, III, 372.)

9. At Belleville, New Jersey.

10. The Liberty party had been formed early in 1840 by political abolitionists under the leadership of such men as Gerrit Smith, William Goodell, Elizur Wright, James Birney, Myron Holley, and Joshua Leavitt. Birney and Thomas Earle were chosen as candidates for President and vice-president of the United States. Their platform pledged their opposition to slavery, with full use of legislative power under the Constitution, and emphasized abolition of the interstate slave trade as well as of slavery in Washington, D.C. In 1840, Birney received about seven thousand votes, and in 1844, again the Liberty party's candidate for president, he received 62,300 votes. In June 1847, because of a conviction that the Liberty party's antislavery program was too narrow, William Goodell and a number of others seceded from the party and founded the Liberty League, which nominated Gerrit Smith for President on a platform of opposition to slavery, tariffs, land monopoly, the liquor traffic, war, and secret societies. In 1848, the Liberty party supported the candidates of the Free Soil Party, Martin Van Buren and Charles Francis Adams, for President and vice-president respectively and merged with the latter party. A small group, however, refused to support the Free Soil candidates and preferred Gerrit Smith. They met as "the Liberty Party" in convention at Buffalo in June 1848, nominated the candidates of the Liberty League, and adopted the latter's platform. In turn the Liberty League gave up its organization and merged with the "new" Liberty party. (William Goodell, *Slavery and Anti-Slavery, a History of the Great Struggle in Both Hemispheres; with a View of the Slavery Question in the United States*, New York, 1852, reprinted in 1968 by Negro Universities Press, pp. 468–482.)

Garrison's reference to "the seceding portion of the Liberty Party" concerns a division in the Liberty party of New York State in 1852. On August 11, elements of the Free Soil and the original Liberty party had gathered in Pittsburgh, Pennsylvania, under the rubric of "Free Democracy" and had nominated John P. Hale, U.S. senator from New Hampshire, as their candidate for President (see note 12). Among the participants were Henry Wilson of Massachusetts, Frederick Douglass, Lewis Tappan, Gerrit Smith, and Charles Francis Adams.

Shortly afterward, on September 2, the Liberty party met at Canastota, New York, and voted to support Hale's candidacy. A minority withdrew and nominated William Goodell as their candidate for President. Apparently, however, the endorsement of Hale was conditional. It depended upon a series of questions that were submitted to Hale, the answers to which would result either in confirmation of the nomination or its reversal. Hale apparently did not reply. It was therefore decided to hold another Liberty party convention at Syracuse on Thursday, September 30, with the understanding that the delegates to the convention would attend the celebration of the anniversary of the rescue of Jerry on the following day. The convention did take place on the appointed day and nominated Goodell for President. (*The National Anti-Slavery Standard*, September 23, 1852, October 7, 1852; *Life*, III, 369–370.)

11. Gerrit Smith and several other leaders of the Liberty party had written the following letter to Hale:

"CANASTOTA, Sept. 2d, 1852.

"HON. JOHN P. HALE — *Dear Sir*: The National Convention of the Liberty Party has, this day, appointed a committee consisting of ourselves. One of our duties is to inquire:

"1st. Whether you believe that Civil Government is instituted for the purpose of maintaining all the political rights of all its subjects, male or female, black or white; and therefore, that every political party is to regard itself as organized for the purpose of securing this equal justice at the hands of Civil Government?

"2d. Whether you believe that Slavery, so far from being capable of legalization, is a naked piracy, around which there can be no possible legal covering; a matchless crime and fraud, to which no Constitution, nor Legislature, nor Judiciary, can afford the least possible shelter?

"We had expected that, long ere this time, you would, in the terms of your acceptance of your nomination to the Presidency of the United States, have made so explicit an avowal of your political creed, as to render any inquiries into the character of that creed quite superfluous. So far, however, is this expectation from being fulfilled, that we are not yet aware that you have accepted the nomination.

"Permit us to express the hope that you will favour us with an early answer, directed to Gerrit Smith, Peterboro, Madison Co., N. Y.

GERRIT SMITH
STILLMAN SPOONER
ABRAM PAYNE
WASHINGTON STICKNEY
B. F. REMINGTON

(*The National Anti-Slavery Standard*, September 23, 1852.)

12. John P. Hale and George W. Julian, Presidential and vice-presidential candidates, respectively, of the "Free Democratic Party."

John Parker Hale (1806–1873) of New Hampshire, a lawyer and political figure, served in the Twenty-eighth Congress, 1843–1845, as a Democrat, and "refused to vote for the annexation of Texas, although instructed to do so by the legislature." Elected to the United States Senate as the first antislavery candidate, he served from March 4, 1847, to March 3, 1853. He was defeated as candidate for President on the Free Soil ticket in 1852, receiving 156,149 votes. He was reelected to the Senate in 1855 and again in 1859, serving until 1865. He was minister to Spain from 1865 to 1869 and lived his last years in Dover, New Hampshire. (*BDAC.*)

George Washington Julian (1817–1899) of Indiana, lawyer, politician and author, was a delegate to the Buffalo Free Soil Convention in 1848, and was elected to Congress as a Free Soiler, serving from 1849 to 1851. He was defeated as the Free Soil candidate for vice-president in 1852. He was a delegate to the Republican National Convention in 1856 and was elected as a Republican to Congress in 1860 and several times thereafter, serving from 1861 to 1871. He was surveyor general of New Mexico, by appointment of President Cleveland, from 1885 to 1889. His last years were spent in Irvington, a suburb of Indianapolis, Indiana. (*BDAC.*)

13. The Latin for "never satisfied."

---

4 8

TO SAMUEL J. MAY

Boston, Sept. 27, 1852.

My dear S. J. May:

Thanks for your letter. You say "come," and the travelling expenses shall be paid. This is very kind. I strongly desire to be at the "Rescue" meeting on Friday next; but I cannot persuade myself that my presence will justify such a tax on the friends of the anti-slavery cause. So, even at this moment, I am hesitating in my mind as to what I ought to do. But you want a definite answer, and it shall be this — I will be with you. My plan is, to leave Boston on Wednesday morning,[1] and lecture in Albany that evening, in compliance with a request of some friends in that city; and on Thursday morning[2] to proceed to Syracuse, arriving in your city, I suppose, by 1 or 2 o'clock. Perhaps it might be well, on that evening, to have a social but somewhat select meeting of friends, to confer together as to the next day's order of proceedings; for the occasion will be one of vast responsibility and importance, and we need great wisdom to direct as well as courage to execute. Every document, and all the resolutions, to be submitted to the meeting, should be most carefully prepared and critically examined, both in a moral and legal point of view.

There ought to be a reliable report of the proceedings,[3] cost what it may; for we may anticipate any amount of misrepresentation on the part of such pro-slavery papers as the "Star," [4] &c. &c.

I sincerely hope that Giddings will not disappoint you,[5] though I hardly expect to see him at the meeting. But as for John P. Hale, though I see his name advertised in your call, I have no idea that he will allow himself to be caught at such a meeting.[6] He is altogether too politic for that, or I am greatly mistaken. Of course, I do not know what promise he has made to you; but such is my feeling.

So utterly unimportant does my presence seem to me, that, much as my social feelings would be gratified by being with you, I should prefer to remain at home, and send you a letter as a substitute, rather than tax the friends to the extent of my travelling expenses. Now, if you feel assured of sufficient help for the occasion without me, what I desire is that, on the receipt of this to-morrow, (Tuesday,) you will telegraph me to that effect; but if I hear nothing from you, then I shall take it for granted that I must go, and will accordingly take the cars on Wednesday morning, as already stated.[7]

Theodore Parker has put into my hands an admirable letter from his pen, to be read to the meeting, provided any one can decipher his manuscript, who shall undertake to read it.[8]

Yours, most affectionately,

Wm. Lloyd Garrison.

Rev. S. J. May.

ALS: Garrison Papers, Boston Public Library. A portion of this letter is printed in *Life*, III, 373.

1. September 29, 1852.
2. September 30.

3. *National Anti-Slavery Standard,* October 7, 1852, carried a report of the proceedings, as did *The Liberator,* October 8, 1852.

4. The Syracuse *Star* was the lineal descendant of the Democratic newspaper, *The Freeman,* which had begun publication in 1844 and had changed its name to the *Star* shortly thereafter. In 1852, S. Corning Judd became its editor and proprietor and was succeeded in October 1853 by Edward Hoagland, who changed its name to the Syracuse *Republican.* (Dwight H. Bruce, *Memorial History of Syracuse,* New York, Syracuse, 1891, p. 555.) Garrison's apprehensions about the hostility of the *Star* and other newspapers in Syracuse toward the "Rescue" meeting were borne out by the account of the meeting in the *Star.* See *The Liberator,* October 8, 1852, which reprinted the *Star's* hostile story of the meeting.

5. The report of the proceedings does not mention the presence of Joshua Giddings.

6. Hale does not appear to have been present.

7. Garrison did attend. He delivered an address and participated in other ways, too.

8. The reports of the proceedings in the *Standard* and *The Liberator* indicate that letters were received from Theodore Parker, Salmon P. Chase of Ohio, Richard Hildreth of Boston, and others. Some but not all were read. It is quite likely that Parker's letter was not read because of an inability to decipher his handwriting, which was notoriously illegible.

49

TO JOSEPH A. DUGDALE

Boston, Oct. 16, 1852.

My Dear Friend:

As I am just starting on my visit to Pennsylvania, (via Northampton,) I have barely time to acknowledge the receipt of your kind letter, — to express my sympathy with you in regard to your late severe illness, and gratification to hear that you are convalescent, — and to say that I shall be happy to comply with your request to be with you at the Kennett Square gathering at the time specified by you,[1] — provided the friends in Philadelphia have not committed me to be at some other place, and I presume they have not done so.

With loving regards to all the friends, and special remembrances from Helen to you and yours, I remain,

Yours, in the bonds of everlasting love,

Wm. Lloyd Garrison.

Joseph A. Dugdale.

ALS: Friends Historical Library, Swarthmore College.

Joseph Dugdale was an antislavery Quaker of Kennett township, in Pennsylvania, near the Delaware border, about ten miles from Wilmington. (R. C. Smedley, *History of the Underground Railroad in Chester* . . . , Lancaster, Pennsylvania, 1883, p. 256.) Garrison, in writing of his visit to Kennett, where he participated in the quarterly meeting of the Society of Friends, said as follows: "Among those who participated in the discussion were Joseph A. Dugdale, formerly of Ohio, now of Kennett, and well known to the readers of the *Liberator* — a thorn in the side of Quaker Hunkerism, and a troubler of its peace, but possessed of a loving and reverent spirit, aspiring after all that is beautiful and good, and a practical reformer on a world-wide scale." (*The Liberator*, December 24, 1852.)

It may also be of interest to cite Garrison's description of Joseph Dugdale's mother. "Another revered friend, whom it was our happiness to greet at Kennett, was Ruth [Garrison errs here. She was Sarah. Dugdale's *wife* was Ruth] Dugdale, the mother of Joseph, and long an accredited minister of the Society of Friends. She was present at the memorable division of the American Anti-Slavery Society, at New York, in 1840, (caused by sectarian and clerical influences,) having been one of a company of faithful abolitionists, who rode all the way from Ohio in an open vehicle, called 'The Liberator,' in order to prevent the betrayal of the Society into the hands of those whose love of supremacy was paramount to their sympathy for the slave, and whose abolitionism was subordinate to their sectarianism. She is remarkable for her strength and clearness of mind, her interesting conversational powers, her benign and dignified carriage, and her motherly qualities." (*The Liberator*, December 31, 1852.)

Dugdale had been born on November 10, 1810, at Bristol, Pennsylvania, and died at Mt. Pleasant, Iowa, March 5, 1896. Of Quaker parentage, he was a farmer, school teacher, minister and reformer, active in antislavery, peace, temperance, and various other reforms. He was "a close friend and laborer with Charles Sumner, Lucretia Mott, William Lloyd Garrison, Wendell Phillips, Lydia Maria Child, Samuel J. May, and many other faithful workers." (*Friends' Intelligencer and Journal*, Philadelphia, 53:190, March 21, 1896.)

1. Garrison was in Kennett for three days. For additional details of the trip, especially his various speaking engagements following his stay in Kennett, see *The Liberator*, December 31, 1852.

---

5 0

TO D. P. HARMON

Boston, Oct. 16, 1852.

My Dear Friend:

Your "specimen of horticultural success," in the shape of a very generous quantity of superb grapes, came duly to hand, in perfect order. One of the bunches weighed two pounds, and seemed to be too precious to touch, while perfectly irresistible to the appetite. My numerous family enjoyed the feast as though they were partaking of the fruits of Paradise. If better grapes grew before "the fall of Adam and Eve," they were a lucky couple; but I have my doubts on that point.

What was even more gratifying than the fruit itself was the very kind note accompanying it, expressive of your personal regard, and warm appreciation of my humble labors in the cause of oppressed humanity universally. Such a testimony is strengthening to my spirit.

The united regards of my family are proffered to you and yours, with many thanks for your kind present.

I am just starting on a tour to Pennsylvania, to be absent about three weeks.¹ Whether at home or abroad, I am, my dear friend,

Yours, in the bonds of everlasting love,

Wm. Lloyd Garrison.

D. P. Harmon.

ALS: University of California Library, Berkeley.

Possibly David Porter Harmon (b. Peterboro, New Hampshire, March 11, 1800; d. Haverhill, Massachusetts, November 11, 1869), wealthy shoe manufacturer and lumber merchant in Haverhill. He was married to Elmira Sargent and had four sons and one daughter. (Artemas C. Harmon, *The Harmon Genealogy*, Washington, 1920, p. 253; George W. Chase, *The History of Haverhill*, Haverhill, 1861, p. 534.)

1. Garrison left Boston on Saturday, October 16, going to Pennsylvania by way of Northampton, Massachusetts, where he took part in antislavery meetings during the afternoon and evening of Sunday, October 17, and remained until the morning of Wednesday, October 20. Arriving in New York that afternoon, he remained until Friday, October 22, when he traveled to Philadelphia, where he stayed with James and Lucretia Mott. On Saturday evening, October 23, he occupied the pulpit of Henry D. More, pastor of the "Independent Chapel" on Thirteenth Street, and delivered a sermon on slavery. On Sunday, October 24, he spoke on the same subject at Franklin Hall in Philadelphia and later that day attended Cherry Street Meeting of Friends, where Lucretia Mott spoke. The primary purpose of Garrison's trip was to attend the annual meeting of the Pennsylvania Anti-Slavery Society which was held in West Chester, Pennsylvania, about thirty miles from Philadelphia, from October 26 to 27. He traveled from Philadelphia to West Chester by train, with more than a hundred delegates from the former city. Unfortunately, during the convention and for several days after his return to Boston, Garrison suffered from severe "hoarseness," which he attributed to "influenza," and which limited his participation in the convention's proceedings. "It was peculiarly trying to our feelings," he noted in his description of the convention, "to be suddenly caught in this manner, when we never had a stronger desire to be in voice, both in regard to public speaking and to private social intercourse; and this hoarseness clung to us not only during the remainder of our sojourn in the State, but some time after our return home, so that we voted — unanimously — to consider our visit measurably a failure, and that, *Deo volente*, we would try to make it up at no distant day." (*The Liberator*, December 10, 1852.) While in West Chester, he stayed at the home of an antislavery Quaker named J. Hoopes. From West Chester Garrison proceeded to Kennett, Pennsylvania, where he spent three days and participated in a quarterly meeting of Friends. Thereafter, Garrison spoke or spent time with friends in Philadelphia, Norristown, Byberry, and Wrightstown. For the account of Garrison's trip, we are indebted to a series of essays by Garrison in *The Liberator*, November 12, 26, December 3, 10, 24, 31, 1852.

5 1

TO ADELINE ROBERTS

Boston, Oct. 16, 1852.

Respected Friend:

Please convey to Mrs. William Ives [1] my grateful acknowledgments for her proffered hospitality, which it will give me very great pleasure to accept.

I am rejoiced to hear that the lectures, thus far delivered, have been fully attended, and equally interesting and instructive. May the whole series exceed in utility the highest anticipations of your Society.

You should have terminated the course with a climax; and therefore should have allowed some other one to give the last lecture than

Your un-oratorical friend,

Wm. Lloyd Garrison.

Miss Adeline Roberts.

ALS: Essex Institute, Salem, Massachusetts.

1. Mrs. William Ives (b. Hingham, Massachusetts, February 10, 1800; d. Chicago, Illinois, October 19, 1882) was the daughter of Perez Gardner of Hingham. She married William Ives of Salem on May 12, 1824. (*Vital Records of Salem, Mass.*, Salem, 1924, III, 539; *History of the Town of Hingham, Massachusetts*, Cambridge, 1893, II, 251.)

III CONVENTIONS AND TRIPS WEST: 1853

T HE YEAR WAS NOTABLE for Garrison's two trips to the West. The first, in April, was marked by visits to Cleveland and Cincinnati, where he attended an antislavery convention on April 19, 20, and 21. The visit to Cincinnati was his first to that city. As *Life*, III, 378, remarks, "On the day appointed he stood on the banks of the Ohio, and beheld for the first time the slave-cursed soil of Kentucky." Unfortunately, his trip, which was to include Michigan, was cut short by a sharp pleuritic attack which sent him to bed and forced him to return home.

The second trip, in October, was primarily a visit to Michigan by way of Ohio. Leaving Boston on October 3, he attended the fourth national Woman's Rights Convention in Cleveland, Ohio, on October 5, 6, and 7, in which he took an active part, visiting Adrian, Michigan, during the following days, where he spent some time at the grave of Elizabeth Chandler, the antislavery poet, and then going on to Detroit, crossing the Detroit River and stepping on Canadian soil at Windsor. Returning to Adrian on October 22 and 23, he helped found the Garrisonian Michigan Anti-Slavery Society and went back to Boston by way of Jefferson, Ohio, where his host was Joshua R. Giddings.

Between these trips there occurred the American Anti-Slavery convention in New York on May 11, where Henry Ward Beecher appeared for the first time on an abolitionist platform; the New England Anti-Slavery Convention in Boston at the end of May, where, on May 26, he delivered "his best considered and most effective speech" of that year [1]; the Bible convention at Hartford, Connecticut, from Thursday, June 2 to Sunday, June 5, "for the purposes of freely and fully canvassing the origin, authority, and influence of the Jewish and Christian Scriptures"; [2] the celebration of West India Emancipation on August 4, at Flushing, Long Island, under the sponsorship of the New York City Anti-Slavery Society; and a visit to New York City to attend the Whole World's Temperance Convention on September

1 and 2, followed on succeeding days by attendance at a stage performance of *Uncle Tom's Cabin* at the National Theatre, and, on the following day, by an address at the New York City Anti-Slavery Society. The year ends with an exchange of letters between Garrison and Harriet Beecher Stowe and Garrison's visit with Mrs. Stowe at Andover, Massachusetts, in December.

1. *Life*, III, 383.
2. *Ibid*.

5 2

TO LYDIA MARIA CHILD

Boston, Jan. 20, 1853.

My dear Mrs. Child:

Thanks for your letter. You will do me a great deal of honor, should you copy my Sonnet to that truly great and good man, Isaac T. Hopper,[1] into the Biography which you are preparing for the press.[2] Most readily do I consent to the alterations in it which you suggest, as they are obviously improvements. If his name be dropped, however, the first line will be two syllables short, which you may supply according to your own good judgment.[3] I am equally thankful and rejoiced to know that his precious memory is in your care, biographically speaking; and I shall look impatiently for the volume, confident that it will be of surpassing interest, and most skilfully executed.

Late as it is, allow me to proffer to you and your esteemed husband, the congratulations and best wishes of the New Year.

Yours, with high and grateful regards,

Wm. Lloyd Garrison.

Lydia Maria Child.

ALS: New York Historical Society.

Lydia Maria Child (1802–1880), prominent author, editor, and antislavery spokesman, had edited the *National Anti-Slavery Standard* in New York City from the spring of 1841 to the spring of 1843. During that time she stayed at the home of Isaac T. Hopper, the antislavery Quaker, philanthropist, and prison reformer who was also business manager of the *Standard*. After resigning as editor she remained in New York, writing articles for newspapers and books for children. From 1847 to 1849 she lived a good part of the time in New Rochelle, New York, at the home of a Quaker abolitionist and participant in the Underground Railroad, David Carpenter. In 1849, she and her husband, David — they had been married since 1829 — moved into a house at West Newton, rented to them by the Boston abolitionist, Ellis G. Loring. At the beginning of 1853, they were still living in West Newton, but at the end of the year they moved to a farm in Wayland, Massachusetts, where they shared a home with Mrs. Child's father, who was then in his late eighties. She and her husband David lived there for the remainder of their lives. (Milton Meltzer, *Tongue of Flame, The Life of Lydia Maria Child*, New York, 1965, *passim*; *Letters*, I and II, provide information about the earlier years of Lydia and David Child. See also *Notable American Women*.)

1. Isaac Tatem Hopper (b. Deptford Township, Gloucester County, New Jersey, December 3, 1771; d. New York City, May 7, 1852), had lived during his youth in Philadelphia, where he learned the tailor's trade. There, too, he joined the Quakers and participated actively in the Pennsylvania Abolition Society and in many other philanthropic and humanitarian endeavors. In 1829 he moved to New York, where he managed a Hicksite Quaker bookstore. After returning to New York from a visit to Britain in 1830, while continuing to manage the bookstore, he devoted his time during the ensuing years to prison and prisoner reform.

With a decline in demand for Hicksite books, he became treasurer and book-agent for the American Anti-Slavery Society in 1841, holding these positions until 1845 when he resigned to devote all his time to the work of the Prison Association, with which he had been connected for many years. It was soon after Hopper's death in May 1852 that Lydia Maria Child began to write his biography.

2. Mrs. Child's biography, *Isaac T. Hopper: A True Life*, was published in Boston, in 1853, by John Jewett and Company. Garrison's sonnet appears on p. 448 and reads as follows:

> "Thou kind and venerable friend of man,
>   In heart and spirit young, though old in years!
>   The tyrant trembles when thy name he hears,
> And the slave joys thy honest face to scan.
> A friend more true and brave, since time began,
>   Humanity has never found: her fears
>   By thee have been dispelled, and wiped the tears
> Adown her sorrow-stricken cheeks that ran.
> If like Napoleon's appears thy face,
>   Thy soul to his bears no similitude.
> He came to curse, but thou to bless our race.
>   Thy hands are pure; in blood were his imbrued.
> His memory shall be covered with disgrace,
>   But thine embalmed among the truly great and good."

3. Garrison's sonnet in the original differed somewhat from that printed by Mrs. Child. Its first four lines, in which the changes occurred, read as follows:

> "Hopper! thou venerable friend of man,
>   In heart and spirit young, though old in years;
>   The tyrant trembles when thy name he hears,
> And the slave joys thy countenance to scan."

The entire sonnet was printed in *Selections from the Writings and Speeches of William Lloyd Garrison* (Boston, 1852), p. 368.

It may also be of interest that the title page of Mrs. Child's volume carried the following four lines of poetry by Garrison:

> "Thine was a soul with sympathy imbued
> Broad as the earth, and as the heavens sublime;
> Thy godlike object, steadfastly pursued,
> To save thy race from misery and crime."

53

TO THOMAS WENTWORTH HIGGINSON

Boston, Feb. 1, 1853.

My Dear Friend:

Yours is just received. I will endeavor to hold myself in readiness for either the 18th or the 25th inst.[1] We have received a parcel at the office, to-day, for Mr. Douglass, from Rochester; so that it is probable he is on his way, and will be able to give his lecture on the 18th.[2]

Myself out of the question, you have an attractive corps of lectures, as designated in the advertisement, which I will publish in the next Liberator.[3]

Your speech,[4] as reported by Mr. Yerrinton,[5] was sent to you this morning by Mr. May.[6] Allow me to judge, and to pronounce it excellent in manner, matter and spirit. You can alter or add to it, *ad libitum.*

Yours, with much regard,

Wm. Lloyd Garrison.

Rev. T. W. Higginson.

ALS: Collection of Richard Maass, White Plains, New York.

Thomas Wentworth Higginson was then president of the "recently formed" Worcester City Anti-Slavery Society. (*The Liberator*, February 11, 1853.)

1. Garrison spoke before the Worcester City Anti-Slavery Society on Friday evening, February 25. (*The Liberator*, February 25, 1853.)

2. Frederick Douglass was scheduled to speak before the Worcester City Anti-Slavery Society on Friday evening, February 18. (*The Liberator*, February 18, 1853.) According to Tilden Edelstein, Douglass failed to appear and Higginson "instead read to the audience from the speeches of Wendell Phillips." (Tilden G. Edelstein, *Strange Enthusiasm, A Life of Thomas Wentworth Higginson*, New Haven and London, 1968, p. 139.) Higginson, in a letter to Garrison, dated February 23, 1853, noted that "Douglass failed us: & you come next." (Antislavery Letters to Garrison and Others, Boston Public Library.)

3. *The Liberator*, February 4 and 11, 1853, listed the following speakers, but not in chronological order, except for the first: Horace Greeley, Garrison, John Pierpont, Theodore Parker, Horace Mann, Frederick Douglass, and Henry Ward Beecher.

4. The reference is to a speech by Higginson at the Twenty-First Annual Meeting of the Massachusetts Anti-Slavery Society, held in Boston on January 26–28, 1853. In a one-sentence summary of his speech, *The Liberator* (February 4, 1853) noted that he "spoke in favor of the most thorough agitation of the community on the subject of slavery, and according to the principles and methods of this Society; — while he declared himself to be a member of the Free Democratic party." The text of Higginson's speech appeared in *The Liberator* on February 11, 1853.

5. James Manning Winchell Yerrinton (1825–1893), the son of James Brown Yerrinton, who had been printer of *The Liberator* from 1841 to 1865, was a printer and stenographer who assisted in the printing of *The Liberator* and was the official stenographer and reporter of the Massachusetts Anti-Slavery Society. (*Life*, I, 124; IV, 169, 325, 425.)

Nationally known for his stenography (often called phonography), in which he was a pioneer, he was born in Providence and came to Boston when very young and was educated in the Boston schools. After leaving school, he assisted his father on *The Liberator*. In 1847, he and five others began the publication of a Sons of Temperance newspaper, called *Excelsior*, which he edited with Charles W. Slack, a Boston abolitionist. In 1849, he sold his interest in the paper and joined his father in printing *The Liberator*, while mastering the art of stenography. During the ensuing years he gained his national reputation as a stenographer, his services being called for throughout the country, North and South. For nearly twenty-five years he was official stenographer of the Superior Criminal Court in Massachusetts. (Obituary, *Boston Transcript*, October 21, 1893.)

6. Samuel May, Jr., who was assistant secretary of the convention.

5 4

TO J. MILLER McKIM

Boston, March 19, 1853.

My dear McKim: —

I hasten to reply to your letter, just received.

It really causes me a great deal of joy to hear that you have concluded to go over to England this spring.[1] My best wishes and aspirations will go with you. I wish I could go myself! — You could not make a transatlantic trip at a time more opportune for our noble cause. My opinion of your qualifications is, that you are admirably fitted to meet British abolitionists face to face, and to remove very many of their erroneous and most injurious notions about us. The work to be done over there is more in the social circle than in public meeting, and no man in our ranks is better qualified to instruct and enlighten in this manner, than yourself. Of course, you will address some public meetings; and you have no occasion to hesitate, or feel abashed, on that score. Like the Welshman's rabbit, you are good any way you can be served up. And you will have such a pleasant time, and will have such a welcome from such friends! But it is not right to envy any body, and so I will *try* not to envy you. But it is so hard to be absolutely resigned in such a case!

There are four persons abroad, with whom you can confer, as to your course, in all confidence as to the soundness of their judgment: — George Thompson in London, John B. Estlin in Bristol,[2] Andrew Paton in Glasgow,[3] and Richard D. Webb in Dublin.[4] You will find many other reliable and highly intelligent friends, but these are specially "booked up" in regard to our cause on both sides of the Atlantic.

You express a hope that I may go to Cincinnati, by the way of Philadelphia. My intention has been, to go by the way of Buffalo, Cleveland, &c.; but mainly with reference to meeting Sallie Holley at Buffalo. I am sorry to say, she has concluded not to go to Cincinnati; and so I may make up my mind to take the southern route,[5] that I may have the pleasure of seeing you before you leave.

You ask what time in May the London anniversaries are held. The very first week — or from the 1st to the 10th of the month inclusive — I believe; so that, if you intend being present at any of them, you ought not to be detained here later than the middle of April.

There is here in Boston, a very worthy colored young man, (a fugitive slave from Maryland,) who has a sister at Baltimore, also a slave, and so white that she would easily pass any where as a white person. She is very intelligent, can read and write, and is in frequent correspondence with her brother. She is ready to leave the city at any moment, in order to come to Boston; and means to do so, as soon as she can procure a ticket. Her brother, therefore, wishes me to ascertain, whether you could probably get some friend, going to Baltimore, to buy a ticket for Philadelphia after his arrival, and enclose it in an envelope, to be left at a certain house in that city, as directed. There would be no risk of detection whatever. All that she needs is the ticket, and she will find her way here. If this can be arranged, the money shall be forwarded to you at once.

We are all well at home. Helen j[oins] with me in loving regards to your wife, yours[elf], and children.

Yours, in great haste,

Wm. Lloyd Garrison.

J. Miller McKim.

ALS: University of Rochester Library.

1. McKim sailed for England from New York on Saturday, April 30, 1853. *The National Anti-Slavery Standard*, May 5, 1853, printed the following item about his trip: "Visit to Europe. — Our friend J. M. McKim, of Philadelphia, sailed, from this port, for England in the Steamer Arctic, on Saturday last, with the purpose of passing several months in Europe. We rejoice, as, we are sure, all Mr. McKim's friends do, that he has concluded to take this season of recreation and rest from the arduous duties of his office, the agency of the Pennsylvania Anti-Slavery Society, to which, for so many years, he has devoted himself with unflagging zeal and industry, almost without a week's intermission. Though his visit abroad is not an official one, he will, of course, meet with many, perhaps with most, of the friends of the Anti-Slavery cause in Great Britain and Ireland; and it is not improper to say, by way of ecumenical introduction, that he is a representative of the American Abolitionists of whom they may be justly proud. . . ." *The Liberator*, May 20, 1853, reprinted this item and added its own felicitations and best wishes to McKim.

2. John Bishop Estlin (1785–1855), a well-known ophthalmic surgeon, was also a reformer and abolitionist.

3. Andrew Paton (1805–1884) was an abolitionist and friend of William Smeal. Garrison, while in Glasgow during his third English mission, in 1846, was the guest of Paton. The latter supported the North during the Civil War. With Smeal and others, Paton "prevented the sailing from the Clyde of a Confederate war vessel that would have been more formidable than the *Alabama*." Their friendship was lifelong. (*Life*, III, 175; IV, 67, 222–223, 283.)

4. Richard Davis Webb was an Irish reformer, Garrison's lifelong friend, and biographer of John Brown. (See *Letters*, II, 684.)

5. As Garrison's letter to Helen, April 18, 1853, indicates, he did not take the southern route.

Concerning the trip, *Life* (III, 378) says the following: "An anti-slavery convention had been called in Cincinnati for April 19, 1853, by the women of that city, and he was invited to attend. The scene was new to him, and he could visit on the way the friends in Cleveland to whom he had owed his life in 1847. On the day appointed he stood on the banks of the Ohio, and beheld for the first time the slave-cursed soil of Kentucky."

The Liberator, in a paragraph signed "Q" (Edmund Quincy, who edited the paper in Garrison's absence), noted that "Mr. Garrison left town last week for Cincinnati, where he proposed to attend the Anti-Slavery Convention now in session. We trust that the excursion will be beneficial to his health, as we are sure it will to the Anti-Slavery Cause. There is, perhaps, no man in the country so well abused and so grossly misrepresented as he, and there is certainly none before whose face prejudice and slander more swiftly flee away and hide themselves. His personal presence, in public and private, is the best antidote and reply to the poisonous calumnies aimed through him at the cause he incarnates in the eyes of pro-slavery America. His friends, and those of the slave, therefore, should rejoice at his occasional visits to distant fields of labor, even though it should be their own immediate loss. . . ." (April 22, 1853.)

5 5

TO HELEN E. GARRISON

Cleveland, April 18, 1853.
Monday Morning.

Dear Wife:

"I take my *pencil* in hand to let you know that I am well, and hope these few lines will find you enjoying the same blessing."

Our ride from Boston to Springfield (100 miles) [1] was accomplished in two hours and three quarters — and the time seemed to be much less than this, with so pleasant a companion as Wendell [Phillips] by my side. The remainder of the ride to Albany (the same distance) was tedious and snail-paced enough, occupying between seven and eight hours. On arriving at the Greenwich [2] depot, I expected (as did every other passenger) the usual means of conveyance across the Hudson river to the city — i.e., a steam ferry-boat. But there was nothing of the kind. Our only alternative was to take a small row-boat, at our own expense, my part of which was 62½ cents! Most shameful sponging, and a most shameful arrangement. I went to the Delevan House, where I paid one dollar for a bed (which I occupied but three hours) and a breakfast as meagre as though Albany had no provision market. So unexpected was this ride into the morning, and so excessively wearied did I feel, that I came very near taking the cars for Boston instead of Buffalo — knowing that, if I continued on, I should have to ride *all* the next night, and fearing I should be completely "used up." However, I concluded to go on, and therefore took the half past 7 A.M. [3] train for Buffalo, arriving at the same hour in the evening. At Syracuse, I saw Mr. Sedgwick [4] at the depot, but no one else that I knew, except Henry B. Stanton, [5] whom I did not care to salute.

We left Buffalo at half past 8 in the evening, and arrived at this place at half past 4 in the morning, (Sunday,[6]) having had a most uncomfortable night — our car being crowded with a set of noisy "Ethiopian" vagrants, and the atmosphere quite intolerable, as not a window was lifted during the night.

Thoroughly jaded out, I went directly to the "New England Hotel," longing and expecting to get a bed immediately; but I had to wait more than three hours before I could get accommodated, the house was so full. At last, I was furnished with one of the largest and best rooms in the hotel, and have had nothing to complain of since. About 9 o'clock I went to bed, and slept soundly until dinner-time. After dinner, I sat down in my room to make some "skeleton" preparation for the Convention at Cincinnati, presuming I should be secure from intrusion; but I soon heard a knock at my door, and found on opening it, Mr. W. H. Day,[7] a very intelligent colored young man, formerly a student at Oberlin, and now about starting a newspaper in behalf of his race.[8] The barber who shaved me in the morning found out who I was, and informed him — so I was no longer *incog.* He remained some time. In the evening, I visited my old friends who watched over me in my sickness, Mr. and Mrs. Jones,[9] and spent an hour with them very pleasantly. Also an hour with Edward Wall,[10] another kind friend. Joseph Barker is in town, but I have not been able to see him yet. Perhaps he is here to take the cars for Cincinnati — though, as he has his wife with him, I fear he is not going.[11]

The weather has been fair all the way, and this morning every thing is brilliant in the extreme. In the course of another hour, I shall leave for Cincinnati,[12] where I shall probably arrive at seasonable bed-time.[13]

So much for the jaunt, thus far. I detest travelling, and like home infinitely better than any other place in the world. More I have not a moment to add.

Yours, lovingly,

Wm. Lloyd Garrison.

H. E. G.

ALS: Garrison Papers, Boston Public Library.

1. This was the beginning of Garrison's trip to Cincinnati — his first visit to that city — to attend the Anti-Slavery Convention on April 19, 20 and 21. He left Boston on Friday afternoon, April 15. Another account of the journey, "Visit to Cincinnati," is to be found in *The Liberator*, May 6, 1853.

2. In his *Liberator* account of the journey, Garrison mentions arriving at "Greenbush, opposite Albany," where he had to hire a row-boat to cross the Hudson River. Since Greenwich, New York, is too far north of Albany to have been the place of crossing, and Greenwich, Connecticut, is ruled out by geography, one can only conclude that Garrison erred here in mentioning "Greenwich" rather than Greenbush.

3. April 16.

4. Most likely Charles Baldwin Sedgwick (b. Pompey, Onondaga County, New York, March 15, 1815; d. Syracuse, February 3 or 7, 1883), a well-known lawyer, who graduated from Hamilton College in 1834, was admitted to the bar in 1837, came to Syracuse in 1842, and formed a law partnership with Peter Outwater. He was originally an antislavery Democrat, was active in the Free Soil movement in 1848 and in the Buffalo convention which nominated Van Buren for President, and in 1854, joined the Republican Party at its inception. In 1858, he was elected to Congress and served from 1859 to 1863. A friend of Abraham Lincoln, he spent the next two years as chairman of the Naval Committee and then of the U.S. Commission to revise the naval code. (Dwight L. Bruce, *Memorial History of Syracuse, New York*, Syracuse, 1891, pp. 109–110; *BDAC*; the latter incorrectly dates Sedgwick's admission to the bar as 1848.) *Weld-Grimké Letters*, I, 464, mentions a Mr. Sedgwick, without further identification, as one of several agents of the American Anti-Slavery Society in 1837 who were retired after one year because of a shortage of funds.

5. Henry Brewster Stanton had broken with Garrison in the late 1830's on the issue of abolitionist political organization, had seceded from the American Anti-Slavery Society in 1840, and had participated in the formation of the rival American and Foreign Anti-Slavery Society, of which he was a secretary. He married Elizabeth Cady during the same year and set sail immediately for England where he participated as a delegate to the World's Anti-Slavery Convention. On his return, he studied law, was admitted to the bar, and practiced law in Boston for several years. A member of the Liberty party at its formation in 1840, he later joined the Free Soil party, helping to draft its platform at Buffalo in 1848, and was a founder of the Republican party in New York State in 1855. In 1847 he moved to Seneca Falls, New York, whence he was elected to the state Senate in 1849. Reelected in 1851, he was not again a candidate. Campaigning for Frémont in 1856, he remained a Republican until Grant's administration, during which he joined the Democrats. After the Civil War, he devoted most of his time to journalism, serving as editor of the New York *Sun* from 1868 until his death.

The relationship between Stanton and Garrison, which began to deteriorate in the late 1830's over the question of abolitionist political action, was exacerbated by the disunion in abolitionist ranks in 1840, with Stanton joining the secession from the American Anti-Slavery Society, and became increasingly embittered with the passing years. With the outbreak of the Civil War, a reconciliation began which culminated in Stanton's participation in the annual meeting of the American Anti-Slavery Society in New York in 1863, and Stanton's tribute to Garrison and *The Liberator* in the New York *Tribune* on January 4, 1866. (*Life*, IV, 78, 175.)

6. April 17.

7. William Howard Day (b. New York City, October 16, 1825; d. Harrisburg, Pennsylvania, December 3, 1900), Negro orator, editor, and leader of his people, prepared for college in Northampton, Massachusetts, where he also learned the art of printing, and entered Oberlin College in 1843. He graduated in 1847, the only black man in his class of fifty. He began speaking on behalf of black civil rights as early as 1845, participated, as an elected representative, in black organizations and conventions, and aided in the repeal of Ohio's "Black Laws" in 1849. For a while, he earned his livelihood as a compositor for the Cleveland *True Democrat* (later the *Leader*), then as mailing clerk and local editor for the same paper. At the end of 1852 (Garrison's letter would seem to indicate the beginning of 1853), in Cleveland, he established *The Aliened American*, a weekly newspaper which he edited until 1855, and during the same year, he was chairman of the committee of citizens of Cleveland to greet Louis Kossuth and present him with money to purchase muskets for Hungary's freedom. Because of ill health, he went to Canada in 1857, where he continued his efforts on behalf of his black brethren. In 1859 (William H. Egle gives 1861 as the date), together with the Reverend William King of Canada, he visited England, Ireland, and Scotland to raise money

for the black settlement at Buxton, Canada. Although King returned to Canada, Day remained in England until the end of the Civil War. In 1866, Day became editor of the secular department of *Zion's Standard and Weekly Review* of New York City, a black newspaper. The following year, he became superintendent of schools for Maryland and Delaware, for the Bureau of Refugees, Freedmen and Abandoned Lands. In later years, he continued, with undiminished vigor, his efforts on behalf of Negro education and civil rights. He was the first black man elected to the school board of Harrisburg, Pennsylvania, and served from 1878 to 1883. He received an honorary degree of Doctor of Divinity from Livingstone College in May 1887. (William J. Simmons, D.D., *Men of Mark: Eminent, Progressive and Rising*, 1887, reprinted by Arno Press and the New York Times, New York, 1968, pp. 978–984; Wm. Henry Egle, *History of the Counties of Dauphin and Lebanon in the Commonwealth of Pennsylvania* . . . , Philadelphia, 1883, p. 568; *The Alumni Catalogue of 1926*, published by Oberlin College, Oberlin, Ohio, 1927, p. 189.)

8. In his *Liberator* account, Garrison says that Day "has recently issued the first number of a weekly paper, entitled 'The Aliened American,' the prospects of which are encouraging."

9. In the *Liberator* account, Garrison notes that "In the evening I called upon my esteemed friend THOMAS JONES, at whose house I was so long confined by a dangerous illness in 1847, and was happy to take him and the dear members of his family again by the hand. Their kindness, during my sickness, makes one of those debts that admits of no adequate compensation." Thomas and Marion Jones, the parents of the future Senator John Percival Jones of Nevada, who served in the Senate from 1873 to 1903, migrated to the United States from Herefordshire, England, in 1829, and settled in Cleveland. Thomas Jones was a marble cutter. (*Life*, III, 207; *The Liberator*, October 29, 1847; *BDAC*; *The Liberator*, May 6, 1853.)

10. Unidentified.

11. After mailing this letter, Garrison did meet Joseph Barker and his wife on the train to Cincinnati. The following is his account of their journey together as well as his remarkable tribute to Barker:

"On Monday morning, I took the train for Cincinnati, and, on entering one of the cars, had the unspeakable satisfaction to find my attached English friends, Joseph Barker and his wife, among the passengers. They had been to Salem, Columbiana county, (where he has purchased a farm, and intends to remove, with his family, in the fall,) and were on their way home to Millwood. We rode together about one hundred miles before we separated, and, of course, made the most of the time and the distance in exchanging thoughts and opinions on various matters. I strongly urged him to accompany me to the Convention, but his domestic affairs required his presence at home. Possibly, there would have been some fluttering if he had gone, not on account of his anti-slavery views or foreign extraction; but because of his religious 'heresies.' As a body, abolitionists are in advance of all others in the land — probably in the world — in mental development and religious liberality; but they are yet too much trammelled, and need to have a more absolute trust in the immortal nature of truth.

"Joseph Barker is comparatively a stranger among us, but in due season he will be seen, heard and felt, on an extended scale. In England, he is widely known as one of the sturdiest and ablest champions of the working classes, incapable of intimidation, and beyond purchase. Born and brought up under the most depressing circumstances, he has conquered difficulties which seemed insurmountable, and by patient industry and untiring research has accumulated a large amount of solid information on a great variety of subjects. He has a large and active brain, a generous and world-embracing heart. It is true, he has seen cause to change his theological views more than once, — growing more and more 'heretical'; but, in every instance, the change has been to his own hurt, in a worldly sense, bringing upon himself fresh opprobrium and ruthless persecution. Thus he has shown a willingness to suffer to any extent, rather than to sacrifice his conscientious convictions. . . . While I am not prepared to endorse all his peculiar views, as he cannot accept all that I entertain, I reverence his moral courage, his bold utterance, his fidelity to his own conscience, and his hearty espousal of the reformatory movements of the age." (*The Liberator*, May 6, 1853.)

12. A detailed account of the convention, which met on April 19, appeared in *The Liberator*, May 6, 1853, under the heading, "Grand Anti-Slavery Convention at Cincinnati."

13. He arrived in Cincinnati on Monday evening, April 18, at 9 o'clock, was met at the depot by A. H. Ernst and Christian Donaldson, and was brought in a carriage "to the beautiful residence of the former at Spring Grove . . . about three miles from the city. Here I was most hospitably entertained during my sojourn, and shall ever cherish the most grateful recollections for the kindness extended to me. It is no disparagement to others to say, that Mrs. Ernst is the soul of anti-slavery in that region. . . . The Female A. S. Circle, with which she is connected, is a vital organization, and working in various ways most effectively." (*The Liberator*, May 6, 1853.)

---

5 6

TO JOSEPH A. DUGDALE

BOSTON, May 19th, 1853.

BELOVED FRIEND: — Nothing keeps me from your gathering of free and truth-loving spirits, to assemble at Old Kennett on the 22d instant, but the close proximity of the New England Anti-Slavery Convention.

I regard your meeting as one of deep interest and universal importance. Its object, as set forth in the Call,[1] commends itself to my understanding and my heart. It is to form a model religious organization, in which unity shall be attained without constraint, — the spirit of progress recognized as without limitation, — the claims of humanity made paramount to all other considerations, — and free speech and free inquiry conceded as the right of every soul, essential to growth 'in knowledge and in grace,'[2] and the best preservative against heresy, whether real or imaginary.

Whether your movement be successful or not, it is worthy of commendation, — a sign of the times equally cheering and prophetic. I see no insuperable difficulty in the way of success, provided the truly catholic spirit evinced in the Call brood over and pervade your deliberations. Of course, every religious association will be what its members are collectively; if they are upright, fearless, honest, and progressive, so will it be. The greater includes the less; the stream cannot rise higher than the fountain.

The questions naturally arise, — How shall this new association be organized, and what shall be its claim? Of whom shall it be composed? What shall be its distinctive object? To what extent shall conformity be required? What is implied by connection therewith? And what shall be its creed and discipline?

In attempting to answer these questions very briefly, (for I write in haste, being straitened as to time, and would not infringe upon that of your meeting,) I do so in no spirit of dogmatism, but with all deference to the opinion of others, and simply as an expression of my own sentiments.

1. 'How shall this new association be organized, and what shall be its claim?'

I answer — It must be purely voluntary, withdrawal from which, at any time, without reproach, shall be the right of every member. It must lay claim to no special divinity. It must not indulge the idle dream of perpetuating itself from age to age, and hence make its safety and growth the chief object of its solicitude; for, in the nature of things, all human agreements, compacts, alliances and organizations, are mutable, and tend to decay. It must be regarded simply as a means to an end — and that end the personal liberty and religious improvement of every human being. It must not predicate any thing of piety or philanthropy upon the mere fact of membership; for 'all are not Israel who are of Israel.' [3]

It must not assume to be the one true, infallible and impeccable Church, or even a branch of it, which it is a religious duty to join, and out of the pale of which, there are none but heretics. It must not go back to the past — not even to apostolic times and usages — to determine what shall be its form or order; for what in one age may be truly serviceable, in another may prove positively detrimental.

2. 'Of whom shall it be composed?' It must recognize no distinction as to complexion or sex. 'Whosoever will, let him come.' [4]

3. 'What shall be its distinctive object?' Practical righteousness; the discovery of truth, and its application ('without partiality and without hypocrisy') [5] to individuals and communities, to customs and institutions, to sects and parties; the acknowledgment of the Fatherhood of God and the Brotherhood of Man.

4. 'To what extent shall conformity be required?' Not in matters of taste and amusement; not in a distinctive outward garb or mode of speech; not in theological opinions; not in regard to religious rites or ceremonies; but only an approval of the object, in the promotion of which every human being has an everlasting interest.

5. 'What is implied by connection therewith?' A friendly and loving spirit, but not necessarily an endorsement of the religious character or opinions of any member; for as the association is to be without sectarian exclusiveness, so it is not to exercise sectarian discipline; and,

therefore, it must leave with its members, in their individual capacity the responsibility for their course. 'So, then, every one of us must give account of himself unto God.' [6]

6. 'What shall be its creed and discipline?' No other creed is needed, no better one can be devised, than that which Jesus gave in his day: — 'Thou shalt love the Lord thy God with all thy heart, and thy neighbor as thyself' [7] — 'Whatsoever ye would that men should do to you, do ye even so to them.' [8] No discipline will work so effectively, or keep the association so pure and vital, as untrammelled speech and the largest liberty of discussion; for these are incompatible with superstition, tyranny, corruption, ambition, phariseeism, worldliness, and crime. Where these are really enjoyed, as well as conceded in the abstract, no bull of excommunication will ever be found necessary. 'The wicked flee when no man pursueth, but the righteous are as bold as a lion.' [9] True, such liberty may be abused, and in some instances will be abused; true, it may subject us to hearing some sentiments distasteful, offensive, and even highly reprehensble. True, some may attempt to run before they are sent, and essay to speak when they ought to be silent; but the evil is only incidental, and will prove efficacious in enabling us all to 'possess our souls in patience.' [10]

Such, briefly, are the suggestions which occur to me at this moment, and which I deferentially submit for the consideration of your meeting. I shall be with you in spirit; I regret that I cannot be so in bodily shape and presence. 'Grace, mercy and peace be with you all.' [11]

Yours, for the world's redemption,

WM. LLOYD GARRISON.

Joseph A. Dugdale, of the Committee.[12]

ALS: Friends Historical Library, Swarthmore College. It was printed in *The Liberator*, July 1, 1853. The text printed here is from *The Liberator*.

1. The Call was entitled "Call for a General Conference, with a View to the Establishment of a Yearly Meeting in Pennsylvania." It announced that "we cordially invite not only the members of the Society of Friends, but all those who feel the want of social and religious cooperation, and believe that a Society may be formed, recognizing the *Progressive Element* which will divorce Religion from *technical theology*, to meet with us in General Conference, at Friends' Meeting-House at Old Kennett, in Chester County, Pennsylvania, on First day, the 22d of Fifth month, 1853, at half past 11 o'clock, A. M. . . ." (*The Liberator*, May 20, 1853.)

2. II Peter 3:18.
3. Romans 9:6.
4. See Revelation 22:17.
5. James 3:17.
6. Romans 14:12.
7. Luke 10:27, which combines Deuteronomy 6:5 and Leviticus 19:18.
8. Matthew 7:12.
9. Proverbs 28:1.

10. Luke 21:19.

11. A variation of II John 1:3, I Corinthians 1:3, and similar verses in the New Testament.

12. *The Liberator*, July 1, 1853, carried a summary of the proceedings of the convention and printed letters to the convention from Garrison, Theodore Parker, Samuel J. May, Thomas Wentworth Higginson, and Gerrit Smith.

---

5 7

TO FRIENDS OF THE AMERICAN
ANTI-SLAVERY SOCIETY

New York, May 30, 1853.

Dear Friend:

The *Executive Committee* of the AMERICAN ANTI-SLAVERY SOCIETY respectfully ask your attention to a subject closely connected, indeed identical, with the interests of the Society and the great cause it represents. We address you as a friend of the principles on which our organization is based, and therefore feel at liberty to proceed at once to the business we have in hand, — the increase of the subscription-list of THE NATIONAL ANTI-SLAVERY STANDARD, and the methods by which its circulation may be made most effective in the Slave's behalf. Notwithstanding the great merits of the paper, we could hardly expect, unless by much outlay of labor, that its circulation should be extensive. Apart from the disadvantages under which it was originally started, and apart also from the unpopularity of Anti-Slavery Truth, uttered "without concealment and without compromise," — [1] in which motto resides alike the secret of the Society's smallness and success, — *The Standard* has to contend against two circumstances, which, though at first view not very apparent or influential, are yet potent as respects its subscription-list.

First. — Its local influences are highly unfavorable. The opposition to it in the city of New York is most bitter and inveterate, while its friends there are so few as hardly to be appreciable. As the organ of an enterprise including in its sphere of action our whole immense country, it is impossible that it should be a vehicle of the merely *local* intelligence which finds its proper place in *The Liberator, The Pennsylvania Freeman,*[2] and *The Bugle*.[3] This fact, as everyone must see on a moment's reflection, has a tendency to prevent *The Standard's* circulation among those friends of the cause whose means may not permit them to take more than one Anti-Slavery newspaper, since they will naturally prefer the one published in their more immediate neighborhood.

Second. — *The Standard,* being the organ of the National Anti-Slavery Society, — a Society composed of persons of all sects and parties, — is under obligation to keep itself aloof from other questions of reform, and to forego the advantages to its circulation which might be derived from enlarging the sphere of its discussions. Common sense and good faith alike dictate its course in this respect; but while Abolitionists and their friends, who generally belong to the most active class in society, continue to feel a deep interest in reformatory views on other subjects, and ma[n]y of them prefer on that account to take journals whose field of discussion is unlimited, it is manifest that *The Standard's* chances for obtaining a large circulation must be somewhat diminished thereby. We allude to this not by way of complaint, but that the position of the paper may be fully understood.

These two circumstances, taken in connection with another, common to every genuine Anti-Slavery periodical, viz. "'the offence of the cross" — [4] never more bitter than at present, notwithstanding the diluted Anti-Slavery doctrines partially permeating the North — may amply account for the fact that the most uncompromising fidelity and great literary excellence have failed to secure for *The Anti-Slavery Standard* the number of subscribers necessary to its highest efficiency and usefulness. We earnestly invoke your assistance in increasing its circulation, and that you may act intelligently, beg leave to make the following statement.

The Standard has for many years been conducted by Mr. *S. H. Gay,* assisted by Mr. *Edmund Quincy* as Corresponding Editor. Mr. *Gay,* during the nine years he has been the only official servant of the American Anti-Slavery Society in N. York, has been obliged to assume responsibilities and duties, distinct from his editorial labors, from the weight of which he should be relieved. With a view of doing this, and at the same time increasing the efficiency of the paper and extending the operations of the Society, the Committee have secured the services, as Associate Editor, of Mr. *Oliver Johnson,* late of *The Pennsylvania Freeman;* so that *The Standard* will hereafter be conducted by Messrs. *Gay* and *Johnson,* as Resident Editors, assisted by Mr. *Quincy* as Corresponding Editor. Of their devoted and unwearying zeal in the Slave's cause, evinced by years of disinterested and laborious toil, their wide and ample knowledge of the cause in all its bearings, their tact, judgment, discretion, and eminent literary qualifications, we will not speak at length, believing that those qualities have been sufficiently tested and made apparent to all who have watched the progress of this incomparably important movement. Nor will we doubt that you appreciate the importance of maintaining a

National Anti-Slavery organization, as the appropriate representative of the cause in other countries, and a point of union and co-operation on the part of Abolitionists in the various States of the American Confederacy. We are sure that you, in common with every intelligent friend of the cause, would regard the overthrow of the American Anti-Slavery Society and its organ as a calamity most deeply to be regretted, and as leaving a breach in our ranks which no other Society and no other paper could adequately fill.

Various circumstances indicate the present as a favorable occasion for extending the sphere of the Society's operations. An increased circulation of *The Standard* will, more than any other mode of action, tend to produce this result. May we hope that you will assist us in this undertaking, either by subscribing for the paper yourself, if not already a subscriber, or by taking a copy or copies for circulation among such friends of the cause as may be unable, or such enemies as may be unwilling, to subscribe for themselves; or will you make such donation in its behalf to the National treasury as shall permit us, as the servants of the Society, to take measures for such gratuitous circulation among people at large as the scantiness of our resources has not heretofore permitted?

We have addressed you as a sincere well-wisher to the cause of the Slave. If each individual with whom we thus communicate will return to us an *immediate* and *favorable* response, if it were only such as easily falls within the scope of a single will, if informed by the spirit of an earnest humanity and genuine self-sacrifice, the aggregate will be such as to aid and encourage us most abundantly in our difficult and yet inspiriting and glorious undertaking.

In behalf of the Executive Committee of the *American Anti-Slavery Society,*

WM. LLOYD GARRISON, President.

Wendell Phillips, Secretary.

Typed copy of form letter: Anti-Slavery Letters to Garrison and Others, Boston Public Library.

This letter was enclosed in a letter from Sydney H. Gay to Richard D. Webb dated August 5, 1853.

1. The motto of the *National Anti-Slavery Standard,* with its first issue, appeared directly beneath its name. An explanation of the choice of this motto appeared in the second issue of the *Standard,* June 18, 1840.

2. The *Pennsylvania Freeman* first appeared in March 1838 as the successor to the *National Enquirer,* established two years earlier by Benjamin Lundy. Originally edited by John Greenleaf Whittier, the *Freeman* became the official organ of the Eastern Pennsylvania Anti-Slavery Society. In December, 1841, the Society voted "the temporary suspension of the *Freeman* in favor of the *Standard*" (*Life*, III, 18) and the transfer of the *Freeman's* subscription to the *Standard* (Letters, III, 60). The *Freeman* was reestablished in January 1844, as the organ of the

Eastern Pennsylvania Anti-Slavery Society, under the editorship of Charles C. Burleigh and J. M. McKim. Later editors included Mary Grew and Oliver Johnson. (*Life*, III, 101.) It continued publication until June 1854. (Oliver Johnson, *William Lloyd Garrison and His Times*, Boston, 1880, pp. 323–324; Louis Filler, *The Crusade Against Slavery, 1830–1860*, New York, Evanston, and London, 1963, p. 105.)

3. The *Anti-Slavery Bugle*, published in Salem, Ohio, was founded in 1845 as the "disunionist organ" of the Ohio American Anti-Slavery Society. It was edited by Benjamin Smith Jones (1812–1862) and his wife, Jane Elizabeth Jones (b. 1813) until 1849 when they were succeeded by Oliver Johnson, who was in turn succeeded by Marius Robinson. It continued in existence until 1861. (*Life*, III, 135, 204, 392; *Letters*, III, 517.)

4. Galatians 5:11.

58

TO SAMUEL J. MAY

Boston, May 31, 1853.

My Dear Friend:

Peter Still[1] has been in this region for some time past, and as far down East as Brunswick,[2] slowly but perseveringly accumulating a portion of the extortionate sum needed to obtain the ransom of his wife and children. He is as modest as he is untiring, and as patient and hopeful as he is affectionate and upright. Poor man! his is an up-hill work, of the severest kind; but I hope it will not be in vain. I feel a fire in all my veins to think of such a man being robbed of his wife and family, as coolly and heartlessly as though he were a mere beast, and they were literally but pieces of merchandise — robbed according to law, according to the American Constitution, and according to *American* Christianity. Nor is he allowed to have them, as any slave trader can have them, at "a fair market" value — say, $2500, — but *he*, *because he is the husband and the father*, and because they attempted to make their escape in order to be with them,[3] is required to pay $5000 for them — and then to regard it as a special favor on the part of the miscreant who claims them as his property![4] How revolting!

Peter has collected about eleven hundred dollars, in addition to the two hundred in your possession. He leaves here on his way home this afternoon, and desires me to request you to send the sum in your hands to Dr. Joseph Parrish,[5] Burlington, N. J., in such manner as may be safest and best.

Our Executive Committee have had a meeting, and unanimously agreed to comply with your suggestion, to hold a special meeting of the American Anti-Slavery Society at Syracuse, on the 29th and 30th of September next, with reference to a grand co-operation at the

"Jerry rescue" celebration on the 1st of October. We shall leave the arrangements, as to the place of meeting, and the price of tickets, (if it be deemed best to have any, whether for the day-time or the evening,) to your discretion, and that of the other friends whom you may consult — wishing the aim to be, to secure as full an attendance as practicable.

Our New England A. S. Convention, just terminated,[6] has been a very interesting one, and gave very great satisfaction. The chief topic discussed was the pro-slavery character of the U.S. Constitution, and the duty of repudiating all allegiance to it.

We are all highly favored with health at home. I hope your dear wife [7] finds her own health more and more improving. Helen unites with me in the kindest regards to her and Charlotte,[8] and all the children. As for yourself, we are both

Yours, with boundless affection,

Wm. Lloyd Garrison.

Samuel J. May.

ALS: Garrison Papers, Boston Pulic Library.

1. Peter Still, with his brother, was kidnapped as a child from an area on the banks of the Delaware River, not far from Philadelphia, and sold into slavery, first in Kentucky, then in Alabama. After forty years, Still succeeded in purchasing his freedom with the help of two German Jewish businessmen, Joseph and Isaac Friedman, of Tuscumbia, Alabama, where he was employed. Upon returning to Philadelphia in November 1850, where William Still, a brother, and other members of his family lived, and following an abortive attempt by a white abolitionist, Seth Conklin, to rescue Still's wife and children — Conklin died in the attempt — Still was offered the opportunity in August 1851 — reaffirmed in August 1852 — to purchase his wife and children from their master for the sum of $5,000. In November 1852, Still embarked upon a campaign to raise the necessary amount, making personal appeals in numerous communities before thousands of people, individually and at mass meetings, throughout New England, New York, New Jersey and Pennsylvania. Those who assisted him included Harriet Beecher Stowe, Gerrit Smith, Horace Greeley, Ellis Gray Loring, Leonard Bacon, Samuel J. May, and many others. After almost two years of effort, he raised the necessary amount and purchased their freedom. On the last day of December 1854, Peter Still greeted his freed wife and children in Cincinnati. (The story of Peter Still has been told by Mrs. Kate R. Pickard, in *The Kidnapped and the Ransomed. Being the Personal Recollections of Peter Still and His Wife 'Vina,' After Forty Years of Slavery*, with an introduction by the Reverend Samuel J. May and an Appendix by William H. Furness, D.D., Syracuse: William T. Hamilton. New York and Auburn: Miller, Orton and Mulligan, 1856. The volume was reprinted in New York in 1941; more recently, in Philadelphia in 1970, by the Jewish Publication Society of America, with an introductory essay by Maxwell Whiteman.)

2. Brunswick, Maine, is northeast of Portland, Maine.

3. Garrison obviously meant to write "him." The escape attempt, as has already been noted, was made under the guidance of Seth Conklin and failed.

4. Their owner was Bernard McKiernan, of South Florence, Alabama. (Kate Pickard, *The Kidnapped and the Ransomed*, 1970 ed., p. 307 and *passim*.)

5. Dr. Joseph Parrish (b. Philadelphia, 1818, fl. Burlington, N.J., 1882), son of Dr. Joseph Parrish of Philadelphia (d. 1840), a Friend and president of the

Pennsylvania Society for the Abolition of Slavery, had graduated from the University of Pennsylvania medical school in 1844 and married Lydia Gaskill, of Burlington, New Jersey, where he set up his practice. He established the *New Jersey Medical Reporter*, which became the official organ of the New Jersey Medical Society and soon achieved national renown. In 1853, he accepted a chair of obstetrics and diseases of women and children at the Philadelphia College of Medicine, and removed to Philadelphia the following year. Thereafter, as a result of ill health, he took a trip to Europe and while in Rome prevailed upon the pope to correct abuses in the treatment of the insane in that city. Returning to Philadelphia, he assumed control of an institution for the training of idiots at Germantown, Pennsylvania. He participated in the work of the Sanitary Commission during the Civil War and in that of the Freedman's Commission immediately after the war. Thereafter he was involved in efforts for the treatment of alcoholics. In 1875 he returned to Burlington where he continued his extensive practice. (Major E. M. Woodward and John F. Hageman, *History of Burlington and Mercer Counties, New Jersey* . . . , Philadelphia, 1883, p. 86.)

6. The New England Anti-Slavery Convention met on Wednesday and Thursday, May 25 and 26, 1853. Its proceedings were reported in *The Liberator*, June 3, 1853.

7. Lucretia Flagge Coffin married Samuel J. May in 1825. (*Letters*, II, 62 *et passim* offers additional information.)

8. Charlotte Coffin, Samuel J. May's sister-in-law, sister of Lucretia Coffin May.

59

TO WENDELL PHILLIPS

Boston, June 25, 1853.

Dear Phillips:

I have just received a letter from our friend, Colonel Whiting,[1] of Concord, desiring me to inform you of the change that has been made in regard to the railroad train for that place. It will leave on Thursday, at half past 12 o'clock, instead of 1 — so do not be behind your time, on any account. They are calculating upon something of a gathering — and you must do your best — in a slaveholding sense, your worst. Col. Whiting desires me to say, that he expects you to be his guest.

Mary Grew will go with us.

Best love to Ann [2] and Phebe.[3]

Yours, devotedly,

Wm. Lloyd Garrison.

Wendell Phillips.

ALS: Taconic Foundation, New York City.

1. Colonel William Whiting (b. Sterling, Mass., October 20, 1788; d. Concord, September 27, 1862) established a harness and carriage-making shop in Concord *ca.* 1808, which became a thriving business by 1831, despite a fire which destroyed his home and shop in 1823. He became an active Mason in 1819; he helped establish the Concord Academy in 1822 and was active in the Concord Lyceum as well as the Social Circle. He was a lieutenant-colonel of artillery in the militia. Reli-

giously active, he taught Sunday School, advocated temperance and equality of education for boys and girls. In politics he was successively a Federalist, National Republican, Whig, Free Soiler, and Republican. A Garrisonian in his antislavery views, he was a constant reader of *The Liberator* from 1835, and for a number of years was president of the Middlesex County Anti-Slavery Society and vice-president of the Massachusetts Anti-Slavery Society. Garrison, Wendell Phillips, and John Brown were guests at his house. He helped the latter financially during the difficulties in Kansas, was a liberal contributor to the antislavery cause in general, and often helped runaway slaves. (E. Rockwood Hoar, *Memoirs of Members of the Social Circle in Concord, Second Series, 1795–1840*, Cambridge, 1888, pp. 247–265; his obituary was printed in *The Liberator*, October 10, 1862.)

2. Ann Terry Greene (1813–1886), wife of Wendell Phillips. For further information see *Letters*, II, 490–491.

3. Phebe Garnaut was the daughter of Eliza Jones (1810–1849) of Wales, and Richard Garnaut, "the son of a French emigrant, a mechanic of great taste and ability." The Garnauts had been married in England, and emigrated immediately thereafter to the United States, where Richard Garnaut and their eldest child died three years after their marriage. Eliza Garnaut was left alone with her infant daughter, Phebe. During the ensuing years, living in Boston, Eliza was especially active in the Moral Reform Society of Boston, as well as in "education, social reorganization, anti-slavery, the amelioration of punishments, the advancement of woman." She died in Boston in 1849 of the cholera. (Wendell Phillips, "Mrs. Eliza Garnaut," *The Liberator*, October 12, 1849.)

With her mother's death, Phebe was left alone. She was immediately adopted by Wendell Phillips and became known as Phebe Phillips. (Oscar Sherwin, *Prophet of Liberty: The Life and Times of Wendell Phillips*, New York, 1958, p. 305.) "The presence of this vivacious teen-aged girl," writes Irving H. Bartlett, "made life at 26 Essex Street considerably brighter. When Wendell was off lecturing, Phebe's sunny influence helped overcome Ann's loneliness, and the challenge of supervising the girl's education kept Ann from brooding over poor health." (*Wendell Phillips, Brahmin Radical*, Boston, 1961, p. 138.) Ralph Korngold writes in *Two Friends of Man, The Story of William Lloyd Garrison Garrison and Wendell Phillips and their Relationship with Abraham Lincoln* (Boston, 1950, p. 174), that Phebe was twelve years old when her mother died, and "was never legally adopted, but was considered so much a member of the household that people referred to her as 'Phebe Phillips.'" Moreover, "Phebe remained with them eleven years, until her marriage, in 1860, to George W. Smalley, a journalist. She followed her husband to England where he became London correspondent of Greeley's New York *Tribune*."

George Smalley (b. Franklin, Mass., June 4, 1833; d. 1916) graduated from Yale in 1853 and studied law in Worcester and at the Harvard Law School from 1853 to 1856, when he was admitted to the bar and began the practice of law in Boston. He went to South Carolina as war correspondent of the *New York Tribune* in November 1861, returned to New York in October 1862, and was thereafter connected with the *Tribune*, editorially, in New York, and then in London as the *Tribune*'s English correspondent. He married Phebe Garnaut on December 25, 1862 (Korngold's date is in error). A daughter was born to them in October 1863. (*Yale College Class of 1853*, printed for members of the class, 1883, p. 207; see also Emet Crozier, *Yankee Reporters, 1861–65*, New York, 1956, *passim*.)

6 0

TO SYDNEY HOWARD GAY(?)

Boston, July 25, 1853.

My Dear Friend:

I have the inexpressible satisfaction to introduce to you my valued friend — the friend of the American abolitionists — the friend of freedom in every clime for all peoples — William H. Ashurst,[1] Esq. (alias "Edward Search,") of Muswell Hill, near London. This is his first visit to America, and, consequently, he is now "a stranger in a strange land."[2] Being alone, and at his period [in] life, he should receive special attention; and I am sure you will do every thing in your power, during his brief sojourn in your city, to make his visit delightful. More I need not add.

Yours, to serve and bless,

Wm. Lloyd Garrison.

ALS: Columbia University Library.

Since the letter is to be found in the Gay Collection at Columbia University, we believe it probable that it was addressed to Gay. However, nowhere in the letter is Gay's name mentioned. Kenneth A. Lohf, Librarian for Rare Books and Manuscripts, Columbia University, in a letter dated March 3, 1972, has written the following: "In response to your letter of February 28, we have examined the letter, written by William Lloyd Garrison on July 25, 1853. There is no evidence in the letter that the recipient was Sydney Howard Gay. Apparently our cataloguer felt that it was written to Gay since all the other letters in the series were."

1. William Henry Ashurst (1792–1855), a London solicitor and philanthropist who contributed to *The Liberator* under the pseudonym "Edward Search." (For further information about him see *Letters*, II, 666.)

2. Exodus 2:22.

6 1

TO ADELINE ROBERTS

Boston, Aug. 26, 1853.

Respected Friend:

I have just received your letter, inviting me to give the closing lecture of the next course, designed by your Society, on the evening of 20th Nov. Your invitation is most cherfully accepted; and, so far as it may be in my power to give "words of cheer and kind advice," on that occasion, I will aim to do so. It is a post of honor that I have occupied so long, that it may seem to some like monopolizing it, and they may think that "rotation in office" is not less desirable than equitable. In this opinion, I entirely concur; and therefore wish you to put a "new broom" in place of the old one, if you can possibly find one. If not, use me as hitherto.

Myself out of the question, I am truly glad that your Society is resolved upon another course of lectures; and I trust it will be marked with the same good results, and the same cheering attendance, as each preceding one has been. All the signs of the times are auspicious.

Allow me to suggest the utility of advertising the course as soon as the list of speakers is completed,[1] so as duly to apprise the citizens of Salem and its vicinity.

Yours, to usher in the jubilee,

Wm. Lloyd Garrison.

Miss A. Roberts.

ALS: Essex Institute, Salem, Massachusetts.

1. The course of lectures, with names of speakers and dates, was announced in *The Liberator*, September 23, 1853. Garrison was listed as speaking on October 20, and as in the past, last.

6 2

TO THE ABOLITIONISTS OF THE UNITED STATES

[August 29, 1853.]

The Executive Committee of the American Anti-Slavery Society appeal to all its members and friends, in every part of the Union, for aid to sustain their operations during the coming Autumn and Winter.

The field of our action is continually enlarging. The demand for the faithful preaching of Anti-Slavery principles is greater than we can meet. From Maine to Wisconsin, the call for those who can speak the words which will first awaken, and then purify and heal, this guilty land, is earnest and loud. What we can do, to answer this call, shall be done. We need not say that our ability, in this respect, will be in proportion to the self-sacrificing contributions of the individual members of the Society, and friends of the cause.

The Committee have already commenced operations for the season, in the Western States. Three of our truest friends and ablest speakers have already gone into that field — viz.: Parker Pillsbury, Stephen S. Foster, and Abby K. Foster. Mr. Garrison is contemplating a visit to Central New York, and to Michigan. Others will precede or follow him; and, joining with the speakers resident at the West, will, we hope, by the first of October, together constitute the largest and strongest corps of Anti-Slavery labourers, which has been in the field for many years.

To carry on the work more particularly in the State of New York, and the States west of it, a generous friend of the cause in Boston has already pledged the sum of One Thousand Dollars. With this encouraging beginning, we appeal with the more confidence to our friends to come forward and sustain this special work. Let us take advantage of the aroused attention, and awakening conscience of the land, and publish the saving truths of uncompromising Anti-Slavery everywhere. It is the truth — and the truth alone — which shall make this people free.[1] Fettered by no sect or party, we will proclaim it, as God shall give us strength.

We address ourselves to every Auxiliary Society — to every Anti-Slavery neighborhood — to every true mind and heart. We have been blamed, by some of our friends, for so seldom calling upon the Abolitionists of the country for pecuniary aid. Certainly we have not pressed them with frequent demands. We have preferred to think that the eminent importance and sacredness of our cause would make all its friends prompt and unsolicited givers. But we feel that the *present* and *future* demand of us greater efforts than we have ever put forth. It is not for us to tire of the work, and throw the burden upon other shoulders. Let *no one* look back, who has put his hand to the Anti-Slavery plough.

We earnestly ask immediate attention to this appeal. Donations of money, or pledges of sums to be paid at any time between this and the first of January next, should be sent to the Treasurer, FRANCIS JACKSON, Boston; or to the Assistant Treasurer, SYDNEY HOWARD GAY, 142 Nassau St., New York.

For the Executive Committee.

WM. LLOYD GARRISON, *President.*

WENDELL PHILLIPS, *Rec. Secretary.*

Boston, August 29, 1853.

Printed in *The Liberator*, September 9 and 16, 1853; also in the *National Anti-Slavery Standard*, September 3 and 10, 1853.

1. A paraphrase of John 8:32.

---

6 3

TO HELEN E. GARRISON

New York, Sept. 5,[1] 1853.

Dear Wife:

You see, by the blot I have made,[2] that I supposed I was in Boston, instead of New York; which is another proof that I always endeavor to make myself at home. And it may seem to you, by not getting a letter from me, on Saturday,[3] (as I intended you should,) that I have indeed forgotten that I have a very pleasant residence in Boston, with a very dear wife and well-beloved children. But, with the hurry and confusion of such a city as this to distract one's mind — with the numerous meetings I have had to attend and address — with the multitude of friends, from various parts of the country, who have desired to see and converse with me — my time has been thoroughly "used up." Each night (to use a Hibernian form of expression,) I have not retired to rest till morning. The weather has been oppressively sultry; without any change or mitigation.

I write now in haste, as in a few minutes I am going to [Sydney] Gay's, at Staten Island, to see Mr. [William H.] Ashurst, where he has been tarrying for a few days past. He still continues in feeble health, and is to sail for home on Wednesday, from this city. It is a prudent step, and I am glad he has engaged his passage. I have had no chance to talk with H. C. W[right], — only to take him by the hand in a public meeting last evening.

Let me begin with the beginning. I arrived here on Thursday afternoon,[4] at 5 o'clock, thoroughly fatigued and overcome by the ride, as it was a very warm day, and the dust, and coal smoke, and cinders, were almost suffocating. In the evening, I attended the Temperance Convention,[5] and at the close was kindly invited to make my abode under the roof of James S. Gibbons,[6] more than two miles "up town." I have been there ever since, and had a very delightful visit.

The Temperance Convention was held Thursday and Friday, and was well attended, although very few clergymen and no dignitaries were present. The women took a prominent part in it — Lucretia Mott, Lucy Stone,[7] Antoinette Brown,[8] Mrs. Gage,[9] Mrs. Nicholes,[10] Miss Clark,[11] +c. I only spoke once, and only for fifteen minutes; of course, I made no speech. The Convention, as a whole, exceeded my anticipations.[12]

On Saturday, I spent several hours in the Crystal Palace, with Joseph A. Dugdale and wife,[13] Mary Ann Johnson,[14] Miss Cannan,[15] and a large number of other friends. In the evening, I went to see Uncle Tom's Cabin played at the National Theatre. It was pretty well done, but, in some respects, I like the Boston performance better.[16]

Sunday forenoon, I went to the Metropolitan Hall, to hear Antoinette Brown preach a regular sermon. Nearly four thousand persons were present. She acquitted herself very acceptably.

In the afternoon, we had an anti-slavery meeting in the same hall;

12½ cts. admission. About 1200 people present. The speakers were C. C. Burleigh, Sojourner Truth,[17] and myself.

In the evening, we had another meeting in the same hall — two thousand persons present, including a large number of Southerners, evidently bent on a disturbance. The meeting was addressed by Oliver Johnson, Lucretia Mott, and Lucy Stone, who were more or less interrupted as they proceeded. At half past 9, we adjourned, as the rowdies were determined that no other person should be heard. It was an effective meeting, and Lucy never acquitted herself better.[18] We are all in fine spirits.

This evening, the women are to have a temperance meeting at the Broadway Tabernacle.[19] To-morrow and next day are to be devoted to the Woman's Rights Convention.[20] On Thursday night, I shall try to be in Boston; so "look out when the bell rings."

I suppose all the children are now at home. A father's love to them all. Last evening, I took tea with George + Catharine,[21] Dr. Roton [22] and Anna.[23] George is better.

Good bye!

W. L. Garrison.

ALS: Garrison Papers, Boston Public Library.

1. "5" is in pencil, perhaps inserted by a later hand.

2. On the dateline, underneath the letters "Ne" of New York, Garrison had written "Bo" but had caught himself, crossed out the letters, and over them had written the correct city.

3. September 3, 1852.

4. September 1.

5. On May 12, 1853, a World's Temperance Convention had assembled in New York City. A substantial number of women attended. When it was proposed that women be placed on the credentials committee, a debate arose in which the organizers of the convention not only turned down that proposal, but succeeded in excluding women entirely from the convention. Thereupon, the Reverend Thomas Wentworth Higginson led a secession whose participants met separately and issued a public protest against the exclusion. (*Life*, III, 388; Lucy Stone, "World's Temperance Convention," *The Liberator*, May 20, 1853.)

Subsequently, a fall World's Temperance Convention was called, by the same group that had earlier excluded women, for September 6 and 7. Thereupon, the seceders issued a call for a counter-Whole World's Temperance Convention, on September 1 and 2. The latter call read as follows:

"Whereas, in response to a call for a preliminary meeting of the friends of Temperance in North America, to make arrangements for a World's Temperance Convention in the city of New York, during the World's Fair, a meeting assembled in that city, on the 12th of May, 1853, which assumed the power to exclude several regularly elected delegates, because they were women;

"And, whereas, a portion of the members of that meeting retired from it, regarding it as false both to the letter and the spirit of the Call;

"The undersigned, consisting in part of such seceding delegates, hereby invite all those in favor of a World's Temperance Convention, which shall be true to its name, to meet in the city of New York, on Thursday and Friday, the 1st and 2d September next, to consider the present needs of the Temperance Reform.

"New York, July 15, 1853."

Signers of the convention call included Higginson, Horace Greeley, Joshua R. Giddings, Theodore Parker, James and Lucretia Mott, Francis Jackson, Stephen Foster, Lucy Stone, Samuel J. May, Oliver Johnson, Garrison, Wendell Phillips, Susan B. Anthony, and many others. (The call was printed in *The Liberator*, July 22, 1853, and in subsequent issues.)

6. James S. Gibbons (1810–1892), Quaker, merchant, and abolitionist, was a son-in-law of Isaac T. Hopper, a close friend of Garrison, and an ever-ready supporter, financially and otherwise, of the abolitionist cause. He had moved to New York from Philadelphia in 1835. (For further information see *Letters*, II, 613.)

7. Lucy Stone (1818–1893), born near West Brookfield, Massachusetts, graduated from Oberlin College in 1847, and began lecturing on woman's rights that year. She became a lecturer in 1848 for the Massachusetts Anti-Slavery Society but did not confine her efforts to that state, speaking throughout New England, the West, and Canada on abolition and woman's rights. She was a leader in calling the first national woman's rights convention at Worcester, Massachusetts, in 1850. She married Henry Browne Blackwell, a Cincinnati merchant and abolitionist, in 1855, but retained her own name. After the Civil War, she helped form the American Woman Suffrage Association; in 1870, she became co-editor of the newly-founded *Woman's Journal* in Boston, of which she was editor-in-chief from 1872 until at least 1888. (*Notable American Women.*)

8. Antoinette Louisa Brown (1825–1921), author and minister, abolitionist and woman's rights leader, graduated from Oberlin College in 1847 and subsequently completed a course of theological studies at Oberlin in 1850. Although she was denied the license to preach, usually given to theological students, she preached on her own responsibility. After participating in the woman's rights convention in Worcester, Massachusetts, in 1850, she became a prominent leader in the movement. In 1853–1854, she served as the ordained pastor of an orthodox Congregational church in Wayne County, New York. She married Samuel C. Blackwell in 1856. Later in life she became a Unitarian. Her books include *Studies in General Science*, New York, 1869; *The Sexes Throughout Nature*, 1875; and *The Physical Basis of Immortality*, 1876.

9. Frances Dana Barker Gage (October 12, 1808–November 10, 1884), author, lecturer and reformer involved in temperance, antislavery and woman's rights, was born in Ohio and married James L. Gage of McConnelsville, Ohio, lawyer and ironfounder, in 1829. By the early 1850's, she was a frequent contributor to the *Ladies' Repository* of Cincinnati, and a leader in the woman's rights movement in Ohio. In 1853, the Gages moved to St. Louis, Missouri. Despite the hostile environment, she continued her reform activities. In 1860, they settled in Columbus, Ohio, where Frances Gage was associate editor of two farm publications, the *Ohio Cultivator* and *Field Notes*. During the Civil War, she worked for a time with the freedmen on Parris Island, South Carolina, and also did a great deal of lecturing in the North about their problems and needs. After the war, she published a volume of *Poems* and a temperance novel, *Elsie Magoon*. In 1865, she moved to Lambertsville, New Jersey. After suffering a paralytic stroke in 1867, she remained paralyzed for the remainder of her life, dying in Greenwich, Connecticut. (*Notable American Women.*)

10. Mrs. Clarina Irene Howard Nichols (not Nicholes) (1810–1885), of Vermont, was an editor and woman's rights leader. After a first marriage and divorce, she married the publisher and printer of the *Windham County Democrat* of Brattleboro, Vermont, George W. Nichols, twenty-five years her senior, in 1843. She had begun writing for the paper in 1840 and later became its editor, making it more receptive to various reforms, including abolition, Fourierism, temperance, and woman's rights. She became active in the woman's rights movement in 1847 and several years later spoke to the Vermont state legislature on a measure to allow women to vote in district school meetings. In the early 1850's she spoke at woman's rights conventions and local lyceums in Vermont, New Hampshire, Massachusetts,

New York, and Pennsylvania. Because of her husband's ill health, the paper was suspended in 1853 and they moved to Kansas, where her husband died in 1855. In Kansas she wrote for the Lawrence *Herald of Freedom* and the Topeka *Kansas Tribune* and continued her activity on behalf of woman's rights. She later moved to California, where she died. (*Notable American Women.*)

11. Miss Emily Clark, otherwise unidentified. See note 19 of this letter.

12. The convention proceedings were reported in *The Liberator*, September 9, 16, 1853.

13. Ruth Dugdale. She died on September 4, 1898, in her ninety-seventh year. (*Friends' Intelligencer*, 55:747, 1898.)

14. Mary Ann Johnson (b. Westmoreland, New Hampshire, August 24, 1808; d. New York, June 8, 1872), daughter of the Reverend Broughton White, a Congregational minister, and wife of abolitionist Oliver Johnson, had married Johnson in Boston in 1832. He was then the editor of the *Christian Soldier*. She was, for a time, assistant matron at the female state prison at Sing Sing, New York. She was active in various reform movements, and later lectured to women's groups on anatomy and physiology. (*Letters*, II, xxvi *et passim*; *Columbian Centinel*, September 8, 1832; Elmira L. White, *Genealogy of the Descendants of John White*, Haverhill, 1905, vol. III, pp. 143–146.)

15. An Anne Cannan was a member of the Finance Committee of the First of August celebration at Abington, Massachusetts, in 1862, and sometimes helped the Garrisons with sewing. She died early in 1874. (See Garrison's letter to Fanny Garrison Villard, March 5, 1874, Houghton Library, Harvard University; *The Liberator*, August 8, 1862; for interesting conjectures, see *Letters*, III, 596.)

16. *The Liberator*, November 26, 1852, announced that "*Uncle Tom's Cabin* has been dramatized, and is now greeted by crowded houses at the Boston Museum." Forrest Wilson, in *Crusader in Crinoline: The Life of Harriet Beecher Stowe* (Philadelphia, London, New York, 1941, p. 325), notes that "a dramatization of *Uncle Tom's Cabin* had begun in August to be played in the Museum Theatre in Boston and another at the National Theatre in New York — separate versions in neither of which did Harriet have any financial interest, as she did not in any of the myriad dramatizations which followed. An author's copyright did not protect dramatic rights until 1870. From the autumn of 1852 until 1931, at least, *Uncle Tom's Cabin* was never 'off the boards' in America."

The Liberator (September 9, 1853), in an item entitled "'Uncle Tom' on the Stage," by a New York correspondent, printed a different view of the two dramatizations. "I went on Saturday evening to see the play of *Uncle Tom's Cabin*, at the National Theatre, invited thereto by the description of the *Times*, which appeared in a late *Standard*. That description does no more than justice to the play. It is better by one hundred percent than the version of the Boston Museum. If the shrewdest abolitionist amongst us had prepared the drama with a view to make the strongest anti-slavery impression, he could scarcely have done the work better."

17. Sojourner Truth (*c*. 1797–1883), black abolitionist, lecturer, and reformer, was born a slave in Ulster County, New York, and belonged to several successive masters until she was set free after 1827, with the end of slavery in New York. As a free woman, she was to use the courts to reclaim her son who had been illegally sold into the South. After living in New York City for several years, she left in 1843 "to travel up and down the land," at the same time changing her name from Isabella Van Wagener (the surname was that of her last owner, who freed her) to Sojourner Truth. After spending some time at a communitarian settlement in Northampton, Massachusetts, where she became personally acquainted with abolitionists, she traveled throughout the West, speaking against slavery. Her primary financial support came from the sale of her book, *The Narrative of Sojourner Truth*, written for her by her friend, Olive Gilbert, with a preface by Garrison and a later preface by Harriet Beecher Stowe. One of the best-known anecdotes about her involves an encounter with Frederick Douglass, who was

advocating armed revolt against slavery as the only recourse left to blacks, when Sojourner rose and asked, "Frederick, is God dead?" During the Civil War, Lincoln appointed her "Counselor" to the blacks in Washington, D.C. One of her achievements there was the integration of the capital's streetcars.

18. The two meetings of which Garrison writes, one in the afternoon and the other in the evening, were sponsored by the New York City Anti-Slavery Society on Sunday, September 4. A report of the meeting appeared in *The Liberator*, September 9, 1853. It notes that "the evening meeting was seriously disturbed by the patriotic and valorous Capt. Rynders, and a select band of his rowdy compeers, who invaded the Hall, and insulted, in the most outrageous manner, the speakers and audience. The *Evening Post* says some of the speakers 'were continually interrupted with profane insults, requests for a lock of their hair, . . . etc., so that the Convention was compelled to adjourn in utter disorder. The whole disturbance was a disgrace to our city.'"

19. Concerning this meeting, *The Liberator* (September 16, 1853) reported that "On Monday evening, a meeting was held in the Broadway Tabernacle, in aid of the funds of the N. Y. State Temperance Society, which was very ably addressed by Mrs. Vaughn, the President of the Society, Miss Emily Clark, Mrs. Amelia Bloomer, and Mrs. H. A. Abbro. No attempts were made to disturb the meeting."

20. Two accounts of the meeting, one of which was reprinted from the *New York Tribune*, appeared in *The Liberator*, September 16, 1853.

21. George W. and Catherine Benson, Garrison's brother-in-law and his wife. Since 1850, they had been living in Williamsburgh, Long Island, where George had started a laundry business. In 1855, they moved to New York City. (*Letters*, II, xxiii–xxiv.)

22. Dr. Edward Rotton (later Edward Rotton Percy; d. Brooklyn, N.Y., Jan. 4, 1875), graduated from the College of Physicians and Surgeons, with an M.D. degree, in New York, in 1850. (Milton Halsey Thomas, compiler, *Columbia University Officers and Alumni, 1754–1857*, New York, Columbia University Press, 1936, p. 219; *Medical Register of New York, New Jersey and Connecticut: 1875–76*, p. 203.) I am indebted to Dr. John B. Blake, Chief, History of Medicine Division, Department of Health, Education, and Welfare, National Library of Medicine, Bethesda, Maryland, and Elizabeth M. Holloway, Associate Curator, Historical Materials, Library of the College of Physicians of Philadelphia, for this information.

23. Anna Benson, George and Catherine Benson's daughter (b. Providence, R.I., Sept. 23, 1834; fl. 1877) married Dr. Edward Rotton Percy, September 23, 1852, in Williamsburgh, Long Island. They had one child, Charlotte Helen, born July 17, 1860, who died in Kansas, January 7, 1870. (W. P. Garrison, *The Benson Family of Newport, Rhode Island*, New York, 1872, p. 54.)

---

6 4

TO SAMUEL MAY, JR.

Boston, Sept. 17, 1853.

My Dear Friend:

As I am allowed a choice as to the evening I will speak at Worcester, please have it understood by the Managers of the Bazaar that I will be "on hand" on Friday evening.[1] On Saturday, I shall probably go to Haverhill, to attend the quarterly meeting of the Essex County

A. S. Society.[2] After that, I must make no more engagements, but be making my arrangements to depart for Michigan.[3]

I have conferred with Wendell Phillips as to the expediency of wholly postponing our semi-annual meeting at Syracuse,[4] and he is decidedly in favor of postponement.[5] To hold it in November will bring it so near the Decade meeting as to make it very inconvenient for both meetings to be attended by those whom we are anxious should participate in the proceedings. Not to have our full strength at Syracuse would be a great disappointment in that region.[6] Not to have it at Philadelphia would be a still greater disappointment. — I will endeavor to deliver an address at Syracuse on my way home.[7] Mr. May, at S.,[8] shall be apprised of this change, as well as the Standard, Freeman, and Bugle,[9] without delay.

Yours, with the highest regard,

Wm. Lloyd Garrison.

S. May, Jr.

ALS: Antislavery Manuscripts, Boston Public Library.

1. The Fifth Worcester (Massachusetts) Anti-Slavery Bazaar was scheduled for Tuesday morning, September 20, to Saturday evening, September 24. During the last three evenings, speeches were to be delivered by Garrison, Wendell Phillips, and others. (*The Liberator*, September 16, 1853.)

2. *The Liberator*, September 16, 1853, carried a notice that "a quarterly meeting of the Essex County Anti-Slavery Society will be held at Haverhill on Saturday evening, and on Sunday, day and evening, September 24 and 25, agreeably to adjournment."

3. The reference is to a tour by Garrison of the West, "with special reference to Michigan," which began on October 3, with Cleveland as his "first halting-place." (*Life*, III, 391.) Garrison, in *The Liberator*, September 23, 1853, announced that "It is our intention to make an anti-slavery tour to the West, in the course of a few days, having been irresistibly importuned to do so by the friends of the cause in that great field of labor. We expect to be absent about six weeks. We shall endeavor to be present at the National Woman's Rights Convention, which is to be held at Cleveland, Ohio, on Wednesday and Thursday, Oct. 5th and 6th; and to arrive in Adrian, Michigan, on the evening of Saturday, Oct. 8th."

4. The semiannual meeting of the American Anti-Slavery Society was originally announced for September 29 and 30, 1853. It was then postponed to November 2 and 3. (*The Liberator*, September 16, 1853.)

5. *The Liberator*, on September 23, 1853, carried an announcement that the meeting which had been postponed to November 2 and 3 had been canceled entirely "in consequence of its proximity to the Second Decade Meeting of the Parent Society, which is to be held in Philadelphia on the 2d and 3d of December, and at which it is desirable to concentrate the anti-slavery strength and talent of the country, as far as practicable."

6. The reason for the disappointment at Syracuse was that the American Anti-Slavery Society meeting of September 29 and 30 was to precede the "Jerry Rescue Celebration" at Syracuse on October 1, so that those attending the former would stay for the latter celebration.

7. From his western tour.

8. Samuel J. May, at Syracuse.

9. The *National Anti-Slavery Standard*, the *Pennsylvania Freeman*, and the *Salem* (Ohio) *Bugle*.

6 5

TO SAMUEL J. MAY

Boston, Sept. 17, 1853.

My Dear Friend:

In consequence of your strongly enforced opinion as to the expediency of postponing the semi-annual meeting of the American A. S. Society to a later period, on account of the Rescue trials, our Committee concluded to name Wednesday and Thursday, Nov. 2d and 3d, as you will see by the last Liberator, as the time for holding the meeting. On further consultation, however, we have come to the conclusion not to hold the meeting at all, as it will certainly conflict with the Decade meeting at Philadelphia, on the 3rd and 4th of Dec. — a meeting of much more importance, and at which we want all the available strength and talent possible. Our prominent speakers cannot attend both meetings, and the Syracuse meeting, therefore, would be very likely to prove a failure, by the non-attendance of some you specially desire to see present. All things considered, it is wiser and better to concentrate all our forces at the Decade gathering at Philadelphia. I presume you, and the friends in your region, will be greatly disappointed at this conclusion; but, on further reflection, I think you will all be reconciled to it.

On my way to the Woman's Rights Convention,[1] I mean to stop at least one night with you. My loving regards to dear Mrs. May and all the family.

Yours, as a brother,

Wm. Lloyd Garrison.

Rev. S. J. May.

ALS: Garrison Papers, Boston Public Library.

1. In Cleveland, Ohio, on October 5 and 6.

6 6

TO SARAH H. EARLE

Boston, Sept. 20, 1853.

Dear Madam:

Mr. May wishes me to inform you, by return mail, whether I will speak at your Bazaar [1] on Thursday or Friday evening. It will be more convenient to me to speak on Friday evening, and so please let it be understood.

Mr. May wishes me to secure Mr. Phillips for Thursday evening. I will try to do so — with what success, you shall know to-morrow evening, by mail.[2]

Hoping your Fair will be highly successful, I remain,

Yours, to break every yoke,

Wm. Lloyd Garrison.

Mrs. Sarah H. Earle.

ALS: Harvard College Library.

Sarah Hussey Earle (b. Nantucket, Mass., August 26, 1799; d. Worcester, Mass., March 9, 1858), daughter of Tristram and Sarah Folger Hussey, married John Milton Earle, of Worcester, journalist, editor, political figure, and owner of the Worcester *Spy*, June 6, 1821. The mother of nine children, two of whom died young, she was an early antislavery sympathizer and activist. (*The Liberator*, March 12, 1858; Pliny Earle, *Ralph Earle and His Descendants*, Worcester, 1888, pp. 205, 209; see also *Letters*, II, 454.)

1. The Fifth Worcester Anti-Slavery Bazaar, mentioned earlier.

2. Apparently Garrison succeeded, for *The Liberator* (September 23, 1853) announced that Wendell Phillips would speak.

67

TO SAMUEL J. MAY

Boston, Sept. 23, 1853.

My Dear Friend:

Your letter of the 21st has just been received, and I have barely time to write a few words, before the mail closes.

I must give up all hope of being at the Rescue celebration, and therefore cannot be with you on the evening of the 30th, according to your desire. I trust, however, that Lucy Stone will deliver an address on that evening, and she will need no aid from any quarter.

The most I can hope to do is to leave Boston on Saturday, the 1st Oct., and arrive at Syracuse by the midnight train; in which case, I will spend the Sunday with you, and perhaps, if it be thought desirable, lecture in the evening; though, after Lucy's meetings, and the Rescue meetings, it would be "carrying coals to Newcastle." It is quite probable, however, that I shall not be able to start till Monday, the 3rd, though I shall make strenuous efforts to leave on Saturday, in order to make my journey to the West less hurried and fatiguing.[1]

I am sorry there has been any confusion about our semi-annual meeting; but, in view of the Decade meeting in Philadelphia, we have done wisely, I think, to omit it altogether. Next year, we will endeavor to hold it at Syracuse, without fail.

I see our brave and noble friend, Gerrit Smith,[2] means to "beard the lion in his den"[3] — in other words, to "agitate, agitate, agitate,"[4] in the very presence of the Judiciary and the teeth of the Government. That is the way to do battle for the Lord, and to make tyranny bite the dust. I wish I could be at Canandaigua.[5]

With Douglass, the die seems to be cast. I lament the schism, but it is unavoidable.[6]

Yours, with my whole soul,

Wm. Lloyd Garrison.

Rev. S. J. May.

ALS: Garrison Papers, Boston Public Library.

1. See Letter 64, to Samuel May, Jr., September 17, 1853, note 3.

2. Gerrit Smith had been elected to the U.S. House of Representatives as an independent candidate in 1852 and served from March 4, 1853 to August 7, 1854. (*BDAC.*)

3. Sir Walter Scott (1771–1832), *Marmion.*

4. "Lord Melbourne. In TORRENS — *Life of Lord Melbourne.* Vol. I. p. 320, and in WALPOLE's *History of England from Conclusion of the Great War*, Vol. III. p. 143." (*Hoyt's New Cyclopedia of Practical Quotations*, New York and London, 1923, p. 612.)

5. Canandaigua is in west central New York, at the north end of Canandaigua Lake and southeast of Rochester.

The reference is to the United States government's final effort to prosecute some of those involved in the Jerry rescue of October 1, 1851, in Syracuse. Samuel J. May writes that "The last attempt to procure a conviction was made at Canandaigua, before Judge Hall, of the United States District Court, in the autumn of 1852. . . . The United States Attorney, Mr. Garvin, found that he could not empanel a jury upon which there were not several who had formed an opinion against the law. So he let all the 'Jerry Rescue Causes' fall to the ground forever" (*Some Recollections of Our Antislavery Conflict*, Boston, 1869, pp. 381–382, 383). Actually, the government's efforts continued into 1853. As late as September 5, 1853, in a letter of reply to the committee which had invited him to preside at the "Jerry Rescue" celebration in Syracuse on October 1, 1853, Gerrit Smith noted that "the trials of persons, charged with rescuing Jerry, will be going on in the U. S. Court at Canandaigua, at the same time that we are celebrating his rescue. . . ." (*The Liberator*, September 16, 1853.) On October 7, 1853, *The Liberator* published an editorial by Edmund Quincy remarking that "It seems that the Government is not yet ready to try the men who dared and did this deed. The defendants have been always ready for trial; but have been compelled to dance attendance on the Courts for *Eight* Sessions, at distant points of the State, and the District Attorney has not got his case ready yet! This is Speedy Justice, with a vengeance! Such a perversion of the tribunals of Justice, as they call themselves, to the indirect punishment of persons obnoxious to the Government, whom it does not hope to convict (for this can be the only explanation of the fact,) is a thing unknown in England, or in any country making any pretensions to Free government. . . ."

6. On September 16, 1853, *The Liberator*, in its "Refuge of Oppression," reprinted an essay from *Frederick Douglass's Paper*, entitled "Opposition from Professed Friends." The essay was a strong attack upon several Garrisonian abolitionists, including at least three blacks. In the following week's issue, *The Liberator*

replied in kind. This was the first public attack upon Douglass in *The Liberator.* For a history of the break between Garrison and Douglass, see Benjamin Quarles, *Frederick Douglass* (Associated Publishers, 1948), *passim*; also, Quarles, "The Break Between Douglass and Garrison," *Journal of Negro History*, 23:144–154 (April 1938).

---

6 8

TO CAROLINE C. THAYER

Past midnight.[1]
[Oct. 3, 1853.]

My dear friend:

"The Lord *preserve you*,"[2] and bless you abundantly, for your many kind gifts to me and mine — (in which petition, or invocation, little Franky[3] will join with a full heart) — every one of which is gratefully appreciated by us all. The quince sent this afternoon is delicious, and the flowers sent for Franky this morning made his eyes sparkle with pleasure.

I shall be off at 9 o'clock this morning for the great West, via Philadelphia, on a crusade for Justice, Liberty and Equality, without regard to sex or complexion.

Hoping to find you well and prosperous or my return, and assuring you afresh of my warmest regards, I remain,

Yours, indefinitely,

Wm. Lloyd Garrison.

Miss Caroline Thayer.

ALS: Massachusetts Historical Society.

1. Two notations, "Oct.?" and "1853?," not in Garrison's hand, and probably written by one of his sons, are to be found above "Past midnight." We have inserted Oct. 3, 1853, as the date of this letter, since Garrison left Boston for his western tour on that day. (See "Mr. Garrison's Tour to the West," *The Liberator*, October 7, 1853.)
2. Psalms 121:7.
3. Francis Jackson Garrison.

---

6 9

TO J. M. W. YERRINTON

Boston, Oct. 3, 1853.

Dear Winchell —

Please read the proofs as carefully and as frequently as you can —

select news items, and watch the articles in the Anti-Slavery papers for selections, in addition to those I have rolled up — and oblige [1]

Everlastingly yours,

Wm. Lloyd Garrison.

ALS: Arlington Historical Society, Arlington, Mass.

1. Last-minute instructions from Garrison to Yerrinton, with regard to *The Liberator*, prior to Garrison's departure for the West.

---

7 0

TO HELEN E. GARRISON

Cleveland, Oct. 8, 1853.

My Dear Wife:

I take it for granted that you have been expecting a line from me, mail after mail, and experienced something of disappointment at receiving nothing till now. You know I told you, before leaving home, that I expected to be so circumstanced, on my route, as to find it difficult to jot down any account of my progress; and this has proved to be the fact. Even now, I have only a few moments (before leaving for Adrian, Michigan) to tell you how I have got along.

All the way from Boston to this city, our trains were much behind their time. We were two hours late at Albany, and in the same proportion all the way through; so that, instead of reaching Buffalo on Tuesday morning, we did not arrive till one o'clock; so that we lost the morning train for Cleveland. At Rochester, Mrs. Burtis,[1] Miss Susan Anthony,[2] Rev. Antoinette Brown, and several other friends, joined us on their way to the Convention, and we had a very pleasant time. I was a good deal fatigued by my "all night's ride," on getting to Buffalo, but concluded I would go on with the friends on the next night to this city. Accordingly, at nine o'clock in the evening, I got into the cars for that purpose, but, just before starting, concluded to beat a retreat, and stay all night at the hotel. During the night, a large fire broke out, burning over four acres in extent, though the buildings were not valuable. I do not fancy the place. In the morning, I left for Cleveland, and on the way, at Erie, had a tremendous thunder-storm, accompanied with hail that speedily covered the ground. I arrived here in the afternoon,[3] and in the evening went to the Women's Rights Convention,[4] where I found James and Lucretia Mott, C. C. Burleigh, Joseph Barker, wife and daughter, Lucy Brown,[5] S. S. and A.K. Foster,[6] and a host of others. Nine meetings were held in succession, the hall being filled to overflowing, and the behaviour of the audience all that could be desired, with few exceptions. The women speakers have acquitted themselves with great ability, and carried off the palm.

Nothing has transpired of special interest to me, except that, yesterday, I had my nose pulled by a brother of the Rev. Dr. Nevin,[7] for calling the latter to his face, in meeting, a rowdy and a blackguard — of which, "particulars hereafter." My nose is still in working order, no harm whatever have [*sic*] been done.[8]

I meant to have filled the sheet, if possible, but I am interrupted every moment by company, and my time is up. I am [in] good health and spirits, and anticipate a pleasant time in Michigan.

Love to all the children and Eliza.[9] Hoping to hear from you at Adrian, I remain,

Yours, lovingly,

Wm. Lloyd Garrison.

ALS: Garrison Papers, Boston Public Library.

1. Mrs. Lewis Burtis (b. Sarah Anthony, Saratoga, N.Y., 1810; d. 1900), a second cousin of Susan B. Anthony, married Lewis B. Burtis (*ca.* 1793–1868), a stove manufacturer and abolitionist of Rochester, in 1839. Abolitionists such as Garrison, Wendell Phillips, Frederick Douglass, and others often visited their home, which also served as a station on the Underground Railroad. In 1848, Mrs. Burtis was secretary of the first woman's rights convention at Seneca Falls, New York. (Material provided by Mrs. Paul T. Shannon, Rochester Historical Society, Rochester, New York; see also *Rochester Union and Advertiser*, June 16, 1868, cited in *Letters*, III, 111, note 6.)

2. Susan Brownell Anthony (February 15, 1820–March 13, 1906), Quaker, woman's rights leader, abolitionist, and temperance advocate. A teacher until about 1848, she thereafter helped to manage the family farm near Rochester, New York. Beginning in 1848, she was active for several years in the Daughters of Temperance, leaving it in 1852 to form the New York State Temperance Society, of which Elizabeth Cady Stanton was president. During the latter year, she participated in her first woman's rights convention, at Syracuse. She was one of the organizers of the Whole World's Temperance Convention. In the years that followed, her activities on behalf of woman's rights earned her William Henry Channing's title of "the Napoleon of the woman's rights movement." She was also "the principal New York agent" of the American Anti-Slavery Society from 1856 to the Civil War. During the Civil War she organized the Women's Loyal National League, which sponsored a petition campaign calling for Negro emancipation. After the Civil War, most of her efforts centered upon the furtherance of the woman suffrage movement. (*Notable American Women.*)

3. Wednesday afternoon, October 5. *Life*, III, 391, and Elizabeth Cady Stanton, Susan B. Anthony, and Matilda Joslyn Gage, *History of Woman Suffrage* (New York, 1881), I, 124, are in error in citing the dates of the convention as October 6, 7, and 8. It began on Wednesday, October 5, and ended Friday, October 7. (See *The Liberator*, September 30 and October 7, 1853.)

4. On Wednesday evening, Garrison introduced the following resolutions to the convention:

"1. *Resolved*, That the natural rights of one human being are those of every other; in all cases equally sacred and inalienable; hence, the boasted 'Rights of Man,' about which we hear so much, are simply the 'Rights of Woman,' about which we hear so little; or, in other words, they are the Rights of Humankind, neither affected by nor dependent upon sex or condition.

"2. *Resolved*, That those who deride the claims of woman to a full recognition of her civil rights and political equality, exhibit the spirit which tyrants and usurpers have displayed in all ages towards the mass of mankind — strike at the foundation of all truly free and equitable government — contend for a sexual aristocracy, which is as irrational and unjust in principle, as that of wealth or hereditary descent — and show their appreciation of liberty to be wholly one-sided and supremely selfish.

"3. *Resolved*, That for the men of this land to claim for themselves the elective franchise, and the right to choose their own rulers, and enact their own laws, as essential to their freedom, safety and welfare, and then to deprive all the women of all these safe guards, solely on the ground of a difference of sex, is to evince the pride of self-esteem, the meanness of usurpation, and the folly of a self-assumed superiority.

"4. *Resolved*, That woman, as well as man, has a right to the highest mental and physical development — to the most ample educational advantages — to the occupancy of whatever position she can reach in Church and State, in science and art, in poetry and music, in painting and sculpture, in civil jurisprudence and political economy, and in the varied departments of human industry, enterprise and skill — to the elective franchise — and to a voice in the administration of justice and the passage of laws for the general welfare.

"5. *Resolved*, That to pretend that the granting of these claims would tend to make woman less amiable and attractive, less regardful of her peculiar duties and obligations as wife and mother, a wanderer from her proper sphere, bringing confusion into domestic life, and strife into the public assembly, is the cant of Papal Rome, as to the discordant and infidel tendencies of the right of private judgment in matters of faith — is the outcry of legitimacy of the incapacity of the people to govern themselves — is the false allegation which selfish and timid conservatism is ever making against every new measure of Reform — and has no foundation in reason, experience, fact or philosophy.

"6. *Resolved*, That the consequences arising from the exclusion of woman from the possession and exercise of her natural rights and the cultivation of her mental faculties have been calamitous to the whole human race — making her servile, dependent, unwomanly — the victim of a false gallantry on the one hand, and of tyrannic subjection on the other — obstructing her mental growth, crippling her physical development, and incapacitating her for general usefulness, and thus inflicting an injury upon all born of woman; and cultivating in man a lordly and arrogant spirit; a love of dominion, a disposition to lightly disregard her comfort and happiness, all of which have been indulged in to a fearful extent, to the curse of his own soul, and the desecration of her nature.

"7. *Resolved*, That so long as the most ignorant, degraded and worthless men are freely admitted to the ballot-box, and practically acknowledged to be competent to determine who shall be in office, and how the government shall be administered, it is preposterous to pretend that women are not qualified to use the elective franchise, and that they are fit only to be recognized, politically speaking, as *non compos mentis*." (*The Liberator*, October 28, 1853.)

5. This may have been Lucy E. Brown, the wife of Henry E. Brown, a minister and professor at Oberlin. After the Civil War, they both worked for the American Missionary Association in Alabama. (Letter from Merton L. Dillon, January 29, 1973.)

6. Stephen S. and Abby Kelley Foster.

7. The Reverend Edwin Henry Nevin (1814–1889), clergyman and author, graduated from Princeton Theological Seminary in 1836, and thereafter served Presbyterian churches at Portsmouth and Poland, Ohio from 1836 to 1841. Elected president of Franklin College in New Athens, Ohio, at the age of twenty-six, he served until 1844, when he resigned and accepted a pastorate in Cleveland. He

retired from the active ministry in 1875 after having served churches in Ohio, Pennsylvania, and New England. His books included *Mode of Baptism* (1847), *Warning Against Popery* (1851), *Faith in God, The Foundation of Individual and National Greatness* (1852), and others.

8. Joseph Barker had characterized the Bible as opposed to woman's rights and as teaching the inferiority of woman. He announced that he would rather renounce the authority of the Bible than accept its teaching concerning the inferiority of women. This aroused the ire of the Reverend Edwin H. Nevin, who demanded and was given the floor for a reply to Mr. Barker. In his remarks he called Barker a "renegade priest" and "an infidel from foreign shores, who had come to teach Americans Christianity." After several unsuccessful attempts by Barker to explain his own views to Nevin, and by others, including Garrison and Stephen Foster, to correct Nevin in his evaluation of Barker, Garrison, speaking from his seat, said: "It is utterly useless to attempt to correct the individual. He is manifestly here in the spirit of a blackguard and rowdy." (*Life*, III, 391–392; Stanton, Anthony, and Gage, *History of Woman Suffrage*, I, 140.)

The incident involving the tweaking of Garrison's nose, which occurred after the meeting on Friday evening, October 7, was described by the *Anti-Slavery Bugle* and reprinted in *The Liberator* (November 4, 1853):

"Mr. Garrison, who, after the adjournment, had delayed to pass from the Hall till the whole audience had retired, met at the door, as he passed out, some three or four men waiting his appearance. Said one of them, a brother of Dr. Nevin:

"Mr. Garrison, I wish to speak to you.

"Mr. G. Will you walk into this room?

"Brother. You said Dr. Nevin had the spirit of a rowdy and a blackguard, did you?

"Mr. G. I did.

"Brother. He is a brother of mine.

"Mr. G. Ah!

"Brother. Did you mean what you said.

"Mr. G. Certainly. I always mean what I say.

"Brother. You said it, did you?

"Mr. G. Yes.

"Brother. [With courage up to the snubbing point.] 'You did, ha! Well then, take that,' — thrusting his hand in Mr. Garrison's face, and giving his nose a friendly tweak.

"Mr. G. You call that a defence of your brother, do you?

"Brother. Yes.

"Mr. G. Well, I am satisfied, if you are. [And Mr. Garrison passed on.]

"In relating the circumstance, Mr. Garrison remarked that he considered this cowardly personal assault as far more honorable than the course of the Reverend Doctor. A decision in which I most cordially concur."

9. Probably the housekeeper. See Letter 112, to Helen Garrison, June 15, 1855.

71

TO HELEN E. GARRISON

Adrian, Oct. 10, 1853.

Dear Helen:

I wrote you a hurried apology for a letter just as I was leaving Cleveland on Saturday morning[1] for this place. I arrived here that evening at 8 o'clock, in company with Marius R. Robinson,[2] the

Editor of the Anti-Slavery Bugle, and Phebe Merritt,[3] an interesting young Quakeress belonging to Battle Creek,[4] a place where I am to lecture next Thursday evening,[5] about seventy miles from here. From thence, I am to go to Detroit, to lecture there on Sunday next, thence to Ann Arbor, and thence to this place on the 22d and 23d inst., to attend a State Convention,[6] at which S[tephen] S. and Abby K. Foster will be present. After that, I shall go back to Ohio, and labor there till the 7th of November, and hope to reach home about the 10th.[7] All my appointments are made up to that time — (the 7th.)

At the depot here, I found waiting for us with his team, Thomas Chandler,[8] the brother of the lamented Elizabeth M. Chandler,[9] who took us to his home, about five miles from this city — for a city it is, having a mayor, board of common councilmen, &c., although it has a population something less than five thousand. The place is finely located, and is growing rapidly. It is the great thoroughfare to the South and the far West. The soil is not like that of Ohio, being light and sandy, but it produces excellent crops of wheat, corn, &c. There is any quantity of fruit in this region, and the peach crop has been enormous.

Friend Chandler lives in a very pleasant and retired spot, having a fine farm of 160 acres. It is furnished with every thing to make a comfortable living. He has an estimable wife, (the sister [10] of Phebe Merritt,) and two boys. He reminds me a good deal of bro. George [Benson], and is worthy of all possible esteem. I was received with all the cordiality of Western hospitality.

Yesterday, (Sunday,) we had two meetings in a commodious hall, capable of holding nearly a thousand persons. It was crowded most densely, and many could find no entrance. Over the platform was placed the name of "Garrison," in well-executed letters in evergreen, surrounded with a wreath. On one side of the room were inscribed the words, "I am an abolitionist," in a similar manner, and on the other side, "Our country is the world — our countrymen are all mankind." I forgot to add in its place, that, under my name, were two hands clasped together, one white, the other black. All this was done by a young lad named Charles Hunt.[11] I spoke at considerable length at both meetings, and was listened to with the most profound attention; and my remarks seemed to be generally well received. It is impossible to say anything new here on the subject of slavery, as they have had all our able lecturers in superabundance. It is almost like "carrying coals to Newcastle," and I felt it to be so.

I was agreeably surprised, while speaking in the afternoon, to see Sallie Holley come into the meeting, with her travelling companion, Miss Putnam,[12] She has been laboring with great success in Detroit and other places, and will probably be induced to remain in the State a short time longer. She put into my hands $31.75, in payment for subscribers she has obtained for the Liberator, and forwarded to Mr. Wallcut. She is a most efficient and acceptable laborer.

After the meeting last evening, I stopped with Dr. Owen,[13] under whose hospitable roof I am now writing my letter. It is an English family, composed of his wife, two children, her mother (Mrs. Ellington) and sister. Mrs. Owen and her sister are very intelligent and pleasing ladies; the mother is a remarkably fine old lady; and the Doctor is a most estimable man. They were all formerly Methodists, but are now thoroughgoing "Garrisonian abolitionists," and foremost in every reform. The "spiritual manifestations" have filled the whole place; and the old lady has occupied this forenoon in giving me some very surprising particulars of the interviews she has had with her husband, sons, and daughters, as well as other persons, in the spirit world, through her son, who is a speaking medium, and is wonderfully operated upon by the spirits, speaking in the tones and imitating the manners of the deceased. It is difficult for the stoutest skepticism to refrain from giving credence to such testimony; though I know you are a "hard case," a Mrs. "unbelieving Thomas," on this subject.

My health continues good, and I am enjoying myself finely. My meetings have been so arranged as not to work me too hard, and every thing planned in accordance with my own wishes. But it is difficult for me to get any retirement, even to write you a hasty note, so many are calling to see and converse with me; and you know I cannot refuse them.

I trust you and all at home are well. I was hoping to get a line from you to-day, but have been disappointed. Perhaps I shall get one to-morrow. I am anxious to hear from you as to the health of my dear and venerated friend, Francis Jackson, which I hope is entirely restored. Tell the children to behave as well as they can, so as to give you as little trouble as possible. I will remember them on their return home. A kiss for the little folks — Fanny,[14] Sarah,[15] and Franky.[16]

This afternoon, I am going ago [*sic*] to Thomas Chandler's, accompanied by Miss Holley, Miss Putnam, and Marius R. Robinson, to spend the night and to-morrow.

Affectionately yours,

Wm. Lloyd Garrison.

N.B. Letters can be sent to me at Adrian from Boston as late as the 18th inst. Has the rent been paid for?

ALS: Garrison Papers, Boston Public Library. A portion of this letter appears in *Life*, III, 392–393.

1. October 8.

2. Marius Racine Robinson (b. Dalton, Massachusetts, July 29, 1806; d. Salem, Ohio, December 8, 1878) was a student at Lane Seminary during the famous debates there on slavery and withdrew from the seminary in the winter of 1834 as one of the famous "Lane Rebels." Robinson, who had been teaching classes for Negroes in Cincinnati, continued to do so through 1836. When the *Philanthropist* began publication in Cincinnati under the editorship of James Birney and the auspices of the Ohio Antislavery Society, Robinson joined its staff. Immediately prior to that step, he had been ordained an evangelist by the New York Central Evangelical Association of Jamestown, New York. After marrying Emily Rakestraw of Ohio on November 19, 1836, he joined the "Seventy" agents of the American Anti-Slavery Society as a result of Weld's influence and his desire to be useful in the antislavery movement. He was commissioned to work in Ohio and made his first speaking trip as an agent from December 1836 to February 1837. He continued his agency until the beginning of 1839, when ill health and the loss of his voice compelled him to resign. At the same time, he severed his connection with the church. Thereafter, he retired to a farm near Putnam, Ohio, where he lived for almost ten years. In May 1851, Robinson was persuaded to assume the editorship of the (Salem, Ohio) *Anti-Slavery Bugle*, the official organ of the Western Anti-Slavery Society. His wife, Emily, became the paper's publishing agent. The paper's policy was Garrisonian, and it supported temperance and woman's rights, disunionism, and pacifism. Because of ill health, Robinson retired as editor in February, 1859, and went into business as the owner of a hat store. During the Civil War, he actively supported the northern war effort. Afterwards, he became president of the Ohio Mutual Life Insurance Company, and a respected and honored citizen of Salem, Ohio. (Russell B. Nye, "Marius Robinson, A Forgotten Abolitionist Leader," *The Ohio State Archaeological and Historical Quarterly*, 55:138–154 (1946); *Life*, IV, 409; *Salem* [Ohio] *Republican*, December 12, 1878; *Salem Daily News*, July 31, 1897. The date of Robinson's death is incorrect in the Nye essay.)

3. Phebe Merritt (b. January 24, 1827 at Halfmoon, Saratoga County, New York) was the daughter of Phebe Hart and Joseph Merritt, a Quaker farmer and flour miller who came from Saratoga County, New York, to Battle Creek, Michigan, in 1837. Jane Merritt, Phebe's sister, married Thomas Chandler. Phebe Merritt married Franklin Gray Stickney, a fruit grower, on June 2, 1862. They later moved to Painesville, Ohio. The *Standard*, April 25, 1863, carried a letter datelined "Battle Creek, Mich., April 14," from Phebe H. M. Stickney, on behalf of Sojourner Truth, thanking various donors who had contributed financially in aid of the latter. (I am indebted to Merton Dillon for providing a part of this information in a letter dated February 24, 1972; the date and place of birth of Phebe Merritt were provided by Mrs. Eleanor Mayer, of the Friends Historical Library of Swarthmore College, in a letter dated March 6, 1972; *Biographical Review of Calhoun County, Michigan . . .* , Chicago, 1904, p. 62; I am indebted to Dennis R. Bodem, State Archivist, Michigan Department of State, Lansing, Michigan, for additional information about the Merritt family; Mathew Adams Stickney, *The Stickney Family*, Salem, Mass., 1869, pp. 333, 416; *Michigan Pioneer Collections*, V, Lansing, 1884, 270–271.)

4. Michigan.

5. October 13.

6. This state convention met for the purpose of organizing the Michigan Anti-Slavery Society. The society was voted unanimously. The speakers included Marius Robinson, Sallie Holley, Stephen and Abby Foster, and Garrison. The society adopted the Garrisonian platform. The resolutions that were adopted were formulated and presented by Garrison. The first resolution was disunionist in nature and read as follows:

"Resolved, That as the motto of the American slaveholders is, 'No union with the abolitionists, religiously or politically,' so the uncompromising friends of the slave are bound to reverse the motto, and extend neither religious nor political fellowship to slaveholders." ("Another State Anti-Slavery Society," *The Liberator*, Nov. 11, 1853.)

The Michigan State Anti-Slavery Society had been organized originally on November 10–11, 1836, at Ann Arbor. Although opposed to the formation of a separate abolitionist political party as late as the spring of 1840, its policy changed in the summer of 1840 when "control passed from the founders to a politically oriented group located for the most part in southeast Michigan." From 1841 to 1848, *The Signal of Liberty* was the organ of the Liberty party of Michigan as well as of the Michigan Anti-Slavery Society. Apparently, both organizations were then under more or less identical leadership. The Michigan Anti-Slavery Society passed out of existence with the demise of the state Liberty Party and *The Signal of Liberty*, which suspended publication on February 5, 1848. (I am indebted for this information to a letter from Merton Dillon, who cites the following sources in his letter of May 16, 1972: Arthur R. Kooker, "The Antislavery Movement in Michigan 1796–1840: A Study in Humanitarianism on an American Frontier," Ph.D. dissertation, University of Michigan, 1941; John R. Kephart, "A Voice for Freedom: The Signal of Liberty, 1841–1848," Ph.D. dissertation, University of Michigan, 1960; and a variety of newspapers including the Jackson *Michigan Freeman*, July 2, 1839; *The Liberator*, November 15, 1839; the Cincinnati *Philanthropist*, April 21, 1840; and *The Signal of Liberty*.)

7. He arrived home on Saturday, November 5 (*The Liberator*, November 11, 1853).

8. Thomas Chandler (b. Centre, Delaware, April 15, 1806; d. Hazelbank Homestead, Lenawee County, near Adrian, Michigan, July 29, 1881) moved to Hazelbank in 1830, with his sister, Elizabeth Chandler, and their aunt, Ruth Evans. A farmer throughout his life, he was a Garrisonian abolitionist and helped organize the Michigan Anti-Slavery Society in 1836. He married Jane Merritt (b. Saratoga County, New York) on February 16, 1843. They had three children, one of whom died in 1851. The remaining two were Merritt (b. 1843) and William (b. 1845). In 1853, Chandler helped to organize anew the Garrisonian Michigan Anti-Slavery Society and was elected its president. In 1857, he was a delegate to the National Disunion Convention at Cleveland, and was president of the Michigan Anti-Slavery Convention at Ann Arbor in January, 1861, that was assaulted by a mob. Such abolitionists as Garrison, Henry C. Wright, Parker Pillsbury, Charles C. Burleigh, and other Garrisonian lecturers made Hazelbank their home when they visited Lenawee County, which was a Quaker settlement and a center of Garrisonian sentiment. (*A Record of the Descendants of George and Jane Chandler* . . . , published by the Chandler Family Reunion Committee, 1937, p. 470; Harriet Brown, "cemetery Records of Lenawee County, Michigan," typescript, Library of Congress; *National Anti-Slavery Standard*, November 12, 1853, October 17, 1857, February 16, 1861. A portion of this material was generously provided by Professor Merton L. Dillon, in a letter dated February 23, 1872.)

9. Elizabeth Margaret Chandler (December 24, 1807–November 2, 1834), antislavery author, was a regular contributor to Benjamin Lundy's *Genius of Universal Emancipation* from 1826 until her death. Beginning in 1829, she conducted the "Ladies Repository" of the *Genius*, which consisted, for the most part, of her own essays and poetry. Upon Garrison's association with the *Genius*, she accepted his viewpoint, that of immediate emancipation, and rejected colonization and gradualism. In 1830, she, her brother, Thomas Chandler, and her aunt, Ruth Evans, moved to the farm, named Hazelbank, to which Garrison refers later in this letter. In 1836, Lundy edited a volume of her *Poetical Works*, for which he wrote a short biographical sketch, and a separate volume of her *Essays, Philanthropic and Moral*. (*Notable American Women*.)

10. Jane Merritt Chandler. She was the sister of Phebe Merritt and the daughter of Joseph and Phebe Hart Merritt.

11. Perhaps Charles J. Hunt (b. Shiawassee County, Michigan, *ca*. 1830; d. Ann Arbor, Michigan, 1905), a graduate of the University of Michigan at Ann

Arbor, who began the practice of law in 1849, and during the Civil War served in the Union Army until wounded. After the war, he practiced law in New York until 1873, and thereafter lived in Detroit where he engaged in business. (Richard Edwards, compiler, *Industries of Michigan. City of Detroit, historical and descriptive review* . . . , New York, 1880, p. 152; letter dated March 23, 1972, from Mary Jo Pugh, Assistant Curator, Michigan Historical Collections, University of Michigan, Ann Arbor, Michigan.)

12. Writing of this meeting, John White Chadwick, in *A Life for Liberty, Anti-Slavery and Other Letters of Sallie Holley* (New York and London, 1899), p. 93, notes that "It was at an anti-slavery convention in Adrian, Michigan, that Miss Putnam met Garrison for the first time, — October 9, 1853. She writes:

" 'What a revelation it was — his broad, human principles and their application to American slavery. Never was the Bible more glowingly quoted than in his rendering of 55th Isaiah, "Break every yoke and let the oppressed go free." We stood with him beside the grave of Elizabeth Margaret Chandler whose tender verse Miss Holley used to quote so lovingly when pleading for the slave mother: —

' "While woman's heart is bleeding
Shall woman's voice be hushed?" ' "

Caroline Putnam (d. Lottsburg, Virginia, January 14, 1917, in her ninety-first year) was born in Massachusetts, daughter of a physician and a descendant of General Israel Putnam, and studied at Oberlin College in 1848–1851, where she met Sallie Holley. She never graduated, but became an ardent abolitionist and a close friend of Miss Holley. With the latter's graduation and entrance into the antislavery movement as a lecturer, Miss Putnam became Miss Holley's traveling companion for many years. After the war, Caroline Putnam, Emily Howland, and Sallie Holley founded the Holley School at Lottsburg, Northumberland County, Virginia, for the education of the freedmen. The three women devoted the remainder of their lives to this cause. For many years, too, Caroline Putnam was the postmaster of Lottsburg. The New York *Evening Post*, January 27, 1917, in a short obituary wrote that "Her principles, Equal Rights for All and the World is My Country, made her unswerving in active interest for the cause of the colored, for peace, for woman suffrage, for the protection of birds, and for prohibition, and even at the age of eighty-eight she drove about her county getting pledges to help make Virginia 'dry,' besides aiding with generous contributions. Her high intellectual attainments and her extraordinary memory made her conversation and her letters unusually interesting up to a very short time before her death, and her influence for good must be of lasting benefit to the people among whom she worked." See also the Richmond, Virginia, *News-Leader*, October 21, 1949, for a short news item, "Negro Church Honors 3 White Educators." Much more information about Miss Putnam is to be found in John White Chadwick, *A Life for Liberty, Anti-Slavery and Other Letters of Sallie Holley*, passim. The failure of *Notable American Women, 1607–1950* (Cambridge, Massachusetts, 1971, 3 vols.) to include an essay on Caroline Putnam is one of the few lacunae in that superb collection.

13. Dr. Woodland Owen (b. Woodchurch, Kent, England, February 28, 1819; fl. 1879) was trained in chemistry, pharmacology, and dentistry and served as a dispensary chemist and dentist in various places in England, especially Norfolk and Kent. In May 1842, he and his brother, John G. Owen, came to the United States. The former opened an office in Rochester where he remained until 1844. After wandering through the Midwest for several years, he settled in Adrian, Michigan, in 1848, where he practiced his profession. He was prominent in antislavery efforts in the early 1850's, his home often serving as a stopping-place for Garrison, Henry C. Wright, Stephen and Abby Kelley Foster, J. W. Walker, and others. He was active in the re-creation of the Michigan Anti-Slavery Society in 1853. He was a Republican in politics with the formation of that party in 1854, and, in 1861, was elected an alderman of the Third Ward of Adrian. He was also active in the local and state horticultural and dental societies.

On August 28, 1843, he married Jane Parton Illendon (b. Woodchurch, Kent, England, December 21, 1822). Of four children, they had two surviving sons, Frank W. and Henry E. Owen.

Mrs. Owen's mother was not "Mrs. Ellington," as Garrison erroneously suggests, but Mrs. Richard *Illendon* (born Sarah Grant, in St. Nicholas Isle, Kent, England, December 11, 1782; d. Three Rivers, Michigan, January 29, 1866). She married Richard Illendon of Woodchurch in 1805. They came to the United States with eight children in 1830, settling on a farm in Pembroke, New York, where her husband died in 1837. When she was a little girl she often sat on John Wesley's knee when he visited her father's house in St. Nicholas Isle. Her biographer writes that after she came to the United States she "often astonished and delighted ministers and laymen by her clear and logical reasoning, and pure christian demeanor. She was a woman of noble attainments, possessing the rarest and sweetest virtues. . . ."

Mrs. Owen had five sisters. We are unable to say which of these is referred by by Garrison.

The "speaking medium," the son of the "old lady" and the brother of Mrs. Owen, was Richard Illendon 2nd (b. Canterbury, England, July 8, 1824; fl. 1879). He was a farmer and lived on his father's farm until 1844, when he came to Michigan. In 1854, he purchased a farm in Adrian, sold it in 1865, and purchased another farm near Three Rivers, Michigan, residing there until 1874, when he returned to Adrian. He joined the Methodist Episcopal Church at sixteen, and remained a member until its division over the issue of slavery. He participated in the convention at Lockport, New York, in 1843, which formed the Wesleyan Methodist Church, but was disappointed in the organization. He became a Garrisonian in the 1840's, and thereafter participated in various reform movements. Antislavery men and women often stayed at his home. He was treasurer of the Michigan Anti-Slavery Society after its reorganization in 1853. In his later years, he was a free-thinker. He married Mary Ann Rulon, September 28, 1853. (W. A. Whitney and R. I. Bonner, *History and Biographical Record of Lenawee County, Michigan*, Adrian, 1879, pp. 342–345; 503–505.)

14. Helen Frances Garrison, almost nine years old.

15. Sarah Benson, George W. Benson's youngest daughter, born in Northampton, Massachusetts, October 17, 1846. She married Horace E. Stone, October 13, 1864. (W. P. Garrison, *The Benson Family of Newport, Rhode Island*, New York, 1872, p. 54.)

16. Francis Jackson Garrison, then almost five years old.

72

TO HELEN E. GARRISON

Battle Creek, Oct. 15, 1853.

My Dear Wife:

Up to this hour, I have not had a word of intelligence from home since I left Boston. Possibly you may have written to me at Adrian, and that a letter is waiting for me at that place. If so, I shall not be able to get it till a week hence. It is not my habit to cherish any feelings of uneasiness about you and the children while I am absent; but I begin to be somewhat restless in mind on that point. I wrote to you from Cleveland and Adrian, and presume the letters came safely to hand.

On Tuesday last,[1] I spent the day (with Mr. Robinson of the Bugle, Sallie Holley and Caroline Putnam,) at Thomas Chandler's, the brother of the lamented Elizabeth M. Chandler, whose memory deserves to be held in lasting remembrance for her early and heroic espousal of the anti-slavery cause. The farm consists of 160 acres, and is beautifully situated — about five miles from Adrian. T. C.'s wife[2] is a very amiable woman, and the daughter of Joseph and Phebe Merritt,[3] of this place, with whom I am now abiding. I spent an hour alone at the grave of Elizabeth, (the remains of her aunt[4] lying besides those of her own,) and pencilled a Sonnet[5] on the post of the railing erected around the deceased, expressive of my estimate of her virtues, and the feelings of my heart. — Sallie Holley had previously paid a brief tribute with her pencil to the exalted worth of the departed. There was nothing else to identify the persons whose remains were lying beneath the sod. They are buried on a rising elevation in a large wheat field, which is seen conspicuously at a considerable distance — half a dozen young and thrifty oak trees standing in a row on one side of the enclosure. To me it was hallowed ground, and while standing there, I renewed my pledge of fidelity to the cause of the enslaved while life continues. Thomas reminds me somewhat of dear brother George [Benson]. His heart was well-nigh buried in Elizabeth's grave, and his reverence for her memory carries an air of solemnity about it, as though she had been an angelic visitant from another sphere. He has an estimable friend and neighbor in Jacob Walton,[6] like himself a "birthright" Friend, and, like him, free from every outward sectarian trammel. I was sorry to leave so consecrated a spot.

On Wednesday morning,[7] I left Adrian in the cars for Jonesville, (38 miles,) in company with Miss Holley and Miss Putnam, who were going still further to a place called Coldwater. At Jonesville, I took the stage (a long-bodied wagon) for Marshall, (28 miles,) and had a fine opportunity by the side of the driver to see the face of the country. The "lay of the land" in Michigan, as far as I have seen it, is extremely beautiful. It is generally of a rolling character, but without any hills. Immense fields of wheat and corn are to be seen in every direction. The soil is light and sandy, yet easily cultivated, and very productive. The road between Jonesville and Marshall was so sandy as to remind me of Cape Cod. Some of the land was as thickly covered with stones as any part of Massachusetts, but they are generally of a small size, hardly suitable for stone-walls.

At 5 o'clock, P.M., I arrived at Marshall, stopping at the hotel till 10 o'clock. The place has about 3000 inhabitants, and, like Jonesville, presents a very attractive appearance. Its streets are nobly wide, and laid out at right angles, and its plank side-walks extend for miles, making a most delightful promenade. There are no abolitionists in the place. At 10 o'clock, P.M., I went to the depot to wait for the train for this place, a distance of only thirteen miles; but I had to wait till after 12 o'clock, (my usual luck,) before the train came along; so that it was after 1 o'clock in the morning on arriving here. At the depot, I was met by my young friend Richard Merritt,[8] whom I saw at the Women's Rights Meeting in New York,[9] and who had just returned home only a few hours before my arrival. I was sorry to have given him all this trouble, but the arrangement was made without my knowledge, as I designed to go to a hotel. Richard conveyed me to his father's residence, a very neat and beautiful one, where at breakfast I was warmly welcomed by his parents, and his young sister Phebe, who came on with me from Cleveland to Adrian. Battle Creek is extremely beautiful in every direction. It has a population equal to Marshall, but is a more enterprising place. The buildings are neat, the streets spacious, though not so regular as at Marshall, and every thing is attractive to the eye. There has been considerable anti-slavery work done here by Henry C. Wright, Parker Pillsbury, Stephen S. Foster, James W. Walker,[10] and other efficient laborers; but not much impression has been made upon the place, owing to the strength of religious bigotry, all the meeting houses being closed against the slave's advocates — except the Methodist's, which, a short time since, was opened once to Miss Holley, but I am refused admission into it, being every where regarded at the West as an infidel of the most dangerous stamp.

In the evening, I addressed a crowded and an attentive audience in the Friends' meeting-house, a very small one, and succeeded in reversing the preconceived opinions of my person and principles to a very satisfactory extent. Many expressed their surprise that they had been so grossly deceived in regard to myself, and a strong reaction in my favor was the consequence.

Yesterday, I spent the forenoon and dined with Henry Willis and his wife,[11] in company with a few friends. It was a very pleasant interview. Mrs. Willis is a sister of the late Abigail Mott,[12] who died in this place, and "of whom the world was not worthy." [13] Mr. Willis [14] is a rough, energetic, enterprising farmer, going extensively into the nursery business; but his wife has once separated from him, on account of his ungovernable temper. He is an outspoken abolitionist, but a man without any influence, and one of those injudicious friends who do a great deal more harm than good to any cause they are so unlucky as to espouse. Still, he has many good traits, and only needs more restraint upon his feelings.

Last evening, I again lectured in the Friends' meeting-house, to a crowded audience, and was listened to with profound attention for two hours. A very favorable impression appears to have been made. This afternoon, I leave for Detroit, where I am to speak to-morrow afternoon and evening. There is a good deal of excitement in that place, caused by the recent meetings held there by S. S. and Abby K. Foster. The Detroit papers are full of pro-slavery slang, especially the Free Soil paper,[15] which has assailed our friends after the style of [James Gordon] Bennett's Herald. I expect to be slandered, caricatured and assailed, in the worst manner; but no matter. One of the Detroit papers exults that my nose was pulled at Cleveland! — From Detroit I go to Ypsilanti and Ann Arbor, thence back to Adrian on Friday next, to attend a state convention.

Yours, lovingly,

Wm. Lloyd Garrison.

☞ My health is first rate, except that I have a slight attack of sore throat. Ever since I have come into Michigan, the weather has been clear and beautiful, with ravishing moonlight evenings. It is a very dry season, but extremely healthy.

[Ask friend Wallcut to send the Liberator to John G. Hoyt,[16] Battle Creek, Michigan, and enclose a receipt for six mos. — $1,25 — and charge the same to me.]

☞ Should my health continue, I shall not be at home probably till the middle of November, or near that time. I wish to speak at Buffalo, Rochester, Syracuse, and Albany, if I can.

ALS: Garrison Papers, Boston Public Library.
A portion of this letter is printed in *Life*, III, 393. A large portion, with minor editorial changes and one important omission, appeared in *The Liberator*, December 2, 1853, in Garrison's account of his "Tour to Ohio and Michigan."

1. October 11.
2. Jane.
3. Joseph Merritt (1792–1863) and Phebe Hart Merritt (b. New York City, 1791; d. Battle Creek, 1870) were the parents of Jane, Phebe, Richard, and Charles Merritt. Joseph Merritt, a Quaker farmer and flour miller, came from Saratoga, New York to Battle Creek, Michigan in 1836 or 1837. He bought a large farm near Battle Creek, and, with Mr. Hart, an interest in the original plat of the city. He built a large residence, planned part of the town, laid out some of its streets, and planted maples along the edges of what came to be named Maple Street. He died an honored citizen. (*Portrait and Biographical Album of Calhoun County, Michigan*, Chicago, 1891, p. 564; "Oak Hill Cemetery Records," Battle Creek, Calhoun, Michigan, typed in 1946 by the Genealogical Society, Salt Lake City, Utah, carbon of typescript in the New England Historic Genealogical Society, Part III, p. 389; *Michigan Pioneer Collections*, V, Lansing, 1884, 270–271. I am indebted to Professor Merton Dillon for providing the information from the latter source in a letter dated February 24, 1972; *The Liberator*, December 2, 1853.)
4. Ruth Evans, who died soon after Elizabeth Chandler.
5. In *The Liberator*, December 2, 1853, Garrison explains how he came to write his sonnet at Elizabeth Chandler's grave: "Her mortal remains lie entombed

on a commanding elevation (selected by herself for that purpose,) near the spot where she died, a neat white railing enclosing them, and some half a dozen young and thrifty oak trees standing in a row on one side of it. I visited the spot several times alone: to me it was 'all-hallowed ground.' It was a pilgrimage that I had yearned to make for many years. . . . I found that my friend, Miss SALLIE HOLLEY, had preceded me in visiting the burial-place, and inscribed with her pencil upon one of the posts a touching tribute to her memory. Another inscription had been made by a fugitive slave. I could do no less than pay my homage in the following lines, written *impromptu* on the spot: —

"TRIBUTE TO THE MEMORY

OF

ELIZABETH MARGARET CHANDLER.

"In thee what glorious attributes combined,
  To make thy life, (though all too brief in years,)
A blessing to the lowliest of mankind,
  That earth no more might be a vale of tears!
Intrepid heroine in the noble cause
  Of outraged nature and the rights of man,
Shunning no cross, and seeking no applause;
  In every conflict always in the van!
Here rests thy body — dust to dust returned —
  What soul more pure e'er took its flight to heaven?
A deathless fame most nobly hast thou earned —
  All honor to thy memory be given!
I consecrate anew, beside thy grave,
  My life to bring redemption to the slave."

6. Jacob Walton (b. Buckingham, Pennsylvania, February 10, 1818) migrated to Saline, Michigan, in 1834. In 1851, he moved to Raisin, Lenawee County, where he was still living in 1887. A farmer by occupation, he represented Lenawee County in the state legislature from 1869 to 1870 and 1873 to 1874. He was a Republican. (*Michigan Biographies* . . . , Michigan Historical Commission, Lansing, 1924, II, 402.)

7. October 12.

8. Richard Merritt (b. 1822; d. Battle Creek, Michigan, September, 1892), son of Joseph and Phebe Merritt. (Oak Hill Cemetery Records . . . , Part III, p. 389.)

9. During the first week in September, 1853.

10. James W. Walker (d. New Lyme, Michigan, April 4, 1854), of Leesburg, Ohio, was a general agent of the Western Anti-Slavery Society. (*Life*, III, 195.) *The Liberator*, April 28, 1854, reprinted from the *Pennsylvania Freeman* a short notice of Walker's death, which mentioned the (Salem) *Anti-Slavery Bugle* as the source of its information, noting that "he filled an important position and did excellent service in the anti-slavery field at the West. But though his labors were mostly confined to that section, the report of his fidelity had won him the esteem and fraternal regard of the Abolitionists of the whole Country. . . ." In a letter to Garrison datelined "Newburgh (Ohio), April 9, 1854," Henry C. Wright wrote that Walker "was hunted from England as a Chartist — a friend of the toiling masses. He was among the Methodists, till he was forced, for conscience sake, to come out of all churches. . . . He has left his mark in Ohio and Michigan. . . ." (*The Liberator*, April 21, 1854.) An obituary in *The Liberator* remarked that Walker "was settled over a flourishing Methodist church and congregation at Cleveland [Ohio], where he was greatly beloved and in much repute," but that "as soon as he perceived that the American Church was the bulwark of slavery, and the American Union a covenant with death, he publicly renounced them both" and joined the abolitionists. It praised his ability as a "public debater and lecturer" and as a frequent contributor to the *Anti-Slavery Bugle*. (*Ibid.*; see also the

remarkable tribute to Walker by Abby Kelley Foster, in a letter dated April 25, 1854, reprinted from the *Anti-Slavery Bugle* in *The Liberator*, May 26, 1854; for some additional information see the *Pennsylvania Freeman*, April 27, 1854.)

11. Henry Willis (b. Philadelphia, November, 1801; d. Battle Creek, Michigan, December 19, 1886), was the son of Thomas Willis, an English cabinet-maker who had immigrated to the United States, and Elizabeth Evans, of Philadelphia. His parents having died while he was quite young, he worked variously as a farmer, from age seven to sixteen, as a shoemaker for the next five years, again as a farmer, and finally as a builder and superintendent of railroads. He settled near Battle Creek, Michigan, in 1839, as a pioneer of the county, cleared much land, and built many farm buildings. He was raised as a Quaker but became a Spiritualist. He was one of the committee of five that organized the National Republican Party at Harrisburg, Pennsylvania, in 1854. He was a radical abolitionist and active in the Underground Railroad. In 1824, he married Hannah Marsh, with whom he had five children and who died in 1833. In 1839, he married Phebe Mott of Albany, New York, with whom he had two sons. (*American Biographical History of Eminent and Self-Made Men . . . Michigan Volume*, Cincinnati, Ohio, 1878, Third District, pp. 103–104; "Oak Hill Cemetery Records, Battle Creek, Calhoun, Michigan," Part IV, p. 624.)

Mrs. Henry Willis, the former Phebe Mott (b. Albany, New York, May 12, 1805) was the ninth of the ten children of Daniel and Amy Mott of Albany, New York. (Thomas C. Cornell, *Adam and Ann Mott: Their Ancestors and Their Descendants*, Poughkeepsie, New York, 1890, pp. 218–219.)

12. Abigail Mott of Albany (b. Albany, New York, May 12, 1803; d. Battle Creek, Michigan, September 5, 1850), was the eighth child of Daniel and Amy Mott of Albany, New York. (Cornell, *Adam and Ann Mott*, pp. 218–219.) Her obituary in the *Standard* read in part:

"At Battle Creek, Mich., at the house of her sister, with whom she was passing the summer, ABIGAIL MOTT of Albany, aged 47. . . .

"The large circle of Anti-Slavery friends to whom ABIGAIL MOTT's brilliant countenance and joyous voice [were] so cheering from year to year in the Anniversary meetings, Conventions and Bazaars in New York, and occasionally in other places, cannot but be saddened that her personal presence is withdrawn. But who shall rise up to do that work which her quiet, unremitting, private exertions, in behalf of the down-trodden and crushed, were effecting on the community wherever she moved?

"O! may her life be to us all an incentive to greater devotion in the work of the slave's redemption.

A. K. F."

(*National Anti-Slavery Standard*, October 10, 1850; *The Liberator*, September 13, 1850.)

13. Hebrews 18:38.

14. The following lines, until the end of the paragraph, were omitted in *The Liberator* article.

15. The Detroit *Free Democrat* (*Life*, III, 393).

16. Otherwise unidentified.

---

7 3

TO HELEN E. GARRISON

Detroit, Oct. 17, 1853.

Dear Wife:

A fortnight, to-day, I left home; and although my time has been busily and pleasantly occupied, it seems a very long period since I bade you adieu. How much, by the almost miraculous aid of steam power, can now be crowded into two weeks! I have traversed almost the entire length of Massachusetts and New York, a large portion of Ohio, and hundreds of miles in Michigan, stopping several days by the way, attending meetings, delivering lectures, &c. I am now a long distance from you. This is a very finely located city, almost equal to Cleveland, well-built, with some of the widest streets I have ever seen, and very cleanly. It contains upwards of thirty thousand inhabitants. Sallie Holley has recently lectured here, to very general acceptance, as she does every where — her addresses being of a religious character, without dealing with persons, churches and parties, in a way to probe them to the quick, yet doing good service to the cause. More recently, our friends the Fosters have held four or five meetings in the City Hall, which were well attended, and which created a good deal of excitement and discussion. They are acting, in various places, as my forerunners; and by their solicitation, I came this long distance from Battle Creek, (about 140 miles,) on Saturday,[1] with my friend Marius R. Robinson, — they having left a few days previous, — thinking I should find all the necessary arrangements made for my lecturing on Sunday afternoon and evening. But, lo! on our arrival, we found nothing had been done — or, rather, that not a hall in the place could be obtained for me, "for love or money." Stephen and Abby [Foster], instead of facilitating my progress, appear to have given me an Irish hoist, "a peg lower." Indeed, the last evening they lectured here, they were enabled to get into the City Hall, only by some persons breaking the lock, and taking possession of it without leave — a measure I would not have sanctioned. The notices of their meetings and persons, by the Detroit papers, (especially the Free Soil organ,) [2] were abusive, untruthful and scurrilous, to the last degree. Every where the press in this country is as foul as the gutter, and as unprincipled as the father of lies. Most of the proprietors and editors more richly deserve a place in the penitentiary than many of its inmates; for they sin as with "a cartrope," and on the largest and most comprehensive scale. It is a terrible sign of general corruption.

Well, no one met us at the depot to welcome us, or to proffer us a particle of hospitality. Marius was as much a stranger in Detroit as myself. Neither of us knew a single person in the city. We drove to "Finney's Temperance Hotel," on "Woodward Avenue," where we are still stopping — a house very well conducted, though not of the first class.

On Sunday morning, Mr. Osborne [3] (who married the amiable and gifted poetess, Lucy A. Colby,[4] of Danvers, Mass., recently deceased,) called upon us, and gave us the first intimation we had received as to the impossibility of procuring a hall for me. He is a very gentlemanly man, and belongs to Salem, but has resided in this city seventeen years. Had he not broken up housekeeping, in consequence of the death of his beloved wife, we should have been kindly welcomed to his home. Opposite Detroit, (a magnificent river, three quarters of a mile wide, separating our national boundary from that of Canada,) resides Henry Bibb,[5] in a rude and impoverished village called Windsor, where he prints "The Voice of the Fugitive"; but, unfortunately, on Wednesday night last, his office was entirely destroyed by fire — press, types, every thing, though I am glad to hear they were insured. The fire is supposed to have been an incendiary act on the part of some of his enemies. Having nothing better to do, we all went over to Windsor, and called at Bibb's residence, a very poor and inferior building, but he was not at home, having come over to the city an hour or two before. We spent half an hour with his wife,[6] whom Samuel J. May helped to educate. She is ladylike and accomplished in her manners, and devotes a portion of her time to teaching. We then walked to Sandwich, (also on the Canada side,) about two miles below, where there is a colored settlement, as also one at Windsor, composed almost wholly of fugitive slaves, though we had no opportunity to converse with any of them. At Sandwich, we saw the barracks (formerly occupied by British soldiers,) which, winter before last, were opened to shelter the crowd of fugitive slaves then hastening to that spot, to prevent them from perishing. It is an old, dilapidated, forsaken building, yet it served a very useful purpose in sheltering the hunted fugitives. We returned to our hotel about 2 o'clock, pretty thoroughly tired by our long jaunt. I forgot to say, in its place, that Sandwich is a small village, a little more civilized in its appearance than Windsor. The inhabitants are chiefly composed of French Canadians, having a large infusion of colored blood in their veins. They are ignorant, poor, and without enterprise. They have a large and modern built Catholic Church, and as it was service time, we had an opportunity to see a large crowd of them, and their appearance was quite unique, with their Canadian ponies, and vehicles of the rudest and queerest shape imaginable; "'spects they growed," like Topsey. Near the new structure was an old Church, long since abandoned, huge, and unshapely, and propped up by long pieces of timber, to prevent its tumbling to the ground.

There are several hundred colored persons in Detroit, who have three places of worship. In the course of the afternoon, I was invited to address them in the Methodist Church in the evening, and did so for an hour and a half, the house being filled, with a sprinkling of whites. They responded to all I said with great enthusiasm, and voted me their thanks by acclamation.

To-day, strenuous efforts are making to procure a hall for me this evening. Should this fresh attempt fail, (as it probably will,) I shall again speak in the same Church,[7] to such as may come to hear me, and leave in the morning train (first, shaking off the dust from my feet, and there is nothing but dust here, the drought being excessive) for Ann Arbor,[8] 40 miles distant, on my way to the Convention at Adrian on Saturday and Sunday next,[9] where I hope to receive tidings from home. No letter from Boston has yet reached me. I trust all is well at home. My love to all the children, and fatherly benediction.

Ever yours, Wm. Lloyd Garrison.

[☞ Friend Wallcut will credit Joseph Watrous,[10] Mystic River, Ct., $2.50, on his Libr. and charge it to me. George C. Smith [11] wishes the direction of his Libr. to be changed from Canandaigua, Ontario Co., N. Y. to Chapinville in the same County and State.]

☞ I do not expect to write any thing about my tour for the Liberator until I return home.[12] What I send you is simply to keep you informed of my movements.

ALS: Garrison Papers, Boston Public Library. A portion of this letter is printed in *Life*, III, 394.

1. October 15, 1853.
2. The Detroit *Free Democrat*.
3. David S. Osborn (usually spelled without the "e") is listed in the city directories of Detroit as a baker in 1845, 1846, 1851, 1853, and 1854 and as a nurseryman in 1869. (I am indebted to Holly B. Ulseth, Curator, the Detroit Historical Commission, letter dated May 18, 1972, and Mrs. Alice C. Dalligan, Detroit Public Library, letter dated May 31, 1972, for this information.)
4. Lucy A. Colby Osborn (d. in Danvers, Massachusetts, August 31, 1853, aged twenty-one years, five months) had been married to David Osborn but six months when she died of consumption. She was his second wife; his first wife, Marie H. Robie, having died in October 1852 (Mrs. Dalligan, letter, note 3). *The Liberator*, on September 9, 1853, printed a short notice of her death in a letter to Garrison from Martha O. Barrett, dated Danvers, September 5, 1853. The letter included the following comments: "You will remember seeing Mrs. Osborne at the Convention at Lynn, in June, shortly after her arrival from her Western home. She came here, hoping to regain her health in New England; but even then, Consumption had set his seal upon her. From that time, she failed constantly. . . .

"Our dear friend's was a peculiarly loving character. Gifted with no ordinary talents, we saw in her the blending of a fine intellect with child-like simplicity and artlessness, and a heart overflowing with love. Indeed, love was her predominant trait; love of nature, and a keen perception of its beauties, and love unbounded for the human race. She sympathized deeply with the suffering and oppressed every where. The slave found in her an earnest friend. Many of her finest strains were called forth by his wrongs. She ever loved the *Liberator* and *Standard*, and preferred them as mediums for her poetical effusions. She was willing to devote her highest efforts for the good of the bondman. His friends always found in her a friend. A few days before her death, I stood beside her; she looked up, and a beautiful smile lighted her pale face, as she said, 'I would like to have seen Mr.

Garrison and Mr. Pillsbury once more before I die; but you will give them my love, will you not?'

"I enclose a copy of her last poem. She left it, penned with a feeble hand, 'For the Liberator.' "

The Liberator printed the poem, "Lay of the Invalid," immediately below the letter.

An earlier poem by Mrs. Osborn, "The Slave-Mother's Choice," appeared in *The Liberator*, April 1, 1853.

5. Henry A. Bibb (b. Shelby County, Kentucky, May, 1815; d. Windsor, Canada West, August 1, 1854), the son of a slave mother and a white father, was an incorrigibly refractory slave who was sold at least six times because of his perverseness. Beginning in 1835, he made numerous attempts to escape with his wife and child. He finally escaped alone, making his way through Missouri, Ohio, Michigan, and Detroit. He attended a convention of free colored people in Detroit in 1843, and in 1844 became active as a speaker in support of the Liberty party candidates in Michigan. Bibb's most important work began in 1850 with the passage of the Fugitive Slave Law, which impelled numerous escaped slaves and other free blacks to go to Canada, the number reaching several thousand by the end of the year. Bibb formed a colonization society "to assist the refugees from American slavery to obtain permanent homes and to promote their social, moral, physical and intellectual development." To promote his views he established a bimonthly newspaper, *The Voice of the Fugitive*, in 1851. In May 1851, the Refugee's Home Society was organized in Detroit with the aim of securing a grant of land from the Canadian government, or purchasing land from private sources, to be distributed to the refugees in twenty-five-acre plots. By 1854, the society had purchased nearly 2,000 acres of land, and had placed twenty families thereon.

Bibb was also active in the antislavery movement generally. He helped form the Anti-Slavery Society of Canada in 1851 and was elected one of its vice-presidents in 1852. He was also the first president of the Windsor branch of the Anti-Slavery Society. He died in August 1854 after an illness of sixteen weeks.

(Fred Landon, "Henry Bibb, Colonizer," *Journal of Negro History*, 5:437–447, 1920; see also *The Narrative of the Life and Adventures of Henry Bibb, an American Slave, written by himself, with an introduction by Lucius Matlack*, New York, 1849. *The Liberator*, August 11, 1854, contains the notice of Bibb's death.)

6. Mary Bibb, who was also an active leader in the Negro community. (Robin W. Winks, *The Blacks in Canada, A History*, New Haven and London, 1971, pp. 205, 372.)

7. In the *Liberator* article describing his tour (December 2, 1853), Garrison reports as follows:

"On Monday, several colored friends renewed their efforts to procure a hall for me, but they were again foiled; so they put out a handbill, stating that freedom of speech was struck down in Detroit, and announcing that I would lecture in the colored Methodist church that evening. The house was crowded at the time specified, a portion of the white citizens being present. The audience were greatly pleased with the lecture, especially the colored portion."

8. In *The Liberator* (December 2, 1853) Garrison reported leaving Detroit with Marius Robinson on Tuesday morning, October 18, and traveling to Ypsilanti, "a thriving village of about 3,000 people, (forty miles distant)" where Garrison spoke in the evening for an hour and a half and was followed by Robinson who delivered "a few well-timed remarks."

On Wednesday morning, they traveled to Ann Arbor, Michigan, about nine miles distant, "a county seat, and full of sectarianism and pro-slavery. . . ." Apparently, exceeding his expectation, Garrison was warmly received that evening at a crowded meeting in the Court House, where he spoke for two hours.

9. This was to be the Michigan State Anti-Slavery Convention, called for October 22 and 23, which Garrison attended and at which he spoke. A summary of the convention proceedings appeared in *The Liberator*, November 11, 1853.

Garrison returned home by way of Ohio, spending one night with Joshua R. Giddings, at Jefferson, Ashtabula County, Ohio. (*Life*, III, 395; *The Liberator*, December 2, 1853.)

10. Joseph Watrous (1800–1875). Unidentified except for the dates of his birth and death, which were provided by Mrs. Elizabeth Knox, Secretary and Curator, the New London County Historical Society, New London, Connecticut, from the Stonington Cemetery Records and the *Mystic Press*.

11. Otherwise unidentified.

12. The article about his tour appeared in *The Liberator*, December 2, 1853.

7 4

TO JOHN P. HALE

Boston, Nov. 10, 1853.

Hon. John P. Hale,

Dear Sir,

The Twentieth Anniversary of the formation of the American Anti-Slavery Society will be celebrated in Philadelphia, on the third and fourth December next. As one of the speakers on that occasion, untrammelled in regard to thought or speech, you are respectfully invited by the Executive Committee to its platform, — earnestly desirous, as you are, for the speedy and eternal overthrow of chattel slavery in our land, which is the specific object of the Society, by all rightful instrumentalities, and divorced from all other questions.

In case your personal attendance should be impracticable, a letter from you, to be read at the meeting, would serve the cause, and excite general interest.[1]

In behalf of the Executive Committee,

We are, Respectfully, Yours,

Wm. Lloyd Garrison, President of the Society.

Wendell Phillips, ⎫
Edmund Quincy, ⎬ Secretaries.
S. H. Gay,   ⎭

ALS: Society for the Preservation of Old Webster, Webster, New Hampshire; signed but not written by Garrison. An almost identical letter to George W. Julian, which omits "In behalf of the Executive Committee, We are, Respectfully, Yours," and substitutes "Yours, for universal emancipation," is also extant, in the Joshua R. Giddings and George W. Julian Papers of the Library of Congress. A third letter, identical with that to Julian but addressed to Theodore Parker, is in the Garrison Papers, Boston Public Library.

1. The record of the proceedings, printed in the *National Anti-Slavery Standard*, December 10, 1853, and *The Liberator*, December 9, 1853, does not include a speech or a letter by Hale. Letters from Gerrit Smith, Cassius M. Clay, Thomas Wentworth Higginson, and George W. Julian were read and printed in the record.

75

TO SAMUEL J. MAY

Boston, Nov. 22, 1853.

My dear friend May:

Lucretia Mott informs me, by letter, that it is your intention to be at the Decade Meeting in Philadelphia [1] — at which tidings we are all very glad in this quarter. Do not let the expense attending your visit to Philadelphia hinder you from going; for I am authorised to say to you, that whatever portion of it, even to the sum total, you feel unable to bear, shall be paid over to you from the treasury of the American A.S. Society. I write in great haste, and can add nothing more, except love to your wife and household.

Yours, most lovingly,

Wm. Lloyd Garrison.

Samuel J. May.

ALS: Garrison Papers, Boston Public Library.

1. May attended and participated actively in the sessions.

76

TO FRANCIS JACKSON

8, Dix Place,
Sunday Afternoon.
[Nov. 27, 1853.]

Dear friend Jackson:

If not otherwise engaged, and it will be both convenient and agreeable to you, please come with George Sunter, [1] and take tea with us this evening — say by 5 o'clock — and gratify my wife, and

Your attached friend,

Wm. Lloyd Garrison.

Francis Jackson,
7 Hollis Street.

ALS: Garrison Papers, Boston Public Library. The date has been penciled in by a later hand.

1. *The Liberator*, December 9, 1853, published three letters from George Sunter, Jr. The first, datelined Boston, November 26, 1853, explained the occasions for the writing of the other two. The first of the latter, datelined Derby, November 4, 1852, had appeared in the *Glasgow Sentinel* and was entitled "Sunday Observance." In it, Sunter had objected to "the anti-christian and demoralizing doctrine

of the peculiar holiness of the first day of the week." The second, datelined Derby, March, 1853, had been sent to the London *Leader* but had been "refused insertion. The occasion of its being written," Sunter explained, "was, that paper's out and out commendation of Franklin Pierce, when in his inaugural address he expressed his determination to execute the Fugitive Slave Law." In subsequent years, *The Liberator* continued to publish a variety of letters from Sunter. George Sunter, Jr. (aged thirty-nine in 1851), was born in Gunnerside, Yorkshire, England, and was an engine driver. In 1851, he was living in Derby, England, with his parents and sisters. (Letter from R. E. Marston, Borough Librarian, County Borough of Derby, March 22, 1972, which lists information from the 1851 Census.)

---

7 7

TO WENDELL PHILLIPS

8, Dix Place,
Sunday Afternoon.
[November 27, 1853.]

Dear Phillips:

Do come and take tea with us this evening — say at half past 5 o'clock — with Francis Jackson and our English friend George Sunter. I am extremely anxious to see you about the Decade Meeting — have sundry letters to show you, one from Cassius M. Clay [1] — &c. &c. Come to tea, if possible. If not, then spend an hour with us after that. But, in neither case, to your own inconvenience; for I remember that you are to lecture to-morrow evening before the Mercantile Library Association.[2]

I meant to have called to see Ann [Phillips] yesterday, but was foiled in my purpose. Will call soon. Best remembrances.

Yours, ever,

Wm. Lloyd Garrison.

Wendell Phillips.

ALS: Morristown National Historic Park.

1. Cassius Marcellus Clay (October 19, 1810–July 22, 1903) was a southern abolitionist. Born and raised in Kentucky, a distant relative of Henry Clay, he graduated from Yale College in 1832, and represented Madison County, Kentucky, in the state legislature in 1835 and 1837. In 1840, after moving to Lexington, he was again elected to the state legislature for one term. Clay's antislavery views dated back to his days at Yale, where he heard Garrison speak. In 1845, he established the *True American,* an antislavery newspaper, at Lexington. When a vigilante group of Lexingtonians sent his equipment, in his absence, to Cincinnati, he continued publishing the paper at the latter place, but then changed its name to the *Examiner* and published it in Louisville, Kentucky. He fought in the Mexican War, and was taken prisoner, though he had opposed the annexation of Texas. In 1848, he supported Zachary Taylor for President, but sought to organize an antislavery party in 1849, running for governor of Kentucky and gaining several thousand votes. He joined the Republican party at its inception, and supported

Frémont and Lincoln in 1856 and 1860, respectively. In 1861 and again in 1863, Lincoln appointed him minister to Russia, a post that he held until 1869. He supported Greeley in 1872, Tilden in 1876, and Blaine in 1884.

The letter from Cassius Clay to which Garrison refers was read to the anniversary antislavery convention in Philadelphia and printed in the proceedings. The letter, regretting Clay's inability to attend the convention, affirmed that "You are right when you class me with those who contend for 'the speedy and eternal overthrow of slavery in our land, by all rightful instrumentalities.' I value it above all other questions. You fight outside of the Union; I within it. So long as we agree in purpose, we will agree to disagree in the means. I love the union as much as the 'Silver Grays' or Southern canters; but I love it not for itself. I love it as the means to an end. I love it as the exponent and conservator of the principles of man's equality and self-government. I love it as the legacy of fathers who avowed that government had only its authority from the consent of the governed. I love it as the guardian also of religious liberty. . . . I love the Union as the banner-bearer of the aspirants of freedom of all lands and nations — lovely in order to be loved. But when it fails in these 'glorious' ends . . . then, say I, *let it perish forever.*

"And as thus I love it, I shall make eternal war upon all those canting scoundrels, whether in Church or State, who would pervert its true prestige to the retainment of slavery, and its extension and perpetuity. I return the war of lynchers and 'respectable' mobs! I return the war of those, however powerful, whose main business it is in these States, to 'crush out Abolitionism!' . . . With a manly heart, which may be beaten down, but never conquered, I stand by you and all true men; and my voice shall ever be, 'don't give up the ship.'

"I am, truly your friend,

C. M. CLAY."

(The Liberator, December 9, 1853.)

2. Justin Winsor, in his chapter on "Libraries in Boston," Justin Winsor, ed., *The Memorial History of Boston* (Boston, 1881, 4 vols.), IV, 283, notes that "To Boston belongs the credit of having started the first of a class of libraries which were of parallel growth with the movements in education that characterized the early half of the present century, — libraries which were intended mainly to help the self-education of the younger members of the commercial classes. The Boston Mercantile Library was begun in 1820, antedating by a few months the similar institution in New York, and by a year that in Philadelphia, both still flourishing; while the Boston institution, after many mischances, having the helpful encouragement at times of eminent men, and floated for some years by the most popular system of public lectures in the town, succumbed in 1877 (when it contained twenty-three thousand volumes) before the progressive work of the Public Library, and became the nucleus of its South End branch."

---

7 8

[TO HARRIET BEECHER STOWE]

BOSTON, Nov. 30, 1853.

ESTEEMED FRIEND:

You frankly say — 'In regard to you, your paper, and in some measure your party, I am in an honest embarrassment. I sympathise with you in many of your positions: others I consider erroneous, hurtful to liberty and the progress of humanity.' Still, you believe us to be 'honest and conscientious' in our opinions.

What those erroneous opinions are, you do not state. I am not able, therefore, to make any reply, on that score. The ground we occupy, as abolitionists, is simply this: — *'Immediate emancipation is the duty of the master, and the right of the slave.'* Our motto is, *'No Union with Slaveholders, religiously or politically.'* This is only the practical application of our principles to whatever sanctions or upholds slavery, in Church or State. I am not disposed to conclude that you regard such sentiments as 'hurtful to the liberty and progress of humanity'; and yet, as these are comprehensively all that we entertain and promulgate, for the overthrow of the slave system, I can only vaguely conjecture to what else you have reference. Believing, as I do, that none of the positions assumed by the American Anti-Slavery Society can be successfully assailed, — and desirous of having them tested as severely as possible, — permit me to say that if, in any particular, you think they are indefensible, I shall esteem it both an honor and a privilege to publish whatever you may feel inclined to write, by way of animadversion or protest.

Of THE LIBERATOR you speak in a friendly spirit, and profess to admire 'its frankness, fearlessness, truthfulness and independence.' I thank you for this tribute. 'At the same time,' you add, 'I regard with apprehension and sorrow much that is in it.' Why are you thus apprehensive? It seems to me a suspicious symptom. Are not the righteous 'as bold as a lion'? [1] The Psalmist could exclaim — 'The Lord is my light and my salvation; whom shall I fear? The Lord is the strength of my life; of whom shall I be afraid?' [2] Your alarm indicates a want of confidence in the truth; nay, I will not say in the truth, but in the soundness of your own opinions. In the truth, your mind is serene; in regard to certain theological views, it is confessedly perturbed. In saying that there is much in THE LIBERATOR which you 'regard with apprehension and sorrow,' am I not correct in surmising that you make no reference to the pro-slavery matter which occupies so liberal a portion of its columns? You would not, I think, have me refuse a hearing to slaveholders or their abettors. I doubt not you appreciate my paper all the more for granting them fair play, and feel no solicitude as to the effect of this course upon the popular mind. 'Let the discussion go on,' you will exclaim, and 'God speed the right.' And yet, what heresy has ever been broached in THE LIBERATOR, which, for impiety and barbarity, will compare with the defence of man-stealing as a divine institution? And why are you not troubled on this account? Shall I answer my own question? It is because of your faith in the absolute and eternal rectitude of the anti-slavery cause: you are sure that no weapon that is formed against it can prosper. It is only the slaveholder who is alarmed in view of a full investigation of this subject. He wishes only his side of it presented. Now, how does it happen, my friend, that, touching the discussion of another subject, you participate in his uneasiness? I mean nothing invidious by this illustration. It seems to me that what, in THE LIBERATOR, you 'regard with apprehension and sorrow,' should fill your bosom with composure, and elicit from you high commendation — namely, that I allow no topic to be introduced into its columns, without giving both sides an impartial hearing. To this rule I have adhered with such fidelity, that no one charges me with its violation. Especially have I ever taken pains to lay before my readers, whatever I have found in print in opposition to my own views, whether relating to Anti-Slavery, Non-Resistance, the Bible, the Sabbath, Women's Rights, &c. &c. In what do you discover the 'frankness, fearlessness, truthfulness and independence' of THE LIBERATOR, if not in this treatment of all conflicting opinions? That you occasionally find in the paper sentiments distasteful to you, at variance with your ideas of right, is not at all surprising. *So do I.* But what then? Is not this inseparable from free discussion? And may not 'error of opinion be safely tolerated, where truth is left free to combat it'? [3] Your objection is fatal to the freedom of the human mind — to the existence of a free press.

You say — 'Were the *Liberator* circulated only among intelligent, well-balanced minds, able to discriminate between good and evil, I should not feel so much apprehension.' So says the Romish Church in regard to the indiscriminate circulation of the Bible among the laity. So says Absolutism, respecting the diffusion of intelligence among the masses. I am surprised at the narrowness of your limitation. Are the people not to be trusted? Are the Pope,[4] and Nicholas [5] and Francis Joseph,[6] right in the conclusions to which they come? Would you have the laws of nature repealed, because they are so often violated, either ignorantly or wilfully? Shall not a beneficent Creator continue to spread the table of his bounty for all, because so many surfeit themselves? Does he err in causing his sun to rise on the evil and on the good, and his rain to fall on the just and on the unjust? Besides, I believe the patrons of THE LIBERATOR will be found to possess remarkably 'intelligent, well-balanced minds,' and to be interested in all the great reforms of the age; and I have yet to hear of any person who has been made less humane, just, Christ-like, by his candid perusal of it. On the contrary, thousands gratefully acknowledge that they have been deeply indebted to it for higher and nobler views of God, of human brotherhood, of life and duty. What other journal in this country is so feared and hated, so proscribed and anathematized, by slave-traffickers and slave-owners, trimming politicians and profligate demagogues, hireling priests and religious formalists, mercenary journalists and servile publishers, — all that is tyrannical in the Government, and corrupt in the Church? How is it habitually characterized by 'the Satanic press' — *Bennett's Herald*, the *New York Observer*, the *New York Express*,[7] &c. &c.? Can such a journal be 'hurtful to liberty and the progress of humanity,' in any rational sense? Can it be safely trusted only 'among intelligent, well-balanced minds, able to discriminate between good and evil'?

Ah! here is the cause of your disquietude! — 'What I fear is, that it will take from poor Uncle Tom [8] his Bible, and give him nothing in its place.' And you say significantly, 'You understand me — do you not?' Frankly, I do not. First — I do not understand, if the Bible be all that you claim for it, and if every adverse criticism upon it in THE LIBER-ATOR is allowed to be met by a friendly one, why you should be anxious as to its just appreciation. The more the anti-slavery coin is rubbed, the brighter it shines — does it not? The more 'Uncle Tom's Cabin' is assailed, the more impregnable it is seen to be. And the more the Bible is sifted, the more highly it will be prized, if it be all holy and true.

Second — I do not understand how any one can 'take from poor Uncle Tom his Bible,' if that book be really a lamp to his feet, and a light to his path, and the word of the living God to his soul; and it seems to me that you throw positive discredit upon his religious ex-perience and inward regeneration, by making such a proposition. If the infernal cruelty of a Legree could not shake his trust in his God and Saviour, do you really think a full discussion of the merits of the Bible, pro and con, might induce him to throw that volume away?

Third — I do not understand how it follows, even if Uncle Tom, or any body else, should be led astray by reading THE LIBERATOR, because it allows both sides of every question to be discussed in its columns, that such a 'frank, fearless, truthful and independent' sheet, as you conclude it to be, ought no longer to possess these characteristics, but should be one-sided, narrow, partial.

Finally — I do not understand why the imputation is thrown upon THE LIBERATOR as tending to rob 'Uncle Tom' of his Bible. I know of no writer in its pages, who wishes to deprive him of it, or of any com-fort he may derive from it. It is for him to place whatever estimate he can upon it; and for you and me to do the same; but for neither of us to accept any more of it than we sincerely believe to be in accordance with reason, truth, eternal right. How much of it is true and obligatory, each one can determine only for himself; for on Protestant ground, there is no room for papal infallibility. All Christendom professes to believe in the inspiration of the volume; and, at the same time, all Christendom is by the ears as to its real teachings. Surely, you would not have me disloyal to my conscience. How do you prove that you are not trammelled by educational or traditional notions as to the entire sanctity of the book? Indeed, it seems to me very evident that you are not free in spirit, in view of the 'apprehension and sorrow' you feel, because you find your conceptions controverted in THE LIBERATOR. Else why such disquietude of mind? 'Thrice is he armed who hath his quarrel just.' [9]

Again you say — 'It is a grief and sorrow of heart to me, that any who are distinguished in the Anti-Slavery cause should be rejecters of that Bible, on which I ground all my hopes of the liberties, not only of the slave, but of the whole human race.' Remember that the Anti-Slavery platform is one to which all are cordially invited, without regard to their scriptural or theological opinions, and on which no person is to be arraigned for anything else but compromising the rights of the slave. Who shall oracularly decide what constitutes a rejection of the Bible? Not you or me — not anybody. Who are the rejecters of that book, to whom you refer? I know of none. If, however, there are such, it is not as abolitionists, but as men. The widest dissent from your opinion, or from mine, in regard to the authority and value of the Bible, it [sic] is not necessarily heresy, — unless the great Protestant right of private judgment be heretical, as Papal Rome says it is. You and I are as likely to err as others, and may make no higher claim to infallibility than others. I must respectfully protest, therefore, against your invidious thrust at 'any who are distinguished in the Anti-Slavery cause,' or who are not distinguished, because they do not endorse your opinions concerning the plenary inspiration of the Bible. You might as properly express 'grief and sorrow of heart,' because there are Unitarians, Universalists, Quakers, &c. &c, — those who reject the ordinances, those who deny the doctrine of everlasting punishment, those who do not believe in the trinity, — to be found among the abolitionists, and all are not Orthodox.

You say it is on the Bible you ground all your hopes of the liberties, not only of the slave, but of the whole human race. How does it happen, then, that, in a nation professing to place as high an estimate upon that volume as yourself, and denouncing as infidels all who do not hold it equally sacred, there are three millions and a half of chattel slaves, who are denied its possession, under severe penalties? Is not slavery sanctioned by the Bible, according to the interpretation of it by the clergy generally, its recognized expounders? What, then, does the cause of bleeding humanity gain by all this veneration for the book?

My reliance for the deliverance of the oppressed universally is upon the nature of man, the inherent wrongfulness of oppression, the power of truth, and the omnipotence of God — using every rightful instrumentality to hasten the jubilee.

Again you say — 'I cannot but regard the admission, by some abolitionists, that the Bible sanctions slavery, as equally unwise and groundless.' But if this is their honest conviction, would you not have them express it? And, thus believing, are they not to be commended for their unswerving fidelity to principle, in refusing to accept it as the inspired word of God? If such were your understanding of any portion of the book, would you not reject it as barbarous and immoral — especially if it consigned you, and your husband, and your children, and your father and mother, and your brothers and sisters, and all your relatives and friends, to the horrible doom of 'Uncle Tom'? I am sure you would, even though you should be branded as infidel by all the clergy and all the churches in Christendom.

For myself, I do not know of a single member of the American Anti-Slavery Society, who admits that the Bible sanctions such a system as that of American slavery. In any meeting of that Society, I believe such an interpretation of the Bible would be unanimously rejected. Ever since its organization, it has uniformly wielded that volume against the impious practice of chattelizing men, women and children; and one of its heaviest and most frequent accusations against the slave system has been, that it makes the Bible an unlawful book in the hands of the slaves.

Possibly, in this particular, you may be better informed than I am as to the Biblical views of the 'Garrisonian abolitionists.' Possibly, some of them may believe that American slavery is sanctioned in some parts of the Bible; yes, in both the Old and the New Testament. What then? First — in this opinion, they are sustained by nine-tenths of the evangelical clergy in the United States, and so cannot be heretical, if the latter are soundly orthodox. Second — so believing, they (unlike the clergy) declare the record to be *false to that extent*, and hold it to be 'a self-evident truth, that all men are created equal and endowed by their Creator with an inalienable right to liberty.' They fill you with 'grief and sorrow,' and you cannot refer to them without registering your protest against their course. But you can, and do, recognize the clergy aforesaid as the ministers of Jesus Christ, and sit at the same communion table with them, and have never called for their expulsion from the pulpit or the church, though they say and teach, first, that chattel slavery is sanctioned by the Bible; and, second, that therefore it cannot be sinful. How marvellously inconsistent is your conduct, as between these parties! Third — whatever may be the convictions of a few individuals in the anti-slavery ranks, as to the pro-slavery character of some parts of the Bible, the American Anti-Slavery Society entertains no such views of the book, as all its official proceedings will testify. A few years since, it twice offered to place five thousand dollars in the treasury of the American Bible Society, provided that Society would agree to expend that sum, with some additional appropriations, in circulating the Bible among the slave population; but the offer was rejected.[10] Moreover, it is a remarkable fact, that the American Anti-Slavery Society is the only organization in this country, that has ever caused to be written, and circulated broadcast through the land, a defence of the Bible against all its pro-slavery interpreters. [See that masterly and unanswerable work, *Weld's Bible Argument*.[11]] Ought not your solicitude, as to the book, to be given to the American Bible Society, and to the great body of the orthodox clergy, rather than to the American Anti-Slavery Society, or to any of its friends?

You do me but simple justice in expressing your belief that I shall be well-pleased with your frankness and sincerity; and I will cherish the hope that you will be equally well-pleased with mine, as exhibited in this reply.

Yours, with high regards,

WM. LLOYD GARRISON.

Printed in *The Liberator*, December 23, 1853.

The Liberator prefaced this letter with the following paragraph: "As many persons are still confused in their minds as to the freedom of the Anti-Slavery Platform, and the safety and propriety of allowing free discussion in *The Liberator*, on all subjects mooted in its columns, — and also as for what we are justly to be held responsible, in conducting an independent and impartial journal, — it may be serviceable to lay before all such the following Letter, written in reply to a private note sent to us by a highly esteemed friend, who is deeply interested in the cause of the oppressed, and sincerely desirous that nothing should be said or done, by any of its advocates, needlessly to alienate any from its support."

The letter itself was headed, in bold caps:

"THE LIBERATOR — FREE DISCUSSION —
THE BIBLE QUESTION."

A perusal of *Life*, III, 395–401, which prints several letters from Harriet Beecher Stowe to Garrison, makes it clear that this letter was written to Mrs. Stowe. She had been invited to attend the Twentieth Anniversary Celebration of the American Anti-Slavery Society but had replied that she could not do so because of her ideological differences with the society. Her official reply was accompanied by an explanatory note to Garrison, which gave the essence of her position as follows:

"I am a constant reader of your paper, and an admirer of much that is in it. I like its frankness, fearlessness, truthfulness, and independence. At the same time I regard with apprehension and sorrow much that is in it. Were it circulated only among intelligent, well-balanced minds, able to discriminate between good and evil, I should not feel so much apprehension. To *me* the paper is decidedly valuable as a fresh and able exposé of the ultra progressive element in our times. What I fear is, that it will take from poor Uncle Tom his Bible, and give him nothing in its place. You understand me — do you not?

"In this view I cannot conscientiously do anything which might endorse your party and your paper, without at the same time entering protest against what I consider erroneous and hurtful. With this view I have written the letter of reply to your invitation, and I imagine that I give you the greatest possible proof of esteem and regard by thus frankly telling you my whole mind, and expecting you to be well pleased with my sincerity. . . ."

She closed her letter with the suggestion that "For many reasons, I should like to have an opportunity of free conversation with you. Could you not come and make us a call one of these days? If you will appoint a time, I will be sure to be at home." (*Life*, III, 396.)

Garrison in turn responded with a private letter, which Mrs. Stowe acknowledged in a letter dated November 30, and in the public letter in *The Liberator*, which did not reveal the identity of the recipient except as a "highly esteemed friend." Since Garrison's private letter to Mrs. Stowe is not available, it is impossible to compare his two letters. But there is little doubt that the public letter was either identical with or an elaboration of his private letter.

Mrs. Stowe replied privately to the public letter, in part as follows: "I see you have published your letter to me in the *Liberator*. I did not reply to that letter immediately because I did not wish to speak on so important a subject *unadvisedly* and without proper thought and reflection. The course I pursued was to make up my file of the *Liberator*, and give it a general investigation as to its drift and course of thought for the past summer. . . .

"I do not answer this letter in the paper, because I think a more private discussion of the matter likely to prove more useful. . . ." She then discussed her differences with the *Liberator*. (*Life*, III, 398–400.)

Life, III, 401, notes that Mrs. Stowe's invitation to Garrison to visit her was accepted and that "the friendly meeting at Andover cannot be exactly dated, but it probably took place in the second week of December. 'I was dreadfully afraid of your father,' Mrs. Stowe has since said to one of Garrison's children; but the conference under her roof dispelled that feeling forever. His spirit captivated her as it had done many another of like prejudices. 'You have,' she wrote to him on December 12, 1853, 'a remarkable tact at conversation.'" Thereafter there were many visits between the two, both at the Garrisons' and at the Stowes'.

Harriet Beecher Stowe (1811–1896), daughter of Lyman Beecher, the prominent orthodox Congregational clergyman, and sister of Henry Ward Beecher, married, in 1836, Calvin Ellis Stowe, a widower, professor of biblical literature at Lane Theological Seminary and the author of an *Introduction to the Criticism and Interpretation of the Bible*. In 1850, the family, with a household of small children, moved to Maine where Calvin had received an appointment at Bowdoin College, his alma mater. *Uncle Tom's Cabin* was written in 1851 as a series of installments for the *National Era*, an antislavery newspaper in Washington, D.C., and was published as a book in 1852. During the latter year, Calvin Stowe was appointed professor of sacred literature at Andover Theological Seminary, and the family moved to Andover, Massachusetts.

In 1853, to meet the attacks upon her novel in the South, Mrs. Stowe published *A Key to Uncle Tom's Cabin* which provided the documentation for the view of slavery presented in the novel. A second antislavery novel, *Dred*, appeared in 1856, but without the acclaim of *Uncle Tom's Cabin*. Thereafter, her other books, none of which dealt with slavery, included *The Minister's Wooing*, serialized in 1858–59 in the *Atlantic Monthly*, *Agnes of Sorrento* (1862), *The Pearl of Orr's Island* (1862), *Oldtown Folks* (1869), and *Poganuc People* (1878). Indeed, between 1862 and 1884, she wrote an average of at least a book a year.

After Calvin Stowe's retirement from teaching, the family moved to Hartford, Connecticut, in 1864, where Calvin Stowe died in 1886 and Harriet Stowe ten years later. (*Notable American Women.*)

1. Proverbs 28:1.

2. Psalms 27:1.

3. Thomas Jefferson, *First Inaugural Address*, 1801.

4. Pius IX was then the reigning pontiff. In 1848, he promulgated the doctrine of the Immaculate Conception of the Virgin Mary.

5. Nicholas I (1796–1855) was the Russian emperor from 1825 to 1855.

6. Francis Joseph (1830–1916) was emperor of Austria from 1848 to 1916. His empire became the Austro-Hungarian Monarchy in 1867.

7. The *New York Express*, a Whig newspaper founded in 1836 by James and Erastus Brooks. During the 1850's, it became a Democratic paper, and remained so until its demise in 1881. (Frank Luther Mott, *American Journalism, 1690–1960*, 3d. ed., New York, 1971, pp. 261–262.)

8. The reference, of course, is to the Uncle Tom of Harriet Beecher Stowe's *Uncle Tom's Cabin*, used as a synonym for the religious slave.

9. Shakespeare, *II Henry VI*, III, ii, 233.

10. The offer was made in 1834 and again in 1835. (*Life*, I, 478 and 478n.) The American Bible Society had been formed in 1816 in New York at a meeting of delegates of between fifty and sixty local Bible societies from throughout the Union. Elias Boudinot was its first president. The society's purpose was to "encourage a wider circulation of the Holy Scriptures without note or comment." (*HEUSH*.)

11. The exact title of Weld's pamphlet — although his name did not appear as author, he did write it — was *The Bible Against Slavery*, New York, American Antislavery Society, 1837. Weld had developed a "Bible argument against slavery" early in his antislavery career. It was an argument which he transmitted to other antislavery agents and lecturers and which he was finally prevailed upon to put into print, although anonymously, in the *Quarterly Anti-Slavery Magazine*, in April, 1837, with the title "Is Slavery from Above or Beneath." As Weld's biographer has noted, the popularity of the article impelled Weld to prepare it as a pamphlet, published later in 1837. "In less than a year it had gone through three editions, and the national society continued to bring out new editions for several years. Antislavery papers quoted it extensively, some of them reprinting the whole pamphlet in serial form. *The Philanthropist* rated it 'the most comprehensive and condensed, the clearest and most conclusive, of any we have seen on the subject.'" (Benjamin P. Thomas, *Theodore Weld, Crusader for Freedom*, New Brunswick, New Jersey, 1950, pp. 126, 277n.) Dwight L. Dumond reports that "after passing through four editions this was out of print for twenty years. It was republished by the Presbyterian Board of Publications in 1864, following Lincoln's Emancipation Proclamation." (*A Bibliography of Antislavery in America*, Ann Arbor, 1961, p. 9.)

IV THE KANSAS-NEBRASKA ACT — THE CONFLICT INTENSIFIES: 1854

THE EARLY MONTHS of 1854 witnessed the national debate over Stephen Douglas' Kansas-Nebraska Act, which proposed to repeal the Missouri Compromise and to open the territory north of 36°30′ to slavery, with "popular sovereignty" to be the ultimate determinant as to the legality of slavery there. Two days after the passage of the act in the House on May 22, Anthony Burns was arrested in Boston as a fugitive slave and, despite an attempt to free him by storming the courthouse, sent back to slavery, with his route to the point of embarkation lined with troops and policemen.

One direct result of the Kansas-Nebraska Act was the organization in the East of "Emigrant Aid" societies to increase the number of Free-State settlers in Kansas and Nebraska. Another was the emerging tendency of all northerners who opposed the extension of slavery to unite into one party. In Massachusetts, antislavery Democrats and Free Soilers, following the Ohio example, combined to form the Republican party.

Of more direct significance to Garrison and other abolitionists, Garrison's biographers point out, was that "the newest and most formidable encroachment on the rights and liberties of the North . . . secured a greater toleration in that section for the abolitionists. . . ." Thus, Garrison's address in New York City on February 14, given at the height of the debate over the Kansas-Nebraska Act, at the invitation of the New York City Anti-Slavery Society, was attended by a large audience despite "execrable" weather, and was "warmly applauded." At the close, the editors of the *New York Times* asked him for the manuscript of his speech, and published it entire the next morning, "occupying more than four columns of the smallest type." As he observes in his letter of

February 16, 1854, to his wife, "Was not that marvellous, as a work of despatch, and as a sign of the times?"

It was on July 4, 1854, that one of the better-known incidents in Garrison's life took place, at Framingham, Massachusetts, when he burned the Constitution as "a covenant with death and an agreement with hell" and exclaimed "So perish all compromises with Tyranny! And let all the people say, Amen!" At which point, "A tremendous shout of 'Amen!' went up to heaven in ratification of the deed, mingled with a few hisses and wrathful exclamations from some who were evidently in a rowdyish state of mind, but who were at once cowed by the popular feeling." (*Life*, III, 412.)

During the latter part of the year, a petition campaign initiated by the abolitionists to remove Judge Edward Loring as judge of probate for his part in sending Anthony Burns back into slavery gained momentum, although it did not achieve success until several years later.

The year closed with Garrison's western speaking tour of about three weeks, beginning at the middle of October. His trip included participation and addresses at antislavery and woman's rights meetings in Syracuse, New York City, Philadelphia, and Westminster, Pennsylvania.

---

7 9

TO HENRY WIGHAM, JR.

Boston, Jan. 1, 1854.

My Dear Friend:

I wish you could hear me shouting to you across the Atlantic, "A Happy New Year to you and yours!" As the distance is too great for me to be heard orally, I must depute my attached friend, and faithful anti-slavery coadjutor for the last twenty years, Parker Pillsbury,[1] to give to you (in case he should visit your renowned and most beautiful city) the best wishes and warmest congratulations of the season, in my behalf. Mr. Pillsbury has been one of the ablest and truest advocates ever raised up to plead the cause of the slave, and truly has he "remembered them that are in bonds as bound with them." No man has been more maligned by the pro-slavery spirit so prevalent in our land, because no one has dealt heavier blows upon it, or done better service in behalf of universal emancipation. You will find him great in his gentleness, in his modesty, in his moral courage, in the noblest attributes of a man. He has somewhat affected his health by his arduous public labors, and seeks to recover it fully by a voyage across the Atlantic. He deserves, and I trust will receive, a hearty welcome at the hands of all those abroad, who take a lively interest in the struggle going on in our land for the utter and speedy abolition of slavery.

With my loving regards to all the dear friends around you, I remain, Your attached friend,

Wm. Lloyd Garrison.

Henry Wigham, Jr.

ALS: New York Public Library.

1. *The Liberator*, February 10, 1854, printed a letter from Parker Pillsbury to Garrison, datelined "Liverpool, Jan. 18, 1854," announcing that he had landed in England that day. Pillsbury returned to Boston, after an absence of more than two years, on May 22, 1856. (*The Liberator*, May 23, 1856.)

---

8 0

TO CAROLINE C. THAYER

8 Dix Place,
Jan. 13, 1854.

My Dear Friend:

Your "cup of kindness," sent to us as a token of friendship, on the advent of the New Year, with the note expressive of your loving regards and desires for our happiness, was most gratefully appreciated, and will excite pleasurable emotions hereafter "for auld lang syne," and in remembrance of the giver. Most warmly do we reciprocate your good wishes.

Our dear friends, Mr. and Mrs. Ayers,[1] of Newton, are to take tea with us this afternoon, and also to spend the evening. Henry C. Wright will also be with us. Can you not, with your mother and sisters, be of our company? Please all come, if you can, that our "cup" may overflow with enjoyment. We shall have tea about 6 o'clock; but come as much earlier as convenient.

Yours, truly,

Wm. Lloyd and Helen E. Garrison.

Miss C. C. Thayer.

ALS: Massachusetts Historical Society.

1. Probably John Ayres (d. June 14, 1888), who was a member of Theodore Parker's congregation and Parker's close friend. One of Parker's last letters from Italy, before his death, was to John Ayres. (John White Chadwick, *Theodore Parker, Preacher and Reformer*, Boston and New York, 1920, pp. 370–371.) Ayres was a clerk in Boston who lived in West Newton until 1862, when he moved to Charlestown, Massachusetts. By 1867, he was treasurer of the Union Sugar Refinery of Boston and was living in Medford, Massachusetts. In 1875, he was again a clerk. (Boston *Directories*, 1841–1889.)

8 1

TO HELEN E. GARRISON

New York, Feb. 16, 1854.

Dear Wife:

I got through to this city, on Tuesday afternoon,[1] at 5 o'clock — therefore in ample season for the evening lecture.[2] I was just "as busy as a bee" with my pencil, the whole distance, writing the remainder of my address, which I finished just before my arrival, not removing from my seat, but for a moment, from Boston to New York. The jolting of the cars was often so great as to make it exceedingly difficult to write a word, and therefore my labor was very great. Of course, with my spinal trouble upon me, I was very much exhausted on my arrival, and felt more like going to bed than delivering a speech.

I found Oliver Johnson at the depot, and went home with him to tea. The weather was perfectly execrable — rainy, foggy, dispiriting — and the walking something less than knee-deep in mud. No evening could have been more unpropitious for my lecture — my usual luck. The Williamsburgh, Brooklyn, Jersey, and other ferry boats, found navigation difficult and dangerous, in consequence of the dense fog; and the result was, that hundreds who intended to be at my lecture, were deterred from coming over. I was prepared, therefore, to see "a beggarly account of empty boxes,"[3] on my going to the Tabernacle, but was agreeably surprised to find a large and substantial audience waiting for my appearance, who warmly applauded me as I walked down the aisle. I got through with reading my lecture quite as well as I expected, though my voice was somewhat hoarse. My language was strong, and my accusations of men and things, religion and politics, were very cutting; but, strange to say, not a single hiss or note of disapprobation was heard from beginning to end, but some of my strongest expressions were the most loudly applauded. At the close, at the request of the editors of the New York *Times*, through their reporter, I gave my manuscript entire to be published in that widely circulated daily; and the next morning, it was published entire in that paper, occupying more than four columns of the smallest type. Was not that marvellous, as a work of despatch, and as a sign of the times? The Executive Committee of the A.S. Society purchased five hundred copies of the *Times* for distribution. The address is to be published in the *Standard*,[4] and they have ordered five hundred copies of that paper. Finally, they will print it in a small tract, and so I shall have delivered it to a large number of people, in spite of the bad weather. It seemed to give great satisfaction universally.

Catharine [Benson] and aunt Charlotte[5] were at the lecture, but I could only see them for a moment that evening. Yesterday, I was so hindered at the Anti-Slavery Office, in various ways, that I had no time to call upon George [Benson]; for early in the afternoon, I had to go over to Jersey city, and take the cars for Paterson, to fulfil my appointment for that evening. The weather was even more unpropitious than the previous evening, and I thought the meeting must inevitably prove a failure. But, though the walking was so bad that only three or four females were present, the hall was crowded with men. They have had no anti-slavery teaching or lecturing in the place, and my effort was an experiment. It succeeded beyond all expectation. I spoke precisely two hours, and was continually applauded throughout. Not a note of disapprobation was heard yet I spared "nothing and nobody."

This morning I returned to the city, and am now with George and Catharine at their rooms. George has been poorly for several days past, but is looking better than I expected, and seems in good spirits. Catharine is quiet, calm, and angel-like, as usual. Tommy[6] was very much pleased with Franky's[7] valentine, and sends his thanks to the dear boy. George[8] is here also, and all are making inquiries about you all — especially dear little Sarah,[9] whom they greatly long to see, and of whose health, and happiness, and improvement, it gives them much joy to hear.

This evening, I am going with the Gibbonses[10] to see some spiritual manifestations;[11] and shall probably be with you tomorrow at tea-time, but may not till Saturday evening.

Ever yours,

W.L.G.

ALS: Garrison Papers, Boston Public Library. The major portion of this letter is printed in *Life*, III, 406–408.

1. February 14.
2. Garrison delivered his lecture in the Broadway Tabernacle, on February 14, 1854, at the invitation of the New York City Anti-Slavery Society. (*Life*, III, 406.)
3. Shakespeare, *Romeo and Juliet*, V, i, 45.
4. The address appeared in the *National Anti-Slavery Standard* on February 25, 1854. *The Liberator* printed it on February 24, 1854. On February 18, the *Standard* printed a report of the lecture, noting that "In spite of the abounding mud in the streets, a dense fog and a penetrating mist, the audience was large, thus showing that many of the citizens of New York were not only willing but anxious to see and hear the man whose trumpet-tones first startled the nation from the guilty slumber that followed the contest of 1820. For the first time in many years Mr. Garrison delivered a written discourse, but the reading was marked by all the earnestness of extemporaneous eloquence, and the attention of the audience was riveted by his impressive words for an hour and a half, interrupted only by the hearty applause which followed some of the most striking passages." It also commented that "one of the most extensively circulated of our daily journals (the *Times*) solicited the privilege of spreading his address, with all its 'ultraism' and

'fanaticism,' before its numerous readers, interlarded with no invidious or qualifying commentary, but copied faithfully and at full length from his own manuscript."

5. Charlotte Newell, William Lloyd Garrison's mother's youngest sister.

6. George and Catherine Benson's fifth child and third son, Thomas Davis Benson, born in Northampton, Massachusetts, September 1, 1842. (W. P. Garrison, *The Benson Family of Newport, Rhode Island*, New York, 1872, p. 54.)

7. Francis Jackson Garrison.

8. Another Benson son, George, born Brooklyn, Connecticut, January 7, 1839. (*The Benson Family of Newport, Rhode Island*, p. 54.)

9. The Bensons' youngest daughter.

10. James S. Gibbons and wife.

11. *Life*, III, 408, has the following footnote:

"See Mr. Garrison's account of these in *Lib.* 24:34. The impersonations were of Isaac T. Hopper (father of Mrs. Abby H. Gibbons), deceased in 1852, and of Jesse Hutchinson (one of the famous singers), deceased in 1853. Various articles in the room were displaced or concealed. 'Jesse' beat a march very true, and also beat time to tunes sung by the company; and, at Mr. Garrison's request, held the latter's foot down and rapped *under* it vibratingly, and then patted his right hand held between his knees — all other hands being on the table. The medium was Mrs. Leah Brown, one of the Fox sisters."

---

8 2

TO PARKER PILLSBURY

[March 21, 1854.]

March 21st. My dear Pillsbury — I send you my heart's tenderest sympathies, in view of your ill state of health, (which I trust will soon be fully restored,) at the same time congratulating you on your rare good fortune in being in such kind hands as those of my revered friend, Mr. Estlin, and his peerless daughter, Mary.[1] If I could fly, like a strong eagle, I would soon be by your side, in bodily presence, as I am now, and shall be continually, in spirit. Your thoughts must be of home, and of the dear ones left behind; but, assured of their health and safety, you will try to give your mind no anxiety on their account. A wide circle of friends, to whom you are so justly endeared, will look with much concern for the next intelligence from Bristol; and a mighty pressure will be taken from their hearts, on learning that you are convalescent. Be exceedingly prudent, and do not attempt to use the pen until all danger is past.

I will try to drop you a line by the steamer which sails from Boston next week.

With deep yearnings of heart for your speedy recovery, and my unbounded regards for dear Mr. Estlin and Mary, I remain,

Yours, lovingly,

Wm. Lloyd Garrison.

ALS: Colby Jr. College.

1. Mary Estlin (b. Bristol, England, 1820; d. Clifton, England, November 14, 1902) was the daughter of John Bishop Estlin, the British ophthalmologist, Unitarian, reformer, and abolitionist friend of Garrison. Her mother having died when Miss Estlin was two, she was raised by her father, and as she matured became his constant companion and aide in all his various activities, especially in the antislavery movement. With the death of her father in 1855, she moved to Durham Down and devoted her life to the causes which he cherished: the Eye Dispensary in Orchard Street, the Hospital for Women in Berkeley-Square, the education of destitute girls and the children of impoverished parents, woman's rights and suffrage, and other reform movements. (*The Inquirer*, November 22, 1902.)

83

TO MRS. CHARLOTTE NEWELL

Boston, April 7, 1854.
14, Dix Place.

My Dear Aunt:

By a letter just received from bro. George W. Benson, he informs me that you have left your situation at the Carleton House, and are now temporarily boarding with Catharine and himself. My object in writing is to invite you to come immediately to Boston, and to make my home yours as long as it may be agreeable to you; for while I have a place to shelter my own head, or a crust of bread to eat, you shall share it with me. You know that I have expressed to you the desire that you would stay with us, any time it might prove unpleasant or undesirable for you to remain where you have been living; and now that you have left, I renew the invitation, and beg you not to hesitate to come at once to my house. You can take the morning train, by the way of New Haven and Springfield, and be in Boston before tea-time. I will be at the depot on your arrival, if you will apprise me of the time of your coming. — My house is 14 Dix Place, in Washington Street.

I am glad to hear that you are somewhat improved in health, and trust the coming warm weather will fully restore you. It is also gratifying to hear that dear George is better, and is soon to remove to better quarters in Williamsburgh. May you both long live to experience much happiness below.

Yours, with much sympathy and love,

Wm. Lloyd Garrison.

Mrs. Charlotte Newell.

ALS: Garrison Papers, Boston Public Library.

8 4

TO ROBERT PURVIS

Boston, April 9, 1854.

My dear Purvis:

I am requested, by the unanimous vote of the Executive Committee of the American Anti-Slavery Society, to invite and strongly urge you to be one of the speakers at the approaching anniversary of the Society,[1] to be held in the Rev. Dr. Chapin's church,[2] in New York city. I trust you will send me an affirmative answer. Let no feelings of diffidence induce you to decline. You can choose your own topic — colonization, colorphobia, the claims of the colored population to freedom and equality in the land of their birth, or any other subject that may suggest itself to your mind. No one can acquit himself more acceptably than yourself; and as a month will intervene before the meeting, you will have time to mature what you might deem pertinent to the occasion. Believe me, this invitation is not made by our Committee as a matter of form, or civility, or friendship even, but for the cause's sake, and so we pray you not to decline it. We are expecting a stirring anniversary.

My wife desires to be affectionately remembered to Mrs. Purvis, yourself, and the children. Of course, my loving regards are mingled and transmitted with hers. All the members of my numerous family are happily in good health, as I trust are the members of your own. Write soon.

Yours, with unbounded esteem,

Wm. Lloyd Garrison.

Robert Purvis.

Transcript: in possession of Walter M. Merrill, Drexel University, Philadelphia, Pennsylvania.

Robert Purvis (b. Charleston, South Carolina, November 4, 1810; d. April 14, 1898) was an almost-white Negro, whose father was an English cotton merchant who came to this country about 1790, whose mother was a mulatto, and whose grandmother had been a "pure Moorish woman" of Morocco, kidnapped by slave catchers and sold in Charleston. Purvis was left a comfortable legacy by his father and devoted his life to helping his people. He made his first public speech against slavery at the age of seventeen, he provided financial support to help Garrison launch *The Liberator* in 1831, and he was a founder of the American Anti-Slavery Society in 1833 in Philadelphia. He married Harriet, the daughter of James Forten, the well-known and well-to-do Negro sailmaker of Philadelphia, in 1834. He visited Europe in 1834, and met with antislavery men and women, including Thomas Clarkson and General Lafayette. On his return to Philadelphia, he continued his efforts on behalf of his people. These included participating in the Underground Railroad, vigilant efforts to prevent the recapture of escaped slaves, activities in the American and Pennsylvania Anti-Slavery Societies, including efforts to integrate the public schools of Philadelphia and to eliminate discrimination against blacks in various areas of society, and in more general reform movements such as penal reform, woman's rights, and temperance. (Joseph A. Borome, "Robert Purvis and His Early Challenge to American Racism," *The Negro History Bulletin*, 30:8–10, May 1967.)

1. This was to be the twentieth-anniversary convention of the American Anti-Slavery Society, in New York City, on Wednesday, Thursday, and Friday, May 10, 11, and 12, 1854.

2. The Reverend Dr. Chapin's church was on Broadway, between Spring and Prince Streets (*The Liberator*, April 7, 1854). The Reverend Dr. Edwin Hubbell Chapin (b. Union Village, New York, December 29, 1814; d. New York City, December 26, 1880) began his ministry in 1837 as pastor of the Independent Christian Church in Richmond, Virginia. He was pastor of the Universalist Church in Charlestown, Massachusetts, from 1840 to 1846 and associate pastor with Hosea Ballou of the School Street Universalist Church from 1846 to 1848. He then went to the Fourth Universalist Society of New York City, which he served until his death. His religious views were influenced by William Ellery Channing's writings. (J. Alexander Patten, *Lives of the Clergy of New York and Brooklyn*, New York, 1878, pp. 83–87; obituary, *New York Times*, December 28, 1880.)

---

8 5

TO SYDNEY HOWARD GAY

Boston, April 21, 1854.

My dear Gay:

I have received a letter from Wm. Henry Burr,[1] the Reporter, at Washington, in which he says — "I shall be glad of an opportunity to report, for the Standard, the annual meeting of the American A. S. Society, at the usual rate of $30 for the morning session, and $3 per column for whatever subsequent proceedings you may want reported, whether in full or in brief." The result of his application he desired me to communicate to you.

Please inform him, therefore, that his overture, so far as the morning session is concerned, is accepted. The Executive Committee have concluded not to have the other proceedings reported; but I deem this a very poor piece of economy, and think that the American Society, doing so little at present for the cause in other respects, should at least make as much of the entire series of meetings as possible, by having all that is interesting reported, not, of course, with the fulness of the first meeting, though somewhat copiously. If you agree with me in this opinion, please make a suggestion to that effect to our Committee, who will undoubtedly be favorably influenced by it. I think our wisest and best expenditure is in having a pretty full report of the proceedings at our great anniversaries, as they are *the* occasions which attract the attention of the whole country; and especially in view of the disposition of the New York press to caricature and misrepresent us most foully, or, if not unfriendly, to pass us by in the mass without particular notice.

The persons who are pledged to speak for us in Dr. Chapin's Church are — Rev. Dr. Furness, of Philadelphia; Rev. Theodore Parker; Wendell Phillips; Lucy Stone; and Robert Purvis. Please announce these in the next *Standard*.[2]

Some time since, our Committee unanimously voted to give Mr. Chapin a cordial invitation to be one of the speakers at the anniversary;[3] and I believe Mr. Hall,[4] Mr. Johnson, and yourself, were appointed to see him, and secure him, if possible, for that occasion. As yet, we hear nothing in regard to his case; though as he has been absent from the city a portion of the time, no opportunity for seeing him may have presented itself. It is not best, however, to delay the publication of the other names any longer on his account, as his own can be added subsequently, should he give an affirmative answer. It is very desirable to secure him, on many accounts. Let him know who else are to speak, and that we give him a *carte blanche* to speak as the spirit shall give him utterance on any phase of our great question, and we may perchance obtain a favorable answer. Indeed, it is time for him to make somewhere a distinct anti-slavery speech. If, now, we could also secure Henry Ward Beecher for the same occasion, what a bill of attractions would be held out to the great public! Is it not *possible* to do this? Pray try, and see.[5]

As it is, we shall have "a strong team," and I trust a glorious anniversary.

My warm regards to Mrs. Gay. If Oliver has returned, remember me affectionately to him.

Yours, truly,

Wm. Lloyd Garrison.

Sydney H. Gay.

ALS: Columbia University Library.

1. William Henry Burr (b. Gloversville, New York, April 15, 1819; d. February 28, 1908) graduated from Union College, Schenectady, New York, in 1838 and later received an honorary M.A. from his alma mater. A resident of Washington, D.C., for many years and an active citizen, he was first assistant on the Union Corps of reporters of the U.S. Senate from 1848 to 1854. From 1861 to 1863, he was a stenographer in the Supreme Court of New York City, and from 1865 to 1869, a stenographer in the U.S. House of Representatives. He was also a portrait painter, a spiritualist, and an author, called by Robert Ingersoll "the great literary detective." His writings include *Bacon and Shakespeare* (1886), and *Thomas Paine — Was He Junius?* (1890). (Henry B. F. Macfarland, *District of Columbia, 1908–1909*, Washington, D.C., 1908, p. 63; Charles Burr Todd, *A General History of the Burr Family*, New York, 1902, pp. 321, 371; obituary, *New York Times*, February 29, 1908.)

2. These names were listed in the *Standard*, April 29, 1854. However, at the last moment, Theodore Parker and Lucy Stone were unable to attend.

3. The *National Anti-Slavery Standard* did not list Dr. Chapin as a speaker, either on April 29 or May 6, 1854.

4. Either William A. Hall, a member of the executive committee and a vice-president of the New York Anti-Slavery Society, or J. Mortimer Hall, a member of its executive committee. (*Annual Report, American Anti-Slavery Society*, May 9, 1855, p. 152.)

5. Beecher did not speak at the meeting.

---

8 6

TO ROBERT PURVIS

Boston, April 21, 1854.

My dear Purvis:

Your letter is received, and we are all very much gratified that you have given an affirmative answer to our invitation to speak at our approaching anniversary at New York. Your acceptance is made with your characteristic diffidence; but you really have no occasion to feel the least embarrassed. Seize hold of some phase of pro-slavery or colonization scoundrelism as a point on which to try the lightning of your moral indignation, *and blaze away*. But I need suggest nothing. You know every rope in the ship, and a better sailor never yet trod upon a plank than yourself.

With Dr. Furness, Theodore Parker, Wendell Phillips, Lucy Stone, and yourself, our anniversary cannot fail to prove highly attractive, and to be deeply interesting. We are not without hope that either E. H. Chapin or Henry Ward Beecher will also consent to speak on the same occasion.

Our cause has recently met with a severe loss at the West, in the death of one of our lecturing agents, James W. Walker. He was the Parker Pillsbury of the West, only more active and energetic; sometimes a little injudicious, perhaps, but always unfaltering, and "faithful unto death." It seems hard to part with one so efficient, especially as the true laborers are so few.

Please give to your dear wife the loving remembrances of my own partner, and also of myself.

Yours, devotedly,

Wm. Lloyd Garrison.

Robt. Purvis, Esq.

ALS: Weston Papers, Boston Public Library.

8 7

TO AN UNKNOWN CORRESPONDENT

Boston, April 21, 1854.

Dear Sir:

Your letter, requesting my autograph, has not been intentionally neglected, but mislaid, and therefore unattended to till now. It is well for your personal safety, doubtless, that your request is made to me north of Mason and Dixon's line; otherwise, it might subject you to the tender mercies of Judge Lynch.

Yours, for universal freedom,

Wm. Lloyd Garrison.

ALS: Ohio State University Libraries.

8 8

TO CAROLINE C. THAYER

14 Dix Place,
June 20, 1854.

Master Francis Jackson Garrison (by proxy paternal) desires to return his juvenile thanks, — to which years can add nothing of heartfelt value, — to his very kind and very attentive friend, Miss Caroline Thayer, for so frequently strewing his pathway with flowers, which, though perishable in their nature, will make his journey through life all the more pleasant and fragrant.

He also wishes her to accept his thanks for her refreshing gift of currants fresh from the country — of cocoa nut cakes — &c. &c., in which Fanny, the boys, and father and mother participated, in honor of the giver, whose friendship is prized by them at the highest value.

F. J. G. hopes that, as he advances in life, he also shall be known by his good *fruits*, like Miss. T., and be, like her, light to the blind, comfort to the suffering, and a blessing to all.

He wishes her a long life here without sorrow, and a blissful immortality as an angel hereafter.

his
Francis Jackson   X   Garrison.
mark.

AL: Massachusetts Historical Society; written by Garrison in his son's name.

8 9

TO CHARLES SUMNER

Boston, June 27, 1854.

Dear Sir:

If you have some enemies on this side of the Atlantic, you have many friends in the old world. Your enemies here are among the vilest of the vile; your friends there are among the best and noblest of mankind. Some of the latter I wish to introduce to you, from Scotland. They are highly respected citizens of Glasgow — namely, Mr. and Mrs. Robert Smith,[1] their daughter and son-in-law, and a gentleman intimately related to them. None of them have been to America before. In the course of a somewhat extended tour, they intend visiting Washington; and as they have long been interested in the anti-slavery cause, they have a desire to be personally introduced to you, as one who has given his reputation and all he can offer upon the altar of freedom, so that not a slave shall be left to clank his chains upon our soil. I am sure you will heartily reciprocate their feelings.

Accept my grateful acknowledgments for the various congressional documents you have kindly forwarded to me, from time to time.

Yours, for universal freedom,

Wm. Lloyd Garrison.

Hon. Charles Sumner.

ALS: Harvard College Library.

Charles Sumner (1811–1874), the great antislavery statesman and scholar, was then United States senator from Massachusetts, having been elected in 1851, and continuing in office until his death.

1. Robert Smith (1801–1873) was a founder of the great ship-owning Glasgow firm of George Smith & Sons and an active social reformer. At the time of their visit to the United States in 1854, Mrs. Smith was a joint vice-president of the Glasgow Female Anti-Slavery Society which sent " 'contributions of Ladies Work, etc., to the American National Anti-Slavery Bazaar, held annually at Boston at Christmas.' " (I am indebted to Elizabeth G. Jack, Reference Librarian, The Library, University of Glasgow, letter dated June 23, 1972, for the above information. She cites Scottish *Notes and Queries*, 5:40, 1891–92, and the Glasgow Post Office Directory, 1854–55, Appendix, p. 124, as her sources.)

9 0

TO H. I. BOWDITCH

Boston, July 13, 1854.

Dr. H. I. Bowditch:

Dear Sir — Allow me to introduce to you my greatly respected friend, Dr. Jefferson Church,[1] of Springfield, Mass., whom I have known and highly esteemed for many years, who has been a subscriber to the Liberator since the memorable mob of "gentlemen of property and standing" in 1835, who has borne a faithful anti-slavery testimony all that time, nobly stemming a pro-slavery public sentiment, and never making principle subordinate to expediency. In his profession, he is much regarded, and is one of the few men who dare to think and investigate for themselves. He would like to confer with you in regard to a valuable medical work, by Dr. Tully,[2] which he is publishing in a series of numbers, some of which may already have fallen under your observation. Any aid or information you can give him, by which his enterprise may be successfully completed, I am sure will be gratefully appreciated, and will no doubt advance the cause of medical science. Like yourself, Dr. Church is a modest man, and not disposed to intrude upon any one, or to make any personal display. More I need not add.

Yours, with high regards,

Wm. Lloyd Garrison.

ALS: Columbia University Library.

Henry Ingersoll Bowditch (b. Salem, Mass., 1808; d. Boston, 1892), physician and abolitionist, graduated from the Harvard Medical School in 1832 and studied medicine in France until 1834, when he returned to Boston and began the practice of medicine. He had first turned toward abolition as the result of the influence of Wilberforce, whose funeral he attended during a short stay in England. His conversion was completed as a result of his subsequent contact in Boston with Garrison and *The Liberator*. As an abolitionist, he assisted runaway slaves and supported the antislavery movement in other ways. His contributions to medicine were outstanding. These included work on diseases and surgery of the chest, and a lifelong interest in tuberculosis. Perhaps his most notable contribution was in the field of public hygiene, in which he wrote *Public Hygiene in America*, published in 1877. As a result of his efforts the first Massachusetts State Board of Health was established in 1869. He was associated with the Massachusetts General Hospital from 1838 until his death; he was Jackson professor of clinical medicine at the Harvard Medical School from 1859 to 1867; and he helped found the Boston Medical Library.

1. Dr. Jefferson Church (1802–1885), of Springfield, Massachusetts, practiced medicine in Springfield for nearly fifty years. He edited and published, together with Dr. Edwin Seeger, Tully's *Materia Medica*. (See *Letters*, II, 720.)

2. William Tully (b. Saybrook Point, Connecticut, November 18, 1785; d. Springfield, Massachusetts, February 28, 1859), physician, was described by a col-

league as "the most learned and thoroughly scientific physician of New England." His career included the practice of medicine, beginning in 1811, in numerous towns and cities in Connecticut, Albany, New York, and from 1851 until his death, in Springfield, Massachusetts. He was president and professor of medicine at the Vermont Academy of Medicine, at Castleton, Vermont, from 1824 until 1830, when he retired as president. Thereafter, for eight more years, he continued as "professor of materia medica and therapeutics." In 1829, he was appointed professor of medicine at Yale, and while continuing to teach at Castleton, moved to New Haven and taught there until 1842 when he resigned. The "valuable medical work" to which Garrison refers, must have been Tully's *Materia Medica, or, Pharmacology and Therapeutics* (1857–1858, 2 vols.), which comprised more than 1500 pages.

---

9 1

TO CAROLINE C. THAYER

14 Dix Place,
August 6, 1854.

My dear Miss Thayer:

The note and the flowers you sent me yesterday pleased me very much; so I wish to return my thanks, which I would gladly accompany with some kisses, if they could be carried by the hand; but when we meet, you shall have a taste of my *two lips* in exchange for your pretty posies. It is all I have to offer. Perhaps brother Willie will be able to find a flower or two in his little garden; and if so, will you please accept them, in addition to what I have promised?

I think you must like little children very much, and I am sure they must love you, or they cannot be good children.

I do not know how God can make such pretty flowers; but is he not kind to do so? There is none so good as he, but we must try to be like him. So father and mother say, and so thinks and feels

Your grateful little friend,

his
Francis Jackson X Garrison.
mark.

Miss Caroline Thayer.

AL: Massachusetts Historical Society; written by Garrison in his son's name.

9 2

TO CAROLINE C. THAYER

14 Dix Place,
Aug. 10, 1854.

Dear Miss Caroline:

My father tells me some persons think the "forbidden fruit" of the garden was apple, and therefore not a pair; only it was a pair, (Adam and Eve,) he says, who were told not to eat it. But such pairs as you were so kind as to send me, to-day, in that cunning little basket, are to be eaten without scruple, whether in Paradise or at 14 Dix Place. I am not yet old enough to understand what you mean by these pairs growing on "a good orthodox tree"; but father knows, I guess, for he smiled as he read your note, and said he was sure you were sound in the faith, and that you looked upon heretics and heresy in the right light. All I know about it is, the pairs were first rate. If orthodoxy always produces such fruits, I go for it; if not, then for some other doxy.

You are very kind indeed, and put yourself to a great deal of trouble to gratify a little boy like me; for this afternoon you sent me another pretty boquet [*sic*] of flowers, so that I am a highly favored child. And now, dear Miss Caroline —

As you have sent me such nice pairs,
So generously spared,
O, may your path be strewed with flowers,
And you likewise be *paired*.

his
Francis Jackson   X   Garrison.
mark.

Miss Caroline Thayer.

AL: Massachusetts Historical Society; written by Garrison in his son's name.

---

9 3

TO MRS. CHARLOTTE NEWELL

Brooklyn, Conn., August 19, 1854.
Saturday morning.

Dear Aunt — We arrived at our friend Scarborough's,[1] on Thursday evening, at half past 7 o'clock, precisely four hours from the time we left the depot in Boston. In my courting days, before an inch of railroad had been made, the same journey used to occupy some fifteen hours or more. Then, it was tedious beyond all expression — except as relieved by the loving expectation of seeing Helen on my arrival. Now, it was performed without any fatigue, and, what was better than formerly, I had Helen all the way with me.

It is fourteen years, I believe, since we were in Brooklyn last. So little is the change that has taken place, that it seems as though time had not fled at all, and that, after all, it is a delusion to suppose that any change has taken place in ourselves, or that we are any older.

Rain is wanted here exceedingly, and perhaps we shall have some to-morrow *when I lecture*. Everything, however, is looking finely, and we are enjoying ourselves very much. I could not long, however, be contented with the quietude of the country, unless I had withdrawn from public life.

Tell George [T. Garrison] he must rusticate a week at Hopedale, [Massachusetts] as I am sure Mr. and Mrs. Fish will be much pleased to have him with them, as he is a favorite of theirs. If he would like to go before my return, he can get two dollars from Mr. Wallcut to pay his expenses, on my account. He might drop a line at once to Mr. Fish, so as to make all sure, and ascertain what day to start. I really hope he will go. He ought to have some recreation as well as the rest of the boys.

I am to lecture twice, to-morrow, (Sunday,) on slavery, in the Unitarian church — forenoon and afternoon — and also at a village, called Killingly, about six miles from here, on Thursday afternoon next. So I shall still be at work for the slave, but not very laboriously.

I hope everything at home goes along safely and pleasantly. See that you get all the supplies needed. Remember me to Eliza and to *Polly* [2] — and ask the latter whether she is as "pretty" as ever, and whether "Polly Hopkins" has yet told her how she does.

Yours, affectionately,

W.L.G.

ALS: Garrison Papers, Boston Public Library. This letter by Garrison is a continuation of one by Helen to Garrison's aunt, Mrs. Charlotte Newell, a widow, who was then staying at the Garrisons' home.

1. Philip Scarborough, a farmer of Brooklyn, Connecticut, and a friend of the Bensons and Garrisons. (Letters, II, 269.) He died in Brooklyn on May 24, 1865, at the age of seventy-seven, and his obituary was printed in *The Liberator* on June 2.

2. It is likely that "Polly" and "Polly Hopkins" were the same, both referring to a parrot in the Garrison home.

9 4

TO MARY ESTLIN

Leicester, [Mass.,] August 27, 1854.

Dear Miss Estlin:

For the first time for many years, I am enjoying, with my wife and children, a short recreation in the country. We are on our way home from a visit to Connecticut, and are tarrying with our dearly beloved friends, Mr. and Mrs. [Samuel] May, [Jr.] in this very pleasant village.

Mr. May has kindly put into my hands the last letter received from you, in which was enclosed a letter (copied) from Mr. Chamerovzow,[1] to yourself, in relation to what the latter deemed an unkind fling made by Mr. Pillsbury at himself personally, and at the British and Foreign Anti-Slavery Society as an association,[2] in a letter published in the Liberator in June last.[3] As you express a wish to hear what may be my view of the matter, in connection with the entire question of anti-slavery conciliation and co-operation, I improve a few moments to send you a few words on this subject.

Of Mr. Chamerovzow, I know nothing personally, and nothing to his disadvantage, excepting that he is the successor of Mr. John Scoble,[4] who was the subtle and deadly enemy of the American Anti-Slavery Society, and who at all times seemed to receive the complete endorsement of the B. & F. A. S. Society, as its recognized Agent and official Secretary. Elected by the Committee of that Society to fill the situation made vacant by the resignation of such a determined foe, Mr. Chamerovzow must not be surprised to find that we are cautious in giving him our confidence and fellowship, and that we regard his election as at least exceedingly enigmatical, if not quite incomprehensible, as our professed friend and coadjutor, by a Committee so long, so bitterly, and so undisguisedly hostile to the American Anti-Slavery Society. *Prima facie*, it has a suspicious look; and where there is ground for suspicion, there is necessarily an absence of entire trust. In the sincerity, integrity, and catholic spirit of Mr. C. towards us and our organization, you and your dear father (how inexpressibly dear in his present afflictive state!) express the utmost confidence; and, certainly, I should be wanting in justice and magnanimity, if I did not readily acknowledge that, since he has had the management of the *Reporter*,[5] the organ of the B. & F. A. S. Society has been characterized by a far better spirit towards us, as well as much greater ability, than formerly. Moreover, your concurrent opinions of Mr. C. impress me strongly and favorably. Nor, as yet, do I see any reason for doubting his sincere desire to see those variances which exist between the professed friends of the slave in England forever terminated, and a hearty union effected on a common basis. Still, avowedly, no change has taken place in the attitude of the B. & F. A. S. Society towards the American A. S. Society; and, at best, it occupies a negative, rather than a co-operative position.

Perhaps I ought to state, to remove any suspicion to the contrary, that no one, on your side of the Atlantic, has at any time, either directly or indirectly, tried to give my mind an unfriendly bias respecting the course pursued by Mr. Chamerovzow. Neither Mr. [George] Thompson, nor Mr. Chesson,[6] nor Mr. W. W. Brown,[7] nor any other person, has communicated to me, nor to any one else in Boston, a single syllable adverse to Mr. C.

As for the criticism, in Mr. Pillsbury's letter, upon the proceedings at the anniversary of the B. & F. A. S. Society, I published it in the Liberator, just as I publish every thing else contained in its columns, on the ground of free judgment and personal independence; and because, as it was Mr. P.'s real opinion, and as I thought it embodied a merited rebuke, it seemed to me proper to do so. If, in those proceedings, (as Mr. P. stated,) the very existence of the American Anti-Slavery Society was ignored, and no reference whatever was made to that Society even in the annual Report, whilst the more superficial anti-slavery action in this country was carefully noticed, and the compromising actors were warmly eulogized, it was pertinent, and not personal, for Mr. Pillsbury to record the fact as palpably significant, and right for me to print it. Under such circumstances, how *could* Mr. P. regard it as specially complimentary to himself to be invited to speak on such an occasion? And was it not natural for him to say of Mr. Chamerovzow — "He seems not to understand that I belong to an anti-slavery movement and society which are utterly ignored, or remembered only to be reviled, by those who have made him their principal medium of communication"? Carefully adding, however — "I know nothing of him personally."

Mr. C. is comparatively young in the cause. He knows little of the *animus*, malignant and proscriptive in the highest degree, which actuated the B. & F. A. S. Society in reference to the American A. S. Society, and particularly in regard to myself, from the time of the sectarian secession from our ranks in 1840, till the day of the resignation of John Scoble, its Secretary; and, therefore, he is not qualified to sit in judgment upon us, or to ask us to change our policy. Indeed, policy is a word not known in our vocabulary. We resort to no tactics, we deal in no stratagems, we attempt to reconcile no antagonisms; but, with a platform free to all persons and all opinions, with an impartial and magnanimous press presenting every side of the question, and with minds ever open to conviction, — inexorable in our regard for principle, and uncompromising in our application of it to sects, parties, and institutions, — we leave affinities to find themselves by a natural law, indifferent whether praise or blame be our lot, letting consequences shape themselves as they may, and at all times endeavoring to remember those in bonds as being bound with them.

I will not doubt, for one moment, the catholic feelings and excellent intentions of Mr. C., in regard to "the old organization." But I will frankly say, that, in my judgment, he is lacking in moral discernment, and, as yet, only "sees men as trees walking"; [8] that he is putting himself to a great deal of unnecessary trouble, anxiety, labor and expense, to effect an *impossible* fraternization; that, between straightforward, radical, courageous abolitionists, whose position is higher than that of Church or State, and who make the deliverance of the slave paramount to all other questions, and round-about, compromising, timid friends of emancipation, who treat the subject sentimentally and act upon it spasmodically, there can be no real union of heart or will, no unity of purpose or action, no vital organization in common. "Let the dead bury their dead." [9] Let the living press on to the mark of their high calling. Needless division sometimes there may be in the promotion of a good cause, and it is ever to be deplored; but that alienation is natural, which arises from a difference of spirit and principle, and can never be reconciled. The British and Foreign A. S. Society and the American A. S. Society have not been divided upon slight grounds; they have not misunderstood each other; they have no mutual concessions to make. The former is the aggressor, and utterly without excuse. The latter has never given any cause for distrust or ill-will, and yet it has been treated as wholly untrustworthy and beneath consideration. Nor is this to beg the question. Let Mr. C., or any one else, show, if he can, when or where we have been the assailants; in what particular we have been discourteous or uncharitable; when we have exhibited a contentious spirit, except in defence of principle; or wherein we have evinced a lack of Christian magnanimity. We are branded as "infidels," because some in our ranks hold objectionable views on other subjects not connected with our cause, or because we are not willing to recognize a pro-slavery religion as genuine. We are denounced as "anarchists" or "disorganizers," because we are unwilling to sustain a government which is cemented with the blood of the slave. And by whom, in this country? Not only by the bitterly pro-slavery party, but by many who claim to be the true friends of the slave. So it is in England. It is the element of religious sectarism which is at the bottom of all these variances, on both sides of the Atlantic, and it is useless to think of propitiating it.

In his letter to you, Mr. Chamerovzow speaks of such as you and your father "having more confidence in Anti-Slavery that is exclusively Garrisonian, than in Anti-Slavery which he (Mr. C.) regards as more particularly catholic." This shows that he is not yet with us, and that he does not yet understand us. How we can be more catholic, where there is no principle involved, than we now are, and have ever been, I am utterly at a loss to imagine. We require no other test of membership in our Society than an assent to the duty of immediate emancipation, and to the inherent sinfulness of slavery; we have no form of discipline or excommunication; our public meetings are as free to those who dissent from our course as to ourselves; our journals publish both sides of the Anti-Slavery question, and particularly the worst things that are said against us — and generally without comment. Indeed, the American A. S. Society has set an example of true catholicity without a parallel, and worthy of all imitation. It recognizes every form of anti-slavery at its true value, is ever ready to give credit to whom credit is due, and never refuses to co-operate with others where this is possible without sacrificing principle. But it believes in no half way measures; it is no respecter of persons, cliques, sects or parties; it places no reliance upon numbers, but only upon what is absolutely right; it has no policy; it regards as the highest expediency the sternest adherence to duty; and it is thoroughly in earnest.

My dear Miss Estlin, I do not think it is possible for our position and course here, to be generally understood or appreciated on your side of the Atlantic. There is considerable anti-slavery *sentiment* in England, but it needs to be crystallized into *principle*. It must naturally and inevitably, by the force of elective affinity, side with what is simply emotional in feeling, and compromising or spasmodic in action, against slavery, in America, than with what is inflexible and radical. We must be content to be misunderstood, misrepresented, and unappreciated, excepting by the very few whose country is indeed the world, and whose countrymen are all mankind; whose religion is anti-sectarian, and ever progressive; and whose reverence for the right is paramount to all concern for the safety of the Church, or the permanence of the State. The motto of all such is, "*Fiat justitia, ruat cœlum.*" [10] We shall gratefully appreciate whatever testimony may be borne in England against our dreadful slave system, and whatever aid may be extended to us, directly or indirectly; but we have no overtures to make, no compromises to suggest, no plans of conciliation to propose, no steps to retrace. Please say all this, for me, to Mr. Chamerovzow, in the spirit of brotherly kindness, and it may save him much unnecessary trouble, not to say deep regret and mortification at the failure of his attempt to unite what in the nature of things can never be reconciled.

And now, dear friend, (for whom I entertain the highest regard,) I have only room to thank you for the admirable letter I received from you some time since; to beg you to convey to your venerated father my warmest sympathies, and best wishes as to his health and happiness; and to assure you that no one more highly appreciates your labors than

Your admiring friend and faithful co-worker,

Wm. Lloyd Garrison.

Miss Mary Estlin.

ALS: Anti-Slavery Papers, Boston Public Library.

1. Louis Alexis Chamerovzow (d. *ca.* 1876) was appointed secretary to the British and Foreign Anti-Slavery Society, as successor to John Scoble, at the end of 1852, for a period of six months. He was appointed permanently in July 1853. He continued as secretary until late in 1869, when he resigned. On May 2, 1870, *The Anti-Slavery Reporter* announced that the Committee of the British and Foreign Anti-Slavery Society, at a general meeting on March 4, 1870, had adopted a resolution recognizing "the zeal and ability with which Mr. L. A. Chamerovzow, lately Secretary of the Society, has served the Anti-Slavery cause for a period of about eighteen years, during which time he has taken the deepest interest in the abolition both of the Slave-Trade and Slavery. . . ." The announcement added that several friends of the society had contributed toward a testimonial gift of more than £600 for Chamerovzow. (Annie Heloise Abel and Frank J. Klingberg, *A Side-Light on Anglo-American Relations, 1839–1858*, The Association for the study of Negro Life and History, Inc., 1927, p. 327, letter dated August 7, 1079, from J. D. S. Hall, Superintendent, Rhodes House Library, Oxford, England.)

2. The British and Foreign Anti-Slavery Society had been founded in 1839 and had called the World's Anti-Slavery Convention in London in 1840. It sided with the anti-Garrisonians following the 1840 split in the ranks of American abolitionists. (*Letters*, II, 592.)

3. The letter of Parker Pillsbury, mentioned here, appeared in *The Liberator*, June 23, 1854. It referred to Pillsbury's attendance on May 22, 1854, at the anniversary of the British and Foreign Anti-Slavery Society in Exeter Hall, London. Pillsbury had been invited to speak and he was listed on the program as a speaker. The following are his relevant comments in the letter:

"The proceedings and speaking, for an anti-slavery meeting, were generally beneath criticism. What mischief I have ever perpetrated, that should have subjected me to an invitation to take part in them, is more than I can imagine. But so it was. I declined peremptorily, on account of ill health; but my letter miscarried, and so I was announced at a venture. For some reason, the old Secretary has, *unfortunately*, disappeared within the last year or two, and a new one has been appointed, inveigled, or seduced, and from him my invitation came. I know nothing of him personally. But he seems not to understand that I belong to an anti-slavery movement and society which are utterly ignored, or remembered *only to be reviled*, by those who have made him their principal medium of communication. At the Exeter Hall meeting, the name of the American Anti-Slavery Society was not mentioned, nor one of its friends, except Gerrit Smith. . . . But neither did the Secretary in his Report, nor did one of the speakers, British or American, make the most distant allusion to the American Anti-Slavery Society, its supporters, its newspapers, its agencies, or any of its operations. . . .

"Most of the speakers exhibited an utter ignorance of the whole subject for which the meeting professes to be called. . . . To me it all appeared a farce — a mere make-believe; and I thought it was generally so regarded. . . . I have no hesitation in giving it as my own conviction, that the only real obstacle to the spread of anti-slavery light and truth on this side the Atlantic, is the British and Foreign Anti-Slavery Society. . . ."

4. John Scoble (b. *ca.* 1810), a British clergyman and abolitionist, was Garrison's friend during the 1830's, but sided with Garrison's opponents after the division of 1840. He was appointed secretary of the British and Foreign Anti-Slavery Society in 1842. While secretary, he helped edit the *Anti-Slavery Reporter*. He migrated to Canada in 1852, and remained there until 1867 when he returned to England. (*Letters,* I, 344; II, 528; Abel and Klingberg, p. 101.)

5. The official organ of the British and Foreign Anti-Slavery Society. Its official title was the *Anti-Slavery Reporter and Aborigines' Friend.* It began publication in 1840 as the successor to the *British Emancipator.* (*Union List of Serials.*)

6. Frederick William Chesson (b. Rochester, England, November 22, 1833; d. London, April 29, 1888), George Thompson's son-in-law, journalist, and reformer, was pro-Garrison in his sympathies and was secretary of the London Emancipation Committee, formed several years before the Civil War "to excite public interest in the American anti-slavery movement and to maintain active alliance and cooperation" with Garrison. The London Emancipation Committee became the nucleus of the Emancipation Society in London, formed at the end of 1862, for the purpose of publicizing the issues involved in the Civil War and creating sympathy for the North. The enlarged society included John Stuart Mill, John Bright, Richard Cobden, Goldwin Smith, Herbert Spencer, Prof. J. E. Cairnes, and other outstanding Englishmen. The "organizer and tireless spirit of the movement," notes *Life* (IV, 66), "was Mr. Chesson, to whose wide acquaintance with public men, unfailing tact and address, thorough information, and extraordinary industry and executive ability, a very large measure of credit for its success was due." Chesson was at various times editor of the *Dial*, a weekly journal, and, with Justin McCarthy, of the *Morning Star*. (*Life*, IV, 65, 66, 67, 71, 194, 196–199, 273.)

7. William Wells Brown (*ca.* 1816–November 6, 1884), Negro historian and reformer, escaped from slavery in 1834, acquired an education during the ensuing years, was employed as a lecturer of the Western New York Anti-Slavery Society and the Massachusetts Anti-Slavery Society and involved himself in temperance, woman's suffrage, and prison reform. In August 1854, he was in England, having gone to Europe in 1849, where he remained until September 1854. His books include *Narrative of William W. Brown, a Fugitive Slave* (1847), *Three Years in Europe* (1852), *Clotel, or The President's Daughter, a Narrative of Slave Life in the United States* (1853), *The Black Man, His Antecedents, His Genius, and his Achievements* (1863), *The Negro in the American Rebellion, His Heroism, and His Fidelity* (1867), and *The Rising Son: or, the Antecedents and the Advancement of the Colored Race* (1874). *The Liberator*, September 22, 1854, prints a letter from Brown dated August 29, which tells of his plans to return to the United States. He was able to return, as *The Liberator*, May 26, 1854, explained, because "the friends of Mr. Brown in England have kindly contributed the amount necessary to secure his ransom from bondage, so that he can return to his native land without being subjected to the terrible liability of being seized as a fugitive, and scourged to death on a Southern plantation."

8. Mark 8:24.

9. Matthew 8:22.

10. "Let justice be done, though heaven fall."

9 5

TO SAMUEL J. MAY

Boston, Sept. 1, 1854.

My dear Mr. May:

Truly, you are *the* watchman upon the walls of our Anti-Slavery Zion; while we, in this region, are without vision, and losing our memory. Had it not been for your quickening letter, just received, I am pretty sure the fact would have been overlooked by us all, that, at New York, last May, we agreed to hold a special meeting of the Parent Society in Syracuse, on the 29th and 30th of Sept. It is singular that none of us here should have remembered that vote. I am not able to consult our Committee, in regard to the matter; for [Wendell] Phillips is in Milton, [Edmund] Quincy at the West, A[nne] W[arren] Weston at Weymouth, Lowell [1] at Cambridge — &c. &c. But as there is no time to be lost, I herewith send you a Call [2] to be inserted in the Syracuse Daily Chronicle,[3] (and also in the Journal,[4] if you think proper,) some half a dozen times perhaps, prior to the meeting — the bill for which shall be promptly liquidated. I have already sent the Call to the Anti-Slavery Standard, the Bugle, and Frederick Douglass's Paper, and have requested Oliver Johnson to get it inserted in the [New York] Tribune.

Of course, it is my intention to be at the meeting. I trust Phillips and Lucy Stone will be there also. I have not yet seen Theodore Parker, but almost despair of securing his attendance, as he has been absent several weeks from the city, and next Sunday commences his regular services at the Music Hall.[5] Be assured, I shall do my best to persuade him to comply with our earnest wishes, and also with your proposal to have him preach for you on the ensuing Sunday. I am anxious for an uncommonly good meeting.

As for our place of meeting, it must be left to your own good judgment in the premises. I have conferred with our friend Francis Jackson, and he says we must leave every thing in your hands (in which I am agreed) as to the hall, price of admission, placards, anti-slavery hymns, &c. We incline to the opinion that, with tickets, the Town Hall will be sufficiently commodious for our *day* meetings — perhaps for the evening also. If not for the latter, then let either the Corinthian or Dr. Wieting's Hall be secured for that purpose. I much prefer to have a *crowded* meeting in a hall of moderate dimensions, than a thin one in a hall of the first class — the magnetic and popular effect is better. I fear there will be very few delegates from the West, in consequence of the Ohio anniversary (just held at Salem) [6] being so near to our contemplated gathering; and I presume there will not be more than half a dozen from this section of the country; so that we shall have to rely mainly, for our audience, upon Syracuse in special, and Central and Western New York in general. You kindly urge me to bring Helen with me, and much would it gratify me to do so, and glad would she be to see you all again, face to face; but the travelling expenses are too great to be added to those we are daily compelled to look in the face.

As for a reporter, if we have any, it will be Mr. [J. M. W.] Yerrinton; but I think our Committee will hardly feel willing to incur so much expense. We will have a meeting soon about it.

I trust our friend Gerrit Smith will be [with] us, on the occasion. I am glad, however, that he has resigned his seat in Congress,[7] and greatly lament the effect of his strange speech about the annexation of Cuba to our country, slavery and all.[8]

You say nothing about the celebration of the "Jerry Rescue." The 1st Oct. is Sunday — do you intend to pass over the anniversary, or to observe it on the 1st, or on the 2nd?[9] It ought to [be] kept, either on Sunday or Monday — though neither Parker nor Phillips could be detained long enough for the latter day.

Love to your dear wife and family.

Yours, affectionately,

Wm. Lloyd Garrison.

ALS: Garrison Papers, Boston Public Library.

1. James Russell Lowell had been converted to abolition by his wife, Maria White, whom he married in December 1844. During the early months of 1845, he was an editorial writer for the *Pennsylvania Freeman*. He formed a connection with the *National Anti-Slavery Standard* in 1846, to which he contributed an occasional poem in the next two years. In March 1848, he became the *Standard's* "corresponding editor," which involved his writing a weekly article — poetry or prose — for which he was to receive $500 a year. In 1849, he was asked to share the "weekly article" and fee with Edmund Quincy, each to alternate in fortnightly articles. At the end of the year, it was agreed that for the future, Lowell would again reduce his commitment to the *Standard* by writing only an occasional piece. This arrangement lasted until the summer of 1852, when the Lowells left for Europe. Although in September 1854 Lowell was a member of the Executive Committee of the American Anti-Slavery Society and a vice-president of the Massachusetts Anti-Slavery Society, an office that he held for several years, his official association with the movement did not long survive the death of his wife, Maria, on October 27, 1853. (Martin Duberman, *James Russell Lowell*, Boston, 1966, pp. 109–110, 113–115, 134; *The Liberator*, February 3, 1854.)

2. The Call to the special meeting of the American Anti-Slavery Society appeared in *The Liberator*, September 8, 1854 and in the succeeding issues prior to the meeting. It was signed by Garrison as president and Wendell Phillips and Sydney Howard Gay as secretaries.

3. The Syracuse *Daily Chronicle* was preceded by the Syracuse *Free Democrat*, founded in 1852 by J. E. Masters. In 1853, Masters changed the name to the Syracuse *Chronicle*, a weekly, and started the *Evening Chronicle*, a daily. George Barnes was the proprietor in 1854 and 1855. After an office fire in 1856,

the paper merged with the Syracuse *Journal*. (Franklin H. Chase, *Syracuse and Its Environs*, New York and Chicago, 1924, II, 665.)

4. The Syracuse *Journal* was the oldest daily newspaper in Onondaga County, New York. On July 4, 1844, Silas F. Smith began publishing the Syracuse *Daily Journal*. Its owner in 1854 was Thomas F. Truair; its editor, Andrew Shuman. (Chase, II, 663–667.)

5. This was where Theodore Parker ordinarily conducted his services.

6. The anniversary meeting of the Western Anti-Slavery Society was held in Salem, Ohio, on Saturday and Sunday, August 27 and 28. A letter from Henry C. Wright describing the sessions appeared in *The Liberator*, September 8, 1854.

7. Gerrit Smith resigned his seat as of August 7, 1854. The text of Smith's public letter of resignation, "To my Constituents," dated Washington, June 27, 1854, appeared in *The Liberator*, July 7, 1854.

8. *The Liberator*, July 21, 1854, reprinted an editorial article on Gerrit Smith, from the *National Era* (undated). The article includes passages from Smith's speech on Cuba, from which we quote the following:

"Let Cuba come to us, if she wishes to come. She belongs to us by force of her geographical position. Let her come, *even if she shall not previously abolish her slavery*. I am willing to risk the subjection of her slavery to a common fate with our own. Slavery must be a short-lived thing in this land. Under our laws, rightly interpreted, and under the various mighty influences at work for liberty in this land, slavery is to come to a speedy termination. God grant that it may be a peaceful one!

"I would not force Cuba into our nation, nor pay $250,000,000 for her, nor $200,000,000 — no, nor even $100,000,000. But when she wishes to come, *I would have her come*; and that I may be more clearly understood on this point, I add, that I would not have her wait, always, for the consent of the Spanish government. Now, if this is *filibusterism*, then all I have to say is, 'Make the most of it!' "

Garrison's distress at this statement is easily understandable.

The address was delivered in Congress on June 27, 1854, and was reprinted in its entirety in *The National Era* of July 20, 1854.

9. *The Liberator*, September 15, 1854, printed the following notice: "We learn from Syracuse, that the 'Jerry Rescue' Committee held a meeting on the evening of the 8th ult., and after much deliberation, voted unanimously to celebrate the Rescue on Saturday, Sept. 30th, (forenoon and afternoon,) provided the American Anti-Slavery Society would give way for that purpose. This arrangement has been cordially agreed to. The meetings of the Society, therefore, will be held on Friday forenoon, afternoon and evening — and again on Saturday evening — and perhaps again on Sunday evening. Among the speakers expected to be present are SAMUEL J. MAY, LUCY STONE, WM. LLOYD GARRISON, ABBY KELLEY FOSTER, CHARLES LENOX REMOND, ANDREW T. FOSS, and WILLIAM WELLS BROWN, who is now probably on his passage to America, no longer a slave, but legally redeemed from his fetters through British benevolence. As our friend GERRIT SMITH will no doubt be at the 'Rescue' celebration, it is hoped he may also find it convenient to attend the meeting of the American A. S. Society. We regret that we cannot hold out any expectation that WENDELL PHILLIPS will be present, in consequence of other engagements on his hand."

9 6

TO LUCY STONE

Boston, Sept. 1, 1854.

My Dear Friend:

"A rolling *stone*," it is said, "gathers no moss"; but what need has it of moss, if it be a diamond of the first water? Motion is the law of vitality; and so this is preliminary to giving you no rest. The Executive Committee of the American Anti-Slavery Society desire me to say to you, that, in accordance with a vote passed at the last annual meeting in New York, a special meeting of the Society is to be held at Syracuse on the 29th and 30th instant, at which your presence is deemed extremely desirable, for many reasons, and therefore they wish you to allow them to announce that you will be among the speakers on that occasion, they bearing your travelling expenses, etc.

Mr. May, with other friends in Syracuse, is very anxious that you should be with us; so am I. Now, please send me an affirmative answer, and make your arrangements accordingly. Say not we can do without you, because we really need you more than ever in the absence of so many from the lecturing field. I will not multiply words, for you do not need them. Paradoxical as it may seem, our hearts are still flesh, though turned to *Stone*.

I presume the Jerry Rescue celebration will come off on the 1st of October, as usual.

It is gratifying to hear of the improved state of health of Mr. Pillsbury in England.[1] His reception appears to be of the most generous character. *You* must see England at no distant day.

Yours to be *stoned*

Wm. Lloyd Garrison

Transcript: Library of Congress.

1. Parker Pillsbury had been seriously ill almost from the day of his arrival in England on January 14, 1854. He stayed at the home of R. D. Webb, from January 16 to February 8, when he seems to have partially recovered his health. On his way to London, by way of Bristol, he again fell ill, and thereafter for several months, stayed at the home of J. B. Estlin, in Bristol, where he was nursed by Estlin's daughter, Mary, Estlin himself being an invalid. Pillsbury described his illness as "a flow of water to the chest [Hydrothorax]." "For a number of days, my disease wore a most alarming aspect. My own expectation of recovery was small. I had the best medical advisers the country affords, one visiting me twice a day for nearly a month, and bringing with him, for the first two weeks another, whose judgment and skill are esteemed of the very highest character." (Letter from Parker Pillsbury to Wendell Phillips, dated "Bristol [Eng.] April 4, 1854," printed in *The Liberator*, April 28, 1854; for additional reports from and about Pillsbury see *The Liberator*, May 26, June 23, July 14 and 28, 1854.)

9 7

TO SAMUEL J. MAY

Boston, Sept. 11, 1854.

My Dear Friend:

Yours of the 9th is just received. It comes opportunely; for your cousin S. M., Jr., Mr. Phillips and myself were seriously proposing to announce to you, by telegraph, our conclusion not to attempt a meeting of the American A. S. Society at Syracuse. And for this reason — the prospective and probable lack of effective speakers. Theodore Parker cannot attend — Wendell Phillips cannot — and Lucy Stone says she has made her engagements to lecture on Woman's Rights, in Vermont, at that time, so that it will be extremely difficult for her to get to Syracuse; still, if her presence is *imperatively* demanded, she will go there. Your cousin cannot go. So that, the only reliable persons are Lucy and myself. It is possible, and not improbable, that William Wells Brown will arrive in season (indeed, we expect him here in the course of another week) from England, and doubtless he can be prevailed to go with us. Then, your cousin thinks Remond, and also the Rev. Mr. Foss,[1] can attend, on their way to the West. Our indefatigable friend, Abby Kelley Foster, means also to be present. If all these should assemble, of course with your help, and that of others in your region, we should be able to get along; especially if (as you suggest in your letter) Saturday forenoon and afternoon be consecrated to the Jerry Rescue Celebration; which arrangement is perfectly agreeable to us — therefore, let it be made.

As for your kind offer of your pulpit on the ensuing Sunday, I dare not promise, now, to fill it for one service, and cannot say whether Lucy Stone would feel like accepting your offer, after so many meetings in succession, but trust she will do so. This matter we will determine when we meet. If neither of us should feel prepared for the service, perhaps you would like to have Rev. Mr. Foss (should he be with us) preach for you. I presume he would readily and acceptably do so.

No appointments must be made for me in your region. I shall be necessitated to return home on the ensuing Monday, as, in a few days afterward, I am bound to start for Pennsylvania, and then onward to Cincinnati, Ohio.

Now let me add, that if, in view of all contingencies, you think it best (seeing that neither Parker nor Phillips can attend) that our meeting should not be held, just say so at once *by telegraph*, and we will omit it — and glad shall I be to be let off, much as I desire to see you and yours, face to face, as well as some other dear friends in Syracuse.[2]

I will give Mr. Parker your message at the earliest opportunity. You are aware that, unlike myself, he is not *"spiritually* minded." [3] Alas for the heretic!

We congratulate Charlotte [4] on her marriage, and wish her and her beloved all conceivable happiness.

Our united love to your dear wife, to Bonny,[5] and John,[6] &c. &c.

Yours, with deathless affection,

Wm. Lloyd Garrison.

Rev. Samuel J. May.

ALS: Garrison Papers, Boston Public Library.

1. The Reverend Andrew Twombly Foss (b. Dover, New Hampshire, October 3, 1803; d. Manchester, New Hampshire, April 14, 1875), a Baptist minister, was ordained in 1827 and thereafter served as pastor in Dover, New Hampshire, South Parsonsfield, Maine, Hopkinton and New Boston, New Hampshire, and Manchester, New Hampshire. In 1847, he became an agent of the Anti-Slavery Society of the Baptist Church North and later served as an agent of the American and Massachusetts Anti-Slavery Societies, lecturing in the northern and western states until the abolition of slavery. During his later years he was both a believer in spiritualism and a rationalist in theology. (Guy S. Rix, compiler, *Genealogy of the Foss Family in America*, carbon copy in the New England Historic Genealogical Society, pp. 68, 135.)

2. As the next letter makes clear, the meeting was not canceled.

3. The reference is to Garrison's interest and belief in "spiritual manifestations."

4. Samuel J. May's daughter, Charlotte Coffin (b. April 24, 1833), married Alfred Wilkinson, a merchant and banker in Syracuse, New York, on July 15, 1854. The marriage ceremony was performed by May. (*The Liberator*, September 1, 1854; Samuel May, John Wilder May, John Joseph May, *A Genealogy of the Descendants of John May*, Boston, 1878, p. 46.)

5. Bonny was the nickname of May's youngest son, George Emerson May, born September 25, 1844. (*A Genealogy of the Descendants of John May*, Boston, 1878, p. 23; letter from Jane H. Pease, University of Maine, Orono, Maine, dated January 15, 1973.)

6. Probably John Edward May (b. October 7, 1829), Samuel J. May's eldest son. (*A Genealogy of the Descendants of John May*, pp. 22–23.)

98

TO LUCY STONE

Boston, Sept. 11, 1854.

My Dear Friend:

"The die is cast." Wendell Phillips has just announced that he cannot attend our meetings at Syracuse on the 29th and 30th. So the greater need of your presence, and the more indispensable your services on that occasion. Do not fail us, I beseech you on bended knee. I know you cannot help being "stoney-hearted," but at the same time you are the kindest of the kind. Besides, the absence of W. P. will be a relief to you, as your veneration will not be taxed by the presence of any other person!

I have just received a letter from Samuel J. May, saying that the Jerry Rescue Committee had concluded to celebrate that event on Saturday, the 30th, (during the day) provided we would adjourn our meeting from Friday evening to Saturday morning. Mr. May took the responsibility of saying that we would cordially agree to the arrangement, and I have just written to him that we endorse what he has done.

Mr. May wishes you to occupy his pulpit one service on the ensuing Sunday. I hope you will do so.

Yours to pull down and build up,[1] #

Wm. Lloyd Garrison.

With the right kind of *Stone*, of course.

Transcript: Library of Congress.
1. See Jeremiah 1:10, 24:6.

---

9 9

TO SAMUEL J. MAY

Boston, Sept. 24, 1854.

My Dear Friend:

I shall leave Boston on *Wednesday* morning for Syracuse, hoping to arrive in your city a little after midnight. I shall go to the Temperance Hotel on my arrival, and get a few hours' rest, and then go to your house to breakfast. This I shall do to avoid the necessity (if I should leave here on Thursday morning) of going into the meeting, Friday forenoon, completely jaded out by the previous day's ride, and loss of sleep.

It is now very uncertain whether Mr. Remond will be able to attend the meeting. He has been quite unwell for a fortnight past, and is looking very miserably.

Lucy Stone writes from Vermont, that if the cholera is in Syracuse, she shall deem it advisable to stay away.

Under these circumstances, I shall make a fresh effort to secure the attendance of Wendell Phillips —[1] though I can give you no encouragement in regard to his going to Syracuse.

I see there is to be a Liberty Party Convention at S. on Thursday. As a political meeting, it is simply absurd; and I wonder that our friend Gerrit Smith, affirming that no party can be national without being pro-slavery, should still give his countenance to any political action looking in that direction.[2]

When shall we have a Convention of the Free States with reference to a peaceful dissolution of the Union?

Yours, for the destruction of Babylon,

Wm. Lloyd Garrison.

N.B. If I should not happen to reach Syracuse at the early date I have named, be not uneasy about my coming. But I hope to see you Thursday morning, without fail.

ALS: Garrison Papers, Boston Public Library.

1. The speakers at the American Anti-Slavery Society meeting included Samuel J. May, Remond, Foss, William Wells Brown, Garrison, Gerrit Smith, Beriah Green, and Frederick Douglass. (*The Liberator*, October 6, 1854.)

2. An article in *The Liberator*, October 6, 1854, probably by Garrison, described the Liberty party convention:

"On Thursday, the Liberty party, which avows its determination to disregard every law and compact in support of slavery, and which is unable to discover any slaveholding provisions in the U. S. Constitution, held a convention in the City Hall, for the purpose of nominating state officers for the ensuing election. The attendance was small: indeed, the rank and file of the party, politically speaking, are scarcely sufficient to constitute 'a corporal's guard,' but they make up in sturdy persistency what they lack in numbers. . . . The principal speakers were Gerrit Smith, Beriah Green, Leonard Gibbs, and Frederick Douglass. William Goodell was nominated for Governor, and Austin Ward for Lieutenant Governor."

100

TO THOMAS DAVIS

Boston, Oct. 6, 1854.

Dear Friend:

I do not know what is the state of your business, or whether you take any boys as apprentices; but I venture to make an inquiry.

I am desirous of finding a suitable trade for my oldest son, George Thompson, which shall be adapted to his taste and peculiar characteristics; and it has occurred to Helen and myself, that an initiation into your line of business would be just the thing for him. For the last eight months, he has been in G. P. Reed's music store, in this city, with a design to act in the capacity of an assistant book-keeper; but he is not sufficiently quick at figures, or in the use of his pen, (though a good penman,) to fill such a situation; consequently, he is now out of employment. He is eighteen and a half years old — is "slow, but sure," and at all times reliable — "steady as the days are long" in mid-summer

— eminently conscientious, honest, and exact — exceedingly methodical in whatever he undertakes, and has a large bump of order — so that he can hardly fail to succeed in any mechanical business where delicacy of hand, neatness of arrangement, and skill in combination are required. George is very diffident, and too distrustful of his own ability, and therefore is not as yet so well prepared as some other boys of his age to "push his way through the world." But he is kind, faithful, steady, upright — a good boy in all respects — though not calculated for a bustling, *driving* business.

Are you so situated that you would be willing to give him a trial in the manufacture of jewellery, &c. &c.? If so, it would give us great pleasure to have him under your supervision — his remuneration to be graduated according to the worth of his services, after a fair trial.

George (as diffident young men are apt to be) is somewhat discouraged, and talks of either going to Kansas or to sea; but we cannot consent to his doing either. He is quite willing, however, to try some mechanical employment, and yours would suit him, we all think, better than almost any other.

Perhaps if you have no need of an additional boy in your service, it may be in your power to suggest where he will be likely to find a situation in some other establishment.

Helen joins me in kindest regards to yourself and Pauline.

Your much obliged friend,

Wm. Lloyd Garrison.

Hon. Thomas Davis.

☞ An answer as soon as convenient will be duly appreciated.

ALS: Massachusetts Historical Society.

Thomas Davis was a jewelry manufacturer in Providence, Rhode Island, who was also involved in politics. A friend of the Garrisons — his first wife Eliza J. Chace was an especially close friend of Helen Garrison — he was an antislavery Democrat who was a representative in Congress from 1853 to 1855. At this time, he was married to Pauline Wright, a widow and friend of Elizabeth Cady Stanton and of Stephen and Abby Kelley Foster, whom he had married after the death of Eliza Chace. (*Letters*, II, 308.)

101

TO FRANCIS JACKSON

Monday Morning. [Oct. 9, 1854.]

My dear friend Jackson:

Enclosed, you will find $60, in part payment for my last quarter's rent. I will give you the balance immediately on my return from the

West, — regretting that there should be any delay about it, especially as you are called to meet the expense of the new range at this time.

Yours, as a very great debtor in many ways to you,

Wm. Lloyd Garrison.

Francis Jackson.

ALS: Garrison Papers, Boston Public Library. The date has been penciled in by a later hand.

---

1 0 2

TO HELEN E. GARRISON

Philadelphia, Oct. 19, 1854.

Dear Wife:

Surrounded by all sorts of friends, in James Mott's parlor, I will try to pencil a few lines to you, to report progress thus far.

On arriving at the depot in New York on Monday evening,[1] I found Dr. Rotton and Oliver Johnson both waiting for me. Our train was nearly an hour beyond the time. After exchanging a few words with Oliver, and ascertaining that he would be at the West Chester meeting, I went with Dr. R. over to Brooklyn, where I found Anna looking very well, and very pleasantly situated in a handsome house, neatly furnished, and well located. Of course, I had a warm welcome. After tea, two nieces of Mary Ann Bowers[2] came in, and sang and played on the piano very creditably — Isaac Swasey[3] and his wife, and friend Truesdell[4] and John O. Wattles,[5] also came in, with two or three others, and we passed the time very agreeably till near midnight. Particular inquiries were made after you and the children, and much love desired to be sent. Little Tommy[6] came over from Williamsburgh, saying that father and mother desired me to come over in the morning, and take breakfast with them; but Dr. R. and Anna thought I had better get my breakfast with them, and then take the cars for W[illiamsburgh, L.I.], which is three miles from B[rooklyn]. After a night's sound sleep, I took an early breakfast, and rode over to George's. Catharine had gone to the Washington Establishment, where she is again located, so that I did not see her. George I found looking very poorly. He had had a very severe attack of dysentery, which at one time looked very threatening, but he is nearly recovered, though still weak. Poor fellow! how many depressing circumstances attend him! What can a sick man do, in the way of breasting both wind and tide? Spending an hour with George, he went over to the city with me, and saw me off in the 10 o'clock train for this city. On board of the cars,

I found Lucy Stone, Susan B. Anthony of Rochester, Lydia Mott of Albany, E. D. Draper of Hopedale, and other friends going to the Woman's Rights Convention — including our English friend George Sunter. Lucy, and Susan, and her sister,[7] and half a dozen others, went with me to friend Mott's,[8] where we found many more already located — a house full. James and Lucretia greeted us in their characteristic manner, — the latter looking in very good health, and the former kissing Lucy repeatedly in a most fatherly manner.

Yesterday, at 10 o'clock, our Convention opened in Sansom street Hall, and held three sessions during the day and evening.[9] These were well attended by a choice body of men and women, a large proportion of the latter being Quakers. The speaking was generally excellent. Those who spoke were, Ernestine L. Rose,[10] (the President of the Convention,) Mrs. Frances D. Gage of Missouri, Mrs. Coe,[11] Miss Anthony and Miss Gage of New York,[12] Lucy Stone, Mrs. Cutler of Illinois,[13] Lucretia Mott, Thomas W. Higginson of Worcester, and myself. Deep interest was manifested in all that was said and done, and this will doubtless increase to the end.

Last evening, Oliver and Mary Ann Johnson arrived from New York. Charles F. Hovey also came yesterday. I cannot begin to enumerate the friends who are in the city. Our West Chester friends, Joseph A. Dugdale, and wife, Hannah Cox,[14] Hannah M. Darlington,[15] &c. &c. are all here. Joseph sends a warm and loving kiss for his darling Fanny.

On Tuesday evening, Wm. Wells Brown had an enthusiastic reception by the colored people.[16] The church was so crowded, that it was with extreme difficulty I could get up to the pulpit. My reception was extremely gratifying. Robert Purvis presided. It was a delightful occasion.

Mary Grew is looking very poorly indeed. She wished to know all about you and the children, and whether I had a letter for her from you — said she should try to write to you soon. Miller McKim and wife send their united love. She is in very good condition.

With abundance of love to the dear children and yourself, I remain,
    Ever yours,

                       W.L.G.

P.S. My cold is no worse, & I feel very well.

ALS: Garrison Papers, Boston Public Library.

1. October 16. This was the beginning of Garrison's western speaking tour of about three weeks' duration. *The Liberator* described the trip in the November 10, 1854 issue.

2. Mary Ann Bowers was the daughter of John and Rosamond Bowers of Kent County, Maryland. The historian of Quakerism in Maryland refers to her as "the last 'traveling friend' in Cecil Monthly Meeting," and notes that she "made

several visits to Delmarva and Pennsylvania Friends in 1849 and 1850. . . ." She married John Needles, an abolitionist of Baltimore, in 1851, but apparently Garrison continued to refer to her by her maiden name. (Kenneth Carroll, *Quakerism on the Eastern Shore*, Maryland Historical Society, 1970, pp. 182, 279.)

3. Isaac Nathaniel Swasey (b. Bath, Maine, February 28, 1820; d. Brooklyn, New York, 1874) married Lucy Amanda Richardson (b. Waltham, Massachusetts, 1825; d. Orange, New York, June 30, 1905) on December 2, 1844. He studied and practiced medicine for a while, but most of his career was devoted to coffee importing and wholesaling in New York City. The first of their children, born in Newburyport in 1846, was named Frederick Garrison Swasey. (Benjamin Franklin Swasey, *Genealogy of the Swasey Family, Cleveland*, 1919, pp. 426–463.)

4. Thomas Truesdell, a Negro abolitionist of Brooklyn, New York. (*Letters*, II, 353.)

5. John Otis Wattles was a graduate of Yale and a resident of Mercer County, Ohio, where he and other members of his family, notably Augustus Wattles, his oldest brother, helped freed southern blacks establish themselves on their own land. He also helped in the creation of schools for blacks in Mercer County. His brother, Augustus, went to Kansas in 1855. John Otis followed in 1857. Both were among the incorporators of Moneka, in Linn County, Kansas, in February 1857. John O. Wattles, who was an abolitionist, has also been characterized as "an ardent advocate of Spiritualism, a non-resistant, an enthusiastic educator and an optimist of the most pronounced type." He died in Moneka in 1859. (Letter from Nyle Miller, Executive Director, Kansas State Historical Society, Topeka, Kansas, November 13, 1972; William Ansel Mitchell, *Linn County, Kansas: A History*, Kansas City, 1928, pp. 139–140; *Kansas Historical Collections*, XII, 1911-1912, 429.)

6. Thomas Davis, son of George W. and Catherine Benson.

7. Mary S. Anthony (1827–1907) is described by Elizabeth Cady Stanton as "a most successful teacher in the public schools of Rochester for a quarter of a century, and a good financier, who with her patrimony and salary had laid by a competence, took on her shoulders double duty at home in cheering the declining years of her parents that Susan might do the public work in the reforms in which they were equally interested. Now, with life's earnest work nearly accomplished [1898], the sisters are living happily together illustrating another of the many charming homes of single women, so rapidly multiplying of late." (*Eighty Years and More, Reminiscences 1815-1897*, 1898, paperback reprint, Schocken Books, New York, 1971; also letter dated June 2, 1972, from Mrs. Robert Shenton, Assistant to the Director, the Arthur and Elizabeth Schlesinger Library on the History of Women in America, Radcliffe College, Cambridge, Massachusetts.)

8. The home of James and Lucretia Mott.

9. *The Liberator*, October 27, 1854, reprinted from the Philadelphia *Ledger* a report of the convention, which met as "the annual National Convention for the advancement of Women's Rights." A later issue of *The Liberator*, January 12, 1855, offers a more detailed report of the proceedings under the title of the "Fifth Annual National Woman's Rights Convention." The convention was held on October 18, 19, and 20.

10. Ernestine Louise Siismonde Potowski (January 13, 1810—August 4, 1892), antislavery and woman's rights leader, was born in Poland, the daughter of a rabbi. A born rebel, she became a free thinker at an early age. She left Poland in 1827, stayed in Berlin two years, was in Paris during the Revolution of 1830, and went to England in 1831 where she was influenced by Robert Owen and other radicals, joining him in 1835 in founding a reform society named the Association of All Classes of All Nations. She married William Rose, a silversmith and jeweler, in 1836; together they came to the United States during the same year. Her activities for woman's rights began in 1836, while her participation in the American free-thought movement began soon afterward. The first national woman's rights convention that she attended was in 1850 at Worcester,

Massachusetts; thereafter, for the next twenty years, her biographer points out, "she missed few of the national conventions and spoke at many of the state ones." It was during the 1850's that she became widely known as an antislavery speaker. In 1869, Mrs. Rose and her husband returned to Europe, and settled in England, returning once to the United States in 1873 for a short stay. Ernestine Rose survived her husband by ten years. (*Notable American Women*; Yuri Suhl, *Ernestine L. Rose and the Battle for Human Rights*, New York, 1959.)

11. Mrs. Emma R. Coe, often referred to in *The Liberator* as of Ohio, was registered on January 12, 1855, at the office of the District Court in Philadelphia, as a student at law in the office of William T. Pierce, who was a member of the Philadelphia bar. She is also referred to as "one of the leaders in the woman's rights movement." In 1851, *The Liberator* announced lectures by her on woman's rights in Abington and Worcester, Massachusetts. (*The Liberator*, February 2, 1855; October 17, 1851). *The Liberator* of November 10, 1854, prints a part of her speech at the Pennsylvania Anti-Slavery Society's Seventeenth Anniversary Convention, and identifies her as being "of Buffalo."

12. Probably Matilda Joslyn Gage (1826–1898). Although Garrison refers to her as "Miss," an article in *The Liberator* (November 3, 1854), reprinted from the *New York Tribune*, refers to her as "Mrs. Gage, of New York." It also says that she "seemed inexperienced in public oratory, but said some good things." Matilda Gage's biographer, Elizabeth B. Warbasse, remarks that in her first public address in September 1852, she spoke "trembling in every limb," and "so softly that few could follow her remarks; even with subsequent improvement she never developed an outstanding platform personality." Born in Cicero, New York, Matilda Joslyn married a Cicero merchant, Henry Gage, in 1845. They finally settled in Fayetteville, New York. Henry Gage died in 1884. Matilda Gage's first public appearance was at the National Woman's Rights Convention, at Syracuse, New York, in September 1852. Thereafter, she became an important figure in the woman's rights movement, primarily as a writer and organizer. (*Notable American Women.*)

13. Hannah Maria Conant Tracy Cutler (1815–1896), physician and woman's rights leader, married John Martin Tracy, a theology student and, later, an anti-slavery lecturer, in 1834. Her husband died in 1844, leaving her with three children to support. She moved to Rochester, Ohio, then the home of her father, and wrote for Ohio newspapers to support herself. After a year of study at Oberlin College (1847–1848), where she met Lucy Stone, she became matron of the Ohio Deaf and Dumb Asylum at Columbus, Ohio, and was next appointed principal of the "female department" of a public high school in Columbus, Ohio. She became active in the woman's rights movement in the 1850's. In 1852, she married Colonel Samuel Cutler, owner of a farm in Dwight, Illinois, where she carried on much of the farm work. In the late 1860's, she received an M.D. degree from Women's Medical College (homeopathic) in Cleveland, Ohio, after a year of study and went into medical practice in Cleveland and, thereafter, in Illinois and California. (*Notable American Women.*)

14. Hannah Cox (November 12, 1797–April 24, 1876), of Longwood, Chester County, Pennsylvania, was the daughter of Jacob Pierce, a Quaker. In 1823, she married John Cox (March 12, 1786–February 22, 1880), a Quaker. They were both influenced by reading *The Liberator*, became active abolitionists, and conducted a station of the Underground Railroad at their farmhouse. They first became acquainted with Garrison at the time of the burning of Pennsylvania Hall in 1838 and remained warm friends thereafter, Garrison frequently stopping at their home. John Cox was president of the Kennett Anti-Slavery Society, and he and his wife were frequently delegates to the state and national anti-slavery conventions. Hannah Cox was a member of the Progressive Friends of Longwood and was also active in the temperance, peace, and anti-capital punishment movements. (Gertrude Bosler Biddle and Sarah Dickinson Lowrie, *Notable Women of Pennsylvania*, Philadelphia, 1942, pp. 124–125; R. C. Smedley, *History of the*

Underground Railroad in Chester . . . , Lancaster, Pa., 1883, pp. 33, 273–281.)

15. Hannah M. Darlington (October 29, 1808–January 1, 1883), of Kennett Township, Chester County, Pennsylvania, was the daughter of James and Hannah Monaghan. She married Chandler Darlington, November 21, 1832. Her husband was a farmer. Both were known for their antislavery views and were active in the Longwood Progressive Friends Meeting. Hannah Darlington moved from Kennett to the nearby town of West Chester, after her husband's death in March 1879. (Gilbert Cope, *Genealogy of the Darlington Family*, West Chester, Pa., 1950, p. 141; Smedley, p. 308.)

16. *The Liberator*, October 13, 1854, had carried an announcement by Garrison that "the colored citizens of Philadelphia intend giving Wm. Wells Brown, who has so creditably represented them and their cause abroad for the last five years, a public reception on Tuesday evening next, Oct. 17. C. L. Remond will be among the speakers. We shall endeavor to be present, and also at the Woman's Rights Convention, which commences in that city on Wednesday next."

103

TO CAROLINE C. THAYER

Christmas Day, 1854.

My dear Miss Thayer,
I do declare
Your gift for "little Franky,"
So pretty 'tis,
Deserves a kiss,
With many a grateful "thank 'ee."

The box you send,
My generous friend,
Of sealing-wax for letters,
And wafers too,
White, red and blue,
Makes him the chief of debtors.

"God bless you," too,
And shower on you
His blessings without ceasing;
May peace and joy,
Without alloy,
Be yours, for aye increasing.

F. J. G.

Sarah Benson desires her uncle to return her heart-felt thanks to her kind friend, Miss Caroline Thayer, for the beautiful doves, in alabaster, presented to her as a Christmas gift; assuring Miss T. that they will be kept with the utmost care, not only because they are so pretty, but for the sake of the giver, whose kindness she hopes ever to remember, and with whose benevolent spirit she desires to be animated as she grows up to womanhood, that her life, too, may be a blessing to all around her.

And Fanny Garrison wishes her grateful acknowledgments to be conveyed to Miss T., for the beautiful basket, with its contents, which she has received, as a fresh token of love at the hands of her dear friend. If "it is more blessed to give than to receive," then Miss T. must indeed feel very happy to day, as she has made all the recipients of her benevolence to leap and sing for joy. For her goodness here, may she fill an angelic sphere hereafter.

14 Dix Place, Dec. 25, 1854.

AL: Massachusetts Historical Society.

The poem was written to Caroline Thayer by Garrison on behalf of his son Frank. The letter was on behalf of his niece, Sarah Benson, and his daughter Fanny.

V THE RADICALIZATION OF MASSACHUSETTS —
WARFARE IN KANSAS: 1855

T HE YEAR WITNESSED the unfolding of events whose roots lay in 1854 and earlier. After holding hearings, in which the abolitionists played a leading part, the legislature of Massachusetts voted in favor of the removal of Edward Greely Loring as judge of probate for his part in the forcible return of Anthony Burns to slavery. The action of the legislature was vetoed, however, by Governor Henry J. Gardner.

The legislature also passed a strengthened Personal Liberty Law which extended the Personal Liberty Act of 1843 to the Fugitive Slave Law of 1850. It provided for habeas corpus for the alleged fugitive, placed the burden of proof on the claimant, prohibited state office-holders, attorneys, judges, as well as sheriffs, jailers, and policemen, from helping to apprehend or return a fugitive, and forbade the use of the state militia on behalf of the claimant. Vetoed by Governor Gardner, it was passed over his veto. As Lawrence Lader points out, the new law "virtually made the Fugitive Law unexecutable in Massachusetts. President Pierce was well aware that an army of fifty thousand men would have trouble removing a slave from Boston now, and neither he nor Buchanan dared to take the risk again." [1]

The struggle in Kansas, the focus of ever-increasing efforts by pro- and antislavery forces, was marked by invasions from Missouri by southern armed bands who terrorized the Free-State inhabitants there, stuffed ballot boxes, and elected a pro-slavery legislature. With the beginning of resistance by Free-State settlers, a state of guerrilla war ensued.

Garrison's activities included a privately sponsored speech on March 1, at the Tremont Temple in Boston, in reply to a pro-slavery address by Senator Sam Houston on February 22, one of a series of lectures sponsored by a committee consisting of Dr. Samuel Gridley Howe and others. Later in the year, when invited by the committee to lecture in the series, Garrison refused and issued a public letter on November 12, sharply critical of the committee's policy of sponsoring southern slaveholders and apologists for slavery as speakers in the series.

Several noteworthy events occurred during the latter part of the year. In October, Garrison was able to purchase his home at Dix Place from Francis Jackson, from whom he had been renting it. On October 21, the twentieth anniversary of the Boston mob of 1835 was celebrated in Boston by the abolitionists and their friends, with Garrison, of course, as the center of the ceremonies.

October and November were marked by serious illnesses for both Garrison and Francis Jackson. The latter, especially, was not expected to recover. But both did.

On November 2, Captain Warren Weston of Weymouth, Massachusetts, the father of Maria Weston Chapman and a dear friend of the Garrisons, died. Shortly thereafter, Maria Weston Chapman, Garrison's close friend and co-worker, returned to the United States from an extended stay of several years in Europe.

1. Lawrence Lader, *The Bold Brahmins: New England's War Against Slavery* (*1831–1863*) (New York, 1961), p. 216.

1 0 4

TO EDWIN BARROWS

Boston, Jan. 1, 1855.

Dear Sir:

Let this note, after so long a period from the date of your letter, requesting my autograph, bear me witness that I have not intended any slight toward yourself — as my silence has been wholly unintentional, your letter having been mislaid till now. I can never refuse a request made in such a friendly spirit, and trust this explanation will be satisfactory.

Proffering to you the warmest salutations of the season, and wishing you in no formal terms "a happy new year," — happy beyond any thing in your experience hitherto, — I remain,

Yours, to write down slavery,

Wm. Lloyd Garrison.

Edwin Barrows.

ALS: Wichita State University Library.

Edwin Barrows (b. Norton, Massachusetts, January 24, 1834; fl. 1896), graduated from Yale in 1857. He taught at a private school in Norton and was later a bookkeeper for several years for Taylor, Symonds and Co., wholesale drygoods, of Providence, Rhode Island. He served in the Civil War, as private, quartermaster-sergeant and under General Banks in Louisiana, until his honorable discharge after a year of service. After the war he became an insurance executive and bank director. Politically, he was a Republican. (Alfred M. Williams and William F. Blanding, *Men of Progress . . . in the State of Rhode Island*, Boston, 1896, p. 5.)

---

1 0 5

TO OLIVER JOHNSON

Boston, Feb. 7, 1855.

Dear Johnson:

In answer to yours just received, I have to say, that Mr. Burlingame [1] has been consulted; that he would like to fill the gap for you next week, if he can, and you can get no one else; but he cannot say definitely, today, whether he will go, because he is to lecture before the Mercantile Library Association in this city the next evening after yours, (Wednesday,) and he has not yet written his lecture. I think, however, he will make an effort to go. Still, let us know at once what your success is in other directions. Our beloved friend, Samuel J. May, of Syracuse, has prepared an elaborate and admirable lecture on the rise and progress of the A.S. movement since 1830, and is anxious to deliver it in as many places as possible. Samuel May Jr. has heard it, and says it is uncommonly felicitous. Its delivery in your city would be a good antidote to the poisonous tirade delivered by Douglass [2] at the Tabernacle.[3] I presume you could get Mr. May to come, if you should telegraph him to that effect.

I have been quite ill for a fortnight past, and am still very feeble, and "good for nothing."

In great haste,

Yours, ever, to serve,

Wm. Lloyd Garrison.

Oliver Johnson.

Transcript: Garrison Papers, Boston Public Library.

1. Anson Burlingame (b. New Berlin, Chenango County, New York, November 14, 1820; d. St. Petersburg, Russia, February 23, 1870), lawyer, politician, and diplomat, lived variously as a youth, with his family, in Seneca County, Ohio, and Detroit and Branch, Michigan. He graduated from Harvard University Law School in 1846, practiced law in Boston, and became active in the Free Soil party in 1848, soon after its formation. He was elected to the Massachusetts Senate in 1852, joined the American ("Know-Nothing") party at its creation in 1854, and, as its candidate, was elected during that year to Congress, serving three terms, from March 4, 1855, to March 3, 1861. He was antislavery in his views and was recognized in Congress as "one of the ablest debaters on the anti-slavery side of

the House." He helped in the formation of the Republican party and was that party's successful candidate for his third and final term in office. After failing in a bid for reelection in 1860, he was rewarded by Lincoln for his service to the Republican party by appointment, in March 1861, as minister to Austria. When he proved unacceptable to the Austrian government because of his views regarding Hungary and Sardinia, he was appointed, instead, as minister to China, serving from 1861 to 1867. Thereafter, he served the Chinese government as its appointee at the head of an official delegation to negotiate treaties with foreign powers.

2. The reference is probably to Frederick Douglass' address, "The Anti-Slavery Movement," which he had been delivering to audiences in the East, including Maine, Massachusetts, and New York. In it, he blamed the Garrisonians for the split in the antislavery movement in 1840, and was severely critical of Garrison's and the American Anti-Slavery Society's disunionist policies. Concerning the Society's slogan of "no union with slaveholders," he remarked, "This I hold to be an abandonment of the great idea with which that Society started. It started to free the slave. It ends by leaving the slave to free himself." Moreover, "defined, as its authors define it, it leads to false doctrines, and mischievous results. It condemns Gerrit Smith for sitting in Congress, and our Saviour for eating with publicans and sinners." The final straw was Douglass' insistence that the Liberty party was "the *only* abolition organization in the country, except a few local associations. It makes a clean sweep of slavery everywhere. It denies that slavery is, or *can* be legalized. . . ." (For the full text of the address, see Philip S. Foner, *The Life and Writings of Frederick Douglass,* New York, 1950, II, 333–359. For a short summary of the address, as delivered in Maine and Massachusetts, see *The Liberator,* January 26, 1855.)

3. Probably the Broadway Tabernacle in New York City.

---

1 0 6

TO J. M. W. YERRINTON

14 Dix Place,
Feb. 20, 1855.

Dear Winchell:

Wendell Phillips, I understand, is to lead off this afternoon in the arraignment of Judge Loring.[1] It seems to me that his speech ought to be reported *verbatim* for the Liberator *this week.* Can you possibly do it? If so, you shall be paid at your usual prices. The Committee meets at 3 o'clock.

Yours, for a good verdict,

W. L. G.

ALS: Arlington Historical Society, Arlington, Massachusetts.

1. On Wednesday, May 24, 1854, Anthony Burns, a fugitive slave who was employed in a clothing store in Boston, was arrested by a United States Deputy marshal and six assistants, on a charge of having escaped from slavery in Virginia. The warrant had been issued by United States Commissioner Edward G. Loring, before whom Burns was brought the next morning. However, Loring adjourned the hearing to Monday morning, May 29. In the interval, a group led by Thomas Wentworth Higginson sought to rescue Burns by force but failed, against the

armed might of more than fifty guards, one of whom was killed. When the hearing took place on Monday, one historian notes, "the courthouse looked like a fortress, two companies of United States Artillery and a corps of Marines forming a cordon around the building and stationed at every floor and window." Commissioner Loring's decision, given on Friday, June 2, required that Burns be sent back to slavery. It was carried out with the use of large military force to prevent any further attempt at rescue. Several days later, Higginson, Theodore Parker, Wendell Phillips, and several others were indicted for participating in the assault on the courthouse, but because of technicalities, the indictments were quashed. Shortly thereafter, Burns's freedom was purchased, he returned to Boston à free man, and subsequently studied at Oberlin College for the Baptist ministry.

As for Loring, the immediate aftermath of his decision was a public demand, led by the abolitionists, who circulated petitions which gained thousands of signatures, for his removal from the office of probate judge for Suffolk County, an office to which he had been appointed in 1847 by Governor George N. Briggs. His office as judge was in addition to that of commissioner of the Circuit Court in Massachusetts, to which he had been appointed in 1841. (See "Remonstrance of Judge Loring," *The Liberator*, February 16, 1855.) The demand for his removal gained momentum during the early part of 1855, so that by February 9, *The Liberator* was able to announce that "Petitions from all parts of the State are pouring into the Legislature, asking for the removal of Judge Loring, for his atrocious conduct in the case of Anthony Burns. . . . Send in the petitions."

The petitions were received by the Joint Standing Committe on Federal Relations of the legislature, which held a public hearing on them on Tuesday afternoon, February 20, in the Representatives' Hall, which was filled to capacity, with additional hundreds of persons turned away for lack of room. Seth Webb, Jr., of Dedham, Wendell Phillips, and Charles M. Ellis appeared for the petitioners. (*The Liberator*, February 23, 1855, printed a summary of their testimony. A stenographic report of Phillips' entire testimony appeared in *The Liberator*, March 2, 1855.) Judge Loring did not appear, but sent a letter (printed in *The Liberator*, February 23, 1855) in reply to the notification of the hearing. Further hearings were held on Wednesday, February 28, and on Tuesday, March 6, 1855. (For summaries, see *The Liberator*, March 9, 1855.) Subsequently, the Committee on Federal Relations voted to recommend the removal of Judge Loring by Henry J. Gardner, governor of Massachusetts. The committee's report appeared in *The Liberator*, April 6, 1855. Although both the Senate and the House voted for Loring's removal, the measure was vetoed by Governor Gardner. (The public outcry persuaded Harvard not to renew Loring's lectureship at the Law School.) After three additional votes by the legislature and vetoes by the governor, the legislature in 1858 again voted removal, under Nathaniel Banks as governor, and Loring was removed. (Lawrence Lader, *The Bold Brahmins: New England's War Against Slavery [1831–1863]*, New York, 1961, pp. 203–216.)

Edward Greely Loring (b. Boston, January 28, 1802; d. Winthrop, Massachusetts, June 19, 1890), graduated from Harvard College in 1821, studied law, entered the law office of his cousin, Charles Greely Loring, and was admitted to the Suffolk Bar in 1824. He later opened his own law office. In 1840, he was appointed a commissioner of the United States Circuit Court. He was a member of the Boston School Committee in 1846–1847. During the latter year, he was appointed lecturer at the Harvard Law School, and judge of probate for Suffolk County. In April 1851, Thomas Sims, an alleged fugitive slave, was taken before him, and defended by Charles Greely Loring. Judge Loring ordered Sims returned to slavery. Not long after his removal President Buchanan appointed him a justice of the United States Court of Claims at Washington, D.C., an office which he held until 1877. (Charles Henry Pope, *Loring Genealogy*, Cambridge, 1917, pp. 170–172.)

1 0 7

TO OLIVER JOHNSON

Boston, Feb. 23, 1855.

My dear Johnson:

Last evening, Gen. Houston [1] gave his lecture on slavery, to a crowded auditory.[2] In every point of view, it was a feeble effort, and went for slavery eternally, by a law of "necessity." He has furnished me with some nuts to crack in my lecture at the Tabernacle on Tuesday evening.[3] On Thursday evening, I am to reply to Houston at the Temple; [4] so I must return home from your city on Wednesday morning.

I intend leaving here on Monday morning. Dr. Rotton expects me to spend the evening and night with him in Brooklyn; and my friend James S. Gibbons has written a letter, cordially inviting me to abide with him. I have replied to him, that I will probably go home with him after my lecture, and take the Boston train at the station near his house the next morning. If, however, you have made other arrangements for me, I ought to hold myself subject to your wishes, and will endeavor to do so.

Yours, ever,

Wm. Lloyd Garrison.

ALS: Garrison Papers, Boston Public Library.

1. Samuel Houston (1793–1863), a Democrat, military man, and political figure, represented Tennessee in the United States Congress from 1823 to 1827, and was governor of the state from 1827 to 1829. As commander-in-chief of the Texan army, in its war against Mexico, he defeated Santa Anna at the Battle of San Jacinto in 1836, thereby securing Texan independence. He served as first president of the Texas Republic from 1836 to 1838, and again from 1841 to 1844. After the annexation of Texas to the United States, he represented the state in the United States Senate from 1845 to 1859. He was elected governor of Texas in 1859, but was removed because of his refusal to go along with secession.

2. *The Liberator*, February 16, 1855, carried a notice that "General Houston, it is said, is now actually coming to Boston to deliver one of the course of lectures upon slavery. A correspondent of the Detroit *Advertiser* says he will take the ground that the South is not aggressive, and that all she requires is a faithful observance of her rights under the Constitution." The address was given in the Tremont Temple.

Garrison's opinion of Houston's address appeared in *The Liberator*, March 2, 1855. "It was a stolid defense of slavery, as a necessity, and utterly devoid of all reason and principle — of course. To the disgrace of Boston, he was loudly applauded at the beginning and at the close of it. On Friday evening [February 23], he delivered a lecture at the Temple, in defence of the Texas revolution; and a more shuffling and deceptive address was never listened to."

3. February 27, in New York City. Garrison's address was the fourteenth and concluding lecture of what was entitled an "Anti-Slavery Course." According to

the *Standard* (March 3, 1855), Garrison's address in Boston was to be a repetition of his address in New York.

4. *The Liberator*, March 2, 1855, carried the following announcement: "This (Thursday) evening, March 1, at the Tremont Temple, commencing at half-past 7, William Lloyd Garrison will Review the Lecture on Slavery, delivered by General Houston, of Texas, on the evening of the 22d ult." The complete text of Houston's speech appeared in the same issue of *The Liberator*. *The Liberator*, March 9, carried a brief summary of Garrison's talk.

---

1 0 8

TO J. M. W. YERRINTON

14 Dix Place,
Thursday, March 22, 1855.

Dear Friend:

Please not to forget that the *final* hearing [1] before the Committee on Capital Punishment will be had this afternoon, (probably at 3 o'clock,) in the Hall of the House of Representatives. Pray, be "in at the *death*," if you can.

Yours, to hang the gallows,

AL: Garrison Papers, Boston Public Library. The bottom of the page is cut off.

The letter does not bear the name of the recipient. However, since it refers to the hearing on capital punishment on March 22, 1855, and since the phonographic report was made by J. M. W. Yerrinton, it seems probable that the letter was addressed to Yerrinton to remind him to be at the hearing and to report it.

1. The reference is to a petition campaign for the abolition of capital punishment that was then being conducted in the state. The petitions were referred to the Committee on Capital Punishment, which conducted hearings. Wendell Phillips testified before the committee on March 16, 1855. *The Liberator* (March 23, 1855) noted that "the Committee of the Legislature, to whom were referred the petitions for the abolition of capital punishment in Massachusetts, have granted every indulgence on the score of an impartial hearing, to those who have desired to be heard on this grave question, whether *pro* or *con*. The discussions have been protracted and have elicited a deep interest." The same issue of *The Liberator* reprinted Phillips' testimony on March 16. At the hearing on March 22, John A. Andrew, the prominent Boston lawyer and later governor of Massachusetts, testified. Andrew's testimony was reported verbatim in *The Liberator*, April 6, 1855, with credit given to "Phonographic Report by J. M. W. Yerrinton." The committee's report opposed the abolition of capital punishment. (*The Liberator*, May 11, 1855.)

1 0 9

TO JOSHUA B. SMITH

Boston, March 23, 1855.

Dear Friend Smith:

I send the bearer of this to you, in order that you may inquire into his case, which, if genuine, comes within the objects of the Vigilance Committee.[1] Who "H. Cole," of Hartford, (who writes the enclosed letter,) is, I do not know. On examining the bearer, you will be able to determine what ought to be done for him, and will inform him accordingly.

Yours, truly,

Wm. Lloyd Garrison.

ALS: Child Papers, Boston Public Library.

Joshua Bean Smith (b. Coatsville, Pennsylvania, November 3, 1813; d. Cambridge, Massachusetts, July 5, 1879), reputedly born of an Indian mother and an English father, was sent to public school by a wealthy Quaker woman in Philadelphia. In 1837, he came to Boston as head waiter at the Mt. Washington House in South Boston. He later worked in the household of Francis G. Shaw, wealthy Boston businessman, abolitionist, and father of Robert Gould Shaw, who was killed during the Civil War while commanding the Negro Massachusetts 54th Regiment. He was next employed by Mr. Thacker, "the leading colored caterer of the time," but then went into business on his own, catering for many of the important people of the area, winning many influential friends, and earning the title of "the Prince of Caterers" in the Boston-Cambridge area. It is said that he refused to cater a banquet in honor of Daniel Webster, because of the latter's role in the passage of the Fugitive Slave Law. He became a very good friend of Charles Sumner, who left him a painting in his will called "The Miracle of the Slave." During the war he was active in recruiting black soldiers for the northern army and generously aided soldiers and their families in need. After the war, he was an active Free Mason and was the first Negro to hold a seat in the Grand Lodge of Massachusetts. From 1873 to 1874, he represented Cambridge in the Massachusetts legislature and was chairman of the Committee on Federal Relations. He was active in helping fugitive slaves to reach Canada and was especially active in the cases of Shadrach and Sims. The one affliction of his life, which was a constant source of grief, was the death of his daughter at an early age, who was said to have died of a broken heart resulting from the racial taunts of a classmate at school. John Daniels, *In Freedom's Birthplace: A Study of the Boston Negroes* (Boston and New York, 1914), p. 449, describes Smith as "a fugitive from North Carolina in 1847," but offers no evidence or documentation. (Boston *Daily Advertiser*, July 7, 1879; Boston *Daily Evening Traveller*, July 5, 1879; Daniels, *In Freedom's Birthplace*, pp. 101, 449, 453, 454; Carleton Mabee, *Black Freedom: The Nonviolent Abolitionists from 1830 through the Civil War*, London, 1970, pp. 104, 197, 295.)

1. The reference is to the Boston Vigilance Committee, which had been set up in the 1840's to help defend fugitive slaves and did yeoman work during the 1850's, after the passage of the Fugitive Slave Law. Among its leaders were Lewis Hayden, Theodore Parker, chairman of the executive committee, Francis Jackson, Charles List, a Boston lawyer, who was its secretary, and others. Among

its financial backers were Amos Lawrence, Francis G. Shaw, and George R. Russell, mayor of West Roxbury.

---

1 1 0

TO JAMES N. BUFFUM

Boston, May 18, 1855.

Dear Buffum:

I have imitated the example of General Andrew Jackson, and "taken the responsibility" [1] — that is, in regard to putting the admirable bust of our noble Phillips in marble, hoping it will ultimately, in the revolution of public sentiment, find an abiding place in Faneuil Hall. The artist is now chiseling it. On the preceding page, I give you a copy of the circular [2] I am sending to a few select friends, and trust it will be responded to without much delay, to the extent needed. Please send me the subscription list you took with you, as I can get some names to be appended to it. Whatever aid you can raise in Lynn, by suggesting the matter to kindly and generous persons, will be gratefully appreciated as though it were a *personal* favor done to myself. Accept any amount, however small. Indeed, large sums are not expected.

William [3] will be ready for you at such time as you may be ready for his services.

My warm regards to your wife & Lizzie.[4]

Ever yours,

Wm. Lloyd Garrison.

James N. Buffum.

ALS: Smith College Library.

1. President Andrew Jackson, during his conflict with the Bank of the United States, had written to William J. Duane, the Secretary of the Treasury, on June 26, 1833, presenting the policy which he intended to pursue toward the Bank. The President closed his letter with the following statement:

"As the subject of this letter belongs principally to your Department, the President has thought it proper to communicate to you in writing the course of policy appertaining to it which he desires to have pursued, as well as to enable you thoroughly to understand it, as to take upon himself the responsibility of a course which involves much private interest and public considerations of the greatest magnitude." (John Spencer Bassett, ed., *Correspondence of Andrew Jackson*, Washington, D.C., 1931, V, 1833–1838, 128.)

2. The text of the circular is that of Letter 111, to Oliver Johnson, June 4, 1855.

3. William Lloyd Garrison, Jr., who was then seeking employment and staying with the Buffums for a while. See Letter 113, tto William Lloyd Garrison, Jr., June 19, 1855.

4. Lizzie was probably James N. Buffum's daughter.

1 1 1

TO OLIVER JOHNSON

Boston, June 4th, 1855.

Esteemed Friend:

Mr. John A. Jackson,[1] a very promising sculptor in this city, (recently returned from Italy,) having moulded a most admirable bust of Wendell Phillips, which will probably never be surpassed, if again equalled, as a likeness of this eloquent orator and gifted advocate of freedom, (whose features deserve to be handed down to posterity along with his growing fame,) it is deemed highly desirable to have it put into marble, to be placed in some public institution in Boston, as may hereafter be agreed upon. The artist's regular price, in such cases, is $400 — one hundred of which he generously contributes towards securing the marble semblance of so noble a man, leaving $300 to be raised by subscription. This sum it is proposed to solicit of a select number of Mr. P's friends, (of course, without his knowledge,) in such proportion as they may feel disposed to give, without taxing any one unduly. The money collected will be paid over to Francis Jackson, as Treasurer, and duly acknowledged. Should you approve of the object, any sum you may be inclined to give, however small, will be thankfully accepted, and may be forwarded to Mr. Jackson, Hollis Street, or to the subscriber, 21 Cornhill, Boston.

Yours, with much respect,

Wm. Lloyd Garrison.

Oliver Johnson.

Form letter, signed but not written by Garrison: Anti-Slavery Manuscripts, Boston Public Library. "Oliver Johnson" is in Garrison's hand.

This letter was sent by Garrison to a select group of friends. See Letter 110, to James Buffum, May 18, 1855.

1. John Adams Jackson (1825–1879), eminent sculptor, famous for portraiture, received his earliest training as a youth in Boston, and completed his studies in Paris. Among those who sat for him were Dr. Lyman Beecher, George S. Hillard, and Wendell Phillips. The bust of Phillips is owned by the Boston Athenaeum.

---

1 1 2

TO HELEN E. GARRISON

Boston, June 15, 1855.

Dear Wife:

Your absence, with that of Franky and Willie, so reduces our number, and makes us all so quiet, that Eliza declares, in the exaggerated

Hibernian style, that "it seems as if nobody was at home." After I shall have left for Abington to-morrow, what superlative will she then use?

I took my first sitting (an hour long) for my portrait yesterday afternoon. Mr. Pope [1] is a very handsome, gentlemanly man, and it is revolting to think that, whether from a mistaken sense of duty or otherwise, he had a hand in the recapture of poor Anthony Burns, as a member of one of the military companies. But such is the slavish subserviency of the soldier to the summons of the government. He is taught to know nothing but OBEDIENCE.

To-morrow forenoon, I am to give him a long sitting. I am not exactly a free agent in this matter, and so cannot honorably "back out" from my engagement, under all the circumstances. I am sorry, however, that I did not know what I now do in regard to him, before I agreed to have my portrait painted by him. There is nothing that *looks* like pro-slavery about him; but I shall waive all controversy for the present at least. I hope he will get a good likeness, but I despair of seeing one, after so many failures.

I called in to see Mr. Wilson [2] yesterday. He says he must have a cloudy day on which to revise my portrait, as the light in his new room is different in effect from what it was in the old one. I shall wait upon his convenience. — How far he may be induced to make alterations, remains to be seen.

Mr. Carleton [3] called this afternoon, and left a letter from Miss C.,[4] enclosing $24 as the sum she had been able to collect — $10 of which were given by Mr. Pope. I believe in such *Popery* as that, Protestant and heretic as I am.

Mr. [Charles Fox] Hovey called to see me this morning. In regard to our 4th of July banner, he says, "Don't wait — go ahead with it!"

I saw Mr. Phillips [5] yesterday afternoon. He came to say he had found a place for Mary Ann's brother.[6] He is to learn the carpenter's trade. Wendell [Phillips] said Ann [Phillips] enjoyed her ride to Lynn, and all got safely down. He is having his house repaired.

Dr. Taft [7] says Dorah [8] has not had any opportunity to see Dr. Stone,[9] in regard to George [T. Garrison], since her return home, but will probably do so in a few days.

Mr. Jackson [10] has caused some new steps to be placed at our back door in the yard. They are quite an improvement.

Yesterday, George [T. Garrison] went to see the great war steamship launched at the Navy Yard.[11] It is estimated there were fifty thousand spectators present. No accident occurred. Think of *Christian* people building such a vessel, for such a purpose, in the nineteenth century!

"Do they miss me at home?" you will ask. The answer is, you know,

"Yes — at morning, at noon, and at night." — If I were disposed to make a pun, or you to be critical, the query might be raised "How can one who is a *Mrs.*, at the same time be *a miss?*"

I hope you are greatly enjoying your visit. All desire to be lovingly remembered to you and Franky, and all the household. I join in the general salutation. Adieu!

Lovingly yours,

W.L.G.

ALS: Garrison Papers, Boston Public Library.

1. John Pope (1820–1880), portrait, landscape and genre painter, was born in Gardner, Maine, and raised as a farmer. He went to Boston at about 1836 to study painting. He began to exhibit at the Boston Athenaeum in 1843 and exhibited there often until 1869. He went to California in 1849, remained there a few years, returned to Boston, where he stayed for a while, and then went to Europe, continuing his studies of art in Rome and Paris. He was back in Boston by 1855, exhibited in the Athenaeum in 1855, 1856, 1857, and 1858, and by 1857 had established a studio in New York City where he remained until his death. His best known work was a portrait of Daniel Webster for the town of Charlestown, Massachusetts. (George C. Groce and Davis H. Wallace, *New-York Historical Society's Dictionary of Artists in America, 1564–1860*, New Haven and London, 1957, p. 511; Mabel Munson Swan, *The Athenaeum Gallery, 1827–1873*, Boston, 1940, p. 264.)

2. Matthew Wilson (b. London, July 17, 1814; d. Brooklyn, New York, February 23, 1892), portrait painter and miniaturist, came to the United States in 1832 and settled in Philadelphia where he studied with Henry Inman. He went to Paris in 1835, thence to Brooklyn, New York. He became an associate of the National Academy in 1843. In 1847, he went to Baltimore, where he lived for at least two years. In the early 1850's, he was in Ohio, and in Boston from 1855 to 1860. He painted a portrait of Lincoln in 1865, and thereafter made his home in Brooklyn, New York. (Groce and Wallace, p. 694; Swan, p. 288.)

3. Perhaps William Tolman Carlton (1816–1888), an American painter who exhibited in the Athenaeum in 1836, 1842 and 1855 (Swan, p. 209). He was then living in Dorchester, Massachusetts, his family having moved there in his youth. During the Civil War, an oil painting by Carlton, "Waiting for the Hour," representing a Watch Meeting of slaves on December 31, 1862, the eve of the Emancipation Proclamation, was presented to Lincoln by citizens of Boston (*Life*, IV, 131–132; *New England Historical and Genealogical Register*, vol. 46, pp. 95–96).

4. Probably Henrietta M. Carlton, who seems to have been William Tolman Carlton's sister. A letter from R. Leighton, of Washington, D.C., addressed to Henrietta Carlton in Dorchester, mentions Carlton's painting "Waiting for the Hour," which had been presented to Lincoln but not yet acknowledged by him. Miss Carlton had previously written to Leighton enquiring about the failure to acknowledge it. The *Index to the Probate Records of the County of Suffolk, 1636–1893*, lists Harriette (sic) M. Carlton's will as probated in 1875.

5. Perhaps Stephen Clarendon Phillips (1801–1857), of Salem, Massachusetts, lawyer, businessman, and Conscience Whig. He served in Congress as a Whig from 1834 to 1838, and was mayor of Salem from 1838 to 1842. After retiring from public office in 1849, he engaged in the lumber business in Canada and died in a fire on a steamer on the St. Lawrence River.

6. No identification of either Mary Ann or her brother. Mary Ann may have been a servant girl in the Garrison household.

7. Dr. Augustine Calvin Taft (b. May 11, 1817; d. February 17, 1857), of

Framingham, Massachusetts, began the practice of medicine in Uxbridge, Massachusetts. There he joined the Orthodox church but withdrew in 1845 because of its pro-slavery policy. Soon afterward, he practiced medicine in East Boston. From 1847 to 1855, he devoted himself to the responsibilities of general agent of the Boston Society for Aiding Discharged Convicts, ceasing his efforts only as a result of ill health. (*The Liberator*, February 20, 1857; *Vital Records of Uxbridge, Mass.*, Boston, 1916, pp. 149, 313.)

8. Deborah M. Taylor, the eldest daughter of Father Edward Taylor, the sailor-preacher of Boston, married Dr. Taft on September 29, 1839. She was called Dorah by her friends. (Gilbert Haven and Thomas Russell, *Father Taylor, The Sailor Preacher*, Boston, 1873, pp. 69, 327; Letter 163, to Helen Garrison, February 21, 1857.)

9. Dr. Henry Orne Stone (b. Salem, Massachusetts, March 7, 1818; d. Framingham, December 13, 1909) graduated from Harvard Medical School in 1841 and practiced medicine in Boston and Concord for ten years. About 1850, he settled in Framingham, where he practiced medicine and also engaged in farming. He was on the committee of arrangements for the Fourth of July celebration in Framingham sponsored by the Massachusetts Anti-Slavery Society. (J. Gardiner Bartlett, *Gregory Stone Genealogy*, Boston, 1918, p. 356; *The Liberator*, July 13, 1855.)

10. Francis Jackson, from whom Garrison was renting the house. See Letter 119, to Francis Jackson, October 11, 1855.

11. The reference is to the launching of the United States steam frigate *Merrimac* at the Charlestown Navy Yard at 11:30 a. m., June 14, 1855. The Boston *Transcript* estimated that there were 100,000 spectators and declared that the launch was "altogether the most beautiful and perfectly artistic we ever witnessed." (The Boston *Daily Evening Transcript*, June 13, 14, 1855.)

113

TO WILLIAM LLOYD GARRISON, JR.

Boston, June 19, 1855.

My dear Son:

You intimated, in your letter to Wendell [Garrison], a desire to be furnished with some postage stamps. Enclosed, I send you a few, and will send you more whenever wanted. I am glad you have promised Wendell that he shall have a letter from you at least once a week, and I have no doubt he will be prompt to reciprocate the favor. I will try to send you a line, now and then; but you know I am given to procrastination on the score of epistolary correspondence. I will not ask you to write to me in return, provided we hear from you through some one of the family.

Your mother made a short visit to Providence last week — leaving home on Thursday, with little Franky, and returning on Saturday evening. She would have staid till Monday, if she had not had her face badly swollen by an ague.

I was at Abington on Sunday, with Mr. Remond, of Salem.[1] The day was very beautiful, and our meetings at the Town Hall were very successful. The object was to redeem the pledge of $150, made at the New England Anti-Slavery Convention. Two hundred and fifty dollars were promptly subscribed on the spot. Philander Shaw [2] gave $100 — Col. Hunt [3] $50 — Lewis Ford $20 — &c. &c. This was nobly done.

Wendell desires me to say, that he wrote to you yesterday by Wigglesworth,[4] who told him to-day that he had not been able to see you. You will probably get it to-morrow.

I presume you will wish to be with us at Framingham, July 4th.[5] If you can do so, without interfering with your business duties, come up to the city the previous evening. If not, the morning train will arrive in ample season — as our special train will not leave Boston for F. until half past 9 o'clock.

Have you had any feelings of home-sickness since you went to Lynn? Or don't you think much about 14 Dix Place? Or is every thing so pleasant with you, that you have no time to indulge in idle grief? I trust this last is the case.

It seems that, as yet, you have found no boarding-house, and so remain at Mr. Buffum's. I hope you will strive in every way to make as little trouble as possible. Every new addition to a family adds to the care thereof.

Be faithful in the discharge of your duties. Punctuality, order, despatch, accuracy — these are qualities to be cultivated by every one engaging in active business. Perform every task with cheerfulness and alacrity, and remember the Golden Rule constantly — "Do as you would be done by." Character is almost every thing. Be careful with whom you associate, and shun evil company as you would flee from the cholera. Indulge in no vicious habit, and look well after your health and morals, in order that you may be happy, and set an example worthy of imitation. Whenever or wherever you can be useful, be prompt to assist, even though at some inconvenience or trouble.

Recollect that you bear my whole name — you alone of all my children. Make it a better one than I have been able to do.

Give my warmest regards to Mr. and Mrs. Buffum, and Lizzie [Buffum]; and believe me to be,

Ever your affectionate father,

Wm. Lloyd Garrison.

P.S. Wendell desires me to add, that he will send the directions to Lizzie in regard to the Grecian Paintings.

☞ When you come to Boston, I will get you a pair of shoes, as desired. Be careful of your clothes.

ALS: Smith College Library.

1. *The Liberator*, June 22, 1855, carried the following announcement: "An anti-slavery meeting was held in the Town Hall at Abington, on Sunday last,

for the purpose of redeeming the pledge of one hundred and fifty dollars made in behalf of the abolitionists in that town at the late New England A. S. Convention. After addresses by Messrs. Garrison and Remond, not only was the entire pledge made up in the course of a few minutes, but one hundred dollars were generously added to it. The abolitionists in that flourishing town are widely known for their faith and their works." A more detailed description of the meeting appeared in *The Liberator*, June 29, 1855.

2. Philander Shaw (b. February 28, 1818; d. Boston, September 24, 1879) of East Abington, now Rockland, Massachusetts, married Betsy Hunt in 1836. At about 1860 he invented an improved boot crimping machine. (Daniel Turner, "Shaw," typescript, New England Historic Genealogical Society, 1936, p. 36; *Vital Records of Abington, Mass.*, Boston, 1912, p. 191; letter from William D. Coughlan, dated Abington, July 6, 1972.)

3. Thomas Jefferson Hunt (b. February 28, 1805), of Abington, was a shoe manufacturer and, later, a wholesale boot and shoe dealer, who married Sarah P. Howe in 1829. He was the son of Captain Thomas Hunt, who introduced the shoe business to Abington in 1793. The shoes he manufactured were called moccasins, and were made from buffalo hides. (T. B. Wyman, Jr., *Genealogy of the Name and Family of Hunt*, Boston, 1862–63, pp. 319, 320; Benjamin Hobart, *History of the Town of Abington*, Boston, 1866, p. 405; letter from William D. Coughlan, dated Abington, July 6, 1972.)

4. Edward Wigglesworth (b. Boston, December 30, 1840; d. Boston, January 23, 1896), was a classmate at Harvard of Wendell Phillips Garrison, class of 1861. After spending eight months at the Harvard Medical School, he joined the Union Army and served until July 1863, when his regiment was mustered out. In 1864, he served as a volunteer surgeon with the Army of the Potomac. He received his M.D. from Harvard Medical School in 1865, spent five years in Europe studying medicine, and returned to Boston where he specialized in diseases of the skin. He was lecturer on syphilis at Harvard Medical School from 1871 to 1881 and founded the Boston Dispensary for Skin Diseases in 1872. (*Fifth Report, Harvard Class of 1861*, New York, 1892, pp. 131–135.)

5. This was to be the annual Fourth of July celebration sponsored by the Massachusetts Anti-Slavery Society in the form of an outdoor picnic at the Framingham Grove. The speakers included Garrison, Phillips, Remond, Stephen S. Foster, Edmund Quincy, and others. (*The Liberator*, June 29, 1855.) William Coughlan writes, in the previously cited letter (note 3), that "Garrison spoke thirteen times at Island Grove from 1846 to 1865. We have one of the few memorials erected to Garrison and the abolitionists. A bronze tablet in a boulder stands on the site of the speaker's stand. It was erected by the late Moses N. Arnold, a local shoe manufacturer, in 1909."

114

TO WENDELL PHILLIPS

Boston, June 26, 1855.

Dear Phillips:

I have just received a letter from our friend, Col. Whiting, of Concord, desiring me to inform you of the change that has been made in regard to the railroad train for that place. It will leave on Thursday,[1] at half past 12 o'clock, instead of 1 — so do not be behind your time, on any account. They are calculating upon something of a gathering[2]

— and you must do your best — in a slaveholding sense, your worst. Col. Whiting desires me to say, that he expects you to be his guest.

Mary Grew will go with us.

Best love to Ann and Phebe.

Yours, devotedly,

Wm. Lloyd Garrison.

Wendell Phillips.

ALS: Merrill Collection of Garrison Papers, Wichita State University Library.

1. June 28, 1855.
2. This was to be the Annual Meeting of the Middlesex County Anti-Slavery Society, scheduled for Friday afternoon, June 29, in the Town Hall, Concord. Phillips and Garrison were listed as speakers. (*The Liberator*, June 29, 1855.)

115

TO ELLIS G. LORING

Boston, Aug. 13, 1855.

My Dear Friend:

Should it be perfectly convenient and agreeable to you and Mrs. Loring [1] to have wife and I, (with perhaps our two youngest children, Fanny and Frank,) visit you on Thursday, we will take the 12 o'clock train on that day, for Beverly, and remain with you until Friday evening or Saturday morning. On Saturday afternoon, I must leave Boston for Haverhill, to attend a series of anti-slavery meetings in that town, in company with Wendell Phillips.

I was not aware, when I addressed a note to you, a few days since, that you had badly sprained your ankle. But I trust you are daily improving in that respect.

Mrs. Loring, I trust, has fully recovered her health.

We pray you not to allow us to come this week, unless entirely convenient to yourselves; for we know your liability to have company suddenly come upon you, and we can again postpone our visit without any difficulty.

Yours, with the highest regards,

Wm. Lloyd Garrison.

Ellis G. Loring, Esq.

ALS: New York Public Library.

Ellis Gray Loring was a Boston lawyer, abolitionist, and friend of Garrison. See *Letters*, II, 57.

1. Louisa Gilman Loring (1797–1868) was an active abolitionist. See *Letters*, II, 79.

116

TO ELIZABETH BUFFUM CHACE

Boston, Sept. 6, 1855. Your letter is just received. I lament to hear of the illness of your beloved father, but trust he will have fully recovered by the time this reaches you.

In its earliest and most critical days, the Anti-Slavery Cause was most deeply indebted to him for the moral courage he displayed, and the eloquence he used in its behalf; and manfully did he uphold its banner 'through evil report,' [1] and many perils, and a thousand fiery trials.

Ever since, that cause has received his zealous aid; and his testimony has never been wanting in behalf of the oppressed, cost what it might to him or his interests.

Though we have differed somewhat as to means, we have never been divided on the vital question of immediate and unconditional emancipation.

May his declining years be rendered in the highest degree felicitous by the remembrance of what he has done for the liberation and improvement of a race 'meted out and trodden under foot.' [2] Give him my kindest salutations, my most grateful recollections, and my best wishes for his complete recovery. God grant we may all live to witness the emancipation of all in bondage! But how portentious and awful is the present aspect of our national affairs! 'What shall the end of these things be?' [3]

You write with reference to my speaking in Providence. Indeed, Providence is a city hard to be affected. I never go to it with an elastic spirit, as I do to many other places. There seems to be a general determination not to hear. Still, that is no reason why we should 'give up the ship,' — and I admire your zeal and perseverance in that direction. Nevertheless, I pray thee have *me* excused, if possible.

Excerpt, printed in Lillie Buffum Chace Wyman and Arthur Crawford Wyman, *Elizabeth Buffum Chace, 1806–1899, Her Life and Its Environment* (Boston, 1914), I, 159–160.

Elizabeth Buffum Chace (b. Providence, Rhode Island, December 9, 1806; d. Central Falls, Rhode Island, 1899) was the daughter of Arnold Buffum, a Quaker, farmer and hat manufacturer, and a founder (in 1832) and first president of the New England Anti-Slavery Society. In 1828, she married Samuel Buffington Chace, a Quaker and son of a Fall River, Massachusetts, cotton manufacturer. Profoundly antislavery, in 1835 she helped form the Fall River Female Anti-Slavery Society, of which she became vice-president. In 1840, she moved with her family to Valley Falls, Rhode Island, where her husband developed a prosperous cotton manufacturing business and where she continued her antislavery efforts. She was a Garrisonian abolitionist and her home served as a station on the Underground

Railroad. She was also active in the woman's rights movement and prison reform. In 1867, she helped found, with Emerson and others, the National Free Religious Association. (*Notable American Women.*)

For additional information about Arnold Buffum see *Letters*, I and II, *passim*.

1. II Corinthians 6:8.
2. Isaiah 18:2.
3. Daniel 12:8.

117

TO CHARLES F. HOVEY

Boston, Sept. 15, 1855.

My dear Hovey:

The nature of the generous communication you have made to Helen and myself,[1] respecting the future, demands something more than a mere verbal expression of thankfulness. Your kind intentions, so frankly and confidingly revealed to us, indicate alike the strength of your friendship, and the abiding interest you take in the cause of reform. It is more blessed, I know, to give than receive; and so you have the advantage of us to that extent; but your benefaction is doubly gratifying — alike as a proof of your personal regard and confidence, and of your desire to sustain me in my efforts to put down governmental corruption and religious imposture, so long as I remain faithful and uncompromising.

"So long," &c. That stipulation you have not made, and you have nobly exacted no conditions; and yet, this must be the condition on which, at any time, I should be willing to receive either interest or principal. And you must reserve to yourself the most absolute freedom to decide whether my future course shall meet your general approbation; and in case it should not, you will as promptly withhold your aid, as you have offered it. I believe I know your heart, and I trust you know mine. Our object is one — freedom of conscience, freedom of speech, freedom of the press, freedom for all in all things, and no truce with cant, imposture, bigotry, priestcraft, or political chicanery.

Every thing in this world is mutable. You will revoke what you now intend in regard to us, both as to interest and principal, should any unforeseen pecuniary pressure in your business operations make it inconvenient to yourself, or embarrassing to those dependent upon you, to carry out your wishes. Less than this I cannot say, to relieve my mind of the anxiety and embarrassment that otherwise would accompany the grateful remembrance of your kindness. Remember — we regard you as pledged to nothing, in consequence of what you have communicated, beyond what for the time being you really take a pleasure in doing; reserving to yourself to change your purposes, as circumstances may seem to demand at your hands.

As the world goes, it is dangerous to personal integrity and independence to be indebted to others, however friendly and generous. But, though often sorely pressed and straitened in my circumstances, I have never yet solicited assistance for myself individually, or my family collectively, to the amount of a farthing. I began the Liberator without a subscriber; I have never in a single instance personally asked any one to subscribe for it; and, "survive or perish," it must be inflexibly independent to the end. Of course, such has been the nature of the struggle which I commenced, and so mighty the opposition with which I have had to contend, that, without the generous pecuniary co-operation of a few friends, (voluntarily offered,) to keep the Liberator afloat, it would have been impossible for me to have "continued to this day." [2] Those friends, it gives me pride and pleasure to believe, while they will not charge me with any lack of appreciation of their kindness, will acknowledge that I have turned neither to the right hand nor to the left, for the sake of avoiding giving offence, or securing the continuance of any co-operation in the anti-slavery cause.

In this expression of my feelings, respecting your kind promise to us both, Helen entirely unites; trusting that the fact of your having communicated to us your friendly purpose will never for a moment restrain your freedom to revoke it, in case of any alteration of views or feelings, or change of circumstances.

Your attached and much obliged friend,

Wm. Lloyd Garrison.

Charles F. Hovey.

ALS: Garrison Papers, Boston Public Library.

1. Charles Hovey had notified the Garrisons that "he proposed to pay them annually a sum equal to the interest on a contemplated legacy. This aid was gratefully accepted by Garrison, on condition that it should be freely revoked at any time, for any reason, and saving his own independence of thought and action." (*Life*, III, 429.) Some months earlier, Hovey had asked Mrs. Garrison to accept a gift of a barrel of flour. " 'I see you have a houseful of people. . . . Your husband's position brings him many guests and expenses which do not belong to him' (M.S.)." Hovey also contributed to a fund for the purchase of Garrison's home in Dix Place, which he had rented from Francis Jackson. (*Life*, III, 428n, 429.)

2. A paraphrase of Acts 26:22.

1 1 8

TO E. A. WEBB

Boston, Sept. 25, 1855.

Dear Friend:

Your letter of the 20th was duly received.

Next Sunday, I am engaged to lecture in East Princeton.[1]

You may consider me engaged to lecture in Keene on Saturday evening, and on Sunday afternoon and evening, Oct. 6th and 7th.[2] Perhaps Saturday and Sunday evening would suffice, omitting Sunday afternoon; but of this you must judge according to circumstances. I should not like to address four meetings successively, and so propose no meeting on Sunday forenoon. Should it be probable that but few comparatively would attend on Sunday afternoon, it might be best not to have a meeting at that time.

Whether Mr. May will be able to accompany me, I cannot now tell, as he is absent from the city; but you shall be seasonably apprised of his coming, in case he gives his consent.

I have long been desirous of seeing your beautiful village, (for such it is always represented to be) — and though I cannot hope to induce many of your citizens to accept all my views on the subject of slavery, I trust their prejudices against me will be somewhat mitigated, after giving me a candid hearing, which is all I ask.

Perhaps you will suggest to me some points to touch upon, which will be hitting the nail upon the head, locally speaking. What does Keene need?

Yours, to break every yoke,

Wm. Lloyd Garrison.

E. A. Webb.

ALS: New Hampshire Historical Society.

Edward A. Webb was a founder of the Keene Public Library, Keene, New Hampshire, in 1859. From 1884 to 1890 he was overseer of the weaving room of Faulkner & Colony, wool dealers, with whom he was associated as early as 1871. (S. G. Griffin, *A History of the Town of Keene*, Keene, 1904, p. 461; Hamilton Child, *Gazetteer of Cheshire County, N.H., 1736–1885*, Syracuse, N.Y., 1885, Part I, p. 234; Part II, p. 178; letter from Mrs. N. B. Lacy, New Hampshire Historical Society, Concord, New Hampshire, October 28, 1972.)

1. This was to be a quarterly meeting of the Worcester County North Anti-Slavery Society, at East Princeton, Massachusetts, on Sunday, September 30.

2. Apparently, Garrison spoke in Keene, New Hampshire, a week later. *The Liberator*, October 12, 1855, announced that "A series of anti-slavery meetings will be held in Keene, commencing on Saturday evening next, Oct. 13, at 7 o'clock; and continuing on Sunday afternoon and evening.

"Wm. Lloyd Garrison and Samuel May, Jr., on behalf of the American Anti-Slavery Society, will attend these meetings."

Garrison's description of his visit to Keene appeared in *The Liberator*, October 26, 1855.

On November 2, *The Liberator* reprinted a short item from the Keene *Sentinel* which described the Sunday evening session.

119

TO FRANCIS JACKSON

Boston, Oct. 11, 1855.

My dear friend Francis Jackson:

Enclosed is the amount due you on the last quarter's rent, ending September 30, 1855, which, under the new arrangement, terminates the further lease of the house, on your part.[1]

In consenting to the arrangement referred to, you have given fresh evidence of your friendly regard for me, and mine, inclusive. Though you speak of it as simply a business transaction, I am not ignorant, but gratefully conscious, of the fact, that, in selling the house for the precise amount which it has cost you, you have, in truth, made a donation to me of a very generous sum, over its actual cost, which unquestionably you could have realized for it, had you disposed of it to any other person. Such is the view which all the friends, who have been made acquainted with it, take of the transfer; and they appreciate the deed accordingly.

My indebtedness to you, in many ways, during the period of our acquaintance, has been great. Of course, it is such as cannot be liquidated. It must, therefore, ever be a part of my memory, not to depress my spirit, but to stimulate me to "love and good works." [2] A profusion of thanks would be most distasteful to you, and foreign to my nature; for, "the thankless oft are noisiest in their thanks," wherein no gratitude is mingled, but only a display of selfishness is made. It is doubly gratifying to my feelings to know that your kindness has not only been based upon personal regard to me as a friend, but has had reference to making my hands strong, and my heart light, in the fearful and long-protracted struggle with the Slave Power. The blessing of those who are ready to perish shall rest upon your head.

To the friends who have joined their contributions to an amount sufficient to secure the house now occupied by my family for our possession, I can only return our poor, stammering acknowledgments. Possessing free, courageous, progressive spirits themselves, they will never consider me under any restriction, in consequence of what they have done, in regard to liberty of thought and expression, but will continue their respect and confidence only so far as they shall see me faithful to my own highest convictions of duty. We may not always all see alike, respecting doctrines or measures, or as to the precise course to be pursued; but I trust that, in spirit and purpose, we shall remain one to the end of our earthly pilgrimage — yes, in all the everlasting future beyond the grave — one to seek the happiness of all, and the detriment of none, at whatever cost to ourselves.

I trust your valuable life may be preserved to a very ripe old age. None can love and esteem you more than

Your grateful friend and faithful co-worker,

Wm. Lloyd Garrison.

Francis Jackson, Esq.

ALS: Garrison Papers, Boston Public Library.

1. A movement to raise funds to enable Garrison to buy his own home had begun in 1847. By January 1, 1849, the fund had reached $2,289.79. Garrison and his family moved into their home at Dix Place, near Hollis Street, in 1853, as tenants of Francis Jackson, their friend and neighbor. By 1855, the original fund had grown sufficiently to enable Garrison to purchase the house from Jackson, who sold it at its original cost, which was substantially lower than it was then worth. (*Life*, III, 265, 428–429.)

2. Hebrews 10:24.

120

TO ADELINE ROBERTS

Boston, Oct. 18, 1855.

Dear Friend:

In accordance with your suggestion, consider me pledged to lecture before your Society on the evening of Dec. 6th. I am not certain whether you have not written 16th.[1] If I have made a blunder, please let me know.

Your co-worker,

Wm. Lloyd Garrison.

Adeline Roberts.

ALS: Essex Institute, Salem, Massachusetts.

1. Since the lectures, sponsored by the Salem Female Anti-Slavery Society, were held on Sunday nights, the correct date was probably December 16, a Sunday, rather than the 6th, a Thursday. (See *The Liberator*, October 19, 1855.)

121

TO SAMUEL J. MAY

Boston, Oct. 26, 1855.

My dear friend S. J. May:

The bearer of this is Mr. George Marshall,[1] (formerly a fugitive slave,) who has just returned from Australia via Liverpool, bringing me a warm commendatory letter from my colored friend Wm. P. Powell, formerly of New York city. Mr. Marshall, you will see, has very high recommendations given to him before he left America, by gentlemen of the medical profession, and others, in Pittsburgh, Buffalo, &c. &c. He contemplates locating himself in Syracuse, if he can find sufficient encouragement in the line of his profession. I have intimated to him that you would be ready to give him such information as he might need, in regard to men and things in your city; and, doubtless, an introduction to one or two of your physicians. Mr. Marshall is evidently a bright, gentlemanly and energetic man, who means to "hoe his own row," and be thoroughly independent, and no burden upon any one. His life has been so eventful that it has been written out in England, and is to be published there in a volume. I hope he will succeed in Syracuse.

A short time since, I received a letter from you, in regard to the lecture you have prepared on the rise and progress of the Anti-Slavery cause, and believe I have secured a hearing for you in Salem and Providence. Probably you have already heard from the parties interested. I have also written to Haverhill, but, as yet, have received no reply. I will do what I can for you elsewhere.

The "Radical Political Abolition Convention" in this city, I did not attend.[2] It amounted to nothing, and may be set down as a failure. The whole movement is made up of strange compounds.

Gerrit Smith took breakfast with me yesterday, in company with Phillips, [Charles F.] Hovey, your cousin S. May, Jr., Oliver Johnson, and others. We had a very frank talk, and a very agreeable time.

I write in great haste, and can add no more, except that I am

Ever yours, truly,

Wm. Lloyd Garrison.

S. J. May.

ALS: Garrison Papers, Boston Public Library.

1. Not further identified.

2. The convention took place at the Melodeon on Tuesday, Wednesday, Thursday, October 23, 24, and 25. Its purpose was to discuss "the *illegality and uncon-*

stitutionality of Slavery, and the power of the Federal Government over slavery in the United States.

"Also, to provide means for propagating the sentiments and advocating the measures of 'Radical Political Abolitionists,' and, if judged best, to organize for that object, A National Abolition Society." William Goodell and James McCune Smith were the committee on arrangements. Expected speakers included Gerrit Smith, Lewis Tappan, S. S. Jocelyn, Frederick Douglass, and L. C. Matlock. (*The Liberator*, October 19, 1855.)

A short item in *The Liberator*, October 26, 1855, noted that "this Convention appeared to excite no attention, and was thinly attended throughout."

122

TO ELIZA FRANCES EDDY

Saturday morning, Nov. 3. [1855.]

My dear Mrs. Eddy:

I beg you to convey to your dear, noble father, all the warm sensibilities and grateful emotions of my soul, for his prompt and truly characteristic reply (through you) to my letter last evening. The grapes were delicious to my taste, and surprisingly sweet. But the quantity sent was over-liberal. Your father is literally as well as playfully exact in saying, that they are a very different kind of "grape" from that which Gen. Taylor [1] ordered Capt. Bragg to give the Mexicans. Had that old war-dog stormed them in this manner, they would have surrendered at discretion, acknowledged his invasion to have been exactly to their taste, drank his health with a relish, pronounced his assault productive of excellent fruit, and *grape*-fully swallowed his prescription.

Gen. Taylor wanted to give the Mexicans "hell." Your father desires to give the whole human race heaven — nothing but heaven. The difference is infinite.

Last night was a sleepless one to me throughout, and I feel much exhausted this morning; but I cannot refrain from sending you this brief note. Of course, your dear father was constantly in my thoughts.[2] I lived twenty years of my life over again, associated with him in counsel and effort. His personal kindness to me and mine — his generous support to the cause of the slave — his unbounded hospitality to its advocates and friends — his frequent sheltering beneath his roof the homeless wanderer and the trembling fugitive — his solid judgment, rare discrimination of character, and grand integrity of life — his cheerful surrender of office, popular favor, and "respectable" standing in the community, for the sake of universal freedom and eternal right — his prompt disposition to "hoist the banner on the outer wall," and to take his stand in "the deadly, imminent breach," [3] with heroic courage and sublime self-forgetfulness — &c. &c.; all these, and a thousand other considerations, growing out of the probable nearness of his removal to the world beyond us, occupied my mind during the silent watches of the night, and rendered sleep impossible.

Your father tenderly refers to the regret he feels in leaving his old friends and comrades, for a short time; but desires me to know that he "is under no depression of spirit." Perhaps that last remark was elicited by my reference to the natural effect of severe dyspeptic attacks upon the animal spirits. I did not for one moment suppose, that your father had any anxiety or concern as to the future — that his mind was not serene and philosophically self-possessed — and that he did not feel himself

"Dressed for the flight, and ready to be gone,"
for on these points I had no doubt.

My dear Mrs. Eddy, you have had a loving father, and you have been to him a dear, good child. Your souls are most closely knit together, and the impending separation cannot but be painfully felt by you both. But you have much of your father's resignation, strength of endurance, "patience of hope and labor of love," [4] and will therefore add nothing to that unavoidable sadness that nature has a right to exact in every such case. Behind the cloud, the sun is shining still; and the portals of the grave are but the opening of the gates of glory to the upright of heart.

Helen sends you her warmest sympathies in this your trial-hour. She desires her love and gratitude to be given to your father, whose life she hopes may yet be prolonged beyond, far beyond what seem to be the probabilities of the case, unless Dr. Bigelow [5] greatly errs in his judgment. She will try to see you soon; and if I am possibly able, I will endeavor to-morrow to call also.

Yours, with a full heart,

Wm. Lloyd Garrison.

☞ Please make no reply to this. — I am sorry that Wendell Phillips has gone to Chicago. Hope your father is easier this morning.

ALS: Garrison Papers, Boston Public Library. A portion of this letter appears in *Life*, III, 429–430. The year has been added by a hand other than Garrison's.

Eliza Frances Eddy (b. Boston, January 13, 1816; d. there, December 29, 1881) was the daughter of Francis Jackson. She married Charles D. Merriam of Boston, November 3, 1836. He died in 1845. She married James Eddy, September 21, 1848. Originally a skilled engraver who had studied in Europe, he became a purchaser and seller of paintings and other art objects. She had three children by her first marriage and four by her second. (Charles Henry Pope, *Merriam Genealogy*, Boston, 1906, p. 250; Ruth S. D. Eddy, *The Eddy Family in America*, Boston, 1930, p. 331.)

1. The reference is to the battle of Buena Vista during the Mexican War. The battle occurred on September 22 and 23, 1847, and the incident to which Garrison

alludes involved General Zachary Taylor (1784–1850), who was to be the twelfth President of the United States, and Captain Braxton Bragg (1817–1876), who served as Confederate general during the Civil War. As Taylor's biographer recounts the story, "Captain Bragg and his battery of six-pounders were hard pressed by the enemy on the second afternoon of the battle and the Captain was preparing to retire in order to save his pieces. Major Mansfield of the Engineers Corps, believing it would be fatal for Bragg to abandon his position, sought out General Taylor to urge him not to allow the battery to move. Taylor replied: 'No sir! no sir! not at all! Tell him not to move one inch, but to give them grape and canister.' A few minutes later Taylor quietly rode up behind Bragg and said, 'A little more grape, Captain Bragg!' " These words inspired Bragg and his men to increase their fire and defeat the enemy. (Brainerd Dyer, *Zachary Taylor*, Baton Rouge, 1946, p. 238. Dyer points out, however, that although the story was publicized throughout the country, it may never have happened. See p. 238n.)

2. *Life*, III, 429, writes that at this time "both Francis Jackson and Mr. Garrison fell ill — the former dangerously, so that his life was despaired of. Neither could visit the other, though but a short distance apart."

3. Shakespeare, *Othello*, I, iii, 136.

4. Variation of I Thessalonians 1:3.

5. Dr. Jacob Bigelow (1787–1879), botanist and physician, was professor of materia medica at the Harvard Medical School from 1815 to 1855, a member of the American Academy of Arts and Sciences for sixty-seven years, and its president from 1847 to 1863. His published writings include *American Medical Botany*, in three volumes, 1817–1820; *Discourse on Self-Limited Diseases*, 1835; *Nature in Disease*, 1854; and *Brief Expositions of Rational Medicine*, 1858.

---

1 2 3

TO ANNE WARREN WESTON

Boston, Nov. 3d, 1855.

My dear friend:

Having been confined to my bed and room, since Monday last, by a violent rheumatic attack, attended with some fever upon the brain, (though now improving,) I have been brought into very close sympathy with all who are sick; and my thoughts, therefore, have gone in the direction of Weymouth, and clustered around the case of your dear father,[1] of whose condition I have heard nothing for some time past. Is he improving? or gradually failing? What are your hopes or fears? Be assured you all have my warmest sympathies in this dark hour of affliction. To your father, give my tenderest remembrances, and the earnest expression of my heart's desire that his present sickness may not be unto death. But if it be decreed otherwise, by a Power to which we must all submit, then I can only trust that he will apprehend the change to be no calamity in itself, but only the carrying out of an all-wise and beneficent arrangement of an all-gracious God, to result in his own higher development and exaltation.

To your mother,[2] give my warm regards, and tell her that though (if your father be as ill as I fear he is) she has a peculiarly heavy cross to bear, I have no doubt that she is amply sustained by her trust in God, "who doeth all things well."

To Deborah and your brother,[3] remember me affectionately and sympathetically.

In these requests, my dear Helen cordially unites; for through what bereavements have we not both passed?

My dear friend, I have most afflicting intelligence to communicate to you. Our dear and noble friend, Francis Jackson, it is declared by his medical adviser, Dr. Bigelow, has only a few days more to live on earth. The fact was communicated to him yesterday, and he received it with that serenity and unfaltering strength of soul which have ever characterised him in time of peril. He is quietly making preparations for his departure; but, of course, little remains to be done, for he is one whose house has long been set in order, and he is not taken by surprise — though the blow will come with sudden and astounding effect upon all his friends. He is very cheerful, and will pass away as nobly as he has lived. But how can we give him up? How spare one of the pillars [of] our anti-slavery temple? Who can fill his place? Ah! our refuge, at such a time, can only be found in the beneficence of God, whose interest in the welfare of the universe is infinite, and who alone sees the end from the beginning. His will be done, not ours. No righteous cause is dependant for its triumph upon an arm of flesh.

It will be a singular, and by no means infelicitous occurrence, if presiding at the 20th anniversary of the Boston mob of 1835, shall prove the last public act of so long-tried and faithful a friend of the oppressed as Francis Jackson.[4] That crown will cover his head resplendently.

When do you expect Maria [Weston Chapman] home? My heart leaps almost wildly to see her again face to face. God preserve her to us and the world for many, many years!

Your sympathising friend,

Wm. Lloyd Garrison.

Anne W. Weston.

—

Dear Anne: Feeling too weak to use the pen comfortably myself, I employed my son Wendell to jot down what is written above, at my dictation; but, since it was finished, and just as I am preparing to mail it, Phebe Garnaut[5] has called in, bringing the sad intelligence of the decease of your father last evening, after much suffering. What more can I add? "The soul knoweth its own grief,"[6] and there are times when none should intermeddle therewith. My heart is bowed with yours — I feel most deeply and tenderly for you all — more than this I must not add now. Adieu!   W. L. G.

Letter dictated by Garrison to his son Wendell, with signature and postscript in Garrison's hand: Child Papers, Boston Public Library.

1. Captain Warren Weston of Weymouth, Massachusetts, father of the five Weston sisters, including Anne Warren Weston and Maria Weston Chapman, died on November 2, at the age of seventy-five. (*Letters*, II, 57.)

2. Ann Bates Weston, Captain Weston's second wife, died in Weymouth, May 18, 1878. (*Ibid.*)

3. Deborah Weston (b. 1814) and Hervey Eliphaz Weston. (*Ibid.*)

4. The anniversary meeting was held on October 21, 1855.

5. The adopted daughter of Wendell Phillips.

6. A variation of Proverbs 14:10.

124

TO FRANCIS JACKSON

14 Dix Place, Nov. 3rd. [1855.]
Saturday eveg.

My dear friend Jackson:

The affectionate and strengthening lines,[1] traced by your own hands this afternoon, which, in spite of medical injunction to the contrary, you were moved to send me, I shall prize and cherish as more precious than any Sibylline leaf. They seem next to your own presence in my chamber; and, though voiceless, had a power to thrill me through and through. I am glad, and yet most sorry, that you felt impelled to make such an effort, in your prostrate condition, by what I had written; — glad, because it has given me the last epistolary token from your own hand I may ever receive; most sorry, because it affects me to think of the pain it must have caused you, to a still further prostration of your system. I write to say this much, because I can do no less; but not on any consideration to prompt you to do the same thing over again. Indeed, in my note to Eliza [F. Eddy], I expressly desired her not to think of making a reply to it, appreciating as I did the heavy pressure which must be continually weighing upon her spirit, through so much anxiety and watchfulness.

Happy am I, if, in any manner, I have been of any service to you, during our long and endearing acquaintance. But you had nothing to learn of me, in regard to the sacred rights of conscience, the freedom of the mind, and the duty of standing by the right, at all hazards, whether solitary or backed up by a multitude. These things I found to be a part of your own nature. Moreover, it was your good fortune to throw off, at a much earlier period in life than I did, the fetters of that terrible theology which has so long held mastery over the New-England mind, making one universal blight of human existence here below, and filling a future state of existence with inconceivable dangers and unutterable horrors. The Fatherhood of God was a doctrine early accepted by you, and at a time when it required the greatest moral courage to do so. Happily, you have lived to see it grow and extend in every direction; and of its ultimate acceptance by the whole human family, you and I have no reason to doubt. God shall be all, and in all; which is saying, in other words, that nothing but goodness is immutable, all-conquering, everlasting.

I dwell, dear friend, with inexpressible satisfaction upon the fact, that your last public act in the service of the slave was that of presiding at the 20th anniversary of the memorable mobocratic 21st of October, 1835.[2] It will constitute a fitting crown of honor to a well-spent life. Nothing could have been more felicitous, or more beautifully and historically, as well as personally appropriate.

I have to communicate to you the death of Capt. Weston of Weymouth. He finished his voyage of life last evening, and has entered into the haven of rest. I have dictated a letter to Anne [W. Weston], conveying my sympathy to the family, in view of their bereavement, and communicating to them, also, the sad intelligence of your own dangerous illness. It will add much to their weight of sorrow, I know; but, at the same time, I felt sure they would wish to be apprised of the fact without any delay.

The reference, in your note, to your parched lips, is very touching. My own are somewhat affected by the little fever I have had; but I am getting better, while you are growing worse. However, this is saying that you are nearer your heavenly home, and that the troubles and cares of life with you are nearly ended.

In life, in death, and ever, yours,

Wm. Lloyd Garrison.

Francis Jackson, Esq.

Letter signed by Garrison and dictated by him, probably to his son Wendell: Garrison Papers, Boston Public Library. The year seems to have been inserted later. A portion of this letter is printed in *Life*, III, 430–431.

1. Francis Jackson's letter to Garrison, dated November 3, is printed in *Life*, III, 430. Since it expresses Jackson's relationship to Garrison, and is yet brief, it merits being quoted in full: "Dear Garrison: Among the choicest cordials the nurse brings to my parched lips are your very kind letters, which I should like very much to reply to; but my physician counsels me to put aside all business, forego to meet old friends, even, and keep very quiet. I am now violating his injunctions, but I must send you a word. It has been one of the most fortunate circumstances of my life that I was thrown so near your teaching and influence. I am very greatly indebted to you. It has for many long years been one of the aims of my life to

stand by you — how well, it is not for me to say. I want to write more, but cannot; I cannot see you now, but I send you my love."

2. Accounts of the anniversary appeared in *The Liberator*, October 26 and November 2, 1855. The meeting was held in Stacy Hall, 46 Washington Street, Codman's Block, "the identical spot which was the scene of the ever memorable outbreak of 1835." Garrison called the meeting to order and, in his introductory remarks, made the following comment: "I think, if I were to take your suffrages as to the man who of all others ought to preside . . . on this occasion, you would all agree that it is the man who, after the Female Anti-Slavery Society was driven from this place, offered them the use of his house, at the risk of having it pulled down over his head. I allude to our friend Francis Jackson. He 'still lives,' and long may he live; and I propose that he preside on this occasion. Those who are in favor of this proposition will manifest it." Garrison's motion carried by a unanimous vote and Jackson presided.

125

TO FRANCIS JACKSON

14 Dix Place, Nov. 4, 1855.
Sunday Evening.

My Dear Friend:

Mr. [Theodore] Parker and Mr. [Charles F.] Hovey have comforted me greatly, to-day, by the intelligence that you had a good night, and appear much improved, being able not only to take, but to retain nourishment in your system. Let us hope that you have been going through a crisis, the peril of which has passed, and that you will continue to mend — and so be preserved to your children and friends some years longer. Whether this be possible or not, I am glad indeed that this has proved to you a sabbath of rest from the suffering of previous days.

This morning, a pressure was upon my brain; and, throwing myself upon my bed, I soon went into a deep sleep, lasting three hours; upon awaking from which, I found my brain relieved, and my whole system greatly refreshed. I now feel only in need of strength. My violent rheumatic pains are gone, my head begins to feel regulated, and my appetite is good. I have been impatient to see you; but it has not been deemed prudent for me to expose myself to the bitter easterly air to-day; and having repeatedly heard from you, and that you are much more comfortable, and knowing that you have already seen more persons than prudence might deem advisable, I shall wait contentedly another day or two at the longest, when I shall hope to take your hand, and find you gaining in strength, appetite, and bodily repose.

In the long run of ages, the duration of individual life a few years, more or less, is of the smallest conceivable importance. In a period so vast, social, communistic, national and world-embracing existence is as the small dust in the balance. There is no sorrow, no suffering, no oppression, no calamity, no curse, either colossal or overwhelming as against Time, which is the conqueror of all things, which makes history itself at last only a myth, and which alone, with ever increasing age, has always the freshness of youth about it, garlanded with flowers, and buoyant with hope. The living mass of mankind, in this mundane sphere, constitutes only a fraction of what has been, but gone before, to that

— "undiscovered bourne,
Whence no traveller returns," [1]

at least none once more to take up his sojourn on earth. The line is continually forming on the other side. What tribes, what races, what generations, have led the way! Immortality is not only sublime in its nature, but in its multitudinous existencies. The march of Eternity is the grand march of the universe, and soul-inspiring.

"Through what new scenes and changes must we pass!" [2]

No matter what "shadows, clouds and darkness" rest upon the future. Enough!

"The soul, secure in her existence, smiles
At the drawn dagger, and defies its point"; [3]

for it "shall flourish in immortal youth —
Unhurt amid the war of elements,
The wreck of matter, and the crush of worlds." [4]

While I would have you, my dear friend, draw no unwarrantable inferences of ultimate recovery from your present relieved condition, I beg you to consider no single opinion of your medical adviser to be absolute in your case, as to the hopelessness of a cure. He may greatly err, however sagacious or discriminating, ordinarily. Let the matter rest in your mind (indeed, I am quite sure it will) with entire composure, because this will make your recovery probable, if it be possible. What is possible in every such case, nature knows a great deal better than any physician; and all she asks is, not to be hindered in her operations. It is for the mind to cooperate with her, and to say, "Do the best you can; and if you cannot succeed, no blame shall attach to you, and I am content."

If you shall lead the way to the spirit-land, (which I am desirous of exploring, in God's good time,) your old associates will be certain to follow you, in due order; and I trust we shall experience no difficulty in finding each other, but shall "meet to part no more." However this may be, I will not any longer weary you with my thoughts and speculations; but, invoking upon you whatever strength and comfort can be vouchsafed to you from above, hoping you will have a night of sweet repose, and praying for your steady restoration to health, I remain, my dear friend,

Yours, "world without end," [5]

Wm. Lloyd Garrison.

Francis Jackson, Esq.

ALS: Garrison Papers, Boston Public Library.

1. "The undiscovered country, from whose bourne / No traveller returns." Shakespeare, *Hamlet*, III, i, 79–80.
2. From *Cato*, Act V, Scene i, a tragedy by Joseph Addison (1672–1719), English classical scholar and author.
3. Addison, *Cato*, Act V, Scene i.
4. *Ibid.*
5. *The Book of Common Prayer*, "Gloria."

126

TO ANNE WARREN WESTON

Boston, Nov. 6, 1855.

My Dear Friend:

As I have not yet been out of the house, although I feel nearly recovered from my late violent attack, lacking only my usual strength, it is deemed prudent for me not to go to Weymouth to-day; though I find it very difficult to restrain myself from so doing. It would have been a mournful satisfaction to me to have been with you in this dark hour of affliction, and to have shown by my presence my respect for the memory of your excellent father. Though it was not often that he and I met, I shall never forget his kindly greeting, or the smile that constantly illuminated his fine countenance. He has seen "the last of earth" — his voyage of life is completed — he has reached his haven of rest. We may serenely leave him, and all our beloved dead, in the hands of Him "who doeth all things well," and "whose tender mercies are over all the works of his hands," [1] now and evermore. No one cares for us, living or dying, so much as the ever-blessed God; and that love which is eternal, can never ultimately be defeated as to its object.

I shall be with you all in spirit to-day, blending my feelings with yours, and participating in your sadness; yet, with you, through the dark cloud seeing the face of a heavenly Father, and throngs of blissful spirits. My special regards and condolence to your dear mother.

Yours, with deepest sympathy,

Wm. Lloyd Garrison.

Anne W. Weston.

ALS: Child Papers, Boston Public Library.

1. Psalms 145:9.

---

1 2 7

TO DR. SAMUEL G. HOWE, AND OTHERS, COMMITTEE

BOSTON, Nov. 12, 1855.

GENTLEMEN: — Your letter of October 1st, 1855, inviting me to deliver one of the lectures of the course on slavery, to be given at the Tremont Temple, was not received by me till to-day. I hasten to reply to it, and to give you my reasons for most respectfully declining your courteous invitation.

In the first place, you state that 'a large number of gentlemen [alias men-stealers] from the South will be invited to favor (!) us with the views prevalent in their vicinity'; and I perceive on the list of pledged lecturers, the names of 'Hon. Henry W. Hilliard, of Alabama,' 'Hon. Robert Toombs, of Georgia,' and as probable substitutes, 'Hon. A. P. Butler, of South Carolina,' and 'Dr. William A. Smith, of Virginia.' [1] I understand, moreover, that your invitation was also sent to that lawless ruffian, the leader of the Missouri-Kansas bandits, David R. Atchison — that desperate demagogue and Iscariot traitor to liberty, Stephen Arnold Douglas, of Illinois — that unmitigated blackguard and shameless bully, Henry A. Wise, of Virginia — and that monster in human form, John M. Mason, the infamous framer of the Fugitive Slave Law, also of Virginia. [2] All these stand committed before the world as the most malignant enemies of the anti-slavery cause, the most bitter contemners of the North, (especially of Massachusetts,) and the most ferocious defenders of the accursed slave system to the end of time — as well as actual slaveholders, whose souls are steeped in pollution, whose hands and garments are dripping with the blood of enslaved millions, and who, instead of being politely invited and handsomely paid by you to utter their blasphemies against the God of freedom and the rights of man, deserve to be capitally executed, 'without benefit of clergy,' [3] (if capital punishment be permissible in any case, which I do not believe,) even under the law of Congress which they themselves endorse, making it a piratical act, worthy of death, to enslave any native-born African, by bringing him to this country for that purpose; for the crime consists solely in the act of enslavement, no matter on what pretence. That they are not to lecture is simply owing to their refusal — their consistent refusal, I will add, however uncivil may have been the language used by them, as in the case of Mr. Wise. *You* invited them in good faith, and in the same terms that you invited all the others.

Gentlemen, you are an Anti-Slavery Committee. You profess to regard slavery as 'the sum of all villanies,'[4] and seek its utter overthrow. Pardon me if I express my astonishment, that you should so far forget what is due to your self-respect, your moral consistency, the dignity of the cause you have espoused, and the common sense of mankind, as to extend to some of the most worthless as well as most fiendish supporters of slavery, an offer to give them a liberal remuneration, if they will come to Boston, and do what in them lies to make this pro-slavery community yet more hostile to freedom, and therefore more zealous in the service of the Slave Power.

I took occasion, in my public reply to Gen. Houston last year, to enter the same protest against a similar invitation extended to him; and I sincerely cherished the hope, that we should be spared the repetition of an absurdity so glaring, and an act so offensive.

Gentlemen, I wish to do full justice to your motives. You doubtless reasoned in this wise: — By inviting the most inveterate slaveholders of the South to defend their slave system before a Boston audience, additional interest will be given to the course of lectures — a more wide-spread discussion of the subject will be the consequence — our cause has nothing to fear, but every thing to gain, from the closest scrutiny — it will be returning good for evil — we shall exhibit true magnanimity, and set an example that will put to shame the whole South for their barbarous treatment of the abolitionists.

Gentlemen, it would mortify me to believe that there lives the man who goes beyond me in a profound appreciation of what justly pertains to a noble, fearless and magnanimous course of conduct — to free discussion — to an untrammelled platform. If there be a journal more free, independent and impartial than THE LIBERATOR, I know not of its existence. If there be an organization which has more consistently maintained freedom of speech for all who attend its meetings than the American Anti-Slavery Society, I have yet to learn its name.

But, gentlemen, 'there is but one step from the sublime to the ridiculous.'[5] Magnanimity, generosity, a good spirit, are all commendable virtues; but so are sound discretion, moral propriety, fidelity to principle. It is not required by the spirit of Christianity, it is not in accordance with the eternal fitness of things, to invite men guilty of 'the highest kind of theft' to come from a remote part of the country, and accept our proffered civilities, that they may show us the utility and excellence of robbing millions of our countrymen of their inalienable rights — of turning them into perishable property and articles of merchandize — of forcing them to live in a state of beastly uncleanness, by abolishing the sacred institution of marriage — of perpetrating upon their bodies and spirits all conceivable outrages; and then to remunerate them liberally, out of the anti-slavery treasury, for this inexcusable and horrible act of villany! Why, gentlemen, this is to run charity and good will into the ground. It has no parallel among straight-forward and earnest men. It almost gives an air of caricature to your entire proceedings. It is not freedom of speech, but inconsiderateness; it is not generosity, but improvidence; it is not overcoming evil with good, but placing good and evil in the same category, making them equally deserving of public courtesy, and equally dubious as to which should prevail!

What is particularly surprising is, that you should have selected from among the slaveholders, and defenders of slavery, the most insolent, depraved, and desperate of them all — Atchison, Wise, Douglas, Mason, Toombs and Butler — the last men, even among slaveholders, (for there are grades among felons,) deserving of notice, much less of special consideration. I have already properly described all but the two last; and beg leave simply to remind you, that Toombs has insultingly boasted that he will marshal his slaves around Bunker Hill Monument, and bid Massachusetts to liberate one of them at her peril. Mr. Butler is the incarnation of South Carolina overseeism, and represents the State which imprisons, and sells into interminable slavery, such colored citizens of Massachusetts as venture upon her soil, and which expelled from her limits our venerable and much-respected fellow-citizen, Hon. Samuel Hoar,[6] though clothed with all the official authority of the Commonwealth to seek in a constitutional manner, and by 'due process of law,' to save those victims of Southern perfidy from their horrible doom. If we must allow our politeness to run in that direction, let us at least select the most decent and candid, not the most abandoned and malignant, among the men-stealers of the South, 'to *favor* us with the views prevalent in their vicinity,' on the subject of chattel slavery. With all possible respect for you, gentlemen, individually and collectively, I, for one, shall keep aloof from any such mixture. Not even to find a tempting opportunity to plead for those in bondage will I consent to recognize the propriety of such a procedure. My aim is to stain the character and render infamous the conduct of the slaveholder, throughout the civilized world. I am for his immediate exclusion from the professedly Christian church, and from every honorable position in the State. As long as he is allowed to hold his head up in society — is deemed worthy of public consideration — is permitted to fill offices of trust and emolument — is recognized as a friend of his country, and animated by the spirit of true piety — and, especially, as long as those who claim to be the representatives and advocates of the slave treat him with marked attention — so long will he continue to rob and oppress the victims of his cupidity. He must be made to feel, as does the foreign slave-trader, the overwhelming power of public sentiment — that he is a 'sinner of the first rank,' utterly without excuse, and deserving of universal abhorrence. Is your invitation to him, gentlemen, at all calculated to produce any such feeling?

Gentlemen, an act wholly unnecessary is labor lost. The adage, that 'it is not worth while to carry coals to Newcastle,' though trite, is in this connection both pertinent and instructive. Is the Anti-Slavery cause, even in its mildest phase, so popular in Boston — are the apologists and defenders of Southern slavery so few and odious — that you deem it a meritorious act to import the leading slaveholders of Virginia, Georgia, Missouri, and South Carolina, to sustain their horrible slave system against such overwhelming odds? How much farther advanced, in principle, on this subject, is Boston than Charleston, Richmond, or Savannah? What of the pulpits and churches of this city? What is the animating spirit of the *Daily Advertiser*, the *Courier*, the *Journal*, the *Traveller*, the *Chronicle*, the *Post*, and other newspapers? [7] While, therefore, the pulpit and press, the wealth, respectability, commercial strength, popular sentiment, and religious influence of Boston, are all actively combined to 'crush out' every vestige of anti-slavery feeling and action, is it judicious or wise for those who are the victims of this all-prevailing pro-slavery sentiment, to put their hands into their pockets, and proffer a liberal pecuniary bribe and every civility to induce the human-flesh-mongers, south of Mason and Dixon's line, to add their diabolism to the general corruption among us? To ask is to answer the question.

Gentlemen, what would be thought of the sanity of the American Board of Commissioners,[8] if, instituting a course of lectures for the subversion of idolatry, they should invite some of the most subtle and malignant worshippers of Brahma to come over, and 'favor us with the views prevalent in their vicinity' — offering not only to give them enough to defray their expenses across the Atlantic, but to put a handsome sum into their pockets? All Christendom would resound with mingled cries of derision and shouts of laughter. When it shall be deemed proper to hire burglars, highwaymen, counterfeiters, and pirates, to show that honesty, justice and mercy ought to be treated as fanaticism, madness and treason, then no objection can consistently be raised to securing the services of slaveholders in opposition to the sacred cause of human liberty.

How reads the Declaration of Independence? 'We hold these truths to be SELF-EVIDENT: — that ALL MEN are created EQUAL; that they are endowed by THEIR CREATOR with certain INALIENABLE RIGHTS; that among these are life, LIBERTY, and the pursuit of happiness.' The right of a human being to his own body and soul, therefore, is not a debatable question. It is to be affirmed and maintained, not argued or proved. No slaveholder needs to be enlightened on that point. No man living is more conscious of his perpetual injustice to his victims. The blood-reeking slave code which he has enacted is the confession, if not the full measure, of his criminality. His guilt makes him a coward as well as a ruffian. Whatever may be his spirit or his manners, when his right to hold slaves is unquestioned, the moment that right is denied, it operates like the touch of Ithuriel's spear, which caused the dissembling toad to assume its true shape, that of a devil.[9] He is then transformed into a wolf or tiger. His passions are 'set on fire of hell.' He spurns all barriers, and defies all restraints. He is ready for imprisoning, tarring and feathering, hanging, assassinating, or lynching in any form, the daring Nathan who has accused him of violence and robbery. His resort is to gags, padlocks, scourges, bowie knives, revolvers, and other instruments of torture and death. His trained bloodhounds are the embodiment of his own spirit. It is not light that he needs, but a heart of flesh. He aspires, in the exercise of his tyrannical power over his slaves, to exalt himself 'above all that is called God,' and is filled with Satanic pride. What is the South but one vast graveyard, in which lie buried all noble aspirations, all reverence for human rights, all freedom of speech, all respect for justice? Truly,

> 'The planters of Columbia
>   Are gods beneath the skies!
> They stamp the slave into the grave,
>   They feed on famine's sighs!
> They curse the land, the wind, the sea —
>   Lord! have they conquered thee?
> With a frown looking down,
>   They curse the land and sea: —
> They rival hell, they libel heaven,
>   But have not conquered thee!' [10]

There are many questions, about which men may honestly differ; but the inherent turpitude of slavery is not one of them. The love of liberty is instinctive in the human breast. In the eloquent language of Lord Brougham: —

'There is a law above all enactments of human codes: it is the law written by the finger of God upon the heart of man; and by that law, unchangeable and eternal, while men despise fraud, and loathe rapine, and abhor blood, they shall reject with indignation the wild and guilty fantasy, that man can hold property in man.'

This sentiment is confirmed by a distinguished Virginian, Judge James G. M'Dowell, when he says: —

'You may place the slave where you please — you may dry up to your utmost the fountain of his feelings, the springs of his thoughts — you may close upon his mind every avenue to knowledge, and cloud it over with artificial night — you may yoke him to labor as an ox which liveth only to work, and worketh only to live — you may put him under any process, which, without destroying his value as a slave, will debase and crush him as a rational being — you may do this, and the idea that he was born free will survive it all. It is allied to his hopes of immortality — it is the ethereal part of his nature, which oppression cannot reach — it is a torch lit up in his soul by the hand of Deity, and never meant to be extinguished by the hand of man.' [11]

Slavery, therefore, is a heinous sin, not a debatable question. 'If a man should propose to me,' said DANIEL O'CONNELL on a certain occasion in Exeter Hall, 'a discussion on the propriety of picking pockets, I would turn him out of my study, for fear that he should carry his theory into practice. But he who thinks he can vindicate the possession of one human being by another — the sale of soul and body — the separation of father and mother — the taking of the mother from the infant at her breast, and selling the one to one master, and the other to another, is a man whom *I will not answer with words.* . . . When an American comes into English society, let him be asked, 'Are you one of the thieves, or are you an honest man? If you are an honest man, then you have given liberty to your slaves. If you are among the thieves, the sooner you take the outside of the house, the better.' [12]

I may be told, gentlemen, that, in declining your courteous invitation, I display as intolerant a spirit as Mason, Wise, Atchison and Douglas, and stand rebuked with them by the readiness of Messrs. Toombs and Hilliard to take up the gauntlet flung down to them. My reply is, that the former act entirely consistent with their slaveholding theory; while the latter are clearly conceding it to be a matter of controversy, and therefore one of uncertainty. Would they gravely discuss the question, whether there can be any property in merchandise, houses, ships, or other productions of human industry? And do they not declare that God and nature make property in man as sacred as any other property? Why then allow it to be an open question? 'If the Lord be God, serve him; if Baal, then serve him.' [13]

I may be reminded, that none of the distinguished speakers, who are to appear in defence of freedom, have thought of objecting to the invitation to Southern slaveholders. Perhaps they have not thought at all about it, and may yet regret that they had not done so before committing themselves. 'To their own master, they stand or fall.' [14]

I condemn them not. It is for each one to 'be fully persuaded in his own mind,' [15] and to act accordingly. Far be it from me to dictate the course for others to pursue, under such circumstances: — mine is clear, and I must be true to my convictions, even at the risk of giving offence, or being grossly misunderstood and misrepresented by the enemies of impartial liberty.

Not doubting your earnest desire to promote the cause of universal emancipation — believing you have acted from the best motives, though unwisely — thanking you for your kind overture — and convinced that the most effective lecture I can deliver is to record this frank and honest testimony, I remain, gentlemen, with high consideration,

Yours, for no union with slaveholders,

WM. LLOYD GARRISON.

Dr. Samuel G. Howe, and others, *Committee.*

Printed in *The Liberator*, November 16, 1855.

Dr. Samuel Gridley Howe (1801–1876), Boston-born, graduated from Brown University in 1821 and from the Harvard Medical School in 1824. He participated in the war for Greek independence (1824–1830), returned to the United States in 1827, gathered food and clothing, and distributed these among the Greeks. In 1832, he founded a school for the blind, later called the Perkins Institution, of which he was superintendent until 1876. He married Julia Ward in 1843. He was defeated as a candidate of the "Conscience" Whigs for Congress in 1846; he helped to found the Massachusetts school for idiotic and feeble-minded youth in 1851; and from 1851 to 1853, edited, with his wife, the *Commonwealth.* Although a Free Soiler and Republican politically, he was a moral and financial supporter of John Brown in Kansas and, later, at Harpers Ferry. During the Civil War he was an active member of the Sanitary Commission.

In addition to Samuel G. Howe, whose name headed the list, the members of the committee were Samuel May, Thomas Russell, Nathaniel B. Shurtleff, John M. Clark, Joseph Story, Philo Sanford, James W. Stone.

The committee sent out some of its invitations to speakers as early as the beginning of August, which indicates that Garrison was a late choice. Indeed, on October 5, 1855, *The Liberator* published a letter of invitation dated August 2, that had been sent to Senators Stephen Douglas and A. P. Butler, with the replies of both men, the former refusing to speak, the latter accepting the invitation. Since Garrison refers to the contents of the letter of invitation, its publication here should prove helpful.

"BOSTON, Aug. 2, 1855.

"DEAR SIR: A series of lectures on the subject of slavery was initiated and very successfully conducted here during the past winter, as you may have learned from the papers of the day. The audiences were large and intelligent, and the card enclosed will indicate to you the character of the lecturers.

"During the next season, a large number of gentlemen from the South will be invited to favor us with the views prevalent in their vicinity; thus, in connection with others, presenting, during the course, every shade of opinion on this question. The respectful attention accorded to Gen. Houston last winter, gives assurance that arguments and opinions from that quarter will be carefully heard and duly appreciated.

"You are hereby respectfully invited to deliver one of the lectures of the course on slavery at the Tremont Temple, in this city, on Thursday evening, February 6th, 1856; or, if that time will not suit your engagements, please mention at once what Thursday evening between the middle of November and the middle of March next will best accommodate you.

"The amount paid to each lecturer will be one hundred dollars, he bearing his own expenses. Please favor with an immediate answer, and at your earliest convenience thereafter transmit the particular phase of the subject that you will present.

"Your obedient servants,

> S. G. HOWE,
> SAMUEL MAY,
> THOMAS RUSSELL,
> NATHANIEL B. SHURTLEFF,
> JOHN M. CLARK,
> JOSEPH STORY,
> PHILO SANFORD,
> JAMES W. STONE.

"Hon. Stephen A. Douglas."

On November 9, *The Liberator* published the list of speakers and their dates, as follows:

"LECTURES ON SLAVERY. This course of Lectures will be delivered in the TREMONT TEMPLE, at 7 1-2 o'clock, on THURSDAY EVENINGS, in the order indicated in the following list:

Nov. 22 — Hon. HORACE MANN, of Ohio.
Nov. 29 — JOHN G. WHITTIER, Esq. — *Poem.*
Dec. 6 — Mrs. Harriet Beecher Stowe's Drama,
        Read by Mrs. M. E. WEBB.
Dec. 13 — Hon. JOSEPH M. ROOT, of Ohio.
Dec. 20 — Hon. HENRY J. RAYMOND, of New York.
Dec. 27 — Hon. LEWIS D. CAMPBELL, of Ohio.
Jan. 3 — Hon. HENRY W. HILLIARD, of Ala.
Jan. 24 — Hon. ROBERT TOOMBS, of Geo.
Jan. 31 — Hon. HENRY B. STANTON, of New York.
Feb. 7 — WENDELL PHILLIPS, Esq.
Feb. 14 — Dr. WILLIAM ELDER, of Pa.
Feb. 21 — Hon. JAMES BELL, of N. H.
Mar. 6 — EDWIN P. WHIPPLE — Esq.

PROBABLE SUBSTITUTES.

Hon. A. P. BUTLER, of S. C.
WILLIAM LLOYD GARRISON, Esq.
Dr. WILLIAM A. SMITH, of Va.
Rev. HENRY WARD BEECHER, of N. Y."

On November 16, the list of speakers in *The Liberator* no longer included Garrison's name as a "probable substitute." What is most interesting is that Wendell Phillips accepted the invitation to speak on February 7, 1856, and despite Garrison's letter did not withdraw his name.

1. Henry Washington Hilliard (1808–1892), lawyer, author, and politician, represented Alabama as a Whig in the United States Congress from 1846 to 1851, left the Whigs and became a Know-Nothing in 1854, joined the Democrats in 1857, and supported the Bell-Everett Constitutional Union ticket in 1860. He opposed secession at the Alabama Convention in 1861, but then served in Braxton Bragg's army as a colonel until his resignation at the end of 1862. He made his home in Atlanta, Georgia, after the war, was unsuccessful as a candidate for Congress in 1876, and was minister to Brazil from 1877 to 1881.

Robert Toombs (1810–1885) was United States senator from Georgia from 1853 to 1861 and a leader of secession. During the war, he was variously a congressman, secretary, and brigadier-general.

Andrew Pickens Butler (1796–1857) was United States senator from South

Carolina from 1846 until his death. It was his vituperative attack upon Charles Sumner in the Senate that evoked an appropriate reply from Sumner, which led to the cowardly beating of Sumner by Butler's nephew and congressman from South Carolina, Preston Brooks.

Dr. William Andrew Smith (1802–1870), Methodist Episcopal clergyman and prominent preacher, was president of Randolph-Macon College, at Ashland, Virginia, from 1846 to 1866, where he was also professor of moral and intellectual philosophy. In 1856 there appeared his volume, *Lectures on the Philosophy and Practice of Slavery as Exhibited in the Institution of Domestic Slavery in the United States, with the duties of Masters to Slaves.*

2. David Rice Atchison (1807–1886), of Missouri, United States Senator from 1843 to 1855, was influential in the passage of the Kansas-Nebraska Bill and the repeal of the Missouri Compromise, and played a prominent part in the raids by the Missouri "border ruffians" into Kansas Territory in 1855–56. He later supported the Confederate cause.

Stephen Arnold Douglas (1813–1861), Democrat, was then a United States Senator from Illinois, an office which he held from 1847 to 1861. He advocated the Compromise of 1850, and he reported the Kansas-Nebraska Bill, which initiated the troubles in Kansas.

Henry Alexander Wise (1806–1876) was a Virginia representative in Congress from 1833 to 1844, minister to Brazil from 1844 to 1847, and governor of Virginia from 1856 to 1860. The John Brown raid on Harpers Ferry occurred during his administration. While in Congress, he was the foremost antagonist of John Quincy Adams, in the latter's efforts to repeal the "Gag Law" against antislavery petitions.

James (not "John") Murray Mason (1798–1871) was a United States senator from Virginia from 1847 to 1861 and the author of the Fugitive Slave Law of 1850.

3. In his annual message to the South Carolina legislature in December 1835, Governor George McDuffie had declared that interference by abolitionists with slavery should be punishable by death "without benefit of clergy." (See *Letters*, II, 10.)

4. John Wesley, *Journal*, February 12, 1772.

5. Thomas Paine, "One step above the sublime makes the ridiculous, and one step above the ridiculous makes the sublime again." *Age of Reason*, Part II, note. Napoleon's celebrated comment, "From the sublime to the ridiculous there is but one step," may have been derived from Paine.

6. Samuel Hoar (1778–1856), an eminent Massachusetts lawyer, served in the state Senate from 1825 to 1833, and as a representative in Congress from 1835 to 1837. Originally a Federalist and then a Whig, he helped form the Free Soil party in Massachusetts and in 1848 his name headed the electoral ticket of that party in Massachusetts. He was also a leading figure in the organization of the Republican party in Massachusetts in 1854 and 1855. In 1844, he was sent by the Massachusetts legislature to South Carolina to test the constitutionality of that state's acts which authorized the imprisonment of all free colored persons who entered the state. Many colored seamen of Massachusetts, on vessels entering South Carolina ports, had been seized, jailed, kept in jail until their vessel sailed, and even sold into slavery for not paying their jail fees. Hoar's arrival in Charleston caused great excitement. On December 5, he was ordered expelled from Charleston, and left that day under threat of violence from a mob that had surrounded his hotel. (Moorfield Storey and Edward W. Emerson, *Ebenezer Rockwood Hoar, A Memoir*, Boston and New York, 1911, pp. 4–5.)

7. The Boston *Courier* had been founded in 1824 by Joseph T. Buckingham, who edited it until 1848. It reflected the views of the Whig party. (*Letters*, II, 221.)

The Boston *Journal*, a daily Whig newspaper, was founded in 1833 as the *Mercantile Journal*. John S. Sleeper was its editor from its beginning until 1854, and was succeeded by Stephen N. Stockwell. The *Journal* was one of the most prosperous newspapers in Boston. (Frank Luther Mott, *American Journalism*, 3d. ed., New York, 1971, p. 218.)

The Boston *Traveller* was first established in January 1825 as the *American Traveller* with Royal L. Porter as editor. In 1845, the Boston *Evening Traveller*, a daily newspaper, superseded the *American Traveller*, which became the semi-weekly issue of the new paper. (Frederic Hudson, *Journalism in the United States*, New York and Evanston, 1969, pp. 382–384.)

The Boston *Daily Chronicle* was published from 1852 to 1857, and then merged with the Boston *Traveller*. (*Union List of Newspapers*.)

The Boston *Morning Post* was founded in 1831 by Charles G. Greene, who was its editor for almost fifty years. "It was a strong Democratic paper, and it soon became the undisputed leader of its party's press in Massachusetts, if not throughout all of New England." (Mott, *American Journalism*, pp. 217–218.)

8. American Board of Commissioners for Foreign Missions, founded in 1810, "the oldest missionary society in the United States."

9. See Milton, *Paradise Lost*, Book IV, line 810.

10. Unidentified.

11. James McDowell (1796–1851) was a member of the Virginia legislature which, in 1832, debated the abolition of slavery in that state. He then advocated the gradual abolition of slavery. He was governor of Virginia from 1842 to 1846 and was elected to Congress as a Democrat in 1846, serving until 1851. In Congress, while supporting state's rights, he strongly opposed slavery "and is said to have done more to impress upon the south the superior economy as well as philanthropy of abolition than any other from Jefferson till his own day" (*BDAC*). The selection quoted by Garrison is from McDowell's speech in the House of Delegates of Virginia, delivered on January 21, 1832. (See Joseph Clarke Robert, *The Road From Monticello: A Study of the Virginia Slavery Debate of 1832*, Durham, N.C., 1941, p. 103.)

12. From Daniel O'Connell, "Slavery Not a Debatable Question," an address later printed in *Daniel O'Connell Upon American Slavery* (New York, published by the American Anti-Slavery Society, 1860), p. 47.

13. I Kings 18:21.

14. Romans 14:4.

15. Romans 14:5.

128

TO MARIA W. CHAPMAN

Boston, Nov. 24, 1855.

My dear Mrs. Chapman:

Now that the joyful event is made certain, I avail myself of the earliest opportunity to congratulate you upon your safe arrival home, after so long an absence from your native land.[1] The fact, that you are really with us again, only needs to be generally known, to excite the liveliest emotions of pleasure in ten thousand hearts, bound up with yours in the most vital and far-reaching movement of the age, and cherishing for you the warmest regard and the highest appreciation, as one of the earliest, most clear-sighted, uncompromising, and efficient advocates of the imbruted slave. The delight I feel in the anticipation of seeing you, face to face, in due season, is inexpressible: it will be almost like a resurrection from the dead, or a return from a higher plane of spiritual existence, so far as your bodily presence is concerned. From a particular stand-point, it seems a whole age since you left us. Seven years is, indeed, a long period to have been absent, considering the brevity of life; but, in the activity and tumult of a desperate campaign, where no time is left for leisure, meditation or retirement, they seem reduced to a single point. How extraordinary and multitudinous have been the events, directly connected with the anti-slavery cause, within this term! What changes in sects, parties, and whole sections of country, on the right side! What rapid strides, startling achievements, and boundless aims, on the part of the Slave Power! In what a close death-grapple are Liberty and Slavery found!

Though absent in body, we know you have been with us unceasingly in spirit since you left us; that nothing which occurred, affecting either the integrity or success of our glorious cause, has escaped your observation; that you have not only improved, but created opportunities to aid us, on British and on French soil, by speech, testimony, personal influence, the press, the preparation of circulars and tracts, a generous pecuniary co-operation, multitudinous letters, and well-directed blows, struck at the right time, and with irresistible force. For all these efforts and sacrifices, we are immensely indebted to you; to say nothing of antecedent years of unequalled industry and labor at home, under the most trying circumstances, and in the midst of all-abounding obloquy, proscription and danger. I will not put up the superfluous petition, "May the blessings of those who are ready to perish rest upon your head!" — because they do now rest upon it. I will not add, "God bless you!" — as it might seem to imply that he had been "slack concerning his promises," and was growing forgetful. "Blessed *are*," not *shall* be, "the merciful. Blessed *are* they who are persecuted for righteousness' sake" — &c. &c. The reward is ever in the performance of the deed.

Welcome home again — a thousand times welcome! Welcome to whatever of unpopularity yet attaches to inflexible and incorruptible abolitionism! Welcome to a still further participation in a cause, which, notwithstanding its grand advances, has yet to contend with Church and State, and all that is rich, strong and powerful in the land! You have a place in our heart of hearts: we already feel the magnetism of your spirit, and the quickening influence of your presence.

How deeply do I regret that you did not arrive in season to be at the twentieth anniversary of the memorable twenty-first of October, 1835, held on the very spot where the mob of "gentlemen of property and standing" achieved such a ruinous victory! It was a most thrilling occasion, as you may readily suppose, and full of heart-stirring reminiscences.

Three weeks ago, we were expecting the speedy and inevitable departure to the Spirit Land of our well-tried and noble friend, Francis Jackson — his physician having oracularly pronounced his disease incurable, warranting no hope of his continuance beyond a fortnight. Now we are rejoicing that, almost as by superhuman power, he is convalescent, and looking and feeling much better than he has done for a year past! How happy he will be to take you by the hand, and you not less so to reciprocate congratulations!

It must have deeply saddened your heart to find that your beloved father was no longer of earth; for, though "no strange thing has happened" to you, seeing that all are mortal, and the most endearing ties of life are constantly sundered — and though death is but the transition to a superior state of existence — still, "some natural tears" are pardonable, and it is hard, very hard, to part with those so near and dear. You have my warmest sympathies, as well as every other member of the family, in view of this bereavement.

Hoping to see you at a day not distant, and wishing to be kindly remembered to you mother, sisters and brother, I remain

Your attached friend,

Wm. Lloyd Garrison.

Mrs. Maria W. Chapman.

P.S. Helen desires me to unite her congratulations with mine on your safe arrival. We shall be most happy to see you, at any time, at our residence, 14 Dix Place, Washington Street, between Elliot and Hollis Streets.

Please say to Anne [W. Weston], that she shall certainly have my article for the Liberty Bell [2] in the course of this coming week. I trust you will find time to write something also.

Transcript: Garrison Papers, Boston Public Library. Most of this letter is included in *Life*, III, 431–433.

1. Mrs. Chapman arrived in Boston on Saturday, November 24, 1855, in the steamer *Canada* from Liverpool, England, "after a residence of more than seven years at Paris." "Though, in consequence of her long absence from the country, she has not been so prominently before the public eye in America as formerly, her labors have been none the less assiduous and serviceable, securing many co-workers and generous contributions to our cause in England, France, Germany, and other parts of Europe." (*The Liberator*, November 30, 1855.)

2. Garrison's article, dated "Boston, 1855," was entitled "The 'Infidelity' of Abolitionism," and appeared in the *Liberty Bell* for 1856, pp. 139–158.

1 2 9

TO HARRIET MARTINEAU

Boston, Dec. 4, 1855.

My dear Miss Martineau:

It is impossible for me to convey to you the pleasure I feel, in common with all our little anti-slavery band, at the safe arrival, in this city, of our beloved Mrs. Chapman, after an absence of more than seven years. Her voyage was a rough one homeward; but she appears quite as young and elastic as she did before she left us. Time really seems to have made no impression upon her, and such is the verdict of all who have seen her. As I presume she has already written to you, I need not give you any particulars of the death and burial of her father, a short time before she reached Boston. My appreciation of her genius, intuition, far-sightedness, moral heroism, and uncompromising philanthropy, as well as of her rare literary taste and culture, is equalled only by my profound regard for your own exalted intellectual and moral endowments, your life and history.

I hasten to thank you, with a heart overflowing with sympathy and gratitude, for the admirable little hymn, by W. J. Fox,[1] which you were so kind as voluntarily to transcribe for me, though so ill; which contains a volume in each verse; which I had never seen before; and which I shall preserve, for your sake, with all possible care, among my choicest treasures.

My indebtedness to you is of long-standing, and very great. Be assured, I have never for one moment forgotten, though, alas! I shall never be able to repay it. It would press heavily upon my spirit, did I not believe that "it is more blessed to give than to receive," — though I, too, would like the luxury of giving in return, if I had any thing better than my poor thanks to offer you. But I am not in a situation to be of any real service to you. No word or act of mine is needed on your part. But, twenty years ago, caricatured, reviled, hated and ostracised as I was universally, because I would not be dumb in regard to the all-pervading crime and curse of chattel slavery, words of sympathy and approval were to me as cold water to the thirsty spirit in a land of drought. Those you gave me at that time while here, with equal courage and generosity, at the risk of social outlawry, popular contempt and indignation, and pecuniary loss, all which you speedily realized. It was not for my sake as an obscure individual, but for Humanity's sake as represented in the sacred cause which I was then humbly striving to advocate, that you thus sublimely took up the cross, "despising the shame,"[2] and have ever since been the unfaltering championess of justice, humanity and freedom, on a world-wide scale.

I remember, with great delight, my visit to you at Tynemouth in 1840, and deeply regretted your absence from the country when I was last in England, in 1846. It does not seem probable that we shall ever again meet on earth; but, whatever the future may have in reserve for us, here or hereafter in another sphere, "the past at last is secure," and as long as memory shall last, it will be equally pleasant and strengthening to review the struggles through which we have passed, and the victories we have won.

I need not say how much I regret to hear that you are probably near the termination of your earthly sojourn; though, after so laborious and self-sacrificing a life, you are entitled to a respite. But there are so few to stand by the cause of suffering humanity, in an unselfish and brave spirit, that none can be spared without a pang.

"The flesh *will* quiver when the pincers tear." [3]

Mrs. Chapman says you are not only resigned and patient, but accept joyfully the destiny which awaits you. This is most consolatory. I know what you have dared to brave, what you have suffered, by the frank avowal of what a hireling priesthood and a corrupt church have branded as atheistical sentiments. Though my belief in immortality is without a peradventure, I desire to tell you that your skepticism, or lack of evidence, on that point, has never altered my confidence in the goodness of your heart, and the nobleness of your character, a hair's breadth, since it was publicly avowed by you. I respect and admire conscientious dissent and honest doubt, to any extent, in any direction — it is so rare in this traditional, dissembling, cowardly world of ours! Conformity is never a virtue, *per se*. Heresy is the only thing that will redeem mankind. You remember the fine lines of James Russell Lowell: — [4]

> "My soul is not a palace of the past,
> Where outworn creeds, like Rome's grey senate, quake,
> Hearing afar the Vandal's trumpet hoarse,
> That shakes old systems with a thunder-fit.
> The time is ripe, and rotten ripe, for change:
> Then let it come! I have no dread of what
> Is called for by the instinct of mankind;
> Nor think I that God's world will fall apart,
> Because we tear a parchment more or less.
> Truth is eternal, but her effluence,
> With endless change, is fitted to the hour;
> Her mirror is turned forward to reflect
> The promise of the future, not the past."

I have no doubt of your being an angel, on seeing "the last of earth";

but, whether this be "the be-all and the end-all here," [5] or whether we ascend to a higher and nobler plane of existence when we yield up our mortal breath, I am sure you have acted well *your* part, and so are prepared for whatever is to come. My hope is, that your valuable life will be prolonged very much beyond your own expectations, or those who watch over you; and to this end, let me entreat you not to continue to overwork that too active brain, which is so disproportionate to your bodily powers.

Neither room nor time will allow me to give you any intelligence on the subject of slavery. Beyond a doubt, the cause of freedom is advancing; but a desperate and bloody struggle is to come, and it is not far off.

Accept my dear wife's blessing, and my own.

Yours, "world without end,"

Wm. Lloyd Garrison.

Harriet Martineau.

ALS: Birmingham Library, Birmingham, England.

Harriet Martineau (1802–1876), prominent British author, who had been in the United States from 1834 to 1836, was one of Garrison's staunchest defenders in England, as is to be seen in her volume, *The Martyr Age in America* (London, 1838). Although deaf and in feeble health most of her life, her health deteriorated even further in 1854. Suffering from irregular action of her heart and difficulty in breathing, as well as various other symptoms, she was led to believe by her physician early in 1855 that her death was imminent because of a diseased heart. For twenty years she was an invalid, remaining in her room but writing as much as ever. (Vera Wheatley, *The Life and Work of Harriet Martineau*, Fair Lawn, New Jersey, 1957, pp. 347–358; *Letters*, II, 16.)

1. Garrison printed the piece, by the Reverend W. J. Fox, entitled "Hymn," in *The Liberator*, December 7, 1855. The first of its four stanzas reads as follows:

> A little child in bulrush ark
> 　　Came floating on the Nile's broad water: —
> The child made Egypt's glory dark,
> 　　And freed his tribe from bonds and slaughter.

The Reverend William Johnson Fox (1786–1864), English Unitarian minister, author, and leader of English rationalism, was a political activist on behalf of Free Trade and the Anti-Corn Law League. He was Member of Parliament for Oldham from 1847 to 1863.

2. Hebrews 12:2.

3. Edward Young (1683–1765), English poet, *The Revenge*, Act V.

4. James Russell Lowell, "A Glance Behind the Curtain," in *Poems* (Boston, 1853, 2 vols.), I, 171–172.

5. Shakespeare, *Macbeth*, I, vii, 5.

1 3 0

TO SAMUEL AARON

Boston, Dec. 7, 1855.

Dear Sir:

Yours of the 4th is just received. It will afford me great pleasure to deliver one of the course of Anti-Slavery lectures referred to in your letter, at your convenience after the middle of January.

Mr. Phillips is now in the State of Maine, but will return to-morrow. I feel very sure that his engagements are such that he will not be able to lecture for you next week, or for some time to come. But he will answer for himself as soon as he returns.

Theodore Parker says he can lecture in Norristown on Tuesday evening, March 25th; but his engagements are such that he cannot do so at an earlier period. He, too, will write to you without delay.

I am to be in Philadelphia, next week, to attend the annual meeting of the Penn. A. S. Society. It it should prove compatible with your arrangements, I would give the desired lecture from me, either on Thursday or Friday evening, to suit your convenience. In that case, so much additional travel would be saved, and I would deduct fifteen dollars from the $40 proffered in your letter. If this arrangement cannot be made, then I will endeavor to be with you in January.

I thank you for your approval of my letter to the Lecturing Committee in this city.[1] That letter will do more good than any lecture I could have delivered here.

Truly yours,

Wm. Lloyd Garrison.

Rev. Saml. Aaron.

ALS: Arthur G. Mitten Collection of the Indiana Historical Society Library.

The Reverend Samuel Aaron (b. New Britain, Bucks County, Pennsylvania, 1800; d. Mount Holly, New Jersey, April 11, 1865), educator and Baptist minister, was ordained and became pastor of a church in New Britain, Pennsylvania, in 1829. He "took charge" of the Burlington, New Jersey, high school, in 1833, serving also as pastor of a Baptist church in that city. In 1841, he accepted a pastorate in a church in Norristown, Pennsylvania, where he remained three years. Thereafter, he founded and directed the Treemount seminary near Norristown, which became known "for the thoroughness of its training and discipline." He left the institution in 1857, as a result of financial difficulties, and accepted the headmastership of the Mt. Holly, New Jersey, institute, where he remained for the rest of his life. He was a temperance advocate and an early supporter of the anti-slavery movement.

1. *The Liberator*, December 14, 1855, carried the following item:

"That most eloquent and fearless advocate of the slave, Rev. Samuel Aaron, of Norristown, (Pa.) writes to Mr. Garrison as follows: — 'For myself, I am gratified by your truthful letter to the Boston Committee, in regard to their invited Southern lecturers. There is neither prudence, dignity nor justice, in sticking such black spots among the stars of light.'"

VI THE ATTACK UPON SUMNER AND THE CANDIDACY OF FRÉMONT: 1856

THE YEAR WITNESSED an exacerbation of feeling between North and South. In Kansas, southern guerrilla bands spread death and destruction, including the burning of the Free-State city of Lawrence, until they were met with the John Brown reprisal, against "a nest of harborers of Border Ruffianism." The executions, numbering five, were carried out on May 25, 1856, at Pottawatomie, Kansas. This was followed at Black Jack Creek, on June 2, by "the first regular battle fought between free-State and pro-slavery men in Kansas" (*Life*, III, 436).

The warfare in Kansas, combined with the violent and cowardly attack by Representative Preston S. Brooks of South Carolina upon Senator Charles Sumner of Massachusetts, who was attacked from behind and beaten into insensibility as he sat at his desk, convinced many northerners that southern pro-slavery aggressiveness had to be stopped, peacefully if possible but through forceful resistance if necessary. One result was an emphasis upon arming the Free-State settlers in Kansas. Another was an increase in support for the Republican party and its standard bearer, John Charles Frémont, whose platform was one of opposition to the extension of slavery. Garrison, who believed Frémont and the Republican party to be superior to the Democratic and Whig parties and their candidates, nevertheless believed it his duty to continue to urge the abolition of slavery in the South, and disunion as the best means toward that end.

131

TO GRACEANNA LEWIS

Boston, Jan. 4, 1856.

Dear Friend:

I have received two letters from you, inquiring whether I have received "a letter of invitation from the Secretary of a Committee on Lectures for the Borough of Phœnixville, Chester Co., Pa." *No such letter has ever come to hand.* I delayed answering your first inquiry, thinking the letter referred to by you would reach me in the course of a few days.

You further inquire, whether I could lecture in that place "sometime during the present winter," or early in March. It would gratify me to be able to do so; but the distance is so great, and the expense of travelling so considerable, that I could not feel warranted in undertaking such a journey merely to give a single lecture.

Yours, to liberate the enslaved,

Wm. Lloyd Garrison.

Grace Anna Lewis.

ALS: Friends Historical Library, Swarthmore College.

Graceanna Lewis (b. near Kimberton, Chester County, Pennsylvania, August 3, 1821; fl. 1907), an eminent reformer and naturalist, was the daughter of John and Esther Fussell Lewis, who were early abolitionists; she was an enthusiastic abolitionist, supporter of woman's rights and a temperance worker. As a naturalist and an artist of note, she wrote on the relationship of birds to the animal kingdom. She also wrote *Microscopic Studies, Water Color Painting of Wild Flowers,* and *Studies in Forestry* and published a number of important charts. Her organizational affiliations included the Academy of Natural Sciences, Rochester Academy of Science, American Philosophical Society, Women's Anthropological Society, and the Delaware County Institute of Science. With her two sisters, Mariann and Elizabeth, she made the Lewis house near Kimberton an important center of the Underground Railway. She later moved to Media, Pennsylvania. (Gertrude Bosler Biddle and Sarah Dickinson Lowrie, *Notable Women of Pennsylvania,* Philadelphia, 1942, pp. 161–162.)

[January 10, 1856.

The letter of this date, which Garrison dated incorrectly, and the actual date of which is February 10, has been placed in its correct chronological order.]

1 3 2

TO SAMUEL J. MAY

Boston, Jan. 27, 1856.

My Dear Friend:

On Saturday, Feb. 9th, I shall leave this city for Albany, where I shall tarry till Monday, when I shall take the cars for Rochester, passing through Syracuse without stopping. On Tuesday evening, Feb. 12th, I shall lecture in Rochester; and in Buffalo on the next evening, 13th. This will complete my engagements.

When you were here, you very kindly expressed your readiness to try to procure me a hearing in some other places along the route. But I am reluctant to give you any trouble of this kind — you, who are so constantly overworked to subserve the interests of our common humanity. If you think a lecture from me on slavery, in Syracuse, (say on Thursday evening, Feb. 14th,) would not be "carrying coals to Newcastle," and would be likely to cover the expenses of the hall, advertising, &c., I will deliver one with much pleasure. Then, if an arrangement could be made for me to speak at Utica on Friday evening, Feb. 15th, I would proceed thither. Probably, in no place would *Saturday* evening be a good one to secure an audience. On Sunday and Monday evenings, I could also speak, if on the line of the Railroad. What would be my chance on the last named evening at Schenectady?

You spoke of my going to Skaneateles. It would give me much gratification to do so, on account of friend J. C. Fuller's [1] family; but, as it [is] off from the railway track several miles, (I know not how many) and as the travelling will be very uncertain, I am rather afraid to run the risk. However, I leave every thing in your own hands, to the extent of the time I have named; and therefore "do with me as seemeth thee good." [2]

Perhaps, should I not hear from you before that time, that either you, or some friend in your stead, will meet me at the depot in Syracuse, on the arrival of the morning train from Albany, on Monday, Feb. 11th, so as to apprise me of the nature of the programme you may have made.

Let it be understood that I wish to burden no one pecuniarily, and therefore make no conditions beyond having my travelling expenses met. Of course, I shall not object to some compensation, should the attendance warrant it.

We have just closed the annual meeting of our State Society,[3] but, in consequence of the severity of the weather, and our hall being located so far up on the Neck as Dover Street, the attendance was not so numerous as on some other occasions. But the discussions were animated, interesting and instructive. We were unanimous in the opinion, that Disunionism must be pressed with increasing persistency and boldness.

I regret to see that, in the great fire which recently destroyed your noble Wieting Hall,[4] John [5] was among the number burnt out, but I trust he was pretty fully insured.

We are all in the enjoyment of health under our roof, and trust it is well with you all at home.

To-morrow, I go to Bangor, and shall probably be absent till Friday. Helen sends her love to you and yours. Mine is included, of course.

Ever yours,

　　　　　　　　　　　　　　　　　　Wm. Lloyd Garrison.

S. J. May.

ALS: Garrison Papers, Boston Public Library.

1. James Cannings Fuller (1793–1847), an English Quaker, settled in Skaneateles, New York, in 1834. He was an early participant in antislavery and other reform movements. *The Liberator*, in an obituary notice, December 10, 1847, wrote that "His character was a rare union of many of the traits which ennobled the early Friends. Indomitable enthusiasm wedded to good practical sense; unfaltering self-reliance; fidelity to his own convictions; frankness of speech; plain, manly understanding; great quickness of apprehension, and a directness of purpose hard to baffle or deceive. . . . His heart had room for all the movements, which seek to relieve and elevate mankind, and to lessen the evils or redress the wrongs of society. . . ." (See *Life*, III, 71; *Letters*, III, 47.) In the summer of 1855, according to the New York State Census of that year, Fuller's wife, Lydia, aged seventy, was living in the homestead, with her daughter, Hannah Fuller, twenty-six, and granddaughters, Lydia M., eight, and Laura E., five, and three servants. The granddaughters were the daughters of Dr. James Fuller of Syracuse, New York, whose wife, Mary, had died in 1855. The children had been living with their grandmother for the past five months. (Letter, dated September 26, 1972, from Richard N. Wright, president, Onondaga Historical Association, Syracuse, New York.)

2. Judges 10:15; II Samuel 15:26.

3. The Twenty-Third Annual Meeting of the Massachusetts Anti-Slavery Society was held at Williams Hall, at the corner of Dover and Washington Streets, on Thursday and Friday, January 24 and 25. (*The Liberator*, January 25, 1856.)

4. Dr. John M. Wieting of Syracuse built Wieting Block and Wieting Hall, within the block, in 1849–1850. The entire block burned to the ground twice, the first time, on January 5, 1856, in subzero temperature. By December 1856, Dr. Wieting rebuilt the block, which burned down again in July 1881. For many years the hall was a famous meeting place for political and social conventions, lectures, concerts and gala affairs of all kinds. (Dwight H. Bruce, ed., *Memorial History of Syracuse, New York*, Syracuse, 1891, pp. 171, 183, 689–690.)

5. May's son, John Edward.

133

TO HELEN E. GARRISON

Albany, Sunday morning, [Feb.] 10. [1856.] [1]

Dear Wife:

You will wish to learn what was my luck in getting to this place yesterday. Well, I succeeded, and I failed — in this wise.

Leaving our depot in Boston at half past 8 o'clock, I found our friend [Charles F.] Hovey in the car, on his way to Framingham, and told him whither I was journeying. Anxious to know what were the probabilities in the case, we consulted the conductor, who said confidently that the train would arrive seasonably at Albany. As the train was due at Albany at 5 o'clock, and the meeting was not to be held till half past 7 o'clock, (a margin for delay of two hours and a half,) I felt that all was safe; especially as the track appeared to be entirely unobstructed. We arrived at Springfield in very good time; but, alas and alack! we had to wait there one whole hour for the down train. Still, I was consoled to think there was an hour and a half left of leeway, in regard to the other half of the distance, and so possessed my soul in patience. At Pittsfield, we were detained half an hour! Still an hour extra left. At the State Line, we were detained an hour more — the down train getting off the track, and therefore being out of time. The remainder of the journey was slowly performed; and, "to make the story short," it was precisely 8 o'clock when I reached the door of our esteemed friend Lydia Mott. She had gone to the meeting, which I had given up in despair. — Immediately, my colored friend William H. Topp [2] came in, and said he was just going up to dismiss the meeting, and asked me to go with him, to let them see that I had actually arrived; but I was cold and exhausted, and begged him to excuse me. He did so, and I sat down, and put on my slippers, taking the matter as settled; but, in the course of fifteen minutes, he was on hand with a sleigh, and said the audience (a large one) filled the Representative Hall, and would not take no for an answer. So, I hurried on my shoes, and hurried to the meeting without any refreshment, and was warmly welcomed on my appearance. It was then half past 8 o'clock. I spoke for an hour, with no sign of uneasiness, and the most perfect attention. I spoke chiefly on the popular religion and the Colonization Society, but not at all to my satisfaction; for every thing was in a whirl with me. But the kindness and patience of the audience were wonderful.

To-night, Sunday, I am to lecture in a fine hall — the weather is pleasant — and I hope we shall have a good audience.

In the morning, I shall leave for Syracuse and Rochester.
More I cannot add, except that I am
Ever your loving husband,

Wm. Lloyd Garrison.

H.E.G.

ALS: Garrison Papers, Boston Public Library.

1. Garrison, absentmindedly and erroneously, dated the letter "Jan. 10." and omitted the year. A later hand inserted the correct month, February, as well as the year.

2. William H. Topp (d. Albany, New York, December 11, 1857, aged forty-five), a black abolitionist and tailor, with whom Garrison often dined while in Albany, was an officer of the Philomathian Society of Albany (a black self-improvement society) and an active leader of his people in Albany and New York State (Quarles, *Black Abolitionists*, pp. 21, 104, 172, 211, 219.) A letter from Aaron M. Powell to Garrison, dated "New York, Dec. 14, 1857" (*The Liberator*, December 18, 1857) reported Topp's death and commented: "He was a devoted philanthropist, a fond husband and parent, a beloved friend, a truly good and noble man. Few there are whose lives have been characterized by a more steadfast devotion to the interests of humanity, — especially to the well-being of the outraged American bondmen, and the nominally free, but persecuted and proscribed colored people of this country. . . . I mourn his loss from our immediate circle, as a dearly beloved personal friend."

In its issue of January 8, 1858, *The Liberator* reprinted an obituary notice from the New York *Christian Inquirer* which threw further light upon Topp's character and reputation. After noting that he had died of consumption, it quoted the Albany *Evening Journal*'s comment that " 'by his industry, enterprise, taste, intelligence and manly deportment, he had acquired a handsome property, and the confidence and friendship of all who knew him.' "

134

TO HELEN E. GARRISON

Rochester, Feb. 12, 1856.
Tuesday Morning.

Dear Wife:

I wrote you a few lines, on Sunday, at Albany, which I suppose will reach you this forenoon. On Sunday morning, I went to hear the Rev. Mr. Mayo,[1] a Universalist minister, preach, in company with Lydia Mott, and a Mrs. Jaques,[2] a friend of hers, residing in a neighboring village. The discourse was an excellent one, breathing an elevated and reformatory spirit throughout. Mr. Mayo read the notice of my evening lecture, and Lydia thinks very highly of him.

In the afternoon, we all went and took tea with William H. Topp and family, and had a very cordial welcome. He is one of the most estimable and gentlemanly men one can meet with in a long journey, and is highly respected in Albany, in spite of the general prejudice against color. He has several interesting children, and they have a good mother. He was formerly very strongly attached to Douglass, but no longer gives him his confidence and regard as he once did.

On Sunday evening, I lectured for two hours to a pretty large and thoroughly attentive audience in Van Vechten's hall, in State Street; and though I tore down the star-spangled banner, and repudiated the Constitution as a blood-stained instrument, and put the Union beneath my feet, and criminated almost every religious and political party in the land, I was frequently applauded, ("Sabbath evening" though it was,) and not a single note of disapprobation was heard.

Yesterday morning, (Monday,) at 7¼ o'clock, I left Albany for Rochester, and arrived here at 5, P.M. At Syracuse, dear S. J. May met me at the depot, and treated me to a dish of excellent oysters in the refreshment room — telling me what arrangements he had made for me, and informing me that they were all well at home. The recent fires in Syracuse have seriously embarrassed it, and the lecturing season has not been a prosperous one. Douglass lectured there a few evenings since, and he always succeeds in securing an audience. Mr. May told me that his congregation had recently made him the generous donation of five hundred dollars. I told him I wished it had been ten times that amount. I am to return to Syracuse to-morrow, and in the evening go with him to a large social party. My lecturing programme is as follows: — This evening, in Rochester; Thursday evening, in Syracuse; Friday evening, in Buffalo; Saturday evening, in Skaneateles; Sunday evening, in Auburn; Monday evening, in Troy; Tuesday evening, (perhaps,) in Springfield; and Wednesday evening, 20th inst., I hope to find myself safely at home.[3]

Last night the wind was high, and early this morning it looked very dismal out of doors, the snow falling and blowing in all directions, and threatening to put an extinguisher upon my evening meeting. The sun is now showing us his countenance occasionally, but the wind continues high and blustering, making it one of the most uncomfortable days to be about. In addition to this drawback, there is to be a general meeting of the citizens this evening, with reference to their city election and some municipal reforms. So I am expecting a slim attendance, and, consequently, very limited receipts at the door to meet the expenses.

I am very well, except a little cold in the head. I hope my voice will not fail me, or become hoarse before I get through; for it is very embarrassing to attempt to speak under such circumstances. But I am talking incessantly, as you may readily suppose, and shall be fortunate if I do not break down.

I have seen but one Rochester paper this morning, and find in it the following reference to my lecture: — "Wm. Lloyd Garrison lectures this evening. He is always worth hearing. The ladies intend to be on hand, in battalions, and, of course, the gents will be with them." To which I will add — "wind and weather permitting."

I am stopping with the Anthonys,[4] and expected to find Susan at home; but she has been absent three weeks, and will not reach here 'till to-day at 1 o'clock. I have not yet seen Isaac or Amy Post,[5] but shall take tea with them this afternoon.

My love to the dear boys and to Fanny, and regards to Eliza. If Lydia is with you, give her my warmest remembrances.

Lovingly yours,

Wm. Lloyd Garrison.

ALS: Garrison Papers, Boston Public Library.

1. Amory Dwight Mayo (b. Warwick, Massachusetts, January 31, 1823; d. Washington, D.C., April 8, 1907), clergyman and educator, was ordained in the ministry of the Universalist church in 1846 and served the Independent Christian Society of Gloucester, Massachusetts, until 1854. He served in Cleveland from 1854 to 1856, in Albany from 1856 to 1863, in Cincinnati from 1863 to 1872, and in Springfield, Massachusetts, from 1872 to 1880. He left the ministry in the latter year, devoting the next two decades to the advancement of public education in the South for white and black. He wrote many works on theology, education, and the social and political issues of the day.

2. Unidentified.

3. On his return to Boston, Garrison summarized some of his difficulties on this trip in *The Liberator*, February 29, 1856: "Our lecturing excursion to western New York, recently, was attended with some drawbacks not put down in our programme. The weather proved to be freezing cold and stormy throughout, the mercury ranging at zero, and frequently far below it, and the snow obstructing all railroad travelling for several days; in consequence of which, we had to recall meetings appointed for us at Troy, Syracuse, Skaneateles, and other places. We lectured twice in Albany to large audiences — once in the Representatives' Chamber, and once in Van Vechten's hall. Also at Rochester, (on a most inclement evening,) Buffalo and Auburn. Everywhere our reception was truly gratifying. . . ."

4. Daniel and Lucy Read Anthony, the parents of Susan B. Anthony. Daniel Anthony (d. Rochester, New York, November 25, 1862, aged sixty-nine) was raised as a Quaker, but left that denomination in his adult years. He was active in temperance as early as 1827, when he organized a Temperance Society in Washington County, New York. He was a devoted antislavery man and a friend of the Negro, and interested in the woman's rights movement. (Obituary, *The Liberator*, December 5, 1862.) Lucy Read Anthony died in 1880 at the age of eighty-six. (*Biographical Record of the City of Rochester, Monroe County, N.Y.*, New York and Chicago, 1902, p. 106.)

5. Isaac Post (1798–1872), abolitionist and spiritualist, lived in Rochester from 1836 until his death. He was originally a farmer, but then entered the drug business, in which he remained for thirty years. A devoted abolitionist, he was a warm friend and adherent of Garrison. A member of the Hicksite branch of the Quakers, he left that body in 1845 because he felt that his membership therein interfered with his abolitionist efforts. His home served as a way-station on the Underground Railroad. He was converted to spiritualism by the Fox sisters in 1848. In 1852, he published *Voices from the Spirit World, being Communications from Many Spirits, by the hand of Isaac Post, Medium.*

Amy Kirby Post was Isaac's second wife, whom he married in 1828. She shared his enthusiasms for antislavery, temperance, woman's rights, and spiritualism. She died on January 20, 1889, at the age of eighty-seven. (*Landmarks of Monroe County, New York*, Boston, 1895, p. 154.)

1 3 5

TO MARIA W. CHAPMAN

14 Dix Place, March 11. [1856?]

Dear Mrs. Chapman:

On leaving you this afternoon, wife understood you to say that you had not been able to obtain any Shaker apple-sauce. We found some at the store of Mr. Meriam,[1] a reliable man, who deals directly with the Shakers, and therefore sells the genuine article. We send you a specimen of it, and hope it will prove acceptable. Please also accept, for dear Mary,[2] a little fresh peach, which we have just taken from a sealed can. May all the good angels be with her to strengthen and raise her up!

Ever truly yours,

Wm. Lloyd Garrison.

ALS: Villard Papers, Harvard College Library.

Since Maria W. Chapman returned from Europe in November 1855, after an absence of several years, during which time the Garrisons moved to 14 Dix Place, this letter could not have been written earlier than 1856. Mrs. Chapman's apparent inability to obtain Shaker applesauce suggests her lack of familiarity with the stores of Boston resulting from her stay abroad and slightly reinforces 1856 as the probable date, but does not preclude a later date in the 1850's or even the early 1860's.

1. Either Jonas Meriam (b. Boston, March 10, 1805; d. February 23, 1866), whose grocery store was at 95 Leverett Street, Boston, and who lived in Billerica, Massachusetts; or Silas Parkhurst Meriam (b. December 31, 1801; d. 1885), a wholesale grocer at 39–40 South Market Street, Boston. (Boston *Directory*, 1857; Charles H. Pope, *Meriam Genealogy*, Boston, 1906, pp. 362–363, 225–226.)

2. Mary Gray Chapman (d. Boston, November 8, 1874, in her seventy-sixth year), Henry Grafton Chapman's sister. (*Life*, IV, 361.)

1 3 6

TO THE EDITOR OF THE *ANTI-SLAVERY ADVOCATE*

Boston, March 18th, 1856.

DEAR FRIEND — It is seldom I am induced to make a public refutation of any of the malicious allegations which are brought against the American Anti-Slavery Society, whether by open pro-slavery enemies or the pseudo friends of negro emancipation, at home or abroad; because they are all most effectually answered by an unswerving adherence to the cause of the oppressed; and because to notice them in detail would be an endless task. But, in view of the insidious efforts making on your side of the Atlantic to destroy all confidence in this society, through unprincipled emissaries from the United States, aided by those who, under an anti-slavery garb, affect to be religiously concerned for the integrity of the movement to which my life is consecrated, I can do no less than to send you a brief letter, explanatory and defensive, — not for my sake personally, but to disabuse the minds of the truly pure and good, that may have been poisoned by the hand of malice, or alarmed by the tocsin of bigotry.

Hitherto, the American Anti-Slavery Society has received generous aid from England and the Continent, which it has gratefully appreciated and faithfully applied in the manner designed by the donors. Why should not the same co-operation be continued? Has the society any other object in view than the abolition of chattel slavery? No. Has it at any time turned aside from its legitimate work to subserve an ulterior purpose? No. Has it yielded one jot or tittle of the rights of the slave, to screen any sect or party from merited condemnation? No. Has it ever been a respecter of persons? No. Has it ever been found wanting in moral intrepidity, personal self-sacrifice, untiring vigilance, or laborious effort? No. Has it presumed to arraign any man, or any body of men, religiously or politically, on any other than a pro-slavery charge, sustained by overwhelming evidence? No. Has it ever attempted to discuss or settle any theological opinions or denominational views, aside from the question of slavery? No. Is it possible for an organization to be more true, disinterested, or impartial, in the prosecution of its specific work? No. Has it ever shrunk from the closest scrutiny "before all Israel and the sun"? [1] No.

The questions I have asked and answered, and answered truly, are sufficiently definite and comprehensive to meet every calumny circulating among you against the society. Why, then, is it not still deserving the generous sympathy and aid of every true friend of freedom?

To the charge that is made, in certain quarters, that it is an "infidel" society, I reply, first, that this is an old device of priestcraft and despotism to put down every righteous reform; secondly, that, in the sense in which it is used, and designed to be understood, it is a most wicked misrepresentation; thirdly, that it is coined and circulated either through deadly enmity to the anti-slavery movement, or by sectarian intolerance, or personal malevolence or selfishness; and, finally, that the society has ever vindicated Christ and his gospel as inimical to oppression in every form, and therefore properly denied that the slave-breeding and slave-hunting religion of this guilty land is genuine christianity.

The manner in which it is attempted to sustain this slanderous imputation is equally impudent and absurd. For example: — in an editorial article in the Glasgow *Chronicle*,[2] of January 30th, I find the American Anti-Slavery Society denounced as clearly "infidel," because I, its president, on a certain occasion, attended a convention held in Hartford, (Connecticut),[3] to consider the question of the plenary inspiration of the Bible, and offered and sustained a series of resolutions in opposition to the popular dogma respecting that volume! The *Chronicle* falsely styles it an *"Anti-Bible* Convention" — how falsely, let the following extract from the call [4] for the convention decide: —

"TO THE FRIENDS OF FREE DISCUSSION.

"The undersigned hereby invite all who are friendly to free discussion, to attend a Convention to be held at Hartford, Conn., on Thursday, Friday, Saturday and Sunday, 2d, 3d, 4th, and 5th June next, for the purpose of freely and fully canvassing the *Origin, Authority and Influence of the Jewish and Christian Scriptures.*

"This invitation is not given to any particular class of philosophers, theologians or thinkers, but is in good faith extended to all who feel an interest in the examination of the question above stated. There are many who believe that a supernatural revelation has been given to man; many others who deny this, and a large number who are afflicted with perplexing doubts — trembling between the silent scepticism of their reason and the fear of absolute denial. In issuing a call for a Convention, we have in view the correction of error, by which party soever entertained, and the relief of those who stand between doubt and fear, from their embarrassing position.

"Some may have no doubt that the Jewish and Christian Scriptures have subserved an important end, and yet believe that their mission is nearly completed and must be superseded by a new dispensation; some may believe that their influence has been prejudicial in every respect, and that they have been a curse rather than a blessing to mankind; others may believe them a perfect record of the Divine will to man — good in the past and for all time to come; and others still may deny the plenary inspiration of the Bible, discarding much of the Old Testament, and receiving most or all of the New. Still, such diversity of opinion, instead of prejudicing the interest and good results which ought to attend such a Convention, will rather tend to increase its interest and enhance its value to the cause of truth.

"Doubtless a free interchange of thought is the best mode of exciting inquiry and of arriving at the truth.

'He who has a truth and keeps it,
Keeps what not to him belongs;
But performs a selfish action,
And his fellow mortal wrongs.' [5]

"We invite, therefore, all who feel an interest in this question, without distinction of sex, colour, sect or party, to come together, that we may sit down like brethren in a communion before the altar of intellectual and spiritual freedom."

Now, that I was present at this convention, and did what the *Chronicle* alleges, is true; but not as President of the American Anti-slavery Society, nor as an abolitionist, but simply as a man, on my own responsibility, and *so explicitly declaring at the time*. Who but a bigot in heart, or a despot in spirit, will question my right to attend such a convention, and to be true to my own convictions? Or who but a simpleton or a knave will maintain that the American Anti-Slavery Society is to be held responsible for an act with which it had no more to do than with the attack upon Sebastopol? Or who but one assuming to wear the robes of papal infallibility will presume to set me down as a heretic or an infidel, because I will not surrender my reason, judgment and conscience at his dictation, and allow him to play the usurper over me? Who the editor of the *Chronicle* is, I neither know, nor care to know, beyond what is clearly manifest to my mind in his case — and that is, that not one drop of genuine *Protestant* blood is running in his veins; that, had he lived in the days of Jesus, he would have piously clamored for his crucifixion, having "heard his blasphemy," [6] and seen that he was "not of God," [7] because he did not keep the sabbath-day; that he is hostile alike to the rights of man and the gospel of freedom; and that he is not an avowed Romanist only because he happens to reside in Scotland, and not in Italy. I judge him as Jesus did certain godly pretenders when he exclaimed, "Woe unto you, scribes and pharisees, hypocrites! because ye build the tombs of the prophets, and garnish the sepulchres of the righteous, and say, if we had been in the days of our fathers, we would not have been partakers with them in the blood of the prophets. Wherefore ye be witnesses unto yourselves, that ye are the children of them which killed the prophets. Fill ye up the measure of your fathers!" [8]

Whatever my religious sentiments may be, (and this is neither the time nor the place to state or defend them) I cherish them with the deepest sincerity, conscientiously believing that they are strictly in accordance with the angelic song, "Glory to God in the highest; on earth peace; good will towards men" [9] — and reverently accepting the apostolic declaration, "So, then, every one of us shall give account of himself to God," [10] not to any human tribunal.

The cry of "infidelity" from Protestant lips, on account of a difference of religious belief to any extent whatever, is an express repudiation of the grand fundamental Protestant doctrine of the right of private judgment and individual conscience, against all papal domination and ecclesiastical authority. The Romish church consistently includes all Protestants in its category of heretics and infidels, from *Martin Luther* to *Thomas Paine*, and justly laughs to scorn the pharisaical sectarian pretensions which exist among dissenters. Concede the right of every soul to decide for itself what is true, or what is inspired, and no man can be an infidel, except he be false to his own standard, or his own professions or pledges. This opprobrious epithet, therefore, should be banished from the vocabulary of all Protestants; and no lover of mental freedom, no just and upright mind, will ever resort to it, to destroy the influence or stain the character of any one. To be in error, theologically or religiously, is no proof of infidelity; for if the errorist be sincere, and true to his own conscience, there is no higher fidelity beneath the stars. The Protestant who shouts "infidel" is a Papist in disguise; just as a democratic advocate of chattel slavery is an absolute tyrant in principle.

But, with all this, the American Anti-Slavery Society has no concern. It is a simple association, organized for a specific object, on a common platform, requiring as the condition of membership only an assent to the doctrine that slaveholding is under all circumstances inexcusable, and that immediate emancipation is the duty of the master and the right of the slave. It has no theological or party test. It takes, and can take, no cognizance of the peculiar religious or political views of its members; it is not responsible for any thing they may say or do in their individual capacity; it leaves them as free to promulgate their distinctive opinions on all subjects, outside of its own chosen sphere, as the air of heaven to circulate. In all these respects, it is precisely like the temperance, peace, suffrage, anti-corn law, and other general movements for the promotion of the common welfare; like them, amenable only for what it does in its official capacity, but made up of persons of all conflicting opinions on other subjects, who surrender nothing by coming together, and who endorse nothing but the rectitude of the object they aim to accomplish. It is a low device, therefore, on the part of its enemies, and indicative of any thing but true sympathy for the fettered slave, to make it responsible for my views, or those of any other officer or member, respecting the Bible, the sabbath, or any other controverted question. When it is "infidel" to the cause of the oppressed — when it misapplies the funds contributed to its treasury — when, for the sake of numbers, means, or popularity, it compromises its principles or weakens its testimonies — then let it be abandoned by all genuine abolitionists; but not till then.

More I have not time to add before the mail closes. What more need be added?

For your faithful co-operation with us, my dear friend, "through evil report and through good report," [11] I remain, gratefully,

Yours, to break every yoke,

Wm. Lloyd Garrison.

Printed in *The Liberator*, March 21, 1856, and in *The Anti-Slavery Advocate*, London, May 1, 1856.

The Anti-Slavery Advocate, a monthly published simultaneously in London and Dublin, was first issued in October 1852. *The Liberator*, in an editorial essay which described the new publication, wrote that "Richard D. Webb of Dublin is announced as the printer and publisher of the paper. No more devoted, faithful, and steadfast friend of the American slave can easily be found, on either side of the water, than Mr. Webb." Webb was Garrison's friend and sympathetic to his views, and apparently founded the monthly to provide a pro-Garrisonian view of American antislavery efforts. (*The Liberator*, October 22, 1852; the same issue of *The Liberator* reprinted the "Introductory Notice" of the first issue of the *Advocate*.)

1. II Samuel 12:12.
2. *The Liberator*, March 14, 1856, printed the editorial from the Glasgow *Chronicle* in its "Refuge of Oppression" section. The same issue carried an editorial entitled "The Malice of Bigotry" which sharply refuted the *Chronicle*'s allegations.
3. The reference is to the Hartford Bible Convention, which met on June 2–5, 1853. For a summary of the convention see *Life*, III, 383–388.
4. The call appeared in *The Liberator*, April 22, 1853.
5. Unidentified.
6. Matthew 26:65.
7. John 8:47.
8. Matthew 23:29–32.
9. Luke 2:14.
10. Romans 14:12.
11. II Corinthians 6:8.

137

TO SAMUEL AARON

Boston, March 21, 1856.

Dear Sir:

I am requested, by a unanimous vote of the Executive Committee of the American Anti-Slavery Society, to invite you to be one of the speakers at the anniversary of the Society, in the city of New York, in May next — 6th.[1] In extending this invitation, they wish you to exercise as much freedom of thought and speech as you would in addressing a meeting of your own in Norristown, and therefore to frame your own resolution and to select your own topic, *ad libitum*. You will be expected to speak as an independent advocate of the slave, not as endorsing the views and measures of the Society itself. They hope that you will see your way clear to give an affirmative answer. Such, also, is the hope of

Your friend and fellow-laborer,

Wm. Lloyd Garrison.

Rev. Samuel Aaron.

ALS: Charles Roberts Autograph Collection, Haverford College, Haverford, Pennsylvania.

1. The report of the convention, printed in *The Liberator*, May 16, 1856, does not refer to Aaron either as speaker or participant.

138

TO SAMUEL J. MAY

Boston, March 21, 1856.

Beloved Friend:

Your letter gives me the assurance of your convalescence, and hence my heart is full of gladness; for a rumor had reached me that you were seriously ill, which, though contradicted by a telegraphic despatch received from John [1] by your cousin,[2] left an apprehension in my mind, in regard to your case, that nothing could so effectually remove as the sight of your handwriting. I meant to have written to you at a much earlier day, but circumstances have hindered. You have so uniformly enjoyed good health since I first knew you, that I had concluded you bore a charmed life, and could not be in any danger. Then, there is such an all-pervading magnetism about you, and in all your acts, that the idea of your removal from earth, as a possible event, at any time, has not occurred to me. I trust that event will be long delayed — not for your sake, (for I feel assured that for you to die will be gain to yourself,) but for the sake of your own family, your own people, our guilty country, and every righteous cause struggling for supremacy. Take all possible care of your health, and run no risk in prematurely resuming your wonted cares and duties. I feel more than a friendly solicitude, more than a brother's love, in your case. You are the Israelite in whom I have never found any guile; ever animated by the spirit of Jesus, hearing testimony against all wrong, seeking to save the lost, and doing good continually. It is not my habit to praise those whom I love and admire, to their faces; but if I could fill the remainder of this sheet with expressions of my esteem and reverence for you, — one of my earliest and most faithful co-workers in the cause of the wretched bondman, — it would be an immense relief to my breast. But I know your shrinking nature, and therefore forbear.

What a series of mishaps I encountered, after our pleasant interview at the Syracuse depot, before my return home! I lectured at Rochester the most inclement evening of this most inclement winter, and, then suffering from an attack of influenza, found myself the next day voiceless! You remember I had engaged to return to Syracuse that day, and spend the evening with you at a social gathering. My cold was so bad, and my lungs so inflamed, and unable to speak, I deemed it prudent not to take the journey, but to keep mostly to my bed and room, hoping that I might be able to be with you on the subsequent day, and fulfil my appointment. But, "I grew no better fast," and Thursday found me worse than ever. So I had no other alternative than to send you a telegraphic message, announcing my inability to lecture. Whatever regret you or others felt at the disappointment, be assured mine was very great — not on my own account personally, not at all, but because every preparation having been kindly made for the meeting, it must have caused considerable trouble and expense. As to the expense that may have been incurred on my account, I cannot feel reconciled to your bearing it, as I fear you have done, exclusively; and, therefore, if you will let me know what you had to pay, I will send you the amount without delay — as there is no reason why I should not do so.

Of course, it will give me great pleasure, should an anti-slavery course of lectures be attempted in Syracuse next winter, as you suggest, to be one of the lecturers, if all be well with me.

Allow me to suggest, that, in view of the severity of our wintry climate, it would be far better to commence the course as early at least as the first of November, and to get it completed by the first of January. I do not understand the policy too generally pursued, to take that portion of the winter which is sure to be the coldest and stormiest, seeing that even by the first of October, the evenings are amply long for the delivery of lectures.

The fate of Kansas is still apparently in suspense; but my own conviction remains unshaken, that Kansas will be a slave State, and that "border ruffian" legislation will be enforced, if need be, by all the military power of the General Government. Pres. Pierce's last message, on that question, is "a settler" — and he is ready to do all that the Slave Power demands at his hands.[3] The dissolution of the Union must first precede the abolition of slavery.

You see that such men as Gerrit Smith, Ward Beecher, and Theodore Parker are finding in Sharp's rifles more than in the peaceful gospel of Christ to aid the cause of right and freedom! They will cause many professed friends of peace to apostatize from their principles, and give a fresh stimulus to the war spirit. I think this is the time for radical peace men to review their testimonies, dealing as tenderly as possible with the settlers in Kansas, (whose situation is undeniably a trying one,) but repudiating a resort to carnal weapons as wrong *per se.*

Through the machinations of that double-and-twisted worker of iniquity, Julia Griffiths,[4] the hue-and-cry of "infidelity" is raised afresh in England and Scotland, by various religious cliques, against the American Anti-Slavery Society, in order to prevent any further contributions being made to the National Bazaar. Douglass is impudently held up as the Christian champion who is nobly battling our "infidel" abolitionism,[5] and every effort is made to extend the circulation of his paper on this account. He connives at all this villany, being utterly unscrupulous in carrying out his own designs. You will be more and more convinced of this, I am confident.

I see that Lewis Tappan,[6] Douglass, McCune Smith,[7] Goodell and Gerrit Smith have called a convention for the purpose of nominating candidates for the Presidency and Vice Presidency of the United States!![8] Can any thing more ludicrous than this be found inside or outside of the Utica Insane Asylum? It is really sad to see so good a man as Gerrit Smith befooled in this manner.

The tone of the Republican party is becoming more and more feeble and indefinite, in order to secure a large vote in the approaching Presidential struggle. At Pittsburgh,[9] they resolved to vote for the admission of Kansas into the Union as a free State! — Wonderful! "Put not your trust in" — politicians!

At home, we are all well as usual. Helen rejoices in your restoration, and desires to be most affectionately remembered to you all. Give my warmest regards to your wife, to the two Charlottes, and to all the boys.

Ever your most attached friend,

Wm. Lloyd Garrison.

Rev. Samuel J. May.

ALS: Garrison Papers, Boston Public Library.

1. John Edward May, Samuel J. May's son.
2. Samuel May, Jr.
3. The reference is probably to President Franklin Pierce's "Proclamation" of February 11, 1856, calling for the maintenance of law and order in Kansas, and ordering the dispersal of "unlawful combinations against the authority of the Territory of Kansas or of the United States." Since the constituted territorial legislature had been elected by pro-slavery fraud and violence this meant that President Pierce was taking the side of pro-slavery elements in Kansas.
4. Julia Griffiths, an Englishwoman, had met Frederick Douglass at Newcastle-on-Tyne during Douglass' stay in England. She came to Rochester in 1848, resided, for a while, in Douglass's home, and played an important role in the early success of *Douglass' Monthly,* which had been established in 1847. She handled the book reviews, taught Douglass "the rules of grammar" and "literary precision," and

helped him place his newspaper on a solid financial basis. Benjamin Quarles writes that "it was largely due to Miss Griffiths' efforts that Douglass was able to issue a periodical for sixteen years." Devoting her time and effort to the paper for almost eight years, "without her effective and energetic management the paper would have been another short-lived abolitionist sheet." She returned to England late in 1855, married H. O. Crofts, a clergyman, and remained in England during the remainder of her life. After her husband's death in the late 1870's, she conducted a school for girls. Her correspondence with Douglass continued throughout her latter years. (Benjamin Quarles, *Frederick Douglass*, Athenaeum, New York, 1969, original edition 1948, pp. 87–88, 91–95, 103–107, 306, 322.)

5. The *Glasgow Chronicle* article on January 30 had closed with the following statement about Frederick Douglass: "We are glad to find that Frederick Douglass, who has established himself as a newspaper editor at Rochester, is vigorously pursuing the sound course which he has chalked out for himself, and, while rebuking the faithlessness of those professors of Christianity who palliate or defend the practice of slavery on the one hand, is, on the other, bearing his testimony against those whose views are apparently tending to the overthrow of all authority, either human or divine." (*The Liberator*, March 14, 1856.)

6. Lewis Tappan (1788–1873), the anti-Garrisonian abolitionist who broke with Garrison in 1840. With his brother, Arthur, and others he formed the American and Foreign Anti-Slavery Society. He was also a supporter of the Liberty party. (See *Letters*, II, xxix, for a short biographical sketch.)

7. James McCune Smith, Negro physician, antislavery leader and author. (*Letters*, II, 354–355.)

8. The convention was that of the Radical Abolitionist party which had been formed in June 1855 at Syracuse, New York, in response to a call signed by William Goodell, Lewis Tappan, Gerrit Smith, Frederick Douglass, and J. McCune Smith. The purpose of the new party was the emancipation of the slave through political action. As Benjamin Quarles indicates, "The Radical Abolitionist party was the Liberty party by another name." J. McCune Smith presided at the convention, which adopted a "Declaration of Sentiments" and an "Exposition of the Constitutional Duty of the Federal Government to Abolish Slavery." The *Radical Abolitionist* was established as the new party's official organ. A subsequent national meeting was held in Boston, in October, 1855, with a very disappointing turnout, and no official resolutions were adopted or political decisions made. Early in 1856, a call was issued for a Radical Abolition nominating convention to meet in May at Syracuse. The convention nominated Gerrit Smith for President and Samuel McFarland of Virginia for vice-president. Although Douglass and Lewis Tappan were present at the convention and supported Gerrit Smith's nomination, they later withdrew their support and voted for Frémont. The Radical Abolitionist party polled a total of 165 votes in all of New York State. In 1857 the party went out of existence. (Quarles, *Frederick Douglass*, pp. 156–164; Bertram Wyatt-Brown, *Lewis Tappan and the Evangelical War Against Slavery*, Cleveland, 1969, p. 334.)

9. "Feb. 22, 1856; the convention which paved the way for that at Philadelphia on June 17 (*Lib.* 26:38)." (*Life*, III, 443n.)

139

TO AUSTIN STEWARD

[BOSTON, MASS., June 1856.]

DEAR SIR:

You state that Rev. N. Paul,[1] as agent for the Wilberforce Settlement, U. C.,[2] in rendering his accounts on his return from England, charged the Board of Managers with the sum of two hundred dollars, paid by him to me while in England; that said sum was allowed by the board; adding that you do not recollect of my acknowledging or giving credit to the Settlement for it.

In reply, I can only assure you that there must be a mistake in regard to this item. I borrowed no money, nor had I any occasion to ask a loan of my friend Paul,[3] my expenses being defrayed by funds contributed by friends in this country; nor could I with propriety receive, nor he give me any part of the money contributed for the benefit of the Wilberforce Settlement; hence a loan or gift from him, could have been nothing more than a personal matter between ourselves. Moreover, had he at that time or any other, given me in good faith the sum named as belonging to the Settlement, (believing that as we were laboring together, for the interest of one common cause, the board would not hesitate to allow it,) he would certainly have demanded a receipt, which it would have pleased me to give, of course, that he might satisfy the board that their liberality had been disbursed according to their wishes, or his judgment. But receiving no money from your agent, will be a sufficient reason for not acknowledging it, or giving due credit to the Settlement. I can account for this charge on his part, in no way, except that as he was with me a part of the time I was in London, and we travelled together a part of the time, during which, he ably and effectively assisted me in exposing that most iniquitous combination, "The American Colonization Society," — he charged me, (that is, to my mission) sundry items of expense which he undoubtedly believed justly incurred by his helping me to open the eyes of British philanthropists to the real design of that society; and I shall ever remember with gratitude, his heartiness and zeal in the cause and in my behalf. I owe much to the success that so signally crowned my mission, to his presence, testimony, and eloquent denunciation of the colonization scheme. I, however, received no money from him, and can but think that the above explanation was the occasion of his making the charge, and which I trust will leave on his memory, no intentional wrong.

WM. L. GARRISON.

BOSTON, MASS., June 1856.

Printed in Austin Steward, *Twenty-Two Years a Slave, and Forty Years a Freeman* . . . (Rochester, N.Y., 1857), pp. 205–206.

Austin Steward, an escaped slave who had taken up residence in Rochester, New York, where he succeeded in business as a grocer, moved to the Negro colony of Wilberforce, near Lucan, Ontario, in Upper Canada, in the early thirties. Steward was a leader of the colony for several years, serving as chairman of the Board of Managers until 1837, when he returned to Rochester. Back in business, he was not very successful, his career as a businessman ending with the burning of his establishment. In later years, he was a schoolteacher in Canandaigua, New York and an agent for the *National Anti-Slavery Standard*. Thereafter, he seems to have dropped out of sight. (Robin W. Winks, *The Blacks in Canada, A History*, Montreal, New Haven, and London, 1971, pp. 158–159, 161, 162, 241; William H. and Jane H. Pease, *Black Utopia, Negro Communal Experiments in America*, Madison, Wisconsin, 1963, pp. 15, 48–61.) In 1857 there appeared his autobiography, *Twenty-Two Years a Slave, and Forty Years a Freeman: Embracing a Correspondence of Several Years, While President of Wilberforce Colony, London, Canada West* (Rochester, N.Y., 221 pp.).

Garrison's letter to Steward was in response to a letter from Steward, dated Canandaigua, New York, May, 1856, which read as follows:

"In a recent examination of the business transactions between the Board of Managers of the Wilberforce Colony, and their agent Rev. N. Paul, I find a charge made by him, and allowed by the board, of the sum of two hundred dollars, which he paid to yourself. Finding no receipt or acknowledgment from you, I write to ask you to favor me with one, or an explanation of the facts in the case, either of which will greatly oblige me, as I design to make it public."

1. The Reverend Nathaniel Paul, a Negro, had gone to England in December 1831 to raise funds for the Negro colony at Wilberforce. Although he remained four years, collecting over $8,000, he returned to Wilberforce empty-handed, explaining that his expenses had equaled his revenues. It was in 1833 that Garrison, in England for several months, had been in contact with Paul. For a detailed account of Garrison's financial relationships with Paul, which also involved the New York Abolitionists, Arthur and Lewis Tappan, see the letter dated Brooklyn, Connecticut, December 17, 1835, from Garrison and Knapp to Lewis Tappan (*Letters*, I) and Garrison's letter to Lewis Tappan, dated Brooklyn, February 29, 1836 (*Letters*, II).

2. Upper Canada.

3. Garrison's memory seems to have failed him in this instance. He did borrow money from Paul in 1833, but the matter had been settled soon afterward.

140

TO WILLIAM LLOYD GARRISON, JR.

Tuesday Morning.
[June 1856]

Dear Willie — Your letter to Wendell, with the coat, has just been received. We regret the latter is too small for you. Whether it will suit Wendell, we do not yet know, as he is absent at school. Mother declines getting you another, without first knowing what you would like; and, accordingly, sends you the enclosed patterns to look at, either of which would make an excellent summer garment. Should you fancy either, return the sample chosen in a letter, and we will get the cloth, and have Mr. Curtis make the coat at once — i.e., if he has your measure correctly; or are you still expanding?

Your affectionate father,

Wm. Lloyd Garrison.

ALS: Smith College Library. The date was added by a later hand.

141

TO THE EDITOR OF THE BOSTON *EVENING TELEGRAPH*

ANTI-SLAVERY OFFICE, 21 Cornhill, June 17, 1856.

To the Editor of the Evening Telegraph:

SIR — In your paper of last evening, you published a petition for a dissolution of the Union, now circulating in this Commonwealth, and appended to it some comments of a most extraordinary character — sagaciously branding it as a 'New Game of the Border Ruffian Party,' (!) and declaring that 'there is but one explanation of this matter which seems to us reasonable,' (!) and that is, that 'the Buchanan leaders, frightened at the general indignation excited against them by the atrocious proceedings in Kansas, have resorted to a desperate expedient to create a reaction in their favor,' (!) and, finally, saying, 'The supporters of border ruffianism doubtless regard this as a very clever trick, and have great hope of profit from it. They are demented.'

It is difficult to believe that you are serious in this case; for, if so, it implies a stultification of mind, on your part, little short of what you term 'demented' — if otherwise, the wit of it is of the very poorest quality.

The petition which has elicited such a ludicrous commentary from your pen was carefully prepared, under the sanction of the Executive Committee of the American Anti-Slavery Society,[1] for general circulation, and bears first upon its list of signers the honored name of FRANCIS JACKSON, of this city, followed by those of WENDELL PHILLIPS, THOMAS WENTWORTH HIGGINSON, and others of high moral worth and eminent philanthropy. It has appeared two weeks successively in the *Liberator*, and once in the *National Anti-Slavery Standard* at New York, accompanied by an urgent appeal to every true friend of freedom to sign it without delay, for the weighty and unanswerable reasons therein set forth. Some years ago, a similar petition (succeeded by many others) was presented to Congress by JOHN QUINCY ADAMS,[2] throwing the bullying South into convulsions, and causing every slave-holding ruffian in the House of Representatives to foam at the mouth. For the last fifteen years, the American Anti-Slavery Society and its auxiliaries have been constantly proclaiming, through their organs, lecturing agents and tracts, that the Union is 'a covenant with death' and 'an agreement with hell,' which ought to be instantly annulled. Indeed, this is the one great issue they present to the understanding, conscience and heart of every one who claims to 'remember them that are in bonds as bound with them,' believing every other to be temporising and delusive. 'The supporters of border ruffianism' are too well satisfied with the Union to circulate any petition for its dissolution, even as 'a very clever trick,' and will be very sure to destroy every copy of the one you have printed that they can lay their hands upon.

The recommendation appended to the petition, to have it sent to 'either Senators Wilson, [John Parker] Hale, Wade, Seward, Collamer, and Fessenden, or to Messrs. [Joshua Reed] Giddings, [Anson] Burlingame, Campbell,[3] or any other suitable Representative, at Washington,' was made solely on the ground that these gentlemen believe in the sacred right of petition, and, as honorable men, will recognize it in this instance — *though not one of them is in favor of the object prayed for.*

Yours, to suppress 'border ruffianism,' and therefore for NO UNION WITH SLAVEHOLDERS,

WM. LLOYD GARRISON.

Printed in *The Liberator*, June 20, 1856.

The letter was printed in *The Liberator* with the following superscription: "The following letter, elicited by a very absurd editorial article which appeared in the Boston *Evening Telegraph* of Monday, was sent to that paper for publication, but only a small portion of it was inserted."

1. The petition, addressed to both houses of Congress, read in part as follows:

"That the South, having declared it to be not only her right and purpose to eternize her slave system where it now exists, but to extend it over all the territories that now belong or may hereafter be annexed to the Republic, come what may; and having outlawed from her soil the entire free colored population of the North, made it perilous for any Northern white citizen to exercise his constitutional right of freedom of speech in that section of the country, and even in the national capital, and proclaimed her hostility to all free institutions universally:

"We, therefore, believe that the time has come for a new arrangement of elements so hostile, of interests so irreconcilable, of institutions so incongruous; and we earnestly request Congress, at its present session, to take such initiatory measures for the speedy, peaceful, and equitable dissolution of the existing Union as the exigencies of the case require — leaving the South to depend upon her own resources, and to take all the responsibility, in the maintenance of her slave system, and the North to organize an independent government in accordance with her own ideas of justice and the rights of man." (*The Liberator*, June 20, 1856.)

2. This petition was offered by John Quincy Adams on January 24, 1842. It was from Haverhill, Massachusetts, and called for a peaceful dissolution of the Union. "It was the first of the kind that had ever reached Congress, and, curiously enough, it did not proceed from professed abolitionists: the first signer was a Locofoco (*alias* Democrat) of high standing. . . . Moreover, Mr. Adams moved the reference of the petition to a committee with instructions to report *adversely*." It was the offering of this petition that evoked an unsuccessful attempt by the pro-slavery members of the House to censure Adams. (*Life*, III, 46–47.)

3. Henry Wilson (1812–1875) was an antislavery senator from Massachusetts from 1855 to 1873, when he resigned to become vice-president of the United States, having been elected on the Republican ticket with President Grant. He served until his death on November 22, 1875.

Benjamin Franklin Wade (1800–1878), antislavery senator from Ohio, served from 1851 to 1869. Wade was originally elected as a Whig but then joined the

Republican party and was reelected under that party's banner beginning in 1856. (*BDAC.*)

William Henry Seward (1801–1872), antislavery senator from New York, was elected to the Senate as a Whig in 1849 and reelected as a Republican in 1855, serving until 1861, when he became secretary of state in Lincoln's cabinet. (*BDAC.*)

Jacob Collamer (1792–1865), antislavery senator from Vermont, was elected to the Senate in 1855, as a Republican, and reelected in 1861, serving until his death. (*BDAC.*)

William Pitt Fessenden (1806–1869), antislavery senator from Maine, was elected as a Whig to the Senate and served from 1854 to 1864, when he resigned to become secretary of the treasury in Lincoln's Cabinet. He was later again elected to the Senate, where he served from 1865 until his death. (*BDAC.*)

Lewis Davis Campbell (1811–1882), Whig representative from Ohio, served from 1849 to 1857. He was chairman of the Committee of Ways and Means in the Thirty-fourth Congress and opposed the repeal of the Missouri Compromise. (*BDAC.*)

142

TO THEODORE PARKER

Wednesday Evening,
July 2, 1856.

Dear Friend:

I have just received a letter from Mr. [Thomas Wentworth] Higginson, dated at Detroit, stating that he is on his way to Chicago, in regard to Kansas matters, and, therefore, deeply to his regret, it will not be in his power to be at our Framingham celebration on the 4th.[1] This will be a serious disappointment to many, and I feel very sorry, almost sad, about it. Now, you intend to rest on the 4th — you ought to have rest — and ought not to be importuned to the contrary. — But — but — what shall we do? Who but yourself can fill the vacancy thus unexpectedly made? Will you have compassion on the multitude, and come and give us half an hour's *talk* (we will not ask for a formal speech) at the Grove on the 4th, either at our forenoon or afternoon service, as may be most convenient for you?[2] You shall make your visit as brief as you please; only show us the light of your countenance, and let us have a word from your mouth; especially in view of our great perplexity, arising from the absence of Mr. Higginson.

"And as in duty bound, will ever pray."

Yours, in joy and in trouble,

Wm. Lloyd Garrison.

Rev. Theodore Parker.

ALS: Garrison Papers, Boston Pubic Library.

1. The annual Fourth of July meeting of the Massachusetts Anti-Slavery Society

at Framingham Grove. The speakers announced for the occasion included Garrison, Phillips, Higginson, Edmund Quincy, Charles Lenox Remond, and Stephen S. Foster. (*The Liberator*, June 27, 1856.)

2. *The Liberator*'s accounts of the meeting in the issues of July 11 and 18 do not mention Theodore Parker's presence.

143

TO SAMUEL MAY, JR.

Boston, July 15, 1856.

Dear Mr. May:

I have several reasons for desiring to be excused from going to Providence on the 3rd of August.[1]

It comes too near the 1st of August. After that celebration,[2] to go immediately to Providence would not allow sufficient time to recover from the fatigue incurred thereby.

My head still gives me some trouble; and, at this season, I ought to be specially cautious in regard to mental excitement.

I am not at any time magnetically drawn towards Providence; it is a hard place, and the people are not "come-at-able," for some reason or other; still, it ought not, on this account, to be wholly given over — only, just at this time, it helps to make me feel indisposed to visit that city.

Besides, you know it is not long since I attended a series of meetings in Providence. It will be better for me to go at a later period, I think.

The expenses of the hall, &c. are usually heavy, and the contributions barely sufficient to cover them, without reference to the expenses of speakers — as you will recollect.

As Mr. Pillsbury is going to P. so soon, it seems to me this should suffice for a time.

Yours, disliking to say, "I must beg off,"

Wm. Lloyd Garrison.

ALS: Garrison Papers, Boston Public Library.

1. *The Liberator*, August 1, 1856, listed an antislavery meeting at Providence, Rhode Island, scheduled for Sunday, August 3, with Charles Lenox Remond as the speaker.

2. The anniversary celebration of British West India Emancipation, sponsored by the Massachusetts Anti-Slavery Society, at Abington, Massachusetts, on August 1. Garrison was to be one of the speakers.

144

TO SAMUEL MAY, JR.

Boston, August 1, 1856.

My dear Mr. May:

My disappointment is very great in not being able to be at your commemorative meeting, to-day; [1] but, though not seriously ill, I am suffering too much bodily pain, and am too much affected by a pressure upon the brain, to make it either prudent or pleasurable for me to participate in your proceedings, or to be even only a mere witness of them. Fortunately, the presence of so many able and eloquent advocates of freedom will render my absence of no account whatever. Still, I deeply regret that I cannot listen to their stirring words, and again see the old and tried friends of our glorious movement, face to face.

With yours, my spirit will be comforted and refreshed to think of the wonderful deliverance of eight hundred thousand human beings from the most frightful bondage, of which this day is the anniversary. History records no event so marvellous and soul-thrilling, in relation to a change in human condition. All praise and honor to British philanthropy, which, against throne and parliament at home, and the whole body of West India planters, dared singlehanded to grapple with the demoniacal power of Slavery, and, after a tremendous and long-protracted struggle, succeeded in vanquishing them all — opening the prison-doors, and setting every captive free beneath the British flag! Everlasting disgrace to America, which, in the face of her Declaration of Independence and the Gospel of Christ, still holds in a bondage equally cruel and degrading four millions of victims, derides all appeals to conscience and the "higher law," persists in extending her bloody sway, and planting chattel slavery as her one cherished and "peculiar institution" wherever her flag advances!

But God reigns, and is omnipotent, and either through moral power inducing repentance, or by fire and blood in the way of divine retribution upon the heads of the oppressors, will yet effect a greater jubilee and ransom a still more numerous host. Yes —

> "The end will come — it will not wait —
> Chains, yokes and scourges have their date;
> Slavery itself must pass away,
> And be a tale of yesterday!" [2]

Yours, to break every yoke,

Wm. Lloyd Garrison.

Rev. Samuel May, Jr.

Garrison Papers, Boston Public Library; printed in *The Liberator*, August 8, 1856.

1. The West India Emancipation celebration at Abington.
2. James Montgomery (1771–1854), English antislavery poet, "A Cry from South Africa: On building a Chapel at Cape Town, for the Negro Slaves of the Colony, in 1828," in *The Poetical Works of James Montgomery* (Boston, 1858), IV, 181–182. Maria W. Chapman, in *Songs of the Free and Hymns of Christian Freedom* (Boston, 1836), p. 99, entitles the poem "The Day is at Hand."

145

TO ANN R. BRAMHALL

Boston, August 8, 1856.

My dear Mrs. Bramhall:

Your kind letter of the 29th ult. was next to the pleasure of taking you by the hand, and talking with you face to face. I would have tried to answer it promptly, but, for the last ten days, I have been confined to the house, and most of the time prostrated upon my bed, — my brain and spine both being badly affected. But I am now greatly relieved of my pain, and improve the first opportunity to thank you (with wife) for your interesting epistle.

You portray, in a graphic and touching manner, the solitariness of your situation in Newark, as pertaining to the anti-slavery cause in special, and the cause of reform universally. Be assured, you have our warmest sympathies. Newark is famous for the number of its churches, and the multitude of its religious observances: why should it not be cold and indifferent to the emancipation of those who are grinding in the Southern prison-house? It manufactures coaches for the nabobs of the South, and whips for the backs of their slaves. It believes in a religion in which the "rulers" believe, which "walks in silver slippers," which is filled with pharisaical pride and exclusiveness, and which strains at a gnat, and readily swallows "a whole caravan of camels." Of course, you will find in such a community but few to sympathize with you in your affinity for what is unpopular and persecuted. It is thus by standing alone that we are brought into closest sympathy with the despised Nazarene.

But it is mournful to see a whole community thus blind and besotted. How shall we make ourselves understood? where shall we obtain audience? who will see if there be any good thing that can come out of Nazareth? Alas for those who have eyes, and see not — ears, and hear not! What then? Can they repeal the law of gravitation? Is the earth never to move? Are they so strong — is God so weak — that we may hang down our heads in despair? Far otherwise. Truth *is* mighty, and will not only maintain its ground, but drive Error to the wall. The Right is ever victorious.

I trust you will at last find that there are some hearts in your city not wholly dead to the claims of suffering humanity — some minds sufficiently enlightened to distinguish between "the *form* of godliness and the *power* thereof," between genuine and spurious faith in God. Complete isolation is far from being a desirable state; the soul is made for personal communion; the heart wants a living presence. Still, if we *must* stand alone, or compromise our principles, there is no alternative: — having done all, God helping us, we will so stand.

You ask whether Kansas is to be sacrificed to the demon slavery. For one, I have no hope in that direction — none whatever. Slavery is planted in Kansas; "border ruffianism" is in the ascendant there, backed up by all the resources of the U. S. Government; freedom lies trodden in the dust, or wanders as an outlaw; the Slave Power has no cause to tremble while the Union lasts, but will find therein whatever it needs for safety, extension and perpetuity.

As between the contending political parties, my feelings and wishes are with the Republican party, of course, because it occupies a position relatively anti-slavery; still, it is made up of very incongruous elements, and will certainly be cheated or defeated in the end. Think of the New York Herald coming to its support! — and yet as bitter and vile against genuine abolitionism as ever.

What a change in the pacific disposition of Gerrit Smith! His faith in God, and in "the foolishness of preaching," [1] has given place to Sharpe's rifles. He is not only for fighting the "border ruffians," but the U. S. government which sustains them in their nefarious acts.[2] In this, I like his consistency. But he is setting an evil example, and measurably throwing his money away; though I have no doubt that he is true to his own present convictions of duty.

Our First of August celebration at Abington was more numerously attended than ever before, and the proceedings were uncommonly interesting. You will see, in the Liberator of this week,[3] the speeches of Higginson and Phillips, delivered on the occasion, and will peruse them with deep interest. I was not able to be present, in consequence of my illness, much to my regret.

Of home matters, there is little of interest to communicate. Our little Franky has had the scarlatina, but is now convalescent. Fanny leaves us to-morrow, to spend a part of her vacation with her cousins at Providence. Wendell will go to Lynn next week, to be with William a little while. George remains at the printing-office, using his fingers to "help the cause along."

Our "help" is just leaving us, and we have no girl in prospect as a substitute; so, wife has more than her hands full, and desires me to say thus much to you, and that she will write to you with as little delay as possible.

We remember the many kindnesses of yourself, and your beloved husband, shown to us through years of friendship, with the deepest gratitude. We regret the distance that separates you from us, but trust to see you once more located in this region, and at no distant day.

The children send their love to you, and desire to be specially remembered to Marcia.[4] As she is one of my favorites, you will give her my love with theirs.

It is not unlikely that you may see me in Newark, in all next week, as I have been urged to visit your city for a special purpose. In case I come, I will not fail to find you. I need a journey of some kind, and hope this will prove beneficial to my health.

I write in galloping haste, and have not begun to say what it is in my heart to write, touching a multitude of matters. Our warmest regards to your husband.

Ever truly yours,

Wm. Lloyd Garrison.

Mrs. Ann R. Bramhall.

Garrison Papers, Boston Public Library.

Ann Rebecca Reed, the daughter of William Reed, married Cornelius Bramhall, of the Boston firm of Manley and Bramhall, in December, 1834. They lived in Dorchester for many years until the end of 1855 when Bramhall opened a business in New York and moved his family to Newark, New Jersey. Later in the year they moved to Jersey City, New Jersey, and by 1863 they were in Orange, New Jersey. In 1865, Bramhall was a partner in a company which manufactured kitchen stoves and water furnaces in New York City. Both Bramhalls were active in the anti-slavery movement. Ann Rebecca Bramhall is listed as a sponsor of the National Anti-Slavery Bazaars. Mr. Bramhall is listed as a dues-paying member of the Massachusetts Anti-Slavery Society as early as 1838, and as a member of the Board of Governors of the Massachusetts Anti-Slavery Society from 1843 to 1855, when he resigned because of his departure from Massachusetts. He thereafter served on the Board of Governors of the American Anti-Slavery Society. (Anti-Slavery Manuscripts, Boston Public Library; *Columbian Centinel*, December 24, 1834; *Annual Reports, American Anti-Slavery Society*, New York, 1856–1860; *Annual Reports, Massachusetts Anti-Slavery Society*, Boston, 1838, 1843–1856.)

1. I Corinthians 1:21.

2. Gerrit Smith supported John Brown and other Free-State settlers in Kansas and helped provide them with arms.

3. August 8.

4. Probably her daughter, but otherwise unidentified.

146

TO THEODORE PARKER

Anti-Slavery Office, 21 Cornhill,
Friday, Sept. 5, 1856.

Dear Mr. Parker:

My excellent friend, Mr. Sprague, of Abington,[1] will explain to you the situation in which the Anti-Slavery ladies of that town and vicinity find themselves, by the unexpected inability of Mr. Phillips to speak at their Fair on Friday evening next.[2] I hope it will be in your power to go in his stead; for I am sure your presence would be greeted by an approving audience, and it would be most serviceable to our cause and the Fair.

Your attached friend,

Wm. Lloyd Garrison.

Rev. Theodore Parker.

ALS: Garrison Papers, Boston Public Library.

1. Elbridge Sprague (b. March 15, 1816), a druggist, married Sarah French of South Braintree and was a staunch pro-Garrisonian abolitionist and friend of Garrison, Phillips, George Thompson of England, and others. (Warren B. Sprague, *Sprague Families in America*, Rutland, Vt., 1913, p. 378.)

2. *The Liberator*, August 29 and September 5, 1856, carried announcements concerning the fair. It was to be held in the Manamooskeagin Hall, at East Abington, in aid of the Massachusetts Anti-Slavery Society. The later issue announced the address by Wendell Phillips. A report of the fair, printed in *The Liberator*, October 10, 1856, indicates that the fair was held from Tuesday, September 9 through Friday, September 12 and that Wendell Phillips did speak on Friday evening.

147

TO AN UNKNOWN CORRESPONDENT

Boston, Oct. 11, 1856.

Dear Friend:

The state of my health is such that it is doubtful whether I shall be able to attend the anniversary of the Pennsylvania A. S. Society,[1] next week, at Norristown. Should I be there, however, it would not be convenient for me to visit Philadelphia so soon after my return home, to give you the desired lecture on the evening of November 2d. Aside from this consideration, and my wish to avoid public lecturing for some time to come, I should not like to attempt to address any public assembly, on the subject of slavery, and expect to obtain a candid hearing in the very midst of a political whirlwind [2] which will then be sweeping over your city, state, the nation. We must bide our time, and "wait a little longer."

AL: Essex Institute, Salem, Massachusetts. Only the first page of this letter seems to have been preserved.

1. The meeting was to be held on October 16 and 17.
2. The presidential election of 1856.

148

TO JAMES MILLER McKIM

Boston, Oct. 14, 1856.

J. MILLER McKIM — *My Dear Friend*: Having been for a few weeks past suffering from ill-health, I reluctantly deem it prudent to forego being at the approaching annual meeting of the Pennsylvania Anti-Slavery Society — deeply regretting to cause any disappointment on account of my absence, and especially that I must be deprived of the unspeakable pleasure of once more seeing, face to face, those whom I regard as among my dearest friends and most reliable coadjutors, whose presence is ever to me an inspiration, and "of whom the world is not worthy." [1]

But my absence will be of little consequence, not only because there will in all probability be no lack of speakers, but because this is not the hour for any of us to obtain a candid hearing, while the community is in a high fever, and a political earthquake is shaking the land to its centre. It is only after the earthquake that the "still, small voice" of truth can be heard, and we must patiently bide our time.

The crisis is full of temptation to swerve from the straight line of rectitude, in order to avert an impending calamity, and to drive back the minions of despotism. Our ranks are again to be thinned, [2] through the pressure of a terrible exigency. Once more, like wheat, we are thoroughly to be sifted. It is difficult to speak so as not to be misunderstood, or to have our language perverted through party trickery. Nevertheless, we may not be wholly dumb. If we may not hope to gain any converts at this hour, we can at least renew our testimonies, "whether men will hear or forbear."

What, then, is our duty as Abolitionists in the present crisis?

First — what it is *not*.

It is not to abandon our principles, for they are immutable and eternal. It is not to lessen our demands, for they are just and right. It is not to lose sight of, or postpone to a more favourable period, the glorious object we have ever had in view — to wit, the total and immediate extinction of slavery — for this would be fatuity. It is not to substitute the non-extension for the abolition of slavery, for this would be to wrestle with an effect, while leaving the cause untouched — to seek to avert the penalty of sin, while allowing the sin itself to go unrepented of. It is not to lower our standard, in order to propitiate the time-serving and cowardly, or to carry any measure however desirable, for this would be certain defeat. It is not to concentrate our forces upon any geographical or side issue with the Slave Power, for this would be a fatal diversion. It is not to plead for the white labourer to the forgetfulness of the black labourer, nor to concern ourselves exclusively with consecrating to freedom any particular portion of the American soil, for ours is neither a complexional nor a sectional movement. It is not to act upon the jesuitical maxim, that the end sanctifies the means, for this is the all-corrupting sin in every part of this rebellious world. It is not to seek what is most available for the hour, or temporary success upon a false basis, for this is to rely upon numbers, and not upon God — upon policy, and not upon principle.

Our duty is first personal, in regard to ourselves. We are to see to it that we make no truce with slavery, either directly or by implication; that we give to it no religious or political sanction in any form, or to any extent; that our hands are clean, and our consciences without condemnation; that we "remember them that are in bonds as being bound with them."

This duty performed, our next is to call to repentance our guilty land; to impeach, criticise, admonish, entreat, rebuke every sect, every party, every person, in affiance or sympathy with the oppressors, or indifferent to the claims of the perishing bondmen; to reject all half-way measures, while hailing with gladness the smallest indications of progress; to be as inexorable as justice, as contumacious as truth, as unbending as the pillars of the universe; to "put on the whole armour of God, and, having done all, TO STAND." [3]

Where, then, is our proper place in the political struggle which is now convulsing the nation, and exciting an unparalleled anxiety in the breasts of the people?

Surely, not with the Democratic party; beyond all question, the most corrupt, the most shameless, the most abandoned, and the most desperate party in existence. From the beginning, "the natural ally of slavery," it has continued to wax worse and worse, till now it is thoroughly Satanic in spirit and purpose; the embodiment of border-ruffianism; its rank-and-file made up largely of the ignorant, the besotted, the mobocratic, the intensely depraved, the utterly lawless, the horribly profane, the fearfully misguided — and governed by the vilest demagogues, the most dangerous conspirators, and the most bloody-minded tyrants; avowing sentiments more derogatory to human nature, more hostile to human liberty, more insulting to Heaven, than have been promulgated by all the tories of Europe for a thousand years; laughing to scorn the "self-evident truths" of the Declaration of Independence, and impudently branding them as self-evident lies; perfidious to all its pledges, prostrating every barrier of freedom, trampling in the dust the Constitution it has sworn to maintain, and making it a crime worthy of imprisonment and death for freemen to defend their lives and property against the murderous assaults of roving bandits and merciless cut-throats. Language is inadequate to describe the transcendent wickedness of the Democratic party, in its present position and under its present guidance. Its mask is off, and INFERNALISM is stamped upon its countenance. Very many of its adherents are to be pitied, for they are duped through their excessive credulity and ignorance; but the intelligent in its ranks, and at its head, are utterly without excuse. They are manifestly destitute of all honesty, traitors to the cause of liberty, and bent on the overthrow of all our free institutions, to subserve their own ends, and forever to establish the bloody supremacy of the slave power over the whole land — ay, over this whole continent. Under the administration of this party, the government has been overthrown, by a *coup d'etat* of the slave oligarchy in the person of Franklin Pierce,[4] assisted by such conspirators as Caleb Cushing,[5] Jefferson Davis,[6] Stephen Arnold Douglas, Lewis Cass, and the whole body of Kansas ruffians — Atchison, Stringfellow,[7] Lecompte,[8] Shannon,[9] Geary,[10] and their associates — and prompted by such lords of the lash and the bludgeon as Butler and Brooks [11] of Carolina, Wise of Virginia, and Toombs of Georgia. It is mockery now to talk of constitutional guarantees on the side of liberty. We are living under a usurpation as absolute as it is detestable; and the fact that the traitorous occupant of the Presidential chair goes unimpeached and unpunished is demonstrative evidence of the general degradation of the people.

All that this party has done, all that it proposes to do, in the way of fillibustering and slavery extension, by armed invasion and through fire and blood, its candidate for the Presidency, James Buchanan, most cordially sanctions; and yet while I am writing, it is thought to be more than probable that he will obtain the vote of Pennsylvania,[12] and thus secure his election! How much better, then, is Pennsylvania than Georgia or Carolina?

No — no friend of the slave, no enemy of slavery extension, can give his support to the Democratic party or its nominee.

As for the American party,[13] it is based upon proscription, and thoroughly pro-slavery. Its candidate, Millard Fillmore, the infamous signer of the execrable Fugitive Slave Law, openly incites to rebellion, on the part of the South, if the North shall achieve a constitutional triumph in the election of Fremont at the pending election! He is playing a most factious part, animated by that spirit which would "rather reign in hell than serve in heaven," [14] and reveals himself to be more and more the supple tool of the slave oligarchy.

Where stands the Republican party, and to what extent is it deserving of commendation or censure?

1. Unquestionably, it embodies the whole *political* anti-slavery strength of the country — the legitimate product of the *moral* agitation of the subject of slavery for the last quarter of a century; for it is not conceivable that any voter desirous of frustrating the aim of the Slave Power at universal dominion will bestow his suffrage upon either Buchanan or Fillmore. In general intelligence, virtuous character, humane sentiment, and patriotic feeling — as well as in the object it is seeking to accomplish — it is incomparably better than the other rival parties; and its success, *as against those parties*, will be a cheering sign of the times.

2. It is sincerely, strenuously, and against the combined forces of the slave oligarchy, wielded with diabolical malignity, endeavoring to prevent the vast territories of the West from becoming a slaveholding empire, divided into manifold slave States; and to this extent, it is favourable to the cause of freedom.

3. It is allowed no foothold at the South, but is everywhere furiously ostracised, so that no meeting can be safely held to advocate its claims, no electoral ticket favourable to the election of its candidates can be formed, no slaveholder, even, can declare his adhesion to it without imperilling his life, and every vial of slaveholding wrath is poured out upon it, and upon all who are identified with it; notwithstanding its constant disavowal of all wish or intention to interfere with slavery where it now exists.

4. It divides the nation by a geographical line, but without any sectional feeling on its own part; this division being caused solely by its just defence of the rights of the North against the daring invasions of the Slave Power, which is determined to "crush out" every sentiment of freedom in the land, and to punish opposition to its monstrous designs as summarily in Massachusetts as in Virginia or Alabama.

5. It helps to disseminate no small amount of light and knowledge in regard to the nature and workings of the slave system, being neces-

sitated to do this to maintain its position; and thus, for the time being, it is moulding public sentiment in the right direction, though with no purpose to aid us in the specific work we are striving to accomplish — namely, the dissolution of the Union, and the abolition of slavery throughout the land.

All this may be fairly set down to the credit of the Republican party; and it is a wise apostolic injunction to give "credit to whom credit is due." Let us be clear in our discrimination, and just in our award, without yielding one jot or tittle of principle, or moving a hair's-breadth from the path of duty.

Because of this marked difference between these parties, ought we therefore to vote for Fremont [15] and Dayton? [16] Can we vote at all?

As a matter of moral consistency, certainly not — for the following among other considerations:

1. For more than twelve years, in our organized capacity as well as individually (accepting the collective and uniform judgment of the nation respecting the character and design of the instrument), we have solemnly proclaimed the Constitution of the United States to be "A COVENANT WITH DEATH, AND AN AGREEMENT WITH HELL," in consequence of its pro-slavery guarantee, and, therefore, that no oath should be taken to uphold it, either by ourselves or by our representatives. We have persistently called for its repudiation on the ground of its inherent wickedness, and its utter overthrow as the bulwark of the slave system. We have traced to it the amazing growth and omnipresent power of the slave system, and found in it the cause of that corruption and vassalage which pervade the entire North. But, aside from any question touching the letter or the spirit of the Constitution, we have constantly declared it to be an axiom of common sense, as well as of fundamental morality, that between freemen and slaveholders there can be no true union; that it is as easy for Christ and Belial to coalesce as it is for Liberty and Slavery; that the institutions and interests of the North are necessarily hostile to those of the South, and *vice versa* — exciting ever increasing jealousies and leading to continual collisions, as our national history plainly demonstrates; that, without the existing Union, the South would be compelled, for self-preservation, and from necessity, speedily to liberate all her bondmen; and thus the overthrow of this blood-stained compact would lead to the formation of a "solemn league and covenant" between all the States, based upon universal freedom, with no root of bitterness to poison our cup; that, by perpetuating this Union, the Slave Power will grow stronger and stronger, more and more exciting, and be able to consummate its boldest designs; that to call those who make merchandise of their fellow-men, and who vindicate the eternal fitness of slavery to the Southern soil

and climate, Christians and Democrats is as insulting to reason as to talk of honest thieves and sober drunkards — and to think of keeping their company without strife or debate, unless degraded to their own abysmal level, is complete infatuation; that they constitute an oligarchy more tyrannical in spirit, more hostile to human development, more barbarous in their conduct, and more shameless in their villany, than any that has ever cursed mankind; that to separate from them, in form and in fact, is due to self-respect, to true manhood, to the cause of freedom universally, to sound morality, to the Christian religion as exemplified by its glorious founder. Finally, we have faithfully protested against turning aside to attend to some local issue, but have always made the slave the skeleton at every feast — Banquo's ghost that will not down at the bidding or entreaty of any party or sect — the test of statesmanship and true patriotism; insisting that any struggle which leaves his deliverance out of the question, or throws him into the background, is essentially defective, and unworthy of our support.

Now, under all these circumstances, for us to rally to the polls in support of an incidental issue with the Slave Power — to become the partisans of a man who simply prefers that the Western territories should be cultivated by free labourers rather than by slaves — to endorse a party which declares itself ready to carry out all the pro-slavery compromises of the Constitution, and wholly indisposed to meddle with the institution of slavery in the Southern States, merely because it is trying to secure a free homestead for white men — would be the grossest inconsistency, in utter disregard of all our professions, and such a glaring violation of our principles that the whole land would regard us with pity, if not with contempt. Unless it is right to do evil that good may come, we are excluded from the polls, in such a contest, by an insuperable moral barrier. The ballot which is stained with the blood of four millions of slaves is not fit to be handled by a freeman. If we can save Kansas only by first swearing to maintain "A COVENANT WITH DEATH," then God absolves us from all responsibility for its loss. We shall do best for Kansas, best for the South, best for the Republic, by a stern adherence to our principles, and refusing to compromise with sin. Our feet are planted upon the Eternal rock: why should we place them upon a sandy foundation? "If God be for us, who can be against us?" [17]

2. The dissolution of the Union is not to leave the slaves to the mercy of their masters: it is to withdraw from those masters all the resources and instrumentalities now furnished to them by the North, without which they are powerless. It is admitted on all sides, and especially by the leaders of the Republican party, that it is madness for the South to threaten a dissolution of the Union; for it is only

through the Union she is enabled to keep her millions of slaves in their chains. Let her cut the connection, and she will be struck with paralysis. This is true. How unspeakably awful, then, is such a Union! Whatever else a party may be, whatever else it may be trying to do that is praiseworthy, how great must be its guilt in conspiring to make perpetual the enslavement of a population equal to the whole of New England!

3. Let us remember that though there has been a Union in theory, there has never been one in fact, between the free and the slave States; that, from the organization of the government till now, the slave oligarchy has had the reins in its own hands; that the breach widens as the spirit of liberty increases in courage and strength at the North; that a Union still continues to exist in form only because the vassalage of the North is unbroken.

4. What an absurdity it is for those who cannot hold a public meeting at the South in favour of freedom, and who would be lynched if they should make the attempt — for Seward, Hale Sumner, Banks,[18] Wilson, and Giddings — to declare that they will stand by the Union to the last! Padlocks are upon their lips in one-half of the Union; yet they insist on its preservation! Where is their manhood — their self-respect — their love of liberty?

But I will add no more. Let us stand by our cause, by the slave in his chains, by the standard of right, leaving the event in the hands of an all-wise God, who alone sees the end from the beginning.

Yours, for no Union with Slaveholders,

WM. LLOYD GARRISON.

Printed in the *National Anti-Slavery Standard*, October 25, 1856. A portion of this letter is printed in *Life*, III, 444–446.

This letter was read by Oliver Johnson at the Twentieth Annual Meeting of the Pennsylvania Anti-Slavery Society, held at Norristown on Thursday and Friday, October 16 and 17, 1856.

1. Hebrews 11:38.
2. Many abolitionists, Samuel J. May among them, were urging support for John C. Frémont as the presidential candidate of the Republican party. See May's letters, dated August 20 and October 14, 1856, in *The Liberator*, October 24, 1856.
3. Ephesians 6:13.
4. Then President of the United States.
5. Caleb Cushing (1800–1879) had been a Whig representative from Massachusetts from 1835 to 1843, envoy extraordinary and minister plenipotentiary to China from 1843 to 1845, colonel of a Massachusetts regiment in the Mexican War; he was appointed brigadier general in 1847. He was subsequently an unsuccessful Democratic candidate for governor in 1847 and 1848, mayor of Newburyport, Massachusetts, in 1851 and 1852, and appointed attorney general of the United States by President Pierce on March 7, 1853, serving until March 3, 1857. He was chairman of the Democratic National Conventions at Baltimore and Charleston in 1860. (*BDAC*.)
6. Jefferson Davis was then secretary of war in Pierce's cabinet, a position which he held from 1853 to 1857. (*BDAC*.)

7. There were two Stringfellows, brothers, among the "border ruffians" in Kansas. The older, General Benjamin F. Stringfellow (1816–1891) was born in Fredericksburg, Virginia. A graduate of the University of Virginia, he was admitted to the bar in 1835, and moved to Missouri in 1838, where he continued to practice law. He was a member of the state legislature from 1844 to 1845, and thereafter attorney general of the state for four years. He formed a partnership with Colonel P. T. Abell at Huntsville, Missouri, and afterwards at Weston, Missouri. With the opening of Kansas, he took an active part in organizing Missourians, called "border ruffians" by the Free-State men, to dominate the political life of the territory, helping to form the Platte County Self-Defensive Association in 1854 and holding the office of secretary. In 1854, he issued a pamphlet entitled *Negro Slavery no Evil, or, the North and the South; the effects of negro slavery as exhibited in the census, by a comparison of the condition of the slaveholding and non-slave-holding states, considered in a report made to the Platte County Self-Defensive Association, St. Louis, 1854.* He moved to Atchinson, Kansas, in 1858, where he acquired large property interests. For many years, he was the chief attorney of the Kansas City, St. Joseph & Council Bluffs railroad. (William H. Coffin, "Settlement of the Friends In Kansas," *Kansas State Historical Collections*, VII, 1901–1902, 331n; obituary, *The Patriot* [Kansas], May 2, 1891.)

The younger brother, Dr. John H. Stringfellow (b. 1819; fl. 1894) was born in Culpeper County, Virginia, and received his medical degree from the University of Pennsylvania in 1845. He practiced medicine in Missouri until the opening of Kansas to settlement, when he crossed into the territory and helped found the town of Atchison. He was founder and editor of the *Squatter Sovereign* and speaker of the first territorial House of Representatives. In February 1856 he was commissioned captain of the Atchison company, Third Regiment of militia, and in April 1856, colonel of the Third Regiment. He served in the Confederate Army as a surgeon during the Civil War, returning to Atchison in 1871, and moving to St. Joseph, Missouri, in 1876, where he remained the rest of his life. (*Kansas State Historical Collections*, VII, 331n.) According to one writer, "the newspapers, particularly the Eastern newspapers, never knew any difference between the Stringfellows, but J. H. seems to have been more active in early Kansas history; he had made the Stringfellow name known in Kansas while B. F. Stringfellow was peacefully practicing law in Missouri. From what we can learn, wherever you encounter the word Stringfellow in Kansas history, J. H. is usually meant. B. F. was the most pugnacious of the two, but J. H. the most active." (*Atchison Daily Globe*, July 16, 1894.)

8. Samuel Dexter Lecompte (1814–1888), originally of Maryland, was appointed chief justice of Kansas Territory on October 3, 1854. He was residing with his family at Shawnee Mission in 1855. He first enunciated the doctrine of "Constructive Treason," whereby opposition to Kansas Territorial legislation was considered opposition to federal legislation and *ergo* either treason or "constructive treason." It was under this doctrine that many Free-State settlers were arrested and imprisoned. (William E. Connelley, *History of Kansas State and People*, Chicago and New York, 1928, I, 328, 386; James C. Malin, "Judge Lecompte and the 'Sack of Lawrence,' May 21, 1856," *Kansas Historical Quarterly*, 20:465–494, 553–597, August 1953; Oswald Garrison Villard, *John Brown, 1800–1859, A Biography Fifty Years After*, New York, 1943, pp. 100, 109, 142.)

9. Wilson Shannon (1802–1877), lawyer and politician, was appointed governor of Kansas Territory on August 10, 1855, a post which he held until August 1856. His sympathies were with the pro-slavery settlers.

10. John White Geary (1819–1873), an officer and participant in the war with Mexico, succeeded Wilson Shannon as governor of Kansas Territory in September 1856 and held the post until March 4, 1857, when he resigned. He was far less partial than his predecessor to the pro-slavery forces, which earned him their enmity, evoked threats against his life, and led to his resignation.

11. Preston Smith Brooks (1819–1857), Democratic representative from South

Carolina from March 1853 to July 1856 and from August 1856 until his death in January 1857, beat Charles Sumner into insensibility on May 22, 1856.

12. Buchanan did carry Pennsylvania.

13. The American party had been founded in 1854, as a secret political organization whose emphasis was antiforeign and anti-Catholic. Because of its secrecy, its members were known as "Know-nothings." The party's candidate in 1856 was Millard Fillmore, the ex-President, who received 874,534 popular and eight electoral votes. It made no nomination in 1860 but supported the Constitutional Union ticket of Bell-Everett. (*HEUSH.*)

14. John Milton, *Paradise Lost*, Book I, line 261.

15. John Charles Frémont (1813–1890), son-in-law of Senator Thomas Hart Benton, explorer, soldier and politician, was nominated by the newly formed Republican party at Philadelphia in June 1856. He was defeated by Buchanan by an electoral vote of 174 to 114 and a popular vote of 1,838,169 to 1,341,264.

16. William Lewis Dayton (1807–1864), of New Jersey, lawyer and antislavery Whig, served in the United States Senate from 1842 to 1851, where he opposed the treaty for the annexation of Texas, the Mexican War, the extension of slavery and the Compromise of 1850, especially the Fugitive Slave Act. He was Frémont's vice-presidential running mate.

17. Romans 8:31.

18. Nathaniel Prentiss Banks (1816–1894), newspaperman, lawyer and politician, was elected to the Thirty-third Congress as a coalition Democrat, to the Thirty-fourth Congress as a candidate of the American party, and to the Thirty-fifth Congress as a Republican, serving from March 1853 to December 1857, when he resigned to become governor of Massachusetts. He held the latter office until January 1861. In Congress, he was regarded as "the very bone and sinew of Free-soilism" and vigorously opposed the Kansas-Nebraska bill. After a long contest, he was elected Speaker of the House in February, 1856. His election was regarded "as the first defeat of slavery in a quarter of a century."

149

TO ELMINA K. ROBERTS

Boston, Nov. 4, 1856.

Dear Friend:

I will endeavor to hold myself in readiness to lecture on Sunday evening, Nov. 23,[1] before your Society, in case you fail to secure some one else for that occasion. — Nov. 30th, I am engaged to be at Worcester.

Yours, truly,

Wm. Lloyd Garrison.

Miss Elmina K. Roberts.

ALS: Essex Institute, Salem, Massachusetts.

Elmina K. Roberts, probably the sister of Adeline Roberts, was a librarian at the Salem Athenaeum. Elmina and Adeline lived in the same house, at 13 Cedar Street, Salem. (Salem *Directory*, 1869.)

1. Garrison was scheduled to speak before the Salem Female Anti-Slavery Society on that date. (*The Liberator*, November 10, 1856.)

150

TO ELIZABETH BUFFUM CHACE

Boston, Nov. 7, 1856. I thank you for your kind invitation to spend Saturday night at Valley Falls and will do so.

I will inform my friend, Mr. Fairbanks,[1] at Providence, of this arrangement.

Excerpt, printed in L. B. C. Wyman and Arthur Wyman, *Elizabeth Buffum Chace, 1806–1899, Her Life and Its Environment* (Boston, 1914), I, 185.

1. Asa Fairbanks (b. Franklin, Massachusetts, July 24, 1795; d. Providence, Rhode Island, summer of 1876) was a prominent merchant in Providence, first in the hat and cap business, then in the grocery trade and later in cotton. He lectured on behalf of the antislavery cause, he helped fugitive slaves, and his house was always open to antislavery people. In 1845, he married Anna Talbot Richmond, whose brother, William E. Richmond, was a staunch antislavery man and close friend of Garrison, Phillips, and Charles Sumner. (Lorenzo Sayles Fairbanks, *Genealogy of the Fairbanks Family in America*, Boston, 1897, p. 491.)

151

TO MISS ROBERTS

Boston, Nov. 18, 1856.

Miss Roberts:

You may consider me engaged to lecture on Sunday evening next, before the Female Anti-Slavery Society.

Yours, truly,

Wm. Lloyd Garrison.

ALS: Essex Institute, Salem, Massachusetts.

Garrison's letter does not specify Miss Roberts' given name. In view of his letter of November 4, 1856, it is probable that he was again writing to Elmina Roberts.

152

TO RALPH WALDO EMERSON

Boston, Nov. 20, 1856.

Dear Sir:

Mr. C. H. Brainard,[1] of this city, the enterprising publisher of the admirable portraits of Seward, Sumner, Banks, Wilson, Burlingame, &c., &c., (by Grozelier,)[2] intends publishing, very shortly, "a mag-

nificent lithographic print, of the size and style of the Champions of
Freedom," in which will be presented the portraits, drawn from daguerreotypes taken expressly for the purpose, of Theodore Parker, Wendell
Phillips, Joshua R. Giddings, Gerrit Smith, Samuel J. May, &c. He
(as well as such of the parties concerned as have been consulted) is
very desirous that your portrait should be among the number designated; and, accordingly, he wishes me to inquire of you, in his behalf,
whether you are willing to allow him to put your likeness among the
others; and, if so, whether you have a good daguerreotype portrait of
yourself, which you would kindly permit the artist to copy from, on
condition of its being safely returned to you again. May I express the
hope that you will not lay any prohibition upon him in this particular,
his object not being a mercenary one, for he is deeply imbued with the
spirit of liberty and progress, and has a profound admiration of your
genius and character. Should you consent, and yet have no satisfactory
likeness of yourself, should you visit the city in the course of a fortnight, arrangements can be made for a sitting to one of our best
daguerreotypists.

You remember what Byron says of fame: —
    "It is to get a wretched picture, and worse bust"; — [3]
but, in this case, you will be sure of a capital portrait,[4] such as will
delight and satisfy your multitudinous friends and admirers; for Grozelier holds the pencil of a master, in the line of his profession.

Yours, with the highest regards,

Wm. Lloyd Garrison.

Ralph Waldo Emerson, Esq.

ALS: Harvard College Library.

1. Charles H. Brainard (b. Newburyport, Massachusetts; d. Washington, D.C.,
February 4, 1885), self-educated, was at various times a messenger, photographer,
auctioneer, lecturer, writer, and printer. For several years he maintained an art
gallery in Boston. He was well known for his elocutionary skill, especially in
readings of Whittier's poetry. From 1881 until the end of his life he was employed
in the Pension Office at Washington, D.C. (Lucy Abigail Brainard, *The Genealogy
of the Brainerd-Brainard Family in America, 1649–1908*, Hartford Press, 1908,
Miscellaneous Record, p. 152.)

2. Leopold Grozelier (1830–1865) was born in France and came to the United
States in the early 1850's. He worked as a portrait artist in New York in 1852 and
as a lithographic artist in Boston from 1854 until his death in 1865. (George C.
Groce and Davis H. Wallace, *New-York Historical Society's Dictionary of Artists
in America, 1564–1860*, New Haven and London, 1957, p. 278.)

3. George Gordon Noel Byron (1788–1824), *Don Juan*, Canto I.

4. *The Liberator*, December 10, 1858, printed the following item:

"PORTRAIT OF RALPH WALDO EMERSON. C. H. Brainard, of this city, has just
published a very admirable and life-like portrait of Mr. Emerson, after the style
of Theodore Parker, Wendell Phillips, Charles Sumner, Henry Wilson, Wm. H.
Seward, &c. &c., by Grozelier, though by another artist, T. M. Johnston, (son of
D. C. Johnston,) a young genius who at one leap takes his position with the most
skilful in the line of his profession, and is yet to be famous, we predict. . . ."

Elizabeth Pease, about 1851

Helen Benson Garrison, about 1853

Charles Fox Hovey, about 1852

Charles Sumner, at the age of forty-two

153

TO HELEN E. GARRISON

Philadelphia, Dec. 17, 1856.

Dear Wife:

I seize a moment, before going to the Convention [1] this morning, to report progress since I left home.

On leaving the depot in Boston, I commenced reading the "Autobiography of a Female Slave," [2] (the volume I loaned to Mrs. Otis,) [3] and was entirely absorbed in the perusal of it until I arrived at the depot in New York, exactly finishing the volume at that moment. I found it to be a most touching and soul-harrowing description of the unescapable horrors of slavery, surpassing any thing of the kind yet presented to the public; and my heart was as heavy as lead when I got through with it, and the world seemed to be clothed in funereal drapery. O, the blessings of personal freedom! O, the happiness of homes made sacred by love, and safe by general reverence for all parental and filial ties! To realize the blessings we enjoy, we must understand what it is to be the "property" of others.

I found Oliver [Johnson] waiting for me at the depot, with a fine young man named Tilton, [4] connected with the N.Y. *Independent,* [5] who is beginning to take a vital interest in radical abolitionism. Mr. Tilton took us over to his residence in Brooklyn, where we took tea, (Mrs. [Mary Ann] Johnson being with us,) and afterward spent the evening at Mr. Judson's, [6] in company with some thirty or forty ladies and gentlemen, (mostly members of Henry Ward Beecher's church,) including Mr. Beecher himself, his brother William, [7] the Rev. Dr. Marsh, [8] and some prominent Fremont men. Oliver brought with him the first volume of the Liberator, and at the request of Ward Beecher, my dedication to the Cause, in the first number, was read by Mr. Tilton, at the conclusion of which, the whole company joined in clapping their hands, and applauded enthusiastically. Then I was called out, and made an exposition of my views, religiously, politically, and governmentally — a very interesting conversational discussion following, chiefly between Dr. Marsh, Ward Beecher, and myself. I have not time to go into particulars; but the result of the interview was mutually gratifying, Beecher behaving nobly, and all exhibiting the utmost respect and kindness towards me personally. At 10 o'clock, we had a most elegant entertainment served up — tea, coffee, varieties of cake, ice cream, oysters, fruits, &c. &c., in liberal profusion. It must have been quite expensive to Mr. Judson; and though I gratefully appreciated it as a personal compliment, I would have preferred the entire omission of it. Oliver thought my remarks would do more good than any public speech I had made in New York.

I slept at Mr. Tilton's, in company with Oliver.

The next morning, I went to the Anti-Slavery Office, prior to leaving for this city, but had no time to call upon bro. George. I left the bundle for him with Oliver, and expect to see him on my way back. Our friend Bramhall met me at the office, took me down to his store, and accompanied me to Jersey City, where he and his wife now reside. He talks of changing his business, and informed me that Mrs. Bramhall was to be at our Bazaar; so we shall enjoy the pleasure of seeing her in her place on that occasion.

I forgot to state that Miss Wait [9] was at our Brooklyn gathering.

I arrived in this city yesterday afternoon; and found Lucretia [Mott] had carefully preserved my share of the dinner, in anticipation of my coming. She and James are as well as usual, and their house is full of guests. Their daughter Martha [10] has been seriously afflicted with erysipelas in the head and face, but is now convalescent.

Last evening, the Fair opened, and presented a handsome appearance, though the company was not so large as last year. I was surrounded with friends, all eager to take me by the hand, and making special inquiries after you and the children — among others, Joseph A. Dugdale and wife, Mary Grew, Margaret Burleigh,[11] Mrs. Purvis,[12] the daughter of Hannah Cox, &c. &c. To-night I have got to speak at the Fair, as Lucy Stone has failed to be here.

Our Convention begins this morning. My time is up, and I must close by sending to the children my dearest love, and to you all that an affectionate heart can prompt. Remember me kindly to Mary-Ann.

Ever yours,

Wm. Lloyd Garrison.

ALS: Garrison Papers, Boston Public Library.

1. Garrison was in Philadelphia to attend the Twenty-first Pennsylvania Anti-Slavery Fair, held in Philadelphia on December 16, 17, 18, and 19, 1856, and an Anti-Slavery Convention arranged in connection with the fair, which began on December 17 at 11 a.m., and continued through the next day. (See the *National Anti-Slavery Standard*, December 6, 1856.)

2. *The Liberator*, November 28, 1856, carried a short notice and review of the book, "Autobiography of a Female Slave. Redfield, 34 Beekman Street, New York, 1857." It described the book as of "400 pages . . . without preface or explanation." "Having had no time to give it a critical examination, but only rapidly to turn over its pages, we can now only say that we are impressed to recognize it as the production of an elevated mind and a philanthropic heart, admirable in narration and powerfully descriptive, characterised by artistic skill, and full of stirring incident, and as worthy to take its place in the first rank of anti-slavery publications. We cannot even surmise the name of its author, nor yet whether it has a masculine or feminine origin."

A later issue of *The Liberator*, January 9, 1857, printed an extract from the book and explained that it was actually a biography of a slave, written by a white southern woman. "The author of this remarkable work is Miss Mattie Griffith, of Kentucky, (the daughter of a deceased slaveholder,) a young lady of rare personal accomplishments and of brilliant promise, who, ignorant of the radical abolition movement at the north, out of the depths of her own soul brought forth this thrilling testimony against the hideous slave system."

A note accompanying a daguerreotype of Mattie Griffith in the Boston Public Library states the following: "The noble Kentucky girl who emancipated the slaves she inherited and came to the North to escape the atmosphere of slavery. She . . . married Albert G. Browne, private secretary to Gov. John A. Andrew," of Massachusetts. She died on May 25, 1906. She was the daughter of Thomas and Martha (Young) Griffith of Kentucky. J. Stoddard Johnson, in *Memorial History of Louisville (Ky.)* . . . *to the Year 1896*, II, 80, states that she moved to Boston in 1860, and wrote poems and tales for Boston and New York journals. In 1853, she had written a volume, *Poems*, dedicated to "the great people of Kentucky. . . ." On June 27, 1867, she married Albert Gallatin Browne, who later became a prominent journalist and banker. (*Report of the Harvard Class of 1853*, Cambridge, 1913, p. 51.)

3. Lucinda Smith was the daughter of Barney and Hannah Smith of Milton, Massachusetts. She married George Alexander Otis (1781–1863) on September 15, 1802, and settled in Boston. Mrs. Otis was a devoted abolitionist whose home was often visited by Garrison, Phillips, Charles Sumner, and other antislavery men and women. George Otis was an author and translator of several books, including Botta's *History of the War of American Independence*. They had many children, including Lucinda (b. 1808), Mary Amy Georgina (b. Quincy, November 11, 1823; d. Boston, 1908), who was usually referred to as Georgena, and James Eugene (b. Boston, March 5, 1827; d. New Bern, North Carolina, November 8, 1864). (William A. Otis, *A Genealogical and Historical Memoir of the Otis Family in America*, Chicago, 1924, pp. 173, 289.)

4. Theodore Tilton (1835–1907) was the antislavery managing editor of the New York *Independent*, the Congregationalist journal of Henry C. Bowen, from 1856 until early in the Civil War when he became editor-in-chief, holding that position until 1871. As a result of the scandal involving Tilton's wife and Henry Ward Beecher, Tilton's close personal friend, who, for a time, was Tilton's associate as editor of the *Independent* and of whose Plymouth Church Tilton was a member and the superintendent of its Sunday School, Bowen dismissed Tilton from the *Independent* in 1871. Ultimately, Tilton sued Beecher but lost the case. He left the United States in 1883 and spent the remainder of his life in Europe, writing books and articles.

5. The New York *Independent* was a weekly Congregational newspaper, with strong antislavery leanings, founded in 1848, edited first by Henry Ward Beecher and then by Theodore Tilton. Henry C. Bowen, a New York merchant, was one of its founders and later became its publisher and sole owner. It continued in existence until 1928. (Frank Luther Mott, *American Journalism, A History: 1690–1960*, 3d. ed., New York, 1962, p. 378.)

6. Charles G. Judson, a merchant dealing in rubber goods, was a member of the Reverend Henry Ward Beecher's church from 1858 to 1863. His wife, Fanny, was a member from 1853 to 1862. (Noyes L. Thompson, *The History of Plymouth Church*, New York, 1873, p. 259; letter from James J. Heslin, The New York Historical Society, November 24, 1972.)

7. William Henry Beecher (b. January 15, 1802; d. 1889), the eldest son of Lyman Beecher and, like his father and brother, a Congregationalist minister, was for many years a home missionary on the Western Reserve, and held pulpits in Ohio and Massachusetts. Barbara M. Cross, ed., *The Autobiography of Lyman Beecher* (Cambridge, Mass., 1961, 2 vols.), I, 90, notes that William "served as itinerant preacher until his father got him a parish in Newport. He had trouble holding churches, and seven pastorates ended in dismission. For a time he served

as agent for the Sabbath School Union. His last church was in a small town in Mass., where he served as village postmaster as well."

8. John Marsh (1788–1864), clergyman and temperance worker, was pastor of the First Congregational Church in Haddam, Connecticut, for many years, beginning in 1818. He became secretary of the Connecticut temperance society which was organized in 1829, and delivered temperance lectures throughout the state. He continued his temperance activities in Philadelphia in 1833, and in New York City in 1836, where he edited the *Temperance Journal*.

9. Unidentified.

10. Martha Mott, the Motts' youngest child, was born in 1828 and, in 1853, married George W. Lord. (Anna Davis Hallowell, ed., *James and Lucretia Mott. Life and Letters*, Boston, 1884, pp. 91, 337.)

11. Margaret Burleigh, originally Margaret Jones of Philadelphia, married Cyrus Moses Burleigh, the abolitionist and temperance advocate, on February 3, 1855. Her husband died on March 7 of the same year. (*Letters*, II, 610.)

12. Harriet Forten, the daughter of James Forten, married Robert Purvis in 1834. She was active in the Philadelphia Female Anti-Slavery Society, especially in its social and fund-raising activities, and each year served on the society's annual fair committee. She was later involved in the movement to end racial segregation on Philadelphia's street cars. John Greenleaf Whittier wrote a poem entitled "To the Daughters of James Forten." (Sylvia G. L. Dannett, *Profiles of Negro Womanhood*, Yonkers, 1964, Vol. I, *1619–1900*, pp. 82–85.)

VII INTENSIFIED CALLS FOR DISUNION: 1857

T HE YEAR OPENED with an observance on January 2 at Faneuil Hall of the twenty-fifth anniversary of the founding of the Massachusetts Anti-Slavery Society, and a Massachusetts Disunion Convention in Worcester, Massachusetts, on January 15. The supporters of the convention were limited to abolitionists, with a scattering of Republicans. The convention "Resolved, That the sooner the separation takes place, the more peaceful it will be; but that peace or war is a *secondary consideration*, in view of our present perils. Slavery must be conquered, 'peacefully if we can, forcibly if we must.'" A state committee, with Thomas Wentworth Higginson as chairman, was formed to publicize the movement for disunion within the state. The spirit of disunion was further strengthened by the Dred Scott decision, issued on March 6, by Chief Justice Roger Taney.

In July, a call to a northern disunion convention was issued under the signatures of Thomas Wentworth Higginson, Wendell Phillips, Garrison, Daniel Mann, and Francis W. Bird. The convention was to inquire into the feasibility of disunion, without committing anyone in advance to the doctrine itself, and was to be held in Cleveland, Ohio, on October 28 and 29. Unfortunately, the financial panic played havoc with the arrangements, and the convention could not be held.

In August, Garrison learned that there was $387.75 on deposit in a Baltimore bank, in an old account of his mother and that he was entitled to the money, less a deduction for the care of his mother's and sister's graves in Baltimore. The final sum, $350, arrived in September, about two weeks before the death of Charlotte Newell, Garrison's mother's youngest sister, who was living with the Garrisons, and helped to cover some of her medical and burial expenses.

154

TO THEODORE TILTON

Boston, Jan. 17, 1857.

My Dear Friend:

I thank you for your note, acknowledging the receipt of the volume of my writing,[1] which I had the pleasure to forward to you by our mutual friend Johnson. With all my heart, I reciprocate the hope you express, that our acquaintance may ripen into a closer intimacy and an enduring friendsip.

In reading the volume referred to, you will remember that it is largely composed of editorial articles very hastily written, with no expectation whatever of their subsequent appearance in a book form. While, however, I do not wish to have any literacy test applied to it, I am willing that the principles and doctrines which it inculcates should be subjected to the most fiery ordeal.

Yours, for eternal progression,

Wm. Lloyd Garrison

Theodore Tilton.

ALS: New York Historical Society.

1. The volume must have been *Selections from the Writings and Speeches of William Lloyd Garrison,* published at Boston by R. F. Wallcut in 1852.

155

TO FRANCIS JACKSON

Sunday Evening. [February, 1857.]

Dear Friend Jackson:

Our friend Wendell Phillips's admirable bust, in marble, being now completed, I wish to pay the artist the sum you have in your possession for that purpose. I will then put into your hands a complete list of the names of all the donors, with the entire receipts given at various times by the artist for value received. Should you be at the office tomorrow, or on any subsequent day, you can leave the money with him, should I not happen to be there.

Truly yours,

Wm. Lloyd Garrison.

ALS: Garrison Papers, Boston Public Library. The date has been inserted by a later hand.

1 5 6

TO LYDIA MARIA CHILD

Boston, Feb. 6, 1857.

My dear Mrs. Child:

I am just on the wing for western New York, to attend a series of Anti-Slavery Conventions in that quarter,[1] and must send you a very brief answer to your interesting and suggestive letter.

I own the three volumes of Abdy's [2] Travels in the U.S., and they are at your service for any length of time you may desire. I shall leave them in the care of my wife, to be given to you when you come to the city, as I shall be absent at that time.

I thank you for calling my particular attention to the manner in which you have treated the subject of slavery, in your admirable work on the Progress of Religious Ideas; [3] and on my return home, (probably about the 23d instant,) I will gladly make suitable extracts for the Liberator.

I shall say nothing to any one about your inquiries on the subject of Spiritual Manifestations. I am a firm believer in the reality of those Manifestations, after the many things I have witnessed, and the various tests I have seen applied; yet I am not a credulous man, nor at all given to the marvellous, and seldom exercise my ideality. True, there are many discrepancies, incongruities, and absurdities attending these Manifestations; but nothing do I find so puerile, or so preposterous, as the various theories which are started to account for them, short of a spiritual origin: I regret that I am to be absent from the city at the time you are to be here, and so can make no arrangement with you to test the matter.

I do not greatly wonder at your "distrust of professional *paid* mediums"; and yet, is it unreasonable if I ask a person to give me his time, his room, &c., for him to require some remuneration, especially when (as is generally the case) he is very poor? Beyond a doubt, some mediums are base imposters, and are pursuing the business merely as selfish adventurers.

The best medium I have ever seen is a Mrs. Tribou,[4] of Hanover, in this State, who comes to this city occasionally, and has just returned home. I wish you could see her, because I have no doubt you would obtain what you so much desire. She is most reliable, and remarkable as a writing, rapping, tipping, healing, and personating medium — being manifold.

Mrs. Eddy [5] will be a good person to consult when you come to the city.

With warm regards to Mr. Child,[6] and unbounded esteem for yourself, I remain,

Ever truly yours,

Wm. Lloyd Garrison.

ALS: Garrison Papers, Boston Public Library.

1. Garrison was scheduled to speak at a series of Anti-Slavery Conventions scheduled for the following dates, under the auspices of the American Anti-Slavery Society: Rochester, Tuesday and Wednesday, February 10 and 11; Syracuse, Friday and Saturday, February 13 and 14; Utica, Monday and Tuesday, February 16 and 17.

A New York State Anti-Slavery Convention was to be held in Albany, on Friday, Saturday, and Sunday, February 20, 21 and 22. (*The Liberator*, February 6, 1857.)

A detailed report of the Rochester convention appeared in *The Liberator*, February 27, 1857. A rather sketchy account of the various conventions was given by Garrison in *The Liberator*, March 6, 1857.

2. Edward Strutt Abdy (1791–1846), fellow of Jesus College, Cambridge, England, was the author of *Journal of a Residence and Tour in the United States of North America, from April, 1833 to October, 1834* (London, 1835, 3 vols.).

3. *The Progress of Religious Ideas Through Successive Ages* (London, 1855, 3 vols.).

4. Mary Tilden (July 3, 1791–December 9, 1879) of Hanover, New Hampshire, married John Tribou in 1810. They had eight children, of whom three sons were married by this time, thus giving us three more Mrs. Tribou's. The precise identity of Mrs. Tribou, the spiritualist mentioned by Garrison, eludes us. (Jedidiah Dwelley and John F. Simmons, *History of the Town of Hanover*, Hanover, 1910, pp. 410, 419.)

5. Eliza Frances Eddy.

6. David Lee Child (1794–1874), journalist, teacher, lawyer, member of the Massachusetts legislature and former editor of the *National Anti-Slavery Standard*. (*Letters*, I, 41 *et passim*; II, 134 *et passim*; III, *passim*.)

157

TO HELEN E. GARRISON

Albany, Feb. 8, 1857.
Sunday forenoon.

Dear Wife:

You will see, by the date of this letter, where I am, and that I was wise enough to rest here over night, and not continue my journey. Nevertheless, if our train had not been two hours behind its regular time from Boston, (waiting at different stations for the "down trains," for the want of a double track,) I should have taken the 6 o'clock train, last evening, for Syracuse, according to my original design, which train I intend to take this evening. I came directly to my esteemed friend Lydia Mott's residence, and found her and her sister Jane [1] at home, and well, who were somewhat expecting to see me. Having sat up so late the night previous, I was exceedingly weary, and at 10 o'clock found an excellent bed, and enjoyed a most refreshing repose till 8 o'clock this morning.

I saw only one person in the cars whom I knew — Benjamin Snow,[2] of Fitchburg, who was going to Pittsfield with his wife and child, on a visit. I did not see her, as she was in another car — he coming to me, and chatting awhile.

The rail-road was in a better condition than I expected to find it, though somewhat affected by the late severe cold and frost. The weather seemed as mild as April, rendering a fire unnecessary; and to-day it is warm and genial, though the sky is overcast as though a change is at hand — the water rushing in torrents down the gutters. By the time our convention comes off at Rochester, I expect we shall have plenty of snow for rain, and the mercury indicating freezing instead of melting weather. But I have no controversy with the maker of the weather.

I am writing on the half of a sheet which contains a letter written for Mary-Ann [3] by Fanny,[4] to her sister, almost a month ago. How it got into my bag, I do not know. Did Fanny miss it, and write another at the time? Or was none sent at all? If the latter was the case, and Mary-Ann would still like to have the letter sent, this sheet can be torn in two, and her half of it enclosed in an envelope, and directed to her sister, with an explanation accompanying it.

Tell George [Thompson Garrison] to remind Mr. [Robert] Wallcut to send Seth Hunt,[5] of Northampton, half a dozen copies of the Liberator containing his letter, explaining his position on the Disunion question. I need not ask George to look after the cat during my absence, for he is my natural successor in that line — only he must not give her too much at a meal.

I hope Fanny is less troubled with her cough. If it should get no better, I wish you would ask Mrs. Edmund Jackson [6] about the cough syrup she makes use of, and try its virtues in Fanny's case. Possibly, you may deem it necessary to consult Dr. Geist: [7] if so, don't hesitate about doing so.

Tell my dear and venerated friend, Mrs. Otis, that I am thinking of her all along my journey, and feel as if her spirit were accompanying me like a benediction. — May her sick chamber be the favorite resort of angelic and ministering spirits. My regards to Georgena and James.[8]

As many kisses for Fanny and Franky, in my behalf, as you please. Remember me to Mary-Ann. Tell Henry [C. Wright] to be sure and abide under my roof.

Yours, most lovingly,

W. L. G.

☞ Lydia and her sister send their warm regards.

ALS: Garrison Papers, Boston Public Library.

1. Jane Mott of Albany, New York (b. October 17, 1793), the fifth child of Daniel and Amy Mott (Thomas C. Cornell, *Adam and Ann Mott: Their Ancestors and Their Descendants*, Poughkeepsie, New York, 1890, p. 219).

2. Benjamin Snow, Jr., of Fitchburg, a director of the Worcester County, North, Anti-Slavery Society (*The Liberator*, April 24, 1857), died in the Worcester Insane Asylum on May 15, 1892, at the age of seventy-eight. He was a paper manufacturer and real estate dealer. He was one of the leaders of the antislavery withdrawal from the Calvinistic Congregational Church and a founder of the Trinitarian Congregational Church, built on Fox Flats, which became a station on the Underground Railroad. He helped many fugitive slaves escape from Boston to Montreal, often using his own house as a shelter. He was also a farmer, with an apple orchard and garden. Garrison and Phillips were often guests at his house. (Doris Kirkpatrick, *The City and the River*, Fitchburg, 1971, pp. 166, 192, 193, 259–260, 262–264, 285, 297; obituary, Boston *Evening Transcript*, May 16, 1892.)

3. Probably a servant in the Garrison household.

4. Helen Frances, Garrison's daughter.

5. Seth Hunt's letter, dated "Northampton, Feb. 2, 1857," appeared in *The Liberator*, February 20, 1857. Seth Hunt (1814–1893), a devotee of temperance and vegetarianism, was an employee of the Connecticut River Railroad Company from 1844 to the end of his life. (*Daily Hampshire Gazette*, July 3, 1893.)

6. Edmund Jackson married Mary H. Hewes in 1827. They had eleven children, five of whom died in infancy or by the age of three. (Letter from Ruth E. Cannard, Director-Curator, Jackson Homestead, Newton, Mass., November 17, 1972.)

7. Dr. Christian F. Geist (1806–1872), a homeopathic physician, had his office in his home at 49 Essex Street, Boston. He practiced in Boston from 1842 to 1872. (Boston *Directory*, 1846–1874; see also *Letters*, III, 356, 357, 367, 404, 538 and 550.)

8. The children of Lucinda Smith Otis. See Letter 153, to Helen Garrison, December 17, 1856, note 3.

158

TO HELEN E. GARRISON

Rochester, Feb. 9, 1857.

Dear Wife:

I wrote a few lines to you yesterday forenoon at Albany. After closing my letter, the Rev. Mr. Mayo (a progressive Universalist clergyman settled in A.) and his wife [1] called to see me at Lydia Mott's, dined with us, and spent the afternoon in a very pleasant interchange of feelings and sentiments. He has been a subscriber to the Liberator for the last two years, though he is not quite ready to subscribe to the doctrine of Disunion. Mrs. Mayo is a sister of Grace Greenwood,[2] but does not resemble her at all. She reminded me of Abby Kelley Foster, of Miss Carleton,[3] and of Lydia Spooner [4] — three in one — looking more like Lydia than either of the others, as a whole. She is a firm believer in Spiritualism, and a partial medium, and related to me many interesting facts as occurring within her knowledge.

I left Albany last evening, (Sunday,) in the 6 o'clock train, for Rochester, in the midst of a pouring rain — the weather being almost as warm as in June. The Hudson river had risen six feet, and it was feared that some of the railroad bridges between Albany and Rochester might be carried away by the flood, or so weakened as to make the travelling somewhat perilous. However, we fortunately met with no serious obstruction; but the change in the weather, on the route, was most extraordinary — seemingly making a difference of 50 degrees in the course of three or four hours; so that, from Syracuse to this place, we were all shivering in the cars, in spite of a good fire in the stove, and Jack Frost was busy in covering all the panes of glass with his curious handiwork. Our train arrived here this morning at half past 4; and at 5, I was in a good bed at the hotel, where I slept till 10 o'clock, having enjoyed a very refreshing slumber. I am now in the parlor of my beloved friends, Isaac and Amy Post. Charles L. Remond and sister [5] are here also, and in good health and spirits, — though they have had a hard time of it for the last two months.

I have not yet seen Susan B. Anthony, but expect she will be here this afternoon. Mr. May [6] I did not see on my way at Syracuse, but we hope to have him with us to-morrow. Considerable disappointment is felt at the absence of Parker Pillsbury, and they wish that he had come here, if he could not have spoken elsewhere.

How we shall get along with our convention, I do not know. Six meetings look to me very formidable, especially as I do [not] as yet feel in the mood for speaking at all. Should Mr. May fail us, we shall be short-handed. Douglass,[7] I am told, intends to show fight, but I trust and advise that no reply may be made to any thing he may say of us.

I am still anxious about Fanny's cough. Let her be careful of herself; for, "of all the little girls I see," &c. &c.

Franky must grow as strong and stout as possible while I am gone. Wendell must not study too hard.

Give my kindest remembrances to dear Mrs. Otis.

I write in haste, as usual, and have no more time left, except to subscribe myself,

Your loving husband,

W. L. G.

☞ Remember me to Mary-Ann.

ALS: Garrison Papers, Boston Public Library.

1. Lucy Caroline Clarke married the Reverend Amory Dwight Mayo, as his second wife, on June 7, 1853.

2. Grace Greenwood was the pen name of Sara Jane Clarke Lippincott (1823–1904). Poet, editor, author of children's books, she wrote for many journals and newspapers of the day, including *Graham's, Sartain's,* the *Union Magazine, Na-*

tional Era, and the *Saturday Evening Post.* Her *Greenwood Leaves* (1850), a collection of magazine pieces, was a best seller, and her volume *Poems* (1851) was widely praised. Her volume of reports of her trip to Europe in 1852–1853, *Haps and Mishaps of a Tour in Europe* (1854), was extremely popular. Her children's books included *Merrie England* (1855) and *Bonnie Scotland* (1861). In 1853, she married Leander K. Lippincott, a young Philadelphian. The marriage was apparently an unhappy one. In 1876, Lippincott, under indictment for fraudulent Indian land claims, fled the country to escape trial. (*Notable American Women.*)

3. See Letter 112, to Helen Garrison, June 15, 1855.

4. Lydia E. Sylvester (1828–1867) married John Spooner in 1851. John was the son of Hannah and Bourne Spooner, the abolitionists of Plymouth, Massachusetts. The Bourne Spooners and the Garrisons were close friends. At the time of Lydia's death in 1867, Garrison wrote as follows: "You can easily imagine how surprised, pained and shocked we were by the intelligence of the death of Lydia Spooner; and we still find it hard to credit the fact. You know how kind and loving she always was to Fanny, and with what affection Fanny has ever regarded her. Lydia was also much attached to our whole family. She was remarkable for her personal beauty and attractions, and, of course, was praised and flattered to a perilous extent; but she never exhibited any vanity, and retained her ingenuousness and self poise in an admirable manner. It was always a pleasure to me to meet her, she was so kind, bright, cheerful, companionable. Poor John must feel the blow heavily; and as for our dear, stricken friends, Mr. and Mrs. Bourne Spooner, they must be overwhelmed by this terrible bereavement. I shall write to them by this mail, expressive of my sympathy and grief at the sad event." (Letter to Helen Garrison, June 7, 1867, Garrison Papers, Boston Public Library; I am indebted to Allen D. Russell of Plymouth, Massachusetts, letter dated July 31, 1972, for biographical information about the Spooner family.)

5. Sarah Parker Remond (1826–1887?), black abolitionist and physician of Salem, Massachusetts, sister of abolitionist Charles Lenox Remond, was active in the Salem Female Anti-Slavery Society, and the Essex County and Massachusetts Anti-Slavery Societies. In 1856, she became an agent of the American Anti-Slavery Society. In 1859 she went to Europe, first England, then Florence, Italy, where she continued her education, spoke and wrote about American slavery and, after the Civil War, studied and practiced medicine. She lived in Florence until her death. (*Notable American Women;* see also Letter 256, to the Editor of the *Anti-Slavery Advocate,* December 28, 1858.)

6. Samuel J. May.

7. Frederick Douglass was opposed to Garrison's disunionism and favored the use of the political process to end slavery.

159

TO HELEN E. GARRISON

Syracuse, Feb. 12, 1857.

Dear Wife:

I have just arrived from Rochester, in company with dear Samuel J. May, who was with us through our meetings in that place, and did us excellent service.[1] Those meetings were not very well attended, but they were highly spirited and interesting, and a deep impression was manifestly produced in regard to our principles and measures.

About seventy-five dollars were raised by contribution and the sale of tickets. Douglass was fortunately absent at Philadelphia, and so we were spared any display of malevolence on his part. Watkins [2] took his place, (though not in his spirit,) and made the best defence he could — and it was ably done — in behalf of the Anti-Slavery character of the Constitution. A leading Republican (Mr. Stebbins) [3] occupied an hour and a half on the same side, in a very jesuitical manner — followed by Samuel R. Porter; [4] but there was no difficulty in disposing of them all. At times, the discussion was quite spicy, attended by some humorous incidents. Our Rochester friends were delighted with the convention throughout — the only regret felt being on account of the thinness of the attendance. Their hospitality was, as usual, all that could be desired. I stopped with friend Post, and Mr. May with a Unitarian Republican acquaintance, Mr. Fogg. [5] Remond and his sister were also at friend Post's. Sarah spoke but once in our meetings, but acquitted herself admirably. She only needs a little more confidence and a little more practice to make her a good lecturer. Charles spoke eloquently and to the point, and was much applauded. Aaron M. Powell [6] made two or three capital speeches in a very impressive manner. I spoke a great deal, and took the laboring oar upon me. At present, I am feeling very well, though I have had comparatively little sleep, and shall probably get little till my return home.

Susan Anthony came on with us this forenoon, and has gone to Utica to make arrangements for us in that place, where we shall probably have a very small attendance of the people, or else a large and rowdyish one — it is a hard place.

I called at the post-office, on my arrival here, to see if there were a line from home, but obtained nothing. I shall expect to hear from you between now and Monday, when I shall leave for Utica. I meant to have inquired for a letter at the post-office in Rochester before leaving, but failed to do so; but I do not suppose you have written to me at that place.

I am now stopping with my friends, Mr. and Mrs. Savage [7] — she being a sister of the late venerable and excellent Stephen Smith. [8] Mr. May intended to take me directly to his house, supposing that Charlotte and her husband had left for Glen Haven, [9] on a visit to Joseph, [10] who is there at the Water Cure, to remain a short time, being still greatly debilitated. Should they leave to-day, I shall change my quarters. I have not yet seen any of Mr. May's family, but he told me in Rochester that his wife was in good health and spirits.

Parker Pillsbury has not yet arrived, but will probably be here this evening.

I scarcely know what has transpired in any direction since I left home, not having seen the papers. The Tribune of last Saturday is the latest paper that has been received from New York, in consequence of the damage that has been done by the flood to the Hudson river railroad. Had I been one day later, I could not have got to Rochester in season for the convention, owing to a similar rise of the Mohawk river.

At Rochester, we had cold and stormy weather from the beginning to the close of our convention. This has always been my luck in that place. Theodore Parker is to lecture there this evening. He was to have lectured here on Tuesday evening, and succeeded in getting here in season; but as it was supposed he could not possibly arrive, he lost his lecture in consequence.

With a father's love to the children, and a husband's love to you, I remain,

Ever yours,

W. L. G.

ALS: Garrison Papers, Boston Public Library.

1. The account of the Rochester meetings, of February 10 and 11, appeared in *The Liberator*, February 27, 1857.

2. *The Liberator* account reported that "Mr. W. J. Watkins then took the stand, and declared himself to be an unadulterated, uncompromising Abolitionist. But there is, said he, a difference of opinion among the friends of emancipation as to the means to be made use of to accomplish abolition. Could I see that the Constitution is 'a covenant with death, and an agreement with hell,' I should so declare it, and trample it under foot. But it is easier to *call* it such than to *prove* it to be so.

"He held that the Constitution, viewed in the light of the rules of legal interpretation, is an anti-slavery document. Not that such was the opinion or intention of the framers, but such we find it."

William J. Watkins is listed in the Rochester city directory for 1855–1856 as an associate editor of *Frederick Douglass' Paper*. The 1857–1858 directory lists him as "assistant editor." The New York State census for 1855 lists him as being twenty-seven years old, a native of Maryland, a resident of Rochester for two years, and profession as "none." He was active in the Underground Railroad. (Letter dated September 13, 1972, from Karl Kabelac, assistant librarian, Department of Rare Books, Manuscripts and Archives, University of Rochester Library.)

3. The *Standard*, February 21, 1857, in its account of the Rochester convention, mentions that "J. W. Stebbins defended the anti-slavery purposes of the Republican party, and the anti-slavery character of the Constitution."

John W. Stebbins (b. Herkimer County, New York, 1819; d. Rochester, July 30, 1905) moved to Rochester in 1850 and was admitted to the bar shortly thereafter. He was a member of the state legislature in 1856 and a number of years *later* was postmaster of Rochester. (Ralph Stebbins Greenlee and Robert Lemuel Greenlee, *The Stebbins Genealogy*, Chicago, 1904, p. 1112; William F. Peck, *History of Rochester and Monroe County*, New York and Chicago, 1908, p. 124.)

4. *The Liberator* reported that "Mr. Samuel D. Porter (of Rochester) here desired to present three propositions embracing the constitutional question for discussion this evening. He proceeded at some length to state his propositions, defining his position to be that of firm belief in the anti-slavery character of the Constitution."

Samuel D. (Garrison's "R" is incorrect) Porter (d. March 6, 1881) came to Rochester in 1827 and earned his livelihood as a bookseller. He was originally an active member of the American Anti-Slavery Society and later supported the

Liberty party, running for mayor many times on that party's ticket despite the paucity of votes cast for him. In 1848, he was a Free Soiler of the Myron Holley-Gerrit Smith school of abolition. He was a friend of the Frederick Douglasses, helping Douglass in 1857 to open Rochester's public school to black children. His barn was for many years a station on the Underground Railroad. (Amy Hamner-Croughton, "Anti-Slavery Days," in Edward R. Foreman, *Rochester Historical Society Publication Fund Series*, Vol. XIV, Rochester, 1936, pp. 121–122, 125, 130; also Vol. II, Rochester, 1923, pp. 59, 122–123.)

5. James P. Fogg, a dealer in seeds, was then living in Rochester. He is listed in the 1850 census as being thirty-seven years old and a native of New Hampshire. His wife, Emily, also thirty-seven, was born in Massachusetts. Fogg is first listed in the Rochester city directory in 1844. He lived in Rochester until about 1862. In addition to being a Unitarian Republican, Fogg was also a temperance supporter. (Karl Kabelac, Department of Rare Books, Manuscripts and Archives, University of Rochester Library, Rochester, New York, letter dated November 2, 1972.)

6. Aaron Macy Powell (b. Clinton, Dutchess County, New York, March 26, 1832; d. May 13, 1899) was a lecturing agent for the American Anti-Slavery Society from 1852 to 1865, and editor of the *National Anti-Slavery Standard* from 1865 to 1870 and of the *National Standard* from 1870 to 1872. From 1872, for the remainder of his life, he devoted much of his time to temperance and prison reform. He was the author of *State Regulation of Vice*, published in 1878. His *Personal Reminiscences of the Anti-Slavery and Other Reforms and Reformers* appeared posthumously in 1899.

7. Richard Savage (b. Syracuse, 1817; d. there, 1885) was a canal captain early in life. He built and managed the St. Charles Hotel in Syracuse and later engaged in the lumber trade. (Dwight H. Bruce, ed., *Memorial History of Syracuse, New York*, Syracuse, 1891, p. 243.)

8. Stephen Smith (b. New Bedford, Massachusetts, October 25, 1776; d. Syracuse, New York, April 23, 1854) was well known as a business man and reformer in Syracuse, where he lived for more than thirty years. In October 1850 he signed a call for a meeting to protest the Fugitive Slave Law. His obituary noted that "his irreproachable morals, kindly and unpretending manners, and unswerving integrity, endeared him to every one who had the pleasure of his acquaintance. His business capacity was inferior to none, and in every benevolent enterprise and reformatory movement, he was among the foremost. . . ." His occupations and business enterprises included that of blacksmith and employee of Messrs. Minturn & Champlin, a large shipping house in New York City, a job which involved an extended trip to Europe and another to India, as supercargo on a ship. He subsequently engaged in the manufacture of salt from sea water. (Syracuse *Daily Standard*, April 25, 1854; letter from Richard N. Wright, President, Onondaga Historical Association, Syracuse, New York.)

9. A summer resort at the southeast end of Lake Skaneateles in Cayuga County, New York. The water cure at Glen Haven had been established by the abolitionist and physician James Caleb Jackson, with Dr. Silas O. Gleason, in the late 1840's. (*Letters*, II, 577.)

10. Son of the Reverend and Mrs. Samuel J. May. See *Letters*, II, 25.

1 6 0

TO HELEN E. GARRISON

Utica — Tuesday — noon.
Feb. 17, 1857.

Dear Wife:

Here I am, on my way homeward. At Syracuse, I was glad to get a letter from Wendy, informing me about home affairs. To-day, I have received a letter from you, and dear Fanny, and my beloved friend H. C. Wright — a trinity in whom I believe, and for whom I could lay down my life. I was delighted to hear from you all, and, though troubled a little about her cough and feverish symptoms, I felt somewhat relieved about Fanny on reading your letter. Still carefully watch her symptoms, and see that she does not unnecessarily expose herself. How much I love that child — how dear she is to my soul! Not simply because she is ours, but because I see in her a most affectionate and generous spirit, and the most promising elements of a noble character. And my dear Franky — is he not also a part of my existence — a child beyond his years, and combining the most excellent traits? Do I not love you all — wife and children dear — beyond the power of utterance? Heaven keep you all, and enable me soon to embrace you under our own roof.

Our meetings were a failure in Syracuse, (as at Rochester,) as to numbers, but they were deeply interesting to those who attended, nevertheless. Gerrit Smith was present at some of them, and some sharp collisions occurred between us in the debate, of an unpleasant nature. I was made sad by some of the developments of his mind and nature on that occasion. His moral philosophy is shambling, and he is as slippery as an eel in discussion. However, notwithstanding his personal popularity in that region, his commanding personal presence, and his oracular manner, he gained nothing, but lost much, by the encounter with us. Douglass was present at the meetings, but wisely and fortunately remained dumb throughout. I did not and would not speak to him. Stephen S. Foster was unexpectedly present, to advocate his Utopian doctrine about forming a new anti-slavery political party; but he made no converts, but was as one beating the air. He spoke ably and effectively, however, on the relations of the church and clergy to slavery. Mr. May presided over our deliberations, and seems now to be prepared to adopt our Disunion views. To adopt and enforce them, I apprehend, would cost him his pulpit in Syracuse, and I fear there are breakers ahead for him, for attending these Disunion Conventions.

I staid all the time at Mr. Savage's and was most comfortably accommodated in all things. He and his wife, though formerly disbelievers in immortality, are now Spiritualists, and have striking manifestations frequently. — I was at several sittings of the circles, and saw and heard many interesting things, all confirming my faith in spiritual agency. But as this is a disagreeable subject to your mind, I will add no more.

We arrived here yesterday, (Monday) forenoon, and commenced our meetings at once, under no favorable circumstances. We held three sessions yesterday — have just completed the fourth — and are to have another this afternoon and evening, to complete the series. Mr. May and Mr. Pillsbury were advertised to be with us, but neither has come, and neither is now expected; consequently, the labor of speaking has devolved upon Powell, Remond and myself. This morning, Powell left us for the Hudson Convention [1] — so that Remond and myself have to do all the talking — the laboring oar being in my hands. I am very weary and exhausted, as you may suppose, for my soul enters warmly into my work, yet I have no cold, and am in good health. I am stopping at Bagg's hotel, not knowing where to go when I came; but, since, two or three persons have invited me home, among them the Presiding Elder of the Methodist Episcopal Church! [2] I have concluded not to change my quarters, and shall leave in the morning for Albany, where I hope again to hear from you. On Thursday evening, Remond and myself will speak in Troy — then will come the three days' meetings in Albany — and on Monday evening next, I am to be at Springfield, with Parker Pillsbury, to address the people — and I trust on Tuesday evening, at tea-time, shall be once more, where I am ever most happy to be, by your side. Love to all the children, Henry, and Mary-Ann, and dear Mrs. Otis.

Ever yours,

W. L. G.

ALS: Garrison Papers, Boston Public Library. The date has been inserted by another hand.

1. *The Liberator*, February 6, 1857, carried the following announcement: "Hudson Convention, at the New York City Hall, Wednesday, Feb. 18. . . . Wendell Phillips, Parker Pillsbury, and Aaron M. Powell, to be in attendance." Hudson is in Columbia County, New York. This was one of a series of county antislavery conventions sponsored by the American Anti-Slavery Society. (See the *Standard*, January 24, 31, 1857.)

2. The Reverend Mr. Parks of Utica, New York. See Letter 161, to Helen, February 18, 1857.

1 6 1

TO HELEN E. GARRISON

Utica, Feb. 18, 1857.

Dear Wife:

I sent you a line by last evening's mail, and this morning, while waiting for the train to take me to Albany, sit down to add a few words more.

Our Convention here terminated last evening. We had three satisfactory meetings during the day and evening, though the attendance was meagre, and without the presence of friends from West Winfield, Rome, and one or two adjacent places, would not have warranted us to proceed. Utica is crammed with orthodox piety, but is as dead and corrupt as a grave-yard respecting the cause of the oppressed, and reformatory movements generally. The newspaper press, of every description, has held us up to ridicule and opprobrium in the meanest way, caricaturing our proceedings, and deceiving the people in the basest manner. Yet I have never attended a series of meetings with more satisfaction to myself. I have never felt more strongly moved by the spirit to speak, and it seemed to be "in demonstration of the spirit, and with power." [1] My strongest points were most warmly endorsed by the assembly, and no exception was taken to any thing that fell from my lips. Remond was extremely felicitous and truly eloquent in all his speeches, and was listened to with great attention and applause. Those present were highly intelligent, and of the very best material. Yesterday afternoon, we had short, but co-operative speeches from Rev. Mr. Karcher,[2] of Rome, (a young and promising Universalist preacher,) and Rev. Mr. Skinner,[3] of Little Falls, a Massachusetts man, and also a Universalist preacher. In the evening, Rev. Mr. Parks, the Presiding Methodist Elder, (who invited me to stay with him,) took some exceptions to some remarks made by Susan B. Anthony, to whom I replied in a manner that elicited no further defence on his part, and was very acceptable to the audience. I am sure we have not visited Utica in vain. Indeed, I am satisfied that the whole series of Conventions projected in this State will prove a capital investment for our cause, notwithstanding the pecuniary outlay required.

What our meetings will be at Albany, remains to be seen. No doubt we shall be vilely aspersed by the press, and in some cases by the pulpits also. I presume there will be a number of reporters present. I forgot to mention, that the New York Herald sent one of its reporters all the way to Utica, to report (i.e. caricature) our proceedings. Let George preserve the Heralds for me till I get back. Republicanism we find to be very poor stuff every where, and yet it is the best there is outside of our own ranks. Disunionism, as we present it, silences every opponent, and makes a powerful impression — there is no escape from the moral pressure we bring to bear upon the question. It is the only vital issue of the times, and must be pushed with all boldness and confidence.

Mr. May was not with us yesterday, but I hope he will be at Albany.

I hardly know what has transpired in the country since I left home, as I keep no run of the papers. Every thing will be disjointed with me till I am once more at my office.

I have not yet seen the Liberator of Friday, and do not know that a single copy of it is taken in this place. I shall find it at Lydia Mott's, in Albany.

It is possible, on getting to Albany this afternoon, that I may slip down to Hudson, (some 30 miles,) and attend the evening meeting with Phillips and Parker Pillsbury. Pillsbury having had a very bad cold at Syracuse, and failing to be with us here, may not be at Hudson; which makes my presence there a little more desirable. Powell is very anxious to have me there; but I must not attempt too much. This morning, I feel quite refreshed, and should like to have a dance with Fanny and Frank, to whom (and George and Wendell) I send a father's love.

You did not say, in your letter, what success Lizzie had in taking your likeness. Probably, it was too early to tell.

Have you seen my bust?

Remember, I am to be at Springfield on Monday evening, and on Tuesday evening, at 14 Dix Place, if permitted.

Give my constant remembrances to dear Mrs. Otis.

Ever lovingly,

W. L. G.

ALS: Garrison Papers, Boston Public Library. Garrison originally dated the letter "Feb. 17," but the 17 was later crossed out and "18" inserted above it, whether by Garrison or by someone else it is uncertain.

1. I Corinthians 2:4.
2. Otherwise unidentified.
3. Possibly Otis Ainsworth Skinner (b. Royalton, Vermont, July 3, 1807; d. Napierville, Illinois, September 18, 1861), a Universalist minister who served churches in Boston and New York between 1831 and 1857. He then moved to Elgin, Illinois, and was elected president of Lombard University at Galesburg. The following year he became pastor of the church of Joliet, Illinois. (Newton Bateman and Paul Selby, *Biographical and Memorial Edition of the Historical Encyclopedia of Illinois*, Chicago, 1915, p. 482.)

1 6 2

TO HELEN E. GARRISON

Albany, Feb. 19, 1857.

Dear Wife:

Before starting for Troy, this afternoon, to speak there with Remond this evening, I seize my pencil to send you an additional hasty scrawl.

We arrived here safely, yesterday, at 4 o'clock, P.M., from Utica, all of us pretty thoroughly jaded, though in good spirits. Charles and Sarah [Remond] are stopping at Mr. Topp's,[1] and Susan B. Anthony and myself at Lydia Mott's, where we are having a refreshing time, of course. Search the world over, and no better woman can be found than Lydia Mott — none more true to principle, none more clear-sighted, none more morally courageous, none more hospitable to the friends of the slave, and of reform generally. Her pecuniary means must be as limited as her heart is large, as she has to work very industriously with her needle to make a livelihood for herself and her eldest sister,[2] who is wholly dependant upon her. To proffer her any thing for her hospitality, in the shape of remuneration, would not be agreeable to her; and yet she must be heavily taxed, in this way, in the course of a year, by the many persons who call upon her. If anyone ever deserved the scriptural panegyric, "She hath done what she could," it is Lydia Mott.[3]

Phillips came down in the early morning train of cars from Utica, yesterday, with Susan, on his way to attend the Hudson Convention, having lectured the evening before in Buffalo, and rode (as usual) all night. He spoke at Cortland, (where Wm. H. Fish is preaching,) on Saturday afternoon and evening and three times on Sunday! It is surprising how much labor and fatigue he can bear, and look so well. Parker Pillsbury was with him, or, rather, preceding him at Hudson, somewhat relieved of his cold. To-morrow we shall know what sort of a time they had. Phillips will not be able to speak here till Saturday evening, even if he have no detention by the way.

This morning, I went down to the river side, to see the wide-spread inundation, which, though not so great as it was last week, exceeds every thing that I ever saw. Front street is entirely under water — hundreds of houses and stores are abandoned, and more or less filled with water up to the second story — boats are plying in the streets as if on the river — and the damage to property and business is immense. — Last night it rained very heavily till morning, thus increasing the volume of water, and extending the freshet. It was lucky for us that we got through yesterday, as no train has come from the West to-day, in consequence of bridges having been swept away since we passed.

The weather is still lowering, threatening rain, and will probably be stormy for us at Troy. The travelling on the ordinary roads was never worse, and the walking is everywhere execrable.

What our Convention will prove here, as to attendance and interest, is beyond conjecture. Owing to the peculiar state of things, we have no right to expect a numerous assembly; but, where two or three are gathered together in the name of Liberty, there it is ever pleasant and profitable to be, in the furtherance of her cause.

A morning paper, announcing our Convention, says that "the notorious Garrison is to be the principal speaker." A Republican paper announced me, at Utica, as "an able man, but a fanatic constitutionally." It is in this way the people are induced (?) to come to our meetings. We must not be astonished that more of them do not come.

I have been to the Post-Office, hoping I might get a letter from home, but was a little disappointed, though I shall look for one on my return from Troy. If you sent more than one letter to me at Utica, then the second remains uncalled for there. That is the only one I have received from you since I left Boston. But, pleasant as it is to hear from you, beloved one, I do not wish you to exert that dislocated arm to write often to me; for the effort, I know, must be very painful to you. Having been the unfortunate cause of that dislocation, I ought to be willing to release you from all obligation to write to me when I am abroad. I presume all is well at home, where, I need not add, I am yearning to be as soon as possible.

I am much obliged to dear H.C.W. [Henry C. Wright] for the letter he sent to me at Utica, and hope he is still under our roof.

Susan B. Anthony will be at our house next week, on her way to Bangor [Maine]. She is a noble woman, and has worked indefatigably in the present series of conventions.

I hope to find dear Mrs. Otis at least as comfortable as when I left her. Give my warmest remembrances to her, to Miss [Henrietta] Sargent, Mrs. [Wendell] Phillips, and others of "the household of faith." [4] Boundless love to all the children. Regards to Mary-Ann.

Forever yours,

W.L.G.

ALS: Garrison Papers, Boston Public Library.

1. William H. Topp of Albany.
2. Mary Mott, born August 30, 1791. (Thomas C. Cornell, *Adam and Ann Mott: Their Ancestors and Their Descendants*, Poughkeepsie, New York, p. 219.)
3. Mark 14:8.
4. Galatians 6:10.

163

TO HELEN E. GARRISON

Albany, Feb. 21, 1857.

Dear Wife:

I was made happy by receiving your letter yesterday, on my return from Troy, where Remond and myself addressed a highly respectable audience the previous evening, the meeting lasting till 10 o'clock. That "great gun" of orthodoxy, Rev. Dr. Beman,[1] was present, together with his colleague, also Rev. Mr. Buckingham [2] and one or two other clergymen. I made a clean breast of it, in regard to the guilt of the church and clergy, and gave them my Disunion views in the most radical manner. Frequent applause showed that my hits told. I trust a very good impression was made. Troy, however, in regard to the cause of reform, is a grave-yard. Every where, "the whole head is sick, and the whole heart faint." [3]

Poor dear Doctor Taft has got his release from earth, and is now a ransomed spirit. Undoubtedly, it is to him a most happy transition. I deeply sympathize with Dora,[4] and yet, as the case was incurable and grievous, rejoice that the heavy burden has been taken from her. I will either see or write to her on my return home.

We held three meetings here yesterday. They were comparatively small, but a number of excellent friends from the surrounding country were in attendance. In the evening, a number of southern law-students were present, and behaved as well as could be expected — occasionally manifesting a disposition to be boisterous; but we had an excellent meeting, nevertheless. To-day, we are to have three more meetings, and three more to-morrow! Phillips will probably be with us this evening. Mr. May will not be able to come from Syracuse, but has sent us a long letter to be read.

Who should look in upon us, last evening, but our true-hearted friend, C. F. Hovey, on his way to New York! He was most cordially greeted by us all, but thinks he must leave here in the evening train, as he wishes to spend Sunday at Staten Island. He told me that he parted from you at Framingham, and also of your disappointment in regard to the funeral of Dr. Taft being at Uxbridge. I am glad you went up to see Dora, and regret my absence on the occasion.

I am in very good health and spirits, and sustain the fatigues of this campaign better than I expected. Pillsbury is getting better of his cold, though it is still troublesome. Powell and Remond are the other speakers. I long to get through, and to be on my way home, though every thing has gone pleasantly since I left.

I am glad to hear of the comfortable state of mind and body of my venerated friend, Mrs. Otis. Long may her valuable life be preserved; for, though its activity is necessarily ended, yet her sweet serenity and ever-progressing spirit, in her sick chamber, are most edifying to all who see her. Of course, you will not fail to give her my best remembrances, and also Georgena, among the best of all daughters.

This morning, I am to have an ambrotype likeness taken of myself, by request; and as the time is at hand for me to sit, I must now lay down my pencil.

Tell Fanny and Franky they are in my thoughts continually. Love to George and Wendell, and regards to Mary Ann.

Most affectionately yours,

W. L. G.

ALS: Garrison Papers, Boston Public Library.

1. The Reverend Nathaniel Sydney Smith Beman (1785–1871) was pastor of the Presbyterian Church in Troy, New York, for forty years. (*Letters*, II, 251.)
2. The Reverend Edgar Buckingham was pastor of the First Unitarian Church of Troy from April 27, 1853 to 1867. He married Sally Anne Hart in 1855. (Arthur J. Weise, *Troy's One Hundred Years*, Troy, 1891, p. 353; letter from Mrs. Frederick R. Walsh, Director, Rensselaer County Historical Society, October 27, 1972.)
3. Isaiah 1:5.
4. Dorah Taft, Augustine Taft's wife.

164

TO JOHN BURT

Boston, Feb. 26, 1857.

Dear Sir:

Having just returned from a tour to Western New York, I find a complimentary letter from you, in regard to my labors in behalf of the enslaved in this land, and desiring me to send you my autograph. I comply with your request, with great pleasure.

Yours, truly,

Wm. Lloyd Garrison.

John Burt.

ALS: Villard Papers, Harvard College Library.

John Otis Burt (b. Syracuse, New York, 1835; d. 1894), son of Aaron and Eleanor Burt, graduated from Harvard in 1858, and traveled in Europe with Joseph May, Samuel J. May's son, who was in the class ahead of him. He served in the Union Army as an assistant surgeon from 1861 to 1863. In 1864, he married Helen Narcissa Moulton, of Oneida County, New York, and during the same year graduated from the College of Physicians and Surgeons of Columbia University in New York. Thereafter, he practiced medicine in Syracuse and taught at the

Syracuse University Medical School. (*Report of the Class of 1858 of Harvard College*, Boston, 1898, pp. 20–22.)

165

TO HELEN E. GARRISON

New York, May 13, 1857.

Dear Wife:

I seize a few moments before breakfast to give you a brief report of our meetings yesterday.[1]

The morning session was largely attended — though not quite so largely as I had hoped to see, as the immense hall in which we met would have held many more, and requires an army to fill it. It is as beautiful, too, in its adornments as it is immense. The speakers were Higginson, Pillsbury, Purvis, and Phillips. It was a most successful meeting throughout; but it was eclipsed in point of interest and enthusiasm by the meeting last evening, which was a very numerous one, and addressed by Rev. Mr. Sloane,[2] of this city, a Covenanter, who made a most impressive speech of a most radical character; Rev. Dr. Furness, of Philadelphia, who was extremely beautiful in his remarks; Remond, who gave us a brief, energetic, rousing talk, which was most warmly responded to; and Phillips, who surpassed himself in a magnificent speech of upwards of an hour. It is as cheering as it is astonishing to see what a change has come over the public mind within the last three years. Never have we had such bold utterances as now in regard to the criminality of the Church and the rottenness of the State, and the duty of overthrowing the Union; and yet, from beginning to end, not only has there been no token of rowdyism, or even restiveness, but the strongest declarations have been the most enthusiastically applauded. Yet there must have been a large number of southerners in the audience; but not one of them dared to peep or mutter.

Among the number present, last evening, was Mr. J. C. Underwood,[3] a Virginian of high respectability, who was compelled to flee from Virginia, a few months since, to save his life, leaving wife, and children, and property, and business behind him, simply for the crime of having favored the election of John C. Fremont to the Presidency! I was introduced to him, and to another Virginian, a Fremonter, both of whom were highly pleased with our proceedings.

Yesterday I took dinner at brother George's, and spent a couple of hours with the family. They have a very pleasant situation on Grand Street, every thing about the premises looking extremely neat and respectable. George and Catherine [Benson], and Mary [4] and Sarah,[5] were present at the morning session. George is comfortably well at this time, but his attacks of neuralgia are frequent and severe, and I know how, in a very slight degree, to sympathize with him. (By the way, my knee gave me no trouble in walking yesterday, and this morning feels comparatively easy, though the pain is still there, and will probably last for some time.)

I saw Mr. and Mrs. Bramhall last evening, whose inquiries after you all were particular; also Miss Safshefka,[6] (Dr.) whose Women's Institution was inaugurated yesterday afternoon; but I could not be present, (to her disappointment,) as I had to attend a private meeting of the delegates and friends of the cause, to consult about the work to be done during the ensuing year. We had a very pleasant interview. Remarks were made by Mr. Foss, Mr. McKim, Mr. May, Abby Kelley Foster, Thomas Whitson,[7] and others. We voted to raise $30,000 for the American A. S. Society during this year, and I trust we shall do it.

A goodly number of friends are present from other places — Mrs. Jones of Troy,[8] Lydia Mott, Susan B. Anthony, the Posts [9] from Long Island, and many others.

I have yet taken no part in speaking, though I am expected to speak this forenoon and this evening. I shall probably speak only this evening, as there are so many others desirous of being heard. Rev. O. B. Frothingham [10] is to speak to us this forenoon.

I forgot to say, that Lucy Stone made a short speech at our meeting yesterday forenoon.

The weather has been superb throughout. I hope to hear from you before I leave for Philadelphia, and that aunt [11] is still improving in health. My heart's love to all the dear ones.

Ever your own,

Wm. Lloyd Garrison.

H. E. G.

ALS: Garrison Papers, Boston Public Library.

1. Garrison was in New York City to attend the Twenty-Fourth Annual Meeting of the American Anti-Slavery Society, held on Tuesday and Wednesday, May 12 and 13 in the City Assembly Rooms, at 446 Broadway, between Howard and Grand Streets.

2. James Renwick Wilson Sloane (b. Topsham, Orange County, Vermont, May 29, 1833; d. Alleghany City, Pennsylvania, March 6, 1886), clergyman and educator, graduated from the Reformed Presbyterian seminary in northwestern Ohio in 1853, and served a pastorate at Rushsylvania, Ohio in 1854, and in New York City as pastor of the Third Reformed Presbyterian (Covenanter) Church, from 1856 to 1868. He was professor of systematic theology and homiletics in Alleghany theological seminary from 1868 until his death.

3. John Curtiss Underwood (1809–1873), a native of Litchfield, Herkimer County, New York, graduated from Hamilton College in 1832, studied law in Virginia, and returned to New York where he practiced law for a while. In 1839,

he married Maria Gloria Jackson of Clarksburg, Virginia, in whose home he had served as a tutor during his previous sojourn in Virginia. They made their home in Clarke County, where they acquired about eight hundred acres of land.

Underwood, a Free-Soiler, was a delegate to the Republican National Convention of 1856. Because of his support of Fremont and his attacks upon slavery, he soon found it necessary to leave Virginia. He was also a delegate to the Republican National Convention of 1860, and traveled across the Eastern States on behalf of Lincoln's candidacy. He served as fifth auditor of the treasury from August 1861 to January 1864, when he was appointed judge of the district court of Virginia. Throughout his lifetime, he remained a devoted defender of equal rights for the freedmen.

4. Mary Benson, the Bensons' daughter, was born in Northampton, Massachusetts, October 18, 1843. She was married on June 17, 1863, in Kansas, to William L. G. Soule. (W. P. Garrison, *The Benson Family of Newport, Rhode Island,* New York, 1872, p. 54.)

5. Sarah Benson, another daughter of the George W. Bensons.

6. Marie Elizabeth Zakrzewska (Garrison's spelling is incorrect) (1829–1902) was a pioneering physician, born in Berlin, Germany, where she had been chief midwife and professor at the Charité hospital's school for midwives. She came to the United States in May 1853, and received her M.D. degree from Cleveland Medical College in 1856. On May 1, 1857, she opened the New York Infirmary for Women and Children, the "Women's Institution" to which Garrison refers, "the country's first hospital staffed by women." She later founded the New England Hospital for Women and Children in Boston, which opened in July 1862. (*Notable American Women.*)

7. Thomas Whitson (b. July 2, 1796; d. West Tallowfield, Pennsylvania, November 24, 1864) was one of the founders of the American Anti-Slavery Society. (*Life,* I, 398; IV, 87, 422.) In 1863, at the third decade meeting of the Society, in Philadelphia in 1863, J. Miller McKim described his appearance at the founding convention in December, 1833: "Among the speakers . . . were two who interested me particularly. One was a countryman dressed in the plainest garb, and in appearance otherwise not particularly calculated to excite expectation. His manner was angular, and his rhetoric not what would be called graceful. But his matter was solid, and as clear as a bell. It had the ring of the genuine metal, and was, moreover, pat to the point in question. When he sat down — which he did after a very brief speech — the question was asked, 'Who is that?' and the answer came, 'Thomas Whitson, of Lancaster County, in this State.'" (Anna Davis Hallowell, *James and Lucretia Mott. Life and Letters,* Boston, 1884, pp. 112–113.) His obituary in *The Liberator,* December 9, 1864, states that he was "an earnest and acceptable minister in the Society of Friends." He was also active in the Underground Railroad for many years. (R. C. Smedley, *History of the Underground Railroad in Chester* . . . , Lancaster, Pa., 1883, pp. 67–70.)

8. A Mrs. Clementina Jones was a teacher at a "select school," apparently her own private school, during the 1850's and 1860's. (Letter from Mrs. Frederick R. Walsh, Director, Rensselaer County Historical Society, October 27, 1972.)

9. Joseph and Mary W. Post of Westbury, Long Island. Joseph Post (b. Westbury, Long Island, 1803; d. there January 11, 1888), the brother of Isaac Post of Rochester, was a member of the Society of Friends, a philanthropist and reformer, and a close personal friend of James and Lucretia Mott. In 1828, he married Mary W. Robbins. Their one child was a daughter, Elizabeth. (Their portraits accompany their biographical sketch in William S. Pelletreau, *A History of Long Island,* New York and Chicago, 1903, III, 221; Aaron M. Powell, *Personal Reminiscences of the Anti-Slavery and Other Reforms and Reformers,* New York, 1899, pp. 155–156.)

10. Octavius Brooks Frothingham (1822–1895), Unitarian clergyman and author, a native of Boston, was at this time pastor of a newly organized Unitarian society in Jersey City, which he served from 1855 to 1859, when he became pastor

of the Third Congregational Unitarian Society in New York City. He remained there for twenty years. In 1867, in Boston, he helped found the Free Religious Association and was its first president until 1878. He wrote numerous works, including *Theodore Parker: A Biography* (1874); *Transcendentalism in New England: A History* (1876); *Gerrit Smith: A Biography* (1877); and *Recollections and Impressions, 1822–1890* (1891).

11. Charlotte Newell.

---

1 6 6

TO HELEN E. GARRISON

Longwood,[1] May 18, 1857.
Monday Evening.

Dear Wife:

The mail is just in, and, to my great surprise and disappointment, I receive no intelligence from you; nor have I received a line since I left home! I am persuaded you must have written, and my perplexity of mind is very great. I must console myself with the saying, that "no news is good news" — and so I hope that aunt is getting along comfortably, and that you are all as well as usual.

On Friday, Oliver Johnson and I took the 11 o'clock train for Philadelphia, hoping to reach that city in season for the afternoon train for Westchester,[2] (Mary Ann having preceded us in an earlier train,) but we arrived about 15 minutes too late; and, accordingly, staid over night at a hotel in Arch street, — called the Ashland House, — James Mott having sold his residence, and living at Germantown.

I called, with Oliver, upon Mary Grew and Margaret Burleigh, and had a short but very pleasant interview. They made many inquiries about you and the children, as a multitude of others have done. Mary is slowly recovering from her long and severe indisposition, but she looks very frail. Her father was too unwell to see us.

In the evening, we went to Sansom Street Hall, to hear William Wells Brown recite his drama.[3] It was well delivered and well received; but the number present was very small, and the expenses must have been much beyond the receipts. We saw a number of our Philadelphia friends present — James Mott, Sarah Pugh,[4] Abby Kimber,[5] and Mattie Griffith,[6] the author of the Autobiography of a Female Slave. She has been very ill since I saw her last, and has still a harassing cough, and looks very pale. Her case, in regard to her slave relations, is a very trying one, as she has no reliable pecuniary resources, and has her sister with her three children to support.

On Saturday morning, we started for Westchester, and from thence took carriage to this place, arriving at Joseph Dugdale's, at dinner time, (Betsey Cowles,[7] of Ohio, accompanying us,) where we had a very warm reception. Joseph's venerable mother embraced me with great affection, and we kissed each other as lovingly as though we were both in the honeymoon of wedlock! You will not be jealous, I know. Of course, I had to answer any number of inquiries about you. After dinner, I went over to the house of my dear friends, John[8] and Hannah Cox, where I have since been, in company with others enough to fill a large hotel. This anniversary is a tremendous tax upon the hospitality of the friends in this vicinity, but it is borne with great cheerfulness.

Sunday morning, we commenced the first of the series of meetings of Progressive Friends.[9] The day, fortunately, proved to be as fair and beautiful as could possibly be desired; and the attendance was truly astonishing, and altogether unprecedented — not less than three thousand — six times larger than could get into the meeting-house could hold [*sic*], and the house densely crowded. I never in my life [saw] such a turnout of vehicles of every kind, nearly all of them commodious and in good condition: — I counted upwards of five hundred, and others made the number upwards of 650! Think of that in a region of country where no populous place is to be found. I had to address the multitude out-doors, as well as the crowd inside. It was a sublime scene, and the occasion of the deepest interest, surpassing any thing that has been seen or felt in any previous year.

We have had four meetings, and free discussion has been the order of the day. We have had sufficient differences of opinion to make the discussion lively and piquant, but a most excellent spirit has pervaded all the deliberations. Lucretia Mott has been with us, and has borne some admirable testimonies. I have used great plainness of speech, and been "favored" in spirit, and my remarks appear to have given very general satisfaction. Indeed, I do not know that any one has taken umbrage at anything I have uttered. To-morrow, however, we are to grapple with the Disunion question and expect a lively time.

Wednesday evening, I am to lecture in Wilmington, Delaware. I hope to be with you in the midnight train on Thursday night. Leave the key out for me.

Lovingly yours,

W. L. Garrison.

☞. The Coxes send their kindest remembrances. I am very anxious to get home, especially on Aunt's account. Kisses for dear Fanny and Franky, and a father's love to Wendell.

☞ Last evening, we had a circle at friend Cox's, and who should reveal themselves but Charley[10] and sister Mary?[11]

ALS: Garrison Papers, Boston Public Library.

1. Pennsylvania.

2. Pennsylvania.

3. *The Liberator*, May 22, 1857, carried the following notice: "A Novel Dramatic Reading (says the Philadelphia *Daily Evening Bulletin*) took place last evening at Sansom Street Hall, by Wm. Wells Brown, the dramatic colored writer, which was highly entertaining, and well received by an intelligent and appreciative audience. The drama is very laughable, and had our citizens been aware of its character, the hall would have been crowded. Mr. Brown has another drama, written by himself, entitled 'The Escape, or a Leap for Freedom,' which he is to give at the same place on Monday evening next."

The dramatic reading to which Garrison refers was probably *The Dough Face*, which Brown wrote prior to *The Escape*.

4. Sarah Pugh (1800–1884) was a teacher, abolitionist, and advocate of woman's rights. Beginning in 1829, in Philadelphia, she conducted her own elementary school for more than a decade. She became an immediate emancipationist and follower of Garrison in 1835, and was thereafter an active participant and leader in the Philadelphia Female Anti-Slavery Society, the Pennsylvania Anti-Slavery Society, and the American Anti-Slavery Society. She remained a Garrisonian after the abolitionist split in 1840, and was one of the delegates to the World's Anti-Slavery Convention in 1840. After a year and a half in Europe during the early 1850's, where she spoke on behalf of the American antislavery cause, she returned to Philadelphia, where she continued her antislavery activities. (*Notable American Women.*)

5. Abby Kimber (1804–March 22, 1871), of Philadelphia, was the daughter of Emmor Kimber, an abolitionist and educator, who had founded a school for girls at Kimberton, Chester County, Pennsylvania, in 1818. Abby Kimber became a teacher in her father's school at the age of fourteen and continued to teach for thirty years, earning the love and admiration of generations of her students. She was an early and consistent abolitionist, holding, at various times, the offices of president, vice-president, and recording secretary of the Philadelphia Female Anti-Slavery Society. For many years, she was a member of the executive committee of the Pennsylvania Anti-Slavery Society and was a delegate to the World's Anti-Slavery Convention in 1840. (R. C. Smedley, *History of the Underground Railroad in Chester* . . . , Lancaster, Pa., 1883, pp. 202–203.)

6. See Letter 153, to Helen, December 17, 1856, note 2.

7. Betsey Cowles (b. February 9, 1810; d. Austinburg, Ohio, July 25, 1876) was the youngest daughter of the Reverend Giles H. Cowles, who had come to Austinburg, in 1810, as the first pastor of its church. She began teaching school in 1825 and thereafter taught in a variety of infant schools, the predecessors of the kindergarten. She graduated from Oberlin College in 1840 and helped organize and conduct the state normal school at Bloomington, Illinois. She later had to leave teaching because of blindness. She was active in woman's rights and antislavery, especially in Ashtabula County, Ohio, where Austinburg is located. (Gertrude Van Rensselaer Wickham, *Memorial to the Pioneer Women of the Western Reserve*, Cleveland, 1896, Part I, pp. 79–80; *The Alumni Catalog of 1926*, Oberlin College, 1927, p. 186; Calvin D. Cowles, *Genealogy of the Cowles Families in America*, New Haven, 1929, I, 128.)

8. See Letter 102, to Helen, October 19, 1854, note 18.

9. This was the Fifth Yearly Meeting of the Progressive Friends of Pennsylvania, which convened in the Longwood meeting-house, Chester County, on Sunday, May 17 and was expected to continue for three days. (*The Standard*, April 11 and subsequent issues, 1857.)

10. Charles Follen Garrison (1842–1849), the Garrison son who was accidentally scalded to death. (*Life*, III, 262–263.)

11. Mary Benson, Helen Garrison's sister, who had died in 1842. (*Letters*, II, xxii.)

167

TO WILLIAM LLOYD GARRISON, JR.

Boston, May 23, 1857.

Dear Willie:

I arrived safely home from my trip to New York and Pennsylvania yesterday morning, in better health than when I left, having attended many meetings, spoken in public many times, and enjoyed myself in the highest degree — especially among the Progressive Friends at Longwood, near old Kennett. Last Sunday, at that place, there were no less than seven hundred vehicles on the ground, and such a concourse of people that not one fourth of the number assembled could get into the meeting-house. We held our meetings for three days. Oliver Johnson and Lucretia Mott were present.

On Wednesday evening, I lectured on slavery in Wilmington, Delaware,[1] (the first slave State in which I have ever attempted to give an address,) to a small but highly respectable audience, who gave me the closest attention for upwards of an hour. There was no excitement in the place whatever, but rather a lack of curiosity. A few moments before I closed, some rogue turned the gas off, and left us in total darkness; but all remained quiet in their seats, and we closed in good order.

You will have already seen that our meetings at New York were eminently successful. I suppose you will hardly be able to leave, so as to be present during the New England A. S. Convention, on Wednesday and Thursday next.

I have just this moment received a letter from George, announcing his safe arrival at Nininger,[2] with which place he seems to be much pleased. He had no difficulty on the route. He is boarding at William Reed's,[3] and has gone to work in the blind and sash factory, belonging to William's father. His letter is dated May 10th, but does not appear to have been mailed till the 12th — so that his letter has been eleven days in reaching Boston.

I found all well as usual at home. Aunt Charlotte seemed to have somewhat improved, and is sanguine that she is soon to get well; but of this there is little probability. She is a good deal emaciated, and her dropsical swellings are symptomatically bad; yet at times she has a voracious appetite, and with her tenacity of will may remain a long time — or she may expire at any moment. To-day she is very feeble; yesterday she was very bright.

I was sorry that I could not be at the birth-day celebration of my attached friend, Mr. Buffum.[4] Wendell says you all had a first-rate time.

Sarah Anthony [5] is to be married in Providence on Tuesday next. Probably Wendy and Fanny will be present at the wedding. They want to see us all.

To-day is the Latin School Exhibition at the Lowell Institute. It is time for me to be there. Hastily,

Your loving father,

Wm. Lloyd Garrison.

ALS: Smith College Library.

1. Garrison's account of his lecture in Wilmington appeared in *The Liberator*, June 12, 1857.

2. Nininger, Dakota County, Minnesota.

3. William Bayliss Reed (b. August 22, 1834) had gone to Nininger, Minnesota, from Milford, Massachusetts, with his parents in 1856. He married Amanda Bunnell in 1859. His father, Anthony Reed (b. July 10, 1805; d. June 8, 1878) was born in Dighton, Massachusetts, which he helped to develop. He moved to Milford, Massachusetts, in 1854 and two years later to Nininger, where he was one of the early white settlers. There he engaged in building and manufacturing. He was a Free Soiler, a Republican, and a Universalist. He later moved to Hastings, Minnesota, where he died. (John L. Reed, *The Reed Genealogy*, Baltimore, 1901, pp. 137, 211–212.)

4. James N. Buffum.

5. Sarah Anthony (b. 1832; d. August 1, 1895), the daughter of Charlotte and Henry Anthony of Providence (*Letters*, II, xxiii), married James Tillinghast, the son of Charles F. and Lusanna Tillinghast on May 26, 1857. (Charles L. Anthony, *Genealogy of the Anthony Family from 1495 to 1904*, Sterling, Illinois, 1904, pp. 239, 240.)

168

A LETTER TO SEVERAL FRIENDS

Boston, June 18, 1857.

Dear Friend:

I am trying to obtain some charitable assistance from a few friends for a very impoverished family, whose case has recently been brought to my notice; and, knowing your benevolence of heart, and your readiness to aid where you have good assurance that your charity will be wisely and mercifully applied, I venture to lay the facts before you.

The case is this. On receiving a well-written, respectful and touching representation of his unfortunate situation, I was recently induced to go to an obscure basement room at No. 20, Williams street, in this city, where I found an intelligent, educated and worthy Irishman, Mr. Michael Sheehy,[1] with his wife, (an uncommonly good looking woman,) and an interesting little girl about ten years of age, in a state of utter destitution, without even a bed to lie upon. Mr. Sheehy arrived in this country in 1853, from Ireland, having at home been "the pupil and friend of O'Connell," an active teetotaller with Father Mathew,[2] and an earnest laborer for the redemption of his ill-fated country. The means he brought with him gradually became exhausted, as he failed to procure steady and remunerative employment; and at last, by a sucession of disappointments and misfortunes, he has been reduced to absolute want; though he has nobly adhered to his temperance and anti-slavery principles, under circumstances calculated to shake the firmest soul. Sorrowful and indignant at the pro-slavery spirit and conduct of his countrymen here, he wrote a lecture on "O'Connell, the Emancipator of the British West India Slaves — the eloquent Advocate of Freedom for all of every color, caste and clime," and delivered it at his own expense, until he could proceed no further, in Taunton, Fall River, New Bedford, Boston, &c.; but he was frowned upon by the Catholic priests, and thereby alienated himself from Catholic sympathy and friendship. Subsequently, he was burnt out in Congress street, losing what little he had, together with eighteen dollars in money in a book, with which he was about to discharge a debt for clothing. Last spring, he was taken down with a violent rheumatic fever, (no marvel, in view of his wretched damp abode,) from which he has not yet fully recovered. Besides this, he has a malformation of his right foot. To add to his misfortunes, his wife had to be in the hospital a long time, on account of a dangerous tumor in her jaw. A man of true self-respect, of genuine sensibility of soul, of honorable pride of character, he has kept his sufferings very much to himself — parting with one article of furniture after another to obtain food. As in his own country, he moved in very respectable society, and at one period was in more than comfortable circumstances, this reversal of fortune is all the more pitiable; for they who are born in degradation and poverty know nothing of the bitterness of such an experience. I feel the more interested in Mr. Sheehy, because he has maintained his anti-slavery integrity to his own cost, where almost all his countrymen have proved recreant. Indeed, I know not when I have seen a suffering family that has impressed me so favorably, or that has so excited my sympathy.

Mr. Sheehy has excellent credentials from Father Mathew and others, as to his character, and competency as an accountant, scrivener, &c. Father Mathew styles him his dear friend, and commends him "with confidence as a virtuous, well educated, and most zealous teetotaller, and an excellent man," in whose success he professes the deepest interest. John O'Connell [3] addresses him a complimentary letter, as one of a committee on the death of Daniel O'Connell. He was employed by the Trustees of the Killarney Savings Bank as an accountant to wind up its affairs, and has a certificate that, "in the discharge of his duties, he gave great satisfaction; both Lord Kenmare[4] and Mr. Herbert,[5] M. P., expressing themselves well pleased with the manner the business was conducted." Thomas Rowean,[6] Justice of the Peace, in this city, certifies that he is "in great distress," and that he has heard him "spoken of as one who enjoyed affluence and respect in his native country"; and, further, that "he gave some free lectures with ability on O'Connell as the advocate of the slave, without any pecuniary benefit resulting to himself." — Quincy A. Shaw,[7] Esq. says — "I certify that the letters of character and the credentials of ability as an accountant which Mr. Sheehy, late of Killarney, produced to me, were given him by parties who knew him for years. I know them to be authentic and trustworthy. Boston, May 28, 1853." Mr. Sheehy was for a time connected with the press in Ireland as a reporter, and is a ready and accurate writer, a good penman, book-keeper, &c. &c.

Some clothing and pecuniary aid (together with a bed) are what his family pressingly need at this moment; and next, and chiefly, he wants some steady employment that shall enable him to subsist by his own toil — for he is no beggar, no drone, and has by no misconduct been thus reduced in life. If you can give him, or procure for him, any situation or transient job, it will be a great boon. Any money or clothing, for himself, his wife, or his child, you may feel disposed to give, I will see it promptly and sacredly applied, as it will be gratefully acknowledged.

With your well-known and characteristic kindness of heart, I am aware that applications for your charities are constant, and that the drain is large, and at times quite exhaustive; but I am also aware that you take pleasure in doing good to the afflicted, and are never weary in this beneficent work — knowing by experience that "it is more blessed to give than to receive."

Yours, to aid the suffering.

Wm. Lloyd Garrison.

Anti-Slavery Office, 21 Cornhill.

ALS: Garrison Papers, Boston Public Library.

Garrison apparently sent several copies of this letter to a number of his friends. There is extant another copy of it with only minor variations. It is dated June 20, 1857, and is to be found in the Garrison Papers, Boston Public Library.

1. On September 11, 1857, *The Liberator* printed a letter from Sheehy to Mr. Patrick J. O'Brien, dated Boston, September 1, 1857, calling for an end to slavery and support for the antislavery movement. See also Garrison's letter to Sheehy, No. 170 in this volume.

2. The Reverend Theobald Mathew (1790–1856), priest and temperance reformer, signed the total abstinence pledge in 1838 and advocated it throughout Ireland. He traveled in the United States from 1849 to 1851.

3. John O'Connell (1810–1858), Irish politician and son of Daniel O'Connell, was M.P. for various constituencies from 1832 to 1857.

4. Thomas Bourne (b. January 15, 1789; d. December 26, 1871) was sheriff of Kerry, Ireland, in 1836. On his father's death in 1853, he became Earl of Kenmare and in 1856 was created Baron Kenmare of Killarney, County Kerry. (H. A. Doubleday and Lord Howard DeWalden, eds., *The Complete Peerage*, London, 1929, VII, 115–116.)

5. Sidney Herbert, first Baron Herbert of Lea (1810–1861) was the conservative M.P. for South Wiltshire from 1832 to 1860. He was secretary to the admiralty from 1841 to 1845, and war secretary under Peel, Aberdeen, and Palmerston. He was created a peer in 1860.

6. Thomas Rowean is listed in the Boston *Directory*, from 1848 to 1872, as employed in the Naturalization Office at 123 Federal Street, Boston. It is stated in William T. Davis, *Bench and Bar of the Commonwealth of Massachusetts* (Boston, 1895), vol. I, p. 502, that "he was an Irishman by birth or extraction, and studied law for a time but was never admitted to the bar. He was largely engaged in the business of naturalization, and his frequent presence in the courts led to the inference that he was a member of the bar."

7. Quincy Adams Shaw (b. Boston, February 8, 1825; d. Jamaica Plain, Mass., June 11, 1908) was the son of the wealthy Boston merchant Robert Gould Shaw and himself a financier. After graduating from Harvard in 1845, he accompanied his cousin, Francis Parkman, the historian, on a journey through the Indian country in the northwest, which Parkman later described in his *Oregon Trail*, dedicated to Shaw. He afterward went to Europe and Egypt with George William Curtis. In the 1850's he became interested in copper mining in Michigan and organized a number of mining companies. In 1871, four of his mining companies were joined into one, the Calumet and Hecla Mining Company, one of the famous copper producers in the country, of which he became president. Although resigning as president in 1872, he directed the operations of the company until 1894. He was a supporter of philanthropic and educational enterprises, donated generously to the Harvard Museum of Comparative Zoology, was a lover and collector of art, and had the largest collection in America of the paintings of the Barbizon school. In March 1860, he married Pauline Agassiz, the daughter of the naturalist, who was herself an educator and philanthropist.

169

TO SUSAN B. ANTHONY

Boston, June 19, 1857.

My Dear Friend:

I seize a moment to thank you for your letter, giving an account of your anti-slavery meetings in Dutchess county,[1] and of the meeting of the "Friends of Progress"[2] in   .[3] I am highly gratified to learn [that] the latter followed the example of the "Progressive Friends" at Longwood, in favor of a dissolution of our blood-stained American Union. I meant to have sent you, in season, some resolutions or "testimony" on the subject, but circumstances prevented; but I felt perfectly satisfied that all would go right, with you, and Aaron,[4] and Oliver Johnson present, to enforce the true doctrine. You must have had a soul-refreshing time at that gathering; and though there appear to have been what Emerson calls "the fleas of a convention" present, still, there was no lack of keen intellect, sound sense, and solid worth.

It was certainly ill-judged, though unquestionably kindly meant, on the part of L. B.,[5] to advertise the meeting in advance, that I was the author of the testimony upon which they were about to act; for, where there is more or less of personal prejudice, in a given case, and where an unbiassed de[cis]ion is desirable, it is better to let things stand upon their own merits. However, the adoption of the document, under such a pressure, is peculiarly gratifying.[6]

I am glad that Andrew Jackson Davis and his wife [7] were at the meeting, and participated so acceptably in its proceedings. Have you seen his Autobiography? [8] Critically speaking, there are some things in it that, perhaps, might as well have been omitted; but it is a very readable volume, full of the lights and shadows of an eventful life and an extraordinary experience. I hope yet to be better acquainted with Mrs. Davis, who impressed me very favorably when here, and of whom you speak in high terms.

With all my heart, I endorse your eulogy of A. M. P.,[9] and regard him as a model young man, and far beyond his years in clearness of vision, maturity of judgment, and depth of moral conviction. May the sharpness of the blade not prematurely destroy the scabbard. I hope he will forego mental effort as much as possible during the hot season, (provided there is to be [one]) and seek greatly to invigorate his physical frame.

I read your account of the interview you had with the "spirits" at Albany, with less of surprise than interest; for, after what I have seen and known, I am constrained to believe in spiritual agency, notwithstanding there are still many things to perplex, and some of the phenomena are any thing but satisfactory. Great allowance must be made for differences of opinion on this subject; and as there is really no moral principle involved in it, there is ample scope for charity and toleration. Some will doubtless believe too much — some, too little.

Wife is indebted to you for your letter, and sends her kindest regards; and so do all the rest of the household, — Wendell, Fanny, Franky, and aunt Charlotte. Aunt is still weak and emaciated, dispirited and hopeful by turns, with no marked changes, but evidently not long for this world. I wish she had less dread of the future; [but] her caution is very large, and her faith very weak; and so she is naturally apprehensive about going to "that bourne whence no traveller returns" [10] in bodily shape of flesh and blood.

George [Thompson Garrison] writes to us that he is much pleased with his location in Minnesota.

On Wednesday, there was a great popular demonstration in this city and on Bunker Hill, with reference to the inauguration of the statue of Warren.[11] The civic and military display served to demonstrate the fact, that "men are but children of a larger growth." [12] Think of Mason, of Virginia, being one of the speakers on Bunker Hill — the author of the Fugitive Slave Bill!

Please remember me lovingly to your parents, to Isaac and Amy Post, and the other beloved friends in R.

Truly yours,

Wm. Lloyd Garrison.

ALS: Yale University Library.

The letter does not bear the name of the recipient. However, since Susan B. Anthony spoke at the antislavery meeting in Dutchess County and the meeting of the "Friends of Progress" in New York, and since she and her parents (see last paragraph of this letter) were then living in Rochester, New York, it is probable that she was the recipient of this letter.

1. The *National Anti-Slavery Standard*, May 9, 1857, carried the following announcement: "An Anti-Slavery Convention, for Dutchess County, under the auspices of the 'American Anti-Slavery Society,' will be held at Washington Hollow, in the County Fair Building, on Saturday and Sunday, May 16th and 17th, 1857.

"Parker Pillsbury, Charles Lenox Remond, Aaron M. Powell, Susan B. Anthony and others will address the Convention." An account of the occasion appeared in the *Standard*, May 30, 1857.

2. The annual meeting of the "Friends of Human Progress," to which Garrison refers, was held in Waterloo, Seneca County, New York, on June 7. The announcement of the meeting in the *Standard*, May 9, 1857, explained that "on behalf of the Yearly Meeting, we invite all who feel that true and acceptable worship consists in something better than empty creeds and stereotyped forms to mingle with us on this occasion.

"Our object in thus assembling ourselves together is not to create a wordy form of Religion, but, in the social communion of soul with soul, endeavor to eliminate [sic] Truth and bring it to bear upon the evils that so crush humanity in this age."

3. The blank is in the original.

4. Aaron Powell.

5. Probably Lewis Burtis of Rochester.

6. *The Liberator*, June 19, 1857, in its account of the meeting, reported that the business committee had offered a number of resolutions to the meeting, including one on slavery, "a very clear and forcible testimony, which was adopted at the recent annual meeting of the Pennsylvania Progressive Friends.

"Aaron M. Powell then addressed the meeting on the subject of Slavery, advocating thorough and uncompromising action, — the dissolution of the Union, — and recommended the adoption of the testimony. . . ."

The testimony, reported in *The Liberator*, was discussed and then adopted, "not unanimously, but by a very large majority."

7. Andrew Jackson Davis (1826–1910), spiritualist, was a failure both as a shoemaker and merchant but had his "psychic flight through space" in 1844. His attempts at healing were not very successful and in 1845 he turned to writing. His books include *Principles of Nature, Her Divine Revelations, and a Voice to Mankind* (1847), *The Great Harmonia* (1850–1852), and *The Philosophy of Spiritual Intercourse* (1856). His biographers note that "he preached social reconstruction as going hand in hand with spiritual regeneration."

Davis was married twice. His first wife died in 1853. He married his second wife, Mrs. Mary (Robinson) Love, a divorcée, in 1855.

8. *The Magic Staff: An Autobiography of Andrew Jackson Davis* (New York, 1857, 552 pp.).

9. Aaron M. Powell.

10. Shakespeare, *Hamlet*, III, i, 79–80.

11. Joseph Warren (1741–1775), physician of Boston, was a prominent Massachusetts patriot, member of the Committee of Correspondence, president of the Provincial Congress of 1774, and chairman of the Committee of Public Safety. He had been made a major-general by the Massachusetts Provincial Congress, but fought as a private soldier at the Battle of Bunker Hill, where he was killed on June 17, 1775. His statue, "Gen. Joseph Warren at Bunker Hill," by Henry Dexter, the prominent Massachusetts sculptor, was inaugurated at Bunker Hill on June 17, 1857. Senator James M. Mason of Virginia was a principal speaker. (See *The Liberator*, June 26, July 24, 1857.)

12. John Dryden (1631–1700), English poet, *All for Love*, Act IV, Scene i.

170

TO M. J. SHEEHY

[June-July, 1857.]

Mr. M. J. Sheehy:

Dear Sir — To-day you are to ⟨emerge from⟩ *exchange* [1] your ⟨dusky,⟩ *contracted,* dismal, cellar room ⟨, and⟩ for a decent and convenient habitation, located where you will have the clear sunshine & pure air of heaven without stint, ⟨and⟩ where the prospect to the eye is as beautiful and picturesque as it is extensive, *⟨(hardly surpassed in Mass.)⟩* and where you and your family will be delivered from those repulsive surroundings ⟨to⟩ which misfortune and penury have compelled you to encounter. Instead of being utterly destitute of all household ⟨necessities and⟩ utensils and conveniences, you will be furnished with such a supply *(scanty though it be)* as will enable you to get along quite comfortably for the present. The contrast to you all will be ⟨a⟩ scarcely less bewildering than pleasant; and in your happiness at this unexpected turn of things, be assured that Mrs. Garrison and I will very deeply participate. *Indeed,* When ⟨you first made⟩ your ⟨appeal⟩ *case was first made known* to us, ⟨when⟩ *we* hardly knew what to do, or where to look for assistance, *in view of burdens already imposed upon us in other directions.* Your destitution was so great, ⟨that⟩ it seemed beyond immediate mitigation, to any appreciable extent; and ⟨so almost fell [?] like⟩ while our sympathy was active, our ⟨depression⟩ ⟨as though it were of⟩ hope of success was almost in a state of paralysis. But we have been most unexpectedly ⟨and⟩ as well as *most* kindly aided by a few benevolent ⟨spirits⟩, *friends,* whose names ⟨you⟩ shall duly be communicated to you, and to whom you are ⟨specially⟩ *almost entirely* indebted for whatever of comfort you shall find in your new situation — we being ⟨nothing⟩ *little* more than the medium through which their benefaction ⟨comes⟩. *flows.* You cannot be much more joyous than ⟨we feel⟩ *ourselves* at this change of circumstances in your condition; and we trust and believe that we shall have no cause to regret what has been achieved in your behalf as a suffering family.

It is proper that you should know on what conditions you enter upon your new premises, and how far you may dismiss *corroding* anxiety from your mind.

Acting as the agent, for others to whom I ⟨hold myself⟩ *am* responsible for the judicious expenditure and prudent supervision of the means put into my hands, ⟨as a sacred trust⟩, I am authorized to say, that, in order to prevent any legal attachment of them of them [2] as against yourself personally for any pecuniary liability to which you ⟨may⟩ *are* now or *may* hereafter be unfortunately exposed, *all* the goods and utensils which you will find in your new abode are to be at your service, and for the convenience of your family, just as much as though they were formally presented to you, while at the same time they are lawfully to be in my possession, and subject to ⟨any⟩ *such* discretionary alteration which circumstances may seem to require. This will be a safe and desirable arrangement on all sides, ⟨and will⟩ without in the least interfering with your liberty of use, or making you responsible beyond the necessary wear and tear of the household appurtenances aforesaid. ⟨I trust this is⟩

I trust this is only "the beginning of the end," and that you will ere long find some kind of employment whereby you will be able to earn an independent subsistence, and to furnish yourself and family with comforts which it is not now in my power to procure for you. Indeed, it is indispensable that you should find something to do, for *individual* charity is soon exhausted, and toil is the price that *the poor* must ⟨be paid⟩ *pay* for bread. I need no assurance, *dear sir,* that you are ready and eager to do whatever your hands *(2)* or head *(1)* can ⟨find to employ them;⟩ *grasp;* and you need none that I shall do what I can by inquiring and recommendation, to find ⟨you [?]⟩ *you such* a situation as you require, though you must not rely too much on my efforts in that direction, as I have *a* very limited business acquaintance.

As for your rent, you need not give yourself any uneasiness about it for the present. I will see it paid with all due punctuality, until I give you further notice. At no time shall it be burdensome to you ⟨, while you remain in your new abode,⟩ by an exchange of places.

And now, ⟨dear Mr. Sheehy,⟩ in answer to the inquiry that may arise in your mind, why I have taken so marked an interest in your case, allow me to say — I have done so, first, because your family was in a state of extreme destitution, obviously through no misconduct, but by a succession of calamities. Second, because as you were once in better circumstances, I felt a special sympathy for you as an intelligent and educated man, ⟨compelled to⟩ not born to ignorance and degradation. Third, because you were ⟨of⟩ *an* Irish *man,* ⟨extraction⟩, which, in this country, is next to being of African extraction. Fourth, because you have long been an earnest teetotaller, and still ⟨hold fast to⟩ *keep* the ⟨principle⟩ *pledge* under circumstances calculated to cause you to swerve from it through despondency of mind. Finally, because, unlike nearly all of your countrymen here, you have *steadily* adhered to the cause of impartial liberty, and *laudably* attempted to interest ⟨your⟩ them in the A. S. ⟨cause,⟩ *struggle,* though with little success. May you ever retain a character for uprightness, and be willing to die of starvation rather than sell your manhood to obtain food or favor!

Be ⟨[then?]⟩ of good cheer. Join with your wife and Maria in a song of thanksgiving, and "hope on, hope ever."

Your friend,

W. L. G.

P. S. Please keep these matters to yourselves, for various reasons. While Mrs. G. has ⟨done⟩ been active in your service, she unites with me in the desire that you will not feel yourselves called upon to multiply your acknowledgments. Of course you are thankful, *as we should be similarly circumstanced.*

ALS: Garrison Papers, Boston Public Library.

This is probably the first draft of the letter. It was written in pencil, with corrections in ink, on a piece of memorandum paper of the New England Mutual Life Insurance Company. All changes, corrections, and insertions have been reproduced here as closely as practicable, as an example of Garrison's method of revising letters. Angle brackets (⟨⟩) enclose Garrison's cancellations. Words within asterisks are Garrison's insertions, usually written above cancellations.

This letter, of course, indicates that Garrison's fund-raising letters of June 18 and 20, on behalf of Mr. Sheehy, proved successful.

1. Words enclosed within asterisks were inserted above the line.
2. In original.

171

TO THE ANTISLAVERY MEN AND WOMEN
OF THE NORTH

WORCESTER, July 8, 1857.

DEAR SIR, — The State Disunion Convention, held at Worcester, Mass., January, 1857, recommended a Northern Convention, based on the same principles, during the present year.[1] Your attention is respectfully invited to the accompanying Call, prepared by a sub-committee designated for that purpose.

The results of the Worcester Convention were important. It established the question of union or disunion *as an open question*, among a large and influential class who have hitherto shrunk from the consideration of the subject. The able correspondents [2] of the Convention, who deprecated Disunion, still recognized it as a legitimate matter of discussion. This was a great step. A great blow was struck at the popular, unreasoning idolatry. Such blows must be repeated. The Slave Power will have lost its chief weapon when the North has learned to calculate the value of the Union. Until that is done, there will always be a means of crushing us into submission.

It may seem, to some, that the present is not a peculiarly favorable period for such a Convention. The year after a Presidential election is always a period of lull. 'Optimists and quietists' represent that the character of the new Administration and the new Congress are not yet definitely indicated. At present, affairs in Kansas look more propitious,[3] while new light dawns in Missouri, and even, it is thought, in Virginia. The memory of the Sumner outrage is softened by the twin deaths of its author and its occasion.[4] The Fugitive Slave Law and the repeal of the Missouri Compromise have ceased to be novelties; and the Dred Scott decision [5] is acquiesced in, by many, as a merely abstract grievance.

But all this is merely a truce, not a peace. We have no indemnity for the past, no security for the future. Not a wrong is yet redressed; Kansas is not yet saved; Sumner is not yet restored; Missouri is not yet freed; Virginia is not yet colonized. The future, in all these cases, is still clouded by uncertainties. If the Dred Scott case be an abstraction, it is one of those abstractions whose practical consequences convulse the world. For all our efforts, there is not yet an inch of truly Free Soil in the nation. — The great State of Ohio, under the ablest Republican government, has just been the scene of bloody and successful slave-hunts.[6] That the new Administration will be thoroughly subservient to the Slave Power is a foregone conclusion. The existence of slavery is aggression, and new ingenuities of outrage may, at any moment, be sprung upon us.

From *mere* Politics there is little to be expected. — The Slave Power has always commanded just votes enough to carry its measures, and, under our present organization, always will. If the Republican party told the truth, last November, the Presidential election transferred the balance of power, more than ever, to the side of slavery. It has four years of corruption, conquest and annexation before it, and it remains to be proved that any merely political combination can defeat it. On the other hand, the attitude of the Republican leaders is now, as always, one of timidity and compromise. They deprecate, with profuse caution, the charge of any disposition to interfere with slavery *as it is*, and claim the support of Southern men for their nominations, as affording undiminished security to slavery. It is evident that the mass of Republican voters, in many States, are becoming more radically anti-slavery. And nothing will do so much to promote that desirable change as the fearless discussion we propose. Undoubtedly, the first object is, to create a united and determined North. But if there is even a chance that the ultimate result of that effort is to be Disunion, every one must admit the necessity of being prepared for it.

In view of these facts, we regard the present as an opportune period for our Convention. We wish to act with calmness, not with impetuosity; to be controlled, not by impulse, but by mature conviction. — It is not strange that such a Convention should be proposed in a period of excitement. That it should be held, in a period of comparative quiet, is a fact of momentous significance.

Such a Convention appeals to three distinct classes of persons: —

1. Those who repudiate the United State Constitution as essentially pro-slavery, and hence abjure all union under it.

2. Those who, not accepting this view of the Constitution, still concur in the opinion that there can be no permanent union between Free and Slave States, and that the only practicable solution will be found, sooner or later, in a separation.

3. Those who, believing in the ultimate triumph of Freedom, without Disunion, still approve of the agitation of the subject, because they admit Disunion to be a *possible* result; and because the discussion will tend, in any case, to strengthen and consolidate the North on the side of Freedom.

It has been determined to summon the Convention by means of a Call,[7] to be signed by such persons as may, from either of the motives above indicated, sympathize with its object. By obtaining many such names, from every free State, the existence and wide distribution of this sentiment will be exhibited, and increased interest will be given to the Convention.

You are therefore respectfully invited to append to this Call your own signature, and to obtain such others as may be within your reach. It is believed that any effort, so bestowed, will be useful anti-slavery work. All copies of the Call should be returned, (with signatures, and a memorandum of the place where obtained,) to JOSEPH A. HOWLAND,[8] Worcester, Mass., on or before September 1st, 1857.

THOMAS WENTWORTH HIGGINSON,

WENDELL PHILLIPS,

DANIEL MANN,[9]

WILLIAM LLOYD GARRISON,

F. W. BIRD.[10]

Printed in *The Liberator*, July 24 and August 21, 1857.

The publication of this letter in *The Liberator* on July 24, 1857, was accompanied by the following explanation, which refers to the letter as a "Circular."

"Below we give an important Circular just issued by a subcommittee of the State Disunion Convention, held at Worcester last January; appended to which is a Call for a Convention of ALL THE FREE STATES, to be held at a central point in October next, 'to consider the practicability, probability and expediency of A SEPARATION BETWEEN THE FREE AND SLAVE STATES.' This will be sent to some of the most reliable friends of impartial freedom, in various parts of the North, for their consideration — no doubt whatever being entertained that they will take a lively interest in the measure proposed, and will exert themselves to procure as many signatures to the Call as practicable, in accordance with the request contained in the Circular.

"It will be seen that the Call is so worded that no one signing it will thereby commit himself in favor of Disunion, its object being to convene a mass meeting of such of the people of the Free States as sympathise with the oppressed, declare their purpose to be true to the cause of freedom, and are convinced that it is impossible to unite hostile interests and institutions under any form of government — a mass meeting of the best heads and hearts to be found at the North, for the purpose of examining the structure of the American Union, its legitimate and inevitable results, its past history and present condition, its future bearings upon the liberties of the world, and determining what is the wisest and safest course to be pursued in regard to it. Under these circumstances, therefore, it is hoped that no Anti-Slavery man or woman will object to signing the Call, — the Convention being one for inquiry and deliberation, and such action as, after the fullest discussion, a majority of its members shall deem it proper to recommend."

1. The State Disunion Convention met on January 15, and had been called by citizens of Worcester headed by Thomas Wentworth Higginson and Thomas Earle. When the convention opened, Francis W. Bird of Walpole was in the chair and Garrison was one of the vice-presidents.

2. A number of prominent Republican leaders sent letters to the convention in which they took issue with the proposal of disunion. They included Senator Henry Wilson, Charles Francis Adams, and Joshua Giddings. (*Life*, III, 451–452.)

3. Robert J. Walker had been appointed the new governor of Kansas Territory by President Buchanan in March 1857 and was inaugurated on May 26. His inaugural address, which emphasized that the residents of the Territory would determine its future, that no fraud or violence would be tolerated, and that slavery was unsuited for Kansas because of climate and would be unprofitable there, was interpreted by southerners as being hostile to slavery and partial to the Free-State

cause. An increase in Free-State immigration to Kansas added to the favorable antislavery prospects in the Territory. (James A. Rawley, *Race and Politics: 'Bleeding Kansas' and the Coming of the Civil War*, Philadelphia and New York, 1969, pp. 204 ff.)

4. Representative Preston S. Brooks of South Carolina, who had beaten Sumner, died on January 27, 1857. Andrew Pickens Butler, the senator from South Carolina and the "occasion" of the beating, died on May 25, 1857. (*BDAC.*)

5. The Dred Scott decision had been issued by Chief Justice Taney on March 6, 1857.

6. For several instances of attempted resistance to capture by fugitive slaves in Ohio, see *The Liberator*, June 19, July 13, 17, 1857.

7. The text of the Call read as follows:

"Whereas, it must be obvious to all, that the American Union is constantly becoming more and more divided, by Slavery, into two distinct and antagonistic nations, between whom harmony is impossible, and even ordinary intercourse is becoming dangerous;

"And, whereas, Slavery has now gained entire control over the three branches of our National Government, Executive, Judiciary, and Legislative; has so interpreted the Constitution as to deny the right of Congress to establish freedom even in the territories, and by the same process has removed all legal protection from a large portion of the people of the free States, and has inflicted, at many times and places, outrages far greater than those which our fathers rose in arms to repel;

"And, whereas, there seems no probability that the future will, in these respects, be different from the past, under existing State relations;

"The undersigned respectfully invite their fellow-citizens of the Free States to meet in Convention, at ————, in October, 1857, to consider the practicability, probability, and expediency of a separation of the Free and Slave States, and to take such other measures as the condition of the times may require.

LEGAL VOTERS.   OTHER PERSONS."

(*The Liberator*, July 24, 1857.)

8. "Joseph A. Howland, of Worcester, a lecturing agent of the Massachusetts A. S. Society (*Lib.* 28:35), and one of the signers of the call for the Disunion Convention of Jan. 15 (*Lib.* 27:2)" (*Life*, III, 460n). Joseph Avery Howland (d. December 20, 1889, aged sixty-nine) was a businessman, active in local politics and woman suffrage. He was occupied with the manufacture of machinery as treasurer of the Woodland Light Machine Company. During the last decade of his life, he engaged in the construction of water works under the firm name of Howland and Ellis. (Obituary, *Boston Evening Transcript*, December 21, 1889.)

9. "A Boston dentist residing in Worcester Co., Mass., possessed of much shrewdness of character, and a racy and forcible writer. See the *Liberator* of this period *passim*." (*Life*, III, 460n.) Daniel Mann, in a letter to Dr. Rufus W. Griswold, dated Boston, January 26, 1856, writes: "Permit me to recall to your remembrance our brief but pleasant acquaintance some twenty years since in Calais, Maine. I was there in the prime of life and you a boy. We have changed positions. I am in my second childhood. . . . I have written a book called Wolfsden, and requested the Publishers to send you a copy. . . . My residence is at Oakdale, Mass., though I spend the winter in Boston. . . ." (Anti-Slavery Letters to Garrison and Others, Boston Public Library.) Dr. Mann's book was entitled *Wolfsden: An Authentic Account of Things There and Thereunto Pertaining, As they Are and Have Been*, by J. B. (Boston, 1856). He is listed as a dentist in the Boston *Directory*, intermittently, from 1839 to 1854, and as a physician in 1857 and 1858. By January 1859, he was in Painesville, Ohio. He was still there in June 1860, but returned to Massachusetts shortly thereafter. During his later years, he lived in Sterling, Mass. His wife, Maria Mann, died in Sterling in 1892, at the age of eighty-five. (Letter dated June 2, 1973, from Mrs. George Otis Tapley, Curator, Sterling Historical Society; letter from Daniel Mann to

Lysander Spooner, January 16, 1859, Anti-Slavery Letters, Boston Public Library; *The Liberator*, June 22, 1860.)

10. Francis W. Bird (b. Dedham, October 22, 1809; d. 1894), of Walpole, graduated from Brown University in 1831. He went into business in 1833, bought the family paper mill from his brother, Josiah, in 1834, went bankrupt in 1842, but in a few years paid all his debts and was back in business. He was elected a member of the state legislature in 1847, 1848, 1867, 1869, 1877, and 1878. He was a member of the state executive council in 1852 and from 1863 to 1865, and of the constitutional convention in 1853, and was state senator in 1871 and Democratic candidate for governor in 1872. He was a "Conscience" Whig during 1846–1848, a Free-Soiler after 1848, and a Republican with the formation of that party. In 1850, he arranged the coalition between Democrats and Free-Soilers which thereafter elected Charles Sumner as United States Senator. He opposed the Know-nothings and any political alliance with them during 1853–1856. (D. Hamilton Hurd, *History of Norfolk County, Mass.*, Philadelphia, 1884, pp. 729–730.)

172

TO ELIZABETH BUFFUM CHACE

Boston, July 13, 1857. It happens, unfortunately, that I am engaged to be at South Danvers, with Parker Pillsbury, on Sunday next, and so cannot be with you, in Providence, on that day, unless I can get excused. I have just written to South Danvers to see if I may be excused.

It surprises and delights me to see how long your series of meetings has been kept up.

Excerpt, printed in L. B. C. Wyman and Arthur Wyman, *Elizabeth Buffum Chace, 1806–1899, Her Life and Its Environment* (Boston, 1914), I, 192.

173

TO ELIZABETH BUFFUM CHACE

Boston, July 15, 1857. I have just apprised our friend Mr. [Asa] Fairbanks that I will lecture twice in Providence on Slavery, on Sunday next, July 19, as I have got excused from South Danvers.

Excerpt, printed in Wyman and Wyman, *Elizabeth Buffum Chace*, I, 192.

174

TO AN UNKNOWN CORRESPONDENT

Boston, July 20, 1857.

Dear Friend:

The bearer of this is an anti-slavery friend, formerly of Littleton, N. H., (Mr. Charles Hazeltine,) [1] who visits your region to see what he can find to do in the line of his profession. He is a competent tuner of piano-fortes, and has been employed for this purpose by Lemuel Gilbert & Co., and he also teaches music. As you will probably know who are most likely to have pianos in their houses in your town, I should esteem it a favor if you would furnish him with the names of such. I have no doubt he will give entire satisfaction.

Yours, truly,

Wm. Lloyd Garrison.

ALS: Villard Papers, Harvard College Library.

1. Charles Hazeltine (b. April 8, 1826; d. Pawtucket, Rhode Island, July 8, 1910) was the son of Enoch Hazeltine, a well-known chair-maker and devoted abolitionist. Charles was a musician who led a church choir and played the tenor viol. He resided in Littleton from 1847 to 1865. For a while he conducted the family business of furniture-making with his elder brother Frederick. After his brother's death in 1864, he moved to New Bedford, Massachusetts. He married Lillias Clough in 1852. After her death in 1860, he married Abby Ottiwell. He was listed in the New Bedford *Directory* from 1867 to 1878 as a piano dealer, repairer, and tuner. He spent the last years of his life in Pawtucket, Rhode Island. (James R. Jackson, *History of Littleton, New Hampshire*, Cambridge, 1905, II, 145–146; III, 255; letter dated September 1, 1972, from Richard C. Kugler, Director, Old Dartmouth Historical Society Whaling Museum, New Bedford, Massachusetts.

175

TO MARIA W. CHAPMAN

Boston, July 23, 1857.

My dear Mrs. Chapman:

Yours of the 21st is received. I think (with yourself and Mrs. Shaw) [1] that it might be serviceable to the cause of humanity for the Executive Committee of the American A. S. Society to enter a public protest against the African importation scheme,[2] which is, unquestionably, the old slave trade in a new form, essentially. You suggest that a meeting of the Committee might be held at the Abington [3] gathering on the 1st of August; but I do not think we shall be able to get a majority, or even a quorum of the members present on that occasion. For one, I am engaged to be at Hopedale on that day.[4] As soon, however, as Mr. May returns from his visit to Montreal, I will confer with him about it, and have the Committee brought together at the earliest convenient period. In the mean time, will you do us all the favor to draw up a series of suitable resolutions for adoption, as you have the English newspapers in your possession?

If I were P. P.,[5] I should hardly feel like going to England again, after interrogating the friends there on the subject, unless they gave me their clear conviction that my presence was very desirable, and would do the anti-slavery cause service. It is a very delicate matter, all round, and I do not know what to advise about it.

I am much obliged to you for your congratulations upon my son's scholastic success. All I can desire to add is, that he is in all respects as good a son as a father could wish to have. His examination at Harvard gave him a clean ticket.[6]

Please give my high regards to your dear mother,[7] and remember me kindly to Deborah [Weston] and your brother.[8]

I am yearning in spirit to see Anna [9] again face to face, as well as Caroline [Weston] and all the absent ones. "When shall we all meet again?" [10]

Yours, ever, absent or present,

Wm. Lloyd Garrison.

Mrs. M. W. Chapman.

ALS: Weston Papers, Boston Public Library.

1. Mrs. Sarah Blake (Sturgis) Shaw (b. August 31, 1815; d. New York, December 29, 1902) was the daughter of Nathaniel R. Sturgis and Susan Parkman. In 1835, she married Francis George Shaw, a businessman, son of Robert Gould Shaw of Boston, who retired from business substantially wealthy in 1840. After living in Boston and West Roxbury — they were also interested in Brook Farm — they moved to Staten Island, New York, in 1849. Her husband translated George Sand's *Consuelo* and *The Countess of Rudostadt* and Zschokke's *History of Switzerland*. They had five children. In 1857, Mrs. Shaw was listed in *The Liberator* (July 17, 1857) as a member of a committee of thirty-one antislavery women, who served as sponsors of the Twenty-Fourth National Anti-Slavery Bazaar, which was to open in Boston on December 17. (*The New England Historical and Genealogical Register*, Boston, 1883, vol. 37, p. 116; Roger F. Sturgis, *Edward Sturgis of Yarmouth, Mass.*, Boston, 1914, p. 51; obituary, *Boston Evening Transcript*, December 30, 1902; Henry W. Sams, ed., *Autobiography of Brook Farm*, Englewood Cliffs, N.J., 1958, *passim.*)

2. *The Liberator*, July 31, 1857, reprinted an article from the London *Times*, which asserted that "the French government, hitherto an active ally in the suppression of the slave trade, has adopted a scheme for exporting 10,000 negroes from the coast to their colonies in the West Indies; and, — what is still more astonishing, — that there is a party in this country urging our government to follow the example of France, and supply our West India colonies with labor in the like manner. . . . We are told that the negroes are to be shipped and transported as emigrants. I deny that it is possible fairly and honestly to ship a thousand

men from the coast of Africa as free emigrants, under any temptation whatever. . . . Indeed, except in the towns and villages of the European settlements,
there is not a free negro on the West coast of Africa. There is not a man, dependent
on his own labor for his support, at liberty to go to the West Indies of his own
free will. . . . The fact is, the proposed system is the old slave-trade in a new
form. . . ."

3. The Massachusetts Anti-Slavery Society was sponsoring its annual West
India Emancipation Celebration at Abington, Massachusetts, on August 1.

4. Garrison was scheduled to speak at the West India Emancipation celebration
at Hopedale, Massachusetts, on August 1.

5. Parker Pillsbury.

6. Wendell Phillips Garrison, Harvard 1861.

7. Ann Bates Weston.

8. Hervey Weston.

9. Ann or Anna Warren Weston.

10. Shakespeare, *Macbeth*, I, i, 1, slightly altered.

176

TO WENDELL PHILLIPS GARRISON

Boston, July 23, 1857.

My dear son:

Rain — rain — rain. You are as unfortunate as was your father in
visiting Newburyport; and I seize my pen to say, (provided this reaches
you before it is too late,) do not think of returning home before Saturday night or Monday forenoon, on the supposition that you will need
some extra washing done before you go to the White Mountains; for
your mother says you are well enough off in that particular, and she
wishes you to remain longer in N. than you contemplated, in order
that you may see its beauties and get a little acquainted with its location, as you cannot do in weather like this; for I take it for granted
that such a storm as we are having reaches far below Newburyport
eastward.

Mr. May left us this afternoon for Syracuse, much to our regret. If
there ever was "an Israelite indeed in whom there was no guile," [1] he
is that man. My soul cleaves to his as did the soul of David to that
of Jonathan.

Dr. Geist is now carefully examining the case of aunt Charlotte,
who has desired to have him called in. She is looking and feeling very
wretchedly, and it seems to me cannot survive many weeks. But I shall
not be able to get the Doctor's opinion of her case in season to tell you
what it is.

You will give our kindest remembrances to Mr. and Mrs. Ashby [2]
and Anna, to whom we feel specially indebted. May you enjoy yourself
to the brim! Don't forget to look "at the house where I was born," in

461

School street. Be sure, too, and visit Mr. and Mrs. Horton,[3] and remember us warmly to them.

Ever your affectionate father,

Wm. Lloyd Garrison.

W. P. Garrison.

ALS: Garrison Papers, Boston Public Library.

1. John 1:47.
2. Mr. and Mrs. William Ashby. William Ashby (1787–1881) of Newburyport was in the iron business for many years, and was a supporter of woman suffrage and of the antislavery movement and a long-time friend of the Garrisons. Garrison attended his eightieth birthday party and stayed with him during the woman suffrage convention in Newburyport in 1869. He was interested in various philanthropic causes, including the Newburyport Library. (John J. Currier, *History of Newburyport, Massachusetts*, Newburyport, 1909, II, 137, 416; obituary, *Boston Evening Transcript*, January 31, 1881.)
3. Jacob Horton (1797–1876), of Newburyport, Massachusetts, was a selectman of Newburyport in 1838, and in 1857 incorporated the Merchants Mutual Marine Insurance Company, in which he was a partner until its dissolution in 1872. He was active in antislavery and was the husband of Harriet Farnham, in whose parents' home in Newburyport Garrison's father and mother had rented a few rooms. Garrison was born under the same roof with Harriet, both growing up together as children, playing together and treating one another as brother and sister. She died on November 28, 1867, in Newburyport, of typhoid fever. (Currier, *History of Newburyport, Massachusetts*, II, 167, 601; letter from Garrison to Jacob Horton, Esq., Roxbury, December 14, 1867, Garrison Papers, Boston Public Library; see *Letters*, I, 82–83.)

177

TO J. M. HAWKS

Boston, July 24, 1857.

Dear Sir:

Pardon me for the delay that has occurred in answering your letter of the 3d instant, relative to my giving an anti-slavery lecture in Manchester. At this season of the year, the evenings are too short for such a lecture after dark; and Sunday seems to offer the only available occasion. If desired, I think I could arrange it so as to speak twice in your place on Sunday, August 15th; and yet, if a single lecture would answer, and you think by that time, or a little later, I could secure an audience on the evening of some other day,[1] I should prefer not to be away from home over Sunday. Shall I hear from you again?

Yours to free the oppressed,

Wm. Lloyd Garrison

Transcript made by Ralph G. Newman, Chicago, Illinois, from ALS in his possession in 1952. Since then the original letter has changed hands, and its location is unknown to us.

Dr. John Milton Hawks (b. in Bradford, New Hampshire, November 26, 1826; fl. 1906), graduated in medicine from the Cincinnati Medical College in 1847, and practiced medicine in Manchester, New Hampshire, from 1848 to 1862. From 1862 to 1865, he was volunteer physician to the freedmen at Edisto Island, South Carolina. After the Civil War, he was variously at Port Orange, Florida (1866–1870), Hyde Park, Massachusetts (1873–1876), and Hawks' Park, Florida (1876 until at least 1906). (Granville P. Conn, *New Hampshire Surgeons in the War of the Rebellion*, Concord, New Hampshire, 1906, pp. 286–288.)

1. *The Liberator*, August 14, 1857, announced that Garrison would "lecture on American slavery in Manchester, (N. H.) on Sunday next, August 16, afternoon and evening."

178

TO E. F. BURNHAM

Boston, Aug. 5, 1857.

Dear Friend:

After dropping my letter into the Post Office this morning, in reference to my lecturing in your place on Sunday next,[1] I received yours, making an inquiry about the same matter, with particular reference to Mr. Pillsbury. He is to lecture in *Portsmouth*, N. H., next Sunday, and so cannot be with me. I will speak twice for you, — on Sunday afternoon, and again in the evening, — and come down in the manner I indicated in my other note — on Sunday morning, to Salem, in the stage.

Yours, in haste,

Wm. Lloyd Garrison.

E. F. Burnham.

ALS: Essex Institute, Salem, Massachusetts.

Eli F. Burnham (b. October 13, 1805; d. March 28, 1885), of Peabody, Massachusetts, married Mary Eveleth in 1831 and Mrs. Edith Eveleth in 1866 (Peabody *Directory*, 1886; *Vital Records of Danvers, Mass.*, Salem, 1909, p. 54; Roderick H. Burnham, *Genealogical Register of Thomas Burnham, the Emigrant*, Hartford, 1884, pp. 350, 382.)

1. Garrison was scheduled to speak in South Danvers, Massachusetts, on Sunday, August 9.

179

TO FRANCIS JACKSON GARRISON

14 Dix Place, Aug. 8. [1857]

Dear Franky:

You made us all very happy by your letter, announcing your safe arrival at Oakdale,[1] and how you and Birney[2] concluded to change sides in your sleep, without being conscious that you entered into any such arrangement. It was very funny, certainly. Though "one good turn deserves another," I don't believe you can do it over again. Do you?

I have no doubt you will be very happy in your new abode. You gravely inform us that you are "not ready to come home yet" — which indicates that you are really quite a witty young man. But you know I like a good joke, and I accept yours on the score of blood relationship.

I might caution you about not doing this, or not going there — about being very careful not to hurt yourself, or to run into danger — and equally careful to give as little trouble as possible to Mrs. Mann — &c. &c.; but I am going to take it for granted that you will be abroad, as you have been at home, a very careful young man, and a very good boy. Be useful as you can about the house, and help the Doctor and Birney as far as in your power. I wish I could be with you, but I am tied to the city, and can only break away on Sunday, to plead for the poor slave, whose cause has but few to uphold it. Tell the Dr. when the jubilee takes place, I shall try to come to Oakdale, and we will shout "Amen!" "Glory!" in a style that will astonish all the Methodist brethren.

We don't want you to fatigue yourself in writing to us again, but we shall be very glad to get another little note from you before your return.

With my best regards to Dr. M. and his wife, and Birney, I remain,
Your delighted father,

Wm. Lloyd Garrison.

ALS: Massachusetts Historical Society. The year was inserted by a later hand.

1. Francis Garrison was visiting Dr. and Mrs. Daniel Mann for a while.
2. Birney Mann (b. *circa* 1847; d. Clinton, Mass., 1903), the son of Dr. and Mrs. Daniel Mann, studied at Boys Latin School in Boston, where he may have been a classmate of Francis Jackson Garrison. Birney Mann was a fine organist and music teacher. (Letter dated June 21, 1973, from Mrs. George Otis Tapley, Curator, Sterling Historical Society, Sterling, Mass.)

1 8 0

TO THE EDITOR OF THE BOSTON *TRANSCRIPT*

[Aug. 13, 1857.]

'Beware of DOGS.'

'Tray, Blanche, and Sweetheart, all.' [1]

To the Editor of the Transcript:

SIR, — It would be an endless task for Abolitionists to undertake to contradict the numberless misrepresentations concerning their course, which are maliciously circulated in every part of the land; and, therefore, they seldom attempt any correction. But, sometimes, an accusation may be brought, of such a nature, and under such circumstances, as to demand a prompt denial, in order that the libeller may be put to open shame, and the cause of the oppressed in our land may receive no injury.

The *dog*-ged perseverance of 'Sigma,' [2] in renewing and reiterating the exploded libel against Mr. Parker Pillsbury, that, 'some years ago, he performed, in public, the ceremony of baptizing three dogs, in the name of the Father, Son and Holy Ghost,' calls for a fresh protest against such flagrant injustice. In support of his foul charge, 'Sigma' quotes a lying statement which appeared in the Salem *Register*,[3] made by an anonymous scribbler, and a most vindictive enemy of the Anti-Slavery cause — to this effect, namely, that 'on a Sabbath afternoon, Mr. Pillsbury went through a mock ceremony of taking several dogs into the church — that he questioned them as to their doctrinal opinion, and made them give replies satisfactory to himself that he propounded them — and finally administered the ceremony of baptism in the following words: "I baptize thee, Bose, in the name of the Father," &c.; "I baptize thee, Tiger," &c. — 'the object of the performer being,' adds 'Sigma,' 'in consonance with his opposition to the Sabbath, *to bring the ordinance of baptism also into contempt*'!

Now, Mr. Editor, I aver that, of all wilful perversions of facts, this has not been surpassed since the time when it was said of another notable disturber of the peace, 'He hath spoken blasphemy; what further need have we of witnesses? behold, now ye have heard his blasphemy.' [4] I testify, 'as an eye and ear witness,' having been at the meeting alluded to, and heard every word uttered by Mr. Pillsbury on that occasion. The facts are these: In the course of one of the most impressive speeches to which I ever listened, Mr. Pillsbury referred to the awful indifference with which the horrible act of reducing millions of immortal beings to the level of brutes, and the condition of property, was every where regarded in the land; and he then proceeded to reverse the case by asking, *what would be said* of the clergyman who should bring sundry dogs into the broad aisle of his church on a communion Sunday, and, professing to regard them as rational and accountable beings, should read to them the creed, and then, affecting to consider them as having given their assent to it, should proceed to baptize them in the name of Father, Son, and Holy Ghost? 'Would not a thrill of horror,' said Mr. Pillsbury, 'run through the community, in view of such a blasphemous procedure? And yet, which is the more blasphemous act — to hurl down those who are made a little lower than the angels among four-footed beasts, or to attempt to elevate dogs to the position of men? But who thrills with indignation, or who lays it to heart, that so many of our fellow-creatures are thus dehumanized? While the canine farce, which has been hypothetically imagined, would excite universal disgust and horror, the terrible tragedy which is going on at the South causes no sensation — elicits no rebuke!'

Now, what could be more pertinent, more striking, or more effective than such an illustration? It certainly made a powerful impression upon the audience at the time, and helped to heighten their conception of the blasphemous nature of chattel slavery, to intensify their abhorrence of it, and to quicken their zeal for its eternal overthrow. How satanic must have been the spirit of the wretch, who, through the Salem *Register*, caricatured all that was said and done on the occasion, representing Mr. Pillsbury as having actually brought a troop of dogs into the church, and baptized them in mockery of religion! And how malignant must be the man who will persist in quoting such a slanderer as authority, and reiterating the infamous allegation!

'Sigma' says: 'We have, on our files, letters writters at that period, from gentlemen of Danvers,[5] of the first respectability, confirming the statement, *in all its minute particulars*, (*!!*) upon the testimony of eye and ear witnesses.' Now, sir, I challenge the production of any one of those letters, or of any one of those eye and ear witnesses.* Against them, I will array hundreds of unimpeachable persons, who heard what Mr. Pillsbury said, and who will readily testify that he has been most shamefully belied.

Let 'Sigma' remember how it turned out in another case —

'The *man* recovered of the bite —
The *dog* it was that died.' [6]

Yours, for the truth,

WM. LLOYD GARRISON.

14 Dix Place, Aug. 13, 1857.

* In reply to this, Sɪɢᴍᴀ brings forward the same old libeller in the Salem Register!!

Printed in *The Liberator*, August 21, 1857.

As printed in *The Liberator*, the letter bore the following heading:
"From the Boston Transcript of August 13.
"THE STORY OF THE THREE BLACK
CROWS OUTDONE."

1. Shakespeare, *King Lear*, III, vi, 62 (modified).

2. The article by "Sigma" appeared in the Boston *Transcript* on Saturday, August 8, 1857. In the course of an attack upon the metropolitan railroad for carrying passengers on Sunday from Boston to Roxbury and upon the city fathers of Boston for permitting the cars to run on a Sunday, in violation of the Sabbath, Sigma added the following comment:

"The religion of the people has far less to apprehend from direct assaults than from insidious approaches. When Parker Pillsbury, some years ago, performed, in public, the ceremony of baptizing three dogs, in the name of the Father, Son, and Holy Ghost; and when, at the Anti-Sabbath Convention, held in this city, a barbarian from Worcester, named Foster, openly denounced the Sabbath; and stated, that, to show his contempt for it, it had been his practice to saw wood, in the view of those who were passing his dwelling, on their way to the meeting-house; we had no fears on account of such abominations. The awful wickedness and absurdity were too palpable for the production of any ill effect. On the contrary, it is quite likely, that some, who were prepared for what they considered a reasonable amount of rascality, recoiled from this clotted mass of stupidity and sacrilege. (!!!)

"We say there is little to be feared from such bold, brutal assaults upon the religion of any people. But the case is very different when the Mayor and Aldermen of Boston fold their official arms, and look composedly upon a palpable desecration of the Sabbath — a perfectly clear and intelligible violation of the laws of God and man!" (Quoted in *The Liberator*, August 14, 1857.)

The same issue includes a letter from Samuel May, Jr., replying to the *Transcript*. See also *The Liberator*, August 21, 1857, for additional letters from Parker Pillsbury and Samuel May, Jr.

3. The *Salem Register* began publication in 1800, under the direction of William Carlton, who was succeeded by Warwick Palfray in 1805. (Frederic Hudson, *Journalism in the United States, from 1690 to 1872*, New York and Evanston, 1969, p. 170).

4. Matthew 26:65.

5. The meeting at which Pillsbury spoke had taken place in Danvers, Massachusetts, several years previously.

6. Oliver Goldsmith, *Elegy on the Death of a Mad Dog*.

181

TO FRANCIS JACKSON GARRISON

Boston, August 13, 1857.

My dear Franky:

Another letter has just been received from you, enclosing a few lines kindly written by Mrs. Mann and the Doctor. We are sorry that you did not get our letters at an earlier date, in consequence of misdirection. I had supposed that Oakdale [1] was a part of Sterling, as Hopedale is of Milford; and so, to "make assurance doubly sure," [2] I directed the letters to "Oakdale, Sterling"; but I shall not make that blunder again. It is good to be growing in knowledge every day, and then to do the right thing as it is made known to us; for who would wish to be in the wrong? How foolish it would be for me now to send you another letter, inscribed "Oakdale, Sterling"! So, whenever we find that we are in the wrong, we must turn away from it, and go in the right direction. Hurrah, then, for Oakdale, independent of Sterling! And hurrah for the *sterling* people that belong to it, and all its *Mannly* inhabitants!

We are glad to hear that you are very happy, and enjoying yourself finely. It will probably be a whole year before you will again go into the country, and you must make the most of your present opportunity. How beautiful must every thing look around you? What is Dix Place for a prospect, compared with the Dr's residence? What is rattling, noisy, crowded, sweltering Boston, compared with quiet, peaceful, lovely Oakdale? If I had the wings of a bird, would I not at once take my flight for your place, and be by your side some hours in advance of the mail which will carry this letter? Yes!

Wendell is now at Nahant, spending a few days with his school-mate, Samuel Phillips.[3] He has not written to us since he left home, almost a week ago; so he is not half so attentive as you have been. Indeed, I think you must be called "the young letter-writer" — perhaps the youngest, just now, in the old Bay State. We must write letters to our friends just as we would talk to them if they were sitting by our side, and then it will come very easy to us.

William came home on Saturday last, and remained with mother till Monday morning. I was absent on Sunday at South Danvers, and did not get home till after he left. He was well and happy.

I believe we have not received any letter from George since you went to Oakdale, but we hope to receive one from him in the course of a few days. I wonder if he does not feel sometimes a little home-sick? Do you know what that feeling is? But you are not very far from Boston, while George is perhaps seventeen hundred miles from us.[4]

Fanny is still at Newburyport, — no doubt as happy as a lark. She has written to us but once; but then, I ought not to complain, for I have not written to her a single line; but I must send her a good long letter to-morrow. We do not know when she thinks of coming home.

We are very lonely without you, and Fanny, and Wendell, and shall be very glad to see you all again around the family table. You think of returning next Wednesday. Come whenever you wish to, and it is perfectly convenient for the Doctor to send you; or stay, if you prefer to.

Aunt Charlotte remains about the same, very weak, but in pretty good spirits. Dr. Geist holds out strong encouragement of her getting well, and feels confident that he can cure her. I hope he is not mistaken, though I have very great doubts, at times, as to how the case will turn.

The kittens have grown very much since you left, and I know not what to do with them. I think I shall keep them all until you return home, hoping that you will be able to give them away; for it is very unpleasant to think of drowning them.

Do you find plenty of berries to pick? And which do you like best — to pick or to eat them?

How I wish I had been with you, and Birney, and the dog, and all the rest of your company, when you went to the Wachusett mountain! Did you know that I went up to the top of it, a few years ago, in company with my friend Joshua T. Everett,[5] of Princeton? So, you see, father and son have stood on the same spot, and been quite elevated in their day. *Excelsior*!

I am now going, with mother, to spend the evening with our dear aged friend, Mrs. Otis. We shall tell her all about you, and your visit to Oakdale.

Mother sends her warmest love to "dear little Frank" — and we both desire to be most kindly remembered to Dr. and Mrs. Mann, Birney, and all the household.

Your loving father,

Wm. Lloyd Garrison.

Francis J. Garrison.

ALS: Massachusetts Historical Society.

1. Oakdale is several miles southwest of Sterling. Both are north of Worcester, Massachusetts.

2. Shakespeare, *Macbeth*, IV, i, 83.

3. Samuel Dunn Phillips was the son of Thomas W. Phillips of Boston. He graduated from Harvard in the class of 1861, and worked among the black freedmen at Port Royal, South Carolina, soon after graduation. He took ill and died there on December 5, 1862. His obituary in *The Liberator*, December 19, 1862, was written by his classmate, Wendell Phillips Garrison.

4. He was then at Nininger, Minnesota.

5. Joshua Titus Everett (b. Princeton, January 6, 1806; d. Westminster, February 10, 1897), of Princeton, Massachusetts, was president of the Worcester County North Division Anti-Slavery Society for many years, and an early abolitionist and reformer. (*Letters*, II, 576.) He was widely known in Worcester County and elsewhere in Massachusetts for his interest in agriculture. His home was a haven for fugitive slaves. He contributed financially to *The Liberator* from time to time. In 1834 and 1835 he was a selectman and assessor in Princeton, and a member of the Massachusetts legislature from 1833 to 1835. (Francis Everett Blake, *History of the Town of Princeton*, Princeton, 1915, p. 99.)

182

TO FANNY GARRISON

Boston, August 14, 1857.

My dear Fanny:

You know that, of all my *daughters*, I love you the best; and yet I have not indicated this in the way of letter-writing, since you left us. Every day I have *intended* to send you an epistle, and every day I have failed to do so, owing to a multiplicity of cares and engagements. What are good intentions worth, unless they are reduced to practice? It is something, perhaps, to know that we are remembered, though no token be received; and to forget you, my darling, is impossible.

We have just received your letter, enclosing one to Franky, which I have directed to him at Oakdale, Mass., and which he will be very proud to receive. He has written us several letters, "short and sweet," and may properly be called "the young letter-writer." Next Wednesday is the time he has set for returning home, but he may possibly remain a few days longer, as he is having a very merry time of it.

I am really afraid you are staying too long for the convenience of our dear friends, Mr. and Mrs. Ashby; though their kindness is inexhaustible. I intended to have gone down to Newburyport, yesterday, or to-day, after you; but circumstances have put it out of my power. To-morrow I must go to Manchester, N. H., where I must lecture on Sunday; so that I cannot visit Newburyport before Thursday or Friday next; and that would protract your visit too long, we fear. Mother will accompany me, if she can.

I am glad you are going to see Mr. Whittier,[1] the poet of whom America has the most reason to be proud, and who has done much to quicken the consciences and touch the hearts of the people, in behalf of the poor oppressed slaves. Give my special regards to him, his mother and sister.

So! you have seen "the house where I was born." Not a princely palace, to be sure, but sufficiently large to accommodate me at the time of my birth. I have many sacred memories clustering about it.

I want to be with you, to stroll about over the places where I used to fly my kite, play marbles, and bat the ball, when I was even younger than you are now.

Mother had scarcely dropped her letter into the post-office, chiding you a little for not writing, when yours was received, making us all very much pleased.

Wendell is spending a few days with his school-mate, Samuel Phillips, at Nahant. He writes us no letters. William came up on Saturday, and remained over till Monday morning.

I am engaged to spend this evening at Mrs. Dall's,[2] and my time is more than "up." Aunt sends her love, with mother's, and says she misses her little nurse greatly. She is very weak, but slightly improved.

I send a whole ream of kind regards, for mother and myself, to dear Mr. & Mrs. Ashby, and Anna.

Your loving father,

Wm. Lloyd Garrison.

Fanny Garrison.

ALS: Villard Papers, Harvard College Library.

1. Garrison, when editor of *The Free Press* in Newburyport, Massachusetts, in 1826, had first discovered John Greenleaf Whittier and published his poems in several issues of the paper (see *Letters*, I, 82).

2. Caroline Wells Healey Dall (1822–1912), author and reformer, operated a nursery for the children of working women in Boston's North End from 1837 to 1842, was vice-principal of Miss English's School for Young Ladies in Georgetown, D.C., from 1842 to 1844, and married the Reverend Charles Henry Appleton Dall, a Unitarian minister and Harvard Divinity School graduate, in 1844. They lived in Toronto, Canada, where Charles Dall served a Unitarian congregation, from 1850 to 1854, when, as a result of Dall's illness, they returned to Boston, occupying a home in West Newton. A year later, Dall went to India, and remained there for thirty-one years, returning for occasional visits to the United States. Although alone with two growing children, Caroline Dall continued her interests in public affairs and writing. She helped organize a woman's rights convention in Boston in 1855, and the New England Woman's Rights Convention in Boston in 1859. Her published works include *Historical Pictures Retouched* (1860), *The College, the Market, and the Court; or Woman's Relation to Education, Labor, and Law* (1867), and *Egypt's Place in History* (1868). (*Notable American Women.*)

183

TO JOHN NEEDLES

Boston, Aug. 14, 1857.

Esteemed friend John Needles:

I do not know but I may have passed almost entirely out of your recollection, but you have not been forgotten by me at any time since our first acquaintance, when I was associated with Benjamin Lundy in editing the "Genius of Universal Emancipation," at Baltimore.[1] Your life has been signally devoted to the cause of suffering humanity, particularly with reference to a race "peeled, meted out, and trodden under foot," [2] on account of their color — and the blessings of those who are ready to perish will ever rest upon your head. It would give me unspeakable pleasure to see you face to face, but that pleasure I cannot now enjoy.

As I have not heard from you for a long time, it is possible that you may have changed your location, and, therefore, that this letter may not reach you. Should you receive it, I wish to secure your kind offices in the following case.

My mother died in Baltimore, in the autumn of 1823, after a lingering illness. She was a member of the Baptist church, and found warm friends in the person of the late Deacon Carnighan,[3] (I think his first name was John,) and his household. I have recently received a letter from W. W. Carnighan,[4] (a son of the Deacon, and now a resident of Cincinnati,) informing me that his mother has in her possession at Baltimore, the Bank-Book belonging to my own mother, which shows a balance of $387.75, and which sum belongs to me as the only surviving heir. This sum, I presume, is the result of thirty-four years' interest upon a few dollars deposited in the Savings Bank before her death. It strikes me as very singular that I have never been apprised of this fact before; though I have no reason to doubt that every thing has been done with the strictest honesty. But as no other child survives, except myself, of course, I am legally entitled to whatever is in the Bank, in my mother's name. Her whole name was Frances Maria Garrison.

W. W. Carnighan writes — "I suppose the correct course to be pursued to obtain the money would be for you to place the matter in the hands of some competent Attorney in Baltimore, giving him an order on my mother for the Bank-Book, and empowering him by your power of attorney to act for you"; — and he suggests either Brantz Mayer [5] or Hon. J. Morrison Harris [6] as a suitable and reliable attorney. But as a lawyer in this case may not be necessary — as it is possible that the gentlemen named may be strongly prejudiced against me on account of my abolitionism — I take the liberty to ask you if you will be so kind as to confer with Mrs. Carnighan, (her present residence in the city I am unable to give you,) and inform me whether the matter cannot be satisfactorily arranged through you, by my sending you a power of attorney, which will be necessary without my personal presence. Perhaps it may be necessary to take out letters of administration, but I trust that formality will not be required. You may give every assurance at the Bank that I am the only surviving heir; and should they want any security from you, by giving it I will see that you are amply compensated.

Struggling as I have been for so many years against the colossal wrong of our country, it will be a timely relief to me to receive the sum aforesaid. Please let me hear from you soon.

Your old and attached friend,

Wm. Lloyd Garrison.

P. S. W. W. Carnighan writes to me, also, that, "in consequence of a road being cut through the grave-yard of the first Baptist Society in Baltimore, it became necessary to remove the bodies lying in our lot — a part of which was cut off by the road. The removal has taken place, and my mother thinks that a proportion of the expense[s] ought to be borne by you. That proportion she states in her letter to be $20." He refers to the body of my mother, which was interred in the lot aforesaid.

Of course, I am ready to meet any necessary expense of the kind; and should the Bank matter be satisfactorily arranged, a deduction might be made accordingly. But it surprises me that the city should seize upon a portion of a grave-yard belonging to a religious society, in order to construct a road through it, and then not only make no remuneration, but compel relatives to remove the bodies at their own expense; whereas, justice obviously requires that the city should make some remuneration.

ALS: Villard Papers, Harvard College Library.

John Needles (b. eastern shore of Maryland, October 4, 1786; d. there, July 18, 1878) was an antislavery Quaker and an early supporter of Benjamin Lundy and Garrison. (*Life*, I, 145; III, 464; IV, 113, 399.) In Baltimore, he worked for many years as a cabinet maker and undertaker. When Benjamin Lundy founded the *Genius of Universal Emancipation*, Needles purchased the printing press and type for him. In 1850, he became a minister of the Society of Friends and traveled through Pennsylvania and Ohio. In addition to antislavery, one of his major interests was the Prisoners' Aid Association. (Hester Rich, Librarian, Maryland Historical Society, letter dater August 3, 1972.)

1. From 1829 to 1830.

2. See Isaiah 18:2.

3. A John Carnighan died of yellow fever on October 18, 1838, at the age of thirty-four. (Hester Rich, Librarian, Maryland Historical Society, letter dated August 3, 1972.) A rather dubious identification, but the best we can do.

4. Unidentified.

5. Brantz Mayer (b. Baltimore, September 27, 1809; d. February 23, 1879) was a practicing lawyer in Baltimore. In 1841, he interrupted his practice to become the secretary of the United States legation in Mexico but resumed it several years later. He contributed frequently to the daily press and various journals and for a time edited the Baltimore *American*, a mercantile journal. He supported the North during the Civil War and was president of the Union State Central Committee of Maryland until he received a commission as colonel from the United States Army. He was a founder of the Maryland Historical Society in 1844 and was elected its president in 1866. His writings include *Mexico as It Was and Is*; *Captain Canot, or Twenty Years in the Life of an African Slaver*; and *A Memoir of Jared Sparks*. (*The Biographical Cyclopedia of Representative Men of Maryland and District of Columbia*, Baltimore, 1879, pp. 679–680.)

6. James Morrison Harris (b. Baltimore, November 20, 1817; d. there, July 16, 1898) was admitted to the bar in 1843. He was elected to Congress from the Third Congressional District of Maryland, as the candidate of the American party, in 1854, and reelected twice, serving from 1855 to 1861. He declined renomination in 1860 and returned to the practice of law and to educational and religious work. (*Ibid.*, pp. 645–646; *BDAC.*)

184

TO FRANCIS JACKSON GARRISON

Boston, Aug. 17, 1857.

My Dear Franky:

I am going to send you a *long* [1] letter, (as you will see by the length of this slip of paper, on which I write, because just at this moment I can find nothing better,) in reply to yours of Saturday, which came to hand this morning.

It seems to me, from your accounts, that, what with picking berries, roasting potatoes and eggs, playing with the dog, going in swimming, and the like, that you and Birney must be having a first rate time. I almost wish I was again a little boy — just for a day or two — so as to make a third one among you. — When I *was* a boy, no one was more fond of bat and ball, or flying the kite, or playing at marbles, or jumping "hop scotch," or paddling in the water, &c. &c., than myself; and though I have outgrown all those amusements, it ever gives me the greatest delight to see "the rising generation" following in the footsteps of their "illustrious predecessors," in this particular.

Yesterday, (Sunday,) I was in Manchester, N. H. I never saw a more perfect day, in all respects. My visit was a very pleasant one. I lectured on slavery in the afternoon and in the evening, to very good audiences, and had a very candid hearing. It is very sad to think how few persons there are to pity the poor slaves; and still more sad to see how many there are who take the part of the slaveholders, because they are strong and powerful. You, my dear boy, I trust, will grow up a good abolitionist; and should your father's voice be hushed in death before the wretched slaves are set free, you must lift up, in the loudest tone, your own voice, saying —

"I am an abolitionist —
　　Then urge me not to pause,
For joyfully do I enlist
　　In freedom's sacred cause:
A nobler strife the world ne'er saw,
　　Th'enslaved to disenthral;
I am a soldier for the war,
　　Whatever may befall.[2]

Marie Addie [3] has written a long letter to Fanny, (who is still at Newburyport,) giving an account of her visit to Provincetown, which she describes as a very funny looking place — the people also looking very queer. She was very sea-sick going down in the boat from Boston, just as your father is whenever he crosses the ocean.

Don't you think it is a little too bad that Wendell has not sent us a single letter since he went away? If he has done so, it has never reached us; and so I cannot tell you how he is enjoying himself. But I take it for granted that he is well, and very happy.

I think of going to Newburyport, after Fanny, on Thursday (Aug. 20) [4] afternoon, and remaining til Saturday; and I should like to have you go with me. So, if it will not be too much trouble for Dr. Mann to put you on board of the cars on Wednesday, — or if he cannot, then on Thursday, — so that you can get here before I go to Newburyport, it will give me a great deal of pleasure to have your company. I will be at the depot, looking out for you.

It is now raining hard, and a very great change has taken place in the weather, it being quite cool. We must take what comes, and be thankful for it — remembering that the good God, our Creator and Father, knows best what is needed, and is always seeking the happiness of the universe.

If I had not engaged to go to Newburyport, it would have given me great pleasure to have accepted the kind invitation of Dr. Mann, to spend Saturday and Sunday at Oakdale, making a visit to Wachusett. You must let him know how very much obliged we feel to him, to Mrs. Mann, and to Birney, for the unwearied pains they have taken to make your visit a gladsome one. May peace and joy be ever with them!

Mother sends her warmest love to you, and longs to embrace you. She joins me in kindest regards to all the family.

Your loving father,

Wm. Lloyd Garrison.

F. J. Garrison.

ALS: Massachusetts Historical Society.

1. This letter was written on a long narrow sheet of blue paper, about a foot and a quarter, or a half, long.

2. The second stanza of "Song of the Abolitionist," composed by Garrison more than fifteen years earlier. (William Lloyd Garrison, *Sonnets and Other Poems,* Boston, 1843, pp. 21–23.)

3. We have not been able to identify Marie Addie, but we do know that Frederick Eugene Anthony, the son of Helen Garrison's sister Charlotte Benson Anthony, married Julia Perkins Adie of Providence in 1872. Unfortunately, we have learned nothing further about the relationship between Marie Addie and Julia Adie. (W. P. *The Benson Family of Newport, Rhode Island,* New York, 1872, p. 44.)

4. The date is inserted in pencil, probably by Garrison.

1 8 5

TO FANNY GARRISON

Boston, Aug. 19, 1857.

My dear Fanny:

Since I wrote to you last evening, I have continued quite unwell, and now feel very feeble and feverish, though I am slightly better of my complaint.

Your mother and I have just returned from the Worcester depot, where we expected to meet Franky, on his return from Oakdale, but we were disappointed. He will probably come in the course of to-morrow.

Uncle Henry Anthony and aunt Charlotte [1] have been making us a visit to-day, together with Henry's brother John [2] and his wife, from Cincinnati. They returned to P. in the afternoon train.

Should I be well enough, I shall endeavor to take the first train for Newburyport, on Friday morning — 7.30 — and shall hope to see you a little after 9 o'clock.

Aunt [3] had quite an ill turn to-day, after dinner, bleeding very freely at the nose. She looks wretchedly, and yet Dr. Geist encourages her to believe that she will recover. I see no change, except for the worse, since he came the first time.

Our loving regards to Mr. and Mrs. Ashby, and Anna.

Your loving father,

Wm. Lloyd Garrison.

Fanny Garrison.

ALS: Garrison Papers, Boston Public Library.

1. Charlotte Benson Anthony, Helen Garrison's older sister, had married Henry Anthony (1802–1879) of Providence, Rhode Island, in 1826. They lived thereafter in Providence. (*Letters*, II, xxiii, 7–8.)

2. John Gould Anthony (1804–1877), zoologist, a native of Providence, Rhode Island, moved to Cincinnati, Ohio, with his parents when he was twelve years old. He went into business at an early age. On October 16, 1832, he married Anna W. Rhodes. On making the acquaintance of Jared Kirtland and other naturalists, he became interested in natural history, especially fresh-water mollusks, and corresponded with mollusk students in the United States and Europe. Retiring from business in 1851 as a result of eye trouble, he embarked upon a pedestrian tour of Kentucky, Tennessee, and Georgia in 1853 during which he collected mollusks and restored his health. He published his results on mollusks from 1854 to 1860.

3. Charlotte Newell, Garrison's mother's sister.

1 8 6

TO J. M. HAWKS

Boston, Aug. 20, 1857

Dear Sir:

On reaching home, I found that I had left my night shirt.[1] You can send it to my address, Anti-Slavery office, 21 Cornhill, Boston, by express, when convenient.

I see you refer to it in your letter, enclosing the notice of my lectures by the *American*, for which accept my thanks.

I had no room to make any allusion to my visit to Manchester in this week's Liberator, in consequence of the pressure of matter.

Give my grateful remembrances to Mrs. Hawks,[2] and believe me

Your much obliged friend,

Wm. Lloyd Garrison

Dr. J. M. Hawks

Transcript: in possession of Walter M. Merrill, Drexel University, Philadelphia, Pennsylvania.

1. Garrison had lectured in Manchester, New Hampshire, on August 16, but was already home on August 17, as the letter of that date indicates.

2. Esther Hill Hawks (b. Hooksett, New Hampshire, August 4, 1833; fl. 1906) married Dr. John Milton Hawks on October 4, 1854. She began the study of medicine soon after her marriage, graduated from the New England Female Medical College in Boston in 1857, and immediately began the practice of medicine in Manchester, New Hampshire. In 1863, she accompanied her husband to South Carolina, where she also served as physician among the freedmen and colored troops. During the thirty years prior to 1906 and perhaps later, she resided in Lynn, Massachusetts. (Granville P. Conn, *New Hampshire Surgeons in the War of the Rebellion*, Concord, New Hampshire, 1906, pp. 288–289.)

1 8 7

TO THE EDITOR OF THE BOSTON *TRANSCRIPT*

[Sept. 8, 1857.]

To the Editor of the Transcript:

SIR — In the *Transcript* of the 13th ult., I declared, both as an eye and ear witness, that the charge brought by Sigma against Parker Pillsbury, of having publicly baptized three dogs, in mockery of religion and its ordinances, was base, malicious, and utterly destitute of truth. In reply to his declaration, that he had 'letters from gentlemen of Danvers, of the first respectability, *confirming the statement, in all its minute particulars*, upon the testimony of eye and ear witnesses,'

I challenged him to produce either witness or letter in a tangible shape. How has he met the challenge? By renewing his atrociously wicked accusation, without presenting a particle of evidence; and by making the columns of the *Transcript*, week after week, a sewer through which to discharge upon my head a torrent of malignant invective and personal defamation.

Ribaldry like this — 'cursing like a very drab' [1] — is beneath serious refutation. Remember, Sigma plumes himself upon being both a Christian and a gentleman! Never was self-delusion ever greater. To reach his abyssmal position, in order to stand on his own level and to meet him with his own weapons, one must make a lower descent than did the rebellious angels: —

    '—— Headlong themselves they threw
    Down from the verge of heaven: nine days they fell.' [2]

Convicted of slander, Sigma seeks to change the issue, and to escape the scorn and indignation of all upright men, by acting the part of the cuttle-fish, and riling the waters, so as not to be transfixed. It is an old and scaly trick, but it will not answer his purpose. No matter what shape he assumes — whether he

    'O'er bog or steep, through strait, rough, dense or rare,
    With head, hands, wings, or feet, pursues his way,
    And swims, or sinks, or wades, or creeps, or flies' — [3]

his exposure is inevitable — his capture certain.

The point in dispute is not whether I am an 'infidel,' or a 'bully,' or 'a pernicious citizen,' or 'foolish and frantic,' or 'a notorious blasphemer,' or 'the devil's printer,' — nor does it relate to my biblical or sabbatical views, — but it is solely as to the truth of the following accusation made by Sigma against one, the latchets of whose shoes he is 'not worthy to unloose': —

'Parker Pillsbury, some years ago, performed, in public, the ceremony of baptizing three dogs, in the name of the Father, Son, and Holy Ghost.'

This was Sigma's original, naked, unqualified charge — leading every unsuspecting reader of the *Transcript* naturally to suppose that, to outrage the religious feelings of the community, Mr. Pillsbury actually and literally did the absurd and monstrous thing attributed to him! Subsequently, Sigma adds that Mr. P. did it 'in consonance with his opposition to the Sabbath, to bring the ordinance of baptism also into contempt'!! His first witness is, the anonymous author of the story in the Salem *Register*, who dares not to avow himself under his own proper signature, and upon whose lying statement all the changes that have since been rung upon Mr. Pillsbury's 'blasphemy,' by the enemies of the Anti-Slavery cause, have been based! His next witness is a 'Mr.

——,' (all in the dark again!) who said, 'he was POSITIVE that Pillsbury *offered the dogs bread and wine*, after he had baptized them, and taken them into the church.' What next? Pushed to the wall, Sigma coolly says — '*Of course*, neither dogs, nor bread, nor wine, were actually present.' What! all gone into thin air! Since the days of veracious Jack Falstaff, has there ever been story-telling equal to this? No dogs, no bread, no wine! 'A hundred upon poor four of us . . . I am a rogue, if I were not at half-sword with a dozen of them two hours together . . . Sixteen, at least, my lord . . . If I fought not with fifty of them, I am a bunch of radish; if there were not two or three and fifty upon poor old Jack, then I am no two-legged creature . . . Four rogues in buckram let drive at me; I made no more ado, but took all their seven points in my target thus . . . These nine men in buckram, that I told thee of — with a thought, seven of the eleven I paid.'[4] Well, to the fabrications of Sigma and his anonymous backer may be justly applied the language of Prince Henry to Falstaff's asseverations: — 'These lies are like the father that begets them; gross as a mountain, open, palpable.'[5]

But Sigma has another dodge: — 'It is well understood that this was a *mock* ceremony throughout'! Nothing left of the story but a mockery! But this representation is equally false. Mr. Pillsbury has denied it, in the most explicit manner, in the *Transcript*, in addition to my own positive contradiction. *Of the hundreds who were present, not one comes forward to contradict our statements, or in support of Sigma.* No 'mock ceremony,' with or without dogs, was performed on the occasion. All that Mr. Pillsbury did — after showing how slavery degrades man to the level of a beast, and in order to give a new and thrilling view of its enormity — was, to put the question to the audience, with true solemnity of feeling and manner, '*What would be said of the clergyman*, [ay! let Sigma answer!] who should bring certain dogs into the church, and proceed to baptize them, one by one, as Bose, Tiger, or Lion, in the name of the Father, Son, and Holy Ghost?' And he promptly added, 'Would not a thrill of horror run through the community, in view of *such a blasphemous procedure*? — And yet, which is the more blasphemous act — to turn men into brutes, or ceremonially to treat brutes as though they were men?' — a question which Sigma will please to answer, if he dare! This was the sum and substance of all that Mr. Pillsbury said and did; and if Sigma can see no pertinency, nay, nothing but 'blasphemy' in the illustration, then, if he were 'brayed in a mortar seven times, yet would not his foolishness depart from him.'[6] Mark how plain a tale puts him down, and subjects him to infinite ridicule! And now, Sigma, 'what trick, what device, what starting-hole, canst thou now find out, to hide thee from this open and apparent shame?' [7]

Before dismissing him and his canine pets, let me again ask, upon what evidence does Sigma charge Mr. Pillsbury with the grave offence of casting ridicule upon one of the sacraments of the Christian religion, which he urges upon him in terms so offensive? A statement made in an anonymous communication in the Salem *Register*, and written by an enemy, which has been contradicted and disproved as often as it has come to the knowledge of Mr. Pillsbury or his friends! Does Sigma mean to be understood that the assertions, — even the uncontradicted assertions, — of newspapers are to be received as evidence of the truth of the charges conveyed in them? It must be in his recollection, as it is in that of multitudes of our fellow citizens, that the Boston *Times*,[8] in an article published on the —day of May, 18—, made charges, with specifications, against himself, of the gravest offences against morality and the law. Does Sigma mean to have it understood that these charges are to be taken as true, because made in a newspaper? And yet the article was not anonymous, like that against Mr. Pillsbury, but written by a responsible editor, who, it is understood, expressed not merely his willingness, but his wish to be proceeded against, either for damages or by way of indictment. And I have never heard of any contradiction or denial on his part. I do not affirm that those charges were true, on this account; but I do say, that such an inference might be made far more reasonably, on his own rule of evidence, than his impeachment of Mr. Pillsbury can be sustained by any proof he has yet brought forward.

Sigma aspires, in company with Capt. Isaiah Rynders and his band of ruffians, to be the champion of the Union, the Bible, the Christian Sabbath, and the ordinances of religion! They are all terribly shocked at my treasonable and irreligious sentiments — one party going for knocking down and dragging out the heretic, the other for an indictment on the part of the Grand Jury, and consignment to the penitentiary! This is a rare exhibition of godliness and patriotism commingled, and an interesting clustering of saints! With your leave Mr. Editor, I shall have something to say on this subject in another number; and, as Sigma has been allowed to fill many of your columns without a word in reply, as your readers will wish and expect to see fair play in this controversy, I take it for granted that you will be just and equal to all the parties, — promising that I will occupy far less space than you have already conceded to Sigma.

Yours, still for the truth,

WM. LLOYD GARRISON.

14 Dix Place, Sept. 8, 1857.

Printed in *The Liberator*, September 11, 1857.

As printed in *The Liberator*, this letter was preceded by the following paragraph:

"The following reply to Sigma has been denied a place in the *Transcript*, though that old vilifier has been permitted to use its columns without stint, number after number, with his malignant attacks upon Mr. Pillsbury and ourselves. Such editorial favoritism, where character is assailed, is meaner than picking pockets or robbing hen-roosts; but Sigma requires it, and his royal displeasure must not be incurred. Shame on such truckling!"

The letter itself carried the legend, "SIGMA AND THE DOGS MUZZLED."

1. Shakespeare, *Hamlet*, II, ii, 591.
2. John Milton, *Paradise Lost*, Book VI.
3. Milton, *Paradise Lost*, Book II.
4. Shakespeare, *I Henry IV*, II, iv.
5. *Ibid.*, lines 230–231.
6. Proverbs 27:22.
7. Shakespeare, *I Henry IV*, II, iv, 267.
8. The Boston *Daily Times* first appeared in 1836 as a penny daily, under George Roberts and William H. Garfield, and lasted twenty-one years. (Frank Luther Mott, *American Journalism, 1690–1960*, 3d. ed., New York, 1971, p. 238.)

188

TO SAMUEL MAY, JR.

Boston, Sept. 10, 1857.

My Dear Mr. May:

I enclose a letter which I have just received from our friend Rev. Claudius Bradford,[1] at Montague, which I have answered to this effect. — 1. That I had promised to go to Cummington with you, via Northampton, and as you were absent at Leicester, I should have to consult you as to the change — saying it would give me great pleasure to lecture in Montague, if I could. 2. That I did not know how I could get from Montague to Cummington on Saturday, in season for the afternoon meeting. 3. That my aunt is so very ill, that her dissolution may take place at any time; and it is possible I may not be able to go even to Cummington. Therefore, I told him not to commit me until he heard from me again. What do you think I had better do? As for lecturing at Montague, on my return from Cummington, I could not feel it right to stop by the way a single hour, especially if aunt should then be living.

To save a long and tedious ride by land, I am inclined (in case Montague is out of the question) to go on the Western railroad to Hinsdale, which cannot be more than half a dozen miles from Cummington, I should think, on examining the map. Or, in case we go to Northampton, why could not our friends there get us up an anti-slavery meeting Friday evening? Will you give me your advice?

The Transcript, as you will see by the Liberator, basely refuses to let me be heard in reply to "Sigma."!

Yours, truly,

W. L. Garrison.

ALS: Antislavery Manuscripts, Boston Public Library.

1. The Reverend Claudius Bradford (d. Yellow Springs, Ohio, February 3, 1863, aged sixty-two) spent the latter years of his life as a teacher of modern languages at Antioch College, in Yellow Springs. His obituary in the New York *Christian Inquirer*, reprinted in *The Liberator*, February 20, 1863, noted that "he was formerly a settled minister in Massachusetts, where he had a large circle of relations and friends. . . . At a time when there were but few open advocates of universal freedom, he was pleading the cause of the slave. His mind was original and richly stored. . . ." Garrison added his own comment that "Mr. Bradford was on our list of highly esteemed friends, and we hear of his loss with regret. He early gave to the Anti-Slavery cause his sympathy and countenance, and took a heartfelt interest in its success." He and his wife, Maria Bradford, were descended from Governor Bradford of Massachusetts. (George W. Knight and John R. Commons, *The History of Higher Education in Ohio*, Washington, D.C., 1891, p. 135.)

189

TO SAMUEL J. MAY

Boston, Sept. 14, 1857.

My Dear Friend:

Yours of the 12th is just received. I thank you for your criticism upon my criticism, and for your reproof of my censure of Gerrit Smith.[1] It is another proof of your friendship, and more to be prized than a personal panegyric. But the right which you thus assert, I also claim for myself; and though, in its exercise, I may at times greatly err, still, I must use it on my own responsibility.

In the half a dozen lines of comment which I made on Mr. Smith's appearance at Burritt's Compensation Convention, I concentrated what might have been diluted to the extent of a column. You say "it was contemptuous, and therefore not fitted to do him or any body else any good." In my judgment, it was *descriptive*, and not contemptuous, and therefore warrantable. It did not impeach his motives, his philanthropy, or his anti-slavery intentions: it described him as eccentric, unstable, inconsistent. Have I not a right to say this in plain terms? And if this is to hold him up to ridicule, is it my fault? or am I therefore to say nothing about it?

But you add, "More than that — it was untrue." What is untrue? The charge that Mr. Smith's course has been erratic? I think not. Even you admit — "On several points, Mr. Smith's opinions seem to me strange and inconsistent." I say the same thing, in a little different phraseology. It may be true, that he has always been a conpensationist: but this does not disprove my general statement. — I cannot possibly reconcile his various declarations and positions, and give up the attempt as hopeless. What if he is "sincere"? I have never raised that question. Sincerity does not make what is crooked straight.

I thank you for your plainly expressed opinion of my dealings with Mr. Smith at Syracuse. You think I treated him very unjustly, and say it alienated friends from me. It is neither my design nor wish to alienate any one from me, or from the anti-slavery cause; nor would I consciously be guilty of injustice to any one; but there are occasions when even a Peter is to be sharply reproved to his face, and strong moral displeasure is to be displayed. I was true to my convictions of duty on that occasion, and performed it, painful as it was; and both in the manner and language of Mr. Smith, I thought I saw ample justification for what fell from my lips. He seemed to me to be playing fast and loose with unchanging principle, and to be lowering the anti-slavery standard to a very low point, in endorsing and embracing slaveholders as Christian brethren. But I have neither time nor room to go into this matter.

I thank you, also, for enclosing Mr. Smith's letter to you, for my perusal. It is evident that my brief criticism has very deeply wounded his feelings. His love of approbation is overmastering at times, and he is too sensitive to rebuke. When he intimates that it is cruel in me to censure or satirize his course, *because he has always eulogized me* — and when he says that abolitionists ought to have confidence in one another, — I feel all the more inclined to criticise, to avoid the appearance of a friendly bias. But I postpone other remarks till I send you his letter. "Sixty years old" — are you? Think of Adam in 1857! You are young yet!

Lovingly yours,

W.L.G.

ALS: Garrison Papers, Boston Public Library.

1. On September 4, 1857, Garrison had printed in *The Liberator* a report of the proceedings of the "Compensation Emancipation Convention," which had been held in Cleveland, Ohio, on August 25. The convention organized a National Compensation Emancipation Society, whose constitution declared that "the object of this society shall be the extinction of slavery by a system of compensation to the slaveholder." Among the resolutions adopted by the convention, *The Liberator* reported, were the following:

"1. Resolved, That in the opinion of this Convention, it is highly desirable that the people of the North should co-operate, in a generous and brotherly spirit, with the people of the South, and share liberally with them in the expense of putting an end to so great a moral and political evil as American slavery.

"2. Resolved, That the American people should make their common Government their agent in this matter, and should call on Congress to pay to each State that shall abolish Slavery, a sum not exceeding two hundred and fifty dollars for each and every slave emancipated, each State providing for any additional remuneration that it may deem proper.

"3. Resolved, That the American people, when helping the emancipators, should help the emancipated also. No measure of aid in this direction could exceed our wishes. Nevertheless, the small sum of twenty-five dollars to each of these wronged and destitute ones would go far toward supplying them with humble homes upon this continent, or upon another, should they prefer so wide a removal from the land of their birth."

After presenting these, and several other resolutions that had been adopted, Garrison commented as follows:

"Among the most prominent speakers at this Convention were Elihu Burritt, Rev. John Rankin of Ohio, and Gerrit Smith. This is the latest (not the last) of the eccentricities, gyrations and somersets of Mr. Smith, whose powers of reasoning and of moral discrimination seem to be getting more and more obfuscated. His step from 'the Jerry Rescue level,' and also from the position that slaveholders are 'pre-eminent pirates,' to the compensation of the Southern men-stealers as a just and obligatory act on the part of the North exceeds the stride from 'the sublime to the ridiculous.' What the next turn of his kaleidoscope may present, it is impossible to conjecture. For many grave considerations, we protest against this Compensation movement."

190

TO WENDELL PHILLIPS GARRISON

14 Dix Place,
Sept. 15, 1857.

My dear Son:

The bearer of this is Albert Gray,[1] of New York city, a young man of highly respectable parentage, who wishes to see what Harvard has to present to the eye and mind. Miss Mary G. Chapman wished me to give him a line to you, asking your kind attentions in his behalf, as far as it may be in your power, without interfering with your studies. She travelled in Europe with his parents, and his mother is now with her in Chauncy Place. After seeing the grounds, buildings, &c., on the college premises, he will take the cars for Mount Auburn, and you will please put him on the right track. I suppose it will not be in your power to accompany him thither, owing to your recitations; but if it should, I should be glad to have you do so.

Aunt has been a little relieved to-day, but this evening she feels worse, and thinks she is fast failing. I saw Dr. Geist to-day, in regard to her case. It is his opinion that she will continue some time longer.

No letter yet from George. Write to him soon.

Your affectionate father,

Wm. Lloyd Garrison.

Wendell P. Garrison.

☞ Should Wendell be absent, if Samuel Phillips will be kind enough to show Albert the premises, &c., he will much oblige me.

ALS: In the possession of Mr. and Mrs. John W. Coolidge, Jr., Marblehead, Massachusetts.

1. Otherwise unidentified.

191

TO JOHN NEEDLES

Boston, Sept. 22, 1857.

Dear Friend:

Your letter of the 18th was duly received to-day, with a draft on the Shawmut Bank, of this city, for three hundred and fifty dollars, on account of the deposit in the Baltimore Savings' Bank, made by my deceased mother. The draft was promptly paid, on its presentation at the Shawmut Bank.

Of course, I desire Mrs. Carnighan to be paid the $20, which you have retained, subject to her order, to meet the expense of the removal and re-interment of the remains of my mother and sister.

You speak of transmitting whatever may remain as a balance in your hand, after settling with the Orphans' Court. It can be but a mere trifle, in itself, which I beg you to retain for the trouble I have given you; and if you will allow me to add something thereto, I should wish to do so.

The promptness, as well as fidelity, with which you have discharged this trust, excites in my bosom the liveliest gratitude.

Nothing could be more opportune than the possession of the amount transmitted to me by you; for, without it, I should be in deep pecuniary embarrassment at this time, and therefore greatly straitened. I believe I mentioned to you, in a previous letter, that my aunt (my mother's youngest sister, now about 64 years of age,) has long been lying under my roof, extremely ill, and in an incurable consumption, and she seems to be near her earthly dissolution, though she may linger some time longer. She was rendered helpless as long ago as last January, and her sickness will absorb *more than all the money left by my mother* — for nursing, medical attendance, and numerous other expenses. As she has not a farthing of her own, the whole burden of this falls upon me, in addition to the expenses of a large family; and it looks almost like a providential occurrence, that my beloved mother's little deposit should have been left to accumulate interest to the present time, till the sum total will suffice to meet a considerable portion of the expenses arising from the sickness (and ultimate burial) of her youngest sister, to whom she was tenderly attached, and who has now none to care for her but myself. If my mother can take cognizance of what I am doing in this matter, her heart will thrill with delight to perceive to what a use her bequest is put.

I transmit to you, by mail, a volume of my writings; and, also, a well executed lithographic portrait of myself, which is generally deemed the best that has yet been taken of me. Please accept these as slight tokens of my grateful appreciation of your kindness, and my love and reverence for your character.

Your attached friend,

Wm. Lloyd Garrison.

John Needles.

ALS: Villard Papers, Harvard College Library.
See Letter 183, August 14, 1857.

192

TO WENDELL PHILLIPS GARRISON

14 Dix Place, Oct. 2. [1857]

My Dear Son:

This morning, (Friday,) at quarter past 7 o'clock, the event which we have been so long anticipating was realized in the decease of my aunt Charlotte. Her exit was a peaceful one, though yesterday she suffered a good deal of distress. The translation, under such circumstances, to "another and a better world," is desirable and beneficent.

The funeral will take place to-morrow afternoon, at 3 o'clock — a remarkably fortunate coincidence for you, as it will not interfere with any of your duties at Cambridge. I shall write to William to come up from Lynn, and remain over Sunday.

Your affectionate father,

Wm. Lloyd Garrison.

Wendell P. Garrison.

ALS: Garrison Papers, Boston Public Library. The year was added by a later hand.

193

TO WILLIAM LLOYD GARRISON, JR.

14 Dix Place, Oct. 2, 1857.

My Dear Son:

After a wasting illness of nine months, aunt Charlotte has taken her flight to "another and a better world." She expired this morning, (Friday,) at a quarter past 7 o'clock, without a struggle. For a few days past, she has suffered a good deal, in consequence of her extreme emaciation, any and every position being one of great pain; but she is now beyond the reach of mortal suffering.

We want you to come up, and attend the funeral, which will take place to-morrow (Saturday) at 3 o'clock. You had better leave in the 1.10 train, in order to be here in season.

Yours, lovingly,

Wm. Lloyd Garrison.

W. L. Garrison, Jr.

ALS: Smith College Library.

194

TO CAROLINE C. THAYER

14 Dix Place, Oct. 2, 1857.

My dear Miss Thayer:

After a lingering illness of nine months' duration, my poor aunt was released from her bodily sufferings yesterday morning, and entered into rest. The funeral will take place this (Saturday) afternoon, at 2 o'clock; and we should be pleased to have you, and any of your dear household, present on the occasion, if perfectly convenient and agreeable.

Mr. Parker [1] will be with us.

Your attached friend,

Wm. Lloyd Garrison.

Miss Caroline Thayer.

ALS: American Antiquarian Society.

1. Theodore Parker.

195

TO THEODORE PARKER

14 Dix Place, Oct. 3. [1857]

Dear Mr. Parker:

To accommodate the undertaker, and in view of the distance to the Forest Hill Cemetery, and the shortness of the afternoon, we have altered the time for the funeral from 3 to 2 o'clock, P. M., to-day. We hope it may be in your power to be with us, without serious inconvenience to yourself.

My aunt was my mother's sister, and the youngest of thirteen children — a large family. She was ever most exemplary in her life, of an excellent disposition, and always full of sympathy for the suffering, and ready to do all in her power to aid the wretched and relieve the sick. Her illness was long protracted, (nine months,) which she bore with rare patience and fortitude.

Yours, truly,

Wm. Lloyd Garrison.

Theodore Parker.

ALS: New York Public Library. The year was added by a later hand.

196

TO ADELINE ROBERTS

Boston, Oct. 12, 1857.

Dear Miss Roberts:

You inquire, whether I will lecture before the Salem Female Anti-Slavery Society on the evening of Dec. 6th.[1] "Providence permitting," I will.

Allow me to add, that you are henceforth at liberty to put my name down among the lecturers in your programme, whenever wanted, to the end of the conflict, without any other specification, except to indicate the time when I shall be wanted.

I owe an apology to Miss Chase for unintentionally omitting to reply to her letter of inquiry, received some time since, and shortly afterward mislaid.

Yours, truly,

Wm. Lloyd Garrison.

Adeline Roberts.

ALS: Essex Institute, Salem, Massachusetts.

1. This date must have been changed afterward. On December 4, *The Liberator* announced that Garrison would deliver an address on temperance in Boston on Sunday evening, December 6.

197

TO WENDELL PHILLIPS

Sunday Morning. [Oct. 18, 1857.]
14 Dix Place.

Dear Phillips:

I have this moment received the accompanying note from Higginson. You see the conclusion to which he has come.[1] No doubt, our Ohio and Michigan friends will be greatly disappointed. As you and I will be mainly responsible for the postponement, the least we can do is to send to the Convention a good long letter, embodying our Disunion views. You will write something in the course of a week — won't you?

Yours ever,

W. L. G.

ALS: Garrison Papers, Boston Public Library. The date was added by a later hand.
The Call for a Convention of the Free States on October 28 and 29, in Cleveland, Ohio, issued by Garrison, Higginson, *et al.*, on July 8, 1857 (see letter of that date), to discuss the question of disunion, had gathered momentum, had received more than six thousand signatures (*The Liberator*, October 16, 1857), and had evoked great interest throughout the North. But apparently there was difficulty in securing a large representation at the convention itself because of the sudden economic depression of 1857, and both Phillips and Garrison seem suddenly to have been unable to attend. On October 17, Higginson, Phillips, and Garrison issued a formal announcement that "in view of the sudden paralytic shock which has fallen upon the whole country, in regard to its financial and business operations — which, at the present time, absorbs the attention and tries the resources of all classes — and which renders it certain that only a local gathering could be secured under such depressing circumstances — the Committee of Arrangements have reluctantly assumed the responsibility of postponing (*pro tempore*) the Northern Convention. . . ." (*The Liberator*, October 23, 1857.)

1. The letter from Thomas Wentworth Higginson, dated "Saturday night," but written in part on October 17 and in part on October 18, recommended postponement. (Thomas Wentworth Higginson to "Dear Sir," October 18, 1857, Garrison Papers, Boston Public Library.)

1 9 8

TO SAMUEL J. MAY

Boston, Oct. 18, 1857.

My dear S. J. May:

In view of the earthquake shock which all the business operations of the country have received, and the absorption of all minds in the deep pecuniary embarrassments of the times, — and, therefore, the palpable inexpediency of attempting to hold a Convention of *the Free States* (as hitherto contemplated) at Cleveland, on the 28th and 29th inst. — Mr. Higginson, Mr. Phillips, and myself, after grave and serious consideration, have assumed the responsibility of postponing our projected Northern Convention until a more auspicious period — at the same time, letting an informal convention be held at Cleveland at the time specified, of such as can make it convenient to be present, so as not to create too great a local disappointment. All our Agents will be there, and no doubt they will make it a stirring meeting. But, in the present paralyzed state of things, it would be absurd to try to secure anything like a representation from the several States, and so we shall go for postponing *the* Northern Convention. I am the more reconciled to this, because Phillips could not have gone to it, if it had been held this month.

Theodore Parker, Phillips, Higginson, &c., will send letters to the meeting at Cleveland, expressive of their views on the Disunion question, which will help to mitigate the disappointment that will be felt by our Ohio friends at their non-attendance. I shall also send a letter; and I hope you will do the same, in case you shall conclude not to go to Cleveland, after what I have written.

When you were in Boston, you very kindly suggested your readiness to write a good word for my son Wendell to Pres. Walker,[1] at Cambridge, in order to secure for him (if practicable) a certain pecuniary benefit of scholarship, to enable him to meet his expenses. I do not know on what conditions the allowance is granted, but it would certainly be a great relief to me if it could be obtained. Wendell has gone through the ordeal of an examination triumphantly — ranking the second scholar out of ninety-five classmates, and coming within 2-7ths of a mark of taking the lead of all. I mention this, as it may possibly have something to do with his getting the desired aid.

Perhaps Pres. Walker may suppose that I have the means to carry Wendell through, without difficulty; but I wish you to let him know that it is only by friendly and charitable assistance that I have ventured to allow him to go to Cambridge. Pecuniarily, I am always "struggling

490

against wind and tide," [2] and can sympathize with you in often finding myself "in a tight place." It *costs* something, in more senses than one, to be notorious for "fanaticism" or philanthrophy.

After a wasting sickness of nine months' duration, (more than six of which were passed under my roof,) my aunt Charlotte saw "the last of earth" on the 2d inst. I rejoice that I was able to give her every attention, and to do all in my power to relieve and save her; but her illness has thrown upon me a heavy pecuniary load, — some hundreds of dollars additional, — and this makes me the more desirous in regard to Wendell's case. Will you be so kind as to write to Pres. Walker about him?

Love to your dear wife, Joseph, "aunt Charlotte," and all your household.

Yours, ever,

Wm. Lloyd Garrison.

☞ Your daughter Charlotte [3] called upon us a day or two since. She is now at Hingham, I believe, with the Thaxters,[4] but we shall to have [*sic*] a visit from her.

ALS: Garrison Papers, Boston Public Library.

1. James Walker (1794–1874) was president of Harvard University from 1853 to 1860.
2. Shakespeare, *III Henry VI*, IV, iii, 59.
3. Charlotte Coffin May (b. April 24, 1833) married Alfred Wilkinson on July 15, 1854. He was a merchant and banker of Syracuse, New York. (Samuel May, John Wilder May, John Joseph May, *A Genealogy of the Descendants of John May*, Boston, 1878, pp. 23, 46.)
4. Probably Daniel and Lucy Thaxter. Daniel Thaxter (b. Hingham, August 11, 1816; d. November 14, 1879) was an optician in Boston, but lived in Hingham. His second wife was Lucy P. Scarborough (b. April 16, 1816), of Brooklyn, Connecticut, an old friend of the Benson and Garrison families. Daniel Thaxter's parents, Joseph B., a silversmith, and Sally Gill Thaxter, were also living in Hingham at the time. (*History of the Town of Hingham*, published by the town, 1893, III, 237; *Boston Directory*, 1857; *Letters*, II, 269.)

199

TO THE PENNSYLVANIA ANTI-SLAVERY SOCIETY

BOSTON, Oct. 20, 1857.

DEAR FRIENDS: When I promised to attend your annual meeting, it was my expectation that the Northern Convention, with reference to a dissolution of the Union, would be held at Cleveland, at the time originally contemplated; but as it has been deemed advisable to postpone that Convention for the time being, on account of the paralysis with which the whole country has been struck in regard to all its financial operations and business relations, and which renders it impossible, therefore, to obtain such an expression of Northern feeling and sentiment upon that question as its importance demands, I beg you to excuse my absence, especially as I have been troubled for a fortnight past with feverish symptoms, which admonish me to be careful of all unnecessary mental excitement.

Yet I can do no less than to send you an expression of my warm regards for you personally and collectively, and my testimony as to the state of our cause, and the work that remains to be done.

From a dizzy height of prosperity, which seemed to rest upon an indestructible basis, the nation has been instantaneously hurled into an abyss of bankruptcy, suffering and ruin, as though the seventh angel had poured out his vial into the air, and great Babylon had come in remembrance before God, to give unto her "the cup of the wine of the fierceness of his wrath." [1] In view of its centuries of bloody oppression — its incorporation of chattel slavery into its constitutional existence — its robbery of one-seventh portion of the people of all their rights as human beings, and reducing them to the level of beasts — its atheistical contempt for the "higher law" of God, and idolatry for the lower law of the bottomless pit — its systematic and universal disregard of all the principles of justice and humanity, whereby the foundations of confidence, as between man and man, have been utterly removed — its hot malignity against the divine command to "proclaim liberty throughout all the land unto all the inhabitants thereof" [2] — its fierce persecution of such as have been raised up to "plead the cause of all such as are appointed to destruction," [3] and shameless regard for wolves in sheep's clothing and profligate demagogues in the garb of patriotism — its extraordinary growth and abounding prosperity, nevertheless, causing it impiously to exclaim, "Who shall bring me down to the ground?" [4] and its sudden fall to the earth, in its triumphal hour, as though smitten by a thunderbolt from a clear sky, causing "men's hearts to fail them for fear," [5] and the knees of the stoutest to smite together, and the strength of the strongest to become as infantile weakness — it is as though a voice from heaven were saying, "Come out of here, my people, that ye be not partakers of her sins, and that ye receive not of her plagues; for her sins have reached unto heaven, and God hath remembered her iniquities. How much she hath glorified herself, and lived deliciously, so much torment and sorrow give her; for she saith in her heart, I sit a queen, and am no widow, and shall see no sorrow. Therefore shall her plagues come in one day; for strong is the Lord God who judgeth her. Rejoice over her, thou heaven, and ye holy apostles and prophets; for God hath avenged you on her." [6]

Of course, in this day of calamity, speculation is busy in tracing the causes of this wide-spread derangement of all our business affairs. The facts are obvious to the most superficial — that the strongest establishments have been crushed like cob-houses, "in the twinkling of an eye" [7] — that millionaires have found themselves swallowed up in a vortex of indebtedness — that failures in every department of trade are taking place unceasingly — that specie payment has been suspended everywhere, indicating a universal inability of the banks to meet their "promises to pay," which means, in other words, universal insolvency — that factories are fast being curtailed in their operations, or wholly closed — that tens of thousands of artisans, operatives and labourers, have been thrown out of employment, and are threatened with a winter of extreme destitution — and that, in regard to all industrial pursuits and enterprises, congestion of the brain and paralysis of the limbs indicate the exact condition of our land, in this day of retributive judgment.

Now, as to the cause of this astounding state of things, there are various opinions — such as that they are to be found in female extravagance, in excess of foreign importation, in fondness for display and high living, in the creation of fictitious stock, *ad infinitum*, in the enormous expansion and sudden contraction of paper currency, in the abandonment of agriculture for traffic, in the vast indebtedness of the West, in speculation run mad, in the practice of giving general and extended credit, in excess of expenditure beyond all possibility of income, in taxing certain raw materials from abroad for home manufacture, and thus rendering it impracticable for our manufacturers to compete in the market with those in other lands — &c., &c., &c. No doubt, all these suggestions are worthy of consideration, and embody a great deal of truth. But the solution of the problem is contained in two words — NATIONAL DEMORALIZATION.

We are a wicked nation and a "fast" people. Our pride, our vanity, our ambition, are paralleled only by our impudence, our barbarity, and our oppression. The god whom we serve is "Manifest Destiny"; the Moloch at whose shrine we kneel is the Slave Power, who causes all, "both small and great, rich and poor, free and bond, to receive a mark in their right hands, or in their foreheads"; [8] and commands that "no man buy or sell save he that hath the mark, or the name of the beast, or the number of his name." [9] Like the ancient Jews, our feet run to evil, and we make haste to shed innocent blood; our lips have spoken lies, our tongue hath muttered perverseness; we conceive mischief, and bring forth iniquity; we hatch cocatrice eggs, and weave the spider's web; the act of violence is in our hands; we have made crooked paths, and there is no judgment in our goings; we wait for light, but behold obscurity; for brightness, but we walk in darkness; we grope for the wall like the blind, and we stumble at noon-day as in the night.[10] Their confession must be ours, in the spirit of hearty repentance: "Our sins testify against us; and *as for our iniquities, we know them*; in transgressing and lying against the Lord, and departing away from our God, SPEAKING OPPRESSION AND REVOLT, conceiving and uttering from the heart words of falsehood." [11]

Every nation has its peculiar source of corruption, misery and ruin. Ours is to be found in that Vesuvius of crime, that maelstrom of blood, that pandemonium of oppression, the slave system. Until that be destroyed, there is no peace, no prosperity, no safety, no permanence for our misnamed republic. For a time, as hitherto, we may "wax fat and kick," [11a] and audaciously echo the words of Pharaoh, "Who is the Lord, that I should obey his voice to let Israel go? I know not the Lord, neither will I let Israel go"; [12] but there shall come upon us, in their order, those terrible plagues which shall make both man and beast cry out for suffering, and cause our soil to be red with blood.

Let others talk of the immediate causes of the present chaotic state of things as they may; for one, I believe it is owing to the existence, growth, extension and supremacy of slavery, in a preëminent degree. Dishonesty must be an essential characteristic of a slaveholding people; and when was worldly success or Heaven's blessing ever promised in that direction? History, whether sacred or profane, teaches me only this as pertaining to despotism — that it curses the soil, fetters industry, paralyzes inventions, destroys wealth, shrivels population, impairs strength, incites to vengeance, spreads pollution, debauches conscience, stultifies intellect, and breeds exterminating judgments. It teaches me, also, that in the train of freedom, — true, impartial, all-abounding freedom — there follow light, and health, and large increase — prosperity like the waves of the sea, and the abundance of peace. Hence, by my reverence for God — by my love of man — by my regard for the welfare and glory of the land of my birth — by my heartfelt desire to see all forms of despotism for ever abolished, and universal brotherhood prevail, I am for the immediate abolition of slavery, and for the removal or destruction of whatever stands in the way of emancipation.

American slavery is upheld by two mighty props — Church and State, religion and government — and when these are overthrown, that foul system shall fall to rise no more. The popular religion is undeniably hostile to the Anti-Slavery movement, and horribly perverse in its teachings and practices. It cheats, steals, commits adultery, enforces concubinage, wields the slave-driver's lash, prosecutes the domestic slave traffic, and sanctions every enormity. Its climax of wickedness is in claiming to be the religion of Him who came to open the prison-doors, and to set the captives free; whose injunction is, "Whatsoever ye would that men should do to you, do ye even so to them," [13] which lays the axe at the root of all injustice; and whose spirit breathed nothing but love and good-will to all mankind. A slaveholding religion is my scorn and abhorrence; and, instead of being deterred from assailing it because it has taken to itself the name of Christianity, I would all the more boldly tear off its mask, and seek its extirpation, on that account.

We have, however, no national religion, or institution of religion, as such; so that the various bodies which make up what we comprehensively call the American Church are to be arraigned in detail, each by itself, none being responsible for the deeds of another. Thus, the American Tract Society,[14] which now, through its Committees and Secretaries, avows its determination not to publish a solitary word against the admitted moral evils and cruelties of slavery, because it would lose THE PRICE OF BLOOD which the South now casts into its polluted treasury, is to be held responsible on its own ground, and pronounced worthy of universal execration. To contribute to its support, under these circumstances, with an intelligent knowledge of its position, is a more guilty act than that of highway robbery. Let it be accursed, in the name of God and his Christ!

A similar condemnation should be bestowed upon that bloated, pharisaical, and self-perpetuating oligarchy, the American Board of Commissioners for Foreign Missions,[15] and upon all the great religious sects and organizations in the land. By affinity of spirit, by selfishness of purpose, they are all with the oppressor, "on whose side there is power," [16] and governed, not by the Prince of Peace, but by "the prince of the power of the air." [17] Spiritual wickedness is inaugurated by them in high places; and they have no other God, no other law, no other standard of judgment, than that of public opinion: in other words they are thoroughly ATHEISTICAL, in the most awful sense of that word. They recognise man-stealing as compatible with a Christian profession; they receive the slave-breeder to their communion as a brother in the Lord; they profess to find in the Bible, which they claim to be the inspired word of God, ample justification for making man the property of man, and make this test conclusive; thus revealing themselves to be "cages of unclean birds,[18] and synagogues of Satan." [19]

But while, religiously, support of slavery is an individual or denominational act, it becomes national by incorporation with the government from which it mainly derives its sustenance and protection. Our fathers committed a fearful sin for themselves and their posterity, when they consented to those slaveholding compromises in the Constitution of the United States, whereby that instrument was made "a covenant with death, and an agreement with hell," from which have come all our woes as a people. We shall bring a heavier load of guilt upon our own souls, if we do not repudiate that Constitution with horror, and pronounce its requirements to be disloyalty to Heaven, and treason to the cause of human liberty universally. We see what our fathers did not see; we know what they did not know; and if for them there can be found a shadow of excuse, in the terrible exigencies by which they were surrounded, none can possibly be found for us, if we imitate their example.

The great pressing duty of the hour, then, is to seek the separation of the North from the South, the free States from the slave States — first, on the ground that we must not "strike hands with thieves, nor consent with adulterers" — and secondly, because, both by a physical and geographical necessity, that separation will inevitably give the death blow to the whole slave system, and thus terminate our arduous struggle in glorious victory, to the joy of heaven and earth. If, as the venerable Josiah Quincy [20] says, "the Union is the slaveholder's main strength, and its continuance his forlorn hope"; [21] if, as John Quincy Adams says, "The bargain between Freedom and Slavery, contained in the Constitution of the United States, is morally and politically vicious, and inconsistent with the principles on which alone our revolution can be justified," then our watch-word should be, "LET THE COMPACT PERISH! NO UNION WITH SLAVEHOLDERS!"

Here is solid ground — from this entrenchment we can never be driven — this embodies all the issues with the Slave Power in one. It must be made the test of genuine patriotism, of incorruptible integrity, of enlightened piety, and of Anti-Slavery fidelity. While the Union stands as it is — while the Constitution remains what it is — the slave oligarchy will continue to wield the destinies of the nation, and nothing can prevent the success of their machinations.

Yours, to smite a slaveholding Union to dust,

WM. LLOYD GARRISON.

Printed in *The Liberator*, October 23, 1857 and in the *National Anti-Slavery Standard*, October 31, 1857.

The Pennsylvania Anti-Slavery Society held its twenty-first anniversary at West Chester on October 22 and 23, 1857. *The Liberator*, November 6, 1857, carried a brief report of the proceedings.

1. Revelation 16:19.
2. Leviticus 25:10.
3. Proverbs 31:8.
4. Obadiah 3.
5. Luke 21:26.
6. Revelation 18:4–5, 7–8, 20.
7. I Corinthians 15:52.
8. Revelation 13:16.

9. *Ibid.*, 13:17.

10. This sentence is composed of Isaiah 59:7 and 59:3–6, 8, 9–10.

11. Isaiah 59:12–13.

11a. Deuteronomy 32:15.

12. Exodus 5:2.

13. Matthew 7:12.

14. The American Tract Society was formed in 1825 by representatives of tract societies throughout the country. By 1850, the society's annual budget was $258,000 and it was publishing 5,000,000 tracts annually. The society was Protestant but nondenominational, and carried the message of Christian salvation. Louis Filler points out that "although it strictly cut out any passages opposing slavery in its writings, it was less strict about the printing of proslavery expressions." (*The Crusade Against Slavery, 1830–1860*, New York, Evanston, and London, 1963, p. 261; see also Dwight Dumond, *Antislavery: The Crusade for Freedom in America*, Ann Arbor, 1961, pp. 156–157.)

15. The American Board of Commissioners for Foreign Missions had been founded in 1810. One of its principal founders was the Reverend Lyman Beecher, "an early advocate of the missionary and Bible movements by which the word of God was to spread across the globe." The organization was the most conservative of the evangelical Protestant organizations. It was generally antiabolitionist in its policies, and "its missionaries to the Cherokee and Choctaw tribes condoned slaveholding as well as polygamy." (Bertram Wyatt-Brown, *Lewis Tappan and the Evangelical War Against Slavery*, Cleveland, 1969, pp. 28–29, 313–314.)

16. Ecclesiastes 4:1.

17. Ephesians 2:2.

18. Revelation 18:2.

19. Revelation 2:9 and 3:9.

20. Josiah Quincy (1772–1864), father of Edmund Quincy, the abolitionist and close friend of Garrison, was a member of Congress from 1805 to 1813 and of the state Senate from 1813 to 1820. He was mayor of Boston from 1823 to 1829, and president of Harvard University from 1829 to 1845. (*BDAC.*)

21. On October 23, 1857, *The Liberator* devoted its entire front page to quotations from statements by several American political figures on "What are the relations and compromises of the U. S. Constitution appertaining to American Slavery?" These included Alexander Hamilton, James Madison, William Ellery Channing, Judge Joseph Story, Daniel Webster, Josiah Quincy, Sr., and John Quincy Adams. The statement by Quincy, which evaluated the possibility of secession by the South, emphasized: "Are the slaveholders fools or madmen? They go out of this Union for the purpose of maintaining the subjection of their slaves? Why, *the arm of the Union is the very sinew of that subjection!* It is the slaveholder's main strength. *Its continuance is his forlorn hope.*" He then went on as follows, citing the remarks of John Quincy Adams, which Garrison quotes in his letter.

"Many years ago, John Quincy Adams related a conversation which he once had with John C. Calhoun on this very subject. . . . 'The impression which it produced upon my mind,' said Mr. Adams, 'is, that *the bargain between Freedom and Slavery, contained in the Constitution of the United States*, is morally and politically vicious, inconsistent with the principles on which alone our revolution can be justified, cruel and oppressive. . . .' "

2 0 0

TO A FRIEND IN NEW BEDFORD

Boston, Nov. 1, 1857.

Dear Friend:

The bearer of this — a very worthy woman, once a slave, but for several years past a resident of Brooklyn, N. Y. — Pomona Brice,[1] visits New Bedford for two reasons: first, hoping to find a nephew of hers — and secondly, with a view to get some pecuniary assistance to enable her to ransom her daughter, and her daughter's children, who are now in Alabama. The wretched state of the times (affecting your own city, I believe, with special severity) renders it hopeless for her to raise funds beyond what may be needed in charity to unable her to get back to Brooklyn.

I hope she will succeed in finding her nephew; and that she may do so, will you be so kind as to put her in the way of seeing the colored ministers, who will be likely to know whether such a person is at present in New Bedford?

The death of our beloved friend Joseph Congdon [2] is an occurrence so sudden and unexpected to me, that I can scarcely bring my mind to realize the fact. No one stood higher in my esteem than he did. Will not some one in N. B. write an obituary notice for the Liberator, setting forth his excellent qualities?

Yours, truly,

Wm. Lloyd Garrison.

ALS: Merrill Collection of Garrison Papers, Wichita State University Library.

1. Otherwise unidentified.

2. On October 30, 1857, *The Liberator* reprinted the following notice from the New Bedford *Mercury* of October 27: "One of our best known and most widely esteemed citizens died yesterday, after a long course of usefulness and industry in this community. We allude to Joseph Congdon, Esq., so long the Cashier of the Mechanics' Bank, which place he had held since the establishment of the bank, a period of no less than twenty-six years. Mr. Congdon was aged fifty-seven years and eleven months. He was a gentleman of exact probity, plain and un-assuming address, of a highly cultivated mind, and well acquainted with literature and science. He was also devoted to benevolent and charitable enterprises, and a most conscientious man. Such men are rare, and their loss creates a void not readily filled. His health has been for some time declining."

2 0 1

TO THEODORE PARKER

14 Dix Place, Nov. 8, 1857.

Dear Mr. Parker:

Permit me to introduce to you two French refugees, who have had a marvellous escape from Cayenne, (the victims of the despotism of the French usurper, Louis Napoleon,[1]) one of whom has with him an account of their escape,[2] as published in the Salem Register,[3] which cannot be read without the deepest commiseration for their unhappy fate. Is it in your power to suggest to them a mode to find friends or employment for the time being, until they can have time to adjust themselves to our usages? They will tell you their story, and I know that you will listen to it not only with respect, but interest. Cannot something be done to procure some temporary assistance? Are there not those who will contribute to their necessities, who might not be willing to aid an unpopular movement?

AL: Garrison Papers, Boston Public Library.

1. Napoleon III, Charles Louis Napoleon Bonaparte (1808–1873), was elected president of France in December 1848. In December 1851, he dissolved the French Assembly and then carried out the bloody *coup d'état* which made him dictator. In December 1852, he was proclaimed emperor of the French. His downfall came with the defeat of the French armies in the Franco-Prussian War in 1870.

2. *The Liberator*, December 25, 1857, printed a news item headed "Liberty for All Mankind." It began as follows: "During the last summer, several French political refugees (the victims of the despotic power of Louis Napoleon) fortunately succeeded in making their escape from Cayenne, and, after encountering many perils and hardships, safely arrived at Salem. One of their number, Leon Chautard, has written a thrilling narrative of their sufferings and escape, making a pamphlet of 63 pages, which it is hoped will be readily purchased in order to administer to their necessities." There then follows an extract from the pamphlet.

The pamphlet was entitled *Escape from Cayenne*, and was printed in Salem, at the Observer Office, 1857.

3. *The Liberator*, December 18, 1857, reprinted a short item about the refugees from the Salem *Register*. The story, as printed in the pamphlet, had originally appeared in an earlier issue of the Salem *Register*.

2 0 2

TO SARAH H. EARLE

Boston, December 25th, 1857.

Dear Mrs. Earle: Will you allow us, your friends in various degrees of intimacy, though with but one degree of appreciation — the highest — of what is worthy of all appreciation, to entreat your acceptance of this little gift in token of what we feel of admiration and reverence, affection and gratitude, to one whose unswerving fidelity and unequalled perseverance in the cause, from the time that its standard was first uplifted, have ever been our strength and our example.

Eliza Lee Follen,	Mary May,[2]
Wendell Phillips,	Charles F. Hovey,
Samuel May, Jr.,	Sarah Russell May,[3]
Edmund Quincy,	C. Lenox Remond,
Charles E. Hodges,[1]	Wm. Lloyd Garrison,
Abby K. Foster,	Francis Jackson.

Printed in the *National Anti-Slavery Standard*, March 27, 1858.

The *National Anti-Slavery Standard* printed this letter following Mrs. Earle's death on March 0, 1858, with the following explanation.

"We are favoured with the following letter, copied on request by her daughter, from the original among her papers. Written with no thought of publicity or coming bereavement, to accompany a little gift from the Twenty-fourth Anti-Slavery Festival, it marks the depth of the impression her life made on hearts worthy of her own — an impression so profound and beautiful that it placed *her*, in their estimate, beyond the application of the general warning, to 'call none happy while yet they live'."

See also the text of Garrison's eulogy at the funeral service for Mrs. Earle, in *The Liberator*, April 9, 1858.

1. The Reverend Charles E. Hodges (b. Boston, December 22, 1824; d. there, June 14, 1870), an active Massachusetts abolitionist, graduated from Harvard College in 1847, and from the Harvard Divinity School in 1850. He was ordained pastor of the Unitarian Church in Barre, Massachusetts, in 1851. However, his antislavery preaching and activities evoked opposition among his parishioners and he resigned in 1854. After preaching in Watertown Massachusetts, during the winter of 1854–55, he left the ministry in the spring of 1855 and soon after began the manufacture of chemicals at South Boston, which he continued until his death. (Almon D. Hodges, Jr., *Genealogical Record of the Hodges Family of New England*, Boston, 1896, p. 57.)

2. Samuel May, Jr.'s mother, Mary Goddard May.

3. Samuel May, Jr.'s wife.

VIII THE REMOVAL OF JUDGE LORING: 1858

T HE FINANCIAL DEPRESSION which had begun in 1857 continued well into the new year. Sydney Gay withdrew from his editorial duties on the *National Anti-Slavery Standard*, which were assumed by Oliver Johnson. The spring of 1858 was marked by final victory in the abolitionist campaign to secure the removal of Judge Edward Loring, as judge of probate, with the necessary legislation enacted by the legislature and approved by newly elected Governor Nathaniel Banks. Garrison may well be pardoned for boasting about the abolitionists' success. In May, the antislavery cause in New England lost one of its pioneers and mainstays with the death of Ellis Gray Loring. During the middle of August, Garrison and his son William spent about a week in a tour of upstate New York, the Catskills and New York City, followed, at the end of August, by Garrison's lecture tour of Vermont which lasted twelve days, from the end of August to the first week in September. Almost the entire month of October was spent in a speaking tour of Pennsylvania, Ohio, New York, and Massachusetts on the way back to Boston.

203

TO JOHN ADAMS JACKSON

[Beginning of 1858?] [1]

My dear Mr. Jackson —

I am extremely sorry again to disappoint you, but it would be too hazardous for me to leave the house to-day, as I have not been off my bed since day before yesterday, except to have it made, till this forenoon. My head is better, and I feel somewhat relieved of my severe pains; so that I confidently hope to give you a sitting to-morrow, either in the forenoon or afternoon, as you may prefer. I will try to make up for lost time, as I regret to keep you waiting a single hour.

Yours, truly,

Wm. Lloyd Garrison.

J. A. Jackson, Esq.

ALS: Wellesley College Library.

1. Garrison's bust by John Adams Jackson was essentially completed by the beginning of May 1858 (see Letter 215, to Oliver Johnson, May 1, 1858). The sittings were, therefore, prior to May.

204

TO WILLIAM LLOYD GARRISON, JR.

Boston, Jan. 7, 1858

My Dear Willie:

I promptly received your kind letter of the 3d inst., and should have answered it as promptly, if it had not been for my engagements. It is not too late, however, to reciprocate all its loving expressions, or to "wish you a happy new year," and your mother, and Fanny and Franky, warmly join with me in so doing. I need not say that its perusal gave me the highest pleasure. Accept my thanks for the check on the Exchange Bank, as your New Year's gift; and as it exactly pays for the stout winter over-coat made me by Mr. Curtis,[1] it will cover me like a garment — though it will never become thread-bare. It was very considerate, on your part, in sending it at this time; for you rightly surmised that I might find it difficult to meet my entire indebtedness.

In spite of all my anxiety and care, my expenses annually are quite large; and during the past year, they have been considerably larger than ever before — owing to a variety of causes, (the fitting out of George and Wendell, the sickness and interment of aunt Charlotte, &c.,) with which you are familiar. I have still a number of bills to meet, but hope there will be enough on the Liberator account to enable me to liquidate them. In a day or two, I shall see where I am.

Far more valuable than any sum you could enclose were the expressions of affection, of gratitude, and of high resolve and earnest purpose on your part, contained in your letter. My pride and comfort in you, and in all the other children, are without alloy; and my confidence in your wish and determination to live a manly life, to set an example worthy of imitation, to leave the world better than you found it, is absolute. So that when you say, "It is something that I strive continually to remember, [the bearing of my name,] and endeavor to make my deportment such that nothing shall happen which would cause you to blush," I am sure it is the language of your heart.

As a father, my aim has been to set a good example to you all, rather than to exercise a rigorous discipline or to drill you doctrinally. If we do not teach by our lives, we teach in vain. An occasional admonition, words of caution, the language of reproof, all have their place; but an affectionate disposition, a benevolent spirit, a true daily life, are worth them all. Happy and favored shall I be, if my children shall derive from me aught of virtue or goodness to develop their moral nature, to inspire them to deeds of kindness, to enable them to discriminate between truth and error, and to make them prize what is right and just above all worldly wealth, popularity or renown.

In a little more than a year, you will have reached your majority, and will then assume all the responsibilities of that untried position. Act well your part, from day to day, and you may leave the future to shape itself, without an anxious thought. No matter whether you ever acquire any worldly reputation, but an unsullied character is more to be prized than all that earth can give.

It seems your salary is to be raised in the course of the present year. Lay up whatever you can prudently, and consider money and its use as much to be morally accounted for as any other trust committed to you. Never seek wealth, in the love of it, as a passion or pursuit; neither be reckless of the means of competence, and ever bear in mind that it is chiefly by economy that those means are obtained. Between extravagance and meanness, there is a noble medium.

Be assured that you were not forgotten by any of us on Christmas and New Year's day, and most happy should we have been to have had you with us at the family board. Some tokens of love, in the shape of gifts for the season, would have been gladly forwarded to you; but my indebtedness admonished me to spend as little as possible for mere presents.

Your mother was delighted with your letter, and sends a mother's love. We are glad you are so attentive to George.

Your affectionate father,

Wm. Lloyd Garrison.

ALS: Smith College Library.

1. John Curtis, Jr., had a clothing store with G. P. Atkins, at 6 North Street, Boston. (Boston *Directory*, 1858.)

2 0 5

TO SAMUEL J. MAY

Boston, Jan. 8, 1858.

Beloved Friend:

By a brief letter received from you yesterday, (dated erroneously Dec. 5, 1857, instead of Jan. 5, 1858,) I am delighted to learn that you have left the Water Cure at Glen Haven, and are once more at "home, sweet home," measurably restored to health, and in good spirits. I meant to have sent you a letter at G. H., thanking you, with a full heart, for the kindly interest you have taken in Wendell's case at Harvard, and for writing in his behalf to Pres. Walker; and also for the letter of Pres. Walker, enclosed in one of yours to me, announcing the result of the correspondence. In how many ways have I been indebted to you since our long and cherished acquaintance! But I am only one of a great multitude, whose deep indebtedness runs in the same direction. Within a few days, Pres. Walker has signified to Wendell that he will undoubtedly be one of ten scholars to participate in the interest on the bequest of the late John E. Thayer; [1] and though the proportionate amount will be small the first year, (about $25,) it will be increased afterward. Wendell feels very grateful (as well as his father and mother) for what you have done in his behalf.

It is not too late to wish you, and your dear wife, and all the members of your beloved family, — "aunt Charlotte" never to be forgotten, — "a happy new year"! As health is so essential to happiness, may yours continue steadily to improve, and every vestige of disease be removed from your system! I beseech you to be careful of "the outward man," and not let the inner man do him any injury through excess of mental or moral effort. Advancing in life as we are, we need to be admonished that we cannot labor and expose ourselves with the same impunity that we could in our younger days. I cannot bear to think of your removal for many a year to come, even though it be to "another and a better world," — for this world is so disordered as imperatively to need your presence to the latest possible hour of mortality. God bless and watch over your entire household!

At home, we commence the new year in good health and spirits. George continues to reside in Minnesota, and seems to be perfectly contented in his new position. William remains in the Bank at Lynn, and gives entire satisfaction. We take great comfort in all our children, and there is not a particle of bitterness in our cup of bliss. They all seem to be animated by one spirit of affection, and to desire to live without a blemish. I mean to try to correspond with you, by letter, more frequently than I have hitherto done. Be assured that both in the "letter" and in the spirit, I am ever

Your faithful, attached and admiring friend,

Wm. Lloyd Garrison.

P. S. I deeply regret that the health of your dear Joseph is not yet restored, so as to warrant his return home. Give him my tenderest sympathies and my warmest remembrances. He is indeed a noble youth. — Helen sends her most loving regards to you all.

ALS: Garrison Papers, Boston Public Library.

1. John Eliot Thayer (1803–1857), the son of the Reverend Nathaniel Thayer of Lancaster, Massachusetts, was a well-known Boston banker who, at his death, left a scholarship fund of $50,000 to Harvard. (Mary C. Crawford, *Famous Families of Massachusetts*, Boston, 1930, p. 352; Samuel Eliot Morison, *Three Centuries of Harvard, 1636–1936*, Cambridge, 1936, p. 296; Henry S. Nourse, ed., *The Birth, Marriage and Death Register . . . of Lancaster, Massachusetts*, Lancaster, 1890, p. 341.)

---

2 0 6

TO SYDNEY HOWARD GAY

Boston, Jan. 15, 1858.

My dear Gay:

Your letter, announcing your purpose to withdraw from your editorial connection with the Standard, on the 1st of March next, was duly received; and yesterday it was laid before a special meeting of the Executive Committee, and, after a full interchange of sentiment, your resignation was accepted — accepted solely because the reasons set forth by you for resigning your present trust *seemed to present no alternative* — to wit, inadequacy of salary, and physical inability to perform all the duties expected, after the retirement of Mr. Johnson.[1] If the Committee could have felt warranted in raising your salary, they would have earnestly solicited you to remain at your post, and deferred final action until they could have heard from you again; but as this was deemed impracticable, when retrenchment has become so imperative, in view of the financial condition and prospects of the Society and Standard for the ensuing year, they felt that they had no right to urge you to remain, after your positive declaration that you must seek more remunerative employment, in justice to your family.

Your letter took us all by surprise, for not one of us had dreamed of such a separation; and if regret could avail anything to avert this necessity, it would assuredly not be lacking. As for the stipend which you and Mr. Johnson have received, from year to year, it has not been at all proportionate to your services, or adequate to meet your current expenses; but it was all the income of the Society would allow.

Mr. May [2] will send you, by to-day's mail, the resolutions which were unanimously adopted by the Committee,[3] in consequence of your resignation.

Mr. Quincy will leave for New York this afternoon, and will doubtless see you to-morrow, so that he will be able to communicate to you any particulars you may wish to learn respecting the action of the Committee.

I cannot close this letter, without expressing to you my high appreciation of the fidelity which you have exhibited to the Anti-Slavery cause, in its most radical phase, ever since you have espoused it; and for nearly fourteen years you have borne aloft its *Standard*, "without concealment and without compromise." The paper, in your hands, has always been "as true as the needle to the pole," without even a vibration, and I have ever felt the utmost reliance upon your clearsightedness, firmness, persistency, and indomitable spirit. I believe it has been your aim to make the Standard an honor to the Society, and a most efficient instrumentality in the furtherance of our glorious cause; and I think you have succeeded in doing so.

Of course, in the hard necessity which requires you to look to more remunerative employment, with a due regard to your family, you have my best wishes for your health, happiness and prosperity. Wherever you are, or however engaged, we are all persuaded that the Anti-Slavery cause will ever be dear to your heart, and its success an object of paramount interest.

Wishing to be fraternally remembered to Mrs. Gay, I remain,

Yours, in unbroken bonds,

Wm. Lloyd Garrison.

Sydney Howard Gay, Esq.

ALS: Columbia University Library.

1. Oliver Johnson had been associate editor of the *Standard* since 1853. Contrary to the implication of this sentence, Johnson did not retire but became senior editor of the *Standard*.

2. Samuel May, Jr.

3. The resolutions, expressing regret at Gay's resignation and appreciation for his past services, appeared in *The Liberator*, March 26, 1858, together with a "Valedictory" from Gay.

2 0 7

TO NATHAN R. JOHNSTON

BOSTON, Jan. 25, 1858.

REV. N. R. JOHNSTON:

DEAR SIR — Though circumstances will prevent my bodily presence at the Anti-Slavery Convention, to be held in Bradford, this week, I shall assuredly be there in spirit, responding to every true word uttered against 'the sum of all villanies,' exulting in every indication of a firm and resolute purpose to seek its eternal overthrow, and rejoicing in every advance towards unity of feeling and action, with reference to the sacred cause of impartial liberty.

I rejoice that the Convention opens its doors to all who may wish to attend, and offers them in good faith a free platform, whatever may be their views on the subject of slavery. 'Let there be light.' Let the discussions be free, earnest, manly, yet kind and fraternal, and characterized throughout by candor and impartiality. Let truth be the object sought — the path of duty honestly inquired for, and courageously welcomed, lead where it may; for it can never lead in a wrong direction. Let there be no evasion, no dust-throwing, no side-issue, no compromise, no attempt to palliate or excuse, no verbal quibbling, no metaphysical hair-splitting, no special pleading, no sanctimonious cant, no cowardly apprehension of 'consequences.' Let the question be clearly stated, intelligently understood, and thoroughly canvassed. It is not, on the part of the North, simply one of self-defence; or pertaining to Kansas, or to the territorial extension of slavery, or to the Fugitive Slave Bill, or to the Dred Scott decision, or to the designs of the Slave Power upon Mexico, Cuba, Central America, St. Domingo, or to the guilt of the South generally. It includes all these, and a great deal more. It is, primarily — 1st. What is American Slavery, in its origin, spirit, history, assumption, and purpose? What is it, judging it by its own code, and testing it by its own fruits? 2d. Who, and how many are its victims, and what is their physical, mental and moral condition? 3d. Who are responsible for their enslavement, and of whom shall their blood be required? 4th. What is the religious relation sustained by the North, through its churches and various other ecclesiastical bodies, to the slave system? 5th. To what extent is the North responsible for the continuance of that system, through its political and governmental relations to the South? 6th. Ought the watchword throughout the North to be, *'No Union with Slaveholders?'*

Briefly I will say, that Slavery originated in man-stealing, by violence and blood, and, as it cannot change its character, is man-stealing to this hour. Its spirit is brutal, sensual, devilish — at war with God and man, and merciless in its treatment of all those who call its rectitude in question. Its history is one of perfidy, usurpation, lust, cruelty, blasphemy, and every conceivable sin and crime — crowded with horrors and reeking with blood. Its assumption is, that it is God-ordained and God-approved — sanctioned alike under the Old and under the New Dispensation — the normal condition of the laboring classes, without regard to race or complexion — never to be abolished, but, on the contrary, to be cherished, strengthened, extended, perpetuated, at whatever sacrifice or hazard. Its purpose is, avowedly, to seek the overthrow of all existing free institutions, to subjugate the entire country to its bloody sway, to tolerate nothing which does not bow down to its behest, and to claim the right of universal dominion. Its code is, the repeal of all the commands of the Decalogue, and all the injunctions of the Gospel — the concentration of all injustice, the culmination of all villany, the acme of all impiety, sundering as it does all human ties, subjecting its victims to every species of torture, degrading them to a level with beasts and perishable property, compelling them to live in a state of uncleanness and pollution surpassed by nothing in Sodom or Gomorrah, and making the traffic in their bodies and souls one of the most active branches of commerce. Its fruits are unbounded profligacy, horrible profanity, wholesale robbery, infernal barbarity, and thronging woes and curses innumerable. Earth shudders at its existence — Heaven cries out against it — Humanity execrates and flees in terror from it — God, and angels, and the spirits of the just made perfect above, and all noble and Christ-like souls on earth, demand its immediate and utter extinction.

The number of those who are clanking their chains in our land, 'without God, and without hope,' it is frightful to contemplate. Think of it! it exceeds the entire population of the six New England States! It is equal to one seventh portion of all the inhabitants in America! Its increase, by natural generation, is not less than one hundred thousand annually! Every five minutes, a fresh victim is added to the immense throng who are doomed to toil, and suffer, and bleed, without redress and beyond all conception! They are systematically degraded, brutalized, heathenized. These are our brethren, according to the flesh — made of the same 'one blood,' [1] 'a little lower than the angels' [2] — under the same law to God — entitled to the hopes and privileges of the same gospel — as dear to the common Father as ourselves — invested by creation with the same inalienable rights — destined to the same immortality — and accountable to the same tribunal.

Where lies the responsibility for their awful fate? Upon every religious denomination which does not bear an uncompromising testimony against Slavery. Upon every church which recognizes slaveholders as of the household of faith, and disciples of Christ. Upon every political party which gives any quarters to Slavery, whether in Kansas or in Carolina. Upon all the people of the North, comprehensively speaking, through their persistent and willing complicity with the slaveholders and slave-traffickers at the South, in every variety of action and combination. Upon the Constitution of the United States, with its iniquitous slaveholding compromises, as 'a covenant with death and an agreement with hell,' and upon all who swear allegiance to it. Upon the American Union, which makes every State slave-hunting ground, and renders it possible for three hundred and fifty thousand Southern taskmasters to hold in iron bondage four millions of the children of God!

What, then, is our common duty? Repentance, in sackcloth and ashes — confession of sin — unwavering adherence to the cause of freedom — *no Union with Slaveholders*!

Yours, to break every yoke,

WM. LLOYD GARRISON.

Printed in *The Liberator*, March 19, 1858.

The Liberator, in printing Garrison's letter, accompanied it with two paragraphs. The first, signed "M" (Samuel May, Jr.), reads as follows:

"The *Green Mountain Freeman* has at length published Mr. Garrison's Letter to the Vermont Anti-Slavery Convention, — which letter had been entrusted to it for publication some six weeks previously. For the knowledge of this fact, we are indebted to a friend, for of late the *Freeman* is not sent to this office in exchange for the *Liberator*, which is mailed regularly to it. Is this intentional?"

The second paragraph reads:

"The following is the letter referred to. In printing it, the *Freeman* (either designedly or through inexcusable carelessness, as the manuscript was very legible) makes numerous errors — among them, for 'Christ-like souls,' substituting the unmeaning words, 'Cabinet-like souls,' etc.!!"

The *Green Mountain Freeman* was "the leading Republican journal of the State." (*The Liberator*, March 12, 1858.)

The Reverand Nathan Robinson Johnston (b. Hopedale, Ohio, October 8, 1820; fl. Oakland, California, 1884) was pastor of the Covenanter Church at Topsham, Vermont. (*Life*, III, 482, 504; IV, 389; Anti-Slavery Manuscripts, Boston Public Library.) Parker Pillsbury once referred to him as "an excellent minister of the Old School Scotch Covenanter Church, the only denomination of the country that occupies genuine Anti-Slavery ground." (Letter from Parker Pillsbury to Garrison, dated February 5, 1858, printed in *The Liberator*, February 12, 1858.)

1. Acts 17:26.
2. Psalms 8:5.

2 0 8

TO AN UNKNOWN CORRESPONDENT

Boston, Feb. 6, 1858.

Dear Friend:

I have taken a very deep interest in the case of M. L. C.[1] & his 2 companions,[2] French refugees from the despotism of L[ouis] N[apoleon], who arrived at S[alem, Massachusetts] last summer, homeless, penniless, friendless, strangers in a strange land, among a people of a strange speech. They are sufferers & martyrs in the cause of E[uropean] freedom — or, rather, freedom for all mankind, for they are ablst. in principle, & argue for the rights of the black man as they do for their own — as you will see, & be glad to see, on reading the thrilling N[arrative] of their escape from C[ayenne], written by Mr. C., & published in pamphlet form [3] — 25 copies of wh. I herewith send to your care, with the hope & belief that you will be able to dispose of them, as an act of charity, among your friends & acquaintance, at 25 cts. each. Mr. C. is an accomplished gent., & of a highly respectable family in France. He thought of going to your place to see whether he could find purchasers for his N[arrative]; but, his diffidence & foreign accent being hindrances to his success, I have feared that he would not be able to sell copies enough to cover his travelling expenses, & so I have undertaken to save him from all risk & uncertainty, by making up packages of 25 copies each, & sending them to reliable & kind-hearted friends, (as in your own case,) in various towns, asking their benevolent co-operation to this extent.

The N. is perfectly authentic, & highly recommended by some of the most respectable citizens in Salem, as you will see by referring to the printed cover [4] of the pamphlet. Those who buy it will get their money's worth, & also do a most charitable deed; for two of these unfortunate men cannot speak a word of English — and as for employment in these "hard times," they cannot find any — so that they are in a state of complete destitution.

My wife, by exerting herself, has already succeeded in selling one hundred copies.

I know, my dear friend, you will not only excuse me for taking this liberty, but be glad to give your co-operation to this extent.

Yearning to see the day when the tyranny of Europe & the slavery of America shall be thoroughly "crushed out," I remain,

Yours, for universal freedom,

W. L. G.

ALS: Garrison Papers, Boston Public Library.

    1. Leon Chautard. Garrison probably uses the "M" for Monsieur.

    2. The two companions were named Paon and Bivors.

    3. Leon Chautard, *Escape from Cayenne* (Salem: Printed at the Observer Office, 1857).

    4. The outside of the back cover listed the names of fifteen outstanding citizens of Salem who had subscribed for the pamphlet and were recommending it for purchase.

---

2 0 9

TO SUSAN B. ANTHONY

Boston, Feb. 9, 1858.

My Dear Friend:

    I am very sorry to give you any trouble, or to cause any derangement, in regard to your appointments of Anti-Slavery Conventions at Hudson, Poughkeepsie,[1] and elsewhere; but my spinal difficulty still remains, though somewhat mitigated, and it would be highly imprudent for me to think of leaving home as soon as an attendance at the meetings you have advertised would require on my part.

    Your letter of the 6th is just received, and I am much relieved in mind to know that you have concluded upon a temporary postponement. You wish to know, however, when I may be certainly expected, and suggest the first week in March in which to hold two conventions — one in Hudson, the other in Poughkeepsie. I hope to be able to carry out this last proposition; but, of course, I cannot now foresee what may be my spinal condition at that time, and I could not think of appearing, especially as "a Garrisonian abolitionist," without a backbone. Trusting that I shall be sufficiently restored, I am willing (if you think best) that you should appoint those two conventions, and advertise me among the speakers — letting the first meeting be called for Tuesday afternoon, March 2d, and continuing until Wednesday night by adjournment (either in Hudson or Poughkeepsie,) and then holding the second convention on Thursday evening, and holding over till Friday night by adjournment. Pray don't have any longer sessions than here marked out.

    Let your convention at Albany be called on Monday AFTERNOON as well as evening, (March 8th,) in order that two addresses, instead of one, may be got out of Phillips; and let him be specially advertised for the two meetings. As Parker Pillsbury thinks of being at the Albany Convention, if you think it best to have it extended two days longer, I suppose we cannot [*sic*] stagger through with the load.

I can add no more, for lack of time; but what I have written will be sufficiently explicit, I hope.

Love to Aaron and Lydia,[2] and all the other "saints."

Yours, truly,

Wm. Lloyd Garrison.

Susan B. Anthony.

ALS: Huntington Library, San Marino, California.

1. Both in upstate New York.
2. Aaron M. Powell and Lydia Mott.

210

TO THE JOINT SPECIAL COMMITTEE
OF THE LEGISLATURE

To the Joint Special Committee of the Legislature, to whom have been referred the petitions for the removal of Judge Loring.

[March 5, 1858.]

GENTLEMEN:

The undersigned, petitioners for the removal of EDWARD GREELEY LORING from the office of Judge of Probate for Suffolk county, respectfully beg leave to submit, in reply to the invitation extended to them to show cause why their prayer should be granted —

That they deem it wholly superfluous to re-open a case which has twice been fully examined in all its bearings, and elaborately argued, before two Committees of the Legislature, upon whose Reports, in the affirmative, the Legislature has twice voted, by a very large majority in both branches, in favor of the object prayed for; and which the popular sentiment of this Commonwealth, deep-rooted and unconquerable, demands to be met in a prompt, manly and satisfactory manner, both by the Senate and House of Representatives, and by the Governor and Council. The time has gone by for hesitancy or doubt, for argument or procrastination. Not an additional ray of light can be needed, on your part, to guide you to just conclusions. The subject has been discussed from Barnstable to Berkshire, for the last three years, at every fire-side, in the social circle, in the public assembly, in every newspaper, and wherever men congregate. It requires no repetition of words, no new evidence, but only ACTION, in conformity with the will of the people, expressed through multitudinous petitions from year to year, and by the twice-recorded verdict of their representatives, in General Court assembled.

Twice have the people of Massachusetts had their solemn decree defeated, respecting the removal of Judge Loring, by a Governor [1] whom they have been unwilling any longer to tolerate in office; and they now look confidently to the present Chief Magistrate,[2] that he will promptly comply with their wishes, if requested to do so on the part of this Legislature. They ask that this case may be met upon its merits, and by a direct vote; and not be superseded, or evaded, or jeoparded, by any other question. They regard this as paramount in importance to all other matters now before the Legislature, because it relates directly to the honor, the dignity, and the sovereignty of the State, and to the imperilled cause of liberty throughout the land. It is not a local concern, affecting only the county of Suffolk, but is as broad as the Commonwealth, and full of significance and interest to the whole country. What is to be gained, gentlemen, by resisting what they so strongly demand? They are permanent — official station is easily changed — and they will allow no incompetency or treachery to defeat their irrevocable purpose. If, for the third time, they shall find themselves baffled, their moral indignation will burn with new intensity, and a deeper agitation will follow. Is it desirable to prolong this excitement?

It has been artfully attempted, by those whose sympathies are wholly *Southern* in their tendencies, to excite odium against the movement for the removal of Judge Loring, by representing it as limited to 'a fanatical association.' Let the numerous petitions before the Committee be examined; and it will be seen that those whose names are appended to them touch every rank in life, every variety of calling, and are irrespective of party lines — including a considerable portion of the women of Massachusetts. They represent no anti-slavery organization, but truly indicate the all-prevailing sentiment of THE PEOPLE. It is a popular, not an abolition demonstration.

The grounds on which the removal of Judge Loring is demanded are various, in the public mind, but in the petitions they are narrowed to one single specification, because that admits of no evasion, and relates to the sovereignty of the State, and to the enforcement of its laws. It is as follows:

That by a law passed May 21, 1855, by the Legislature of Massachusetts, it was declared —

'No person who holds any office under the laws of the United States, which qualifies him to issue any warrant or other process, or to grant any certificate under the acts of Congress named in the 6th section of this act, or to serve the same, shall, at the same time, hold any office of honor, trust or emolument under the laws of this Commonwealth.'

That in open defiance of this law, and of the voice of the people of Massachusetts, as expressed (without distinction of party) by the action of two separate Legislatures for his removal, but twice rendered inoperative by Executive nonconcurrence, Edward Greeley Loring, while acting as a Commissioner of the United States, continues to hold the office of Judge of Probate for the county of Suffolk; thus setting an example of contumacy unbecoming a good citizen, and wantonly disregarding the moral convictions of the people of this State as pertaining to the enforcement of the odious Fugitive Slave Bill.

They, therefore, earnestly pray the General Court again to recommend to the Governor and Council, the removal of said Edward Greeley Loring from the office of Judge of Probate; and thus enforce a wholesome law of the Commonwealth, which it is his declared purpose to disregard, and thereby vindicate the sovereignty of the people of this Commonwealth.

The law here referred to was passed by the Legislature in connection with the Personal Liberty Bill, (a Bill, the adoption of which was hailed with exultation by the friends of freedom throughout the North, and which has given intense dissatisfaction to the 'lords of the lash' at the South,) in consequence of the deep moral repugnance of the people of this Commonwealth to the odious Fugitive Slave Law, which they regard as equally inhuman and unconstitutional; and also on account of the summary manner in which Judge Loring, as United States Commissioner, remanded Anthony Burns back to chains and bondage, against law and against evidence, to his own disgrace, and to the shame and sorrow of Massachusetts — thereby fearfully endangering the public peace, and bringing this great community to the verge of bloody violence and horrid massacre. While the law forbids no citizen from filling the office of Slave Commissioner, who chooses to act in that capacity, it expressly declares that no person holding any office of honor, trust or emolument, under the laws of this Commonwealth, shall at the same time be a Commissioner of the United States, to carry into execution the Fugitive Slave Law.

Judge Loring has continued to violate this law ever since its enactment, and openly defies the Commonwealth. He will neither retire from his office as Judge of Probate, nor yield up his office as Slave Commissioner. If he had not been apparently lost to all self-respect — if he had had any considerations for the moral convictions and humane feelings of the people of this State — he would long since have voluntarily vacated his judicial position, and given place to some other person, against whom no such aversion existed. This he would have done as an act of magnanimity, and to show that he was not animated by any selfish motive, even though believing that he had faithfully discharged a most unpleasant duty as Commissioner. But his is a contumacious and defiant spirit. He triumphs over the law, and tramples it under his feet. He declares that he will never obey it, and that he will not only be Slave Commissioner, but Judge of Probate also, any law of this Commonwealth to the contrary notwithstanding.

Gentlemen of the Committee, this is the issue you are called upon to meet, and in reference to which you are to make your report to the Legislature. This is the issue upon which the Legislature itself must act — the Governor and Council also. Either enforce the law, or repeal it. The people will tolerate no repeal, and they demand its execution. Shall they, or a solitary individual, rule the old Bay State? As legislators, of what avail will your enactments prove, if every factious spirit is to be allowed to disregard them with impunity? Vindicate, then, the insulted majesty of the State, give heed to the voice of the people, and thereby confer upon this Legislature and the present State administration lasting honor, secure the public repose, and promote public justice. 'God save the Commonwealth of Massachusetts!'

For the petitioners,

> SAMUEL MAY,[3]
> FRANCIS JACKSON,
> WM. LLOYD GARRISON,
> THEODORE PARKER,
> WENDELL PHILLIPS,
> SAMUEL MAY, JR.,
> ROBERT F. WALLCUT,
> JAMES JACKSON.[4]

Printed in *The Liberator*, March 5, 1858.

1. Henry Joseph Gardner (1818–1892), originally a Whig, was first elected governor of Massachusetts in 1854 as candidate of the Know-Nothing party. He was reelected in 1855 and 1856 but was defeated in 1857 by Nathaniel P. Banks, the Republican candidate. Although presumably antislavery, in 1855 he vetoed the Personal Liberty Bill, which was passed by the legislature over his veto. He also vetoed the legislature's resolution for the removal of Judge Loring.

2. Nathaniel Banks.

3. Samuel May (b. December 4, 1776; d. February 3, 1870), of Boston, was the father of Samuel May, Jr., the abolitionist. At the age of twenty-one, he opened a hardware store and later built a warehouse on Broad street, where he and his sons continued the business for sixty-six years. He built a branch of the business at Montreal, Canada, and through agents carried on a fur trade at Buffalo, New York. In later years, he became involved in cotton manufacturing, and in 1825 joined the woolen mills in Salisbury, Massachusetts, continuing his association for twenty-three years. In 1857, he was almost overwhelmed by losses, but managed to recoup his fortune during the ensuing years. He declined public office, yet was involved in religious affairs and public service. He was a deacon of the Hollis Street Church and a member of Theodore Parker's church, an overseer of the poor for many years, an officer of the Boston Dispensary; he was associated with Dr. Samuel G. Howe in establishing the Massachusetts Asylum for the Blind and was an original proprietor of the Boston Athenaeum. (Samuel May, John Wilder May, John Joseph May, *A Genealogy of the Descendants of John May*, Boston, 1878, pp. 15–16.)

4. Probably James Jackson (1777–1867), a prominent Boston physician, who

had been professor of medicine at the Harvard Medical School, "the first in America to investigate vaccination in a scientific spirit," and a founder of the Massachusetts General Hospital. He was married to Elizabeth Cabot and, after her death, to her sister Sarah. They were the daughters of Lydia and Andrew Cabot, who was the brother of Samuel Cabot, the father of Eliza Cabot Follen, the abolitionist and reformer. His *Letters to a Young Physician* (1855) is "one of the classics of American medical literature." (L. Vernon Briggs, *History and Genealogy of the Cabot Family, 1475–1927*, privately printed by Goodspeed's, Boston, 1927, I, 270–271.)

211

TO SAMUEL J. MAY

BOSTON, March 6, 1858.

MY DEAR FRIEND:

I am sorely disappointed that the state of my health is such as to render it imprudent for me to attend the Convention at Albany; though, as you will have the powerful aid of Mr. Phillips, Mr. Remond, and other efficient speakers, my absence will be of very little consequence.

If I were present with you, I might feel disposed to say, among other utterances —

O, citizens of the Empire State! what power of speech can stir your blood, what trumpet-tone summon you to action, in the most perilous crisis the nation has known since the days of your revolutionary fathers? Are not the skies crowded with fiery portents? Does not the earth quake beneath your feet? Is not the blackness of darkness gathering over the land, the precursor of a storm of divine retribution, before which your mightiest bulwarks of defence shall be as chaff before the whirlwind? Is this a time for the indulgence of party strife, or sectarian rivalry, or foolish prejudice, or venal selfishness? Is it a time to mock at justice, to hinder the proclamation of truth, to decry virtue, to bow submissively to high-handed usurpation, to inaugurate the reign of terror? What and where are your own liberties? Are they more real than the spectres of a distempered imagination? You are Americans, forsooth! Over your heads proudly floats the star-spangled banner! Your country spreads from the Lakes to the Gulf, and from the Atlantic to the Pacific! Yet who, among your swarming millions, can exercise freedom of speech or of the press in all the South, in reprobation of its horrible slave system, without being compelled to accept the alternative of banishment or death? In this particular, and to this extent, wherein do you differ from the subjugated masses in Russia, Austria, Italy, Naples, France? But what right have you to complain of this? As you sow, shall you not also reap? Have you not wickedly assisted to bind the galling fetters of slavery upon the limbs of four millions of your countrymen, by religious and political complicity with their remorseless oppressors? by constitutional compromises and governmental arrangements? by complexional proscription and deliberate agreement? by ridiculing the doctrine of inalienable human rights, as applied to those whose skins are not colored like your own, and branding as visionaries and fanatics those who demand, in the name of the living God, the instant emancipation of all who are pining in bondage?

O, people of New York! wide are the boundaries of your state, embracing a whole empire! Why is it that you allow the poor trembling fugitive slave, who flies to your soil for refuge, to be hunted with impunity like a wild beast, and captured and returned to stripes and torture? Why do your knees smite together and your hands become palsied, in the presence of the slave-hunter or his loathsome representative? Is it because it is so written in the bond? Is it because this is a part of the price which your fathers paid to secure the existing Union between the North and South? Is this your justification? What, then, is such a compact but "a covenant with death"? What is it, if it be not "an agreement with hell"? Are you so blind as not to perceive, so infatuated as not to understand, that "when judgment is laid to the line, and righteousness to the plummet, the hail shall sweep away your refuge of lies, and the waters overflow the hiding-place; and your covenant with death shall be annulled; and your agreement with hell shall not stand; and that when the overflowing scourge shall pass through, then ye shall be trodden down by it"?[1] Of what avail will be your temple-worship, your sabbatical observance, your religious rites and offerings, your missionary efforts abroad, your proselyting spirit at home? While you are preying upon the outcast and the oppressed, is your praying to God any thing better than a solemn mockery? Do you not know that you cannot strike hands with thieves, nor consent with adulterers, without participating in the guilt, the shame, and the retribution?

To what else are you giving your consent, whereby your hands are made red with innocent blood? Do you not concede to the three hundred and fifty thousand slaveholders at the South the right to represent three fifths of four millions of slaves in Congress, for the exclusive benefit of a liberty-hating slave oligarchy, and to render hopeless the delivery of those captive millions? Was there ever a worse conspiracy against justice and the rights of man than this?

But this is not all. What if the slaves at the South, goaded to desperation, and inspired by the irrepressible spirit of freedom, should rise in arms, as did your revolutionary sires, and seek to win their liberty through blood? What if you should be summoned, by the

President of the United States, in such an emergency, to shoulder your muskets and buckle on your knapsacks, and march to the South for the purpose of reducing those heroic insurgents again to chattel servitude? In that case, you would obey! Your plea would be, "It is so written in the bond! The Union, it must and shall be preserved!" [2]

And for all these things, shall not a righteous God bring you into judgment?

By all that is precious in the blood of Christ — by all that is sacred in "the glorious gospel of the blessed God" [3] — by all the holy commands and binding precepts of a pure religion — by every consideration of justice, honor, humanity, self-respect, and self-preservation — by reverence for the higher law of God, and unfaltering faith in a stern adherence to principle, as the highest expediency and the wisest policy — cease to give any countenance or aid to the traffickers in slaves and the souls of men, make the Empire State free to every bondman who shall plant his weary feet upon its soil, dissolve the hateful ties which connect you with the South, and on your banner inscribe the glorious motto, "*No Union with Slaveholders!*"

Yours, for universal freedom,

WM. LLOYD GARRISON.

REV. SAMUEL J. MAY.

Printed in *The Liberator*, March 26, 1858.

1. Isaiah 28:17, 18.
2. President Andrew Jackson's toast at the Jefferson Birthday celebration, April 13, 1830 was "Our Federal Union: it must be preserved."
3. I Timothy 1:11.

212

TO SUSAN B. ANTHONY

Boston, April 14, 1858.

My Dear Friend:

The bag of dried peaches, enclosing a smaller parcel for our dear friend Francis Jackson, and your kind letter accompanying it, were duly received, and most gratefully appreciated by us all. It was just like your generous nature to send us so large a quantity, at so much trouble and expense. Will you allow us in some way to reciprocate your kindness? The peaches prove to be excellent, and they are greatly relished by all the household. Helen desires me to proffer you her special acknowledgments, and to say that the gift was very opportune, as all her preserves had been used up, and it was difficult to know what to get for a "relish."

Excuse my procrastination. It may almost have justified you in supposing that I was waiting for another crop of peaches to grow, to be "cut and dried," and thoroughly tested, before sending you our household vote of thanks. Both Helen and myself have been intending, each day, to send you a good long letter; but something or other has occurred to prevent us. Please put us down, therefore, as persons of the best intentions, who are too apt to leave others to take the will for the deed.

I thank you for your kind solicitude in regard to my health, and have endeavored to comply with your advice to abstain from public speaking. To-morrow (Fast Day)[1] I go to Plymouth[2] with Remond to hold three meetings, and, having been silent so long, shall feel it somewhat difficult to "resume the thread of my discourse." I am not wholly relieved of my spinal complaint, though considerably better than when you were here. I tell my friends that I have been constantly improving since the removal of Judge Loring; and this is no joke. As soon as the deed was done, I felt a load taken from my shoulders, as Christian did in "Pilgrim's Progress," when he came in sight of the Cross, and I was ready to leap for joy. It was indeed a great triumph for us, obtained after a most protracted struggle. Truly does the Boston *Courier* declare, that it was effected solely through the persevering efforts of our little band of abolitionists; for, had it not been for our holding a rod *in terrorem* over the heads of the Republicans, (now the dominant party in this Commonwealth,) and doing all the work of preparing and circulating petitions, and using all our influence with members of the Legislature during the session, they would have done nothing about it. Indeed, very many of them wished to have nothing to do with it, and refused to put their names to the petitions, fearing it might injure the popularity of Gov. Banks. I was very apprehensive that we should be again defeated — in which case, we should have had no opportunity to make another trial, in consequence of a new arrangement of our courts, and Judge Loring, alias the Slave Power, would have triumphed over the State. But, happily, the righteous cause prevailed, justice was meted out to the refractory slave-catching Judge, and the whole North was electrified and strengthened by the act. So much for the "do-nothing Garrisonian abolitionists," who give no votes, and lack practicality! So much for moral suasion, and its connection with political action!

After you left us, our beloved friend, Abby Kelley Foster, remained with us awhile, with poor dear Alla[3] suffering from her diseased spine. She writes to us, since her return home, that Alla has considerably improved, and that the new mechanical apparatus which she is using is producing a marked and most salutary effect upon her whole system. Doubtless Abby keeps you informed upon this subject, and I need not go into particulars.

For the last ten or twelve days, Helen Pillsbury, the only daughter of Parker and Sarah, has been lying at "death's door," in consequence of a severe attack of scarletina, after having just recovered from the measles. A letter from Parker, received yesterday, states that there are some slight hopes of her recovery; but a few days will determine her case. His own health is greatly impaired, and the family are truly in affliction. The death of their darling Helen would prove a terrible blow.

Mr. May's little Bessie [4] is down with the measles, and his own health, and that of his wife, is very much impaired.

For a week past, Fanny has been confined to the house with a slow fever, but is now convalescent. Frank is well, and studious as usual; and both send their loving regards to you. Mary-Ann reciprocates your kind remembrance.

I will try to make a speech, if desired, at the Woman's Rights Convention, and to draw up a series of Resolutions, but fear I shall not succeed. [5]

Hoping to greet you at the approaching anniversary and wishing to be kindly remembered to father and mother, and all the household, I remain,

Your attached friend,

Wm. Lloyd Garrison.

Susan B. Anthony.

ALS: Merrill Collection of Garrison Papers, Wichita State University.

1. "A day usually in the spring appointed by the magistrates and governors of some of the New England colonies and states as a holiday for the purpose of fasting and prayer." (*Webster's Third New International Dictionary*, unabridged, 1967.) *The Liberator*, April 2, 1858, announced that the governor of New Hampshire had appointed Thursday, April 8, "to be Fast"; and Governor Banks had appointed Thursday, April 15, for "Fast in this State."

2. This was to be a quarterly meeting of the Old Colony Anti-Slavery Society, which was to convene on Thursday, April 15, at Plymouth, Massachusetts.

3. Paulina Wright Foster, nicknamed "Alla," Abby Kelley Foster's only child, was born in May 1847. She suffered from a severe curvature of the spine. After graduating from Vassar in 1872 she did postgraduate work at Cornell, and subsequently lived and taught school in Roxbury, Massachusetts. ("Abigail Kelley Foster" in *Notable American Women*; Reginald Foster, *Foster Genealogy*, Chicago, 1899, Part I, p. 366.)

4. Samuel May, Jr.'s daughter, Elizabeth Goddard, born April 21, 1850.

5. Garrison is referring to the Ninth National Woman's Rights Convention, which was to be held in New York City, on Thursday and Friday, May 13 and 14, 1858. The announcement of the convention in *The Liberator* on April 30 listed Garrison as one of the speakers.

213

TO ADELINE ROBERTS

Boston, April 14, 1858.

Dear Friend:

Your favor of the 10th is received.

It will give me great pleasure to give the closing lecture of the next course of Anti-Slavery Lectures before your Society, at the time specified by you — Dec. 5th.

Hoping that the course will prove the most successful of the whole series, I remain,

Yours, to free the enslaved,

Wm. Lloyd Garrison.

Miss Adeline Roberts.

ALS: Essex Institute, Salem, Massachusetts.

214

TO JOHN W. LE BARNES

Boston, April 29, 1858.

Dear Sir:

I deem it an honor to have received an official invitation to be present, this evening, at the meeting at Turner's Hall, to commemorate the memories of Orsini [1] and his associates, who have recently been beheaded by the decree of a remorseless tyrant in the person of Louis Napoleon, because it implies that you believe my sympathies and aspirations are with the oppressed throughout the world, without regard to race, color or clime. You rightly judge my character. I am not only an abolitionist for the chattelized slave, but an emancipationist for the whole human race. I am no advocate for one-sided liberty, or mere national independence; but, wherever tyranny exists, I loathe and execrate it, and proclaim liberty to be the inalienable right of every human being — liberty of person, of locomotion, of thought, of speech, of the press — liberty in all things, under all circumstances, in all lands, for all peoples, through all time, and to all eternity. For more than a quarter of a century, I have publicly inscribed on my flag this motto — 'My country is the world; my countrymen are all mankind.' This sentiment is in my heart, and circulates with every drop of blood in my body; and when I prove recreant to it, let my tongue cleave to the roof of my mouth. [2] Therefore it is that I deeply sympathize with your gathering, this evening, because it is a heartfelt protest against the cowardly, perfidious blood-stained usurper who has crushed the liberties of France, perpetrated innumerable crimes and atrocities, and is seeking to aid every form of European despotism. It is true, I do not believe in killing any man — not even so great a monster as Louis Napoleon — because I believe in the inviolability of human life, and that the weapons of death are the legitimate weapons of tyranny; while those of liberty are thought, speech, intellectual enlightenment, protest, contumacy, non-conformity, untiring persistency, indomitable purpose, unconquerable will, moral rebellion, abiding faith in the right, the divine spirit of martyrdom. Nevertheless, judging from the stand-point of patriotism as manifested at Bunker Hill and at Yorktown, at Bannockburn and Thermopylae, and during the famous 'three days' in Paris, when the Republic was inaugurated, with 'LIBERTY, EQUALITY, FRATERNITY,' for its watchwords, I am bound to say, (that I may not be misunderstood by any one,) that Orsini was no assassin in spirit or purpose, but a brave man, true to his convictions of duty, his hatred of oppression, and his desire for the reign of freedom throughout Europe; and that it was the wholesale murderer Louis Napoleon who deserved to be beheaded, rather than Orsini.

Your meeting will receive no sanction from the American press, people, or government. How can America sympathize with any struggle for freedom in the old world? She holds every seventh person of her vast population in fetters of iron, as a brute beast, as an article of merchandize. With four millions of slaves in her ruthless grasp, she has not only lost all reverence for human rights, but she ridicules and rejects her own Declaration of Independence; and hence, her instincts and feelings are with every tyrant in Europe, and against its downtrodden masses; and such will be her state and attitude until she breaks every fetter, and liberates every slave, on her own soil: then shall she lead the nations of the earth to universal freedom.

Much more I could add, for my heart is full, and I 'could pour it out like water'; — but I must pause. Let me conclude with this sentiment: —

Liberty for France, for Germany, for Italy, for all nations! Liberty for the slaves in America, for the serfs in Russia, for all peoples who are held in thraldom; Defiance and resistance to despots, come what may, and success to treason as against bloody usurpation!

Accept this testimony as a substitute for my bodily presence, and believe me, dear sir.

Yours, to break every yoke,

WM. LLOYD GARRISON,
Editor of the *Liberator.*

Printed in *The Liberator*, May 7, 1858.

The Liberator printed this letter as part of an account of the meeting which Garrison had been invited to attend. It reported that "on Thursday evening of last week, a public meeting was held in Turner's Hall, 677 Washington Street, in this city 'in honor of Orsini and Pierri, the noble martyrs of liberty,' who were recently beheaded in Paris for attempting the death of Louis Napoleon, the perjured usurper, and for killing and wounding several of his retinue by certain destructive materials used on the occasion. The meeting was chiefly composed of Frenchmen, Germans, and Italians, many of them exiles for their love of republican freedom."

It announced, too, that John W. Le Barnes was president of the committee of arrangements and chairman of the meeting. Le Barnes read Garrison's letter to the assemblage, which greeted it "with frequent and spirited demonstrations of approval."

John W. Le Barnes, of Boston, was born in 1828 and was employed at the Boston Waterworks Company. He was later a supporter of John Brown and sought to engineer Brown's escape after the Harpers Ferry episode. It was at his suggestion and expense that George Henry Hoyt, a recently graduated lawyer, went to Harpers Ferry in 1859, ostensibly as Brown's counsel, but actually to provide information for the effectuation of a plan by Le Barnes, Higginson, and others to secure Brown's escape. During the Civil War Le Barnes was lieutenant of a German company in the Twentieth Massachusetts Infantry. He was admitted to the Suffolk bar and began the practice of law in 1864. In 1894, he was practicing law in Washington, D.C. (Manuscripts Relating to John Brown, Collected by Thomas Wentworth Higginson, Boston Public Library; the collection includes fifteen letters from Le Barnes to Higginson about John Brown. Tilden G. Edelstein, *Strange Enthusiasm: A Life of Thomas Wentworth Higginson*, New Haven and London, 1968, pp. 229–230, 235–236; Richard J. Hinton, *John Brown and His Men; With Some Account of the Roads They Traveled to Reach Harper's Ferry*, New York, 1894, pp. 365–366, 372, 377, 520–526; Thomas Wentworth Higginson, *Cheerful Yesterdays*, Boston and New York, 1898, pp. 231–232, 240; William T. Davis, *Bench and Bar of the Commonwealth of Massachusetts*, Boston, 1895, I, 628.)

1. Felice, Count de Orsini (1819–1858), an Italian patriot and revolutionist. Together with other conspirators, he attempted to assassinate Napoleon III, by exploding bombs in Paris on January 14, 1858, in revenge for the French occupation of Rome. He and his accomplice, Pieri, were guillotined.

2. Psalms 137:6.

215

TO OLIVER JOHNSON

Boston, May 1, 1858.

My dear Johnson:

Your letter, containing a check for $15, to pay for the bust, and its transportation to New York, was received yesterday; and it gave me real pleasure to be able to put the money into the hands of Mr. Jackson, the artist, because I know how straitened he is in his pecuniary affairs, having received no encouragement at all proportionate to his merits — confirming the old declaration, "A prophet hath no honor in his own country," he being a Boston mechanic originally, and so the aristocracy are bound to ignore his claims. He is trying to get to Rome and Florence, where he ought to be, and where he would unquestionably win renown as a sculptor.

It was wholly for his sake that I ventured (though with great reluctance, and only because I was sure you would appreciate the motive) to make the suggestion to you about the bust; for the bust being a personal matter, I cannot properly do anything about it — whereas, in the case of Wendell Phillips, I could readily exert myself, both to procure the means to have his bust put into marble, and to multiply copies of the plaster cast.

The bust will be sent to you in all next week, only the original cast having yet been taken, it being necessary that the mould should be first thoroughly dried before taking additional copies. How it will strike you as a likeness, remains to be seen; but there are very conflicting opinions about it among the friends here, as usual in regard to such matters. It is astonishing how differently the same object strikes different persons, who are equally well acquainted with the original of which that is intended to be a similitude. Thus, friend Wallcutt thinks he should hardly recognize the bust, in a promiscuous group; while Henry C. Wright pronounces it to be admirable in all respects — the best likeness that has ever been taken of me, or probably ever will be. On the whole, the friends generally are very well satisfied with it. Helen likes it much better than she anticipated, and I think well of it, as far as I can judge of my own face. One thing is certain, for some reason or other, I have one of the most difficult faces in the world to take, (owing, probably, to its changeableness of expression,) all artists, at home and abroad, having failed to get a likeness generally satisfactory to my personal friends. Out of a hundred daguerreotypes that have been taken of me, not one is worth looking at a second time. The failure is absolute, whether it be Brady,[1] in your city, or Southwick[2] or Whipple,[3] here. Jackson[4] acknowledges that he has never had one sit to him, whose living expression it has been so difficult to catch, as in my own case; nor has he ever had one sit to him so many times, or for whom he has exerted himself so laboriously to achieve success. Besides, there is an inherent difficulty with which he has had to contend, and which it is not possible for even genius to surmount, in making a bust of me. My spectacles are a part of my face — few even see me for a moment without them — and they greatly modify the appearance of my eyes, and my general expression of countenance. In fact, when I lay them aside, I am almost another man. Now, no bust is ever provided with spectacles; consequently, whoever looks at mine will see me under conditions perhaps never before contemplated, and so will naturally fail to see a striking likeness, as in the case of Phillips, which I think can never be excelled. Jackson has seen me longer, and scanned my face more minutely, without my glasses, than any other person, except my own wife; and if, after all, he has not achieved what my friends have so long desired to see, I am satisfied that none will ever be able to get a striking and satisfactory likeness of me while in the body.

The front view of a bust is generally the least satisfactory — (as it is in Phillips's.) A profile or two-thirds view is best. Mine, all concede, is much the best as seen standing on *the right side of it*, a little distance off; and if you can place it in the office in that position, on a bracket, it will be the best disposal you can make of it. But please critically examine, and judge for yourself; and if you can say anything about it, that may encourage the artist, (you remember his masterly likeness of Dr. Beecher,[5] Blagden,[6] &c., and he has since taken a capital one of Longfellow,[7]) I shall be glad, and will copy it into the Liberator for his benefit.

Pardon me for dwelling so minutely on this matter, for you know it is not often I "get upon a *bust*." I heartily thank you for your characteristic kindness in procuring the means to purchase, for the office, a copy of the bust, and also every one who contributed to make up the fifteen dollars. It may be an object of curiosity to strangers to look at it, even though the "horns" are missing.

I am very sorry to hear of the illness of Victoria Knight,[8] and trust it will not be "unto death."

Winchell Yerrinton has just lost, by measles and scarlatina, a fine little boy, three and a half years old, who is to be buried this day. It is a sad affliction.

I am glad to learn that Theodore Parker is to be with you at your next Progressive Friends' meeting. Certainly, if he wishes me to speak in Music Hall, during his absence, I will cheerfully do so. But, as yet, he has said nothing to me on the subject.

Are we to have a social meeting on Monday evening, prior to the anniversary,[9] at your office? If so, I will go down to it, before going to my friend, John Hopper's,[10] where I am to make my headquarters, as usual — though the Neills,[11] from Belfast, have kindly invited me to stay with them. After the Woman's Rights meeting, I may go to Staten Island, and accept a renewed invitation from Mrs. Shaw,[12] and remain over Sunday.

Parker Pillsbury's daughter has been fearfully ill, but I believe she is now out of danger.

My own health is better, but I am daily affected by my spinal difficulty. Helen and the children are well. We all send loving regards to Mary Ann and yourself.

Ever yours,

Wm. Lloyd Garrison.

Transcript: Garrison Papers, Boston Public Library.

1. Mathew B. Brady (1823–1896) was the pioneer photographer, who had established a portrait studio in New York City in 1842 or 1843 and whose work was patronized by thousands. In 1849 he received the first gold medal awarded for daguerreotypes. He published his *Gallery of Illustrious Americans* in 1850, and in 1851 he received the prize medal for American daguerreotypes at the World's Fair in London, for a collection of forty-eight American portraits. After 1855, he abandoned the daguerreotype for the photograph. His photographs of the Civil War were justly famous.

2. The transcriber seems to have erred in spelling the name. Garrison's reference is probably to Albert Sands Southworth (b. March 12, 1811; d. March 3, 1894), who resided in Charlestown, Massachusetts, and was a photographer in Boston. (Samuel G. Webber, *A Genealogy of the Southworths* [*Southards*], Boston, 1905, p. 261.)

3. John Adams Whipple (b. Grafton, Massachusetts, September 10, 1822; fl. 1884), inventor, was the first to manufacture the chemicals used in the daguerreotype process. In time, he devoted all his attention to photography, wherein he made numerous improvements. He invented crayon daguerreotypes and daguerreotypes on glass, and also performed the first successful experiment in stellar photography. In 1884, he was living in Cambridge, Massachusetts, and publishing religious tracts in Boston. (George S. Mann, *Genealogy of the Descendants of Richard Mann of Scituate, Mass.*, Boston, 1884, p. 116.)

4. John Adams Jackson, the sculptor.

5. Dr. Lyman Beecher (1775–1863) was the eminent clergyman, former pastor of the Hanover Street Congregational Church in Boston, former president of Lane Theological Seminary, and father of Henry Ward Beecher and Harriet Beecher Stowe. (See *Letters*, II, 66.)

6. The Reverend George Washington Blagden was pastor of the Old South Church in Boston from 1836 to 1872, overseer of Harvard from 1854 to 1859, and husband of Wendell Phillips's sister, Miriam. (*Letters*, II, 110.)

7. Henry Wadsworth Longfellow, the poet.

8. Jennie Victoria Knight, the daughter of Holland Lorenzo Knight and Mary Ann (Mrs. Oliver) Johnson's sister, Jane Charlotte. Originally of Cambridge, Massachusetts, she married Dr. Henry Smith, editor of the *Homeopathic Review*, on April 7, 1859, and moved with him to Longwood, Pennsylvania. She died on May 30, 1865. Garrison, in a letter to Helen, dated June 8, 1865, writes that "at sundown . . . we committed to the grave the mortal remains of Victoria Smith. . . . You will recall the bright little girl whom we used to see daily at Cambridgeport, when we resided in her father's house at Cambridgeport. She grew up to be beautiful in person and in mind, and was greatly endeared to those who knew her intimately. A year ago, at this time, she acted as Clerk of the Meeting here; . . . in April she went with her husband to the island of Bermuda, (her difficulty being of a pulmonary nature,) when she remained till the 30th of May, on which day her spirit took its flight to the regions of bliss. She was a believer in Spiritualism, and occasionally a trance medium. . . ." (Garrison Papers, Boston Public Library; *National Anti-Slavery Standard*, April 15, 1859.)

9. The Twenty-fifth Annual Meeting of the American Anti-Slavery Society was to be held in New York City, on Tuesday and Wednesday, May 11 and 12.

10. John T. Hopper (b. Philadelphia, 1815; d. Milton, Ulster County, New York, July 18, 1864), son of Isaac T. Hopper, was a devoted abolitionist. He was

mobbed at Savannah, Georgia, in 1836, barely escaping with his life, when it was learned that he was Isaac Hopper's son. In 1836, too, he was admitted to the bar in New York, where he practiced law for many years. During the last twenty years of his life, he was an agent of the New England Life Insurance Company in New York. Although a Quaker, he supported the vigorous prosecution of the Civil War. (Obituary, *The New York Times*, July 21, 1864; Lydia M. Child, *Isaac T. Hopper: A True Life*, Boston, 1860, pp. 319, 322–327.)

11. Robert Neill (1804–1864), a watchmaker and jeweler, opened his own business in 1803. He married Margaret Riddle in 1828. They had two sons and a daughter: John (1829–1881), Henry James (1831–1891), and Isabella (1836–1898). I am indebted to Mr. J. W. Vitty, Librarian, Belfast Library and Society for Promoting Knowledge, who provided a photocopy of the Neill family tree, whence this information was gleaned. The Belfast *Telegraph*, April 12, 1950, printed a letter (undated) from Colin Johnston Robb, Longhall County, Armagh, which provides additional information, some of it slightly at variance with the family tree. I am also indebted to Mr. H. Russell, Local History Librarian, City of Belfast Public Libraries, for certain items of information.

12. Mrs. Sarah Blake Shaw.

216

TO HELEN E. GARRISON

New York, May 12, 1858.

Dear Wife:

Notwithstanding we had so much rain in Boston, I found the ride to this city (especially after leaving Hartford) as dusty as though there were not a drop of moisture in the universe, and, consequently, was covered with dust on my arrival, which I shook off, not exactly as a testimony against the city, but with a very considerate regard for my appearance. Francis Jackson, [Charles F.] Hovey, H. C. Wright, Miss Cabot,[1] Mrs. Follen and Charles,[2] Mr. May,[3] Remond, Sarah, and Miss Forten,[4] Mrs. [Caroline Wells Healey] Dall, &c. constituted our party. Of course, we had a very pleasant conversational time of it, though a party of our company, (Mrs. Follen, Miss Cabot, and Charles Follen,) were in another car from our own. I met young George Benson [5] at the depot, who is always prompt to meet me on such occasion, and he accompanied me to John Hopper's residence, where I received a most hearty welcome, of course. Rosalie [6] soon put the babe into my arms, and a fine little fellow [he] is, most certainly — just six weeks old to a day, though as bright as though he were double that age. I gave him lots of kisses and my benediction, which he took in excellent part. Rosa's nurse is to leave her to-day, so that the entire care of little Willie will devolve upon her; and how great such a care is, in the case of the first-born, you know by experience. I gave Rosa and John your congratulations, adding that you thought a baby girl to match, in due season, would be just the next best thing.

Yesterday we had our usual ill luck about the weather — it not only raining, but pouring, all the afternoon and evening. Nevertheless, our anniversary meeting in the forenoon was a large one, and every thing went off satisfactorily.[7] I made no speech,[8] but simply read my long series of resolutions,[9] which were listened to with deep interest, and elicited frequent applause. One of them, however, branding the revival generally as deceptive and spurious,[10] roused up all the serpents in the galleries, and hisses came thick and fast, accompanied by the strongest manifestations of approval. Those furious hisses indicated, in the most unmistakable manner, the exact truthfulness of the resolution. Remond made the opening speech, and was well received. He was followed by Phillips, who made, as usual, a telling speech. Miss Watkins [11] made the closing speech, and it produced an excellent impression.

At the time of adjournment, it rained so violently that I did not venture out (for did I not have "a bran new hat" to spoil?) even to get a lunch, and so remained in the hall without any thing to eat or drink until nearly 7 o'clock — occupying the interim in conversation with Dr. Furness, Mattie Griffith, Mrs. Bramhall, Lydia Mott, Susan B. Anthony, and many others, all kindly inquiring after you and the children. Catharine [Benson] was also present. She said that she had just had a letter from bro. George, dated at St. Louis. He was on his way to Lawrence, Kansas, and is probably there by this time. He had had several attacks of neuralgia, and had been a good deal exposed in travelling, having very unwisely left his overcoat at home, though Catharine strenuously urged him to take it with him. He went to Virginia, to do some business for a gentleman in this city, and succeeded in doing it satisfactorily, I believe, and will ultimately derive some pecuniary advantage from it. If he can see an opening in Kansas, he will doubtless locate himself there, taking Catharine and the boys with him.

Yesterday afternoon was devoted to business, and was not a public meeting. We got into an earnest discussion with three Covenanter ministers about some remarks made by Mr. Foss in regard to Christ and the Bible, and had a lively time of it. I do not believe we shall receive much aid from the Covenanters, after all; for though they are comparatively radical on the subject of slavery, I fear they think more of sect than of the slave.

In the evening, the hall was well filled, many being disappointed at the non-attendance of Theodore Parker — one man having walked seven miles to hear him. Edmund Quincy made the opening speech, but the audience at last grew impatient, and were not disposed to listen any longer. His forte is with the pen, not as a public speaker.

I followed him in an off-hand speech, which seemed to be relished throughout, and was followed briefly by Phillips.

To-day, the great conflict is to come off in the Tract Society,[12] and it will be an exciting time. I wish I could be present.

I am a little uncertain about the time of returning home, but think I shall stay over Sunday, as they are confidently expecting me at Staten Island. A father's love to Fanny and Franky.

Your loving husband,

Wm. Lloyd Garrison.

ALS: Garrison Papers, Boston Public Library.

1. Susan Copley Cabot (b. Boston, January 19, 1794; d. Brookline, Massachusetts, January 22, 1861) was the daughter of Samuel and Sally Cabot, and the sister of Eliza Follen. She was an occasional contributor to the *Liberty Bell*. She never married. (L. Vernon Briggs, *History and Genealogy of the Cabot Family, 1475–1927*, privately printed by Goodspeed's, Boston, 1927, I, 228.)

2. Charles Christopher Follen (b. 1830; d. 1872), the only child of Charles and Eliza Lee Follen. He graduated from Harvard in 1849. He was a fervent abolitionist, a member of the executive committee of the Massachusetts Anti-Slavery Society, and a warm friend of Garrison and his associates. He fought in a Massachusetts battalion during the Civil War. (*The Quinquennial Catalogue of the Officers and Graduates of Harvard University, 1636–1895*, Cambridge, 1895, p. 596; draft of a eulogy by Maria W. Chapman, Anti-Slavery Manuscripts, Boston Public Library.)

3. Samuel May, Jr.

4. Charlotte L. Forten (1837–1914), a Negro teacher and author, was the daughter of Robert and Mary Forten of Philadelphia. Her grandfather, James Forten, sailmaker and antislavery leader, was one of Garrison's principal backers in the early years of *The Liberator* and the American Anti-Slavery Society. In 1854, she went to Salem, Massachusetts, where she continued her education, while living at the home of Charles Lenox Remond. She graduated from the Higginson Grammar School in February 1855, and then completed a one-year course at the Salem State Normal School. She taught in the Epes Grammar School in Salem, from July 1856 to March 1858, the first Negro to teach white children in that school. Because of illness, she lived much of the next three years in Philadelphia. During the Civil War, she participated as a teacher in the Port Royal undertaking from 1862 to 1864. In 1878, she married Francis James Grimké, the new pastor of the Fifteenth Street Presbyterian Church in Washington, D.C., where she had been living and working since 1871. (*Notable American Women.*)

5. George W. Benson's son.

6. John Hopper's wife.

7. An account of the proceedings appeared in *The Liberator*, May 14, 21, 1858.

8. Garrison, president of the American Anti-Slavery Society, called the convention to order and presided.

9. For the text of the resolutions see *The Liberator*, May 14, 1858.

10. This resolution read as follows: "Resolved, that the 'revival of religion,' which has swept over the country with contagious rapidity during the last three months, is manifestly delusive and spurious, exceptional cases to the contrary notwithstanding; because it has expressly excluded the millions in bondage from all consideration — has multiplied its converts as readily at the South as at the North — has excited no opposition in the midst of universal, all-abounding corruption and profligacy — has received the sanction and cooperation of the most pro-slavery divines and journals in the land — has operated (as it was evidently

designed) to strengthen a Church which is 'the bulwark of slavery,' and to divert attention from the work of practical righteousness."

11. Frances Ellen Watkins (1825–1911), of Baltimore, Maryland, Negro author and lecturer, was the niece of the Reverend William Watkins, by whom she was raised and educated. Her earliest collection of poetry and prose, *Forest Leaves*, was published in 1845. Another volume of verse, *Poems on Miscellaneous Subjects*, appeared in 1854. The same year, she delivered her first antislavery lecture, "Education and the Elevation of the Colored Race," in New Bedford, Massachusetts. Its success led to her being engaged as a lecturer by the Maine Anti-Slavery Society for two years. She subsequently continued to lecture throughout much of the North. She married Fenton Harper in Cincinnati, in 1860, and lived with him on a farm near Columbus, Ohio, until his death in 1864, when she resumed her lecturing. She lived the last years of her life in Philadelphia. (*Notable American Women*.)

12. The reference is to the anniversary meeting of the American Tract Society, held in New York City. A small group within the society had planned to protest the society's policy of avoiding any statement or publication on slavery and to attempt to replace the society's executive board. However, the attempt failed. (See *The Liberator*, May 21, 1858.)

217

TO LOUISA LORING

14 Dix Place, May 24, 1858.
3 o'clock, P. M.

My dear Mrs. Loring:

My friend Mr. Jackson has just communicated to me the sad and startling intelligence of the death of your beloved husband, of whose illness I had not heard a syllable. O, how much more stunning, how utterly overwhelming will it be to you and your dear Anna,[1] — deepened in intensity by the distressing circumstance of your absence at the time in a distant city! What your feelings must be, I can only faintly imagine by my own. My heart is oppresively full, my eyes are swimming in tears, and I feel pressing upon me the weight of a great bereavement. I have a long list of cherished and honored friends; but they are nearest and dearest to me, who, at the earliest period of the long-protracted struggle for the liberation of a race, "peeled, meted out, and trodden under foot"[2] in our land, gave to that struggle their public countenance and earnest support, serenely confronting the most virulent opposition, and continuing steadfast and immovable, at whatever personal disadvantage; and who extended to me a friendly hand and an approving voice when I stood before the nation almost friendless and alone. Of these, your estimable husband was one, — your own benevolent spirit sweetly mingling with his, the twain being one. My indebtedness to him was large at that time, on the score of counsel and generous co-operation; and how much he did for the Anti-Slavery cause, during a period covering at least a quarter of a century, by his brave example, his unflinching testimony, his spotless life, and his pecuniary contributions, I need not state to you, who knew him better than any other being in the world.

I wish it were in my power to say anything that would help to bind up your lacerated heart. Alas! what are words, however well chosen, under such circumstances? Consolation can alone be found in the reflection, that what we call death is but a translation — a spiritual birth — one of the links in the chain of eternal progression — a part of the divine arrangement of Him "who doeth all things well"; that, in itself, it is neither an evil nor a mysterious dispensation of Providence; that with us all, the event is only a question of time, for we are all mortal; and that, in the sweep of ages, a few years more or less dwindle to an imperceptible point. I not only believe in immortality, but I as firmly believe that our departed loved ones and friends are around and with us, though unseen by mortal eyes, endeavoring to comfort and strengthen us in the hour of trial, and under every bereavement. The spirit of your husband is with you and Anna; he was never more near than now; your souls are still undivided — still one. May heavenly light be vouchsafed to you in the midst of earthly darkness, and angels minister unto you in your mortal agony!

My dear wife mingles her tears with yours and mine. Twice has our household been visited in a similar manner.[3] There are two vacancies in the family group that can never be filled. We therefore know how to weep with those who weep, and to participate in the sorrows of others.

Your afflicted and sympathizing friend,

Wm. Lloyd Garrison.

Mrs. Louisa Loring.

ALS: Schlesinger Library, Radcliffe College.

1. Anna Loring (b. November 10, 1830; d. 1896), Ellis and Louisa Loring's daughter. In 1863, she married Otto Dresel, a German pianist and composer. Lydia Maria Child dedicated *Fact and Fiction* (1846), a collection of stories about fallen women, to Anna Loring. She was vice-president of the Sanitary Commission in Boston during the Civil War and was also president of the Vincent Hospital in Boston. (Charles Henry Pope, *Loring Genealogy*, Cambridge, 1917, p. 256.)

2. Isaiah 18:2.

3. The Garrisons had lost two children.

2 1 8

TO FRANCIS JACKSON

14 Dix Place, May 25, 1858.

Dear Friend Jackson:

I know you will pardon me for raising the inquiry, whether our worthy friend, Mrs. Lucy N. Coleman,[1] of Rochester, N.Y., can be accommodated with a bed at your house *to-night*, as we happen to be full. She has just arrived from Springfield, and has some acquaintance in Roxbury, but hardly knows how to find them this evening. I presume you will be full after to-night, and perhaps it will be really inconvenient to entertain Mrs. C. to-night. If so, you will frankly say so, and we will try to arrange matters for her somehow at home.

Ever yours,

W. L. G.

ALS: Garrison Papers, Boston Public Library.

1. Mrs. Lucy Newhall Colman (she dropped the "e" in Coleman some time after her husband's death) (b. Sturbridge, Mass., July 26, 1817; d. January 18, 1906), teacher, abolitionist and participant in the woman's rights movement, married John Mabrey Davis at the age of eighteen, and resided in Boston until her husband's death six years later. She then married Luther N. Coleman, a railway engineer and musician, who was killed in a railroad accident in 1852. At the time of her husband's death, they were living in Rochester and had a daughter seven years old. After her husband's death, she taught at a school for black children in Rochester. She had already, some years since, become interested in the antislavery movement, woman's rights, and the abolition of corporal punishment in the schools. During the 1850's, she abandoned teaching for an appointment as antislavery lecturer, and served as agent for the American and Western Anti-Slavery Societies. Her "dearest" friend in Rochester was Amy Post. She was also a friend of Susan B. Anthony, with whom she participated in the woman's rights movement. After the beginning of the Civil War, she served as matron of the National Colored Orphan Asylum at Washington. After 1873, she made her home in Syracuse, New York. (Letter from Mary R. [Mrs. Paul T.] Shannon, Rochester Historical Society, Rochester, New York; Lucy Colman, *Reminiscences*, Buffalo, New York, 1891, *passim*.)

2 1 9

TO THEODORE PARKER

14 Dix Place, May 26. [1858]

Dear Mr. Parker:

I was so interrupted by company to a late hour last night, that I have found it impossible to look over your manuscript, though I tried to do my best. You say it is written so plain that he who runs may read it — "if he can." I can say, on an examination of it, that its chirography is such as to furnish a very strong inducement for any man to run who attempts to read it!

However, I trust that, by the aid of your good wife,[1] Miss Stephenson,[2] Wendell Phillips, Samuel May, Jr., Robert F. Wallcut, Winchell Yerrinton, and a few others, we shall be able to decipher it, so as to print it in the Liberator [3] without any serious blunders.

Your puzzled friend,

Wm. Lloyd Garrison.

Rev. Theodore Parker.

ALS: Garrison Papers, Boston Public Library. The year has been inserted by a hand other than Garrison's.

1. Lydia Cabot (b. Boston, September 12, 1813; d. there April 9, 1880), daughter of John Cabot of Newton, married Parker on April 20, 1837, (L. Vernon Briggs, *History and Genealogy of the Cabot Family, 1475–1927*, privately printed by Goodspeed's, Boston, 1927, II, 643).

2. Hannah E. Stevenson (b. *c.* 1807; d. 1887) moved into the Parkers' household soon after they had moved to Boston from West Roxbury in the late 1840's. (John White Chadwick, *Theodore Parker, Preacher and Reformer*, Boston and New York, 1900, pp. 292–293.) Henry Steele Commager writes of her that "she was a tart old lady, and some of Parker's friends were afraid of her, but she got along famously with Lydia [Parker's wife] and was devoted to Theodore, a little jealous of some of the other ladies who fluttered around him . . . she was secretary, companion, and housekeeper, all in one; she was indispensable" (*Theodore Parker, Yankee Crusader*, Boston, 1936, p. 106). For Garrison's opinion of her, see Letter 260, to Theodore Parker, January 15, 1859. Her obituary appeared in the *Boston Evening Transcript*, June 11, 1887.

3. The manuscript was the text of an address Parker had delivered at the New England Anti-Slavery Convention, in Boston, on the morning of May 26. It was printed in *The Liberator* in two installments, on June 4 and 11, 1858.

220

TO THE SIXTH YEARLY MEETING OF
PROGRESSIVE FRIENDS

BOSTON, May 28, 1858.

MY DEAR FRIEND: The recollection of what I saw, what I heard, what I enjoyed at your last annual meeting, makes my heart throb with such pleasurable emotions that I know not how to be absent from your approaching anniversary. But circumstances constrain me to remain at home, and I can only send you all my loving remembrances and fervent benediction.

As a matter of friendly accommodation, I have consented to act as a substitute for my friend Theodore Parker, in Music Hall, on Sunday next — not to fill his place, of course, for who but himself can do that? but to make it convenient for him to be with you. Of his rare culture, his scholarly proficiency, his mental force, his liberal mind, his philanthropic and progressive spirit, and his massive brain (in which a whole Alexandrian library of knowledge appears to be stored, not for mere ornament or selfish accumulation, but for constant use and circulation), I need say nothing. He is too widely known in Christendom to need an introduction in any part of it. He has been with you before, and you will deem it a high privilege to have him with you again.

I take it for granted that the noble testimonies borne at your last gathering will be substantially reiterated this year, with whatever emphasis and enlargement the times may seem to require. But let us remember that we live in deeds, not in words. Let us be careful to lay down no principle to violate it ourselves, or to wink at its violation in others. Moral consistency of action is, alas! very difficult to be found, and not very easy to attain; yet it remains eternally true that we cannot serve God and Mammon, nor embrace Christ and Belial, at the same time. Wherever duty points the way, there let us walk unfalteringly, nor dread the lions that may threaten to devour us. Let our song be, "God is our refuge and strength; a very present help in trouble. Therefore will not we fear, though the earth be removed, and though the mountains be carried into the midst of the sea." [1]

Yours, fraternally,

WM. LLOYD GARRISON.

Printed in the *National Anti-Slavery Standard*, June 12, 1858.
This letter was read at the Sixth Yearly Meeting of Progressive Friends, at Longwood, Chester County, Pennsylvania, which met from May 30 to June 2. Parker delivered four addresses there, two on each of the first two days of the meeting.

1. Psalms 46:1.

221

TO THEODORE PARKER

14 Dix Place, June 3, 1858.

My dear Mr. Parker:

I am greatly obliged to you for your kind note, — so characteristic of your catholic spirit in all matters pertaining to an honest and conscientious difference of opinion. — Be assured, if I had supposed you would have felt averse to a religious presentation to your people of my views on the subject of peace, I should not have done so. Be true to your own convictions, and I will try to be true to mine — holding the mind open to receive any new light that may be shed in any direction.

As to the pecuniary "consideration" enclosed in your note for my discourse, I return it with thankfulness. —

1. Because I never thought, and cannot think, of receiving a farthing on that score.

2. Because I informed your people that I stood in your place as an act of friendship, to enable you to dispense "the word" in a distant State; and, therefore, not as a matter of contract. And,

3. Because, on the score of favors, I am still very much your debtor, especially for your consoling services in times of affliction and bereavement by death.

"May grace, mercy and *peace*" be with you and yours, now and evermore!

Yours, with high regards,

Wm. Lloyd Garrison.

Rev. Theodore Parker.

ALS: Garrison Papers, Boston Public Library; also printed in *Life*, III, 474–475.

On May 30, Garrison had occupied Parker's pulpit, permitting the latter to speak at the meeting of the Progressive Friends in Pennsylvania. On June 3, Parker wrote Garrison the following letter (*Life*, III, 474):

"My Dear Mr. Garrison: I owe you many thanks for standing in my place and preaching the able discourse of last Sunday. I am glad, also, that you took that theme on which we probably differ most; for though I don't think with you thereon, I yet wish your views to be ably set forth before those who listen to me.

"Please accept the pecuniary *consideration*, also, with the hearty thanks of Yours faithfully,

Theodore Parker."

Garrison's letter of the same date was in reply to Parker's.

---

2 2 2

TO THEODORE PARKER

14 Dix Place,
June 17, 1858.

My dear Mr. Parker:

I return you the volume of the writings of James Nayler,[1] which I took the liberty to borrow from your library during your absence in Pennsylvania, — thanking you for the use of it.

I wish to renew to you the expression of my grateful acknowledgments for the handsome and valuable present of five volumes of the "Dictionary of Greek and Roman Biography and Mythology" to my son Wendell, who also appreciates it with the deepest gratitude. In this, you have most generously circumvented me, in regard to my Music Hall discourse, and, as a "non resistant", I readily submit — only, however, with this understanding, that your gift to Wendell is wholly gratuitous on your part.

My dear wife hardly feels reconciled to your taxing yourself so heavily, when you have so many expenses, and so many calls upon your benevolence; but the gift will be a lasting memorial to us all of your friendship, and will be carefully preserved by him to whom it was given, probably long after you and I shall have "put on immortality."

I am delighted to know that you are willing to say something in merited praise of that wonderful old man, Humboldt,[2] at our gathering at Framingham, on the 4th of July.[3] I hope nothing will occur to prevent your doing so; for it is not possible for any one to do it so well as yourself. We will have your tribute carefully reported, printed, and transmitted to that scientific prodigy and veteran philanthropist. Perhaps you will draw up a resolution, to be adopted by acclamation on the occasion.

Your much obliged friend,

Wm. Lloyd Garrison.

Rev. Theodore Parker.

ALS: Garrison Papers, Boston Public Library.

1. James Nayler (1618–1660), English Puritan, adopted Quakerism in 1651 and came to believe that he was the new incarnation of Christ. He was imprisoned in 1653 and 1655. In 1656, he was convicted of blasphemy, sentenced to be whipped, branded on the forehead with a "B" for blasphemer, had his tongue bored with a red-hot iron, and was imprisoned for two years. A collected edition of his *Tracts* appeared in 1716.

2. Friedrich Heinrich Alexander, Baron von Humboldt (1769–1859), German naturalist and traveler, initiated the era of scientific exploration with his expedition to Cuba, Central, and South America from 1799 to 1804, which was characterized by systematic observation. He is regarded as having laid the foundation of the sciences of physical geography and meteorology. His great work on natural science was *Cosmos* (5 volumes, 1845–1862).

3. This was a celebration sponsored by the Massachusetts Anti-Slavery Society on Monday, July 5 (not 4) at the Grove in Framingham. (*The Liberator*, July 2, 1858.) An account of the celebration appeared in *The Liberator*, July 9, 1858. Parker apparently did not speak, because of ill health, but *The Liberator* did print his "Tribute to Baron Von Humboldt" (July 9, 1858), which he was unable to deliver.

2 2 3

TO SAMUEL MAY, JR.

Boston, July 20, 1858.

My dear Mr. May:

I have received a second letter from our friend, Rev. N. R. Johnston, of Topsham, Vt., urging me to attend an Anti-Slavery Convention at West Randolph, on the 24th and 25th of August, whether [Wendell] Phillips can accompany me or not; and I have given him an affirmative answer, stating that I should urge you to be with me on that occasion. Will you do so? It will be very gratifying to me to have your company and co-operation.

After the Convention, I shall probably lecture in some three or four places in Vermont before my return home.

I have agreed to attend the anniversaries of the Pennsylvania and Ohio A. S. Societies in October next.

I must give up the idea of going to Brookfield [Massachusetts]. At present, I am suffering from my periodical brain attack, originating in the desperate fever I had in Ohio in 1847.

We have had a sick household, all of us receiving medical treatment — wife, Fanny, Wendell, Franky, and myself. Fanny is now at Lynn, but still troubled with a cough. Franky has also a cough, with a slow fever, and no appetite. Wendell is now convalescent, but he has had a severe throat attack, which prevented his being at the examination of his class last week at Cambridge. He had a special examination yesterday, which will be finished to-day. To-morrow, he will go to the summer retreat of Mr. and Mrs. Forbes,[1] (of Milton,) at the island of Naushon, beyond New Bedford, to spend two or three weeks.

Francis Jackson has purchased the house next to ours — 12 Dix Place — formerly occupied by Mr. Morton.[2] He intends renting it.

I yesterday had an interview with Helper,[3] the author of the Impending Crisis. He is evidently in earnest, and will not quail. I urged him to be with us at our Abington celebration on the 31st inst.,[4] and think he will do so.

Fortunately for us, we are to have the presence and testimony of the Rev. Mr. Bleby,[5] an intelligent and courageous missionary from Barbadoes, who has been 27 years in the West Indies — has been tarred and feathered, had his chapel torn down, &c. (in the days of slavery,) and can testify to the beneficent workings of emancipation. He will also go to Milford.[6]

Yours, truly,

W. L. Garrison.

ALS: Antislavery Manuscripts, Boston Public Library.

1. John Murray Forbes (1813–1898), a businessman active in public affairs, had accumulated a substantial fortune during several years in the Orient by the time he was twenty-four. Returning to Massachusetts, he continued to prosper in business during the ensuing decade, at the end of which he turned to railroad building and management in the West. In 1834, he married Sarah Hathaway of New Bedford, Massachusetts, with whom he had six children. From 1857, the island of Naushon at the entrance of Buzzard's Bay was their summer home, of which Forbes's biographer writes that "he made the place memorable by the simple yet generous hospitality that he exercised and the distinguished men and women who were his guests."

2. Joseph F. Morton is listed in the Boston *Directory*, intermittently, from 1843 to 1859, as a clerk. From 1861 to 1864, he is listed as being in the metals business, with a home in North Cambridge.

3. Hinton Rowan Helper (1829–1909) was the North Carolina-born author of *The Impending Crisis of the South*, published in 1857. The book was an attack on slavery as an economic evil, injurious to the interests of the nonslave-holding South. Helper was United States Consul at Buenos Aires from 1861 to 1867. Several of his books on the American Negro, published after the Civil War, were viciously racist.

4. The celebration of the anniversary of British West India Emancipation, under the auspices of the Massachusetts Anti-Slavery Society, at Abington, Massachusetts. (*The Liberator*, July 30, 1858.)

5. The Reverend Henry Bleby (1809–1882), according to *The Liberator* (July 30, 1858), "has been a resident missionary in Jamaica and Barbadoes for the last twenty-seven years." The text of his speech appeared in *The Liberator*, August 6, 1858, *The Standard* in a biographical note reported that he had been a missionary among the blacks in the West Indies "both before and since their emancipation. His object in coming to this country is to receive such contributions as the liberality of the friends of the Negro race may prompt them to bestow, to assist in the erection of schools, that the advantages of education may be more widely extended amongst the colored children of Barbadoes, where he now exercises his ministry. Mr. Bleby was one of the missionaries whose places of worship were destroyed by the opponents of Negro instruction during the severe struggle which preceded the abolition of slavery in the British Colonies, and he sustained indignities and outrages in his person and family similar to those which Southern intolerance inflicts upon the faithful friends and teachers of the slaves; and once, after being covered with tar, narrowly escaped burning to death." (July 24, 1858.)

Bleby was the author of several books, including *Death Struggles of Slavery*, London, 1853; *Scenes in the Caribbean Sea: Being Sketches from a Missionary's Notebook*, London, 1854; *Josiah, the Maimed Fugitive*, London, 1873; *A Missionary Father's Tale*, London, 1876; *Romance Without Fiction: Or, Sketches from the Portfolio of an Old Missionary*, London, 1872. (*National Union Catalogue, Pre-1956 Imprints*, London, 1969, vol. 61, p. 81.)

6. The West India Emancipation celebration at Milford, Massachusetts, was held on August 2, with both Garrison and Bleby, among others, present as speakers. (*The Liberator*, August 6, 1858.)

2 2 4

TO AARON M. POWELL

Boston, July 25, 1858.

My dear Powell:

I am made very sad by reading, in the last *Standard*, a notice of the great bereavement which your parents, your sister, and yourself have been called to experience, in the removal by death of the dear and noble boy [1] who made your household so bright and full of promise. In every such case, " 'tis the *survivor* dies." I take it for granted that the departed never have cause to lament their translation; nor would they again return to the earth, in the flesh, if they could; while I am persuaded that our beloved ones, thus removed from our sight, are drawn to us by magnetic affinity, and are more or less frequently by our side, sharing our sorrows and participating in our joys. To me this conviction is very strengthening.

I did not know your stricken brother, but I have no doubt he was a boy of uncommon promise, and that all that is said of him in the *Standard* was justly merited. How loving and promising was my own little boy, Charles Follen, and how suddenly he was taken from me! [2] Having had the same cup of bitterness put to my lips which you are now called upon to drink, I know how to sympathize with you all. Yet I am comforted by the reflection, that you need nothing from me to convince you that "it is well with the lad"; [3] that it is a natural event, and neither a dark nor mysterious dispensation; that what is seemingly your loss, will be a gain in the end; and that, while the heart may bleed and the tears of affection may fall, a sweet spirit of resignation should be dominant in the breast.

What is the state of your own health? Are you taking as much recreation, and making as little mental effort, as a due regard for your constitution demands? I know it is true, as Dr. Young says —

"That life is long which answers life's great end" [4] —

yet I would (if it may be so) have you live to venerable age, more for the sake of others than for your own sake — with reference to extended usefulness in opposing popular corruption, liberating the oppressed, and helping to shape the destiny of this vast empire, now stretching from ocean to ocean. I hope, therefore, that you are at present thinking a great deal more of sunshine, and air, and exercise, and diversion, than you are of books, of politics, or even of the anti-slavery cause. At least, knowing how susceptible you are to bronchial and lung difficulties, I trust you are making no efforts whatever at public speaking, but rather wisely remaining both quiet and dumb, so as to be full-toned and vigorous during our next fall and winter campaign.

We have had our share of sickness at home, during the last three months. My wife has been prostrated by a general congestion of her system — Fanny has been without appetite, and much debilitated by a nervous cough — Franky has had a slow gastric fever — Wendell has had a violent throat attack, of a glandular nature, so as to be compelled to leave Cambridge before his term expired — while I have been troubled with my annual difficulty about the brain, the result of my Western fever in 1847. Happily, we are all now convalescent, though not fully restored.

William (my second son) and I think of making a trip shortly, via Ghent, the Catskill mountains, and the Hudson river, to New York, as a matter of recreation; in which case, if convenient and agreeable, we should like to spend twenty-four or forty-eight hours with you, and in your vicinity — leaving Boston somewhere about the 10th of August, and completing our excursion in six or seven days, as after that I have engaged to go on a short lecturing tour to Vermont. Perhaps we may go to New York first, and then go up the Hudson to your place. You shall hear from me again about it.

I desire to be most kindly remembered to your parents and sister, proffering to you all my heart-felt sympathies, which are fully shared by my dear wife.

Yours, with the warmest regards,

Wm. Lloyd Garrison.

A. M. Powell.

ALS: Merrill Collection, Wichita State University.

1. Edward Powell, a younger brother of Aaron M. Powell, was slightly less than thirteen years old when he died at his father's home in Ghent, Columbia County, New York. He had been in ill health for several years and, as reported in the *Standard*, died of "catarrhal fever and dropsy on the brain." (The *Standard*, July 24, 1858.)

2. Charles Follen Garrison (b. 1842) had died in 1849.

3. II Kings 4:26, somewhat altered.

4. Edward Young (1683–1765), English poet, *Night Thoughts*, Night V.

225

TO WILLIAM LLOYD GARRISON, JR.

Boston, July 27, 1858.

My dear William:

In consequence of my engagement to go to Vermont on Monday, August 23d,[1] I find it will not be possible for me to take our contemplated trip at the time we agreed upon; for, in that case, we should not arrive home until Saturday night, or Sunday morning, Aug. 21st or 22d, which would allow me no time to make my arrangements to go to the Green Mountains. Hence, we must go earlier or later. I am to be at Fitchburg on Sunday, August 8th,[2] and could leave home with you on Thursday, Aug. 12th, for a week; or we could wait till about the 10th of Sept.

As I am to make an excursion to Vermont, which may combine a little recreation with some labor, I think, on the whole, you had better take your own time, and go without me in whatever direction you think best. Perhaps Ritchie [3] will consent to be your travelling companion; and as his father [4] is in the city of New York, I dare say he would like to go there, and so up the North River to the Catskill mountains, &c., &c. Or if you should go alone, I could give you a letter to Powell, at Ghent, so that you would have no difficulty on the way.

Your attached father,

Wm. Lloyd Garrison.

W. L. G., Jr.

ALS: Smith College Library.

1. Garrison was scheduled to speak at an antislavery convention at West Randolph on Tuesday and Wednesday, August 24 and 25.

2. Garrison was to speak in Fitchburg on Saturday and Sunday, August 7 and 8.

3. John Ritchie (d. Jackson, New Hampshire, July 11, 1919, aged eighty-two) graduated from Harvard in 1861 and was a great traveler throughout most of his life, traveling in the United States and Europe. During the Civil War, he was a member of the Quartermaster's Corps of the 54th Massachusetts Regiment. He was considered a Bostonian, living on Beacon Hill when not traveling. He was interested in astronomy and in the manufacturing of violins. In later years, he was on the executive committee of the Anti-Imperial League and was a member of the Boston Scientific Society and a fellow of the American Academy. He lived in Dresden, Germany, from 1895 to 1908. (Obituary, Boston *Evening Transcript,* July 12, 1919.)

4. Uriah Ritchie (d. Boston, October 11, 1865, aged sixty-six) came to the United States from Ireland in 1823 with his younger brother, John. The brothers engaged in business in Boston as masons and house-builders for about forty years. (*Fifth Report, Harvard College Class of 1861,* New York,, 1892, pp. 95–98; Florence Osgood Rand, *A Genealogy of the Rand Family in the United States,* New York, 1898, p. 77; obituary of John Ritchie, Boston *Evening Transcript,* December 8, 1883.) *The Liberator,* in an obituary on October 20, 1865, wrote that Ritchie "was one of the earliest and most uncompromising friends of the anti-slavery cause in Boston — a most industrious, enterprising and esteemed citizen — an independent and conscientious thinker — and that 'noblest work of God, an honest man'."

2 2 6

TO WENDELL PHILLIPS GARRISON

Boston, July 28, 1858.

My Dear Son:

Mr. [Charles F.] Hovey has just called in to inquire after your health, and wishes me to write to you, and say, that he and his son William [1] are going to make a tour to the White Mountains next week, and he would be glad of your company, and strongly hopes you will accompany them — he cheerfully paying all expenses, &c. William, he says, will want a companion in his rambles, and selects you as number 1, if you deem it best to go. They will start either on Wednesday or Thursday next, as may be most convenient for you. The overture on Mr. H's part is kind and generous. You are now, I doubt not, most happily situated, and may wish to remain where you are. Let me hear from you at once, as Mr. Hovey must get another companion for William, in case you conclude to remain at N[aushon]. I leave the matter entirely with you.

Your loving father,

W. L. G.

W. P. Garrison.

ALS: Smith College Library.

1. William Alfred Hovey (b. Boston, December 21, 1841; d. February 18, 1906) was educated in the public schools of Boston. After graduation in 1860, he spent nearly two years in Italy, Germany, and France, studying languages and culture. On his return, he joined the Sanitary Commission. After the Civil War, he worked for several years as an engineer and superintendent of coal mines in Pennsylvania. In the 1870's, he returned to Massachusetts, devoted himself to journalism, and, after one or two other ventures, edited the Boston *Evening Transcript* for six years. During the last twenty years of his life he was employed by the Bell Telephone Company. (*The Hovey Book*, Haverhill, Massachusetts, 1913, pp. 342–343.)

2 2 7

TO AARON M. POWELL

Boston, August 9, 1858.

My dear Powell:

I have been out of the city to attend some anti-slavery meetings, or I should have answered your letter (which I read with deep interest and sympathetic emotion) on Saturday.

Having received an urgent invitation from dear Lydia Mott to visit Albany on our tour, William and I have concluded to do so. Our programme is as follows: — Leave Boston on Thursday morning next for Albany; remain there till Saturday morning; then go to Ghent, and remain with you over Sunday; on Monday, go to Catskill, and (if practicable) get to New York that evening, or early the next day, and leave there for Boston Wednesday afternoon — a quick, and somewhat hurried trip.

It just occurs to me that this will leave too little time for William to see the city of New York. I therefore think we had better take the morning boat at Albany, on Saturday, for Catskill, (should the day prove pleasant,) and return that evening to Ghent, and so spend Sunday with you. Then go direct to New York on Monday morning.

We should be exceedingly happy to have your company at Catskill, on Saturday; but do not put yourself to any trouble or fatigue to be with us, as we shall be able to find our way to Ghent. Perhaps we may receive a line from you at Albany.

I write in the utmost haste, and can only beg to be sympathizingly remembered to all at home.

Your attached friend,

Wm. Lloyd Garrison.

A. M. Powell.

ALS: Merrill Collection of Garrison Papers, Wichita State University.

228

TO SAMUEL MAY, JR.

Boston, Aug. 11, 1858.

My dear Mr. May:

A line was received from you to-day, containing notices enclosed, &c. The paper is so crowded, every inch of it, that I could not find room even for the notice of our friend D. S. Whitney,[1] which you thought it might be well to republish, with additions. I was sorry not to have room for the sketch of Mr. Foss's remarks at Abington,[2] which you kindly sent, but it can be given next week. Heywood[3] wrote out his own speech entire. Some illustrations in it will be familiar to our friend Wendell Phillips; but it reads well as a whole. He does not wish to be reported again very soon.

We had a pleasant time at Fitchburg,[4] and received the hospitality of Mr. Snow,[5] who is about the only one in the place willing to be identified with us. We had a good meeting in Mr. Davis's Church [6] on Saturday evening, a small but attentive audience being present. On Sunday (third service) meeting was a large one, the great Town Hall being nearly filled — some eight or nine hundred persons as listeners — but *no collection*, owing to a blunder, so that I had to pay my own travelling expenses, and suppose Heywood was left in the same predicament. The blunder happened in this wise: — On going to the meeting, I said to Heywood, the collection to defray expenses must not be forgotten. Our friend Snow went to the meeting in advance of us. So, before I commenced, I beckoned to him to come to the platform, and said it would be necessary to have a collection to meet the expenses of the hall, &c, &c. He replied that those expenses had been already provided for, which left me to infer that it was deemed best not to take up a collection. After the meeting, he came up and expressed his regret that no collection had been taken up for the cause. I then told him that he had given me no encouragement to take one up, and therefore concluded some other arrangement had been made to raise the money. It seems he had assumed the expense of the hall, advertising, handbills, &c, and only meant that I need not be concerned on that score. For want of this explanation at the time, we lost perhaps a good collection, as so many people were present. I was very sorry, and so was Heywood.

I leave in the morning, with William, for Ghent, and a trip to the Catskill mountains — then down the Hudson to New York city, where we shall spend a couple of days — calculating to reach Boston on Thursday night, next week. Should you wish to write to me, a letter addressed to the care of Oliver Johnson will be in season, should it arrive any time during Wednesday.

None of the Petitions [7] have yet been sent out. The delay is a serious one, as no time ought to be lost.

Nell has gone West,[8] and nothing can be done about the affidavits desired by Mrs. Chapman.

Our friend Mr. Johnston, of Topsham, Vt., writes to me that he finds it very difficult to get a hearing for me, so strong is the prejudice against me in the various towns. As a specimen of the letters he is receiving, he sends me the one herewith enclosed. Please save it. He asks whether he shall go forward, neverthless, and incur the expense of halls, advertising, &c., &c, on account of our Society. I have not time to answer his letter; but I do not feel inclined to have any such expenses incurred at this time. I care very little about the State, and will not sue for a hearing, nor appear to be anxious to thrust myself upon it.

For your kindness to Fanny and Frank, accept our special thanks. Hurrah for the Atlantic cable! [9]

Truly yours,

W. L. Garrison.

ALS: Antislavery Manuscripts, Boston Public Library.

1. On August 6, 1858, *The Liberator* did print the following notice:

"Daniel S. Whitney, at present in Iowa, has been appointed a Lecturing and Collecting Agent of the American Anti-Slavery Society.

"He is expected to be travelling to Massachusetts, and subscriptions for the *National Anti-Slavery Standard* and *The Liberator* may be paid to him."

Daniel S. Whitney (b. Danvers, now Peabody, February 4, 1810; fl. Southboro, Massachusetts, 1889) was a reformer at an early age, taking the temperance pledge when he was twenty years old. In 1836, he was converted to abolition by a lecture by Samuel J. May, at Salem, Massachusetts. He was ordained an evangelist by the Massachusetts Association of Restorationists and occupied pulpits as a substitute for several years. He was connected with the Hopedale Community at Milford for eight years, until 1850. In 1853, he was chosen a delegate from Boylston, Massachusetts, to the state constitutional convention. Soon after, he moved to Southboro, Massachusetts. He helped fugitive slaves and was a Garrisonian abolitionist. During the last year of the Civil War, he worked on the Sanitary Commission. (D. Hamilton Hurd, *History of Worcester County, Mass.*, Philadelphia, 1889, I, 101.)

2. The celebration of West India Emancipation was held at Abington, Massachusetts, on July 31. Andrew T. Foss's remarks appeared in *The Liberator*, August 20, 1858.

3. *The Liberator*, August 6, 1858, in describing the West India Emancipation meeting at Milford, Massachusetts, on August 2, at which Heywood spoke, referred to him as "E. H. Heywood, of Hubbardston, (recently a graduate of Brown University, and a young man of brilliant promise,) whose uncompromising arraignment of parties and sects caused a most ludicrous fluttering among certain clerical gentlemen, but was loudly applauded by the audience." Heywood also spoke at Abington on July 31. His speech at that meeting appeared in *The Liberator*, August 13, 1858. Ezra Hervey Heywood (b. Princeton, Massachusetts, September 29, 1829; d. Boston, May 22, 1893) graduated from Brown University in 1856, became an agent of the Massachusetts Anti-Slavery Society, and was founder and editor of *The Word*. He wrote many essays on labor and the emancipation of women. (*Historical Catalogue of Brown University, 1764–1904*, Providence, Rhode Island, 1905, p. 243.)

4. Garrison and Heywood spoke at Fitchburg, Massachusetts, on Saturday and Sunday, August 7 and 8.

5. Benjamin Snow of Fitchburg.

6. The Reverend Elnathan Davis (b. 1807; d. 1881) became pastor of the Trinitarian Congregational Church in Fitchburg at about 1850 and remained there for more than fourteen years. Previously, he had been active in missionary work in northern Indiana and southern Michigan, had been a minister in Massachusetts, and had participated in the work of the American Peace Society. He subsequently continued his efforts in missionary work and for peace. (Obituary, Boston *Evening Transcript*, April 11, 1881.)

Davis's church in Fitchburg had been formed by seceders from the Calvinistic Congregational Church in 1843 who were antislavery in spirit and practice. It was a way-station on the Underground Railroad to Canada. The church disbanded after the Emancipation Proclamation. (William A. Emerson, *Fitchburg, Mass., Past and Present*, Fitchburg, 1887, p. 298.)

7. *The Liberator*, August 20, 1858, carried the following announcement:

"All who have received, or who may receive, copies of the Petition to the next Legislature, asking that the soil of Massachusetts may be made free, and that kidnapping shall be forever prohibited thereon, are urgently requested to give immediate attention to the circulation of the same in their respective towns, and so to organize the movement, that every man and every woman throughout each town of this Commonwealth shall have an opportunity to sign the same."

8. William Cooper Nell (1816–1874) of Boston was a Negro author, abolitionist, and friend of Garrison. In May 1851, he published a pamphlet on *Services of Colored Americans in the Wars of 1776 and 1812*. In 1855, there appeared his book, *The Colored Patriots of the American Revolution*, with an introduction by Harriet Beecher Stowe. He was appointed a clerk in the post office in Boston in 1861, thus becoming "the first colored man to hold a post under the federal government." He played a leading part in eliminating Negro segregation in the public schools in Boston in 1855. (See Louis Ruchames, "Race and Education in Massachusetts," *Negro History Bulletin*, December 1949, pp. 53–58, 71.)

9. The Atlantic Cable was completed and messages relayed through it in August 1858. The announcement of the successful laying of the cable was made on August 5. (See *The Liberator*, August 13, 1858.) However, it soon broke down. The first real success was in 1866.

---

2 2 9

TO WENDELL PHILLIPS GARRISON

[Boston, August 20, 1858.]

Dear Wendell — If you can do so, without too great a sacrifice in regard to time, I wish you would accept Mrs. Gibbons's [1] kind invitation, even if only for 24 or 36 hours. I tried hard to see her, with William, when we were in New York, but was baffled by circumstances, much to my regret. Enclosed, I send you $2.00, to pay for washing, &c. Should you need more before your return, let me know, and the amount needed shall be forwarded.

Give my kindest regards to Capt. De Peyster [2] and family, whose kindness we shall long remember.

Lovingly yours,

Father.

P. S. Oliver Johnson will tell you how to get to Mrs. Gibbons's. Mr. Gay ditto.

ALS: In possession of Walter M. Merrill.

Garrison's note is written at the end of a letter from Helen Garrison to Wendell Phillips Garrison dated August 20, 1858.

1. Abigail Hopper Gibbons (1801–1893) was the daughter of the veteran antislavery Quaker Isaac Tatem Hopper and Sarah Hopper. When only twenty, she established a day school for Quaker children in Philadelphia and maintained it for almost ten years. Abigail moved to New York in 1830, a year after her father had moved there with his second wife, Abigail's mother having died in 1822. In 1833, she married James S. Gibbons, who was more than eight years her junior,

a Philadelphia dry goods merchant, banker, and fervent antislavery man. After two years in Philadelphia, they made their home in New York City. She became active in the antislavery movement in New York, in temperance, opposition to capital punishment, the rehabilitation of prisoners and help for the poor. When, in 1841, and again in 1842, the New York Monthly Meeting of Friends (Hicksite) disowned her father and husband because of their abolitionist activities, she resigned from the society. (*Notable American Women.*)

2. Captain Frederick Augustus De Peyster (b. *c.* 1790–92; d. before 1877) was commander of a packet line from New York to Liverpool until 1845, when he retired and became governor of Sailor's Snug Harbor at Staten Island. His second daughter, Justine Watts De Peyster, 1820–1891, married Charles F. Hovey, the abolitionist, in 1837. Helen Garrison's letter, to which W. L. Garrison's note is appended, mentions as Wendell Garrison's friend, William Hovey, the son of Justine and Charles F. Hovey and grandson of Captain Frederick A. De Peyster. The letter is addressed to Staten Island, where Wendell was staying.

The reader should not confuse Captain Frederick A. De Peyster with his brother, Captain James Ferguson De Peyster (1794–1874), who also lived in New York, where he was prominent in business, social, and political affairs. (Waldron Phoenix Belknap, Jr., *The De Peyster Genealogy*, Boston, 1956, p. 96; Frank Allaben, *John Watts De Peyster*, New York, 1908, I, 22, 23, 186.)

230

TO HELEN E. GARRISON

West Randolph,[1] Aug. 26, 1858.

Dear Wife:

I arrived in this village on Monday, at 3, P.M., having intersected our friend, Mr. May,[2] at Nashua [New Hampshire], and enjoying his company the remainder of the long ride. We were joined on the way by the Rev. N. R. Johnston, our Covenanter friend, who has exerted himself so assiduously to get up the present series of anti-slavery meetings in the State. I found at the depot, a young lad waiting for me, to carry me in a wagon some four miles to the home of Benjamin W. Dyer,[3] an old anti-slavery friend, and a free and independent thinker on all subjects, especially pertaining to reform. He was absent from home on my arrival, but got back before bedtime, and gave me a very cordial welcome. He has one of the finest farms in this region, and owns a great number of sheep and cattle. I find much prejudice against him, on account of his radical views, prevailing here, but his character is without blemish, and he is the President of the Temperance Society. His wife was formerly as radical as himself, I am told, but with her the pendulum has swung to the other extreme, and she now seems to be quite averse to all reformers.

Our meetings commenced on Tuesday forenoon,[4] and ended last evening. We could not obtain any meeting-house in the place, so "anti-Garrisonian" are the churches here, and so we had to go into a hall connected with the tavern, used for dancing and other purposes. The seats were rough boards, which made it somewhat annoying to the ladies with their hoops and crinolines, but the hall was tolerably spacious, and answered very well, though at times uncomfortably crowded. Persons were present from various towns in the region round about, drawn together from various motives, that of curiosity, in regard to myself, being dominant. Our discussions covered the whole ground – the principal speakers being Mr. Pillsbury, Mr. May, Mr. Johnston, and myself. The type of anti-slavery, in this State, being almost wholly Republican, a good deal of uneasiness is felt by the leaders of the party lest we shall damage it; and we all did our best to that end, and I trust to some purpose. No one appeared in defence of the party, except an old Baptist clergyman, of Braintree, by the name of Baldwin, who exhibited a very good spirit, but was very easily disposed of.[5] Throughout the meetings, the audience behaved with great propriety, except at the closing meeting, last evening, when a few disorderly spirits at the door tried to make some confusion, but their success was small. Mr. Pillsbury ploughs deeper than any of us, or else there is something in his manner of expressing himself that repels many from him. My own remarks were generally received with favor, and I am assured, on all hands, that my visit to Vermont will produce a most favorable impression, and remove much unfounded prejudice. I trust, for the sake of that cause which is so dear to my heart, that this may prove true; though I have no doubt that both pulpit and press will do their worst to misrepresent and caricature my views.

I have found no one here to proffer me any hospitality, and so have had to ride, after each evening meeting, some three or four miles, to a neighboring village, with an antislavery friend, in order to find lodging. In fact, though I have dated this letter "West Randolph," I am writing it in Braintree, at the home of James Hutchinson,[6] a young married man, of more than common intelligence and energy, with whom Miss Holley and Miss Putnam tarried while here, and who, though an earnest Republican, is a subscriber to the Liberator, and an efficient anti-slavery laborer. I think he will be a Disunionist ultimately — just as soon as he understands the question in all its bearings.

We have had the loveliest weather possible since we left home — cool enough for a fire, and for blankets at night — a state of the atmosphere that would suit you exactly. The Green Mountains are dressed in their greenest attire, and present every phase of beauty and grandeur. This is a singularly picturesque and beautiful region, where "only man is vile." [7] I wish you were here to enjoy it.

This afternoon, we shall take the cars — some 25 miles — to Montpelier, the capital of the State, where we are to hold two meetings to-morrow.[8] The papers there are all hostile to us, and will be sure to abuse us; nevertheless, truth is stronger than all the powers of darkness, and we fear nothing.

Have Fanny and Franky yet got home? I have not seen them so long, that I feel a deep sense of bereavement, and long to embrace them, almost as though they had been lost, but were at last found.

Tell Wendell not to sit too long at the desk, but to take all the exercise he can before he goes over to Cambridge.

Should you write to me, send your letter to the care of Rev. N. R. Johnston, Topsham, Vt., unless you have something important that ought to reach me sooner.

Your loving husband,

Wm. Lloyd Garrison.

(☞ Don't forget the cat and kitten.)

ALS: Garrison Papers, Boston Public Library.

1. Vermont. *The Liberator*, September 10, 1858, carried Garrison's report of his visit to Vermont. An account of the convention at West Randolph appeared in *The Liberator*, September 3, 1858.

2. Samuel May, Jr.

3. Benjamin W. Dyer of Randolph, Vermont, was a member of the resolutions and nominating committees of the antislavery convention at West Randolph (*The Liberator*, September 3, 1858). Born in Vermont, he was a farmer and was forty-two years old in 1850. (Reidun D. Nuquist, Assistant Librarian, Vermont Historical Society, letter dated September 14, 1972.)

4. August 24.

5. *The Liberator*'s account of the meeting carried the following report of Baldwin: "Rev. Mr. Baldwin was called upon to speak. He said he had not expected to speak. He had long heard of some of the speakers here, especially of Mr. Garrison. He had never seen Mr. G. until yesterday; he had heard him with pleasure, and could say a hearty *Amen* to nearly all that he said; a majority of his speech he endorsed in full; his arguments they could not gainsay. I have, said Mr. B., regarded myself for a long time as an abolitionist, and I should like to tell you just where I stand. I have long been connected with the Baptist Church, and see no necessity of leaving it. Should a slaveholding Baptist, D. D. or otherwise, come to my church, I would not ask him to my pulpit, nor to sit with me in the desk, — I would not. The press is a great lever, and Mr. Garrison is using it powerfully. The ballot box is another lever, which many are using well. I belong to the Republican party, and I believe that, had it not been for the Republican party, Kansas would have been admitted as a slave State. Mr. B. spoke at length and approvingly of the course of the Republicans in Congress."

Mr. Baldwin has not been further identified.

6. James Hutchinson (b. Randolph, Vermont, January 1, 1826; fl. 1903) taught school for three years and then settled as a farmer on his ancestral homestead in Braintree, Vermont, where he remained until 1869, when he moved with his family to West Randolph. He was an early supporter of the Republican party and active in the antislavery movement. He was subsequently an associate judge of the county, state senator, county commissioner, and postmaster at West Randolph. (Hiram Carlton, *Genealogical and Family History of the State of Vermont*, New York and Chicago, 1903, II, 39–40.)

7. Reginald Heber (1783–1826), English bishop, "From Greenland's Icy Mountains," a hymn.

8. Garrison's schedule of speeches was listed in *The Liberator*, August 27, 1858, as follows:

At Montpelier,	Friday,	August 27
West Brookfield,	Sunday,	" 29
Topsham,	Monday,	" 30
St. Johnsbury,	Wednesday,	September 1
McIndoes Falls,	Thursday,	" 2
Bradford,	Friday,	" 3

231

TO HELEN E. GARRISON

Montpelier, August 28, 1858.

Dear Wife:

This is the capital of the State, and a very pretty place it is, of some three or four thousand inhabitants, lying in one of the handsomest valleys in the State, and surrounded by the loftiest hills, and in the distance by a circular chain of mountains, making the prospect sublime and beautiful indeed. On our arrival here on Thursday afternoon, we found no one to welcome us, except Mr. Claflin,[1] a mechanic, who is at work on the new State House, and who belongs to Northfield. We had no alternative, therefore, but to go to Burnham's hotel. After disposing of our luggage, we ascended a high hill just before sunset, and enjoyed one of the finest views we ever beheld. One of the distant mountains is called "The Camel's Hump," and looks very much like it. A range lying toward the North looked so much like the Catskill mountains as to create the illusion, for a moment, that I was actually gazing upon them. The whole region here is truly romantic and grand. The spirit of Liberty ought to be found here, "to the manor born," [2] but, alas! appearances are often deceitful.

There is a small meeting-house in the town, called the Free Church, which we were enabled to procure for our meetings, at a cost of five dollars, being unoccupied at present. All the other churches were, of course, inaccessible. We did not anticipate a warm reception on coming to Montpelier, as it is the head-quarters of political demagogueism, and we have not been disappointed. Our first meeting, yesterday afternoon, was thinly attended, the most of the audience being those who had come from a distance, and only two females being present. Mr. May made an excellent speech. As I am every where in this State assailed on account of my religious views, I took occasion to sift the charges of "infidelity," "anti-Bible," "anti-Church," "anti-Sabbath," &c. &c., and made clean work of it. There were two Methodist ministers, and also one Episcopal, present. We invited the freest interrogation and discussion, but no one had any objection to propound. A very favorable impression appeared to be made. Last evening we held another meeting, which was much better attended, though there were not more than half a dozen women present. We had lawyers, ministers, editors, and judges present, and I went into Disunionism with all my "soul, mind and strength," [3] and, on concluding, was most warmly applauded! Our collection amounted to nearly seven dollars, and considering that not a soul in the audience pretended to be a "Garrisonian" abolitionist, and that we gave no quarters to Church or State, to priests or politicians, we thought it was doing pretty well. I trust our coming here will not have been wholly in vain.

To-day, (Saturday,) we leave for West Brookfield, via Northfield — ten miles by rail-road, ten miles by land-carriage, "uphill and downhill." It has rained hard all night, and is still raining, so that we shall be sure to have no rain, though we may get a little wet. To-morrow we hold two meetings at West Brookfield, and, should the weather prove fair, we expect to have a good gathering.

I wrote a few lines to you at West Randolph, and hope to hear from you before I get home. I am somewhat weary, not having had any sleep for two nights past, owing to lying upon a feather bed.

I shall be glad when I get through, as "there is no place like home." A father's love to such of the children as are at home, and my kind regards to Mary-Ann.

Yours, truly, ever,

Wm. Lloyd Garrison.

ALS: Garrison Papers, Boston Public Library.

1. William Henry Harrison Claflin (1815–1895), of Northfield, was listed as a carpenter, contractor, builder, in the *Business Directory of Washington County, Vermont* (Syracuse, N.Y., 1889). (Charles Henry Wight, *Genealogy of the Claflin Family*, New York, n.d., p. 149.)
2. "To the manner born," Shakespeare, *Hamlet*, I, iv, 15.
3. A variation of Deuteronomy 6:5.

232

TO STEPHEN S. AND ABBY K. FOSTER

Boston, Sept. 7, 1858.

My Dear Friends:

I am glad that my friend William Robson [1] is to receive a welcome at your hands, under your roof, as he is in all respects worthy — being an uncompromising abolitionist, a vigorous and independent thinker, and a very conscientious and deeply religious man, strongly inclined to Swedenborgianism theologically, though by education a Unitarian. He was the friend of Henry C. Wright and Parker Pillsbury when they were in England. As postmaster at Warrington, he occupies a highly respectable and influential position at home; and I doubt not that his visit to this country will furnish him with the materials to aid our cause quite efficiently on his return home. He is anxious to make the acquaintance of the most noted abolitionists, so that he may be able to speak of them intelligently on his return. You will find him an honest, sincere, outspoken man.

I have just returned from my visit to Vermont, having enjoyed the trip exceedingly, attended eighteen meetings in twelve days, and spoken at every one of them, in company with our friend Mr. May.[2] We hope something has been done to "help the cause along."

A thousand thanks for your kind and generous entertainment of Fanny and Franky, who have returned home greatly improved in their looks and health. We hope to find some opportunity to reciprocate your kindness.

It gives us joy to hear that dear Alla's health is gaining steadily. May her shadow never be less, but a great deal more, in womanly expansion!

I am writing "on time," and can add no more, except that wife sends her kindest regards and warmest acknowledgments to you both.

Ever truly yours,

Wm. Lloyd Garrison.

S. S. and A. K. Foster.

ALS: Kelley-Foster Collection, Worcester Historical Society.

1. William Robson (b. Warrington, England, *ca.* 1805; fl. Lymm, 1892), the youngest son of Robert and Margaret Robson of Warrington, was postmaster at Warrington in the 1840's and 1850's and a member of the Warrington Anti-Slavery Society as well as of the local temperance and bible societies. In November 1858, after his return from the United States, he gave a lecture to the Warrington Mechanics Institution on his "Travels in America." In 1859, he helped to arrange a series of lectures by Sarah P. Remond on American Slavery. Following these lectures, the Warrington Anti-Slavery Society was formed, with Mrs. Robson as a co-treasurer and William Robson as a founding member. (I am indebted for this information to George A. Carter, Chief Librarian, Municipal Library, County Borough of Warrington, letter dated September 28, 1972.) *The Liberator* of September 10, 1858 printed a letter from Robson under the title "Thoughts of a Stranger on the Church in the United States."

In August 1877, Garrison visited Robson at Lymm (near Warrington), England, where Robson tendered him a banquet. (*Life*, IV, 284.)

2. Samuel May, Jr.

2 3 3

TO J. MILLER McKIM

Boston, Sept. 11, 1858.

My Dear McKim:

Yours of the 4th is received. The time you designate for holding the anniversary of your State [1] A. S. Society, Oct. 6th, 7th and 8th, will suit me very well; and I hope nothing will interpose to prevent my being with you on that occasion. I hear nothing, as yet, from our Ohio friends, but presume they will appoint their anniversary on the subsequent week — say on Friday, Saturday and Sunday, 15th, 16th, and 17th, as I presume they will wish to include Sunday as usual.

It would give me great pleasure to spend Sunday, the 10th, either at Longwood, or with our friend Thomas Whitson. If there could be a meeting appointed for me at Pittsburg, on my way to Salem,[2] — say on Tuesday evening, 19th Oct., — I should like to lecture in that place on the subject of slavery; but I do not know any persons in P., and cannot, therefore, solicit the necessary co-operation. It is many years since I addressed an audience in that city, and then it was composed mostly of colored persons.

My recent trip to Vermont, with Mr. May, was very pleasant, and, as far as could be judged, highly successful. It is a region full of marvellous beauty and wild romance. I returned with improved health, though I made eighteen long speeches in the course of twelve days. No one appeared to contest our doctrine of disunionism, or to defend the Church from our strongest accusations.

How much pleasure it will give me to see my dear Pennsylvania friends again face to face! You know that I visit no other part of the country with quite so much pleasure as your own. There is something about progressive Quakerism for which I feel a special attachment.

I hear that the health of James and Lucretia Mott continues excellent. May their days on the earth be very long! And so of you and yours.

Wife has had an interesting letter from our dear and cherished friend Mary Grew, who belongs to the household of *our* saints, and to which she will try to reply soon.

Your attached friend,

Wm. Lloyd Garrison.

J. M. McKim.

ALS: Garrison Papers, Boston Public Library.

1. Pennsylvania.
2. Ohio.

2 3 4

TO J. MILLER McKIM

Boston, Sept. 25, 1858.

My dear McKim:

I lose no time in replying to your letter, just received.

I do not think it worth while for me to attempt giving an anti-slavery address in Philadelphia. I shall not arrive in your city till Tuesday afternoon, Oct. 5th, when I shall make my way directly to the Anti-Slavery office, and will then go out to your residence, or that of James and Lucretia Mott, and spend the night, if thought best by you. Wednesday morning we must be off for Westchester.

At the request of Thomas Whitson, I have agreed to go to Christiana immediately after the close of your anniversary, and give a lecture on Sunday, Oct. 10th, at Bart,[1] on my way to Ohio. If arrangements could be made for me satisfactorily, I should like to speak at Harrisburg and Pittsburg *en route.* I could also speak at one or two other places, perhaps, in the State, if the meetings were arranged consecutively, so as to lose no time. I must be in Salem, Ohio, as early as Oct. 15th — Friday.

I feel very happy at the thought of so soon meeting you and my other dear Pennsylvania friends, face to face.

Plan for me as you may think best, and I will try to act in conformity therewith.

With warm regards to your wife, and all "the household of faith," I remain,

Yours, faithfully,

Wm. Lloyd Garrison.

J. Miller McKim.

ALS: Garrison Papers, Boston Public Library.

1. A post hamlet of Lancaster County, Pennsylvania, about fifty miles west of Philadelphia.

---

2 3 5

TO WILLIAM H. FISH

Boston, Sept. 30, 1858.

My Dear Friend:

I owe you ten thousand thanks for the many kind and urgent overtures you have made to me, directly and indirectly, from time to time, to visit Cortland — and twice ten thousand apologies for not having answered all your letters seriatim. Be assured, I have felt the strongest desire to comply with your solicitations, but circumstances have conspired to rend this impracticable. In a letter to Mr. May, recently received, you again raise the inquiry whether it will not be possible for me to lecture in your village on my return home from Ohio. It gives me great pleasure to answer in the affirmative. Leaving Rochester on Saturday morning, Oct. 23d, for Cortland, I hope to be with you that day, and to spend Sunday, the 24th, with you — speaking three times on that day, if desired, on anti-slavery, peace, and religious freedom. Saturday evening, if thought best, we might have a social gathering for conversation. Or, if preferred, I would lecture on slavery that evening, and also again on Sunday evening — speaking on other topics during the day. I do not know how my voice will hold out, or in what condition I may be on my return from Ohio; and this makes me hesitate about promising to give four consecutive lectures in Cortland. However, consider me in your hands. I will try to comply with the arrangements you may deem it best to make. On Monday, 25th, I must go to Syracuse, on my way home.

Please write to me at Salem, Ohio, (care of Marius R. Robinson,) and let me know whether it will be agreeable to you to have me come at the time specified.

After the many lectures and addresses you have had on slavery in C., I can present nothing new or specially interesting; but if the people see that I have neither hoofs nor horns, perhaps some prejudices may be removed, and the cause of the oppressed thereby advanced.

You see, therefore, that I avail myself of the first convenient opportunity to visit your place; and I shall hope to find you and Mrs. Fish in the enjoyment of good health.

My wife sends her warm regards to you both. If George were here, he would assuredly do the same thing. William is in the Leighton bank, at Lynn, and Wendell is at Harvard. Fanny and Frank are the only children at home. All well.

Your attached friend,

Wm. Lloyd Garrison.

Wm. H. Fish.

ALS: Villard Papers, Harvard College Library.

The Reverend William H. Fish had come from Hopedale, Massachusetts, to central New York, the area in which Cortland is located, in 1855.

2 3 6

TO HELEN E. GARRISON

Philadelphia, Oct. 6, 1858.

Dear Wife:

On the eve of starting for West Chester,[1] I seize [my] pencil to announce my safe arrival here; and to [say] that, on arriving at the depot in New York, I found [young] George Benson waiting, as usual, to greet me, and [ta]ke me home to Grand Street. In the same train came Mr. Eldridge,[2] wife, and four daughters, on their way to Lawrence, Kansas, all destined to George's residence. It was a sudden and complete "Kansas invasion," but George and Catherine took every thing quietly, as though they had the Revere House[3] in which to accommodate any number of visitors. I found them all well, except Mary, who had sprained her ankle by stepping off as you did at Mr. Hovey's door, supposing she was on the pavement. Dr. Rotton and Anne were present, and we all had a fine set down together. Seeing that to find beds for so many would be impracticable, I went up after tea, and spent the evening and night at the Gibbonses — found them all at home, and all well — and had a warm reception. Mrs. Sedgwick,[4] the famous school teacher of Lenox, was also there, and a very interesting woman she is.

Oliver Johnson was coming on with me, but could not do so, in consequence of a violent diarrhoea. In his stead, we have the Rev. Mr. Bleby, to our surprise and gratification.

Last evening, I was at Miller McK[im's,] where I spent the night, at Germantown. W[e had] a large circle of friends present — James & [Lu]cretia Mott, Edw. M. Davis and wife,[5] Ab[by] Kimber, Sarah Pugh, and many others — a[ll] asking about you and the children, and a[ll] delighted to look at your daguerreotypes. [We] had a very pleasant interview.

My time is up. Love and kisses for the children. Regards to Mary Ann.

Your loving husband,

W. L. G.

ALS: Garrison Papers, Boston Public Library.
    A tear in the page renders part of the letter illegible.

1. Pennsylvania. For Garrison's account of his trip to New York, Pennsylvania and Ohio see his letter to *The Liberator* dated Salem, (Ohio), October 15, 1858.
    2. Shalor Winchell Eldridge (1816–1899), a native of Springfield, Massachusetts, engaged in business as a railroad contractor at Southampton, Massachusetts. He married Mary Norton in 1839. In 1855, he began to manage and later bought the Gillis House in Kansas City, Missouri, which was originally the headquarters

of the New England Emigrant Aid Company for their emigrants to Kansas. In 1856 he leased the Free State Hotel in Lawrence, Kansas, which was burnt by a pro-slavery posse in May 1856, and was a factor in provoking the John Brown killings at Pottawatomie. He was a Free-Stater and a Republican party leader in Kansas. He was a quartermaster and, subsequently, an army paymaster during the Civil War. After the war he was a building contractor and in the 1870's engaged in mining in Colorado and Arkansas. His first wife died in 1869. Eldridge had three brothers, James M., Edward S., and Thomas B., all of whom were involved in the early history of Kansas. His four daughters were Mary S., Alice M., Evangeline L., and Josephine P. (Letter dated September 12, 1972, from Nyle Miller, Executive Director, Kansas State Historical Society, Topeka, Kansas.)

3. The Revere House, in Revere, Massachusetts, was built in 1845 as the Neptune House, by Cornelius Ellis. After being burnt, it was remodeled and called the Revere House. (Benjamin Shurtleff, *The History of the Town of Revere*, Boston, 1937, pp. 312, 335.)

4. Catherine (also Catharine) Maria Sedgwick (b. Stockbridge, Massachusetts, 1789; d. near Roxbury, Massachusetts, 1867), author and educator, undertook the management of a private school for young ladies on her father's death in 1813 and continued it for fifty years. She wrote novels, biographies, and books of moral uplift.

5. Edward M. Davis married Maria, a daughter of James and Lucretia Mott, in 1836. In 1850, the Davises and Thomas Mott, brother of Maria, and his family, bought a farm several miles from Philadelphia and moved there with their families. Davis was an abolitionist and a nonresistant. (See *Letters*, II, 334.)

---

2 3 7

TO HELEN E. GARRISON

Christiana, Oct. 9, 1858.

Dear Wife:

I pencilled a few hurried lines to you at Philadelphia, but had not time to put it into the mail before leaving the city, and so dropped it into the post office at West Chester.

Our meetings at West Chester [1] were not quite so well attended as usual, but, as the "Friends" are apt to say, it was a "strengthening" occasion, and one of "great enlargement" of spirit. We were disappointed in not having Dr. Furness with us; and there was no speaker from abroad besides myself, except Mr. Bleby, whose narrative of the workings of West India Emancipation, though previously read by many present as reported in the Standard and Liberator, was listened to with thrilling interest. He remained throughout the meetings, excepting the last, and seemed to be highly gratified. It was an assembly perfectly unique to him, so almost entirely made up of Quaker materials, of the most "progressive" stamp. I did not have much speaking to do; for there is much more disposition for general discussion at this anniversary than at ours. Besides, Quakers are very slow and methodical in all that they do, and consume three fold more time in transacting their business than we do. There was great unity of sentiment, and the resolutions that I presented,[2] written in my usual "strong" style, were unanimously adopted, except one, relating to the Republican party, there being two negative votes. Lucretia Mott and Mary Grew made excellent speeches; so did McKim, Thomas Whitson, Henry Grew, Joseph A. Dugdale, and Benj. Collier.[3] At the close, it was declared to have proved their very best anniversary; though I think they have had others not less so. The last impressions are always the most vivid.

Multitudinous inquiries were made after you and the children, all regretting that you were not with me, and all desiring to be affectionately remembered to you. The best thing I could do was to let them see your daguerreotype, and those of the children; and many eagerly examined them who had never seen you or any of the family.

I stopped at our friend Simon Barnard,[4] with Mr. Bleby, each of us having a good room and an excellent bed, and finding the most cordial hospitality. The Longwood friends were particular in their inquiries after you and the family. Our dear friends the Coxes were as hearty as ever, and I have agreed with Hannah to be her beau to Boston next year, if nothing happens to prevent, and to take her husband John along with us, if he will come.

J.A. Dugdale's mother is in Indiana.

Bayard Taylor's [5] father and mother were at our meeting. Bayard is expected home next week from his foreign tour, bringing his wife and babe with him.

Our meeting at West Chester closed yesterday at 1 o'clock. At 3, P. M. I took the same train in which our Philadelphia friends left, got out at the Paoli station, nine miles below, then took the cars for Christiana, and arrived here at early tea time, and am now under the roof of my quaint and excellent friend Thomas Whitson. This evening I am to give a lecture on Disunionism in this place. To-morrow (Sunday) afternoon, I am to speak in the Quaker meeting-house at Bart. Whether I am to lecture any where else before reaching Salem, I do not know,[6] but hope to speak in Pittsburgh.

My health is good, and the weather is beautiful. Trusting all goes on well at home, and sending kisses for the children, and kind regards to Mary Ann, I remain, in life and evermore,

Your loving husband,

W.L.G.

ALS: Garrison Papers, Boston Public Library.

1. The convention at West Chester began on Wednesday, October 6, and ended on Friday, October 8.

2. Fourteen resolutions were adopted, of which three were Garrison's. His numbered 9, 11, and 12, and read as follows:

"9. Resolved, That as far as the Constitution of the United States is concerned, in regard to all its slaveholding compromises there is no difference whatever between the Democratic and Republican parties; the blood of four millions of imbruted slaves is upon them both; they both consent to a slave oligarchy in Congress, to the hunting of fugitive slaves, and to the use of the military and moral power of the nation for the suppression of slave insurrections, and they are equally zealous in declaring their loyalty to a Union which, so far as the victims of slavery are concerned, is fitly described as a 'covenant with death and an agreement with hell.'

"11. Resolved, That Pennsylvania ought to be free soil to every fugitive slave who may come within her borders; that while she consents to the enforcement of the Fugitive Slave law or to the rendition of any one who has escaped from chains and slavery, she is guilty of the crime of kidnapping; that she is solemnly bound to decree that no human being shall be put on trial, before any tribunal upon her soil, to determine whether he is the property of another. Therefore,

"12. Resolved, That it should be a prominent object of this society to circulate petitions throughout the State asking the Legislature to pass the decree aforesaid, and thus to put an end to all slavehunting within her limits."

(The *National Anti-Slavery Standard*, October 16, 1858, printed a detailed report of the proceedings of the convention, including the resolutions.)

3. See Letter 242, to *The Liberator*, October 15, 1858.

4. Simon Barnard (b. Newlin, Pennsylvania, August 7, 1802; fl. 1883), born into an antislavery family, was an active participant and leader in the antislavery movement in the southern section of Chester County, as well as in the Underground Railroad. He married Sarah Darlington in 1827. He was engaged in farming in Newlin until his fiftieth year, when he and his family moved to West Chester, Pennsylvania, where he went into the lumber business and the building of houses. In 1863, he moved to Philadelphia, where he manufactured bricks and invested in real estate. (R. C. Smedley, *History of the Underground Railroad in Chester* . . . , Lancaster, Pa., 1883, pp. 282–288.)

5. Bayard Taylor (1825–1878), author, poet, translator of *Faust*, and traveler, was brought up as a Quaker at Kennett Square, Chester County, Pennsylvania, by his parents, Joseph and Rebecca Bauer (Way) Taylor. His first wife, who died in December 1850, after two months of marriage, was Mary Agnew of Kennett Square. He then married Marie Hansen, daughter of the Danish astronomer Peter Andreas Hansen, at Gotha on October 27, 1857, and returned to the United States in 1858, where he established himself on a farm near Kennett Square and built a house called Cedarcroft. Bayard and Marie Taylor's "babe" was a daughter, Lillian Bayard.

6. Garrison did speak in Harrisburg, Pennsylvania, on Monday evening, October 10. For his experience in that city see Letter 242, Letter to *The Liberator*, October 15, 1858.

---

2 3 8

TO SAMUEL J. MAY

Christiana, Oct. 9, 1858.

My Dear Friend:

I am here, under the hospitable roof of my friend Thomas Whitson, on my way to Salem, Ohio, having attended a very satisfactory anniversary of the Pennsylvania Anti-Slavery Society at West Chester.

I have just received a letter from William H. Fish, at Cortland, informing me that the Spiritualists have engaged Prof. S. B. Brittan [1] to lecture in that place on Spiritualism, on Sunday, 24th. inst., the time I thought of being there, and suggesting some weighty reasons for postponing my visit until some time in November; adding, however, that he would try to get the engagement of Prof. Brittan postponed, if possible, provided I could not come in November. I have written to him that I will postpone my visit accordingly; and I now write to you to say, that I would like to alter my arrangement for Syracuse, so as not to lecture on Monday evening, the 25th inst., but to spend Saturday and Sunday, the 23d and 24th, with you, and, if you wish, speak on some other subject to your people once in the day time on Sunday, and give my anti-slavery lecture in the evening, and then pass on to Albany the next morning.

I do not wish to give you any trouble; this change may not be convenient to you; if not, then let the first arrangement stand for a meeting on Monday evening, if that be thought worth while.

I have requested Mr. Fish to let you know whether I am to be at Cortland on the 23d and 24th, as originally agreed upon, or otherwise. If otherwise, then you may expect to see me on Saturday from Rochester, instead of on Monday from Cortland. A line addressed to me at Rochester, to the care of Susan B. Anthony, will make all plain, and I will endeavor to be governed by it.

Our friend Whitson sends you his cordial regards, and entertains a lively appreciation of your moral worth and large-hearted philanthropy.

What queer ideas of government infest the brains of Gerrit Smith! And how deluded he is to suppose that he is to roll up a large vote for Governor! [2]

Trusting to find you in improving health, and all the family well, I remain,

Yours, evermore,

Wm. Lloyd Garrison.

Saml. J. May.

ALS: Garrison Papers, Boston Public Library.

1. S. B. Brittan of New York, a spiritualist, had participated as a speaker in the Rutland Free Convention, at Rutland, Vermont, June 25–27, 1858. The convention ranged over an entire gamut of issues, including free trade, slavery, woman's rights, spiritualism, the Sabbath, the Bible, immortality, land reform, marriage, and maternity. Brittan's talk, on "The Natural Evidences of Immortality," cited Robert Owen as a skeptic who had finally been won over to the belief in immortality. Ernestine Rose, a close friend of Owen for more than twenty-five years, replied that "if Robert Owen should tell me that he had seen a mouse draw a three-decker through the streets of New York, I would say, 'I cannot believe it.' . . ." (Yuri Suhl, *Ernestine L. Rose and the Battle for Human Rights*, New York, 1959, pp. 193, 195–196.)

2. Gerrit Smith was twice a candidate for governor of New York: in 1840 and again in 1858. During the latter year, his nomination was "on a platform of abolition and prohibition," and he received 5,446 votes. *The Liberator*, on September 24, 1858, carried a letter by Henry C. Wright, which reported on a public interview given by Smith for his constituents on September 8, 1858, at the Rochester Court House. Smith answered numerous questions about his platform. Frederick Douglass was chairman of the meeting. In noting Smith's "queer ideas of government" Garrison was probably referring to, among other things, Smith's condemnation at his interview of "all governmental schools. Compulsory schools are absurd and oppressive. Government should have no concern with education or religion. . . . Schools should be supported voluntarily, as churches and ministers are." (*Ibid.*) Smith's biographer speaks of "the immense fatigues of a Gubernatorial campaign in which he spoke fifty-three times, each averaging two hours and a half." (Octavius Brooks Frothingham, *Gerrit Smith, A Biography*, New York, 1878, p. 244.)

239

TO HELEN E. GARRISON

Altoona, Oct. 13, 1858.

Dear Wife:

On arriving at Harrisburg from Christiana, I found waiting for me at the depot, my old friend Dr. William W. Rutherford,[1] with whom I stopped when I was in H. ten years ago, and who has been a subscriber to the Liberator since 1836. His wife is a kind, lady-like woman. I was very hospitably entertained. He said a meeting had been notified for me that evening, (though I presume few knew of it, as no handbills had been issued,) but as it was the evening before the day of election, he presumed it would be a failure; and so it turned out, for not more than twenty-five persons were present, (the smallest audience I ever addressed,) some five or six of these being colored. Nevertheless, I gave them a speech an hour and a half long, (!) just as though I were speaking to twenty-five hundred persons. I was suffering from hoarseness and irritation of the throat when I began, and you may readily suppose I was effectually "talked out" of voice when I ended. I am still so hoarse that I can hardly speak above a whisper, and I am afraid I shall be in a voiceless condition at the Salem anniversary. Nevertheless, my remarks at Harrisburg seemed to be highly relished by the few who were present, and to stimulate their interest in the cause afresh.

I arrived here last evening from H. at 7 o'clock, and stopped over night at one of the best hotels there is in the country. Altoona is situated in a wild and picturesque region, in the vicinity of mountain scenery, and is getting to be quite a village. It is the usual stopping place between Philadelphia and Pittsburg, on the part of those who do not wish to ride all night.

I shall leave in the train for Pittsburgh in the course of a few minutes. I am in a "quandary," not knowing whether meetings have been appointed for me in Pittsburgh and Allegheny, (I sincerely hope they have not, on account of my hoarseness,) not having received any answer to my letter to Mr. McIntosh.[2] If I knew no meeting was to be held in either place, I could continue on to Salem, and arrive there this evening at tea-time. — On the whole, however, I suppose it is my duty to be sure on this point, and so I shall tarry at Pittsburgh, and ascertain what is the state of the case, as a letter from Mr. McIntosh may have failed to reach me.

I have had no time, as yet, to send any sketch to the Liberator, but will try to do so when I get to Salem, before the anniversary comes off.

It rained hard all day yesterday, and was very gloomy; but as I was riding in the cars, it was of little consequence. The whole ride was through wild, beautiful and sublime scenery. But I hardly saw a decent house the entire distance. The country dwelling houses look very shabby universally, the people caring more for large and commodious barns.

This morning it is somewhat lowering, but it looks as if it would clear off by noon. I have had a long night's rest, but am still very hoarse; for I do not easily recover my voice when once gone. In other respects, I feel very well.

I have kissed you and all the children this morning, as ambroty [pes], and hope to do so by the living contact on the evening of Nov. 1st.

Your ever loving husband,

W. L. G.

ALS: Garrison Papers, Boston Public Library.

1. Dr. William Wilson Rutherford (b. Dauphin County, Pennsylvania, November 23, 1805; d. March 13, 1875) graduated from Jefferson Medical College in 1832, married Eleanor Reed Crane in the same year, and was a well-known physician and surgeon in Harrisburg, Pennsylvania. (William K. and Anna C. Rutherford, *Genealogical History of the Rutherford Family, Shawnee Mission, Kansas,* 1969, p. 159.)

2. Mr. L. McIntosh (b. Nairn, Scotland, 1811; fl. Shaler Township, Pennsylvania, 1889) of Allegheny, Pennsylvania, was a shoemaker in his native town prior to coming to the United States in 1838. He settled in Allegheny, where he continued his shoemaking for twenty-eight years. He was married twice. The only child of his second marriage was named Lucretia Mott. In 1873 he purchased land in Shaler Township and went to live there. (*History of Allegheny County, Pennsylvania,* Chicago, 1889, Part II, p. 490.)

2 4 0

TO HELEN E. GARRISON

Salem, (Ohio,) Oct. 14, 1858.

Dear Wife:

I wrote to you a few lines, yesterday morning, at Altoona, stating that I expected to stop in Pittsburgh, and give a lecture, and perhaps also one in Allegheny, (which is connected with P. by a long bridge,) on my way to this place; but as I had heard nothing from Mr. McIntosh, and saw nothing of him at the Pittsburgh depot, and could find nothing about a lecture from me in any of the P. papers of that day, and knew not upon whom to call, and it was raining tremendously, bidding *fair* for a very *foul* and dismal evening, I concluded to keep on my journey to this place — exceedingly glad, in consequence of my extreme hoarseness, to escape in this manner, as it will give me time fully to recover my voice in season for the anniversary here. After leaving Pittsburgh, the weather cleared up, the sun shone brilliantly, and the ride by the side of the beautiful Ohio river became very exhilarating. The distance from Pittsburgh to Salem is about 70 miles. A gentlemanly looking person sat by my side, some ten or fifteen miles, and was communicative. He proved to be one [who] had been, in his early days, a missionary among the Indians, and for many years afterwards among the Hindoos; and he gave me considerable information concerning the state of things in India. I did not learn his name, and have no reason to suppose that he knew mine.

I arrived here about 5 in the evening, and was welcomed at the handsome and commodious residence of our friends Benjamin and Jane Elizabeth Jones.[1] They were not expecting me until to-day or to-morrow. They rent their house, and take board with the family.

Marius R. Robinson called in on his way home, not knowing that I had arrived. He has lately sold his residence, (about two miles from the village,) intending to remove into town, but every thing with them is at this moment in a state of confusion. To-day, the remains of his daughter,[2] which were buried on his own little estate, are to be disinterred, and consigned to the town cemetery. It will probably cause some fresh pangs, and open some wounds which time had measurably healed.

I find the friends are almost entirely discouraged here as to our cause in general, and the Bugle in particular. The love of some has waxed cold; some have moved away; some have failed in business; some have been drawn into politics; and hardly any are left to sympathize with and sustain our radical position. There is little or no money at the West. I do not think our friends here are able to pay one farthing towards defraying my travelling expenses; so that my visit to them must be a contribution on the part of the American Anti-Slavery Society — for you know I am not able to travel nearly two thousand miles at my own charge. For my lectures, I get and ask no remuneration, and make no charge.

This morning I had the happiness to receive your letter of the 10th inst., and read it with great interest, glad to get all the particulars recorded therein. It is the only one I have received from any one since I left home. I shall hope to get another letter from you at Rochester, and perhaps another at Syracuse.

You will doubtless continue to have more or less company until my return home, and, of course, afterward; for, while we remain in the city, we shall inevitably be more and more taxed in this manner, as there will be more and more a desire on the part of distant friends, visiting Boston, to call upon us; and in cases when I have received freely of their hospitality, it necessarily subjects me to the obligation to return such kindness, though it also subjects me to an expense which I cannot well bear — being all the time pressed pecuniarily to keep out of debt — for debt is my dread, and yours not less.

I am glad to hear that Franky is so well developing at the gymnasium, as he only needs a healthy body to make himself a useful man. — Fanny, too, I doubt not, will improve very much by such exercises; but let her be careful not to attempt too much. A father's benediction be upon all the household!

Ever truly your loving husband,

W. L. G.

☞ My warmest remembrances to our dear friend Mr. Hovey, and the friends in general.

ALS: Garrison Papers, Boston Public Library.

1. Benjamin Smith Jones (b. Philadelphia, February 13, 1812; d. Kennett Square, Pennsylvania, October 7, 1862) and Jane Elizabeth Hitchcock Jones (b. Vernon, Oneida County, New York, March 13, 1813; d. Vernon, New York, January 13, 1896) had been co-editors of the *Anti-Slavery Bugle*, in Salem. Ohio, from September 1845 until June 1849, when they were replaced by Oliver Johnson. Benjamin Smith Jones was a Philadelphia Quaker who married Jane Elizabeth Hitchcock on January 13, 1846. Their one child, Ella Honora, was born in 1848. Mr. and Mrs. Jones were both active in the Western Anti-Slavery Society and Mrs. Jones conducted an antislavery book agency in Salem. The latter was also active in the cause of woman's rights. After her husband's death at Kennett Square, Pennsylvania, she returned to Vernon, New York, with her daughter, and lived there the remaining years of her life. Benjamin Jones's obituary in *The Liberator,* October 24, 1862, noted that "in the East and in the West he labored long and faithfully, both as a public speaker and an editor, in behalf of the Anti-Slavery cause, and in him unpopular truth found an earnest champion, and popular wrong a faithful censor." (*Life,* III, 197, 204, 207; IV, 389; *Notable American Women.*)

2. Cornelia, the daughter of Marius R. and Emily Robinson, had died on May 15, 1854, aged fifteen and a half years. (*The Pennsylvania Freeman*, May 25, 1854.)

---

2 4 1

TO WILLIAM LLOYD GARRISON, JR.

Salem, (Ohio,) Oct. 15, 1858.

My Dear Son:

I was very much pleased to receive a letter from you last evening, dated the 11th inst., though the contents of it, in relation to George, took me somewhat by surprise. It was just like your generous nature and brotherly affection to send George the fifty dollars necessary to get him to Kansas, and I do not doubt it will be most gratefully appreciated by him in such a trying emergency, or that he will refund you the amount as soon as it is in his power. I approve of what you have done; and for the words of cheer which you have sent to George, as well as the substantial aid, I give you my benediction. No doubt, George is wise in leaving Nininger; not that it may not be a flourishing place some time in the great hereafter, (and so of the whole State of Minnesota,) but its present prospects are depressing in the extreme. The fact is, the whole great West is "dead broke." Speculation has cursed it like a mildew. The unscrupulous haste to get rich has brought with it the inevitable divine retribution. All prosperity must have a reliable basis; otherwise it is an attempt to walk upon water, or build castles in the air. It is of little use to try to anticipate posterity, and expect a value to be given to land where there are neither inhabitants nor money.

My own impression is, that George had better return home; but as it is not his, nor yours — as he seems to "bate not a jot of heart or hope," [1] but feels resolute in trying his fortune in Kansas — of course, I shall not urge him to come back at present. If he is to continue to be a journeyman printer, (and I do not believe he will get into any business, though he may,) I should think he would incomparably prefer to be at home, and in the office of the Liberator. But of this he must judge.

Your expression of confidence in his rectitude of conduct and sound principles is well-founded. I have always felt that he may be trusted in any part of the world; and yet it will be necessary for him to be very watchful over himself, for he will be exposed to great temptations, and the state of society around will be rather calculated to drag down than to elevate. I trust he will ever remain true as steel to his anti-slavery and temperance principles, and be animated more and more by the divine spirit of peace, especially as he will be associated with so many who have been made warlike, and almost ferocious, by border ruffian invasion. I write with special reference to his residence in Kansas, where he may be liable to insult or peril simply on account of being my son. I shall feel much more solicitous for his safety in Kansas than in Minnesota.

I have had a very pleasant tour thus far, though I have made myself quite hoarse by too much speaking.

To-morrow, the anniversary of the Ohio Anti-Slavery Society will commence in this place, and continue three days.[2] The attendance will probably be much less than usual,[3] as the season is so far advanced. The friends of our cause are a good deal discouraged here, but I shall try to inspire them with fresh hope.

Give my warm regards to Mr. and Mrs. Buffum and family, to aunt Miriam, to Charles and Lizzie, and my respects to Mr. Mudge,[4] whose kindness to you I shall ever gratefully appreciate. Be zealous in the discharge of every duty, and seek to know and do what is right, above all else.

Your loving father,

Wm. Lloyd Garrison.

ALS: Smith College Library.

1. John Milton, "Sonnet. To Cyriack Skinner."

2. This was to be the Sixteenth Annual Meeting of the Western Anti-Slavery Society (also called the Ohio Anti-Slavery Society), which met on October 16–18. A report of the proceedings appeared in the *National Anti-Slavery Standard*, October 30, 1858.

3. The attendance was much better than expected. The report of the proceedings noted that "the meeting was well-attended; so well, indeed, that the Town Hall was far too small for the occasion, being crowded at times to its utmost capacity, while some who desired to enter were unable to do so. The spirit of the meeting, too, was such as to afford encouragement for the present and inspire hope for the future." (*Ibid.*)

4. Probably Benjamin Franklin Mudge (b. Orrington, Maine, August 11, 1817; d. Manhattan, Kansas, November 21, 1879) who moved to Lynn with his parents in 1818. At the age of fourteen, he became a shoemaker, a trade which he followed for six years. After teaching school in Topsfield and Lynn, Massachusetts, he graduated from Wesleyan College in 1840. He then studied law privately, passed the bar in 1842, and practiced law in Lynn until 1859. In 1852, he was elected mayor of Lynn, where he was also active in public affairs, in antislavery and temperance. From 1859 until the outbreak of the Civil War, he lived in Kentucky, where he worked as a chemist for a coal and oil company. With the onset of the war, he moved to Kansas, where he received an appointment as state geologist. In 1865, he was appointed professor of geology and associated sciences at the State Agricultural College in Manhattan, Kansas. (James R. Newhall, *Centennial Memorial of Lynn* . . . , Lynn, 1876, pp. 147–150; James R. Newhall, *History of Lynn*, Lynn, 1897, I, 426, II, 177.)

2 4 2

TO THE LIBERATOR

Salem, (Ohio,) Oct. 15, 1858.

Leaving home on the 4th inst. for a rapid anti-slavery tour to Ohio, through Pennsylvania, — with special reference to the Anniversaries of the Pennsylvania and Ohio Anti-Slavery Societies, — it is time to send at least a hasty sketch of the incidents by the way for the *Liberator.*

The railroad ride from Boston to New York was, as usual, very pleasant and expeditious, excepting always that portion of the route which lies between New Haven and the great city, and which for the quantity and penetrating quality of its dust is unequalled in any other part of the country through which I have travelled. The desert of Sahara can hardly surpass it, in this particular. So constant and serious an annoyance to such multitudes of travellers should be remedied, either by daily watering of the road, or by some other process. When shall we have cars so constructed, or with such contrivances, as to wholly abate the nuisance?

I remained in the city over night, partaking of the ever generous hospitality of those long cherished friends, JAMES S. and ABBY H. GIBBONS, for which I have been so often indebted to them.

Mrs. SEDGWICK, the estimable and renowned teacher at Lenox, (Mass.,) was also a guest there at the same time, whose acquaintance it was gratifying to make. Next to seeing that departed venerable friend of humanity, ISAAC T. HOPPER, is seeing Mrs. GIBBONS, his daughter, who, in all the sympathetic and benevolent qualities of her mind, closely resembles her father, as well as in some of her features. And, truly —

> 'There's nought in this bad world like sympathy;
> 'Tis so becoming to the soul and face —
> Sets to soft music the harmonious sigh,
> And robes sweet friendship with angelic grace.' [1]

On going to the Anti-Slavery office the next day, I had the unexpected pleasure of meeting that devoted and amiable man, HENRY BLEBY, the English Wesleyan missionary from Barbadoes, on his return from a short tour to Canada, prior to his departure for his sea-girt home. It was doubly gratifying to be informed by him that he intended to be at the Anniversary of the Pennsylvania Anti-Slavery Society at West Chester, in accordance with an earnest invitation extended to him by its Executive Committee. It was a source of mutual regret that we could not take the same train to Philadelphia that day, I having by agreement to go at an earlier hour — arriving in that pleasant city at 3, P. M., and immediately leaving it, with my beloved friend, J. MILLER McKIM, to partake of his hospitality, and spend the night under his roof at Germantown. He has a very pleasant residence — most richly is he deserving of it — long may he and his dear family live to enjoy it! A large party assembled at tea, such as cannot easily be gathered, for moral worth and active philanthropy, in any given district — among them, JAMES and LUCRETIA MOTT, SARAH PUGH, ABBY KIMBER, EDWARD M. DAVIS, and other well known friends in the Anti-Slavery cause. My pulses always leap in the presence of such, and of others like them in this State, who were among the first to give me words of encouragement and steadfast support in the terrible and long-protracted struggle for the abolition of slavery. JAMES and LU-CRETIA MOTT had evidently improved in their appearance since their removal from the city to Germantown, having thus measurably divested themselves of a mountainous burden of 'visitation' which their philan-thropic conspicuity had brought upon them. While they are living, it is not for me to say of them what my heart dictates.

> 'But there are deeds which should not pass away,
> And names that must not wither;' [2]

and, surely, theirs are of this character. May time continue to deal gently with them!

The anniversary at West Chester commenced on Wednesday, 6th inst., at 10 A. M., and ended on Friday, at 1 P. M. Though a highly respectable number were present throughout, and very 'weighty' in respect to intelligence, moral excellence, and gravity of deportment, the attendance was not quite so large as usual. One reason for this was, we were told, that a horticultural fair had just been held in the place, which had been largely attended, and consequently, the farming population could not find any more leisure time just then. Success to every horticultural fair! But, first of all, success to the cause of liberty! It has been always so, in every place, in our great struggle. No matter how inferior or subordinate, every thing else is preferred to the Anti-Slavery cause. It is never said, 'We have just had an immense gathering to see what can be done to deliver our land from its terrible oppression, and therefore the small attendance to witness this exhibition, or to promote this measure.' But let us hope that this will not always be so; for

> 'Tis liberty alone that gives the flowers
> Of fleeting life their lustre and perfume,
> And we are weeds without it. * * *
> Hence slaves, that once conceive the glowing thought
> Of freedom, in that hope itself possess

All that the contest calls for; spirit, strength,
The scorn of danger, and united hearts,
The surest presage of the good they seek.' [3]

There will one day be a common gathering of the people of the North to effect a common deliverance; when, forgetting their religious and political differences of opinion, — as men do in the midst of a vast conflagration, or when scourged by pestilence or famine, or in view of an impending earthquake, or overtaken by a sudden inundation, — they shall unite the instinct of self-preservation to the sense of a high religious duty, and concentrate their energies to achieve the safety and liberty of the entire republic.

The spirit of this anniversary was never more harmonious, though the attitude of the Society was never more uncompromising. Doubtless you will see in the *Standard*, this week, the series of resolutions adopted on the occasion, and hence be able to judge of the accuracy of my statement. The testimony of the Society has long been clearly registered in favor of a dissolution of the Union, for the highest moral and religious considerations, and with reference to the guilty complicity of the North with the South in the matter of chattel slavery; but a considerable number of its members and friends still, on pressing occasions, continue to exercise the elective franchise, reconciling the act to their consciences as best they may, and consoling themselves with the reflection that they have tried to do something politically to thwart the machinations of the Slave Power. I cannot find it in my heart to impeach their motives, though I am surprised that they do not see more clearly what is necessarily and inevitably involved in their vote. Here and there, one of them makes a strenuous effort to shield himself behind 'the Gerrit Smith theory' of the Anti-Slavery character of the U. S. Constitution [4] — a theory which Mr. Smith himself has never reduced to practice; which, in the face of seventy years of legislation, and against the concurrent views of twenty-five millions of people, is utterly absurd and preposterous; and which can never be imposed upon the South, except through fire and blood, and then never successfully. From the beginning till now, the pro-slavery compromises of the Constitution have never been misunderstood in any part of the nation. Perhaps no parts of that instrument have been quite so clearly apprehended. Whatever construction may have been placed by parties, sects, legislatures and courts, upon this article or that section, they have never questioned the right of slave representation (in the proportion of three-fifths) in Congress, or the right of the slave-holder to recover his fugitive slave in any quarter of the Union, or the right and duty of the U. S. Government to put down a slave insurrection, in case of an appeal for aid on the part of the Executive of any slave State. I find, in all cases, that those who assume the Constitution to be anti-slavery, in order to rebut the charge of sustaining slavery by voting, regularly vote the Republican ticket so far as this Society is concerned: — that is, they endeavor to elect men to office, who utterly reject their interpretation of the Constitution as historically false and morally fraudulent, and heartily accept that which this nation has placed upon the instrument ever since its adoption! This is glaringly inconsistent, and self-condemnatory. A large proportion of those who still vote, however, do not attempt to deny the pro-slavery character of the Constitution, but claim that, somehow or other, they only vote to prevent the extension of slavery, as a distinct issue, and not for the instrument itself, under which they exercise the elective franchise. But this is certainly a delusion. The Kansas or territorial issue is but the incident of the hour; the Constitution and Government are 'in permanent session,' and the primary and essential object of voting is to secure their constant operation. The representative elected must take oath or affirmation to sustain the Constitution, not to 'save Kansas,' or perform any other meritorious act; and that oath or affirmation throws around the slave system, for its maintenance and security, the military and naval power of the whole country. What can be plainer than this?

I am astonished that any member of the Society of Friends could ever have felt justified in voting to uphold the Constitution of the United States, in view of his religious conviction that war in all cases is anti-christian, immoral and inhuman; for, by that instrument, the whole war system is explicitly sanctioned and provided for — army, navy, militia, letters of marque, and all the terrible enginery of war. Moreover, the awful power is committed to Congress to declare war whenever that body (perhaps unparalleled for its corruption and profligacy) shall deem it expedient to do so — Congress being the sole judge of the exigencies which render the war necessary. How can a Quaker — or, indeed, any one professing to be religiously opposed to fighting — vote for such a war-sustaining instrument? How can he do so without being condemned out of his own mouth? What if the Constitution contained an article forbidding the worship of one God and the preaching of the Gospel of Christ — could any Christian vote for any man to maintain it in Congress or elsewhere, without denying his own faith, and condemning his religious profession by his practice?

It is no answer to reply that 'we must have a government' — that to act upon this principle would be to leave the legislation of the country in the hands of the unscrupulous and lawless — that, complicated with difficulties as voting is, the consequences of non-voting would be still more disastrous. It is no answer, because this is the jesuitical doctrine of Rome, that 'the end sanctifies the means,' and 'we may do evil that good may come.' It is no answer, because the command is, 'Let the dead bury their dead' [5] — and even a heathen could exclaim, 'Let justice be done, though the heavens fall!' [6] It is ever the most expedient, the wisest, safest, best, to obey God, and do what is right. O, blessed are they who belong to 'a kingdom that cannot be shaken,' [7] and whose song at all times is, 'God is our refuge and strength, a very present help in trouble; therefore will not we fear, though the earth be removed, and though the mountains be carried into the midst of the sea; though the waters thereof roar and be troubled, though the mountains shake with the swelling thereof.' [8]

Excellent speeches were made at West Chester by LUCRETIA MOTT, J. MILLER McKIM, MARY GREW, THOMAS WHITSON, HENRY GREW, BENJAMIN COLLIER, and others — all well calculated to edify, quicken and encourage all present to renewed efforts in the cause of the oppressed; so that, at the close of the anniversary, it was the universal feeling that it had been 'a strengthening occasion,' and 'a season of great enlargement,' to borrow the expressive language of Friends. The narrative of the operations and results of the great experiment of West India emancipation, by Rev. HENRY BLEBY, — though in substance known to many persons, through the report of it in the *Standard* and *Liberator*, — was listened to with the profoundest attention and the most thrilling interest, causing all hearts to be filled with a joy and a thankfulness for which no adequate expression could be found in words. Its repetition in every town and village would do much to remove prejudice, to enlighten ignorance, to repel slander, to turn disgust into admiration, and to advance the cause of emancipation in this country; and it is much to be regretted that Mr. Bleby must speedily return to Barbadoes, he not supposing, on leaving the island, that there would be any necessity for him to bear witness in this manner to the successful workings of the most beneficent act in the history of England. On landing in America, he found, to his astonishment, that every where emancipation in the British colonies was proclaimed to be a failure! Hence, the readiness with which he has stood forth, — perhaps the most competent witness living, — to testify to the facts as they exist, which triumphantly refute the scandalous misstatements of a pro-slavery press. It is to be hoped that he will fully realize the sum he has wished to raise, to enable him to erect some additional school-houses in Barbadoes for the instruction of the numerous children under his fatherly charge. It will be a good investment for the cause of freedom, at home and abroad. Mr. Bleby seems to be admirably adapted to fill the responsible post he occupies, and long may his valuable life be preserved.

One of the speakers at West Chester — BENJAMIN COLLIER — is a native of England, though a resident of this country for several years past. He alternately works at his trade as a mechanic, and 'dispenses the word' as an independent Methodist preacher. He speaks in a simple, direct, telling manner, from the heart to the heart, and loses no opportunity to plead for those in bonds. In behalf of an absent friend of the cause, and in accordance with his own convictions, he urged upon the Society the importance of introducing suitable songs and hymns into its meetings, and cultivating a taste for melody, and thus giving additional variety and attractiveness to the proceedings. I confess, the recommendation, made as it was almost exclusively to a body of sedate but unmusical Friends, considerably excited my organ of mirthfulness — it seemed so much like suggesting to a company of cripples the utility of performing a pirouette, or joining in a country dance! Something like a ludicrous sensation must have been felt by all present; and our friend Mr. McKim seemed to think the suggestion quite inopportune, under the circumstances. Nevertheless, I am for singing as well as speaking noble thoughts and inspiring sentiments, and hold the faculty of music to be divinely bestowed for human enjoyment and improvement.

> 'Music the fiercest grief can charm,
> And fate's severest rage disarm;
> Music can soften pain to ease,
> And make despair and madness please!
> Our joys below it can improve,
> And antedate the bliss above.' [9]

But our adult Quaker friends are too old, and as yet retain too much of their traditional opposition to melodious sounds, to regard with interest or favor the proposition submitted to them by Mr. Collier.

Our Kennett and Longwood friends — the Coxes, the Darlingtons, the Barnards,[10] the Dugdales, the Agnews,[11] the Peirces,[12] &c., &c., — were present 'in the spirit of love and of a sound mind,' full of resolution to persevere to the end, and resolved to know no weariness in this blessed cause. My previous arrangements were such as to prevent my acceptance of their urgent invitation to accompany them home, and spend a few days in that beautiful region.

Leaving West Chester on Friday afternoon — largely indebted to Simon Barnard and family for their kind entertainment, — I took the cars for Paoli,[13] (a locality full of revolutionary incidents,) [14] and from thence to Christiana, the residence of Thomas Whitson, one of the signers of the 'Declaration of Sentiments' at Philadelphia, in 1833, with a strong and an original mind, remarkable for 'pith o' sense' and quaintness of expression, and imbued with the spirit of reform on a scale commensurate with the wants and necessities of mankind. I was most happy to find myself once more under his hospitable roof, and the large family circle unbroken since my last visit, and in good health. On Saturday evening, I addressed a small audience in the school-house, the weekly lyceum kindly voting to postpone their usual discussion. On Sunday, I spoke at considerable length in the Friends (Hicksite) meeting-house at Bart, about five miles from Christiana — a queer looking house that, like Topsy, appeared to have 'growed,' and, in comparison with which, 'the most ancient heavens' seemed just created. It is beautifully located, however, and we had a solid gathering. On returning from the meeting, we passed near the spot — hereafter to be historically famous, and ever an object of curiosity to the passing traveller — where the Methodist slave-hunter, Gorsuch,[15] from Maryland, was shot dead by one of his slaves whom he was attempting to arrest, and who succeeded in making their escape to Canada. It was Bunker Hill and Lexington on a limited scale. I had the satisfaction to place my feet upon the threshold and to sit down in a room of the dwelling of ELIJAH LEWIS, a most blameless and worthy member of the Society of Friends, who, with CASTNER HANWAY, was ruthlessly seized and conveyed to prison on the charge of 'TREASON,' where he remained 'in durance vile' for several months. Posterity shall place both of these sufferers among 'those of whom the world was not worthy.'

> 'Affliction is the wholesome soil of virtue,
> Where patience, honor, sweet humanity,
> Calm fortitude, take root and strongly flourish.'[16]

On Monday, 10th, I proceeded on my way to Harrisburg, where I was met at the depot by my old friend, Dr. W. W. RUTHERFORD, and cordially welcomed to his residence. He has been a subscriber to the *Liberator* for more than twenty years, and never flinched at his post. A lecture from me had been advertised for that evening, but as it was the evening before the day of the State election, when the political excitement was at fever heat, no appointment could have been more unpropitious. Besides this, a circus had come into town that day; and a fat woman, weighing several hundred pounds, three living male skeletons, and a huge boa-constrictor, were on exhibition! Moreover, the place has a large foreign population, wholly inaccessible, and the bluest kind of orthodoxy holds mastery over the popular mind. What chance had the cause of four millions of imbruted slaves against such odds? My audience was the smallest I ever addressed on any occasion — some twenty-five persons; but I occupied an hour and a half, as though twenty-five hundred persons had been present — remembering, for my encouragement, the story of Dr. Lyman Beecher once having preached a sermon, and performed the usual religious exercises, on a stormy Sunday, with only one man (a stranger,) besides the sexton, for an audience, whose conversion he effected, and who subsequently became an eminent preacher.

Harrisburg is situated on the banks of the Susquehannah, and is surrounded with scenery mingling the sublime and the beautiful in equal proportion.

From Harrisburg I proceeded on my way to Altoona, resting over night at one of the largest and best hotels to be found in the Union, and on Wednesday, at 2 o'clock, arrived at Pittsburgh, where I had some expectation of lecturing that evening; but hearing nothing from the friend to whom I had written on the subject, seeing no reference to any meeting in any of the morning papers that I was able to procure, and the rain pouring down in torrents, making the aspect of the place black and dismal beyond description, and being utterly unfit to make a speech in consequence of extreme hoarseness, (which three days of rest have not yet removed,) I concluded to continue my journey to Salem, arriving here early in the evening, glad to find repose in the quiet home of BENJAMIN S. and JANE ELIZABETH JONES, whose fidelity to our cause, and efficient services in its behalf, are so widely known.

The West is everywhere in a state of great depression, and there are few hopeful spirits to be found in any direction. Our cause is suffering severely for the want of means, and the prospect of immediate relief is extremely dubious. The circulation of the *Bugle*, though deserving of many thousand subscribers, is more limited than ever, and its continuance can be effected only by the most strenuous efforts. Much anxiety is felt by the Executive Committee as to the result of the approaching anniversary of the State Anti-Slavery Society; for without money little or nothing can be done by them, and money at this juncture is not to be obtained, except at considerable self-sacrifice on the part of many.

The recent elections in this State and in Pennsylvania indicate a growing North, and a general public sentiment, more favorable to our movement than formerly, is unquestionably in process of a solid and reliable formation; so that the South has no reason for exultation, even though our Anti-Slavery instrumentalities are somewhat crippled by the pressure of the 'hard times.'

Trusting that a fresh impetus will be given to our movement by the anniversary which is to commence to-morrow, I remain,

Yours, in the assurance of ultimate victory,

WM. LLOYD GARRISON.

Printed in *The Liberator*, October 22, 1858; also in the *National Anti-Slavery Standard*, October 30, 1858.

1. Unidentified.

2. Lord Byron, *Childe Harold*, Canto III, stanza lxvii.

3. William Cowper (1731–1800), English poet, *The Task*, Book 5, "The Winter Morning Walk," lines 446–448, 374–378.

4. An example of Gerrit Smith's "theory" was expressed in one of a series of resolutions which he presented at a state Liberty party convention, at Cazenovia, July 3, 1849. It read as follows:

"Resolved, That the Federal Constitution clearly requires the abolition of every part of American slavery; and that the Phillipses, and Quincys, and Garrisons, and Douglasses, who throw away this staff of anti-slavery accomplishment, and chime in with the popular cry, that the constitution is pro-slavery, do, thereby, notwithstanding their anti-slavery hearts, make themselves practically and effectively pro-slavery."

(Octavius Brooks Frothingham, *Gerrit Smith, a Biography*, New York, 1878, p. 188; a more developed expression of his theory appears in a letter by Smith to Edmund Quincy, November 23, 1846, which is printed, *ibid.*, pp. 201–208.)

5. Matthew 8:22.

6. William Watson (*ca.* 1559–1603), English conspirator and author, *Ten Quodlibetical Questions Concerning Religion and State* (1601).

7. Hebrews 12:28: "a kingdom which cannot be moved."

8. Psalms 46:1–2.

9. Alexander Pope, "Ode on St. Cecilia's Day."

10. Simon and Sarah Barnard. Several other Barnards were also active in the antislavery movement in Chester County, Pennsylvania. These were Simon's brother, Richard M. Barnard, whose farm adjoined Simon's and who was an accountant, mathematician, surveyor, and politician; Eusebius Barnard, who was a Quaker, and active in the Underground Railroad, and William Barnard, Eusebius's brother, also a Quaker, whose second wife was Benjamin Lundy's sister, Mary. (R. C. Smedley, *History of the Underground Railroad in Chester . . .* , Lancaster, Pa., 1883, pp. 288–300.)

11. Allen and Maria Agnew were active in the Underground Railroad (Smedley, *Underground Railroad*, p. 32). John Agnew, a farmer, is also known to have lived in Kennett Township at the time, and is described as having been "a man of energy and character." His son, Lewis, was born in 1832, and married Maria Louisa Taylor. (Gilbert Cope and Henry B. Ashmead, *Genealogical and Personal Memoirs of Chester and Delaware Counties, Pennsylvania*, New York and Chicago, 1904, II, 316.)

12. Gideon Peirce of Ercildoun, Chester County, Pennsylvania, was active in the Underground Railroad. (W. W. Thomson, *Chester County and Its People*, Chicago and New York, 1898, pp. 345–346.) Sidney Peirce was clerk of the Pennsylvania Yearly Meeting of Progressive Friends in 1853. The relationship between the two has not been established. (Letter from Dorothy B. Lapp, Librarian, Chester County Historical Society, West Chester, Pennsylvania, September 15, 1972.)

13. Paoli, Pennsylvania, near Valley Forge.

14. One such incident, which occurred on the night of September 20, 1777, was the defeat, in a surprise attack by the British under General Charles Grey, of a force of 1,500 men under General Anthony Wayne. About 150 men, after surrendering, were killed in cold blood by the British and Hessians. A monument of marble commemorates the dead.

15. For the story of the Christiana affair, involving Gorsuch, Elijah Lewis, and Castner Hanway, see Letter 34, to J. Miller McKim, October 4, 1851, note 2.

16. Unidentified.

2 4 3

TO HELEN E. GARRISON

Salem, Monday, Oct. 18, 1858.

Dear Wife — I believe I wrote to you that, before leaving Boston, I wrote to Mr. McIntosh at Allegheny, Pa., saying that I would lecture either in that place or in Pittsburgh, (connected by a bridge,) or in both, on my way through to this town, if he wished me to; requesting him to send me word to West Chester, Pa. As I got no tidings from him at W. C., and was rendered quite incapable of public speaking thro' hoarseness, I did not stop at Pittsburgh, supposing no appointment had been made. Saturday, Marius R. Robinson received a letter from Mr. McIntosh, inquiring after me, saying that he wrote two letters to me, directed to West Chester, and that a hall was engaged for me on one of the evenings I had specified. It seems an audience of fifteen hundred persons gathered to hear me lecture, and gathered in vain — notwithstanding the Republicans were holding a jubilee meeting over their recent political victory. The disappointment, as you may suppose, was very great, and an expense thrown upon Mr. McIntosh, and perhaps one or two others, of seventeen dollars. I am very sorry it so turned out.

The anniversary of the Ohio A. S. Society commenced here in the town hall on Saturday forenoon. It is usually held about the first of September, in order to accommodate the farmers; and our friends feared that, in consequence of the lateness of the season, the attendance would be greatly diminished. Six meetings have already been held, all crowded to overflowing, many unable to obtain an entrance, and a most refreshing occasion it has been. A fine magnetic spirit has seemed to pervade all hearts, and a very hopeful feeling awakened in all breasts. The proceedings have elicited lively demonstrations of satisfaction; our standard has been kept erect; disunionism has been enforced with all fidelity, and the religion of the land exposed in all its corruption; but there has been no wincing — not a single note of disapprobation. I have spoken five times, and find myself in better voice than when I began. Miss Watkins has spoken twice, to great acceptance. Dr. Brooks [1] has also spoken, and Marius R. Robinson, and Josephine Griffing; [2] but the speaking has chiefly devolved upon me. We shall have one, perhaps two more sessions to-day. The weather has been perfect throughout — clear, mild, and lovely as possible, and the moon has shone brilliantly each evening. Nothing in this particular could be more delightful, and all hearts are made glad. Delegates are here from a wide range of towns, and from various States. I have received the warmest welcome, on all hands, and many are the applications made to me to visit various places, and lecture to the people; and great is the regret to find that I am not to remain longer in this State. To-morrow I shall go to Cleveland, and lecture there on Wednesday evening, arrangements having been made for that purpose. On Thursday I shall proceed to Rochester, where I hope to receive another letter from you.

I was pleasantly surprised to see Mary Ann Johnson come into our first meeting, and was hoping to see Oliver behind her. She is on a visit to friends in Canton, and is looking very well.

I am very glad that I brought with me the daguerreotypes of yourself and the children, as many of the friends have felt great satisfaction in looking at them.

I received a letter from William, stating that George was determined to get to Lawrence, Kansas, and that he had forwarded $50 to him. Willie is a noble boy, and loving and true to his brothers. I wish George would return home, but he must decide for himself. Kisses for Fanny and Franky.

Adieu, love!

W. L. G.

ALS: Garrison Papers, Boston Public Library.

1. Dr. Martin L. Brooks (b. Berlin, Connecticut, December 7, 1812; d. Cleveland, Ohio, June 10, 1899) went to Ohio at the age of six, and attended Oberlin for two years. He was influenced by Garrison and on July 4, 1833, delivered the first abolitionist speech ever made at Oberlin. After Oberlin, he taught school at Cincinnati and at Gallipolis, Ohio, where he taught a school for blacks, some of whom were freed slaves. He participated in the Underground Railroad and helped many fugitive slaves to Canada. For a while he studied at the Medical College of Ohio in Cincinnati, but with the exhaustion of his funds he engaged in business in Kaskaskia, Illinois, for several years, where he came into close contact with Abraham Lincoln. In 1842, he returned to Cincinnati and completed his medical studies, graduating in 1844. After a few years in Patriot, Indiana, he settled in Cleveland, Ohio, in 1848, where he carried on a large and respected medical practice as a general practitioner for more than forty-five years. Originally a Whig, he joined the Republican party at its inception. (*A History of Cleveland, Ohio*, Chicago and Cleveland, 1910, III, 127–129.)

2. Josephine Sophia White (1814–1872), originally of Hebron, Connecticut, married Charles Stockman Spooner Griffing, a machinist, in 1835, and moved with him, around 1842, to Litchfield, Ohio. Josephine Griffing was influenced by Garrisonian abolition, accepted the slogan, "no union with slaveholders," and opened her home to fugitive slaves. She was a member and officer of the Western Anti-Slavery Society, a contributor to the *Anti-Slavery Bugle*, and a paid agent of the society between 1851 and 1855. She was also a woman's rights and temperance advocate. (*Notable American Women*.)

2 4 4

TO SAMUEL J. MAY

Salem, Oct. 19, 1858.

My Dear Friend:

Your letter is just received. After all, I shall not be able to go to Syracuse on Saturday and Sunday next, but our friend William H. Fish holds me to my original engagement, and I must therefore be in Cortland on those days. I asked him to write to you about it, and suppose he has done so, ere this. I am sorry that I can be with you only on Monday, for I would like to spend two or three days with you and your dear family.

And now as to Monday evening next. You will understand that I have no particular desire to give an Anti-Slavery lecture in Syracuse at that time, as the people have had so much on the subject, and especially as we could spend the evening socially together; yet, of course, I will most cheerfully speak to the people that evening, if you think it worth while. I submit the whole matter to your own good judgment: — do as you think best.

I have given your kind message to Marius R. Robinson and Benjamin S. Jones, and their wives, and it was very gratifying to them; and they unitedly desire me to send you their loving and admiring remembrances. Marius was particularly pleased with your commendation of the Bugle. He is a very modest man, and always disposed to underrate himself; and such a well-merited compliment as you sent to him is very strengthening to him.

We have just concluded the anniversary of the Ohio A.S. Society. It has been a magnetic occasion; all hearts have melted and mingled together; every one is encouraged to go forward; and a strong inpulse has been given to the cause.

I go to Cleveland today, and shall lecture there to-morrow evening. On Thursday I shall leave Cleveland for Rochester. If you have occasion to write to me again, please direct your letter to the care of Susan B. Anthony, Rochester.

The weather is ravishingly beautiful, and the moonlight evenings brilliant and exhilarating.

I am glad you think of going to Europe, not merely with a view to the improvement of your health — a matter of first importance — but also that many true friends of freedom and humanity there may see and know you personally; and you become better acquainted with them.

With much love to Mrs. May, the two Charlottes, and all the dear household, and regards to Mr. Wilkinson [1] if he is at home, I remain, in haste,

Ever your most loving friend,

Wm. Lloyd Garrison.

Samuel J. May.

N.B. Your letter did not reach me promptly, as you directed it to "Salem, Columbiana, N.Y.," and it first went to Salem in your State, and then was sent here at a venture. I lose no time in answering it.

ALS: Garrison Papers, Boston Public Library.

1. Alfred Wilkinson (1831–1886), Charlotte May's husband, was a graduate of the Rensselaer Polytechnic Institute and a merchant and banker in Syracuse, New York. (Samuel May, John Wilder May, John Joseph May, *A Genealogy of the Descendants of John May*, Boston, 1878, p. 46; Dwight H. Bruce, *Memorial History of Syracuse, N.Y.*, Syracuse, 1891, Part II, p. 248.)

245

TO HELEN E. GARRISON

Cleveland, Oct. 20, 1858.

Dear Wife:

I left Salem yesterday at noon, and arrived here at 4 o'clock, where I am enjoying the hospitality of my friend William F. Parker,[1] who used to be an active member of the Northampton "Community," and who has a promising son bearing my name, 17 years of age, and a fine family consisting of six children. Special inquiries were made after you and the children. Mr. P's mother is living with them. He is about the only abolitionist in all Cleveland.

Our anniversary at Salem closed on Monday afternoon, at 5 o'clock, the day having been spent in short, telling speeches, chiefly in reference to the question of funds; and, though the company present was not large, and the financial state of things is at the lowest point, and the abolitionists very much straitened in special, between five and six hundred dollars were obtained in money and pledges. How far the latter may be redeemed remains to be seen. But the prevailing spirit was excellent, and everybody seemed to be filled with gladness.

Monday evening, a very large and choice company of anti-slavery friends assembled in the spacious parlors of our friends Benjamin and J. Elizabeth Jones, for social interchange of thought and feeling; and a very pleasant time we had of it. To enjoy the friendship of such souls would repay a century of popular odium and proscription.

At the request of my friend Joseph Heaton,[2] I sat for my photograph before leaving; but, though the artist was skilful at his business, and tried three or four times, he was as unsuccessful as all others invariably are. I am satisfied that, from some unexplainable cause, a good likeness of me cannot be procured by the daguerreotype and photographic process. I am glad that you have a portrait of me, (by Wilson,[3]) which is satisfactory to your mind.

Last evening, some of Mr. Parker's neighbors, with their wives, (one of them with a sweet, bright little babe, a year old,) came in to see me, and we had a pleasant conversational time of it. This evening I am to lecture in Chapin Hall, but expect to have a very small audience, as Cleveland has almost as little anti-slavery feeling as a grave-yard. I intend to find my old friends, Mr. Jones[4] and family, (at whose house I was so dangerously ill,[5]) and shall probably take tea with them.

I have just received a letter from Susan B. Anthony, saying that it would be useless for me to attempt to lecture in Rochester on Friday evening, as on that day Ira Stout[6] is to be hung, and a tremendous excitement is prevailing in the place. You saw Aaron M. Powell's letter in the Liberator,[7] in regard to the mobocratic tumult growing out of this case, at a meeting called in R. in opposition to capital punishment. I want rest, and am very glad I am not to lecture in Rochester.

On arriving here, Mr. Parker put a letter from you and Fanny into my hands, much to my comfort, the contents of which were eagerly perused. Tell Fanny I have given her daguerreotype an additional kiss for her note, and Franky one more also for his remembrances of father. I deeply regret to hear that Mr. Hovey continues so afflicted with his rheumatism, and beg to be remembered to him in a most sympathizing spirit. I wonder whether he has tried the medicine I bought for him; if not, I wish he would consent to make the experiment. I am also very sorry to hear that our dear friend Mrs. Phillips is still so unwell, both for her sake and Wendell's. Remember me to them most lovingly. Also to dear friend Wallcut and family, the Yerrintons, Mr. Whipple,[8] Mr. [Francis] Jackson, Mrs. [Eliza Frances] Eddy, Mr. and Mrs. Parker, &c. &c..

I am glad to hear that Fanny is advancing in her musical studies, and long to be in the parlor, listening to her new performances. I am enjoying myself very much, but "there is no place like home." Regards to Mary Ann. Am glad to hear from the cat.

Ever yours,

W.L.G.

☞ I am to be in Syracuse, on the 25th — in Albany, on the 26th — in Springfield, on the 27th — in Northampton, on the 28th, on my way to Cummington.

ALS: Garrison Papers, Boston Public Library.

1. William F. Parker (b. Reading, Massachusetts, November 20, 1811) was the son of Benjamin and Susan F. Parker. He married Rebecca Macy of Nantucket in 1836. They and their two children joined the Northampton Association of Education and Industry in October, 1842. Their six children were William Harrison, Lloyd Garrison, Albert M., Rebecca, Alexander, and Abby. Parker and his family probably moved to Cleveland in 1851 or 1852, as his name appears for the first time in the Cleveland *City Directory* in 1852–1853, where he is listed as a carpenter at Wasson's car factory. (Charles A. Sheffield, *The History of Florence, Massachusetts,* Florence, 1895, pp. 67–68; *Vital Records of Nantucket,* Boston, 1927, IV, 258; letter from Edouard A. Stackpole, Nantucket, Massachusetts, March 29, 1971; letter from Virginia R. Hawley, The Western Reserve Historical Society, April 24, 1971.)

2. There is a possibility that Joseph Heaton and Joseph Oriel Eaton, who was to gain fame as a painter, were one and the same person. Members of the original Heaton family which went to Ohio sometimes changed their name to Eaton; a Joseph Heaton is mentioned in the 1840 census for Ohio as living in Newark, Licking County, Ohio; and Joseph Oriel Eaton was born in Newark, Licking County, Ohio. Eaton or Heaton may have wanted the photograph taken for his own use in doing a painting of Garrison. In any event, Joseph Oriel Eaton (1829–1875) spent his early years in Ohio, living in Cincinnati from 1857 to 1860, and his last years in Yonkers, New York, where he died. (Letter dated September 23, 1972, from Virginia Hawley, General Reference Supervisor, The Western Reserve Historical Society, Cleveland, Ohio; *Cincinnati, the Queen City,* Chicago and Cincinnati, 1912, vol. 3, pp. 590–591.)

3. Matthew Wilson.

4. Thomas Jones.

5. In 1847.

6. Marion Ira Stout was hanged in Rochester on October 22, 1858, for the murder of his sister's husband, Charles W. Littles, on November 19, 1857. Stout and his sister Sarah, who had been having an incestuous relationship which had apparently been discovered by Sarah's husband, had beaten Littles to death and then thrown his body over a cliff. As they threw the body, they too fell over the cliff and were severely injured. They were arrested and charged with murder several weeks later. The sister was convicted of manslaughter in the second degree and Stout was convicted of first degree murder and sentenced to death. A petition was circulated urging the commutation of the death sentence to life imprisonment on a variety of grounds: the tyrannical and debauched character of the deceased, the lightness of the sentence of Stout's sister, and the conditions of Stout's upbringing, his father having been known as a professional criminal. Stout tried to commit suicide on October 13, but did not succeed. A number of local liberals, radicals, and Quakers, including Frederick Douglass, Isaac Post, and Susan B. Anthony, tried to rally support for Stout and for the commutation of his sentence, but failed. *The Last Writings of Marion Ira Stout* was published in Rochester in 1858. (*The New York Times,* September 21, October 11, 19, 23 and 25, 1858; Blake McKelvey, *Rochester, The Flower City,* Cambridge, 1949, p. 31.)

7. Aaron M. Powell's letter, dated Rochester, New York, October 8, 1858, appeared in *The Liberator,* October 15, 1858. It reported that "In the Monroe County Jail is a young man, Ira Stout, condemned to be hung on the 22d of this month for the crime of murder. Deprecating the influence of capital executions upon the community, and radically opposed to the execution of the revolting statute, in any case, however guilty the criminal, the opponents of the Death Penalty issued a Call for a public meeting to be held in the City Hall last evening, for a protest against capital punishment, under any circumstances, and with a view to secure, in the case of the young man now condemned to death, a commutation of the sentence to imprisonment for life." The letter then notes that a crowd of 1,500 filled the hall to capacity, with an equal number turned away. Handbills

had been circulated earlier denouncing the meeting and its participants. Among
the crowd were many who came to break up the meeting. Their efforts, including
noisy demonstrations, succeeded. Among the speakers were Frederick Douglass,
Powell, a Rev. Mr. Tuttle, and Susan B. Anthony.

8. Charles K. Whipple, nonresistant, abolitionist, and author, also helped to
edit *The Liberator*. (*Letters*, II, 438.)

---

2 4 6

TO HELEN E. GARRISON

Rochester, Oct. 22, 1858.

Dear Wife:

I take Susan B. Anthony's pen in hand "to let you know that I am
well, and hearty as a buck, and hope these few lines will find you
enjoying the same blessing."

On arriving here last evening, (Thursday,) at half past 8 o'clock,
I found friend Post, Aaron M. Powell, Susan and her brother,[1] waiting
to greet me at the depot; and jumping into a vehicle, with Susan and
Aaron, was driven out to Mr. Anthony's[2] country residence, (a very
neat and pretty one,) about three miles from the city, where we all
sat down to a late, but excellent supper — not retiring to rest till eleven
o'clock. Susan's father and mother are away on a journey. Aaron has
been here for the last seven weeks, preaching every Sunday to the
Unitarians, in their church — a singular fact. I believe his ministrations
have been very acceptable. Next Sunday he gives his farewell discourse. His health, he says, has decidedly improved since he has been
here, though he still looks delicate. He tells me Lizzie[3] has been appointed school teacher at Ghent, near their residence. She is at present
in Albany, at Lydia Mott's, where I expect to be on Tuesday evening.

Susan is looking very well, and sends any amount of affectionate
regard to you, desiring me to say to you how much she would delight
to have you here at this time. Shouldn't I be still more delighted? And
am I not feeling happier and happier as the time for my being at home
approaches nearer and nearer? Most assuredly.

My lecture at Cleveland was almost a failure as to attendance — not
more than a hundred and fifty being present. It began to rain (my
usual luck) about an hour before meeting time, and has rained from
that time till now, and is still raining, the weather being mild, but the
atmosphere so foggy that nothing is visible beyond a few rods. Very
little notice was given of the meeting, so that the great mass of the
people knew nothing about it. It is absurd to attempt to hold a meeting
under such circumstances. However, those who were present seemed
to be much pleased, and I trust some good was done, however limited.

Among my auditors was A. E. Newton,[4] the editor of the New England Spiritualist, who is on a lecturing tour out West in behalf of Spiritualism. He told me that he had recently parted company with Henry C. Wright, but I do not remember where he said Henry was going.

At Buffalo, one or two hundred rowdies and vagabonds came on in the train to Rochester, having been over to the Canada side to see the brutal prize fight between Morrissey and Heenan; [5] but they occupied cars by themselves, as their company was unendurable.

To-day there will be great excitement in this city, growing out of the execution of Ira Stout for the murder of his brother-in-law. Military companies are ordered out to prevent a rescue, but this is ridiculous, as all the ruffianism in the city is clamorous for the hanging of Stout.

I had a letter, last evening, from Saml. J. May, expressing regret that I must go to Cortland on Saturday and Sunday, but wishing me to dine with him on Saturday, on my way to C. I shall do so, and return to Syracuse Monday, to lecture that evening.

The weather has been so mild that I have had no occasion for my shawl; and glad am I that I did not take my overcoat. It would have been a sweltering incumbrance.

I am not to speak publicly, either at Albany or Springfield, as circumstances pertaining to the State election are unfavorable; so that I shall get plenty of rest.

I am gratified to hear that the new furnace works well, though if the weather has been in Boston what it has been in Ohio, you must have had little occasion for a furnace fire.

I had some washing done — a dozen pieces — in Salem, but every one of the shirts was badly smooched on the bosom, and it was throwing away seventy-five cents in paying for it. But I shall get along pretty well till I get home.

It is not improbable that I may not be able to get back from Cummington to Northampton, on Monday, Nov. 1st, in season to connect with the train, and get home that evening. Should I fail to do so, do not be uneasy; as you may confidently look for me on Tuesday. Nevertheless, I hope to embrace you all at tea-time on Monday evening.

It is a great comfort to me to have the daguerreotypes of yourself and the children with me. I must not travel any distance from home without them. Besides, they are examined with great interest by all the friends.

Aaron sends his kindest remembrances to you and the children.

Salute Fanny and Franky each morning with a kiss for my sake. A father's love for Willey and Wendy.

Adieu, love!

W. L. G.

ALS: Garrison Papers, Boston Public Library.

1. Susan Anthony had two brothers, both of whom were then living in Kansas. One of them was apparently visiting Rochester at this time.

Daniel Read Anthony (1824–1904) taught school for several years, engaged in the insurance business, visited Kansas in 1854 with the first colony sent out by the New England Emigrant Society, and assisted in the founding of Lawrence, Kansas. He returned to Rochester in the fall of 1854, and settled in Leavenworth, Kansas, in 1857. He was mayor of Leavenworth in 1863, postmaster for several years, and at the beginning of the Civil War fought in the Union Army. After 1871, he was proprietor and editor of the Leavenworth *Times*.

Jacob Merritt Anthony (1834–1900) worked on the family farm in Rochester until the age of twenty-two when he went to Kansas, enlisted in John Brown's band, and fought at the battle of Osawatomie. In April 1858, he married Mary Almira Luther at Osawatomie. During the Civil War he fought in the Union army. He died suddenly of heart failure in Fort Scott, Kansas in 1900. (Charles L. Anthony, *Genealogy of the Anthony Family from 1495 to 1904*, Sterling, Illinois, 1904, pp. 173, 185–186, 189; Katharine B. Anthony, *Susan B. Anthony: Her Personal History and Her Era*, New York, 1954, pp. 19, 32, 83, 135–137, 188, 456–457.)

2. Susan B. Anthony's father, Daniel Anthony.

3. Elizabeth Powell (b. 1841), was Aaron Powell's sister, several years his junior. (Aaron M. Powell, *Personal Reminiscences*, New York, 1899, pp. xix, 219.) She married Henry Bond in 1872 and also became a dean of Swarthmore College, Pennsylvania. (Charles S. Powell, *History and Genealogy of the Powells in America*, St. Petersburg, Fla., 1935, p. 117.)

4. Alonzo Elliot Newton (b. Marlboro, Westmoreland County, New Hampshire, February 23, 1821; d. Arlington, Massachusetts, April 12, 1889) moved to Boston in 1844, and remained there for about twenty years as a printer, proofreader, and journalist. In 1863, he was a clerk of the War Department at Washington, D.C., and also helped organize and superintend the colored schools in Washington, for about five years. (Ermina Newton Leonard, *Newton Genealogy*, De Pere, Wisc., 1915, p. 372.)

5. The prize-fight between John Morrissey and John C. Heenan, two Irish-Americans, took place on October 19, 1858. Morrissey was the victor in eleven rounds. It may be noted that it was customary at the time for the victor to kiss the hand of the loser. Concerning the crowd, *The New York Times*, on October 22, 1858, remarked that "it would be difficult . . . to select a crowd in any part of the world whose features were more deeply seethed with every bad and foul passion that belongs to man. . . ." (*The New York Times*, October 18, 21, 22, and 23.)

247

TO HELEN E. GARRISON

Cortland, Oct. 25, 1858.

Dear Wife:

On Friday evening, a large circle of anti-slavery friends assembled in Rochester at the house of Isaac and Amy Post, to give me their welcome, and a very agreeable time we had. I stopped at friend Post's that night, in order to be near the depot in the morning, as Susan B. Anthony's home is at least three miles in the interior.

On Friday afternoon, Susan and Aaron[1] took me in a carriage to Mount Hope Cemetery, which is a very fine one in its natural features, and which, like Mount Auburn, has an observatory, from the top of which the view is even more extensive than that obtained at Mount Auburn, and in some respects superior.

Saturday morning, I took the cars for Syracuse, arriving there at noon. Mr. May had sent Bonny[2] down to the depot with a carriage to carry me up to his house, but we missed of each other. Mr. May is looking better than I expected, but his gait is less firm, and he is evidently lacking in vigor. He has made up his mind to go to Europe, just as soon as Joseph returns, unless that should be in mid winter, as he does not feel like leaving Mrs. May alone. Charlotte Wilkinson and her husband are to take charge of Mr. Wilkinson's[3] residence, during the absence of Mr. W. and family on their European tour. Charlotte has a beautiful baby,[4] and is herself looking remarkably well. Her husband is absent at the West. Mrs. May seems in good spirits, and was kind as usual in her attentions. Charlotte Coffin is still the excellent Charlotte, but time is evidently making some impression upon her. Bonny has grown up quite tall, and will make a smart and energetic business man, I think. He has no taste for books. He is going to Theodore D. Weld's school at Raritan Bay.[5] Mr. May will take Bonny with him on Tuesday, accompanying me as far as Albany. You may expect to see Mr. May in Boston before you will see me — say on Friday or Saturday. He thinks of stopping in the city a week or ten days. Of course, I proffered him our hospitality during that time; but he will go to his uncle's in Hollis street, if they can accommodate him; if not, he will stay with us. Be sure and tell him he is welcome to our home.

Saturday afternoon, I left Syracuse for Cortland, arriving just in time for the evening meeting; and so, merely swallowing a cup of tea, I went to the Stone Church, where our friend W. H. Fish, regularly officiates, and found a large assembly gathered to hear me. I spoke on the religious aspects of our cause, and was listened to with great interest and manifest satisfaction. Yesterday I made three long speeches, on Inspiration, the Bible, Ancient and Modern Tests of Piety, and the relations of our cause to the government and Union. The house was thronged — many persons coming from abroad, in all directions — some as far as twenty-five miles in their carriages. It was a noble body of men and women to look in the face, and they gave me the most gratifying attention. — My views of the Bible elicited a great deal of interest and discussion.

Cortland is one of the neatest and pleasantest villages in the United States. I have seen nothing surpassing it, except St. Johnsbury, in Vermont. Our friend Fish has done a great work in this region, and is greatly beloved. He and his wife send their cordial regards to you.

I received a letter from you at Syracuse, and was very glad to get it. Am very sorry to hear of Mr. Parker's illness, and that Mr. Phillips is looking so unwell, but trust they are both now convalescent.

Do give my kindest remembrances to my venerable friend Mr. Otis,[6] whom I am anxious to see again in that sacred room, and also to Georgina. Kisses for the dear ones.

Ever yours,

W.L.G.

☞ I go to Syracuse this morning, and shall lecture there this evening.

ALS: Garrison Papers, Boston Public Library.

1. Aaron M. Powell.
2. Samuel J. May's youngest son, George Emerson May.
3. John Wilkinson (b. Skaneateles, New York, September 30, 1798; d. Syracuse, New York, September 1862), Alfred Wilkinson's father, was admitted to the bar in 1819, the first lawyer to settle in Syracuse. He was appointed the first postmaster in Syracuse in 1820, and was elected clerk of the village in 1825. For several years he was president of the Syracuse and Utica Railroad and later president of the Michigan Southern Railroad. He was also a banker and a member of the state assembly. He married Henrietta Wilhelmina Swart in 1825. They had eight children. (Dwight H. Bruce, *Memorial History of Syracuse, New York*, Syracuse, 1891, Part II, p. 76; Franklin H. Chase, *Syracuse and Its Environs*, New York and Chicago, 1924, III, 184.)
4. Alfred, born June 9, 1858. (Samuel May, John Wilder May, John Joseph May, *Genealogy of the Descendants of John May*, Boston, 1878, p. 46.)
5. New Jersey.
6. Mrs. Lucinda Smith Otis.

---

2 4 8

TO *THE LIBERATOR*

SYRACUSE, Oct. 25, 1858.

The anniversary of the Western Anti-Slavery Society having been notified to be held six weeks later in the season than usual, it was feared, by some, that the attendance would be greatly lessened, as no mass meeting could be held out of doors; but, though the number present was somewhat diminished, it was too large to find accommodation in the town hall, which, on Sunday, was crowded to excess, and could easily have been twice filled. Delegates were present from various parts of the West, reliable, true-hearted, and indomitable in spirit. The anniversary opened on Saturday morning, 16th inst., and continued, by successive meetings, until Monday evening. If, before it was held, there was some despondency of feeling, in regard to the aspect of affairs, through the general pecuniary depression which exists so extensively at the West, no sooner did its sessions commence than all this was dissipated, and all present seemed to be inspired by a common sentiment of hope and courage. The Annual Report of the Executive Committee, drawn up and read by J. ELIZABETH JONES, the Corresponding Secretary, was an impressive statement of the condition of our cause, especially in Ohio, and gave the key-note to the entire proceedings. It was evident that deeds, rather than words, were wanted, and that unless the spirit of benevolence and self-sacrifice came to the rescue, the existence of the *Bugle* would be imperilled, and the operations of the Society measurably suspended. On the last day, that spirit was earnestly appealed to, and most generously responded, considering the crippled condition of many in their business affairs. Thirty-six new subscribers were obtained for the *Bugle*. The amount received in cash was upwards of four hundred dollars, and the pledges to the Society amounted to about five hundred dollars. All hearts were made glad at the result. A portion of the time, the discussion was general, earnest, and of a very practical character. Speeches were made — such as the times demanded — by the President, MARIUS R. ROBINSON, and by Dr. A. BROOKE,[1] FRANCES ELLEN WATKINS, WILLIAM HOISINGTON,[2] (the blind preacher,) JOSEPHINE GRIFFING, BENJAMIN S. JONES, JEHU HALLIDAY,[3] BENJAMIN BOWN,[4] T. B. McCORMICK,[5] THOMAS BROWN,[6] and others. These were listened to with earnest and unfaltering attention, as though a great and solemn crisis was at hand, and every one must gird up his loins to meet it. Miss WATKINS, as usual, made a very marked impression upon those who listened to her pathetic and eloquent words; and, though identified by complexion with a proscribed race, and young in years, produced the general conviction that scarcely a white young lady in the land, however favored with scholastic advantages, could be found to match her in the gift of speech and the power of literary composition. The speech of Mrs. GRIFFING was an admirable effort, full of soul and feeling, tersely expressed, and highly effective. But I have not time to go into the particulars.

The resolutions adopted were of a high-toned character, and had the ring of the true metal in them. I never saw a gathering more magnetically drawn together; and the temper of the discussions (at times very spirited) was admirable throughout. Rely upon it, the abolitionists of Ohio will not be found wanting in any hour of trial, as compared with those of any other State.

Since the anniversary, I have lectured in Cleveland once, and in Cortland, in this State, four times. This evening, I shall address a public meeting in this place, and to-morrow evening another in Albany, on my way home, via Northampton and Cummington. Further particulars must be left till my return.

My visit to Cortland, on Saturday and Sunday, (where our esteemed and efficient coadjutor, WILLIAM H. FISH, is located,) was uncommonly interesting.

I am now partaking of the hospitality of my early and beloved friend, SAMUEL J. MAY, who intends to be with his friends in Boston next week, and who contemplates a voyage to Europe for his health.

W.L.G.

Printed in *The Liberator*, October 29, 1858.

1. Dr. Abraham (also Abram) Brooke was the son of Samuel and Sarah Garrigus Brooke, of Philadelphia. In 1830, he and his brother, William, migrated westward and settled in Marlborough Township, Ohio. He was active in the antislavery cause, was on the executive committee of the Western Anti-Slavery Society and corresponded with various antislavery leaders. (William Henry Perrin, *History of Stark County*, . . . *Ohio*, Chicago, 1881, p. 921; *The Standard*, October 30, 1858.)

2. The Reverend William Henry Hoisington (b. near Buffalo, New York, April 10, 1813; d. Rochelle, Illinois, July 1, 1899) was an assistant teacher in the preparatory department at Oberlin College from 1837 to 1838 and a Congregational minister and lecturer. In 1845, he married Rachel Coleman of Wayne, Ashtabula County, Ohio. Later, he married Loretta H. Cutter, also of Wayne, Ohio. (Harry Hoisington, "The American Family Hoisington," Boston, 1934, carbon copy of typescript in New England Historic Genealogical Society, No. 64; *The Alumni Catalogue of 1920*, Oberlin College, 1927, p. 157.)

3. Jehu Halliday was a member of the Business Committee of the Western Anti-Slavery Society. (*The Standard*, October 30, 1858.)

4. Benjamin Bown of Ohio was at this time an officer of the American Anti-Slavery Society and of the Western Anti-Slavery Society, which had its headquarters in Salem, Ohio. (In *The Liberator* his name was mistakenly spelled "Brown.")

5. An extant broadside, in the possession of the Ohio Historical Society, announced that T. B. McCormick would be speaking at Eaton, Ohio, on April 30, 1857, on the "Unconstitutionality of American Slavery, and the Duty and Power of the General Government to Abolish it. . . ." It identifies McCormick as "the clergyman for whom the Governor of Kentucky made a requisition upon the Governor of Indiana, charging him with aiding in the escape of fugitive slaves. The warrant was issued and Mr. McCormick is thereby exiled from his home." A letter from T. B. McCormick to George Whipple, dated December 8, 1865, Princeton, Indiana, is to be found in the archives of the American Missionary Society. A "Rev. McCormack" is listed as an Underground Railroad operator in Gibson County, Indiana by Wilbur H. Siebert, *The Underground Railroad from Slavery to Freedom* (1898, reprinted by Peter Smith, Gloucester, Mass., 1968), p. 407. Since Princeton is in Gibson County, Indiana, Siebert must have been referring to T. B. McCormick, despite the slight variation in spelling. (I am indebted to Merton L. Dillon, letter dated January 29, 1973, for this information.)

6. Thomas Brown, a peddler originally of Cincinnati, Ohio, had been released from prison in Kentucky in 1857 after serving three years for transporting fugitive slaves. After his release, he lectured about his experience. In 1858, he published a pamphlet entitled *Brown's Three Years in the Kentucky Prisons from May 30, 1854 to May 18, 1857* (Indianapolis, 1858), 19 pp. (I am indebted to Mrs. Virginia R. Hawley, General Reference Supervisor, The Western Reserve Historical Society, Cleveland, Ohio, for information about Brown and for a photocopy of his pamphlet.)

2 4 9

TO HELEN E. GARRISON

Syracuse, Oct. 26, 1858.

Dear Wife:

I gave my lecture, last evening, in Convention Hall, a very neat and commodious room. Expecting only a baker's dozen present, in consequence of the pending State election, and the excitement growing out of it,[1] I was agreeably surprised to find assembled some three or four hundred persons — a majority of them, however, being ladies. I did not touch upon politics, but confined myself wholly to the religious aspects of our cause. The attention was all I could ask, and my remarks, though strong and pointed, were repeatedly applauded. I feel fresh and strong this morning, notwithstanding my four long consecutive speeches at Cortland; and I hope to get home in as good condition as I was when I went away.

It is one of the loveliest mornings of the season. The sun is shining brilliantly, and it would seem as if there were nothing but peace and good-will in all the world. Mrs. May has just brought to me some ice to look at, the first of the season, as it was quite cold last night.

Mr. May, and Bonny, and myself, will start for Albany toward noon — they going down the Hudson river to-night, in the steam-boat, to New York, and I stopping at Lydia Mott's. I expect, so far as attendance is concerned, that my meeting at Albany, this evening, will prove a dead failure. There is no abolitionism in that city; and as Albany is the seat of government, it is a thoroughly corrupt and selfish place. Besides, the State election is to come off in the course of a few days, and there is no disposition to hear about any thing else. I tried to dissuade Lydia from attempting a meeting, but she has deemed it best to go forward, and so we must "run for luck." Had it not been for Mr. May's personal influence and large circle of friends, and under his own signature in the papers urging the people to attend the lecture here, I should have had an empty hall, beyond all doubt.

A week from this morning I hope to be at home. I do not see how I shall be able to reach home on Monday evening, at tea-time, according to my original calculation; for I believe that Cummington is some twenty or twenty-five miles from Northampton, which must be travelled in a private carriage over a very hilly road; so that the best thing I can do will be to try to intersect with the afternoon train at Springfield from New York to Boston, arriving home at mid-night, or a little after. You may therefore leave the key outside of the door in the usual place; so that if I come at that time, I need make no disturbance. It will not be necessary to leave any light burning for me, as I can easily find the match-box on the kitchen shelf. And, besides, it is possible I may not get home until Tuesday evening at tea-time.

You will probably see Mr. May on Saturday. He expects to stop at his uncle's,[2] if they can accommodate him; if not, he will be with us. As soon as Joseph [3] returns, he (Mr. May) will go directly to Paris, where John Edward [4] will be waiting for him, and they both will travel through Switzerland, Italy, &c., until next spring, when John will return home, and Mr. May will go to England, and there spend the summer. I think he will take a new lease of life in so doing. Glad indeed am I that he has found kind and generous friends to make up a purse to defray his travelling expenses. To this end Gerrit Smith has generously contributed fifty dollars.

My remembrances cluster around the hallowed chamber of my dear and venerated friend, Mrs. Otis — the pattern of all that is patient, meek, and morally excellent, and a marvel for the fresh and lively interest she takes in all that concerns the progress and redemption of our race. Convey to her and Georgina my most affectionate regards.

Hoping to find my dear friends, Mr. and Mrs. Phillips, Mr. Hovey, and Mr. Hovey, [sic] in a convalescent state, and all well at home, and rejoicing to hear how well the dear children have behaved, I remain,

Ever yours,

W.L.G.

ALS: Garrison Papers, Boston Public Library.

1. The candidates for the office of governor of New York State were Edwin D. Morgan, Republican, Amasa J. Parker, Democrat, Lorenzo Burrows, American party, and Gerrit Smith, candidate of the People's State Ticket. Edwin D. Morgan emerged the victor by a majority of 17,440 votes over his Democratic rival. (Glyndon G. Van Deusen, *William Henry Seward*, New York, 1967, 193, 196.)

2. Samuel May, the father of Samuel May, Jr.

3. Samuel J. May's son.

4. John Edward May, son of Samuel J. May, born October 7, 1829, at Brooklyn, Connecticut. (See *Letters*, II, 5.)

250

TO OLIVER JOHNSON

Syracuse, Oct. 26, 1858.

Dear Johnson:

Please to see that William Robinson [1] of Pulaski township, Lawrence Co., Pa., is duly credited for the enclosed seven ($7.00) dollars, as payment on his subscription to The Standard. Let a receipt be sent to him in his paper.

I have had a most delightful time since I left home. Everywhere I have been greeted with great kindness, and in all meetings I have attended, there has been the utmost cordiality evinced. What a marvellous change since the early mobocratic days of the anti-slavery cause!

I lectured here to a good house last evening, and am to lecture tonight in Albany. You will probably see Mr. May in New York on Friday.

Ever truly yours,

Wm. Lloyd Garrison.

Transcript: Garrison Papers, Boston Public Library.

1. Probably the son of Samuel and Elizabeth Jane Robinson, of Pulaski township, Pennsylvania. The father was one of the pioneers in the area, a Whig, and a Republican at that party's birth. William settled at Georgetown, later Sheakleyville, Mercer County, Pennsylvania, and had died by 1909. (J. G. White, *A Twentieth Century History of Mercer County, Pennsylvania,* Chicago, 1909, p. 584.)

---

2 5 1

TO WILLIAM LLOYD GARRISON, JR.

Northampton, Oct. 26, [28,] 1858.

My dear Willey:

I was very much gratified to receive a letter from you at Albany, accompanying one from your mother. I gave the leaves you enclosed to Lizzie M. Powell,[1] and could you have seen how much pleasure it gave her, you would have felt like sending her a whole forest — at least,
  "When Birnam woods do come to Dunsinane."[2]
She seems to be much delighted with your letters, and I dare say hers are as pleasant to you. She is a remarkable girl for her years, and I was glad to see her in an improved state of health. She accompanied me to Chatham Four Corners, where she met her parents, and went to Ghent.[3] I believe she commences her school next week. I cautioned her "to teach the young ideas how to shoot,"[4] so as to kill nobody. She will do so. Would that every other teacher in the land would do the same! How soon would the war-spirit be mitigated throughout our wide domains!

It gave me more pleasure than I can express to learn that you had ventured to give an address upon Non-Resistance; because I believe that doctrine to be more comprehensive and glorious, more reconciling and redeeming, more philosophical and Christian, than any other that the world has known. It includes the inviolability of human life — the abolition of the gallows and all war — the overthrow of all national pride and rivalry — the conquest of all fear of man and all human selfishness — the godlike returning of good for evil, and blessing for cursing — the brotherhood of man — the establishment of universal peace and good will. Of course, it can neither be understood nor received by those who are led by the spirit of this world and the customs of the age; but is and must be to the priest "a stone of stumbling," [5] and to the politician "a rock of offence," [6] but to those who apprehend and adopt it, it will prove to be "the power of God and the wisdom of God unto salvation." [7] I shall be glad to hear more about the discussion that followed when I see you.

I have just arrived here, having had about the pleasantest tour in my life. Every where I have met with marked respect and kindness, generous hospitality, and many warm and attached friends. How utterly different from the state of things twenty years ago! Not a sign of disapprobation, not a note of opposition, have I seen or heard in any of the numerous meetings I have addressed since I left home. No one appears to deny or contest any thing advanced. A great change has certainly taken place in the public sentiment of the North, and is still going on, with silent but irresistible power, notwithstanding the leaders of the Republican party are, nationally speaking, modifying and diluting the issue to be presented in 1860. But, oh! how much still remains to be done!

I read the report of G. W. Curtis's [8] lecture on "Fair Play for Women," as reported in the number of the Bee [9] which you forwarded to Lizzie, with much satisfaction. I like its straightforward thoroughness and manly tone, even more than its rhetorical beauty, which I fully appreciate. May his moral development keep pace with his mental culture!

I am to lecture in Northampton this evening, in the spacious town hall — expecting nothing better than "a beggarly account of empty boxes," [10] on the score of attendance — for this is a place noted for orthodox narrowness and bigotry; and where these are dominant, conscience is in a state of moral paralysis; and one might as well attempt to "create a soul under the ribs of death," [11] as to galvanize such a community.

To-morrow I shall go to Cummington, and hope to be safely at home on Monday night. Probably you will be up the next Saturday.

Wishing to be kindly remembered to Mr. and Mrs. Buffum, Lizzie [Buffum], Charles, Mr. Mudge, &c., I remain,

Your loving father,

Wm. Lloyd Garrison.

ALS: Smith College Library. Garrison misdated this letter "Oct. 26." October 28 is the correct date. He was in Syracuse on October 26, and only arrived in Northampton on October 28.

1. Aaron M. Powell's sister.
2. Shakespeare, *Macbeth*, V, v, 44–45.
3. New York.
4. James Thomson, *The Seasons*, "Spring," line 1,150.
5. Isaiah 8:14.
6. *Idem.*
7. I Corinthians 1:24; Romans 1:16.
8. George William Curtis (1824–1892), originally of Providence, Rhode Island, man of letters and orator, friend and follower of Ralph Waldo Emerson, was the author of *Nile Notes of a Howadji* (1851) and *The Howadji in Syria* (1852), both books of travel, and of *Lotus Eating* (1852) and *Potiphar Papers* (1853). He was an associate editor of *Putnam's Monthly* until 1856, when that journal went into bankruptcy. In 1863, he became the editor of *Harper's Weekly*. He was vigorously antislavery, an advocate and supporter of the woman's rights movement, and an early advocate of civil service reform.
9. The reference is to the Boston *Atlas and Daily Bee*. The Boston *Daily Bee* began publication in 1842. In May 1858, it united with the Boston *Daily Atlas* to form the *Atlas and Daily Bee*. (*Union List of Newspapers*.) *The Liberator*, October 29, 1858, published extracts of Curtis' lecture on "Fair Play for Women" from the *Atlas and Bee*.
10. Shakespeare, *Romeo and Juliet*, V, i, 45.
11. John Milton, *Comus*, line 560.

252

TO HELEN E. GARRISON

[Northampton, Oct. 28, 1858.]

I found Lydia and her excellent sister [1] (the types of earnestness and meekness blended) looking remarkably well, and increased my large indebtedness to them on the score of hospitality. — Lizzie M. Powell was there, having staid a week longer to see me, and returning home with me to Ghent the next morning, (yesterday,) where she is to keep school during the winter, near her father's residence. She is much improved in health, and is very superior in her mental and moral constitution, and warm in her affectional nature. I find that she and Willie are in frequent correspondence, to the mutual gratification of both, I have no doubt — of one, *herself*, I am quite certain. If nothing else grows out of it, it will strengthen the bonds of friendship, and help to make them experts in literary correspondence. Certainly, I think Lizzie has no superior for her years, in all that constitutes solid worth. Her father and mother met us at the depot in Chatham, and warmly grasped me by the hand.

I felt very grateful to you for another letter which I received at

Albany, enclosing an interesting one from Willie. The letter you sent to Rochester was duly received by me before leaving that city; so that I have missed nothing you have sent me since I left home.

I arrived in Springfield yesterday at 2, P.M., and found at the depot my attached friend and warm admirer, Mr. E. W. Thwing,[2] by whom I was taken to his pleasant, but unpretentious residence on Crescent Hill, (just beyond the residence of Mrs. Gordon's [3] parents,) [4] where I was most kindly entertained by himself and wife. They have but one child — a fine, intelligent and handsome boy, eight years old, bearing my name. Last evening, several friends came in to see me, and we all had a very pleasant interview.

This morning, (Thursday,) I came to Northampton — was met at the depot by my friend Seth Hunt, and taken to his sweet home. This evening I am to lecture in the spacious Town Hall, but presume the audience will be very thin. It was deemed best, in Albany, not to attempt a meeting. Douglass and Pryne [5] spoke that evening, in favor of Gerrit Smith. Adieu!

Ever yours,

W.L.G.

☞ Tell the children I carry them in my heart and memory. Remembrances to Mary Ann.[6] My good will to the cat. Love to all the friends.

ALS: Garrison Papers, Boston Public Library. The first part of the letter seems to be missing, and the dateline has been inserted by a hand other than Garrison's.

1. Lydia Mott of Albany and her sister Abigail.
2. Ebenezer Withington Thwing (b. November 9, 1806; fl. 1883) was the son of Nicholas and Lydia Thwing. He married Nancy Appleton in 1830. She died in 1845. In 1846, he married Anna Marks, of Burlington, Connecticut. Their child, William Lloyd Garrison Thwing, was born in Springfield, Massachusetts, March 20, 1850. The Springfield *Directory* for 1858 lists E. W. Twing (no "h") as the owner of a variety store. By 1883, E. W. Thwing was living in Naples, New York. (Walter E. Thwing, *Thwing: A Genealogical, Biographical and Historical Account of the Family*, Boston, 1883, p. 94.)
3. Rebecca Ames Gordon (1827–1912) was the granddaughter of David Ames, Superintendent of the Springfield Armory and a paper manufacturer. Her husband was Solomon Jones Gordon, a native of Plymouth, Massachusetts and a Harvard graduate, "who became a prominent and successful patent lawyer in New York." (Letter from Juliette Tomlinson, Director, Connecticut Valley Historical Museum, Springfield, Massachusetts, dated January 26, 1973; *Springfield Republican*, July 5, 1912.)
4. Mrs. Gordon's parents were David Ames, Jr. (1791–1883) of Springfield, Massachusetts, a paper manufacturer, and Mary O. Mitchell (1801–1861) of Bridgewater, Massachusetts. David and Mary Ames resided at 241 Maple Street, Springfield. (Charles Wells Chapin, *Sketches of the Old Inhabitants and Other Citizens of Old Springfield*, Springfield, Mass., 1893, pp. 18–21. I am indebted to Dorothy Mozley, Genealogy and Local History Librarian, Springfield City Library, for part of this information.)
5. The Reverend Abraham Pryne (d. Williamsport, New York, September 20, 1862, at forty years of age) was an antislavery clergyman, admirer of Gerrit Smith,

and a leader of the Liberty party in New York State. He was an editor of the *Progressive Christian* and a contributor to Frederick Douglass's paper. He was elected to the New York State Assembly by the Republicans of the western district of Wayne County. His death was by suicide, following a long illness. (*The Liberator*, October 3, 1862, reprints an obituary from the *Syracuse Journal* of September 24, 1862.)

6. Probably the Garrisons' servant girl.

2 5 3

TO HELEN E. GARRISON

Northampton, Oct. 29, 1858.

Dear Wife:

My lecture, last evening, was attended by about two hundred persons — more than twice the number I had anticipated, though the larger portion came from Florence and other places, — the mass of the people here being too bigoted, and too much under the control of the clergy, to be disposed to give any countenance to "infidel" anti-slavery meetings. I was not sparing in my denunciations of the popular religion, and had the satisfaction of seeing that my shots took effect by several wounded birds flying out of the room. I know of no place more dead than Northampton, and deem labor here almost wholly thrown away. Yet some good may grow out of the meeting, beyond what is apparent. Were it not for the position of the clergy and the churches every where, how speedily would the Anti-Slavery cause be triumphant in all the North! Surely, a fearful responsibility is resting upon them; and to them is applicable all the righteous denunciations of the prophets to the oppressive and obdurate Jews.

Our Florence friends came down in a great omnibus load, and without them the meeting would have looked thin indeed in the spacious town hall. Mr. and Mrs. Hammond [1] took tea with me at Mr. Hunt's. Mr. Hammond came afterward. Many inquiries were made about you and the children — the daguerreotypes of you all were looked at with great pleasure — and I was complimented as looking "as good as new." Indeed, wherever I have travelled on my present tour, I have had constant expressions of surprise made in regard to my unaltered looks for many years past. I was never feeling better than now.

How I am to get to Cummington, to-day, I do not yet know. There seems to be no one going from this place or Florence, Mr. Hunt being unable to leave, much to his regret. I shall probably have to hire a vehicle, and go alone, unless Mr. Hayward [2] should arrive in the half past 1 o'clock train from Springfield to-day; but I have not heard from him or Mr. May since I left, and fear we shall fail to connect. — I am sorry we did not have a mutual understanding about the matter.

The beautiful cases which contain the children's daguerreotypes, and your own, were made at Florence. Mr. Hill [3] is interested in the manufacture of such, and I hope is doing well. I shall go through Florence on my way to Cummington.

Yesterday afternoon, I went through the new Insane State Asylum, and was surprised and delighted at the immense scale on which it is laid out, and the almost unequalled beauty of its location. The view from the top of the Observatory is one of the finest in the country — the grand and the beautiful blending in all directions — Mount Tom and Mount Holyoke being almost within hailing distances seemingly. The whole region is full of sublimity and romance.

Is it not singular that I saw nothing of Dr. Mann [4] 'at Cleveland? Or did he get discouraged at the prospect, and return home?

I am still hoping to be with you all at tea-time on Monday evening, but may miss the train; in which case leave the key out at the door, for I shall be home at midnight. Love and kisses for Fanny and Franky.

Faithfully and ever yours,

W.L.G.

ALS: Garrison Papers, Boston Public Library.

1. Elisha Livermore Hammond (1799–1882) and Eliza Preston Hammond. A farmer and artist, Elisha Hammond was a confirmed abolitionist and temperance man and, for a while, a member of the Northampton Association of Education and Industry. He painted a portrait of Garrison in 1844. He continued to live in the area until almost the end of his life. (Letters, III, 246–249, to Helen Garrison, January 12, 1844; Charles A. Sheffield, *The History of Florence, Massachusetts,* Florence, 1895, pp. 221–224.)

2. Josiah Hayward, originally of Salem, Massachusetts, a black abolitionist, joined the Northampton Association in March, 1843 and stayed there for a year. He also sent his daughter to the Northampton Association as a boarding scholar. In 1872, a Josiah Hayward was listed in the Springfield *Directory* as a cabinet maker. He died in 1874. (Letter from Garrison to Oliver Johnson, April 21, 1874, Garrison Papers, Boston Public Library; Sheffield, *History of Florence,* pp. 67–68.)

3. Samuel L. Hill (b. Smithfield, Rhode Island, July 30, 1806; d. Citronelle, Alabama, December 13, 1882) had been overseer of a cotton factory in Willimantic, Connecticut, where he was also active as a deacon in the Baptist church until an incident involving Wendell Phillips, who was driven out of the church by another deacon. He was a founder of the Northampton Association in 1842 and was assistant director of the silk manufacturing department. After the breaking up of the association, he engaged in the manufacture of silk. He was particularly interested in schools and education. (Sheffield, *History of Florence,* pp. 205–211.)

4. Dr. Daniel Mann had moved to Painesville, Ohio, shortly before Garrison's trip to Cleveland. (See Letter 171, July 8, 1857.)

2 5 4

TO THEODORE BOURNE

Boston, Nov. 18, 1858.

My Dear Friend: — It gave me the greatest gratification to receive and read your letter of the 8th inst. It seemed next to receiving an epistle from your venerated father,[1] whose memory will ever be dear to me, and whose labors, sacrifices, and perils in the cause of the millions in our land who are "appointed to destruction" [1a] ought to be biographically chronicled and perpetuated.

I confess my early and large indebtedness to him for enabling me to apprehend with irresistible clearness the inherent sinfulness of slavery under all circumstances, and its utter incompatibility with the spirit and precepts of Christianity.

I felt and was inspired by the magnetism of his lion-heart soul, which knew nothing of fear, and trampled upon all compromises with oppression, yet was full of womanly gentleness and susceptibility; and mightily did he aid the anti-slavery cause in its earliest stages by his advocacy of the doctrine of immediate and unconditional emancipation, his exposure to the hypocrisy of the colonization scheme, and his reprobation of a negro-hating slaveholding religion. He was both "a son of thunder" [2] and "a son of consolation." [3] Never has slavery had a more indomitable foe or freedom a truer friend.

You inquire whether your father was not the author of the work entitled "Slavery Illustrated in its Effects upon Woman," published in this city in 1837, by Isaac Knapp.[4] He was, as every line of it bears witness. I wish it could be republished, and a million copies of it distributed broadcast. . . . . I thank you for sending me a copy of the Constitution of the "African Civilization Society," [5] and the pamphlet by Benjamin Coates,[6] which I have briefly noticed in the *Liberator* of this week.[7] I am not prepared to state my views of this new movement at length; but I heartily wish prosperity to every benevolent effort to increase the growth of free cotton, whether in Africa, India, or elsewhere, and thus to strike a heavy blow at slavery pecuniarily. I am in hopes, however, that we are nearer the jubilee than such a movement would seem to imply.

Still, let every just instrumentality be used for the eternal overthrow of slavery.

Yours, to break every yoke,

Wm. Lloyd Garrison.

Mr. Theodore Bourne.

Printed newspaper clipping: Garrison Papers, Boston Public Library.

Theodore Bourne (d. March 21, 1910, aged eighty-nine), the son of the pioneer abolitionist, George Bourne, was ordained a Presbyterian minister but had to give up the ministry because of a throat affliction. Before the Civil War, he was a professor of languages at the Huguenot Institute on Staten Island, New York, and helped his father with lectures in the antislavery cause. After the Civil War he was the founder and first secretary of the Society for the Prevention of Crime in New York. (Obituary, *The New York Times*, March 23, 1910.)

1. The Reverend George Bourne (1780–1845), antislavery pioneer and author. (*Letters*, II, 35.)

1a. Proverbs 31:8.

2. Mark 3:17.

3. Acts 4:36.

4. Garrison's early associate on *The Liberator* and in the antislavery movement. (See *Letters*, II, xxvi.)

5. The African Civilization Society was founded in 1858 by Henry Highland Garnet, a black colonizationist, with "the avowed purpose of bringing about 'the civilization and Christianization' of the Dark Continent." Garnet favored emigration to Liberia. (Quarles, *Black Abolitionists*, pp. 216–217.)

6. Benjamin Coates (d. March 8, 1887, aged eighty-one) was a member of the firm of Coates Bros., wool merchants, in Philadelphia, Pennsylvania, and, at one time, a special partner in the publishing house of Porter & Coates. He was active in the antislavery movement, but was a colonizationist as well as an abolitionist. He took an active part in building the Republic of Liberia. Coates's pamphlet was entitled *Cotton Cultivation in Africa: Suggestions on the Importance of the Cultivation of Cotton in Africa, in Reference to the Abolition of Slavery in the United States, Through the Organization of an African Civilization Society*, published in 1854 and again in 1858. (Boston *Evening Transcript*, March 10, 1887; *National Union Catalogue of Pre-1956 Imprints*, vol. 113, p. 226.)

7. November 19.

255

TO OLIVER JOHNSON

Boston, Nov. 18, 1858.

Dear Johnson:

You know I have taken a deep interest in the success of a very promising sculptor of this city, John Adams Jackson, whose bust of Wendell Phillips you have in the Anti-Slavery office, as well as my own. You will recollect, also, the admirable busts he made of old Dr. Beecher [1] and Dr. Blagden. [2] Yesterday he called to say to me, that he is very desirous of trying his luck in New York, if he can get a head or two to mould, by way of showing his artistic ability, and to warrant him in beginning the experiment. Circumstances are such as make it important for him to know whether there will be any chance for him in that direction, *without delay*. I told him that I would write to you on the subject. He is willing to take any head, *pro tempore*, for fifty dollars — half his usual price, until he makes himself known to the public. Could not Horace Greeley [3] be persuaded to sit for a bust? Or Ward Beecher, or E. H. Chapin, [4] their friends and admirers making up the necessary $50? Would not William Cullen Bryant [5] make an admirable Socratic bust? and could he not, as a lover of art, and an appreciater of genius, be induced to patronize Jackson? Doubtless he has friends who would be willing to meet the expenses.

It would be necessary to have two or three busts engaged, to warrant Mr. Jackson to take a room. He deserves any amount of patronage, and is a fine fellow, modest as talented.

I am much obliged to you for taking the trouble to look after my night shirt, which I carelessly left at West Chester. It was safely received.

Ought there not to be petitions sent from your office, and circulated particularly in Central and Western New York, such as we are circulating in this State, against slave hunting and slave trials? [6] Could not your City Society do something about it?

Wife has been quite ill for a fortnight past, with a sort of rheumatic or congestive fever. She is now better, but has a troublesome cough, and will need to be very careful.

My oldest son, George Thompson, who has been in Minnesota for a year and a half past, will return home shortly, every thing at the West being in a state of collapse.

I hope you and Mary Ann are well. Next to a good conscience, what is there to compare with good health? In haste,

Yours, ever,

Wm. Lloyd Garrison.

ALS: Garrison Papers, Boston Public Library.

1. Dr. Lyman Beecher.
2. Dr. George Washington Blagden.
3. Horace Greeley (1811–1872), the editor of the New York *Tribune.*
4. The Reverend Dr. Edwin Hubbell Chapin.
5. William Cullen Bryant (1794–1878), the noted poet and editor of the New York *Evening Post* for almost half a century.
6. The text of the Massachusetts petition read as follows:
   "*To the Honorable Senate and House of Representatives*
   of the Commonwealth of Massachusetts: —
"The undersigned, citizens of Massachusetts, respectfully ask you to enact that no person, who has been held as a slave, shall be delivered up, by any officer or court, State or Federal, within this Commonwealth, to any one claiming him on the ground that he owes 'service or labor' to such claimant by the laws of one of the Slave States of this Union." (*The Liberator*, October 1, 1858.)

2 5 6

TO THE EDITOR OF THE *ANTI-SLAVERY ADVOCATE*

Boston, December 28th, 1858.

My Dear Friend,

To-morrow, Samuel J. May of Syracuse, (a cousin of Samuel May, jr.,) and Sarah P. Remond of Salem, intend embarking for the old world, in the Liverpool steamer, from this city. Mr. May, I understand, will make no delay in England, but will proceed at once to the Continent, in order to spend the winter in Italy with his eldest son,[1] who is now in Paris. Miss Remond goes forth on her own responsibility, not representing any society, but identified by complexion and destiny, by sisterly sympathy and generous philanthropy with the millions in this country who are punished worse than white criminals for the color of their skin — for being the descendants of Africans — though none the less the children of God. She is much esteemed and beloved by all who know her; and she will carry with her the best wishes of them all for her safety and happiness. I can easily imagine how unutterable must be her feelings on finding herself, for the first time in her life, in a land where this dreadful spirit of caste is quite unknown; where she can travel on terms of equality with others, with no liability to insult or ostracism; where she will be estimated according to her moral worth and intellectual force. It will be to her almost like a resurrection from the dead, and to that extent a foretaste of the heavenly state. It will a thousand times repay her for all the discomforts and dangers of the Atlantic voyage. I have had no conference with her in regard to her transatlantic journey, and therefore do not know how far she thinks of attempting to lecture abroad on the subject of slavery. She is comparatively new in the lecturing field, but only needs practice to become a pleasing and impressive public speaker. Her appeals are to the conscience and the heart, and always made with dignity and earnest conviction. She is capable of gracing any circle, and will be her own best recommendation wherever she travels. She has been so long interested in the anti-slavery movement that she is thoroughly posted upon all matters pertaining to it, and I doubt not will be able to remove many unfounded prejudices against it and its advocates, as she shall have opportunity.

* * * For myself, I am not so young by twelve years as when I last bade you adieu at Liverpool. On the 10th inst. I completed my fifty-third year. Thirty years of that period I have given to the cause of the enslaved millions in this land; for it was in 1828 that I first became their public advocate. I wish I could tell you about what time to expect the jubilee; but this is certain — the event "is nearer than when we believed." At present the slave power seems to have unwonted dominion; and yet never were its foes so numerous, never was it so consciously weak, as at the present time. The South stands thoroughly unmasked. She audaciously maintains the moral rectitude and eternal fitness of slavery, insists that slave property is to be recognized every where like other property, goes for the extension of the system in every direction, and, finally, has reopened the African slave trade, in bold defiance of the law of the land. All this is needed to make up a speedy and final issue between the North and the South.

How is my dear friend James Haughton? Still busily engaged in his philanthropic labors, and bearing many a faithful testimony for the right, "whether men will hear or forbear." [2] I am indebted to him for Dublin papers from time to time, containing sensible and well written essays from his pen, which I read with much interest and pleasure. May his days "be long in the land!" [3] I shall hardly forgive him, however, if he does not make a flying visit to the United States ere long.

Ever your attached and faithful friend,

WM. LLOYD GARRISON.

Printed in *The Anti-Slavery Advocate*, London, February, 1859.

1. John Edward.
2. Ezekiel 2:5, 7.
3. Exodus 20:12.

257

TO WILLIAM LLOYD GARRISON, JR.

Boston, Dec. 31, 1858.

Dear William:

Though it is the last day of the year, there is no reason why I, and your mother, and Fanny and Franky, should not wish you a happy new year. May you be happily preserved from all "the ills that flesh is heir to," [1] and continue daily to "grow in knowledge and in grace." [2] May you ever keep in the right path, shun the very appearance of evil, be superior to every evil temptation, and reverently seek to know and do the will of God. May your moral vision ever be clear to discern the right from the wrong, your conscience ever clean and vital, your heart ever tender and affectionate, your spirit ever pure and elevated. May you be prudent and economical without being parsimonious, and generous and philanthropic without being credulous and inconsiderate. May your interest in all the reforms of the day, — especially in the cause of the imbruted slave, — grow more and more vital, impelling you to the performance of high moral achievements in behalf of suffering humanity, and making your life a blessing to the world. May you be delivered from "that fear of man which bringeth a snare," [3] in sustaining what is just, following what is good, and adhering to what is right. May you never go with the multitude to do evil, but be willing to stand alone, if need be, with God and the truth, even if it bring you to the cross or the stake. May you be known for your integrity of character, and aim at perfection in all noble qualities. My heart-felt benediction, mingled with your mother's, is upon you; and may the benediction of "our Father in heaven" be added thereto!

Thus far, my happiness in my children has been without alloy. George has always been circumspect and exemplary in his conduct, to a remarkable degree; and I feel that he may be safely trusted, even at the far West, where great temptations beset young men, though I would much prefer to have him with us at home. Wendell has always been a model boy, mature beyond his years, unexceptionable in deportment, amiable and affectionate in spirit, and full of promise for the future. Fanny is a dear child, specially dear because she is the only daughter, of a most generous and loving nature, full of sensibility, and promising to make a noble woman. Franky is the Benjamin of the flock, around whom my heartstrings very closely twine, gentle, conscientious, most affectionate, laudably ambitious, studious and thoughtful, sensitive to blame, with a large brain and a large heart for a little boy. As for yourself, I am delighted with your ingenuousness, kindness of heart, self-forgetfulness, loving disposition, and generous regard for every member of the family. In a few days you will complete your twenty-first year, and take upon yourself the responsibilities of manhood. Let us have a little celebration of the event, at home, that evening, if you can leave seasonably, or on the subsequent evening, (Saturday,) remaining with us till Monday. Do not fail to come.

I send the accompanying volume to Mr. Mudge, with a letter accompanying it, to which no written reply is needed.

Your loving father,

Wm. LLoyd Garrison.

W. L. G., Jr.

ALS: Smith College Library.

1. Shakespeare, *Hamlet*, III, i, 63.
2. 2 Peter 3:18.
3. Proverbs 29:25.

IX DEATH, MARRIAGE, AND DIVISION
AMONG THE GARRISONIANS: 1859

TWENTY-EIGHT YEARS had passed since *The Liberator* first began to appear and twenty-seven years since the formation of the New England Anti-Slavery Society in 1832. Time was now beginning to take its toll among abolitionist leaders. Arnold Buffum died in March, Charles F. Hovey in April, and Effingham Capron and Samuel Philbrick in September. Theodore Parker, who had suffered from tuberculosis for some time, took a turn for the worse at the beginning of the year and sailed for the West Indies, on February 4, in an unsuccessful attempt to restore his health.

But if some abolitionists were yielding to the infirmities of age and illness, others were witnessing the marriages of their children and the births of grandchildren. On June 23, two antislavery families were united when the son of Maria and Henry Grafton Chapman married the daughter of John and Eleanor Jay.

In February, Garrison appeared before a committee of the Massachusetts legislature to urge passage of a bill to prohibit slave-catching in the state of Massachusetts. Despite a strong petition campaign and much public support, the bill did not pass the legislature.

The growth of the Republican party created serious problems for the Garrisonian abolitionists. To certain radical abolitionists, the Republican party, with its limited antislavery program and its emphasis on nonextension rather than abolition of slavery, and its ability to capture the votes and support of many devoted antislavery persons, including abolitionists, represented the greatest obstacle to the abolition of slavery.

In view of that judgment, the great need of the moment, according to such as Stephen and Abby Kelley Foster and Parker Pillsbury, was for abolitionists to concentrate their attacks upon the Republicans. To Garrison, however, the Republican party, despite its limited platform and faults, represented a movement of public opinion in the direction of antislavery. It was the Democratic party, with its pro-slavery stand, which constituted the true menace. These political differences, and others which stemmed from them, led to an exacerbation of feelings and personal rifts among the abolitionists, especially between Garrison and the Fosters.

The end of the year witnessed John Brown's attack upon Harpers Ferry in October, his sentence of death on November 2, and his hanging on December 2. Garrison, despite his nonresistance philosophy, after the first shock of the report of the attack, gave full support to Brown. On the evening of Brown's hanging, Garrison spoke at Tremont Temple in Boston, emphasizing that he was a nonresistant, and had "labored unremittingly to effect the peaceful abolition of slavery, by an appeal to the reason and conscience of the slaveholder," yet "Whenever there is a contest between the oppressed and the oppressor, — the weapons being equal between the parties, — God knows that my heart must be with the oppressed, and always against the oppressor. Therefore, whenever commenced, I cannot but wish success to all slave insurrections. I thank God when men who believe in the right and duty of wielding carnal weapons, are so far advanced that they will take those weapons out of the scale of despotism, and throw them into the scale of freedom. It is an indication of progress, and a positive moral growth. . . . Rather than see men wearing their chains in a cowardly and servile spirit, I would, as an advocate of peace, much rather see them breaking the head of the tyrant with their chains." (*Life*, III, 491–492.)

---

2 5 8

TO FRANCIS JACKSON

Boston, Jan. 2, 1859.

Dear Friend:

I am much gratified to learn by your note, in reply to mine, that the book I sent to you, as a very slight token of my loving regards, was peculiarly acceptable. As I have another copy, it will not be necessary for me to borrow it, for a careful examination of its contents.

For the sentiments so kindly and felicitously expressed towards me, I thank you with an overflowing heart. With characteristic modesty, you assign me hereafter, in the spirit-life, a higher sphere than your own. Welded together as our spirits are, in oneness of feeling and purpose, in friendship and love, I trust we shall ever be found *side by side*, neither separated by distance nor divided by location, but cheerfully running "the race that is set before us," [1] and pressing equally onward in the path of duty as it shall open before us, which is the path of immortal blessedness.

The verse you quote from "the old Methodist hymn" cannot be altered for the better, and stirs the soul like a trumpet-call from the skies. It is kindred to that grand one of Dr. Watts: [2]

> "I'll praise my Maker with my breath,
> And when my voice is lost in death,
>   Praise shall employ my nobler powers;
> My days of praise shall ne'er be past,
> While life, and thought, and being last,
>   *Or immortality endures.*"

All is bright in the future. "There is no death." [3] Paul says of the mortal body, — I think with wonderful prophetic accuracy, as well as rare felicity of illustration, — "It is sown in weakness, it is raised in power.[4] It is sown in corruption, it is raised in incorruption; [5] it is sown a natural body, it is raised a spiritual body." [6] Hence, let all the human race join with him in the triumphant interrogation, "O Death! where is thy sting? O Grave! where is thy victory?" [7]

Your note discloses to me, most unexpectedly, a large augmentation of my indebtedness to you. I felt greatly obliged for your taking so much trouble to see that the needed alteration in my furnace was properly made, but expected to-morrow to receive Herman & Bryant's bill for the same for payment, concluding they had been disposed to give me a liberal credit. It seems, however, that you have made the necessary settlement, and desire me to accept it as a "labor of love," and a fresh gift at your hands, in addition to the other repairs made under your kind supervision, which I was also expecting to liquidate, as they were much needed. This is to be tried *in* (at least *with*) a new furnace, but certainly not a furnace of affliction! You have not only said to me and mine, "Be ye warmed," but have provided the means. For this we shall try to give you a warm reception as often as you look in upon us. Your gift relieves me, at this time, from a financial pressure. The new furnace works admirably. This is the first winter we have been comfortable in more than one room, a considerable portion of the time, since we came to Dix Place: now, dining room, entry and parlors are all as genial and summer-like as we can desire.

Please accept a slice from an excellent cheese from the dairy of my Connecticut friend Philip Scarborough.

Your greatly obliged friend,

Wm. Lloyd Garrison.

Francis Jackson.

ALS: Garrison Papers, Boston Public Library.

1. Hebrews 12:1.
2. Dr. Isaac Watts (1674–1748), English dissenting clergyman and writer of hymns. The quotation is from his versification of Psalm 146, printed in *Church Psalmody, A Collection of Psalms and Hymns, Adapted to Public Worship, selected from Dr. Watts and other authors* (Boston, 1848), p. 241.
3. Henry Wadsworth Longfellow (1807–1882), "Resignation," stanza 5, *Poems* (Boston, 1857), II, 254.
4. I Corinthians 15:43.
5. *Ibid.*, 15:42.
6. *Ibid.*, 15:44.
7. *Ibid.*, 15:55.

259

TO ELIAS RICHARDS

Boston, Jan. 11, 1859.

My Dear Friend:

Your letter is just received, and I lose no time in replying to it.

When I proposed to you to lecture in Weymouth next Sunday evening, I quite forgot that I was engaged on that evening to lecture before the Salem Female Anti-Slavery Society. So that I must ask for a postponement of one week from Sunday, if that will be agreeable to Mr. Mellen [1] and the friends. If not, we will agree upon some other time as mutually convenient.

Yours, with warm regards,

Wm. Lloyd Garrison.

Elias Richards.

ALS: Merrill Collection of Garrison Papers, Wichita State University Library.

Elias Richards (b. January 23, 1802; d. September 20, 1887) of Weymouth, Massachusetts, a businessman, was listed in the Weymouth *Directory* for 1870–71 as secretary and director of the Weymouth and Braintree Mutual Fire Insurance Company, and was a founder in 1879 and president of the Weymouth Historical Society. He also helped to found the Weymouth and Braintree Union Lyceum. He was a supporter of the antislavery cause. *The Liberator* (February 11, 1859) lists him and his wife, E. Hunt Richards, as contributors to the Massachusetts Anti-Slavery Society. (George W. Chamberlain, *History of Weymouth, Mass.*, Weymouth, 1923, II, 758–760; IV, 600; Gilbert Nash, *Historical Sketch of the Town of Weymouth*, Weymouth, 1885, p. 134.) Edmund S. Hunt, *Weymouth Ways and Weymouth People: Reminiscences* (Boston, 1907), p. 30, writes that "Mr. Richards was a prominent abolitionist and prohibitionist and a hard fighter for what he thought right (always in the front with Garrison and Thompson)." I am indebted to Harry C. Belcher, former president, Weymouth Historical Society, for this quotation.

1. The Reverend Charles Mellen was pastor of the First Universalist Society of Weymouth, Massachusetts, from April 1855 to April 1860. (Nash, *Weymouth*, p. 119.)

2 6 0

TO THEODORE PARKER

Boston, Jan. 15, 1859.

Dear Mr. Parker:

In common with a host of warmly attached personal friends, and a great multitude of enlightened and grateful admirers of your character and labors, I am made very sad to hear that your bodily indisposition is of so serious a nature as not only to preclude you from exercising your public functions at Music Hall, but also to require, at this wintry season, an ocean voyage and a residence in a foreign clime, as essential to your restoration to health.[1] You have fought long and bravely against disease, and by high resolve and heroic purpose endeavored to expel the enemy. Doubtless, the conflict has been too long protracted on your part; and now that the fleshly nature is compelled to yield, though the mind is as clear and vigorous as ever, I trust you will give it all possible chances of recovery, by taking absolute rest from all mental excitement, and summoning as much determination to get well, as you have shown not to consider yourself sick.

As an act of friendly consideration, I have forborne calling to see you, knowing you need to be kept very secluded, and rejoicing to hear that you are so well guarded in this respect; yet I hope it may be possible for me to give you the parting hand, and my benediction at the same time, without burdening you, before you leave the city. Of that, you and Mrs. Parker must be the judge.

I shall try to look wholly on the bright side, and hope for the best results in regard to your voyage and a change of climate. Life with you, I am sure, is mainly desirable that you may continue your labors in the field of humanity, and for the good of all mankind. How much you have done for the freedom of the human mind, for the exposure of political corruption, for the removal of theological error, for the suppression of religious bigotry and superstition, for the overthrow of injustice, for the slave in his fetters, for the prisoner in his cell, for "the perishing classes" of every description, it is not for you to know, it is not for me to compute. You have touched, quickened, inspired thousands of minds, which in their turn shall impregnate other minds with generous and noble sentiments, down through the centuries to come, — an ever widening circle, on both sides of the Atlantic. "The past, at least, is secure." [2] What the future has in store, only the Infinite Father knows. His will be done!

I thank you for the many kind words you have spoken in my behalf, and for various acts of kindness done to me and mine. As I have nothing to offer in return but my grateful acknowledgments, I must ever remain your debtor. If, however, at any time or in any way, I can be of service to you, it will give me great pleasure to perform it.

I proffer my heartfelt sympathies to your dear wife in this time of trial. I have ever admired her meek and quiet spirit, her sweet and gentle nature, her benevolent disposition, her domestic consecration, and felt that you were singularly fortunate in your choice of such a partner for life. She belongs to my calendar of living saints. — May all the disembodied ones, and all the good angels, watch over you both, and a gracious Providence prolong your lives to "a green old age"!

I send my warm regards to dear Miss Stevenson, entertaining as I do for her the highest respect in regard to her rare womanly culture, her intellectual vigor, her moral excellence, and her sympathetic nature, drawing her closely to the side of the distressed and suffering, the poor and perishing. Tell her she is in my eyes very beautiful, in the highest and noblest sense of the term.

To all that I have written, my own dear wife most heartily responds.

Mrs. Hamilton Willis [3] made us a visit yesterday, and desired me to say to you that in case Dr. Howe [4] could not go with you abroad, and it would be agreeable to you, her husband would esteem it both a privilege and a pleasure to be your travelling assistant and companion.

Please make no attempt to answer this.[5]

Your attached and sympathizing friend,

                                Wm. Lloyd Garrison.

Theodore Parker.

ALS: Garrison Papers, Boston Public Library. A portion of this letter is printed in *Life*, III, 480–481.

1. At the beginning of January 1859, Parker's tuberculosis took a turn for the worse. His physicians predicted that his chance of recovery was but one in ten. A trip to the West Indies and then to Europe was decided upon. His congregation voted him a year's leave of absence, with his salary to be continued. Parker left Boston on February 3, accompanied by his wife, Miss Stevenson, and George Cabot. They set sail for Santa Cruz from New York on February 8. Dr. and Mrs. Samuel Gridley Howe joined them for the first part of their cruise, leaving them at Havana, Cuba, on March 3. (John White Chadwick, *Theodore Parker, Preacher and Reformer*, Boston and New York, 1900, pp. 350–354.)

2. Daniel Webster, "Second Speech on Foote's Resolution," January 26, 1830.

3. Mrs. Hamilton Willis (née Louisa Winship, d. New York, November 24, 1862, aged forty-three) was a devoted supporter of the antislavery cause. Her husband was a successful merchant and stockbroker in Boston, who retired on a competency in 1853. He was the son of Benjamin and Elizabeth Sewall Willis, the latter having been the daughter of Colonel Joseph May, the father of Samuel J. May. Hamilton Willis also contributed articles to the Boston press. *The Liberator*, December 5, 1862, printed an obituary of Mrs. Hamilton Willis which referred to her as "pure in heart, gentle and affectionate in spirit, faithful in performance of duty and unfaltering in her convictions of right." The information about Mr. Willis

is from the *New England Historical and Genealogical Register*, XXVII, 118, XXXIII, 132.

4. Samuel Gridley Howe.

5. Parker replied on January 31, 1859. His letter included the following noteworthy passage: "I knew *you* long before you ever heard of me, and often heard you speak — never without instruction and admiration. Three men now living have done New England and the North great service. They are quite unlike, but all are soldiers in the same great cause — Wm. L. Garrison, Horace Mann, and R. W. Emerson. You took the most dangerous and difficult part, and no soldier ever fought with more gallant hardihood, no martyr ever more nobly bore what came as the earthly reward of his nobleness. The great work of a great man — *Himself*, his *character* — that is sure to do its work though his special labors fail of immediate triumph. I am to thank you for what your character has taught me — it has been a continual Gospel of Strength. I value Integrity above all human virtues. I never knew yours fail — no, nor even falter. God bless you for it." (*Life*, III, 481.)

261

TO JOHN GREENLEAF WHITTIER

Boston, Feb. 12, 1859.

Dear Whittier:

I believe I mentioned to you, on Friday, that I am to deliver a lyceum lecture in Newburyport, on Friday evening, 25th inst. *You* and your *poetry* are to constitute my theme on that occasion. Will you oblige me by giving me a few particulars as to your early life — the date and place of your birth — the names of your parents in full — what education you obtained — how much you worked at the shoe-making business — &c.? I do not ask for any thing more than a very brief statement (*inter nos*) of these little particulars, because I do not wish to give you any trouble; but I ought to be "posted" to that extent, in professing to give a sketch of your history. Was it not in 1833 that you openly espoused the Anti-Slavery cause,[1] during my absence in England? Did you ever edit any other journals, except the American Manufacturer[2] and the New England Weekly Review?[3] Am I right in the impression that your excellent father rather discouraged your youthful poetical efforts, as not being sufficiently practical? How was it with your sainted mother in this matter? Send me what you please.

I was much gratified to spend an hour with you yesterday, and hope to see you more frequently than hitherto. Please give my warm regards to your sister.

Your attached friend,

Wm. Lloyd Garrison.

J. G. Whittier.[4]

ALS: Garrison Papers, Boston Public Library.

1. Whittier did openly espouse the antislavery cause in 1833, as a result of Garrison's influence.

2. Whittier edited the *American Manufacturer* of Boston for seven months, beginning in January 1829. Garrison helped him secure the position.

3. Whittier was editor of the *New England Weekly Review*, published in Hartford, Connecticut, from June 1830 to January 1832.

4. For Whittier's reply to this letter, see John B. Pickard, ed., *The Letters of John Greenleaf Whittier* (Cambridge, 1975), vol. II, Letter No. 864.

262

TO SEVERAL AMERICAN FRIENDS OF
GEORGE THOMPSON

BOSTON, February 15, 1859.

DEAR FRIEND:

You are aware, doubtless, that our esteemed friend, and the early, self-sacrificing, intrepid, and eloquent advocate of universal emancipation, GEORGE THOMPSON, ESQ., returned from India to England some months ago, with ruined health and paralysis of all his limbs, so as to be helpless as a babe. Fearing, from his long protracted illness abroad, and his inability to do anything for his family since his return home, and also from his characteristic unwillingness to let his necessities be known to any one, that he might be in a straitened condition as to his means of daily subsistence, we requested our beloved coadjutor, REV. SAMUEL J. MAY, of Syracuse, now in England, to call upon Mr. Thompson, as soon as he arrived in London, and ascertain the exact situation of our afflicted friend. A long and very touching letter has just been received from Mr. May, dated London, Jan. 17, 1859, giving full particulars of the causes of Mr. Thompson's illness abroad, his terrible sufferings on his homeward voyage, his present somewhat improved state of health, and his pecuniary destitution. We make a brief extract. Mr. May says: —

"Mr. and Mrs. Thompson occupy a cottage in Surrey, at a rent of £50. I saw him on the 14th, walking to meet us, but looking much emaciated. Both his hands are still partially paralyzed, and somewhat misshapen. He cannot put them naturally and easily to his head. He cannot write any, nor can he dress and undress himself alone. Still, he has recovered much more, I am assured, than it was expected he ever would, even by his physicians; though he is but a wreck of what he was when we first knew him. . . . I think, however, he might be wholly restored to health, were it not for his pecuniary embarrassment, and the treatment he is receiving from the company in whose service he went to India, who refuse to pay the balance of his salary, because he left his post as the only means of saving his life, at the advice of his physicians in Calcutta. *He has no means of subsistence.* 'Indeed,' said he, 'I had not enough to pay the funeral expenses of my dear mother, who died about a fortnight ago.' *I wish his American friends would send him one thousand dollars.*"

This intelligence is distressing, and will awaken the liveliest sympathy and the most generous feelings in the breast of every one who is personally acquainted with Mr. Thompson; who remembers with admiration his unparalleled efforts in behalf of West India emancipation, and his subsequent labors in this country in the ANTI-SLAVERY cause, during the perilous times of 1834–5 — a mission of love and disinterested philanthropy, on his part, the results of which, in the furtherance of that beneficent cause, in a thousand particulars, are beyond sober estimate. To think of one so gifted, so thoroughly tried, so alive to the claims of suffering humanity, so dead to all selfish and personal considerations, so faithful and unswerving in his devotion to the right, so unobtrusive and uncomplaining when stricken and helpless, suffering for the means of daily subsistence, with his dependent family! It must not and will not be so long. We feel assured that his case only needs to be known to those to whom we send this private circular — private because a due regard to Mr. Thompson's feelings makes publicity undesirable — to induce them gladly to contribute something for his immediate relief. Any sum will be duly appreciated, and in due time gratefully acknowledged. A list of the donors will be forwarded to Mr. Thompson, for his gratification, and to quicken his reminiscences of persons and places in America.

Mr. May suggests that one thousand dollars should be raised for this purpose. This sum ought to be easily and promptly obtained, without severely taxing any one, among Mr. Thompson's many friends and admirers on this side of the Atlantic. It will be the means of saving him from sharp distress and sore privation, at least for a time; and it may, and doubtless will, exert a powerful influence in restoring him to health and public usefulness. It should be remembered that, for his spendid services in this country in behalf of impartial freedom, Mr. Thompson has never yet received a special token of the regard and gratitude of American abolitionists, such as his helpless situation makes it now so desirable to proffer him and his family.

Letters, enclosing aid for Mr. Thompson, may be addressed to either of the undersigned, or to FRANCIS JACKSON, ESQ., 27 Hollis Street, Treasurer of the American Anti-Slavery Society, who will see that the money is safely forwarded to Mr. T. at the earliest moment.

Wm. Lloyd Garrison,
Wendell Phillips
Maria Weston Chapman.

Printed form letter, signed by Garrison, Phillips and M. W. Chapman: Huntington Library, San Marino, California (enclosed in Garrison's letter to Susan B. Anthony of February 21, 1859).

---

2 6 3

TO MARIA W. CHAPMAN

Boston, Feb. 18, 1859

Dear Mrs. Chapman:

Herewith you will find the printed Circular in regard to the case of dear George Thompson. I have signed *all* the copies I send to you, and Phillips a large portion of them, and he will sign the remainder when received from you. Will you please add your signature, and return the package, if convenient, by the express to-morrow? I am impatient to get the letter off, and especially to get the needed returns, that Thompson may be relieved as speedily as possible. Keep as many copies as you choose, and oblige me by letting me know to whom you will send this appeal, so as to prevent a needless repetition in any case. Wendell has written to Gerrit Smith and Edward Harris.[1]

And so, dear Anne,[2] I hear, is soon to leave us for Europe. I wish I could go with her, but wishing is vain. May the voyage, and the sojourn abroad, restore her sight in full, and in every respect be a blessing to her! Being a married man, my admiration of her is not that of a lover; but it comes as near that as the case will admit!

My warm regards to her, and your mother, and Deborah,[3] and Hervey;[4]

Yours, ever for the right,

Wm. Lloyd Garrison.

Mrs. M. W. Chapman.

Transcript: Garrison Papers, Boston Public Library.

1. Edward Harris (b. Lime Rock, now Lincoln, Rhode Island, October 3, 1801; d. Woonsocket, Rhode Island, November 24, 1872), businessman, wool manufacturer, and banker, was also well known for his philanthropies. He was a temperance and antislavery advocate and liberally supported the abolitionist movement. After John Brown's raid on Harpers Ferry, he wrote a letter to Brown in jail, to which Brown responded. He helped Brown's family financially after the execution. (*Biographical Encyclopedia of Representative Men of Rhode Island*, Providence, 1881, Part I, pp. 228–230.)
2. Anne Warren Weston, Maria W. Chapman's sister.
3. Deborah Weston, another sister.
4. Hervey Weston, her brother.

2 6 4

TO SUSAN B. ANTHONY

Boston, Feb. 21, 1859.

Dear Friend:

I send this circular to you, not to tax your generosity, which is so overtaxed at all times, but to solicit your co-operation, by showing it to such of our friends in Rochester as may feel desirous to contribute to this fund, to any extent, by their sympathy with and regard for dear suffering George Thompson. Perhaps Mr. T. [may] have some admirers outside of your little anti-slavery circle, who, on knowing his situation, would readily make a donation for his relief.

Ever since I parted from Aaron,[1] at Hudson, until within a few days, I have been quite unwell, and wholly "used up" as to public speaking, through loss of voice.

Wife is in tolerable health, but not as I wish to see her, strong and vigorous. All send their kindest regards to you.

Yours, in every good work,

Wm. Lloyd Garrison.

Susan B. Anthony.

ALS: Huntington Library, San Marino, California.

1. Aaron M. Powell.

---

2 6 5

TO JOSEPH A. DUGDALE

Boston, Feb. 21, 1859.

Dear Joseph — I send this circular to you, not to tax your generosity which is so constantly overtaxed, although with very limited means, but thinking there may be some in your neighborhood, who, on hearing it read, or reading it for themselves, might be willing to contribute their mite, and esteem it a privilege to do so, toward the amount we are endeavoring to raise, as speedily as possible, for dear suffering George Thompson.

Wife and myself have been both quite unwell for a month past, but are now somewhat better. We send our loving regards to you and your wife, and to all the Longwood friends. In haste,

Ever faithfully yours,

Wm. Lloyd Garrison.

J. A. Dugdale.

ALS: Friends Historical Library, Swarthmore College (enclosing circular of February 15 about George Thompson).

---

2 6 6

TO JAMES FREEMAN CLARKE

Anti-Slavery Office, 21 Cornhill,
March 5, 1859.

Dear Sir:

The bearer of this is Mr. Casseres,[1] a most accomplished pianist, whose recommendations are of the best character, and who recently gave a very successful matinée in this city. He intends giving a public concert, in case he can get a sufficient number of tickets pledged in advance to warrant the undertaking, so as not to incur an expense which he cannot conveniently meet. You will see by his list of subscribers as commenced, that he starts under highly respectable auspices: — Gov. Banks,[2] Mr. Hillard,[3] Mr. Hale,[4] even Mr. Cushing,[5] (!) leading the way. Thinking it possible that you may be able to give him some names, &c., and knowing your hearty interest in every thing pertaining to a race "peeled, meted out, and trodden under foot"[6] in our land, I give him this introductory note; assuring him that, such is your "freedom in the Lord," such your conviction that it is always "lawful to do well on the sabbath day,"[7] you would not deem it out of time and place, at the conclusion of your forenoon services to-morrow, to have the matter broken to you.

On Tuesday, Mr. Nell[8] will take such names as Mr. Casseres can procure, and call upon them to ascertain how many of them will be willing to take tickets. The Concert cannot fail, if held, to prove a great success on the part of Mr. C.

I am very glad to see your article on the condition of the free colored population, in the last Christian Examiner.[9] I shall try to copy it entire in the Liberator as soon as practicable; probably in two numbers.

Can you let me have your excellent speech made at the State House before the Committee on Federal Relations, against slave-catching in this State — say, by Tuesday forenoon?[10] It was not reported by Mr. Yerrinton, as he thought you probably had the main portion of it written, and would prefer to prepare it for the press.

I spent a very agreeable evening with your mother,[11] last evening, at my venerated friend Mrs. Otis.

Yours, with high regards,

Wm. Lloyd Garrison.

Rev. J. F. Clarke.

ALS: Houghton Library, Harvard University.

James Freeman Clarke (1810–1888), prominent Boston Unitarian clergyman, graduated from the Harvard Divinity School and received his ordination in 1833. He was minister of a Unitarian church in Louisville, Kentucky, from 1833 to 1840, during part of which period he also edited the *Western Messenger*. In 1841, in Boston, he founded a new Unitarian church, the Church of the Disciples, of which he was pastor for the remainder of his life, except for the period from August 1850 to January 1, 1854, when he was absent because of ill health. In his later years, Clarke was a member of the State Board of Education, a trustee of the Boston Public Library, a nonresident professor at the Harvard Divinity School, and a member of the Board of Overseers of Harvard College. His reform activities included antislavery, temperance, and woman suffrage. Among his numerous published works were *The Christian Doctrine of Forgiveness of Sin* (1852), *The Christian Doctrine of Prayer* (1854), *Orthodoxy: Its Truths and Errors* (1866), *Ten Great Religions* (1871 and 1883), and *Anti-Slavery Days* (1884).

1. Señor Louis de Casseres, "of Spanish-African blood, a native of Jamaica." *Dwight's Journal of Music*, on Saturday, January 22, 1859, printed a review of a recital by Casseres, ending with, "Altogether the occasion was a very pleasant one, and Señor Casseres won the sympathies and the respect of his audience. . . ." See also the short item in *The Liberator*, February 25, 1859, entitled "An Accomplished Colored Pianist."

2. Governor Nathaniel P. Banks of Massachusetts.

3. George Stillman Hillard (1808–1879) of Boston, lawyer, orator and scholar, was a close friend of Charles Sumner, with whom he opened a law practice in 1834, and a well-known public figure. (*Letters*, II, 62.)

4. Nathan Hale (1784–1863) of Boston was a lawyer, journalist, and civic leader, editor of the Boston *Daily Advertiser* from 1814 to 1854, supporter of the Republican party, the first president of the Boston & Worcester Railroad from 1831 to 1849, chairman of the commission that established the Boston water system, and a founder of the *North American Review* in 1815. His son, Edward Everett Hale, had been pastor of the South Congregational Church in Boston since 1856, a position which he held for forty-three years, and was also to achieve distinction as an author.

5. Caleb Cushing.

6. Isaiah 18:7.

7. Luke 6:9; Mark 3:4.

8. William C. Nell.

9. Clarke's essay, "Condition of the Free Colored People of the United States," had appeared in the March issue of the *Christian Examiner*. It was reprinted in *The Liberator* on March 18 and 25, 1859.

The *Christian Examiner* of Boston, a Unitarian publication and one of the most important American religious journals of its time, had been founded in 1824 by, among others, Nathan Hale, the editor of the Boston *Advertiser*. In 1859, it was edited by Edward Everett Hale and Frederick Henry Hedge. Theodore Parker called it "the best religious periodical in America." (Frank Luther Mott, *A History of American Magazines*, vol. I, *1741–1850*, Cambridge, 1957, pp. 284–292.)

10. *The Liberator*, March 4, 1859, reported that "On Thursday evening, last week, another hearing was granted in the Representatives' Hall, by the Committee on Federal Relations, to the petitioners for the passage of a law, giving liberty and

protection to every fugitive slave coming within the limits of the Commonwealth. Notwithstanding the inclemency of the weather, the Hall was well filled by a deeply interested audience, whose feelings were evidently wholly with the object of the petitions. The speakers on this occasion, were Samuel E. Sewall, Esq., Rev. James Freeman Clarke, Francis W. Bird, Esq., Wm. Lloyd Garrison, and Rev. Samuel May, Jr. The speeches of Mr. Clarke and Mr. Bird we hope to be able to print next week. . . . The hearings being now closed, it is hoped, and reasonably expected, that the Committee having this matter in charge, will make a favorable report without delay, and that the Legislature will promptly meet the case, in the right manner, by an overwhelming vote." Clarke's address, delivered on February 24, was printed in *The Liberator*, March 11, 1859.

11. Rebecca Parker Hull (b. February 7, 1790; d. 1865) was a daughter of General William Hull. She married Dr. Samuel Clarke, of Newton, Massachusetts, on May 18, 1805. (Colonel Charles H. Weygant, *The Hull Family in America*, n. p., 1913, pp. 493, 512.)

---

2 6 7

TO JOHN W. HUTCHINSON

Boston, March 15, 1859.

Dear Friend:

Yours, of yesterday, is just received. I regret that you had the trouble of calling twice at the Anti-Slavery Office, without seeing me, especially on so kind and generous an errand. What you propose for the benefit of G[eorge] T[hompson] meets my warm approval; only I think, with you, that no public announcement of your *intention* should be made, as it might be individually commented upon in certain quarters, and perhaps make *him* a little sensitive, as he is one of the last men in the world to make any appeal for assistance in any direction, however straitened as to his circumstances. We will let our anti-slavery friends in the city privately know what your plan is, and I trust you will have a crowded hall on each evening. I am to lecture in Fall River on Tuesday evening, and so shall be deprived of the pleasure of seeing and hearing you.

Yours, for universal liberty,

Wm. Lloyd Garrison.

N. B. You may easily imagine how, in common with a great multitude of his friends and admirers, I was made sad, beyond expression, at the sudden termination of the earthly life of dear, impulsive, noble Judson, in the manner it happened. Of course, he knew not what he did. But he no longer sees "through a glass darkly" [1] — every fetter is broken — his spirit is free — and *all is well*! I should like to hear the songs he is now singing in "Jerusalem, my happy home!"

In the great struggle which has been going on so long to deliver our land from the tyrannous dominion of the Slave Power, and from the curse of slavery, and to make liberty the heritage and possession of every human being on our soil, the intelligent and impartial historian can never forget the disinterested and powerful aid rendered to it by "the Hutchinson Family." May you and yours, and Asa and family, long be preserved, to sing the songs of freedom and humanity in the ears of the people, and to see the triumph of the right!

ALS: Lynn Historical Society, Lynn, Massachusetts.

John Wallace Hutchinson (b. Milford, New Hampshire, January 4, 1821; fl. 1896), baritone and violinist, was a member of the famous "Hutchinson family" of singers, closely identified with the antislavery and temperance movements. The father, Jesse Hutchinson (b. Middleton, Massachusetts, February 3, 1778; d. Milford, New Hampshire, February 16, 1851) married Mary Leavitt of Mt. Vernon, New Hampshire, in 1800 and lived on a farm in Milford for several years. Of their sixteen children, three died in infancy and all had musical talent. Parents and children frequently sang in chorus at prayer-meetings and at home, and were constantly urged to appear in public. In 1841, the four youngest children, Judson, John, Asa, and Abby, formed a quartet which made a successful concert tour in New England. In 1842 and thereafter they worked closely with the abolitionists, singing at antislavery meetings and helping to spread the antislavery message. In 1845, they toured Europe and met with great success. Following Abby's marriage in 1849, the original quartet disbanded and various members of the family appeared in concerts. They gave concerts coast-to-coast in the United States during the election campaigns of 1856 and 1860, forming several groups from different members of the family, including the third generation. They were especially active during the Civil War at recruiting stations and army camps. In 1855, John, Judson, and Asa went to Minnesota and founded the town of Hutchinson, about sixty miles from St. Paul.

Abby Hutchinson (b. Milford, New Hampshire, August 29, 1829; d. New York City, November 24, 1892), the contralto, married Ludlow Patton of New York City in 1849, and thereafter retired from the group. Other members of the family continued to appear in concerts in various combinations.

Judson (b. Milford, New Hampshire, March 14, 1807; d. Lynn, Massachusetts, January 10, 1859), a tenor, was the leader of the quartet and the humorist of the troupe. He composed much of the music that they sang. Next to Abby, he was most beloved by the family and the public. As a result of financial and various other personal difficulties, including severe states of depression, Judson hanged himself.

Asa was the youngest son. He sang bass and was the executive. He married Elizabeth B. Chase of Nantucket in the late 1840's and had five children. He died in Hutchinson, Minnesota, November 25, 1884.

(John W. Hutchinson, *History of the Hutchinson Family*, 1893, I, 362–363; II, 255–260, 261–269.)

1. I Corinthians 13:12.

2 6 8

TO OLIVER JOHNSON

Boston, April 16, 1859.

My Dear Johnson:

Yours of yesterday is just received. I will not delay an answer to it. I do not wonder that you have felt a disappointment in not hearing from me before this, in reply to other letters that you have written; [1] but, the truth is, for a month past, I have been "good for nothing" — a mere "cumberer of the ground" [2] — in consequence of ill health; for the most part of the time lying upon my back, with a severe spinal attack, which assumed a neuralgic form; accompanied with a slow fever which still courses through my whole system, and renders me unfit for any kind of mental or physical effort. Hence I have omitted nearly all correspondence, though day after day hoping to be able to meet it. I am somewhat relieved, but still far from feeling well. Ill as I was, I should have made an effort promptly to answer your first letter, in regard to an increase of your salary, had I felt I could be warranted in giving you any hope of success in your application. But I said nothing to the Committee about it, because I know it would be useless to do so — not for lack of a just appreciation of your valuable services and arduous labors, not because yours is an adequate salary, but because the expenses of the Standard are already so great, that they keep our Committee divided on the question of continuing it any longer. Besides, before your letter came, we had just voted to accept the proposition to enroll Harriet Martineau among the regular correspondents of the Standard, at an expense of £50 per annum — an acquisition to us, for many reasons, worth a great deal more than the cost; one or two of our Committee, however, demurring even to this arrangement. My hope is, that the Standard will so increase its subscription list as hereafter to make an increase of your salary a more than probable event.

I know how you labor, and can imagine the endless interruptions and annoyances to which you are subjected, in your daily routine. I know, too, how expensive city living is, and how that expense is augmenting rather than diminishing. My own experience is very convincing on that point; for my house is a semi-hotel, with the numerous anti-slavery friends and visitors whom I am called to entertain, and whose presence is ever welcome. Do what I will, my annual expenses are large, as my situation here exposes me to these liabilities, unavoidably. I am never so far in funds as to have a spare dollar by me, using what economy I can.

The obituary notice of our departed friend Arnold Buffum [3] was very well prepared, if it *was* written by Lewis Tappan; yet I suppose I should not have copied it into the Liberator, if I had known or suspected that it came from the pen of L.T. It seems he is angry because I omitted the fact, that friend Buffum was a member of the Executive Committee of the American and Foreign A.S. Society; but I took that liberty, because I never felt that A.B. was at all animated by the new organization *spirit*, though I always thought he was culpable in consenting to remain in such a connexion; and he always seemed to me to be singularly obfuscated in supposing or pleading that his justification was to be found in his willingness to work with everybody in behalf of the slave. You describe his characteristics accurately. If you think I had better insert what I left out, I will do so; but, in that case, I shall have to make some comments which I would rather not be forced to print.[4]

Your solicitude in regard to our approaching anniversary is largely shared by myself. I am not aware, however, that anyone is thinking of making an issue with me, or with our Society, on that occasion; but we, in some sort, must always "run for luck" at our anniversary. If we "cut and dry" every meeting, we shall be sure to have a storm raised in the quarter, and by the persons, to whom you refer; yet, as far as practicable, our Committee will be disposed to make the needful arrangements. As yet, we do not know, certainly, who will consent to speak, beyond the Rev. Mr. Milligan [5] of Pennsylvania. Phillips we must calculate upon, of course. I hope Dr. Furness will be with us. Rev. O. B. Frothingham has promised to do so, conditionally. Whether I shall be able to take my part in the proceedings, I cannot now tell. We shall be glad to have Mr. Giddings, if he be in the city at that time.

Victoria and her husband [6] passed through Boston, a day or two since, for New Bedford. I saw Mr. Smith, for a few moments, at the office, and expected to see them both at my house, by agreement, in the afternoon, but a hail storm prevented. Lasting bliss be theirs!

Warmest regards to Mary Ann.

W.L.G.

☞ Mr. Burr [7] has offered to be our reporter this year, but Mr. Yerrinton is engaged for this anniversary.

Transcript: Garrison Papers, Boston Public Library.

1. Oliver Johnson had first written to Garrison about an increase in his salary on March 3, 1859. He was receiving a slary of $1,000 a year and was barely able to make ends meet. He pointed out that he had no means for dentistry and was "somewhat pinched to meet ordinary expenses." Theodore Tilton, who had a lesser position on the *Independent*, was earning $1,500 a year and ordinary reporters on New York's daily papers earned more than he. The letter was written in confidence and emphasized that Johnson would accept Garrison's advice in the matter, what-

ever it might be. (Antislavery Letters to Garrison and Others, Boston Public Library.)

2. Luke 13:7.

3. The first notice of Arnold Buffum's death appeared in *The Liberator*, March 18, 1859. In reporting the death, it noted that Buffum was "the first President of the New England (now the Massachusetts) Anti-Slavery Society, and the first to enter the lecturing field in their behalf. He died at Eagleswood, Perth Amboy, N. J., on Monday last, after a short but severe illness, at the ripe age of 77. His end was peace — his mind bright — his faith firm."

Two obituaries of Buffum were reprinted from the *Standard* in *The Liberator*. The first appeared in *The Liberator*, March 25, 1859, and was reprinted from the *Standard* of March 19, 1859. A longer and more detailed obituary appeared in the *Standard*, March 26, 1859, and was reprinted in *The Liberator*, April 8, 1859. There were omissions from both.

4. The first omission was as follows: "After the secession of 1840, he acted for some years with the New Organization; but he has often said that he did this, not from any want of confidence in his former associates, but because the new Society afforded him, as he thought, a very desirable opportunity for serving the cause, in the circumstances in which he was then placed. We, of course, must regard this as a great error of judgment on his part, but we have no reason to doubt that he acted conscientiously; and certainly he has never faltered in his testimony against slavery." The omission from the second obituary mentioned Buffum's membership on the executive committee of the American and Foreign Anti-Slavery Society.

5. The Reverend Alexander McCloud Milligan (April 6, 1822–May 7, 1885), the son of a minister, classical scholar and abolitionist, was a precocious child who read the Bible in Hebrew and Greek before he was thirteen, and graduated from Duquesne College in 1843 and from the Reformed Presbyterian Theological Seminary in Allegheny, Pennsylvania, in 1847. He was ordained and installed as pastor at New Alexandria, Pennsylvania, in 1848, and remained there until 1853, when he was called to the Third Reformed Presbyterian Church in Philadelphia, where he stayed until 1856. From 1856 to 1866, he served several churches in New Alexandria, Clarksburg, and Greensboro, Pennsylvania. His last congregation, which he served beginning in 1866, was the Eighth Street Pittsburgh congregation. He was a prominent abolitionist, was assaulted twice by mobs and narrowly escaped with his life. Kossuth said of him that he was "the ablest natural orator he ever heard on either side of the Atlantic." Milligan also corresponded with John Brown after the latter's capture at Harpers Ferry. (John N. Boucher, *Old and New Westmoreland*, New York, 1819, II, 624–626. See also *Letters*, II, 112; the source there, probably incorrectly, gives 1827 as the date of Milligan't birth.)

6. Henry Mitchell Smith (1835–1901), a native of New York City, had married Jennie Victoria Knight on April 7, 1859. He graduated from the New York Medical College in 1860 and joined the American Institute of Homoeopathy during the same year. His obituary notes that in 1856 "in the Fremont campaign he took considerable interest in politics, and at about that time made the acquaintance of Wm. Cullen Bryant, Wm. Lloyd Garrison, Richard McCormick, Horace Greeley, and other well-known men." Smith occupied the chair of physiology in the New York Medical College for Women from 1865 to 1866 and the same chair in the New York Homoeopathic Medical College from 1866 to 1868, and made many contributions to the literature of homoeopathy. (*Biographical Cyclopaedia of Homoeopathic Physicians and Surgeons*, Chicago, 1893, p. 88; Eugene H. Porter, ed., *Transactions of the Fifty-Seventh Session of the American Institute of Homoeopathy, held at Richfield Springs, N.Y., June 18, 1901*, New York, 1902, pp. 918–920; *Transactions of the Homoeopathic Medical Society of the State of New York for the Year 1902*, XXXVII, 310–311; letter dated February 15, 1973, from John B. Blake, Ph.D., Chief, History of Medicine Division, National Institutes of Health, Bethesda, Maryland; also see Letter 215, May 1, 1858.)

7. William Henry Burr.

2 6 9

TO WILLIAM H. FURNESS

Boston, April 21, 1859.

Dear Mr. Furness:

At a meeting of the Executive Committee of the American Anti-Slavery Society, a few days since, I was unanimously requested to give you a most cordial and brotherly invitation to be one of the speakers at the approaching anniversary of that Society in New York — May 10th and 11th — leaving you to choose any one of the four public meetings that will be held, to suit your own convenience; though preferring to have you speak at the opening meeting on Tuesday forenoon, if agreeable to you. We know how unfeigned is your diffidence in regard to appearing on such a platform — your habit of preparing your Sunday discourses as for the press — and that you have again and again complied with a similar request on our part, which nothing but the deepest sympathy with the fettered slaves in our land could have induced you to do; and, therefore, we would not be deemed importunate, as though we thought great urgency were needed. What we desire to say is, that your presence is ever inspiring, your words ever most acceptable, and we strongly wish to see you and hear you as often as our anniversary recurs. I need hardly say that all your expenses to New York, and home again, will be cheerfully paid by the Society.[1]

It has given me the greatest pleasure to publish in this week's Liberator the whole of your most timely, and pertinent, and morally impressive, and eloquent discourse on "Religion and Politics." I wish it could find millions of readers.[2]

What a scene, what a struggle, and what a triumphant result you have had in Philadelphia, in regard to the last fugitive slave case! But how guilty is Pennsylvania, and Massachusetts, and every Northern State, in allowing a human being to be placed on trial to determine the question whether he has a right to himself, or is owned by another! [3]

Yours, with the warmest regards,

Wm. Lloyd Garrison.

Rev. Wm. H. Furness.

ALS: University of Pennsylvania.

1. Dr. Furness accepted Garrison's invitation. *The Liberator*, April 29, 1859, listed him as one of the speakers. His address appeared in *The Liberator*, May 20, 1859.

2. This address was printed in *The Liberator*, April 20, 1859. Dr. Furness had delivered it in the First Congregational Unitarian Church in Philadelphia, Sunday, March 20, 1859.

3. Garrison refers to the freeing of an alleged fugitive slave named Daniel Webster by United States Commissioner J. Cooke Longstreth in Philadelphia on April 6. He was freed on the basis of unproven identity. (*The Liberator*, April 15, 1859.)

270

TO JAMES MONROE

Boston, April 22, 1859.

Dear Sir:

I take the liberty of inquiring of you, whether there is any chance for an amiable and worthy colored youth, (handsome, and but slightly tinctured with African blood, about 19 or 20 years of age,) to obtain an education at your Oberlin institution, he paying his way by some sort of manual labor. He can read and write, but has a strong desire to be taught other branches of learning, so that he in turn may become a teacher, or in some other way useful to those who are identified with him in complexion and destiny. He has no knowledge of any mechanical trade, having been a house-servant; but he is willing to do any manual service whereby he may be able to secure what he so much desires. He is modest, gentle, and pleasing in his manners. I told him I would write to you on the subject; assuring him that his complexion would be no barrier to his getting a favorable response to his application at Oberlin, if nothing else stood in the way.

He would be very useful in a hotel, if a place could be found for him in O.

He is very anxious to get an immediate answer; and as, through illness, I have delayed writing to you some two or three weeks, since first he made known his wishes to me, I shall feel under special obligation to you if you will answer this at your earliest convenience. I hope it will be in your power to return a favorable answer.

What a humiliating spectacle is presented to the world in the trials [1] now going on at Cleveland of your humane and Christian citizens who so nobly "delivered the spoiled out of the hands of the oppressor"! [2] Of course, as the jury has been constituted, their conviction is inevitable. What a work of moral regeneration yet remains to be done in Ohio, in Massachusetts, throughout the North, in opposition to slavery and slave-hunting! But this very prosecution will give a fresh impetus to our noble cause.

Yours, with warm regards,

Wm. Lloyd Garrison.

Prof. James Munroe. [3]

ALS: Monroe Papers, Oberlin College Library. A portion of this letter is quoted in Robert Samuel Fletcher, *A History of Oberlin College, From its Foundation to the Civil War* (Oberlin, Ohio, 1943), p. 414.

James Monroe (b. Plainfield, Connecticut, July 18, 1821; d. Oberlin, Ohio, July 6, 1898) was an antislavery lecturer in Connecticut and neighboring states before studying at Oberlin College, where he graduated in 1846. He was professor of rhetoric and belles lettres at Oberlin from 1849 to 1862. He was also a member of the Ohio House of Representatives from 1856 to 1859 and of the Ohio Senate from 1860 to 1862. He served as United States consul to Rio de Janeiro from 1863 to 1869. He was elected to Congress in 1870 and served from 1871 to 1881. He spent most of his later years, 1883–1896, as professor of political science and modern history at Oberlin. (Fletcher, *A History of Oberlin College*, pp. 390–391, 899, 903.)

1. On September 13, 1858, John Rice, a black man, living in Oberlin, Ohio, was arrested near Oberlin by a deputy United States marshall and his assistant, and two Kentuckians who claimed him as a runaway slave from Kentucky. He was taken to Wellington, Ohio, the nearest station on the Cleveland and Columbus railroad, and held in a tavern awaiting a train for his journey back to Kentucky. As news of the arrest spread throughout the area a crowd of people from both Oberlin and Wellington gathered and demanded that Rice be freed. His captors, fearful of the crowd, released him and he was quickly spirited away to safety.

On December 6, a United States grand jury, sitting at Cleveland, indicted thirty-seven alleged participants in the rescue, most from Oberlin, some from Wellington. These included Professor Peck of Oberlin, a number of theological students, and some of the most prominent residents of both towns. The first to be tried was Simeon Bushnell, the driver of the wagon in which Rice drove off. His trial began on April 5, 1859. The abolitionists charged that the jury was carefully selected so as to return a guilty verdict, which it did ten days later. Next to be tried was Charles H. Langston, who was also pronounced guilty. Thereupon, the antislavery men of the area retaliated through a grand jury indictment and arrest of those involved in Rice's arrest. However, one day before their trial, an agreement was reached whereby all pending prosecutions were abandoned "and all the unconvicted prisoners were at once set free." (*Annual Report of the American Anti-Slavery Society, by the Executive Committee, For the Year Ending May 1, 1859*, New York, 1859, pp. 91–97; also, . . . *For the Year Ending May 1, 1860*, pp. 63–74.)

2. Jeremiah 21:12, 22:3.
3. The correct spelling is Monroe.

271

TO HELEN E. GARRISON

New York, May 12, 1859.

My dear Wife:

Our anniversary meetings being terminated, I take a breathing spell, and sit down the first thing this morning to report progress. And first, as to our Monday's ride to this city. The day, you will recollect, was as sultry as in July or August — the mercury ranging as high in the shade as 88 or 90 deg., with a burning sun, a cloudless sky, and any quantity of dust to smother and annoy us, especially over that portion of our route which lies between Hartford and New York. Our anti-slavery company in the cars consisted of Francis Jackson, Phillips, Quincy, Remond, and Mrs. Severance [1] and Mrs. Dall, with the two last of whom I rode all the way, and, of course, had a very agreeable social chit-chat on matters and things in general. On arriving here, I went immediately to bro. George's,[2] where I had a warm greeting, and spent the night. Bro. G. has had some very severe attacks of neuralgia, but he is now better, though unable to predict what a day will bring forth in regard to that strange, mysterious, and intolerable disease. Sarah Benson [3] has grown nearly as tall as Fanny, straight as an arrow, and looking fresh and handsome as a rose. Mary is quite tall, but is looking thin and cadaverous, as though she were going into a decline. George and Tommy are fine young men, and board with the family. The Washing and Bathing Institution has not been in operation, to any extent, for several months past, and it is very doubtful what will be done with it, as it needs repairs to the extent of five or six hundred dollars. Of course, not being in operation, Catharine [Benson] has had no connection with it all that time, and, consequently, has been cut off from the stipend she has usually received in that direction. How the family has contrived to live, I do not know; but, at times, they must be sorely pressed for means. I think, Catharine would like to get on a farm, if one could be obtained, but is ready to do any thing, and to go any where, that may hold out the prospect of a comfortable subsistence. Bro. G. did intend to make another visit to Kansas, but, for the present, at least, will remain at home. He says that Henry Egbert writes from Lawrence that he has abandoned the idea of going to Pike's Peak, and thinks George Thompson [Garrison] has concluded not to go. Perhaps you have had a letter from the latter since I left home. If so, I hope he sends relief to all our minds by confirming what Henry writes.

Next, as to the weather we have had. You know that I predicted we should not escape without a cold, dreary, Northeasterly rain-storm; for I do not *remember* an exception to this, for twenty-five years, during anniversary week; yet on Monday evening, hot, sweltering as it was, a genuine dog-day, nothing seemed more unlikely to happen. But on rising the next morning, presto! and what a change! "As cold as Greenland" — every body shivering and shaking — a dismal storm, which has continued without abatement to this hour. Rain, rain, rain, and mud and nastiness *ad nauseam,* and in any quantity. It was lucky indeed that you insisted on my bringing along with me my great-coat, for I have had to wear it continually, and hardly been comfortable at that. My rubber over-shoes have also been needed as much as at any time of the year. Every thing has been extremely dreary.

Next, as to our anniversary. The weather, of course, has been against us, from beginning to end, and our great and magnificent hall altogether more spacious than we needed. Still, the attendance throughout was respectable in character and numbers, and, on the whole, more numerous than ever before. The meetings were all interesting and high-toned, and the speaking generally very good. I made no speech, but, as presiding officer, had occasion to make a few incidental remarks, now and then. Among other speakers were two Unitarian ministers, Rev. Mr. Longfellow [4] and Rev. Mr. Noyes.[5] Lucretia Mott was not able to be with us till the second day. Last evening's meeting, in spite of the dismal storm, was a very large one, Dr. Cheever [6] being among the auditors. Phillips made a great effort, as he did at our first meeting, and every thing ended in the best manner. This afternoon and evening, the women are to have their Convention.[7]

Next, as to my health. I have got along far better than I had any right to suppose I could, and think the journey will prove advantageous, judging by my present feelings. So, you need not feel any uneasiness on my account. I still intend going to Eagleswood [8] on Saturday, remaining over Sunday, and getting to Boston Monday, in the midnight train.

I have had a warm welcome at John Hopper's, kissed the baby, and had a good time generally.

Ever so many inquiries are made after you and the children.

Hoping to hear from you before my return, and sending a father's love to the children, I remain,

Ever your devoted husband,

Wm. Lloyd Garrison.

N.B. What has been the conclusion in regard to Mary Ann? I hope she is better than when I left.

ALS: Garrison Papers, Boston Public Library.

1. Carolina Maria Seymour (1820–1914), a native of New York, married Theodoric Cordenio Severance, a young Ohioan born in New England, in 1840, and moved to Cleveland, Ohio, where Severance entered the banking business. Their home was a gathering place for abolitionists, woman's rights and temperance people, and a variety of other reformers. Carolina Severance became especially active in woman's rights during the 1850's. In 1855, the family moved to Boston, where Mrs. Severance attended Theodore Parker's church and became active in the antislavery movement. In 1875, she and her husband moved to Los Angeles, California, where she continued her reform and cultural activities. (*Notable American Women.*)

2. George W. Benson.

3. Sarah, Mary, George, Tommy, and Henry Egbert were George W. Benson's children. (See *Letters*, II, xxiv.)

4. The Reverend Samuel Longfellow (1819–1892) attended and graduated from the Harvard Divinity School in the 1840's and was ordained a Unitarian minister at Fall River, Massachusetts, in February 1848. In 1853, he received a call to the Second Unitarian Church in Brooklyn, New York, where he remained

until 1860. Longfellow wrote poetry, composed hymns, and published a two-volume biography of his brother Henry Wadsworth Longfellow in 1886, and a sequel, *Final Memorials of Henry Wadsworth Longfellow,* in 1892.

5. The *National Anti-Slavery Standard,* April 9, 1859, carried the following notice: "We learn, also, that still another free pulpit is to be immediately set up in this city, by the Rev. George R. Noyes, late pastor of the Unitarian Church in Chicago. Mr. Noyes repudiates every sectarian name, and hopes to gather a congregation of spirits akin to himself, to whom he may be useful as a religious teacher. . . . He has come to New York, not upon anybody's invitation, but from a conviction of duty — a belief that this is the field appointed for him by Providence; and he proposes, we understand, to commence preaching at his own charge, trusting to find, in due time, all needed sympathy and support. The inaugural service, we learn, will be held in Hope Chapel tomorrow (Sunday) afternoon, at half-past 3 o'clock. Mr. Noyes will preach an anti-slavery gospel."

6. George Barrell Cheever (1807–1890), a native of Maine, clergyman and reformer, was ordained at the Howard Street Congregational Church in Salem, Massachusetts, in 1833, served as pastor of the Allen Street Presbyterian Church in New York from 1838 to 1844, as editor of the New York *Evangelist* in 1845, and as pastor of the Church of the Puritans, Union Square, New York, from 1846 to 1867. He was actively antislavery and a prolific writer on theology, poetry, and the evils of slavery, his books including *God Against Slavery* (1857) and *The Guilt of Slavery and the Crime of Slaveholding, Demonstrated from the Hebrew and Greek Scriptures* (1860).

7. The National Woman's Rights Association held its annual meeting in New York City on Tuesday evening, May 12, in Mozart Hall. A report of the meeting appeared in the *Standard,* May 21, 1859.

8. Eagleswood, New Jersey, the site of Theodore Weld's home and school.

272

TO DR. C. F. GEIST

Boston, May 23, 1859.

Dr. C. F. Geist:

Dear Sir — I feel honored by the invitation of the Committee of Arrangements to be present at a dinner to be provided in Faneuil Hall, on the 2d of June, complimentary to the members of the American Institute of Homoeopathy,[1] and trust nothing will occur to prevent my compliance with it.

Mrs. Garrison hopes to be able to be with me at the Social Levee and Promenade Supper in the evening.

Rejoicing at the extension and triumph of the Homoeopathic[2] as against the nauseous and destructive Allopathic[3] treatment, I remain,

Yours, for freedom and progress,

Wm. Lloyd Garrison.

ALS: New York Historical Society.

1. The American Institute of Homoeopathy was organized in 1844 and is the oldest national medical organization in the United States. (*HEUSH.*)

2. Homoeopathy: "a system of medical practice that treats a disease esp. by

the administration of minute doses of a remedy that would in healthy persons produce symptoms of the disease treated." (*Webster's Seventh New Collegiate Dictionary*, 1967.)

　　3. Allopathy: "a system of medical practice that combats disease by remedies producing effects different from those produced by the disease treated." (*Ibid.*)

---

2 7 3

TO PARKER PILLSBURY

Boston, June 3, 1859.

My Dear Friend:

　A whole week has transpired since you put your explanatory letter into my hands, when I did not mean to allow twenty-four hours to elapse before answering it. So much for continual interruptions and engagements.

　At our annual meeting in January,[1] I was surprised at what seemed to me the sombre and discouraging views of the state of our cause taken by Mrs. Foster, Mr. Higginson, and yourself;[2] and, in order to give a more cheerful tone to the meeting, I indulged in a little pleasantry — not dreaming of giving any offense, or exciting any feeling, in any breast. On leaving the platform, however, Mr. Higginson followed me into the ante-room, and exhibited a good deal of excitement — accusing me of attacking *him* personally, and attempting to throw ridicule upon him. All that I could do was to protest that I had not singled him out for invidious criticism as he had declared, and that I only aimed to throw a little sunshine upon what I thought was a depressing state of the atmosphere. He did not seem willing to accept my explanation, but left me in an inflamed mood of mind, averring that I had made *him* the special target of my ridicule — &c. I was greatly surprised at his sensitiveness, and especially at his unwillingness to receive my statement as satisfactory; but I could do no more in the premises.

　In the afternoon of the same day, you made a rejoinder to my speech — a speech which I understood you to say you did not hear — wherein you held me up to the audience, (so I understood your remarks at the time, and so did all with whom I then conversed,) as singling out for scurrilous abuse and low ridicule Abby Kelley Foster; and intimating that, at some future day, in view of "her cracked voice and gray hairs," having worn herself out in the service of the slave, it would be no very pleasant recollection to me that I had sought to make her a laughing-stock — &c. Your aim seemed to be to excite for her the deepest sympathy of the audience, and the most indignant feelings against myself. I thought you manifested a perturbed state of mind, and a good deal of personal feeling on the occasion. No single occurrence ever took me more by surprise, or filled me with greater astonishment; no rebuke ever seemed to me more uncalled for, no impeachment more gratuitous and unjust. At the conclusion of your remark, I rose, and, expressing my surprise at what had fallen from your lips, and that you could conceive it possible for me to hold up to ridicule the "cracked voice and gray hairs" of one I so loved and honored as A. K. F., (who has not a gray hair in her head, I am told,) I emphatically disclaimed the charge, and cast it from me wide as the poles asunder; saying that if you had heard my speech, you could not possibly have thrown such an imputation upon me.[3] Mrs. Foster followed me, exonerating me from the imputation, and declaring that she took no offense at my language.[4] Under these circumstances, I was greatly surprised and pained that you did not come forward, and express your gratification to find that you had got a wrong impression of what had fallen from my lips in your absence from the meeting; and I felt your silence most keenly.

In your letter, you say that you protested against the construction I had placed upon your criticism, both while sitting upon the sofa behind me, and afterwards openly in remarks before the meeting. To this, I can only say that I have no recollection of any distinct disclaimer on your part as touching the substance of your impeachment — that is, holding Abby up to ridicule, with her "cracked voice," &c. She herself, at the close of the anniversary, begged me to overlook it, — apologizing for you that you were sick, and consequently in a somewhat morbid state. *I followed her advice,* and let it pass; though, as Mr. Phillips told you, (not only without my consent, but in opposition to my express injunction to say nothing to you on the subject,) I very keenly felt the severe and unmerited rebuke you gave me on that occasion.

Referring to this unpleasant collision, (which to me came "like hail from a clear sky,") you say, "Now it seemed to me at that time, that *I was the injured party.* You put most severe & unjust words into my mouth, which I did not utter, could not utter, and then commented upon them with very great harshness indeed." Though I may not have given your language *verbatim,* do I understand you to say that you did not represent me as acting in an unfeeling and cruelly satirical manner toward Abby — nor mean any such thing? What, then, did you mean and say? How is it that every body present understood you as I did? Can you recall your words? For *what* was I censurable? I used no names, I cast no personal reflections, but only spoke of the unusually lugubrious speeches that had been made that day, and tried to relieve the sombre shading of the picture — nothing more. The effect was certainly instantaneous — the relief universal.

I heartily accept the expression of your "deep regrets and deeper sorrow" that you should have "seemed" to do me injustice; and I as freely say that I am not less regretful if I have at any time, in your judgment, misrepresented or misinterpreted your words or actions. It has not been in my heart to do so; and I sincerely wish "bygones to be bygones."

A word on another subject. You say — "From my stand-point, and with my experience, I am compelled to differ with you in my estimate of the Republican party," &c. And you add — "Certainly, I cannot possibly regard that party, as you pronounced it, *'the hope of the country.'* " This quotation does me gross injustice, and I am sorry to see it in your letter. It is part of a dislocated sentence — a fraction of a very cautious and definite statement. After saying, "My hope is in the Republican party," I added with emphasis — "Mark me! not the Republican party where it now stands, or as to its non-extension policy, but as to its MATERIALS, — embodying as it does the intelligence, virtue, moral sentiment, and political A. S. feeling of the North, — in contrast to the thoroughly demoralized, pro-slavery Democratic party, which is ready to do any thing demanded by the Slave Power; and so, out of those MATERIALS, working up the Northern mind to our stand-point of Disunion." If I had said, "My hope is in the Republican party," and left the remark unexplained, I should have falsified all my declarations against it, in regard

AL: Garrison Papers, Boston Public Library; apparently a first draft. The letter is unfinished, with many corrections, insertions, etc. Where Garrison has corrected his grammar or has substituted one word for another, with the original crossed out, only the final phrasing has been retained.

1. The twenty-seventh annual meeting of the Massachusetts Anti-Slavery Society, held in Boston on January 27 and 28, 1859.

2. Parker Pillsbury, Abby Kelley Foster, and Thomas Wentworth Higginson had spoken, in that order, in what seemed indeed to be a "sombre" mood and had attacked the Republican party as being equally hostile and detrimental, with the Democratic party, to the antislavery movement. Pillsbury had begun the attack with resolutions which asserted that "the subtle and fiendish spirit of hostility to the Anti-Slavery cause, that was at first exhibited through colonization schemes, clerical appeals, and a liberty party, (falsely so called,) is now acting with far more power and hope of success in the Republican party, and calls for more vigor and watchfulness on the part of the genuine friends of the slave, than did any of its earlier manifestations," and that "the Republican party, in protecting slavery where it is, and in all its pledges, promises and oaths to support and prolong the Union, is quite as reprehensible as the Democratic party in seeking to extend it; and acting, as it does professedly as a party opposed to slavery, is becoming far more dangerous to the cause of freedom than its opponents with a more open policy and course of action."

Abby Kelley Foster seconded Pillsbury's resolutions and made the following comments: "The Republican party are so near us that we find it difficult to apply to them the needed rebuke and opposition for their unfaithfulness to the principles we hold in common. Nevertheless, such rebuke ought to be given. I call upon every member of the Republican party to cease from his present coöperation with the slave-hunter and the kidnapper. The Republican party voted the money that re-enslaved Anthony Burns, and every voter in it is responsible for the guilt of that act.

"Self-gratulation is yet premature with us. Nothing has been done, while anything remains to be done. The present is the most dangerous crisis to which Anti-Slavery has ever been subjected. We were more secure when our foes were open and undisguised. At present, the Republican party is stealthily sucking the very blood from our veins.

"Our work is to be done over again. We must convert those who think they are already converted. Henry Wilson boasted that the Republicans fought the Democrats on every new issue. We must add to that, that they unite with the Democrats on all the more vital and essential old issues. . . ."

Higginson, for the most part, spoke in a similar vein. "The quiet of the present period forebodes great and imminent danger. Here we are, meeting in peace, not persecuted, only neglected. This indifference is worse than the howling of angry multitudes. Any one can mount guard well in time of open opposition; the period of quiet requires yet more resolution, more vigilance. The unanimity of the Republican party is the surest token of its doom. . . .

"The slave power stands behind all parties and all measures. We have cleared away many new issues, settled many new questions; but slavery still stands there, silent, but mighty. We have not yet grappled with that. When will the actual struggle come?

"The time is coming when our premature congratulations will be checked by disgraceful defeat. . . ."

Garrison is reported in *The Liberator* as having commented on the remarks of the previous speakers as follows: "Mr. Garrison thought the tone of the remarks this afternoon unduly desponding and lugubrious. Was it dangerous to our cause to admit that we had made progress? Was the recognition of this fact an assumption that nothing more was to be done? It is well for us occasionally to review our course, and to rejoice in what we have gained. We have no occasion to speak in desponding tones. I think the signs of the times cheerful and hopeful.

"As to the Republican party, every political party will be proportionate to the character of the people. This one is a time-serving, a temporizing, a cowardly party; yet it is plainly distinguishable in some respects from the Democratic party. The Republican is a pie-bald, a heterogeneous party, very diverse in the constituents which compose it. It has never professed, as the old 'Liberty party' did, to be an Anti-Slavery party. It claims only to oppose the extension of slavery, and it does oppose it. It has really tried to do the work which it has claimed to undertake." (For a detailed report of the proceedings, see *The Liberator*, February 4, 1859.)

3. Although speeches by Pillsbury and Garrison, delivered during the afternoon in question, are reported in apparent detail, there is no reference in them or in the remainder of the procedings to the personal altercation between the two men concerning Mrs. Foster.

4. These remarks were not reported in *The Liberator*.

2 7 4

TO G. LYMAN DWIGHT

Boston, June 12, 1859.

Dear Sir:

No apology was needed, on your part, for soliciting of me my auto-graph. I should have complied with your request at an earlier date, had I not been absent from the city for several days past.

Yours, truly,

Wm. Lloyd Garrison.

G. Lyman Dwight.

ALS: Brown University Library.

Gamaliel Lyman Dwight (b. February 3, 1841; fl. Providence, Rhode Island, 1874) was the son of Gamaliel Lyman Dwight, a lawyer in Providence, who died in 1854. The young Dwight was a freshman at Brown University when the Civil War broke out and joined a Rhode Island battery, leaving the army in 1864 as a captain. He then studied medicine at Harvard Medical School and Berlin, Germany, married Anne Ives Carrington in 1871, and was living in Providence in 1874, although not practicing medicine, because of his health. (Benjamin W. Dwight, *The History of the Descendants of John Dwight of Dedham, Mass.*, New York, 1874, I, 485.)

2 7 5

TO LYDIA MARIA CHILD

Boston, June 14, 1859.

My dear Mrs. Child:

Yesterday morning, I put a letter to you into the post-office, and last evening received one from you, not in reply to mine, of course, but kindly inviting wife and myself to spend next Sunday with you and David, at Wayland. The state of my throat and lungs is the only thing that makes me hesitate to send you an affirmative answer; and yet, I want to see you so much with particular reference to the work that I suggested in my letter, that I will venture to make the engagement, (provided the weather be not stormy) — and therefore you may expect to see me on Saturday evening, on the arrival of the stage.

Wife desires me to send you her kindest regards and warmest thanks, and to say that she would be most happy to accompany me to Wayland; but she has been away from home so much of late, that she feels as if she ought to look after the children at home; though she may alter her mind. She is, however, anticipating with much pleasure a visit from you and your husband at no distant day, at our house.

You say you have had an attack of rheumatism in the foot, and ingenuously confess, "That comes of working in my garden on Sunday." No doubt of it! And this might be a very serious matter indeed, to be most gravely considered, if no such consequence were ever known to follow working in a garden on Monday, Tuesday, or any other "secular" day of the week. How Nature, by her constant and unerring operations, satirizes and explodes the dogma, that one day in seven is more holy than another! But you very consolingly remark, that *if* God commanded men to be stoned to death for picking up sticks on Sunday, you ought to consider yourself "let off very cheaply to have only a lame foot for setting out plants three hours, on his holy day." I think so too; but, in that case, where is the justice or impartiality of that Being who is said to be "no respecter of persons"? This making fish of one, and flesh of another, it is hard to reconcile. It must be left among "the divine mysteries"!

I would rather have your rheumatism, incurred by treading under foot a superstitious notion, than to be exempt from it by compliance with that folly. When shall the conception of a jealous and vindictive God be banished from the earth? Not while a priest remains above ground.

With my high regards to Mr. Child, I remain,

Yours for physical, mental and spiritual freedom,

Wm. Lloyd Garrison.

L. Maria Child.

☞ I pray you not to put yourself to the slightest trouble on my account, on the score of eating and drinking. I am "one of the family."

ALS: College of the Holy Cross, Worcester, Mass.

276

TO MR. AND MRS. JOHN JAY

Boston, June 21, 1859.

Dear Mr. and Mrs. Jay:

For the kind invitation extended to us to be of the company at your sweet homestead on Thursday next, to witness the wedding rites [1] to be performed on that occasion, accept our warmest thanks; and be assured that it would be most gladly accepted by us, if circumstances rendered it convenient. We will not fail at least to remember the hour, and in spirit will try to imagine the scene, and to participate in its joyous festivity. Our best wishes for the bridegroom and the bride, that their union may prove felicitous and enduring to them, a rich blessing to yourselves, and unalloyed satisfaction to all relatives and friends. The former we have known from his childhood. As the worthy son of honored parents, whose friendship we have greatly prized from an early period, we feel a special interest in whatever relates to his well-being and happiness; and though we have not the pleasure of a personal acquaintance with your beloved daughter — soon to be his wedded wife — we have no doubt that he has been most fortunate in his choice, as we trust she will find him ever to be the soul of honor, and governed by the truest affection and the highest integrity; therefore, we give them our heartfelt benediction! Many will be the congratulations showered upon them — many the wishes expressed for their life-long happiness — many the invocations uttered for their preservation and perfect felicity; but, among all these, on the part of friends and acquaintances, none will exceed in heartiness and fervency those of

Yours, with the highest respect,

Wm. Lloyd Garrison,
Helen E. Garrison.

Mr. and Mrs. John Jay.

ALS: Columbia University Library.

John Jay (1817–1894) was the son of Judge William Jay and the grandson of Chief Justice John Jay. He was admitted to the bar in 1839 and practiced law in New York City for almost twenty years, when he retired from practice, devoting the remainder of his life to public service and the care of his estate. He became an antislavery advocate while studying at Columbia College, when he was manager of the New York Young Men's Anti-Slavery Society. He was active on behalf of Negro rights, and acted as counsel for many fugitive slaves after the passage of the Fugitive Slave Law in 1850. He participated in the organization of the Republican party in New York State. During the Civil War, he espoused Negro enlistments in the Northern Army, the Emancipation Proclamation, the Freedmen's Bureau, and the Thirteenth Amendment. He was minister to Austria from 1869 to 1874, and was later active in civil service reform. On June 23, 1837, he married Eleanor Kingsland Field of New York City.

1. The marriage, on Thursday, June 23, 1859, involved Henry Grafton Chapman, the only son of Maria Weston Chapman and Henry Grafton Chapman, and Eleanor Jay, the daughter of John and Eleanor Kingsland Field Jay. The groom was born in Boston in 1833 and died in Manila, Philippine Islands, March 14, 1883. His occupation was banking. In his youth he was affiliated for a time with the English banking firm of Baring Brothers, whose founder, Joshua Bates, was a relative. He was later a member of the banking firm of Ward, Campbell and Company in New York and a member and, for a time, president of the New York Stock Exchange. He made voyages to China, Japan and South America. The bride died in New York on June 8, 1921. (*The New York Times*, March 17, 1883; June 11, 1921; Frederick Clifton Pierce, *Field Genealogy*, Chicago, 1901, pp. 383–384.)

2 7 7

TO HENRY C. WRIGHT

Boston, June 27, 1859.

My dear H.C.W.: —

I have been intending every day for the last fortnight to send you a letter, but something or other has interposed to prevent it. But I must not delay a moment longer.

Mr. Phillips duly communicated to us the letter you sent to him, in which you so gratefully and affectionately express your feelings toward my dear wife and myself; and direct him, whenever he receives the legacy left you by Mr. Hovey,[1] to pay one fourth of it over to us, for our benefit, as a token of your appreciation of our friendship and hospitality. If we decline receiving it for ourselves, then to deposit it for the benefit of Fanny and Franky.

What ever we have done for you, my dear friend, on the score of hospitality, has always been done as to *one of our family*, without thought or desire of remuneration at any time. Hence, we are unwilling to consider the relation a different one, by receiving for ourselves the gift you propose. While we live, and have a roof over us, you shall always find "a home" with us, in health or sickness, in strength or in helplessness.

But your instruction to Mr. Phillips is, that the money you proffer us, if declined by us, is to be deposited in some bank for the benefit of Fanny and Franky. As in this case you will take no refusal, we have conferred together about it, and our conclusion is to accept it in trust — with this proviso, that if, from any unforeseen misfortune or destitution on your part you should need it at any time, it shall be wholly expended for your benefit. Accordingly, it will be safely deposited in the Savings Bank in this city, whenever received.

The legacies of our lamented friend Hovey have attracted a great deal of attention, and made a marked sensation, in various quarters. No doubt the pseudo-religionists and heartless conservatives of our times are much disturbed and chagrined in view of their appropriation. Forty thousand dollars to be expended for the promotion of the most radical and unpopular reforms! Did the world ever hear of such a thing before? Is it not enough to throw all hunkerdom into convulsions? And then, six thousand dollars[2] distributed among such "fanatical," "infidel," "disorganizing" persons as Henry C. Wright, Parker Pillsbury, Stephen S. Foster, and Wm. Lloyd Garrison, and their families! Verily, this is to cause endurance to pass its bounds! It is quite insufferable!

I am more and more struck with the moral courage and deliberate purpose manifested by our departed friend Hovey, in these bequests. He had a host of friends, and many in the Anti-Slavery ranks to whom he was strongly attached, and whom he held in the highest esteem; but no other half a dozen in the land were so proscribed and denounced by the scribes and pharisees and hypocrites in the Church, and by the time-servers and demagogues in the States, as those to whom he specifically gave in his Will the tokens of his respect, confidence, and undying friendship. It was his last and most striking testimony of his interest in the most radical reformers. *We were singled out for no other purpose.* It was his "ruling passion strong in death." [3]

It is a great trust which has been committed to us — the expenditure of eight thousand dollars per annum for five years in cause of anti-slavery, woman's rights, peace, temperance, &c. No doubt we shall be bored with all sorts of applications, from all sorts of persons; indeed, they already begin to pour in. But the estate is not yet settled.

Now, a word in regard to your kind and generous overture to me to join you immediately for a tour at the West, for the benefit of my health. Much should I rejoice to take such a tour with you; but as the difficulty under which I am now laboring is mainly bronchial, requiring abstinence from all speaking as much as possible, and as it would be next to impossible for me to take such a tour without seeing a great many persons, and having a constant strain made upon my vocal organs; I deem it most provident to remain at or near home this summer. I am slowly improving, and by care hope to get my voice again for public lecturing, which I have not attempted for four months past.

To make such a tour as you propose would be very expensive; and though you generously promise me that it shall cost me nothing, I could not consent to tax you, or on any other friends, to that extent, and in that direction, unless I were in a condition to converse and lecture all the way through. I hope yet, in the hereafter, to go to the West with you.

Helen and the children are all well, and send you their united love. Keep me posted as to your movements. Give my kindest remembrances to all my Ohio friends. Take good care of your health, and God bless and save you eternally!

Ever your attached friend,

Wm. Lloyd Garrison.

H.C.W.

☞ The tribute you wrote for the Liberator, to the memory of C. F. Hovey, before the N.E. Convention, accidentally got mislaid at the time, and came to light a few days ago. It is in this week's Liberator. [4]

ALS: Garrison Papers, Boston Public Library; most of this letter is reprinted in *Life*, III, 478–479.

1. Charles Fox Hovey had died in Boston on April 28, 1859. *The Liberator* (May 6, 1859), in its obituary, reported that "By his Will, we understand, he made large bequests to his family, and to several of his friends, and gave the rest of his estate for the promotion of the various reforms to which his life had been devoted, and especially to the Anti-Slavery cause; placing on record a very strong testimony in favor of universal and impartial liberty."

The section in his will which allocated funds to a number of antislavery men and women for the promotion of the antislavery and other causes reads as follows:

"Article 16. After setting aside sufficient funds to pay all legacies and bequests herein made, I direct my said Trustees to hold all the rest and residue of my estate, real, personal and mixed, in special trust for the following purposes, namely; to pay over, out of the interest and principal of said special trust, a sum of not less than eight thousand dollars annually, until the same be all exhausted, to said Wendell Phillips, William Lloyd Garrison, Stephen S. Foster, Abby K. Foster, Parker Pillsbury, Henry C. Wright, Francis Jackson and Charles K. Whipple, and their survivors and survivor, for them to use and expend, at their discretion, without any responsibility to any one, for promotion of the Anti-Slavery cause and other reforms, such as Woman's Rights, Non-Resistance, Free Trade and Temperance, at their discretion; and I request said Wendell Phillips and his said associates to expend not less than eight thousand dollars annually, by the preparation and circulation of books, newspapers, employing agents, and the delivery of lectures that will, in their judgment, change public opinion, and secure the abolition of Slavery in the United States, and promote said other reforms. Believing that the chain upon four millions of slaves, with tyrants at one end and hypocrites at the other, has become the strongest bond of the Union of the States, I desire said Phillips and his associates to expend said bequest by employing such agents as believe and practice the doctrine of 'No union with slaveholders, religiously or politically'; and by circulating such publications as tend to destroy every pro-slavery institution."

(*Annual Report of the American Anti-Slavery Society for the Year Ending May 1, 1859*, New York, 1860, p. 141.)

2. The amount was actually "not less than eight thousand dollars."

3. Alexander Pope, *Moral Essays*, Epistle I, To Lord Cobham.

4. Wright's tribute was in the form of a letter to Garrison, and appeared in *The Liberator*, June 24, 1859. The letter began as follows: "The death of Charles F. Hovey is a deep affliction to me. He was my friend. With few men have I been more intimate, or more identified in the cause of human redemption. From my first acquaintance with him on board the Sheridan, on my voyage to Europe in 1842, to his last sickness, he has been my friend, and has aided me in all my efforts as an advocate of Anti-Slavery, Non-Resistance, Total Abstinence, the Ante-Natal Rights and Education of Children, of Marriage and Parentage, Free Trade, and the Elevation and Happiness of Man. Though I differed from him in some things which are essential elements of life to me, yet on these topics of disagreement in opinion we have held much and pleasant communion."

Henry C. Wright's letter must have been written prior to May 25, which was when the New England Anti-Slavery Convention convened. (*The Liberator*, May 13, 1859.)

2 7 8

TO AARON COOLEY

Boston, July 12, 1859.

Dear Sir,

It is not in my power to obtain for you the sum you wish to raise, either as a gift or a loan. At present, I am straitened in my own circumstances, and therefore am unable to do for you what I otherwise would be glad to do. As to Mr. Phillips, he is absent from the city, having taken up his residence in the country for the summer; but I have occasion to know that he has been so severely taxed, within the past few months, by the appeals that have been made to his benevolence, as well as by the pressure which the Anti-Slavery cause always brings upon him, that it would be useles for me or you to make any application to him for assistance at this time.

If at any time hereafter I can be of service to you, I will not forget you. To whatever extent I may have been indebted to you for my rescue in 1835, I desire to be truly grateful.

Your, truly,

Wm. Lloyd Garrison.

Aaron Cooley.

Transcript: Garrison Papers, Boston Public Library.

Aaron Cooley (b. January 26, 1801) was the son of a well-to-do trucker who had subsequently lost his property. In 1859, Cooley began writing letters to Garrison, Phillips, and others, claiming to have helped rescue Garrison from the mob in Boston in 1835 and asking for financial help in recognition of his assistance to Garrison. Garrison's account of the 1835 riot, in *Life*, II, 21, included the following statement: "I fortunately extricated myself from the rope, and was seized by two or three powerful men, to whose firmness, policy and muscular energy I am probably indebted for my preservation." At this point, a footnote in *Life* makes the following comment: "'They were the Messrs. Daniel and 'Buff' [Aaron] Cooley, an eminent trucking firm on India Street. Their action at this particular juncture was a great surprise to all of their acquaintance, as their associates were nearly all opponents of the abolitionists.' (E. N. Moore, in Boston *Sunday Budget*, Mar. 18, 1883)."

In response to Cooley's importunities, Garrison and Phillips did send him money from time to time. By 1862, this had amounted to more than a hundred dollars. In 1868, Garrison finally wrote him that he would answer no more letters. A comment in a hand other than Garrison's, on a letter from Cooley to Garrison dated September 3, 1866, notes the following: "Memo: Cooley was a man of profligate character, who made no sign or claim for his help in rescuing W. L. G. from the hands of the mob until 25 years later, when he strove to make capital out of it and 'bleed' Mr. G. and his friends." (See also Garrison's letter to Cooley, May 21, 1868; and Garrison's letter to Wendell Phillips, October 27, 1869, Garrison Papers, Boston Public Library; Cooley's letter to Hervey E. Weston, August 4, 1868, Weston Papers, Boston Public Library; and letters from Cooley to Garrison, September 3, 1866, July 22, 1868, Anti-Slavery Letters to Garrison and Others, Boston Public Library.)

2 7 9

TO WENDELL PHILLIPS GARRISON

Boston, July 18, 1859.

My Dear Son, Wendell P. Garrison:

To-day you are to leave home, to spend your college vacation in a pedestrious tour to the western part of Massachusetts, for the purpose of invigorating your health, and improving your mind by a careful observation of Nature in her varied aspects. The route you have chosen mingles as much of the sublime and beautiful as one could desire; and should you, and the worthy companion in your travels, (Mr. John Ritchie,[1]) exercise due care, and not attempt to do more than you are really able to bear in the way of walking and exposure, I have no doubt it will prove to you both a very delightful and beneficial tour, and enable you to enter upon your next term at Harvard with fresh elasticity of spirit and renewed bodily vigor. Books are invaluable in their place; but there is nothing like a practical acquaintance with men and things. Indeed, no more pregnant maxim was ever uttered than this — "The proper study of mankind is man." [2]

I need not suggest to you the utility of jotting down in a note-book whatever you find that is particularly noteworthy, because your habits are methodical; and having taken such pains at the beginning in preparing your maps, &c., you will be no less careful to record the most striking incidents in your tour.

A considerable portion of the region through which you will pass is ground untravelled by me. I have few personal acquaintances, therefore, in that direction; yet I doubt not there are many persons whose sympathy for the slave is deep-rooted, whose interest in the Anti-Slavery struggle is ever enlarging, and who will be happy to show you and your companion any kindness in their power, on communicating your names. Named as you are after my beloved friend and eloquent coadjutor, Wendell Phillips, Esq., on his account you will find those who will take a peculiar pleasure in giving you a friendly welcome. I shall ever feel most grateful for whatever attentions may be paid to you and Mr. Ritchie.

Should you be so unfortunate as to meet with any serious accident, or be overtaken by illness, (which I trust will not be the case,) assure those with whom your lot may be cast for the time being, that I will sacredly discharge all necessary expenses that may be incurred in trying to effect your restoration.

Avail yourself of every suitable opportunity to bear your testimony.

modestly but firmly, in favor of temperance, peace, anti-slavery, and every other progressive movement of the age.

I commend you to the kind consideration and unlimited confidence of all with whom you may come in contact. You have ever been a most dutiful son, and your conduct has been without a stain in any particular; and I am proud to know that, at Harvard, you not only take a high position for scholarship, but are greatly respected for your moral worth. May you ever live to adorn humanity, and elevate and bless mankind, until you are called to enter a higher sphere of existence! The fervent benediction of your father and mother rests upon you.

Mr. Ritchie, your associate, is the worthy son of a worthy father,[3] whom I have long known in the anti-slavery cause. I am glad he is to be with you. God bless and preserve you both!

Your loving father,

Wm. Lloyd Garrison.

ALS: Smith College Library.

1. *The Fifth Report, Harvard College Class of 1861* (New York, 1892, pp. 95–98), which consists of biographical memoirs of members of the class, has the following comment on the Garrison-Ritchie walking tour, in a biographical sketch of Ritchie: "The summer of 1859 was given up to a pedestrian tour with classmate Garrison, which took in portions of the Connecticut, Housatonic, and Hudson River valleys, and terminated with West Point and the Catskills — a walk of some 300 miles."

2. Alexander Pope, *Essay on Man.*

3. Uriah Ritchie.

---

2 8 0

TO ABBY KELLEY FOSTER

Boston, July 22, 1859.

My Dear Friend:

It was my wish and intention to have had a private interview with you at our Framingham celebration on the 4th inst.,[1] in order to talk over various matters; but no opportunity fairly presented itself. In the forenoon, Mr. [Wendell] Phillips was busily engaged in conversation with you at great length; in the afternoon, though I looked for you through the audience, I did not see you, and was therefore unable to execute my purpose.

I have been waiting ever since the New England Convention,[2] hoping to hear (as I think I was entitled to hear) from you in writing; but as you have preserved an unbroken silence up to this hour, I take it for granted that you do not mean to break it until you first hear from me; — so I will not wait any longer.

I have said that I think I was entitled to hear from you, because I understand that you felt grievously wounded in consequence of what fell from my lips at the Convention; [3] and because you left my house, (when I was coming down stairs to greet you as usual.) in a manner that indicated a highly excited state of mind, — avoiding as you did my very presence. Your "sober second thought," I was confident, would lead you to see that you had acted in a manner not compatible with either true self-respect, or personal friendship. Why did you thus shun me? If you had any grievance to complain of, why did you not tell me of it to my face? For, remember, you have neither said nor written a single word to me, whereby I could even surmise that your feelings were wounded. Why, then, have you made the painful revelation to others, and not to me? And why should I be left to obtain through others, what you ought to have frankly communicated to me? Is this becoming an old and tried friend? I think not.

It seems that your duty was to have said to me that morning, in substance — feeling as you did — "I was not able to be at the closing meeting of the Convention last evening; but my husband, on returning from it, gave me such an account of your remarks, in regard to myself, as to excite my grief and astonishment. But, inasmuch as he may have misinterpreted or misunderstood you, I desire to know what you did say, or intended to be understood as saying; for I cannot believe that you would *intentionally* say or do aught to impeach my integrity in the prosecution of the anti-slavery cause." Had you taken this course, an explanation might have been made on the spot, to the removal of all those painful feelings which have followed as a consequence of this omission.

Now, as *you* charge me with nothing, — i.e., face to face or by letter, — what can I plead?

I hear that you believe or suppose that I attributed to you intentional dishonesty in the manner of procuring money of prominent members of the Republican party. [4] Such a thought never entered my mind. It is true that I endeavored to show the inconsistency and *practical* wrongfulness of your course, as it seemed to me, in that particular — without, however, calling you by name; but I neither impeached, nor meant to impeach, your personal integrity. God forbid! I believe you to have always been actuated by the highest and purest motives, however lacking in judgment or consistency. Of all the women who have appeared upon the historic stage, I have always regarded you as peerless — the moral Joan of Arc of the world — and so have expressed myself to friends, far and near, again and again. My admiration of your character and moral heroism, of your self-sacrificing spirit and exhausting philanthropy, has been limited by nothing but the power of speech to express it. Our friendship has been intimate and unbroken for more than a quarter of a century, — through how many fiery trials and strange vicissitudes! — and no one out of my family has been nearer or dearer to me than yourself. My heart has grown liquid with emotion as I have seen your amazing self-denial, courage and perseverance, — ending in making yourself a living sacrifice upon the altar of bleeding humanity. How, then, was it possible for me to accuse you of intentional wrong-doing? Or how could you so readily come to the conclusion, that that was what I did, and what I intended to do?

Let me assure you that, widely as you and Stephen [S. Foster] may differ from me on some points, I believe you both to be actuated by the highest considerations, and that you would both prefer death at the stake to the performance of an action dishonest or hypocritical in your own eyes; and that I am, as from the beginning,

Your true and faithful friend,

Wm. Lloyd Garrison.

Mrs. A. K. Foster.

ALS: Abigail Kelley Foster Papers, American Antiquarian Society, Worcester, Massachusetts; rough draft in Garrison Papers, Boston Public Library.

1. This was the annual July 4 antislavery celebration sponsored by the Massachusetts Anti-Slavery Society at the Framingham Grove.

2. The New England Anti-Slavery Convention met on May 25 and 26, 1859, in Boston.

3. A repetition of the conflict which had occurred at the Massachusetts Anti-Slavery Society convention in January took place at the New England Anti-Slavery Convention at the end of May. The questions involved were whether or not the antislavery movement had made any progress toward the abolition of slavery, whether or not progress had been made in changing public opinion on the nature of slavery, the evaluation of the Republican party as an antislavery organization, and the nature of the relationship that ought to prevail between the Garrisonians and the Republican party. On all of these questions, Stephen and Abby Foster and Parker Pillsbury were on one side, with Garrison on the other. The proceedings of the convention were reported in *The Liberator*, June 3, 1859.

4. Apparently, Abby Foster had asked Republicans to contribute funds for the antislavery movement on the theory that both groups had certain purposes in common and could work together up to a certain point. Garrison objected to her accepting money from them and then characterizing them as the greatest obstacle to the elimination of slavery.

The last session of the convention was on Thursday evening, May 26. The report of this session does not reproduce Garrison's remarks verbatim but merely summarizes them in some detail. There is nothing in the summary to indicate any personal attack upon Abby or Stephen Foster, although Garrison did criticize and condemn the views they held and some of their remarks at the convention. The first sentence of the summary remarked that "Mr. Garrison did not think it necessary to answer the charges made against the Anti-Slavery Society, but would simply say they were all false, unjust, and entirely uncalled for." It may also be noted that Garrison seconded a motion to reconsider certain resolutions that had been introduced at the previous session that day by Stephen Foster and adopted, 22 to 17.

They were reconsidered and apparently voted down, 44 to 5. (*The Liberator*, June 3, 1859.)

---

2 8 1

TO ABBY KELLEY FOSTER

Boston, July 25, 1859.

My Dear Friend:

Your letter, in reply to the one I sent to you on Friday, is before me.[1]

In the first place, let me say, I marked my letter to you "private" on the *envelope*, simply to insure its opening and perusal by yourself; but not meaning thereby that you should keep it from the eye of Stephen one moment, unless you preferred to do so. I will add, that *I* have no objection whatever to your letting any one read the letter, if *you* have none. Only I think the less publicity in regard to the present unhappy misunderstanding, the better.

In the second place, let me say, I know not on what *reasonable* ground *you* have been waiting (as you declare) ever since the New England Convention to hear from *me*. If you had any thing to complain of, respecting my criticism upon your course, at the Convention, why did you not have the frankness and fidelity to let me know it, either by letter or by word of mouth? How can you justify yourself in such a procedure, while pouring your griefs into the ears of others, I do not understand. Why should I have written to *you*, with no impeachment, charge or complaint before me on your part? Unconscious of having done you any wrong, it was not my duty to gather from the lips of others, what your own refrained from conveying to me, and then take the initiative in this correspondence. Yet I have done so; but, instead of my magnanimity being appreciated or perceived, you insist that *you* were entitled to hear from *me*, and hence your long silence! To me, this is a new view of obligations.

In the third place, let me say, the explanation you give why you left my house with such precipitancy is hardly satisfactory, because it was not then seven o'clock; because you heard my wife call me to speak to you — (and, springing at the call, I was in a moment in the entry to give you my hand as usual, but you had vanished!) and because, however hurried you may have been, you certainly were not so much pressed for time that you could not stop even to say good-bye; for did you not afterward make a visit to Mr. [Wendell] Phillips? What else could I infer but that you were in a highly excited state of mind? And why had I not a right to believe that when your "sober second thought" came, you would regret such hastiness, and write me a letter, telling me in what manner, and to what extent, you felt I had done you wrong? You ask — "Did I not tell Mrs. Garrison distinctly, that we were obliged to leave Boston at 8 o'clock, and that previous to that hour, we had got to breakfast, and to *visit Alla's* [2] *surgeon*, and that every moment must be saved?" My wife has no recollection of any reference having been made to seeing Alla's physician, but she vividly remembers how Alla exclaimed, in view of your precipitate departure from the house, "Why, *mother!*" — and, as our own break-fast was all ready, she wished you and Alla to partake of it, without any loss of time. It must have been a very "disagreeable dream," as you admit, under which you were laboring at the time.

In the fourth place, let me say, the readiness with which you came to the conclusion that I *meant* to accuse you of a lack of integrity, — after such an unbroken friendship as ours had been for twenty-five years, — was and still is to me inexplicable. It is the saddest part of it all. You say — "The audience understood you to accuse me of being fraudulent, and of obtaining money under false pretences." I do not believe it. What right have you to say this? You were not present. If you had been, you would have heard — what the audience heard — from my lips, when Mr. [Charles C.] Burleigh, to remove all possi-bility of misapprehension, said to me, "You did not mean to accuse Mrs. Foster of fraudulent intentions?" "Certainly not," I replied; while I still felt constrained to regard your course as unwarrantable, and highly inconsistent. To my disclaimer of any design of imputing "intentional dishonesty" to you, you say, "Can a person be dishonest without intention of being so? So, you still think I have been dishonest, but not intentionally so!" To this I can only reply, that such verbal criticism and such forced construction seem to indicate a determination upon your part to place the worst possible construction upon my lan-guage and motives. In such a state of mind, how can I hope any thing from your candor or charity? Now, I have never doubted that you were justified in your own mind in getting money for our Anti-Slavery treasury of leading Republicans, in the manner you did, and afterward seeking to get them and their party officially branded as the worst and most dangerous obstacles in our path; yet I am persuaded such a pro-cedure is utterly indefensible, and, upon the face of it, would be re-garded "on 'Change," or by any impartial jury, as practically unfair. That was what I said; but I expressly acquitted you of any "intentional" wrong-doing. Why persist in ignoring the fact that I did so? You say that "mutual friends" requested me privately in the ante-room to make "retraction," and I "declined doing so." Retraction implies an admitted wrong. I had nothing to retract; but, in reply to Stephen, and to Mr. Burleigh's inquiry, I explained what I meant, and disclaimed any design to stain your personal integrity. I cannot believe there was an unprejudiced person in the audience who left the hall that evening, understanding me as attacking your character — not one. Hence —

In the fifth place, let me say, your assertion, "It therefore remains true that I stand before the public (!) accused by you of fraud . . . this accusation is on the wings of the press, (!) and is ready to meet me whenever I shall again attempt to serve the slave financially," is baseless, and the result, I charitably believe, of a morbid condition of the mind. So far as the public at large is concerned, it knows nothing of the matter, as no reference was made to it in the published proceedings of the Convention; and had it not been for Stephen dragging it before the meeting, and making a long, exaggerated, lachrymal, and highly injudicious speech upon it, the whole affair would have ended with the occasion, and gone into oblivion.

Finally, let me say, even if I had so utterly changed in spirit towards you as to cruelly assail your integrity, (as you seem too willing to believe,) how does it follow, if your zeal and courage in the Anti-Slavery cause are what they once were, — if that cause is still paramount in your affection over all personal feelings, — that you cannot go West, as you contemplated, and seek pecuniary aid for the Western Anti-Slavery Society as hitherto? You say, (so unlike your former self!) — "Not only will the enemies, but the friends of the cause will distrust me"! Will they? Then, "bide your time." Will they? Why do you thus hastily impeach their discernment, and sense of justice, and personal knowledge of your character? Attribute what you please to me of personal influence, no man can long mislead or deceive the tried abolitionists. Witness "new organization"! [3] Witness Rogers [4] and [Frederick] [*] Douglass! Witness all who have turned aside, or attempted to compromise the cause, in order to propitiate a pro-slavery church or party, or for any other purpose! Your shrinking into nothingness — your paralysis of effort — your conclusion that, by my injustice, your way is henceforth effectually hedged up, and you can do no more for the slave — are all unworthy of your earlier days, and indicate that you are not in spirit as you have been, either through bodily infirmity or some mental hallucination. Let who will wrong you, BE YOURSELF, as of old, still shouting — "I am a soldier for the war, *whatever may befall,*" or whoever may lift his heel against me! This I understand to be normal, healthy, genuine abolitionism. "He that endures *to the end,* the same shall be saved." [5]

If, after all, you are disposed to make this a public matter in the columns of the Liberator, so be it — your course is plain. Send me a letter, over your signature, for publication, stating your belief or apprehension that some persons may suppose that I meant to impeach your honesty at the Convention, notwithstanding my explanation at that time, and see whether I fail to be sufficiently explicit in reply to it. This you should have done at the outset, if (as you say) it is a public, and not a "private" affair. My own conviction is, that a mole-hill has been magnified to a mountainous size, and that a true regard for the cause which is so dear to us will dictate the suppression of all public reference to it. If you think otherwise, I have suggested the method of disposing of it, once for all, in the Liberator. Should you prefer to have Stephen write such a letter, it will be all the same; but deliberately reflect before you act.

I need not add, that we shall be glad to see you all at our house at any time, and that our latch-strings will always be out to you and yours as hitherto. Especially do we desire, both for our pleasure and her convenience, that Alla will make our house her home, during her visits to the city.

I remain, in the bonds of true friendship,
    Yours, to break every yoke,

Wm. Lloyd Garrison.

Mrs. Abby Kelley Foster.

ALS: Abigail Kelley Foster Papers, American Antiquarian Society, Worcester, Massachusetts; rough draft in Garrison Papers, Boston Public Library.

1. Abby Foster's letter to Garrison was dated "At home, July 24, 1859." In view of the importance of the issue involved, especially for Garrison's personal relationship to the Fosters and other abolitionists involved, Mrs. Foster's letter is herewith reproduced in its entirety.
"My dear Friend
"Yours of 22d did not reach me till last evening.
"You 'have been waiting ever since the New England Convention hoping to hear, as you think you was [sic] entitled to hear, from me':
"And I have been waiting ever since the New England Convention hoping to hear as I think I am entitled to hear from *you*, but not '*privately.*'
"No words of yours at that Convention had any effect on my private reputation or relations. And personally I entertain not the least iota of unkind feeling towards you. Had it not been for the circumstances of the previous evening I am confident you never could have put upon the manner of my leaving your house on Friday morning the construction you have given it in your letter. Did I not tell Mrs. Garrison distinctly that we were obliged to leave Boston at 8 o'clock and that previous to that time we had to get breakfast and to visit Alla's surgeon, and that every moment must be saved? But had I had time to see you on that occasion I was not prepared to make any reference to the discussion of the previous evening. It was not to me then a reality but only a disagreeable dream.
"It was not till I had heard from a great variety of minds the impression made on them by your remarks that evening in relation to my course, as well as your exact language taken down on its utterance, that I could fully realize the report.
"As the case has been presented to me it stands thus. The audience understood you to accuse me of being fraudulent and of obtaining money under false pretenses — That my conduct would be thus regarded on change. — 2d That our mutual friends requested you privately in the ante-room to make retraction — That you declined to do so — That my course and character were vindicated on the platform by our mutual friends and then even you made no explanation which

at all relieved me from the imputation of dishonesty — 3 That since the close of the meeting you have been requested by our mutual friends to take back what you then said. (Not to me of course as it is in no way a private matter) 4 That now in your letter to me you say you hear that I believe you attributed to me 'intentional dishonesty.' So you still think I have been dishonest though not intentionally so. Can a person be dishonest without intention of being so? Your terms seem to me an utter confounding of language. Dishonesty necessarily implies moral obliquity. An insane person or an idiot can do without crime that which when done by a person in his senses would be termed dishonesty and for which he would every where be held responsible. It therefore remains true that I stand before the public accused by you of fraud. That public knows I could not do that which, on change, would be regarded as fraud without knowing it. This accusation is on the wings of the press and is ready to meet me whenever I shall again attempt to serve the slave publicly, in the only way in which I now can serve him — financially.

"I had intended to go West this autumn to aid the Western A. S. Society in its present extremity. But I am most effectually shut off from this work. Not only will the enemies but the friends of the cause will distrust me. Your charge remains unretracted, unexplained, and in full force wherever it can harm my influence. You rest under the responsibility, therefore, of removing from the public mind the impression which you unintentionally have made upon it that I am not a woman of integrity — that I am capable of fraud.

"Here then I leave this matter. I have never shunned you. I have had no occasion to do so — But those who do not know me will more than ever shun me unless this matter is fully and fairly cleared up to them.

"Your letter is endorsed 'Private.' No one knows I have received it — not even my husband from whom I am not wont to withhold any thing. I shall be glad to have this correspondence always remain private if you choose it.

"Yours truly and faithfully

A. K. Foster.

W. L. Garrison"

(Abigail Kelley Foster Papers, American Antiquarian Society, Worcester, Massachusetts.)

2. Alla was the Fosters' daughter.

3. The reference is to the secession from the American Anti-Slavery Society in 1840 and the formation of the rival American and Foreign Anti-Slavery Society.

4. Nathaniel P. Rogers (1794–1846), a New Hampshire abolitionist, broke with Garrison during the last years of his life. (See *Letters*, II, pp. 463–464 *et passim*.)

5. Matthew 10:22.

282

TO WENDELL PHILLIPS GARRISON

Boston, Aug. 23, 1859.

Dear Wendell:

William has just been to see Dr. Geist, who pronounces his disease to be the varioloid,[1] and who says William must not think of going to Lynn this week. I have just written to Mr. Mudge to this effect. We have just had a family consultation, (Miss [Mary] Grew included,) and we are united in the opinion that you ought at once to return home, as the seeds of the same disease may be already in your own person, you having slept with him since your return home together. It is due to Mr. Buffum's family that you should leave, because the children may be exposed to the disease, (which is contagious,) through you. On the same ground, Miss McKim [2] must (as an act of wise precaution) forego her contemplated visit to our house, great as our regret will be not to have the pleasure of her company. Miss Grew thinks that, under the circumstances, it would be best for her to return home without unnecessary delay.

It will not be best to have publicity given in Lynn to William's case, but Mr. and Mrs. Buffum ought to know it, and also Miss McKim.

Your loving father,

Wm. Lloyd Garrison.

ALS: Smith College Library.

1. "A modified mild form of smallpox occurring in persons who have been vaccinated or who have had smallpox" (*Webster's Seventh New Collegiate Dictionary*).

2. Lucy McKim (b. Philadelphia, October 30, 1842; d. Llewellyn Park, New York, May 11, 1877), the daughter of J. Miller and Sarah A. McKim. She married Wendell Phillips Garrison on December 6, 1865. They had three children. (Wendell Phillips Garrison, *In Memoriam, Sarah A. McKim*, New York, 1891, privately printed, p. 23.)

---

2 8 3

TO FANNY GARRISON

Boston, Sept. 6, 1859.

Dear Fanny:

We are all anxious to see you once more at home; for, though you are *a young miss*, you are nevertheless *a great miss* from our family circle. It is very pleasant, therefore, to think of your returning to Boston to-morrow with Mr. Heywood; yet we deem it on the safe side of prudence for you to spend a few days at Mrs. Emerson's,[1] until you can be vaccinated by Dr. Geist — as he thinks it best, notwithstanding the failure of the attempt by Dr. Oakie.[2] Franky's vaccination has taken "first rate," and doubtless prevented him from having the small pox. The doctor will probably vaccinate you from his arm.

William is so far recovered that, yesterday, he came down stairs, and sat with us at the dinner-table. He will remain in the house a week longer. I do not think any marks will be left permanently upon his face. He has borne his sickness very patiently. He sends his love to you, and says he is sorry to keep you away from the house.

Saturday afternoon, your mother (who has had a great deal of care and anxiety since Willie's confinement) was taken with shiverings and sickness at the stomach, and forced to take her bed, which she has kept ever since, having had "a run of fever," though she feels considerably better this morning, and I trust is on the mending hand. We were at first apprehensive that she might be coming down with the varioloid, but there seems to be no appearance of it in an eruptive form, and it is nothing more, probably, than a sudden cold, which has put a stop to her natural perspiration, and brought on a congestion of her system, chiefly affecting her head.

It has been very fortunate for us that we have had so kind, willing and courageous a girl as Josephine.[3] She has taken nearly all the care of Willie, and without her, we should have been in a sad plight.

Your visit to Providence has been protracted more than double the period that we first contemplated. Most grateful do we feel to Henry and Charlotte,[4] and all the family, for their great kindness to you and us. That kindness we are most anxious to reciprocate at an early day, by entertaining them under our own roof. Remember us to them with great affection. Also to our much respected friend, Miss Forbes,[5] whose kindness we shall always remember.

Do not forget to give Jemima [6] and the one who has washed your clothes a dollar each, not as payment, (for it is too trifling a sum,) but as a slight token of your appreciation of their kindness. Our regards to Jemima, whom we shall be glad to see in Boston.

I forget Mrs. Emerson's number in Hudson Street. (Franky says it is 32.) Near Kneeland Street. If I am not at the depot on your arrival, let Mr. Heywood put you into a hack, and tell the driver to leave you at 32 Hudson Street.

Be sure and bring all your things, and meet Mr. Heywood at the depot at the time he will name to you.

Your mother sends her heart's love to you, and longs to embrace you. Love to all as one.

Your affectionate father,

Wm. Lloyd Garrison.

☞ We all send our warmest regards to Mary Benson.[7]

ALS: Villard Papers, Boston Public Library.

1. Mrs. Hannah Bradbury Emerson (b. January 10, 1803) was the daughter of Captain Joseph Kingsbury of York, Maine. In 1825, she married Captain August Emerson of York, afterwards of Bangor and Boston. She was active in literary and philanthropic matters in Boston and was one of the editors of *The Friend of Virtue*, published in Boston from 1838 to 1867 by the New England Female Moral Society and the Tolitha Cumi Maternity Home and Hospital. (Mary K. Talcott, *The Genealogy of the Descendants of Henry Kingsbury of Ipswich and Haverhill, Mass.*, Hartford, 1905, pp. 404–405; Boston *Directory*, 1859; *Union List of Serials*.)
2. Unidentified.

3. Unidentified.
4. Henry and Charlotte Benson Anthony, of Providence, Rhode Island.
5. Unidentified.
6. Probably the Anthonys' maid.
7. George W. Benson's daughter.

---

2 8 4

TO ABBY KELLEY FOSTER

Boston, Sept. 8, 1859.

My Dear Friend:

Your letter, in reply to mine of July 25th, is just received. You have taken a long time in which to shape it — so long that I had given up all expectation of hearing from you on the subject. Of this I do not complain. I only regret to perceive that it shows no abatement of heat, inflammation, exasperation of mind on your part; for if I were your enemy, instead of an old and attached friend — if I had purposely wronged and injured you, instead of "unintentionally" having done so, as you admitted in a former letter — I do not see how your apparent alienation of spirit and sharpness of manner could easily be heightened. — This gives me unfeigned pain; but it concerns your own peace of mind, much more than it does my own, and I can only deplore the revelation.

You send me twenty closely written pages, to prove that you are a woman of integrity of purpose in your anti-slavery labors! As I have never "intentionally" designed to impeach your integrity, it is a needless effort. After a careful perusal of all that you have written, and all that has transpired, I have no "retraction" to make, no "apology" to offer, because I do not see or feel that I have been a wrong-doer.

I will not attempt to make an elaborate reply to the various points in your letter, for I am sadly convinced that nothing will satisfy you, except "retraction" and "apology"; and this is a demand I cannot comply with, for the reason above stated; though there is nothing I am not ready to do for you within the bounds of reason and self-respect. Yet, I will briefly refer to two or three particulars; and then, so far as I am concerned, bring this correspondence to a final close.

On the first page of your letter, you group together various expressions of mine, detached from their connection, touching my judgment of your state of mind and course of conduct. As they stand in my letter, I see nothing to alter. It seems there must be no criticism of any thing you may say or do, for it is at once tortured into a personal affront. The sensitiveness which you feel and exhibit on the score of personal censure should admonish you to be more cautious in impeaching the motives and actions of others, who may be as sincerely acting up to their light, and as faithfully attempting to perform their duty as they understand it, as yourself. Believing that you were suffering under "a morbid condition of mind, or some mental hallucination," for the time being, I frankly and charitably said so, meaning to give you no offence thereby. *Why* I thought you had "acted in a manner not compatible with either true self-respect or personal friendship," I fully stated in my former letter, and I need not go over that ground again.

I did not need to be reminded that, ever since its organization, you had not spared either Republicans or the Republican party for their pro-slavery acts. Neither have I been lacking in fidelity in that direction, according to my rule of judgment. Of that I did not complain in my censure of your course in obtaining funds for our anti-slavery treasury. To say of a party that it is weak, timid, compromising — that it does not aim to abolish slavery, but only to stop its advancement into new territories, and to repel the aggressions of the Slave Power upon Northern rights and interests — and therefore is only dealing with a side issue, and is not an anti-slavery party, is one thing; but to attempt to get it branded as either the worst enemy or the most dangerous obstacle to our cause, by the American Anti-Slavery Society, after soliciting and obtaining of its prominent leaders money for the treasury of that Society, on the special ground that the result of its expenditure in the lecturing field would be a diminution of "satanic Democracy," and a consequent increase of "Republicanism," as well as to advance the anti-slavery cause in every direction, is quite another thing — as widely different as the noon of day is from midnight. And therein I think your conduct has been blameworthy, as well as that of some others.

The case, in a nut-shell, stands thus. Your last special financial effort was made in this city and vicinity, at a time when there was a general collapse in business affairs, when there was universal distrust, when money could not be obtained, except at the most exorbitant rates. No period ever seemed to be more hopeless in regard to obtaining funds for our unpopular movement. All the members of our Board deemed it to be so. Even your own indomitable spirit almost quailed, and saw and confessed the desperateness of the case, though resolved to make the attempt. Now, by what process did you propose to touch the feelings and excite the self-denying liberality of the leading Republicans, in order to secure their pecuniary co-operation? Was it to go, and charge them to their faces with being hypocrites, murderers, enemies, or even obstacles in the way of our noble cause — then solicit their money, and assure them it should be expended in branding them with the terms aforesaid, by the very Society they were asked to aid? No. Had you done this, you would assuredly have had "your labor for your pains," and been regarded by them either with displeasure for your presumption, or pity for your weakness. But you did no such thing. On the contrary, you said to me and the Board — "I will show them that, in helping us, they will help the growth of the Republican party" — [not the growth of the greatest obstacle, one more to be feared and deprecated than any thing the South can do!] — "I will remind them of the fact, that where there is the most of 'ultra abolitionism,' there the Republican party finds its strongest support, as a philosophical consequence — I will point them particularly to the 'BLACK BELT' (Democratic) in Pennsylvania, Illinois, Indiana, and other parts of the West, and tell them that, if they will help us, we will endeavor to *whiten it out* before the Presidential election of 1860." This was your plan, and substantially your language, and it made you enthusiastic, and confident of success. You acted upon it to the letter, and the result was, in various instances, liberal donations in good faith to our treasury, from well-known Republicans. All this was right and proper. I entered into your plan with all my heart, and rejoiced that you succeeded so well. You compromised nothing, though I have reason to believe you then waived all personal controversy as to the relative position of the Republican party to our movement.

At last came the New England Anti-Slavery Convention,[1] at which you and Stephen, and Parker [Pillsbury] were particularly, in my judgment unjustly severe upon the Republican party, (as well as upon such men as Dr. Cheever and his associates) — you all sought, with no little heat, to obtain the passage of a resolution, branding that party as more dangerous, and therefore more to be feared and assailed, than even satanic Democracy itself; and there was no lack of accusation or insinuation that the Standard and Liberator, and even the Board itself, if not the Society, were going backward, becoming conservative, and growing unfaithful to the demands of the hour! This resolution I resisted as a matter of conscience, consistency, and fair dealing. Your zeal to get it adopted, in view of your last financial operations in Boston, appeared to me the grossest inconsistency, and elicited the censure I gave, without, however, naming you or any other person. That you were justified to yourself, I did not doubt; but *I* could not find any justification for your course, under the circumstances. Nor do I think it would be justified "on 'change," or by any impartial jury. Certainly, while you are in such a state of mind, I should not feel justified in appointing you, or any other person similarly affected, as a financial agent of the American Anti-Slavery Society.

You ask me why I did not remonstrate with you in private, and add

— "Why, on the contrary, did you go into a public meeting, made up of the friends and the foes of the cause, and there impeach me?" My reply is, that I met the emergency when it arose, and as it seemed to me duty to the cause demanded. I may have been unfortunate in the language I used, and it may have been susceptible of an interpretation I did not mean to give it; but if, unhappily, I did you any wrong, you are right in conceding it to have been "unintentional."

To your reminder, — "You certainly will not plead that you had not opportunity most ample to speak to me on this subject, for I had made your house my home for weeks, while I was specially employed in making these solicitations," — I reply, true; but, at that time, there was no special call for criticism; and I was glad, as well as other members of the Board, to see you in a frame of mind towards the Republican party that indicated a more broad and philosophical view of the various phases of the anti-slavery struggle. Nor did I dream that you would so soon be led into such injustice and inconsistency.

You refer once more to my expressed disappointment in not hearing from you at the outset. You ask — "Why should *I* have written to *you*? *I had nothing to communicate.* The offence of which I complained was public, and already well understood by you. Why should I have repeated what had already been better done by others?" To this my reply is, that I have given you the reasons in my previous letters why you should have written to me in the first instance, and those reasons you have not met. "The offence of which *I* complained was public." But *you* made no complaint — at least, none to me. So far from uttering a word in my hearing, or sending me a line, indicating that you felt I had done you an injury, for which reparation ought to be publicly made, you preserved a long, unbroken silence — except as you made others acquainted with your feelings I insist that this was neither fair nor above-board, and that it was not for me to gather up hearsay gossip in so grave a matter. It was your duty, — a duty that you owed to yourself and me, — to call me to account, in a friendly spirit, by a direct communication. But if you "had nothing to communicate," what had I to answer? It was a "public" matter, forsooth! Then, if it was of such vast importance to your future usefulness in the anti-slavery cause, why did you not promptly take a "public" medium — the *Liberator*, for instance — and ask to be relieved from any false impressions that my remarks may have made upon any one present? But, to this day, had I not opened this correspondence, I have no reason to suppose that I should have heard a syllable from you on the subject, either by epistle or word of mouth! Is this what is due from one tried friend to another? Is this a specimen of your usual anti-slavery fidelity? And why do you decline accepting the overture contained in my last letter?

You take fresh offence at my saying that your plea of a want of time to say farewell when you left my house in such haste, was "hardly satisfactory," in view of all the circumstances; and you sharply bid me ask Mrs. Goodrich [2] sundry questions concerning your movements that morning, prior to your reaching the depot, in order to be convinced that you were not in a too excited frame of mind to see me. I need do no such thing. I am willing and glad to accept your explanation as to my mistaken impressions respecting your feelings on that occasion.

I could comment upon many other points in your letter, but I forbear — having already written more than I intended. I deeply regret this collision, but am consoled to know it was none of my seeking. I will make no parade of the feelings which I still cherish for you, in spite of all that has transpired, but only subscribe myself, as hitherto,

Your faithful friend and co-worker in the cause of the oppressed,

Wm. Lloyd Garrison.

A. K. Foster.

ALS: Abigail Kelley Foster Papers, American Antiquarian Society. A rough draft of this letter is to be found in the Garrison Papers, Boston Public Library.

There is a notation at the top of the letter, in Abby K. Foster's hand, which reads: "No. 3. which has never been answered because I cannot afford to again defend myself against the charge of falsehood. A. K. F."

1. The New England Anti-Slavery Convention was held in Boston on May 25 and 26, 1859.

2. Unidentified.

285

TO SAMUEL J. MAY

Boston, Sept. 19, 1859.

My dear Friend:

Your beloved son, Joseph, informs me that he is preparing a packet to send to you by the steamer on Wednesday, and kindly offers to enclose therein this hasty note. Of his present condition he will, of course, inform you, and I therefore will only say that he seems pretty well.

We have had a "sick house" for the past six weeks, William having had a genuine case of small pox, and his mother an attack of varioloid. Both are now entirely well, and no blemishes will be left by the disease. How William caught it is a mystery to us all. Fanny was fortunately absent on a visit to her aunt in Providence.

I have not attempted to lecture since last February, in consequence of a bronchial difficulty, which, by abstinence from public speaking, is now nearly removed. But I do not expect to occupy the lecturing field again as I have hitherto done. Alas! that the advocates of the oppressed are still so few!

I have read with great interest and pleasure the various letters from your pen that have appeared in print, giving sketches of your European adventures.[1] A thousand times have I rejoiced in spirit that you have been permitted to make such a tour, and I have tried to accompany you every step of the way. To us who are born on this side of the Atlantic, the old world becomes the new, and every thing is as fresh as it is ancient. Bating all the discomforts necessarily incidental to so extended a journey, how great must have been your enjoyment — how many your surprises — how multitudinous your views of the sublime and the beautiful. We, Americans, are said to be deficient in veneration; and it is an excellent method to cultivate that organ; (phrenologically speaking,) by taking a trip to Europe, where every inch of ground is historic, and antiquity is visible in every direction.

I do not learn that you have been seriously indisposed at any time since you left home, and trust you will return greatly invigorated.

On Saturday, Massachusetts was dishonored afresh by the inauguration of the statue of Daniel Webster on the State House grounds, by the permission of our last Legislature.[2] The equinoctial storm raged violently all day, preventing a general parade, and compelling Mr. Everett [3] to deliver his eulogy in Music Hall. We have a petition already printed, and widely circulated, asking the next Legislature to remove the statue, by a due regard for the humanity and self-respect of the Commonwealth. How many will sign it is quite problematical, but a protracted struggle is before us.

You are now in England, and I doubt not have met with a pleasant and hearty reception, not merely from your Unitarian friends, but especially from those who are deeply interested in our anti-slavery struggle, as far as you have seen them; for your name, and long-tried services in that cause, have long been familiar and dear to many of them. O that I could be with you at this moment, in body as in spirit, once more to take by the hand my old and cherished friends!

☞ Richard D. Webb's youngest son [4] is under my roof, having just arrived from California, on his way home. He will remain a short time, make a visit to Ohio, and return in all October. He is in fine health, and strongly reminds me of his father.

Rev. George Ellis [5] (of Charlestown) is just engaged to Lucretia Gould,[6] Ben's [7] sister —

The last intelligence from Theodore Parker is, on the whole favorable; but it is not at all probable that he will ever be able again to speak in Music Hall.

My wife sends her most loving regards to you, as well as all the household.

Be assured that a hearty welcome awaits you on your return.

Your attached friend,

Wm. Lloyd Garrison.

ALS: Garrison Papers, Boston Public Library.

Samuel J. May was in England at this time, having left the United States in December 1858, and arriving in London on January 12, 1859. He visited France, Italy, Germany, Switzerland, Holland, and Belgium. He spent the last three months of his trip in England, where he remained until the end of October, when he sailed for Boston in the steamer *America*, arriving in Boston on November 5 and proceeding immediately to Syracuse. (*The Liberator*, November 18, 1859; *Memoir of Samuel J. May*, Boston, 1873, pp. 196–216.)

1. Many of these letters have been reprinted in *Memoir of Samuel J. May*, pp. 197–215.

2. On September 9, 1859, *The Liberator*, in an editorial entitled "The Statue Must Be Removed," wrote as follows:

"The Webster Statue, in front of the State House, will be inaugurated on the afternoon of the 17th of September. Rev. Dr. Lothrop will offer the prayer, Prof. Felton will deliver the statue into the hands of Mayor Lincoln, representing the city, and His Honor will immediately place it in the custody of the State, Gov. Banks receiving it. Brief addresses will be delivered, and Mr. Everett will then pronounce his oration on Webster."

As to the statue itself, "the grant of a portion of the State House grounds for the erection of this statue, by the last Legislature, was an outrageous abuse of trust, and an insult to the moral and humane feelings of the people of this Commonwealth. It was adroitly obtained at the heel of the session, without debate, in a thin House, through Boston pro-slavery management and the connivance of Gov. Banks, who, since his elevation to the Chair of State, has evidently sought to conciliate the 'cottonocracy,' and to adulterate the little Republicanism he ever possessed, hoping thereby to promote his elevation to a still higher position. . . .

"The people of Massachusetts would, if permitted to register their votes on the question, reject by an overwhelming majority the proposition to erect this Webster statue in the place assigned to it. . . ."

3. Edward Everett (1794–1865), of Boston, Massachusetts, was a Unitarian clergyman, professor of Greek literature at Harvard, orator, editor of the *North American Review*, and politician. A conservative in politics, he represented the Middlesex district in Congress from 1825 to 1835, was governor of Massachusetts from 1836 to 1839, and minister to the Court of St. James from 1841 to 1845. From 1846 to 1849 he was president of Harvard. He was secretary of state for four months, until the close of President Fillmore's administration in March 1853; after being elected for a six-year term to the United States Senate by the Massachusetts legislature, the pressures of office proved too great for him and he resigned before the end of the session. In the election of 1860, he was the vice-presidential candidate of the Constitutional Union party, with John Bell of Tennessee, the presidential candidate.

4. Richard Webb (1835–1882), a printer by trade, traveled to Australia in the 1850's and to the United States in 1859, where he met his father's abolitionist friends, including Frederick Douglass, Stephen Foster, Samuel J. May, and Garrison. He came to the United States again in 1863 and with his father in 1868. He returned to Dublin in 1872 for his father's funeral. (Letter from Douglas C. Riach, Ballsbridge, Dublin, Republic of Ireland, October 27, 1972.)

5. George Edward Ellis (1814–1894), a native of Boston, was pastor of the Harvard Unitarian Church in Charlestown, Massachusetts, for twenty-nine years, beginning in 1840; co-editor of the *Christian Register* from September 1842 to

February 1845, and an editor of the *Christian Examiner* from 1849 to 1855. He held the chair of systematic theology in the Harvard Divinity School from 1857 to 1863. He was passionately interested in American history, wrote biographies of John Mason, Anne Hutchinson, and William Penn for Sparks's *Library of American Biography*, and numerous other books and essays.

Ellis's marriage to Lucretia Goddard Gould on October 22, 1859, was his second; his first wife, Elizabeth Bruce Eager, who bore him one son, having died in 1842.

6. Lucretia Goddard Gould (b. June 14, 1831; d. July 6, 1869). (Benjamin Apthorp Gould, *The Family of Zaccheus Gould of Topsfield*, Lynn, 1895, p. 134.)

7. Benjamin Apthorp Gould (1824–1896), astronomer; a native of Boston, he founded the *Astronomical Journal* in 1849 and continued it until the Civil War. He was in charge of the longitude department of the United States Coast Survey from 1852 to 1867 and from 1855 to 1859 was director of the Dudley Observatory at Albany, New York. With his own private observatory near Cambridge, Massachusetts, erected through the financial assistance of Mary Apthorp Quincy, daughter of Josiah Quincy, whom he married in 1861, he continued his researches and made valuable contributions to astronomy.

---

2 8 6

TO MISS ROBERTS

Boston, Oct. 10, 1859.

Dear Miss Roberts:

I am glad to hear that the Course of Anti-Slavery Lectures is to be kept up by your persevering Society the coming season, as hitherto. And may it be crowned with pre-eminent success!

You ask whether I will lecture in Salem on Sunday evening, Jan. 15, 1860.

I will, with great pleasure — *Deo volente*.

Yours, for immediate emancipation,

Wm. Lloyd Garrison.

☞ Send me your advertisement seasonably for insertion in the Liberator.[1]

ALS: Essex Institute, Salem, Massachusetts.

Garrison did not specify to which Miss Roberts, Adeline or Elmina, the letter was addressed.

1. The advertisment of the lecture series appeared in *The Liberator*, December 2, 1859.

2 8 7

TO ELIZABETH BUFFUM CHACE

Oct. 17, 1859. I can hardly realize that your beloved father has gone; and much did I regret that it was not in my power to be at his interment.

How true and faithful you have been to the cause of the enslaved for many a year past! Heaven bless you and your dear household, and long preserve you in continued well-doing!

Excerpt, printed in Lillie Buffum Chace Wyman and Arthur Crawford Wyman, *Elizabeth Buffum Chace, Her Life and Its Environment* (Boston, 1914), I, 199–200.

It is strange that Garrison would write this note more than half a year after Arnold Buffum's death. It seems to have been occasioned by a note from Elizabeth Buffum Chace.

2 8 8

TO AN UNKNOWN CORRESPONDENT

Boston, Oct. 17, 1859.

Dear Sir:

Since the receipt of your letter, I have been in that state of bodily debility which makes "the grasshopper a burden." [1] This must be my apology for not sending you my autograph more promptly.

Yours, truly,

Wm. Lloyd Garrison.

ALS: In possession of James Lawton, Brookline, Massachusetts.

1. Ecclesiastes 12:5.

2 8 9

TO ELIZABETH PEASE NICHOL

Boston, Oct. 18, 1859

My dear Friend:

You have met with a great bereavement — how great, you alone can tell. The intelligence of the death of your beloved and honored husband [1] is received by us all with sadness. Alas! that it was not my privilege & [2] happiness to enjoy his personal acquaintance! I believe

I never saw him. But my highest conviction of his worth is derived from the fact that my beloved friend, Elizabeth Pease, regarded him as worthy of her life-long love in the nearest and holiest relation of life. You were deserving of all that he was, however excellent & noble. I cannot bear to think of his having passed away from earth before feeling his friendly grasp, & sitting down with you both under your own hospitable roof. I have been dreaming of another visit to Scotland, at no distant day, & in that dream I saw myself at the Observatory, made welcome by you both. The dream can be only partially realized, if at all. *He* will not be there, even should I be permitted to visit your beautiful home; not there in bodily proportion, as a tangible object, with whom to commune, face to face. And yet, in a most living and veritable sense, I believe he will be there — *is* there already — as full of consciousness and affection as ever, with all his faculties and powers untouched by the mysterious change through which he has passed, & as deeply interested in your welfare and happiness. With the strongest assurance of an immortal life, & with what I regard as conclusive evidence that our departed loved ones are often very near to us — as near as souls can ever be together — I have long since regarded what we call death, not only without dismay, not only with resignation, but with a profound perception of its beneficence, as well as its necessity, trying as the separation may be. While I proffer you my tenderest sympathies, I rejoice with you in the hope of immortality — "He is not dead," said Jesus. It is as true of your beloved husband as it was of him to whom those words are applied[3] — There are, as yet, but few particulars given of his illness. It must have been short, and the blow sudden; for "congestion of the brain" tells the whole sad story. Enthusiastic in the promotion of his favorite science — laborious for the enlightenment and good of others, beyond his natural powers — he fell as a martyr, and as such deserves to be crowned. To say that he has not lived in vain is an inadequate expression, for in its broadest sense of few cannot this be said. He had but few peers in the realm of mind, & in gifts & attainments stood conspicuous in the universal crowd of men. His children[4] have reason to be proud of his memory, while they lament his sudden removal in the maturity of his powers. I am too well acquainted with the religiousness of your nature, my dear friend, not to believe that this bereavement will be sustained by you in the spirit of pious resignation to the Divine Will. "Though He slay me, yet will I trust in Him."[5] Not to weep would be unnatural, but behind the cloud, the Sun of Righteousness is shining still. May you be sustained by all holy spirits & all good influences!

I ought not to have waited for an event like this to send you a friendly letter; but, as to epistolary matters, I am always slow to execute, through my aversion to the use of the pen, much as I love and cherish my friends. You are always a part of my memory. Since I first knew you, I have steadily cherished for you the profoundest regard as one of the best of women. All the past rises up before me, and multitudinous emotions overpower me. Your kindness & beneficence — do not suppose that I can ever forget them.

My health has not been good for the past six months, & I need rest & recreation for a while. It is possible I may visit Scotland next Spring, though my aversion to the sea is almost unconquerable. In case I shall make the voyage, there will be none I shall more desire to see than yourself.

Your unaltered & unalterable friend

Wm. Lloyd Garrison.

Elizabeth P. Nichol.

My dear Helen sends you her liveliest sympathies and her warmest regards.

Transcript: Garrison Papers, Boston Public Library.

1. John Pringle Nichol (1804–1859), astronomer, regius professor of astronomy at Glasgow University, had married Elizabeth Pease in 1853. (*Letters*, II, 326–327. *The Liberator*, October 28, 1859, reprinted an obituary from the *Glasgow Commonwealth* of September 24, 1859.)

2. Garrison almost never used the ampersand, which must have been used as shorthand by the transcriber.

3. The reference is probably to an altered version of the story in Matthew 9:18–25, and other Gospels, of the young woman of whom her father said, "My daughter is even now dead." The remark of Jesus was, "Give place: for the maid is not dead, but sleepeth."

4. He had a son and a daughter by a previous marriage.

5. Job 13:15.

290

TO HENRY C. WRIGHT

Boston, Oct. 19, 1859.

Dear Henry:

Such is the state of my throat and lungs that I must forego all public speaking for a long time to come. I am now under medical treatment and advice. I must decline the overture made to me to speak in Portland, Dec. 18th, and shall be very glad, therefore, if you can act as my substitute.

I shall not be able to go to Worcester next Sunday.[1] If you are not otherwise engaged, I think Mr. May would like to have you go there with Remond.

I must recall my promise to be at the Harwich meeting.[2]

I am glad you have written E. P. Nichol and Robson.[3] The name of the Superintendant of the Boston Schools is Philbrick,[4] not Whipple, as you supposed; but Mr. Robson will know to whom you allude.

Shall we not see you at Dix Place Friday or Saturday?

Ever faithfully yours,

Wm. Lloyd Garrison.

H. C. Wright.

☞ Mr. May tells me he has secured the attendance of Adin Ballou and A. T. Foss at Worcester; so your presence will not be needed. You are expected to go to Harwich.

ALS: Garrison Papers, Boston Public Library.

1. This was to be a special meeting of the Worcester County South Division Anti-Slavery Society, on Sunday, October 23. Garrison had been listed as one of the speakers. (*The Liberator*, October 7, 1859.)

2. *The Liberator*, October 14, 1859, had carried the following announcement: "CAPE COD ANNUAL MEETING. — The Annual Anti-Slavery Convention, for Barnstable County, will be held at Harwich, in Exchange Hall, on Saturday and Sunday, November 5th and 6th. . . .

"William Lloyd Garrison, and other speakers to be more particularly named hereafter, will attend the Convention."

3. Apparently, Robson had given some books to the Boston superintendent of schools, who believed them to be a gift. But Robson had assumed that they would be paid for. There was some confusion, and Henry Wright had just written to Robson to explain the problem. A letter from Wright to Garrison, dated October 17, 1859, to which Garrison's letter is a reply, provides additional details of the mix-up. (Anti-Slavery Letters to Garrison and Others, Boston Public Library.)

4. John Dudley Philbrick (b. Deerfield, New Hampshire, May 27, 1818; d. Danvers, Massachusetts, February 2, 1886) was superintendent of public instruction in Boston from 1857 to 1874 and 1876 to 1878. He was also a member of the state board of education for ten years and president of teachers' associations of Massachusetts and Connecticut.

291

TO OLIVER JOHNSON

Boston, Nov. 1, 1859.

Dear Johnson:

Enclosed, you will find a Resolution, adopted by our Executive Committee,[1] to be published in the next Standard and Liberator, and also in the Tribune of Thursday morning. Perhaps having the first publication of it, the Tribune will give it an insertion without charge; but, if not, you are authorised to have it inserted as an advertisement, as it is important, for popular effect, that it should be seen and known as widely as possible, without any delay. It will help to increase the uneasiness of the oppressor, and to strengthen the hands of the friends of freedom, even should the suggestion thrown out not be very generally adopted. But, should there be any thing like a reasonable time allowed between the sentence and the execution of Capt. Brown, it will no doubt be acted upon in various parts of the country, to the furtherance of our good cause.

What Capt. Brown expected to accomplish [2] with only a score of abettors is to me, up to this hour, quite enigmatical. Upon the face of it, his raid into Virginia looks utterly lacking in common sense — a desperate self-sacrifice for the purpose of giving an earthquake shock to the slave system, and thus hastening the day for a universal catastrophe. But, whatever may have been his errors of judgment or calculation, his bearing since his capture and during his trial has been truly sublime, and challenges for him all of human sympathy and respect. Of course, he will be hung, and quite as speedily as decency will allow. In Boston we have thought it would be a master-stroke of policy to urge *the day of his execution* as the day for a general public expression of sentiment with reference to the guilt and danger of slavery. Please say a word with reference to the proposition of the Executive Committee, and urge its adoption by all who claim to deplore and abhor the accursed slave system.

You have doubtless read what our excellent friend, Adin Ballou, has had to say in the last two numbers of his *Practical Christian*, by way of reply to J. M. McKim and Saml. May, Jr., impeaching the spirit and consistency of the American and Massachusetts Anti-Slavery Societies, &c. &c.[3] I am surprised that one so usually clear-sighted as he is should make so much out of so very little, and

"— give to an inch the importance of a mile";

and I cannot but think that he is growing hypercritical, through a morbid state of mind which prevents an extended view and an impartial judgment. But he deserves to be answered (if answered at all) with all possible respect and kindness. His conscientiousness is unquestionable, and his great circumspection will do us no harm.

In the course of a few days, I hope you will see my son George walking into your office from Lawrence, Kansas.

Yours, in improving health,

Wm. Lloyd Garrison.

ALS: Chicago Historical Society.

1. The resolution urged that the day of John Brown's execution, December 2, 1859, be observed publicly, "for the furtherance of the anti-slavery cause" and the abolition of slavery. (*The Liberator*, November 4, 1859.)

2. The reference is to the attack on Harpers Ferry, by John Brown and his group, on October 16, 1859.

3. On September 17, 1859, the *National Anti-Slavery Standard* reprinted an

essay by Adin Ballou, "Practical Christian Anti-Slavery," from the *Practical Christian*. This essay was also reprinted in *The Liberator*, September 16, 1859.

After suggesting that "we have heretofore consorted chiefly with the old American Anti-Slavery Society, sometimes called Garrisonians . . . because their fundamentals seemed to us nearer right than those of any other professedly anti-slavery class. Moreover, we felt that our kind of Christianity, with its non-resistance and non-politics, would be less cramped and more at home on their platform than on others where milito-political or ecclesiastical influences prevailed," he noted his growing estrangement from the Garrisonians. The reasons were the following:

"1. Because the war-principle and spirit are becoming too dominant and rampant for our endurance. The motto is reiterated with general applause, '*Peaceably if we can, forcibly if we must.*' The local governments of the land are persistently instigated to pass penal laws against pro-slavery laws of the general government, and to revolt against its Constitutional supremacy. Red Revolutionism, for the sake of the Anti-Slavery cause, is plainly preached and eloquently urged as the duty of the people. . . .

"2. Because there is a growing disposition among our anti-slavery associates to magnify their movement for the abolition of chattel slavery as including the main substance of Christianity, or a natural religion much purer than Christianity, to the great disparagement of other departments of righteousness, and manifest contempt for really valuable established religious institutions. . . .

"3. We find ourselves in doubt whether to consider the Anti-Slavery platform a desirable resort for us, because of the increasing egotism, extremism, exaggerationism, antagonism and contemptuous personality, which we are obliged to witness. . . ."

In the following week's issue, September 24, 1859, the *Standard's* Philadelphia Correspondent, signing himself "M," for McKim, devoted a column and a half to Ballou's criticism. While conceding that Ballou's "article contains much wholesome and edifying truth," it also denied many of Ballou's charges and urged him to remain within the organization which included a variety of points of view concerning politics and nonresistance. On November 4, *The Liberator* reprinted an essay by Ballou from the *Practical Christian*, entitled "Adin Ballou in Reply to J. Miller McKim."

The gist of the differences between Adin Ballou and Samuel May, Jr. is to be found in the report of a colloquy between the two at a meeting of the Worcester County South Division Anti-Slavery Society, at Worcester, on October 23, 1859. *The Liberator* (November 4, 1859), in reporting the proceedings, wrote as follows: "Adin Ballou again spoke, re-affirming his previous positions, protesting against giving the slightest countenance to physical resistance to the slaveholder, which he thought was done by the resolutions just read. [They had been introduced by May, and were said to represent Garrison's views as well.] He objected to the petitions for a Personal Liberty law in this State, as virtually asking the State to involve itself in a violent contest with the Federal Government and the Slave Power. He objected also to the Petition for the Removal of the Webster Statue, inasmuch as Governor Banks and the Massachusetts Legislature, themselves supporting the United States Constitution, cannot consistently censure Daniel Webster for his support of the Fugitive Slave Law.

"To this Mr. May replied that Mr. Ballou's argument, if sound, would well-nigh render impossible any Anti-Slavery movement; — that we may, and should, ask men to do the right and just thing, even though they have sworn to do the wrong; that the inconsistency is *their* business, not ours; that our request may be the very means of enlightening them as to the guilt of their position and conduct, and of leading them to repentance; and, at all events, that we are bound to call on all men to cease to uphold slavery, or approve the slaveholder, and to do their utmost, in every just and proper way, to bring slavery to an end, and to fasten shame and disgrace, instead of honor, upon all defenders and apologists of 'the vilest system' that ever saw the sun."

292

TO W. H. FURNESS

Boston, Dec. 17, 1859.

Dear Mr. Furness:

Allow me to introduce to you the eldest son [1] of my much lamented friend, Charles F. Hovey. He is named after his father, and for his father's sake you will be happy to take him by the hand. He is a promising young man, and resembles both father and mother in his features.

My heart is drawn more closely to you than ever, if possible, in these momentous times. John Brown has raised up all the fierceness and diabolism of the pit at the South, and among a certain class at the North; but he has also inspired and strengthened millions to abhor slavery, and labor for its overthrow. God bless you and yours abundantly!

Ever your attached friend,

Wm. Lloyd Garrison.

Rev. W. H. Furness.

ALS: University of Pennsylvania Library.

1. Charles A. Hovey (d. Manchester, New Hampshire, June 19, 1886, aged forty-six) was prominent in the temperance cause for many years. At his death he was paymaster of the Stark Manufacturing Company. (Obituary, Boston *Evening Transcript*, June 21, 1886.)

293

TO J. MILLER McKIM

Boston, Dec. 17, 1859.

My dear McKim:

The bearer of this is Charles A. Hovey, the eldest son of our dear departed friend Charles F. Hovey, and very promising withal, having wisely concluded to be a farmer, and to cultivate the earth, instead of being a trader. He has a farm at Framingham. I know it will give you pleasure to take him by the hand for his father's sake, and to introduce him to any anti-slavery friend that may happen to come into the Anti-Slavery Office when he is present.

How much I would like to say about the John Brown affair! But I can only express my profound gratification that you and Wendell were able to take care of the body, and attend the funeral.[1] I would have been with you, if I had not been absent from the city. Your account of the matter in the Tribune will be read by hundreds of thousands with thrilling emotions.[2] I was sorry that I could not publish your excellent remarks at the funeral, in the last Liberator, for lack of room. Indeed, I never was in such a dilemma in regard to the matter on hand for my paper. It is overwhelming, needing a daily sheet larger than the Tribune to dispose of it.

My love to all the dear circle of friends in Philadelphia and vicinity, your estimable wife and beloved children in special; and my warmest thanks for all the kindness shown to my eldest son, G.T.G.

Full of strength and encouragement at the signs of the times, I remain,

Your attached friend,

Wm. Lloyd Garrison.

J. M. McKim.

☞ Please introduce Charles to dear James and Lucretia Mott.

ALS: Garrison Papers, Boston Public Library.

1. Wendell Phillips and J. Miller McKim accompanied John Brown's body from Philadelphia, where it arrived on December 3, the day after the execution, to North Elba, New York, where Brown was buried and the funeral service conducted on December 8. Both McKim and Phillips spoke at the service. (Oswald Garrison Villard, *John Brown, 1800–1859, A Biography Fifty Years After*, New York, 1943, pp. 561–562.)

2. The account, headed "The Burial of John Brown — The Passage of the Body to North Elba — The Funeral — Speeches of Mr. McKim and Mr. Phillips," appeared in the *Standard*, December 17, 1859. It carried a footnote that "though it appeared first in *The Tribune*, [it] was intended for *The Standard* as well. It has been revised by the writer since its publication in the first-named paper." McKim's name does not appear as the author, who is referred to as "Our Special Correspondent."

294

TO AN UNKNOWN CORRESPONDENT

Boston, Dec. 18, 1859.

Dear Sir:

You inquire, whether I will speak in Concord, some evening this week, on the great theme of the times. If agreeable to you and the other friends, I will be with you *on Friday next*, and lecture that evening. Or, should you prefer Monday evening, 26th inst., I will come at that time. As for my terms, they are — my travelling expenses, and any thing beyond that may be raised *without taxing any persons in special*. Let this be understood. If nothing beyond the travelling expenses can be collected, so be it.

I am glad, as is my wife, to hear that dear Mrs. Pillsbury is in a comparatively comfortable state of health. We have thought much of her, and sympathized with her in all her sufferings. Few wives could have been found in this land so self-sacrificing in the way of separating from their husbands, for the slave's sake, as she has shown herself in consenting to Parker's continued absence from home in the lecturing field. God bless and preserve her, and grant her full restoration to health!

Our warm regards to her and Helen.

Please let me know which of the evenings I have named, (if either,) will suit your purpose.

Yours, to break every yoke,

Wm. Lloyd Garrison.

N. B. John Brown executed will do more for our good cause, incomparably, than John Brown pardoned.

ALS: Colby Junior College, New London, New Hampshire.

X ILLNESS, MORE CONVENTIONS, AND
GARRISONIAN ANTISLAVERY REDEFINED: 1860

I LLNESS OF THROAT and lungs plagued Garrison during the early part of 1860 as well as at its end, forcing him to confine himself for the most part to his home and Boston, diminishing the number of his speaking engagements and even his writings for *The Liberator*. On *The Liberator*, he was helped by the editorial assistance of Charles K. Whipple, who assumed much of the burden of the paper. Yet he continued his unsuccessful efforts on behalf of a law to prohibit slave-catching in Massachusetts, participated in the annual meetings of the Massachusetts Anti-Slavery Society in Boston in January, the American Anti-Slavery Society in New York on May 8 and 9, and the New England Anti-Slavery Convention in Boston on May 30. At the end of July and the early part of August, Garrison vacationed in the mountains of New Hampshire and Maine and returned refreshed and strengthened. But his health deteriorated again, so that all speaking engagements had to be canceled for the remainder of the year. In a number of instances, letters from him were read to assembled audiences. It seems almost providential and indeed appropriate that his last extant letter of the year should be that of December 1 to James Redpath, for perhaps more than any other it summarizes his antislavery philosophy and program.

295

TO SAMUEL J. MAY

Boston, Jan. 14, 1860.

My Dear Friend:

I ought to be ashamed of myself — and am — that I have not answered your first letter,[1] without waiting to receive a second one; but

I am so deluged with letters and manuscripts, that many of them get temporarily displaced or mislaid before being attended to; and so — "out of sight, out of mind."

To your kind inquiry as to the state of my health, I am happy to reply that I am feeling quite as well as usual — at no time, however, being free from my catarrhal attacks, which trouble me a good deal. I have scarcely written any thing for the Liberator for some time past, mainly because I have been anxious to record in its columns, as fully as possible, the amazing outpouring of public sentiment — pro and con — in relation to John Brown; and because I am ever disposed to be indulgent to correspondents — especially to "C. K. W." [2] — even to the exclusion of my own articles. I must, however, "turn over a new leaf," as soon as the present extraordinary pressure shall have been removed.

I am very much obliged to you for inviting me to give one of your course of anti-slavery lectures in Syracuse; but the distance is too far, and the travelling expenses too great, to warrant such a journey, unless I could do some anti-slavery labor by the way. At such an inclement season of the year, I feel inclined not to venture far beyond the vicinity of Boston; and I have therefore declined a most pressing invitation to be present at the annual gathering at Albany, Jan. 31, and Feb. 1 and 2.[3]

As the Women's Rights Convention is to be held at Albany, Feb. 3 and 4,[4] I am almost tempted to revoke my decision, and say I will be at Albany, and then on Saturday, Feb. 4th, go to Syracuse, and spend the Sunday with you, and lecture (should the arrangement be agreeable) on Monday evening, Feb. 6th, and return home the next day. But I dare not, now, make any definite pledge, and will revolve the matter over in my mind, and let you know my final conclusion shortly. I long to see you and your dear family again under your own roof.

I trust your own health continues good, and that your European tour will long prove of real service to you in the way of longevity. Do not overwork yourself. As we are advancing in life toward the goal of old age, we ought to remember that we cannot bear the burdens and labors of life as in our younger days.

Our Executive Committee have acted upon your suggestion to send Anti-Slavery books to various parts of England, and will carry it out in a liberal manner. As for agents abroad, we do not see our way clear to make any overtures at present, but we shall not lose sight of the subject.

It is gratifying to hear that our afflicted friend, Gerrit Smith, is nearly restored to his usual state of health. He has had my deepest sympathies, and so has Mrs. Smith. May his days of usefulness yet be many on the earth.[5]

How pleasant it must have been to you to have had such a reception on your arrival home! No man better deserves a host of loving and unswerving friends than yourself, and these abound in all directions.

Helen sends her kindest regard to you, to Mrs. May, the two Charlottes, and all the children. Mine are included in hers.

Lovingly yours,

Wm. Lloyd Garrison.

S. J. May.

ALS: Garrison Papers, Boston Public Library.

1. This must have been the first letter after Samuel J. May's return from Europe. On November 18, 1859, *The Liberator* reported that "After an absence of ten months on a European tour for the benefit of his health (which has been greatly improved by it,) he [May] arrived safely at Boston on the 5th inst., where he was warmly greeted by a social gathering of his relatives and co-workers in the cause of suffering humanity. He then proceeded to Syracuse. Though arriving at eleven at night, he was met by a large crowd at the depot, who gave him a hearty welcome. The next day, he received the congratulations of his friends, and a public reception was arranged for him for the evening. . . ."

2. Charles K. Whipple.

3. This was to be the New York State Annual Anti-Slavery Convention.

4. The New York State Woman's Rights Convention.

5. Following John Brown's attack on Harpers Ferry, Gerrit Smith, who had been one of his chief supporters, had a mental breakdown and was taken to the asylum for the insane at Utica, New York, on November 7. By December 29 he had recovered sufficiently to be released and brought back to his home. (Octavius Brooks Frothingham, *Gerrit Smith, A Biography*, New York, 1878, pp. 245–246.)

296

TO ELIZABETH PEASE NICHOL

Boston, Feb. 22, 1860

My dear Friend:

I have just received your kind letter, which I have perused with the deepest sympathy; and as the steamer sails today for Liverpool, I will lose no time in answering it, however briefly.

The long & painfully interesting epistle which you sent to Mr. Phillips, giving a detailed account of the sickness & death of your lamented husband, & expressing the greatness of your bereavement, I read with indescribable feelings. Surely, Prof. Nichol must have possessed the noblest qualities of mind & soul to have excited in you such unbounded admiration and love; for I know how high is your standard of moral excellence, & what a noble affectionate nature is yours. Alas! that it was not my privilege to know him as a personal friend! O that it were in my power to convey to you, in words, that consolation which you need! But only "the heart knoweth its own bitterness," [1] and speech can do little toward filling "an aching void." [2] I can only mingle my grief with yours, hoping thus to extract some portion of its severity from your bosom. There are some considerations which should serve to break the force of such a separation while allowing the heart full scope for its sorrow.

1. The transition cannot, I feel persuaded, in any case, be a loss to the departed.

2. It is not extinction of being, but occupying a higher plane, under better conditions.

3. It is not a special calamity, rarely experienced, but a universal occurrence & inevitable among those who have no abiding place here.

4. It is a part of the beneficent scheme of Divine Love, & therefore to be accepted as such in the spirit of filial resignation — as in the memorable words of Job — "The Lord gave, & the Lord has taken away. Blessed be the name of the Lord!" [3]

5. In the vast sweep of time, and the multitudinous events in this boundless universe, our losses are utterly imperceptible, though for the hour grievous to be borne, and seemingly irreparable.

6. The departed, though absent in body, are with us in spirit — "not lost, but gone before." [4] In due time, a re-union shall take place, when all tears shall be wiped away, and there shall be no more death.

In regard to my visiting England, I cannot yet write definitely about it. If my desire shall be gratified, I shall certainly hope to see you in the course of next summer, as well as many other dear friends abroad. But my health is now good, & I need not, therefore, try a voyage to the old world to recover it, unless indeed it should again be seriously impaired. Under no circumstances do I expect to leave home before the middle of May; so that I shall not have the melancholy pleasure of seeing you at the Observatory before the expiration of your present lease; probably not till after you are quietly settled in your new residence near Edinburgh. But I dare not make any promise, or even hold out any expectation of my coming. How to leave home I know not, wrapped up as my affections are in a beloved & loving wife & in dutiful children, & from whose society it is a cross to me to be absent even for a few days. There is more or less peril in crossing the ocean; & I suffer exceedingly from sea sickness. Nevertheless, my pulse leaps at the thought of standing again on British soil. I will decide soon. Should I come it is not unlikely that my dear friend, Samuel May Jr., our General Agent, will accompany me. His health is really impaired, & he needs relaxation; & I have no doubt a sea voyage would be of real benefit to him. Together I should hope that we might do something towards deepening the Anti-Slavery sentiment of England, & thus aiding the cause of the millions in bondage here; which is in fact the cause of all mankind.

I wish you could know my wife & children. They all long to see you, & fondly hope that one day they may have this pleasure, even in Boston! No man has been more blessed than myself in regard to these sacred relations. My home is all that I desire, & one spirit animates our entire household — that of unalloyed love.

Should you see the Patons,[5] Andersons,[6] Smeals,[7] &c. &c. tell them they are an undying part of my memory, & bound up in my warmest regards.

Heaven sustain & bless you!

Yours, in fullest sympathy

Wm. Lloyd Garrison

E. P. Nichol.

Charles Sumner considers himself quite restored to health.

Transcript: Garrison Papers, Boston Public Library.

1. Proverbs 14:10.
2. William Cowper, *Olney Hymns*, 1.
3. Job 1:21.
4. Caroline Elizabeth Sarah Norton (1808–1877), English poet and novelist, "Not Lost but Gone Before."
5. Mr. and Mrs. Andrew Paton of Glasgow, Scotland.
6. The Reverend William Anderson (1799–1873), Scottish preacher, was pastor of a congregation in John Street, Glasgow, from 1822 until his death, prominent in political and social reforms and the author of pamphlets and books in theology.
7. William Smeal (1793–1877), British abolitionist and Quaker and Garrison's lifelong friend. (*Letters*, II, 728.)

297

TO WENDELL PHILLIPS GARRISON

Boston, March 21, 1860.

My Dear Son:

The Williamses,[1] at Roxbury, desire you to take tea and spend the evening with them on Friday next. Will you do so? Mrs. Hovey [2] and William Hovey are going out, and wish for your company. Let them have it if you can.

Rev. Mr. Trask,[3] the indefatigable Anti-Tobacco missionary, was in my office, a day or two since, and spoke in very complimentary terms of your essay on Tobacco in the Harvard Magazine.[4] Were you not my son, he said, he would indulge in still stronger panegyric. I am made very happy by the unfolding of your moral nature in connection with your intellectual development; and feel assured that your example at College will be of great value to others.

Your loving father,

Wm. Lloyd Garrison.

W. P. Garrison.

ALS: Smith College Library.

1. Probably Henry Willard Williams (1821–1895) and his family. Williams was a general agent for *The Liberator* in 1842. Soon thereafter he entered the Harvard Medical School, graduated in 1849, and went on to establish himself in Boston as one of the most prominent and scientifically creative ophthalmologists in the country. He was married twice: to Elizabeth Dewe of London in 1848 and to Elizabeth Adeline Low of Boston in 1860. He had six sons. (*Letters*, III, 85–87, to Nathaniel P. Rogers, June 7, 1842.)

2. Mrs. Charles F. Hovey, née Justine Watts de Peyster, whose husband had died the year before. She had married Hovey in 1837. (See Letter 229, to Wendell Phillips Garrison, August 20, 1858, note 2.)

3. The Reverend George Trask (1798–1875), of Framingham, Massachusetts. Trask was also prominent in the peace, temperance, and antislavery movements. (*Letters*, II, 99.)

4. At that time, the essays in the *Harvard Magazine* did not carry bylines. However, the first essay in the issue of March 1860, VI, 169–180, was entitled "The Use of Tobacco in College," and was undoubtedly the one mentioned by Garrison as having been written by his son, Wendell. The essay condemned the use of tobacco.

298

TO WENDELL PHILLIPS GARRISON

Boston, March 22, 1860.

My Dear Son:

William Hovey says that the hour for tea, to-morrow evening, at the Williamses, will be 8 o'clock; so that you will be able to get there seasonably. William and his mother will go out earlier than it will be convenient for you to do.

Nature presents a wintry aspect to-day, but she understands what is her most appropriate attire, and therefore is beyond criticism.

The Committee of the Legislature, to whom our petitions for a Personal Liberty Bill were referred, have reported "leave to withdraw" — which means, let slave-hunters have leave still to pursue their prey on the soil of Massachusetts! [1]

Your affectionate father,

Wm. Lloyd Garrison.

W. P. Garrison.

ALS: Massachusetts Historical Society.

1. *The Liberator*, March 30, 1860, reported as follows concerning the committee's action: "In view of the pending Presidential election, it was hardly expected by the most sanguine that the present Legislature would decree the abolition of slave-hunting in this State, by a two-thirds vote; but, surely, no one dreamed that the committee, having this subject under consideration, would have the cool audacity to 'report that *the petitioners have leave to withdraw.*'!! Yet they have done so, — Hon. Nathaniel H. Whiting, of Plymouth, alone dissenting, — and the Senate has accepted the report!"

299

TO THOMAS WENTWORTH HIGGINSON

Boston, April 6, 1860.

My dear Mr. Higginson:

I take great pleasure in introducing to you the bearer of this, Mr. Louis Wageley,[1] who has been a resident for some time in Milford, in this State, and who has been commended to me by friends in that town as a young man of fine talents, an acquisitive and progressive mind, and excellent character. He thinks of establishing himself in Worcester, for the purpose of teaching the German language, &c., and I hope he will be successful. His manners are pleasing, and he impresses me as one eminently worthy of encouragement. If you can be of any service to him, I think you will readily do so.

Truly yours,

Wm. Lloyd Garrison.

ALS: Harvard College Library.

1. Louis Wageley was a German immigrant. During the Civil War he served in the Union army as a private, and later, as captain. (Abijah P. Marvin, *History of Worcester in the War of the Rebellion*, Worcester, 1870, pp. 65, 98, 100–101, 127, 521.)

300

TO CAROLINE C. THAYER

14 Dix Place, May 19, 1860.

My Dear Friend:

The sad intelligence of the death of your dear and venerated mother reached me during my absence in New York.[1] I need not attempt to describe how strongly I was affected by it. It was only a few days before I left home, that I had the pleasure of meeting her in Washington Street, (with Eliza,[2]) and looking upon her radiant countenance, (which always carried a benediction with it,) and hearing from her lips the expression of her gratification at my recent visit to your home, and her hope that I would renew it speedily. Ah! how could I dream that it was the last time I should be permitted to see her in the flesh? And yet, what prescriptive lease of life have any of us, even though much younger than herself? She had attained a ripe old age; and, happily for her, she passed away without any lingering sickness, almost by an instantaneous translation.

So motherly was she in her nature, that I almost felt in her presence as if I were one of her children.

Her traits of character struck me, from my first acquaintance with her, as admirable. Firmness, dignity, self-respect, humility, reverence, affection, benevolence, sympathy for the suffering, maternal watchfulness and fidelity, and whatever tends to ennoble and bless — these seemed to be inherent, and developed in no ordinary degree. It is but the simplest justice to her memory to say that she was, in the highest sense, a pattern of excellence.

If she thus impressed me and others, who only saw her occasionally, what must have been her worth in your eyes, and those of your brothers and sisters, who received her daily blessing and experienced her unfailing love, and were with her from your cradles to the time of her burial! How great is your bereavement! All the sympathies of my heart, and those of my dear wife, are with you all.

"The Lord gave, and the Lord hath taken away." [3] This is no empty language; for "in him we live, and move, and have our being," [4] and "he giveth to all life, and breath, and all things." [5] Happy for us if we can say, at all times, and under all our afflictions, as Job did, "Blessed be the name of the Lord!" [6]

Alas! sad tidings have come to-day from Florence, in regard to the condition of our dear friend, Theodore Parker. It leaves little or no hope of his recovery; nay, it almost warrants the heart-depressing conclusion, that he has, ere this, seen "the last of earth," so that we shall never behold him again in the flesh. Our solace must be found in the noble life he has lived, and the great example he has set, and the mighty influences for good that have emanated from him.[7]

Give my warmest regards and heart-felt sympathies to your sisters and brother.

Your attached friend,

Wm. Lloyd Garrison.

Caroline Thayer.

ALS: Garrison Papers, Boston Public Library.

1. Susanna T. Thayer had died on May 9. Her obituary appeared in *The Liberator* on June 1, 1860.

2. Eliza Thayer, Carolines sister.
3. Job 1:21.
4. Acts 17:28.
5. Acts 17:25.
6. Job 1:21.
7. Parker had died on May 10, but the news had not yet reached Boston.

301

TO HENRY I. BOWDITCH

Boston, June 18, 1860.

My dear friend Bowditch:

The bearer of this is Richard Steele,[1] Esq., formerly of New Hampshire, a man of collegiate education, strict uprightness, and an old friend of the Anti-Slavery cause. He has been engaged as a copyist in this city for a few years past; but, at present, for lack of employment, is in a destitute condition, especially as he has not been able to get some compensation due him. He is a highminded man, not wishing to be dependant upon the charity of others, and desirous of getting something to do, no matter what, that can give him his bread. He has been a practising physician for many years, and was regularly educated for the profession. Is there any thing within the scope of your benevolence or knowledge that he can probably do or obtain, to keep him from suffering? It is sad to see so worthy and well-educated a man reduced to such an extremity. I trust some way of relief will open to him.

Yours, with warm regards,

Wm. Lloyd Garrison.

Dr. Henry I. Bowditch.

ALS: Villard Papers, Boston Public Library.

1. Richard Steele is listed intermittently in the Boston *Directory* as a physician 1859 to 1871, but was not a member of either the Suffolk County or Massachusetts Medical Society. The 1871 *Directory* lists him as living at the Home for Aged Men, 133 West Springfield Street.

302

TO WENDELL PHILLIPS

Boston, July 5, 1860.

Dear Phillips:

We had a very excellent meeting without you, yesterday, at Framingham,[1] but it would have been better if you had been present. The attendance was very large. H. Ford Douglass [2] made a long and telling speech, and drew out Henry Wilson in explanation and defence of himself, and Abraham Lincoln, and the Republican party. How I wished you had been present! Pillsbury made a long, able, and racy reply. [Edmund] Quincy presided.

Enclosed, I send you an editorial article from the Tribune of yesterday. I shall print it on the first page of the next Liberator,[3] and want you to reply [to] it. Any thing from you by Tuesday will be seasonable.

My loving regards and best wishes to Ann.

Ever yours,

Wm. Lloyd Garrison.

ALS: Collection of Foreman M. Lebold.

1. The meeting was under the auspices of the Massachusetts Anti-Slavery Society. A detailed account appeared in *The Liberator*, July 13, 1860.

2. H. Ford Douglass, a black man, then twenty-eight years old, was of Chicago, Illinois (*The Liberator*, July 13, 1860; his speech, which is printed in its entirety in this issue, gives these facts about himself.) According to John Hope Franklin, during the Civil War "an independent battery at Lawrence, Kansas, was led by Captain H. Ford Douglass and First Lieutenant W. D. Matthews." (*From Slavery to Freedom, A History of Negro Americans*, 3d. ed., New York, 1967, p. 191.) Philip Foner refers to him as "a runaway slave who became a leading Abolitionist orator in the midwest" and as "the most outspoken black critic of Lincoln" during the election of 1860. (*The Voice of Black America, Major Speeches by Negroes in the United States, 1797–1971*, New York, 1972, p. 232. Foner also reproduces Douglass's July 4, 1860, speech at Framingham.) For a while, in the mid-1850's, Douglass was active in the Anti-Slavery Society of Canada, and was an editor of the *Provincial Freeman*, "launched in March 1953, in Windsor, Canada West." (Robin W. Winks, *The Blacks in Canada, A History*, Montreal, New Haven, and London, 1971, pp. 257, 394–395.)

3. The New York *Tribune* editorial appeared in *The Liberator*, July 13, 1860. It consisted of a rebuttal of an article in *The Liberator* by Wendell Phillips, which had called Abraham Lincoln "the slave-hound of Illinois." Phillips's reply appeared in the same issue of *The Liberator*, on the editorial page.

303

TO CHARLES SUMNER

Boston, July 16, 1860.

Hon. Charles Sumner:

Dear Sir — The anniversary of British West India Emancipation will be commemorated, as usual, on the approaching 1st of August, at the Abington Grove, under the direction of the Managers of the Massachusetts Anti-Slavery Society; and I am requested by them to extend to you their most cordial invitation to be present, and bear such testimony to the beneficent workings of this grand event (itself without a parallel in history) as unquestionable facts fully warrant.

Hoping it may be in your power to comply with this invitation, and knowing that such a testimony would be read by thousands with great interest, to the furtherance of the cause of the millions yet waiting for deliverance from the galling chains of slavery in our own land, I remain,

Yours, to break every yoke,

Wm. Lloyd Garrison.

P. S. Allow me warmly to congratulate you upon your complete restoration to health, and upon the successful delivery of your great speech in Congress,[1] the potency of which is seen in the writhings and denunciations of the slaveholding oligarchy and their base Northern allies, quite as much as in the commendations and rejoicings of your numerous friends and admirers.

ALS: Houghton Library, Harvard University.

1. Sumner's speech in the Senate, the first since his brutal beating in May 1856, by Representative Preston S. Brooks of South Carolina, was delivered on June 4, was entitled "The Barbarism of Slavery," and occupied four hours. *The Liberator*, June 8, 1860, carried an editorial about it and announced that "In order that our readers may be put in immediate possession of this masterly speech of Mr. Sumner, we publish it in an extra, which is equivalent to giving them an extra number of *The Liberator*, as it would occupy four pages of our paper in the type ordinarily used by us. Its circulation will be immense, and it will be read by millions. That portion of it which relates to the U. S. Constitution is open to criticism hereafter."

304

TO LYDIA D. PARKER

Boston, July 20, 1860.

My dear Mrs. Parker:

I received, last evening, with grateful and heartfelt emotion, the photographic view of the most cherished portion of your beloved and widely deplored husband's study, (wanting nothing but his own dear presence to be perfect,) and also the neat velvet cap made expressly for his comfort and protection by good Miss Stephenson. These memorials I shall preserve with care and reverence. O that, in wearing the cap, I may catch something of the inspiration of him for whom it was originally intended! Doubtless, I shall find a magnetic influence lingering about it, to incite to fresh exertions, and to quicken new thoughts, with reference to the promotion of truth and right in the earth.

You have had my warmest sympathies in all the severe trials through which you have been called to pass. Multitudes unknown to you have mingled their tears with yours, and mourned a great bereavement. It gladdens my spirit to read in your note respecting Theodore — "He has gone to a more beautiful world, and he comes to me, even now, to strengthen and comfort." That is the true view to be taken of the event. If I needed (as I do not) any assurance of immortal life, I should find it in the removal of one so good and gifted as your husband; for to suppose that all the glorious faculties which he possessed, so capable of everlasting development, terminated with his earthly life, is to libel the Creator, and make creation a failure.

In due time, full justice will be done to the memory of Mr. Parker. Theological bigots may seek to asperse it, but it will shine more and more resplendent as time advances. High on the list of the world's greatest minds and noblest benefactors is his name forever to be inscribed.

I have regarded his union in wedlock with you as most fortunate and felicitous; and in friendship was he equally favored in the rare companionship of Miss Stevenson.[1] I greatly esteem and admire you both.

Wife sends her kind regards and grateful acknowledgments. Mr. Parker was her special favorite.

We are busily engaged in packing up for a few weeks' sojourn among the mountains in New Hampshire, and shall leave with all the children in the morning for Northumberland, via Portland.

Yours, in every good work,

Wm. Lloyd Garrison.

Mrs. Lydia D. Parker.

ALS: Villard Papers, Houghton Library, Harvard University.

1. The "ph" and "v" seem to have been used interchangeably in the spelling of her name.

305

TO EZRA HERVEY HEYWOOD

NORTHUMBERLAND, N. H., July 30, 1860.

MY DEAR HEYWOOD:

Absent from home, seeking invigoration of body and mind among the mountains in New Hampshire, I shall be deprived of the pleasure of participating in the First of August Celebration at Abington; but the day and the occasion will not be forgotten by me. In spirit I shall be with you all, rejoicing in the beneficent results of the abolition of

British colonial slavery, and lamenting the continuance of the same dreadful system of bondage in our own most guilty country.

The act of West India Emancipation has been commonly, but absurdly, styled 'an experiment.' An experiment is something uncertain in itself, which may or may not prove successful, and which is problematical until it is tested. But there was nothing doubtful about the act aforesaid; its consequences were as sure as the law of gravitation, and as glorious as they were sure. None but the most unthinking, or the most perverse, could believe otherwise. Those consequences were truthfully predicted ages ago, in their natural order: — the substitution of light for darkness, of health for disease, of righteousness for iniquity, of the glory of the Lord for the the reign of Satan, of abundance and prosperity for dearth and suffering, of general restoration for universal ruin. [See 58th chapter of Isaiah.] I know that, throughout our slavery-cursed land, every effort has been made, by a venal press, by unscrupulous demagogues, by the enemies of the Anti-Slavery cause universally, to represent the emancipation of the West India bondman as an utter failure — as disastrous to the general prosperity, and tending to the lowest barbarism. Even the London *Times* has repeatedly made the same damaging declarations, which have been eagerly copied into the pro-slavery journals of this country as oracular and conclusive. But I know that all such representations are false, malicious, mercenary, satanic. They are proved to be such by the testimony of West India governors, magistrates, missionaries, resident planters, and intelligent and truth-seeking tourists; by the strictest Parliamentary investigations; by the constantly improving condition of the emancipated laborers, physically, intellectually, morally; BY HUMAN NATURE ITSELF. The London *Times* is no more veracious in this matter than the Charleston *Mercury* or the New Yord *Herald*. It is manifestly the purchased tool of the cottonocracy at home and in the United States; and it grossly and wickedly misrepresents the views and feelings of the British people, who justly glory in their act of negro emancipation.

To say that emancipation in the West Indies has proved a failure, is to declare that a state of unlimited concubinage and beastly amalgamation is more conducive to virtue and purity than sacred marriage, recognized and defended by law; that turning men, women and children into marketable commodities is a better investment than to allow them to develop their faculties and powers as rational and accountable beings; that to substitute the blood-reeking lash for a just compensation, and to drive the laborer to unrequited toil like a beast, is pecuniarily more profitable than the system of mutual compact and the stimulus of the hope of reward; that enforced, unlettered ignorance is better for society than general education; that for an immense mass of human beings to be given over to irresponsible and absolute power, lodged in the hands of mercenary owners and ruthless overseers — to be deprived of all testimony in cases of personal wrong and outrage, which are of daily occurrence — to be stripped of all rights and immunities as completely as though they were on a level with sheep and swine — is better for them, and for the entire community, than though they were protected by law, allowed to testify against those seeking their detriment, and clothed with all the rights of human nature! All such declarations originate either in idiocy or diabolism: they are the subversion of all the rules of morality, all the principles of justice, all the claims of humanity, and indicate either the extinguishment of reason, or a very close approximation to total depravity, on the part of those giving them circulation.

Rejoice, then, abolitionists, in the downfall of British colonial slavery, and mingle your voices of thanksgiving and praise with those of a million freedmen in the isles of the sea! Labor unceasingly to effect, by the help of God and the power of his truth, a still more extended emancipation, and even a more glorious jubilee, in your own country! Be deterred by no obstacle, deceived by no artifice, allured by no compromise, lulled into security by no partial success, satisfied with no half-way measures; but, 'remembering those who are in bonds as bound with them,'[1] and therefore demanding immediate and unconditional emancipation in their behalf, as the imperative duty of those who are exercising unjust dominion over them, press onward in the glorious cause you have espoused, assured of final victory — a victory which shall heal every wound, unite every breach, reconcile every difference, and bless every portion of the land!

Yours, to break every yoke,

WM. LLOYD GARRISON.

Printed in *The Liberator*, August 10, 1860.

1. Hebrews 13:3.

---

3 0 6

TO GEORGE W. STACY

NORTHUMBERLAND, N. H., July 31st, 1860.

DEAR FRIEND, — I am two hundred and fifty miles from Milford, enjoying a little recreation in this mountainous region; so that I shall not be able to attend the celebration on Thursday next,[1] in your town, as I designed doing when I last saw you. But you will have no lack of earnest, faithful, eloquent speakers, and the great historical event of British West India Emancipation will be commemorated, not merely for its own intrinsic moral grandeur, but to the furtherance of the Anti-Slavery struggle in our own land.

Next to the crime of enslaving human beings is the crime of misrepresenting, for slaveholding ends, the results of their emancipation from slavery. Ever since the liberation of the West India bondmen, the most systematic, persevering and unscrupulous means have been resorted to, in every portion of the United States, to create the impression that it has proved a most calamitous act; the object being to reconcile the public mind to the continuance of slavery at the South as far less an evil than its abolition, and to dispirit the friends of impartial liberty in their labors to hasten the day of jubilee here. No fabrication has been deemed too mean, no slander too malignant, no lie too atrocious, to be coined and circulated for this dete table purpose. These forgeries and calumnies have been readily believed, so that there is, probably, but a small portion of the people who see and know that every thing is working well in the emancipated colonies. How, indeed, could it be otherwise? How could the complete suppression of a system embodying 'the sum of all villanies,' [2] be followed by evil consequences in any direction? Whether reference be made to the moral condition or the material prosperity of the colonies, how could freedom fail to prove an inestimable blessing to those who had so long been deprived of it? From the hour they received this boon, on bended knee, with throbbing hearts, and quivering lips, and shouts of thanksgiving to God, up to the present time, they have been steadily advancing in intelligence, sobriety, industry, economy, and all the moral virtues. They have magnanimously cast into oblivion all memory of the terrible wrongs and sufferings they endured while toiling under the yoke, and smarting under the lash; and in no instance have they resorted to any vindictive or retaliatory act. No life has been taken, no blood shed, no plantation fired. In no part of the world has there been seen a more orderly population, or a more pacific and cheering state of things, with so little military or constabulary espionage. Dr. John Davy,[3] brother of the celebrated Sir Humphry Davy,[4] testifies: —
'The abolition of slavery has been in every respect advantageous, to the negroes, to the planters, and to the population generally. Prior to abolition, crime of every kind was prevalent, especially robbery. Since then, [speaking of Barbadoes,] I have not heard of the murder of a white man, nor any instance of revenge taken by the liberated, for cruel treatment inflicted before liberation. The security, as to property, in which the opulent live here, is remarkable. Beggars and want are almost unknown.' The same witness also declares: — 'Three-fourths of

the laborers in Antigua have cottages of their own, and small freeholds. Eighty-seven villages have all been built by emancipated laborers, near the estates on which they were formerly chattels.' The Governor of Tobago says: [5] — 'I deny that the peasantry are abandoned to slothful habits. On the contrary, I assert that a more industrious class does not exist in the world; at least, where they are working for themselves.' Sir Charles Grey,[6] who was Governor of Jamaica in 1850, says: — 'There are few races of men who will work harder, or more perseveringly, than the negroes, when they are sure of getting the produce of their labor.' Thatched hovels, with mud walls, have given place to numerous free villages, regularly laid out, and houses built of stone or wood, with shingled roofs, green blinds, and verandahs, to shield them from the sun. The names of these villages give pleasant indication of the gratitude of the colored people towards their benefactors. They are called Clarkson, Wilberforce, Buxton, Brougham, Macaulay,[7] Thompson, Gurney,[8] Sligo,[9] &c. The names given to their own little homes have almost a poetic interest, so touching and expressive is their simplicity. The following are samples: — 'Happy Retreat,' 'Thank God for It,' 'A Little of my Own,' 'Liberty and Content,' 'Thankful Hill,' 'Come and See.'

The Rev. Henry Bleby, whose visit to this country two years ago will ever be pleasantly remembered, says: — 'As for the moral condition of Barbadoes, I believe the criminal statistics, for the last five years, would compare, without disadvantage, with any country under heaven. I have a membership of 1700 colored persons, and during the last two years, I have not had a single case of intemperance reported to me. Every Sabbath our churches are crowded with people anxious to receive instruction. I know of no people in the world who will make such efforts, and exercise such self-denial, to obtain education for their children as the colored people of Barbadoes. It is a falsehood that emancipation has failed to improve the condition of the colored race. Throughout the West Indies, in every island, the condition of the people is incomparably superior to what it was in slavery. Some say, if it has not ruined the laborers, it has ruined the planters. I deny that statement as plainly as I deny the other. Emancipation has proved a blessing, instead of a curse, to the proprietors.'

Then as to the sugar question. In Barbadoes, between 1842 and 1852, the increase of sugar exported was 27,240 hogsheads. The report for 1851 states: 'There has been more sugar shipped from this island this year, than in any one year since it has been peopled.' The report for 1853 announces 'vast increase in trade.' 'A great increase in the value of exports' is announced in the report of 1858. In one year in the Bahamas, the exports and imports increased half a million of dollars. The report for 1858 in Grenada says: — 'State of finances most satisfactory. A greatly extended surface is covered by sugar cultivation.' The report in 1858, in St. Kitt's, states: — 'A larger quantity of sugar is produced now than in the time of slavery.' In St. Lucia, between the four years ending 1852, and the four years ending 1858, the increase of sugar exported was 1,803,518 pounds. In Trinidad, in 1852, the crop was the largest ever shipped from the island; and it has been extending since. The report for 1853 speaks of 'marked improvement in the cultivation of the sugar estates.' Export of sugar rose from an average of 310,797 cwt. under slavery, to 425,042 cwt. in the seven years ending 1854.

And this testimony could be multiplied indefinitely, given by competent, reliable, authoritative witnesses. Thus are the promises of God fulfilled, as set forth in the 58th chapter of Isaiah,[10] a chapter that ought to be read with emphasis at every celebration of West India Emancipation, as the prelude to whatever addresses the occasion may call forth. 'Alleluia! for the Lord God omnipotent reigneth!' [11]

Inspired by this grand example and these cheering facts, let us renew our efforts for the total and eternal overthrow of slavery in the United States, that the nation may be saved from irremediable ruin, and that all hearts and voices may join in the song of jubilee from the Atlantic to the Pacific, every chain being broken, every bondman set free!

'Ho! children of the brave —
Ho! freemen of the land —
That stamped into the grave
Oppression's bloody band!
Come on — come on — and joined be we
To make the fettered bondman free!' [12]

Yours for universal freedom,

WM. LLOYD GARRISON.

GEORGE W. STACY.

Printed in *The Liberator*, August 17, 1860.

The Reverend George Whittemore Stacy (b. Boston, March 13, 1809; fl. 1882) established the unsuccessful weekly *Groton Herald* in 1829 with the assistance of a young Mr. Rogers, entered a printing co-partnership in 1830 with Adin Ballou in Milford, Massachusetts, and after studying theology was ordained a Restorationist preacher and installed pastor of the First Church in Carlisle, Massachusetts. He was an early abolitionist and a member of the Hopedale Community from its beginning until 1846, when he moved to Milford where he opened a printing and stationery establishment, in which he prospered. In 1867, he was a member of the General Court of Massachusetts and held other public offices as well. (Adin Ballou, *History of the Town of Milford, Worcester County, Mass.,* Boston, 1882, pp. 1025–1026.)

1. The annual West India Emancipaton celebration at Milford, Massachusetts, on Thursday, August 2. George W. Stacy acted as chairman and called the meeting to order. (*The Liberator,* August 17, 1860.)

2. John Wesley, *Journal*, February 12, 1792.

3. John Davy (1790–1868), M.D., physiologist and anatomist, army surgeon and inspector-general of army hospitals, published several works of science and travel. One of these was entitled *The West Indies, Before and Since Slave Emancipation, Comprising the Windward and Leeward Islands' Military Command; Founded on Notes and Observations Collected During a Three Years' Residence* (London, Dublin and Barbados, 1854), 551 pp. The second quotation seems to have been taken from pp. 390–391, although somewhat altered. The first includes phrases and ideas from p. 15, but is sufficiently different to have been taken from another source by the same author.

4. Sir Humphry Davy (1778–1829), celebrated natural philosopher and chemist.

5. The governor of Tobago at this time was Sir Francis Hincks (1807–1885), a Canadian statesman, who was governor of Barbados and the Windward Isles from 1855 to 1862 and of British Guiana from 1862 to 1869.

6. Sir Charles Edward Grey (1785–1865) was governor of Barbados and other islands from 1841 to 1846 and of Jamaica from 1847 to 1853.

7. Zachary Macaulay (1768–1838), philanthropist and prominent English abolitionist.

8. Joseph John Gurney (1788–1847), English Quaker, philanthropist and writer, prominent in the West Indies emancipation movement, had visited the United States, Canada and the West Indies from 1837 to 1840.

9. Howe Peter Browne, Second Marquis of Sligo (b. May 18, 1788; d. January 26, 1845), of Ireland, became marquis of Sligo on his father's death in 1809. He was governor-general of Jamaica, where he owned 20,000 acres of land and many slaves, from 1833 to 1836. With the abolition of slavery in Jamaica, he urged the planters to pursue a conciliatory and humane policy toward their former slaves who had been transformed by law into apprentices. He was a Whig in politics. (Geoffrey H. White, ed., *The Complete Peerage . . . by G. E. C.*, London, 1953, vol. 12, Part I, p. 25; William Law Mathieson, *British Slavery and Its Abolition, 1823–1838*, reprint, New York, 1967, pp. 256 ff.)

10. The sixth verse reads: "Is not this the fast that I have chosen? to loose the bands of wickedness, to undo the heavy burdens, and to let the oppressed go free, and that ye break every yoke?" Verses 10 and 11 read: "And if thou draw out thy soul to the hungry, and satisfy the afflicted soul; then shall thy light rise in obscurity, and thy darkness be as the noon day:
"And the Lord shall guide thee continually, and satisfy thy soul in drought, and make fat thy bones: and thou shalt be like a watered garden, and like a spring of water, whose waters fail not."

11. Revelation 19:6.

12. Unidentified.

307

TO WILLIAM LLOYD GARRISON, JR.

Northumberland, Aug. 1, 1860.

My dear Son:

Wondering that none of us had received a line from you, we were all made glad, yesterday, by receiving your three letters — one to mother, one to Wendell, and one to Fanny. Each one was of interest, showing that you have a facility in epistolary composition. I have no doubt you will be successful as a writer, whether for the private or the public eye.

Your account of the wanderings and adventures of Charles C.[1] was amusing, evincing on his part, as a pedestrian tourist, a determination to *cram* as many incidents into his budget of memory as possible; and also a perseverance, which, if rightly directed, will place him in the front rank of enterprising men of business. But he may "lack ballast," and "carry too much sail" for his tonnage; in which case, his barque will easily be thrown upon its beam-ends.

I was interested in your account of the long interview you had with Francis Merriam,[2] and trust that your hopes as to his future career will be more than realized. The best service that can be done for him is to give him good counsel; and I have no doubt you spoke to him wisely as well as kindly. He deserves sympathy, much charitable allowance, and friendly co-operation and guidance, that he may not become a wreck, either as to his vagaries of mind or his private habits. By the gratitude we owe to Mr. Jackson, and the affection we bear for F's mother, we are bound to do all we can to save and bless the unfortunate young man.

Your suggestion to Wendell, as to the rowdyish conduct of the Harvard boys at Worcester,[3] will be improved by him in due time, as he takes the same just view of it.

We have had much enjoyment crowded into a short space since we have been here; though the weather, on the whole, has been uncomfortably cold — more like October or November in Boston — making daily fires not only very comfortable, but almost indispensable, at least morning and evening. Your mother has not been able to encounter the fatigue of some of our expeditions, and, consequently, has not been able to see as many of the beauties and wonders of this grand region as the rest of us; and though she has enjoyed herself, and found quite as much of cool weather as she desired to exchange for the sweltering heat of the city, she will not regret seeing 14 Dix Place at an early day, which to her (is it not to us all?) is "the dearest spot of all on earth." We shall probably leave here next Wednesday, in which case we shall be able to see you before you take your tour of recreation.

I am just getting over two days of the bowel complaint, which has been pretty severe, and expect to feel all the better for it.

Wendell and Franky will write to you soon. George returns home on Saturday.

I have no time to give you any description of what we have seen, or as to where we have been. New Hampshire is full of grandeur and beauty.

I am writing this in hot haste; the mail is to close immediately.

With the warmest regards to my dear friends, Mr. and Mrs. Buffum, aunt Miriam,[4] &c., I remain, my dear son,

Your loving father,

Wm. Lloyd Garrison.

☞ All send their loving remembrances as one.

ALS: Smith College Library.

1. Probably Charles C. Cram of Boston, who became a second lieutenant in the Sixth Battery Massachusetts Light Infantry and died of disease at Berwick City, Louisiana, October 11, 1863. (*Massachusetts Soldiers, Sailors and Marines in the Civil War*, Norwood, Mass., 1931–1937, vol. 5, p. 416.)

2. Francis Jackson Meriam, or Merriam (b. Framingham, Massachusetts, November 17, 1837; d. New York City, November 28, 1865), grandson of Francis Jackson and son of Mrs. Eliza Francis Jackson Eddy by her first marriage, was a member of John Brown's band at Harpers Ferry. He joined the group on the day before the attack and was left at the Kennedy Farm, to help guard the arms which were left there while the attack on Harpers Ferry was made. As a result, he was able to escape to Canada. Oswald Garrison Villard describes him as "erratic and unbalanced, frail in his physique," "he was forever urging wild schemes upon his superiors, and often attempting them." During the Civil War, he served as captain in the Third South Carolina Colored Infantry. (Oswald Garrison Villard, *John Brown, 1800–1859, A Biography Fifty Years After*, New York, 1943, pp. 421, 685 *et passim*.)

3. On July 25, 1860, following a day of regatta races at Worcester, Massachusetts, in which several colleges participated, "some of the students forgot their good breeding and paraded the streets at unseasonable hours, making hideous noises, breaking windows, and destroying signs and other property." Three Harvard sophomores were arrestetd and released on recognizance after they paid for the damages. (Boston *Daily Evening Transcript*, July 26 and 27, 1860.)

4. Unidentified.

308

TO OLIVER JOHNSON

Boston, August 9, 1860.

My dear Johnson:

I have just returned, with my family, from an excursion to the mountainous regions of New Hampshire, and a residence of nearly three weeks at Northumberland, a little village about thirty miles beyond Gorham, and just as far from Boston as New York. Having unpacked, brushed off the dirt, and obtained a little rest from an intensely sultry ride, I lose no time in taking my pen to give you my warmest thanks for sending me (what I have long wanted) a daguerreotype of yourself, in the best style of the art, and a most satisfactory and admirable likeness it is. If you are not quite so youthful in your appearance as you were thirty years ago, you are at least all the better for the change; as good wine is said to improve, the longer it is kept!

Be assured, I keep step in this matter with you, and, being a little older than yourself, I believe, must of necessity keep the precedence in age. We shall both be venerable, one of these days, if we are not called away prematurely. I am powerfully impressed that something has happened to me since I was married, when I look into the faces of my five children — three of them full-bearded adults! You have no reminder of this kind, but may find them in the grey hairs which are beginning to make their appearance in beard and hair; for time deals very impartially with all mankind, and finds no difficulty in pulverizing them all, in the long run. Is it not something to be able to sing —

"In the days when we went gypsying, a long time ago"? [1]

Onward is the word, whether or no.

Our friendship commenced at [an] early period, and nothing has ever occurred to cast a shadow upon it. Without seeking conformity of thought or action as an end, we have been singularly fortunate in having the same general estimate of men and institutions, and essentially the same views of duty, without losing a particle of our individuality or personal independence.

I feel that we are much nearer to each other than common friends: there is a brotherly feeling between us, which, though not of blood relationship, is of the strongest quality. The cause of reform in its broadest aspects, and the anti-slavery cause in special, is greatly indebted to you for services equally timely, long-continued, and valuable — rendered at all times in a cheerful, unselfish, self-denying spirit. Whether these shall ever be fully recognized or not, the rich consolation must ever be yours that you have "acted well your part." [2]

I wish you could enjoy a respite from your labors at this warm season, and leave the city for a tour or sojourn in the country. You need it and deserve it. For the first time since I was married, I have taken my family with me expressly for recreation; and though our absence from home was somewhat less than three weeks, we are all consciously better for our contact with the glorious mountain scenery in New Hampshire. We did not go to the White Mountains, though we saw them repeatedly to the best advantage. Our residence was ten miles from Lancaster, and we explored the whole Northern portion of the State up to Lake Connecticut, finding everywhere objects of grandeur and beauty, and mountainous elevations whose name is "legion."

Touring with a large family, even for a brief period, and in the most economical manner, is an expensive luxury. It cost me at the rate of fifty dollars a week — the railroad fare alone amounting to that sum, to say nothing of hiring horses and wagons for various excursions from our stopping-place. I should like to have stayed two or three weeks longer, but could not afford to do so, as my house was open to friends during my absence, which augmented my expenses. We had for our companions Mr. & Mrs. (Abby Southwick) Stephenson,[3] of West Newton, with their five children, and really had a very pleasant time together. We ascended the famous Stratford Peaks, Cape Horn, Mount Prospect, the Dixville Notch, &c., and for the time being were "monarchs of all we surveyed."[4] Climbing at 54 years of age is not quite as easy as it used to be at 20. But at what age does one cease aspiring?

My wife is much pleased with your likeness, and thinks it is excellent. We desire to be most affectionately remembered to Mary Ann, whose health, we trust, is fully restored since I saw her in May.

I have not time to write anything about the state of our cause, or national affairs, but every thing looks to me hopeful, even though a pregnant future lies before us. The election of Lincoln seems to be more and more probable. He will do nothing to offend the South.

Ever faithfully yours,

Wm. Lloyd Garrison.

Oliver Johnson.

Transcript: Garrison Papers, Boston Public Library

1. Edwin Ransford (1805–1876), English song-writer, actor, singer and composer, "In the Days When We Went Gypsying."
2. Byron, *Don Juan*, Canto XVI, "So well she acted all and every part."
3. Abigail Southwick (b. September 17, 1819) was the eldest daughter of Joseph and Thankful Hussey Southwick, originally of Maine and later of Boston. She married John H. Stephenson on "February 1, 1859" (*sic*). (James M. Caller and M. A. Ober, *Genealogy of the Descendants of Lawrence and Cassandra Southwick*, Salem, 1881, p. 261.) Abigail's parents were pioneer abolitionists and old friends of the Garrisons. (See *Letters*, II, *passim*.)
John Hubbard Stephenson (b. Lancaster, New Hampshire, 1820; d. Staten Island, New York, December 21, 1888) was a member, early in life, of the firm of Stephenson & Plympton, millinery jobbers in Boston. In 1868, in New York, he founded the importing house of Stephenson Bros. & Co. and became a prominent merchant. (Boston *Evening Transcript*, December 22, 1888.) The *Anti-Slavery Standard*, February 21, 1863, lists Stephenson as a contributor of $10 in the subscription list of the Twenty-Ninth National Anti-Slavery Subscription Anniversary.
4. William Cowper (1731–1800), *Verses Supposed to be Written by Alexander Selkirk*.

309

TO WENDELL PHILLIPS GARRISON

Boston, August 9, 1860.

My dear son Wendell:

Our ride homeward from Northumberland,[1] yesterday, was a very sultry one, and, consequently, somewhat burdensome. We were behind our time on arriving at Portland, as though our steam-engine itself felt the pressure of the heat, and could not make as good time as usual. The dust was not as annoying as I anticipated it would be, but the cinders and stench from the engine attached to our train from Portland to Boston were exceedingly trying. All along our route, it looked very threateningly as to a violent thunder-storm in various directions; and, at last, we had the benefit of a dashing shower, accompanied with thunder and lightning. Fortunately for your mother, she could not distinguish the rumbling of the thunder from the noise of the train. We saw nobody on the way whom we knew, at any of the stopping-places; though, at the Bethel station,[2] we were in hopes to meet with our friend John T. Sargent.[3] At Shelburne,[4] where Winchell Yerrinton and his wife are recreating for a few days, young Laighton,[5] (who accompanied them to S.) of Boston, got into the cars, on his return home, having received a telegraphic despatch to the effect that his father was dangerously ill. On the way from Gorham[6] to Portland, was introduced by Mr. Stephenson[7] to Mr. Benton,[8] a Republican lawyer of Lancaster,[9] who was present at my lecture, and expressed a great deal of satisfaction with it, and said it was generally very well received. Of course, as a politician, and doubtless expecting preferment hereafter, especially if "honest Old Abe" should prove successful, he was not quite ready for a dissolution of the Union. We had an extended conversation on politics, anti-slavery, and matters and things in general. In the course of it, he informed me that he was on his way to Portland to see Neal Dow's daughter,[10] to whom he is engaged, and will probably ere long be married. This fact was communicated by my asking him how many children he had, (!) — supposing him to be a married man. I was much pleased with his intelligence and frankness, and on parting he cordially expressed the hope that I would soon again visit Lancaster, and give the people some additional lectures on slavery.

We passed over the Newburyport bridge a little before sundown. It was very pleasant to me to see my native river, the Merrimack, but I could not see "the house where I was born";[11] though I pointed out to the Stephensons the meeting-house which stands next to the house.

On arriving at Lynn, Willie promptly came into our car as by instinct, and rode with us to the West Lynn depot. On Saturday, he leaves for Ghent.[12]

We arrived in Boston at 8 o'clock, all of us pretty thoroughly tired out. On getting to Dix Place, found every thing right, and a good supper waiting for us. Henry C. Wright was there to give us a hearty greeting. He said it had been the hottest day of the season, and he had never suffered so much from the heat before. The night was too hot and close for refreshing slumber — about as it was the night before at Northumberland. To-day the heat is nearly as great, and perspiration starts easily, especially upon your mother, whose tendency is to be in "the melting mood." [13] It would seem to be just the time to go to the mountains, rather than to leave them for the city. But we are not masters of our destiny always.

On settling with Mr. Stephenson, I found that the sum total of the expenses of our trip was $130 — add to this, household expenses at home, $11 — making the sum $141, with a few incidental expenses besides. Averaging nearly $10 a week for each one of us. Travelling is an expensive luxury, especially for pleasure. This has been my first family excursion; and though it has cost more than I expected, I am very glad indeed that we have made it together. What a pity that Willie was not with us, to make the circle complete! The only regret I have is, that your mother did not have the beautiful ride to lake Connecticut, and back, and also to the Dixville Notch.

Franky left his night-shirt, which you can put into your carpet-bag. He left in our room two or three stones, which he brought from the Notch, and would like to have you put into the same bag, if you have room.

Should you happen to require more money at Bangor, [Maine] it shall be promptly forwarded to you. Enjoy yourself all you can, and be careful of excess in every direction. I wish I could be at Bangor with you. I hope you will be sure to see my excellent friend, Mr. Battles.[14] Perhaps he will introduce you to another old friend of mine, George Kent, Esq.,[15] formerly of Concord, N.H. (the intimate friend of the late N. P. Rogers,) and brother of Gov. Kent.[16]

Mr. Wallcut says he sent the last week's Liberator, but I will re-mail it to you.

Mother, Fanny and Franky and George send their kindest regards. We desire to be unitedly remembered to Mr. and Mrs. Marshall,[17] Mr. and Mrs. Willson,[18] &c.

Your loving father,

Wm. Lloyd Garrison.

ALS: Garrison Papers, Boston Public Library.

1. In northern New Hampshire. Garrison's route was southeastward to Portland, Maine, then southward to Boston.
2. Bethel, Maine, on the way to Portland, Maine.
3. The Reverend John Turner Sargent V (b. Boston, July 12, 1807; d. March 27, 1877), Unitarian minister, was the pastor of the Suffolk-Street Chapel from 1837 to 1844, when he resigned because of dissatisfaction among his parishioners over his invitation to Theodore Parker to speak in his pulpit. In 1846, he was installed as the first minister of the First Unitarian Society of Somerville from which he resigned after two years because of ill health. He next occupied the pulpit of the South Universalist Society in Boston for about a year. He was an early antislavery man, and active in temperance, woman suffrage, and a variety of charities. He was a close friend, from childhood, of Wendell Phillips, who spoke at his funeral. He was married twice. His first wife, Charlotte Sophia White, died

in 1854. On June 4, 1855, he married Mary Elizabeth Fisk, of New Orleans, who was born on January 27, 1827, and died in New York, May 31, 1904. She was a granddaughter of Amos Willard, a Boston clockmaker, and she was "the moving spirit of the famous Radical Club which, formed in the Sargent house in 1867, continued to meet there on Saturdays until it was dissolved in 1880." John Turner Sargent was the society's moderator. (Justin Winsor, *The Memorial History of Boston*, Boston, 1881, III, 482; Emma W. and Charles S. Sargent, *Epes Sargent of Gloucester and His Descendants*, Boston and New York, 1923, pp. 162–165, 169.)

4. Shelburne, New Hampshire, near the border of New Hampshire and Maine.

5. Joshua James Laighton (b. Portsmouth, New Hampshire, October 1837; d. September 1864) graduated from Bowdoin College in 1857 and from Harvard Divinity School in 1861. In 1861–1862, he was instructor in Biblical Literature at Meadville Theological Seminary, Pennsylvania. Thereafter, he became mentally disturbed and died in the McLean Asylum, Somerville, Massachusetts. (*Harvard University Quinquennial Catalogue*, Cambridge, 1930, p. 117; Nehemiah Cleaveland and Alpheus Spring Packard, *History of Bowdoin College* . . . , Boston, 1882, p. 718; *General Catalogue of Bowdoin College* . . . *1794–1950*, Brunswick, 1950, p. 107.)

6. Gorham, Maine, is several miles west of Portland.

7. John H. Stephenson.

8. Jacob Benton (1814–1892), a native of Waterford, Vermont, moved to Lancaster, Coos County, New Hampshire, in 1842, was admitted to the bar, and began practicing law in 1843. He was a member of the state House of Representatives from 1854 to 1856, a delegate to the Republican National Convention in 1860, a brigadier general during the Civil War, and a member of the United States Congress from March 4, 1867 to March 3, 1871. (*BDAC*.)

9. Lancaster, New Hampshire, south of Northumberland.

10. Neal Dow (1804–1897), a native of Portland, Maine, was a prominent temperance reformer of Quaker parentage and training, and the "father of the Maine temperance law," enacted on June 2, 1851, when he was mayor of Portland. In 1830, he married Maria Cornelia Durant Maynard. They had nine children, four of whom died in infancy. Jacob Benton married Dow's daughter, his eldest child, Louisa (b. 1831) on December 12, 1860. (Robert Piercy Dow, *The Book of Dow*, Claremont, New Hampshire, 1929, p. 340.)

11. Thomas Hood (1799–1845), English poet, "I remember."

12. William Lloyd Garrison, Jr., corresponded with Elizabeth Powell, Aaron Powell's sister, who was teaching in Ghent, New York.

13. Shakespeare, *Othello*, V, ii, 349.

14. The Reverend Amory Battles was pastor of the Universalist Church in Bangor, Maine, from January 1851 to March 1872. (*History of Penobscot County, Maine*, Cleveland, 1882, p. 732.) He was one of a group of Bangor citizens who invited Ernestine Rose, the prominent Jewish abolitionist and woman's rights advocate, to participate in a course of lectures at Bangor. The invitation precipitated a public controversy. The committee refused to rescind the invitation and Mrs. Rose spoke to "large and enthusiastic audiences," twice in two successive evenings. For the story of the controversy and the Reverend Mr. Battles' part in it, see Yuri Suhl, *Ernestine L. Rose and the Battle for Human Rights* (New York, 1959), pp. 173–177. The Reverend Mr. Battles' public letter in defense of Mrs. Rose's appearance is reprinted in Suhl, pp. 287–288.

15. George Kent (1796–fl. 1859), of Concord, New Hampshire, was an early antislavery man and friend of Garrison. (See *Letters*, II, 464, for additional information.) From 1852 to 1859, he was associated in a law practice in Bangor with his brother Edward. (*Collections of the Maine Historical Society*, Portland, 1881, VIII, 450.)

16. Edward Kent (1802–1877) was mayor of Bangor from 1836 to 1838 and governor of Maine from 1838 to 1840. From 1849 to 1853 he was United States

consul at Rio de Janeiro and from 1859 to 1873 was associate justice of the state Supreme Court.

17. Perhaps Professor L. Marshall, a musical director of the Penobscot Musical Association (Penobscot County, Maine), organized in 1848. In a letter written on January 11, 1877, to his daughter Fanny, Garrison refers to a Professor Marshall who had "an enthusiastic appreciation of the wonders of Nature," and whose "exhibition of the remarkable features of the Yellow Stone region, by the aid of the stereopticon, cannot but induce travelling to see it. . . ." (Garrison Papers, Boston Public Library.)

18. Perhaps Franklin Augustus Wilson (b. Bradford, Maine, November 6, 1832; fl. 1903), a graduate of Bowdoin in 1854, who studied law and settled in Bangor, where he was a prominent lawyer for many years. He married Mary Elliott Carr, September 1, 1859. She died in 1867. (*American Series of Popular Biographies, Maine Edition*, Boston, 1903, pp. 53–54.)

310

TO J. MILLER McKIM

Boston, Sept. 1st, 1860.

My dear McKim:

I am much gratified by the invitation so cordially extended to me by your Executive Committee, to attend the anniversary of the Pennsylvania A. S. Society at Kennett, on the 24th of October. You may consider me "booked" for the occasion. My heart warms instinctively towards my anti-slavery friends in your State, and I am never more happy than when in their company.

I hope Phillips will also be at your meeting, but, of course, it is almost "hoping against hope." Still, send him an urgent invitation, and I will back it up to the extent of my ability.

With kindest remembrances to your wife and family, and to every member of your Executive Committee, I remain,

Your old and true friend,

Wm. Lloyd Garrison.

J. M. McKim.

ALS: Garrison Papers, Boston Public Library.

The letter was originally dated "Sept. 24," but "24" was crossed out and "1st" was placed underneath it. In view of Garrison's illness later in the month, which would have precluded his accepting an invitation to speak, September 1 seems the more likely date.

311

TO THE PUBLISHERS OF THE *WORLD*

Boston, Sept. 18, 1860.

To the Publishers of the World:

Gentlemen — I thank you for sending me your printed circular.

The state of my throat is such, owing to increasing bronchial difficulties, that I shall be compelled to withdraw from the lecturing field for the coming season; so that I do not wish to have my name inserted in your list of Lyceum lecturers. I have already had to decline various overtures of this kind.

Respectfully yours,

Wm. Lloyd Garrison.

ALS: New York Public Library.

Garrison's letter was in response to a form letter concerning his participation as a Lyceum lecturer during the ensuing year. The letter read as follows:

" 'The World' Office
No. 35 Park Row
New York, September, 1860

"Sir:

If you would like to have your name included in the list of
'Lyceum Lecturers,'
which we shall speedily publish, please notify us to that effect by return of mail, and append the address to which you wish your Correspondents to direct their letters.

Respectfully yours,

The Publishers of 'THE WORLD' "

(Printed copy in New York Public Library.)

The New York *World* was founded by Alexander Cummings, a Philadelphia journalist, as a religious and highly moral daily newspaper. "It excluded theatre advertising, lottery reports, details of criminal trials, divorce proceedings, and everything of a sensational cast. It advertised church and Sunday School supplies, and was itself advertised in the backs of hymnals." Apparently, it also printed lists of prominent speakers who were available for Lyceum lectures.

312

TO GEORGE L. STEARNS

Boston, Sept. 23, 1860.

Dear Sir:

Be so kind as to return the thanks of Mrs. G., and myself and children, to your beloved wife, (and accept them also for yourself,) for the basket of beautiful and delicious pears so kindly and considerately left at our door to-day. Nothing could be more palatable, *except* "free-

dom to a slave," with which nothing is comparable, and which is accompanied with all good fruits.

Mrs. Stearns will oblige me by accepting the volume and tracts contained in the parcel I send, as a slight token of my regards.

My wife wishes me to send her grateful acknowledgments.

Yours, for a fruitful life,

Wm. Lloyd Garrison.

Geo. L. Stearns, Esq.

ALS: New York Public Library.

George Luther Stearns (1809–1867), prominent Boston businessman, Unitarian, supporter of the Free-soil and Republican parties in Massachusetts, provided funds for the purchase of rifles for the Free-State forces in Kansas and was
one of the major backers of John Brown in his raid on Harpers Ferry. During the
Civil War, he recruited Negro soldiers for the 54th and 55th Massachusetts regi-
ments.

313

TO SAMUEL J. MAY

Boston, Sept. 28, 1860.

My Dear Friend:

I ought to have answered your kind letter many days ago, but,
for the last fortnight, I have felt too unwell to do any thing in the
way of correspondence. I have been suffering from a slow fever, a
severe bronchial attack, with congestion of the lungs; and though
partially relieved, am still "good for nothing." The fact is, I have a
growing throat ailment, travelling steadily towards my lungs; so that
my physician (Dr. Geist) seriously warns me, that if I do not withdraw from the lecturing field, I shall certainly meet with the fate of
Theodore Parker at no distant day. Whether there is any peril of this
kind or not, I know I am unable to use my voice as formerly, and I
feel an increasing difficulty in the chest.

Thus situated, I am unable to attend the anniversary of the Jerry
Rescue,[1] as you desire.

But, were I "in speaking order," the fact that Frederick Douglass
is to be present at the celebration, and to participate therein, would
powerfully repel me from attending. I regard him as thoroughly base
and selfish, and I know that his hostility to the American Anti-Slavery
Society and its leading advocates is unmitigated and unceasing. He
has just attended Stephen S. Foster's Political Convention[2] at Worcester, and made it an occasion for fresh misrepresentation of the Society,
and fresh sneers at its friends. His contemptuous treatment of George

Thompson, during his late visit to England, was unprovoked and outrageous. In fact, he reveals himself more and more to me as destitute of every principle of honor, ungrateful to the last degree, and malevolent in spirit. He is not worthy of respect, confidence, or countenance.

We (the Hovey Committee) [3] purchased five thousand copies of your excellent Peace Address,[4] and shall see that they are judiciously distributed. Any number of them will be cheerfully placed at your disposal.

I spoke to Mr. Hinton about your manuscript discourse in reference to Theodore Parker,[5] and he said there had been an unexpected delay in the publication of the work, but that it would soon make its appearance, and that your tribute was in the hands of the printer.

What a farce (politically speaking) is the nomination of Gerrit Smith for the Presidency of the United States by a baker's dozen of adherents at Syracuse! [6] I see that Goodell, in his *Principia*,[7] repudiates the nomination,[8] both on account of the discouraging tone of Smith's letter to the Convention,[9] and because of his theological latitudinarianism!

It is very odd that G. S. should give the Jerry Rescue celebration a cold shoulder, seeing he once said it should be observed to the latest period.

Aside from myself, all under my roof are well, and send loving remembrances to you and Mrs. May. Charlotte, whom we deem it a privilege to have with us, has just received a letter from you, and will write to you soon.

Your affectionate friend,

Wm. Lloyd Garrison.

Rev. S. J. May.

ALS: Garrison Papers, Boston Public Library.

1. The anniversary of the Jerry Rescue was celebrated at Syracuse on October 2, 1860. The Reverend Beriah Green, the pioneer abolitionist, served as chairman. The speakers included Beriah Green, Samuel J. May, Frederick Douglass and Professor James A. Thome. (*The Liberator*, October 19, 1860.)

2. The convention was held on September 19 and 20 and was a continuation of another that had been held on May 29, 1860. The call to the convention, signed by John Pierpont, President, and Stephen S. Foster, Chairman of the Business Committee, announced that "the object of this Convention is to consider the propriety of organizing a *Political Party* upon an Anti-Slavery interpretation of the U. S. Constitution, with the avowed purpose of abolishing slavery in the states, as well as Territories of the Union." (*The Liberator*, September 7, 1860.)

This convention was closely related to an earlier convention of Radical Abolitionists which met at Syracuse, New York, on August 29, and nominated Gerrit Smith for President and Samuel McFarland of Pennsylvania for vice-president. (*The Liberator*, September 7, 1860.)

At the Worcester convention, Douglass emphasized that the American Anti-Slavery Society was not an antislavery but simply a disunionist organization. He was criticized by E. D. Draper of Hopedale and Joseph A. Howland of Boston. The main result of the convention was the adoption of a motion for the formation of an Anti-Slavery Educational Society and of a resolution which affirmed that "the members of this Convention, called to consider the proposition to form a sound Abolition Political Party, extend their earnest sympathy and their hearty God-speed to the little band of faithful Abolitionists which has nominated Gerrit Smith as their candidate to be supported for the Presidency in the coming election." (*The Liberator*, October 5, 1860.) For a Garrisonian report of the Worcester convention, see *The Liberator*, September 28, 1860.

3. Charles F. Hovey, who had died in April 1859, had left a quarter of his estate for the promotion of antislavery and other reform activities. The trustees of this fund were Phillips, Garrison, Stephen S. and Abby K. Foster, Parker Pillsbury, Henry C. Wright, Francis Jackson, and Charles K. Whipple. (*Life*, III, 477.)

4. *The Liberator*, June 1, 1860, carried an announcement that Samuel J. May had delivered "an admirable address before the American Peace Society, on Monday evening last, in Park St. Church."

5. May had preached before Parker's congregation in Boston on June 3, 1860 and, of course, devoted it to Parker. Neither *The Liberator* nor the *Standard* printed the text of the address. This may be the address referred to here. However, I can find no indication that it or any other address by May on Parker was ultimately published. (John White Chadwick, *Theodore Parker, Preacher and Reformer*, Boston and New York, 1960, p. 375. Chadwick does not refer to any published sermon by May on Parker. *Ibid.*, p. xix.)

6. The reference is to the Radical Abolition Convention at Syracuse, New York, on August 29.

7. William Goodell edited *The Principia*, the first isue of which appeared on November 19, 1859. Its subtitle was "First Principles in Religion, Morals, Government, and the Economy of Life." Its "Prospectus" described its object as the promotion of "pure religion, sound morals, Christian reforms; the abolition of slaveholding, caste, the rum-traffic, and kindred crimes — the application of Christian Principles to all the relations, duties, business arrangements, and aims of life. . . ." It was published in New York City and listed Samuel Wilde as its proprietor. It continued to appear until 1866.

8. *The Liberator*, September 28, 1860, reprinted William Goodell's comment in *The Principia*, in which he stated that "We are not pleased with the idea of going into battle under the leadership of a general who tells his army, beforehand, that he has little or no hope of ultimate success in the undertaking. . . . So long as the leader predicts defeat, is it creditable that a victory will be achieved?. . . . We cannot help to carry on a struggle at the ballot-box, with the understanding that it is to be a hopeless one. . . ."

9. Gerrit Smith, in a letter dated August 27, 1860, had written to the Syracuse Convention, which he was unable to attend, that "I trust that your Convention will make a national ticket, and also a New York State ticket. Not that I suppose either will get many votes; but that I warmly desire that the handful who wish to vote in accordance with the claims of absolute rectitude, of justice and mercy, may have the needed facilities for doing so.

"Long ago did I become convinced that the American people have not virtue enough to impel them to vote against slavery and the dram-shop. . . ." (*The Liberator*, September 28, 1860.)

314

TO NATHAN R. JOHNSTON

Boston, Oct. 15, 1860.

My Dear Friend:

Nothing but the lack of voice, in consequence of a bronchial difficulty which compels me to be silent, prevents my attendance at the Bradford Convention.[1] The remembrance of my visit to Vermont, two years ago, is fragrant and pleasurable to this hour. Wherever I travelled, I found kind friends and hospitable treatment, and a disposition to give me a candid hearing on the part of such as came to listen. It is true, very many stood aloof, and would not attend, owing to a deep-seated yet groundless prejudice, which led them to imagine that my sentiments were of a pestilent character, and my purposes subversive of the very foundations of society! Had they done me the simple justice to listen to my testimonies, they would have found them but an earnest reiteration of those which prophets and apostles uttered ages ago, and for which Jesus offered up his life on Calvary. The only abolitionism I have ever advocated is embodied in the 58th chapter of Isaiah — in the Golden Rule — and in the Declaration of Independence. If this is sedition, or fanaticism, or treason, or infidelity, I plead guilty to the charge. I am for breaking every yoke, and letting the oppressed go free. I am for doing unto others as I would be done by. I "hold these truths to be self-evident: that all men are created equal; that they are endowed by their Creator with certain inalienable rights; that among these are life, liberty, and the pursuit of happiness." Hence, my religion forbids me having any complicity with slavery, and my patriotism compels me to inscribe upon my banner the motto, "No Union with Slave-holders!" Hence, whatever stands in the way of the emancipation of those in bondage, no matter what may be its pretensions or claims, is repugnant to justice and at war with the rights of our common humanity; and no quarter should be given to it. Tell me not of the sacredness of a pro-slavery church, or the value of a pro-slavery government: they are both inherently and incurably corrupt, and deserve no countenance, but rather to be execrated. I care not whither the principles of liberty lead, nor to what results. They may cost property, reputation, life itself, but without them there is no hope of human redemption, and Christ will have died in vain. In such a struggle, compromise is the worst policy, and subversive of all right.

The work before us is not the limitation but the extinction of slavery. Ours is not a geographical conscience, "bounded by 36 degrees,

30 minutes, North latitude," [2] but it abhors the claim of property in man as much in Carolina as in Kansas, and the traffic in human flesh between the several Slave States as much as between the coast of Africa and our own shores. While the North remains in religious affiliation with the South, and sustains a Union cemented with the blood of those in bondage, our field of labor is and will be appropriately here. The day that shall witness her hands clean of this appalling iniquity will terminate the conflict and usher in the jubilee!

I salute your Convention with hope and joy. All the omens are with us. FORWARD!

Yours, in every struggle for the right,

Wm. Lloyd Garrison.

Rev. N. R. Johnston.

ALS: Garrison Papers, Boston Public Library; printed in *The Liberator*, November 2, 1860.

This is Garrison's reply to an invitation from N. R. Johnston to attend and address the Fourth Annual Meeting of the Vermont Anti-Slavery Convention at Bradford, Vermont, on Wednesday and Thursday, October 17 and 18, 1860 (*The Liberator*, October 12, 1860). A draft of the opening lines of this letter, substantially the same as the final copy, is to be found in the Garrison Papers, Boston Public Library.

1. A report of the convention's proceedings appeared in *The Liberator*, November 2, 1860.

2. The Missouri Compromise.

315

TO J. MILLER McKIM

Boston, Oct. 21, 1860.

My Dear Friend:

Since I promised to attend the anniversary of the Pennsylvania Anti-Slavery Society, at Kennett,[1] I have been suffering from a severe attack of bronchitis; and though, at the present time, it is considerably mitigated, I am under positive medical prohibition in reference to public speaking, for some time to come. Hence, I must again disappoint my Pennsylvania friends, — most deeply to my own regret and loss; for their magnetic presence is ever most delightful and strengthening to my spirit. I can only beg to be affectionately remembered to them all, and invoke upon their deliberations the blessing of the Infinite Father.

Twenty-five years ago this evening, I was in a cell in the Leverett Street jail in this city, — a device of the city authorities to save my life against the murderous designs of an infuriated mob of (so called) "gentlemen of property and standing," on account of my anti-slavery principles. Previous to my imprisonment, I was in the hands of the rioters for a time, who tore the clothes from my body, as they dragged me through the streets, and who made the most desperate efforts to take me where they could apply a coat of tar and feathers, and commit other outrages as their ungovernable malignity might suggest. Rescued at last by the mayor and his posse, it was deemed indispensable to my personal safety to commit me to prison! This was the only governmental protection that was vouchsafed to me. You remember all the circumstances of that memorable event, and I need not repeat them. Nearly all the prominent actors therein have been called to their final account, but the sacred and glorious cause which they madly attempted to overthrow is now shaping the destiny of the nation!

So far as the North is concerned, a marvellous change for the better has taken place in public sentiment, in relation to the Anti-Slavery movement. The struggle for the freedom of speech and of the press has every where been fought, and the victory won. A general enlightenment has taken place upon the subject of slavery. The opinions of a vast multitude have been essentially changed, and secured to the side of freedom. The conflict between free institutions and slave institutions is seen and acknowledged to be irrepressible — not of man's devising, but of God's ordering — and it is deepening in intensity daily, in spite of every effort of political cunning and religious sorcery to effect a reconciliation. The pending Presidential election witnesses a marked division between the political forces of the North and of the South; and though it relates, ostensibly, solely to the question of the further extension of slavery, it really signifies a much deeper sentiment in the breasts of the people of the North, which, in process of time must ripen into more decisive action.

So far as the South is concerned, she has apparently waxed worse and worse — grown more and more desperate — revealed more and more of savage brutality and fiendish malignity — until her crimes and atrocities, not only as perpetrated upon her dehumanized slaves, but as inflicted upon Northern citizens and strangers within her limits, have become too numerous for record, and almost too horrible for belief.

But all this is the sign that the end is rapidly approaching. Peaceably or by a bloody process, the oppressed will eventually obtain their freedom, and nothing can prevent it. Trusting that it may be achieved without the shedding of blood, I remain,

Yours, for liberty and equality for all mankind,

Wm. Lloyd Garrison.

J. Miller McKim.

ALS: Garrison Papers, Boston Public Library; printed in *The Liberator*, November 9, 1860. *The Liberator* misdates the letter October 11.

1. The meeting was held on Thursday, October 25. Garrison's letter was read to the assemblage. The report of the proceedings appeared in *The Liberator*, November 9, 1860, and, in greater detail, in the *National Anti-Slavery Standard*, November 3, 1860.

316

TO WENDELL PHILLIPS GARRISON

Boston, Nov. 2, 1860.

My Dear Son:

I have just ascertained that Ralph W. Emerson is to speak at Music Hall on Sunday; so you had better invite Thaxter [1] to remain over night. We shall probably be able to give him a separate room.

We shall expect you both to dinner to-morrow.

Fanny will convey to Miss Otis [2] the information you desire.

Am glad to hear that your health is improving.

Hastily, but lovingly,

Wm. Lloyd Garrison.

W. P. G.

ALS: Garrison Papers, Boston Public Library.

1. Sidney Warren Thaxter (b. Bangor, Maine, September 8, 1839; fl. 1901) was a classmate of Wendell Phillips Garrison at Harvard. After graduation he engaged in the flour business with his younger brother. He served in the Union army from October 1861 to 1864, reaching the rank of major. After his discharge, he reentered the flour business. In November 1866, he married Laura May Farnham, of Bangor, who died in 1880. (*Harvard Clas of 1861, Fifth Report*, pp. 124–125; *Sixth Report*, p. 49.)

2. Georgena Otis. See Letter 153, December 17, 1856.

317

TO J. MILLER McKIM

Boston, Nov. 5, 1860.

My dear McKim:

A day or two since, a sister of Thomas Sims [1] called to see me in relation to the case of a young slave girl, about 15 years old, (so white that she passes generally as a white girl,) who is now with a Mr. Scudder [2] of Savannah, Ga. (hired but not owned by him,) at present residing about two miles from Rahway, New Jersey, and who is soon to return South, probably via Philadelphia. Miss Sims requested me to ask you to call at Robert Jones's,[3] No. 5, 8th Street, where you will find Leonora Redding,[4] the aunt of the slave girl, who will give you all the particulars of the case. I know you will readily do so, as it may result in the freedom of this young victim, who, of course, is entitled to her liberty, having been permitted to come North by her owner. Should any thing result from the interview, please let me know.

Since reading the report of the proceedings of your annual meeting at Kennett, in the last *Standard*, I have felt additional regret that I was not able to be present. Who is Dr. Stebbins,[5] and where does he reside? He is evidently a fossilized Quaker, and yet vital with pro-slavery prejudice and hate.[6] I do not wonder that Purvis felt indignant and disgusted at Crozier's talk,[7] especially in the boast of C. that he had slept with a negro, as proof that he had no prejudice! But I am sorry that our friend P. was betrayed into the use of certain epithets in relation to Washington and Jefferson,[8] which, while lacking in force because so common in the streets, will be sure to be circulated through the pro-slavery press, from one end of the country to the other, unnecessarily to the detriment of the anti-slavery cause. Still, I appreciate the noble spirit of R. P., and would be far from screening Washington or Jefferson from condemnation of the severest kind for holding slaves all their lives long. Some of your city papers, I see, are exhibiting the spirit of 1835.[9]

The Annual Report is an admirable document.

With the warmest regards,

Yours, always,

Wm. Lloyd Garrison.

J. M. McKim.

ALS: University of Michigan Library.

1. Thomas Sims was the central figure in a fugitive slave case in Boston in 1851. Seventeen years old at the time, Sims was seized, arrested and claimed as the property of a Georgia planter. He was returned to his owner by the United States commissioner, despite popular indignation which necessitated his being guarded by a company of armed men to forestall any attempt to rescue him. (Quarles, *Black Abolitionists*, pp. 206–207.)

2. Unidentified.

3. The Philadelphia *City Directories* for 1866–1890 list Robert Jones as a colored barber at 5 N. 8th Street. (Letter from Nicholas B. Wainright, Director, the Historical Society of Pennsylvania, February 8, 1973.)

4. Unidentified.

5. Dr. Stebbins had interrupted Anna Dickinson, a speaker who had argued the pro-slavery nature of the Constitution, and cried out, "I differ with the lady. The Constitution does not recognize property in men. I differ entirely with the speaker." The report of the convention included the following comment about his later remarks: "Dr. Stebbins . . . thought the laudation that had been bestowed on the anti-slavery movement had not been deserved, and that the good it had accomplished had been greatly exaggerated. Indeed, he believed that the

Anti-Slavery Societies had been a dead weight on the cause from the beginning. . . . He was present at the formation of the [American Anti-Slavery] Society. He might have had the 'honor' of being handed down to posterity as one of the 'signers,' if he had chosen; but he did not choose. There were too many New England ministers in the body and too much cant for him. . . . It was to the Republican party that we were at this time to look for anything like effective action. They proposed something practical, and had the power and will to accomplish it. Dr. Stebbins continued this train of thought at some length, arguing calmly and decorously against abolitionism and in favor of Republican partyism." (*National Anti-Slavery Standard*, November 3, 1860.)

Dr. Sumner Stebbins (b. Cazenovia, New York, May 12, 1809; d. Kennett Square, Pennsylvania, July 12, 1884) learned the trade of a tailor early in life, then taught school in Kennett Square, studied medicine at the University of Pennsylvania, Philadelphia, and practiced in Chester County, Pennsylvania, until 1856, when he retired and moved to Mt. Pleasant, Iowa, where he studied law and was admitted to the bar but did not practice. In 1859, he moved to Marshall, Michigan, where he practiced medicine and edited the Marshall *Statesman*. He returned to Pennsylvania in 1860 and practiced medicine in Unionville, Chester County, until 1881. He was both an antislavery and temperance advocate and was a member of the Progressive Friends of Longwood, Pennsylvania. (Ralph S. Greenlee and Robert L. Greenlee, *The Stebbins Genealogy*, Chicago, 1904, vol. II, Part II, pp. 1043–1045.) On May 21, 1868, he wrote to Garrison about a prohibition tract that he had written, and signed his letter, "Your Old Friend Sumner Stebbins." (Anti-Slavery Letters to Garrison and Others, Boston Public Library.)

6. Garrison does Stebbins somewhat of an injustice here. However foolish his remarks may have seemed, he seems to have been antislavery in sentiment, although he limited his views to those represented by the Republican party.

7. Hiram P. Crozier of Huntington, Long Island was reported by the *Standard* as saying that "he had never had the consciousness of prejudice against color. He had lived at Peterboro, where little or no distinction was made on account of complexion. He had eaten with black men; he had *slept* with a black man; and this, perhaps, was as severe a test as a man's anti-slavery character could be put to. He had been in terms of intimacy with Henry Highland Garnet, and he considered himself debtor in that intercourse."

Robert Purvis made the following comments on Crozier's remarks: "The gentleman from Long Island made some remarks which suggest to me a few words in reply. I am glad to see the gentleman here. This is a free platform, and we welcome to it speakers of every variety of opinion. But, sir, I utterly repudiate the idea that social intimacy with colored men is a test of anti-slavery character. Sir, what has eating with a man, or sleeping with a man, to do with the question of human rights? This, sir, is novel anti-slavery doctrine; and, in the name of the cause, I utterly, and, in my own name, scornfully repudiate it! Sir, we ask no favors of any man or any class of men, in this contest. A white man may eat and otherwise associate with colored men, without conferring thereby any favor. It is quite possible that the favor may be on the other side!

"Sir, this is a question, not of complexion but of principle. Social intercourse is regulated by irreversible social laws. Every man will find his level. Gentlemen will associate with gentlemen; vulgarity will find its natural place, and true refinement will be respected without regard of color; and that, sir, is what this glorious anti-slavery enterprise is teaching the American people."

Crozier replied that he had been misunderstood. "I did not claim to be conferring a favor in associating with colored men." (November 3, 1860.)

Hiram P. Crozier was the minister of the First Universalist Society in Huntington from April 1859 until about 1865. Earlier, he had been the first minister of the Church of Peterboro, at Peterboro, New York, from 1847 until about 1849, when he was asked to resign because of his "radical atheistic" teachings. The church had been formed under the theory of Gerrit Smith that the true church should be free of "ecclesiasticism and creeds." (*History of Suffolk County, New York*, New York, 1882, Part II, p. 55; John E. Smith, *Our County and Its People, A Descriptive and Biographical Record of Madison County, New York*, Boston, 1899, pp. 395–396; letter from James Hurley, Assistant Director, The Long Island Historical Society, Brooklyn, N.Y., February 6, 1973. Crozier's obituary appeared in the Brooklyn *Eagle*, March 9, 1883.)

8. Later in the meeting, Crozier had defended the antislavery nature of the Constitution and characterized Thomas Jefferson as "a good anti-slavery man." Purvis again replied to him: "I am astonished at the audacity of the gentleman from Long Island, in standing up here and claiming Thomas Jefferson to be an anti-slavery man. Sir, Thomas Jefferson was a slaveholder; and I hold all slaveholders to be tyrants and robbers. It is said that Thomas Jefferson sold his own daughter; this, if true, said Mr. Purvis, raising his voice and speaking in a manner highly impassioned, 'proves him to have been a *scoundrel* as well as a tyrant!' (Sensation.)" Concerning Washington, Purvis said: "I do not share with others in their veneration for the 'Father of our country.' I hold all slaveholders, as such, to be robbers. General Washington was a slaveholder; General Washington tried, under that bill, after it had become a law, to recover from New Hampshire a poor woman, flying through perils and toils (thereby showing a truer courage than ever he did), that she might escape the yoke of slavery on his plantation (hisses near the door)."

9. The year in which Garrison was mobbed.

318

TO JAMES REDPATH

Boston, Dec. 1, 1860.

Dear Sir:

Abstaining by medical advice from all public speaking at present, in consequence of a bronchial difficulty, I can only respond by letter to the invitation extended to me by the committee of arrangements, to participate in the proceedings of the Convention to be held at the Temple on Monday next, in order "to mark the anniversary of the martyrdom of John Brown," and to consider the question, "How can American slavery be abolished?"

My method of abolishing slavery is before the country, and has been for the last thirty years. I see no inducement to change or modify it, in any material respect. Briefly, it is comprised in these particulars: —

1. To brand slavery as essentially, self-evidently and eternally unjust, as applied to any portion of mankind; and, therefore, not to be made a debatable question, nor a matter of policy, nor dependant upon any contingency for its abolition; on the contrary, it is to be abhorred, denounced, assailed, in season and out of season, without forbearance or mercy, without compromise or procrastination, by every legitimate weapon, until it cease to pollute and curse the land.

2. Being a system of unparalleled enormity, its upholders and abet-

tors should be the objects of continual warning, entreaty, expostulation, rebuke, exposure and assault. No religious body, claiming the Christian name, and exercising any discipline whatever, should allow any such to be recognized as competent to membership. None of them should be elevated to any position of public trust and emolument. They should be subjected to universal and social outlawry. Public indignation should burn like fire against them. They are the deadliest enemies of domestic tranquillity, of public order, of sound morality, of sacred law, of general prosperity. Towards the objects of their oppression, they reverse all the rules of justice, all the requirements of humanity, all the axioms of political economy, and consign them to a fate a thousand times more to be dreaded than untimely death. They perpetrate all crimes in the one act of making merchandize of their fellow-creatures, and hence give unbounded scope to licentiousness, brutality, robbery and murder; and when their conduct is called in question, instantly their passions are "set on fire of hell," [1] and they behave like demons. Witness the present state of the South, blending as it does the maniacal ravings of Bedlam with the torments of the damned!

3. For the slave, every demand is to be made that one human being may claim of another. Immediate and unconditional emancipation — the recognition and protection of his manhood by law — the power to make contracts, to receive wages, to accumulate property, to acquire knowledge, to dwell where he chooses, to defend his wife, children, and fireside. Were the patriots of 1776 justified in rising up in insurrection, and resisting British oppression unto death? Then are the slaves of the South to be justified, a thousand times more, in imitating their example, and making "Liberty or Death" their motto — enduring as they do, to quote the language of Jefferson in their case, "a bondage, one hour of which is fraught with more misery than ages of that which we rose in rebellion to oppose." Did our revolutionary fathers deserve foreign sympathy, and was it meritorious on the part of France to aid them to achieve their independence? So do the slaves deserve as much sympathy and aid at the hands of all who believe in the Bunker Hill process of making tyranny bite the dust. Was it to the immortal honor of Lafayette, that he drew his sword and perilled his life for our deliverance? Still more is it to the glory of John Brown and his associates at Harper's Ferry, that they staked all that was dear to them, and nearly all perished, in the attempt to liberate the sable bondmen in Virginia. "*Sic semper tyrannis!*" Brand the man as a hypocrite and dastard, who, in one breath, exults in the deeds of Washington and Warren, and in the next, denounces Nat Turner as a monster for refusing longer to wear the yoke and be driven under

the lash, and for taking up arms to defend his God-given rights. If the doctrine of non-resistance ought to be spurned for oppressed white men, it is equally to be spurned for oppressed black men. Weapons of death for all, or for none, who are struggling to be free. Let Hancock and Adams be covered with infamy, or the black liberators who aided John Brown be honored in history.

Thus do I defend the manhood of the humblest slave as on a level with that of his lordly tyrant, and thus do I place them together on the same equality of natural rights. Thus do I test the nation by its own revolutionary standard, taking Bunker Hill monument for my measuring line. No matter for race or complexion — "a man's a man, for a' that." [2] But, for myself, I believe in the inviolability of human life, and therefore disarm, by my principles, alike the oppressor and the oppressed. I believe in the immense superiority of spiritual over carnal weapons, and so seek not the overthrow of slavery by a bloody process. But, assuredly, were I a convert to the doctrine of '76, that a resort to the sword is justifiable to recover lost liberty, then would I plot insurrection by day and by night, deal more in blows and less in words, and seek through blood the emancipation of all who are groaning in captivity at the South.

Finally, I am for taking away all the props which now sustain the slave system, and thus effecting its speedy and eternal overthrow.

Yours, for no union with slaveholders,

Wm. Lloyd Garrison.

James Redpath, Esq.

ALS: Garrison Papers, Boston Public Library.

James Redpath (1833–1891), journalist, editor, and author, was a native of Scotland who came to the United States with his family in 1850 and settled in Michigan. Between 1854 and 1859 he visited Kansas a number of times as a correspondent of the *New York Tribune*. While in Kansas, he became closely attached to John Brown. In 1859, his book, *The Roving Editor, or Talks with Slaves in the Southern States*, which included some of his earlier articles, appeared. His best-known works, *Echoes of Harper's Ferry*, an anthology of writings about John Brown, and *The Public Life of Captain John Brown*, appeared in 1860, as did *A Guide to Hayti*. The latter was based upon his experience as commissioner of emigration in the United States, to which he was appointed by the president of Haiti in 1859. He also founded the Haitian Emigrant Bureau in Boston and New York, and later became Haitian consul at Philadelphia. He was a correspondent with the Northern armies during the Civil War. After the war, he was superintendent of education at Charleston, South Carolina, and in 1868 he founded the Boston Lyceum Bureau, later called the Redpath Lyceum Bureau.

1. James 3:6.
2. Robert Burns.

Index of Recipients

Index of Names

Index of Recipients

(References are to letter numbers)

Index of Names

The following abbreviations are used: AA–SS, American Anti-Slavery Society; MA–SS, Massachusetts Anti-Slavery Society; WLG, William Lloyd Garrison.

Aaron, Samuel: identified, 374; letters to, 374, 388–89
Abbot, Rev. John S. C., 180; identified, 198
Abbro, Mrs. H. A., 252
Abdy, Edward Strutt, 421; identified, 422
Abington, Mass.: WLG speaks in, 339–41; First of August celebrations in, 401, 398, 399, 400, 459, 461, 537, 538, 543, 545, 675–76, 677–79; mentioned, 32, 403
Abolitionists of the United States, letter to, 246–47
Adams, Charles Francis, 217, 456
Adams, John Quincy: quoted, 162–63, 497; and first disunion petition, 395, 396; mentioned, 194, 496
Adams, Samuel, 704
Addie, Marie, 474; identified, 475
Addison, Joseph, quoted and identified, 357, 358
Adrian, Michigan, 224, 253, 262–63
African Civilization Society, 597; identified, 598
African Repository, 186
Agnews, the (of West Chester, Pa.), 572; identified, 575
Alabama, 135, 165
Albany, N.Y.: WLG to speak in, 219, 587, 589, 591, 594; WLG in, 379, 380–81, 382, 422–23, 424–25, 434–35; antislavery meetings at, 422, 431, 432, 436, 511, 667; WLG's letter to convention at, 516–518; mentioned, 199, 580
Alexandria, Va., 136, 165, 166
Aliened American, The, 233, 234
Altoona, Pa., 561–62, 574
America. *See* United States of America
American, The, 477

American and Foreign Anti-Slavery Society, 113, 233, 619, 620, 644, 646
American Anti-Slavery Society: letter to friends of, 238–40; annual meetings, (1850) 1, 6–7, 9, 10, 11–15 *passim*; (1851) 52–54, 55–57, 67; (1852) 200; (1853) 224; (1854) 296, 297–98; (1856) 388–89, 439; (1857) 444; (1858) 525, 526, 528–29; (1859) 619, 621, 625; (1860) 666; various agents and members of, 7, 8, 11, 15, 28, 37, 54, 61, 77, 92, 214, 233, 259, 264, 296, 313, 428, 588, 651; WLG's image as president of, 9; character of, 13, 97, 159–60, 281, 384, 387, 307–08, 360; and religion, 18–19, 25, 285, 286, 385–388, 391; meetings under auspices of, 56, 241–42, 253, 254, 255–56, 312–319 *passim*, 346, 450; letter to Louis Kossuth signed by WLG as president of, 94, 97–186, 186–87; O'Connell on, 131–32, 142, 144; *Declaration of Sentiments* of, 185, 199, 572; rending of in 1840, 215, 233, 644, 646; finances of, 246–47, 313, 439, 564; Decade Meeting, 253, 254, 255, 277, 278, 280; to distribute speech of WLG, 292; and British and Foreign Anti-Slavery Society, 306–09, 310; criticisms of, 330, 383–88, 391, 661, 662, 693, 694, 700–01; disunion petition circulated by, 395–96; and politics, 650–51
American Bible Society, 286; identified, 288
American Board of Commissioners for Foreign Missions: identified, 368, 497; mentioned, 362, 495
American Colonization Society: WLG

favors resistance, 390; to be at Charlotte Newell's funeral, 487; cosigns letter to Massachusetts legislature, 515; WLG to take place of, 533–35; writes to WLG, 535, 609; health of, 586, 603, 607–08, 654, 673; death of, 674, 676–77; S. J. May's address on, 694, 695; mentioned, 31, 97, 291, 317, 356, 398, 580, 693

Parker, Mrs. Theodore (Lydia Cabot): identified, 533; letter to, 676–77; WLG's appreciation of, 608; mentioned, 580, 607

Parker, William, 93

Parker, William F., 579, 580; identified, 581

Parker, William Lloyd Garrison, 579

Parks, Rev. Mr., 431, 432

Parrish, Dr. Joseph, 241; identified, 242–43

Parry, John Humffreys, 77; identified, 84

"Pastoral Letter," 216

Paterson, N.J., 293

Paton, Andrew, 229, 670; identified, 230

Paton, Mrs. Andrew, 670

Paul, Rev. Nathaniel, 392–94; identified, 394

Paulding, James K., 174; identified, 197–98

Pawtucket, R.I., 30, 32

Payne, Abram, 218

Peace Congresses, 63, 64

Pearl (schooner), 163, 194

Pease, Elizabeth. *See* Nichol, Mrs. John Pringle

Peck, Professor (of Oberlin), 623

Peel, Sir Robert, 124; identified, 191

Peirces, the (of West Chester, Pa.), 572; identified, 575

Pennsylvania: and fugitive slaves, 2, 92–93, 153–54, 559, 621; WLG visits, 67, 96, 220, 222, 321–22, 374, 441–42, 501, 554, 556, 557–59; WLG's affection for friends in, 202–03, 553, 691, 697; call to establish meeting of Progressive Friends in, 235–37; mentioned, 56, 118, 214, 376, 406, 574

Pennsylvania Abolition Society, 15

Pennsylvania Anti-Slavery Society: WLG's letter for, 87–92; letter to, 491–96; annual meetings of: (1851) 67, 92; (1852) 96, 202–03, 214, 222; (1855) 374; (1856) 403, 404, 415, 416; (1857) 491, 496; (1858) 537,

553, 559, 567, 568–72; (1860) 691, 697–98, 699; Fair, 416; mentioned, 230, 240, 241, 296, 443

Pennsylvania Freeman: identified, 240–41; mentioned, 205, 238, 239, 240, 253, 313

Pennsylvania Woman Suffrage Association, 33

People's Charter: identified, 44–45; various Chartists, 58, 83, 84, 110, 113, 271

Percy, Dr. Edward Rotton (formerly Dr. Rotton): identified, 252; mentioned, 249, 321, 332, 556

Percy, Mrs. Edward Rotton (Anna Benson): identified, 252; mentioned, 249, 321, 556

Personal Liberty Law, 327, 513–14

Petersburg Intelligencer, 176

Philadelphia, Pa.: Kossuth in, 154; WLG in, 222, 290, 321–22, 416; AA–SS Decade meeting in, 253, 254, 255, 277, 278; Woman's Rights Convention in, 322, 323; fugitive slave case in, 621, 622; mentioned, 9–10, 33, 135, 220, 229, 257, 374, 403, 427, 441, 554

Philadelphia Female Anti-Slavery Society, 418, 443

Philanthropist, 264, 288

Philbrick, John Dudley, identified, 660

Philbrick, Samuel, 215, 603; identified, 217

Phillips, Phebe. *See* Garnaut, Phebe

Phillips, Samuel: identified, 469; mentioned, 468, 470–71, 485

Phillips, Stephen Clarendon, 337; identified, 338

Phillips, Wendell: identified, 7; letters to, 45–46, 243, 279, 341–42, 489, 674–75; speaks, 2, 28, 31, 32, 34, 62, 65, 243, 255, 298, 299, 341, 342, 366, 398, 401, 403, 434, 438, 511, 528, 529, 619, 625; with WLG in New York, 6, 624; cosigns various letters and calls, 7, 94, 181, 240, 247, 277, 395, 419, 456, 500, 515, 611; to attend meetings, 56, 65, 66, 200, 212, 312, 314, 316, 317, 318, 342, 433, 436, 516, 537, 691; quoted, 184–85; and Burns case, 208, 331; writes to conventions, 214, 490; and Whole World's Temperance Convention, 250; and removal of Loring, 330, 331; and capital punishment, 333; bust of, 335, 336, 420, 524, 525, 598; breakfasts with WLG and others, 349; in Chicago, 351; in Maine, 374;